Third Edition

Financial Statement Analysis & Valuation

PETER D. EASTON
University of Notre Dame

MARY LEA McANALLY
Texas A&M University

GREGORY A. SOMMERS
Southern Methodist University

XIAO-JUN ZHANG
University of California, Berkeley

Cambridge
BUSINESS PUBLISHERS

To my daughters, Joanne and Stacey
    —PDE

To my husband Brittan, and my children Loic, Maclean, Quinn and Kay
    —MLM

To my wife Susan, and my children Christian, Peter and Philip
    —GAS

To my wife Sharon, my daughter Jasmine, and my parents 滕惠清 and 张祥林
    —XZ

Financial Statement Analysis & Valuation, Third Edition, by Peter D. Easton, Mary Lea McAnally, Gregory A. Sommers, and Xiao-Jun Zhang.

Student Edition ISBN 978-1-61853-009-7

Bookstores & Faculty: to order this book, call 800-619-6473 or email customerservice@cambridgepub.com.

Students: to order this book, please visit the book's Website and order directly online.

Printed in Canada.
10 9 8 7 6 5 4 3 2 1

About the Authors

PETER D. EASTON is an expert in accounting and valuation and holds the Notre Dame Alumni Chair in Accountancy in the Mendoza College of Business. Professor Easton's expertise is widely recognized by the academic research community and by the legal community. Professor Easton frequently serves as a consultant on accounting and valuation issues in federal and state courts.

Professor Easton holds undergraduate degrees from the University of Adelaide and the University of South Australia. He holds a graduate degree from the University of New England and a PhD in Business Administration (majoring in accounting and finance) from the University of California, Berkeley.

Professor Easton's research on corporate valuation has been published in the *Journal of Accounting and Economics, Journal of Accounting Research, The Accounting Review, Contemporary Accounting Research, Review of Accounting Studies,* and *Journal of Business Finance and Accounting*. Professor Easton has served as an associate editor for 11 leading accounting journals and he is currently an associate editor for the *Journal of Accounting Research, Journal of Business Finance and Accounting,* and *Journal of Accounting, Auditing, and Finance*. He is an editor of the *Review of Accounting Studies*.

Professor Easton has held appointments at the University of Chicago, the University of California at Berkeley, Ohio State University, Macquarie University, the Australian Graduate School of Management, the University of Melbourne, Tilburg University, National University of Singapore, Seoul National University, and Nyenrode University. He is the recipient of numerous awards for excellence in teaching and in research. Professor Easton regularly teaches accounting analysis and security valuation to MBAs. In addition, Professor Easton has taught managerial accounting at the graduate level.

MARY LEA McANALLY is the Philip Ljundahl Professor of Accounting and Associate Dean for Graduate Programs at the Mays Business School. She obtained her PhD from Stanford University and B. Comm. from the University of Alberta. She worked as a Chartered Accountant (in Canada) and is a Certified Internal Auditor. Prior to arriving at Texas A&M in 2002, Professor McAnally held positions at University of Texas at Austin, Canadian National Railways, and Dunwoody and Company.

Her research interests include accounting and disclosure in regulated environments, executive compensation, and accounting for risk. She has published articles in the leading academic journals including *Journal of Accounting and Economics, Journal of Accounting Research, The Accounting Review, Review of Accounting Studies,* and *Contemporary Accounting Research*. Professor McAnally received the Mays Business School Research Achievement Award in 2005. She is Associate Editor at *Accounting Horizons* and serves on the editorial board of *Contemporary Accounting Research* and is Guest Editor for the MBA-teaching volume of *Issues in Accounting Education* (2012). She is active in the American Accounting Association and its FARS section.

At Texas A&M, Professor McAnally teaches financial reporting, analysis, and valuation in the full-time and Executive MBA programs. Through the Mays Center for Executive Development, she works with corporate clients including Halliburton, AT&T, and Baker Hughes. She has also taught at University of Calgary, IMADEC (in Austria) and at the Indian School of Business, in Hyderabad. She has received numerous faculty-determined and student-initiated teaching awards at the MBA and executive levels. Those awards include the Beazley Award, the Trammell Foundation Award, the MBA Teaching Award (multiple times), the MBA Association Distinguished Faculty Award (three times), the Award for Outstanding and Memorable Faculty Member, and the Distinguished Achievement Award.

GREGORY A. SOMMERS is Director of the Master of Science in Accounting program and Professor of Practice in Accounting in the Edwin L. Cox School of Business at Southern Methodist University. He holds an undergraduate degree in accounting from Fresno Pacific University and a PhD in Accounting and Management Information Systems from The Ohio State University. Professor Sommers is a Certified Public Accountant who practiced in and continues to be licensed in California.

Professor Sommers' research focuses on market-based empirical studies of the relations between currently available accounting data, expectations of future accounting data, expected cost of capital and valuation. His research has been published in *Journal of Accounting Research* and *Journal of Business, Finance, and Accounting*. Professor Sommers serves on the editorial board of *Review of Accounting Studies*.

Professor Sommers teaches financial accounting, including international accounting, in the undergraduate and graduate programs as well as in executive education at Southern Methodist University. He has taught financial statement analysis and valuation for over ten years at the graduate level and his teaching materials were previously utilized as resources for another textbook in this area. Professor Sommers' teaching has earned him numerous awards including Outstanding MBA Teaching as well as recognition from student organizations.

Professor Sommers is an active member of the American Accounting Association and its Financial Accounting and Reporting Section. He has served as chairman of the Trueblood Seminar for Professors sponsored by Deloitte. Professor Sommers is recognized as an expert in the areas of financial reporting, financial analysis, estimation of cost of capital, and business valuation.

XIAO-JUN ZHANG is the E. R. Niemela Associate Professor of Accounting at the Haas School of Business, University of California, Berkeley. He has served as Chair of the accounting group and the Director of the Center for Financial Reporting and Management at the University of California, Berkeley.

Professor Zhang holds an undergraduate degree from Renmin University, and masters degrees from the University of Maryland and Columbia University. Professor Zhang received his PhD from Columbia University.

Professor Zhang's research focuses on financial statement analysis and security valuation. His work has been published in highly respected research journals including *The Accounting Review, Journal of Accounting and Economics, Journal of Accounting Research, and Review of Accounting Studies*. Professor Zhang has served on the editorial board of several journals, and has been a reviewer for many others top journals in the fields of finance and accounting.

Professor Zhang teaches undergraduate, MBA, and PhD courses in accounting and analysis. He is consistently ranked among the best instructors by students at the University of California, Berkeley. Professor Zhang is a respected consultant having performed consulting services for several hedge funds. He has also served as an advisor to the Investment Club at the University of California, Berkeley.

Preface

Welcome to the Third Edition of *Financial Statement Analysis & Valuation*. Our main goal in writing this book was to address the needs of today's instructors and students interested in financial analysis and valuation by providing the most contemporary, engaging, and user-oriented textbook available. This book is the product of extensive market research including focus groups, market surveys, class tests, manuscript reviews, and interviews with faculty from across the country. We are grateful to students and faculty whose insights, suggestions and feedback greatly benefited this Third Edition.

TARGET AUDIENCE

Financial Statement Analysis & Valuation is intended for use in a financial statement analysis and/or valuation course in which profitability analysis and security valuation are emphasized. This book accommodates mini-courses lasting only a few days as well as extended courses lasting a full semester.

INNOVATIVE APPROACH

Financial Statement Analysis & Valuation is applications oriented and focuses on the most salient aspects of accounting, analysis, and valuation. It teaches students how to read, analyze, and interpret financial statement data to make informed business decisions. This textbook makes financial statement analysis and valuation **engaging**, **relevant**, and **contemporary**. To that end, it consistently incorporates **real company data**, both in the body of each module and throughout the assignment material.

FLEXIBLE STRUCTURE

The curricula, instructor preferences, and course lengths vary across colleges. Accordingly and to the extent possible, the 15 modules that make up *Financial Statement Analysis & Valuation* were designed independently of one another. This modular presentation enables each college and instructor to "customize" the book to best fit their needs. Our introduction and discussion of financial statements constitute Modules 1 and 2. Module 3 presents the analysis of financial statements with an emphasis on analysis of operating profitability. Module 4 introduces credit risk analysis. Modules 5 through 10 offer an analysis of accounting numbers and disclosures. The aim of those modules is to help us better interpret financial statements and to adjust those statements as necessary to improve our financial statement analysis. Modules 11 through 15 describe forecasting, cost of capital estimation, and company valuation.

Flexibility for Courses of Varying Lengths

Many instructors have approached us to ask about suggested class structures based on courses of varying length. To that end, we provide the following table of possible course designs. For instructors desiring greater emphasis on accounting analysis, additional time can be spent on

Modules 1 through 10. For instructors desiring greater emphasis on analysis and valuation, additional time can be spent on Modules 11 through 15.

	15 Week Semester-Course	10 Week Quarter-Course	6 Week Mini-Course	1 Week Intensive-Course
MODULE 1 Framework for Analysis and Valuation	Week 1	Week 1 (Modules 1 and 2)	Week 1 (Modules 1 and 2)	Day 1 (Modules 1 and 2)
MODULE 2 Overview of Business Activities and Financial Statements	Weeks 1 and 2			
MODULE 3 Profitability Analysis and Interpretation	Week 3	Week 2	Week 2	Day 2
MODULE 4 Credit Risk Analysis and Interpretation	Week 4	Week 3	Optional	Optional
MODULE 5 Revenue Recognition and Operating Income	Week 5	Week 4	Week 3	Day 3 (Modules 5 and 6)
MODULE 6 Asset Recognition and Operating Assets	Week 6	Week 5	Skim	
MODULE 7 Liability Recognition and Nonowner Financing	Week 7	Optional	Optional	Optional
MODULE 8 Equity Recognition and Owner Financing	Week 8	Optional	Optional	Optional
MODULE 9 Incorporate Entities	Week 9	Week 6	Optional	Optional
MODULE 10 Off-Balance-Sheet Financing	Week 10	Week 7	Skim	Optional
MODULE 11 Forecasting Financial Statements	Week 11	Week 8	Week 4	Day 4 (Modules 11 and 12)
MODULE 12 Cost of Capital and Valuation Basics	Week 12	Week 9	Week 5	
MODULE 13 Cash-Flow-Based Valuation	Week 13	Weeks 9 and 10	Weeks 5 and 6	Day 5 (Modules 13 and 14)
MODULE 14 Operating-Income-Based Valuation	Week 14	Week 10	Week 6	
MODULE 15 Market-Based Valuation	Week 15	Optional	Optional	Optional

INNOVATIVE PEDAGOGY

Financial Statement Analysis & Valuation includes special features specifically designed for the student with a keen interest in analysis and valuation.

Focus Companies for Each Module

Each module's content is explained through the reporting activities of real companies. To that end, each module incorporates a "focus company" for special emphasis and demonstration. The enhanced instructional value of focus companies comes from the way they engage students in real analysis and interpretation. Focus companies were selected based on the industries that business students typically enter upon graduation.

Focus Company by Module

MODULE 1	Berkshire Hathaway	**MODULE 9**	Google
MODULE 2	Apple	**MODULE 10**	Delta Airlines
MODULE 3	Target	**MODULE 11**	Procter & Gamble
MODULE 4	Home Depot	**MODULE 12**	Southern Company
MODULE 5	Pfizer	**MODULE 13**	Johnson & Johnson
MODULE 6	Cisco	**MODULE 14**	Johnson & Johnson
MODULE 7	Verizon	**MODULE 15**	Family Dollar
MODULE 8	Aon	**APPENDIX C**	Kimberly-Clark

Real Company Data Throughout

Market research and reviewer feedback tell us that one of instructors' greatest frustrations with other financial statement analysis and valuation textbooks is their lack of real, contemporary company data. We have gone to great lengths to incorporate real company data throughout each module to reinforce important concepts and engage students. We engage nonaccounting students specializing in finance, marketing, management, real estate, operations, and so forth, with companies and scenarios that are relevant to them. For representative examples, **SEE PAGES 3-10; 5-5; 6-11.**

Decision Orientation

One primary goal of a financial statement analysis and valuation course is to teach students the skills needed to apply their accounting knowledge to solving real business problems and making informed business decisions. With that goal in mind, Analysis Decision boxes in each module encourage students to apply the material presented to solving actual business scenarios. For representative examples, **SEE PAGES 2-12; 5-18; 6-12; 8-9.**

Research Insights

Academic research plays an important role in the way business is conducted, accounting and analysis are performed, and students are taught. It is important for students to recognize how modern research and modern business practice interact. Therefore, we periodically incorporate relevant research to help students understand the important relation between research and modern business. For representative examples, **SEE PAGES 3-18; 5-32.**

Financial Statement Effects Template

As instructors, we recognize that the financial statement analysis and valuation course is not directed solely toward accounting majors. *Financial Statement Analysis & Valuation* embraces this reality. This book highlights **financial reporting**, **analysis**, **valuation**, **interpretation**, **applications** and **decision making**. We incorporate the following **financial statement effects template** to train students in understanding the economic ramifications of transactions and their impacts on financial statements. This analytical tool is a great resource for students in learning analysis and applying it to their future courses and careers. Each transaction is identified in the "Transaction" column. Then, the dollar amounts (positive or negative) of the financial statement effects are recorded in the appropriate balance sheet or income statement columns. The template also reflects the statement of cash flow effects (via the cash column) and the statement of stockholders' equity effects (via the contributed capital and earned capital columns). The earned capital account is immediately updated to reflect any income or loss arising from each transaction (denoted by the arrow line from net income to earned capital). This template is instructive as it reveals the financial impacts of transactions, and it provides insights into the effects of accounting choices. For those desiring a more traditional analysis, journal entries and T-accounts are shown in the margin.

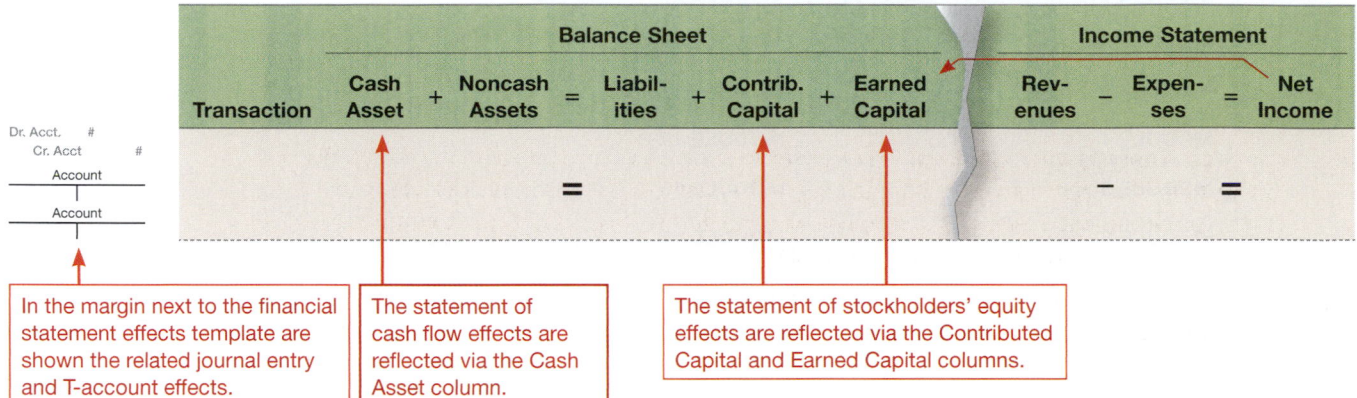

Balance Sheet									**Income Statement**			
Transaction	Cash Asset	+	Noncash Assets	=	Liabil- ities	+	Contrib. Capital	+	Earned Capital	Rev- enues	−	Expen- ses	=	Net Income

Dr. Acct.   #
    Cr. Acct   #
_____
    Account
_____
    Account

In the margin next to the financial statement effects template are shown the related journal entry and T-account effects.

The statement of cash flow effects are reflected via the Cash Asset column.

The statement of stockholders' equity effects are reflected via the Contributed Capital and Earned Capital columns.

Mid-Module and Module-End Reviews

Financial statement analysis and valuation can be challenging—especially for students lacking business experience or previous exposure to finance, management, and other business courses. To reinforce concepts presented in each module and to ensure student comprehension, we include mid-module and module-end reviews that require students to recall and apply the financial statement analysis and valuation techniques and concepts described in each module. To aid students in developing their comparative analysis skills, most of those review problems center on a company or companies that compete with the focus company of that module. For representative examples, **SEE PAGES 3-8; 8-15; 11-37.**

Excellent, Class-Tested Assignment Materials

Excellent assignment material is a must-have component of any successful textbook (and class). We went to great lengths to create the best assignments possible from contemporary financial statements. In keeping with the rest of the book, we used real company data extensively. We also ensured that assignments reflect our belief that students should be trained in analyzing accounting information to make business decisions, as opposed to working on mechanical tasks. Assignments encourage students to analyze accounting information, interpret it, and apply the knowledge gained to a business decision or in a valuation context. There are six categories of assignments: **Questions**, **Mini Exercises**, **Exercises**, **Problems**, **International Applications**, and **Discussion Points**. For representative examples, **SEE PAGES 3-34; 6-45; 10-32.**

THIRD EDITION CHANGES

Based on classroom use and reviewer feedback, a number of substantive changes have been made in the third edition to further enhance the students' experiences:

- **Updated Financial Data:** We have updated all Focus Company financial statements and disclosures to reflect each company's latest available filings. We also explain the SEC's EDGAR financial statement retrieval software and the user's ability to download excel spreadsheets of the financial statements from 10-K filings.

- **Updated Assignments:** We have updated nearly all assignments using real data to reflect each company's latest available filings and have added many new assignments that also utilize real financial data and footnotes.

- **International Financial Reporting Standards (IFRS):** We have updated the IFRS Insight boxes and IFRS Alert boxes throughout the text to introduce students to the similarities and differences between U.S. GAAP and IFRS. We conclude each module with a summary of notable differences between IFRS and U.S. GAAP. We also added a new category of assignments, *IFRS Applications*, that require students to apply IFRS.

■ **New Focus Companies:** We now utilize Target as the focus company of Module 3, and Aon Corporation as the focus company of Module 8.

■ **Value Chain and SWOT:** Module 1 includes new discussion of business analysis, with inclusion of Porter's value-chain and the SWOT analysis to accompany Porter's competitive forces model.

■ **Four-Step Analysis and Valuation Framework:** Module 1 introduces a new 4-step framework to help students visualize the analysis and valuation process; the four steps involve: business environment analysis; assessment of company performance and condition; prediction of company financials; and business valuation.

■ **Treatment of Cash:** We treat cash and cash equivalents as a nonoperating asset to reflect its increased use in a manner similar to short-term marketable securities. This revision reflects changes in practice.

■ **Simplified Treatment of Income Taxes:** We simplified the treatment of the income tax rate in Module 3; this carries through the ROE disaggregation analysis and in many other sections of the book.

■ **Enhanced Credit Analysis:** Module 4 includes new information on accounting adjustments for credit analysis, with reference to S&P's adjustments for Home Depot. It also expands the explanation of credit risk analysis with reference to procedures at S&P and Moody's.

■ **Accounting Quality:** We added a new section on accounting quality in Module 5. It describes measures of accounting quality and factors that mitigate accounting quality. We also provide a check list of items in financial statements that should be reviewed when analyzing financial statements.

■ **Equity Method Implications:** Module 7 provides expanded analysis, with an illustrative scenario, of the financial implications of equity method reporting, including its limitations for ratio analysis.

■ **Intercorporate Investments:** Consistent with recent changes in accounting standards, we have revised Module 9 to emphasize investors' control of securities and deemphasize the percentage of ownership as the determining factor in selecting the method used for financial reporting.

■ **Equity Investments:** We expanded our coverage of equity investments with additional examples and explanation.

■ **Credit Ratings:** We have expanded the section on Credit Ratings in Module 8 to add a discussion on trends in credit ratings. We have also updated the credit rating statistics to reflect the latest publication of Moody's Financial Metrics.

■ **Noncontrolling Interest:** We added expanded discussion of noncontrolling interest, including accounting for noncontrolling interest, how its reported in the balance sheet and income statement, and the interpretation of related disclosures.

■ **Revised Forecasting Module:** We have rewritten Module 11 on forecasting financial statements to help students understand the forecasting process; the revised module uses an actual analyst report on Procter & Gamble, together with the analysts' spreadsheets (from Morgan Stanley) to show how forecasting is performed in practice.

■ **Expanded Valuation Discussion:** Modules 13 and 14 include enhanced discussion of valuation factors, including that for growth rates, the terminal period, mid-year adjustments, reverse engineering, and the use of nominal (risk-adjusted) versus real numbers.

■ **New Case Analysis:** New Appendix C illustrates a case analysis of the financial reporting, forecasting, and valuation of Kimberly-Clark Corporation.

■ **New Regulations:** We highlight pending and proposed accounting standards and their likely effects, if passed. These include pending standards on financial statement presentation and leasing. This edition also reflects all accounting standards in effect since our last edition, including the new business combination and consolidation standard and goodwill impairment testing.

COMPANION CASEBOOK

Cases in Financial Reporting, 7th edition by Ellen Engel (University of Chicago), D. Eric Hirst (University of Texas – Austin), and Mary Lea McAnally (Texas A&M University). This book comprises 27 cases and is a perfect companion book for faculty interested in exposing students to a wide range of real financial statements. The cases are current and cover companies from Canada, France, Austria, the Netherlands, the UK, India, as well as from the U.S. Many of the U.S. companies are major multinationals. Each case deals with a specific financial accounting topic within the context of one (or more) company's financial statements. Each case contains financial statement information and a set of directed questions pertaining to one or two specific financial accounting issues. This is a separate, saleable casebook (**ISBN 978-1-934319-79-6**). Contact your sales representative to receive a desk copy or email **customerservice@cambridgepub.com.**

ONLINE INSTRUCTION AND HOMEWORK MANAGEMENT SYSTEM

 This supplement is ideal for distance/online/hybrid instruction, faculty responsible for large sections, and/or courses requiring independent learning. Available for an additional fee, this Web-based instruction and homework management system enables students to solve select assignments in each module and receive instant feedback. Assignments with a red check mark in the margin next to them are available in the online system. For more information, contact your sales representative.

SUPPLEMENT PACKAGE

For Instructors

Solutions Manual: Created by the authors, the *Solutions Manual* contains complete solutions to all the assignments in the textbook.

PowerPoint: Created by the authors, the PowerPoint slides outline key elements of each module.

Test Bank: Written by the authors, the test bank includes multiple-choice items, exercises, short essay questions, and problems.

Computerized Test Bank: This computerized version of the test bank enables you to add and edit questions; create up to 99 versions of each test; attach graphic files to questions; import and export ASCII files; and select questions based on type or learning objective. It provides password protection for saved tests and question databases and is able to run on a network.

Website: All instructor materials are accessible via the book's Website (password protected) along with other useful links and information. **www.cambridgepub.com**

For Students

Student Solutions Manual: Created by the authors, the student solutions manual contains all solutions to the even-numbered assignment materials in the textbook. This is a **restricted** item that is only available to students after their instructor has authorized its purchase.

Website: Useful links are available to students free of charge on the book's Website.

ACKNOWLEDGMENTS

All three editions of this book benefited greatly from the valuable feedback of focus group attendees, reviewers, students, and colleagues. We are extremely grateful to them for their help in making this project a success.

Kristian Allee, *Michigan State University*
Progyan Basu, *University of Maryland*
Hilary Becker, *Carlton University*
Frank Beil, *University of Minnesota*
William Black, *Case Western Reserve University*
Philip Brown, *Harding University*
Michael Calegari, *Santa Clara University*
Charles Caliendo, *University of Minnesota*
Shelly Canterbury, *George Mason University*
Agnes Cheng, *Louisiana State University*
Mei Cheng, *University of Arizona*
Bob Churchman, *Harding University*
Michael Clement, *University of Texas—Austin*
Daniel Cohen, *University of Texas—Dallas*
Steve Crawford, *Rice University*
Hemang Desai, *Southern Methodist University*
Timothy Dimond, *Northern Illinois University*
Ellen Engel, *University of Chicago*
Patricia Fairfield, *Georgetown University*
Lucille Faurel, *University of California—Irvine*
Mary Fischer, *University of Texas—Tyler*
Karen Foust, *Tulane University*
Margaret Gagne, *Marist College*
Kelly Gamble, *University of Alabama—Huntsville*
Waqar Ghani, *Saint Joseph's University*
Jianxin Gong, *University of Illinois*
Jeffrey Gramlich, *University of Southern Maine*
Umit Gurun, *University of Texas—Dallas*
Robert Halsey, *Babson College*
John Hand, *University of North Carolina*
Trevor S. Harris, *Columbia University*
Robert Holtfreter, *Central Washington University*
James A Howard, *University of Maryland*
Ronald Jastrzebski, *Purdue University*
Rick Johnston, *Ohio State University*
Christopher Jones, *George Washington University*
William Kamas, *University of Texas*
Jocelyn Kauffunger, *University of Pittsburgh*
Elizabeth Keating, *Harvard University*
Myung-Sun Kim, *SUNY University of Buffalo*
Sungsoo Kim, *Rutgers University—Camden*
Bonnie Klamm, *North Dakota State University*
John Kostolansky, *Loyola University*
Gopal Krishnan, *George Mason University*
Ron Lazer, *University of Houston*
Reuven Lehavy, *University of Michigan*
Siyi Li, *University of Illinois—Chicago*
Steve Lim, *Texas Christian University*
Henock Louis, *Penn State University*

Stanimir Markov, *University of Texas—Dallas*
Karen McDougal, *St. Joseph University*
Krishnagopal Menon, *Boston University*
Norman Meonske, *Kent State University*
Birendra Mishra, *California State University- Riverside*
Debra Moore, *Dallas Baptist University*
Erin Moore, *Westfield State University*
Mark Moore, *Texas Tech University*
Haim Mozes, *Fordham University*
R.D. Nair, *University of Wisconsin*
Alex Nekrasov, *University of California—Irvine*
Christopher Noe, *Massachusetts Institute of Technology*
Emeka Nwaeze, *University of Texas—San Antonio*
Donald Pagach, *North Carolina State University*
Shailendra Pandit, *University of Illinois—Chicago*
Ray Pfeiffer, *Texas Christian University*
Chris Prestigiacomo, *University of Missouri*
Larry Prober, *Rider University*
Rama Ramamurthy, *College of William & Mary*
Ken Reichelt, *Louisiana State University*
Jay Rich, *Illinois State University*
Edward Riedl, *Harvard University*
Byung Ro, *Purdue University*
Andrea Roberts, *University of Virginia*
Darren Roulstone, *Ohio State University*
Marc Rubin, *Miami University*
Carol Sargent, *Georgia State University*
Galen Sevcik, *Georgia State University*
Nicholas Seybert, *University of Maryland*
Andreas Simon, *Cal Poly—San Luis Obispo*
Praveen Sinha, *Cal State—Long Beach*
Nancy Snow, *University of Toledo*
Victor Stanton, *University of California—Berkeley*
John J. Surdick, *Xavier University*
Eric Sussman, *UCLA*
Diane Tanner, *University of North Florida*
Gary Taylor, *University of Alabama*
Teresa Thamer, *Brenau University*
Mark Trombley, *University of Arizona*
Andrew VanBusKirk, *Ohio State University*
William Walsh, *Syracuse University*
Charles Wasley, *University of Rochester*
Ralph Welton, *Clemson University*
Clark Wheatley, *Florida International University*
Matt Wieland, *University of Georgia*
Jeffrey Wong, *University of Nevada—Reno*
Lee Yao, *Loyola University—New Orleans*
Yong Yu, *University of Texas*

In addition, we are extremely grateful to George Werthman, Jocelyn Mousel, Jill Fischer, Rich Kolasa, Debbie McQuade, Terry McQuade, and the entire team at Cambridge Business Publishers for their encouragement, enthusiasm, and guidance.

Peter   *Mary Lea*   *Greg*   *Xiao-Jun*
March 2012

Brief Contents

Contents

Module **1**

Framework for Analysis and Valuation   1-2

Module **2**

Overview of Business Activities and Financial Statements   2-2

Module **3**

Profitability Analysis and
Interpretation   3-2

Module **4**

Credit Risk Analysis and
Interpretation   4-2

Module 8

Equity Recognition and Owner Financing   8-2

Module 9

Intercorporate Entities   9-2

Module **12**

Cost of Capital and Valuation Basics   12-2

Module **13**

Cash-Flow-Based Valuation   13-2

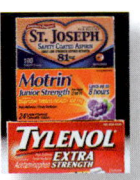

Module **14**

Operating-Income-Based Valuation   14-2

Module **15**

Market-Based Valuation   15-2

Appendix **A**

Compound Interest Tables   A-1

Appendix **B**

Chart of Accounts   B-1

Appendix **C**

Comprehensive Case   C-2

LEARNING OBJECTIVES

1. Identify and discuss the users and suppliers of financial statement information. (p. 1-6)

2. Identify and explain the four financial statements, and define the accounting equation. (p. 1-10)

3. Describe business analysis within the context of a competitive environment. (p. 1-15)

4. Explain and apply the basics of profitability analysis. (p. 1-21)

5. Describe the accounting principles and regulations that frame financial statements. (p. 1-27)

© Getty Images

Framework for Analysis and Valuation

Berkshire Hathaway owns numerous businesses that pursue diverse activities. The legendary Warren Buffett, the "Sage of Omaha," manages the company. Buffett's investment philosophy is to acquire and hold companies over the long run. His acquisition criteria, taken from Berkshire Hathaway's annual report, follow:

> ### BERKSHIRE HATHAWAY

1. Large purchases (and large pretax earnings).
2. Demonstrated consistent earning power (future projections are of *no* interest to us, nor are 'turnaround' situations).
3. Businesses earning good returns on equity while employing little or no debt.
4. Management in place (we can't supply it).
5. Simple businesses (if there's lots of technology, we won't understand it).
6. An offering price (we don't want to waste our time or that of the seller by talking, even preliminarily, about a transaction when price is unknown).

At least three of Buffett's six criteria relate to financial performance. First, he seeks businesses with large and consistent earning power. Buffett is not only looking for consistent earnings, but earnings that are measured according to accounting policies that closely mirror the underlying economic performance of the business.

Second, Buffett focuses on "businesses earning good returns on equity," defined as income divided by average stockholders' equity: "Our preference would be to reach our goal by directly owning a diversified group of businesses that generate cash and consistently earn above-average returns" (Berkshire Hathaway annual report). For management to earn a good return on equity, it must focus on both income (financial performance) and equity (financial condition).

Third, Buffett values companies based on their ability to generate consistent earnings and cash. He focuses on *intrinsic value,* which he defines in each annual report as follows:

> Intrinsic value is an all-important concept that offers the only logical approach to evaluating the relative attractiveness of investments and businesses. Intrinsic value can be defined simply: It is the discounted value of the cash that can be taken out of a business during its remaining life.

The discounted value Buffett describes is the present (today's) value of the cash flows the company expects to generate in the future. Cash is generated when companies are well managed and operate profitably and efficiently.

Warren Buffett provides some especially useful investment guidance in his Chairman's letter from a prior period's Berkshire Hathaway annual report:

(continued on next page)

(continued from previous page)

Three suggestions for investors: First, beware of companies displaying weak accounting. If a company still does not expense options, or if its pension assumptions are fanciful, watch out. When managements take the low road in aspects that are visible, it is likely they are following a similar path behind the scenes. There is seldom just one cockroach in the kitchen.

Second, unintelligible footnotes usually indicate untrustworthy management. If you can't understand a footnote or other managerial explanation, it's usually because the CEO doesn't want you to. Enron's descriptions of certain transactions still baffle me.

Finally, be suspicious of companies that trumpet earnings projections and growth expectations. Businesses seldom operate in a tranquil, no-surprise environment, and earnings simply don't advance smoothly (except, of course, in the offering books of investment bankers).

This book explains Buffett's references to stock option accounting and pension assumptions as well as a host of other accounting issues that affect interpretation and valuation of companies' financial performance. We will analyze and interpret the footnotes, which Buffett views as crucial to quality financial reporting and analysis. Our philosophy is simple: we must understand the intricacies and nuances of financial reporting to become critical readers and users of financial reports for company analysis and valuation.

Sources: Berkshire Hathaway *10-K Reports*, Berkshire Hathaway *Annual Reports; The Wall Street Journal,* January 2012.

MODULE ORGANIZATION

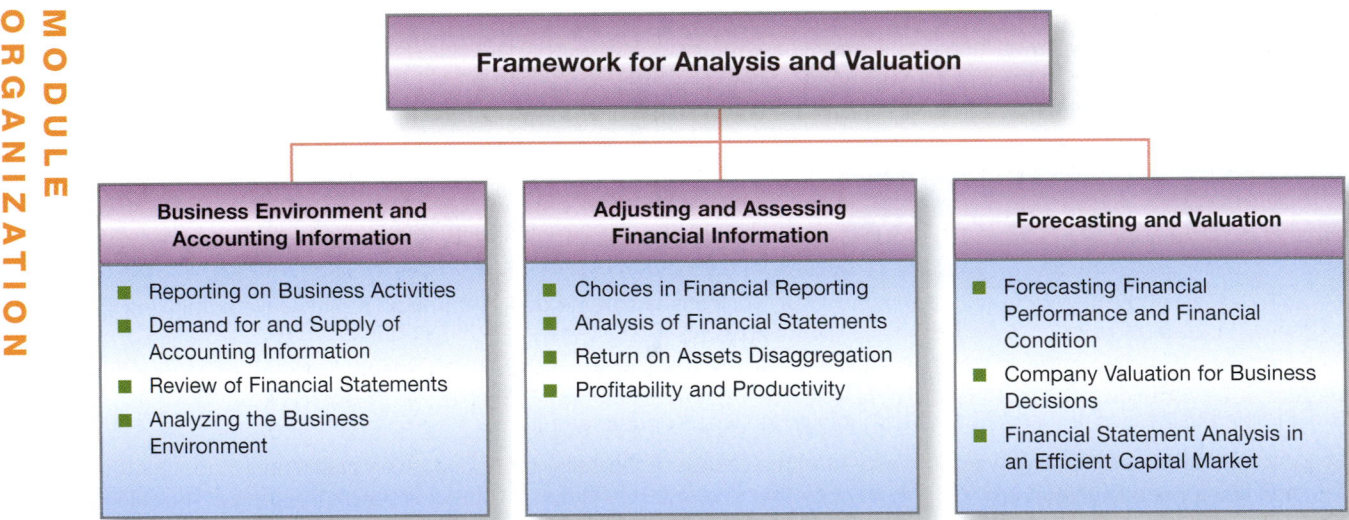

Financial statement analysis is the process of extracting information from financial statements to better understand a company's current and future performance and financial condition. Financial statements serve many objectives. Management uses financial statements to raise financing for the company, to meet disclosure requirements, and to serve as a benchmark for executive bonuses. Investors and analysts use financial statements to help decide whether to buy or sell stock. Creditors and rating agencies use financial statements to help decide on the creditworthiness of a company's debt and lending terms. Regulatory agencies use financial statements to enact social and economic policies and to monitor compliance with laws. Legal institutions use financial statements to assess fines and reparations in litigation. Various other decision makers rely on financial statements for purposes ranging from determining demands in labor union negotiations to assessing damages for environmental abuses.

Valuation is the process of drawing on the results of financial statement analysis to estimate a company's worth (enterprise value). A company's worth can be viewed as a collection of assets, and those assets have claims on them. Owner claims are reflected in equity shares (securities) of a company. Nonowner claims are reflected in obligations and debt shares (securities) of the company. The valuation process seeks to assess the worth of equity shares or debt shares, or both.

Financial statement analysis and valuation is the joint process of scrutinizing a company's financial statements and valuing its equity and debt. The relations between the company (its assets) and the market claims on the company are depicted here:

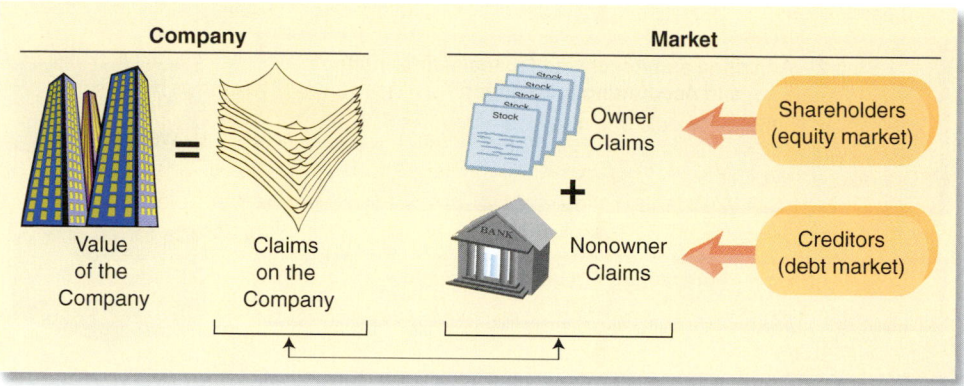

We see that company value equals owner and nonowner claims, where those claims are valued by the equity and debt markets.

This book provides a framework and several tools to help us analyze companies and value their securities. To this end, it is helpful to imagine yourself as a specific user of financial statements. For example, imagine you are a stock investor—how do you identify a stock to buy or whether to sell a stock you own? Imagine you are a bond trader—how do you identify a bond to acquire or whether to dispose of a bond you own? Imagine you are a manager—how do you decide whether to acquire another company or divest of a current division? Imagine you are an equity or credit analyst—how do you assess and communicate an investment appraisal or credit risk report? This focused perspective will enhance your learning process and makes it relevant.

This module begins with an overview of the demand for and supply of accounting information. We then review financial statements and explain what they convey about a company. We provide an introduction to analysis of the business environment, which is a crucial part of understanding the context in which we draw inferences from financial statements. Profitability is described next as it frames much of our analysis of financial statements. In concluding the module, we discuss the application of information garnered from financial statement analysis and business analysis to produce forecasts that are used in valuation. We include (in the appendix) a discussion of the regulatory environment that defines current financial reporting for companies.

The remainder of the book is organized around four key steps in financial statement analysis and valuation. These steps are portrayed graphically at the top of the next page. **Step 1** consists of Modules 1 and 2 where we develop an understanding of the business environment and company-reported accounting information. This helps answer the question: What is the setting in which the company operates? **Step 2** consists of Modules 3 and 4, which introduce both profitability and credit risk analysis, and Modules 5 through 10, which provide tools for adjusting and assessing financial statement information. This step is the core of financial statement analysis; allowing us to adjust financial statements as necessary to improve our analysis and better reflect business performance and financial condition. The adjustments and assessments answer the question: What is the company's current financial performance and condition? **Step 3** consists of Module 11, which applies our knowledge of the business environment and company's current status to form predictions about future financial performance and condition. Forecasting reflects our beliefs of where the company is heading. **Step 4** consists of Modules 12 through 15 and applies the forecasted information in a variety of valuation methods. The valuation estimates based on forecasted numbers help answer the question: What is the company worth? Implicit to all decision making in a business context should be an analysis of value or the change in value. This book teaches the explicit connections that allow us to estimate company value from financial information.

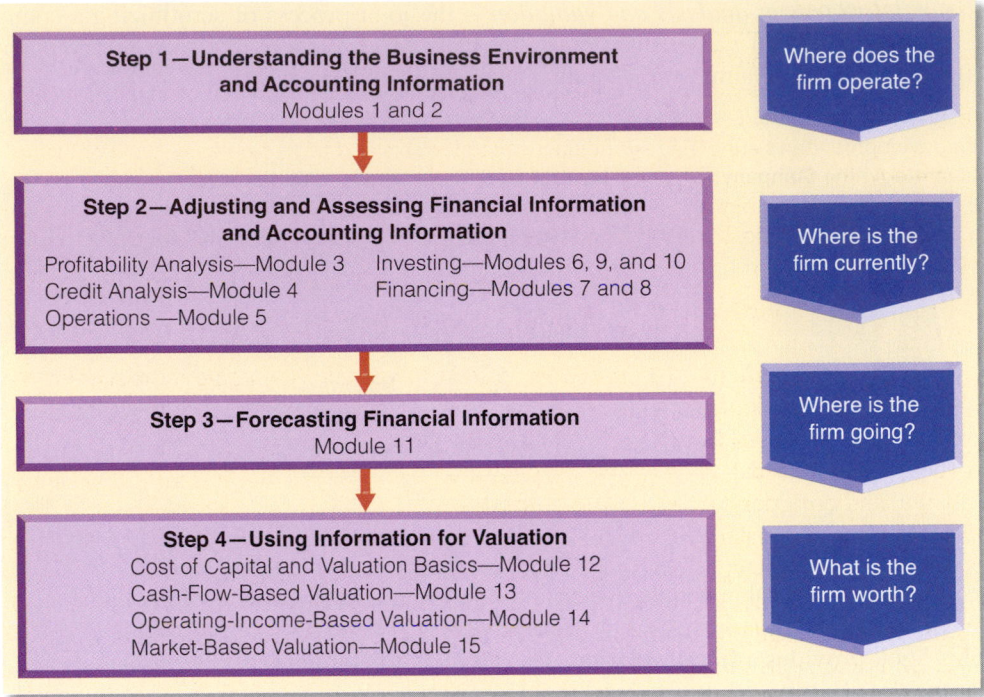

STEP 1—BUSINESS ENVIRONMENT AND ACCOUNTING INFORMATION

Reporting on Business Activities

To effectively analyze a company or infer its value, we must understand the company's business activities. Financial statements help us understand these business activities. These statements report on a company's performance and financial condition, and reveal executive management's privileged information and insights.

Financial statements satisfy the needs of different users. The functioning of the accounting information system involves application of accounting standards to produce financial statements. Effectively using this information system involves making judgments, assumptions, and estimates based on data contained in the financial reports. The greatest value we derive from this information system as users of financial reports is the insight we gain into the business activities of the company under analysis.

To effectively analyze and use accounting information, we must consider the business context in which the information is created—see Exhibit 1.1. Without exception, all companies *plan* business activities, *finance* those activities, *invest* in those activities, and then engage in *operating* activities. Companies conduct all these activities while confronting *business forces*, including market constraints and competitive pressures. Financial statements provide crucial input for strategic planning. They also provide information about the relative success of those plans, which can be used to take corrective action or make new operating, investing, and financing decisions.

Exhibit 1.1 depicts the business activities for a typical company. The outer (green) ring is the planning process that reflects the overarching goals and objectives of the company within which strategic decisions are made. Those strategic decisions involve company financing, asset management, and daily operations. **Apple, Inc.**, the focus company in Module 2, provides the following description of its business strategy in its annual report:

> **Business Strategy** The Company is committed to bringing the best user experience to its customers through its innovative hardware, software, peripherals, services, and Internet offerings. The Company's business strategy leverages its unique ability to design and develop its own

continued

continued from prior page

operating systems, hardware, application software, and services to provide its customers new products and solutions with superior ease-of-use, seamless integration, and innovative industrial design. The Company believes continual investment in research and development is critical to the development and enhancement of innovative products and technologies. In conjunction with its strategy, the Company continues to build and host a robust platform for the discovery and delivery of third-party digital content and applications through the iTunes Store... The Company is therefore uniquely positioned to offer superior and well-integrated digital lifestyle and productivity solutions.

A company's *strategic* (or *business*) *plan* reflects how it plans to achieve its goals and objectives. A plan's success depends on an effective analysis of market demand and supply. Specifically, a company must assess demand for its products and services, and assess the supply of its inputs (both labor and capital). The plan must also include competitive analyses, opportunity assessments, and consideration of business threats.

Historical financial statements provide insight into the success of a company's strategic plan, and are an important input to the planning process. These statements highlight portions of the strategic plan that proved profitable and, thus, warrant additional capital investment. They also reveal areas that are less effective, and provide information to help managers develop remedial action.

Once strategic adjustments are planned and implemented, the resulting financial statements provide input into the planning process for the following year; and this process begins again. Understanding a company's strategic plan helps focus our analysis of financial statements by placing them in proper context.

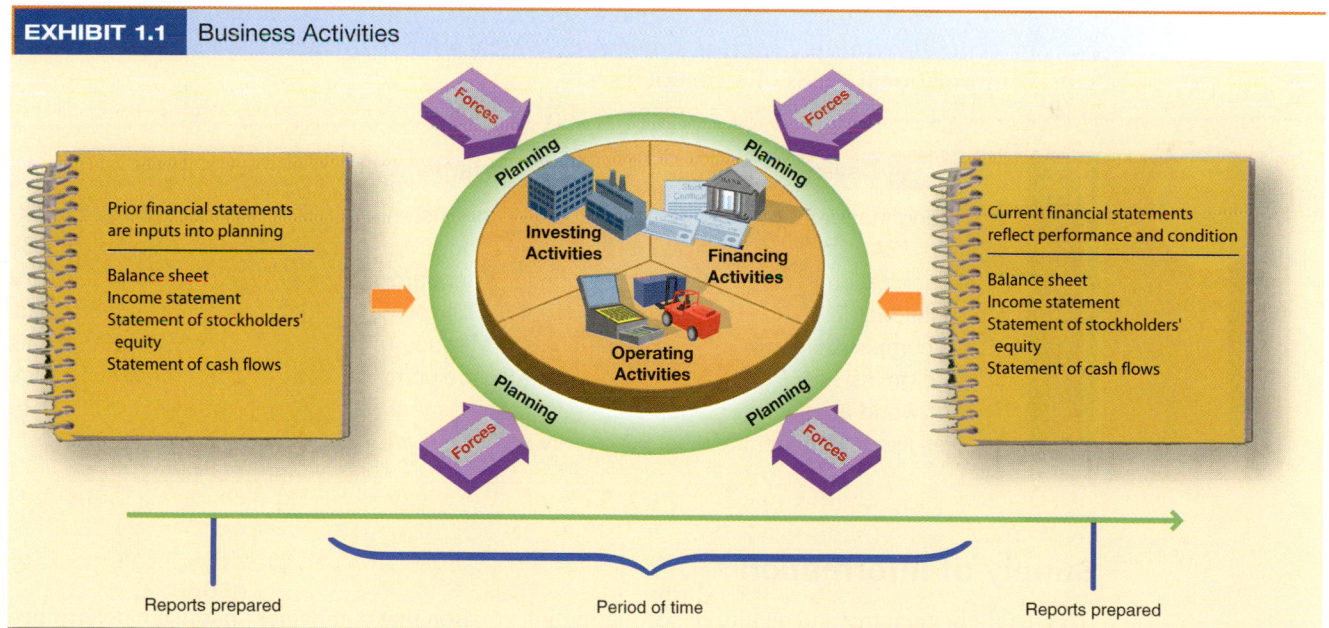

EXHIBIT 1.1 Business Activities

DEMAND FOR AND SUPPLY OF ACCOUNTING INFORMATION

Demand for financial statements has existed for centuries as a means to facilitate efficient contracting and risk-sharing. Decision makers and other stakeholders demand information on a company's past and prospective returns and risks. Supply of financial statements is driven by companies that wish to lower their costs of financing and less obvious costs such as political, contracting, and labor. Managers decide how much financial information to supply by weighing the costs of disclosure against the benefits of disclosure. Regulatory agencies

LO1 Identify and discuss the users and suppliers of financial statement information.

intervene in this process with various disclosure requirements that establish a minimum supply of information.

Demand for Information

The following broad classes of users possess a demand for financial accounting information:

- Managers and employees
- Investment analysts and information intermediaries
- Creditors and suppliers
- Shareholders and directors
- Customers and strategic partners
- Regulators and tax agencies
- Voters and their representatives

For their own well-being and future earnings potential, managers and employees demand accounting information on the financial condition, profitability, and prospects of their companies as well as comparative financial information on competing companies and business opportunities. Investment analysts and other information intermediaries, such as the financial press and business commentators, are interested in predicting companies' future performance. Banks and other lenders demand financial accounting information to help determine loan terms, loan amounts, interest rates, and required collateral. Shareholders and directors demand financial accounting information to assess the profitability and risks of companies. Customers (both current and potential) demand accounting information to assess a company's ability to provide products and/or services as agreed and to assess the company's staying power and reliability. Regulators (such as the SEC, the Federal Trade Commission, and the Federal Reserve Bank) and tax agencies demand accounting information for antitrust assessments, public protection, price setting, import-export analyses, and establishing tax policies. Voters and their representatives to national, state, and local governments demand accounting information for policy decisions. To satisfy these varying demands for and uses of financial information, companies prepare *general-purpose financial statements*, which refer to financial statements aimed to satisfy informational needs of a generic user.

IFRS INSIGHT   Development of International Standards

The accounting standards explained in this book are consistent with generally accepted accounting principles (GAAP) primarily developed by the Financial Accounting Standards Board (FASB). A similar organization, the International Accounting Standards Board (IASB), develops a global set of International Financial Reporting Standards (IFRS) for preparation of financial statements. To increase comparability of financial statements and reduce reporting complexity, the Securities Exchange Commission (SEC), the FASB, and the IASB are committed to a process of convergence to one set of world accounting standards. As we progress through the book, we will provide IFRS Insight boxes like this to identify differences between GAAP and IFRS.

Supply of Information

In general, the quantity and quality of accounting information that companies supply are determined by managers' assessment of the benefits and costs of disclosure. Managers release information provided the benefits of disclosing that information outweigh the costs of doing so. Both *regulation* and *bargaining power* affect disclosure costs and benefits and thus play roles in determining the supply of accounting information. Most areas of the world regulate the minimum levels of accounting disclosures. In the U.S., publicly traded firms must file financial accounting information with the Securities Exchange Commission (SEC). The two main compulsory SEC filings are:

- Form **10-K**: the audited annual report, which provides a comprehensive overview of the company for the past year; includes the four financial statements, discussed below, with explanatory notes and the management's discussion and analysis of financial results along with other important disclosures and for periods in addition to the past year.

- Form **10-Q**: the quarterly report, which provides an interim view of a company's financial position and performance; includes summary versions of the four financial statements and limited additional disclosures.

Additional common SEC financial filings are:

- Form **10-K/A** or **10-Q/A**: the "A" refers to an amended previously filed Form 10-K or 10-Q, respectively, usually due to an accounting change or error correction.

- Form **20-F**: submitted by all "foreign private issuers" to reconcile accounting statements to U.S. GAAP standards.

These forms are available electronically from the SEC Website (see Appendix 1A). The minimum, regulated level of information is not the standard. Both the quantity and quality of information differ across companies and over time. We need only look at several annual reports to see considerable variance in the amount and type of accounting information supplied. For example, differences abound on disclosures for segment operations, product performance reports, and financing activities. Further, some stakeholders possess ample bargaining power to obtain accounting information for themselves. These typically include private lenders and major suppliers and customers.

The information that companies make public is a rich source from which we perform our financial statement analysis. Our understanding of that information provides the basis for evaluating how the company has chosen to operate in its business environment, where the company is currently, and what it plans for the future. This analysis then shapes our expectations of the company's future (our forecasts). Still, as we use the information provided by the company, we must consider the benefits and costs that influence the company's disclosures.

Benefits of Disclosure

The benefits of supplying accounting information extend to a company's capital, labor, input, and output markets. Companies must compete in these markets. For example, capital markets provide debt and equity financing; the better a company's prospects, the lower is its cost of capital (as reflected in lower interest rates or higher stock prices). The same holds for a company's recruiting efforts in labor markets and its ability to establish superior supplier-customer relations in the input and output markets.

A company's performance in these markets depends on success with its business activities *and* the market's awareness of that success. Companies reap the benefits of disclosure with good news about their products, processes, management, and so forth. That is, there are real economic incentives for companies to disclose reliable (audited) accounting information enabling them to better compete in capital, labor, input, and output markets.

What inhibits companies from providing false or misleading good news? There are several constraints. An important constraint imposed by stakeholders is that of audit requirements and legal repercussions associated with inaccurate accounting information. Another relates to reputation effects from disclosures as subsequent events either support or refute earlier news.

Costs of Disclosure

The costs of supplying accounting information include its preparation and dissemination, competitive disadvantages, litigation potential, and political costs. Preparation and dissemination costs can be substantial, but companies have often already incurred those costs because managers need similar information for their own business decisions. The potential for information to yield competitive disadvantages is high. Companies are concerned that disclosures of their activities such as product or segment successes, strategic alliances or pursuits, technological or system innovations, and product or process quality improvements will harm their competitive advantages. Also, companies are frequently sued when disclosures create expectations that are not met. Highly visible companies often face political and public pressure, which creates "political costs." These companies often try to appear as if they do not generate excess profits. For example, government defense contractors, large software conglomerates, and oil companies are favorite targets of public scrutiny. Disclosure costs are higher for companies facing political costs.

The SEC adopted Regulation FD, or Reg FD for short, to curb the practice of selective disclosure by public companies (called *issuers* by the SEC) to certain shareholders and financial analysts. In the past, many companies disclosed important information in meetings and conference calls that excluded individual shareholders. The goal of this rule is to even the playing field for all investors. Reg FD reads as follows: "Whenever an issuer discloses any material nonpublic information regarding that issuer, the issuer shall make public disclosure of that information . . . simultaneously, in the case of an intentional disclosure; and . . . promptly, in the case of a non-intentional disclosure." Reg FD increased the cost of voluntary financial disclosure and led some companies to curtail the supply of financial information to all users.

International Accounting Standards and Convergence

The International Accounting Standards Board (IASB) oversees the development of accounting standards for a vast number of countries outside the U.S. More than 100 countries, including those in the European Union, require use of International Financial Reporting Standards (IFRS) developed by the IASB. For many years, IASB and the FASB operated as independent standard-setting bodies. In the early 2000s, pressure mounted for these two standard-setting organizations to collaborate and create one set of internationally acceptable standards. At a joint meeting in 2002, the FASB and the IASB each acknowledged their commitment to the development of high-quality, compatible accounting standards that could be used for both domestic and cross-border financial reporting. At that meeting, both the FASB and IASB pledged to use their best efforts to (a) make their existing financial reporting standards fully compatible as soon as practicable and (b) to coordinate their future work programs to ensure that once achieved, compatibility is maintained.

In May 2011, the SEC proposed a transition method to incorporate IFRS into the U.S. reporting system. The SEC delineated the perceived benefits and risks of this possibility but did not lay out a definitive timeline for use of IFRS in the U.S. Larger companies have begun to issue IFRS compliant financial statements, and foreign private issuers on U.S. stock exchanges are currently permitted to file financial statements in accordance with IFRS without reconciliation to U.S. GAAP as was previously required.

Are financial statements issued under IFRS substantially different from those issued under U.S. GAAP? At a broad level, the answer is no. Both are prepared using accrual accounting and utilize similar conceptual frameworks. Both require the same set of financial statements: a balance sheet, an income statement, a statement of cash flows, a statement of stockholders' equity, and a set of explanatory footnotes. That does not mean that no differences exist. However, the differences are typically technical in nature, and do not differ on broad principles discussed in this book. Indeed, recent accounting standards issued by the FASB and the IASB, such as the accounting for acquisitions of companies, were developed jointly and issued simultaneously to minimize differences as the two standard-setting bodies work toward harmonization of international standards.

At the end of each module, we summarize key differences between U.S. GAAP and IFRS. Also, there are a variety of sources that provide more detailed and technical analysis of similarities and differences between U.S. GAAP and IFRS. The FASB, the IASB, and each of the "Big 4" accounting firms also maintain Websites devoted to this issue. Search under IFRS and PwC, KPMG, EY and Deloitte; the two standard-setting bodies also provide useful information, see: FASB (**www.fasb.org/intl/**) and IASB (**www.iasb.org/Home.htm**).

BUSINESS INSIGHT   **Accounting Quality**

In the bear market that followed the bursting of the dot-com bubble in the early 2000s, and amid a series of corporate scandals such as **Enron**, **Tyco**, and **WorldCom**, Congress passed the ***Sarbanes-Oxley Act,*** often referred to as *SOX*. SOX sought to rectify perceived problems in accounting, including weak audit committees and deficient internal controls. Increased scrutiny of financial reporting and internal controls has had some success. A report by **Glass, Lewis and Co.**, a corporate-governance research firm, shows that the number of financial restatements by publicly traded companies surged to a record 1,295 in 2005—which is one restatement for each 12 public companies, and more than triple the 2002 total, the year SOX passed. The Glass, Lewis and Co. report concluded that "when so many companies produce inaccurate financial statements, it seriously calls into question the quality of information that investors relied upon to make capital-allocation decisions" (**CFO.Com**). Bottom line: we must be critical readers of financial reports.

Review of Financial Statements

Companies use four financial statements to periodically report on business activities. These statements are the: balance sheet, income statement, statement of stockholders' equity, and statement of cash flows. Exhibit 1.2 shows how these statements are linked across time. A balance sheet reports on a company's financial position at a *point in time*. The income statement, statement of stockholders' equity, and the statement of cash flows report on performance over a *period of time*. The three statements in the middle of Exhibit 1.2 (period-of-time statements) link the balance sheet from the beginning to the end of a period.

LO2 Identify and explain the four financial statements, and define the accounting equation.

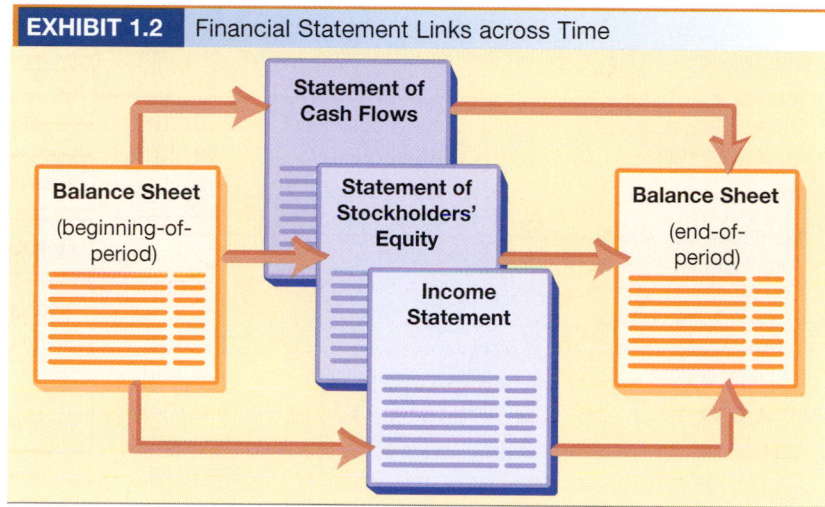

EXHIBIT 1.2   Financial Statement Links across Time

A one-year, or annual, reporting period is common and is called the *accounting,* or *fiscal, year.* Of course, firms prepare financial statements more frequently; semiannual, quarterly, and monthly financial statements are common. *Calendar-year* companies have reporting periods beginning on January 1 and ending on December 31. **Berkshire Hathaway** is a calendar-year company. Some companies choose a fiscal year ending on a date other than December 31, such as when sales and inventory are low. For example, **Best Buy**'s fiscal year-end is always near February 1, after the busy holiday season.

Balance Sheet

A balance sheet reports a company's financial position at a point in time. The balance sheet reports the company's *resources (assets)*, namely, what the company owns. The balance sheet also reports the *sources* of asset financing. There are two ways a company can finance its assets. It can raise money from shareholders; this is *owner financing*. It can also raise money from banks or other creditors and suppliers; this is *nonowner financing*. This means that both owners and nonowners hold claims on company assets. Owner claims on assets are referred to as *equity* and nonowner claims are referred to as *liabilities* (or debt). Since all financing must be invested in something, we obtain the following basic relation: *investing equals financing*. This equality is called the **accounting equation,** which follows:

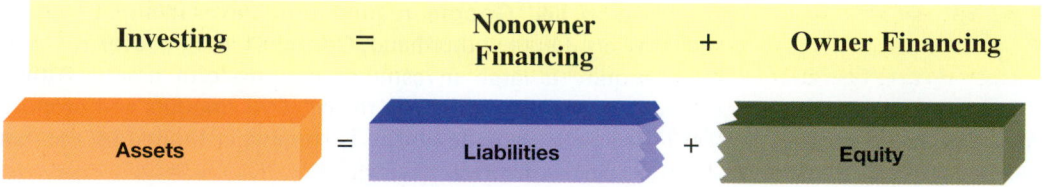

Investing	=	Nonowner Financing	+	Owner Financing
Assets	=	Liabilities	+	Equity

The accounting equation works for all companies at all points in time.

The balance sheet for **Berkshire Hathaway** is in Exhibit 1.3 (condensed). Refer to this balance sheet to verify the following amounts: assets = $372,229 million; liabilities = $209,295 million; and equity = \$162,934 million. Assets equal liabilities plus equity, which reflects the accounting equation: investing equals financing.

Investing Activities

Balance sheets are organized like the accounting equation. Investing activities are represented by the company's assets. These assets are financed by a combination of nonowner financing (liabilities) and owner financing (equity).

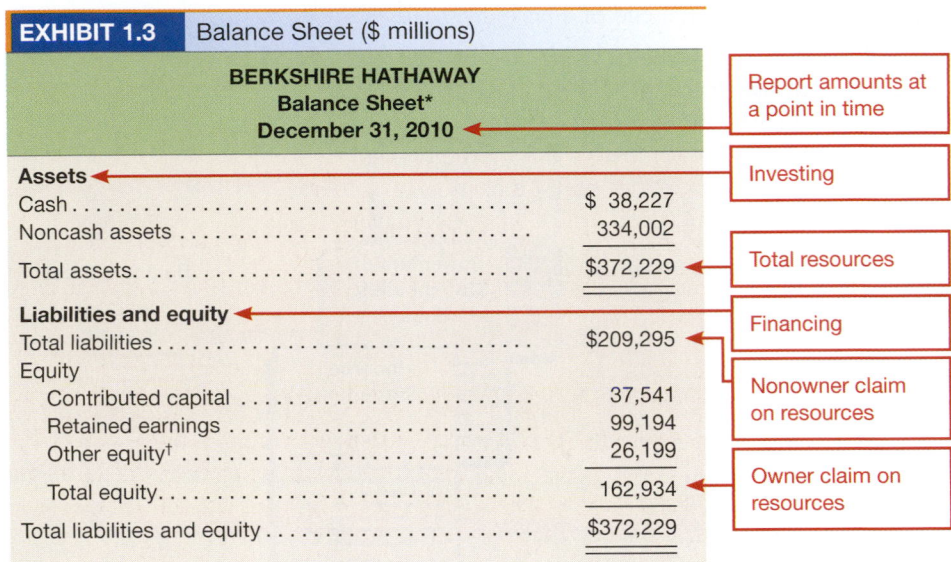

EXHIBIT 1.3   Balance Sheet ($ millions)

BERKSHIRE HATHAWAY
Balance Sheet*
December 31, 2010 ← Report amounts at a point in time

Assets ←	Investing	
Cash		$ 38,227
Noncash assets		334,002
Total assets	← Total resources	$372,229
Liabilities and equity ←	Financing	
Total liabilities	← Nonowner claim on resources	$209,295
Equity		
Contributed capital		37,541
Retained earnings		99,194
Other equity†		26,199
Total equity	← Owner claim on resources	162,934
Total liabilities and equity		$372,229

* Financial statement titles often begin with the word *consolidated*. This means that the financial statement includes a parent company and one or more subsidiaries, companies that the parent company owns.

† For Berkshire Hathaway, other equity includes accumulated other comprehensive income and noncontrolling interests.

For simplicity, Berkshire Hathaway's balance sheet in Exhibit 1.3 categorizes assets into cash and noncash assets. Noncash assets consist of several asset categories (Module 2 explains the composition of noncash assets). These categories are listed in order of their nearness to cash. For example, companies own a category of assets called inventories. These are goods that the company intends to sell to its customers. Inventories are converted into cash when they are sold within a short period of time. Hence, they are classified as short-term assets. Companies also report a category of assets called property, plant and equipment. This category includes a company's office buildings or manufacturing facilities. Property, plant and equipment assets will be held for an extended period of time and are, therefore, generally classified as long-term assets.

The relative proportion of short-term and long-term assets is largely determined by a company's business model. This is evident in the graph to the side that depicts the relative proportion of short- and long-term assets for several companies that we feature in this book. Companies such as **Cisco** and **Google** require little investment in long-term assets. On the other hand, **Comcast** and **Procter & Gamble** require a large investment in long-term assets. Although managers can influence the relative amounts and proportion of assets, their flexibility is somewhat limited by the nature of their industries.

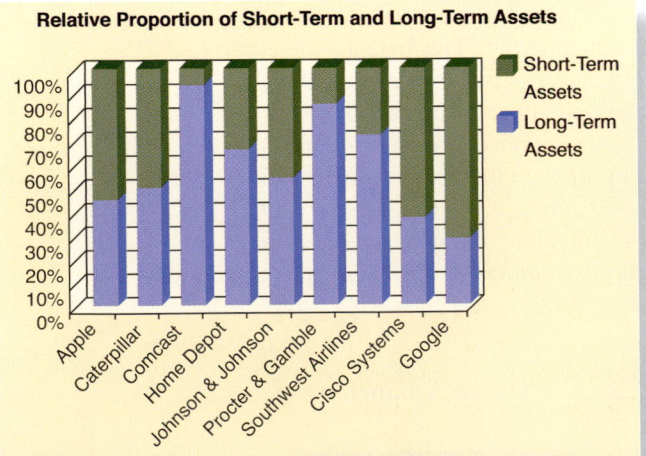

Relative Proportion of Short-Term and Long-Term Assets

■ Short-Term Assets
■ Long-Term Assets

(Apple, Caterpillar, Comcast, Home Depot, Johnson & Johnson, Procter & Gamble, Southwest Airlines, Cisco Systems, Google)

Financing Activities

Assets must be paid for, and funding is provided by a combination of owner and nonowner financing. Owner (or equity) financing includes resources contributed to the company by its owners along with any profit retained by the company. Nonowner (creditor or debt) financing is borrowed money. We distinguish between these two financing sources for a reason: borrowed money entails a legal obligation to repay amounts owed, and failure to do so can result in severe consequences for the borrower. Equity financing entails no such legal obligation for repayment.

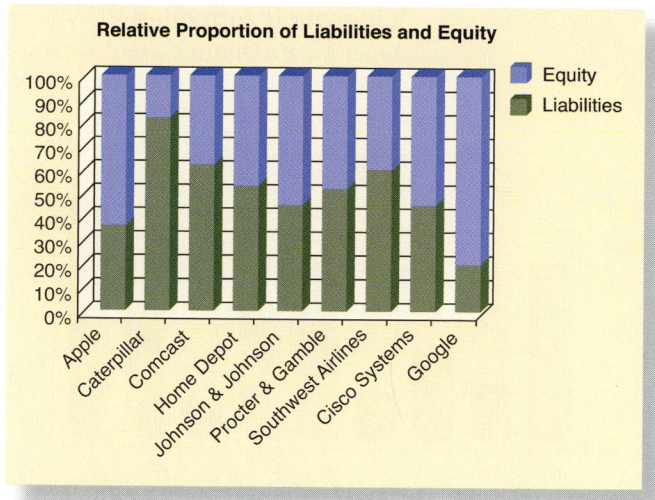

The relative proportion of nonowner (liabilities) and owner (equity) financing is largely determined by a company's business model. This is evident in the graph to the side, again citing many of the companies we feature as focus companies in this book. **Google** is a relatively new company that is expanding into new markets. Its business model is, therefore, more risky than that of a more established company operating in relatively stable markets. Google cannot afford to take on additional risk of higher nonowner financing levels. On the other hand, **Caterpillar's** cash flows are relatively stable. It can operate with more nonowner financing.

IFRS INSIGHT	**Balance Sheet Presentation and IFRS**

Balance sheets prepared under IFRS tend to classify accounts in reverse order of liquidity (lack of nearness to cash). For example, intangible assets are typically listed first and cash is listed last among assets. Also, equity is typically listed before liabilities, where liabilities are again listed in order of decreasing liquidity.

Income Statement

An **income statement** reports on a company's performance over a period of time and lists amounts for revenues (also called sales) and expenses. Revenues less expenses yield the bottom-line net income amount. **Berkshire Hathaway**'s income statement is in Exhibit 1.4. Refer to its income statement to verify the following: revenues = $136,185 million; expenses = $123,218 million; and net income = $12,967 million. Net income reflects the profit (also called earnings) to owners for that specific period.

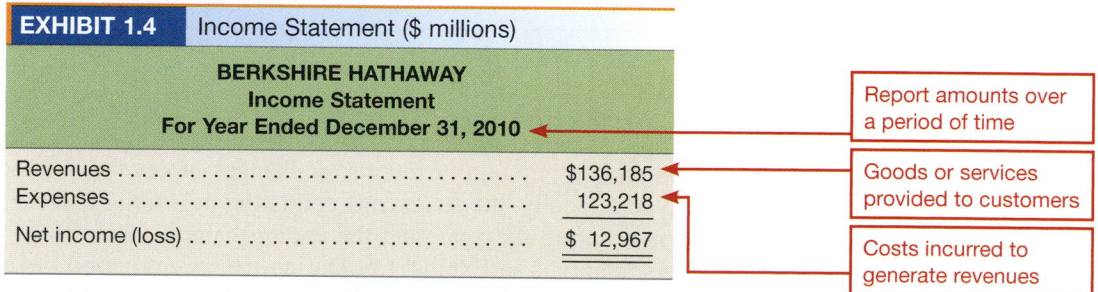

EXHIBIT 1.4	Income Statement ($ millions)

BERKSHIRE HATHAWAY
Income Statement
For Year Ended December 31, 2010

Revenues	$136,185
Expenses	123,218
Net income (loss)	$ 12,967

Report amounts over a period of time

Goods or services provided to customers

Costs incurred to generate revenues

Manufacturing and merchandising companies typically include an additional expense account, called cost of goods sold (or cost of sales), in the income statement following revenues. It is also common to report a subtotal called gross profit (or gross margin), which is revenues less cost of goods sold. The company's remaining expenses are then reported below gross profit. This income statement layout follows:

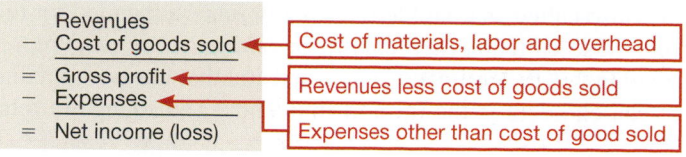

	Revenues
−	Cost of goods sold	← Cost of materials, labor and overhead
=	Gross profit	← Revenues less cost of goods sold
−	Expenses	← Expenses other than cost of good sold
=	Net income (loss)	

Operating Activities

Operating activities use company resources to produce, promote, and sell its products and services. These activities extend from input markets involving suppliers of materials and labor to a company's output markets involving customers of products and services. Input markets generate most *expenses* (or *costs*) such as inventory, salaries, materials, and logistics. Output markets generate *revenues* (or *sales*) to customers. Output markets also generate some expenses such as marketing and distributing products and services to customers. Net income arises when revenues exceed expenses. A loss occurs when expenses exceed revenues.

Differences exist in the relative profitability of companies across industries. Although effective management can increase the profitability of a company, business models play a large part in determining company profitability. These differences are illustrated in the graph (to the side) of net income as a percentage of sales for several companies.

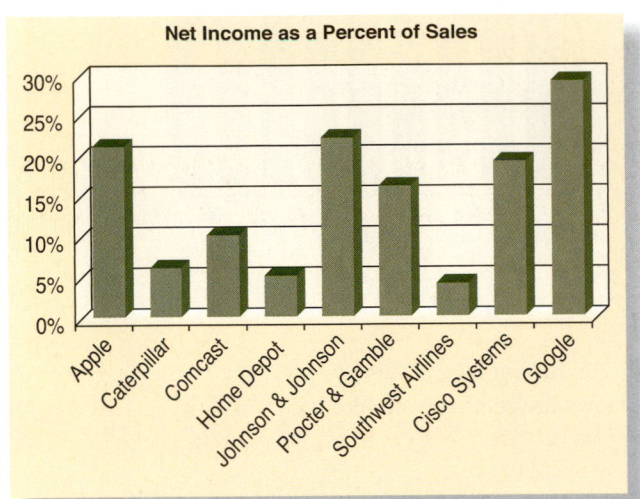

Net Income as a Percent of Sales

Home Depot operates in a mature industry with little ability to differentiate its products from those of its competitors. Hence, its net income as a percentage of sales is low. **Southwest Airlines** faces a different kind of problem: having competitors that are desperate and trying to survive. Profitability will not return to the transportation industry until weaker competitors are no longer protected by bankruptcy courts. At the other end of the spectrum are **Apple**, **Cisco Systems** and **Google**. All three are dominant in their industries with products protected by patent laws. Their profitability levels are more akin to that of monopolists.

BUSINESS INSIGHT | **Warren Buffett on Financial Reports**

"When Charlie and I read reports, we have no interest in pictures of personnel, plants or products. References to EBITDA [earnings before interest, taxes, depreciation and amortization] make us shudder—does management think the tooth fairy pays for capital expenditures? We're very suspicious of accounting methodology that is vague or unclear, since too often that means management wishes to hide something. And we don't want to read messages that a public relations department or consultant has turned out. Instead, we expect a company's CEO to explain in his or her own words what's happening." —Berkshire Hathaway annual report

---

Statement of Stockholders' Equity

The **statement of stockholders' equity** reports on changes in key types of equity over a period of time. For each type of equity, the statement reports the beginning balance, a summary of the activity in the account during the year, and the ending balance. **Berkshire Hathaway**'s statement of stockholders' equity is in Exhibit 1.5. During the recent period, its equity changed due to share issuances and income reinvestment. Berkshire Hathaway classifies these changes into three categories:

- *Contributed capital*, the stockholders' net contributions to the company
- *Retained earnings*, net income over the life of the company minus all dividends ever paid
- *Other*, consists of amounts that we explain later in the book

Contributed capital represents the cash the company received from the sale of stock to stockholders (also called shareholders), less any funds expended for the repurchase of stock. Retained earnings (also called *earned capital* or *reinvested capital*) represent the cumulative total amount of income that the company has earned and that has been retained in the business and not distributed to shareholders in the form of dividends. The change in retained earnings links consecutive bal-

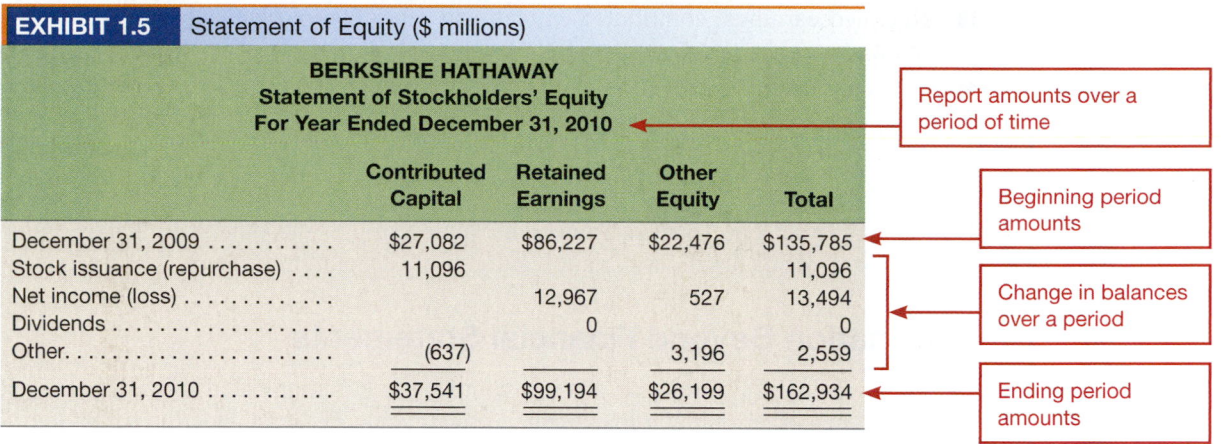

EXHIBIT 1.5 Statement of Equity ($ millions)

BERKSHIRE HATHAWAY
Statement of Stockholders' Equity
For Year Ended December 31, 2010

	Contributed Capital	Retained Earnings	Other Equity	Total
December 31, 2009	$27,082	$86,227	$22,476	$135,785
Stock issuance (repurchase)	11,096			11,096
Net income (loss)		12,967	527	13,494
Dividends		0		0
Other.	(637)		3,196	2,559
December 31, 2010	$37,541	$99,194	$26,199	$162,934

Report amounts over a period of time

Beginning period amounts

Change in balances over a period

Ending period amounts

ance sheets via the income statement: Ending retained earnings = Beginning retained earnings + Net income − Dividends. For Berkshire Hathaway, its recent year's retained earnings increases from $86,227 million to $99,194 million. This increase of $12,967 million is explained by its net income of $12,967 million as Berkshire Hathaway paid no dividends in 2010.

Statement of Cash Flows

The **statement of cash flows** reports the change (either an increase or a decrease) in a company's cash balance over a period of time. The statement reports on cash inflows and outflows from operating, investing, and financing activities over a period of time. Berkshire Hathaway's statement of cash flows is in Exhibit 1.6. Its cash balance increased by $7,669 million in the recent period: operating activities generated a $17,895 million cash inflow, investing activities reduced cash by $18,277 million, and financing activities yielded a cash inflow of $8,051 million.

Berkshire Hathaway's operating cash flow of $17,895 million does not equal its $12,967 million net income. Generally, a company's net cash flow for a period does *not* equal its net income for the period. This is due to timing differences between when revenue and expense items are recognized on the income statement and when cash is received and paid. (We discuss this concept further in subsequent modules.)

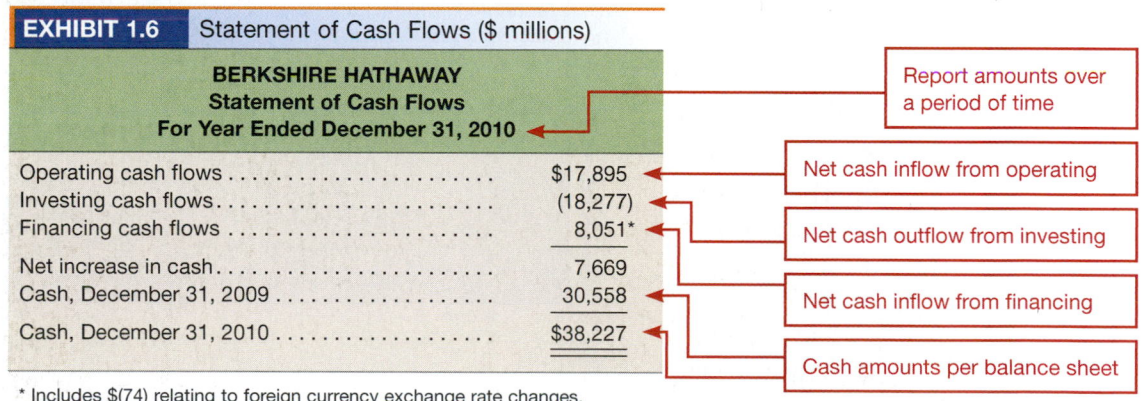

EXHIBIT 1.6 Statement of Cash Flows ($ millions)

BERKSHIRE HATHAWAY
Statement of Cash Flows
For Year Ended December 31, 2010

Operating cash flows	$17,895
Investing cash flows.	(18,277)
Financing cash flows	8,051*
Net increase in cash.	7,669
Cash, December 31, 2009	30,558
Cash, December 31, 2010	$38,227

* Includes $(74) relating to foreign currency exchange rate changes.

Report amounts over a period of time

Net cash inflow from operating

Net cash outflow from investing

Net cash inflow from financing

Cash amounts per balance sheet

Financial Statement Linkages

The four financial statements are linked within and across periods—consider the following:

■ The income statement and the balance sheet are linked via retained earnings. For Berkshire Hathaway, the $12,967 million increase in retained earnings (reported on the balance sheet) equals its net income (reported on the income statement) (see Exhibit 1.5). Berkshire Hathaway did not pay dividends in 2010.

- Retained earnings, contributed capital, and other equity balances appear both on the statement of stockholders' equity and the balance sheet.

- The statement of cash flows is linked to the income statement as net income is a component of operating cash flow. The statement of cash flows is also linked to the balance sheet as the change in the balance sheet cash account reflects the net cash inflows and outflows for the period.

Items that impact one financial statement ripple through the others. Linkages among the four financial statements are an important feature of the accounting system.

Information Beyond Financial Statements

Important financial information about a company is communicated to various decision makers through means other than the four financial statements. These include the following:

- Management Discussion and Analysis (MD&A)
- Independent Auditor Report
- Financial statement footnotes
- Regulatory filings, including proxy statements and other SEC filings

We describe and explain the usefulness of these additional information sources throughout the book.

Analyzing the Competitive Environment

LO3 Describe business analysis within the context of a competitive environment.

To understand a company we must "know the business." A way to formalize that knowledge is through use of Porter's *value-chain model* (see Porter, *Competitive Advantage: Creating and Sustaining Superior Performance*, 1985, and the graphic below). Analysis using the value-chain seeks to identify and understand the activities that create a company's profit margin. Primary activities are:

- Inbound logistics
- Operations
- Outbound logistics
- Marketing and sales
- Servicing

Support activities are:

- Firm infrastructure
- Human resource management
- Technology/ product development
- Procurement

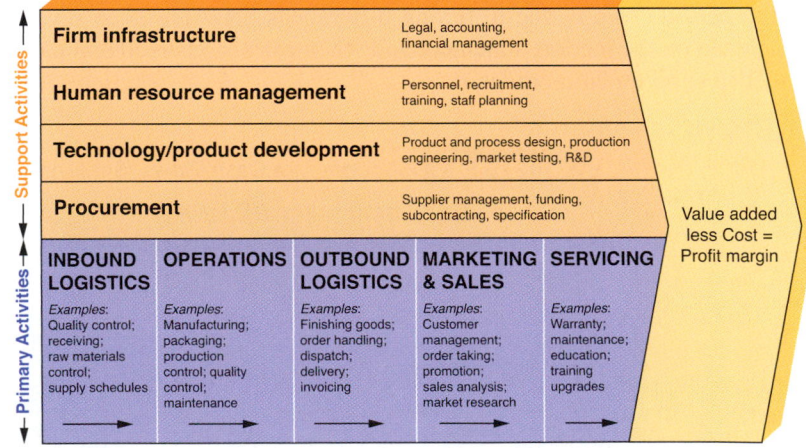

The results of these activities manifest themselves in a company's financial statements and the supporting documents.

A company's primary and support activities are not carried out in isolation but are, instead, influenced by five important forces that confront the company and determine its competitive intensity: (A) industry competition, (B) buyer power, (C) supplier power, (D) product substitutes, and (E) threat of entry (for further discussion, see Porter, *Competitive Strategy: Techniques for Analyzing Industries and Competitors,* 1980 and 1998).

| EXHIBIT 1.7 | Competitive Forces within the Broader Business Environment |

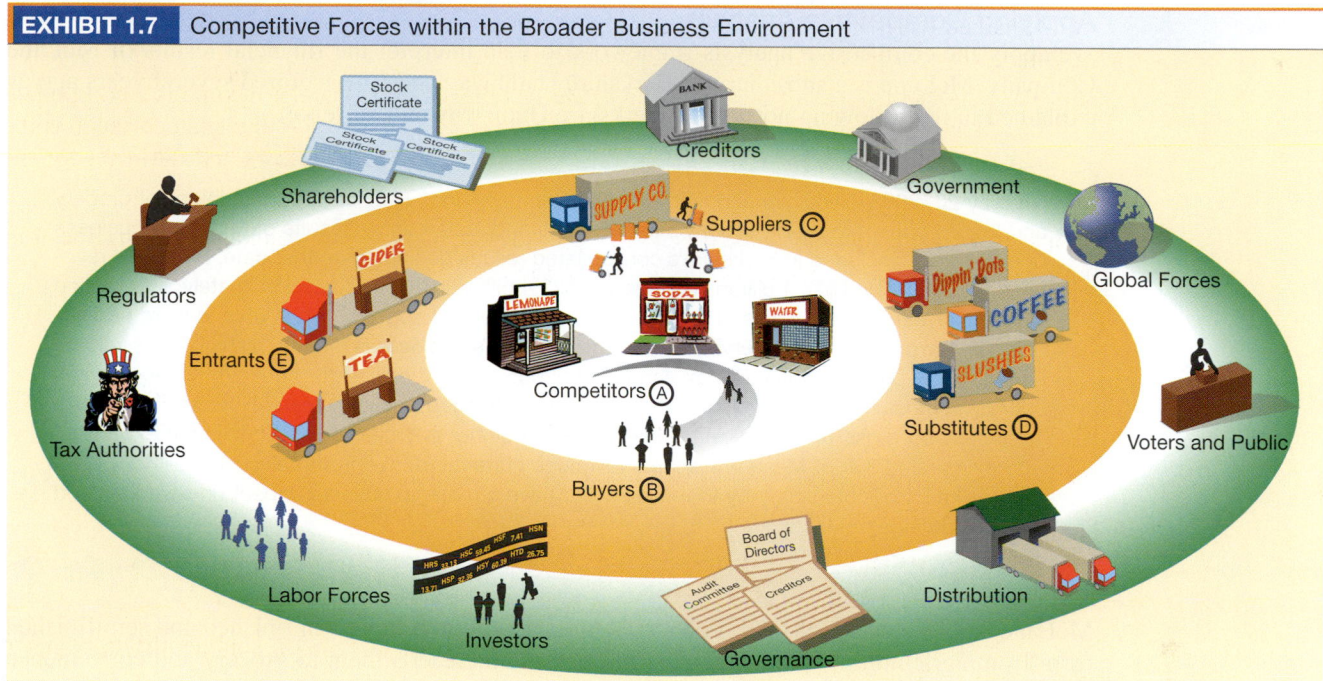

These five forces are depicted graphically in Exhibit 1.7 and are key determinants of profitability.

(A) **Industry competition** Competition and rivalry raise the cost of doing business as companies must hire and train competitive workers, advertise products, research and develop products, and engage in other related activities.

(B) **Bargaining power of buyers** Buyers with strong bargaining power can extract price concessions and demand a higher level of service and delayed payment terms; this force reduces both profits from sales and the operating cash flows to sellers.

(C) **Bargaining power of suppliers** Suppliers with strong bargaining power can demand higher prices and earlier payments, yielding adverse effects on profits and cash flows to buyers.

(D) **Threat of substitution** As the number of product substitutes increases, sellers have less power to raise prices and/or pass on costs to buyers; accordingly, threat of substitution places downward pressure on profits of sellers.

(E) **Threat of entry** New market entrants increase competition; to mitigate that threat, companies expend monies on activities such as new technologies, promotion, and human development to erect *barriers to entry* and to create *economies of scale*.

The broader business environment affects the level of profitability that a company can expect to achieve. Global economic forces and the quality and cost of labor affect the macroeconomy in which the company operates. Government regulation, borrowing agreements exacted by creditors, and internal governance procedures also affect the range of operating activities in which a company can engage. In addition, strategic plans are influenced by the oversight of equity markets, and investors are loathe to allow companies the freedom to manage for the longer term. Each of these external forces affects a company's strategic planning and expected level of profitability.

The relative strength of companies within their industries, and vis-à-vis suppliers and customers, is an important determinant of both their profitability and the structure of their balance sheets. As competition intensifies, profitability likely declines, and the amount of assets companies need to carry on their balance sheet likely increases in an effort to generate more profit. Such changes are revealed in the income statement and the balance sheet.

Applying Competitive Analysis

We apply the competitive analysis framework to help interpret the financial results of McLane Company. McLane is a subsidiary of Berkshire Hathaway and was acquired several years ago as explained in the following note to the Berkshire Hathaway annual report:

On May 23, 2003, Berkshire acquired McLane Company, Inc., ("McLane") a distributor of grocery and food products to retailers, convenience stores and restaurants. Results of McLane's business operations are included in Berkshire's consolidated results beginning on that date. McLane's revenues in 2005 totaled $24.1 billion compared to $23.4 billion in 2004 and approximately $22.0 billion for the full year of 2003. Sales of grocery products increased about 5% in 2005 and were partially offset by lower sales to foodservice customers. McLane's business is marked by high sales volume and very low profit margins. Pretax earnings in 2005 of $217 million declined $11 million versus 2004. The gross margin percentage was relatively unchanged between years. However, the resulting increased gross profit was more than offset by higher payroll, fuel and insurance expenses. Approximately 33% of McLane's annual revenues currently derive from sales to Wal-Mart. Loss or curtailment of purchasing by Wal-Mart could have a material adverse impact on revenues and pre-tax earnings of McLane.

McLane is a wholesaler of food products; it purchases food products in finished and semifinished form from agricultural and food-related businesses and resells them to grocery and convenience food stores. The extensive distribution network required in this business entails considerable investment. Our business analysis of McLane's financial results includes the following observations:

- **Industry competitors** McLane has many competitors with food products that are difficult to differentiate.

- **Bargaining power of buyers** The note above reveals that 33% of McLane's sales are to Wal-Mart, which has considerable buying power that limits seller profits; also, the food industry is characterized by high turnover and low profit margins, which implies that cost control is key to success.

- **Bargaining power of suppliers** McLane is large ($24 billion in annual sales), which implies its suppliers are unlikely to exert forces to increase its cost of sales.

- **Threat of substitution** Grocery items are usually not well differentiated; this means the threat of substitution is high, which inhibits its ability to raise selling prices.

- **Threat of entry** High investment costs, such as warehousing and logistics, are a barrier to entry in McLane's business; this means the threat of entry is relatively low.

Our analysis reveals that McLane is a high-volume, low-margin company. Its ability to control costs is crucial to its financial performance, including its ability to fully utilize its assets. Evaluation of McLane's financial statements should focus on that dimension.

Analyzing the Broader Business Environment

Quality analysis depends on an effective business analysis. Before we analyze a single accounting number, we must ask questions about a company's business environment such as the following:

- *Life cycle* At what stage in its life is this company? Is it a startup, experiencing growing pains? Is it strong and mature, reaping the benefits of competitive advantages? Is it nearing the end of its life, trying to milk what it can from stagnant product lines?

- *Outputs* What products does it sell? Are its products new, established, or dated? Do its products have substitutes? How complicated are its products to produce?

- *Buyers* Who are its buyers? Are buyers in good financial condition? Do buyers have substantial purchasing power? Can the seller dictate sales terms to buyers?

- *Inputs* Who are its suppliers? Are there many supply sources? Does the company depend on a few supply sources with potential for high input costs?

- *Competition* In what kind of markets does it operate? Are markets open? Is the market competitive? Does the company have competitive advantages? Can it protect itself from new entrants? At what cost? How must it compete to survive?

- *Financing* Must it seek financing from public markets? Is it going public? Is it seeking to use its stock to acquire another company? Is it in danger of defaulting on debt covenants? Are there incentives to tell an overly optimistic story to attract lower cost financing or to avoid default on debt?

- *Labor* Who are its managers? What are their backgrounds? Can they be trusted? Are they competent? What is the state of employee relations? Is labor unionized?

- *Governance* How effective is its corporate governance? Does it have a strong and independent board of directors? Does a strong audit committee of the board exist, and is it populated with outsiders? Does management have a large portion of its wealth tied to the company's stock?

- *Risk* Is it subject to lawsuits from competitors or shareholders? Is it under investigation by regulators? Has it changed auditors? If so, why? Are its auditors independent? Does it face environmental and/or political risks?

SWOT Analysis of the Business Environment

As an alternative to Porter-based competitive analysis, some prefer a SWOT analysis of a company. SWOT is an acronym that stands for Strength, Weakness, Opportunities and Threats. This analysis can be applied to almost any organization. This approach is universally applicable and easy to apply, and can be graphically portrayed as follows:

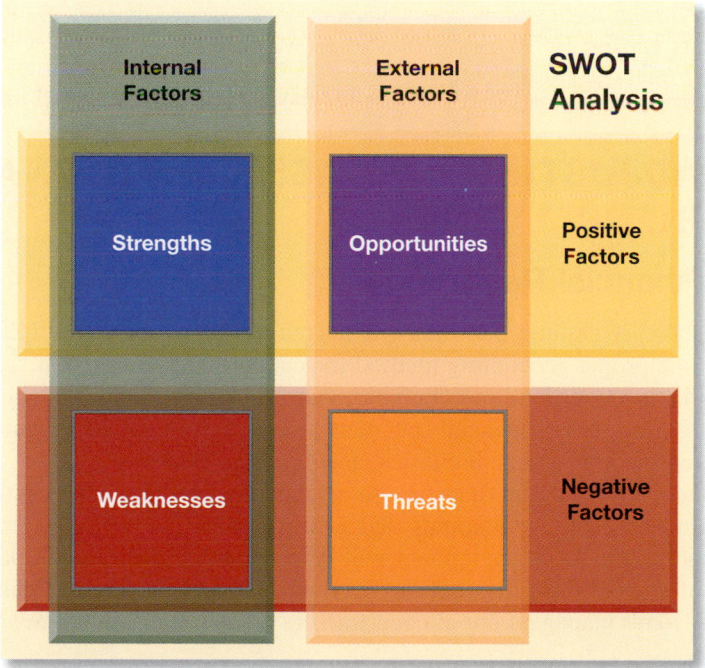

SWOT analysis has two parts. Looking internally, we review a company's Strengths and Weaknesses, while for external purposes we review the Opportunities of and Threats to the company. SWOT analysis then tries to understand particular Strengths and Weaknesses that give rise to specific Opportunities (to exploit the Strengths) and Threats (caused by the Weaknesses). When used as part of an overall strategic analysis, SWOT can provide a good review of strategic options. However, SWOT is sometimes criticized as too subjective. Two individuals can identify entirely different factors from a SWOT analysis of the same company. This is partly because SWOT is intuitive and allows varying opinions on the relevant factors.

In sum, we must assess the broader business context in which a company operates as we read and interpret its financial statements. A review of financial statements, which reflect business activities, cannot be undertaken in a vacuum. It is contextual and can only be effectively undertaken within the framework of a thorough understanding of the broader forces that impact company performance. We should view the above questions as a sneak preview of the types we will ask and answer throughout this book when we read and interpret financial statements for purposes of forecasting and valuation.

MID-MODULE REVIEW

The following financial information is from **Allstate Corporation**, a competitor of Berkshire Hathaway's GEICO Insurance, for the year ended December 31, 2010 ($ millions).

Cash, ending year	$ 562
Cash flows from operations	3,689
Revenues	31,400
Stockholders' equity	19,044
Cash flows from financing	(6,071)
Total liabilities	111,830
Expenses	30,427
Noncash assets	130,312
Cash flows from investing	2,332
Net income	928
Cash, beginning year	612

Required

1. Prepare an income statement, balance sheet, and statement of cash flows for Allstate at December 31, 2010.
2. Compare the balance sheet and income statement of Allstate to those of Berkshire Hathaway in Exhibits 1.3 and 1.4. What differences do we observe?

The solution is on page 1-42.

STEP 2—ADJUSTING AND ASSESSING FINANCIAL INFORMATION

Choices in Financial Reporting

Some people mistakenly assume that financial accounting is an exact discipline—that is, companies select the one proper accounting method to account for a transaction, and then follow the rules. The reality is that GAAP allows companies choices in preparing financial statements. The choice of methods often yields financial statements that are markedly different from one another in terms of reported income, assets, liabilities, and equity amounts.

People often are surprised that financial statements comprise numerous estimates. For example, companies must estimate the amounts that will eventually be collected from customers, the length of time that buildings and equipment will be productive, the value impairments of assets, the future costs of warranty claims, and the eventual payouts on pension plans. Following are examples of how some managers are alleged to have abused the latitude available in reporting financial results.

Company	Allegations
Adelphia Communications (ADELQ)	Founding Rigas family collected $3.1 billion in off-balance-sheet loans backed by Adelphia; it overstated results by inflating capital expenses and hiding debt.
Bristol-Myers Squibb (BMY)	Inflated its 2001 revenue by $1.5 billion by "channel stuffing," or forcing wholesalers to accept more inventory than they could sell to get inventory off Bristol-Myers' books.

continued

continued from prior page

Enron	Created profits and hid debt totaling over $1 billion by improperly using off-the-books partnerships; manipulated the Texas power market; bribed foreign governments to win contracts abroad; manipulated California energy market.
Global Crossing (GLBC)	Engaged in network capacity "swaps" with other carriers to inflate revenue; shredded documents related to accounting practices.
Green Mountain Coffee Roasters (GMCR)	In 2011 Q2, beat the consensus earnings forecast by a wide margin due to recording an unusual negative accrual for sales returns of over $22 million.
Halliburton (HAL)	Improperly booked $100 million in annual construction cost overruns before customers agreed to pay for them.
Qwest Communications International (Q)	Inflated revenue using network capacity "swaps" and improper accounting for long-term deals.
Sears Holding Company (SHLD)	Markedly increased its allowance for uncollectible accounts in a year when earnings were high; in subsequent years when earnings were low, reversals of the allowance allowed it to prop up earnings at a time when losses in its credit card unit were soaring.
Time Warner (TWX)	As the ad market faltered and AOL's purchase of Time Warner loomed, AOL inflated sales by booking revenue for barter deals and ads it sold for third parties. These questionable revenues boosted growth rates and sealed the deal. AOL also boosted sales via "round-trip" deals with advertisers and suppliers.
WorldCom	Overstated cash flow by booking $11 billion in operating expenses as capital costs; loaned founder Bernard Ebbers $400 million off-the-books.

Accounting standard setters walk a fine line regarding choice in accounting. On one hand, they are concerned that choice in preparing financial statements will lead to abuse by those seeking to gain by influencing decisions of financial statement users. On the other hand, standard setters are concerned that companies are too diverse for a "one size fits all" financial accounting system.

Enron exemplifies the problems that accompany rigid accounting standards. A set of accounting standards relating to special purpose entities (SPEs) provided preparers with guidelines under which those entities were or were not to be consolidated. Unfortunately, once the SPE guidelines were set, some people worked diligently to structure SPE transactions so as to narrowly avoid the consolidation requirements and achieve *off-balance-sheet* financing. This is just one example of how, with rigid standards, companies can adhere to the letter of the rule, but not its intent. In such situations, the financial statements are not fairly presented. When financial statements are not fairly presented, it frustrates our attempt at determining where the company is currently. This leads to reductions in our ability to accurately determine where the company is going and impacts our estimate of what the company is worth.

For most of its existence, the FASB has promulgated standards that were quite complicated and replete with guidelines. This invited abuse of the type embodied by the Enron scandal. In recent years, the pendulum has begun to swing away from such rigidity. Now, once financial statements are prepared, company management is required to step back from the details and make a judgment on whether the statements taken as a whole "fairly present" the financial condition of the company as is asserted in the company's audit report (see below).

Moreover, since the enactment of the **Sarbanes-Oxley Act**, the SEC requires the chief executive officer (CEO) of the company and its chief financial officer (CFO) to personally sign a statement attesting to the accuracy and completeness of the financial statements. This requirement is an important step in restoring confidence in the integrity of financial accounting. The statements signed by both the CEO and CFO contain the following declarations:

- Both the CEO and CFO have personally reviewed the annual report.
- There are no untrue statements of a material fact that would make the statements misleading.
- Financial statements fairly present in all material respects the financial condition of the company.
- All material facts are disclosed to the company's auditors and board of directors.
- No changes to its system of internal controls are made unless properly communicated.

The Sarbanes-Oxley Act also imposed fines and potential jail time for executives. Presumably, the prospect of personal losses is designed to make these executives more vigilant in monitoring the financial accounting system. More recently, Congress passed *The Wall Street Reform and Consumer Protection Act* of 2010 (or the Dodd-Frank Act). Among the provisions of the act were rules that strengthened SOX by augmenting "claw-back" provisions for executives' ill-gotten gains.

Analysis of Financial Statements

LO4 Explain and apply the basics of profitability analysis.

This section previews the analysis framework of this book. This framework is used extensively by market professionals who analyze financial reports to evaluate company management and value the company's debt and equity securities. Analysis of financial performance is crucial in assessing prior strategic decisions and evaluating strategic alternatives.

Return on Assets

Suppose we learn that a company reports a profit of $10 million. Does the $10 million profit indicate that the company is performing well? Knowing that a company reports a profit is certainly positive as it indicates that customers value its goods or services and that its revenues exceed expenses. However, we cannot assess how well it is performing without considering the context. To explain, suppose we learn that this company has $500 million in assets. We now assess the $10 million profit as low because relative to the size of its asset investment, the company earned a paltry 2% return, computed as $10 million divided by $500 million. A 2% return on assets is what a much lower-risk investment in government-backed bond might yield. The important point is that a company's profitability must be assessed with respect to the size of its investment. One common metric is the *return on assets* (ROA)—defined as net income for that period divided by the average assets for that period.

Components of Return on Assets

We can separate return on assets into two components: profitability and productivity. Profitability relates profit to sales. This ratio is called the *profit margin* (PM), and it reflects the net income (profit after tax) earned on each sales dollar. Management wants to earn as much profit as possible from sales.

Productivity relates sales to assets. This component, called *asset turnover* (AT), reflects sales generated by each dollar of assets. Management wants to maximize asset productivity, that is, to achieve the highest possible sales level for a given level of assets (or to achieve a given level of sales with the smallest level of assets).

Exhibit 1.8 depicts the disaggregation of return on assets into these two components. Profitability (PM) and productivity (AT) are multiplied to yield the return on assets (ROA). Average assets are commonly defined as (beginning-year assets + ending-year assets)/2.

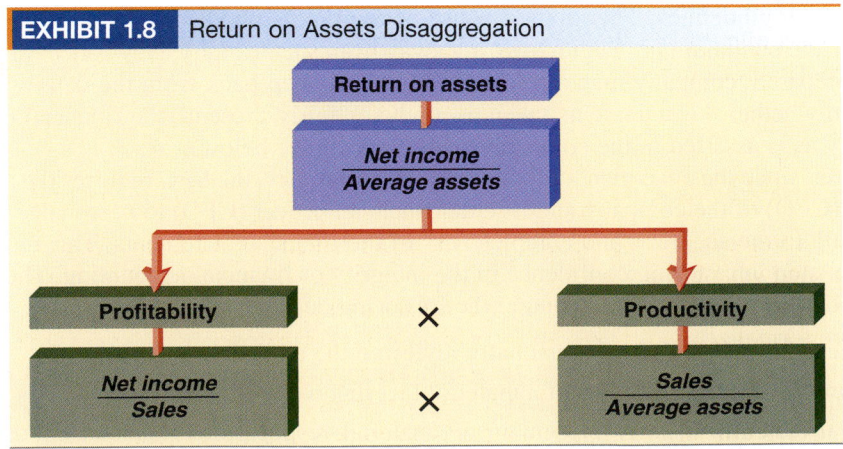

EXHIBIT 1.8 Return on Assets Disaggregation

Profitability and Productivity

There are an infinite number of combinations of profit margin and asset turnover that yield the same return on assets. To illustrate, Exhibit 1.9 graphs actual combinations of these two components for companies that we highlight in this book (each is identified by their ticker symbol). Retailers, like **Costco** (COST), **Best Buy** (BBY) and **TJX Companies** (TJX) are characterized by relatively low profit margins and a high turnover of their assets. The business models for other companies such as the pharmaceuticals [**Johnson & Johnson** (JNJ) and **Pfizer** (PFE)] require a larger investment in assets. These companies must earn a higher profit margin to yield an acceptable ROA. We might be surprised to see technology companies such as **Apple** in the group with high asset investments. Technology companies typically maintain a high level of cash and short-term investments on their balance sheets, which allows them to respond quickly to opportunities. The solid line represents those profitability and productivity combinations that yield about a 10% return on assets.

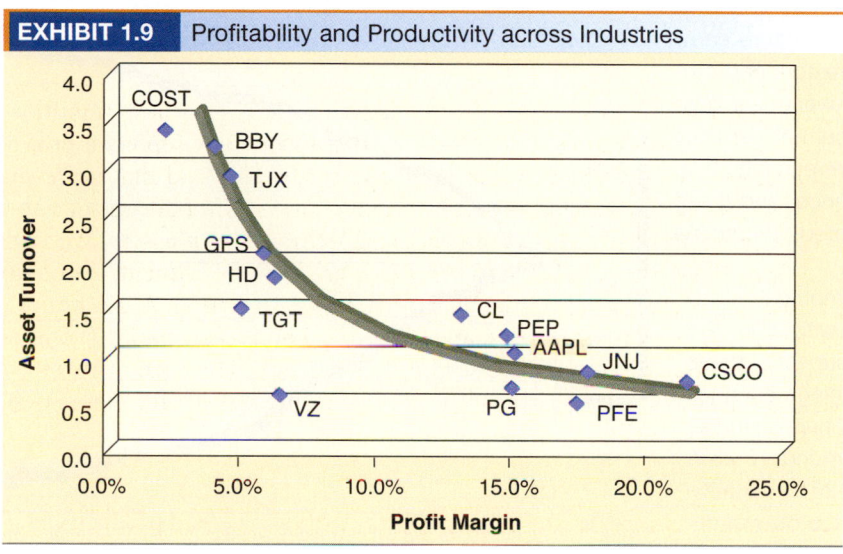

EXHIBIT 1.9   Profitability and Productivity across Industries

Return on Equity

Another important analysis measure is return on equity (ROE), which is defined as net income divided by average stockholders' equity, where average equity is commonly defined as (beginning-year equity + ending-year equity)/2. In this case, company earnings are compared to the level of stockholder (not total) investment. ROE reflects the return to stockholders, which is different from the return for the entire company (ROA).

ANALYSIS DECISION   **You Are the Chief Financial Officer**

You are reviewing your company's financial performance for the first six months of the year and are unsatisfied with the results. How can you disaggregate return on assets to identify areas for improvement? [Answer, p. 1-32]

STEP 3—FORECASTING FINANCIAL NUMBERS

Forecasting is a step where we proceed from our understanding of the company's current environment (Step 1) and what has occurred with the company (Step 2) to a prediction of what will occur next. This step is crucial to decision making and valuation, and it is arguably a very difficult task.

When we formalize predictions and state them in the form of financial projections, the quality of our forecasts is dependent on at least two factors. First, the quality of our analysis performed in Steps 1 and 2 in understanding the business environment and in adjusting and assessing financial information is crucial. If we fail to effectively understand the context in which a company operates, we will not be able to make appropriate estimates going forward. The quality of our adjustments and assessments made to the company's financial information drives the quality of our forecasts. For example, if we fail to realize the existence of off-balance-sheet financing, leverage is likely understated and then anticipated future financing needs are inaccurately forecasted.

Another example would be not recognizing the negative implications for future operations of growing inventory levels combined with flat or declining sales. Second, the quality of our forecasts is dependent on our assumptions being realistic and achievable. For example, is a company, which has recently experienced sales declines, likely to become the industry leader? Can a company increase sales when confronting a new entrant in the industry? Part of our task is to objectively examine what evidence supports, or not, the forecast assumptions we make. In sum, the importance of forecast quality cannot be overemphasized as it is vital to our estimates of where a company is going, which are direct inputs to valuation.

RESEARCH INSIGHT | **Knowledge of Future Earnings Yields Excess Returns**

Evidence shows that knowledge of future earnings is valuable and useful to investors and others. The theoretical linkage between earnings and stock prices is as follows: current earnings predict future earnings, and future earnings help determine expected future dividends, and these future dividends, when discounted, determine current stock price.

Numerous large-sample empirical studies provide evidence consistent with a linkage between earnings and prices. A subset of these studies finds a link between earnings changes and excess stock returns. In general, studies find excess annual returns of around 10-25% for earnings increases, and 10-25% negative returns for earnings decreases. It is no wonder that investors, analysts, and others devote so much time and effort to forecasting.

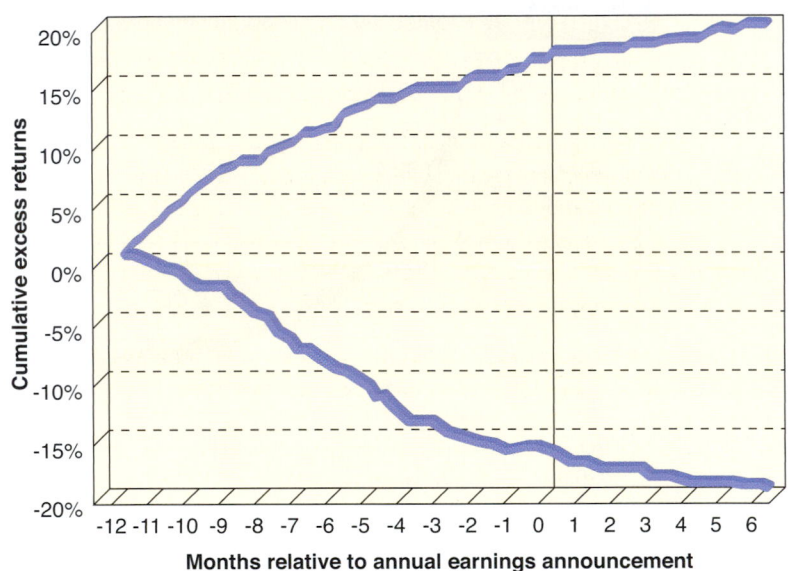

STEP 4—COMPANY VALUATION

When we embark on financial statement analysis, we are motivated by the need to make a financial decision. This could be from an external standpoint such as whether to buy or sell shares as an investor or from an internal standpoint such as evaluating a potential acquisition or change in scope of operations. All financial decisions involve valuation at some level. In making these decisions, we attempt to predict the future. The need for predictions arises from our desire to determine what a company is worth (Step 4). The key to good valuation estimates is accurate forecasts of future payoffs. And, the key to forecasting is having a good understanding of where the firm currently is and the business environment in which it competes.

One method for determining value is to directly examine the worth of the company's assets and liabilities. However, in most cases, we instead think of the worth of a company as the current value of expected payoffs. In Modules 12 to 14, we describe how to compute value using dividends, cash flows, and earnings as the payoffs. We often hear the adage "cash is king," which some then interpret as cash being best for valuation instead of, say, dividends or earnings. However, like earnings, cash reporting is subject to managerial biases and accounting limitations—no more, no less. Yet, there are situations where cash or earnings or dividends can work better for valuation purposes. We must develop the skills to understand where those situations are and where one, or a combination of different metrics, is best for valuation.

Module 15 tackles market-based valuation, which is probably the most frequently used valuation technique in the world today. At first glance, this method appears not to require the analysis performed in Steps 1, 2, and 3, as it generally utilizes market multiples determined from comparable firms. However, this is deceiving. Understanding where the company operates, where the company currently is, and where the company is going also drives valuation using multiples. That is, our financial analysis influences the choice of market multiple, the choice of comparables, and interpretation of the valuation estimate.

RESEARCH INSIGHT   **Are Earnings Important?**

A study asked top finance executives of publicly traded companies to *rank the three most important measures to report to outsiders.* The study reports that:

> "[More than 50% of] CFOs state that earnings are the most important financial metric to external constituents . . . this finding could reflect superior informational content in earnings over the other metrics. Alternatively, it could reflect myopic managerial concern about earnings. The emphasis on earnings is noteworthy because cash flows continue to be the measure emphasized in the academic finance literature."

The study also reports that CFOs view year-over-year change in earnings to be of critical importance to outsiders. Why is that? The study provides the following insights.

> "CFOs note that the first item in a press release is often a comparison of current quarter earnings with four quarters lagged quarterly earnings . . . CFOs also mention that while analysts' forecasts can be guided by management, last year's quarterly earnings number is a benchmark that is harder, if not impossible, to manage after the 10-Q has been filed with the SEC . . . Several executives mention that comparison to seasonally lagged earnings numbers provides a measure of earnings momentum and growth, and therefore is a useful gauge of corporate performance."

Thus, are earnings important? To the majority of finance chiefs surveyed, the answer is a resounding yes. (Source: Graham, et al., *Journal of Accounting and Economics,* 2005)

Financial Statement Analysis in an Efficient Capital Market

Some question the value of financial statement analysis if capital markets are efficient. The idea of market-efficiency is that security prices reflect available information and respond rapidly to new information when it is available. Some people incorrectly believe that this implies there is no gain to engaging in financial statement analysis. However, if our expectations differ from those of other investors there exists an opportunity to make trades based on those beliefs.

Market-efficiency requires effort from people to gather information, interpret it, and then make trades creating supply or demand pressures such that market prices adjust to a new equilibrium reflecting that information. This task of information gathering and processing is the task of financial analysts and investors. In the U.S. capital markets, the existence of a well-functioning capital market, particularly for the largest firms, allows for buy-side and sell-side analysts, institutional investors, and others to fill this role to potentially render prices efficient. For other firms where there is infrequent coverage in the financial press and little following from investors, prices can be less efficient. Academic research has found many anomalies where markets appear to not fully reflect information or reflect it with a lag.

Another facet of this discussion is management incentives. Management often has an incentive to report favorable financial information due to compensation agreements and a desire to maximize share price. While U.S. GAAP and IFRS put some restrictions on what is reported, the financial data can be biased, misleading, or obscuring of reality. Our analysis attempts to recognize and adjust for such possibilities. However, our estimates of value are only as good as the accounting numbers that underlie them. If we are able to perform effective analysis and gain a thorough understanding of where the firm operates, is currently situated, and is going, then even in an efficient market there are gains available through financial statement analysis.

ANALYZING GLOBAL REPORTS

The U.S. is among only a few economically developed countries (such as India, Singapore, and Russia) that do not use IFRS (a list is at **www.iasplus.com/country/useias.htm**). While laws and enforcement mechanisms vary across countries, the demand and supply of accounting information are governed by global economic forces. Thus, it is not surprising that companies under IFRS prepare and disclose the same set of financial statements. While account titles and footnote details differ, the underlying principles are the same. That is, U.S. GAAP and IFRS both capture, aggregate, summarize, and report economic activities on an accrual basis. Given the global economy and liquid transnational capital markets, it is critical that we be conversant with both U.S. GAAP and IFRS. For this purpose, each module includes a summary of any notable differences between these two systems of accounting for topics covered in that module. Also, each module has assignments that examine IFRS companies and their financial statements. By using a wide array of financial information, we will speak the language of accounting in at least two dialects.

MODULE-END REVIEW

Following are selected data from **Progressive Corporation**'s 2010 10-K.

$ millions	2010
Sales............................	$14,963
Net income......................	1,068
Average assets..................	20,600
Average stockholders' equity.........	5,899

Required

a. Compute Progressive's return on assets. Disaggregate the ROA into its profitability and productivity components.
b. Compute Progressive's return on equity (ROE).

The solution is on page 1-43.

APPENDIX 1A: ACCESSING SEC FILINGS

All companies traded publicly in the U.S. are required to file various reports with the SEC, two of which are the 10-Q (quarterly financial statements) and the 10-K (annual financial statements). For filings of companies publicly traded outside the U.S., the regulators of those stock exchanges usually require financial statements to be filed that can be accessed through the exchange Websites. Popular exchanges outside the U.S. include the London, Tokyo, Hong Kong, Frankfurt and Toronto Stock Exchanges. These and other exchanges belong to the World Federation of Exchanges whose Website (**www.World-Exchanges.org**) includes links to the respective exchanges. Following is a brief tutorial to access these electronic filings for firms traded in the U.S. The SEC's Website is **www.sec.gov**.

1. Following is the opening screen. Click on **"Search for Company Filings"** (highlighted below).

2. Click on company or fund name, ticker symbol, CIK (Central Index Key), file number, state, country, or SIC (Standard Industrial Classification).

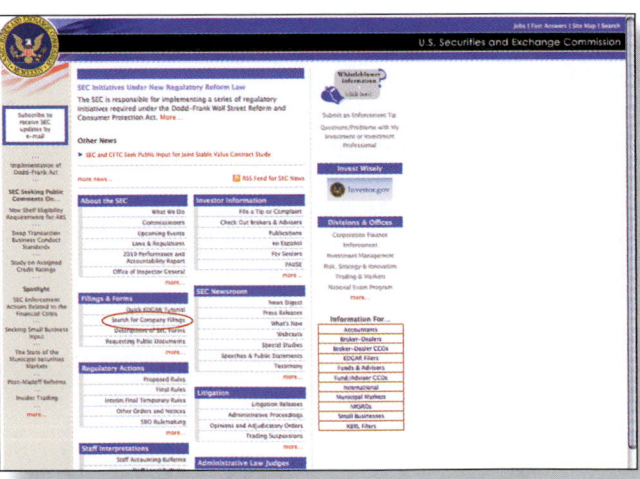

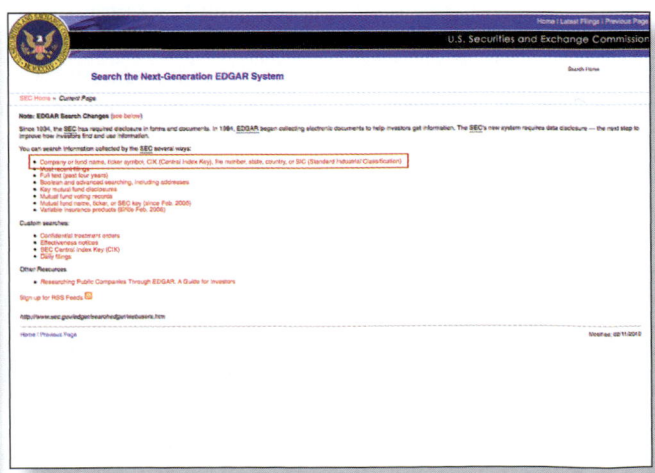

3. In **Company name**, type in the name of the company we are looking for. In this case, we are searching for Berkshire Hathaway. Then click enter.

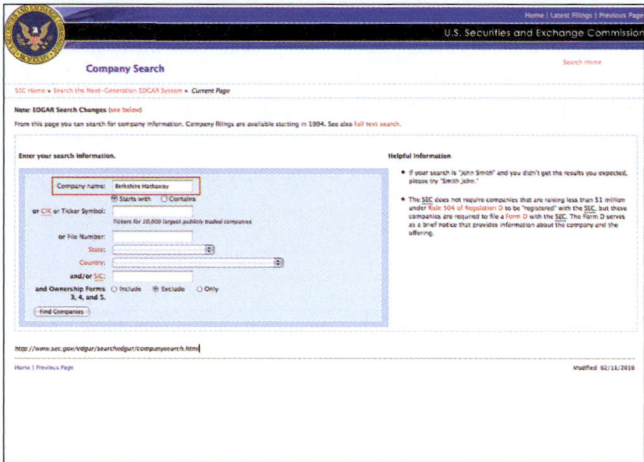

4. Several references to Berkshire appear. Click on the **CIK** (the SEC's numbering system) next to Berkshire Hathaway, Inc.

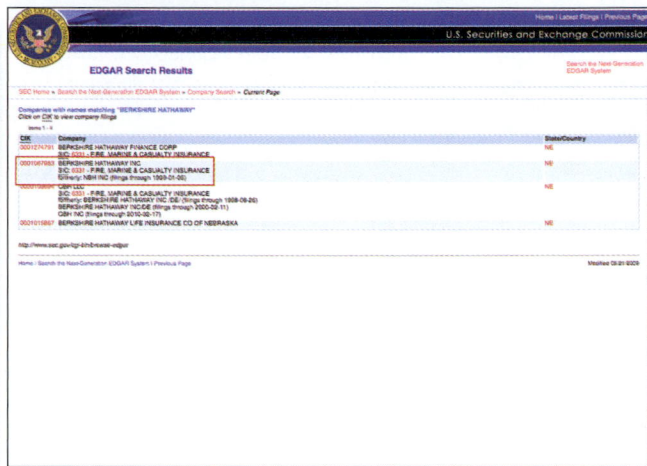

5. Enter the form number under "filing type" that we want to access. In this case we are looking for the 10-K.

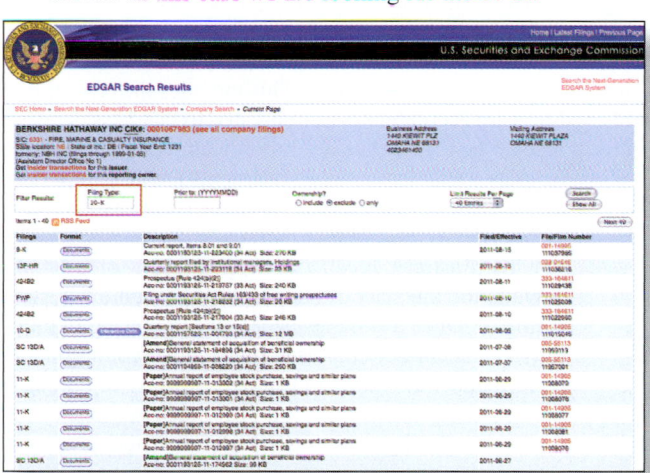

6. Click on the document link for the year that we want to access.

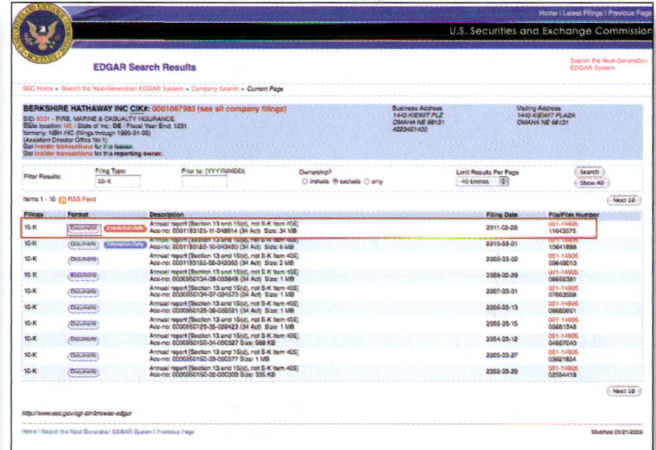

7. Exhibits relating to Berkshire Hathaway's 10-K filing appear; click on the 10-K document.

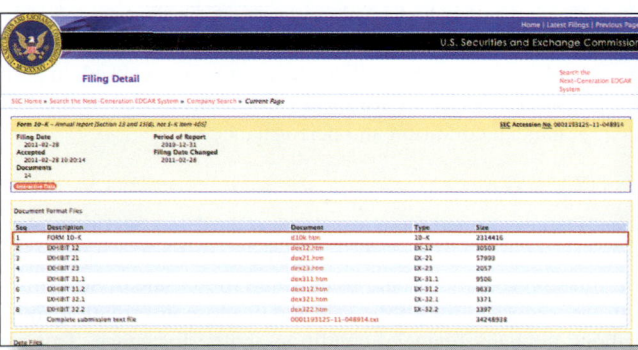

8. The Berkshire Hathaway 10-K will open up; the file is searchable.

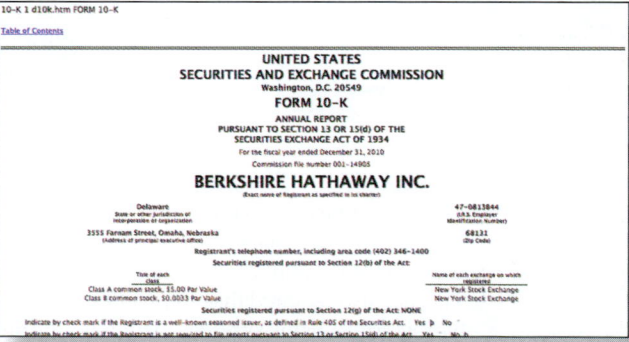

9. Download an Excel file of the data by clicking on "Interactive Data."

10. Click on "View Excel Document" to view or download as a spreadsheet.

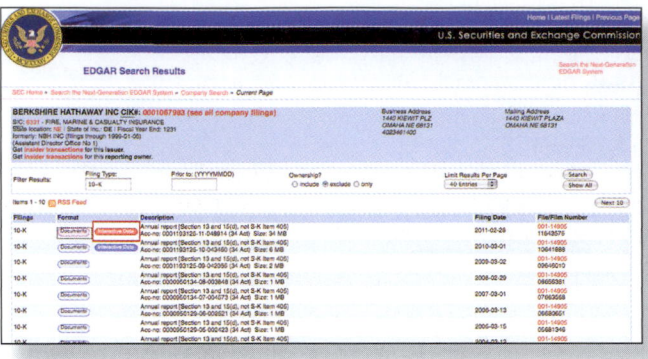
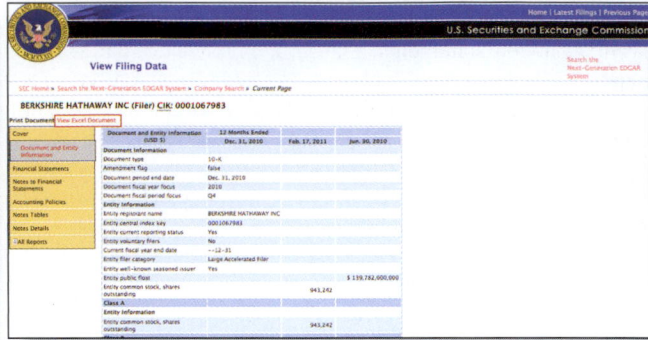

APPENDIX 1B: ACCOUNTING PRINCIPLES AND GOVERNANCE

Financial Accounting Environment

LO5 Describe the accounting principles and regulations that frame financial statements.

Information in financial statements is crucial to valuing a company's debt and equity securities. Financial statement information can affect the price the market is willing to pay for the company's equity securities and interest rates attached to its debt securities.

The importance of financial statements means that their reliability is paramount. This includes the crucial role of ethics. To the extent that financial performance and condition are accurately communicated to business decision makers, debt and equity securities are more accurately priced. When securities are mis-priced, resources can be inefficiently allocated both within and across economies. Accurate, reliable financial statements are also important for the effective functioning of many other markets such as labor, input, and output markets.

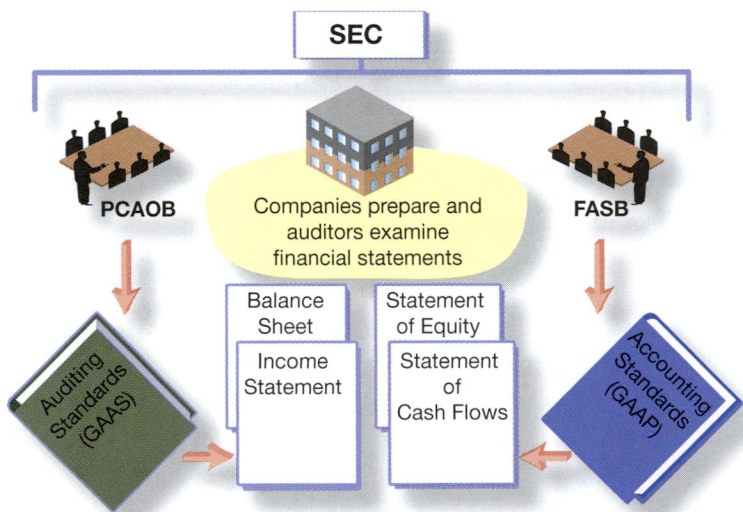

To illustrate, recall the consequences of a breakdown in the integrity of the financial accounting system at **Enron**. Once it became clear that Enron had not faithfully and accurately reported its financial condition and performance, the market became unwilling to purchase Enron's securities. The value of its debt and equity securities dropped precipitously and the company was unable to obtain cash needed for operating activities. Within months of the disclosure of its financial accounting irregularities, Enron, with revenues of over $100 billion and total company value of over $60 billion, the fifth largest U.S. company, was bankrupt!

Further historical evidence of the importance of financial accounting is provided by the Great Depression of the 20th century. This depression was caused, in part, by the failure of companies to faithfully report their financial condition and performance.

Oversight of Financial Accounting

The stock market crash of 1929 and the ensuing Great Depression led Congress to pass the 1933 Securities Act. This act had two main objectives: (1) to require disclosure of financial and other information about securities being offered for public sale; and (2) to prohibit deceit, misrepresentations, and other fraud in the sale of securities. This act also required that companies register all securities proposed for public sale and disclose information about the securities being offered, including information about company financial condition and performance. This act became and remains a foundation for contemporary financial reporting.

Congress also passed the 1934 Securities Exchange Act, which created the **Securities and Exchange Commission** (SEC) and gave it broad powers to regulate the issuance and trading of securities. The act also provides that companies with more than $10 million in assets and whose securities are held by more than 500 owners must file annual and other periodic reports, including financial statements that are available for download from the SEC's database (**www.sec.gov**).

The SEC has ultimate authority over U.S. financial reporting, including setting accounting standards for preparing financial statements. Since 1939, however, the SEC has looked primarily to the private sector to set accounting standards. One such private sector organization is the American Institute of Certified Public Accountants (AICPA), whose two committees, the Committee on Accounting Procedure (1939–59) and the Accounting Principles Board (1959–73), authored the initial body of accounting standards.

Currently, the **Financial Accounting Standards Board (FASB)** sets U.S. financial accounting standards. The FASB is an independent body overseen by a foundation, whose members include public accounting firms, investment managers, academics, and corporate managers. The FASB has published over 150 accounting standards governing the preparation of financial reports. This is in addition to over 40 standards that were written by predecessor organizations to the FASB, numerous bulletins and interpretations, Emerging Issues Task Force (EITF) statements, AICPA statements of position (SOP), and direct SEC guidance, along with speeches made by high-ranking SEC personnel, all of which form the body of accounting standards governing financial statements. Collectively, these pronouncements, rules and guidance create what is called **Generally Accepted Accounting Principles (GAAP)**.

The standard-setting process is arduous, often lasting up to a decade and involving extensive comment by the public, public officials, accountants, academics, investors, analysts, and corporate preparers of financial reports. The reason for this involved process is that amendments to existing standards or the creation of new standards affect the reported financial performance and condition of companies. Consequently, given the widespread impact of financial accounting, there are considerable economic consequences as a result of accounting changes. To influence the standard-setting process, special interest groups often lobby members of Congress to pressure the SEC and, ultimately, the FASB, on issues about which constituents feel strongly.

Audits and Corporate Governance

Even though key executives must personally attest to the completeness and accuracy of company financial statements, markets demand further assurances from outside parties to achieve the level of confidence necessary to warrant investment, credit, and other business decisions. To that end, companies engage external auditors to provide an opinion about financial statements. Further, companies implement a system of checks and balances that monitor managers' actions, which is called *corporate governance*.

Audit Report

Financial statements for each publicly traded company must be audited by an independent audit firm. There are a number of large auditing firms that are authorized by the SEC to provide auditing services for companies that issue securities to the public: **PricewaterhouseCoopers, KPMG, Ernst & Young, Deloitte, RSM McGladrey, Grant Thornton,** and **BDO Seidman,** to name a few. These firms provide opinions about financial statements for the large majority of publicly traded U.S. companies. A company's Board of Directors hires the auditors to review and express an opinion on its financial statements. The audit opinion expressed by Deloitte & Touche, LLP, on the financial statements of **Berkshire Hathaway** is reproduced in Exhibit 1.10.

The basic "clean" audit report is consistent across companies and includes these assertions:

- Financial statements are management's responsibility. Auditor responsibility is to express an *opinion* on those statements.

- Auditing involves a sampling of transactions, not investigation of each transaction.

- Audit opinion provides *reasonable assurance* that the statements are free of *material* misstatements, not a guarantee.

- Auditors review accounting policies used by management and the estimates used in preparing the statements.

- Financial statements *present fairly*, *in all material respects* a company's financial condition, in conformity with GAAP.

If the auditor cannot make all of these assertions, the auditor cannot issue a clean opinion. Instead, the auditor issues a "qualified" opinion and states the reasons a clean opinion cannot be issued. Financial report readers should scrutinize with care both the qualified audit opinion and the financial statements themselves.

The audit opinion is not based on a test of each transaction. Instead, auditors usually develop statistical samples to make inferences about the larger set of transactions. The audit report is not a guarantee that no misstatements exist. Auditors only provide reasonable assurance that the statements are free of material misstatements. Their use of the word "reasonable" is deliberate, as they do not want to be held to an absolute standard should problems be

EXHIBIT 1.10   Audit Report for Berkshire Hathaway

To the Board of Directors and Shareholders of Berkshire Hathaway Inc.

We have audited the accompanying consolidated balance sheets of Berkshire Hathaway Inc. and subsidiaries (the "Company") as of December 31, 2010 and 2009, and the related consolidated statements of earnings, cash flows and changes in shareholders' equity and comprehensive income for each of the three years in the period ended December 31, 2010. We also have audited the Company's internal control over financial reporting as of December 31, 2010, based on criteria established in Internal Control—Integrated Framework issued by the Committee of Sponsoring Organizations of the Treadway Commission. The Company's management is responsible for these financial statements, for maintaining effective internal control over financial reporting, and for its assessment of the effectiveness of internal control over financial reporting, included in the accompanying Management's Report on Internal Control over Financial Reporting. Our responsibility is to express an opinion on these financial statements and an opinion on the Company's internal control over financial reporting based on our audits.

We conducted our audits in accordance with the standards of the Public Company Accounting Oversight Board (United States). Those standards require that we plan and perform the audit to obtain reasonable assurance about whether the financial statements are free of material misstatement and whether effective internal control over financial reporting was maintained in all material respects. Our audits of the financial statements included examining, on a test basis, evidence supporting the amounts and disclosures in the financial statements, assessing the accounting principles used and significant estimates made by management, and evaluating the overall financial statement presentation. Our audit of internal control over financial reporting included obtaining an understanding of internal control over financial reporting, assessing the risk that a material weakness exists, and testing and evaluating the design and operating effectiveness of internal control based on the assessed risk. Our audits also included performing such other procedures as we considered necessary in the circumstances. We believe that our audits provide a reasonable basis for our opinions.

A company's internal control over financial reporting is a process designed by, or under the supervision of, the company's principal executive and principal financial officers, or persons performing similar functions, and effected by the company's board of directors, management, and other personnel to provide reasonable assurance regarding the reliability of financial reporting and the preparation of financial statements for external purposes in accordance with generally accepted accounting principles. A company's internal control over financial reporting includes those policies and procedures that (1) pertain to the maintenance of records that, in reasonable detail, accurately and fairly reflect the transactions and dispositions of the assets of the company; (2) provide reasonable assurance that transactions are recorded as necessary to permit preparation of financial statements in accordance with generally accepted accounting principles, and that receipts and expenditures of the company are being made only in accordance with authorizations of management and directors of the company; and (3) provide reasonable assurance regarding prevention or timely detection of unauthorized acquisition, use, or disposition of the company's assets that could have a material effect on the financial statements.

Because of the inherent limitations of internal control over financial reporting, including the possibility of collusion or improper management override of controls, material misstatements due to error or fraud may not be prevented or detected on a timely basis. Also, projections of any evaluation of the effectiveness of the internal control over financial reporting to future periods are subject to the risk that the controls may become inadequate because of changes in conditions, or that the degree of compliance with the policies or procedures may deteriorate.

In our opinion, the consolidated financial statements referred to above present fairly, in all material respects, the financial position of Berkshire Hathaway Inc. and subsidiaries as of December 31, 2010 and 2009, and the results of their operations and their cash flows for each of the three years in the period ended December 31, 2010, in conformity with accounting principles generally accepted in the United States of America. Also, in our opinion, the Company maintained, in all material respects, effective internal control over financial reporting as of December 31, 2010, based on the criteria established in Internal Control—Integrated Framework issued by the Committee of Sponsoring Organizations of the Treadway Commission.

DELOITTE & TOUCHE LLP

Omaha, Nebraska
February 25, 2011

subsequently uncovered. The word *material* is used in the sense that an item must be of sufficient magnitude to change the perceptions or decisions of the financial statement user (such as a decision to purchase stock or extend credit).

The requirement of auditor independence is the cornerstone of effective auditing and is subject to debate because the company pays the auditor's fees. Regulators have questioned the perceived lack of independence of auditing firms and the degree to which declining independence compromises the ability of auditing firms to challenge a client's dubious accounting.

The Sarbanes-Oxley Act contained several provisions designed to encourage auditor independence:

1. It established the **Public Company Accounting Oversight Board** (PCAOB) to oversee the development of audit standards and to monitor the effectiveness of auditors,
2. It prohibits auditors from offering certain types of consulting services, and requires audit partners to rotate clients every five years, and
3. It requires audit committees to consist of independent members.

Audit Committee

Law requires each publicly traded company to have a board of directors, where stockholders elect each director. This board represents the company owners and oversees management. The board also hires the company's executive management and regularly reviews company operations.

The board of directors usually establishes several subcommittees to focus on particular governance tasks such as compensation, strategic plans, and financial management. Governance committees are commonplace. One of these, the audit committee, oversees the financial accounting system. Exhibit 1.11 illustrates a typical organization of a company's governance structure.

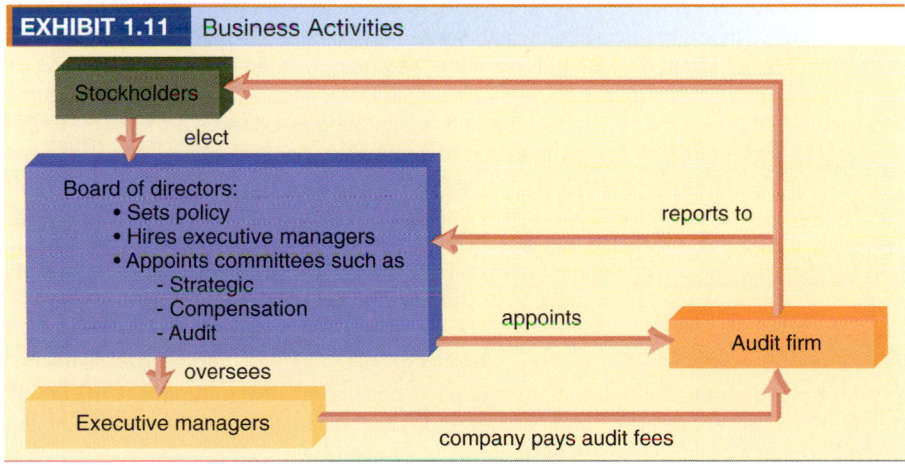

EXHIBIT 1.11 Business Activities

The audit committee must consist solely of outside directors, and cannot include the CEO. As part of its oversight of the financial accounting system, the audit committee focuses on **internal controls**, which are the policies and procedures used to protect assets, ensure reliable accounting, promote efficient operations, and urge adherence to company policies.

Regulatory and Legal Environment

The regulatory and legal environment provides further assurance that financial statements are complete and accurate.

SEC Enforcement Actions

Companies whose securities are issued to the public must file reports with the SEC (see **www.sec.gov**). One of these reports is the 10-K, which includes the annual financial statements (quarterly statements are filed on report 10-Q). The 10-K report provides more information than the company's glossy annual report, which is partly a marketing document (although the basic financial statements are identical). We prefer to use the 10-K because of its additional information.

The SEC critically reviews all of the financial reports that companies submit. If irregularities are found, the SEC has the authority to bring enforcement actions against companies that it feels are misrepresenting their financial condition (remember the phrase in the audit opinion that requires companies to "present fairly, in all material respects, the financial position of . . ."). One such action was brought against **Dell, Inc.** and its executives in 2011. Following are excerpts from the SEC's complaint:

The Securities and Exchange Commission today charged Dell Inc. with failing to disclose material information to investors and using fraudulent accounting to make it falsely appear that the company was consistently meeting Wall Street earnings targets and reducing its operating expenses.

The SEC alleges that Dell did not disclose to investors large exclusivity payments the company received from Intel Corporation not to use central processing units (CPUs) manufactured by Intel's main rival. It was these payments rather than the company's management and operations that allowed Dell to meet its earnings targets. After Intel cut these payments, Dell again misled investors by not disclosing the true reason behind the company's decreased profitability...

The SEC's complaint, filed in federal district court in Washington, D.C., alleges that Dell Inc., Michael Dell, Rollins, and Schneider misrepresented the basis for the company's ability to consistently meet or exceed consensus analyst EPS estimates from fiscal year 2002 through fiscal year 2006. Without the Intel payments, Dell would have missed the EPS consensus in every quarter during this period...

The SEC's complaint further alleges that Dell's most senior former accounting personnel, including Schneider, Dunning, and Jackson engaged in improper accounting by maintaining a series of "cookie jar" reserves that it used to cover shortfalls in operating results from FY 2002 to FY 2005. Dell's fraudulent accounting made it appear that it was consistently meeting Wall Street earnings targets and reducing its operating expenses through the company's management and operations.

According to the SEC's complaint, Intel made exclusivity payments to Dell in order for Dell not to use CPUs manufactured by its rival—Advance Micro Devices, Inc. (AMD). These exclusivity payments grew from 10 percent of Dell's operating income in FY 2003 to 38 percent in FY 2006, and peaked at 76 percent in the first quarter of FY 2007. The SEC alleges that Dell Inc., Michael Dell, Rollins, and Schneider failed to disclose the basis for the company's sharp drop in its operating results in its second quarter of fiscal 2007 as Intel cut its payments after Dell announced its intention to begin using AMD CPUs. In dollar terms, the reduction in Intel exclusivity payments was equivalent to 75 percent of the decline in Dell's operating income. Michael Dell, Rollins, and Schneider had been warned in the past that Intel would cut its funding if Dell added AMD as a vendor. Nevertheless, in Dell's second quarter FY 2007 earnings call, they told investors that the sharp drop in the company's operating results was attributable to Dell pricing too aggressively in the face of slowing demand and to component costs declining less than expected.

The SEC's complaint further alleges that the reserve manipulations allowed Dell to materially misstate its earnings and its operating expenses as a percentage of revenue—an important financial metric that the Company itself highlighted—for over three years. The manipulations also enabled Dell to misstate materially the trend and amount of operating income of its EMEA segment, an important business unit that Dell also highlighted, from the third quarter of FY 2003 through the first quarter of FY 2005.

While not admitting to wrongdoing, Dell agreed to pay a penalty of $100 million to settle the SEC's charges. The SEC's oversight and powers of prosecution are an important check to help insure that companies' reports to investors "present fairly, in all material respects" their financial condition.

BUSINESS INSIGHT	Warren Buffett on Audit Committees

"Audit committees can't audit. Only a company's outside auditor can determine whether the earnings that a management purports to have made are suspect. Reforms that ignore this reality and that instead focus on the structure and charter of the audit committee will accomplish little. As we've discussed, far too many managers have fudged their company's numbers in recent years, using both accounting and operational techniques that are typically legal but that nevertheless materially mislead investors. Frequently, auditors knew about these deceptions. Too often, however, they remained silent. The key job of the audit committee is simply to get the auditors to divulge what they know. To do this job, the committee must make sure that the auditors worry more about misleading its members than about offending management. In recent years auditors have not felt that way. They have instead generally viewed the CEO, rather than the shareholders or directors, as their client. That has been a natural result of day-to-day working relationships and also of the auditors' understanding that, no matter what the board says, the CEO and CFO pay their fees and determine whether they are retained for both auditing and other work. The rules that have been recently instituted won't materially change this reality. What will break this cozy relationship is audit committees unequivocally putting auditors on the spot, making them understand they will become liable for major monetary penalties if they don't come forth with what they know or suspect."

—Warren Buffett, Berkshire Hathaway annual report

Courts

Courts provide remedies to individuals and companies that suffer damages as a result of material misstatements in financial statements. Typical court actions involve shareholders who sue the company and its auditors, alleging that the company disclosed, and the auditors attested to, false and misleading financial statements. Shareholder lawsuits are chronically in the news; although, the number of such suits has declined in recent years. Stanford Law School's Securities Class Action Clearinghouse commented that "Two factors are likely responsible for the decline. First, lawsuits arising from the dramatic boom and bust of U.S. equities in the late 1990s and early 2000s are now largely behind us. Second, improved corporate governance in the wake of the **Enron** and **WorldCom** frauds likely reduced the actual incidence of fraud." Nevertheless, courts continue to wield considerable power. For example, the SEC and the New York District Attorney successfully brought suit against **Adelphia Communications Corporation** and its owners on behalf of the U.S. Government and numerous investors, creditors, employees and others affiliated with the company. The press release announcing the settlement read, in part:

> *Washington, D.C., April 25, 2005*—The Securities and Exchange Commission today announced that it and the United States Attorney's Office for the Southern District of New York (USAO) reached an agreement to settle a civil enforcement action and resolve criminal charges against Adelphia Communications Corporation, its founder John J. Rigas, and his three sons, Timothy J. Rigas, Michael J. Rigas and James P. Rigas, in one of the most extensive financial frauds ever to take place at a public company.
>
> In its complaint, the Commission charged that Adelphia, at the direction of the individual defendants: (1) fraudulently excluded billions of dollars in liabilities from its consolidated financial statements by hiding them on the books of off-balance sheet affiliates; (2) falsified operating statistics and inflated earnings to meet Wall Street estimates; and (3) concealed rampant self-dealing by the Rigas family, including the undisclosed use of corporate funds for purchases of Adelphia stock and luxury condominiums.
>
> Mark K. Schonfeld, Director of the SEC's Northeast Regional Office, said, "This settlement agreement presents a strong, coordinated approach by the SEC and the U.S. Attorney's Office to resolving one of the most complicated and egregious financial frauds committed at a public company. The settlement provides an expedient and effective way to provide victims of Adelphia's fraud with a substantial recovery while at the same time enabling Adelphia to emerge from Chapter 11 bankruptcy."

The settlement terms of this action, and related criminal actions against the Rigas family, resulted in the following:

■ Rigas family members forfeited in excess of $1.5 billion in assets derived from the fraud; the funds were used, in part, to establish a fund for the fraud victims.

■ Rigas family members were barred from acting as officers or directors of a public company.

■ John Rigas, the 80-year-old founder of Adelphia Communications, was sentenced to 15 years in prison; he applied for a Presidential pardon in January 2009 but was denied.

■ Timothy Rigas, the ex-finance chief, was sentenced to 20 years and is currently serving time at a federal correctional complex in North Carolina.

GUIDANCE ANSWERS . . . ANALYSIS DECISION

You Are the Chief Financial Officer Financial performance is often measured by return on assets, which can be disaggregated into the profit margin (profit after tax/sales) and the asset turnover (sales/average assets). This disaggregation might lead you to review factors affecting profitability (gross margins and expense control) and to assess how effectively your company is utilizing its assets (the turnover rates). Finding ways to increase profitability for a given level of investment or to reduce the amount of invested capital while not adversely impacting profitability contributes to improved financial performance.

Superscript ^A(B) denotes assignments based on Appendix 1A (1B).

DISCUSSION QUESTIONS

Q1-1. A firm's planning activities motivate and shape three types of business activities. List the three activities. Describe how financial statements can provide useful information for each activity. How can subsequent financial statements be used to evaluate the success of each of the activities?

Q1-2. The accounting equation (Assets = Liabilities + Equity) is a fundamental business concept. Explain what this equation reveals about a company's sources and uses of funds and the claims on company resources.

Q1-3.   Companies prepare four primary financial statements. What are those financial statements and what information is typically conveyed in each?

Q1-4.   Does a balance sheet report on a period of time or at a point in time? Explain the information conveyed in the balance sheet.

Q1-5.   Does an income statement report on a period of time or at a point in time? Explain the information conveyed in the income statement.

Q1-6.   Does a statement of cash flows report on a period of time or at a point in time? Explain the information and activities conveyed in the statement of cash flows.

Q1-7.   Explain how a company's four primary financial statements are linked.

Q1-8.   Financial statements are used by several interested stakeholders. List three or more potential external users of financial statements. Explain how each constituent on your list might use financial statement information in their decision making process.

Q1-9.   Describe the role of forecasting in valuation. Why is understanding a company's business environment and its accounting information crucial to forecasting?

PROCTER & GAMBLE (PG)

Q1-10.^A   Access the 2011 10-K for **Procter & Gamble** at the SEC's database of financial reports (**www.sec. gov**). Who is P&G's auditor? What specific language does the auditor use in expressing its opinion and what responsibilities does it assume?

Q1-11.^B   Business decision makers external to the company increasingly demand more financial information from companies. Discuss the reasons why companies have traditionally opposed the efforts of regulatory agencies like the SEC to require more disclosure.

Q1-12.^B   What are generally accepted accounting principles and what organizations presently establish them?

ENRON

Q1-13.^B   Corporate governance has received considerable attention since the collapse of **Enron** and other accounting-related scandals. What is meant by corporate governance? What are the primary means by which sound corporate governance is achieved?

Q1-14.^B   What is the primary function of the auditor? In your own words, describe what an audit opinion says.

Q1-15.   Describe a decision that requires financial statement information, other than a stock investment decision. How is financial statement information useful in making this decision?

Q1-16.   Users of financial statement information are vitally concerned with the company's strategic direction. Despite their understanding of this need for information, companies are reluctant to supply it. Why? In particular, what costs are companies concerned about?

Q1-17.   One of Warren Buffett's acquisition criteria is to invest in businesses "earning good return on equity." The return on equity (ROE) formula uses both net income and stockholders' equity. Why is it important to relate net income to stockholders' equity? Why isn't it sufficient to merely concentrate on companies with the highest net income?

Q1-18.   One of Warren Buffett's acquisition criteria is to invest in businesses "earning good return on equity, while employing little or no debt." Why is Buffett concerned about debt?

Assignments with the ✔ in the margin are available in an online homework system.
See the Preface of the book for details.

MINI EXERCISES

DELL, INC. (DELL)

M1-19.   **Relating Financing and Investing Activities**   (LO2)
In a recent year, the total assets of **Dell, Inc.** equal $38,599 million and its equity is $7,766 million. What is the amount of its liabilities? Does Dell receive more financing from its owners or nonowners? What percentage of financing is provided by Dell's owners?

BEST BUY (BBY)

M1-20.   **Relating Financing and Investing Activities**   (LO2)
In a recent year, the total assets of **Best Buy** equal $17,849 million and its liabilities equal $10,557 million. What is the amount of Best Buy's equity? Does Best Buy receive more financing from its owners or nonowners? What percentage of financing is provided by its owners?

 M1-21.   **Applying the Accounting Equation and Computing Financing Proportions**   (LO2)
Use the accounting equation to compute the missing financial amounts (a), (b), and (c). Which of these companies is more owner-financed? Which of these companies is more nonowner-financed? Discuss why the proportion of owner financing might differ across these three businesses.

($ millions)	Assets	=	Liabilities	+	Equity
Hewlett-Packard............................	$124,503	=	$83,722	+	$ (a)
General Mills................................	$ 18,674	=	$ (b)	+	$ 6,612
Target.......................................	$ (c)	=	$28,218	+	$15,487

HEWLETT-
PACKARD
(HPQ)
GENERAL MILLS
(GIS)
TARGET
(TGT)
STARBUCKS
(SBUX)

E. I. DUPONT DE
NEMOURS
(DD)

M1-22.ᴬ Identifying Key Numbers from Financial Statements (LO2)

Access the October 3, 2010, 10-K for **Starbucks Corporation** at the SEC's database for financial reports (**www.sec.gov**). What did Starbucks report for total assets, liabilities, and equity at October 3, 2010? Confirm that the accounting equation holds. What percent of Starbucks' assets is financed by nonowners?

M1-23.ᴬ Verifying Linkages Between Financial Statements (LO2)

Access the 2010 10-K for **DuPont** at the SEC's database of financial reports (**www.sec.gov**). Using its December 31, 2010, consolidated statement of stockholders' equity, prepare a table to reconcile the opening and ending balances of its retained (reinvested) earnings for 2010 by showing the activity in the account during the year.

M1-24. Identifying Financial Statement Line Items and Accounts (LO2)

Several line items and account titles are listed below. For each, indicate in which of the following financial statement(s) we would likely find the item or account: income statement (IS), balance sheet (BS), statement of stockholders' equity (SE), or statement of cash flows (SCF).

a. Cash asset	*d.* Contributed capital	*g.* Cash inflow for stock issued
b. Expenses	*e.* Cash outflow for capital expenditures	*h.* Cash outflow for dividends
c. Noncash assets	*f.* Retained earnings	*i.* Net income

M1-25. Identifying Ethical Issues and Accounting Choices (LO5)

Assume that you are a technology services provider and you must decide on whether to record revenue from the installation of computer software for one of your clients. Your contract calls for acceptance of the software by the client within six months of installation. According to the contract, you will be paid only when the client "accepts" the installation. Although you have not yet received your client's formal acceptance, you are confident that it is forthcoming. Failure to record these revenues will cause your company to miss Wall Street's earnings estimates. What stakeholders will be affected by your decision and how might they be affected?

M1-26.ᴮ Understanding Internal Controls and Their Importance (LO5)

The Sarbanes-Oxley Act legislation requires companies to report on the effectiveness of their internal controls. The SEC administers the Sarbanes-Oxley Act, and defines internal controls as follows:

> "A process designed by, or under the supervision of, the registrant's principal executive and principal financial officers . . . to provide reasonable assurance regarding the reliability of financial reporting and the preparation of financial statements for external purposes in accordance with generally accepted accounting principles."

Why would Congress believe that internal controls are such an important area to monitor and report on?

EXERCISES

E1-27. Composition of Accounts on the Balance Sheet (LO2)

Answer the following questions about the **Target** balance sheet.

TARGET
(TGT)

a.   Accounts Receivable comprises a large proportion of its total assets. Why would a retailer such as Target report accounts receivable on its balance sheet?

b.   Briefly describe the types of assets that Target is likely to include in its inventory.

c.   What kinds of assets would Target likely include in its Property, Plant and Equipment?

d.   Target reports about two-thirds of its total assets as long-term. Given Target's business model, why do we see it report a relatively high proportion of long-term assets?

E1-28. Applying the Accounting Equation and Assessing Financial Statement Linkages (LO2)

Answer the following questions. (*Hint*: Apply the accounting equation.)

INTEL
(INTC)

a.   **Intel** had assets equal to $63,186 million and liabilities equal to $13,756 million for a recent year-end. What was Intel's total equity at year-end? Why would we expect a company like Intel to report a relatively high proportion of equity vis-á-vis liabilities?

JETBLUE
(JBLU)

b. At the beginning of a recent year, **JetBlue**'s assets were $6,549 million and its equity was $1,546 million. During the year, assets increased $44 million and liabilities decreased $(64) million. What was JetBlue's equity at the end of the year?

c. What balance sheet account provides the link between the balance sheet and the income statement? Briefly describe how this linkage works.

E1-29.   Specifying Financial Information Users and Uses   (LO1)
Financial statements have a wide audience of interested stakeholders. Identify two or more financial statement users that are external to the company. For each user on your list, specify two questions that could be addressed with financial statement information.

E1-30.   Applying Financial Statement Relations to Compute Dividends   (LO2)
Colgate-Palmolive reports the following dollar balances in its retained earnings account.

COLGATE-PALMOLIVE
(CL)

($ millions)	2010	2009
Retained earnings	$14,329	$13,157

During 2010, Colgate-Palmolive reported net income of $2,203 million. What amount of dividends, if any, did Colgate-Palmolive pay to its shareholders in 2010? What percent of its net income did Colgate-Palmolive pay out as dividends in 2010?

E1-31.   Computing and Interpreting Financial Statement Ratios   (LO4)
Following are selected ratios of **Colgate-Palmolive** for 2010 and 2009.

COLGATE-PALMOLIVE
(CL)

Return on Assets (ROA) Component	2010	2009
Profitability (Net income/Sales)	14%	15%
Productivity (Sales/Average net assets)................	1.4	1.5

a. Was the company profitable in 2010? What evidence do you have of this?
b. Is the change in productivity (asset turnover) a positive development? Explain.
c. Compute the company's return on assets (ROA) for 2010 (show computations).

E1-32.   Computing Return on Assets and Applying the Accounting Equation   (LO4)
Nordstrom, Inc., reports net income of $613 million for its fiscal year ended January 2011. At the beginning of that fiscal year, Nordstrom had $6,579 million in total assets. By fiscal year-end 2011, total assets had grown to $7,462 million. What is Nordstrom's return on assets (ROA)?

NORDSTROM, INC.
(JWN)

E1-33.   Assessing the Role of Financial Statements in Society   (LO1)
Financial statement information plays an important role in modern society and business.

a. Identify two or more external stakeholders that are interested in a company's financial statements and what their particular interests are.
b. What are *generally accepted accounting principles*? What organizations have primary responsibility for the formulation of GAAP?
c. What role does financial statement information play in the allocation of society's financial resources?
d. What are three aspects of the accounting environment that can create ethical pressure on management?

E1-34.   Computing Return on Equity   (LO4)
Starbucks reports net income for 2010 of $945.6 million. Its stockholders' equity is $3,056.9 million and $3,682.3 million for 2009 and 2010, respectively.

STARBUCKS
(SBUX)

a. Compute its return on equity for 2010.
b. Starbucks repurchased over $285 million of its common stock in 2010. How did this repurchase affect Starbucks' ROE?
c. Why do you think a company like Starbucks repurchases its own stock?

PROBLEMS

    P1-35.   Computing Return on Equity and Return on Assets   (LO4)
The following table contains financial statement information for **Wal-Mart Stores, Inc.**

WAL-MART STORES, INC.
(WMT)

($ millions)	Total Assets	Net Income	Sales	Equity
2009	$180,663	$16,389	$421,849	$68,542
2010	170,407	14,370	408,085	70,468
2011	163,429	13,381	404,254	65,285

Required

a. Compute the return on equity (ROE) for 2010 and 2011. What trend, if any, is evident? How does Wal-Mart's ROE compare with the approximately 20% median ROE for companies in the Dow Jones Industrial average for 2011?

b. Compute the return on assets (ROA) for 2010 through 2011. What trends, if any, are evident? How does Wal-Mart's ROA compare with the approximate 6.7% median ROA for companies in the Dow Jones Industrial average for 2011?

c. What factors might allow a company like Wal-Mart to reap above-average returns?

P1-36. Formulating Financial Statements from Raw Data   (LO2)

Following is selected financial information from **General Mills, Inc.**, for its fiscal year ended May 29, 2011 ($ millions).

✔

GENERAL MILLS, INC.
(GIS)

Revenue	$14,880.2
Cash from operating activities	1,526.8
Cash, beginning year	673.2
Total equity.................................	6,612.2
Noncash assets	18,054.9
Cash from financing activities*..............	(865.3)
Cost of goods sold...........................	8,926.7
Total expenses (other than cost of goods sold).............	4,155.2
Cash, end of year...........................	619.6
Total liabilities.............................	12,062.3
Cash from investing activities................	(715.1)

˙Cash from financing activities includes the effects of foreign exchange rate fluctuations.

Required

a. Prepare the income statement, the balance sheet, and the statement of cash flows for General Mills for the fiscal year ended May 2011.

b. Do the negative amounts for cash from investing activities and cash from financing activities concern us? Explain.

c. Using the statements prepared for part *a*, compute the following ratios (for this part only, use the year-end balance instead of the average for assets and stockholders' equity):
  i. Profit margin
  ii. Turnover of total assets
  iii. Return on assets
  iv. Return on equity

P1-37. Formulating Financial Statements from Raw Data   (LO2)

Following is selected financial information from **Abercrombie & Fitch** for its fiscal year ended January 29, 2011 ($ millions).

ABERCROMBIE & FITCH
(ANF)

Noncash assets	$2,122
Total expenses (other than cost of goods sold).............	2,062
Cash from investing activities................	(93)
Cash, ending year	826
Revenue	3,469
Total liabilities.............................	1,057
Cash from operating activities	392
Cash from financing activities*..............	(143)
Cost of goods sold...........................	1,257
Cash, beginning year	670
Stockholders' equity	1,891

˙Cash from financing activities includes the effects of foreign exchange rate fluctuations.

Required

a. Prepare the income statement, the balance sheet, and the statement of cash flows for Abercrombie & Fitch for the fiscal year ended January 2011.

b. Do the negative amounts for cash from investing activities and cash from financing activities concern us? Explain.

c. Using the statements prepared for part *a*, compute the following ratios (for this part only, use the year-end balance instead of the average for assets and stockholders' equity):

   i. Profit margin
   ii. Asset turnover
   iii. Return on assets
   iv. Return on equity

CISCO SYSTEMS, INC.
(CSCO)

P1-38. **Formulating Financial Statements from Raw Data**   **(LO2)**

Following is selected financial information from **Cisco Systems, Inc.**, for the year ended July 31, 2010 ($ millions).

Cash, ending year	$ 4,581
Cash from operating activities	10,173
Sales	40,040
Stockholders' equity	44,285
Cost of goods sold	14,397
Cash used in financing activities	621
Total liabilities	36,845
Total expense (other than cost of goods sold)	17,876
Noncash assets	76,549
Cash used in investing activities	(11,931)
Net income	7,767
Cash, beginning year	5,718

Required

a. Prepare the income statement, the balance sheet, and the statement of cash flows for Cisco Systems for the fiscal year ended July 31, 2010.

b. Do the negative amounts for cash from investing activities and cash from financing activities concern us? Explain.

c. Using the statements prepared for part *a*, compute the following ratios (for this part only, use the year-end balance instead of the average for assets and stockholders' equity):

   i. Profit margin
   ii. Asset turnover
   iii. Return on assets
   iv. Return on equity

P1-39. **Formulating a Statement of Stockholders' Equity from Raw Data**   **(LO2)**

Crocker Corporation began calendar-year 2011 with stockholders' equity of $100,000, consisting of contributed capital of $70,000 and retained earnings of $30,000. During 2011, it issued additional stock for total cash proceeds of $30,000. It also reported $50,000 of net income, and paid $25,000 as a cash dividend to shareholders.

Required

Prepare the 2011 statement of stockholders' equity for Crocker Corporation.

GAP, INC.
(GPS)

P1-40. **Formulating a Statement of Stockholders' Equity from Raw Data**   **(LO2)**

Gap, Inc., reports the following selected information at January 30, 2010 ($ millions).

Contributed capital, Jan. 30, 2010	$ 2,990
Treasury stock, Jan. 30, 2010	(9,069)
Retained earnings, Jan. 30, 2010	10,815
Accumulated other comprehensive income, Jan. 30, 2010	155

During fiscal year 2011, Gap reported the following:

1. Sale of stock .... $ 4
2. Purchase of stock 1,797
3. Net income 1,204
4. Cash dividends 252
5. Other comprehensive income 30

Required
Use this information to prepare the statement of stockholders' equity for Gap, Inc. for 2011.

P1-41.   **Computing, Analyzing, and Interpreting Return on Equity and Return on Assets**   **(LO4)**
Following are summary financial statement data for **Kimberly-Clark** for 2008 through 2010.

KIMBERLY-CLARK
(KMB)

KIMBERLY-CLARK CORPORATION (KMB)			
($ millions)	2010	2009	2008
Sales.....................	$19,746	$19,115	$19,415
Net income...............	1,843	1,884	1,690
Total assets.............	19,864	19,209	18,089
Equity...................	6,202	5,690	4,261

Required
a. Compute the return on assets and return on equity for 2009 and 2010 (use average assets and average equity), together with the components of ROA (profit margin and asset turnover). What trends do we observe? Which component appears to be driving the change in ROA over this time period?
b. KMB repurchased a large amount of its common shares in recent years at a cost of over $4.7 billion. How did this repurchase affect its return on equity?

P1-42.   **Computing, Analyzing, and Interpreting Return on Equity and Return on Assets**   **(LO4)**
Following are summary financial statement data for **Nordstrom, Inc.** for 2009 through 2011.

NORDSTROM, INC.
(JWN)

($ millions)	2011	2010	2009
Sales.....................	$9,700	$8,627	$8,573
Net income...............	613	441	401
Total assets.............	7,462	6,579	5,661
Equity...................	2,021	1,572	1,210

Required
Compute return on assets and return on equity for each year 2010 and 2011 (use average assets and average equity), together with the components of ROA (profit margin and asset turnover). What trends, if any, do we observe? Which component, if any, appears to be driving the change in ROA over this time period?

P1-43.   **Computing, Analyzing, and Interpreting Return on Equity**   **(LO4)**
Nokia manufactures, markets, and sells phones and other electronics. Total stockholders' equity for Nokia is €16,231 in 2010 and €14,749 in 2009. In 2010, Nokia reported net income of €1,850 on sales of €42,446.

NOKIA
(NOK)

Required
a. What is Nokia's return on equity for 2010?
b. What are total expenses for Nokia in 2010?
c. Nokia used cash to repurchase a large amount of its common stock during the period 2006 through 2008. What motivations might Nokia have for repurchasing its common stock?

P1-44.   **Comparing Abercrombie & Fitch and TJX Companies**   **(LO4)**
Following are selected financial statement data from **Abercrombie & Fitch** (ANF—upscale clothing retailer) and **TJX Companies** (TJX—value priced clothing retailer including TJ Maxx)—both dated the end of January 2011 or 2010.

ABERCROMBIE &
FITCH
(ANF)
TJX COMPANIES
(TJX)

($ millions)	Company	Total Assets	Net Income	Sales
2010	TJX Companies Inc..........	$7,464		
2011	TJX Companies Inc..........	7,972	$1,343	$21,942
2010	Abercrombie & Fitch	2,821		
2011	Abercrombie & Fitch	2,948	150	3,469

Required
a. Compute the return on assets for both companies for the year ended January 2011.
b. Disaggregate the ROAs for both companies into the profit margin and asset turnover.
c. What differences are observed? Evaluate these differences in light of the two companies' business models. Which company has better financial performance?

P1-45. **Computing and Interpreting Return on Assets and Its Components** (LO4)

MCDONALD'S CORPORATION (MCD)

McDonald's Corporation (MCD) reported the following balance sheet and income statement data for 2008 through 2010.

($ millions)	Total Assets	Net Income	Sales
2008	$28,461.5		
2009	30,224.9	$4,551.0	$22,744.7
2010	31,975.2	4,946.3	24,074.6

Required

a. What is MCD's return on assets for 2009 and 2010? Disaggregate MCD's ROA into its net profit margin and its asset turnover.

b. What factor is mainly responsible for the change in MCD's ROA over this two-year period?

P1-46. **Disaggregating Return on Assets over Multiple Periods** (LO4)

3M COMPANY (MMM)

Following are selected financial statement data from **3M Company** for 2007 through 2010.

($ millions)	Total Assets	Net Income	Sales
2007	$24,694	$4,096	$24,462
2008 . . . , ...	25,793	3,460	25,269
2009	27,250	3,193	23,123
2010	30,156	4,085	26,662

Required

a. Compute **3M Company**'s return on assets for 2008 through 2010. Disaggregate 3M's ROA into the profit margin and asset turnover for 2008 through 2010. What trends do we observe?

b. Which ROA component appears to be driving the trend observed in part *a*? Explain.

 P1-47.[A] **Reading and Interpreting Audit Opinions** (LO5)

APPLE, INC. (AAPL)

Apple, Inc.'s 2010 financial statements include the following audit report from **Ernst & Young LLP**.

REPORT OF INDEPENDENT REGISTERED PUBLIC ACCOUNTING FIRM

The Board of Directors and Shareholders of Apple Inc.

We have audited the accompanying consolidated balance sheets of Apple Inc. as of September 25, 2010 and September 26, 2009, and the related consolidated statements of operations, shareholders' equity and cash flows for the years then ended. These financial statements are the responsibility of the Company's management. Our responsibility is to express an opinion on these financial statements based on our audits.

We conducted our audits in accordance with the standards of the Public Company Accounting Oversight Board (United States). Those standards require that we plan and perform the audit to obtain reasonable assurance about whether the financial statements are free of material misstatement. An audit includes examining, on a test basis, evidence supporting the amounts and disclosures in the financial statements. An audit also includes assessing the accounting principles used and significant estimates made by management, as well as evaluating the overall financial statement presentation. We believe that our audits provide a reasonable basis for our opinion.

In our opinion, the financial statements referred to above present fairly, in all material respects, the consolidated financial position of Apple Inc. at September 25, 2010 and September 26, 2009, and the consolidated results of its operations and its cash flows for the years then ended, in conformity with U.S. generally accepted accounting principles.

We also have audited, in accordance with the standards of the Public Company Accounting Oversight Board (United States), Apple Inc.'s internal control over financial reporting as of September 25, 2010, based on criteria established in Internal Control—Integrated Framework issued by the Committee of Sponsoring Organizations of the Treadway Commission and our report dated October 27, 2010 expressed an unqualified opinion thereon.

/s/ Ernst & Young LLP
San Jose, California
October 27, 2010

Required

a.   To whom is the report addressed? Why?

b.   In your own words, briefly describe the audit process. What steps do auditors take to determine whether a company's financial statements are free from material misstatement?

c.   What is the nature of Ernst & Young's opinion? What do you believe the word *fairly* means? Is Ernst & Young providing a guarantee to Apple's financial statement users?

d.   What other opinion is Ernst & Young rendering? Why is this opinion important?

P1-48.   Reading and Interpreting CEO Certifications   (LO5)

Following is the CEO Certification required by the Sarbanes-Oxley Act and signed by **Apple** CEO Steve Jobs. Apple's Chief Financial Officer signed a similar form.

APPLE, INC.
(AAPL)

CERTIFICATIONS

I, Steven P. Jobs, certify that:

1.   I have reviewed this annual report on Form 10-K of Apple, Inc.;

2.   Based on my knowledge, this report does not contain any untrue statement of a material fact or omit to state a material fact necessary to make the statements made, in light of the circumstances under which such statements were made, not misleading with respect to the period covered by this report;

3.   Based on my knowledge, the financial statements, and other financial information included in this report, fairly present in all material respects the financial condition, results of operations and cash flows of the registrant as of, and for, the periods presented in this report;

4.   The registrant's other certifying officer(s) and I are responsible for establishing and maintaining disclosure controls and procedures (as defined in Exchange Act Rules 13a-15(e) and 15d-15(e)) and internal control over financial reporting (as defined in Exchange Act Rules 13a-15(f) and 15d-15(f) for the registrant) and have:

(a)   Designed such disclosure controls and procedures, or caused such disclosure controls and procedures to be designed under our supervision, to ensure that material information relating to the registrant, including its consolidated subsidiaries, is made known to us by others within those entities, particularly during the period in which this report is being prepared;

(b)   Designed such internal control over financial reporting, or caused such internal control over financial reporting to be designed under our supervision, to provide reasonable assurance regarding the reliability of financial reporting and the preparation of financial statements for external purposes in accordance with generally accepted accounting principles;

(c)   Evaluated the effectiveness of the registrant's disclosure controls and procedures and presented in this report our conclusions about the effectiveness of the disclosure controls and procedures, as of the end of the period covered by this report based on such evaluation; and

(d)   Disclosed in this report any change in the registrant's internal control over financial reporting that occurred during the registrant's most recent fiscal quarter (the registrant's fourth fiscal quarter in the case of an annual report) that has materially affected, or is reasonably likely to materially affect, the registrant's internal control over financial reporting; and

5.   The registrant's other certifying officer(s) and I have disclosed, based on our most recent evaluation of internal control over financial reporting, to the registrant's auditors and the audit committee of the registrant's board of directors (or persons performing the equivalent functions):

(a)   All significant deficiencies and material weaknesses in the design or operation of internal control over financial reporting which are reasonably likely to adversely affect the registrant's ability to record, process, summarize, and report financial information; and

(b)   Any fraud, whether or not material, that involves management or other employees who have a significant role in the registrant's internal control over financial reporting.

Date: October 27, 2010

By: /s/ STEVEN P. JOBS
Steven P. Jobs
Chief Executive Officer

Required

a.   Summarize the assertions that Steve Jobs made in this certification.

b.   Why did Congress feel it important that CEOs and CFOs sign such certifications?

c.   What potential liability do you believe the CEO and CFO are assuming by signing such certifications?

P1-49. Assessing Corporate Governance and Its Effects (LO5)

GENERAL ELECTRIC (GE)

Review the corporate governance section of **General Electric**'s Website (find and click on: "Our Company"; then, find and click on: "Governance").

Required

a. In your words, briefly describe GE's governance structure.

b. What is the main purpose of its governance structure?

IFRS APPLICATIONS

I1-50. Applying the Accounting Equation and Computing Financing Proportions (LO2)

The following table contains fiscal 2009 information for three companies that use IFRS. Apply the accounting equation to compute the missing financial amounts (a), (b), and (c). Which of these companies is more owner-financed? Which of these companies is more nonowner-financed? Discuss why the proportion of owner financing might differ across these three companies.

OMV GROUP ERICSSON BAE SYSTEMS

(Amounts in millions)	Assets	=	Liabilities	+	Equity
OMV Group (France)	€ 21,415		€ 11,380		(a)
Ericsson (Sweden).	SEK 269,809		(b)		SEK 141,027
BAE Systems (UK).	(c)		£20,680		£4,727

ASTRAZENECA

I1-51. Computing Return on Equity and Return on Assets (LO4)

The following table contains financial statement information for **AstraZeneca**, which is a global bio-pharmaceutical company focused on discovery, development, manufacturing and commercialization of medicines and is headquartered in London, UK.

($ millions)	Total Assets	Net Income	Sales	Equity
2007	$47,988	$5,969	$29,559	$14,915
2008	46,950	4,224	31,601	16,060
2009	54,920	7,490	32,804	20,821

Required

a. Compute the return on equity (ROE) for 2008 and 2009. What trend, if any, is evident? How does AstraZeneca's ROE compare with the approximately 17% median ROE for companies in the Dow Jones Industrial average for 2009?

b. Compute the return on assets (ROA) for 2008 and 2009. What trends, if any, are evident? How does AstraZeneca's ROA compare with the approximate 6.5% median ROA for companies in the Dow Jones Industrial average for 2009?

c. What factors might allow a company like AstraZeneca to reap above-average returns?

I1-52. Computing and Interpreting Return on Assets and Its Components (LO4)

TESCO PLC

Tesco PLC, which is one of the world's largest retailers and is headquartered in Cheshunt, U.K., reported the following balance sheet and income statement data for 2007 through 2009.

(£ millions)	Total Assets	Net Income	Sales
2007	£24,807	£1,899	£42,641
2008	30,164	2,130	47,298
2009	46,053	2,166	54,327

Required

a. What is Tesco's return on assets for 2008 and 2009?

b. Disaggregate Tesco's ROA metrics from part *a* into profit margin and asset turnover.

c. What factor is mainly responsible for the change in Tesco's ROA over this period?

DISCUSSION POINTS

D1-53.   Strategic Financing   (LO2)

You and your management team are working to develop the strategic direction of your company for the next three years. One issue you are discussing is how to finance the projected increases in operating assets. Your options are to rely more heavily on operating creditors, borrow the funds, or to sell additional stock in your company. Discuss the pros and cons of each source of financing.

D1-54.   Statement Analysis   (LO4)

You are evaluating your company's recent operating performance and are trying to decide on the relative weights you should put on the income statement, the balance sheet, and the statement of cash flows. Discuss the information each of these statements provides and its role in evaluating operating performance.

D1-55.   Analyst Relations   (LO2)

Your investor relations department reports to you that stockholders and financial analysts evaluate the quality of a company's financial reports based on their "transparency," namely the clarity and completeness of the company's financial disclosures. Discuss the trade-offs of providing more or less transparent financial reports.

D1-56.   Ethics and Governance: Management Communications   (LO5)

The Business Insight box on page 1-13 quotes Warren Buffett on the use of accounting jargon. Many companies publicly describe their performance using terms such as "EBITDA" or "earnings purged of various expenses" because they believe these terms more effectively reflect their companies' performance than GAAP-defined terms such as net income. What ethical issues might arise from the use of such terms and what challenges does their use present for the governance of the company by shareholders and directors?

D1-57.[B]   Ethics and Governance: Auditor Independence   (LO5)

The SEC has been concerned with the "independence" of external auditing firms. It is especially concerned about how large non-audit (such as consulting) fees might impact how aggressively auditing firms pursue accounting issues they uncover in their audits. Congress recently passed legislation that prohibits accounting firms from providing both consulting and auditing services to the same client. How might consulting fees affect auditor independence? What other conflicts of interest might exist for auditors? How do these conflicts impact the governance process?

SOLUTIONS TO REVIEW PROBLEMS

Mid-Module Review

Solution

1.

ALLSTATE CORPORATION
Income Statement
For Year Ended December 31, 2010

Revenues	$31,400
Expenses	30,472
Net income	$ 928

ALLSTATE CORPORATION
Balance Sheet
December 31, 2010

Cash	$ 562	Total liabilities	$111,830
Noncash assets	130,312	Stockholders' equity	19,044
Total assets	$130,874	Total liabilities and equity	$130,874

ALLSTATE CORPORATION Statement of Cash Flows For Year Ended December 31, 2010	
Cash flows from operations	$3,689
Cash flows from investing	2,332
Cash flows from financing	(6,071)
Net increase (decrease) in cash	(50)
Cash, beginning year	612
Cash, ending year	$ 562

2. Berkshire Hathaway is a larger company; its total assets are $372,229 million compared to Allstate's assets of $130,874 million. The income statements of the two companies are markedly different. Berkshire Hathaway reports more than four times as much revenue ($135,185 million compared to $31,400 million). The difference in net income is also large; Berkshire Hathaway earned $12,967 million whereas Allstate reported net income of only $928 million.

Module-End Review

Solution

a. ROA = Net income/Average assets = $1,068/$20,600 = 5.2%. The profitability component is Net income/Sales = $1,068/$14,963 = 7.1%, and the productivity component is Sales/Average assets = $14,963/$20,600 = 0.73. Notice that 7.1% × 0.73 = 5.2%. Thus, the two components, when multiplied yield ROA.

b. ROE = Net income/Average stockholders' equity = $1,068/$5,899 = 18.1%.

1. Describe and interpret the elements of and the information conveyed by financial statements. (p. 2-4)

2. Analyze and interpret transactions using the financial statement effects template. (p. 2-19)

3. Analyze and interpret accounting adjustments and their financial statement effects. (p. 2-22)

4. Construct financial statements from account balances. (p. 2-27)

Overview of Business Activities and Financial Statements

In 1985, the board of directors of **Apple** along with the new CEO John Sculley, dismissed Steve Jobs, Apple's co-founder. Fast forward 12 years—Apple is struggling to survive. After a series of crippling financial losses, the company's stock price is at an all-time low. In a complete about-face, the board asks Steve Jobs to return as interim CEO to begin a critical restructuring of the company's product line. True to form, Jobs shows up at his first meeting with Apple senior executives wearing shorts, sneakers, and a few days' beard growth. Sitting in a swivel chair and spinning slowly, Jobs begins quizzing the executives. "OK, tell me what's wrong with this place," asks Jobs. Mumbled replies and embarrassed looks ensue. Jobs cuts them short and jumps up: "It's the products! So what's wrong with the products?" Again, more weak answers and again Jobs cut them off. "The products SUCK!" he roars. "There's no sex in them anymore!"

APPLE

Jobs was right—Apple was mired in a sea of problems, many stemming from a weak product line. The company's decision to design proprietary software that was often incompatible with Windows had relegated Apple to a niche player in the highly competitive, low-margin PC business. Years before, **Microsoft** had replicated the Mac operating system and licensed the software to PC manufacturers such as **Dell**. Apple's cumulative profit from 2001-2003 was an anemic $109 million and its prospects were dim.

That was then; this is now. Apple's iPod and iTunes sales quickly soared and comprised nearly 50% of Apple's revenues. However, today those products account for only 20% of its revenues. iPhone sales now top $25 billion annually, which is over one-third of total revenues. The effects of iPad sales will further reduce that percentage.

Apple's shares (ticker: AAPL) traded around $400 in 2011, a staggering 100 times the $4 they fetched fourteen years earlier when Jobs rejoined the team. Indeed, Apple's stock has more than doubled in price in the past two years, as the following price chart illustrates. The total stock market value of Apple stock (called the market capitalization or market cap) exceeded $373 billion in 2011.

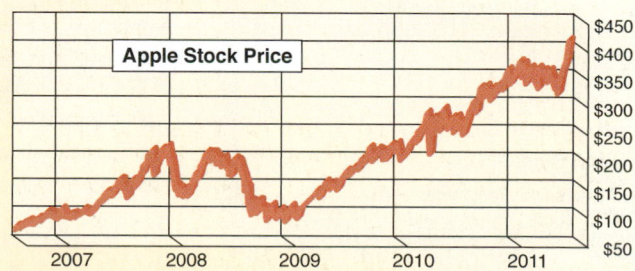

This module defines and explains the components of each financial statement: the balance sheet, the income statement, the statement of cash flows, and the statement of stockholders' equity. Let's begin with a sneak preview of Apple's financial statements.

(continued on next page)

(continued from previous page)

Apple's balance sheet is very liquid as many of its assets can be readily converted to cash. Indeed, Apple holds over two-thirds of its assets in cash and marketable securities. Liquidity is important for companies like Apple that must react quickly to opportunities and changing market conditions. Like other technology companies, much of Apple's production is subcontracted. Consequently, Apple's property, plant and equipment make up only 6% of its assets.

On the financing side of its balance sheet, almost two-thirds of Apple's resources come from owner financing: from common stock sold to shareholders and from past profits that have been reinvested in the business. Technology companies such as Apple, which have uncertain product life-cycles and highly volatile cash flows, strive to avoid high debt levels that might cause financial problems in a business downturn. Apple's nonowner financing consists of low-cost credit from suppliers (accounts payable) and unpaid overhead expenses (accrued liabilities).

Consider Apple's income statement: driven by the popularity and high profit margins of iPods and iPhones, Apple recently reported over $18.3 billion of operating income. This is impressive given that Apple spends three cents of every sales dollar on research and development and runs expensive advertising campaigns.

Yet, companies cannot live by profits alone. It is cash that pays bills. Profits and cash flow reflect two different concepts, each providing a different perspective on company performance. Apple generated over $18.5 billion of cash flow from operating activities, and invested most of this cash flow in marketable securities. We review Apple's cash flows in this module.

Apple pays no dividends and its newly issued common stock relates primarily to executive stock options. These capital transactions are reported in the statement of stockholders' equity.

While it is important to understand what is reported in each of the four financial statements, it is also important to know what is *not* reported. To illustrate, *Fortune* reported that "Jobs cut a deal with the Big Five record companies . . . to sell songs on iTunes, but they were afraid of Internet piracy. So Jobs promised to wrap their songs in Apple's *FairPlay*—the only copy-protection software that is iPod-compatible. Other digital music services such as Yahoo Music Unlimited and Napster reached similar deals with the big record labels. But Apple refused to license *FairPlay* to them. So those companies turned to Microsoft for copy protection. That means none of the songs sold by those services can be played on the wildly popular iPod. Instead, users of the services had to rely on inferior devices made by companies like Samsung and SanDisk that supported Microsoft's Windows Media format."

Apple's copy-protection software described above creates a barrier to competition that allows iPod to earn above-average profits. This represents a valuable resource to Apple, but it is not reported as an asset on Apple's balance sheet. Consider another example. Apple's software engineers write code and create software that will generate profits for Apple in the future. While this represents a valuable resource to Apple, it is not reported on the balance sheet because Apple expenses the software engineers' salaries when the code is written. Finally, Steve Jobs himself was a valuable unrecorded asset for Apple. We discuss these and other issues relating to asset recognition and measurement in this module.

Sources: Apple 2010 10-K; Apple 2010 Annual Report; *BusinessWeek*, 2006; *Fortune*, 2006 and 2012.

MODULE ORGANIZATION

Overview of Business Activities and Financial Statements

Analyzing Components of Financial Statements
- Balance Sheet
- Income Statement
- Statement of Stockholders' Equity
- Statement of Cash Flows
- Retained Earnings Reconciliation

Analyzing Transactions and Accounting Adjustments
- Analyzing Transactions and Assessing Financial Statement Effects
- Interpreting Accounting Adjustments
- Constructing Financial Statements
- Closing Process

The first section of this module defines and explains key elements of financial statements. Our analysis of financial statements is enhanced when we know what is measured and what is not measured by financial statements. This section also discusses some analysis insights that are helpful in our assessment of company performance and financial condition.

INTERPRETING A BALANCE SHEET

The balance sheet is divided into three sections: assets, liabilities, and stockholders' equity. It provides information about the resources available to management and the claims against those resources by creditors and shareholders. The balance sheet reports the assets, liabilities and equity at a *point in time*. Balance sheet accounts are called "permanent accounts" in that they carry over from period to period; that is, the ending balance from one period becomes the beginning balance for the next.

LO1 Describe and interpret the elements of and the information conveyed by financial statements.

Assets

Companies acquire assets to yield a return for their shareholders. Assets are expected to produce economic benefits in the form of revenues, either directly, such as with inventory, or indirectly, such as with a manufacturing plant that produces inventories for sale. To create shareholder value, assets must yield income that is in excess of the cost of the funds used to acquire the assets.

The asset section of the **Apple** balance sheet is shown in Exhibit 2.1. Apple reports $75,183 million of total assets as of September 25, 2010, its year-end. Amounts reported on the balance sheet are at a *point in time*—that is, the close of business on the day of the report. An asset must possess two characteristics to be reported on the balance sheet:

1. It must be owned (or controlled) by the company.

2. It must confer expected future economic benefits that result from a past transaction or event.

The first requirement, owning or controlling an asset, implies that a company has legal title to the asset, such as the title to property, or has the unrestricted right to use the asset, such as a lease on the property. The second requirement implies that a company expects to realize a benefit from the asset. Benefits can be cash inflows from the sale of an asset or from sales of products produced by the asset. Benefits also can refer to the receipt of other assets such as an account receivable from a credit sale. Or, benefits can arise from future services the company will receive, such as prepaying for a year-long insurance policy. This requirement also implies that we cannot record an asset such as a brand name without a transaction to acquire it.

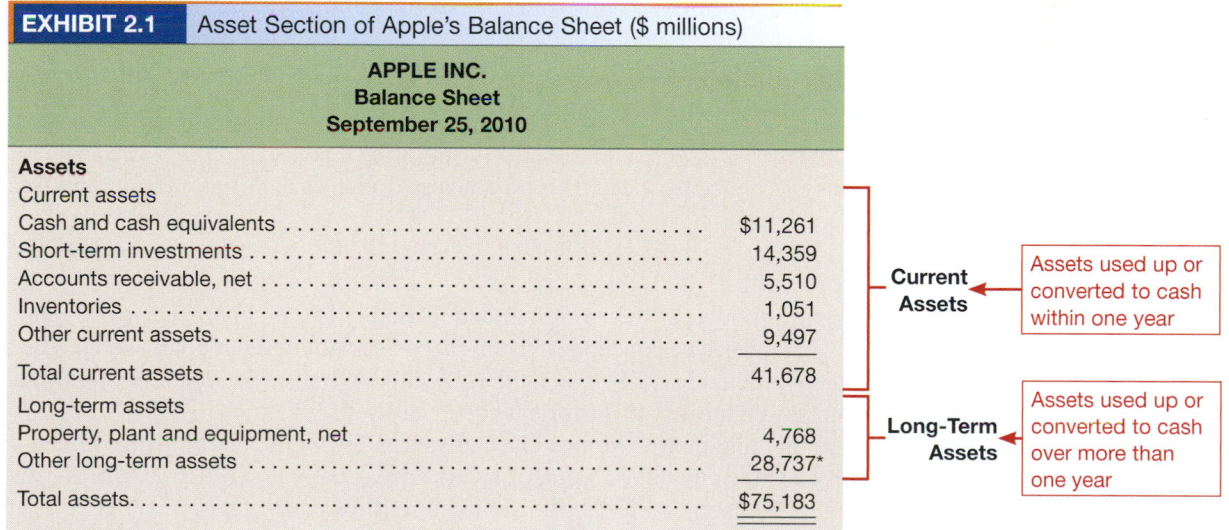

EXHIBIT 2.1	Asset Section of Apple's Balance Sheet ($ millions)

APPLE INC.
Balance Sheet
September 25, 2010

Assets	
Current assets	
Cash and cash equivalents	$11,261
Short-term investments	14,359
Accounts receivable, net	5,510
Inventories	1,051
Other current assets	9,497
Total current assets	41,678
Long-term assets	
Property, plant and equipment, net	4,768
Other long-term assets	28,737*
Total assets	$75,183

Current Assets — Assets used up or converted to cash within one year

Long-Term Assets — Assets used up or converted to cash over more than one year

*Includes $25,391 million of long-term marketable securities

Current Assets

The balance sheet lists assets in order of decreasing **liquidity**, which refers to the ease of converting noncash assets into cash. The most liquid assets are called **current assets** and they are listed first. A company expects to convert its current assets into cash or use those assets in operations within the coming fiscal year.[1] Typical examples of current assets follow:

Cash—currency, bank deposits, and investments with an original maturity of 90 days or less (called *cash equivalents*);

Short-term investments—marketable securities and other investments that the company expects to dispose of in the short run;

Accounts receivable, net—amounts due to the company from customers arising from the sale of products and services on credit ("net" refers to the subtraction of uncollectible accounts);

Inventories—goods purchased or produced for sale to customers;

Prepaid expenses—costs paid in advance for rent, insurance, advertising and other services.

Apple reports current assets of $41,678 million in 2010, which is 55% of its total assets. The amount of current assets is an important measure of liquidity, which relates to a company's ability to make short-term payments. Companies require a degree of liquidity to operate effectively, as they must be able to respond to changing market conditions and take advantage of opportunities. However, current assets are expensive to hold (they must be stored, insured, monitored, financed, and so forth)—and they typically generate relatively low returns. As a result, companies seek to maintain only just enough current assets to cover liquidity needs, but not so much to unnecessarily reduce income.

Long-Term Assets

The second section of the balance sheet reports long-term (noncurrent) assets. Long-term assets include the following:

Property, plant and equipment (PPE), net—land, factory buildings, warehouses, office buildings, machinery, motor vehicles, office equipment and other items used in operating activities ("net" refers to subtraction of accumulated depreciation, the portion of the assets' cost that has been expensed);

Long-term investments—investments that the company does not intend to sell in the near future;

Intangible and other assets—assets without physical substance, including patents, trademarks, franchise rights, goodwill and other costs the company incurred that provide future benefits.

Long-term assets are not expected to be converted into cash for some time and are, therefore, listed after current assets.

Measuring Assets

Most assets are reported at their original acquisition costs, or **historical costs**, and not at their current market values. The concept of historical costs is not without controversy. The controversy arises because of the trade-off between the **relevance** of current market values for many business decisions and the **reliability** of historical cost measures.

To illustrate, imagine we are financial analysts and want to determine the value of a company. The company's value equals the value of its assets less the value of its liabilities. Current market values of company assets (and liabilities) are more informative and relevant to our analysis than are historical costs. But how can we determine market values? For some assets, like marketable securities, values are readily obtained from online quotes or from *The Wall Street Journal*. For other assets like property, plant, and equipment, their market values are far more subjective and

---

[1] Technically, current assets include those assets expected to be converted into cash within the upcoming fiscal year or the company's operating cycle (the cash-to-cash cycle), whichever is longer. **Fortune Brands** (manufacturer of Jim Beam Whiskey) provides an example of a current asset with a cash conversion cycle of longer than one year. Its inventory footnote reports: "In accordance with generally recognized trade practices, bulk whiskey inventories are classified as current assets, although the majority of such inventories, due to the duration of aging processes, ordinarily will not be sold within one year."

difficult to estimate. It would be easier for us, as analysts, if companies reported credible market values on their balance sheet. However, allowing companies to report estimates of asset market values would introduce potential *bias* into financial reporting. Consequently, companies continue to report historical costs because the loss in reliability from using subjective market values on the balance sheet is considered to be greater than the loss in relevance from using historical costs.

It is important to realize that balance sheets only include items that can be reliably measured. If a company cannot assign a monetary amount to an asset with relative certainty, it does not recognize an asset on the balance sheet. This means that there are, typically, considerable "assets" that are not reflected on a balance sheet. For example, the well-known apple image is absent from Apple's balance sheet. This image is called an "unrecognized intangible asset." Both requirements for an asset are met: Apple owns the brand and it expects to realize future benefits from the logo. The problem is reliably measuring the expected future benefits to be derived from the image. Intangible assets such as the Coke bottle silhouette, the iPod brandname, and the Nike swoosh also are not on their respective balance sheets. Companies only report intangible assets on the balance sheet when the assets are purchased. Any internally created intangible assets are not reported on a balance sheet. A sizable amount of resources is, therefore, potentially omitted from companies' balance sheets.

Excluded intangible assets often relate to *knowledge-based* (intellectual) assets, such as a strong management team, a well-designed supply chain, or superior technology. Although these intangible assets confer a competitive advantage to the company, and yield above-normal income (and clear economic benefits to those companies), they cannot be reliably measured. This is one reason why companies in knowledge-based industries are so difficult to analyze and value.

Presumably, however, companies' market values reflect these excluded intangible assets. This can yield a large difference between the market value and the book (reported) value of a company's equity. This is illustrated in the following ratios of market value to book value (averages from 2011): **Apple** is 5.4 and **Target** is 2.3. These market-to-book values (ratios) are greater for companies with large knowledge-based assets that are not reported on the balance sheet, but are reflected in company market value (such as with **Apple**). Companies such as **Target** have fewer of these assets. Hence, their balance sheets usually reflect a greater portion of company value.

Liabilities and Equity

Liabilities and stockholders' equity represent the sources of capital the company uses to finance the acquisition of assets. In general, liabilities represent a company's future economic sacrifices. Liabilities are borrowed funds such as accounts payable and obligations to lenders. They can be interest-bearing or non-interest-bearing.

Equity represents capital that has been invested by the shareholders, either directly via the purchase of stock, or indirectly in the form of *retained earnings* that reflect earnings that are reinvested in the business and not paid out as dividends.

The liabilities and stockholders' equity sections of the **Apple** balance sheet are reproduced in Exhibit 2.2. Apple reports $27,392 million of total liabilities and $47,791 million of stockholders' equity as of its 2010 year-end.

Why would Apple obtain capital from both borrowed funds and shareholders? Why not just one or the other? The answer lies in their relative costs and the contractual agreements that Apple has with each.

Creditors have the first claim on the assets of the company. As a result, their position is not as risky and, accordingly, their expected return on investment is less than that required by shareholders. Also, interest is tax deductible whereas dividends are not. This makes debt a less expensive source of capital than equity. So, then, why should a company not finance itself entirely with borrowed funds? The reason is that borrowed funds entail contractual obligations to repay the principal and interest on the debt. If a company cannot make these payments when they come due, creditors can force the company into bankruptcy and potentially put the company out of business. Shareholders, in contrast, cannot require repurchase of their stock, or even the payment of dividends. Thus, companies take on a level of debt that they can comfortably repay at reasonable interest costs. The remaining balance required to fund business activities is financed with more costly equity capital.

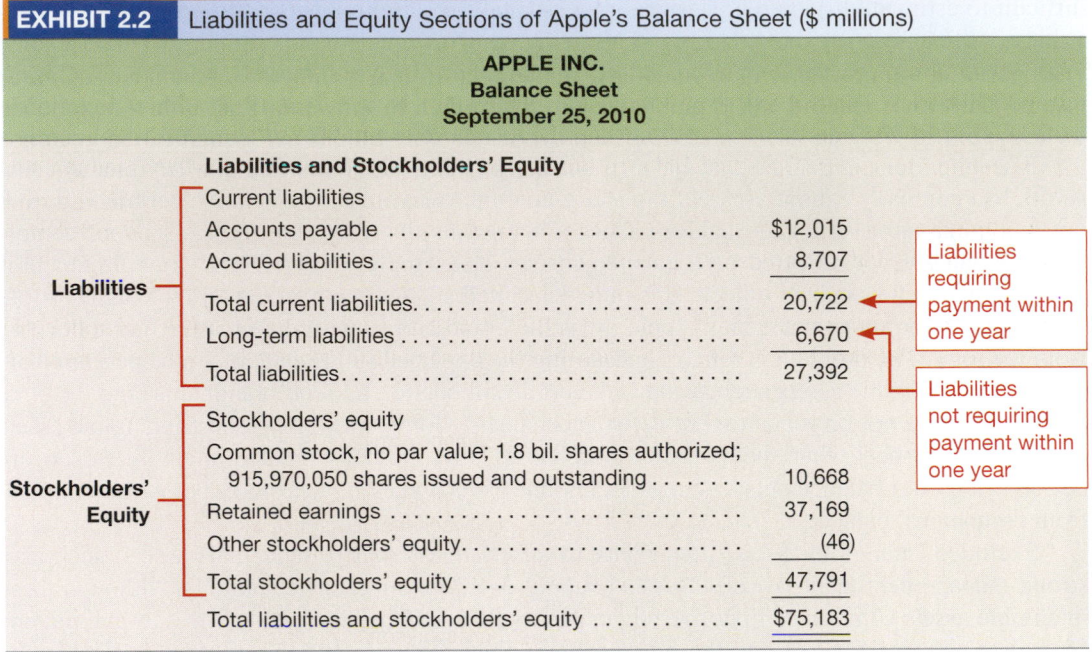

EXHIBIT 2.2   Liabilities and Equity Sections of Apple's Balance Sheet ($ millions)

APPLE INC.
Balance Sheet
September 25, 2010

Liabilities and Stockholders' Equity

Liabilities	
Current liabilities	
Accounts payable	$12,015
Accrued liabilities	8,707
Total current liabilities	20,722
Long-term liabilities	6,670
Total liabilities	27,392
Stockholders' Equity	
Stockholders' equity	
Common stock, no par value; 1.8 bil. shares authorized; 915,970,050 shares issued and outstanding	10,668
Retained earnings	37,169
Other stockholders' equity	(46)
Total stockholders' equity	47,791
Total liabilities and stockholders' equity	$75,183

Liabilities requiring payment within one year

Liabilities not requiring payment within one year

Current Liabilities

The balance sheet lists liabilities in order of maturity. Obligations that must be settled within one year are called **current liabilities**. Examples of common current liabilities follow:

Accounts payable—amounts owed to suppliers for goods and services purchased on credit.

Accrued liabilities—obligations for expenses that have been incurred but not yet paid; examples are accrued wages payable (wages earned by employees but not yet paid), accrued interest payable (interest that is owing but has not been paid), and accrued income taxes (taxes due).

Unearned revenues—obligations created when the company accepts payment in advance for goods or services it will deliver in the future; also called advances from customers, customer deposits, or deferred revenues.

Short-term notes payable—short-term debt payable to banks or other creditors.

Current maturities of long-term debt—principal portion of long-term debt that is due to be paid within one year.

Apple reports current liabilities of $20,722 million on its 2010 balance sheet.

Accounts payable arise when one company purchases goods or services from another company. Typically, sellers offer credit terms when selling to other companies, rather than expecting cash on delivery. The seller records an account receivable and the buyer records an account payable. Apple reports accounts payable of $12,015 million as of the balance sheet date. Accounts payable are relatively uncomplicated liabilities. A transaction occurs (inventory purchase), a bill is sent, and the amount owed is reported on the balance sheet as a liability.

Apple's accrued liabilities total $8,707 million. Accrued liabilities refer to incomplete transactions. For example, employees work and earn wages, but usually are not paid until later, such as several days after the period-end. Wages must be reported as expense in the period that employees earn them because those wages payable are obligations of the company and a liability (wages payable) must be set up on the balance sheet. This is an *accrual*. Other common accruals include the recording of liabilities such as rent and utilities payable, taxes payable, and interest payable on borrowings. All of these accruals involve recognition of expense in the income statement and a liability on the balance sheet.

Net working capital, or simply working capital, reflects the difference between current assets and current liabilities and is defined as follows:

$$\text{Net working capital} = \text{Current assets} - \text{Current liabilities}$$

We usually prefer to see more current assets than current liabilities to ensure that companies are liquid. That is, companies should have sufficient funds to pay their short-term debts as they mature. The net working capital required to conduct business depends on the company's **operating (or cash) cycle**, which is the time between paying cash for goods or employee services and receiving cash from customers—see Exhibit 2.3.

Companies, for example, use cash to purchase or manufacture inventories held for resale. Inventories are usually purchased on credit from suppliers (accounts payable). This financing is called **trade credit**. Inventories are sold, either for cash or on credit (accounts receivable). When receivables are ultimately collected, a portion of the cash received is used to repay accounts payable and the remainder goes to the cash account for the next operating cycle.

EXHIBIT 2.3   Operating Cycle

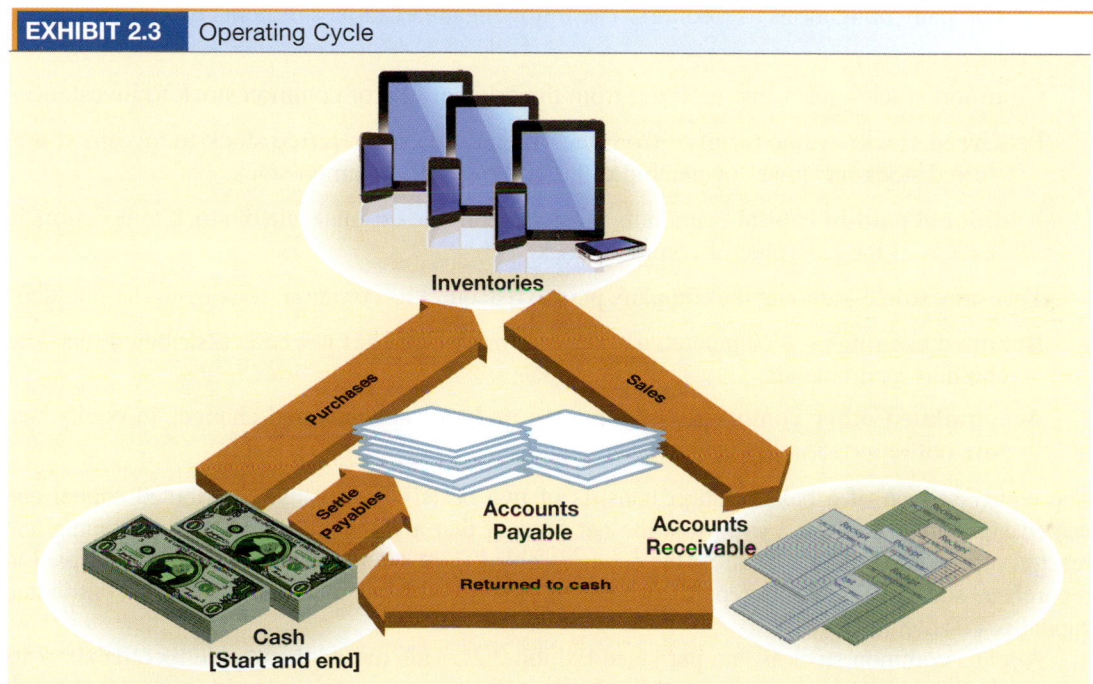

When cash is invested in inventory, the inventory can remain with the company for 30 to 90 days or more. Once inventory is sold, the resulting accounts receivable can remain with the company for another 30 to 90 days. Assets such as inventories and accounts receivable are costly to hold and, consequently, companies strive to reduce operating cycles with various initiatives that aim to:

- Decrease accounts receivable by better collection procedures
- Reduce inventory levels by improved production systems and management
- Increase trade credit to minimize the cash invested in inventories

Analysts often use the "cash conversion cycle" to evaluate company liquidity. The cash conversion cycle is the number of days the company has its cash tied up in receivables and inventories, less the number of days of trade credit provided by company suppliers.

Noncurrent Liabilities

Noncurrent liabilities are obligations due after one year. Examples of noncurrent liabilities follow:

Long-term debt—amounts borrowed from creditors that are scheduled to be repaid more than one year in the future; any portion of long-term debt that is due within one year is reclassified as a current liability called *current maturities of long-term debt*. Long-term debt includes bonds, mortgages, and other long-term loans.

Other long-term liabilities—various obligations, such as pension liabilities and long-term tax liabilities, that will be settled a year or more into the future.

Apple reports $6,670 million of noncurrent liabilities. As is typical of high-tech companies, Apple has no long-term debt. Instead, all of its noncurrent liabilities relate to deferred revenue and deferred taxes. Deferred (unearned) revenue arises when a company receives cash in advance of providing a good or service.

Stockholders' Equity

Stockholders' equity reflects financing provided from company owners. Equity is often referred to as *residual interest*. That is, stockholders have a claim on any assets in excess of what is needed to meet company obligations to creditors. The following are examples of items typically included in equity:

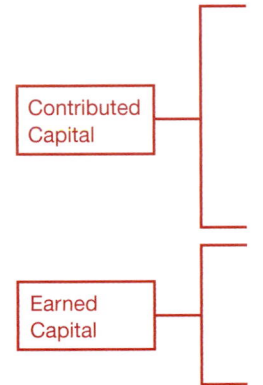

Common stock—par value received from the original sale of common stock to investors.

Preferred stock—value received from the original sale of preferred stock to investors; preferred stock has fewer ownership rights compared to common stock.

Additional paid-in capital—amounts received from the original sale of stock to investors in excess of the par value of common stock.

Treasury stock—amount the company paid to reacquire its common stock from shareholders.

Retained earnings—accumulated net income (profit) that has not been distributed to stockholders as dividends.

Accumulated other comprehensive income or loss—accumulated changes in equity that are not reported in the income statement.

The equity section of a balance sheet consists of two basic components: contributed capital and earned capital. **Contributed capital** is the net funding that a company received from issuing and reacquiring its equity shares; that is, the funds received from issuing shares less any funds paid to repurchase such shares. Apple reports $47,791 million in total stockholders' equity. Its contributed capital is $10,668 million.

Apple's common stock is "no par" (see Exhibit 2.2). This means that Apple records all of its contributed capital in the common stock account and records no additional paid-in capital. Apple's stockholders (via its board of directors) have authorized it to issue up to 1.8 billion shares of common stock. To date, it has sold (issued) 915,970,050 shares for total proceeds of $10,668 million, or $11.65 per share, on average. Apple has repurchased no shares of stock to date.

Earned capital is the cumulative net income (loss) that has been retained by the company (not paid out to shareholders as dividends). Apple's earned capital (titled Retained Earnings) totals $37,169 million as of its 2010 year-end. Its other equity accounts total $(46) million.

Retained Earnings

There is an important relation for retained earnings that reconciles its beginning balance and its ending balance, which is shown in Exhibit 2.4.

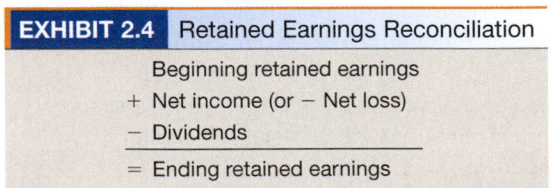

EXHIBIT 2.4	Retained Earnings Reconciliation
	Beginning retained earnings
	+ Net income (or − Net loss)
	− Dividends
	= Ending retained earnings

This is a useful relation to remember. Apple's retained earnings increases (or decreases) each year by the amount of its reported net income (loss). If Apple paid dividends, it would decrease retained earnings, but Apple currently pays no dividends. (There are other items that can impact retained earnings that we discuss in later modules.) After we explain the income statement, we will revisit this relation and show how retained earnings link the balance sheet and income statement.

BUSINESS INSIGHT | **How Much Debt Is Reasonable?**

Apple reports total assets of $75,183 million, liabilities of $27,392 million, and stockholders' equity of $47,791 million. This reveals that it finances 36% of its assets with borrowed funds and 64% with shareholder investment. This is a lower percentage of nonowner financing than other companies such as **Target** and **Procter & Gamble** (P&G). Companies must monitor their financing sources and amounts. Too much borrowing is risky as borrowed amounts must be repaid with interest. The level of debt that a company can effectively manage depends on the stability and reliability of its operating cash flows. Companies such as P&G and Target can manage relatively high debt levels because their cash flows are relatively stable. Apple operates in an industry that changes rapidly. It cannot afford to take on too much borrowing risk.

($ millions)	Assets	Liabilities	Liabilities to Assets ratio	Equity	Equity to Assets ratio
Apple, Inc.	$ 75,183	$27,392	36.4%	$47,791	63.6%
Cisco Systems, Inc.	81,130	36,845	45.4%	44,285	54.6%
Gap, Inc.	7,065	2,985	42.3%	4,080	57.7%
Procter & Gamble Co.	128,172	66,733	52.1%	61,439	47.9%
Target Corporation	43,705	28,218	64.6%	15,487	35.4%

Book Value vs Market Value Stockholders' equity is the "value" of the company determined by GAAP and is commonly referred to as the company's **book value**. This value is different from a company's **market value** (market capitalization or *market cap*), which is computed by multiplying the number of outstanding common shares by the per share market value. We can compute Apple's market cap by multiplying its outstanding shares at September 25, 2010, (915,970,050 shares) by its stock price on that date ($292.32), which equals $267.8 billion. This is considerably larger than its book value of equity on that date of $47,791 million. Book value and market value can differ for several reasons, mostly related to the recognition of transactions and events in financial statements such as the following:

■ GAAP generally reports assets and liabilities at historical costs, whereas the market attempts to estimate fair market values.

■ GAAP excludes resources that cannot be reliably measured (due to the absence of a past transaction or event) such as talented management, employee morale, recent innovations and successful marketing, whereas the market attempts to value these.

■ GAAP does not consider market differences in which companies operate, such as competitive conditions and expected changes, whereas the market attempts to factor in these differences in determining value.

■ GAAP does not usually report expected future performance, whereas the market attempts to predict and value future performance.

Presently for U.S. companies, book value is, on average, about two-thirds of market value. This means that the market has drawn on information in addition to that provided in the balance sheet and income statement in valuing equity shares. A major part of this information is in financial statement notes, but not all. It is important to understand that, eventually, all factors determining company market value are reflected in financial statements and book value. Assets are eventually sold and liabilities are settled. Moreover, talented management, employee morale, technological innovations, and successful marketing are eventually recognized in reported profit. The difference between book value and market value is one of timing.

BUSINESS INSIGHT   **Apple's Market and Book Values**

Apple's market value has historically exceeded its book value of equity (see graph below). Much of Apple's market value derives from intangible assets, such as brand equity, that are not fully reflected on its balance sheet, and from favorable expectations of future financial performance (particularly in recent years). Apple has incurred many costs, such as R&D, advertising, and promotion, that will probably yield future economic benefits. However, Apple expensed these costs (did not capitalize them as assets) because their future benefits were uncertain and therefore could not be reliably measured. Companies capitalize intangible assets only when those assets are purchased, and not when they are internally developed. Consequently, Apple's balance sheet and the balance sheets of many knowledge-based companies are, arguably, less informative about company value.

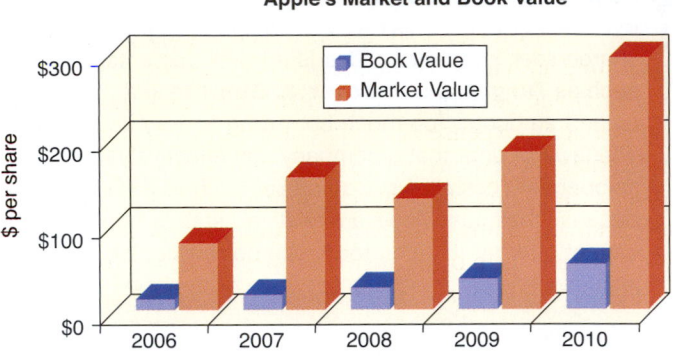

Apple's Market and Book Value

INTERPRETING AN INCOME STATEMENT

The income statement reports revenues earned during a period, the expenses incurred to produce those revenues, and the resulting net income or loss. Apple's income statement from its 2010 10-K is shown in Exhibit 2.5. Apple reports net income of $14,013 million on sales of $65,225 million. This means that about $0.21 of each dollar of sales is brought down to the bottom line, computed as $14,013 million divided by $65,225 million. Apple's net income margin is higher than that of the average publicly-traded company, which reports about $0.06 in profit for each sales dollar. The remaining $0.79 of each sales dollar for Apple (computed as $1 minus $0.21) is consumed by costs incurred to generate sales. These costs include production costs (cost of sales), wages, advertising, research and development, equipment costs (such as depreciation), and taxes.

EXHIBIT 2.5	Apple's Income Statement ($ millions)

APPLE INC.
Income Statement
For Year Ended September 25, 2010

Net sales.	$65,225
Cost of sales.	39,541
Gross margin	25,684
Operating expenses	
Research and development	1,782
Selling, general, and administrative	5,517
Total operating expenses	7,299
Operating profit	18,385
Other revenue and expense	
Interest and other income, net	155
Income before provision for income taxes.	18,540
Provision for income taxes	4,527
Net income.	$14,013

To analyze an income statement we must understand some terminology. **Revenues** (Sales) are increases in net assets (assets less liabilities) as a result of ordinary operating activities. **Expenses** are decreases in net assets used to generate revenues, including costs of sales, operating costs like wages and advertising (usually titled selling, general, and administrative expenses or SG&A), and nonoperating costs like interest on debt. The difference between revenues and expenses is **net income** when revenues exceed expenses, or **net loss** when expenses exceed revenues. The terms income, profit, and earnings are used interchangeably (as are revenues and sales).

Operating expenses are the usual and customary costs that a company incurs to support its operating activities. Those include cost of goods sold, selling expenses, depreciation expense, and research and development expense. Not all of these expenses require a cash outlay; for example, depreciation expense is a noncash expense, as are many liabilities such as wages payable, that recognize the expense in advance of cash payment. **Nonoperating expenses** relate to the company's financing and investing activities, and include interest expense, interest or dividend income, and gains and losses from the sale of securities. Business decision makers and analysts usually segregate operating and nonoperating activities as they offer different insights into company performance and condition.

> **Alert** The FASB has released a preliminary draft of a proposal to restructure financial statements to, among other things, better distinguish operating and nonoperating activities.

ANALYSIS DECISION   **You Are the Securities Analyst**

You are analyzing the performance of a company that hired a new CEO during the current year. The current year's income statement includes an expense labeled "asset write-offs." Write-offs represent the accelerated transfer of costs from the balance sheet to the income statement. Are you concerned about the legitimacy of these expenses? Why or why not? [Answer, p. 2-34]

Recognition of Revenues and Expenses

An important consideration in preparing the income statement is *when* to recognize revenues and expenses. For many revenues and expenses, the decision is easy. When a customer purchases groceries, pays with a check, and walks out of the store with the groceries, we know that the sale is made and revenue should be recognized. Or, when companies receive and pay an electric bill with a check, they have clearly incurred an expense that should be recognized.

However, should Apple recognize revenue when it sells iPods to a retailer that does not have to pay Apple for 60 days? Should Apple recognize an expense for employees who work this week but will not be paid until the first of next month? The answer to both of these questions is yes.

Two fundamental principles guide recognition of revenues and expenses:

Revenue Recognition Principle—recognize revenues when *earned*.

Expense Recognition (Matching) Principle—recognize expenses when *incurred*.

These two principles are the foundation of **accrual accounting**, which is the accounting system used to prepare all GAAP-based financial statements. The general approach is this: first, recognize revenues in the time period they are earned; then, record all expenses *incurred* to generate those revenues during that same time period (this is called matching expenses to revenues). Net income is then correctly reported for that period.

Recognizing revenues when earned does not necessarily imply the receipt of cash. Revenue is *earned* when the company has done everything that it is supposed to do. This means that a sale of goods on credit would qualify for recognition as long as the revenues are earned. Likewise, companies recognize an expense when it is *incurred*, even if no cash is paid. For example, companies recognize as expenses the wages earned by employees, even though they will not be paid until the next pay period. The company records an expense but pays no cash; instead, it records an accrued liability for the wages payable.

Accrual accounting requires estimates and assumptions. Examples include estimating how much revenue has been earned on a long-term contract, the amount of accounts receivable that will not be collected, the degree to which equipment has been "used up," the cleanup costs that a company must eventually pay for environmental liabilities, and numerous other estimates. All of these estimates and assumptions affect both reported net income and the balance sheet. Judgments affect all financial statements. This is an important by-product of accrual accounting. We discuss these estimates and assumptions, and their effects on financial statements, throughout the book.

ANALYSIS DECISION   You Are the CFO

Assume that you learn of the leakage of hazardous waste from your company's factory. It is estimated that cleanup will cost $10 million. Part 1: What effect will recording this cost have on your company's balance sheet and its income statement? Part 2: Accounting rules require you to record this cost if it is both probable and can be reliably estimated. Although the cleanup is relatively certain, the cost is a guess at this point. Consequently, you have some discretion whether to record it. Discuss the parties that are likely affected by your decision on whether or not to record the liability and related expense, and the ethical issues involved. [Answer 2-34]

Reporting of Transitory Items

To this point, we have only considered income from continuing operations and its components. A more complete income statement format is in Exhibit 2.6. The most noticeable difference involves two additional components of net income located at the bottom of the statement. These two components are specifically segregated from the "income from continuing operations" and are defined as follows:

1. **Discontinued operations** Gains or losses (and net income or loss) from business segments that are being sold or have been sold in the current period.
2. **Extraordinary items** Gains or losses from events that are both *unusual* and *infrequent* and are, therefore, excluded from income from continuing operations.

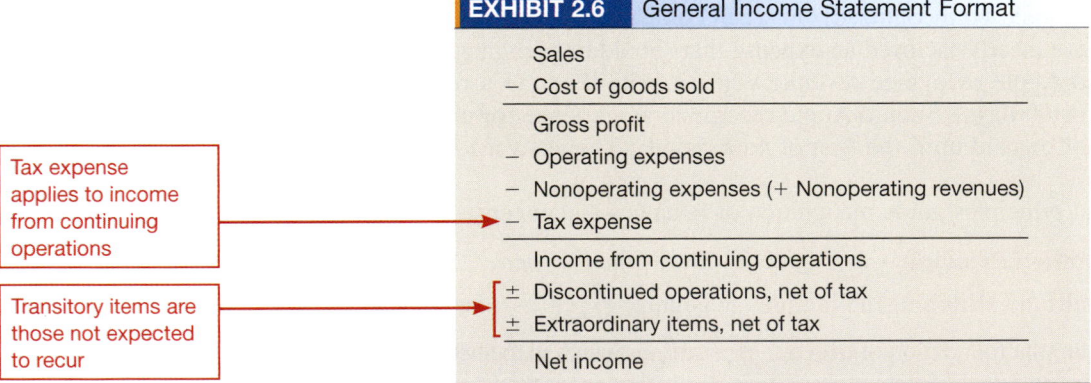

EXHIBIT 2.6   General Income Statement Format

Sales
− Cost of goods sold

Gross profit
− Operating expenses
− Nonoperating expenses (+ Nonoperating revenues)
− Tax expense

Income from continuing operations
± Discontinued operations, net of tax
± Extraordinary items, net of tax

Net income

Tax expense applies to income from continuing operations

Transitory items are those not expected to recur

These two components are segregated because they represent **transitory items**, which reflect transactions or events that are unlikely to recur. Many readers of financial statements are interested in *future* company performance. They analyze current-year financial statements to gain clues to better *predict* future performance. (Stock prices, for example, are based on a company's expected profits and cash flows.)

Transitory items, by definition, are unlikely to arise in future periods. Although transitory items can help us analyze past performance, they are largely irrelevant to predicting future performance. This means that investors and other users tend to focus on income from continuing operations because that is the level of profitability that is likely to **persist** (continue) into the future. Likewise, the financial press tends to focus on income from continuing operations when it discloses corporate earnings (often described as *earnings before one-time charges*).

INTERPRETING A STATEMENT OF STOCKHOLDERS' EQUITY

The statement of stockholders' equity reconciles the beginning and ending balances of stockholders' equity accounts. The statement of stockholders' equity for **Apple** is shown in Exhibit 2.7.

| **EXHIBIT 2.7** | Apple's Statement of Stockholders' Equity |

APPLE INC.
Statement of Stockholders' Equity
For Year Ended September 25, 2010

($ millions)	Common Stock	Retained Earnings	Other Stockholders' Equity	Total Stockholders' Equity
Balance at September 26, 2009......$ 8,210		$23,353	$77	$31,640
Common stock issued.............. 2,458				2,458
Net income......................		14,013		14,013
Dividends......................		0		0
Other.........................		(197)	(123)	(320)
Balance at September 25, 2010......$10,668		$37,169	$(46)	$47,791

Apple's first equity component is common stock. The balance in common stock at the beginning of the year is $8,210 million. During 2010, Apple issued $2,458 million worth of common stock to employees who exercised stock options. At the end of 2010, the common stock account reports a balance of $10,668 million.

Apple's second stockholders' equity component is retained earnings. It totals $23,353 million at the start of fiscal 2010. During the year, it increased by $14,013 million from net income. Apple's retained earnings do not decrease for dividends because Apple pays no dividends; it also reports $(197) million of miscellaneous adjustments. The balance of retained earnings at year-end is $37,169 million.

In sum, total stockholders' equity begins the year at $31,640 million (including $77 million relating to miscellaneous accounts that increase total stockholders' equity) and ends fiscal 2010 with a balance of $47,791 million (including $(46) million relating to miscellaneous accounts that decrease total stockholders' equity) for a net increase of $16,151 million.

INTERPRETING A STATEMENT OF CASH FLOWS

The balance sheet and income statement are prepared using accrual accounting, in which revenues are recognized when earned and expenses when incurred. This means that companies can report income even though no cash is received. Cash shortages—due to unexpected cash outlays or when customers refuse to or cannot pay—can create economic hardships for companies and even cause their demise.

To assess cash flows, we must assess a company's cash management. Obligations to employees, creditors, and others are usually settled with cash. Illiquid companies (those lacking cash) are at risk of failure. Given the importance of cash management, companies must report a statement of cash flows in addition to the balance sheet, income statement, and statement of equity.

The income statement provides information about the economic viability of the company's products and services. It tells us whether the company can sell its products and services at prices that cover its costs and provide a reasonable return to lenders and stockholders. On the other hand, the statement of cash flows provides information about the company's ability to generate cash from those same transactions. It tells us from what sources the company has generated its cash (so we can evaluate whether those sources are persistent or transitory) and what it has done with the cash it generated.

Statement Format and Data Sources

The statement of cash flows is formatted to report cash inflows and cash outflows by the three primary business activities:

- *Cash flows from operating activities* Cash flows from the company's transactions and events that relate to its operations.
- *Cash flows from investing activities* Cash flows from acquisitions and divestitures of investments and long-term assets.
- *Cash flows from financing activities* Cash flows from issuances of and payments toward borrowings and equity.

The combined cash flows from these three sections yield the net change in cash for the period. The three sections of the statement of cash flows relate to the income statement and to different parts of the balance sheet. These relations are highlighted in the table below:

Cash flow section	Information from income statement	Information from balance sheet	
Net cash flows from operating activities. . . .	**Revenues** **− Expenses** **= Net income**	**Current operating assets** Long-term operating and all nonoperating assets	**Current operating liabilities** Long-term operating and all nonoperating liabilities Equity
Net cash flows from investing activities	Revenues − Expenses = Net income	Current operating assets **Long-term operating and all nonoperating assets**	Current operating liabilities Long-term operating and all nonoperating liabilities Equity
Net cash flows from financing activities	Revenues − Expenses = Net income	Current operating assets Long-term operating and all nonoperating assets	Current operating liabilities **Long-term operating and all nonoperating liabilities** **Equity**

Specifically, the three sections draw generally on the following information:

- **Net cash flows from operating activities** relate to the income statement and to the current asset and current liabilities sections of the balance sheet.

- **Net cash flows from investing activities** relate to the long-term assets section of the balance sheet.

- **Net cash flows from financing activities** relate to the long-term liabilities and stockholders' equity sections of the balance sheet.

These relations do not hold exactly, but they provide us a useful way to visualize the construction of the statement of cash flows.

In analyzing the statement of cash flows, we should not necessarily conclude that the company is better off if cash increases and worse off if cash decreases. It is not the change in cash that is most important, but the reasons behind the change. For example, what are the sources of cash inflows? Are these sources transitory? Are these sources mainly from operating activities? To what uses have cash inflows been put? Such questions and answers are key to properly using the statement of cash flows.

Exhibit 2.8 shows **Apple**'s statement of cash flows. Apple reported $18,595 million in net cash inflows from operating activities in 2010. This is substantially greater than its net income of $14,013 million. The operating activities section of the statement of cash flows reconciles the difference between net income and operating cash flow. The difference is due to the add-back of

EXHIBIT 2.8 Apple's Statement of Cash Flows ($ millions)	
APPLE INC. **Statement of Cash Flows** **For Year Ended September 25, 2010**	
Operating activities	
Net income	14,013
Adjustments to reconcile net income to cash generated by operating activities:	
Depreciation, amortization and accretion	1,027
Stock-based compensation expense	879
Deferred income tax expense	1,440
Loss on disposition of property, plant and equipment	24
Changes in operating assets and liabilities:	
Increase in accounts receivable	(2,142)
Increase in inventories	(596)
Increase in vendor non-trade receivables	(2,718)
Increase in other current assets	(1,514)
Increase in other assets	(120)
Increase in accounts payable	6,307
Increase in deferred revenue	1,217
Increase in other liabilities	778
Cash generated by operating activities	18,595
Investing activities	
Purchases of marketable securities	(57,793)
Proceeds from maturities of marketable securities	24,930
Proceeds from sales of marketable securities	21,788
Purchases of other long-term investments	(18)
Payments made in connection with business acquisitions, net of cash acquired	(638)
Payments for acquisition of property, plant and equipment	(2,005)
Payments for acquisition of intangible assets	(116)
Other	(2)
Cash used in investing activities	(13,854)
Financing activities	
Proceeds from issuance of common stock	912
Excess tax benefits from stock-based compensation	751
Taxes paid related to net share settlement of equity awards	(406)
Cash generated by financing activities	1,257
Increase/(decrease) in cash and cash equivalents	5,998
Cash and cash equivalents, beginning of the year	5,263
Cash and cash equivalents, end of the year	$11,261

depreciation, a noncash expense in the income statement, and other noncash expenses, together with year-over-year changes in operating assets and liabilities.

Apple reports a net cash outflow of $13,854 million for investing activities, mainly for investments in marketable securities. Apple also generated $1,257 million from financing activities, mainly cash received when employees exercised their options to purchase common stock.

Overall, Apple's cash flow picture is strong. It is generating cash from operating activities and the sale of stock to employees, and is investing excess cash in marketable securities to ensure future liquidity.

Cash Flow Computations

It is sometimes difficult to understand why certain accounts are added to and subtracted from net income to yield net cash flows from operating activities. It often takes more than one pass through this section to grasp how this part of the cash flow statement is constructed.

A key to understanding these computations is to remember that under accrual accounting, revenues are recognized when earned and expenses when incurred. This recognition policy does not necessarily coincide with the receipt or payment of cash. The top line (net income) of the operating section of the statement of cash flows represents net (accrual) income under GAAP. The bottom line (net cash flows from operating activities) is the *cash profit* the company would have reported had it constructed its income statement on a cash basis rather than an accrual basis. Computing net cash flows from operating activities begins with GAAP profit and adjusts it to compute cash profit using the following general approach:

	Add (+) or Subtract (−) from Net Income
Net income..........................	$ #
Add: depreciation expense	+
Adjust for changes in current assets	
Subtract increases in current assets	−
Add decreases in current assets	+
Adjust for changes in current liabilities	
Add increases in current liabilities	+
Subtract decreases in current liabilities ..	−
Cash from operating activities	$ #

Adjustments for noncash revenues, expenses, gains and losses — [applies to the "Add: depreciation expense" through "Adjust for changes in current assets" rows]

Adjustments for changes in noncash current assets and current liabilities — [applies to the "Adjust for changes in current assets" through "Subtract decreases in current liabilities" rows]

Typically, net income is first adjusted for noncash expenses such as depreciation, and is then adjusted for changes during the year in current assets and current liabilities to yield cash flow from operating activities, or *cash profit*. The depreciation adjustment merely zeros out (undoes the effect of) depreciation expense, a noncash expense, which is deducted in computing net income. The following table provides brief explanations of adjustments for receivables, inventories, and payables and accruals, which are frequent sources of adjustments in this section:

	Change in account balance...	Means that...	Which requires this adjustment to net income to yield cash profit...
Receivables	Increase	Sales and net income increase, but cash is not yet received	Deduct increase in receivables from net income
	Decrease	More cash is received than is reported in sales and net income	Add decrease in receivables to net income
Inventories	Increase	Cash is paid for inventories that are not yet reflected in cost of goods sold	Deduct increase in inventories from net income
	Decrease	Cost of goods sold includes inventory costs that were paid for in a prior period	Add decrease in inventories to net income
Payables and accruals	Increase	More goods and services are acquired on credit, delaying cash payment	Add increase in payables and accruals to net income
	Decrease	More cash is paid than is reflected in cost of goods sold or operating expenses	Deduct decrease in payables and accruals from net income

| BUSINESS INSIGHT | Insights into Apple's Statement of Cash Flows |

The following provides insights into the computation of some amounts in the operating section of Apple's statement of cash flows in Exhibit 2.8 ($ millions).

Statement amount	Explanation of computation
Depreciation, amortization, and accretion $1,027	When buildings and equipment are acquired, their cost is recorded on the balance sheet as assets. Subsequently, as the assets are used up to generate revenues, a portion of their cost is transferred from the balance sheet to the income statement as an expense, called *depreciation*. Depreciation expense does not involve the payment of cash (that occurs when the asset is purchased). If we want to compute *cash profit*, we must add back depreciation expense to zero it out from income. The $1,027 in the second line of the statement of cash flows merely zeros out (undoes) the depreciation expense that was subtracted when Apple computed GAAP net income. Likewise, the next line (Stock-based compensation expense of $879) uses the same concept.
Increase in accounts receivable, $(2,142)	When a company sells goods *on credit*, it records revenue because it is earned, even though cash is not yet received. When Apple sold $2,142 of goods on credit, its revenues and net income increased by that amount, but no cash was received. Apple's cash profit is, thus, $2,142 less than net income. The $2,142 is subtracted from net income in computing net cash inflows from operations.
Increase in inventories, $(596)	When Apple purchases inventories, the purchase cost is reported on its balance sheet as a current asset. When inventories are sold, their cost is removed from the balance sheet and transferred to the income statement as an expense called cost of goods sold. If some inventories acquired are not yet sold, their cost is not yet reported in cost of goods sold and net income. The subtraction of $596 relates to the increase in inventories; it reflects the fact that cost of goods sold does not include all of the cash that was spent on inventories. That is, $596 cash was spent that is not yet reflected in cost of goods sold. Thus, the $596 is deducted from net income to compute *cash profit* for the period.
Increase in accounts payable, $6,307	Apple purchases much of its inventories on credit. The $6,307 increase in accounts payable reflects inventories that have been purchased, but have not yet been paid for in cash. The add-back of this $6,307 to net income reflects the fact that *cash profit* is $6,307 higher because $6,307 of accounts payable are not yet paid.

It is also helpful to use the following decision guide, involving changes in assets, liabilities, and equity, to understand increases and decreases in cash flows.

	Cash flow increases from	Cash flow decreases from
Assets.	Account decreases	Account increases
Liabilities and equity.	Account increases	Account decreases

The table above applies to all sections of the statement of cash flows. To determine if a change in each asset and liability account creates a cash inflow or outflow, examine the change and apply the decision rules from the table. For example, in the investing section, cash decreases when PPE assets increase. In the financing section, borrowing from a bank increases cash.

Sometimes the cash flow effect of an item reported in the statement of cash flows does not agree with the difference in the balance sheet accounts that we observe. This can be due to several factors. One common factor is when a company uses its own stock to acquire another entity. There is no cash effect from a stock acquisition and, hence, it is not reported in the statement of cash flows. Yet, the company does increase its assets and liabilities when it adds the acquired company's assets and liabilities to its balance sheet.

Knowledge of how companies record cash inflows and outflows helps us better understand the statement of cash flows. Determining how changes in asset and liability accounts affect cash provides an analytic tool *and* offers greater insight into managing a business. For instance, reducing the levels of receivables and inventories increases cash. Similarly, increasing the levels of accounts payable and accrued liabilities increases cash. Managing cash balances by managing other accounts is called *working capital management*, which is important for all companies.

MID-MODULE REVIEW 1

Following are account balances ($ millions) for **Dell Inc.** Using these data, prepare Dell's income statement and statement of cash flows for the fiscal year ended January 28, 2011. Prepare its balance sheet dated January 28, 2011.

Cash and cash equivalents, ending year	$13,913	Inventories	$ 1,301
Net cash provided by financing activities	474	Accounts payable	11,293
Long-term debt	5,146	Other stockholders' equity	(28,775)
Property, plant and equipment, net	1,953	Long-term investments	704
Other noncurrent assets	6,921	Other current assets	3,219
Accrued and other current liabilities	7,339	Retained earnings	24,744
Other noncurrent liabilities	6,204	Accounts receivable	10,136
Short-term investments	452	Selling, general and administrative expenses	7,302
Income tax expense	715	Research and development expenses	661
Net cash provided by operating activities	3,969	Cost of revenue	50,098
Paid-in capital	11,797	Net cash used in investing activities	(1,165)
Cash and cash equivalents, beginning year	10,635	Interest expense	83
Revenue	61,494		
Short-term debt	851		

The solution is on page 2-49.

ARTICULATION OF FINANCIAL STATEMENTS

LO2 Analyze and interpret transactions using the financial statement effects template.

The four financial statements are linked with each other and linked across time. This linkage is called **articulation**. This section demonstrates the articulation of financial statements using Apple.

Retained Earnings Reconciliation

The balance sheet and income statement are linked via retained earnings. Recall that retained earnings is updated each period and reflects cumulative income that has not yet been distributed to shareholders. Exhibit 2.9 shows **Apple**'s retained earnings reconciliation for 2010.

EXHIBIT 2.9	Apple's Retained Earnings Reconciliation

APPLE INC. Retained Earnings Reconciliation ($ millions) For Year Ended September 25, 2010	
Retained earnings, September 26, 2009	$23,353
Add: Net income	14,013
Less: Dividends	0
Other adjustments	(197)
Retained earnings, September 25, 2010	$37,169

This reconciliation of retained earnings links the balance sheet and income statement.

In the absence of transactions with stockholders—such as stock issuances and repurchases, and dividend payments—the change in stockholders' equity equals income or loss for the period. The income statement, thus, measures the change in company value as measured by *GAAP*. This is not necessarily company value as measured by the *market*. Of course, all value-relevant items eventually find their way into the income statement. So, from a long-term perspective, the income statement does measure change in company value. This is why stock prices react to reported income and to analysts' expectations about future income.

Financial Statement Linkages

Articulation of the four financial statements is shown in Exhibit 2.10. Apple begins fiscal 2010 with assets of $47,501 million, consisting of cash for $5,263 million and noncash assets for $42,238 million. These investments are financed with $15,861 million from nonowners and

$31,640 million from shareholders. The owner financing consists of contributed capital of $8,210 million, retained earnings of $23,353 million, and other stockholders' equity of $77 million.

Exhibit 2.10 shows balance sheets at the beginning and end of Apple's fiscal year on the left and right columns, respectively. The middle column reflects operating activities for 2010. The statement of cash flows explains how operating, investing, and financing activities increase the cash balance by $5,998 million from $5,263 million at the beginning of the year to $11,261 million at year-end. The ending balance in cash is reported in the year-end balance sheet on the right.

EXHIBIT 2.10   Articulation of Apple Financial Statements ($ millions)

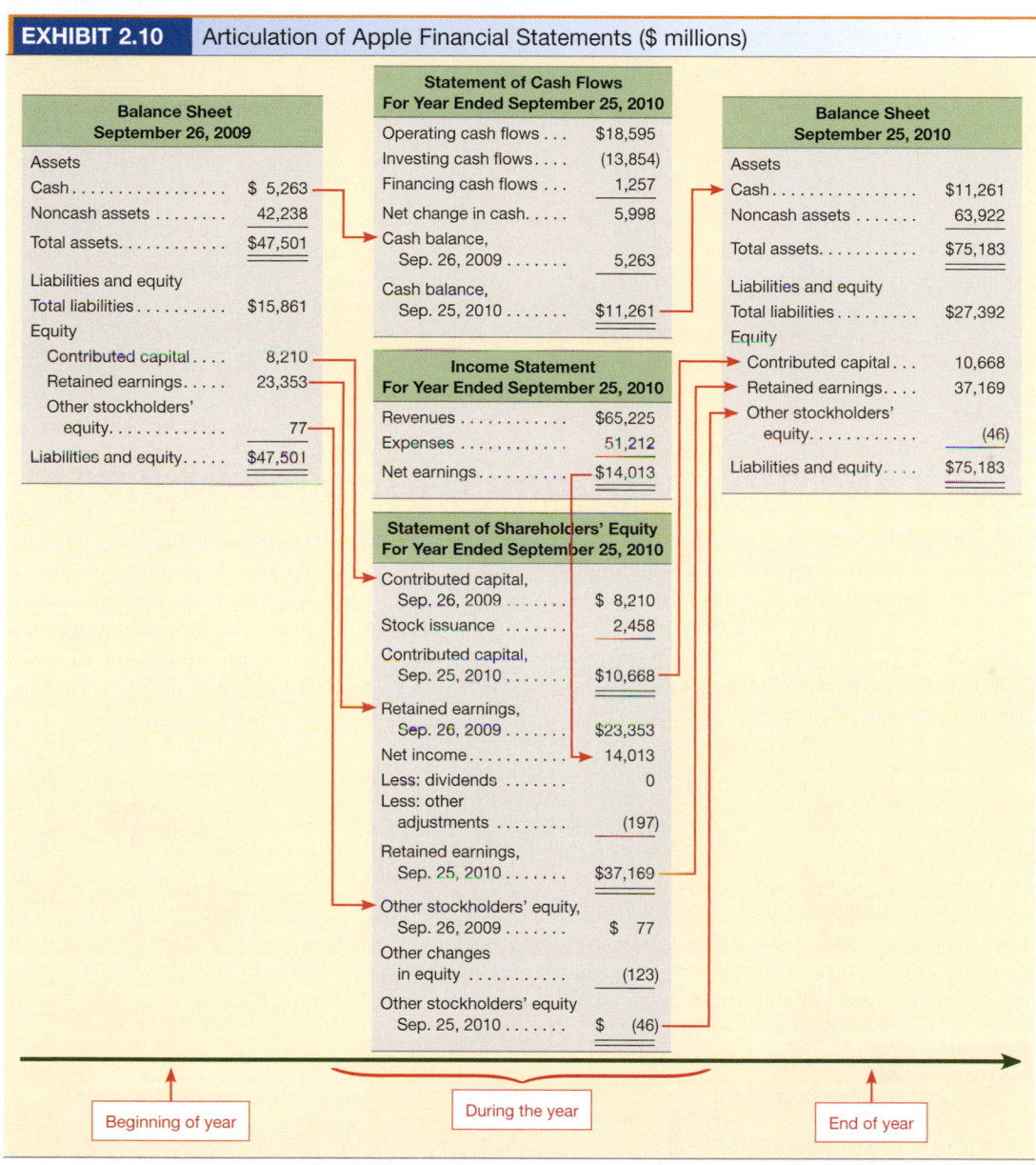

Apple's $14,013 million net income reported on the income statement is also carried over to the statement of shareholders' equity. The net income explains nearly all of the change in retained earnings reported in the statement of shareholders' equity because Apple paid no dividends in that year (other adjustments reduce retained earnings by $197 million).

There is an order to financial statement preparation. First, a company prepares its income statement using the income statement accounts. It then uses the net income number and dividend information to update the retained earnings account. Second, it prepares the balance sheet using the updated retained earnings account along with the remaining balance sheet accounts from the trial balance. Third, it prepares the statement of stockholders' equity. Fourth, it prepares the statement of cash flows using information from the cash account (and other sources).

MID-MODULE REVIEW 2

Refer to information in Mid-Module Review 1; assume that **Dell** reports the following balances for the prior year balance sheet and current year income statement. Prepare the articulation of Dell's financial statements from fiscal years 2010 to 2011 following the format of Exhibit 2.10.

Balance Sheet, January 29, 2010		Income Statement, For Year Ended January 28, 2011	
Assets		Revenues	$61,494
Cash	$10,635	Expenses	58,859
Noncash assets	23,017	Net earnings	$ 2,635
Total assets	$33,652		
Liabilities and Equity			
Total liabilities	$28,011		
Equity			
Contributed capital	11,472		
Retained earnings	22,110		
Other stockholders' equity	(27,941)		
Liabilities and equity	$33,652		

The solution is on page 2-50.

ANALYZING TRANSACTIONS AND ADJUSTMENTS

Financial statements report on the financial performance of a business using the language of accounting. To prepare these statements, companies translate day-to-day transactions into accounting records (called journals), and then record (post) them to individual accounts. At the end of an accounting period, each of these accounts is totaled, and the resulting balances are used to prepare financial statements. After the financial statements are prepared, the temporary (income statement) accounts are "zeroed out" so that the next period can begin anew—akin to clearing a scoreboard for the next game. Permanent (balance sheet) accounts continue to reflect financial position and carry over from period to period—akin to keeping track of wins and losses even when a particular scoreboard is cleared.

The *accounting cycle* is illustrated in Exhibit 2.11. Transactions are first recorded in the accounting records. Each of these transactions is, generally, the result of an external transaction, such as recording a sale to a customer or the payment of wages to employees. Once all of the transactions have been recorded during the accounting period, the company adjusts the accounting records to recognize a number of events that have occurred, but which have not yet been recorded. These might include the recognition of wage expense and the related wages payable for those employees who have earned wages, but have not yet been paid, or the recognition of depreciation expense for build-

EXHIBIT 2.11 Accounting Cycle

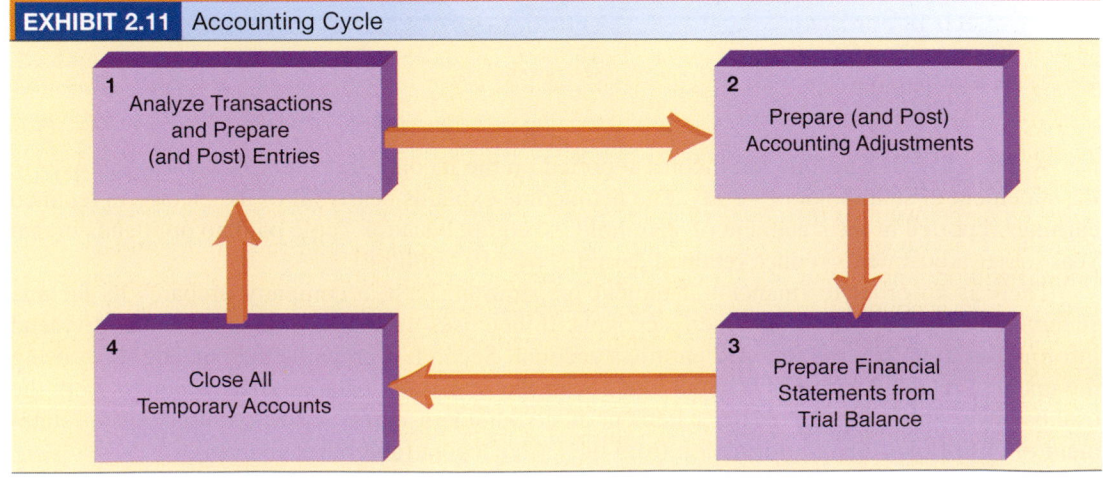

ings and equipment. These adjustments are made at the end of the accounting period to properly adjust the accounting records before the financial statements are prepared. Once all adjustments are made, financial statements are prepared. This module describes the details of this accounting cycle. Understanding the financial statement preparation process requires an understanding of the language used to record business transactions in accounting records. The recording and statement preparation processes are readily understood once we learn that language (of financial effects) and its mechanics (entries and posting). Even if we never journalize a transaction or prepare a financial statement, understanding the accounting process aids us in analyzing and interpreting accounting reports. Understanding the accounting language also facilitates our communication with business professionals within a company and with members of the business community outside of a company.

Transaction Analysis

This section introduces our financial statement effects template, which we use throughout the book to reflect the effects of transactions on financial statements.

LO3 Analyze and interpret accounting adjustments and their financial statement effects.

Apple reports total assets of $75,183 million, total liabilities of $27,392 million, and equity of $47,791 million. The accounting equation for Apple follows ($ million):

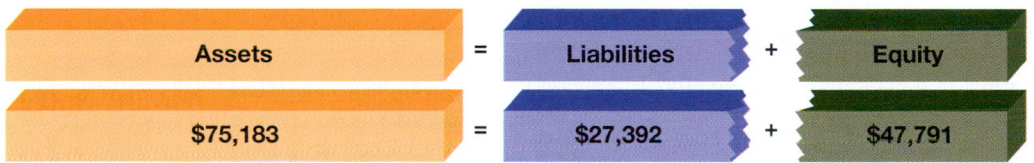

We often draw on this relation to assess the effects of transactions and events, different accounting methods, and choices that managers make in preparing financial statements. For example, we are interested in knowing the effects of an asset acquisition or sale on the balance sheet, income statement, and cash flow statement. Or, we might want to understand how the failure to recognize a liability would understate liabilities and overstate profits and equity. To perform these sorts of analyses, we employ the following **financial statement effects template**:

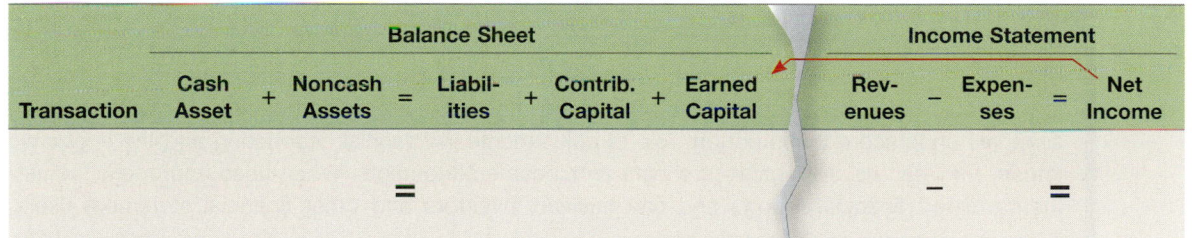

The template captures the transaction and its financial statement effects on the four financial statements: balance sheet, income statement, statement of stockholders' equity, and statement of cash flows. For the balance sheet, we differentiate between cash and noncash assets so as to identify the cash effects of transactions. Likewise, equity is separated into the contributed and earned capital components. Finally, income statement effects are separated into revenues, expenses, and net income (the updating of retained earnings is denoted with an arrow line running from net income to earned capital). This template provides a convenient means to represent relatively complex financial accounting transactions and events in a simple, concise manner for both analysis and interpretation.

In addition to using the template to show the dollar effects of a transaction on the four financial statements, we also include each transaction's *journal entry* and *T-account* representation in the margin. These are part of the bookkeeping aspects of accounting. The margin entries can be ignored without any loss of insight gained from the template. (Journal entries and T-accounts use acronyms for account titles; a list of acronyms is in Appendix C near the end of the book.)

The process leading up to preparing financial statements involves two steps: (1) recording transactions during the accounting period, and (2) adjusting accounting records to reflect events that have occurred but are not yet evidenced by an external transaction. We provide a brief introduction to these two steps, followed by a comprehensive example that includes preparation of financial statements.

Analyzing and Recording Transactions: An Illustration

All transactions affecting a company are recorded in its accounting records. For example, assume that a company paid $100 cash wages to employees. This is reflected in the following financial statement effects template.

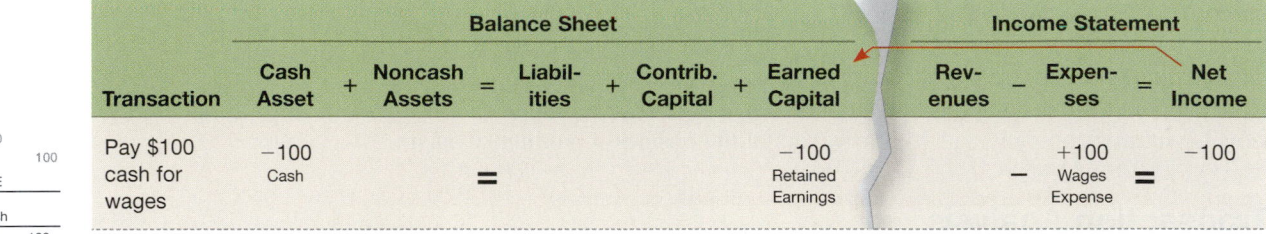

	Balance Sheet						Income Statement		
Transaction	Cash Asset	+ Noncash Assets	= Liabil- ities	+ Contrib. Capital	+ Earned Capital		Rev- enues	− Expen- ses	= Net Income
Pay $100 cash for wages	−100 Cash		=		−100 Retained Earnings			+100 Wages Expense	− = −100

Cash assets are reduced by $100, and wage expense of $100 is reflected in the income statement, which reduces income and retained earnings by that amount. All transactions incurred by the company during the accounting period are recorded similarly. We show several further examples in our comprehensive illustration later in this section.

Adjusting Accounts

We must understand accounting adjustments (commonly called *accruals*) to fully analyze and interpret financial statements. In the transaction above, we record wage expense that has been earned by (and paid to) employees during the period. What if the employees were not paid for wages earned at period-end? Should the expense still be recorded? The answer is yes. All expenses incurred to generate, directly or indirectly, the revenues reported in the period must be recorded. This is the case even if those expenses are still unpaid at period-end. Failure to recognize wages expense would overstate net income for the period because wages have been earned and should be reported as expense in this period. Also, failure to record those wages at period-end would understate liabilities. Thus, neither the income statement nor the balance sheet would be accurate. Adjustments are, therefore, necessary to accurately portray financial condition and performance of a company.

BUSINESS INSIGHT | **Accounting Scandals and Improper Adjustments**

Many accounting scandals involve the improper use of adjustments to manipulate income. The following table highlights three specific adjustment manipulations by companies. These accounting scandals underscore the important role of adjustments in financial accounting and the economic impact they can have on balance sheets and income statements. When used improperly, adjustments distort financial reports and can mislead investors and other financial statement users.
(Source: "Corporate Scandal Sheet," Forbes 2002.)

Company	Allegations	Accounting Adjustment
Halliburton (HAL)	Improperly booked $100 million in annual construction cost overruns before customers agreed to pay for them.	Halliburton recognized revenues before earned. Its accounting entry increased accounts receivable and revenue, thereby inflating net income. It later wrote off the receivables when customers refused to pay.
WorldCom (WCOEQ)	Improperly recorded $11 billion of operating expenses as capital costs (assets).	WorldCom recorded costs as assets on the balance sheet rather than as expenses in the income statement. This inflated both assets and income. It later wrote off the assets (and reduced income) when the transactions were uncovered.
Xerox (XRX)	Overstated net income by $1.5 billion over five years.	Customers purchased copiers and service contracts as one purchase. Xerox allocated most of the "sale" to hardware, thereby recognizing revenues before they were earned under service contracts.

Despite their (generally) beneficial effects, adjustments can be misused. Managers can use adjustments to bias reported income, rendering it higher or lower than it really is. Adjustments, if misused, can adversely affect business and investment decisions. Many recent accounting scandals have resulted from improper use of adjustments. Although outsiders cannot directly observe companies' specific accounting entries, their impact can be detected as changes in balance sheet and income statement accounts. Those changes provide signals for financial statement analysis. Consequently, understanding the accrual process will help us know what to look for as we analyze companies' financial reports.

There are four types of adjustments, which are illustrated in the following graphic. The two adjustments on the left relate to the receipt or payment of cash before revenue or expense is recognized. The two on the right relate to the receipt or payment of cash after revenue or expense is recognized.

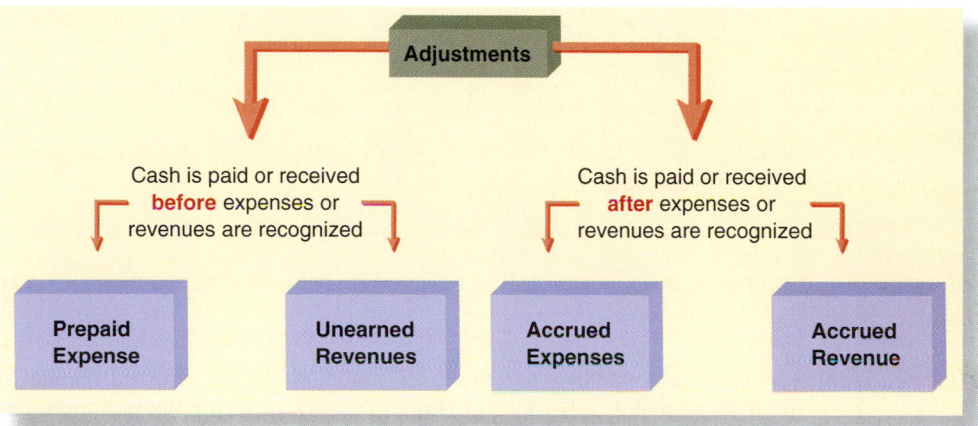

One of two types of accounts arises when cash is received or paid *before* recognition of revenue or expense.

>   ***Prepaid expenses*** Prepaid expenses reflect advance cash payments that will ultimately become expenses; an example is the payment of radio advertising that will not be aired until sometime in the future.

>   ***Unearned revenues*** Unearned revenues reflect cash received from customers before any services or goods are provided; an example is cash received from patrons for tickets to an upcoming concert.

To illustrate the adjustment required with prepaid expenses, assume that Apple pays $3,000 cash at the beginning of this year to rent office space, and that this allows Apple to use the space for the current year and two additional years. When paid, the prepaid rent is an asset for Apple (it now controls the space, which is expected to provide future benefits for its business). At the end of the first year, one-third of the Prepaid Rent asset is used up. Apple, therefore, removes that portion from its balance sheet and recognizes it as an expense in the income statement. The beginning-year payment and year-end expensing of the rental asset are recorded as follows:

			Balance Sheet								Income Statement			
Transaction	Cash Asset	+	Noncash Assets	=	Liabil-ities	+	Contrib. Capital	+	Earned Capital		Rev-enues	−	Expen-ses	=	Net Income
a. Beginning-year $3,000 cash payment in advance of 3-year rent	−3,000 Cash		+3,000 Prepaid Rent	=								−		=	
b. Recognition of 1-year rent expense of $1,000			−1,000 Prepaid Rent	=					−1,000 Retained Earnings			−	+1,000 Rent Expense	=	−1,000

PPRNT 3,000
    Cash   3,000

| PPRNT
3,000 |
      Cash
          | 3,000

RNTE 1,000
   PPRNT 1,000

| RNTE
1,000 |
      PPRNT
          | 1,000

To illustrate unearned revenues, assume that Apple receives $5,000 cash in advance of providing services to a client. That amount is initially recorded as a liability for services owed the client. Later, when Apple provides the services, it can recognize that revenue since it is now earned. The receipt of cash and subsequent recognition of revenue are recorded as follows:

	Balance Sheet						Income Statement		
Transaction	Cash Asset	+ Noncash Assets	= Liabil- ities	+ Contrib. Capital	+ Earned Capital		Rev- enues	− Expen- ses	= Net Income
a. Receive $5,000 cash in advance for future services	+5,000 Cash		= +5,000 Unearned Revenue				−		=
b. Rec-ognition of $5,000 services rev-enue earned			= −5,000 Unearned Revenue		+5,000 Retained Earnings		+5,000 Revenue	−	= +5,000

One of two types of accounts arises when cash is received or paid *after* recognition of revenue or expense.

Accrued expenses Accrued expenses are expenses incurred and recognized on the income statement, even though they are not yet paid in cash; an example is wages owed to employees who performed work but who have not yet been paid.

Accrued revenues Accrued revenues are revenues earned and recognized on the income statement, even though cash is not yet received; examples include accounts receivable and revenue earned under a long-term contract.

To illustrate accrued expenses, assume that $100 of wages earned by Apple employees this period is paid the following period. The period-end adjustment, and subsequent payment the following period, are both reflected in the following template.

	Balance Sheet						Income Statement		
Transaction	Cash Asset	+ Noncash Assets	= Liabil- ities	+ Contrib. Capital	+ Earned Capital		Rev- enues	− Expen- ses	= Net Income
Period 1: Accrue $100 wages expense and liability			= +100 Wages Payable		−100 Retained Earnings		−	+100 Wages Expense	= −100
Period 2: Pay $100 cash for wages	−100 Cash		= −100 Wages Payable				−		=

Wages expense is recorded in period 1's income statement because it is incurred by the company and earned by employees in that period. Also, a liability is recorded in period 1 reflecting the company's obligation to make payment to employees. In period 2, the wages are paid, which means that both cash and the liability are reduced.

To illustrate the accrual of revenues, assume that Apple is performing work under a long-term contract that allows it to bill the customer periodically as work is performed. At the end of the current period, it determines that it has earned $100,000 per contact. The accrual of this revenue and its subsequent collection are recorded as follows ($ 000s):

Transaction	Balance Sheet									Income Statement				
	Cash Asset	+	Noncash Assets	=	Liabil- ities	+	Contrib. Capital	+	Earned Capital		Rev- enues	−	Expen- ses	= Net Income
a. Accrual of $100 of earned revenue			+100 Accounts Receivable	=					+100 Retained Earnings		+100 Revenue	−		= +100
b. Collection of account receivable	+100 Cash		−100 Accounts Receivable	=								−		=

```
AR      100
   REV       100
      AR
   100 |
      REV
         |   100

Cash   100
   AR        100
      Cash
   100 |
      AR
         |   100
```

Adjustments are an important part of the accounting process and are crucial to accurate and informative financial accounting. It is through the accruals process that managers communicate information about future cash flows. For example, from accrual information, we know that Apple paid for a resource (inventories) that it has not yet sold. We know that suppliers have money owed to them (accounts payable) but Apple won't pay them until a future period. We know that revenues have been earned but cash not yet received (accounts receivable). Those accruals tell us about Apple's past performance and, perhaps more importantly, about Apple's future cash flows. When used correctly, accruals convey a wealth of information about the past and the future that is useful in our evaluation of company financial performance and condition. Thus, we can use accrual information to more precisely value companies' equity and debt securities.

Not all managers are honest; some misuse accounting accruals to improperly recognize revenues and expenses. Abuses include accruing revenue before it is earned; and accruing expenses in the wrong period or in the wrong amount. These actions are fraudulent as they deliberately overstate or understate revenues and expenses and, thus, reported net income is incorrect. Safeguards against this type of managerial behavior include corporate governance systems (internal controls, accounting policies and procedures, routine scrutiny of accounting reports, and audit committees) and external checks and balances (independent auditors, regulatory bodies, and the court system). Collectively, these safeguards aim to protect interests of companies' internal and external stakeholders. When managers abuse accounting systems, tough and swift sanctions remind others that corporate malfeasance is unacceptable. Videos of police officers leading corporate executives to jail in handcuffs (the infamous "perp walk") send that message.

RESEARCH INSIGHT   Accruals: Good or Bad?

Researchers use accounting accruals to study the effects of earnings management on financial accounting. Earnings management is broadly defined as the use of accounting discretion to distort reported earnings. Managers have incentives to manage earnings in many situations. For example, managers have tendencies to accelerate revenue recognition to increase stock prices prior to equity offerings. In contrast, other research shows that managers decelerate revenue recognition to depress stock prices prior to the management buyout (where management repurchases common stock and takes the company "private"). Research also shows that managers use discretion when reporting special items to either meet or beat analysts' forecasts of earnings and/or to avoid reporting a loss. Not all earnings management occurs for opportunistic reasons. Research shows that managers use accruals to communicate private information about future profitability to outsiders. For example, management might signal future profitability through use of income-decreasing accruals to show investors that it can afford to apply conservative accounting. This "signaling" through accruals is found to precede stock splits and dividend increases. In sum, we must look at reported earnings in conjunction with other earnings quality signals (such as levels of disclosure, degree of corporate governance, and industry performance) to interpret information in accruals.

Constructing Financial Statements from Transactions and Adjustments

LO4 Construct financial statements from account balances.

We can prepare each of the four financial statements directly from our financial statement effects template. The balance sheet and income statement accounts, and their respective balances, can be read off the bottom row that totals the transactions and adjustments recorded during the period. The statement of cash flows and statement of stockholders' equity are represented by the cash column and the contributed and earned capital columns, respectively.

Illustration: Recording Transactions, Adjusting Accounts, and Preparing Statements

This section provides a comprehensive illustration that uses the financial statement effects template with a number of transactions related to Apple's 2010 financial statements shown earlier. These summary transactions are described in the far left column of the following template. Each column is summed to arrive at the balance sheet and income statement totals that tie to Apple's statements. Detailed explanations for each transaction are provided after the template. Then, we use the information in the template to construct Apple's financial statements.

Transaction Explanation Apple begins fiscal year 2010 with $47,501 million in total assets, consisting of $5,263 million of cash and $42,238 million of noncash assets. It also reports $15,861 million of liabilities and $31,640 million of stockholders' equity ($8,210 million of contributed capital and $23,430 million of earned capital, which includes other equity for this exhibit). During the year, eleven summary transactions occur that are described below.

1. **Owner Financing.** Companies raise funds from two sources: investing from shareholders and borrowing from creditors. Transaction 1 reflects issuance of common stock for $2,458 million. Cash is increased by that amount, as is contributed capital. Stock issuance (as well as its repurchase and any dividends paid to shareholders) does not impact income. Companies cannot record profit by trading in their own stock.

2. **Purchase PPE financed by debt.** Apple acquires $2,005 million of property, plant and equipment (PPE), and it finances this acquisition with a $2,005 million loan. Noncash assets increase by the $2,005 million of PPE, and liabilities increase by $2,005 million of long-term debt. PPE is initially reported on the balance sheet at the cost Apple paid to acquire it. When plant and equipment are used, a portion of the purchase cost is transferred from the balance sheet to the income statement as an expense called depreciation. Accounting for depreciation is shown in Transaction 9. The borrowing of money does not yield income, and repaying the principal amount borrowed is not an expense. Paying interest *on* liabilities, however, is an expense.

3. **Purchase inventories on credit.** Companies commonly acquire inventories from suppliers *on credit* (also called *on account*). The phrase "on credit" means that the purchase has not yet been paid for. A purchaser is typically allowed 30 days or more during which to make payment. When acquired in this manner, noncash assets (inventories) increase by the $40,137 million cost of the acquired inventory, and a liability (accounts payable) increases to reflect the amount owed to the supplier. Although inventories (iPods and iPhones, for example) normally carry a retail selling price that is higher than cost, this eventual profit is not recognized until inventories are sold.

4. **Sell inventories on credit.** Apple subsequently sells inventories that cost $39,541 million for a retail selling price of $65,225 million *on credit*. The phrase "on credit" means that Apple has not yet received cash for the selling price; cash receipt is expected in the future. The sale of inventories is recorded in two parts: the revenue part and the expense part. First, the sale is recorded by an increase in both revenues and noncash assets (accounts receivable). Revenues increase net income which, in turn, increases earned capital (via retained earnings). Second, the cost of inventories sold is removed from the balance sheet (Apple no longer owns those assets), and is transferred to the income statement as an expense, called *cost of goods sold*, which decreases both net income and earned capital by $39,541 (again, via retained earnings).

Transaction	Cash Asset	+	Noncash Assets	=	Liabil-ities	+	Contrib. Capital	+	Earned Capital		Rev-enues	−	Expen-ses	=	Net Income
					Balance Sheet							**Income Statement**			
Bal., Sept. 26, 2009	5,263		42,238	=	15,861		8,210		23,430			−		=	
1. Sell common stock for $2,458	+2,458 Cash			=			+2,458 Common Stock					−		=	
2. Purchase $2,005 of PPE, financed by $2,005 of long-term debt			+2,005 PPE, net	=	+2,005 Long-Term Debt							−		=	
3. Purchase $40,137 of inventories on account			+40,137 Inventories	=	+40,137 Accounts Payable							−		=	
4. Sell inventories costing $39,541 for $65,225 on account			+65,225 Accounts Receivable	=					+65,225 Retained Earnings		+65,225 Sales	−		=	+65,225
			−39,541 Inventory	=					−39,541 Retained Earnings			−	+39,541 Cost of Goods Sold	=	−39,541
5. Collect $63,083 of receivables and pay $31,542 of accounts payable and other liabilities	+63,083 Cash		−63,083 Accounts Receivable	=								−		=	
	−31,542 Cash			=	−31,542 Accounts Payable							−		=	
6. Pay operating expenses and taxes (excluding depreciation) of $9,868	−9,868 Cash			=					−9,868 Retained Earnings			−	+9,868 Operating Expenses	=	−9,868
7. Accrue expenses of $931				=	+931 Accrued Liabilities				−931 Retained Earnings			−	+931 Operating Expenses	=	−931
8. Purchase noncash assets for $18,288	−18,288 Cash		+18,288 Marketable Securities	=								−		=	
9. Record depreciation of $1,027			−1,027 PPE, net	=					−1,027 Retained Earnings			−	+1,027 Depreciation Expense	=	−1,027
10. Record receipt of net investment income of $155	+155 Cash			=					+155 Retained Earnings			−	−155* Investment Income	=	+155
11. Record decrease in Other Assets and AOCI			−320 Other Assets	=					−320 Accumulated Other Comp. Income			−		=	
Bal., Sept. 25, 2010	11,261	+	63,922	=	27,392	+	10,668	+	37,123		65,225	−	51,212	=	14,013

* Apple reports investment income as an "addback" to other expenses.

5. **Collect receivables and settle payables.** Apple receives $63,083 million cash from the collection of its accounts receivable, thus reducing noncash assets (accounts receivable) by that amount. Apple uses these proceeds to pay off $31,542 of its liabilities (accounts payable and other liabilities). Collecting accounts receivable does not yield revenue; instead, revenue is recognized when *earned* (see Transaction 4). Thus, recognizing revenue when earned does not necessarily yield an immediate cash increase.

6. **Pay cash for expenses.** Apple pays $9,868 million cash for expenses. This payment increases expenses, and reduces net income (and earned capital). Expenses are recognized when incurred, regardless of when they are paid. Expenses are both incurred and paid in this transaction. Transaction 7 is a case where expenses are recognized *before* being paid.

7. **Accrue expenses.** Accrued expenses relate to expenses that are incurred but not yet paid. For example, employees often work near the end of a period but are not paid until the next period. The company must record wages expense even though employees have not yet been paid in cash. The rationale is that expenses must be recorded in the period incurred to report the correct income for the period. In this transaction, Apple accrues $931 million of expenses, which reduces net income (and earned capital). Apple simultaneously records a $931 million increase in liabilities for its obligation to make future payment. This transaction is an accounting adjustment, or accrual.

8. **Purchase noncash assets.** Apple uses $18,288 million of its excess cash to purchase marketable securities as an investment. Thus, noncash assets increase. This is a common use of excess cash, especially for high-tech companies that desire added liquidity to take advantage of opportunities in a rapidly changing industry.

9. **Record depreciation.** Transaction 9 is another accounting adjustment. In this case, Apple recognizes that a portion of its plant and equipment is "used up" while generating revenues. Thus, it records a portion of the PPE cost as an expense during the period. In this case, $1,027 million of PPE cost is removed from the balance sheet and transferred to the income statement as depreciation expense. Net income (and earned capital) are reduced by $1,027 million.

10. **Record investment income.** Apple recognizes $155 of investment income in transaction 10. Profit increases by this same amount, resulting in an increase in retained earnings.

11. **Miscellaneous.** The final transaction is a miscellaneous adjustment to noncash assets and an earned capital account called accumulated other comprehensive income, which is distinct from retained earnings.

We can use the column totals from the financial statement effects template to prepare Apple's financial statements (in condensed form). We derive Apple's 2010 balance sheet and income statement from the template as follows ($ millions).

APPLE INC. Condensed Balance Sheet September 25, 2010		APPLE INC. Condensed Income Statement For Year Ended September 25, 2010	
Cash asset	$11,261	Revenues	$65,225
Noncash assets	63,922	Expenses	51,212
Total assets	$75,183	Net income	$14,013
Liabilities	$27,392		
Contributed capital	10,668		
Earned capital	37,123		
Total liabilities and equity	$75,183		

We can summarize Apple's cash transactions from the cash column of the template. The cash column of the financial effects template reveals that cash increases by $5,998 million during the year from $5,263 million to $11,561 million; see the following statement. Items that contribute to this net increase are identified by the cash entries in that column (the subtotals for operating, investing, and financing sections are slightly different from actual results because of simplifying assumptions we make for our transactions example).

APPLE INC. Statement of Cash Flows ($ millions) For Year Ended September 25, 2010	
Operating cash flows (+ $31,541 − $9,868 + $155)	$21,828
Investing cash flows	(18,288)
Financing cash flows	2,458
Net change in cash	5,998
Cash balance, Sep. 26, 2009	5,263
Cash balance, Sep. 25, 2010	$11,261

Apple's statement of stockholders' equity summarizes the transactions relating to its equity accounts. This statement follows and is organized into its contributed capital and earned capital categories of equity.

APPLE INC. Condensed Statement of Stockholders' Equity For Year Ended September 25, 2010			
($ millions)	Contributed Capital	Earned Capital	Total
Balance, September 26, 2009	$ 8,210	$23,430	$31,640
Issuance of common stock	2,458		2,458
Net income		14,013	14,013
Miscellaneous		(320)	(320)
Balance, September 25, 2010	$10,668	$37,123	$47,791

Recall from prior courses that the usual first step in preparing financial statements is to prepare a **trial balance**, which is a listing of all accounts and their balances at a point in time. Also, recall that an *unadjusted trial balance* is one that is prepared prior to accounting adjustments; an *adjusted trial balance* is one prepared after accounting adjustments are entered.

Closing Process

The **closing process** refers to the 'zeroing out' of revenue and expense accounts (the temporary accounts) by transferring their ending balances to retained earnings. (Recall, income statement accounts—revenues and expenses—and the dividend account are temporary accounts because their balances are zero at the end of each accounting period; balance sheet accounts carry over from period to period and are called permanent accounts.) The closing process is typically carried out via a series of journal entries that successively zero out each revenue and expense account, transferring those balances to retained earnings. The result is that all income statement accounts begin the next period with zero balances. The balance sheet accounts do not need to be similarly adjusted because their balances carry over from period to period. Recall the scoreboard analogy.

Our financial statement effects template makes the closing process unnecessary because the template updates retained earnings with each revenue and expense entry. The arrow that runs from net income to retained earnings (part of earned capital) highlights the continual updating.

It is important to distinguish our financial statement effects template from companies' accounting systems. The financial statement effects template and T-accounts are pedagogical tools that represent transactions' effects on the four financial statements. The template is highly stylized but its simplicity is instructive. In practice, managers use journal entries to record transactions and adjustments. The template captures these in summarized fashion. At this point, we have explained and illustrated all aspects of the accounting cycle.

> **BUSINESS INSIGHT**   **Controlling vs Noncontrolling Interest**
>
> Financial statements are prepared on a *consolidated* basis. To consolidate a balance sheet, a company includes all the assets and liabilities of subsidiaries under its control. When a company controls a subsidiary, it directs all (100%) of the subsidiary's operations. But control does not mean 100% ownership; control can occur when a company owns the majority of a subsidiary's voting stock. For example, **Verizon** owns 55% of the voting stock of **Verizon Wireless**, a separate legal entity. This 55% gives Verizon voting control and Verizon is said to have a **controlling interest** in Verizon Wireless. The remaining 45% is owned by **Vodafone**, a UK telecom; Vodafone has a **noncontrolling interest** in Verizon Wireless. Now imagine if Verizon wanted to repaint the trucks in the Verizon Wireless fleet. Verizon would not paint only 55% of the trucks; it "controls" 100% of Verizon Wireless' trucks by virtue of its controlling interest, and it would paint all trucks. Consolidated financial statements reflect this notion of control. Verizon's balance sheet includes 100% of Verizon Wireless assets and liabilities. Because it owns only a 55% interest in Verizon Wireless assets and liabilities, Verizon reports the other 45% in equity as noncontrolling interest. The same logic applies to the income statement; that is, 100% of subsidiaries' revenues and expenses are included, and then the noncontrolling interest portion of net income is separated from net income at the bottom.

ANALYZING GLOBAL REPORTS

Both GAAP and IFRS use accrual accounting to prepare financial statements. Although there are vastly more similarities than differences, we highlight below a few of the more notable differences for financial statements.

Balance Sheet The most visible difference is that the typical IFRS-based balance sheet is presented in reverse order of liquidity. The least liquid asset, usually goodwill, is listed first and the most liquid asset, cash, is last. The same inverse liquidity order applies to liabilities. There are also several detailed presentation and measurement differences that we explain in other modules. As one example, for GAAP-based balance sheets, bank overdrafts are often netted against cash balances. IFRS does not permit this netting on the balance sheet. However, the IFRS statement of cash flows *does* net the cash balance with any bank overdrafts and, thus, the cash balance on the statement of cash flows might not match the cash amount on the balance sheet.

Income Statement The most visible difference is that GAAP requires three years' data on the income statement whereas IFRS requires only two. Another difference is that GAAP income statements classify expenses by *function* and must separately report expenses applicable to revenues (cost of goods sold), whereas IFRS permits expense classification by *function* (cost of sales, selling and administrative, etc.) or by *type* (raw materials, labor, depreciation, etc.). This means, for example, that under IFRS, there is no requirement to report a cost of sales figure. Another difference is that no item can be classified as extraordinary under IFRS. Still another is that for items either unusual or infrequent, but not both, GAAP requires separate presentation in the income statement as a component of earnings from continuing operations. IFRS also requires disclosure of these items, but permits disclosure in notes to financial statements.

Statement of Cash Flows One of the more apparent differences between GAAP and IFRS is that a GAAP-based statement of cash flows classifies interest expense, interest revenue, and dividend revenue as operating cash flows, and dividends paid as financing cash flows. IFRS allows firms to choose from between the following two options:

1. Classify interest expense, dividends paid, interest revenue, and dividend revenue as operating cash flows, or
2. Classify interest expense and dividends paid as financing cash flows, and interest revenue and dividend revenue as investing cash flows.

MODULE-END REVIEW

At December 31, 2010, assume that the condensed balance sheet of **Gateway** shows the following.

Cash.	$ 80,000	Liabilities.	$200,000
Noncash assets	270,000	Contributed capital.	50,000
		Earned capital	100,000
Total assets.	$350,000	Total liabilities and equity	$350,000

Assume the following summary transactions occur during 2011.

1. Purchase inventory of $80,000 on credit.
2. Pay employees $10,000 cash for wages earned this year.
3. Sell inventory costing $40,000 for $70,000 on credit.
4. Collect $15,000 cash from the accounts receivable in transaction 3.
5. Pay $35,000 cash toward the accounts payable in transaction 1.
6. Purchase advertising for $25,000 cash that will air next year.
7. Employees earn $5,000 in wages that will not be paid until next year.
8. Record $3,000 depreciation on its equipment.

Required

a. Record transactions 1 through 8 using the financial statement effects template.
b. Prepare the income statement and balance sheet for 2011.
c. Show linkage(s) between the income statement and the balance sheet.

The solution to the review problem is on page 2-51.

APPENDIX 2A: Additional Information Sources

The four financial statements are only a part of the information available to financial statement users. Additional information, from a variety of sources, provides useful insight into company operating activities and future prospects. This section highlights additional information sources.

Form 10-K

Companies with publicly traded securities must file a detailed annual report and discussion of their business activities in their Form 10-K with the SEC (quarterly reports are filed on Form 10-Q). Many of the disclosures in the 10-K are mandated by law and include the following general categories: Item 1, *Business;* Item 1A. *Risk Factors;* Item 2, *Properties;* Item 3, *Legal Proceedings;* Item 4, *Submission of Matters to a Vote of Security Holders;* Item 5, *Market for Registrant's Common Equity and Related Stockholder Matters;* Item 6, *Selected Financial Data;* Item 7, *Management's Discussion and Analysis of Financial Condition and Results of Operations;* Item 7A, *Quantitative and Qualitative Disclosures About Market Risk;* Item 8, *Financial Statements and Supplementary Data;* Item 9, *Changes in and Disagreements With Accountants on Accounting and Financial Disclosure;* Item 9A, *Controls and Procedures.*

Description of the Business (Item 1)

Companies must provide a general description of their business, including their principal products and services, the source and availability of required raw materials, all patents, trademarks, licenses, and important related agreements, seasonality of the business, any dependence upon a single customer, competitive conditions, including particular markets in which the company competes, the product offerings in those markets, and the status of its competitive environment. Companies must also provide a description of their overall strategy. **Apple**'s partial disclosure follows:

> The Company is committed to bringing the best user experience to its customers through its innovative hardware, software, peripherals, services, and Internet offerings. The Company's business strategy leverages its unique ability to design and develop its own operating systems, hardware, application software, and services to provide its customers new products and solutions with superior ease-of-use, seamless integration, and innovative industrial design. The Company believes continual investment in research and development is critical to

continued

continued from prior page

the development and enhancement of innovative products and technologies. In conjunction with its strategy, the Company continues to build and host a robust platform for the discovery and delivery of third-party digital content and applications through the iTunes Store. . . . Additionally, the Company's strategy includes expanding its distribution to effectively reach more customers and provide them with a high-quality sales and post-sales support experience. The Company is therefore uniquely positioned to offer superior and well-integrated digital lifestyle and productivity solutions.

Management's Discussion and Analysis of Financial Condition and Results of Operations (Item 7)

The management discussion and analysis (MD&A) section of the 10-K contains valuable insight into the company's results of operations. In addition to an executive overview of company status and its recent operating results, the MD&A section includes information relating to its critical accounting policies and estimates used in preparing its financial statements, a detailed discussion of its sales activity, year-over-year comparisons of operating activities, analysis of gross margin, operating expenses, taxes, and off-balance-sheet and contractual obligations, assessment of factors that affect future results and financial condition. Item 7A reports quantitative and qualitative disclosures about market risk. For example, Apple makes the following disclosure relating to its Mac operating system and its iPods, iPhones, iPads and other products.

The Company is currently the only maker of hardware using the Mac OS. The Mac OS has a minority market share in the personal computer market, which is dominated by makers of computers using competing operating systems, most notably Windows. The Company's financial condition and operating results substantially depend on its ability to continually develop improvements to the Mac platform to maintain perceived design and functional advantages. Use of unauthorized copies of the Mac OS on other companies' hardware products may result in decreased demand for the Company's hardware products, and materially adversely affect its financial condition and operating results.

Form 8-K

Another useful report that is required by the SEC and is publicly available is the Form 8-K. This form must be filed within four business days of any of the following events:

- Entry into or termination of a material definitive agreement (including petition for bankruptcy)
- Exit from a line of business or impairment of assets
- Change in the company's certified public accounting firm
- Change in control of the company
- Departure of the company's executive officers
- Changes in the company's articles of incorporation or bylaws

Outsiders typically use Form 8-K to monitor for material adverse changes in the company.

Analyst Reports

Sell-side analysts provide their clients with objective analyses of company operating activities. Frequently, these reports include a discussion of the competitive environment for each of the company's principal product lines, strengths and weaknesses of the company, and an investment recommendation, including financial analysis and a stock price target. For example, **J.P. Morgan** provides the following in its July 2011 report to clients on Apple:

J.P.Morgan

North America Equity Research
20 July 2011

Apple Inc.

Overweight

This Party is Just Getting Started; Upside Parade
Likely to Continue; Lifting Dec-12 PT to $525

AAPL, AAPL US
Price: $376.85

▲ **Price Target: $525.00**
Previous: $450.00

With Overweight-rated Apple's stock, it is time for the value-like multiples to be rerated higher. We expect the stock to move higher in the near to mid term. Consistent with our preview, Apple reported a outstanding June quarter, and there appears no end to the upside parade. We believe the results likely restore the wow factor to the stock. In our view, the return of the wow factor, easing supply constraints, and pending new product cycles should jettison the fear that had been dogging valuation the last couple of months. We are raising our Dec-12 price target to $525, versus $450 previously.

Price Performance

	YTD	1m	3m	12m
Abs	13.4%	16.7%	12.6%	52.2%

- **A ridiculously big June quarter beat.** Apple reported major upside to Street consensus. Apple reported revenue/EPS of $28.6bn/$7.79, versus consensus of $25.0bn/$5.87. GM and OM were up more than 200 bps QoQ. As previewed, revenue upside from iPad and iPhone, combined with better component pricing and improved supply of iPads, drove a solid beat on the unit metrics. APAC growth of 247% was major upside driver, and we expect this trend to continue.

- **Whoa Nellie, those are big numbers.** June quarter unit shipments of 20.3M iPhones and 9.25M iPads beat our significantly above-consensus estimates of 19.6M and 8.7M. With iPhone, we think that carrier, geographic, enterprise, and dual mode GSM/CDMA expansion opportunities offer plenty of headroom for ongoing growth. As for the iPad, we expect the burst in units to ease investor concerns that competition or supply constraints would be a drag on growth. Mac results were in-line, but this performance should be put in perspective given the weak PC market (Mac units outgrow the broader PC market by a factor of five).

Credit Services

Several firms including **Standard & Poor's** (**StandardAndPoors.com**), **Moody's Investors Service** (**Moodys.com**), and **Fitch Ratings** (**FitchRatings.com**) provide credit analysis that assists potential lenders, investors, employees, and other users in evaluating a company's creditworthiness and future financial viability. Credit analysis is a specialized field of analysis, quite different from the equity analysis illustrated here. These firms issue credit ratings on publicly issued bonds as well as on firms' commercial paper.

Data Services

A number of companies supply financial statement data in easy-to-download spreadsheet formats. **Thomson Reuters Corporation** (**ThomsonReuters.com**) provides a wealth of information to its database subscribers, including the widely quoted *First Call* summary of analysts' earnings forecasts. Standard & Poor's provides financial data for all publicly traded companies in its *Compustat* database. This database reports a plethora of individual data items for all publicly traded companies or for any specified subset of companies. These data are useful for performing statistical analysis and making comparisons across companies or within industries. Finally, **Capital IQ** (www.CapitalIQ.com), a division of Standard & Poor's, provides "as presented" financial data that conform to published financial statements as well as additional statistical data and analysis.

GUIDANCE ANSWERS . . . ANALYSIS DECISION

You Are the Securities Analyst Of special concern is the possibility that the new CEO is shifting costs to the current period in lieu of recording them in future periods. Evidence suggests that such behavior occurs when a new management team takes control. The reasoning is that the new management can blame poor current period performance on prior management and, at the same time, rid the balance sheet (and the new management team) of costs that would normally be expensed in future periods.

You are the CFO Part 1: Liabilities will increase by $10 million for the estimated amount of the cleanup, an expense in that amount will be recognized in the income statement, thus reducing both income and retained earnings (equity) by $10 million. Part 2: Stakeholders affected by recognition decisions of this type are often much broader than first realized. Management is directly involved in the decision. Recording this cost can affect the market value of the company, its relations with lenders and suppliers, its auditors, and many other stakeholders. Further, if recording this cost is the right accounting decision, failure to do so can foster unethical behavior throughout the company, thus affecting additional company employees.

Superscript ᴬ denotes assignments based on Appendix 2A.

DISCUSSION QUESTIONS

Q2-1. The balance sheet consists of assets, liabilities, and equity. Define each category and provide two examples of accounts reported within each category.

Q2-2. Explain how we account for a cost that creates an immediate benefit versus a cost that creates a future benefit.

Q2-3. GAAP is based on the concept of accrual accounting. Define and describe accrual accounting.

Q2-4. Analysts attempt to identify transitory items in an income statement. Define transitory items. What is the purpose of identifying transitory items?

Q2-5. What is the statement of stockholders' equity? What useful information does it contain?

Q2-6. What is the statement of cash flows? What useful information does it contain?

Q2-7. Define and explain the concept of financial statement articulation. What insight comes from understanding articulation?

Q2-8. Describe the flow of costs for the purchase of a machine. At what point do such costs become expenses? Why is it necessary to record the expenses related to the machine in the same period as the revenues it produces?

Q2-9. What are the two essential characteristics of an asset?

Q2-10. What does the concept of liquidity refer to? Explain.

Q2-11. What does the term *current* denote when referring to assets?

Q2-12. Assets are recorded at historical costs even though current market values might, arguably, be more relevant to financial statement readers. Describe the reasoning behind historical cost usage.

Q2-13. Identify three intangible assets that are likely to be *excluded* from the balance sheet because they cannot be reliably measured.

Q2-14. Identify three intangible assets that are recorded on the balance sheet.

Q2-15. What are accrued liabilities? Provide an example.

Q2-16. Define net working capital. Explain how increasing the amount of trade credit can reduce the net working capital for a company.

Q2-17. What is the difference between company *book value* and *market value*? Explain why these two amounts differ.

Q2-18. The financial statement effects template includes an arrow line running from net income to earned capital. What does this arrow line denote?

Assignments with the ✔ in the margin are available in an online homework system.
See the Preface of the book for details.

MINI EXERCISES

M2-19. Identifying and Classifying Financial Statement Items (LO1)

For each of the following items, indicate whether they would be reported in the balance sheet (B) or income statement (I).

a. Net income	*d.* Accumulated depreciation	*g.* Interest expense
b. Retained earnings	*e.* Wages expense	*h.* Interest payable
c. Depreciation expense	*f.* Wages payable	*i.* Sales

 M2-20. Identifying and Classifying Financial Statement Items (LO1)

For each of the following items, indicate whether they would be reported in the balance sheet (B) or income statement (I).

a. Machinery	*e.* Common stock	*i.* Taxes expense
b. Supplies expense	*f.* Factory buildings	*j.* Cost of goods sold
c. Inventories	*g.* Receivables	*k.* Long-term debt
d. Sales	*h.* Taxes payable	*l.* Treasury stock

M2-21. Computing and Comparing Income and Cash Flow Measures (LO1)

Penno Corporation recorded service revenues of $100,000 in 2012, of which $70,000 were on credit and $30,000 were for cash. Moreover, of the $70,000 credit sales for 2012, Penno collected $20,000 cash on those receivables before year-end 2012. The company also paid $25,000 cash for 2012 wages. Its employees also earned another $15,000 in wages for 2012, which were not yet paid at year-end 2012. (a) Compute the company's net income for 2012. (b) How much net cash inflow or outflow did the company generate in 2012? Explain why Penno's net income and net cash flow differ.

M2-22. Assigning Accounts to Sections of the Balance Sheet (LO1)

Identify each of the following accounts as a component of assets (A), liabilities (L), or equity (E).

a.	Cash and cash equivalents _____		*e.*	Long-term debt _____
b.	Wages payable _____		*f.*	Retained earnings _____
c.	Common stock _____		*g.*	Additional paid-in capital _____
d.	Equipment _____		*h.*	Taxes payable _____

M2-23. Determining Missing Information Using the Accounting Equation (LO4)

Use your knowledge of accounting relations to complete the following table for Boatsman Company.

	2011	2012
Beginning retained earnings.....	$89,089	$?
Net income (loss)	?	48,192
Dividends	0	15,060
Ending retained earnings	69,634	?

M2-24. Reconciling Retained Earnings (LO4)

Following is financial information from **Johnson & Johnson** for the year ended January 2, 2011. Prepare the retained earnings reconciliation for Johnson & Johnson for the year ended January 2, 2011 ($ millions).

JOHNSON & JOHNSON
(JNJ)

Retained earnings, Jan. 3, 2010......$70,306		Dividends......................	$5,804
Net earnings.................... 13,334		Retained earnings, Jan. 2, 2011	?
Other retained earnings changes..... (63)			

M2-25. Analyzing Transactions to Compute Net Income (LO2)

Wasley Corp., a start-up company, provided services that were acceptable to its customers and billed those customers for $350,000 in 2011. However, Wasley collected only $280,000 cash in 2011, and the remaining $70,000 was collected in 2012. Wasley employees earned $200,000 in 2011 wages that were not paid until the first week of 2012. How much net income does Wasley report for 2011? For 2012 (assuming no additional transactions)?

M2-26. Analyzing Transactions Using the Financial Statement Effects Template (LO2)

Report the effects for each of the following transactions using the financial statement effects template.

a. Issue stock for $1,000 cash.
b. Purchase inventory for $500 cash.
c. Sell inventory in transaction *b* for $2,000 on credit.
d. Receive $2,000 cash toward transaction *c* receivable.

EXERCISES

E2-27. Constructing Financial Statements from Account Data (LO4)

Barth Company reports the following year-end account balances at December 31, 2011. Prepare the 2011 income statement and the balance sheet as of December 31, 2011.

Accounts payable.	$ 16,000	Inventory	$ 36,000
Accounts receivable.	30,000	Land.	80,000
Bonds payable, long-term	200,000	Goodwill.	8,000
Buildings.	151,000	Retained earnings	60,000
Cash.	48,000	Sales revenue.	400,000
Common stock.	150,000	Supplies inventory	3,000
Cost of goods sold.	180,000	Supplies expense.	6,000
Equipment	70,000	Wages expense	40,000

E2-28. **Constructing Financial Statements from Transaction Data** **(LO2, 4)**

Baiman Corporation commences operations at the beginning of January. It provides its services on credit and bills its customers $30,000 for January sales. Its employees also earn January wages of $12,000 that are not paid until the first of February. Complete the following statements for the month-end of January.

Income Statement			Balance Sheet	
Sales.	$		Cash.	$
Wages expense			Accounts receivable.	
Net income (loss)	$		Total assets.	$
			Wages payable.	$
			Retained earnings	
			Total liabilities and equity . . .	$

E2-29. **Analyzing and Reporting Financial Statement Effects of Transactions** **(LO2, 4)**

M.E. Carter launched a professional services firm on March 1. The firm will prepare financial statements at each month-end. In March (its first month), Carter executed the following transactions. Prepare an income statement for Carter Company for the month of March.

a. Carter (owner) invested in the company, $100,000 cash and $20,000 in property and equipment. The company issued common stock to Carter.

b. The company paid $3,200 cash for rent of office furnishings and facilities for March.

c. The company performed services for clients and immediately received $4,000 cash earned.

d. The company performed services for clients and sent a bill for $14,000 with payment due within 60 days.

e. The company compensated an office employee with $4,800 cash as salary for March.

f. The company received $10,000 cash as partial payment on the amount owed from clients in transaction *d*.

g. The company paid $935 cash in dividends to Carter (owner).

E2-30. **Analyzing Transactions Using the Financial Statement Effects Template** **(LO2)**

Enter the effects of each of the transactions *a* through *g* from Exercise 2-29 using the financial statement effects template shown in the module.

 E2-31. **Identifying and Classifying Balance Sheet and Income Statement Accounts** **(LO4)**

STAPLES, INC.
(SPLS)

Following are selected accounts for **Staples, Inc.**

a. Indicate whether each account appears on the balance sheet (B) or income statement (I).

b. Using the following data, compute total assets and total expenses.

c. Compute net profit margin (net income/sales) and total liabilities-to-equity ratio (total liabilities/stockholders' equity).

($ millions)	Amount	Classification
Sales.	$24,545	
Accumulated depreciation	3,566	
Depreciation expense.	498	
Retained earnings	6,492	
Net income.	889	
Property, plant & equipment, net	2,148	
Selling, general & administrative expense	4,913	
Accounts receivable.	1,954	
Total liabilities.	6,960	
Stockholders' equity	6,951	

E2-32. **Identifying and Classifying Balance Sheet and Income Statement Accounts**   **(LO4)**
Following are selected accounts for **Target Corporation**.

a.   Indicate whether each account appears on the balance sheet (B) or income statement (I).
b.   Using the following data, compute total assets and total expenses.
c.   Compute net profit margin (net income/sales) and total liabilities-to-equity ratio (total liabilities/ stockholders' equity).

TARGET CORPORATION (TGT)

($ millions)	Amount	Classification
Total revenues	$67,390	
Accumulated depreciation	11,555	
Depreciation expense.	2,084	
Retained earnings	12,698	
Net income.	2,920	
Property, plant & equipment, net	25,493	
Selling, general & administrative expense	13,469	
Credit card receivables.	6,153	
Total liabilities.	28,218	
Stockholders' equity	15,487	

E2-33. **Comparing Income Statements and Balance Sheets of Competitors**   **(LO4)**
Following are selected income statement and balance sheet data from two retailers: **Abercrombie & Fitch** (clothing retailer in the high-end market) and **TJX Companies** (clothing retailer in the value-priced market).

ABERCROMBIE & FITCH (ANF) **TJX COMPANIES** (TJX)

Income Statement ($ millions)	ANF	TJX
Sales.	$3,469	$21,942
Cost of goods sold.	1,257	16,040
Gross profit.	2,212	5,902
Total expenses	2,062	4,559
Net income.	$ 150	$ 1,343

Balance Sheet ($ millions)	ANF	TJX
Current assets	$1,433	$5,100
Long-term assets	1,515	2,872
Total assets	$2,948	$7,972
Current liabilities	$ 559	$3,133
Long-term liabilities	498	1,739
Total liabilities	1,057	4,872
Stockholders' equity	1,891	3,100
Total liabilities and equity	$2,948	$7,972

a. Express each income statement amount as a percentage of sales. Comment on any differences observed between these two companies, especially as they relate to their respective business models.

b. Express each balance sheet amount as a percentage of total assets. Comment on any differences observed between these two companies, especially as they relate to their respective business models.

c. Which company has a higher proportion of stockholders' equity (and a lower proportion of debt)? What do the ratios tell us about relative riskiness of the two companies?

E2-34. **Comparing Income Statements and Balance Sheets of Competitors** (LO1, 4)
Following are selected income statement and balance sheet data from two computer competitors: **Apple** and **Dell**.

APPLE
(AAPL)
DELL
(DELL)

Income Statement ($ millions)	Apple	Dell
Sales	$65,225	$61,494
Cost of goods sold	39,541	50,098
Gross profit	25,684	11,396
Total expenses	11,671	8,761
Net income	$14,013	$ 2,635

Balance Sheet ($ millions)	Apple	Dell
Current assets	$41,678	$29,021
Long-term assets	33,505	9,578
Total assets	$75,183	$38,599
Current liabilities	$20,722	$19,483
Long-term liabilities	6,670	11,350
Total liabilities	27,392	30,833
Stockholders' equity	47,791	7,766
Total liabilities and equity	$75,183	$38,599

a. Express each income statement amount as a percentage of sales. Comment on any differences observed between the two companies, especially as they relate to their respective business models. (*Hint:* Apple's gross profit as a percentage of sales is considerably higher than Dell's. What aspect of Apple's business do we believe is driving its profitability?)

b. Express each balance sheet amount as a percentage of total assets. Comment on any differences observed between the two companies. Apple has chosen to structure itself with a higher proportion of equity (and a lower proportion of debt) than Dell. How does this capital structure decision affect our evaluation of the relative riskiness of these two companies?

E2-35. **Comparing Income Statements and Balance Sheets of Competitors** (LO1, 4)

Following are selected income statement and balance sheet data for two communications companies: **Comcast** and **Verizon**.

COMCAST
(CMCSA)
VERIZON
(VZ)

Income Statement ($ millions)	Comcast	Verizon
Sales..........................	$37,937	$106,565
Operating costs	29,957	91,920
Operating profit	7,980	14,645
Nonoperating expenses........	4,345	4,428
Net income...................	$ 3,635	$ 10,217

Balance Sheet ($ millions)	Comcast	Verizon
Current assets	$ 8,886	$ 22,348
Long-term assets	109,648	197,657
Total assets.................	$118,534	$220,005
Current liabilities.............	$ 8,234	$ 30,597
Long-term liabilities	65,723	102,496
Total liabilities...............	73,957	133,093
Stockholders' equity*.........	44,577	86,912
Total liabilities and equity	$118,534	$220,005

*Includes noncontrolling interest

a. Express each income statement amount as a percentage of sales. Comment on any differences observed between the two companies.

b. Express each balance sheet amount as a percentage of total assets. Comment on any differences observed between the two companies, especially as they relate to their respective business models.

c. Both Verizon and Comcast have chosen a capital structure with a higher proportion of liabilities than equity. How does this capital structure decision affect our evaluation of the riskiness of these two companies? Take into consideration the large level of capital expenditures that each must make to remain competitive.

E2-36. **Comparing Financial Information Across Industries** (LO1, 4)

Use the data and computations required in parts a and b of exercises E2-33 and E2-34 to compare **TJX Companies** and **Apple Inc.**

TJX COMPANIES
(TJX)
APPLE INC.
(AAPL)

a. Compare gross profit and net income as a percentage of sales for these two companies. How might differences in their respective business models explain the differences observed?

b. Compare sales versus total assets. What do observed differences indicate about the relative capital intensity of these two industries?

c. Which company has the higher percentage of total liabilities to stockholders' equity? What do these ratios imply about the relative riskiness of these two companies?

d. Compare the ratio of net income to stockholders' equity for these two companies. Which business model appears to yield higher returns on shareholder investment? Using answers to parts a through c above, identify the factors that appear to drive the ratio of net income to stockholders' equity.

E2-37. **Analyzing Transactions Using the Financial Statement Effects Template** (LO2)

Record the effect of each of the following transactions for Hora Company using the financial statement effects template.

a. Wages of $500 are earned by employees but not yet paid.

b. $2,000 of inventory is purchased on credit.

c. Inventory purchased in transaction b is sold for $3,000 on credit.

d. Collected $3,000 cash from transaction c.

e. Equipment is acquired for $5,000 cash.

f. Recorded $1,000 depreciation expense on equipment from transaction e.

g. Paid $10,000 cash toward a note payable that came due.

h. Paid $2,000 cash for interest on borrowings.

PROBLEMS

5M COMPANY
(MMM)

P2-38. **Constructing and Analyzing Balance Sheet Amounts from Incomplete Data**   (LO1, 4)

Selected balance sheet amounts for **3M Company**, a manufacturer of consumer and business products, for three recent years follow.

$ millions	Current Assets	Long-Term Assets	Total Assets	Current Liabilities	Long-Term Liabilities	Total Liabilities	Stockholders' Equity*
2008	$ 9,598	$?	$25,793	$?	$9,550	$15,489	$10,304
2009	10,795	16,455	?	4,897	9,051	?	13,302
2010	?	17,941	30,156	6,089	8,050	14,139	?

* Includes noncontrolling interest

Required

a. Compute the missing balance sheet amounts for each of the three years shown.

b. What types of accounts would we expect to be included in current assets? In long-term assets?

P2-39. **Analyzing Transactions Using the Financial Statement Effects Template**   (LO2, 4)

Sefcik Company began operations on the first of October. Following are the transactions for its first month of business.

1. S. Sefcik launched Sefcik Company and invested $50,000 into the business in exchange for common stock. The company also borrowed $100,000 from a local bank.
2. Sefcik Co. purchased equipment for $95,000 cash and purchased inventory of $40,000 on credit (the company still owes its suppliers for the inventory at month-end).
3. Sefcik Co. sold inventory costing $30,000 for $50,000 cash.
4. Sefcik Co. paid $10,000 cash for wages owed employees for October work.
5. Sefcik Co. paid interest on the bank loan of $1,000 cash.
6. Sefcik Co. recorded $500 of depreciation expense related to its equipment.
7. Sefcik Co. paid a dividend of $2,000 cash.

Required

a. Record the effects of each transaction using the financial statement effects template.

b. Prepare the income statement and balance sheet at the end of October.

P2-40. **Analyzing Transactions Using the Financial Statement Effects Template**   (LO2, 3)

Following are selected transactions of Mogg Company. Record the effects of each using the financial statement effects template.

1. Shareholders contribute $10,000 cash to the business in exchange for common stock.
2. Employees earn $500 in wages that have not been paid at period-end.
3. Inventory of $3,000 is purchased on credit.
4. The inventory purchased in transaction 3 is sold for $4,500 on credit.
5. The company collected the $4,500 owed to it per transaction 4.
6. Equipment is purchased for $5,000 cash.
7. Depreciation of $1,000 is recorded on the equipment from transaction 6.
8. The Supplies account had a $3,800 balance at the beginning of this period; a physical count at period-end shows that $800 of supplies are still available. No supplies were purchased during this period.
9. The company paid $10,000 cash toward the principal on a note payable; also, $500 cash is paid to cover this note's interest expense for the period.
10. The company received $8,000 cash in advance for services to be delivered next period.

P2-41. **Comparing Operating Characteristics Across Industries**   (LO1, 4)

Following are selected income statement and balance sheet data for companies in different industries.

TARGET
(TGT)
NIKE
(NKE)
HARLEY-DAVIDSON
(HOG)
CISCO SYSTEMS
(CSCO)

$ millions	Sales	Cost of Goods Sold	Gross Profit	Net income	Assets	Liabilities	Stockholders' Equity
Target Corp.	$67,390	$45,725	$21,665	$2,920	$43,705	$28,218	$15,487
Nike, Inc.	20,862	11,354	9,508	2,133	14,998	5,155	9,843
Harley-Davidson....	4,859	2,749	2,110	147	9,431	7,224	2,207
Cisco Systems	40,040	14,397	25,643	7,767	81,130	36,845	44,285

Required

a. Compute the following ratios for each company.
1. Gross profit/Sales
2. Net income/Sales
3. Net income/Stockholders' equity
4. Liabilities/Stockholders' equity

b. Comment on any differences among the companies' gross profit to sales ratios and net income as a percentage of sales. Do differences in the companies' business models explain the differences observed?

c. Which company reports the highest ratio of net income to equity? Suggest one or more reasons for this result.

d. Which company has financed itself with the highest percentage of liabilities to equity? Suggest one or more reasons why this company can take on such debt levels.

P2-42. Comparing Cash Flows Across Retailers   (LO1, 4)

Following are selected accounts from the income statement and the statement of cash flows for several retailers.

| | | Net | Cash Flows from | | |
$ millions	Sales	Income	Operating	Investing	Financing
Macy's	$ 25,003	$ 847	$ 1,506	$ (465)	$ (1,263)
Home Depot, Inc.	67,997	3,338	4,585	(1,012)	(4,451)
Staples, Inc.	24,545	882	1,446	(472)	(938)
Target Corp.	67,390	2,920	5,271	(1,744)	(4,015)
Wal-Mart Stores	421,849	16,389	23,643	(12,193)	(12,028)

MACY'S
(M)
HOME DEPOT
(HD)
STAPLES
(SPLS)
TARGET
(TGT)
WAL-MART
(WMT)

Required

a. Compute the ratio of net income to sales for each company. Rank the companies on the basis of this ratio. Do their respective business models give insight into these differences?

b. Compute net cash flows from operating activities as a percentage of sales. Rank the companies on the basis of this ratio. Does this ranking coincide with the ratio rankings from part a? Suggest one or more reasons for any differences you observe.

c. Compute net cash flows from investing activities as a percentage of sales. Rank the companies on the basis of this ratio. Does this ranking coincide with the ratio rankings from part a? Suggest one or more reasons for any differences you observe.

d. All of these companies report negative cash flows from financing activities. What does it mean for a company to have net cash *outflow* from financing?

P2-43. Interpreting the Statement of Cash Flows   (LO1, 4)

Following is the statement of cash flows for **Wal-Mart Stores, Inc.**

WAL-MART
(WMT)

WAL-MART STORES, INC.
Statement of Cash Flows
For Year Ended January 31, 2011 ($ millions)

Cash flows from operating activities	
Net income	$ 16,993
Income from discontinued operations, net of tax.	(1,034)
Income from continuing operations	15,959
Adjustments to reconcile income from continuing operations to net cash provided by operating activities:	
Depreciation and amortizations	7,641
Deferred income taxes	651
Other operating activities	1,087
Changes in certain assets and liabilities, net of effects of acquisitions:	
Increase in accounts receivable	(733)
Increase in inventories.	(3,086)
Increase in accounts payable	2,557
Decrease in accrued liabilities.	(433)
Net cash provided by operating activities	23,643

continued

continued from prior page

Cash flows from investing activities	
Payments for property and equipment.	(12,699)
Proceeds from disposal of property and equipment	489
Investments and business acquisitions, net of cash acquired.	(202)
Other investing activities.	219
Net cash used in investing activities of continuing operations	(12,193)
Cash flows from financing activities	
Net change in short-term borrowings.	503
Proceeds from issuance of long-term debt	11,396
Payment of long-term debt.	(4,080)
Dividends paid	(4,437)
Purchase of company stock.	(14,776)
Payment of capital lease obligations	(363)
Other financing activities	(271)
Net cash used in financing activities	(12,028)
Effect of exchange rate changes on cash	66
Net (decrease) increase in cash	(512)
Cash at beginning of year	7,907
Cash at end of year	$ 7,395

Required

a. Why does Wal-Mart add back depreciation to compute net cash flows from operating activities?

b. Explain why the increase in receivables and inventories is reported as a cash outflow. Why do accounts payable provide a source of cash? Explain why the decrease in accrued liabilities is reported as a cash outflow.

c. Wal-Mart reports that it invested $12,699 million in property and equipment. Is this an appropriate type of expenditure for Wal-Mart to make? What relation should expenditures for PPE assets have with depreciation expense?

d. Wal-Mart indicates that it paid $14,776 million to repurchase its common stock in fiscal 2011 and, in addition, paid dividends of $4,437 million. Thus, Wal-Mart paid $19,213 million of cash to its shareholders during the year. How do we evaluate that use of cash relative to other possible uses for Wal-Mart's cash?

e. Provide an overall assessment of Wal-Mart's cash flows for 2011. In the analysis, consider the sources and uses of cash.

P2-44.   Interpreting the Statement of Cash Flows   (LO1, 4)

VERIZON
(VZ)

Following is the statement of cash flows for **Verizon**.

VERIZON Statement of Cash Flows For Year Ended December 31, 2010 ($ millions)	
Cash Flows from Operating Activities	
Net income.	$10,217
Adjustments to reconcile net income to net cash provided by operating activities:	
Depreciation and amortization expense.	16,405
Employee retirement benefits.	3,988
Deferred income taxes	3,233
Provision for uncollectible accounts.	1,246
Equity in earnings of unconsolidated businesses, net of dividends received	2
Changes in current assets and liabilities, net of effects	
from acquisition or disposition of businesses:	
Accounts receivable	(859)
Inventories.	299
Other assets	(313)
Accounts payable and accrued liabilities	1,075
Other, net	(1,930)
Net cash provided by operating activities	33,363

continued

continued from prior page

Cash Flows from Investing Activities	
Capital expenditures (including capitalized software)	(16,458)
Acquisitions of licenses, investments and businesses, net of cash acquired	(1,438)
Proceeds from dispositions	2,594
Net change in short-term investments.	(3)
Other, net	251
Net cash used in investing activities	(15,054)
Cash Flows from Financing Activities	
Repayments of long-term borrowings and capital lease obligations.	$ (8,136)
Increase (decrease) in short-term obligations, excluding current maturities	(1,097)
Dividends paid	(5,412)
Proceeds from access line spin-off	3,083
Other, net	(2,088)
Net cash used in financing activities	(13,650)
Increase (decrease) in cash and cash equivalents.	4,659
Cash and cash equivalents, beginning of year	2,009
Cash and cash equivalents, end of year	$ 6,668

Required

a. Why does Verizon add back depreciation to compute net cash flows from operating activities? What does the size of the depreciation add-back indicate about the relative capital intensity of this industry?

b. Verizon reports that it invested $16,458 million in property and equipment. These expenditures are necessitated by market pressures as the company faces stiff competition from other communications companies, such as **Comcast**. Where in the 10-K might we find additional information about these capital expenditures to ascertain whether Verizon is addressing the company's most pressing needs? What relation might we expect between the size of these capital expenditures and the amount of depreciation expense reported?

c. Verizon's statement of cash flows indicates that the company paid $8,136 million in debt payments. What problem does Verizon's high debt load pose for its ability to maintain the level of capital expenditures necessary to remain competitive in its industry?

d. During the year, Verizon paid dividends of $5,412 million but did not repay a sizeable portion of its debt. How do dividend payments differ from debt payments? Why would Verizon continue to pay dividends in light of cash demands for needed capital expenditures and debt repayments?

e. Provide an overall assessment of Verizon's cash flows for 2010. In the analysis, consider the sources and uses of cash.

P2-45.   Analyzing Transactions Using the Financial Statement Effects Template   (LO2)
On March 1, S. Penman (owner) launched AniFoods, Inc., an organic foods retailing company. Following are the transactions for its first month of business.

1. S. Penman (owner) contributed $100,000 cash to the company in return for common stock. Penman also lent the company $55,000. This $55,000 note is due one year hence.
2. The company purchased equipment in the amount of $50,000, paying $10,000 cash and signing a note payable to the equipment manufacturer for the remaining balance.
3. The company purchased inventory for $80,000 cash in March.
4. The company had March sales of $100,000 of which $60,000 was for cash and $40,000 on credit. Total cost of goods sold for its March sales was $70,000.
5. The company purchased future advertising time from a local radio station for $10,000 cash.
6. During March, $7,500 worth of radio spots purchased in transaction 5 are aired. The remaining spots will be aired in April.
7. Employee wages earned and paid during March total $15,000 cash.
8. Prior to disclosing the financial statements, the company recognized that employees had earned an additional $1,000 in wages that will be paid in the next period.
9. The company recorded $2,000 of depreciation for March relating to its equipment.

Required

a. Record the effect of each transaction using the financial statement effects template.
b. Prepare a March income statement and a balance sheet as of the end of March for AniFoods, Inc.

P2-46. Analyzing Transactions Using the Financial Statement Effects Template (LO4)

Hanlon Advertising Company began the current month with the following balance sheet.

Cash..........................	$ 80,000	Liabilities.....................	$ 70,000
Noncash assets	135,000	Contributed capital.............	110,000
		Earned capital	35,000
Total assets...................	$215,000	Total liabilities and equity	$215,000

Following are summary transactions that occurred during the current month.

1. The company purchased supplies for $5,000 cash; none were used this month.
2. Services of $2,500 were performed this month on credit.
3. Services were performed for $10,000 cash this month.
4. The company purchased advertising for $8,000 cash; the ads will run next month.
5. The company received $1,200 cash as partial payment on accounts receivable from transaction 2.
6. The company paid $3,400 cash toward the accounts payable balance reported at the beginning of the month.
7. Paid $3,100 cash toward this month's wages expenses.
8. The company declared and paid dividends of $500 cash.

Required
a. Record the effects of each transaction using the financial statement effects template.
b. Prepare the income statement for this month and the balance sheet as of month-end.

 P2-47. Reconciling and Computing Operating Cash Flows from Net Income (LO1, 4)

Petroni Company reports the following selected results for its current calendar year.

Net income....................	$130,000
Depreciation expense..........	25,000
Accounts receivable increase....	10,000
Accounts payable increase	6,000
Prepaid expenses decrease.....	3,000
Wages payable decrease.......	4,000

Required
a. Prepare the operating section only of Petroni Company's statement of cash flows for the year.
b. Does the positive sign on depreciation expense indicate that the company is generating cash by recording depreciation? Explain.
c. Explain why the increase in accounts receivable is a use of cash in the statement of cash flows.
d. Explain why the decrease in prepaid expense is a source of cash in the statement of cash flows.

P2-48. Inferring Transactions from Financial Statements (LO1)

THE GAP, INC.
(GPS)

The GAP is a global clothing retailer for men, women, children and babies. The following information is taken from the Gap's fiscal 2011 annual report.

Selected Balance Sheet Data	2011	2010
Inventories	$1,620	$1,477
Accounts Payable	1,049	1,027

a. The Gap purchased inventories totalling $8,918 million during 2011. Use the financial statement effects template to record cost of goods sold for The Gap's fiscal year ended 2011. (Assume that Accounts Payable is used only for recording purchases of inventories and all inventories are purchased on credit.)
b. What amount did the company pay to suppliers during the year? Record this with the financial statement effects template.

IFRS APPLICATIONS

 **I2-49. Comparing Income Statements and Balance Sheets of Competitors** (LO1)

Following are selected income statement and balance sheet data from two European grocery chain companies: **Tesco PLC** (UK) and **Ahold** (The Netherlands).

Income Statements (for fiscal year ended)	Tesco February 26, 2011 (in £millions)	Ahold January 2, 2011 (in €millions)
Sales.	£60,931	€29,530
Cost of goods sold.	55,871	21,610
Gross profit.	5,060	7,920
Total expenses	2,405	7,067
Net income.	£ 2,655	€ 853

Balance Sheet (as of)	Tesco February 26, 2011 (in £millions)	Ahold January 2, 2011 (in €millions)
Current assets	£11,438	€ 5,194
Long-term assets.	35,768	9,531
Total assets.	£47,206	€14,725
Current liabilities.	£17,731	€ 4,092
Long-term liabilities	12,852	4,723
Total liabilities.	30,583	8,815
Stockholders' equity	16,623	5,910
Total liabilities and equity.	£47,206	€14,725

Required

a. Prepare a common-sized income statement. To do this, express each income statement amount as a percent of sales. Comment on any differences observed between the two companies. Ahold's gross profit percentage of sales is considerably higher than Tesco's. What might explain this difference?

b. Prepare a common-sized balance sheet. To do this, express each balance sheet amount as a percent of total assets. Comment on any differences observed between the two companies.

c. Ahold has chosen to structure itself with a higher proportion of equity (and a lower proportion of debt) than Tesco. How does this capital structure decision affect your assessment of the relative riskiness of these two companies?

I2-50. Interpreting the Statement of Cash Flows (LO1)

Following is the statement of cash flows for **AstraZeneca**, a multinational pharmaceutical conglomerate, headquartered in London, UK. The company uses IFRS for its financials and provides a conversion to U.S. $ as a convenience to investors.

ASTRAZENECA Consolidated Statement of Cash Flows For Year Ended December 31, 2009 ($ millions)	
Cash flows from operating activities	
Profit before tax	$10,807
Finance income and expense	736
Depreciation, amortization and impairment.	2,087
Increase in trade and other receivables.	(256)
Decrease in inventories	6
Increase in trade and other payables and provisions.	1,579
Other non-cash movements.	(200)
Cash generated from operations	14,759
Interest paid	(639)
Tax paid	(2,381)
Net cash inflow from operating activities.	11,739

continued

continued from prior page

Cash flows from investing activities	
Movement in short term investments and fixed deposits	$ (1,371)
Purchase of property, plant and equipment.	(962)
Disposal of property, plant and equipment	138
Purchase of intangible assets	(624)
Disposal of intangible assets	269
Purchase of non-current asset investments.	(31)
Disposal of non-current asset investments	3
Interest received.	113
Payments made by subsidiaries to non-controlling interests	(11)
Net cash outflow from investing activities	(2,476)
Net cash inflow/(outflow) before financing activities	9,263
Cash flows from financing activities	
Proceeds from issue of share capital.	135
Repayment of loans	(650)
Dividends paid	(2,977)
Movement in short term borrowings	(137)
Net cash (outflow)/inflow from financing activities.	(3,629)
Net increase/(decrease) in cash and cash equivalents in the period	$ 5,634
Cash and cash equivalents at beginning of the period	4,123
Exchange rate effects.	71
Cash and cash equivalents at the end of the period.	$ 9,828

Required

a. Why does AstraZeneca add back depreciation to compute net cash flows from operating activities?

b. Explain why the increase in trade and other receivables is reported as a cash outflow and the decrease in inventories is reported as a cash inflow. Explain why trade and other payables and provisions are shown as a source of cash.

c. AstraZeneca reports that it invested $962 million in property and equipment. Is this an appropriate type of expenditure for AstraZeneca to make? What relation should expenditures for PPE assets have with depreciation expense?

d. AstraZeneca indicates that it paid dividends of $2,977 million. How do we evaluate that use of cash relative to other possible uses for AstraZeneca's cash?

e. Provide an overall assessment of AstraZeneca's cash flows for 2009. In the analysis, consider the sources and uses of cash.

DISCUSSION POINTS

D2-51. **Inferring Transactions from Financial Statements**   (LO1, 2)

COSTCO WHOLESALE CORPORATION (COST)

Costco Wholesale Corporation operates membership warehouses selling food, appliances, consumer electronics, apparel and other household goods at 582 locations across the U.S. as well as in Canada, the United Kingdom, Japan, Australia, South Korea, Taiwan, Mexico and Puerto Rico. As of its fiscal year-end 2010, Costco had approximately 60 million members. Selected fiscal-year information from the company's balance sheets follows.

Selected Balance Sheet Data ($ millions)	2010	2009
Merchandise inventories	$5,638	$5,405
Deferred membership income (liability)	869	824

a. During fiscal 2010, Costco collected $1,736 million cash for membership fees. Use the financial statement effects template to record the cash collected for membership fees.

b. Costco recorded merchandise costs (that is, cost of goods sold) of $67,995 in 2011. Record this transaction in the financial statements effects template.

c. Determine the value of merchandise that Costco purchased during fiscal-year 2011. Use the financial statement effects template to record these merchandise purchases. Assume all of Costco's purchases are on credit.

D2-52. **Assessing Financial Statement Effects of Adjustments** **(LO2)**
For each of the following separate situations, prepare the necessary accounting adjustments using the financial statement effects template.

a. Unrecorded depreciation on equipment is $610.
b. The Supplies account has an unadjusted balance of $2,990. Supplies still available at the end of the period total $1,100.
c. On the date for preparing financial statements, an estimated utilities expense of $390 has been incurred, but no utility bill has yet been received or paid.
d. On the first day of the current period, rent for four periods was paid and recorded as a $2,800 debit to Prepaid Rent and a $2,800 credit to Cash.
e. Nine months ago, **The Allstate Corporation** sold a one-year policy to a customer and recorded the receipt of the premium by crediting Unearned Revenue for $624. No accounting adjustments have been prepared during the nine-month period. Allstate's annual financial statements are now being prepared.
f. At the end of the period, employee wages of $965 have been incurred but not paid or recorded.
g. At the end of the period, $300 of interest has been earned but not yet received or recorded.

ALLSTATE CORP.
(ALL)

D2-53. **Inferring Transactions from Financial Statements** **(LO1, 2)**
Foot Locker, Inc., a retailer of athletic footwear and apparel, operates about 3,400 stores in the United States, Canada, Europe, Australia, and New Zealand. During its fiscal year ended in 2010, Foot Locker purchased merchandise inventory costing $3,555 ($ millions). Assume that Foot Locker makes all purchases on credit, and that its accounts payable is only used for inventory purchases. The following T-accounts reflect information contained in the company's fiscal 2009 and 2010 balance sheets ($ millions).

FOOT LOCKER, INC.
(FL)

Inventories				Accounts Payable	
2009 Bal.	1,037			215	2009 Bal.
2010 Bal.	1,059			223	2010 Bal.

a. Use the financial statement effects template to record Foot Locker's 2010 purchases.
b. What amount did Foot Locker pay in cash to its suppliers during fiscal year 2010? Explain.
c. Use the financial statement effects template to record cost of goods sold for its fiscal year 2010.

D2-54. **Understanding the Company Operating Cycle and Management Strategy** **(LO1)**
Consider the operating cycle as depicted in Exhibit 2.3, to answer the following questions.

a. Why might a company want to reduce its cash conversion cycle? (*Hint*: Consider the financial statement implications of reducing the cash conversion cycle.)
b. How might a company reduce its cash conversion cycle?
c. Examine and discuss the potential impacts on *customers* and *suppliers* of taking the actions identified in part *b*.

D2-55. **Ethics and Governance: Understanding Revenue Recognition and Expense Recording** **(LO1)**
Revenue should be recognized when it is earned and expense when incurred. Given some lack of specificity in these terms, companies have some latitude when applying GAAP to determine the timing and amount of revenues and expenses. A few companies use this latitude to manage reported earnings. Some have argued that it is not necessarily bad for companies to manage earnings in that, by doing so, management (1) can better provide investors and creditors with reported earnings that are closer to "core" earnings (that is, management purges earnings of components deemed irrelevant or distracting so that share prices better reflect company performance); and (2) can present the company in the best light, which benefits both shareholders and employees—a Machiavellian argument that "the end justifies the means."

a. Is it good that GAAP is written as broadly as it is? Explain. What are the pros and cons of defining accounting terms more strictly?
b. Assess (both pro and con) the Machiavellian argument above that defends managing earnings.

SOLUTIONS TO REVIEW PROBLEMS

Mid-Module Review 1

Solution

DELL INC. Income Statement For Fiscal Year Ended January 28, 2011	
Revenue	$61,494
Cost of revenue	50,098
Gross margin	11,396
Operating expenses	
Selling, general, and administrative expenses	7,302
Research and development expenses	661
Total operating expenses	7,963
Operating income	3,433
Interest expense	83
Income before income taxes	3,350
Income tax expense	715
Net income	$ 2,635

DELL INC. Statement of Cash Flows For Fiscal Year Ended January 28, 2011	
Net cash provided by operating activities	$ 3,969
Net cash used in investing activities	(1,165)
Net cash provided by financing activities	474
Net increase in cash and cash equivalents	3,278
Cash and cash equivalents, beginning of year	10,635
Cash and cash equivalents, ending of year	$13,913

DELL INC. Balance Sheet January 28, 2011			
Assets		**Liabilities and Equity**	
Current assets		Current liabilities	
Cash and cash equivalents	$13,913	Short-term debt	$ 851
Short-term investments	452	Accounts payable	11,293
Accounts receivable	10,136	Accrued and other current liabilities . . .	7,339
Inventories	1,301	Total current liabilities	19,483
Other current assets	3,219	Long-term debt	5,146
Total current assets	29,021	Other noncurrent liabilities	6,204
		Total liabilities	30,833
Property, plant, and equipment, net	1,953	Stockholders' equity	
Long-term investments	704	Paid-in capital	11,797
Other noncurrent assets	6,921	Retained earnings	24,744
		Other stockholders' equity	(28,775)
		Total stockholders' equity	7,766
Total assets	$38,599	Total liabilities and stockholders' equity .	$38,599

Mid-Module Review 2

Solution

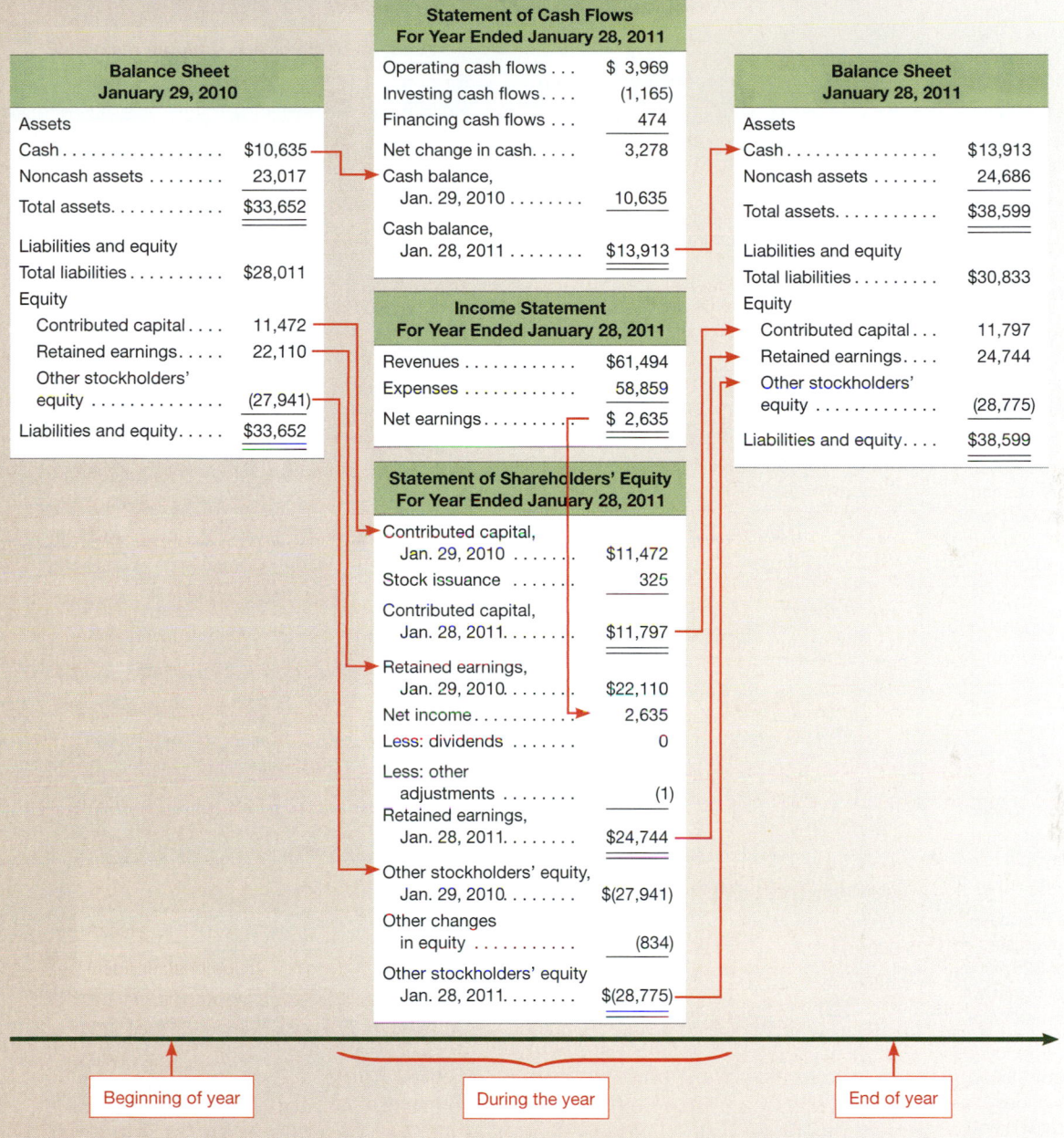

Balance Sheet
January 29, 2010

Assets	
Cash	$10,635
Noncash assets	23,017
Total assets.	$33,652

Liabilities and equity	
Total liabilities	$28,011
Equity	
Contributed capital	11,472
Retained earnings.	22,110
Other stockholders' equity	(27,941)
Liabilities and equity.	$33,652

Statement of Cash Flows
For Year Ended January 28, 2011

Operating cash flows . . .	$ 3,969
Investing cash flows. . . .	(1,165)
Financing cash flows . . .	474
Net change in cash.	3,278
Cash balance, Jan. 29, 2010	10,635
Cash balance, Jan. 28, 2011	$13,913

Income Statement
For Year Ended January 28, 2011

Revenues	$61,494
Expenses	58,859
Net earnings.	$ 2,635

Statement of Shareholders' Equity
For Year Ended January 28, 2011

Contributed capital, Jan. 29, 2010	$11,472
Stock issuance	325
Contributed capital, Jan. 28, 2011.	$11,797
Retained earnings, Jan. 29, 2010.	$22,110
Net income.	2,635
Less: dividends	0
Less: other adjustments	(1)
Retained earnings, Jan. 28, 2011.	$24,744
Other stockholders' equity, Jan. 29, 2010.	$(27,941)
Other changes in equity	(834)
Other stockholders' equity Jan. 28, 2011.	$(28,775)

Balance Sheet
January 28, 2011

Assets	
Cash	$13,913
Noncash assets	24,686
Total assets.	$38,599

Liabilities and equity	
Total liabilities	$30,833
Equity	
Contributed capital . . .	11,797
Retained earnings. . . .	24,744
Other stockholders' equity	(28,775)
Liabilities and equity. . . .	$38,599

Beginning of year

During the year

End of year

Module-End Review

Solution

a.

Transaction	Balance Sheet					Income Statement		
	Cash Asset	+ Noncash Assets	= Liabil- ities	+ Contrib. Capital	+ Earned Capital	Rev- enues	− Expen- ses	= Net Income
Beginning balance	+80,000	+270,000	= +200,000	+50,000	+100,000		−	=
1. Purchase inventory of $80,000 on credit		+80,000 Inventory	= +80,000 Accounts Payable				−	=
2. Pay employees $10,000 cash for wages earned this year	−10,000 Cash		=		−10,000 Retained Earnings		+10,000 Wages Expense	−10,000
3. Sell inventory costing $40,000 for $70,000 on credit		+70,000 Accounts Receivable −40,000 Inventory	=		+70,000 Retained Earnings −40,000 Retained Earning	+70,000 Sales	− +40,000 Cost of Goods Sold	+70,000 = −40,000
4. Collect $15,000 cash from the accounts receivable in transaction 3	+15,000 Cash	−15,000 Accounts Receivable	=				−	=
5. Pay $35,000 cash toward the accounts payable in transaction 1	−35,000 Cash		= −35,000 Accounts Payable				−	=
6. Purchase advertising for $25,000 cash that will air next year	−25,000 Cash	+25,000 Prepaid Advertising	=				−	=
7. Employees earn $5,000 in wages that will not be paid until next year			= +5,000 Wages Payable		−5,000 Retained Earnings		+5,000 Wages Expense	−5,000
8. Record $3,000 depreciation on its equipment		−3,000 PPE, net	=		−3,000 Retained Earnings		+3,000 Depreciation Expense	−3,000
Ending balance	+25,000	+387,000	= +250,000	+50,000	+112,000	+70,000	− +58,000	= +12,000

b.

GATEWAY	
Income Statement	
For Year Ended December 31, 2011	
Revenues	$70,000
Expenses	58,000
Net income.	$12,000

GATEWAY			
Balance Sheet			
December 31, 2011			
Cash	$ 25,000	Liabilities.	$250,000
Noncash assets	387,000	Contributed capital.	50,000
		Earned capital (retained earnings)	112,000
Total assets.	$412,000	Total liabilities and equity	$412,000

c. The linkage between the income statement and the balance sheet is retained earnings. Each period, the retained earnings account is updated for net income less dividends paid. For this period, that updating follows.

GATEWAY	
Retained Earnings Reconciliation	
For Year Ended December 31, 2011	
Retained earnings, Dec. 31, 2010	$100,000
Add: Net income	12,000
Less: Dividends	(0)
Retained earnings, Dec. 31, 2011	$112,000

LEARNING OBJECTIVES

1. Compute return on equity (ROE) and disaggregate it into components of operating and nonoperating returns. (p. 3-4)

2. Disaggregate operating return (RNOA) into components of profitability and asset turnover. (p. 3-12)

3. Explain nonoperating return and compute it from return on equity and the operating return. (p. 3-17)

4. Describe and illustrate traditional DuPont disaggregation of ROE. (p. 3-26)

© Getty Images

Profitability Analysis and Interpretation

Target employs a number of financial measures to assess its overall performance and financial condition. These measures include ratios related to profitability and asset turnover as well as the return on invested capital. Analysts, too, use a variety of measures to capture different aspects of company performance to answer questions such as: Is it managed efficiently and profitably? Does it use assets effectively? Is performance achieved with a minimum of debt?

One fundamental measure is return on capital, which Warren Buffett, CEO of the investment firm **Berkshire Hathaway**, lists in his acquisition criteria cited in Module 1: "Our preference would be to reach our goal by directly owning a diversified group of businesses that generate cash and consistently earn above-average returns on capital." All return metrics follow the same basic formula—they divide some measure of profit by some measure of investment. A company's performance is commonly judged by its profitability. Although analysis of profit is important, it is only part of the story. A more meaningful analysis is to compare level of profitability with the amount of capital that has been invested in the business. The most common return measure is return on equity (ROE), which focuses on shareholder investment as its measure of invested capital. By focusing on the *equity* investment, ROE measures return from the perspective of the common shareholder rather than the company overall. Target's ROE for 2011 was 18.94%, up from 15.26% two years prior.

This module focuses on analysis of return metrics. Beyond ROE, we put special emphasis on the return on net operating assets (RNOA), computed as net operating profit after tax (NOPAT) divided by average net operating assets (NOA). RNOA focuses on operating activities—operating profit relative to investment in net operating assets. It is important to distinguish operating activities from nonoperating activities because the capital markets value each component differently, placing much greater emphasis on operations. Target's RNOA has improved from 8.97% to 11.43% in the past three years.

RNOA consists of two components: profitability and asset productivity. Increasing either component increases RNOA. These components reflect on the first two questions we posed above: Is the company managed efficiently and profitably? Does it use assets effectively?

The profitability component of RNOA measures net operating profit after tax for each sales dollar (NOPAT/Sales), and is called the net operating profit margin (NOPM). Target's NOPM has increased from 4.25% to 5.04% in the past three years.

Asset productivity, the second component of RNOA, is reflected in net operating asset turnover (NOAT). NOAT is measured as sales divided by average net operating assets—it captures the notion of how many sales dollars are generated by each dollar of invested assets. Target has increased its NOAT from 2.11 to 2.27 in the past three years. Increasing the turnover for large asset bases is difficult, and NOAT measures tend to fluctuate in a narrow band. When companies are able to make a meaningful improvement in NOAT, however, it usually has a large impact on RNOA.

RNOA is an important metric in assessing the performance of company management. We can use the RNOA components, NOPM and NOAT, to assess how effectively and efficiently management uses the company's operating assets to produce a return.

The difference between ROE and RNOA is important for our analysis. Specifically, ROE consists of a return on operating activities (RNOA) *plus* a return on nonoperating activities, where the latter reflects how well the company uses borrowed funds.

(continued on next page)

(continued from previous page)

Companies can increase ROE by borrowing money and effectively using those borrowed funds. However, debt can increase the company's risk—where severe consequences can result if debt is not repaid when due. This is why Warren Buffett focuses on "businesses earning good returns on equity while employing little or no debt." For those companies that do employ debt, our analysis seeks to evaluate their ability to repay the amounts owed when due.

Over the years, analysts, creditors and others have developed hundreds of ratios to measure specific aspects of financial performance. Most of these seek answers to the root question: Can the company achieve a high return on its invested capital and, if so, is that return sustainable?

Sources: *Target 10-K, 2011*; *Berkshire Hathaway 10-K,* 2010; *The Wall Street Journal,* January 2011.

MODULE
ORGANIZATION

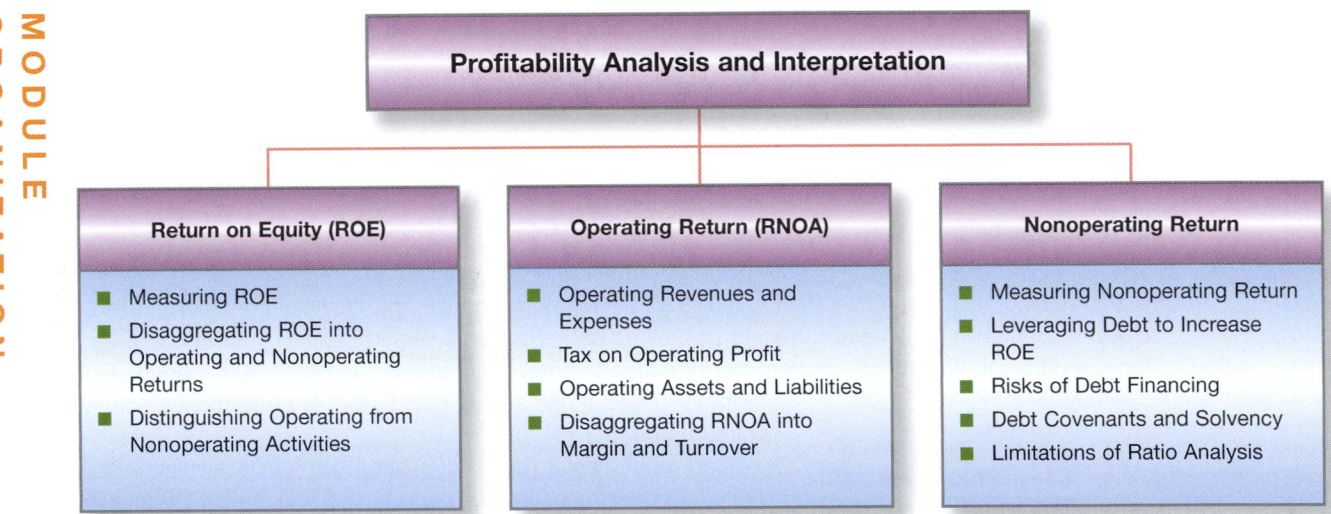

A key aspect of any analysis is identifying the business activities that drive company success. We pursue an answer to the question: Is the company earning an acceptable rate of return on its invested capital? We also want to know the extent to which the company's return on invested capital results from its operating versus its nonoperating activities. The distinction between returns from operating and nonoperating activities is important and plays a key role in our analysis.

Operating activities are the core activities of a company. They consist of those activities required to deliver a company's products or services to its customers. A company engages in operating activities when it conducts research and development, establishes supply chains, assembles administrative support, produces and markets its products, and follows up with after-sale customer services.

The asset side of a company's balance sheet reflects resources devoted to operating activities with accounts such as receivables, inventories, and property, plant and equipment (PPE). Operating activities are reflected in liabilities with accounts such as accounts payable, accrued expenses, and long-term operating liabilities such as pension and health care obligations. The income statement reflects operating activities through accounts such as revenues, costs of goods sold, and operating expenses such as selling, general, and administrative expenses that include wages, advertising, depreciation, occupancy, insurance, and research and development. Operating activities create the most long-lasting (persistent) effects on future profitability and cash flows of the company. Operations provide the primary value drivers for company stakeholders. It is for this reason that operating activities play such a prominent role in assessing profitability.

Nonoperating activities relate to the investing of cash in marketable securities and in other nonoperating investments. Nonoperating activities also relate to borrowings through accounts such as short- and long-term debt. These nonoperating assets and liabilities expand and contract to buffer fluctuations in operating asset and liability levels. When operating assets grow faster than operating liabilities, companies typically increase their nonoperating liabilities to fund the deficit. Later, these liabilities decline when operating assets decline. When companies have cash in excess of what is needed for operating activities, they often invest the cash temporarily in marketable securities or other investments to provide some return until those funds are needed for operations.

The income statement reflects nonoperating activities through accounts such as interest and dividend revenue, capital gains or losses relating to investments, and interest expense on borrowed funds. Nonoperating expenses, net of any nonoperating revenues, provide a nonoperating return for a company. Although nonoperating activities are important and must be managed well, they are not the main value drivers for company stakeholders.

We begin this module by explaining the return on equity (ROE). We then discuss in more detail how ROE consists of both an operating return (RNOA) and a nonoperating return. Next, we discuss the two RNOA components that measure profitability and asset turnover. We conclude this module with a discussion of nonoperating return, focusing on the notion that companies can increase ROE through judicious use of debt.

RETURN ON EQUITY (ROE)

Return on equity (ROE) is the principal summary measure of company performance and is defined as follows:

$$ROE = \frac{\text{Net income}}{\text{Average stockholders' equity}}$$

LO1 Compute return on equity (ROE) and disaggregate it into components of operating and nonoperating returns.

ROE relates net income to the average investment by shareholders as measured by total stockholders' equity from the balance sheet.

Warren Buffett highlights ROE as part of his acquisition criteria: "Businesses earning good returns on equity while employing little or no debt." The ROE formula can be rewritten in a way to better see the point Buffett is making (derivation of this ROE formula is in Appendix 3A):

$$ROE = \text{Operating return} + \text{Nonoperating return}$$

The equation above shows that ROE consists of two returns: (1) the return from the company's operating activities, linked to revenues and expenses from the company's products or services, and (2) the return from the company's use of debt, net of any return from nonoperating investments. Companies can use debt to increase their return on equity, but this increases risk because the failure to make required debt payments can yield many legal consequences, including bankruptcy. This is one reason why Warren Buffett focuses on companies whose return on equity is derived primarily from operating activities.

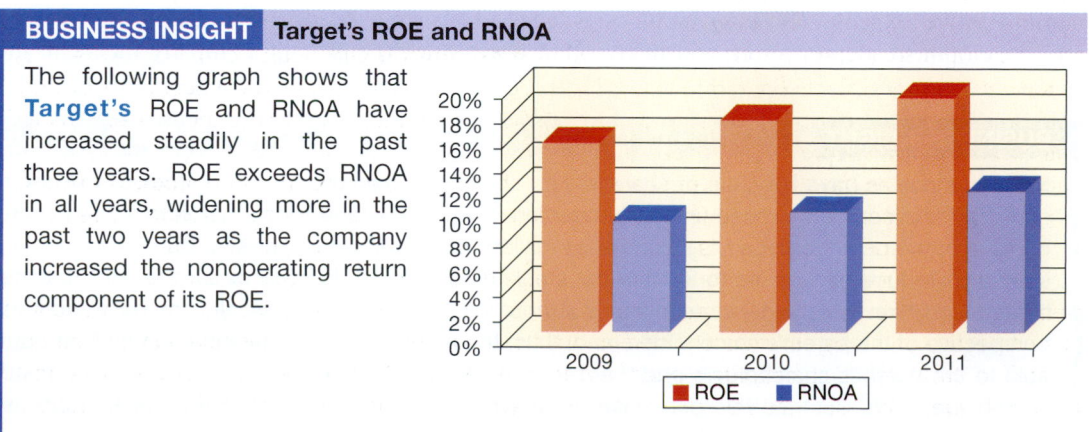

BUSINESS INSIGHT Target's ROE and RNOA

The following graph shows that **Target's** ROE and RNOA have increased steadily in the past three years. ROE exceeds RNOA in all years, widening more in the past two years as the company increased the nonoperating return component of its ROE.

OPERATING RETURN (RNOA)

Operating returns are reflected in the **return on net operating assets (RNOA)**, defined as follows:

$$RNOA = \frac{\text{Net operating profit after tax (NOPAT)}}{\text{Average net operating assets (NOA)}}$$

To implement this formula, we must first classify the income statement and balance sheet into operating and nonoperating components so that we can assess each separately. We first consider operating activities on the income statement and explain how to compute NOPAT. Second, we consider operating activities on the balance sheet and explain how to compute NOA.

Operating Items in the Income Statement —NOPAT

The income statement reports both operating and nonoperating activities. Exhibit 3.1 shows a typical income statement with the operating activities highlighted.

EXHIBIT 3.1   Operating and Nonoperating Items in the Income Statement
Typical Income Statement **Operating Items Highlighted**
Revenues
Cost of sales
Gross profit
Operating expenses
Selling, general and administrative
Asset impairment expense
Gains and losses on asset disposal
Total operating expenses
Operating income
Interest expense
Interest and dividend revenue
Investment gains and losses
Total nonoperating expenses
Income from continuing operations before taxes
Tax expense
Income from continuing operations
Income (loss) from discontinued operations, net of tax (see Appendix 3A)
Consolidated net income
Less: consolidated net income attributable to noncontrolling interest (see Appendix 3A)
Consolidated net income attributable to parent shareholders

Operating activities are those that relate to bringing a company's products or services to market and any after-sales support. The income statement in Exhibit 3.1 reflects operating activities through revenues, costs of goods sold (COGS), and other expenses. Selling, general, and administrative expense (SG&A) includes wages, advertising, occupancy, insurance, research and development, depreciation, and many other operating expenses the company incurs in the

BUSINESS INSIGHT	Which Net Income and Stockholders' Equity to Use?

Many companies have two sets of shareholders: those that own the common stock of the parent company (the company whose financial statements we review) and those that own shares in one or more of the parent company's subsidiaries (called "noncontrolling interest"). Current accounting standards require companies to identify the stockholders' equity relating to each group of shareholders and, likewise, the net income that is attributable to each. ROE is usually computed from the perspective of the parent's shareholders and, thus, the numerator is the net income that is attributable to the parent's shareholders and the denominator is the stockholders' equity of the parent's shareholders. We illustrate this difference for **Walmart** in our Mid-Module Review and discuss noncontrolling interests more fully in Module 9.

ordinary course of business (some of these are often reported as separate line items in the income statement). Companies also dispose of operating assets, and can realize gains or losses from their disposal, or write them off partially or completely when they become impaired. These, too, are operating activities. Finally, the reported tax expense on the income statement reflects both operating and nonoperating activities. Later in this section we use Target's income statement to explain how to separately estimate tax expense related to operating activities only.

Nonoperating activities relate to borrowed money that creates interest expense. Nonoperating activities also relate to investments such as marketable securities and other investments that yield interest or dividend revenue and capital gains or losses from any sales of nonoperating investments during the period. Often companies report income or loss from discontinued operations, which we consider as a nonoperating item on the income statement. ROE analysis is from the perspective of parent-company shareholders; thus, we also consider the portion of consolidated net income that is attributable to noncontrolling shareholders as a nonoperating item on the income statement (but *excluded* from the tax shield defined below).

Following is Target's 2011 income statement with the operating items highlighted. Target's operating items include sales, cost of sales, SG&A, and depreciation expense. Target's pretax operating income is $5,252 million. Its nonoperating activities relate to its borrowed money (mainly interest expense) which yield pretax net nonoperating expense of $757 million.

TARGET Income Statement ($ millions) For Year Ended January 29, 2011	
Sales.	$65,786
Credit card revenues	1,604
Total revenues	67,390
Cost of sales.	45,725
Selling, general and administrative expenses	13,469
Credit card expenses	860
Depreciation and amortization	2,084
Earnings before interest expense and income taxes	5,252
Net interest expense	
Nonrecourse debt collateralized by credit card receivables.	83
Other interest expense	677
Interest income.	(3)
Net interest expense	757
Earnings before income taxes	4,495
Provision for income taxes.	1,575
Net earnings.	$ 2,920

Computing Tax on Operating Profit

Target's income statement reports net operating profit *before* tax (NOPBT) of $5,252 million. But, the numerator of the RNOA formula, defined previously, uses net operating profit *after tax* (NOPAT). Thus, we need to subtract taxes to determine NOPAT.

$$\textbf{NOPAT} = \textbf{NOPBT} - \textbf{Tax on operating profit}$$

The tax expense of $1,575 million that Target reports on its income statement pertains to both operating *and* nonoperating activities. To compute NOPAT, we need to compute the tax expense relating solely to operating profit as follows:

$$\textbf{Tax on operating profit} = \textbf{Tax expense} + (\textbf{Pretax net nonoperating expense} \times \textbf{Statutory tax rate})$$

Tax Shield

The amount in parentheses is called the *tax shield*, which is the taxes that Target saved by having tax-deductible nonoperating expenses (see Tax Shield box on the next page for details). By definition, the taxes saved (by the tax shield) do not relate to operating profits; thus, we must add back the tax shield to total tax expense to compute tax on operating profit. (For companies with nonoperating

BUSINESS INSIGHT Tax Shield

Persons with home mortgages understand well the beneficial effects of the "interest tax shield." To see how the interest tax shield works, consider two individuals, each with income of $50,000 and each with only one expense: a home. Assume that one person pays $10,000 per year in rent; the other pays $10,000 in interest on a home mortgage. Rent is not deductible for tax purposes, whereas mortgage interest (but not principal) is deductible. Assume that each person pays taxes at 25%, the personal tax rate for this income level. Their tax payments follow.

	Renter	Home owner
Income before interest and taxes.............	$50,000	$50,000
Less interest deduction	0	(10,000)
Taxable income	$50,000	$40,000
Taxes paid (25% rate)......................	$12,500	$10,000

The renter reports $50,000 in taxable income and pays $12,500 in taxes. The home owner deducts $10,000 in interest, which lowers taxable income to $40,000 and reduces taxes to $10,000. By deducting mortgage interest, the home owner's tax bill is $2,500 lower. The $2,500 is the *interest tax shield*, and we can compute it directly as the $10,000 interest deduction multiplied by the 25% tax rate.

BUSINESS INSIGHT Tax Rates for Computing NOPAT

In our examples and assignments, we assume the statutory tax rate is 37% as this is the approximate average combined federal and state tax rate for public companies. We can, as an alternative approach, compute a *company-specific* tax rate using the income tax footnote in the 10-K. For example, **Target** provides the following table in its 10-K for the year ended January 29, 2011:

Tax Rate Reconciliation	2011	2010	2009
Federal statutory rate......................	35.0%	35.0%	35.0%
State income taxes, net of federal tax benefit	1.4	2.8	3.8
Other......................................	(1.3)	(2.1)	(1.4)
Effective tax rate.........................	35.1%	35.7%	37.4%

The federal statutory rate is 35.0%, and **Target** pays state taxes amounting to an additional 1.4% (it also reports reductions of 1.3% relating to "other" items). Thus, **Target's** effective tax rate (or average) for *all* of its income is the sum of all its taxes paid less benefits received, or 35.1%. However, the tax shield that we add back in computing NOPAT uses only *federal and state tax rates*. For **Target**, the company-specific tax rate that we can use to compute the tax shield is 36.4% (35.0% + 1.4%). It would be incorrect to use **Target's** 35.1% company-specific effective tax rate to compute NOPAT, as that rate includes both operating and nonoperating items. We discuss income tax more fully in Module 5.

revenue greater than nonoperating expense, so-called *net nonoperating revenue,* the tax on operating profit is computed as: Tax expense − [Pretax net nonoperating revenue × Statutory tax rate]).

Applying this method, we see that Target had a tax shield of $280 million (computed as pretax net nonoperating expense of $757 million times its statutory tax rate of 37%) and tax on operating profit of $1,855 million (computed as $1,575 million + $280 million).[1] We subtract the

---

[1] The statutory federal tax rate for corporations is 35% (per U.S. tax code). Also, most states and some local jurisdictions tax corporate income, and those state taxes are deductible for federal tax purposes. The *net* state tax rate is the statutory rate less the federal tax deduction. The tax rate on operating profit is the sum of the two. On average, the net state tax is about 2%; thus, we use 37% (35% + 2%) as the assumed tax rate on nonoperating expenses and revenues in our examples and assignments at the end of the module. The business insight boxes below explain that the tax rate on pretax profit will usually *not* be the assumed statutory rate (37%).

tax on operating profit from the net operating profit before tax to obtain NOPAT. Thus, Target's net operating profit after tax is computed as follows ($ millions):

Net operating profit before tax (NOPBT)		$5,252
Less tax on operating profit		
Tax expense (from income statement)	$1,575	
Tax shield ($757 × 37%).	+280	(1,855)
Net operating profit after tax (NOPAT)		$3,397

MID-MODULE REVIEW 1

Following is the income statement of **Walmart**.

WALMART Income Statement ($ millions) For Fiscal Year Ended January 31, 2011	
Net sales.	$418,952
Membership and other income	2,897
Revenues, total.	421,849
Costs and expenses	
Cost of sales.	315,287
Operating, selling, general and administrative expenses.	81,020
Operating income.	25,542
Interest	
Debt	1,928
Capital leases	277
Interest income.	(201)
Interest, net	2,004
Income from continuing operations before income taxes	23,538
Provision for income taxes	
Current	6,703
Deferred	876
Provision for income taxes, total	7,579
Income from continuing operations	15,959
Income (loss) from discontinued operations, net of tax.	1,034
Consolidated net income	16,993
Less consolidated net income attributable to noncontrolling interest	(604)
Consolidated net income attributable to Walmart	$ 16,389

Required

Compute Walmart's net operating profit after tax (NOPAT) for its fiscal year 2011. Assume a statutory rate of 37% applies to nonoperating expenses and revenues.

The solution is on page 3-49.

Operating Items in the Balance Sheet —NOA

RNOA relates NOPAT to the average net operating assets (NOA) of the company. We compute NOA as follows:

$$\text{Net operating assets} = \text{Operating assets} - \text{Operating liabilities}$$

To compute NOA we must partition the balance sheet into operating and nonoperating items. Exhibit 3.2 shows a typical balance sheet and highlights the operating items.

| **EXHIBIT 3.2** | Operating and Nonoperating Items in the Balance Sheet |

Typical Balance Sheet
Operating Items Highlighted

Current assets
Cash and cash equivalents
Short-term investments
Accounts receivable
Inventories
Prepaid expenses
Deferred income tax assets
Other current assets
Current assets of discontinued operations

Long-term assets
Long-term investments in securities
Property, plant and equipment, net
Capitalized lease assets
Natural resources
Equity method investments
Goodwill and intangible assets
Deferred income tax assets
Other long-term assets
Long-term assets of discontinued operations

Current liabilities
Short-term notes and interest payable
Current maturities of long-term debt
Accounts payable
Accrued liabilities
Unearned revenue
Deferred income tax liabilities
Current liabilities of discontinued operations

Long-term liabilities
Bonds and notes payable
Capitalized lease obligations
Pension and other post-employment liabilities
Deferred income tax liabilities
Long-term liabilities of discontinued operations

Stockholders' equity
All equity accounts

Noncontrolling (minority) interest

Operating assets are those assets directly linked to operating activities, the company's ongoing (continuing) business operations. They typically include receivables, inventories, prepaid expenses, property, plant and equipment (PPE), and capitalized lease assets, and exclude short-term and long-term investments in marketable securities and any current and noncurrent assets that relate to discontinued operations. Equity investments in affiliated companies and goodwill are considered operating assets if they pertain to the ownership of stock in other firms linked to the company's operating activities (see Module 9). Deferred tax assets (and liabilities) are operating items because they relate to future tax deductions (or payments) arising from operating activities (see Module 5). We assume that "other" assets and liabilities, and "other" revenues and expenses, are operating unless information suggests otherwise. For example, details in footnotes might reveal that "other" includes nonoperating items. Or the company might explicitly indicate the "other" is nonoperating by reporting the item after a subtotal for income from operations. In these cases, we would consider the "other" as nonoperating.

Operating liabilities are liabilities that arise from operating revenues and expenses. For example, accounts payable and accrued expenses help fund inventories, wages, utilities, and other operating expenses; also, unearned revenue (an operating liability) relates to operating revenue. Similarly, pension and other post-employment obligations relate to long-term obligations for employee retirement and health care, which by definition are operating activities (see Module 10). Operating liabilities exclude bank loans, mortgages or other debt, which are nonoperating. Further, companies often use capitalized leases to finance long-term operating assets, and these capitalized lease liabilities are also nonoperating (see Module 10). Lastly, nonoperating liabilities include any current and noncurrent liabilities that relate to discontinued operations.

Nonoperating assets include cash and cash equivalents (see Business Insight box below) and investments in marketable securities, both short- and long-term. Nonoperating liabilities include interest bearing debt, both short- and long-term, and capitalized lease obligations. Finally, we consider all equity accounts nonoperating, including equity relating to noncontrolling interest.

| BUSINESS INSIGHT | Why is Cash a Nonoperating Asset? |

Most analysts consider cash as nonoperating because this account consists almost totally of "cash equivalents," which are short-term investments with a scheduled maturity of 90 days or less. Technically, the amount of cash needed to support routine business transactions is considered as operating and the remainder as a nonoperating short-term investment, similar to investments reported as marketable securities. If we know what portion of the cash balance supports operating activities, we would classify that as operating. Unfortunately, companies do not report that information and most analysts feel that it is probably a small portion. As a result, we, like others, treat the entire cash balance as nonoperating and recognize that we are probably understating net operating assets slightly.

The following is Target's balance sheets for 2011 and 2010. Its operating assets and operating liabilities are highlighted.

TARGET Balance Sheets		
(In millions)	**Jan. 29, 2011**	**Jan. 30, 2010**
Assets		
Cash and cash equivalents	$ 1,712	$ 2,200
Credit card receivables, net of allowance of $690 and $1,016	6,153	6,966
Inventory	7,596	7,179
Other current assets	1,752	2,079
Total current assets	17,213	18,424
Property and equipment		
Land	5,928	5,793
Buildings and improvements	23,081	22,152
Fixtures and equipment	4,939	4,743
Computer hardware and software	2,533	2,575
Construction-in-progress	567	502
Accumulated depreciation	(11,555)	(10,485)
Property and equipment, net	25,493	25,280
Other noncurrent assets	999	829
Total assets	$43,705	$44,533
Liabilities and shareholders' investment		
Accounts payable	$6,625	$6,511
Accrued and other current liabilities	3,326	3,120
Unsecured debt and other borrowings	119	796
Nonrecourse debt collateralized by credit card receivables	—	900
Total current liabilities	10,070	11,327
Unsecured debt and other borrowings	11,653	10,643
Nonrecourse debt collateralized by credit card receivables	3,954	4,475
Deferred income taxes	934	835
Other noncurrent liabilities	1,607	1,906
Total noncurrent liabilities	18,148	17,859
Shareholders' investment		
Common stock	59	62
Additional paid-in-capital	3,311	2,919
Retained earnings	12,698	12,947
Accumulated other comprehensive loss	(581)	(581)
Total shareholders' investment	15,487	15,347
Total liabilities and shareholders' investment	$43,705	$44,533

We assume that Target's "other" assets and liabilities are operating. We can sometimes make a finer distinction if footnotes to financial statements provide additional information. For now, assume that these "other" items reported in balance sheets pertain to operations.

Using Target's highlighted balance sheet above, we compute net operating assets for 2011 and 2010 as follows (recall that Net operating assets (NOA) = Total operating assets − Total operating liabilities).

Target ($ millions)	Jan. 29, 2011	Jan. 30, 2010
Operating assets		
Credit card receivables.	$ 6,153	$ 6,966
Inventory.	7,596	7,179
Other current assets	1,752	2,079
Property and equipment, net	25,493	25,280
Other noncurrent assets	999	829
Total operating assets	**41,993**	**42,333**
Operating liabilities		
Accounts payable.	6,625	6,511
Accrued and other current liabilities.	3,326	3,120
Deferred income taxes	934	835
Other noncurrent liabilities	1,607	1,906
Total operating liabilities.	**12,492**	**12,372**
Net operating assets (NOA).	**$29,501**	**$29,961**

To determine average NOA, we take a simple average of two consecutive years' numbers. Thus, return on net operating assets (RNOA) for Target for 2011 is computed as follows ($ millions).

$$\text{RNOA} = \frac{\text{NOPAT}}{\text{Average NOA}} = \frac{\$3,397}{(\$29,501 + \$29,961)/2} = 11.43\%$$

Target's 2011 RNOA is 11.43%. By comparison, **Walmart**'s (its main competitor) RNOA is 15.63% (this computation is shown in Mid-Module Review 2), and the average for all publicly traded companies is about 8% for the past decade.

Recall that RNOA is related to ROE as follows: ROE = Operating return + Nonoperating return, where RNOA is the operating return. Thus, we can ask how do Target's RNOA and ROE compare? To answer this we need Target's 2011 ROE, which is computed as follows ($ millions).

$$\text{ROE} = \frac{\text{Net income}}{\text{Average stockholders' equity}} = \frac{\$2,920}{(\$15,487 + \$15,347)/2} = 18.94\%$$

In relative terms, Target's operating return (RNOA) is 60% (11.43%/18.94%) of its total ROE, which is slightly less than the average publicly traded company's percent of near 69%. Its nonoperating return of 7.5% (18.94% − 11.43%) makes up the remaining 40% of ROE.

Exhibit 3.3 provides a summary of key terms introduced to this point and their definitions.

EXHIBIT 3.3	Key Ratio and Acronym Definitions
Ratio	**Definition**
ROE: Return on equity.	Net income*/Average stockholders' equity*
NOPAT: Net operating profit after tax.	Operating revenues less operating expenses such as cost of sales, selling, general and administrative expense, and taxes; it excludes nonoperating revenues and expenses such as interest revenue, dividend revenue, interest expense, gains and losses on investments, discontinued operations, and income attributed to noncontrolling interest.
NOA: Net operating assets	Operating assets less operating liabilities; it excludes nonoperating items such as investments in marketable securities and interest-bearing debt.
RNOA: Return on net operating assets. . .	NOPAT/Average NOA
NNE: Net nonoperating expense	NOPAT − Net income*; NNE consists of nonoperating expenses and revenues, net of tax, as well as any noncontrolling interest reported on the income statement. (Noncontrolling interest is *excluded* from the tax shield estimation.)

* Amount attributable to the parent company's shareholders.

RNOA DISAGGREGATION INTO MARGIN AND TURNOVER

Disaggregating RNOA into its two components, profit margin and asset turnover, yields further insights into a company's performance. This disaggregation follows.

LO2 Disaggregate operating return (RNOA) into components of profitability and asset turnover.

$$RNOA = \frac{NOPAT}{Average\ NOA} = \frac{NOPAT}{Sales} \times \frac{Sales}{Average\ NOA}$$

Net operating profit margin (NOPM)

Net operating asset turnover (NOAT)

Net Operating Profit Margin

Net operating profit margin (NOPM) reveals how much operating profit the company earns from each sales dollar. All things equal, a higher NOPM is preferable. NOPM is affected by the level of gross profit the company earns on its products (revenue minus cost of goods sold), which depends on product prices and manufacturing or purchase costs. NOPM is also affected by the level of operating expenses the company requires to support its products or services. This includes overhead costs such as wages, marketing, occupancy, and research and development. Finally, NOPM is affected by the level of competition (which affects product pricing) and the company's willingness and ability to control costs.

Target's net operating profit margin is computed as follows ($ millions).

$$NOPM = \frac{NOPAT}{Revenues} = \frac{\$3,397}{\$67,390} = 5.04\%$$

This result means that for each dollar of sales at Target, the company earns roughly 5.04¢ profit after all operating expenses and taxes. As a reference, the median NOPM for publicly traded companies during the past decade is about 6¢.

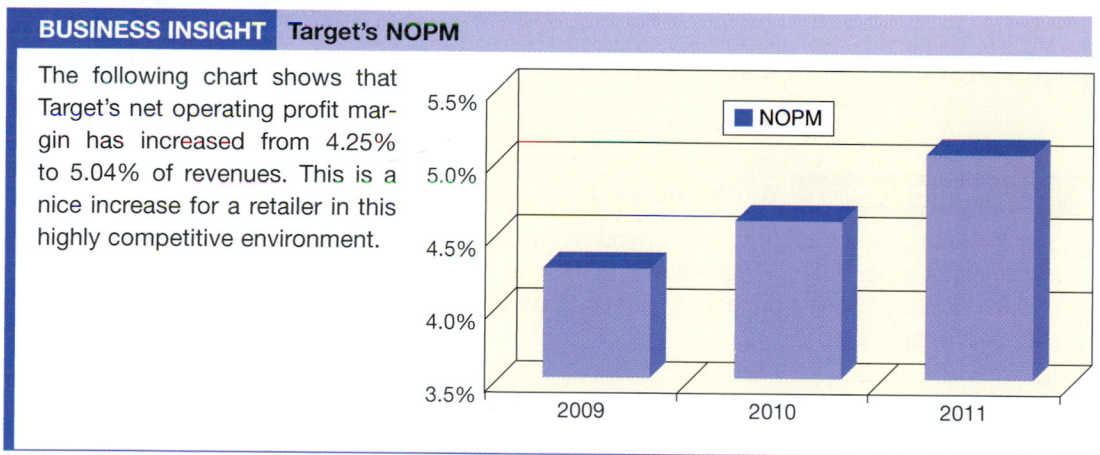

BUSINESS INSIGHT Target's NOPM

The following chart shows that Target's net operating profit margin has increased from 4.25% to 5.04% of revenues. This is a nice increase for a retailer in this highly competitive environment.

Net Operating Asset Turnover

Net operating asset turnover (NOAT) measures the productivity of the company's net operating assets. This metric reveals the level of sales the company realizes from each dollar invested in net operating assets. All things equal, a higher NOAT is preferable. Target's net operating asset turnover ratio follows ($ millions).

$$NOAT = \frac{Revenues}{Average\ NOA} = \frac{\$67,390}{(\$29,501 + \$29,961)/2} = 2.27$$

This result means that for each dollar of net operating assets, Target realizes $2.27 in sales. As a reference, the median for publicly traded companies over the past decade is about $1.40.

NOAT can be increased by either increasing sales for a given level of investment in operating assets, or by reducing the amount of operating assets necessary to generate a dollar of sales, or both. Reducing operating working capital (current operating assets less current operating liabilities) is usually easier than reducing long-term net operating assets. For example, companies can implement strategies to collect their receivables faster, reduce their inventories, and delay payments to their suppliers. All of these actions reduce operating working capital and, thereby, increase NOAT. These strategies must be managed, however, so as not to negatively impact sales or supplier relations. Working capital management is an important part of managing the company effectively.

It is usually more difficult to reduce the level of long-term net operating assets. The level of PPE required by the company is determined more by the nature of the company's products or services than by management action. For example, telecommunications companies require more capital investment than do retail stores. Still, there are several actions that managers can take to reduce capital investment. Some companies pursue novel approaches, such as corporate alliances, outsourcing, and use of special purpose entities; we discuss some of these approaches in Module 10.

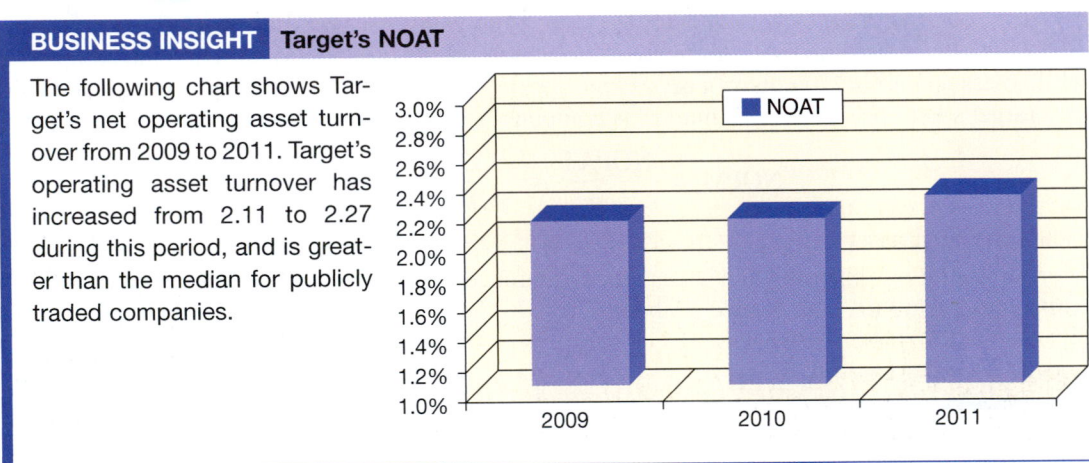

BUSINESS INSIGHT   Target's NOAT

The following chart shows Target's net operating asset turnover from 2009 to 2011. Target's operating asset turnover has increased from 2.11 to 2.27 during this period, and is greater than the median for publicly traded companies.

ANALYSIS DECISION   You Are the CEO

You are analyzing the performance of your company. Your analysis of RNOA reveals the following (industry benchmarks in parentheses): RNOA is 16% (10%), NOPM is 18% (17%), and NOAT is 0.89 (0.59). What interpretations do you draw that are useful for managing your company? [Answer, p. 3-29]

Trade-Off between Margin and Turnover

Operating profit margin and turnover of net operating assets are largely affected by a company's business model. This is an important concept. Specifically, an infinite number of combinations of net operating profit margin and net operating asset turnover will yield a given RNOA. This relation is depicted in Exhibit 3.4 (where the curved line reflects the median RNOA for all publicly traded companies during the most recent decade).

This exhibit reveals that some industries, such as communication and utilities, are capital intensive with relatively low net operating asset turnover. Accordingly, for such industries to achieve a required RNOA (to be competitive in the overall market), they must obtain a higher profit margin. On the other hand, companies such as wholesalers and retailers hold fewer assets

EXHIBIT 3.4   Profitability and Productivity across Industries

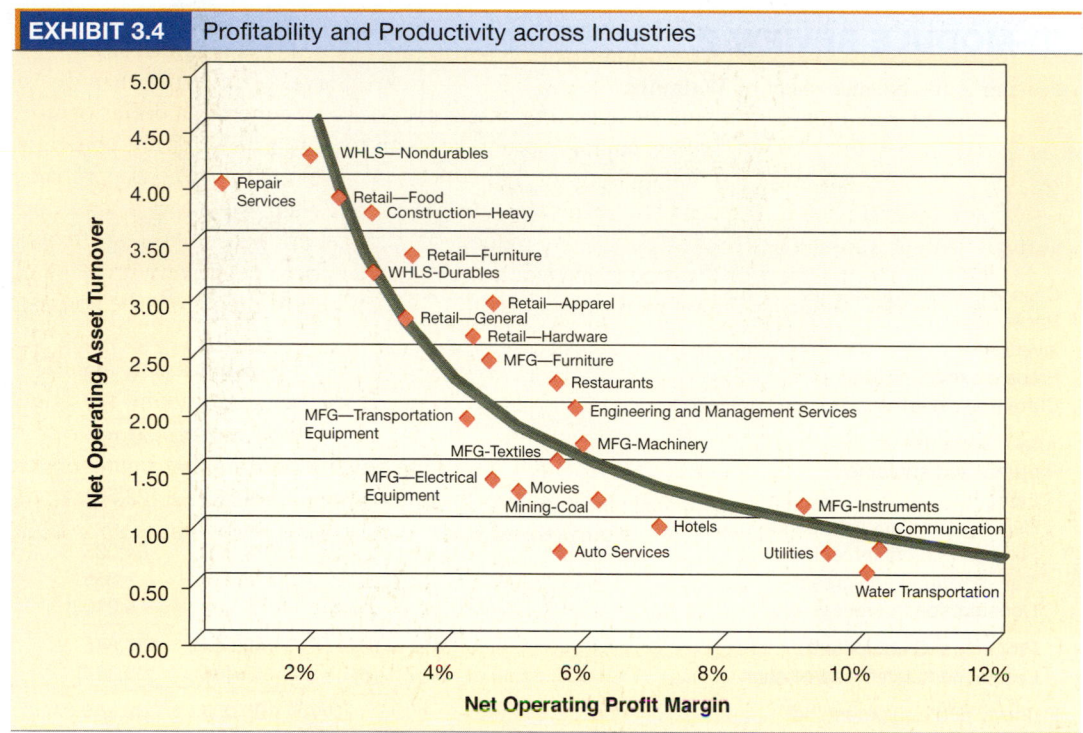

and, therefore, can operate on lower operating profit margins to achieve a sufficient RNOA. This is because their asset turnover is far greater.

This exhibit warns of blindly comparing the performance of companies across different industries. For instance, a higher profit margin in the communications industry compared with the retailing industry is not necessarily the result of better management. Instead, the communications industry is extremely capital intensive and thus, to achieve an equivalent RNOA, communications companies must earn a higher profit margin to offset their lower asset turnover. Basic economics suggests that all industries must earn an acceptable return on investment if they are to continue to attract investors and survive.

The trade-off between margin and turnover is relatively straightforward when comparing companies that operate in one industry (*pure-play* firms). Analyzing conglomerates that operate in several industries is more challenging. Conglomerates' margins and turnover rates are a weighted average of the margins and turnover rates for the various industries in which they operate. For example, **Caterpillar, Inc.,** is a blend of a manufacturing company and a financial institution (**Caterpillar Financial Services Corp.**); thus, the margin and turnover benchmarks for Caterpillar on a consolidated basis are a weighted average of those two industries.

To summarize, ROE is the sum of the returns from operating (RNOA) and nonoperating activities. Further, RNOA is the product of NOPM and NOAT.

RESEARCH INSIGHT   **NOPM and NOAT Explain Stock Prices**

Research shows that stock returns are positively associated with earnings—when companies report higher than expected earnings, stock returns rise. Research also reports that the RNOA components (NOPM and NOAT) are more strongly associated with stock returns and future profitability than earnings (or return on assets) alone. This applies to the short-term market response to earnings announcements and long-term stock price changes. Thus, disaggregating earnings and the balance sheet into operating and nonoperating components is a useful analysis tool. [Source: Soliman, Mark T., Use of DuPont Analysis by Market Participants (October 2007), SSRN: ssrn.com/abstract=1101981.]

MID-MODULE REVIEW 2

Following is the balance sheet of Walmart.

WALMART Balance Sheets		
(millions, except share data)	Jan. 31, 2011	Jan. 31, 2010
Cash and cash equivalents	$ 7,395	$ 7,907
Receivables, net	5,089	4,144
Inventories	36,318	32,713
Prepaid expenses and other	2,960	3,128
Current assets of discontinued operations	131	140
Total current assets	51,893	48,032
Property and equipment		
Land	24,386	22,591
Buildings and improvements	79,051	73,657
Fixtures and equipment	38,290	34,035
Transportation equipment	2,595	2,355
Construction in process	4,262	5,210
Property and equipment	148,584	137,848
Less accumulated depreciation	(43,486)	(38,304)
Property and equipment, net	105,098	99,544
Property under capital leases		
Property under capital leases	5,905	5,669
Less accumulated amortization	(3,125)	(2,906)
Property under capital leases, net	2,780	2,763
Goodwill	16,763	16,126
Other assets and deferred charges	4,129	3,942
Total assets	$180,663	$170,407
Short-term borrowings	$ 1,031	$ 523
Accounts payable	33,557	30,451
Accrued liabilities	18,701	18,734
Accrued income taxes	157	1,347
Long-term debt due within one year	4,655	4,050
Obligations under capital leases due within one year	336	346
Current liabilities of discontinued operations	47	92
Total current liabilities	58,484	55,543
Long-term debt	40,692	33,231
Long-term obligations under capital leases	3,150	3,170
Deferred income taxes and other	6,682	5,508
Redeemable noncontrolling interest	408	307
Equity		
Preferred stock ($0.10 par value; 100 shares authorized, none issued)	—	—
Common stock ($0.10 par value; 11,000 shares authorized, 3,516 and 3,786 issued and outstanding at January 31, 2011 and 2010, respectively)	352	378
Capital in excess of par value	3,577	3,803
Retained earnings	63,967	66,357
Accumulated other comprehensive income (loss)	646	(70)
Total Walmart shareholders' equity	68,542	70,468
Noncontrolling interest	2,705	2,180
Total equity	71,247	72,648
Total liabilities and equity	$180,663	$170,407

Required

1. Compute Walmart's net operating assets for its fiscal year-ends 2011 and 2010.

2. Refer to Walmart's income statement and NOPAT from Mid-Module Review 1. Compute Walmart's return on net operating assets (RNOA) for 2011.
3. Compute Walmart's 2011 ROE. What percentage of Walmart's ROE comes from operations?
4. Disaggregate Walmart's 2011 RNOA into net operating profit margin (NOPM) and net operating asset turnover (NOAT).
5. Compare and contrast Walmart's ROE, RNOA, NOPM, and NOAT with those same measures computed in this module for Target. Interpret the results.

The solution is on page 3-50.

Further RNOA Disaggregation

While disaggregation of RNOA into net operating profit margin (NOPM) and net operating asset turnover (NOAT) yields valuable insight into factors driving company performance, analysts and creditors usually disaggregate those components even further. The purpose is to better identify the specific drivers of both profitability and turnover.

To disaggregate NOPM, we examine the gross profit on products sold and the individual expense accounts that affect operating profit as a percentage of sales (such as Gross profit/Sales and SG&A/Sales). These margin ratios aid comparisons across companies of differing sizes and across different time periods for the same company. We further discuss profit margin disaggregation in other modules that focus on operating results.

To disaggregate NOAT, we examine the individual balance sheet accounts that comprise NOA and compare them to the related income statement activity. Specifically, we compute accounts receivable turnover (ART), inventory turnover (INVT), property, plant and equipment turnover (PPET), as well as turnovers for liability accounts such as accounts payable (APT). Analysts and creditors often compute the net operating working capital turnover (NOWCT) to assess a company's working capital management compared to its competitors and recent trends. (Recall that operating working capital is calculated as current operating assets less current operating liabilities.) These turnover rates are further discussed in other modules that focus on operating assets and liabilities. Exhibit 3.5 provides a broad overview of ratios commonly used for component disaggregation and analysis.

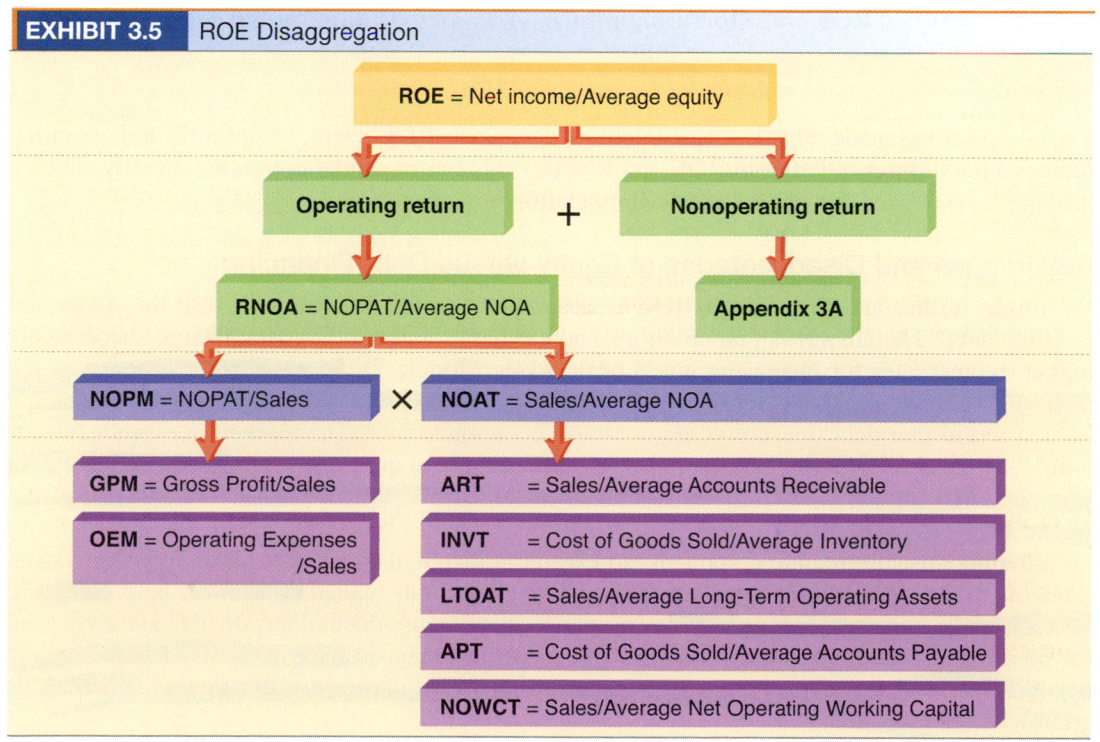

EXHIBIT 3.5   ROE Disaggregation

ROE = Net income/Average equity

Operating return + Nonoperating return

RNOA = NOPAT/Average NOA   Appendix 3A

NOPM = NOPAT/Sales × NOAT = Sales/Average NOA

GPM = Gross Profit/Sales

OEM = Operating Expenses/Sales

ART = Sales/Average Accounts Receivable

INVT = Cost of Goods Sold/Average Inventory

LTOAT = Sales/Average Long-Term Operating Assets

APT = Cost of Goods Sold/Average Accounts Payable

NOWCT = Sales/Average Net Operating Working Capital

NONOPERATING RETURN

LO3 Explain nonoperating return and compute it from return on equity and the operating return.

This section discusses a company's nonoperating return. In it's simplest form, the return on nonoperating activities measures the extent to which a company is using debt to increase its return on equity.

Equity Only Financing

The following example provides the intuition for nonoperating return. Assume that a company has $1,000 in net operating assets for the current year in which it earns a 20% RNOA. It finances those assets entirely with equity investment (no debt). To simplify this example, we assume that taxes are 0%; later, we explain the impact of taxes. Its ROE is computed as follows:

$$
\begin{aligned}
\textbf{ROE} &= \textbf{Operating return} + \textbf{Nonoperating return} \\
&= \qquad 20\% \qquad + \qquad 0\% \\
&= \qquad\qquad 20\%
\end{aligned}
$$

Equity and Debt Financing

Next, assume that this company borrows $500 at 7% interest and uses those funds to acquire additional operating assets yielding the same 20% operating return as above. Its net operating assets for the year now total $1,500, and its profit is $265, computed as follows:

Profit from assets financed with equity ($1,000 × 20%)		$200
Profit from assets financed with debt ($500 × 20%)	$100	
Less interest expense from debt ($500 × 7%)	(35)	65
Net profit.		$265

We see that this company has increased its profit to $265 (up from $200) with the addition of debt, and its ROE is now 26.5% ($265/$1,000). The reason for the increased ROE is that the company borrowed $500 at 7% (and paid $35 of interest expense) and invested those funds in assets earning 20% (which generated $100 of profits). That difference of 13% ($65 profit, computed as [20% − 7%] × $500) accrues to shareholders. Stated differently, the company's ROE now consists of the following.

$$
\begin{aligned}
\textbf{ROE} &= \textbf{Operating return} + \textbf{Nonoperating return} \\
&= \qquad 20\% \qquad + \qquad 6.5\% \\
&= \qquad\qquad 26.5\%
\end{aligned}
$$

The company has made effective use of debt to increase its ROE. Here, we infer the nonoperating return as the difference between ROE and RNOA. This return can be computed directly, and we provide an expanded discussion of this computation in Appendix 3A.

Advantages and Disadvantages of Equity versus Debt Financing

We might further ask: If a higher ROE is desirable, why don't companies use the maximum possible debt? The answer is that creditors, such as banks and bondholders, charge successively higher interest rates for increasing levels of debt (see Module 7). At some point, the cost of the additional debt exceeds the return on the additional assets acquired from the debt financing. Thereafter, further debt financing does not make economic sense. The market, in essence, places a limit on the level of debt that a company can effectively acquire. In sum, shareholders benefit from increased use of debt provided that the assets financed with the debt earn a return that exceeds the cost of the debt.

Creditors usually require a company to execute a loan agreement that places varying restrictions on the company's operating activities. These restrictions, called *covenants*, help safeguard debtholders in the face of increased risk. Covenants exist because debtholders do not have a voice on the board of directors like stockholders do. These debt covenants impose a "cost" on the company beyond that of the interest rate, and these covenants are more stringent as a company increases its reliance on debt financing.

RESEARCH INSIGHT | **Ratio Behavior over Time**

How do RNOA and ROE behave over time? Following is a graph of these ratios (on average for a large set of firms) over the past decade. We see there is considerable variability in these ratios over time. The proportion of RNOA to ROE is greater for some periods of time than for others. Yet, in all periods for this large sample of firms, ROE exceeds RNOA. This is evidence of a positive effect, on average, for ROE from financial leverage.

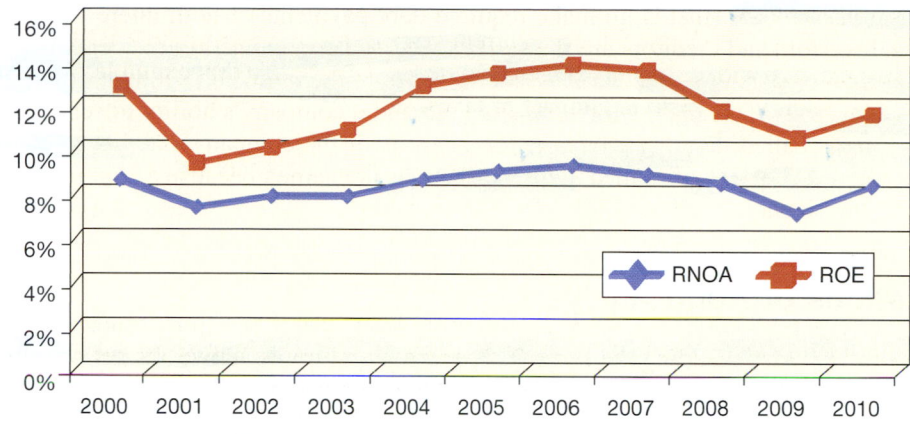

Financial Leverage Across Industries

As we have seen, companies can effectively use debt to increase ROE with returns from non-operating activities. The advantage of debt is that it typically is a less costly source of financing; currently the cost of debt is about 4% versus a cost of equity of about 12%, on average. Although it reduces financing costs, debt does carry default risk: the risk that the company will be unable to repay debt when it comes due. Creditors have several legal remedies when companies default, including forcing a company into bankruptcy and possibly liquidating its assets.

During the past decade, the median ratio of total liabilities to stockholders' equity, which measures the relative use of debt versus equity in a company's capital structure, is about 1.5 for publicly traded companies with sales over $500 million. This means that the average company is financed with about $1.50 of liabilities for each dollar of stockholders' equity. However, the relative use of debt varies considerably across industries as illustrated in Exhibit 3.6.

EXHIBIT 3.6 | Median Ratio of Liabilities-to-Equity for Selected Industries

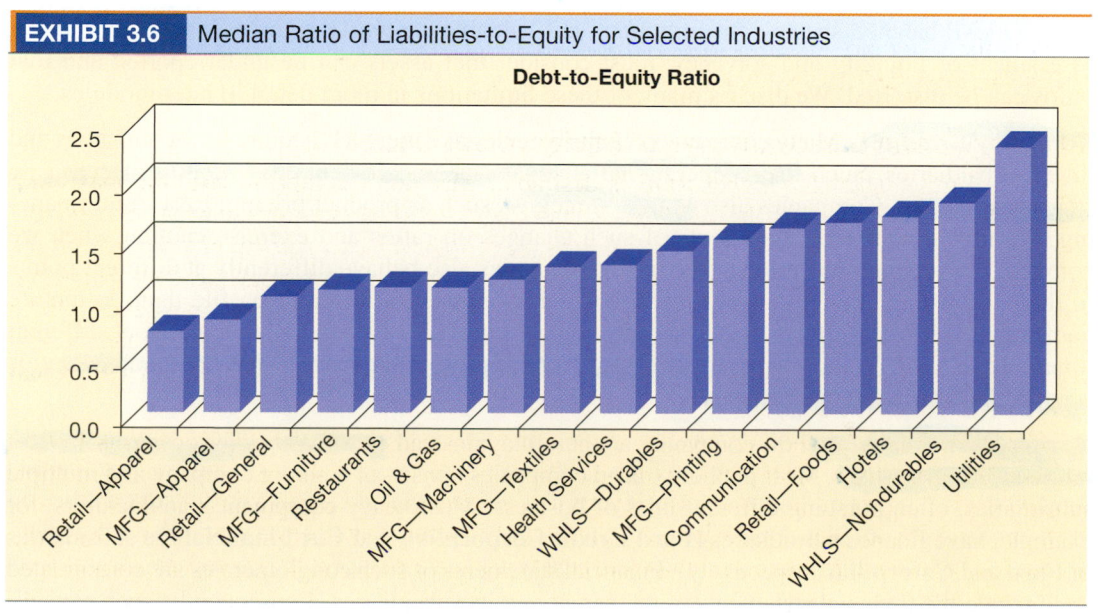

Companies in the utilities industry have a large proportion of debt. Because the utilities industry is regulated, profits and cash flows are relatively certain and stable and, as a result, utility companies can support a higher debt level. The hotel and nondurable wholesale industries also utilize a relatively high proportion of debt. However, these industries are not regulated, their market is more competitive and volatile and, consequently, their use of debt carries more risk. At the lower end of debt financing are retail and restaurant companies.

The core of our analysis relating to debt is the examination of a company's ability to generate cash to *service* its debt (that is, to make required debt payments of both interest and principal). Analysts, investors and creditors are primarily concerned about whether the company either has sufficient cash available or whether it is able to generate the required cash in the future to cover its debt obligations. The analysis of available cash and a company's ability to service its debt in the short run is called *liquidity analysis*. The analysis of the company's ability to generate sufficient cash in the long run is called *solvency analysis* (so named because a bankrupt company is said to be "insolvent").

Limitations of Ratio Analysis

The quality of financial statement analysis depends on the quality of financial information. We ought not blindly analyze numbers; doing so can lead to faulty conclusions and suboptimal decisions. Instead, we need to acknowledge that current accounting rules (GAAP) have limitations, and be fully aware of the company's environment, its competitive pressures, and any structural and strategic changes. This section discusses some of the factors that limit the usefulness of financial accounting information for ratio analysis.

GAAP Limitations   Several limitations in GAAP can distort financial ratios. Limitations include:

1. **Measurability**. Financial statements reflect what can be reliably measured. This results in nonrecognition of certain assets, often internally developed assets, the very assets that are most likely to confer a competitive advantage and create value. Examples are brand name, a superior management team, employee skills, and a reliable supply chain.

2. **Non-capitalized costs**. Related to the concept of measurability is the expensing of costs relating to "assets" that cannot be identified with enough precision to warrant capitalization. Examples are brand equity costs from advertising and other promotional activities, and research and development costs relating to future products.

3. **Historical costs**. Assets and liabilities are usually recorded at original acquisition or issuance costs. Subsequent increases in value are not recorded until realized, and declines in value are only recognized if deemed permanent.

Thus, GAAP balance sheets omit important and valuable assets. Our analysis of ROE and our assessment of liquidity and solvency, must consider that assets can be underreported and that ratios can be distorted. We discuss many of these limitations in more detail in later modules.

Company Changes   Many companies regularly undertake mergers, acquire new companies and divest subsidiaries. Such major operational changes can impair the comparability of company ratios across time. Companies also change strategies, such as product pricing, R&D, and financing. We must understand the effects of such changes on ratios and exercise caution when we compare ratios from one period to the next. Companies also behave differently at different points in their life cycles. For instance, growth companies possess a different profile than do mature companies. Seasonal effects also markedly impact analysis of financial statements at different times of the year. Thus, we must consider life cycle and seasonality when we compare ratios across companies and over time.

Conglomerate Effects   Few companies are pure-play; instead, most companies operate in several businesses or industries. Most publicly traded companies consist of a parent company and multiple subsidiaries, often pursuing different lines of business. Most heavy equipment manufacturers, for example, have finance subsidiaries (**Ford Credit Corporation** and **Cat Financial** are subsidiaries of **Ford** and **Caterpillar** respectively). Financial statements of such conglomerates are consolidated and include the financial statements of the parent and its subsidiaries. Consequently, such consolidated statements are challenging to analyze. Typically, analysts break the financials apart into their component businesses and separately analyze each component. Fortunately, companies must report financial information (albeit limited) for major business segments in their 10-Ks.

Fuzzy View Ratios reduce, to a single number, the myriad complexities of a company's operations. No scalar can accurately capture all qualitative aspects of a company. Ratios cannot meaningfully convey a company's marketing and management philosophies, its human resource activities, its financing activities, its strategic initiatives, and its product management. In our analysis we must learn to look through the numbers and ratios to better understand the operational factors that drive financial results. Successful analysis seeks to gain insight into what a company is really about and what the future portends. Our overriding purpose in analysis is to understand the past and present to better predict the future. Computing and examining ratios is one step in that process.

ANALYZING GLOBAL REPORTS

An important aim of this module is to distinguish between operating and nonoperating items for the balance sheet and income statement. U.S. GAAP and IFRS generally account for items similarly, but there are certain disclosure differences worth noting.

The IFRS balance sheet is similar to its U.S. GAAP counterpart, with the visible exception for the frequent, but not mandatory, reverse ordering of assets and liabilities. However, one notable difference is that IFRS companies routinely report "financial assets" or "financial liabilities" on the balance sheet. We must assess these items. IFRS defines financial assets to include receivables (operating item), loans to affiliates or associates (can be operating or nonoperating depending on the nature of the transactions), securities held as investments (nonoperating), and derivatives (nonoperating). IFRS notes to financial statements, which tend to be more detailed than U.S. GAAP notes, usually detail what financial assets and liabilities consist of. This helps us accurately determine NOA and NNO.

The IFRS income statement usually reports fewer line items than U.S. GAAP income statements and, further, there is no definition of "operating activities" under IFRS. This means we must devote attention to classify operating versus nonoperating income components. Following is a table that shows common U.S. GAAP income statement items and their classification as operating (O) or nonoperating (N). This table also indicates which items are required for IFRS income statements.

Income Statement Line Items	Operating (O) or Nonoperating (N)	Required on IFRS Income Statement
Net sales	O	YES
Cost of sales	O	—
Selling, general and administrative (SG&A) expense	O	—
Provisions for doubtful accounts.	O	—
Nonoperating income	N	—
Interest revenue and Interest expense	N	YES
Nonoperating expenses	N	—
Income before income taxes.	O and N	—
Income tax expense	O and N	YES
Earnings on equity investments (associates and joint ventures). . .	O	YES
Income from continuing operations	O	—
Discontinued operations	N	YES
Income before extraordinary items	O and N	—
Extraordinary items, net of income tax	O or N	—
Net income	O and N	YES
Net income attributable to noncontrolling interest	N	YES
Net income attributable to controlling interest	O and N	YES
Earnings per share (Basic EPS and Diluted EPS)	O and N	YES

There is no requirement to report income from operations, yet many IFRS companies do so. However, items that are considered operating such as gains and losses on disposals of operating assets, or income from equity method investments, are often reported below the operating income line. We must examine IFRS income statements and their notes to make an independent assessment of what is operating. IFRS income statements usually report separately the other nonoperating revenues and expenses even though this is not required. We can better assess the nature of these items by reading the notes.

MODULE-END REVIEW

Refer to the income statement and balance sheet of **Walmart**, from Mid-Module Reviews 1 and 2 earlier in this module.

Required

1. Compute Walmart's nonoperating return for 2011.
2. Compute Target's nonoperating return for 2011 from the information reported in this module. Compare and contrast the nonoperating return for Walmart and Target. Interpret the results.
3. Compute Walmart's liabilities-to-equity ratio for 2011.
4. Compute Target's liabilities-to-equity ratio for 2011 from the balance sheet in this module. Compare and contrast the ratio to Walmart's liabilities-to-equity ratio. Interpret the results.

The solution is on page 3-50.

APPENDIX 3A: Nonoperating Return Component of ROE

In this appendix, we consider the nonoperating return component of ROE in more detail. We also provide a derivation of that nonoperating return and discuss several special topics pertaining to it. We begin by considering three special cases of capital structure financing.

Nonoperating Return Framework

In the module, we infer the nonoperating return as the difference between ROE and RNOA. The nonoperating return can also be computed directly as FLEV × Spread, where FLEV is the degree of financial leverage and Spread is the difference between the assets' after-tax operating return (RNOA) and the after-tax cost of debt.

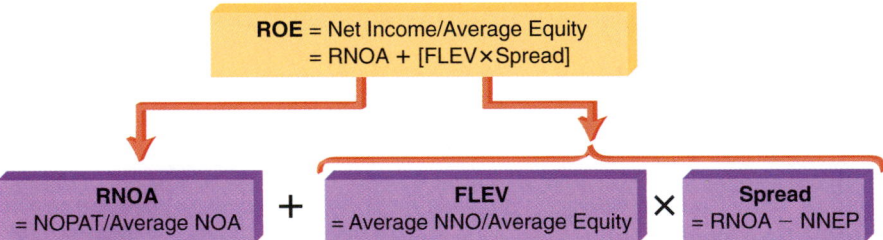

Exhibit 3A.1 provides definitions for each of the terms required in this computation.

EXHIBIT 3A.1	Nonoperating Return Definitions
NNO: Net nonoperating obligations	Nonoperating liabilities (plus any noncontrolling interest reported on the balance sheet) less nonoperating assets
FLEV: Financial leverage	Average NNO/Average equity
NNE: Net nonoperating expense	NOPAT – Net income*; NNE consists of nonoperating expenses and revenues, net of tax, as well as any noncontrolling interest reported on the income statement. (Noncontrolling interest is *excluded* from the tax shield estimation.)
NNEP: Net nonoperating expense percent	NNE/Average NNO
Spread	RNOA – NNEP

* Amount attributable to the parent company's shareholders.

Nonoperating Return—With Debt Financing, but Without Nonoperating Assets

To illustrate computation of the nonoperating return when the company has debt and equity financing (without nonoperating assets), let's refer to our example in this module of the company that increases its ROE through use of debt. (For this first illustration, view FLEV as the relative use of debt in the capital structure, and Spread as the difference between RNOA and the net nonoperating expense percent.) Again, assume that this company has $1,000 of equity, $500 of 7% debt, total assets of $1,500 that earn a 20% return, and a tax rate of 0%. The net income of this firm is $265, computed as follows:

Profit from assets financed with equity ($1,000 × 20%)		$200
Profit from assets financed with debt ($500 × 20%)	$100	
Less interest expense from debt ($500 × 7%)	(35)	65
Net profit.		$265

This company's ROE is 26.5%, computed as $265/$1,000 (assuming income received at year-end for simplicity and average equity is $1,000). Its RNOA is 20%, FLEV is 0.50 (computed as $500 of average net nonoperating obligations divided by $1,000 average equity), and its Spread is 13% (computed as 20% less 7%). This company's ROE, shown with the nonoperating return being directly computed, is as follows:

$$\text{ROE} = \text{RNOA} + [\text{FLEV} \times \text{Spread}]$$
$$= 20\% \quad + [\ 0.50 \quad \times \quad 13\% \ ]$$
$$= 26.5\%$$

We see that when a company's nonoperating activities relate solely to the borrowing of money (without nonoperating assets), FLEV collapses to the ratio of debt to equity, called the debt-to-equity ratio.

Nonoperating Return—Without Debt Financing, but With Nonoperating Assets

Some companies, such as many high-tech firms, have no debt, and maintain large portfolios of marketable securities. They hold these highly liquid assets so that they can respond quickly to new opportunities or react to competitive pressures. With high levels of nonoperating assets and no nonoperating liabilities, the net nonoperating obligations (NNO) has a negative sign (NNO = Nonoperating liabilities − Nonoperating assets). Likewise, FLEV is negative: Average NNO (−) / Average Equity (+). Further, net nonoperating expense (NNE = NOPAT − Net income) is negative because investment *income* is a negative nonoperating expense. However, the net nonoperating expense percent (NNEP) is positive because the negative NNE is divided by the negative NNO. *This causes ROE to be less than RNOA* (see computations below). We use the 2010 10-K of **Intel** to illustrate this curious result (Intel reports no noncontrolling interest).

Intel ($ millions, except percentages)	2010	2009	Average	Computation
NOA	$ 28,652	$ 29,232	$ 28,942	—
NNO	$(20,778)	$(12,472)	$(16,625)	—
Stockholders' equity	$ 49,430	$ 41,704	$ 45,567	—
Net income.	$ 11,464	—	—	—
NOPAT	$ 11,250	—	—	—
NNE (NOPAT − Net income)	$ (214)	—	—	—
FLEV.	(0.3648)	—	—	$(16,625)/$45,567
RNOA	38.87%	—	—	$11,250/$28,942
NNEP	1.29%	—	—	$(214)/$(16,625)
Spread	37.58%	—	—	38.87%-1.29%

Intel's NNO is negative because its investment in marketable securities exceeds its debt. Intel's ROE is 25.16%, and it consists of the following:

$$\text{ROE} = \text{RNOA} + [\ \text{FLEV} \times \text{Spread}\ ]$$
$$= 38.87\% + [\ -0.3648 \times 37.58\% \ ]$$
$$= 38.87\% + \qquad [-13.71\%]$$
$$= 25.16\%$$

Intel's ROE is lower than its RNOA because of its large investment in marketable securities. That is, its excessive liquidity is penalizing its return on equity. The rationale for this seemingly incongruous result is this: Intel's ROE derives from operating and nonoperating assets. Intel's operating assets are providing an outstanding return (38.87%), much higher than the return on its marketable securities (1.29%). Holding liquid assets that are less productive means that Intel's shareholders are funding a sizeable level of liquidity, and sacrificing returns in the process. Why? Many companies in high-tech industries feel the need to maintain excessive liquidity to gain flexibility—the flexibility to take advantage of opportunities and to react quickly to competitor maneuvers. Intel's management, evidently, feels that the investment of costly equity capital in this manner will reap future rewards for its shareholders. Its 25.16% ROE provides some evidence that this strategy is not necessarily misguided.

Nonoperating Return—With Debt Financing and Nonoperating Assets

Most companies report both debt and investments on their balance sheets. If that debt markedly exceeds the investment balance, their ROE will look more like our first example (with debt only). Instead, if investments predominate, their ROE will look more like Intel's. It is important to remember that both the average NNO (and FLEV) and NNE can be either positive (debt) or negative (investments), and it is not always the case that ROE exceeds RNOA. We now compute nonoperating return for Target, a company with both debt and investments.

Nonoperating Return for Target

In Exhibit 3A.1, we define net nonoperating expense (NNE) as NOPAT − Net income. For Target, we can compute NNE as NOPAT of $3,397 million less net income of $2,920 million, which yields $477 million. More generally, NNE can include a number of nonoperating items such as interest expense, interest revenue, dividend income, investment gains and losses, income (loss) on discontinued operations and noncontrolling interest (if any); all net of tax. (Recall that the simple illustration at the beginning of this appendix *ignored taxes*, which meant NNE was equal to the $35 interest paid.)

To compute operating return (RNOA) we divided NOPAT from the income statement, by NOA from the balance sheet. Similarly, to compute the net nonoperating expense percent (NNEP), we divide NNE from the income statement by net nonoperating obligations from the balance sheet (NNO). Exhibit 3A.2 shows how a balance sheet can be reorganized into operating and nonoperating items.

EXHIBIT 3A.2	Simplified Balance Sheet	
	Assets	**Liabilities**
Net operating assets (NOA)	Current Operating Assets	Current Operating Liabilities
(assets − liabilities)	+ Long-Term Operating Assets	+ Long-Term Operating Liabilities
	= Total Operating Assets	= Total Operating Liabilities
Net nonoperating obligations (NNO).	Current Nonoperating Assets	Current Nonoperating Liabilities
(liabilities − assets)	+ Long-Term Nonoperating Assets	+ Long-Term Nonoperating Liabilities
		+ Noncontrolling Interest (if any)
	= Total Nonoperating Assets	= Total Nonoperating Liabilities
		Equity
Equity (NOA − NNO)		Stockholders' Equity (excluding any noncontrolling interest)
	Total Assets	Total Liabilities and Equity

Net nonoperating obligations are total nonoperating liabilities, including any noncontrolling interest, less total nonoperating assets. The accounting equation stipulates that Assets = Liabilities + Equity, so we can adjust it to yield the following key identity:

$$\text{Net operating assets (NOA)} = \text{Net nonoperating obligations (NNO)} + \text{Stockholders' equity}$$

For Target, we compute NNO as follows:

Target ($ millions)	2011	2010
Nonoperating liabilities		
Unsecured debt and other borrowings	$ 119	$ 796
Nonrecourse debt collateralized by credit card receivables	—	900
L-T Unsecured debt and other borrowings	11,653	10,643
L-T Nonrecourse debt collateralized by credit card receivables	3,954	4,475
Total nonoperating liabilities.	15,726	16,814
Nonoperating assets		
Cash and cash equivalents	1,712	2,200
Short-term and long-term investments	0	0
Total nonoperating assets	1,712	2,200
Net nonoperating obligations (NNO)	$14,014	$14,614

Accordingly (drawing on NNE from the income statement and NNO from the balance sheet), we compute the net nonoperating expense percent (NNEP) as follows:

$$\text{Net nonoperating expense percent (NNE)} = \frac{\text{Net nonoperating expense (NNE)}}{\text{Average net nonoperating obligations (NNO)}}$$

The net nonoperating expense percent (NNEP) measures the average cost of net nonoperating obligations. The denominator uses the average NNO similar to the return calculations (such as ROE and RNOA).

In the simple illustration from earlier in this appendix, that company's net nonoperating expense percent is 7%, computed as $35/$500, which is exactly equal to the interest rate on the loan. With real financial statements, NNEP is more complicated because NNE often includes both interest on borrowed money and nonoperating income, and NNO is the net of operating liabilities less nonoperating assets. Thus NNEP often reflects an average return on nonoperating activities. For Target, its 2011 NNEP is 3.33%, computed as $477 million/[($14,014 million + $14,614 million)/2].

Target's 2011 RNOA is 11.43%, which means that net operating assets generate more return than the 3.33% cost of net nonoperating obligations. That is, Target earns a Spread of 8.10%, the difference between RNOA (11.43%) and NNEP (3.33%), on each asset financed with borrowed funds. By borrowing funds, Target creates leverage, which can be measured relative to stockholders' equity; that ratio is called financial leverage (FLEV). In sum, total nonoperating return is computed by the following formula:

$$\text{Nonoperating return} = \frac{\text{Average net nonoperating obligations (NNO)}}{\text{Average stockholders' equity}} \times (\text{RNOA} - \text{NNEP})$$

FLEV   Spread

Two points are immediately clear from this equation. First, ROE increases with the Spread between RNOA and NNEP. The more profitable the return on operating assets, the higher the return to shareholders. Second, the higher the debt relative to equity, the higher the ROE (assuming, of course, a positive Spread).

Target's 2011 Spread between RNOA and NNEP is 8.10%. It has average NNO of $14,314 million [($14,014 million + $14,614 million)/2] and average equity of $15,417 million [($15,487 million + $15,347 million)/2]. Thus, Target's ROE is as follows:

ROE = Operating return + Nonoperating return
    =   11.43%   + [$14,314/$15,417] × [11.43% − 3.33%]
    =   11.43%   +   [0.9285] × [8.10%]
    =   **18.95%** (0.0001 rounding error)

Most companies report both debt and investments on their balance sheets. If that debt markedly exceeds the investment balance, their ROE will look more like our Target example (with net debt). Instead, if investments predominate, their ROE will look more like Intel's (with net investments). It is important to remember that both the average NNO (and FLEV) and NNE can be either positive (debt) or negative (investments), and it is not always the case that ROE exceeds RNOA.

Derivation of Nonoperating Return Formula

Following is the algebraic derivation of the nonoperating return formula, where NI is net income, SE is average stockholders' equity, and all other terms are as defined in Exhibits 3.3 and 3A.1.

$$
\begin{aligned}
\text{ROE} &= \frac{\text{NI}}{\text{SE}} \\[6pt]
&= \frac{\text{NOPAT} - \text{NNE}}{\text{SE}} \\[6pt]
&= \frac{\text{NOPAT}}{\text{SE}} - \frac{\text{NNE}}{\text{SE}} \\[6pt]
&= \left(\frac{\text{NOA}}{\text{SE}} \times \text{RNOA} \right) - \left(\frac{\text{NNO}}{\text{SE}} \times \text{NNEP} \right) \\[6pt]
&= \left(\frac{\text{SE} + \text{NNO}}{\text{SE}} \times \text{RNOA} \right) - \left(\frac{\text{NNO}}{\text{SE}} \times \text{NNEP} \right) \\[6pt]
&= \left[\text{RNOA} \times \left(1 + \frac{\text{NNO}}{\text{SE}} \right) \right] - \left(\frac{\text{NNO}}{\text{SE}} \times \text{NNEP} \right) \\[6pt]
&= \text{RNOA} + \left(\frac{\text{NNO}}{\text{SE}} \times \text{RNOA} \right) - \left(\frac{\text{NNO}}{\text{SE}} \times \text{NNEP} \right) \\[6pt]
&= \text{RNOA} + \left(\frac{\text{NNO}}{\text{SE}} \right)(\text{RNOA} - \text{NNEP}) \\[6pt]
&= \text{RNOA} + (\text{FLEV} \times \text{Spread})
\end{aligned}
$$

Special Topics

The return on equity (ROE) computation becomes a bit more complicated in the presence of discontinued operations, preferred stock, and minority (or noncontrolling) equity interest. The first of these apportions ROE between operating and nonoperating returns, and the other two affect the dollar amount included in the denominator (average equity) of the ROE computation. Recall that ROE measures the return on investment for common shareholders. *The ROE numerator should include only the income available to pay common dividends and the ROE denominator should include common equity only, not the equity of preferred or minority shareholders.*

Discontinued Operations Discontinued operations are subsidiaries or business segments that the board of directors has formally decided to divest. Companies must report discontinued operations on a separate line, below income from continuing operations. The separate line item includes the net income or loss from discontinued operations along with any gains or losses on the disposal of discontinued net assets (see Module 5 for details). Although not required, many companies disclose the net assets of discontinued operations on the balance sheet to distinguish them from continuing net assets. If the net assets are not separated on the balance sheet, the footnotes provide details to facilitate a disaggregated analysis. These net assets of discontinued operations should be treated as nonoperating (they represent a nonoperating "investment" once they have been classified as discontinued) and their after-tax profit (loss) should be treated as nonoperating as well. Although the ROE computation is unaffected, the nonoperating portion of the ROE for the year will include the contribution of discontinued operations.

Preferred Stock The ROE formula takes the perspective of the common shareholder in that it relates the income available to pay common dividends to the average common shareholder. As such, preferred stock should not be included in average stockholders' equity in the denominator of the ROE formula. Similarly, any dividends paid on preferred stock should be subtracted from net income to yield the profit available to pay common dividends. (Dividends are not an expense in computing net income; thus, net income is available to both preferred and common shareholders. To determine net income available to common shareholders, we must subtract preferred dividends.) Thus, the presence of preferred stock requires two adjustments to the ROE formula.

1. Preferred dividends must be subtracted from net income in the numerator.
2. Preferred stock must be subtracted from stockholders' equity in the denominator.

This modified return on equity formula is more accurately labeled return on common equity (ROCE).

$$
\text{ROCE} = \frac{\text{Net income} - \text{Preferred dividends}}{\text{Average stockholders' equity} - \text{Average preferred equity}}
$$

Noncontrolling Interest When a company acquires controlling interest of the outstanding voting stock of another company, the parent company must consolidate the new subsidiary in its balance sheet and income statement (see

Module 9). This means that the parent company must include 100% of the subsidiary's assets, liabilities, revenues and expenses. If the parent acquires less than 100% of the subsidiary's voting stock, the remaining claim of noncontrolling shareholders is reported on the balance sheet as a component of stockholders' equity called noncontrolling interest, and net income is separated into income attributable to company shareholders and that attributable to noncontrolling interests. *The ROE computation, then, should use the net income attributable to company shareholders divided by the average stockholders' equity where equity excludes noncontrolling interest.*

To illustrate the calculation of ROE, FLEV, and Spread in the presence of noncontrolling interest we consider the following selected balance sheet and income statement items from **Walmart** ($ millions).

	2011	2010	Average
Balance sheet items			
Net operating assets (NOA)	$114,040	$106,320	$110,180
Nonoperating liabilities.	$ 50,319	$ 41,719	$ 46,019
Less: Nonoperating assets.	(7,526)	(8,047)	(7,787)
Plus: Noncontrolling interest	2,705	2,180	2,443
NNO including noncontrolling interest	45,498	35,852	40,675
Equity (attributable to Walmart shareholders)	68,542	70,468	69,505
Total NNO and Equity.	$114,040	$106,320	$110,180
Income statement items			
Net operating profit after tax (NOPAT)	$ 17,222		
Net nonoperating expense (NNE).	(833)		
Net income attributable to Walmart shareholders	$ 16,389		

We then compute the following key ratios ($ millions):

RNOA	15.63%	($17,222/$110,180)
ROE	23.58%	($16,389/$69,505)
FLEV.	0.585	($40,675/$69,505)
NNEP	2.05%	($833/$40,675)
Spread	13.58%	(15.63% − 2.05%)

We can also calculate NNE directly as follows ($ millions):

Net nonoperating expenses (excluding noncontrolling interest), pretax	$2,004
Less: Tax shield on net nonoperating expenses (excluding noncontrolling interest), net at 37%	(741)
Net nonoperating expenses (excluding noncontrolling interest), after-tax.	1,263
Less: Income from discontinued operations, after-tax.	(1,034)
Plus: Net income attributable to noncontrolling interest	604
Net nonoperating expense	$ 833

APPENDIX 3B: DuPont Disaggregation Analysis

Disaggregation of return on equity (ROE) into three components (profitability, turnover, and financial leverage) was initially introduced by the **E.I. DuPont de Nemours and Company** to aid its managers in performance evaluation. DuPont realized that management's focus on profit alone was insufficient because profit can be simply increased by additional investment in low-yielding, but safe, assets. Further, DuPont wanted managers to think like investors and to manage their portfolio of activities using investment principles that allocate scarce investment capital to competing projects in descending order of return on investment (the *capital budgeting approach*). The DuPont model incorporates this investment perspective into performance measurement by disaggregating ROE into the following three components:

L04 Describe and illustrate traditional DuPont disaggregation of ROE.

1. Profitability
2. Turnover (asset utilization)
3. Financial leverage

Each of these measures is generally positive, in which case an increase in any one would increase ROE. A focus on these measures encourages managers to focus on *both* the balance sheet and the income statement. Such an analysis typically examines each of these components over time. Managers then seek to reverse adverse trends and to sustain positive trends.

Basic DuPont Model

The basic DuPont model disaggregates ROE as follows:

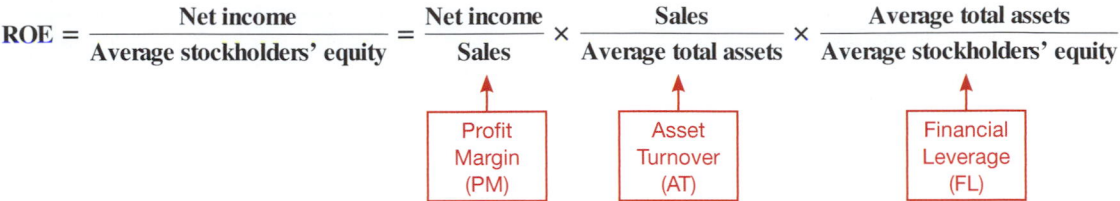

$$\text{ROE} = \frac{\text{Net income}}{\text{Average stockholders' equity}} = \frac{\text{Net income}}{\text{Sales}} \times \frac{\text{Sales}}{\text{Average total assets}} \times \frac{\text{Average total assets}}{\text{Average stockholders' equity}}$$

Profit Margin (PM)   Asset Turnover (AT)   Financial Leverage (FL)

These three components are described as follows:

■ **Profit margin** is the amount of profit that the company earns from each dollar of sales. A company can increase its profit margin by increasing its gross profit margin (Gross profit/Sales) and/or by reducing its expenses (other than cost of sales) as a percentage of sales.

■ **Asset turnover** is a productivity measure that reflects the volume of sales that a company generates from each dollar invested in assets. A company can increase its asset turnover by increasing sales volume with no increase in assets and/or by reducing asset investment without reducing sales.

■ **Financial leverage** measures the degree to which the company finances its assets with debt rather than equity. Increasing the percentage of debt relative to equity increases the financial leverage. Although financial leverage increases ROE (when performance is positive), debt must be used with care as it increases the company's relative riskiness (see our following discussion of financial leverage).

Return on Assets

The first two terms in the DuPont model, profit margin and asset turnover, relate to company operations and combine to yield return on assets (ROA) as follows:

$$\text{ROA} = \frac{\text{Net income}}{\text{Average total assets}} = \frac{\text{Net income}}{\text{Sales}} \times \frac{\text{Sales}}{\text{Average total assets}}$$

Profit Margin   Asset Turnover

Return on assets (ROA)

Return on assets combines the first two terms in the ROE disaggregation, profit margin and turnover. It measures the return on investment for the company without regard to how it is financed (the relative proportion of debt and equity in its capital structure). Operating managers of a company typically grasp the income statement. They readily understand the pricing of products, the management of production costs, and the importance of controlling overhead costs. However, many managers do not appreciate the importance of managing the balance sheet. The ROA approach to performance measurement encourages managers to also focus on the returns that they achieve from the invested capital under their control. Those returns are maximized by a joint focus on both profitability and productivity.

Profitability

Profitability is measured by the profit margin (Net income/Sales). Analysis of profitability typically examines performance over time relative to benchmarks (such as competitors' or industry performance), which highlights trends and abnormalities. When abnormal performance is discovered, managers either correct suboptimal performance or protect superior performance. There are two general areas of profitability analysis: gross profit margin analysis and expense management.

Gross Profit Margin The gross profit margin (Gross profit/Sales) is crucial. It measures the gross profit (sales less cost of goods sold) for each sales dollar. Gross profit margin is affected by both the selling prices of products and their manufacturing cost. When markets are more competitive (or when products lose their competitive advantage), a company must reduce product prices to maintain market share and any increases in manufacturing costs cannot be directly passed on to customers; suggesting managers must focus on reducing costs. This might result in outsourcing of activities to lower labor costs and/or finding lower-cost raw materials. Such measures can yield a loss of product quality if not managed properly, which could further deteriorate the product's market position. Another strategy is to reduce product features not valued by the market. Focus groups of consumers can often identify these non-value-added product features that can be eliminated to save costs without affecting the product's value to consumers.

Expense Management Managers can focus on reducing manufacturing and/or administrative (*overhead*) expenses to increase profitability. *Manufacturing overhead* refers to all production expenses other than manufacturing labor and materials. These expenses include utilities, depreciation, and administrative costs related to manufacturing the product. *Administrative overhead* refers to all expenses not in cost of goods sold such as administrative salaries and benefits, marketing, legal, accounting, research and development. These overhead costs must be managed carefully as they can represent investments. Reductions in spending on advertising and research yield short-run, positive impacts on profitability, but can yield long-run deterioration in the company's market position. Likewise, requiring employees to work harder and longer can delay increases in wage-related costs, but the likely decline in employee morale can create long-run negative consequences.

Productivity

Productivity in the DuPont model refers to the volume of dollar sales resulting from each dollar invested in assets. When a decline in productivity is observed, managers have two avenues of attack:

1. Increase sales volume from the existing asset base, and/or
2. Decrease the investment in assets without reducing sales volume.

The first approach focuses on capacity utilization. Increasing throughput lowers per unit manufacturing costs as fixed costs are spread over a larger sales base. The second approach focuses on elimination of excess assets. That reduction increases cash and also reduces carrying costs associated with the eliminated assets.

Manager efforts to reduce assets often initially focus on working capital (current assets and liabilities). Receivables can be reduced by better credit-granting policies and better monitoring of outstanding receivables. Inventories can be reduced through just-in-time delivery of raw materials, elimination of bottlenecks in production to reduce work-in-process inventories, and producing to order rather than to estimated demand to reduce finished goods inventories. Companies can also delay payment of accounts payable to generate needed cash. Payables management is more art than science, and reductions must be managed with care so as not to threaten valuable supply channels.

Manager efforts to reduce long-term assets are more difficult. Recent years have witnessed an increase in use of corporate alliances, joint ventures, and activities that seek joint ownership of assets such as manufacturing, distribution, service facilities, and information technology (IT). Another strategy is to outsource production to reduce manufacturing assets. Outsourcing is effective provided the benefits from eliminating manufacturing assets more than offset the increased costs of purchasing goods from outsourced producers.

Financial Leverage

The third term in the DuPont model is financial leverage, the relative proportion of debt versus equity in the company's capital structure. Financial leverage in the DuPont model is measured by the ratio of average total assets to average stockholders' equity. An increase in this ratio implies an increase in the relative use of debt. This is evident from the accounting equation: assets = liabilities + equity. For example, assume that assets are financed equally with debt and equity. The accounting equation, expressed in percentage terms, follows: 100% = 50% + 50%, and the financial leverage of the company is 2.0 (100%/50%). If we increase the proportion of debt to 75% (decrease the proportion of equity to 25%), the financial leverage increases to 4.0 (100%/25%). The measure of financial leverage is important because debt is a contractual obligation (dividends are not), and a company's failure to make required debt payments can result in legal repercussions and even bankruptcy. As financial leverage increases, so do the required debt payments, along with the probability that the company is unable to meet its debt obligations in a business downturn.

ROA Adjustment in the Basic DuPont Model

The basic DuPont model is not entirely accurate, and adjusting the return on assets for the effect of interest addresses the inaccuracy.

Return on assets typically focuses on the operating side of the business (profit margin and asset turnover). Further, ROA is typically under the control of operating managers while the capital structure decision (the relative proportion of debt and equity) is not. Accordingly, an adjustment is often made to the numerator of ROA, and sometimes to the denominator. The numerator adjustment adds back the after-tax net interest expense (net of any other nonoperating revenues or expenses) and is computed as follows:

$$\text{ROA} = \frac{\text{Net income} + [\text{Interest expense } (1 - \text{Statutory tax rate})]}{\text{Average total assets}}$$

This adjusted numerator better reflects the company's operating profit as it measures return on assets exclusive of financing costs (independent of the capital structure decision). This adjusted ROA is typically reported by data collection services such as Compustat and Capital IQ, while the unadjusted is not. ("Statutory tax rate" in the ROA formula is the federal statutory tax rate *plus* the state tax rate net of any federal tax benefits; we use the 37% federal and state tax rates as explained in the NOPAT computation.)

The denominator adjustment is less common. That adjustment removes non-interest-bearing short-term liabilities (accounts payable and accrued liabilities) from total assets. The adjusted assets in the denominator are considered to better approximate the net assets that must be financed by long-term creditors and stockholders. In sum, adjustments to ROA move the numerator closer to net operating profit after-tax (NOPAT) and move the denominator closer to net operating assets (NOA). The resulting ROA ratio is then closer to the return on net operating assets (RNOA).

Illustration of DuPont Disaggregation

To illustrate DuPont disaggregation analysis, we use Target's income statement and balance sheet reported earlier in this module. Exhibit 3B.1 shows the computation for each component of the DuPont disaggregation analysis applied to Target.

EXHIBIT 3B.1	Computation of DuPont Disaggregation Analysis for Target	
Ratio Component	**Definition**	**Computation**
Profit margin (PM).	$\dfrac{\text{Net income}}{\text{Sales}}$	$\dfrac{\$2,920}{\$67,390} = 4.33\%$
Asset turnover (AT).	$\dfrac{\text{Sales}}{\text{Average total assets}}$	$\dfrac{\$67,390}{(\$43,705 + \$44,533)/2} = 1.53$
Financial leverage (FL)	$\dfrac{\text{Average total assets}}{\text{Average total equity}}$	$\dfrac{(\$43,705 + \$44,533)/2}{(\$15,487 + \$15,347)/2} = 2.86$
Return on equity (ROE).	$\dfrac{\text{Net income}}{\text{Average total equity}}$	$\dfrac{\$2,920}{(\$15,487 + \$15,347)/2} = 18.94\%$
	or PM × AT × FL	or 4.33% × 1.53 × 2.86 = 18.94
Return on assets (Adjusted).	$\dfrac{\text{Net income} + [\text{Interest expense} \times (1 - \text{Statutory Tax rate})]}{\text{Average total assets}}$	$\dfrac{\{\$2,920 + [\$757 \times (1 - 37\%)]\}}{(\$43,705 + \$44,533)/2} = 7.70\%$

GUIDANCE ANSWERS . . . ANALYSIS DECISION

You Are the CEO Your company is performing substantially better than its competitors. Namely, your RNOA of 16% is markedly superior to competitors' RNOA of 10%. However, RNOA disaggregation shows that this is mainly attributed to your NOAT of 0.89 versus competitors' NOAT of 0.59. Your NOPM of 18% is essentially identical to competitors' NOPM of 17%. Accordingly, you will want to maintain your NOAT as further improvements are probably difficult to achieve. Importantly, you are likely to achieve the greatest benefit with efforts at improving your NOPM of 18%, which is only marginally better than the industry norm of 17%.

Superscript ^A(B) denotes assignments based on Appendix 3A (3B).

DISCUSSION QUESTIONS

Q3-1. Explain in general terms the concept of return on investment. Why is this concept important in the analysis of financial performance?

Q3-2.^A (a) Explain how an increase in financial leverage can increase a company's ROE. (b) Given the potentially positive relation between financial leverage and ROE, why don't we see companies with 100% financial leverage (entirely nonowner financed)?

Q3-3. Gross profit margin (Gross profit/Sales) is an important determinant of NOPAT. Identify two factors that can cause gross profit margin to decline. Is a reduction in the gross profit margin always bad news? Explain.

Q3-4. When might a reduction in operating expenses as a percentage of sales denote a short-term gain at the cost of long-term performance?

Q3-5. Describe the concept of asset turnover. What does the concept mean and why is it so important to understanding and interpreting financial performance?

Q3-6. Explain what it means when a company's ROE exceeds its RNOA.

Q3-7.[A] Discontinued operations are typically viewed as a nonoperating activity in the analysis of the balance sheet and the income statement. What is the rationale for this treatment?

Q3-8. Describe what is meant by the "tax shield."

Q3-9. What is meant by the term "net" in net operating assets (NOA).

Q3-10. Why is it important to disaggregate RNOA into operating profit margin (NOPM) and net operating assets turnover (NOAT)?

Q3-11. What insights do we gain from the graphical relation between profit margin and asset turnover?

Q3-12. Explain the concept of liquidity and why it is crucial to company survival.

Q3-13. Identify at least two factors that limit the usefulness of ratio analysis.

Q3-14.[A] Define (1) net nonoperating obligations and (2) the net nonoperating expense.

**Assignments with the ✔ logo in the margin are available in an online homework system.
See the Preface of the book for details.**

MINI EXERCISES

M3-15. Identify and Compute Net Operating Assets (LO1)

Following is the balance sheet for **Home Depot, Inc.** Identify and compute fiscal year-end 2011 net operating assets.

HOME DEPOT
(HD)

(amounts in millions, except share and per share data)	January 30, 2011	January 31, 2010
Assets		
Current Assets		
Cash and cash equivalents	$ 545	$ 1,421
Receivables, net	1,085	964
Merchandise inventories	10,625	10,188
Other current assets	1,224	1,327
Total current assets	13,479	13,900
Property and equipment, at cost		
Land	8,497	8,451
Buildings	17,606	17,391
Furniture, fixtures and equipment	9,687	9,091
Leaseholder improvements	1,373	1,383
Construction in progress	654	525
Capital leases	568	504
	38,385	37,345
Less accumulated depreciation and amortization	13,325	11,795
Net property and equipment	25,060	25,550
Notes receivable	139	33
Goodwill	1,187	1,171
Other assets	260	223
Total assets	$40,125	$40,877

continued

continued from prior page

Liabilities and stockholders' equity		
Current liabilities		
Accounts payable...	$ 4,717	$ 4,863
Accrued salaries and related expenses...............................	1,290	1,263
Sales taxes payable.......................................	368	362
Deferred revenue	1,177	1,158
Income taxes payable	13	108
Current installments of long-term debt	1,042	1,020
Other accrued expenses	1,515	1,589
Total current liabilities.......................................	10,122	10,363
Long-term debt, excluding current installments	8,707	8,662
Other long-term liabilities...................................	2,135	2,140
Deferred income taxes.....................................	272	319
Total liabilities...	21,236	21,484
Stockholders' equity		
Common stock, par value $0.05; authorized: 10 billion shares; issued: 1.722 billion shares at January 30, 2011 and 1.716 billion shares at January 31, 2010; outstanding: 1.623 billion shares at January 30, 2011 and 1.698 billion shares at January 31, 2010	86	86
Paid-in capital	6,556	6,304
Retained earnings	14,995	13,226
Accumulated other comprehensive income........................	445	362
Treasury stock, at cost, 99 million shares at January 30, 2011 and 18 million shares at January 31, 2010.........................	(3,193)	(585)
Total stockholders' equity	18,889	19,393
Total liabilities and stockholders' equity........................	$40,125	$40,877

HOME DEPOT
(HD)

M3-16. **Identify and Compute NOPAT** **(LO1)**

Following is the income statement for **Home Depot, Inc.** Compute NOPBT—net operating profit *before* tax. (*Hint:* Treat Home Depot's "other" income as nonoperating since the company classifies it as such in its income statement.) Compute NOPAT for 2011 using a combined Federal and State statutory tax rate of 37%.

(amounts in millions)	January 30, 2011
Net sales...	$67,997
Cost of sales..	44,693
Gross profit...	23,304
Operating expenses:	
Selling, general and administrative	15,849
Depreciation and amortization...	1,616
Total operating expenses.................................	17,465
Operating income..	5,839
Interest and other (income) expense:	
Interest and investment income..	(15)
Interest expense...	530
Other...	51
Interest and other, net	566
Earnings before provision for income taxes........................	5,273
Provision for income taxes.................................	1,935
Net earnings..	$ 3,338

M3-17.   Compute RNOA, Net Operating Profit Margin, and NOA Turnover   (LO2)

Selected balance sheet and income statement information for **Nordstrom, Inc.**, a department store retailer, follows.

NORDSTROM, INC.
(JWN)

Company ($ millions)	Ticker	2011 Revenues	2011 NOPAT	2011 Net Operating Assets	2010 Net Operating Assets
Nordstrom, Inc	JWN	$9,700	$693	$3,296	$3,390

a.   Compute its 2011 return on net operating assets (RNOA).

b.   Disaggregate RNOA into net operating profit margin (NOPM) and net operating asset turnover (NOAT). Confirm that RNOA = NOPM × NOAT.

M3-18.   Identify and Compute Net Operating Assets   (LO2)

Following is the balance sheet for **Lowe's Companies, Inc.** Identify and compute its 2011 net operating assets (NOA).

LOWE'S
COMPANIES, INC.
(LOW)

LOWE'S COMPANIES, INC.		
($ millions, except par value)	January 28, 2011	January 29, 2010
Assets		
Current assets		
Cash and cash equivalents	$ 652	$ 632
Short-term investments	471	425
Merchandise inventory—net	8,321	8,249
Deferred income taxes—net.	193	208
Other current assets.	330	218
Total current assets	9,967	9,732
Property, less accumulated depreciation.	22,089	22,499
Long-term investments	1,008	277
Other assets.	635	497
Total assets.	$33,699	$33,005
Liabilities and Shareholders' Equity		
Current liabilities		
Current maturities of long-term debt	$ 36	$ 552
Accounts payable.	4,351	4,287
Accrued compensation and employee benefits.	667	577
Deferred revenue	707	683
Other current liabilities	1,358	1,256
Total current liabilities.	7,119	7,355
Long-term debt, excluding current maturities	6,537	4,528
Deferred income taxes—net.	467	598
Deferred revenue—extended protection plans	631	549
Other liabilities	833	906
Total liabilities	15,587	13,936
Shareholders' equity		
Preferred stock—$5 par value, none issued	—	—
Common stock—$.50 par value; Shares issued and outstanding:		
January 28, 2011, 1,354; January 29, 2010, 1,459	677	729
Capital in excess of par value	11	6
Retained earnings	17,371	18,307
Accumulated other comprehensive income.	53	27
Total shareholders' equity	18,112	19,069
Total liabilities and shareholders' equity.	$33,699	$33,005

M3-19.   Identify and Compute NOPAT   (LO2)

Following is the income statement for **Lowe's Companies, Inc.** Compute its 2011 net operating profit after tax (NOPAT) assuming a 37% total statutory tax rate.

LOWE'S
COMPANIES, INC.
(LOW)

LOWE'S COMPANIES, INC.			
Fiscal years ended (In millions)	January 28, 2011	January 29, 2010	January 30, 2009
Net sales.	$48,815	$47,220	$48,230
Cost of sales.	31,663	30,757	31,729
Gross margin	17,152	16,463	16,501
Expenses			
Selling, general and administrative	12,006	11,737	11,176
Depreciation	1,586	1,614	1,539
Interest—net.	332	287	280
Total expenses	13,924	13,638	12,995
Pre-tax earnings.	3,228	2,825	3,506
Income tax provision	1,218	1,042	1,311
Net earnings.	$ 2,010	$ 1,783	$ 2,195

M3-20.[B] **Compute and Interpret Disaggregation of Dupont Analysis Ratios   (LO4)**

MACYS, INC.
(M)

Selected balance sheet and income statement information for **Macy's, Inc.**, a retailer, follows.

Company ($ millions)	Ticker	2011 Sales	2011 Net Income	2011 Assets	2010 Assets	2011 Stockholders' Equity	2010 Stockholders' Equity
Macy's	M	$25,003	$847	$20,631	$21,300	$5,530	$4,653

a. Compute Macy's 2011 return on equity (ROE).
b. Disaggregate ROE into profit margin, asset turnover, and financial leverage. Confirm that ROE = PM × AT × FL.

M3-21.   Compute RNOA, Net Operating Profit Margin, and NOA Turnover for Competitors   (LO2)

ABERCROMBIE &
FITCH
(ANF)
TJX COMPANIES
(TJX)

Selected balance sheet and income statement information from **Abercrombie & Fitch** and **TJX Companies**, clothing retailers in the high-end and value-priced segments, respectively, follows.

Company ($ millions)	Ticker	2011 Sales	2011 NOPAT	2011 Net Operating Assets	2010 Net Operating Assets
Abercrombie & Fitch...	ANF	$ 3,469	$ 152	$1,032	$1,055
TJX Companies	TJX	21,942	1,364	2,072	1,937

a. Compute the 2011 return on net operating assets (RNOA) for both companies.
b. Disaggregate RNOA into net operating profit margin (NOPM) and net operating asset turnover (NOAT) for each company. Confirm that RNOA = NOPM × NOAT.
c. Discuss differences observed with respect to NOPM and NOAT and interpret these differences in light of each company's business model.

M3-22.   Compute and Interpret Liabilities-to-Equity Ratio   (LO1)

VERIZON
(VZ)

Selected balance sheet and income statement information from **Verizon** follows.

($ millions)	2010	2009
Current assets	$ 22,348	$ 21,745
Current liabilities.	30,597	29,136
Total liabilities	133,093	142,764
Equity	86,912	84,143
Earnings before interest and taxes.	15,207	16,622
Interest expense.	2,523	3,102

a. Compute the liabilities-to-equity ratio for each year and discuss any noticeable change. (The average liabilities-to-equity ratio for the telecommunications industry is 1.67.) Do you have any concerns about Verizon's financial leverage and the company's ability to meet interest obligations? Explain.

b.   Verizon's capital expenditures are expected to increase substantially as it seeks to respond to competitive pressures to upgrade the quality of its communication infrastructure. Assess Verizon's financing risks in light of this strategic direction.

M3-23.   Compute Tax Rate on Operating Profit and NOPAT   (LO2)

Selected income statement information for 2011 is presented below for **Home Depot** and **Lowe's**.

HOME DEPOT
(HD)
LOWE'S
COMPANIES, INC.
(LOW)

Company ($ millions)	Ticker	Net Operating Profit Before Tax	Pretax Net Nonoperating Expense	Tax Expense	Statutory Tax Rate	Sales
Home Depot........	HD	$5,839	$566	$1,935	37%	$67,997
Lowe's	LOW	3,560	332	1,218	37%	48,815

a.   Compute NOPAT for each company.
b.   Compute NOPAT as a percent of sales for each company.

M3-24.[B]   Compute and Interpret Measures for DuPont Disaggregation Analysis   (LO4)

Refer to the 2010 fiscal year financial data of **3M Company** from P3-36 to answer the following requirements (perform these computations from the perspective of a 3M shareholder).

3M COMPANY
(MMM)

a.   Compute the DuPont model component measures for profit margin, asset turnover, and financial leverage.
b.   Compute ROE. Confirm that ROE equals ROE computed using the component measures from part a (ROE = PM × AT × FL).
c.   Compute adjusted ROA (assume a tax rate of 37% and pretax net interest expense of $163).

EXERCISES

E3-25.   Compute and Interpret RNOA, Profit Margin, and Asset Turnover of Competitors   (LO2)

Selected balance sheet and income statement information for drug store retailers **CVS** and **Walgreen** follows.

CVS CAREMARK
CORP
(CVS)
WALGREEN CO.
(WAG)

Company ($ millions)	Ticker	2010 Sales	2010 NOPAT	2010 Net Operating Assets	2009 Net Operating Assets
CVS Caremark	CVS	$96,413	$3,777	$46,360	$45,889
Walgreen Co.........	WAG	67,420	2,145	14,921	14,140

a.   Compute the 2010 return on net operating assets (RNOA) for each company.
b.   Disaggregate RNOA into net operating profit margin (NOPM) and net operating asset turnover (NOAT) for each company.
c.   Discuss any differences in these ratios for each company.

E3-26.   Compute, Disaggregate, and Interpret RNOA of Competitors   (LO2)

Selected balance sheet and income statement information for the clothing retailers, **Abercrombie & Fitch** and **The GAP, Inc.**, follows.

ABERCROMBIE &
FITCH
(ANF)
THE GAP, INC.
(GPS)

Company ($ millions)	Ticker	2011 Sales	2011 NOPAT	2011 Net Operating Assets	2010 Net Operating Assets
Abercrombie & Fitch...	ANF	$ 3,469	$ 152	$1,032	$1,055
The GAP...........	GPS	14,664	1,195	2,419	2,318

a.   Compute the 2011 return on net operating assets (RNOA) for each company.
b.   Disaggregate RNOA into net operating profit margin (NOPM) and net operating asset turnover (NOAT) for each company.
c.   Discuss any differences in these ratios for each company.

E3-27. **Compute, Disaggregate, and Interpret RNOA of Competitors** (LO2)

NORDSTROM
(JWN)
LIMITED BRANDS
(LTD)

Selected balance sheet and income statement information for the clothing retailers **Nordstrom** and **Limited Brands** follows.

Company ($ millions)	Ticker	2011 Sales	2011 NOPAT	2011 Net Operating Assets	2010 Net Operating Assets
Nordstrom	JWN	$9,700	$693	$3,296	$3,390
Limited Brands.......	LTD	9,613	826	2,854	3,103

a. Compute the 2011 return on net operating assets (RNOA) for each company.
b. Disaggregate RNOA into net operating profit margin (NOPM) and net operating asset turnover (NOAT) for each company.
c. Discuss any differences in these ratios for each company. Identify the factor(s) that drives the differences in RNOA observed from your analyses in parts a and b.

E3-28. **Compute, Disaggregate, and Interpret ROE and RNOA** (LO1, 2)

INTEL
(INTC)

Selected fiscal year balance sheet and income statement information for the computer chip maker, **Intel**, follows ($ millions).

Company	Ticker	2010 Sales	2010 Net Income	2010 Net Operating Profit After Tax	2010 Net Operating Assets	2009 Net Operating Assets	2010 Stockholders' Equity	2009 Stockholders' Equity
Intel.......	INTC	$43,623	$11,464	$11,250	$28,652	$29,232	$49,430	$41,704

a. Compute the 2010 return on equity (ROE) and the 2010 return on net operating assets (RNOA).
b. Disaggregate RNOA into net operating profit margin (NOPM) and net operating asset turnover (NOAT). What observations can we make about the company's NOPM and NOAT?
c. Compute the percentage of RNOA to ROE, and compute the company's nonoperating return for 2010.

E3-29. **Compute, Disaggregate and Interpret ROE and RNOA** (LO1, 2)

MACY'S
(M)

Selected balance sheet and income statement information from **Macy's** follows ($ millions).

Company	Ticker	2011 Sales	2011 Net Income	2011 Net Operating Profit After Tax	2011 Net Operating Assets	2010 Net Operating Assets	2011 Stockholders' Equity	2010 Stockholders' Equity
Macy's	M	$25,003	$847	$1,209	$11,491	$11,665	$5,530	$4,653

a. Compute the 2011 return on equity (ROE) and 2011 return on net operating assets (RNOA).
b. Disaggregate RNOA into net operating profit margin (NOPM) and net operating asset turnover (NOAT). What observations can we make about Macy's NOPM and NOAT?
c. Compute the percentage of RNOA to ROE, and compute Macy's nonoperating return for 2011.

E3-30. **Compute, Disaggregate and Interpret ROE and RNOA** (LO1, 2)

CISCO SYSTEMS
(CSCO)

Selected balance sheet and income statement information from the software company, **Cisco Systems, Inc.,** follows ($ millions).

Company	Ticker	2010 Sales	2010 Net Income	2010 Net Operating Profit After Tax	2010 Net Operating Assets	2009 Net Operating Assets	2010 Stockholders' Equity	2009 Stockholders' Equity
Cisco Systems	CSCO	$40,040	$7,767	$7,609	$19,708	$13,971	$44,267	$38,647

a. Compute the 2010 return on equity (ROE) and 2010 return on net operating assets (RNOA).
b. Disaggregate the RNOA from part a into net operating profit margin (NOPM) and net operating asset turnover (NOAT).
c. Compute the percentage of RNOA to ROE. Explain the relation we observe between ROE and RNOA, and Cisco's use of equity capital.

E3-31.   Compute and Interpret Liabilities-to-Equity Ratio   (LO1)

Selected balance sheet and income statement information from **Comcast Corporation** for 2010 and 2009 follows ($ millions).

COMCAST
CORPORATION
(CMCSA)

	Total Current Assets	Total Current Liabilities	Pretax Income	Interest Expense	Total Liabilities*	Stockholders' Equity
2010	$8,886	$8,234	$6,104	$1,735	$74,100	$44,434
2009	3,223	7,249	5,106	2,044	69,922	42,811

*Includes redeemable noncontrolling interests

a.   Compute the liabilities-to-equity ratio for each year and discuss any noticeable change.
b.   What is your overall assessment of the company's financing risks from the analyses in part *a*? Explain.

E3-32.   Compute and Interpret Liabilities-to-Equity Ratio   (LO1)

Selected balance sheet and income statement information from **Verizon Communications, Inc.**, for 2010 and 2009 follows ($ millions).

VERIZON
COMMUNICATIONS,
INC.
(VZ)

	Total Current Assets	Total Current Liabilities	Pretax Income	Interest Expense	Total Liabilities	Stockholders' Equity
2010	$22,348	$30,597	$12,684	$2,469	$133,093	$86,912
2009	21,745	29,136	13,520	3,011	142,764	84,143

a.   Compute the liabilities-to-equity ratio for each year and discuss any noticeable change.
b.   What is your overall assessment of the company's financing risks from the analyses in part *a*? Explain.

E3-33.   Compute and Interpret Liabilities-to-Equity Ratio for Business Segments   (LO1, 2)

Selected balance sheet and income statement information from **General Electric Company** and its two principal business segments (Industrial and Financial) for 2010 follows.

GENERAL ELECTRIC
(GE)

($ millions)	Pretax Income	Interest Expense	Total Liabilities	Stockholders' Equity
Industrial segment	$15,166	$ 1,600	$ 95,729	$123,034
Financial segment	2,172	14,956	538,530	70,148
Other........................	(3,130)[1]	(573)[2]	(7,241)[2]	(68,984)
General Electric Consolidated	$14,208	$15,983	$627,018	$124,198[3]

1 Includes unallocated corporate operating activities.
2 Includes intercompany loans and related interest expense; these are deducted (eliminated) in preparing consolidated financial statements.
3 The consolidated equity equals the equity of the parent (industrial); this is explained in Module 9.

a.   Compute the liabilities-to-equity ratio for 2010 for the two business segments (Industrial and Financial) and the company as a whole.
b.   What is your overall assessment of the company's financing risks? Explain. What differences do you observe between the two business segments? Do these differences correspond to your prior expectations given each company's business model?
c.   Discuss the implications of the analysis of consolidated financial statements and the additional insight that can be gained from a more in-depth analysis of primary business segments.

E3-34.[A]   **Direct Computation of Nonoperating Return   (LO1, 3)**

Refer to the income statement and balance sheet of **Walmart**, from Mid-Module Reviews 1 and 2.

WALMART
(WMT)

a.   Compute the FLEV and Spread for Walmart for 2011.
b.   Use RNOA from Mid-Module Review 2, and the FLEV and Spread from part a, to compute ROE. Compare the ROE calculated in this exercise with the ROE from Mid-Module Review 2.

E3-35.   Compute NOPAT Using Tax Rates from Tax Footnote   (LO1)

The income statement for **TJX Companies**, follows.

TJX COMPANIES
(TJX)

TJX COMPANIES Consolidated Statements of Income	
Fiscal Year Ended ($ thousands)	January 29, 2011
Net sales.	$21,942,193
Cost of sales, including buying and occupancy costs.	16,040,461
Selling, general and administrative expenses	3,710,053
Provision (credit) for computer intrusion related costs.	(11,550)
Interest expense, net	39,137
Income from continuing operations before provision for income taxes.	2,164,092
Provision for income taxes.	824,562
Income from continuing operations	1,339,530
Gain from discontinued operations, net of income taxes	3,611
Net income.	$ 1,343,141

TJX provides the following footnote disclosure relating to its effective tax rate:

	January 29, 2011
U.S. federal statutory income tax rate	35.0%
Effective state income tax rate.	4.1
Impact of foreign operations	(0.5)
All other	(0.5)
Worldwide effective income tax rate	38.1%

Compute TJX's NOPAT for 2011 using its income tax footnote disclosure.

PROBLEMS

3M COMPANY
(MMM)

P3-36.   Analysis and Interpretation of Profitability   (LO1, 2)
Balance sheets and income statements for **3M Company** follow.

Consolidated Statements of Income			
Years ended December 31 (In millions)	2010	2009	2008
Net sales.	$26,662	$23,123	$25,269
Operating expenses			
Cost of sales.	13,831	12,109	13,379
Selling, general and administrative expenses	5,479	4,907	5,245
Research, development and related expenses	1,434	1,293	1,404
Loss from sale of businesses	—	—	23
Total operating expenses	20,744	18,309	20,051
Operating income.	5,918	4,814	5,218
Interest expense and income			
Interest expense.	201	219	215
Interest income.	(38)	(37)	(105)
Total interest expense.	163	182	110
Income before income taxes	5,755	4,632	5,108
Provision for income taxes.	1,592	1,388	1,588
Net income including noncontrolling interest.	4,163	3,244	3,520
Less: Net income attributable to noncontrolling interest . . .	78	51	60
Net income attributable to 3M	$ 4,085	$ 3,193	$ 3,460

Consolidated Balance Sheets At December 31 ($ millions, except per share amount)	2010	2009
Assets		
Current assets		
Cash and cash equivalents.	$ 3,377	$ 3,040
Marketable securities—current.	1,101	744
Accounts receivable—net of allowances of $98 and $109.	3,615	3,250
Inventories		
Finished goods	1,476	1,255
Work in process.	950	815
Raw materials and supplies	729	569
Total inventories	3,155	2,639
Other current assets	967	1,122
Total current assets.	12,215	10,795
Marketable securities—noncurrent.	540	825
Investments	146	103
Property, plant and equipment	20,253	19,440
Less: Accumulated depreciation	(12,974)	(12,440)
Property, plant and equipment—net.	7,279	7,000
Goodwill	6,820	5,832
Intangible assets—net	1,820	1,342
Prepaid pension benefits	74	78
Other assets	1,262	1,275
Total assets	$30,156	$27,250
Liabilities		
Current liabilities		
Short-term borrowings and current portion of long-term debt.	$ 1,269	$ 613
Accounts payable.	1,662	1,453
Accrued payroll.	778	680
Accrued income taxes	358	252
Other current liabilities	2,022	1,899
Total current liabilities	6,089	4,897
Long-term debt	4,183	5,097
Pension and postretirement benefits	2,013	2,227
Other liabilities	1,854	1,727
Total liabilities	14,139	13,948
Equity		
3M Company shareholders' equity: Common stock, par value $.01 per share; Shares outstanding—2010: 711,977,608; Shares outstanding—2009: 710,599,119.	9	9
Additional paid-in capital	3,468	3,153
Retained earnings.	25,995	23,753
Treasury stock.	(10,266)	(10,397)
Accumulated other comprehensive income (loss)	(3,543)	(3,754)
Total 3M Company shareholders' equity.	15,663	12,764
Noncontrolling interest.	354	538
Total equity	16,017	13,302
Total liabilities and equity	$30,156	$27,250

Required

a. Compute net operating profit after tax (NOPAT) for 2010. Assume that the combined federal and state statutory tax rate is 37%.

b. Compute net operating assets (NOA) for 2010 and 2009. Treat noncurrent Investments as a nonoperating item.

c. Compute and disaggregate 3M's RNOA into net operating profit margin (NOPM) and net operating asset turnover (NOAT) for 2010. Demonstrate that RNOA = NOPM × NOAT.

    d. Compute net nonoperating obligations (NNO) for 2010 and 2009. (*Hint:* Include noncontrolling interest from the balance sheet with NNO.) Confirm the relation: NOA = NNO + Stockholders' equity.

    e. Compute return on equity (ROE) for 2010.

    f. What is the nonoperating return component of ROE for 2010?

    g. Comment on the difference between ROE and RNOA. What inference can we draw from this comparison?

3M COMPANY
(MMM)

P3-37. **Analysis and Interpretation of Liabilities-to-Equity** (LO1)

Refer to the financial information of **3M Company** in P3-36 to answer the following requirements.

Required

    a. Compute the liabilities-to-equity ratios for 2010 and 2009. Comment on any noticeable changes.

    b. Summarize your findings about the company's financing risks. Do you have any concerns about its ability to meet its debt obligations?

3M COMPANY
(MMM)

P3-38.[A] **Direct Computation of Nonoperating Return** (LO1, 2, 3)

Refer to the financial information of **3M Company** in P3-36 to answer the following requirements.

Required

    a. Compute its financial leverage (FLEV) and Spread for 2010. Recall that NNE = NOPAT − Net income; remember to use stockholders' equity and net income for 3M's shareholders (excluding noncontrolling interests).

    b. Assume that its return on equity (ROE) for 2010 is 28.74% and its return on net operating assets (RNOA) is 27.88%. Confirm computations to yield the relation: ROE = RNOA + (FLEV × Spread).

    c. What do your computations of the nonoperating return imply about the company's use of borrowed funds?

BEST BUY CO., INC.
(BBY)

P3-39. **Analysis and Interpretation of Profitability** (LO1, 2)

Balance sheets and income statements for **Best Buy Co., Inc.**, follow.

Consolidated Statements of Earnings			
For Fiscal Years Ended ($ in millions)	February 26, 2011	February 27, 2010	February 28, 2009
Revenue	$50,272	$49,694	$45,015
Cost of goods sold.	37,611	37,534	34,017
Restructuring charges—cost of goods sold.	24	—	—
Gross profit.	12,637	12,160	10,998
Selling, general and administrative expenses	10,325	9,873	8,984
Restructuring charges	198	52	78
Goodwill and tradename impairment.	—	—	66
Operating income.	2,114	2,235	1,870
Other income (expense)			
Investment income and other.	51	54	35
Investment impairment.	—	—	(111)
Interest expense	(87)	(94)	(94)
Earnings before income tax expense and equity in income of affiliates.	2,078	2,195	1,700
Income tax expense.	714	802	674
Equity in income of affiliates.	2	1	7
Net earnings including noncontrolling interests.	1,366	1,394	1,033
Net earnings attributable to noncontrolling interests.	(89)	(77)	(30)
Net earnings attributable to Best Buy Co., Inc.	$ 1,277	$ 1,317	$ 1,003

Consolidated Balance Sheets		
($ millions, except per share and share amounts)	February 26, 2011	February 27, 2010
Assets		
Current assets		
Cash and cash equivalents..	$ 1,103	$ 1,826
Short-term investments	22	90
Receivables	2,348	2,020
Merchandise inventories...	5,897	5,486
Other current assets..	1,103	1,144
Total current assets..	10,473	10,566
Property and equipment		
Land and buildings...	766	757
Leasehold improvements	2,318	2,154
Fixtures and equipment	4,701	4,447
Property under capital lease.....................................	120	95
	7,905	7,453
Less accumulated depreciation	4,082	3,383
Net property and equipment...................................	3,823	4,070
Goodwill..	2,454	2,452
Tradenames, net..	133	159
Customer relationships, net	203	279
Equity and other investments.....................................	328	324
Other noncurrent assets...	435	452
Total assets..	$17,849	$18,302
Liabilities and equity		
Current liabilities		
Accounts payable...	$ 4,894	$ 5,276
Unredeemed gift card liabilities	474	463
Accrued compensation and related expenses........................	570	544
Accrued liabilities	1,471	1,681
Accrued income taxes	256	316
Short-term debt	557	663
Current portion of long-term debt	441	35
Total current liabilities	8,663	8,978
Long-term liabilities	1,183	1,256
Long-term debt	711	1,104
Equity		
Best Buy Co., Inc. Shareholders' equity		
Preferred stock, $1.00 par value:		
Authorized—400,000 shares; issued and outstanding—none	—	—
Common stock, $0.10 par value:		
Authorized—1.0 billion shares; issued and outstanding—		
392,590,000 and 418,815,000 shares, respectively	39	42
Additional paid-in-capital	18	441
Retained earnings..	6,372	5,797
Accumulated other comprehensive income..........................	173	40
Total Best Buy Co., Inc. shareholders' equity........................	6,602	6,320
Noncontrolling interests	690	644
Total equity..	7,292	6,964
Total liabilities and equity	$17,849	$18,302

Required

a. Compute net operating profit after tax (NOPAT) for 2011. Assume that the combined federal and state statutory tax rate is 37%.

b. Compute net operating assets (NOA) for 2011 and 2010. (*Hint:* Treat the Equity and Other Investments and the Long-Term Liabilities as operating.)

c. Compute and disaggregate Best Buy's RNOA into net operating profit margin (NOPM) and net operating asset turnover (NOAT) for 2011; confirm that RNOA = NOPM × NOAT. The median NOPM and NOAT for companies in Best Buy's industry are 3.32% and 3.27%, respectively, yielding a median RNOA of slightly over 11%. Comment on NOPM and NOAT estimates for Best Buy in comparison to industry medians.

d. Compute net nonoperating obligations (NNO) for 2011 and 2010. Confirm the relation: NOA = NNO + Stockholders' equity.

e. Compute return on equity (ROE) for 2010.

f. Infer the nonoperating return component of ROE for 2010.

g. Comment on the difference between ROE and RNOA. What does this relation suggest about Best Buy's use of equity capital?

P3-40. Analysis and Interpretation of Liabilities-to-Equity (LO1)

BEST BUY
(BBY)

Refer to the financial information of **Best Buy (BBY)** in P3-39 to answer the following requirements.

Required

a. Compute Best Buy's liabilities-to-equity ratio for 2011 and 2010. Comment on any noticeable change.

b. Summarize your findings about the company's financing risks. Do you have any concerns about Best Buy's ability to meet its debt obligations?

P3-41.[A] **Direct Computation of Nonoperating Return** (LO1, 3)

BEST BUY
(BBY)

Refer to the financial information of **Best Buy (BBY)** in P3-39 to answer the following requirements.

Required

a. Compute Best Buy's financial leverage (FLEV) and Spread for 2011; recall, NNE = NOPAT − Net income.

b. Assume that Best Buy's return on equity (ROE) for 2011 is 19.76% and its return on net operating assets (RNOA) is 18.86%. Confirm computations to yield the relation: ROE = RNOA + (FLEV × Spread).

c. What do your computations of the nonoperating return in parts a and b imply about the company's use of borrowed funds?

P3-42. Analysis and Interpretation of Profitability (LO1, 2)

INTEL
CORPORATION
(INTC)

Balance sheets and income statements for **Intel Corporation** follow. Refer to these financial statements to answer the requirements.

INTEL CORPORATION Consolidated Statements of Income			
(in millions)	2010	2009	2008
Net revenue	$43,623	$35,127	$37,586
Cost of sales	15,132	15,566	16,742
Gross margin	28,491	19,561	20,844
Research and development	6,576	5,653	5,722
Marketing, general and administrative	6,309	7,931	5,452
Restructuring and asset impairment charges	—	231	710
Amortization of acquisition-related intangibles	18	35	6
Operating expenses	12,903	13,850	11,890
Operating income	15,588	5,711	8,954
Gains (losses) on equity method investments, net	117	(147)	(1,380)
Gains (losses) on other equity investments, net	231	(23)	(376)
Interest and other, net	109	163	488
Income before taxes	16,045	5,704	7,686
Provision for taxes	4,581	1,335	2,394
Net income	$11,464	$ 4,369	$ 5,292

INTEL CORPORATION Consolidated Balance Sheets		
(in millions, except par value)	2010	2009
Assets		
Current assets		
Cash and cash equivalents	$ 5,498	$ 3,987
Short-term investments	11,294	5,285
Trading assets	5,093	4,648
Accounts receivable, net of allowance for doubtful accounts of		
$28 ($19 in 2009)	2,867	2,273
Inventories	3,757	2,935
Deferred tax assets	1,488	1,216
Other current assets	1,614	813
Total current assets	31,611	21,157
Property, plant and equipment, net	17,899	17,225
Marketable equity securities	1,008	773
Other long-term investments	3,026	4,179
Goodwill	4,531	4,421
Other long-term assets	5,111	5,340
Total assets	$63,186	$53,095
Liabilities and stockholders' equity		
Current liabilities		
Short-term debt	$ 38	$ 172
Accounts payable	2,290	1,883
Accrued compensation and benefits	2,888	2,448
Accrued advertising	1,007	773
Deferred income on shipments to distributors	622	593
Other accrued liabilities	2,482	1,722
Total current liabilities	9,327	7,591
Long-term income taxes payable	190	193
Long-term debt	2,077	2,049
Long-term deferred tax liabilities	926	555
Other long-term liabilities	1,236	1,003
Stockholders' equity		
Preferred stock, $0.001 par value, 50 shares authorized; none issued	—	—
Common stock, $0.001 par value, 10,000 shares authorized;		
5,581 issued and 5,511 outstanding (5,523 issued and		
outstanding in 2009) and capital in excess of par value	16,178	14,993
Accumulated other comprehensive income (loss)	333	393
Retained earnings	32,919	26,318
Total stockholders' equity	49,430	41,704
Total liabilities and stockholders' equity	$63,186	$53,095

Required

a. Compute net operating profit after tax (NOPAT) for 2010. Assume that the combined federal and state statutory tax rate is 37%.

b. Compute net operating assets (NOA) for 2010 and 2009. (Hint: Assume that trading assets and long-term marketable equity securities are investments in marketable securities and are therefore, nonoperating assets; also, footnotes reveal that the other long-term investments are mainly loan receivables and are, therefore, operating.)

c. Compute RNOA and disaggregate it into net operating profit margin (NOPM) and net operating asset turnover (NOAT) for 2010. Comment on the drivers of RNOA.

d. Compute net nonoperating obligations (NNO) for 2010 and 2009. Confirm the relation: NOA = NNO + Stockholders' equity.

e. Compute return on equity (ROE) for 2010.

f. Infer the nonoperating return component of ROE for 2010.

g. Comment on the difference between ROE and RNOA. What does this relation suggest about Intel's use of equity capital?

NORDSTROM, INC.
(JWN)

P3-43.   **Analysis and Interpretation of Profitability**   **(LO1, 2)**
Balance sheets and income statements for **Nordstrom, Inc.**, follow. Refer to these financial statements to answer the requirements.

NORDSTROM, INC.			
Consolidated Statements of Earnings			
Fiscal Years Ended ($ millions)	**2011**	**2010**	**2009**
Net sales.	$9,310	$8,258	$8,272
Credit card revenues	390	369	301
Total revenues	9,700	8,627	8,573
Cost of sales and related buying and occupancy costs	(5,897)	(5,328)	(5,417)
Selling, general and administrative expenses			
Retail	(2,412)	(2,109)	(2,103)
Credit	(273)	(356)	(274)
Earnings before interest and income taxes	1,118	834	779
Interest expense, net	(127)	(138)	(131)
Earnings before income taxes	991	696	648
Income tax expense.	(378)	(255)	(247)
Net earnings.	$ 613	$ 441	$ 401

NORDSTROM, INC.		
Consolidated Balance Sheets		
($ millions)	**January 29, 2011**	**January 30, 2010**
Assets		
Current assets		
Cash and cash equivalents	$1,506	$ 795
Accounts receivable, net	2,026	2,035
Merchandise inventories	977	898
Current deferred tax assets, net.	236	238
Prepaid expenses and other	79	88
Total current assets	4,824	4,054
Land, buildings and equipment (net of accumulated depreciation		
of $3,520 and $3,316).	2,318	2,242
Goodwill.	53	53
Other assets.	267	230
Total assets.	$7,462	$6,579
Liabilities and Shareholders' Equity		
Current liabilities		
Accounts payable.	$ 846	$ 726
Accrued salaries, wages and related benefits	375	336
Other current liabilities	652	596
Current portion of long-term debt	6	356
Total current liabilities.	1,879	2,014
Long-term debt, net.	2,775	2,257
Deferred property incentives, net.	495	469
Other liabilities	292	267
Shareholders' equity		
Common stock, no par value: 1,000 shares authorized;		
218.0 and 217.7 shares issued and outstanding	1,168	1,066
Retained earnings	882	525
Accumulated other comprehensive loss	(29)	(19)
Total shareholders' equity	2,021	1,572
Total liabilities and shareholders' equity.	$7,462	$6,579

Required

a. Compute net operating profit after tax (NOPAT) for 2011. Assume that the combined federal and state statutory tax rate is 37%.

b. Compute net operating assets (NOA) for 2011 and 2010.

c. Compute RNOA and disaggregate it into net operating profit margin (NOPM) and net operating asset turnover (NOAT) for 2011; confirm that RNOA = NOPM × NOAT. The median NOPM and NOAT for companies in Nordstrom's industry are 4.46% and 2.81%, respectively, yielding a median RNOA of slightly over 12%. Comment on NOPM and NOAT estimates for Nordstrom in comparison to industry medians.

d. Compute net nonoperating obligations (NNO) for 2011 and 2010. Confirm the relation: NOA = NNO + Stockholders' equity.

e. Compute return on equity (ROE) for 2011.

f. Infer the nonoperating return component of ROE for 2011.

g. Comment on the difference between ROE and RNOA. What does this relation suggest about Nordstrom's use of equity capital?

P3-44.   Analysis and Interpretation of Profitability   (LO1, 2)

Balance sheets and income statements for **Kraft Foods, Inc.**, follow. Refer to these financial statements to answer the following requirements.

KRAFT FOODS, INC.
(KFT)

KRAFT FOODS, INC.
Income Statements

Years Ended December 31 (In millions)	2010	2009	2008
Net revenues	$49,207	$38,754	$40,492
Cost of sales.	31,305	24,819	27,164
Gross profit.	17,902	13,935	13,328
Selling, general and administrative expenses	12,001	8,784	8,613
Asset impairment and exit costs	18	(64)	1,024
Losses on divestitures, net.	6	6	92
Amortization of intangibles.	211	26	23
Operating income.	5,666	5,183	3,576
Interest and other expense, net	2,024	1,237	1,240
Earnings from continuing operations before income taxes	3,642	3,946	2,336
Provision for income taxes.	1,147	1,136	658
Earnings from continuing operations.	2,495	2,810	1,678
Earnings and gain from discontinued operations, net of income taxes.	1,644	218	1,215
Net earnings.	4,139	3,028	2,893
Noncontrolling interest.	25	7	9
Net earnings attributable to Kraft Foods	$ 4,114	$ 3,021	$ 2,884

KRAFT FOODS, INC.
Balance Sheets

December 31 (In millions, except per share amounts)	2010	2009
Assets		
Cash and cash equivalents	$ 2,481	$ 2,101
Receivables (net of allowances of $246 in 2010 and $121 in 2009)	6,539	5,197
Inventories, net.	5,310	3,775
Deferred income taxes.	898	730
Other current assets.	993	651
Total current assets	16,221	12,454
Property, plant and equipment, net	13,792	10,693
Goodwill.	37,856	28,764
Intangible assets, net.	25,963	13,429
Prepaid pension assets	86	115
Other assets.	1,371	1,259
Total assets.	$95,289	$66,714

continued

continued from prior page

Liabilities		
Short-term borrowings.	$ 750	$ 453
Current portion of long-term debt	1,115	513
Accounts payable.	5,409	3,766
Accrued marketing.	2,515	2,181
Accrued employment costs	1,292	1,175
Other current liabilities	4,579	3,403
Total current liabilities.	15,660	11,491
Long-term debt	26,859	18,024
Deferred income taxes.	7,984	4,508
Accrued pension costs.	2,382	1,765
Accrued postretirement health care costs	3,046	2,816
Other liabilities	3,416	2,138
Total liabilities.	59,347	40,742
Equity		
Common Stock, no par value (1,996,537,778 shares issued in 2010 and		
1,735,000,000 shares issued in 2009)	—	—
Additional paid-in capital	31,231	23,611
Retained earnings	16,619	14,636
Accumulated other comprehensive losses	(3,890)	(3,955)
Treasury stock, at cost.	(8,126)	(8,416)
Total Kraft Foods shareholders' equity.	35,834	25,876
Noncontrolling interest	108	96
Total equity.	35,942	25,972
Total liabilities and equity	$95,289	$66,714

Required

a. Compute net operating profit after tax (NOPAT) for 2010. Assume that the combined federal and state statutory tax rate is 37%.

b. Compute net operating assets (NOA) for 2010 and 2009.

c. Compute RNOA and disaggregate it into net operating profit margin (NOPM) and net operating asset turnover (NOAT) for 2011; confirm that RNOA = NOPM × NOAT. The median NOPM and NOAT for companies in KFT's industry are 6.22% and 1.66, respectively, yielding a median RNOA of 10.3%. Comment on NOPM and NOAT estimates for KFT in comparison to industry medians.

d. Compute net nonoperating obligations (NNO) for 2010 and 2009. Confirm the relation: NOA = NNO + Stockholders' equity.

e. Compute return on equity (ROE) for 2010.

f. Infer the nonoperating return component of ROE for 2010.

g. Comment on the difference between ROE and RNOA. What does this relation suggest about Kraft's use of debt?

P3-45. **Analysis and Interpretation of Liabilities-to-Equity** **(LO1)**

KRAFT FOODS, INC.
(KFT)

Refer to the financial information of **Kraft Foods, Inc.,** in P3-44 to answer the following requirements.

Required

a. Compute its liabilities-to-equity ratio for 2010 and 2009. Comment on any noticeable change.

b. Summarize your findings about the company's financing risks. Do you have any concerns about its ability to meet its debt obligations?

P3-46.[A] **Direct Computation of Nonoperating Return** **(LO1, 3)**

KRAFT FOODS, INC.
(KFT)

Refer to the financial information of **Kraft Foods, Inc.,** in P3-44 to answer the following requirements.

Required

a. Assume that 2010 net nonoperating expenses (NNE) are $(344) million and that 2010 RNOA is 7.18%. Compute financial leverage (FLEV) and Spread for 2010.

b. Assume that 2010 return on equity (ROE) is 13.33%. Confirm computations to yield the relation: ROE = RNOA + (FLEV × Spread).

c. What do your computations of the nonoperating return in parts a and b imply about the company's use of borrowed funds?

P3-47. **Analysis and Interpretation of Profit Margin, Asset Turnover, and RNOA for Several Companies** (LO2)

Net operating profit margin (NOPM) and net operating asset turnover (NOAT) for several selected companies for the most recent year follow.

	NOPM	NOAT
Abbott Laboratories............	13.83%	1.11
FedEx	3.60%	2.51
CVS Caremark.................	3.92%	2.09
Kraft	7.66%	0.94
Walgreen's	3.18%	4.64
Caterpillar...................	6.79%	1.18
Target	5.04%	2.27
Best Buy......................	2.76%	6.83

Required

a. Graph NOPM and NOAT for each of these companies. Do you see a pattern that is similar to that shown in this module? Explain. (The graph in the module is based on medians for selected industries; the graph for this problem uses fewer companies than in the module and, thus, will not be as smooth.)

b. Consider the trade-off between profit margin and asset turnover. How can we evaluate companies on the profit margin and asset turnover trade-off? Explain.

P3-48.[B] **Compute and Analyze Measures for DuPont Disaggregation Analysis** (LO4)

Refer to the fiscal 2011 financial data of **Best Buy Co., Inc.,** in P3-39 to answer the following requirements.

Required

a. Apply the basic DuPont model and compute the component measures for profit margin, asset turnover, and financial leverage.

b. Compute ROE. Confirm that ROE equals ROE computed using the component measures from part *a* (ROE = PM × AT × FL).

c. Compute adjusted ROA (assume a tax rate of 37%).

P3-49.[B] **Compute and Analyze Measures for DuPont Disaggregation Analysis** (LO4)

Refer to the fiscal 2010 financial data of **Kraft Foods** in P3-44 to answer the following requirements.

Required

a. Apply the basic DuPont model and compute its component measures for profit margin, asset turnover, and financial leverage.

b. Compute ROE. Confirm that ROE equals ROE computed using the component measures from part *a* (ROE = PM × AT × FL).

c. Compute adjusted ROA (assume a tax rate of 37%). Compare the adjusted and unadjusted ROA ratios and explain why they differ.

IFRS APPLICATIONS

I3-50. **Compute, Disaggregate, and Interpret RNOA of Competitors** (LO2)

Shell Oil Company is the U.S.-based subsidiary of **Royal Dutch Shell**, a multinational oil company headquartered in The Hague, The Netherlands. **BP Limited** is a multinational oil company headquartered in London U.K. Selected balance sheet and income statement information and assumptions for both Shell and BP follow.

($ millions)	2009 Sales	2009 NOPAT	2009 Net Operating Assets	2008 Net Operating Assets
Shell Oil Company	$283,164	$11,793	$169,294	$148,070
BP Limited	243,173	16,800	138,275	125,834

a. Compute the 2009 return on net operating assets (RNOA) for each company.

Margin notes (right column):

ABBOTT LABORATORIES (ABT)
FEDEX (FDX)
CVS CAREMARK (CVS)
KRAFT (KFT)
WALGREENS (WAG)
CATERPILLAR (CAT)
TARGET (TGT)
BEST BUY (BBY)

BEST BUY (BBY)

KRAFT FOODS (KFT)

SHELL OIL COMPANY ROYAL DUTCH SHELL BP LIMITED

    b. Disaggregate RNOA into net operating profit margin (NOPM) and net operating asset turnover (NOAT) for each company.

    c. Discuss any differences in these ratios for each company. What drives the differences in RNOA observed in parts *a* and *b*?

I3-51.   **Compute, Disaggregate, and Interpret ROE and RNOA**   (LO1, 2)

OMV GROUP

Headquartered in Vienna, **OMV Group** is Austria's largest oil-producing, refining and gas station operating company. Selected fiscal year balance sheet and income statement information and assumptions for OMV Group follows (€ thousands).

2009 Sales	2009 Net Income	2009 Net Operating Profit After Tax	2009 Net Operating Assets	2008 Net Operating Assets	2009 Stockholders' Equity	2008 Stockholders' Equity
€17,917,267	€716,931	€526,104	€13,002,350	€12,028,024	€10,034,785	€9,363,243

    a. Compute the 2009 return on equity (ROE) and the 2009 return on net operating assets (RNOA).

    b. Disaggregate RNOA into net operating profit margin (NOPM) and net operating asset turnover (NOAT).

    c. Compute the percentage of RNOA to ROE, and compute OMV Group's nonoperating return for 2009.

I3-52.   **Compute and Interpret Liabilities-to-Equity Ratio**   (LO1)

SCHNEIDER ELECTRIC

Schneider Electric is a multinational energy company headquartered in Rueil-Malmaison, France. Selected balance sheet and income statement information and assumptions for 2008 and 2009 follows.

(€ millions)	Total Current Assets	Total Current Liabilities	Pretax Income	Interest Expense	Total Liabilities	Stockholders' Equity
2008	$8,778	$6,444	$2,266	$294	$13,756	$11,051
2009	9,731	6,162	1,208	323	13,761	11,888

    a. Compute the liabilities-to-equity ratio for each year and discuss any noticeable change.

    b. What is the overall assessment of the company's financing risks from the analyses in *a*? Explain.

I3-53.   **Analysis and Interpretation of Profitability**   (LO1, 2)

WM MORRISON SUPERMARKETS PLC

Wm Morrison Supermarkets plc is the fourth largest chain of supermarkets in the United Kingdom, headquartered in Bradford, England. Balance sheets and income statements for Morrison follow.

WM MORRISON SUPERMARKETS plc Consolidated statements of comprehensive income			
52 weeks ended 31 January 2010 (£ millions)	2010	2009	2008
Turnover	£ 15,410	£ 14,528	£ 12,969
Cost of sales.	(14,348)	(13,615)	(12,151)
Gross profit.	1,062	913	818
Other operating income	65	37	30
Administrative expenses	(224)	(281)	(268)
Profits arising on fixed-asset transactions.	4	2	32
Operating profit	907	671	612
Finance costs.	(60)	(60)	(60)
Finance income	11	44	60
Profit before taxation	858	655	612
Taxation	(260)	(195)	(58)
Profit for the period	£ 598	£ 460	£ 554

WM MORRISON SUPERMARKETS plc Consolidated balance sheets		
(£ millions)	**2010**	**2009**
Assets		
Non-current assets		
Property, plant and equipment.................................	£ 7,180	£ 6,587
Lease prepayments	257	250
Investment property[1]	229	242
Other financial assets[2]	—	81
	7,666	7,160
Current assets		
Stocks[3]...	577	494
Debtors[4]	201	245
Other financial assets......................................	71	—
Cash and cash equivalents	245	327
	1,094	1,066
Liabilities		
Current liabilities		
Creditors[5]	(1,845)	(1,915)
Other financial liabilities	(213)	(1)
Current tax liabilities......................................	(94)	(108)
	(2,152)	(2,024)
Non-current liabilities		
Other financial liabilities	(1,027)	(1,049)
Deferred tax liabilities.....................................	(515)	(472)
Net pension liabilities	(17)	(49)
Provisions...	(100)	(112)
	(1,659)	(1,682)
Net assets	**£ 4,949**	**£ 4,520**
Shareholders' equity		
Called-up share capital	£ 265	£ 263
Share premium...	92	60
Capital redemption reserve	6	6
Merger reserve...	2,578	2,578
Retained earnings and hedging reserve........................	2,008	1,613
Total equity attributable to the owners of the Company	**£ 4,949**	**£ 4,520**

[1] Investment property is a nonoperating asset
[2] These are primarily marketable securities
[3] Stocks means inventories
[4] Debtors means accounts receivable
[5] Creditors means accounts payable

Required

a.   Compute net operating profit after tax (NOPAT) for 2010 and 2009. Assume that marginal tax rates are 35.9% for 2010 and 36.0% for 2009.

b.   Compute net operating assets (NOA) for 2010 and 2009.

c.   Compute and disaggregate RNOA into net operating profit margin (NOPM) and net operating asset turnover (NOAT) for 2010 and 2009; assume that 2008 NOA is £4,666 million. Has the company's RNOA improved or worsened? Explain.

d.   Compute net nonoperating obligations (NNO) for 2010 and 2009. Confirm the relation: NOA = NNO + Shareholders' equity.

e.   Compute return on equity (ROE) for 2010 and 2009. (Shareholders' equity in 2008 is £4,378 million.)

f.   What is the nonoperating return component of ROE for 2010 and 2009?

g.   Comment on the difference between ROE and RNOA. What inference can we draw from this comparison?

WM MORRISON SUPERMARKETS PLC

I3-54. Analysis and Interpretation of Liabilities-to-Equity (LO1)

Wm Morrison Supermarkets plc is the fourth largest chain of supermarkets in the United Kingdom, headquartered in Bradford, England. Refer to the financial information for Morrisons in I3-53 to answer the following requirements.

Required

a. Compute liabilities-to-equity ratio for 2010 and 2009. Comment on any noticeable changes.
b. Summarize the findings about the company's financing risks. Do we have any concerns about its ability to meet its debt obligations?

DISCUSSION POINTS

D3-55. Gross Profit and Strategic Management (LO2)

One way to increase overall profitability is to increase gross profit. This can be accomplished by raising prices and/or by reducing manufacturing costs.

Required

a. Will raising prices and/or reducing manufacturing costs unambiguously increase gross profit? Explain.
b. What strategy might you develop as a manager to (i) increase product prices, or (ii) reduce product manufacturing cost?

D3-56. Asset Turnover and Strategic Management (LO2)

Increasing net operating asset turnover requires some combination of increasing sales and/or decreasing net operating assets. For the latter, many companies consider ways to reduce their investment in working capital (current assets less current liabilities). This can be accomplished by reducing the level of accounts receivable and inventories, or by increasing the level of accounts payable.

Required

a. Develop a list of suggested actions that you, as a manager, could undertake to achieve these three objectives.
b. Describe the marketing implications of reducing receivables and inventories, and the supplier implications of delaying payment. How can a company reduce working capital without negatively impacting its performance?

D3-57. Ethics and Governance: Earnings Management (LO1)

Companies are aware that analysts focus on profitability in evaluating financial performance. Managers have historically utilized a number of methods to improve reported profitability that are cosmetic in nature and do not affect "real" operating performance. These methods are subsumed under the general heading of "earnings management." Justification for such actions typically includes the following arguments:

- Increasing stock price by managing earnings benefits shareholders; thus, no one is hurt by these actions.
- Earnings management is a temporary fix; such actions will be curtailed once "real" profitability improves, as managers expect.

Required

a. Identify the affected parties in any scheme to manage profits to prop up stock price.
b. Do the ends (of earnings management) justify the means? Explain.
c. To what extent are the objectives of managers different from those of shareholders?
d. What governance structure can you envision that might inhibit earnings management?

SOLUTIONS TO REVIEW PROBLEMS

Mid-Module Review 1

Solution

Walmart's NOPAT is computed as follows (in $ millions):

$$\text{NOPAT} = \text{Operating profit before tax} - (\text{Tax expense} + [\text{Net nonoperating expenses} \times 37\%])$$
$$= \$25,542 - (\$7,579 + [\$2,004 \times 37\%])$$
$$= \underline{\underline{\$17,222}}$$

Walmart had $604 million of "consolidated net income attributable to noncontrolling interest"; while this amount is defined as part of nonoperating items, *it is excluded from the tax shield estimation* (as it does not limit the company's taxes and it is a simple attribution of income to non-Walmart stockholders).

Mid-Module Review 2

Solution ($ millions)

1.

	Jan. 31, 2011	Jan. 31, 2010
Operating assets		
Receivables, net..	$ 5,089	$ 4,144
Inventories	36,318	32,713
Prepaid expenses and other	2,960	3,128
Property and equipment, net	105,098	99,544
Property under capital leases, net	2,780	2,763
Goodwill...	16,763	16,126
Other assets and deferred charges	4,129	3,942
Total operating assets	173,137	162,360
Operating liabilities		
Accounts payable.......................................	33,557	30,451
Accrued liabilities	18,701	18,734
Accrued income taxes	157	1,347
Deferred income taxes and other........................	6,682	5,508
Total operating liabilities	59,097	56,040
Net operating assets (NOA)............................	$114,040	$106,320

2. $\text{RNOA} = \dfrac{\$17,222}{(\$114,040 + \$106,320)/2} = 15.63\%$

3. $\text{ROE} = \dfrac{\$16,389}{(\$68,542 + \$70,468)/2} = 23.58\%$

   (We use net income and stockholders' equity attributable to Walmart's shareholders.)
   Walmart's RNOA makes up 66% of its ROE, computed as 15.63%/23.58%.

4. $\text{NOPM} = \$17,222/\$421,849 = 4.08\%$

   $\text{NOAT} = \dfrac{\$421,849}{(\$114,040 + \$106,320)/2} = 3.83$

5.

	ROE	RNOA	NOPM	NOAT
Target	18.94%	11.43%	5.04%	2.27
Walmart	23.58%	15.63%	4.08%	3.83

Walmart's higher ROE is driven by higher RNOA as the nonoperating return is similar (7.96% for WMT and 7.51% for TGT). Walmart's higher RNOA is the result of much higher NOAT, which more than offsets its lower NOPM.

Module-End Review

Solution ($ millions)

1. Walmart ROE = Operating return (RNOA) + Nonoperating return
   Using solutions from Mid-Module Review 2, and substituting, we get:
   23.58% = 15.62% + Nonoperating return
   7.96% = Nonoperating return
2. Target's ROE = Operating return (RNOA) + Nonoperating return
   18.94% = 11.43% + Nonoperating return
   7.51% = Nonoperating return

Walmart's ROE is higher than Target's because of its higher RNOA. The nonoperating return is a function of both the relative amount of debt in their capital structures and the spread of the return on net operating assets over the cost of that debt. Both companies are increasing their ROE by the use of financial leverage. Further analysis is warranted to investigate whether either company is taking on too much default risk by their use of debt.

3. Walmart's liabilities-to-equity ratio = Total liabilities/Total equity
   (We use total consolidated equity to be consistent with the consolidated liabilities in the numerator.)
   ($58,484 + $40,692 + $3,150 + $6,682)/$71,247 = 1.53

4. Target's liabilities-to-equity ratio = Total liabilities/Total equity
   ($10,070 + $18,148)/$15,487 = 1.82

While the liabilities-to-equity ratios for both companies are higher than for the average retail company (see: Exhibit 3.6), neither company's ratio is markedly out of line with medians for all publicly traded companies over the past decade. Further analysis is necessary to evaluate if that debt exposure is excessive. That additional analysis will examine the amount of projected debt payments (found in the long-term debt footnote) with projected net cash from operating activities.

1. Understand the demand for and supply of credit. (p. 4-3)

2. Explain the credit risk analysis process. (p. 4-7)

3. Perform a credit analysis, and compute and interpret measures of credit risk. (p. 4-8)

4. Describe the credit rating process and explain why companies are interested in their credit ratings. (p. 4-23)

5. Explain bankruptcy prediction models, and compute and interpret measures of bankruptcy risk. (p. 4-28)

© Getty Images

MODULE

4

Credit Risk Analysis and Interpretation

HOME DEPOT

There are three ways to obtain an asset: borrow it, receive it as a gift, or earn it. In a corporate setting this translates into borrowing money (securing non-owner financing), selling shares (receiving capital from owners), or generating profits. We know it is important to analyze a company's ability to generate operating profits (the third way to obtain an asset). To do this, we divide the income statement into operating and nonoperating items, and then focus on operating items. We similarly divide the balance sheet into operating and nonoperating items to determine the return on *net* operating assets (NOA). The 'net' or 'N' in NOA refers to operating assets less operating liabilities, where the latter refers to borrowing from operating sources (the first way to obtain an asset). In this module we consider borrowing from *non*operating sources such as short-term and long-term debt. We explore the role debt plays and how it figures in companies' credit risk.

Home Depot borrows money from both operating and nonoperating creditors. Its January 2011 balance sheet reveals that some of the borrowed money comes from operating liabilities; trade creditors that have shipped inventory to Home Depot but have yet to be paid. This amounts to $4,717 million. Other borrowed money comes from nonoperating liabilities; primarily long-term debt. While many companies borrow from banks, Home Depot does not. Its debt is publicly traded. In addition, Home Depot reports lease liabilities on its balance sheet which means that the company has borrowed from leasing companies or from sellers that provided financing. Given such a wide range of borrowed money, Home Depot's financial condition is of interest to many types of current and potential creditors, whose overarching concern is whether Home Depot will repay the borrowed money in full and on time. That is, Home Depot's creditors need to assess the company's credit risk.

A credit analysis begins with an understanding of the specific nature of the borrowed money. Suppliers, for example, are naturally concerned with Home Depot's short-term liquidity because invoices from suppliers are generally paid within a few months of the inventory being shipped. To increase liquidity, Home Depot has established several lines of credit. These are funds available from Home Depot's bank as needed. In 2011, Home Depot had backup credit facility with a consortium of banks for borrowings up to $2 billion. The credit facility, which expires in July 2013, provides Home Depot's creditors with some assurance that they will be repaid. Suppliers will consider Home Depot's current level of accounts payable as well as its turnover of both accounts payable and inventory. If Home Depot maintains historic turnover rates, suppliers can determine when they can expect payment. This will help them gauge the risk associated with extending credit to Home Depot.

Lenders are interested in the borrower's ability to repay debt over a longer term. For example, in September 2010, Home Depot issued $1 billion of Senior Notes, half due in 2020 and the other half due in 2040. Because these notes are long-term, debt investors are concerned with longer-term solvency and cash flow. In addition, these potential investors likely analyzed Home Depot's expansion plans with a view to understanding whether the company would have sufficient cash to expand and repay the notes.

Several "third parties" are interested in analyzing Home Depot's creditworthiness as well. In particular, credit-rating agencies assess companies' credit risk to determine bond and issuer ratings. These agencies, including **S&P**, **Moody's**, and **Fitch**

(continued on next page)

(continued from previous page)

Ratings, do not have money at risk, but the accuracy of their ratings affects their corporate reputations. Thus, they are interested in correctly assessing companies' credit risk. In early 2011, the three agencies' ratings of Home Depot were BBB+, A3, and BBB+, respectively. S&P's rating reflects Home Depot's strength ("substantial U.S. store footprint and recognized name, cost reductions initiatives that have limited profit erosion through the economic downturn, and meaningful free cash flow generating ability") as well as its risk factors ("the weak state of the U.S. housing market" and "weak intermediate financial risk profile . . . and our expectation that leverage will increase"). We explain the various types of analyses that contribute to an evaluation of a company's credit quality in this module.

Sources: Home Depot Annual Report and 10-K Filing; Moodys.com/research; StandardAndPoors.com/ratingsdirect.

MODULE ORGANIZATION

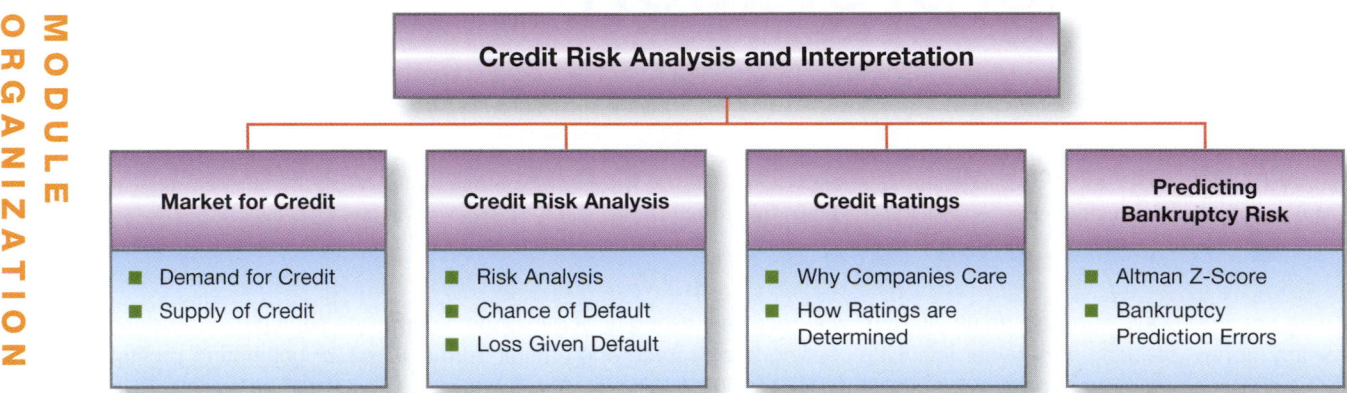

The key to understanding credit risk is to first understand that credit is similar to other commodities—there is a demand for credit and a supply of credit. Firms demand credit for operating, investing and financing activities and numerous parties are willing to meet that demand including creditors, banks, public debt investors, and other private lenders. Each of these parties is concerned with repayment and, thus, must analyze the borrower's creditworthiness. Such analysis follows much of the same model as equity analysis, but the focus is a bit different. While equity investors are concerned with profitability and earning a return, debt investors have far less opportunity for upside. That is, debt investors' maximum return is determined by the interest rate set in the "loan" as well as the prevailing market rate of interest.

This module begins with a discussion of credit markets—the supply and demand for credit. Then we consider credit risk analysis and explain how operating and nonoperating creditors use financial accounting numbers and other information to make lending decisions. We learn how banks make loans to customers and about common loan terms and conditions. The module also discusses how credit-rating agencies assess companies' credit risk to determine credit ratings and how ratings affect bond prices and cost of debt capital.

We use Home Depot as the focus company. We reproduce its balance sheet in Exhibit 4.1 and its debt footnote in Exhibit 4.2.

DEMAND FOR AND SUPPLY OF CREDIT

LO1 Understand the demand for and supply of credit.

To understand the market for credit, we first consider the demand for credit and then the supply of credit.

Demand for Credit

Companies demand credit for various operating, investing and financing activities.

Operating activities Many companies have cyclical operating cash needs. For example, companies that manufacture inventory have to pay for materials and labor months before they will be able to sell their product and collect revenue. This is also the case for seasonal companies

EXHIBIT 4.1	Home Depot Balance Sheet		

Amounts in millions, except share and per share data	January 30, 2011	January 31, 2010
Assets		
Current Assets		
Cash and cash equivalents.	$ 545	$ 1,421
Receivables, net	1,085	964
Merchandise inventories.	10,625	10,188
Other current assets	1,224	1,327
Total current assets.	13,479	13,900
Net property and equipment	25,060	25,550
Notes receivable.	139	33
Goodwill	1,187	1,171
Other assets	260	223
Total assets	$40,125	$40,877
Liabilities and Stockholders' Equity		
Current Liabilities		
Accounts payable.	$ 4,717	$ 4,863
Accrued salaries and related expenses	1,290	1,263
Sales taxes payable	368	362
Deferred revenue	1,177	1,158
Income taxes payable.	13	108
Current installments of long-term debt.	1,042	1,020
Other accrued expenses.	1,515	1,589
Total current liabilities	10,122	10,363
Long-term debt, excluding current installments.	8,707	8,662
Other long-term liabilities	2,135	2,140
Deferred income taxes	272	319
Total liabilities	21,236	21,484
Stockholders' equity		
Common Stock, par value $0.05; authorized: 10 billion shares; issued: 1.722 billion and 1.716 billion shares; outstanding: 1.623 billion and 1.698 billion shares.	86	86
Paid-in capital.	6,556	6,304
Retained earnings.	14,995	13,226
Accumulated other comprehensive income.	445	362
Treasury Stock, at cost, 99 million and 18 million shares	(3,193)	(585)
Total stockholders' equity.	18,889	19,393
Total liabilities and stockholders' equity.	$40,125	$40,877

EXHIBIT 4.2	Debt Footnote for Home Depot		

$ in millions	January 30, 2011	January 31, 2010
4.625% Senior Notes; due August 15, 2010; interest payable semi-annually on February 15 and August 15	$ 0	$ 999
5.20% Senior Notes; due March 1, 2011; interest payable semi-annually on March 1 and September 1	1,000	1,000
5.25% Senior Notes; due December 16, 2013; interest payable semi-annually on June 16 and December 16	1,297	1,258
5.40% Senior Notes; due March 1, 2016; interest payable semi-annually on March 1 and September 1	3,033	3,040
3.95% Senior Notes; due September 15, 2020; interest payable semi-annually on March 15 and September 15	499	0
5.875% Senior Notes; due December 16, 2036; interest payable semi-annually on June 16 and December 16	2,960	2,960
5.40% Senior Notes; due September 15, 2040; interest payable semi-annually on March 15 and September 15	499	0
Capital Lease Obligations; payable in varying installments through January 31, 2055	452	408
Other.	9	17
Total debt	9,749	9,682
Less current installments	1,042	1,020
Long-Term Debt, excluding current installments.	$ 8,707	$ 8,662

such as retailers that purchase merchandise for the end-of-year holiday season. Because these purchases are made long before expected sales, suppliers extend credit to cover the intervening months. Such seasonal cash needs are routine in nature and credit risk is relatively low. The suppliers' past experiences with a company will dictate the credit terms extended to it. In the event that suppliers' credit does not extend far enough, a company might need to arrange short-term loans from their bank.

Cash needed for operating activities is not uniformly "low risk." Contrast cyclical, ongoing operating cash flow needs as discussed above, with cash needed to cover operating losses. If the losses are recurring, a company's cash needs might not be temporary unless it is able to return quickly to profitability. This makes it more difficult for the company to raise capital because of the increased uncertainty about whether and when it will be able to repay the borrowed amounts. A company's need for cash can be critical, and finding a willing lender can be the difference between bankruptcy and continued operations.

Investing activities Companies routinely require large amounts of cash for investments including purchases of new equipment and property (capital expenditures) and for corporate acquisitions. These cash needs vary in timing and amount and are especially important for start-ups and growth companies that need cash to construct or purchase their initial plant and stores. For example, in the year ended January 2011, Home Depot opened two new stores in the U.S. and renovated other stores. They paid more than $1 billion cash for these new assets. As entities mature, they often settle into more predictable patterns of capital expenditures.

Financing activities Companies occasionally need credit for financing activities, such as issuance of debt for repayment of maturing debt obligations or the repurchase of common stock. For example, the $1 billion cash that Home Depot received from the notes issued in September 2010 was used to repay $1 billion of Senior Notes that matured August 15, 2010.

Supply of Credit

There are numerous parties that supply both operating and nonoperating credit to meet companies' demands.

Trade credit Trade credit from suppliers is routine and most often non-interest bearing. Companies apply for credit and provide the supplier with relevant financial information. This is especially important for private companies that want trade credit. Whereas suppliers can use publicly available data to evaluate the credit risk of public companies, such information is not available for private companies. Once approved, customers formally accept suppliers' credit terms that specify the amount and timing of any early payment discounts, the maximum credit limit, payment terms, and other restrictions or specifications. Suppliers tailor these contractual terms to the particular customer's existing and ongoing creditworthiness. For example, suppliers can set lower credit limits for riskier customers or impose interest payments if credit risk worsens.

ANALYSIS DECISION	You Are the Manager

You have been hired to help grow a start-up. It reported sales of $2 million during the past fiscal quarter. Currently, it does not offer trade credit, as the majority of its customers use credit cards. In a bid to expand the business, you are asked to determine whether extending trade credit is a good idea. What factors are important for you in making this decision? [Answer, p. 4–33]

Bank loans Banks structure financing to meet specific client needs. Balancing client needs are the myriad rules and restrictions imposed by bank regulators. For example, bank regulators require that banks hold capital (shareholders' equity) in proportion to their loan portfolio (banks' main asset). The riskier the loan, the more capital a bank must hold for that loan. Holding capital is costly and, therefore, banks carefully assess each and every loan application. Bankers often have long-term relationships with their customers; bankers call this "relationship banking," which provides the bank with access to information needed for detailed credit analysis for different types of loans.

Revolving credit lines are loans that companies draw on as needed. Revolvers, as they are called, are like credit cards because a company takes cash out as needed and makes payments as cash is available (in uneven amounts). Interest rates on revolving credit lines are often floating, which means the bank adjusts the rate up or down according to the prevailing market rate of interest. This adjustable interest rate feature limits the bank's interest-rate risk.

Lines of credit are guarantees that funds will be available when needed. To increase liquidity, companies negotiate lines of credit with their bank or with a consortium of banks. These lines of credit act as backup or interim financing. Often companies use their lines of credit to repay short-term commercial paper (discussed below) until more commercial paper can be sold. Ratings agencies such as **Moody's** and **S&P** will not rate a company's commercial paper unless there is a line of credit to secure the commercial paper. In the year ended January 2011, **Home Depot**'s commercial paper program is supported by a $2 billion backup credit facility with a consortium of banks. Companies pay for lines of credit in two ways. First, the bank charges a percentage for the unused portion of the credit line. This charge ranges from 25 to 100 basis points annually, and compensates the bank for standing ready to honor a company's cash demands. Second, the bank charges interest on the used portion of the line of credit.

Letters of credit facilitate private international transactions. A letter of credit interposes a bank between the two parties to a transaction. The letter provides a guarantee of payment from the buyer, is legally enforceable and, therefore, reduces the credit risk to the seller. The benefit of the letter of credit is that it substitutes the bank's (higher) credit rating for that of the buyer. Letters of credit are used mostly to facilitate transactions when the two parties are in different countries. Recently, letters of credit have been used by land developers to ensure that the proposed infrastructure is built.

Term loans are what we commonly understand by "bank loan." A company applies for the loan and if successful, receives a set amount of cash at the start of the loan (the principal). The loan agreement specifies periodic payments of principal and interest. Interest rates are either fixed or floating and a term loan will usually mature between 1 and 10 years. Many banks actively market small-business term-loan programs that provide companies with needed operating cash or funds to purchase long-term assets such as equipment.

Mortgages are loans secured by long-term assets such as land and buildings, which means that the lender can foreclose on the mortgage and seize the property in the event of default. Mortgage claims are filed with a public register such as local land title offices. Because a mortgage is often a company's largest debt, mortgage lenders perform **due diligence** before lending. For example, a mortgage lender will verify income statement and balance sheet information and run title searches to ensure that there are no prior claims on the property.

Nonbank private financing Companies occasionally borrow from **nonbank private lenders**, usually when they have been turned down for a loan from a traditional bank. Private lenders might fund higher risk ventures because they have a better understanding of the business or a particular market segment. In addition to providing funds, some private lenders will creatively structure loan repayment and sometimes act as an ongoing management consultant to the borrower.

RESEARCH INSIGHT	**Nonbank Private Debt**

Researchers David Denis and Vassil Mihov study companies' choices among public debt, bank debt, and private nonbank debt. They report that public borrowers are more profitable and have higher asset turnover. However, the main determinant of a company's choice is its credit rating. Those with the highest credit quality issue public debt, those with medium credit quality borrow privately from banks, and those with the lowest credit quality (have not established a strong credit reputation) borrow from nonbank private lenders. (Source: *Choice Among Bank Debt, Non-Bank Private Debt and Public Debt: Evidence From New Corporate Borrowings,* http://papers.ssrn.com/sol3/papers.cfm?abstract_id=269129)

Lease financing   An alternate form of borrowing is leasing. Leasing firms finance capital expenditures for equipment such as vehicles, production machinery, and computer equipment. Some leasing firms are associated with the equipment manufacturer (such as **GMAC** or **Ford Credit** or **IBM**'s financial services). Other leasing firms are independent and provide a full range of lease services. The leasing firm analyzes the credit risk associated with the lease, bearing in mind that the leased assets are held as collateral, and that some of the risk can be mitigated by tailoring the lease terms. At the end of January 2011, **Home Depot** reported on its balance sheet lease obligations of $452 million; payable in varying installments through January 31, 2055.

Publicly traded debt   Issuing debt securities in capital markets is a cost-efficient way to raise capital. Companies issue short-term or long-term debt depending on the specific need for funding. **Commercial paper** is short term; because maturities do not exceed 270 days the borrowing is exempt from SEC regulations. Companies use proceeds from commercial paper to finance short-term operating or working capital needs. Commercial paper is issued primarily by financial companies (commercial banks, mortgage companies, leasing companies, and insurance underwriters) although large manufacturers and retailers also issue commercial paper. Home Depot did not have any commercial paper outstanding at year end, January 30, 2011. The year before, it had an average daily commercial paper balance of $55 million but this was repaid by the end of the fiscal year. It is most often the case that companies pay a lower rate of interest for short-term commercial paper than for longer-term bonds or notes. The average interest rate on Home Depot's commercial paper during fiscal 2010 was 1.1%.

To secure longer-term funding, companies issue **bonds** or **debentures**. For example, at January 30, 2011, Home Depot had long-term debt of $ 9,288 million arising from Senior Notes which mature between March 2011 and September 2040. Home Depot's debt footnote, reproduced in Exhibit 4.2, shows that interest rates on those notes range from 3.95% to 5.875%. Debt that is offered for sale to the public is regulated by the SEC even if the company's stock does not trade publicly. Generally, the entire face amount (principal) of the bond is repaid at maturity, and tax-deductible interest payments are made in the interim (nearly always semiannually). After they are issued, corporate bonds can trade on major exchanges but most of the trading is decentralized, as dealers trade the bonds in over-the-counter markets. Investors who buy the bonds when they are issued and in subsequent re-sales, are concerned with the issuing company's ability to meet semiannual interest payments (short-term liquidity) and to repay the principal at maturity (long-term solvency and cash flow coverage).

MID-MODULE REVIEW 1

Rising Sun Company is a successful importer of traditional Japanese food. The company is privately held and has operated since 1982. Revenues and net income for the most recent fiscal year were $82 million and $9 million, respectively. Currently located in San Francisco, the company is considering expansion into the Seattle area. Management has prepared a business plan and estimates that the company needs $15 million to complete the plan, including $6 million to purchase land and construct a storage facility; $2 million for office equipment and leasehold improvements for rented office space; $5 million for inventory purchases; and $2 million to pay permit fees, rent, wages, and other operating expenses in the first few months until revenues are realized.

Required
What sources of financing should Rising Sun Company consider? Discuss each source.

The solution is on page 4-45.

CREDIT RISK ANALYSIS PROCESS

LO2 Explain the credit risk analysis process.

The overarching purpose of credit risk analysis is to quantify potential credit losses so that lending decisions are made with full information. **Expected credit losses** are the product of two factors, the **chance of default** and the size of the **loss given default**. This is algebraically reflected as follows:

$$\text{Expected credit loss} = \text{Chance of default} \times \text{Loss given default}$$

Before we discuss how lenders assess these two factors, consider that the number and types of parties who perform credit risk analysis is broad and varied: trade creditors, banks and nonbank financial institutions, debt investors (including participants in public debt markets), and credit rating agencies. The key distinction among the groups is the nature of the information they use in their analysis. That is, not all lenders have access to the same information and, thus, each group tailors its approach to credit analysis.

Trade creditors acquire additional information via credit applications. Given its size and reputation, Home Depot has little difficulty attracting trade credit, and information is publicly available to potential and existing creditors. But for private companies, the credit application might be the only information available to a potential lender. Trade creditors check applicants' references, including trade references (names of other trade creditors, their respective credit limits, outstanding balances, and any nonpayment information) and bank references (names of bankers and the amounts of any lines of credit). Because trade creditors often extend credit to many customers in the same industry, the chance of default can be highly correlated among customers. Thus trade creditors closely monitor information on industry trends and outlook.

Banks and nonbank financial institutions have access to information that managers do not release to the public. Moreover, bankers typically negotiate the loan and adjust loan terms to fit the chance of default for each client. As well, banks can monitor bank balances and act on early warning signs. Thus, private lenders are in a unique position to refine their credit analysis.

In contrast, public-debt investors have little access to additional information; they can only decide to buy or sell the bond at the current price. They have access to public information including earnings announcements and annual reports (see Research Insight below). Public-debt investors also can avail themselves of debt ratings (which we discuss later), but apart from that, public-debt investors have publicly available information only.

Similar to lenders and investors, credit raters assess credit risk, but their purpose and methods differ in several important respects. First, credit rating agencies have no direct financial involvement with the companies whose credit they are rating; they perform the analysis to provide a publicly available signal to lenders and potential lenders. Second, credit rating agencies have access to more, and often better, information than other lenders. Credit analysts are not subject to Regulation FD and routinely meet with managers both in conference calls and face to face. Thus credit-rating agencies can refine the risk analysis for individual companies and compare statistics and trends across companies. Credit raters have the best, most current information. It is for this reason that other creditors rely heavily on credit ratings. [On August 15, 2000, the SEC adopted Regulation Fair Disclosure (FD) to curb selective disclosure of information by publicly traded companies. Reg FD requires that if a U.S. public company discloses material nonpublic information to a select group (such as equity analysts), the company must simultaneously disclose the information to the public. The regulation levels the information playing field.]

RESEARCH INSIGHT	Accounting Earnings and Bond Prices

Researchers Peter Easton, Steven Monahan, and Florin Vasvari study how companies' earnings announcements affect bond prices. They document large changes in bond prices around earnings announcements and find that these changes are larger for net losses. Thus, companies with public debt have strong incentives to avoid losses because they depress bond prices. These researchers also find that bond-price changes are larger for speculative grade bonds. A main inference is that accounting earnings (and its components) are priced in bond returns. (Source: *Initial Evidence on the Role of Accounting Earnings in the Bond Market*, http://papers.ssrn.com/sol3/papers.cfm?abstract_id=997821)

ANALYZING CREDIT RISK

The main purpose of a credit analysis is to quantify the risk of loss from nonpayment. To quantify expected credit losses, potential lenders must assess the chance of default and the size of

LO3 Perform a credit analysis, and compute and interpret measures of credit risk.

the loss given a default. While lenders have different information sets and use different credit analysis models, there are four common steps to determine the chance of default. We discuss each of these four steps and we consider how creditors might limit their losses in the event of default.

Chance of Default

The **chance of default** depends on the company's ability to repay the debt which, in turn, depends on the company's future performance and cash flow. Different lenders approach credit analysis with different techniques. The following discussion is comprehensive, and not a script that any one creditor follows. As a starting point, the analysis considers the company's past performance and its current financial condition, projects future cash flows, and determines a probability that a company will have insufficient cash to repay the loan.

Step 1: Assess nature and purpose of the loan

A necessary first step for the prospective lender is to determine why the borrower needs the loan. If one cannot be assured of the need for credit, proceeding to the analysis stage is pointless. As we explained, there are many reasons to borrow (for cyclical cash flow needs, to fund temporary or ongoing operating losses, for major capital expenditures or acquisitions, or to reconfigure capital structure). The nature and purpose of the loan affect its riskiness. Lending to a company that needs funds for ongoing operations is riskier than a company that needs funds to expand into a new profitable market segment. In the year ended January 2007, **Home Depot** borrowed almost $9 billion, using some proceeds to repay maturing debt, fund the repurchase of stock, and to acquire **Hughes Supply, Inc.** That year, the company also sold commercial paper to support short-term liquidity needs. The nature and purpose of the loan also affect the focus and depth of the lender's credit analysis. For example, trade creditors will not do as in-depth an analysis as a mortgage lender. Each computes and analyzes the same types of ratios but their emphases will differ.

Step 2: Assess macroeconomic environment and industry conditions

Like financial analysis, credit analysis must consider the broader business context in which a company operates. The nature of the competitive intensity in the industry affects the expected level of profitability. Global economic forces affect the macro economy in which the company operates. Government regulation, borrowing agreements exacted by creditors, and internal governance procedures also affect companies' range of operating activities. Such external forces affect companies' strategic planning and expected short-term and long-term profits. A company's relative strength within its industry, and vis-à-vis its suppliers and customers, can determine both profitability and its asset base. As competition intensifies, profitability likely declines, and the level of assets needed to compete likely increases. These changes in the income statement and the balance sheet can adversely impact operating performance and cash flow and the company's ability to repay its debts. There are several ways to systematically consider broader business forces. We discuss one such framework: Porter's Five Forces (Porter, *Competitive Strategy: Techniques for Analyzing Industries and Competitors*, 1980 and 1998); and we assess each force for Home Depot.

(A) Industry competition Increased rivalry raises the cost of doing business as companies must compete for workers, advertise products, and research and develop new products. **Home Depot**'s industry competition is intense. Its biggest rival is **Lowe's Companies**. In many markets, Lowes and Home Depot compete directly for the same do-it-yourself customer. Smaller hardware stores and lumber yards create additional rivalry (such as **Ace Hardware** and **Sears**). Competition also arises from specialty stores that focus on one aspect of home improvement such as flooring, kitchens, lighting, and roofing. Home Depot's garden center faces competition from national nurseries, and most cities have large local nurseries and garden specialty shops. Increasingly, Home Depot faces competition from online vendors such as **US Appliances**, **iFloor**, and nurseries such as **Autumn Ridge** and **Henry Fields**.

(B) Buyer power Buyers, the customers, with strong bargaining power can extract price concessions and demand a higher level of service and delayed payment terms; further, a company that faces strong customers has decreased profits and operating cash flows. Home Depot's buyer power is low. Home Depot has three types of customers: do-it-yourself (DIY) customers, buy-it-yourself customers (those who like to pick out materials and appliances but want a professional to install them), and the professional customer (contractors, plumbers, landscapers). None of these customers has strong bargaining power with Home Depot, although the company does now offer large-quantity purchases and separate staff to assist professional customers.

(C) Supplier power Suppliers with strong bargaining power can demand higher prices and earlier payments; a company that faces strong suppliers has decreased profits and operating cash flows. Home Depot's supplier power is low. A typical Home Depot store has 40,000 different products purchased from many suppliers. It often accounts for a large portion of a supplier's sales. This decreases the supplier's power and Home Depot can command lower prices and longer payment terms. These sorts of concessions increase Home Depot's margins.

(D) Threat of substitution As the number of product substitutes increases, sellers have less power to raise prices and/or pass on costs to buyers; accordingly, threat of substitution places downward pressure on sellers' profits. At Home Depot, the threat of substitution is low to medium. There are few substitutes for home improvement and the nesting instinct is timeless. Home Depot offers in-store "How To" classes that customers can substitute with online instructions and do-it-yourself videos. In times of economic growth, new-home purchases are a substitute but represent a minimal threat because even new home owners want to decorate, landscape, and make other improvements.

(E) Threat of entry New market entrants increase competition; to mitigate that threat, companies expend monies on activities such as new technologies, promotion, and human development to erect barriers to entry and to create economies of scale. Home Depot faces a weak threat of entry in the form of big-box retailers. New market entrants would find it difficult to compete directly with Home Depot and Lowes. Both companies enjoy economies of scale and are protected by barriers to entry including trained workforce, large capital start-up costs, prime locations, national brand recognition, and customer loyalty. However, threat of entry from online and specialty stores is medium to high.

In sum, the industry in which a company operates dictates much of the company's potential profitability and efficiency. Home Depot does business in a highly competitive market but enjoys low supplier and buyer power. This indicates that, at least in the short run, the company should remain profitable and the chance of default is relatively low.

Step 3: Perform financial analysis

A financial analysis includes calculating ratios. But ratios are only as accurate as the numbers in the numerator and denominator. Thus, it is crucial to begin with high-quality inputs. In later modules we explain adjusting the financial statements to ensure the quality of the numbers. We adjust the financial statement to exclude one-time events or transactions that will not persist and to include all assets and liabilities at proper amounts; both for purposes of increasing the quality of the ratio inputs. From the adjusted financials, we calculate ratios and then compare them to the ratios of competitors as well as to broader industry averages.

Apart from earnings per share (EPS), GAAP does not define ratios. Some ratios (such as current ratio) are universally defined but many more ratios have no unique, commonly accepted definition. For example, the debt to equity ratio is defined as either total liabilities to equity or as total debt (interest bearing liabilities) to equity. Similarly, measures such as free cash flow or EBITDA, which are inputs to ratio calculations, often have more than one definition. One version of free cash flow deducts capital expenditures from operating cash flow. Another version also deducts dividends paid. It is not possible to specify the "correct" way to compute ratios. The best advice is to know what is in the numerator and denominator of any particular ratio and then interpret the quotient accordingly.

Just as no two analysts compute ratios the same, there is little agreement about the best set of ratios to assess credit risk. For example, this module's Appendix shows a list of ratios (along with their definitions) that S&P and Moody's use to prepare credit ratings. The ratios are widely divergent and similar ratios are defined differently by the rating agencies.

For our purposes, we compute three classes of credit-risk ratios: profitability and coverage, liquidity, and solvency. Profitability and coverage ratios are called "flow" ratios because they include cash flow and income statement data. The liquidity and solvency ratios are called "stock" ratios because they use balance sheet numbers only. We use both flow and stock variables to assess credit risk.

Adjusted financial statements As a prelude to the analysis process, we analyze current and prior years' financial statements to be sure that they accurately reflect the company's financial condition and operating performance. Why? The answer resides in the fact that *general-purpose* financial statements prepared in conformity with GAAP do not always accurately reflect our estimate of the "true" financial condition and operating performance of the company. Accordingly, before we begin the analysis process, we analyze historical financial statements to be sure they reflect our estimate of the "true" financial condition of the company and consider adjustments when those reports are inconsistent with reality. Later modules assess

BUSINESS INSIGHT

Prior to its ratio analysis, S&P adjusts companies' balance sheets and income statements for the following:

- Operating leases
- Debt of joint ventures and unconsolidated subsidiaries
- Financial guarantees
- Take-or-pay contracts
- Factored, transferred, or securitized receivables
- Contingent liabilities

The table below shows some of the adjusted numbers S&P used for its credit analysis of Home Depot in 2010. For example, see that S&P adjusts Debt (column 1) to include $4,961 million of operating leases and $940.6 of other items including pension related obligations. We consider these topics in Module 9.

		Reconciliation of Home Depot Reported Amounts with Standard & Poor's Adjusted Amounts Fiscal year ended Jan. 31, 2010							
$ millions	Debt	Operating income (before D&A)	Operating income (before D&A)	Operating income (after D&A)	Interest expense	Cash flow from operations	Cash flow from operations	Capital expenditures
Reported...............	9,682.0	6,656.0	6,656.0	4,949.0	676.0	5,125.0	5,125.0	966.0
Standard & Poor's adjustments								
Operating leases	4,961.0	803.0	418.9	418.9	418.9	384.1	384.1	448.7
Additional items included in debt	940.6	—	—	—	—	—	—	—
Capitalized interest........	—	—	—	—	4.0	(4.0)	(4.0)	(4.0)
Share-based compensation expense..	—	—	201.0	—	—	—	—	—
Reclassification of nonoperating income (expenses)............	—	—	—	18.0	—	—	—	—
Reclassification of working-capital cash flow changes..........	—	—	—	—	—	—	(521.0)	—
Total adjustments........	5,901.6	803.0	619.9	436.9	422.9	380.1	(140.9)	444.7
Standard & Poor's adjusted amounts*	15,583.6	7,459.0	7,275.9	5,385.9	1,098.9	5,505.1	4,984.1	1,410.7
		[Operating income before D&A]*	[EBITDA]*	[EBIT]		[Cash flow from operations]*	[Funds from operations]*	

* Home Depot Inc. reported amounts are taken from financial statements but might include adjustments made by data providers or reclassifications made by Standard & Poor's analysts. Two reported amounts (operating income before D&A and cash flow from operations are used to derive more than one Standard & Poor's–adjusted amount (Operating income before D&A and EBITDA, and Cash flow from operations and Funds from operations, respectively). Consequently, the first section in some tables may feature duplicate descriptions and amounts.

the accounting and measurement of assets and liabilities, from which we will be able to make informed judgments about the adjustments necessary to reflect the true financial condition and performance of the company.[1]

Profitability analysis Profitability is related to credit risk because firms wish to pay interest and repay their debt with cash generated from profits. The more profitable the firm, the less likely it is to default on its debt. S&P's *Rating Methodology: Evaluating the Issuer* lays out an additional consideration, "a company that generates higher operating returns has a greater ability to generate equity capital internally, attract capital externally, and withstand business adversity. Earnings power ultimately attests to the value of the firm's assets as well." To this point, on August 30, 2011, Moody's upgraded Home Depot's rating to A3 from Baa1 because the rating agency was impressed by the company's strong operating performance during the second quarter. "Home Depot's significant improvement in its in-store shopping experience and supply chain will continue to benefit its earnings. The rating also reflects Home Depot's notably improved execution ability which has resulted in its comparable store sales out performing Lowe's for the past nine quarters." (Source: Moodys.com/research/Moodys-upgrades-Home-Depots-senior-unsecured-rating-to-A3—PR_225225.)

Module 3 describes in detail how to analyze a firm's profitability using return on net operating assets (RNOA) and its component parts: net operating profit margin (NOPM), which measures the profit earned on each dollar of sales; and net operating asset turnover (NOAT), which measures the efficiency of operating assets. This type of profitability analysis is applicable for credit analysis.

Home Depot's income statement for the year ended January 30, 2011, is in Exhibit 4.3. Home Depot's net operating profit after tax is $3,696 million, computed as $5,839 million − [$1,953 million + ($566 million × 36.7%)].

EXHIBIT 4.3	Income Statement for Home Depot			
HOME DEPOT				
Income Statement				
Fiscal Year Ended (in millions)		**January 30, 2011**	**January 31, 2010**	**February 1, 2009**
Net sales.		$67,997	$ 66,176	$71,288
Cost of sales.		44,693	43,764	47,298
Gross profit.		23,304	22,412	23,990
Operating expenses				
Selling, general and administrative		15,849	15,902	17,846
Depreciation and amortization.		1,616	1,707	1,785
Total operating expenses.		17,465	17,609	19,631
Operating income.		5,839	4,803	4,359
Interest expense and other, net		566	821	769
Earnings from continuing operations before provision for income taxes.		5,273	3,982	3,590
Provision for income taxes.		1,935	1,362	1,278
Earnings from continuing operations		3,338	2,620	2,312
Earnings (loss) from discontinued operations, net of tax.		—	41	(52)
Net earnings.		$ 3,338	$ 2,661	$ 2,260

Home Depot's net operating assets for 2011 and 2010, respectively, are $27,954 million and $27,621 million.[2] Thus, the company's RNOA for 2011 is 13.3%.[3] RNOA dropped sharply

---

[1] For simplicity, we compute ratios in this module using numbers reported instead of adjusted numbers. We also do this so that we can compare its ratios to other companies' ratios. An alternate, more exact, approach is to recompute all competitors' numbers and create adjusted industry-level ratios.
[2] 2011: ($40,125 million − $545 million − $139 million) − ($21,236 million − $1,042 million − $8,707 million). 2010: ($40,877 million − $1,421 million − $33 million) − ($21,484 million − $1,020 million − $8,662 million)
[3] $3,696 million/[($27,954 million + $27,621 million)/2]

after the fiscal year ended January 2008, after housing starts markedly slowed and the recession kicked in. Since then, profitability has steadily improved but has not returned to pre-recession levels.

Home Depot's return on equity (ROE) for 2011 was 17.4%.[4] Companies can effectively use debt to increase returns to shareholders. By comparing ROE and RNOA (see graphic below) we can see the power of this leverage. During 2011, Home Depot had a nonoperating return of 4.1% (17.4% − 13.3%) because the company borrowed money at an average, after-tax rate of 4% and invested it in profitable operating activities that earned 13.3%. Financial leverage (FLEV) measures companies' relative use of debt to equity. In 2011, Home Depot's FLEV was 0.45, computed as average FLEV for 2011 and 2010. For 2011, FLEV was 0.48: ($1,042 + $8,707 − $545 − $139)/$18,889; and for 2010, FLEV was 0.42: ($1,020 + $8,662 − $1,421 − $33)/$19,393). This means that for every dollar of equity, the company had $0.45 of net nonoperating obligations (primarily short and long-term debt). The higher the FLEV the greater the nonoperating return. However, as companies' debt increases (higher FLEV) so does the risk of default. Companies like Home Depot balance the benefit of leverage with this increased risk.

Ideally, numbers in the RNOA analysis are adjusted to better reflect a company's economic profitability. We exclude items that we expect will not persist to reveal a more accurate picture of the company's future profitability (as well as for liquidity, solvency, and cash flow). All ratios we compute in credit analysis should use these adjusted income statement items as inputs. An examination of Home Depot's income statement and footnotes reveals no material one-time charges.

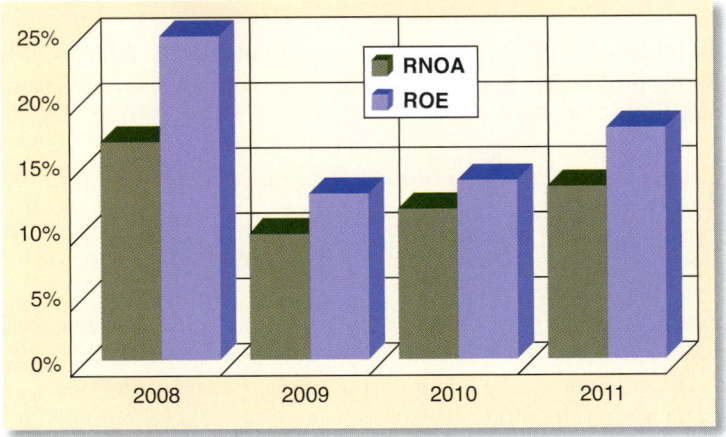

Coverage Analysis Coverage ratios compare operating profits or cash flows to interest and/or principal payments. We use coverage ratios along with RNOA and ROE, to assess the company's ability to generate profit and cash to cover the fixed charges from debt (interest and principal) in the short and long term.

Times interest earned The times interest earned ratio reflects the operating income available to pay interest expense and is defined as follows:

$$\text{Times interest earned} = \frac{\textbf{Earnings before interest and taxes}}{\textbf{Interest expense}}$$

The underlying assumption is that only interest must be paid because the principal will be refinanced. The numerator is similar to net operating profits after tax (NOPAT), but it is pretax instead of after tax. Management wants this ratio to be sufficiently high so that there is little risk of default. Home Depot's 2011 times interest earned ratio is 10.9 ($5,803 million/$530 million). The ratio was 7.0 in 2010 ($4,699 million/$676 million). The 2011 increase is a result of increased profitability coupled with a drop in interest expense.

---

[4] $3,338 million/[($19,393 million + $18,889 million)/2]

EBITDA Coverage Ratio

Earnings before interest, tax, depreciation and amortization (EBITDA) is a non-GAAP performance metric commonly used by analysts and investors. EBITDA coverage is defined as:

$$\text{EBITDA coverage} = \frac{\text{Earnings before tax} + \text{Interest expense, net} + \text{Depreciation} + \text{Amortization}}{\text{Interest expense}}$$

The ratio is similar to times interest earned ratio, but more widely used because depreciation does not require a cash outflow and, thus, more cash is available to "cover" fixed debt charges than GAAP earnings would convey. Other versions of the ratio add back only amortization, or include gross interest expense in the denominator. See the module's Appendix for a list of ratios used by ratings agencies. The EBITDA coverage ratio is always higher than times interest earned (because of the depreciation add back) but measures the same concept: the companies' ability to pay interest out of current profits. The graphic below compares Home Depot's times interest earned ratio to EBITDA coverage.

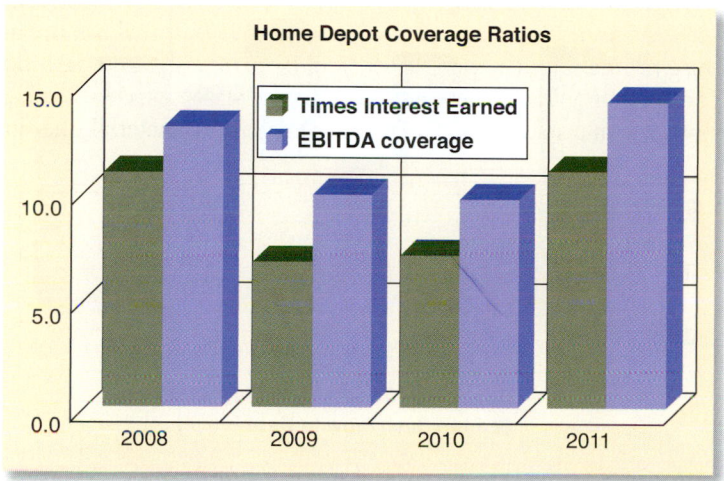

Cash from operations to total debt A company's liquidity depends critically on its ability to generate additional cash to cover debt payments as they come due. The times interest earned and EBITDA coverage ratios assume that the company needs to "cover" interest payments only each year because the principal owing will be refinanced. This is not always a valid assumption. To measure a company's ability to repay principal in the short and longer term, we can use the operating cash flow to total debt ratio. The ratio is defined as follows (related ratios exist that measure a company's ability to generate additional cash to short-term debt and long-term debt):

$$\text{Cash from operations to total debt} = \frac{\text{Cash from operations}}{\text{Short-term debt} + \text{Long-term debt}}$$

For the year ended January 30, 2011, **Home Depot**'s statement of cash flows reported cash from operations of $4,585 million. Home Depot's cash from operations to total debt ratio was 0.47 in 2011 ($4,585 million/[$1,042 million + $8,707 million]). This ratio hovers around 0.5 for Home Depot as the graphic on the next page shows.

Free operating cash flow to total debt Companies must replace tangible assets each year to continue operations. Any excess operating cash flow after cash spent on capital expenditures (CAPEX) is considered "free" cash flow in that the company is free to use the cash for other purposes including debt repayments. Some creditors use the following free cash flow measure as another coverage ratio.

$$\text{Free operating cash flow to total debt} = \frac{\text{Cash from operations} - \text{CAPEX}}{\text{Short-term debt} + \text{Long-term debt}}$$

The free operating cash flow to total debt ratio is argued to reflect a company's ability to repay debt from the cash flows remaining after CAPEX. For the year ended January 30, 2011, **Home Depot**'s statement of cash flows reported cash spent for capital expenditures of $1,096 million. Thus, its free operating cash flow to total debt ratio is 0.36 in 2011 ([$4,585 million − $1,096 million]/[$1,042 million + $8,707 million]). This ratio was higher in 2011 and 2010 compared to the two prior years (see graphic below). This increase has two drivers: (1) Home Depot's CAPEX was much higher before the recession of 2008–09, and (2) the company had more debt in prior years.

There are many variations of liquidity, solvency, and coverage ratios. The basic idea is to construct measures that reflect a company's credit risk exposure. There is not one "best" financial ratio. Instead, as financial statement users, we want to use measures that capture the risk we are most concerned with. It is also important to compute the ratios ourselves to ensure we know what is included and excluded from each ratio.

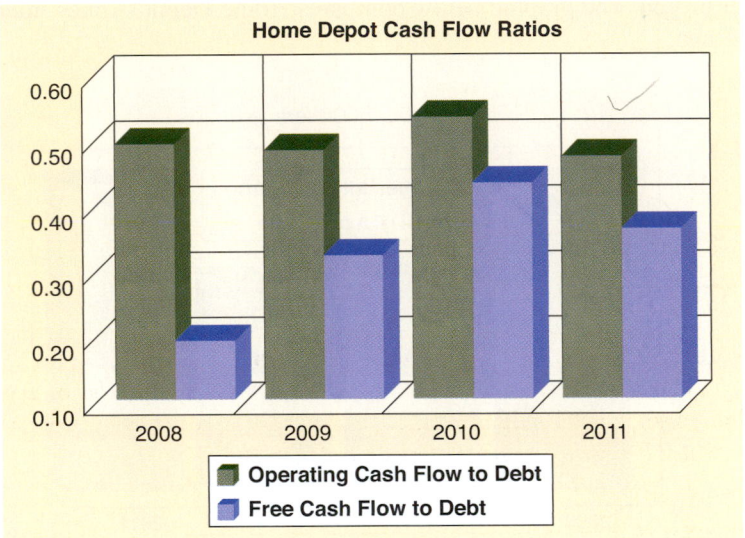

Liquidity Analysis Liquidity refers to cash availability: how much cash a company has, and how much it can generate on short notice. In this section, we discuss several of the most common liquidity measures: the current ratio, working capital, and the quick ratio.[5]

Current Ratio Current assets are assets that a company expects to convert into cash within the next operating cycle, which is typically a year. Current liabilities are those liabilities that come due within the next year. An excess of current assets over current liabilities (Current assets − Current liabilities), is known as net working capital or simply working capital. Positive working capital implies more expected cash inflows than cash outflows in the short run. The current ratio expresses working capital as a ratio and is computed as follows:

$$\text{Current ratio} = \frac{\text{Current assets}}{\text{Current liabilities}}$$

Positive working capital or a current ratio greater than 1.0 both imply more expected cash inflows than cash outflows in the short run. Generally, companies prefer a higher current ratio (more working capital); however, an excessively high current ratio can indicate inefficient asset use. A current ratio less than 1.0 (negative working capital) is not always a bad sign. For example, retailers carry inventory that is about the same value as accounts payable and, thus, working capital is near zero. If the inventory is sold as anticipated, sufficient cash will be generated to pay current liabilities. Other companies are especially efficient at managing working capital by minimizing

---

[5] For simplicity, we compute ratios in this module using numbers reported instead of adjusted numbers. We also do this so that we can compare its ratios to other companies' ratios. An alternate, more exact, approach is to recompute all competitors' numbers and create adjusted industry-level ratios.

receivables and inventories and maximizing payables. **Dell** is the classic example of an efficient manufacturer with little to no working capital.

In 2011, **Home Depot**'s current ratio was 1.33 and it has fluctuated within a range of 1.15 to 1.34 over the previous three years, as shown in the graphic. Home Depot is a cash-and-carry business and, thus, we do not expect its current ratio to be as high as companies that carry a high level of receivables. Given that its current ratio exceeds 1.0, Home Depot seems reasonably liquid.

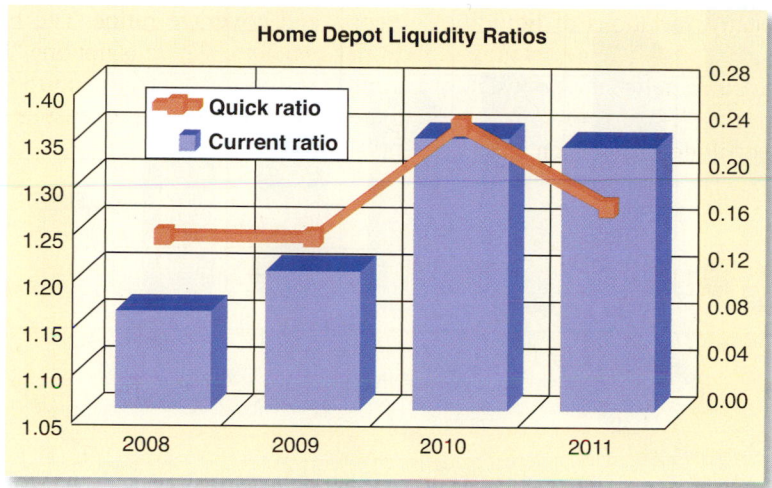

Quick Ratio The quick ratio is a variant of the current ratio. It focuses on quick assets, which are those assets likely to be converted to cash within a relatively short period of time. Specifically, quick assets include cash, marketable securities, and accounts receivable; they exclude inventories and prepaid assets. The quick ratio is defined as follows:

$$\text{Quick ratio} = \frac{\text{Cash} + \text{Marketable securities} + \text{Accounts receivables}}{\text{Current liabilities}}$$

The quick ratio gauges a company's ability to meet its current liabilities without liquidating inventories that could require markdowns. It is a more stringent test of liquidity than the current ratio. **Home Depot**'s 2011 quick ratio is 0.16, computed as ($545 million + $1,085 million)/$10,122 million. It is not uncommon for a company's quick ratio to be less than 1.0. Home Depot's 2011 quick ratio is lower than in 2010 but higher than the previous two years, as the graphic shows. This is due to higher accounts receivable but less cash in 2011 compared to 2010. In 2011, the current ratio remains about the same as the prior year but the quick ratio drops. This signals a potential buildup in inventory, which is something financial statement users should monitor.

Solvency Analysis Long-term **solvency** analysis considers a company's ability to meet its debt obligations, including both periodic interest payments and the repayment of the principal amount borrowed. The general approach to measuring solvency is to assess the level of liabilities relative to equity. There are a variety of ratios used to gauge solvency; all use balance sheet data and assess the proportion of capital raised from creditors. We discuss two solvency ratios: liabilities-to-equity and long-term debt to total capital.

Note: Debt is normally a less costly source of financing vis-á-vis equity financing. Although less costly, debt carries default risk: the risk that a company is unable to repay debt principal and interest when it comes due.

Liabilities-to-Equity The liabilities-to-equity ratio is defined as follows:

$$\text{Liabilities-to-equity ratio} = \frac{\text{Total liabilities}}{\text{Stockholders' equity}}$$

This ratio conveys how reliant a company is on creditor financing compared with equity financing. A higher ratio indicates a less solvent company. The median ratio of total liabilities-to-equity is slightly less than 1.0 for publicly traded companies. This means that the average company is financed with about half debt and half equity. However, the relative use of debt varies considerably across industries as illustrated in Exhibit 4.4.

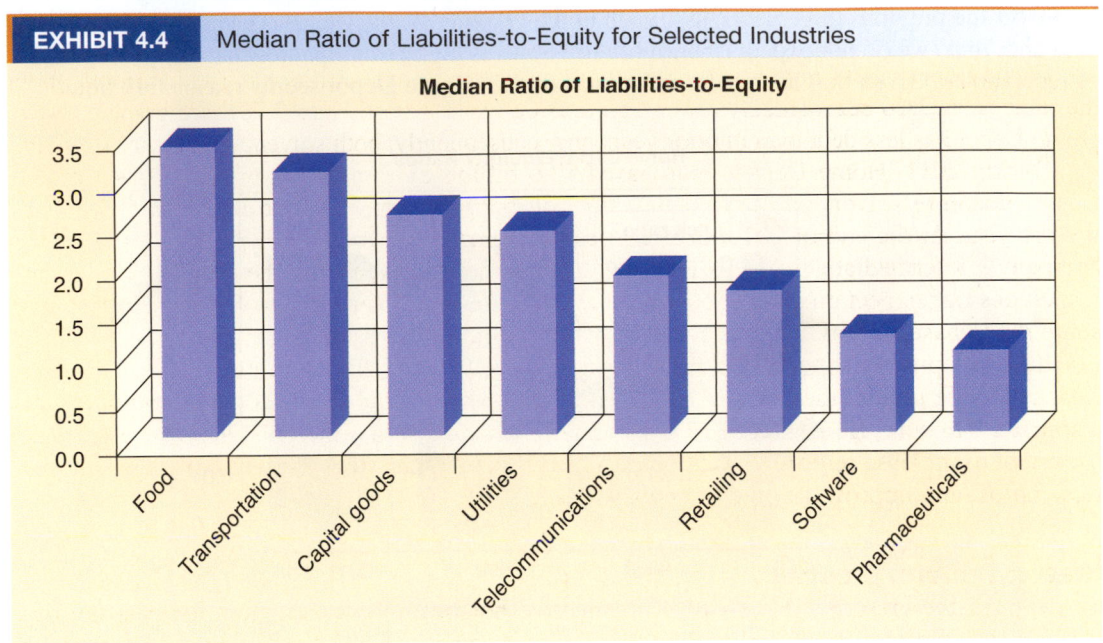

EXHIBIT 4.4   Median Ratio of Liabilities-to-Equity for Selected Industries

Companies in the food, transportation, capital goods, and utilities industries have among the highest proportions of debt. Because the utilities industry is regulated, profits and cash flows are relatively certain and stable and, as a result, utility companies can support a higher debt level. The other three industries also utilize a relatively high proportion of debt. However, these industries are not regulated and their markets are more competitive and volatile. Consequently, their use of debt carries more risk. At the lower end of debt financing are software firms whose profits and cash flows can be very uncertain; and pharmaceutical firms whose persistently high profits and cash flows reduce the need for debt financing.

Home Depot's total liabilities-to-equity ratio is 1.12 in 2011 ($21,236 million/$18,889 million), a marked drop from 1.5 in 2008—see graphic below. Home Depot's ratio is much lower than the average for retailing firms (1.5) and just slightly above 1.0, the average for publicly traded companies.

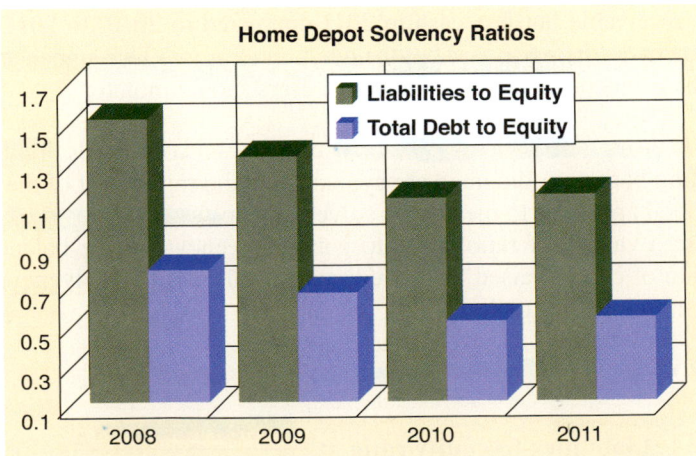

Total debt-to-equity A drawback of the liabilities-to-equity ratio is that it does not distinguish between operating creditors (such as accounts payable) and debt obligations. We can refine our analysis with a solvency ratio such as follows:

$$\text{Total debt-to-equity} = \frac{\text{Long-term debt including current portion + Short-term debt}}{\text{Stockholders' equity}}$$

This solvency ratio assumes that current operating liabilities will be repaid from current assets (so-called self-liquidating) such that lenders should focus on the relative proportions of debt and equity. (Variations of this ratio include only long-term debt in the numerator and/or total capital in the denominator; these solvency ratios differ in their exact definitions but all assess the company's capital structure and measure the relative debt load.)

Home Depot's 2011 ratio was 0.52 [($1,042 million + $8,707 million)/$18,889 million] about the same as in 2010 but markedly lower than in 2008 when the ratio was 0.76—see graphic above. Home Depot has less debt than in prior years and, consequently, both solvency ratios are stronger.

During 2011, Home Depot repurchased $2.6 billion of common stock. The effect of this was to decrease solvency but only by a fraction because Home Depot also repaid debt during the year. At the end of 2010, S&P addressed Home Depot's stock buybacks, saying, "The company's intermediate financial risk profile is somewhat weak for the 'BBB+' rating, and it includes our expectation that leverage will increase due potentially to future debt-financed share repurchase activity. As of Aug. 1, 2010, we estimate the company could add about $3 billion debt to repurchase shares and remain below 2.5x leverage. We currently believe such debt-financed share repurchases would only occur when the company believes the environment has stabilized." In sum, Home Depot's ratio analysis reveals a profitable company that effectively uses debt to increase returns to shareholders, a company with strengthening coverage and cash flow ratios, and improved liquidity and solvency.

Step 4: Perform prospective analysis

To evaluate the creditworthiness of a prospective borrower, creditors must forecast the borrower's cash flows to estimate its ability to repay its obligations. To effectively look forward, we first must look back. That is, the forecasting process begins by adjusting current and prior years' financial statements so that they accurately reflect the company's financial condition and performance. Once we have adjusted the historical results (see Step 3), we are ready to forecast future results.

In Module 11, we explain how to project financial statements. The forecasting process discussed in Module 11 applies to credit analysis as well as to equity valuation. In particular, projected cash flows are especially critical because a company must have sufficient cash in the future to repay debts as they mature and to service those debts along the way. The projected financials should adjust the capital structure to reflect anticipated future debt retirements as they come due over the forecast horizon. Once we have the projected financials, we can compute the ratios we described above (regarding profitability, liquidity, solvency, and coverage) and evaluate changes or trends.

MID-MODULE REVIEW 2

Refer to the fiscal 2011 income statement and balance sheet of **Lowe's Companies, Inc.**, below.

LOWE'S COMPANIES, INC. Income Statement (In millions) For Fiscal Year Ended January 28, 2011	
Net sales.	$48,815
Cost of sales.	31,663
Gross margin	17,152
Selling, general and administrative expense	12,006
Depreciation.	1,586
Interest	332
Total expenses.	13,924
Pretax earnings	3,228
Income tax provision	1,218
Net earnings.	$ 2,010

LOWE'S COMPANIES, INC.
Balance Sheet

(In millions, except par value)	January 28, 2011	January 29, 2010
Assets		
Cash and cash equivalents	$ 652	$ 632
Short-term investments	471	425
Merchandise inventory, net	8,321	8,249
Deferred income taxes, net	193	208
Other current assets	330	218
Total current assets	9,967	9,732
Property, less accumulated depreciation	22,089	22,499
Long-term investments	1,008	277
Other assets	635	497
Total assets	$33,699	$33,005
Liabilities and Shareholders' Equity		
Current maturities of long-term debt	$ 36	$ 552
Accounts payable	4,351	4,287
Accrued compensation and employee benefits	667	577
Deferred revenue	707	683
Other current liabilities	1,358	1,256
Total current liabilities	7,119	7,355
Long-term debt, excluding current maturities	6,537	4,528
Deferred income taxes, net	467	598
Deferred revenue—extended protection plans	631	549
Other liabilities	833	906
Total liabilities	15,587	13,936
Shareholders' equity		
Preferred stock—$5 par value, none issued	—	—
Common stock—$.50 par value; shares issued and outstanding, 2011: 1,354; 2010: 1,459	677	729
Capital in excess of par value	11	6
Retained earnings	17,371	18,307
Accumulated other comprehensive income	53	27
Total shareholders' equity	18,112	19,069
Total liabilities and shareholders' equity	$33,699	$33,005

Required

Compute the following liquidity, solvency, and coverage ratios for Lowe's Companies. Interpret and assess these ratios for Lowe's relative to those previously computed for Home Depot in our text. For 2011, Lowe's statement of cash flows reported cash from operations of $3,852 million and capital expenditures of $1,329 million. Assume Lowe's marginal tax rate is 35%.

1. Return on net operating assets
2. Return on equity
3. Times interest earned
4. EBITDA coverage
5. Operating cash flow to debt
6. Free cash flow to debt
7. Current ratio
8. Quick ratio
9. Liabilities-to-equity ratio
10. Total debt-to-equity ratio

The solution is on page 4-46.

Loss Given Default

Recall that the main purpose of credit risk analysis is to quantify potential credit losses so that credit decisions are made with full information. Expected credit losses are the product of two factors, the chance of default and the size of the loss given a default. The previous section discussed how to analyze financial information to determine the chance of default. In this section, we consider the factors that affect the amount that could be lost if the company defaulted on its obligations, referred to as **loss given default**.

When a company defaults on its obligations (such as failing to make payments or violating loan covenants), creditors seek to claim the remaining assets owed. A creditor's potential loss depends on the priority of the claim compared with all other existing claims. Laws and private contracts determine the order of repayment among all the creditors. Companies must repay senior claims first and the U.S. Bankruptcy Code specifies the priority of other claims. If a company is in default, it is likely that it has fully drawn on lines of credit. This means that it has no means to raise additional cash. For low priority claims (called junior claims), a conservative approach to estimating the potential loss would be to assume that the entire amount will be lost.

One way to minimize potential loss is to structure credit terms for the loan in advance. These credit terms include (1) credit limits, (2) collateral, (3) repayment terms, and (4) covenants to limit the loss in the event of default. This section focuses on each of these four credit terms. It is important to understand the relation between the likelihood of default (as assessed by the analysis above) and credit terms: the higher the chance of default, the stricter the credit terms a lender will impose. For example, if long-term solvency is in question, a lender might structure repayment terms so that the loan is repaid in the short term. However, there is a trade-off, the lender does not want to set credit terms so strict that the terms themselves cause the borrower to default. In general, trade creditors, banks, and other lenders follow standard operating procedures that provide guidelines on credit terms.

BUSINESS INSIGHT | **Quantifying 'Loss Given Default'**

Loss-given-default assessments can be expressed as a percent of principal and any accrued interest that will likely be recouped. For example, **Moody's** assigns a loss-given-default (LGD) rating for each bond issue it rates, using the following scale. (Source: *Moody's Approach to Global Standard Adjustments in the Analysis of Financial Statements for Non-Financial Corporations.*)

Rating	Loss range		Rating	Loss range
LGD1	≥ 0% and < 10%		LGD4	≥50% and > 70%
LGD2	≥10% and < 30%		LGD5	≥70% and < 90%
LGD3	≥30% and < 50%		LGD6	≥90% and ≤100%

Credit limits A **credit limit** is the maximum that a creditor will allow a customer to owe at any point in time. These limits are set based on the lender's experience with similar borrowers as well as firm-specific credit analysis. Some view a credit limit as the maximum amount that a creditor is willing to lose to the customer. By carefully setting credit limits, creditors can minimize their loss in the event of default, which limits credit risk.

Trade creditors commonly set low credit limits for new customers and higher limits for customers with repayment histories. The Bankruptcy Abuse and Consumer Protection Act (2005) offers some protection to ordinary trade creditors. The Act provides that accounts payable for goods shipped to a customer within 20 days before the bankruptcy have a higher priority for payment. This reduces the size of a loss but trade creditors must monitor its customers for signs of bankruptcy and act quickly to limit potential losses.

Banks set credit limits on revolving lines of credit. Banks commonly specify that the credit line will be reduced in size if the customer's credit rating falls (see covenants below). This serves to limit potential losses. In the year ended January 2011, **Home Depot** maintained a $2 billion credit facility with a consortium of banks.

Collateral   To minimize the loss in the event of default, creditors often secure their transaction by taking collateral. **Collateral** is property that the borrower pledges to guarantee repayment. Creditors take real and personal property as collateral.[6] One of the most common forms of collateral is a real estate mortgage, which is typically long-term debt and thus requires substantial collateral (land, buildings, and improvements) to reduce the lender's extended-duration risk. Banks and other creditors take marketable securities, accounts receivable, inventory, and other personal property as collateral. The best collateral is high-grade property such as securities with an active market because the value is known and liquidation is straightforward.

Before taking property as collateral, potential creditors should investigate prior liens. The Uniform Commercial Code (UCC) helps creditors in these investigations. Under the UCC, states have created registry systems that track real and personal property pledged as collateral. (The UCC is a uniform set of rules that govern commercial transactions such as leases, banking transactions, and collateral taken in secured transactions; a uniform set of rules is important especially for transactions across state lines.)

Creditors that take collateral often file a UCC "financing statement," which publicly notifies others that the creditor has a claim (called a security interest) in the debtor's property (the collateral). The financing statement lets the creditor establish priority over the collateral in the event the business owner files for bankruptcy or becomes insolvent. This sort of registry is particularly effective for personal property that is highly mobile, such as automobiles, aircraft, and mobile homes, because ownership transfers of this sort of personal property must also be registered with government agencies (such as departments of motor vehicles). Thus, the creditor's secured interest and the sale or transfer of the collateral are both matters of public record. A full credit analysis should include an assessment of the number of existing liens already in effect for the debtor.

The Bankruptcy Abuse and Consumer Protection Act (2005) offers some protection to ordinary trade creditors who do not routinely take collateral. This Act provides that the seller can reclaim goods shipped within 45 days before bankruptcy to settle an unpaid balance. Any remaining balance is considered a general senior unsecured claim. These protections reduce the size of a loss but creditors must be aware of any bankrupt customers and act quickly to limit potential losses.

In assessing the loss-given-default, collateral will limit the amount of the loss but amounts owing in excess of the fair-value of the collateral will be lost. Moreover, given a default, the time and costs incurred to gain control of and liquidate collateral can be substantial. Thus, even with high-quality collateral, credit risk remains in credit or loan arrangements.

Repayment term   The "term" of a loan refers to the length of time the creditor has to repay the debt. Trade creditors implement time as part of their credit policies and often offer early payment discounts to control the credit risk. Bank and nonbank financing can be either long-term or short-term but the nature of the loan influences the **repayment terms**. Lenders will ordinarily want to match the length of the loan to the useful life of the asset, the period over which the asset generates cash flows. Companies use long-term debt to purchase or improve long-term fixed assets (property, plant facilities and equipment). Short-term debt is often used to raise cash for cyclical inventory needs, accounts payable, and working capital. To assess the loss given default, analysts consider the match between asset lives and liability terms. Also, it is generally the case that interest rates on long-term debt are higher than short-term rates. Thus, the repayment term affects the cost of debt. This is another example of the risk and reward trade-off. The longer the term, the higher the chance of default, the greater the credit risk. To compensate for this increased risk, creditors require a higher return.

Covenants   **Covenants** are terms and conditions of a loan designed to limit the loss given default and thereby control credit risk after the loan is made. In short, lenders add covenants to

---

[6] *Real property* is land and anything built or growing on the land. *Personal property* is any property that is not real property. The distinction between the two types can be confusing because property can be changed from real to personal (for example, agricultural crops are real property until harvested) and from personal to real (for example, lumber is personal property until it is used to construct a building). Fixtures are a special type of personal property—fixtures are firmly attached to real property but can be removed without impairing the real property.

maintain loan quality; that is, to ensure adequate cash flow from the loan (interest and principal payments). Loan covenants can help the lender *detect* deteriorating loan quality as covenants allow the lender to monitor the loan and receive early warnings when borrowers run into financial trouble. Loan covenants can also *prevent* deteriorating loan quality by limiting the borrower's behavior to avoid situations leading to financial trouble. If a borrower violates one or more covenants, the lender can consider the loan in default and change the loan pricing (increase the interest rate) or alter the repayment terms. In the extreme, the lender can demand repayment in full. Weaker borrowers are riskier and their loan covenants would likely be more restrictive. There are three types of common loan covenants.

Covenants that require the borrower to take certain actions Lenders often require that borrowers take certain actions to help the lender monitor the loan quality and to ensure that the borrower continues to operate smoothly and repay the loan in the event of loss of the original collateral or of indispensable owners or managers. Borrowers are often required to:

- Submit financial statements at least annually (or more frequently for riskier borrowers); a variant of this covenant relates to loans collateralized by accounts receivable when the borrower is often required to submit monthly aging schedules for its receivables.
- Maintain hazard and content insurance on inventory, plant, and equipment.
- Pay all taxes and other required operating fees and licenses.
- Avoid any private or governmental liens on the property.

Covenants that restrict the borrower from taking certain actions The lender might use loan covenants to prevent the borrower from taking certain actions unless the lender gives prior approval. Commonly restricted actions include:

- Changing the management team
- Increasing dividends, owners' withdrawals, and management salaries
- Making major investments or capital expenditures
- Merging with or acquiring other entities
- Taking on additional loans or debt to ensure that the borrower does not diminish the quality of the original loan

Covenants that require the borrower to maintain specific financial conditions Lenders often require borrowers to maintain certain levels in key financial ratios such as:

- Minimum working capital, current ratio, or quick ratio (to ensure ongoing liquidity)
- Minimum return on assets or return on equity (to give the lender an early warning and allow the lender to call the loan before financial troubles grow)
- Minimum equity (to limit treasury stock repurchases that would erode firm equity)
- Maximum debt-to-equity or debt-to-assets (to limit the borrower's leverage and ensure long-term solvency)

Companies rarely disclose details about their loan covenants. For example, Home Depot reports the following in footnotes to the financial statements: "The credit facility expires in July 2013 and contains various restrictive covenants. As of January 30, 2011, we were in compliance with all of the covenants, and they are not expected to impact our liquidity or capital resources."

CREDIT RATINGS

LO4 Describe the credit rating process and explain why companies are interested in their credit ratings.

A credit rating is an opinion of an entity's creditworthiness. The rating captures the entity's ability to meet its financial commitments as they come due. In the U.S., a number of firms provide credit ratings and each firm has its own unique method to arrive at a rating. But the credit analysis methods they apply are similar: credit analysts at the rating agencies evaluate financial and nonfinancial data in a manner explained in this module. The analysts consider macroeconomic, industry, and firm-specific information to assess both the chance of default and the ultimate payment in the event of default. Analysts calculate ratios and consider credit terms, such as collateral security and subordination. In the end, they arrive at a rating from their analysis that reflects both the likelihood of default and any financial loss suffered in the event of default.

Credit rating agencies provide ratings on both debt issues and issuers. An issue rating is an opinion about whether a particular debt security will be repaid. The types of debt securities that the rating agencies cover is broad and consists of a wide variety of other debt issues including debentures, asset-backed and mortgage-backed securities, convertible bonds, short-term bonds, medium-term notes, preferred stock, and derivative securities. The credit agencies also provide ratings for specific debt issuers. An issuer rating is a comprehensive opinion of an entity's ability to meet obligations. Agencies provide issuer ratings for corporate families, sovereign nations, municipalities, other public finance issuers, and derivative instrument counterparties.

In early 2006, **Home Depot**'s credit ratings were strong. Moody's long-term rating was Aa3 for Home Depot and S&P's short-term rating was A1+. Both agencies opined that the company was high-grade. However, within two years, both agencies had changed their outlook to "negative" citing recent acquisitions and the deterioration of credit quality resulting from higher financial leverage and decreasing profitability. Much of this was due to the severe drop off in home construction and renovation during the credit crisis of 2008. However, during 2010 and 2011, business began to rebound and by the end of 2011, Home Depot's long-term bond ratings were medium grade: A3 (from Moody's) and A− (from S&P and Fitch).

BUSINESS INSIGHT   **Credit Ratings**

Each rating agency has its own scale to communicate its opinion about the chance of default. The two best-known and most influential rating agencies are **Standard and Poor's** (S&P) and **Moody's Investor Services**. The following summarizes these agencies' long-term issue rating scales. The Appendix discusses the two companies' rating scales in more detail.

	Standard and Poor's	**Moody's**
Investment Grade	AAA, AA: High credit-quality A, BBB: Medium credit-quality	Aaa: Highest rating Aa1, Aa2, Aa3: High-grade A1, A2, A3: Upper-medium grade Baa1, Baa2, Baa3: Medium grade
Non-investment grade	BB, B, CCC, CC: Low credit-quality D: Bonds in default for non-payment of principal and/or interest	Ba1, Ba2, Ba3: speculative elements B1, B2, B3: subject to high credit risk Caa1, Caa2, Caa3: bonds of poor standing Ca: highly speculative, or near default C: lowest rating, typically in default, little prospect for recovery of principal or interest

---

Why Companies Care About Their Credit Rating

Credit rating agencies play an important role in credit markets because they help investors analyze credit risk. But why should companies care about their own credit ratings? There are two main reasons.

First, credit ratings affect the cost of debt. Recall that the cost of debt is the market rate of interest, which is defined as the risk-free rate (the yield on U.S. Government borrowings with maturity that matches the company's own debt), plus a risk premium (also called a spread). The risk premium for a company depends on the company's credit risk which is directly linked to the company's credit rating: riskier bonds have a larger risk premium. This risk premium can be large. For example, in 2005, **Ford Credit Corporation**'s credit ratings deteriorated and its unsecured long-term debt risk premium grew from 165 to 660 basis points. This cost the company millions of dollars in additional interest expense. Exhibit 4.5 shows the yield on risk-free bonds (Treasury bonds), the yield on bonds with Moody's highest credit rating (Aaa), and the yield on bonds with a lower credit rating (Baa).

| **EXHIBIT 4.5** | Treasury and Corporate 10-Year Bond Yields 2000–2010 |

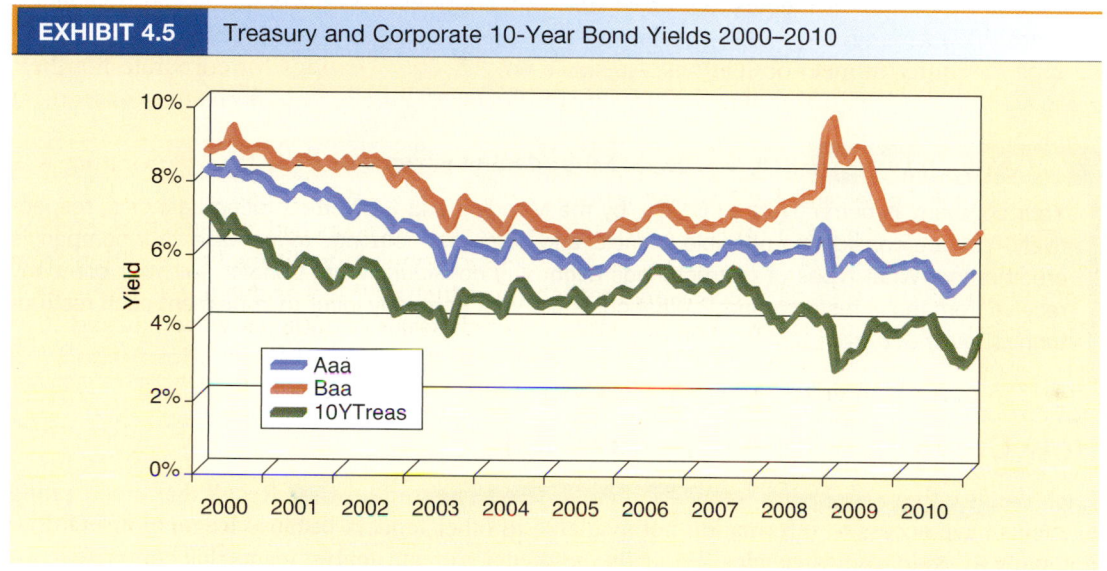

These yields increase (shift upwards) as debt quality moves from Treasury securities (generally considered to be risk free), which is the highest-quality debt reflected in the line nearest to zero, to the Aaa (highest) rated corporates and, finally, to the Baa (lower-rated) corporates. That is, higher credit-rated issuers warrant a lower rate than lower credit-rated issuers. This difference is substantial. For example, in late 2011, the average 10-year Treasury bond yield is 2.17%, while the Aaa corporate bond yield is 2.72% and the average Baa yield is 5.25%.

Higher cost of debt not only increases interest expense, it could limit the number of new investment projects. With a higher cost of debt, some new projects might not yield a return greater than their financing cost. Thus, a decrease in credit rating can restrict a company's growth and future profitability. Although credit ratings are only opinions, they are influential.

To understand the second reason companies care about their credit ratings, we see that both S&P and Moody's provide ratings for "investment grade" bonds versus "non-investment grade" bonds (also called speculative bonds or junk bonds). This is an important distinction for companies because many investors will not, or cannot, purchase non-investment grade bonds. For example, **CALPERS**, the largest pension fund in the country, is prohibited by their board of directors from holding bonds with an S&P rating less than BBB. Companies seek large institutional investors such as CALPERS because they trade more carefully and less frequently than individual investors and liquidity traders. Thus, companies are extremely averse to falling from investment to non-investment grade.

Evidence suggests that companies try to maintain investment grade bond ratings. Following is a graph of the distribution of companies across bond ratings. Ratings of A and Baa account for nearly half of all corporate issuers while those issuers in the top ratings categories (Aaa and Aa) account for 14% of corporate issuers (source: *Moody's Financial Metrics 2010*).

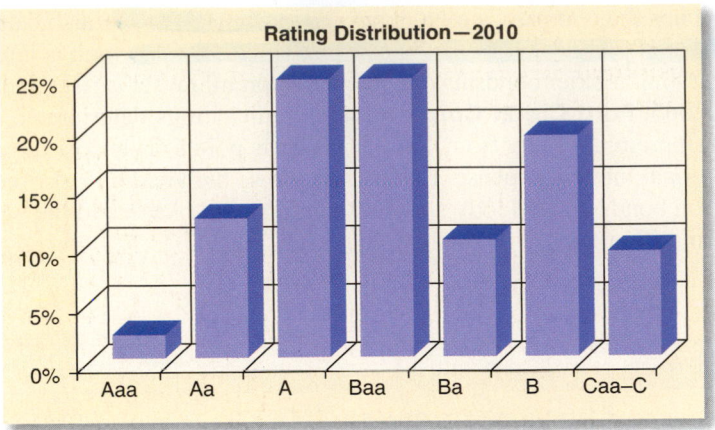

How Credit Ratings Are Determined

Each credit rating agency has its own unique approach to credit rating. Recall that credit rating agencies have access to information not available to other lenders because Regulation FD does not apply to credit rating agencies. Typically the agencies create analyst teams that comprise a primary analyst (team leader) and other analysts and specialists. During the rating process, members of this team often meet face to face with managers of the company being rated. Such meetings can provide insight into managers' expectations about future demand and industry conditions as well as detailed information on operating and investment plans.

Each rating agency has its own proprietary, analytical models and methodologies but these models all include at least three types of inputs: macroeconomic statistics, industry data, and company specific information. It should not be surprising that credit rating agencies employ macroeconomists as economy-wide changes can have a considerable impact on the financial position of individual companies. These economists monitor unemployment statistics, consumer confidence metrics, Federal Reserve Bank announcements (about interest rates and adjustments), regulatory pronouncements, and related events. These macroeconomic events are common across individual issue and issuer ratings.

The analyst team analyzes industry level data in a manner as previously discussed. Each rating agency tailors existing frameworks (such as Porter's five forces or a SWOT analysis) and augments their analysis with in-house quantitative (statistical) models. The agencies have industry experts; that is, analysts who have deep understanding of particular industries.

The analyst team gathers financial statement data to compute and analyze financial ratios such as those we described earlier. A list of the ratios that S&P uses, together with median averages for various risk classes, is in Exhibit 4.6. In examining the ratios, recall that debt is increasingly more risky as we move from the first row Aaa, to the last, C.

The team also seeks firm-specific qualitative information such as the company's history, executives' reputation, number of employees, corporate governance structure, employee turnover, and customer satisfaction. As part of this evaluation, analysts do on-site visits and speak directly with managers and executives. Importantly, the analyst team must determine whether and how historic company-specific information will change in the future. After all, credit ratings are forward-looking assessments of a company's ability to make timely debt payments. To that end, analysts project financial statements and ratios under a number of scenarios and perform sensitivity analysis on their numbers.

EXHIBIT 4.6	Ratio Values for Different Risk Classes of Corporate Debt*

	EBITA/ Average Assets	Operating Margin	EBITA Margin	EBITA/ Interest Expense	(FFO + IntExp) / IntExp	Debt/ EBITDA	Debt/Book Capitalization	FFO/Debt	Retained cash Flow/Net Debt	CAPEX/ Depreciation
Aaa.....	20.6%	22.8%	24.9%	25.6	23.8	0.7	20.7%	129.5%	83.2%	1.2
Aa......	12.6%	20.5%	21.6%	12.5	13.6	1.6	39.3%	51.8%	39.4%	1.2
A.......	11.8%	14.9%	15.0%	7.5	8.3	1.9	43.7%	40.2%	30.7%	1.0
Baa.....	9.0%	12.4%	13.1%	4.4	6.1	2.7	45.4%	27.4%	26.6%	1.1
Ba......	8.3%	10.9%	12.4%	3.1	4.5	3.3	50.8%	22.3%	23.5%	1.1
B.......	6.6%	7.8%	9.1%	1.4	2.6	5.1	73.8%	11.7%	11.6%	0.9
C.......	2.3%	3.1%	2.8%	0.4	1.4	7.7	100.5%	3.1%	3.2%	0.7

*Table reports 2010 median values; from Moody's Financial Metrics™, Key Ratios by rating and industry for North American nonfinancial corporations: December 2010 (reproduced with permission). See Appendix for ratio definitions; approximate definitions are shown below for convenience.

Ratio	Definition
EBITA/Average Assets	EBITA/Average of Current and Previous Year Assets
EBITA/Interest Expense	EBITA/Interest Expense
EBITA Margin	EBITA/Net Revenue
Operating Margin	Operating Profit/Net Revenue
(FFO + Interest Exp)/Interest Exp	(Funds From Operations + Interest Expense)/Interest Expense
FFO/Debt	Funds From Operations/(Short-Term Debt + Long-Term Debt)
RCF/Debt	(FFO − Preferred Dividends − Common Dividends − Minority Dividends)/(Short-Term Debt + Long-Term Debt)
Debt/EBITDA	(Short-Term Debt + Long-Term Debt)/EBITDA
Debt/Book Capitalization	(Short-Term Debt + Long-Term Debt)/(Short-Term Debt + Long-Term Debt + Deferred Taxes + Minority Interest + Book Equity)
CAPEX/Depreciation Exp	Capital expenditures/Depreciation Expense

where: EBITA = Earnings from continuing operations before interest, taxes, and amortization
        EBITDA = Earnings from continuing operations before interest and taxes, depreciation, and amortization
        FFO = Net income from continuing operations plus depreciation, amortization, deferred income taxes, and other noncash items

The analyst team completes its analysis and then presents its findings and recommendations to a rating committee that reviews the team's work. In the end, it is these rating committees that decide the final rating (or rating outcome) for debt issues and issuers. The next step is for the rating agency to inform the issuer of the rating committee's decision. In some cases, issuers disagree with the rating and agencies have procedures for handling appeals. The agency releases ratings via press release and on their Web pages. The analyst team monitors ongoing developments and provides periodic updates about issues and issuers.

BUSINESS INSIGHT	Moody's Approach to Credit Ratings

Moody's applies a holistic approach to credit ratings, which is described from excerpts on its Website as follows [www.Moodys.com/Moodys/cust/AboutMoodys/AboutMoodys.aspx?topic5Rapproach].

Emphasis on the Qualitative: Moody's ratings are not based on a defined set of financial ratios or rigid computer models. Rather, they are the product of a comprehensive analysis of each individual issue and issuer by experienced, well-informed, impartial credit analysts.

Focus on the Long-Term: Since Moody's ratings are intended to measure long-term risk, our analytical focus is on fundamental factors that will drive each issuer's long-term ability to meet debt payments, such as a change in management strategy or regulatory trends. As a rule of thumb, we are looking through the next economic cycle or longer.

Global Consistency: Our analytical team approach also supports consistency by including Moody's directors, along with global industry specialists and analysts with regional and other perspectives, in every rating decision.

Level and Predictability of Cash Flow: Our main emphasis throughout the rating analysis is on understanding strategic factors likely to support future cash flow, while identifying critical factors that will inhibit future cash flow. The issuer's capacity to respond favorably to uncertainty is also key. Generally, the greater the predictability of an issuer's cash flow and the larger the cushion supporting anticipated debt payments, the higher the rating will be.

Common across all rating agencies, is that the rated organizations (corporations, municipalities, sovereign nations) pay the credit rating agencies for a rating. Conceivably this could create a lack of independence or other conflicts of interest. Indeed, credit rating agencies came under attack in the wake of the accounting scandals during the dot com crisis. Critics claimed that the major rating agencies failed investors by not providing reliable ratings on **Enron**, **WorldCom**, and other companies that eventually went bankrupt. Agencies were also cited for abuses including failing to provide timely ratings downgrades, billing companies for unsolicited ratings, and bundling ratings with additional (potentially more lucrative) services. The agencies defended themselves (and the Courts agreed) on the grounds that ratings are merely opinions and thus, protected under the First amendment.

The Credit Rating Agency Reform Act of 2006 established a registration system for credit rating agencies. Under this law, credit rating agencies with three years of experience are allowed to register with the SEC and will be considered *nationally recognized statistical ratings organizations* (NRSROs). Prior to this law, the SEC had sole authority to designate credit rating agencies as NRSROs. Of the more than 130 credit rating agencies, the SEC has designated only ten as NRSROs (see Business Insight box below).

BUSINESS INSIGHT   Competition Among Credit Rating Agencies

When this book went to print, the SEC had designated only ten organizations as nationally recognized statistical ratings organizations (NRSROs). The ten are:

Agency	Headquarters
Moody's Investor Service	U.S.A.
Standard & Poor's	U.S.A.
Fitch Ratings	U.S.A.
A. M. Best Company	U.S.A.
Dominion Bond Rating Service, Ltd.	Canada
Japan Credit Rating Agency, Ltd.	Japan
R&I, Inc.	Japan
Egan-Jones Rating Company	U.S.A.
Kroll Bond Rating Agency	U.S.A.
Morningstar, Inc.	U.S.A.

The Credit Rating Agency Reform Act has detractors and supporters. Some contend that NRSRO designation bestows a competitive advantage to certain agencies. This view is supported by the vigor with which non-recognized agencies seek NRSRO status. On the other hand, the NRSRO designation might have actually increased competition in the industry by providing a "seal of approval" to smaller agencies. Regulation can have another benefit: "Importantly, the new law gives the SEC the tools necessary to hold recognized rating agencies accountable if they fail to produce credible and reliable ratings," declared Jim Kaitz, president of the Association for Financial Professionals.

RESEARCH INSIGHT   Value Relevance of Credit Ratings Upgrades and Downgrades

The SEC enacted Regulation Fair Disclosure (Reg FD) in 2000 which prohibits public companies from selectively disclosing information to favored investment analysts. However, companies are still permitted to make private disclosures to credit rating agencies. Research shows that stock-price reactions to ratings downgrades and upgrades are more pronounced after the new rules came into play. It appears that credit ratings are now a more important source of information because credit analysts at rating agencies have an informational edge over equity analysts under Reg FD. (Source: "Informational Effects of Regulation FD: Evidence from Rating Agencies" Journal of Financial Economics, 2008, by Philippe Jorion, Zhu Liu, and Charles Shi; http://papers.ssrn.com/sol3/papers.cfm?abstract_id=556824).

PREDICTING BANKRUPTCY RISK

Bankruptcy is a worst-case scenario for creditors. Accordingly, creditors are very interested in assessing the likelihood that a company will go bankrupt.

Altman Z-Score

Professor Edward Altman is a leader in this area, which sprung from his study on the use of financial ratios to predict corporate bankruptcy risk (Altman, E., "Financial Ratios, Discriminant Analysis and the Prediction of Corporate Bankruptcy," *Journal of Finance*, September 1968). He developed a model for scoring a company based on various financial indicators and a way to apply that score (called Z-score) to assess a company's bankruptcy risk. To derive the model, Altman used data from many bankrupt and non-bankrupt public companies along with a statistical methodology called Multiple Discriminant Analysis. Altman's weighted model to predict a company's **Z-score** follows:

LO5 Explain bankruptcy prediction models, and compute and interpret measures of bankruptcy risk.

$$\text{Z-Score} = \left[1.2 \times \frac{\text{Working Capital}}{\text{Total Assets}}\right] + \left[1.4 \times \frac{\text{Retained Earnings}}{\text{Total Assets}}\right] + \left[3.3 \times \frac{\text{EBIT}}{\text{Total Assets}}\right] + \left[0.6 \times \frac{\text{Market Value of Equity}}{\text{Total Liabilities}}\right] + \left[0.99 \times \frac{\text{Sales}}{\text{Total Assets}}\right]$$

Each variable in the Z-score model relates to financial strength. The first variable provides a measure of liquidity, while the second and third variables measure long-term and short-term profitability. The fourth variable captures the company's levered status, while the fifth variable reflects its total asset efficiency.

By comparing Z-scores of bankrupt and non-bankrupt companies, Altman derived the following interpretations in Exhibit 4.7.

EXHIBIT 4.7	Z-Scores and Their Interpretation
Z-score	**Interpretation**
Z-score > 3.00	Company is healthy and there is low bankruptcy potential in the short term
2.99 > Z-score > 1.80	Gray area—company is exposed to some risk of bankruptcy; caution is advised
1.80 > Z-score	Company is in financial distress and there is high bankruptcy potential in short term

The cut-offs in this exhibit are shown to predict bankruptcy reasonably accurately up to two years in advance. The model is 95% accurate in the first year and 72% accurate in the second year. For years beyond the second year, the model's predictive ability declines sharply.

Application of Z-Score

To compute a Z-score for **Home Depot**, we use the financial statement information shown in Exhibit 4.8 and as reported (in millions) for the year ended January 30, 2011, from Exhibits 4.1 and 4.3.

EXHIBIT 4.8	Financial Statement Information for Home Depot		
Current assets	$13,479	Shares outstanding, in millions	1,623
Current liabilities.	10,122	× Price per share	$ 36.70
Working capital (WC)	$ 3,357	Market value of equity (MVE)	$59,564
Total assets (TA).	$40,125	Total liabilities (TL)	$21,236
Retained earnings (RE).	$14,995	Sales.	$67,997
EBIT	$ 5,839		

Home Depot's Z-score is computed as 4.464, which is detailed in Exhibit 4.9. Its 4.464 Z-score exceeds the 3.00 lower cut-off for "safe" companies. Thus, we conclude that there is a low risk of Home Depot going bankrupt in the short term.

EXHIBIT 4.9	Z-Score Computation for Home Depot		
Variable	**Financial Ratio**	**Weight**	**Score**
WC/TA	($3,357/$40,125) $\times$	1.2 =	0.100
RE/TA	($14,995/$40,125) $\times$	1.4 =	0.523
EBIT/TA	($5,839/$40,125) $\times$	3.3 =	0.480
MVE/TL	($59,564/$21,236) $\times$	0.6 =	1.683
Sales/TA	($67,997/$40,125) $\times$	0.99 =	1.678
		Z-score =	**4.464**

Bankruptcy Prediction Errors

Predictions are imperfect and errors occur. Two types of errors can arise from the Z-score model: **Type I error** (a false negative) and **Type II error** (a false positive). In Altman's Z-score model, a "positive" indicates bankruptcy. Thus, a Type I error occurs when a company's Z-score indicates the company is healthy, yet the company goes bankrupt. This can happen if, for example, a pending lawsuit was not recognized in the financial statements, or a sudden downturn in the industry forced the company to fail despite adequate recent performance. A Type II error occurs when a company's Z-score indicates the company is likely to go bankrupt, yet the company remains solvent. This can happen if the company is rebounding from a small downturn in business or has recently gone public and its ratios are weak because of the company's age. Exhibit 4.10 shows both types of error.

EXHIBIT 4.10	Z-Score Prediction Errors	
	Predicted Classification	
	Bankrupt	**Non-Bankrupt**
True Classification — Bankrupt	Correct prediction	Type I error
True Classification — Non-Bankrupt	Type II error	Correct prediction

Given the potential for both Type I and Type II errors, a Z-score must be viewed as only one piece of evidence for assessing bankruptcy risk.

Altman twice revised the Z-score model to allow for different industries and firm-age, as well as for privately-held firms. These models are more accurate when applied to those types of companies. Altman and other researchers also developed the ZETA analysis, which adds new variables for the persistence of earnings, the interest coverage ratio (EBIT/interest payments), the current ratio, the company capitalization (MVE/total capital), and the company size (natural logarithm of total assets)—see E. Altman, R. Haldeman, and P. Narayanan, "ZETA Analysis: A New Model to Identify Bankruptcy Risk of Corporations," *Journal of Banking and Finance*, June 1977. With the ZETA analysis, Altman et al. recommend adjustments to financial statement numbers to reflect the true underlying economics. The ZETA model performs similarly with Z-scores in short-term predictive accuracy, but it yields better long-term predictions (up to 70% prediction accuracy five years before bankruptcy).

| BUSINESS INSIGHT | Predicting Bankruptcy for Private Companies |

Moody's KMV RiskCalc™ uses extensive data from 1,600 credit defaults in the private sector. The model provides an example of how credit rating agencies assess the likelihood of default and bankruptcy. Most notably, Moody's model differs in a two-pronged assessment of solvency: financial-statement-only mode and a credit-cycle-adjusted mode. The latter adjusts for a company's stage of the credit cycle and is assessed on an industry-wide and country-wide basis that is updated monthly. The financial-statement-only risk evaluation is quite similar in spirit to Altman's original Z-score model, applying slightly different variables to capture leverage, profitability, liquidity, size, and growth. (Source: Moody's, "RiskCalc™ Private Model: Moody's Default Model for Private Firms," Global Credit Research, 2004.)

MODULE-END REVIEW

Refer to the income statement and balance sheet of **Lowe's Companies, Inc.**, from Mid-Module Review 1 and 2 earlier in this module.

Required

a. Compute and interpret the Altman Z-score for Lowe's Companies for the year ended January 28, 2011. On that date, the company's stock closed at $25.25 per share.

b. How does Lowe's Z-score compare to Home Depot's Z-score computed in the module? Which company has a higher bankruptcy risk? Explain.

The solution is on page 4-46.

APPENDIX 4: Credit Risk Analysis at Two Major NRSROs

Standard & Poor's Credit Risk Analysis **Standard & Poor's** (S&P) considers the following in its credit risk analysis of companies.

- Business risk
- Industry characteristics
- Competitive position (marketing, technology, efficiency, regulation)
- Management
- Financial risk

- Financial characteristics
- Financial policy
- Profitability
- Capital structure
- Cash flow protection
- Financial flexibility

S&P provides long-term and short-term issuer credit ratings (in addition to ratings on specific bond issues, called issue ratings).

S&P classifies its long-term issuer ratings from AAA through CC. This yields eight distinct ratings; their meanings follow:

AAA extremely strong capacity to meet financial commitments.

AA very strong capacity to meet financial commitments; differs from AAA only to a small degree.

A strong capacity to meet financial commitments but somewhat more susceptible to the adverse effects of changes in circumstances and economic conditions.

BBB adequate capacity to meet financial commitments; adverse economic conditions or changing circumstances are more likely to lead to a weakened capacity to meet financial commitments.

BB less vulnerable in the near term than other lower-rated entities; it faces major ongoing uncertainties and exposure to adverse business, financial, or economic conditions which could lead to inadequate capacity to meet financial commitments.

B more vulnerable than BB, but currently has the capacity to meet financial commitments; adverse business, financial, or economic conditions will likely impair the capacity or willingness to meet financial commitments.

CCC currently vulnerable and is dependent upon favorable business, financial, and economic conditions to meet financial commitments.

CC currently highly vulnerable.

Then, for ratings AA through CCC, S&P can modify the rating by adding a plus (+) or minus (−) sign to show relative standing within those ratings. This creates 20 distinct ratings for companies that issue long-term debt.

 S&P classifies its short-term issue ratings from A-1 through C. This yields five distinct ratings; their meanings follow:

A-1 strong capacity to meet financial commitments; within this category, S&P can add a plus sign (+) to indicate that the capacity to meet financial commitments is extremely strong.

A-2 satisfactory capacity to meet financial commitments but somewhat more susceptible to the adverse effects of changes in circumstances and economic conditions.

A-3 adequate capacity to meet financial obligations but adverse economic conditions or changing circumstances are more likely to lead to a weakened capacity to meet financial commitments.

B vulnerable and has significant speculative characteristics; currently has the capacity to meet financial commitments, however, faces major ongoing uncertainties which could lead to inadequate capacity to meet its financial commitments. Ratings of 'B-1', 'B-2', and 'B-3' can be assigned to indicate finer distinctions within the 'B' category; that is B-1, B-2 and B-3 in order of decreasing capacity to meet financial commitments over the short-term.

C currently vulnerable to nonpayment; dependent on favorable business, financial, and economic conditions to meet financial commitments.

Periodically, S&P provides updated information on its ratings to the market in two forms: rating outlooks and CreditWatch. A rating outlook assesses how changes in the macroeconomy can affect a company's long-term credit rating in the intermediate term, typically six months to two years. The economic or business changes in a rating outlook are often generic and trends are still developing. A CreditWatch is more specific than a rating outlook as it focuses on identifiable events and trends that cause the S&P analysis to reevaluate existing ratings.

 Ratings outlooks and CreditWatch take the following forms: "positive" or "negative," meaning that a rating might be raised or lowered, respectively. A "developing" rating outlook or CreditWatch means that the rating can change but S&P does not know the direction. Neither ratings outlooks nor CreditWatch signify that a specific credit rating will change, only that S&P is performing ongoing analysis and that the rating can change.

Moody's Credit Risk Analysis **Moody**'s considers the following four factors in its credit risk analysis of companies.

- ■ Size, Scale and Diversification
- ■ Product Portfolio and Profitability
- ■ Financial Strength
- ■ Financial Policies

Moody's classifies its long-term issuer ratings from Aaa through C. This yields nine distinct ratings; their meanings follow:

Aaa highest quality with minimal credit risk.

Aa high quality with very low credit risk.

A upper-medium grade with low credit risk.

Baa medium grade, moderate credit risk; may possess certain speculative characteristics.

Ba speculative elements with substantial credit risk.

B speculative with high credit risk.

Caa poor standing with very high credit risk.

Ca highly speculative and are in, or very near, default, with some prospect of recovery of principal and interest.

C lowest rated class; in default, with little prospect for recovery of principal or interest.

Then, for ratings Aa through Caa, Moody's can modify the rating by adding a 1, 2, or 3 to show relative standing within that rating category (where a 1 indicates a higher ranking). This creates 23 distinct ratings for companies that issue long-term debt.

 Moody's employs the following four ratings for short-term obligations:

P-1 superior ability to repay.

P-2 strong ability to repay.

P-3 acceptable ability to repay.

NP does not fall within any of the Prime rating categories.

Moody's provides the following reconciliation between its long-term and short-term ratings:

Long-Term vs Short-Term Ratings		
Long Term		**Short Term**
Investment Grade	Aaa	
	Aa1	
	Aa2	
	Aa3	Prime-1 (or P-1)
	A1	
	A2	
	A3	Prime-2 (or P-2)
	Baa1	
	Baa2	Prime-3 (or P-3)
	Baa3	
Speculative Grade (or "High Yield" or "Junk")	Ba1	
	Ba2	
	Ba3	
	B1	
	B2	
	B3	Not Prime
	Caa1	
	Caa2	
	Caa3	
	Ca	
	C	

Below is a list of ratios that S&P and Moody's use to evaluate credit risk and assign credit ratings. The list is not exhaustive, but illustrates the most important ratios used by the two agencies. The two agencies measure similar credit-related qualities but their particular ratios sometimes differ.

		S&P	Moody's
Profitability and Coverage Ratios			
Operating income to revenues	$\dfrac{\text{Sales} - \text{COGS} - \text{SGA} - \text{R\&D expense} + \text{Depreciation included in COGS and SGA and R\&D}}{\text{Sales}}$	✓	
Operating income margin	$\dfrac{\text{Earnings from continuing operations} + \text{Tax expense}}{\text{Sales}}$		✓
EBITA margin	$\dfrac{\text{Earnings from continuing operations} + \text{Interest expense, net} + \text{Tax expense} + \text{Amortization expense}}{\text{Sales}}$		✓
Return on capital	$\dfrac{\text{Earnings from continuing operations} + \text{Interest expense, net} + \text{Tax expense}}{\text{Average of beginning and end of year (Long-term debt} + \text{Current maturities} + \text{Commercial paper} + \text{Short-term borrowings} + \text{Equity)}}$	✓	
EBIT interest coverage	$\dfrac{\text{Earnings from continuing operations} + \text{Interest expense, net} + \text{Tax expense}}{\text{Gross interest expense, before subtracting capitalized interest and interest income}}$	✓	
EBITDA interest coverage	$\dfrac{\text{Earnings from continuing operations} + \text{Interest expense, net} + \text{Tax expense} + \text{Depreciation expense} + \text{Amortization expense}}{\text{Gross interest expense, before subtracting capitalized interest and interest income}}$	✓	
EBITA interest coverage	$\dfrac{\text{Earnings from continuing operations} + \text{Interest expense, net} + \text{Tax expense} + \text{Amortization expense}}{\text{Gross interest expense, before subtracting capitalized interest and interest income}}$		✓
Solvency and Leverage Ratios			
Debt to EBITDA	$\dfrac{\text{(Long-term debt} + \text{Current maturities} + \text{Commercial paper} + \text{Short-term borrowings)}}{\text{(Earnings from continuing operations} + \text{Interest expense, net} + \text{Tax expense} + \text{Depreciation expense} + \text{Amortization expense)}}$	✓	✓

continued

continued from prior page

		S&P	Moody's
Debt to equity	$$\dfrac{\text{Long-term debt} + \text{Current maturities} + \text{Commercial paper} + \text{Short-term borrowings}}{\text{Equity}}$$	✓	
Debt to book capitalization	$$\dfrac{\text{Long-term debt} + \text{Current maturities} + \text{Commercial paper} + \text{Short-term borrowings}}{\left(\begin{array}{c}\text{Long-term debt} + \text{Current maturities} + \text{Commercial paper} \\ + \text{Short-term borrowings} + \text{Deferred taxes} + \text{Minority interest} + \text{Equity}\end{array}\right)}$$		✓
Debt to market value of equity	$$\dfrac{\text{Long-term debt} + \text{Current maturities} + \text{Commercial paper} + \text{Short-term borrowings}}{\text{Year-end market capitalization}}$$	✓	
EBITA to average assets	$$\dfrac{\left(\begin{array}{c}\text{Earnings from continuing operations} + \text{Interest expense, net} \\ + \text{Tax expense} + \text{Amortization expense}\end{array}\right)}{\text{Average of beginning and end of year assets}}$$		✓

Cash Flow Ratios

		S&P	Moody's
Funds from operations to debt	$$\dfrac{\left(\begin{array}{c}\text{Net income from continuing operations} + \text{Depreciation} + \text{Amortization} \\ + \text{Deferred tax expense} + \text{Other noncash items}\end{array}\right)}{\text{Long-term debt} + \text{Current maturities} + \text{Commercial paper} + \text{Short-term borrowings}}$$	✓	✓
Cash flow interest coverage	$$\dfrac{\text{Operating cash flow} - \text{CAPEX} + \text{Interest expense, net}}{\text{Gross interest expense, before subtracting capitalized interest and interest income}}$$	✓	
Funds from operations coverage	$$\dfrac{\left(\begin{array}{c}\text{Net income from continuing operations} + \text{Depreciation} + \text{Amortization} \\ + \text{Deferred tax expense} + \text{Other noncash items} + \text{Interest expense}\end{array}\right)}{\text{Interest expense, net}}$$		✓
Debt service coverage	$$\dfrac{\text{Operating cash flow} - \text{CAPEX} + \text{Interest expense, net}}{\left(\begin{array}{c}\text{Gross interest expense, before subtracting capitalized interest and interest income} \\ + \text{Annual debt principal payment}\end{array}\right)}$$	✓	
Free operating cash flow to debt	$$\dfrac{\left(\begin{array}{c}\text{Operating cash flow} - \text{CAPEX} - \text{Increase in working capital} + \text{Decrease in working} \\ \text{capital (excluding cash, marketable securities, and short-term debt)}\end{array}\right)}{\text{Long-term debt} + \text{Current maturities} + \text{Commercial paper} + \text{Short-term borrowings}}$$	✓	
Retained cash flow to debt	$$\dfrac{\text{Operating cash flow} - \text{Dividends}}{\text{Long-term debt} + \text{Current maturities} + \text{Commercial paper} + \text{Short-term borrowings}}$$		✓

GUIDANCE ANSWERS . . . ANALYSIS DECISION

You Are the Manager There are costs and benefits to extending credit to our customers. On the cost side, you will have to set up a credit-granting policy, decide what your credit terms will be, assign these new credit-granting responsibilities to a staff person. After sales, you will need to implement a system to send bills and establish receivable collections. A significant cost would arise if you had large uncollectible accounts. On the benefit side, granting credit should increase your sales, profit, and cash flow. If all your competitors currently offer credit, your not doing so is a competitive disadvantage. You would need to quantify the costs and benefits and determine which is greater in making your final decision.

You Are the Vice President of Finance You might consider the types of restructuring that would strengthen financial ratios typically used to assess liquidity and solvency by the rating agencies. Such restructuring includes generating cash by reducing inventory, reallocating cash outflows from investing activities (PPE) to debt reduction, and issuing stock for cash and using the proceeds to reduce debt (an equity for debt recapitalization). These actions increase liquidity or reduce financial leverage and, thus, should improve debt rating. An improved debt rating will attract more debtholders because your current debt rating is below investment grade and is not a suitable investment for many professionally managed portfolios. An improved debt rating will also lower the interest rate on your debt. Offsetting these benefits are costs such as the following: (1) potential loss of sales from inventory stock-outs; (2) potential future cash flow reductions and loss of market power from reduced PPE investments; and (3) costs of equity issuances (equity costs more than debt because investors demand a higher return to compensate for added risk and the lack of tax deductibility of dividends vis-à-vis interest payments), which can yield a net increase in the total cost of capital. All cost and benefits must be assessed before you pursue any restructuring.

DISCUSSION QUESTIONS

Q4-1. Companies often borrow money to fund operating activities. Why do lenders distinguish between cyclical cash needs and cash needed to fund operating losses?

Q4-2. Explain how a company's need of cash for investing activities differs over that company's life cycle. Suggest three reasons a company would borrow cash for financing activities.

Q4-3. Identify at least three parties that routinely supply credit to companies.

Q4-4. Distinguish between a line of credit and a letter of credit. Why do companies obtain lines of credit?

Q4-5. Identify and explain at least three means that banks have to extend credit to companies.

Q4-6. What is credit risk? What is the main purpose of performing a credit analysis?

Q4-7. What are the four steps to assess the chance of default for a company?

Q4-8. Why are missing or understated liabilities especially critical for credit analysis?

Q4-9. Explain the concepts of liquidity and solvency. Why is performance on these two dimensions crucial to company survival? How does coverage analysis differ from measures of liquidity and solvency?

Q4-10. What two factors determine a company's level of credit risk? Explain what each factor tries to measure.

Q4-11. Why do lenders require collateral? What are some common types of collateral?

Q4-12. Why do lenders impose debt covenants on borrowers? Explain the three types of debt covenants.

Q4-13. What is a credit rating? Why do companies care about their credit ratings?

Q4-14. Explain in general terms, the Altman bankruptcy prediction model. What do each of the five model variables measure?

Q4-15. With respect to bankruptcy prediction, what is a Type I error? A Type II error? If you are a creditor, which type of error is more costly to you? Why?

**Assignments with the ✅ in the margin are available in an online homework system.
See the Preface of the book for details.**

MINI EXERCISES

M4-16. **Analyzing Notes, Yields, Financial Ratios, and Credit Ratings** (LO2, LO3, LO4)

Comcast Corporation reports long-term senior notes totaling over $31 billion in its 2010 10-K. Following are selected ratios from Exhibit 4.6 computed for Comcast Corp. utilizing its 2010 data. This debt is rated "Baa" by Moody's, which is a lower medium grade. Examine the ratios provided. *(Hint: Compare Comcast's ratios to the ratio values reported in Exhibit 4.6.)* What factors do you believe contribute to Comcast's credit rating being less than stellar?

COMCAST CORP.
(CMCSA)

EBITA/Average assets	7.8%
Operating Margin	21.0%
EBITA Margin	23.9%
EBITA/interest expense	4.8
Debt/EBITDA	3.5
Debt/Book capitalization	30.2%
CAPEX/Depreciation	0.9

M4-17. **Risk Analysis Using Liquidity, Solvency and Coverage Ratios** (LO3)

Following are liquidity, solvency and coverage ratios for **Pfizer** for two recent fiscal years. Is the company more or less risky to creditors in 2006 compared to 2005? Explain.

PFIZER
(PFE)

Ratio	2005	2006
Liquidity ratios		
Current ratio	1.473	2.195
Quick ratio	1.142	1.759
Solvency ratios		
Liabilities-to-equity ratio	0.791	0.609
Long-term debt-to-equity ratio	0.109	0.0877
Coverage ratios		
Times interest earned	32.426	29.865
Cash from operations to total debt	0.821	2.205
Free operating cash flow to total debt	0.704	1.948

BAKER HUGHES
(BHI)

M4-18.   Risk Analysis Using Profitability, Coverage, Liquidity and Solvency   (LO3)

Following are liquidity, solvency and coverage ratios for **Baker Hughes** for two recent fiscal years. Is the company more or less risky to creditors in 2010 compared to 2009? Explain.

Ratio	2010	2009
Profitability and coverage		
RNOA	7.6%	6.8%
ROE..	7.6%	6.0%
Times interest earned....................................	10.05	5.86
EBITDA coverage	17.63	11.54
Liquidity		
Current ratio	2.77	3.86
Quick ratio	1.80	2.43
Solvency		
Liabilities to equity	0.61	0.57
Total debt to equity.......................................	0.27	0.25

PFIZER
(PFE)

M4-19.   Off-Balance-Sheet Financing and Liquidity and Solvency Ratios   (LO3)

Refer to the liquidity and solvency ratios for **Pfizer** in M4-17. Assume that the company had substantial operating leases that represent material off-balance-sheet liabilities and assets. What types of adjustments would we make to the liquidity and solvency ratios to reflect such financing? Explain.

LOGITECH INTL SA
(LOGI)

M4-20.   Bankruptcy Risk and Z-Score Analysis   (LO5)

Following are selected ratios for **Logitech International SA** for the company's 2011 and 2010 fiscal years. Compute and interpret Altman Z-scores for both years.

Ratio	2011	2010
Working capital to total assets.....................................	0.325	0.221
Retained earnings to total assets.................................	0.813	0.879
EBIT to total assets	0.077	0.049
Market value of equity to total assets	1.74	1.79
Market value of equity to total liabilities.......................	4.95	4.77
Sales to total assets..	1.269	1.229

JETBLUE AIRWAYS
(JBLU)

M4-21.   Bankruptcy Risk and Z-Score Analysis   (LO5)

Following are selected ratios for **JetBlue Airways** for two recent fiscal years. Compute and interpret Altman Z-scores for the company for both years. Is the company's bankruptcy risk increasing or decreasing over this period?

Ratio	2010	2009
Current ratio	1.253	1.326
Working capital to total assets.....................................	0.042	0.058
Retained earnings to total assets.................................	0.033	0.019
EBIT to total assets	0.05	0.04
Market value of equity to total liabilities.......................	0.39	0.32
Sales to total assets..	0.573	0.503

EXERCISES

HOME DEPOT
(HD)

E4-22.   Assigning a Long-Term Debt Rating Using Financial Ratios   (LO3, LO4)

Refer to the **Home Depot** 2011 financial statements shown earlier in the module to answer the following requirements.

Required

a. Compute the following seven Moody's metrics for Home Depot. See Appendix for definitions. (*Hint:* Home Depot's amortization expense relates to tangible assets; consequently, treat depreciation and amortization as all depreciation. Operating cash flows are $4,585 million, dividends are $1,569 million, and gross interest expense is $530 million.)

> EBITA to average assets
> Operating margin
> EBITA margin
> EBITA interest coverage
> Debt to EBITDA
> Debt to book capitalization
> Retained cash flow to debt

b. Use your computations from part a, along with measures in Exhibit 4.6, to estimate the long-term debt rating for Home Depot.

E4-23. **Compute and Interpret Liquidity, Solvency and Coverage Ratios** **(LO3)**
Selected balance sheet and income statement information from **Verizon Communications** follows.

($ millions)	2005	2004
Current assets	$ 16,448	$ 19,479
Current liabilities.......................	25,063	23,129
Total liabilities.........................	101,696	103,345
Equity.................................	66,434	62,613
Earnings before interest and taxes..........	12,787	12,496
Interest expense.......................	2,180	2,384
Net cash flow from operating activities	22,012	21,820

Required

a. Compute the current ratio for each year and discuss any trend in liquidity. What additional information about the numbers used to compute this ratio might be useful in helping you assess liquidity? Explain.

b. Compute times interest earned, total liabilities-to-equity, and net cash from operating activities to total liabilities ratios for each year and discuss any trends for each. Do you have any concerns about the extent of Verizon's financial leverage and the company's ability to meet interest obligations? Explain.

c. Verizon's capital expenditures are expected to increase substantially as it seeks to respond to competitive pressures to upgrade the quality of its communications infrastructure. Assess Verizon's liquidity and solvency in light of this strategic direction.

E4-24. **Compute and Interpret Coverage, Liquidity and Solvency Ratios** **(LO3)**
Selected balance sheet and income statement information from **CVS Caremark** for 2008 through 2010 follows ($ millions).

	Total Current Assets	Total Current Liabilities	Pretax Income	Interest Expense	Total Liabilities	Equity
2010	$17,706	$11,070	$5,629	$536	$24,469	$37,700
2009	17,537	12,300	5,913	525	25,873	35,768
2008	16,526	13,490	5,537	509	26,386	34,574

Required

a. Compute times interest earned ratio for each year and discuss any trends for each.

b. Compute the current ratio for each year and discuss any trend in liquidity. Do you believe the company is sufficiently liquid? Explain. What additional information about the accounting numbers comprising this ratio might be useful in helping you assess liquidity? Explain.

c. Compute the total liabilities-to-equity ratio for each year and discuss any trends for each.

d. What is your overall assessment of the company's credit risk from the analyses in (*a*), (*b*), and (*c*)? Explain.

E4-25. Compute and Interpret Coverage, Liquidity and Ratios (LO3)

The table below shows selected balance sheet and income statement information for Tesco PLC and Ahold, two grocery chains based in Europe. The companies report financial statements using International Financial Reporting Standards (IFRS).

	Tesco PLC 26-Feb-11 (in £ millions)	Ahold 2-Jan-11 (in € millions)
Balance Sheet information		
Current assets	£11,438	€ 5,194
Long-term assets	35,768	9,531
Total assets	£47,206	€14,725
Current liabilities	£17,731	€ 4,092
Long-term liabilities	12,852	4,723
Stockholder's equity	16,623	5,910
Total liabilities and equity	£47,206	€14,725
Income Statement information		
Sales	£60,931	€29,530
Depreciation and amortization	1,225	812
Interest expense, net	333	259
Tax provision	864	271
Net income	2,671	853

Required

a. Compute the following profitability and coverage metrics: return on equity, times interest earned, and EBITDA coverage. (Use year-end equity for return on equity calculation.)

b. Compute the current ratio for each company and discuss any differences. Which company is more liquid? What additional information about the accounting numbers in this ratio might be useful in helping you assess liquidity? Explain.

c. Compute the total liabilities-to-equity ratio for each company. Which company is more solvent?

d. What is your overall assessment of the companies' credit risk from the analyses in (a), (b), and (c)? Explain.

E4-26. Compute and Interpret Solvency Ratios for Business Segments (LO3)

Selected balance sheet and income statement information from **General Electric Company** and its two principal business segments (Industrial and Financial) for 2010 follows.

($ millions)	Pretax Income	Interest Expense	Net Income	Total Liabilities	Equity
Industrial segments	$15,166	$ 1,600	$11,644	$ 95,729	$118,936
Financial segments	2,172	14,956	2,155	538,530	68,984
Other	(3,130)[1]	(573)[2]	(2,155)[2]	(7,241)[2]	—
General Electric Consolidated	14,208	15,983	11,644	627,018	118,936[3]

[1] Includes unallocated corporate operating activities.

[2] Includes intercompany loans and related interest expense; these are deducted (eliminated) in preparing consolidated financial statements.

[3] The consolidated equity is the equity of the parent (industrial); this is explained in Module 9.

Required

a. Compute the return on equity (ROE), the times interest earned ratio and the total liabilities-to-equity ratio for 2010 for the company's two business segments and the company as a whole. (Use year-end equity for return on equity calculation.)

b. What is your overall assessment of the company's credit risk? Explain. What differences do you observe between the two business segments? Do these differences correspond to your prior expectations given each company's business model?

c. Discuss the implications of the analysis of consolidated financial statements and the additional insight that can be gained from a more in-depth analysis of primary business segments.

E4-27.   Compute and Interpret Liquidity, Solvency, and Coverage Ratios   (LO3)

Selected balance sheet and income statement information for **Calpine Corporation** for 2004 and 2006 follows.

CALPINE
CORPORATION
(CPN)

($ millions)	2004	2006
Cash.	$1,376.73	$1,503.36
Accounts receivable.	1,097.16	735.30
Current assets	3,563.56	3,168.33
Current liabilities.	3,285.39	6,057.95
Long-term debt	16,940.81	3,351.63
Short-term debt	1,033.96	4,568.83
Total liabilities.	22,628.42	25,743.17
Interest expense.	1,516.90	1,288.29
Capital expenditures	1,545.48	211.50
Equity	4,587.67	(7,152.90)
Cash from operations.	9.89	155.98
Earnings before interest and taxes.	1,589.84	1,877.84

Required

a. Compute the following liquidity, solvency and coverage ratios for both years.

> Current ratio
> Quick ratio
> Liabilities-to-equity ratio
> Long-term debt-to-equity
> Times interest earned
> Cash from operations to total debt
> Free operating cash flow to total debt

b. What is your overall assessment of the company's credit risk? Explain. What differences do you observe between the two years?

E4-28.   Compute and Interpret Z-scores   (LO5)

Following is selected financial information for **Procter & Gamble** and **Johnson & Johnson** for recent financial statements.

PROCTER &
GAMBLE
(PG)
JOHNSON &
JOHNSON
(JNJ)

($ millions)	Procter & Gamble	Johnson & Johnson
Working capital.	$ (5,323)	$ 24,235
Retained earnings	70,682	77,773
Earnings before interest and tax	16,020	17,402
Market value of equity	175,816	243,581
Sales.	82,559	61,587
Total assets	138,354	102,908
Total liabilities.	70,353	46,329

a. Compute and compare the Altman Z-scores for each company.

b. Is either company likely to go bankrupt in the short term? Explain.

E4-29.   Compute and Interpret Altman's Z-scores   (LO5)

Following is selected financial information for **eBay**, for its fiscal years 2005 and 2006.

EBAY
(EBAY)

($ millions, except per share data)	2005	2006
Current assets	$3,183.24	$4,970.59
Current liabilities	1,484.93	2,518.39
Total assets	11,788.99	13,494.01
Total liabilities	1,741.00	2,589.38
Shares outstanding	1,404.18	1,368.51
Retained earnings	2,819.64	4,538.35
Stock price per share	43.22	30.07
Sales	4,552.40	5,969.74
Earnings before interest and taxes	1,445.18	1,439.77

Required

a. Compute and compare the Altman Z-scores for both years. What explains the apparent trend?

b. Is the company more likely to go bankrupt given the Z-score in 2006 compared to 2005? Explain.

PROBLEMS

LOWE'S
(LOW)

P4-30. **Assigning a Long-Term Debt Rating Using Financial Ratios** (LO3, LO4)

Refer to the **Lowe's** 2011 financial statements, shown earlier in Mid-Module Review 2 to answer the following requirements.

Required

a. Compute the following seven Moody's metrics for Lowe's. See Appendix for definitions of Moody's ratios. (*Hint:* Lowe's amortization expense relates to tangible assets; consequently, treat depreciation and amortization as all depreciation. Its gross interest expense was $358 million, cash from operations was $3,852 million, and its dividends paid were $571 million for 2011.)

> EBITA to average assets
> Operating margin
> EBITA margin
> EBITA interest coverage
> Debt to EBITDA
> Debt to book capitalization
> Retained cash flow to debt

b. Use your computations from part a, along with measures from Exhibit 4.6, to estimate the long-term debt rating for Lowe's.

LOCKHEED MARTIN CORPORATION (LMT)

P4-31. **Compute and Interpret Liquidity, Solvency and Coverage Ratios** (LO3)

Balance sheets and income statements for **Lockheed Martin Corporation** follow. Refer to these financial statements to answer the requirements.

Income Statement Year Ended December 31 (In millions)	2005	2004	2003
Net sales			
Products	$31,518	$30,202	$27,290
Service	5,695	5,324	4,534
	37,213	35,526	31,824
Cost of sales			
Products	28,800	27,879	25,306
Services	5,073	4,765	4,099
Unallocated corporate costs	803	914	443
	34,676	33,558	29,848
	2,537	1,968	1,976

continued

continued from prior page

Other income and expenses, net	449	121	43
Operating profit	2,986	2,089	2,019
Interest expense	370	425	487
Earnings before taxes	2,616	1,664	1,532
Income tax expense	791	398	479
Net earnings	$ 1,825	$ 1,266	$ 1,053

Balance Sheet		
December 31 (In millions)	2005	2004
Assets		
Cash and cash equivalents	$ 2,244	$ 1,060
Short-term investments	429	396
Receivables	4,579	4,094
Inventories	1,921	1,864
Deferred income taxes	861	982
Other current assets	495	557
Total current assets	10,529	8,953
Property, plant and equipment net	3,924	3,599
Investments in equity securities	196	812
Goodwill	8,447	7,892
Purchased intangibles, net	560	672
Prepaid pension asset	1,360	1,030
Other assets	2,728	2,596
Total assets	$27,744	$25,554
Liabilities and stockholders' equity		
Accounts payable	$ 1,998	$ 1,726
Customer advances and amounts in excess of costs incurred	4,331	4,028
Salaries, benefits and payroll taxes	1,475	1,346
Current maturities of long-term debt	202	15
Other current liabilities	1,422	1,451
Total current liabilities	9,428	8,566
Long-term debt	4,784	5,104
Accrued pension liabilities	2,097	1,660
Other postretirement benefit liabilities	1,277	1,236
Other liabilities	2,291	1,967
Stockholders' equity		
Common stock, $1 par value per share	432	438
Additional paid-in capital	1,724	2,223
Retained earnings	7,278	5,915
Accumulated other comprehensive loss	(1,553)	(1,532)
Other	(14)	(23)
Total stockholders' equity	7,867	7,021
Total liabilities and stockholders' equity	$27,744	$25,554

Consolidated Statement of Cash Flow			
Year Ended December 31 (in millions)	2005	2004	2003
Operating Activities			
Net earnings.	$1,825	$1,266	$1,053
Adjustments to reconcile net earnings to net cash provided by operating activities:			
Depreciation and amortization.	555	511	480
Amortization of purchased intangibles	150	145	129
Deferred federal income taxes.	24	(58)	467
Changes in operating assets and liabilities:			
Receivables.	(390)	(87)	(258)
Inventories.	(39)	519	(94)
Accounts payable	239	288	330
Customer advances and amounts in excess of costs incurred	296	(228)	(285)
Other	534	568	(13)
Net cash provided by operating activities	3,194	2,924	1,809
Investing Activities			
Expenditures for property, plant and equipment	(865)	(769)	(687)
Acquisition of businesses/investments in affiliated companies.	(564)	(91)	(821)
Proceeds from divestiture of businesses/investments in affiliated companies	935	279	234
Purchase of short-term investments, net.	(33)	(156)	(240)
Other.	28	29	53
Net cash used for investing activities	(499)	(708)	(1,461)
Financing Activities			
Repayments of long-term debt	(133)	(1,089)	(2,202)
Issuances of long-term debt	—	—	1,000
Long-term debt repayment and issuance costs	(12)	(163)	(175)
Issuances of common stock	406	164	44
Repurchases of common stock.	(1,310)	(673)	(482)
Common stock dividends	(462)	(405)	(261)
Net cash used for financing activities.	(1,511)	(2,166)	(2,076)
Net increase (decrease) in cash and cash equivalents	1,184	50	(1,728)
Cash and cash equivalents at beginning of year	1,060	1,010	2,738
Cash and cash equivalents at end of year.	$2,244	$1,060	$1,010

Required

a. Compute Lockheed Martin's current ratio and quick ratio for 2005 and 2004. Comment on any observed trends.

b. Compute total liabilities-to-equity ratios and long-term debt-to-equity ratios for 2005 and 2004. Comment on any trends you observe.

c. Compute times interest earned ratio, cash from operations to total debt ratio, and free operating cash flow to total debt ratios. Comment on any trends you observe.

d. Summarize your findings in a conclusion about the company's credit risk. Do you have any concerns about the company's ability to meet its debt obligations?

P4-32. **Assess Credit Risk** (LO2, LO3)

NEXTERA ENERGY, INC. (NEE)

Balance sheets and income statements for **NextEra Energy, Inc.** follow. Refer to these financial statements to answer the requirements.

Balance Sheets		
(millions)	December 31, 2010	December 31, 2009
Current assets		
Cash and cash equivalents	$ 302	$ 238
Receivables, net	2,582	2,247
Materials, supplies and fossil fuel inventory	857	877
Regulatory assets	686	209
Derivatives and other	831	766
Total current assets	5,258	4,337
Property, plant and equipment		
Electric utility plant in service and other property	48,841	46,330
Nuclear fuel	1,539	1,414
Construction in progress	3,841	2,425
Less accumulated depreciation and amortization	(15,146)	(14,091)
Total property, plant and equipment, net	39,075	36,078
Special use funds	3,742	3,390
Prepaid benefit costs	1,259	1,184
Other investments	971	935
Regulatory assets	910	909
Other assets	1,779	1,625
Total assets	$52,994	$48,458
Current liabilities		
Commercial paper	$ 889	$ 2,020
Current maturities of long-term debt	1,920	569
Accounts payable	1,124	992
Deposits	634	613
Accrued interest and taxes	462	466
Regulatory liabilities	51	379
Derivatives and other	1,824	1,410
Total current liabilities	6,904	6,449
Long-term debt	18,013	16,300
Asset retirement obligations	1,639	2,418
Deferred income taxes	5,109	4,860
Regulatory liabilities	4,259	3,182
Other long-term liabilities	2,609	2,282
Total liabilities	38,533	35,491
Common shareholders' equity	14,461	12,967
Total equity and liabilities	$52,994	$48,458

Statements of Income			
(millions)	2010	2009	2008
Operating revenues	$15,317	$15,643	$16,410
Operating expenses:			
Fuel, purchased power and interchange	6,242	7,405	8,412
Other operations and maintenance	2,877	2,649	2,527
Depreciation and amortization	1,807	1,765	1,442
Taxes other than income taxes	1,148	1,230	1,204
Total operating expenses	12,074	13,049	13,585
Operating income	3,243	2,594	2,825
Other income (deductions):			
Interest expense	(979)	(849)	(813)
Interest income	91	78	72
Other nonoperating income (deductions)	134	119	5
Total other deductions, net	(754)	(652)	(736)
Income before income taxes	2,489	1,942	2,089
Income taxes	532	327	450
Net income	$ 1,957	$ 1,615	$ 1,639

Required

a. Use the financial statements and the information below to compute the following profitability and coverage, liquidity and solvency ratios for 2010 and 2009: RNOA, ROE, times interest earned, free cash flow to debt, current ratio, quick ratio, liabilities-to-equity ratio, and total debt-to-equity ratio. (For simplicity here, use year-end balances for the denominator of RNOA and ROE.) Comment on any observed trends.

	2010	2009
NOPAT	$ 2,447	$ 2,039
Net operating assets (NOA)	31,261	27,937
Cash from operations.	3,834	4,463
CAPEX	2,605	2,522

b. Summarize your findings in a conclusion about the company's credit risk. Do you have any concerns about the company's ability to meet its debt obligations?

 P4-33. Compute and Interpret Z-score (LO5)

LOCKHEED
MARTIN
CORPORATION
(LMT)

Refer to the financial statements for **Lockheed Martin Corporation** in P4-31 to answer the requirements. As of December 31, 2005 and 2004, there were approximately 434,264,432 and 440,445,630 shares outstanding. The company's stock closed at $63.63 on December 31, 2005, and at $55.55 on December 31, 2004.

Required

a. Compute and compare the Altman Z-scores *for both years*. What explains the apparent trend?
b. Is the company more likely to go bankrupt given the Z-score in 2005 compared to 2004? Explain.

P4-34. Compute and Interpret Z-score (LO5)

AT&T INC
(T)

Balance sheets and income statements for **AT&T, Inc.** follow. Refer to these financial statements to answer the requirements.

AT&T INC. Consolidated Balance Sheet ($ millions) June 30, 2011 Unaudited	
Assets	
Current Assets	
Cash and cash equivalents.	$ 3,831
Accounts receivable - net of allowances for doubtful accounts of $908	13,608
Prepaid expenses.	1,563
Deferred income taxes	1,180
Other current assets.	2,057
Total current assets	22,239
Property, Plant and Equipment—Net.	104,606
Goodwill	73,591
Licenses	50,403
Customer Lists and Relationships—Net	3,643
Other Intangible Assets—Net.	5,407
Investments in Equity Affiliates.	5,207
Other Assets.	6,918
Total Assets	$272,014

continued

continued from prior page

Liabilities and Stockholders' Equity

Current Liabilities

Debt maturing within one year	$ 7,910
Accounts payable and accrued liabilities	18,145
Advanced billing and customer deposits	3,804
Accrued taxes	1,130
Dividends payable	2,548
Total current liabilities	33,537
Long-Term Debt	58,663

Deferred Credits and Other Noncurrent Liabilities

Deferred income taxes	25,065
Postemployment benefit obligation	28,350
Other noncurrent liabilities	12,290
Total deferred credits and other noncurrent liabilities	65,705

Stockholders' Equity

Common stock ($1 par value, 14,000,000,000 shares authorized and 6,495,231,088 shares issued)	6,495
Additional paid-in capital	91,687
Retained earnings	33,687
Treasury stock (570,191,742 shares)	(20,786)
Accumulated other comprehensive income	2,720
Noncontrolling interest	306
Total stockholders' equity	114,109
Total Liabilities and Stockholders' Equity	$272,014

AT&T INC.
Consolidated Statement of Income ($ millions)
Six Months Ended June 30, 2011
Unaudited

Operating Revenues

Wireless service	$28,118
Data	14,536
Voice	12,893
Directory	1,709
Other	5,486
Total operating revenues	62,742

Operating Expenses

Cost of services and sales (exclusive of depreciation and amortization shown separately below)	26,735
Selling, general and administrative	14,848
Depreciation and amortization	9,186
Total operating expenses	50,769
Operating income	11,973
Interest expense, net	1,152
Income from continuing operations before income taxes	10,821
Income tax expense	3,695
Income from continuing operations	7,126
Loss from discontinued operations, net of tax	—
Net income	7,126
Less: Net income attributable to noncontrolling interest	(127)
Net income attributable to AT&T	$ 6,999

Required

a. Compute AT&T's current ratio and quick ratio at June 30, 2011. Comment on the results.

b. Compute AT&T's working capital. What is negative working capital? Should a creditor be concerned about AT&T's working capital? Explain.

c. Compute and interpret the company's Altman Z-scores for the second quarter of 2011. Remember to annualize your income statement numbers. The per share market value of AT&T's stock was $31.41 on June 30, 2011.

DISCUSSION POINTS

D4-35.   Management Application: Solvency and Strategic Management   (LO3, LO4)

A company's solvency and ability to meet future debt payments weigh heavily in a credit analysts' evaluation. One way to increase reported solvency and operating profit (and NOPAT) is to use operating leases or to structure lease transactions so that they qualify for operating lease treatment under GAAP.

Required

a. Will using operating leases unambiguously reduce liabilities and increase operating profit? Will such a strategy always improve credit ratings?

b. What consequences might arise if a company focuses on financial reporting outcomes of its lease transactions?

D4-36.   Ethics and Corporate Governance: Meeting Debt Covenants   (LO1)

Companies routinely face debt covenants and occasionally these covenants are binding. That is, the company's financial statements indicate that the covenant has been violated or is close to being violated. Managers have historically used various means to improve their reported numbers to avoid binding covenants, including adjusting accounting accruals, and making "real" operating changes such as decreasing certain discretionary expenses or cutting back on capital expenditures.

Required

a. How do accounting accrual adjustments affect covenants that require minimums for retained earnings or for certain ratios such as the current ratio? Are those effects permanent?

b. How do real operating changes affect covenants that require minimums for retained earnings or for certain ratios such as the current ratio? Are those effects permanent?

c. What consequences might arise if the company focuses on managing reported numbers to avoid violating debt covenants? What parties are affected by such schemes?

SOLUTIONS TO REVIEW PROBLEMS

Mid-Module Review 1

Solution

Rising Sun Company could consider a wide range of financing options including the following:

- *Trade credit* The company should leverage its existing trade credit arrangements to buy the $5 million of inventory. Because this is a new location and not a new business, credit terms should not differ from those extended to its San Francisco operation.
- *Bank loans* Presumably the company has banking relationships with bankers in San Francisco. With a sound business plan, the company should be able to secure bank financing. Ideally, the company could pay off the term loan over a term that matches the life of the storage facility. Alternately, Rising Sun can take a mortgage, which would enable the company to pay the loan off over a longer term. The mortgage might be originated in the Seattle area where lenders are more familiar with real estate prices and risks.
- *Nonbank private financing* The company might explore nonbank private lenders if bank loans are not an option or if the company wants to run the operation with a local partner.
- *Lease financing* Office equipment could potentially be leased or purchased via a long-term capital lease. The company should check with the equipment vendor or manufacturer.
- *Publicly traded debt* Because Rising Sun is a private company, this is most costly and, thus, the least likely source of debt financing. However, it is possible for privately held companies to sell debt in the open market. Registering the debt issue with the SEC, engaging an investment bank or other broker to sell the debt, and complying with regulations are costly, especially when it only needs $15 million.

Mid-Module Review 2

Solution ($ millions)

Ratio ($ in millions)	Home Depot	Lowe's Companies
RNOA	$\dfrac{\$5,839 - \$1,953 + (\$566 \times 36.7\%)}{\begin{array}{c}(\$40,125 - \$545 - \$139) - \\ (\$21,236 - \$1,042 - \$8,707) + \\ (\$40,877 - \$1,421 - \$33) - \\ (\$21,484 - \$1,020 - \$8,662)/2\end{array}} = 13.3\%$	$\dfrac{(\$3,228 + \$332) - \$1,218 + (\$332 \times 35\%)}{\begin{array}{c}(\$33,699 - \$652 - \$471 - \$1,008) - \\ (\$15,587 - \$36 - \$6,537) + \\ (\$33,005 - \$632 - \$425 - \$277) - \\ (\$13,936 - \$552 - \$4,528)/2\end{array}} = 9.8\%$
ROE	$\dfrac{\$3,338}{(\$19,393 + \$18,889)/2} = 17.4\%$	$\dfrac{\$2,010}{(\$18,112 + \$19,069)/2} = 10.8\%$
Times interest earned	$\dfrac{\$5,803}{\$530} = 10.95$	$\dfrac{\$3,228 + \$332}{\$332} = 10.72$
EBITDA coverage	$\dfrac{\$5,273 + \$566 + \$1,616}{\$530} = 14.07$	$\dfrac{\$3,228 + \$332 + \$1,586}{\$332} = 15.50$
Operating cash flow to debt	$\dfrac{\$4,585}{\$1,042 + \$8,707} = 0.47$	$\dfrac{\$3,852}{\$36 + \$6,537} = 0.59$
Free cash flow to debt	$\dfrac{\$4,585 - \$1,096}{\$1,042 + \$8,707} = 0.36$	$\dfrac{\$3,852 - \$1,329}{\$36 + \$6,537} = 0.38$
Current ratio	$\dfrac{\$13,479}{\$10,122} = 1.33$	$\dfrac{\$9,967}{\$7,119} = 1.40$
Quick ratio	$\dfrac{\$545 + \$1,085}{\$10,122} = 0.16$	$\dfrac{\$652 + \$471}{\$7,119} = 0.16$
Liabilities to Equity	$\dfrac{\$21,236}{\$18,889} = 1.12$	$\dfrac{\$15,587}{\$18,112} = 0.86$
Total debt to Equity	$\dfrac{\$1,042 + \$8,707}{\$18,889} = 0.52$	$\dfrac{\$36 + \$6,537}{\$18,112} = 0.36$

Interpretation: Home Depot's profitability metrics are stronger than Lowe's: both RNOA and ROE are significantly higher. In addition, nonoperating return that Home Depot earns (4.1%) is four times as big as that of Lowe's. This implies that Home Depot is better able to use debt to achieve higher returns for shareholders. The companies' coverage ratios are strong and similar in magnitude. Lowe's operating cash flow metric is stronger than Home Depot's, but because Lowe's CAPEX is much higher than Home Depot's in 2011, the free cash flow metrics are similar. Looking at the current and quick ratios, we see that the companies are equally liquid. Home Depot is slightly less solvent but noted earlier, ratios with equity in the denominator were negatively affected by the company's recent stock buybacks. Both companies carry significant debt but appear able to make interest and debt payments as they fall due.

Module-End Review

Solution

a.

Current assets	$ 9,967	Shares outstanding, in millions	1,354
Current liabilities	7,119	× Price per share	$ 25.25
Working capital (WC)	$ 2,848	Market value of equity (MVE)	$34,189
Total assets (TA)	$33,699	Total liabilities (TL)	$15,587
Retained earnings (RE)	$17,371	Sales	$48,815
EBIT	$ 3,560		

	Variable		Weight		Score
WC/TA	($2,848/$33,699)	×	1.2	=	0.101
RE/TA	($17,371/$33,699)	×	1.4	=	0.722
EBIT/TA	($3,560/$33,699)	×	3.3	=	0.349
MVE/TL	($34,189/$15,587)	×	0.6	=	1.316
Sales/TA	($48,815/$33,699)	×	0.99	=	1.434
			Z-score =		3.922

Lowe's Z-score is greater than 3.0, which means the company is not at all likely to go bankrupt in the near term.

b. Home Depot's Z-score of 4.464 is above Lowe's score of 3.922. Both companies have high Z-scores, which means that neither company faces any substantial bankruptcy risk in the near term.

1. Explain revenue recognition criteria and identify transactions of special concern for analysis. (p. 5-5)

2. Describe and analyze accounting for operating expenses, including research and development, and restructuring. (p. 5-13)

3. Explain and analyze accounting for income taxes. (p. 5-19)

4. Explain how foreign currency fluctuations affect the income statement. (p. 5-27)

5. Compute earnings per share and explain the effect of dilutive securities. (p. 5-29)

6. Explain accounting quality and identify areas for analysis. (p. 5-31)

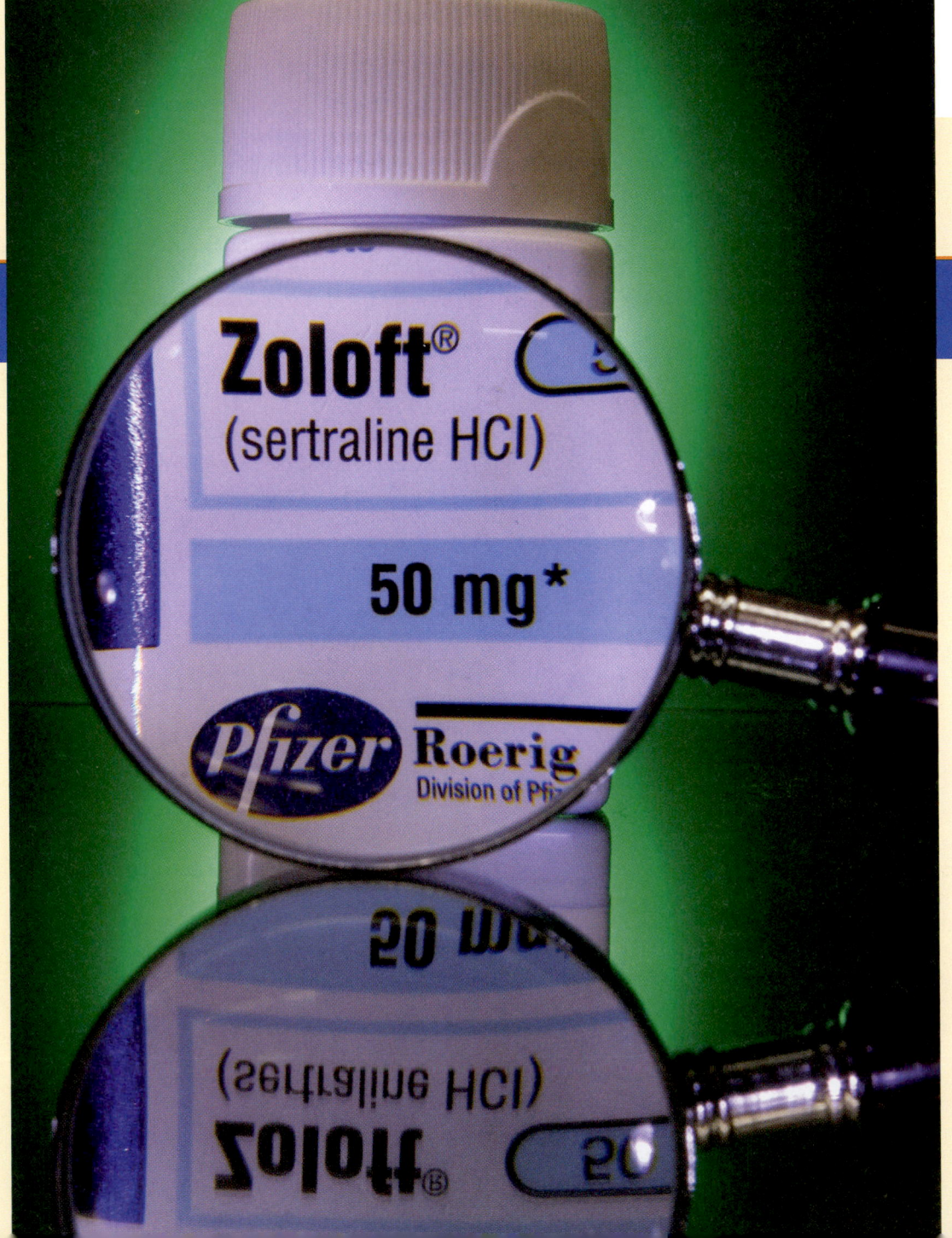

© Getty Images

Revenue Recognition and Operating Income

Pfizer's business is to discover, develop, manufacture and market leading prescription medicines. These endeavors define the company's operating activities and include research and development, manufacturing, advertising, sales, after-sale customer support, and all administrative functions necessary to support Pfizer's various activities.

PFIZER

Accounting for operating activities involves numerous estimates and choices, and GAAP often grants considerable latitude. To illustrate, consider the choice of when to recognize sales revenue. Should Pfizer recognize revenue when it receives a customer order? When it ships the drug order? Or, when the customer pays? GAAP requires that revenues be recognized when *earned*. It is up to the company to decide when that condition is met.

This module identifies several revenue-recognition scenarios that are especially troublesome for companies, their auditors, regulators, and outside stakeholders.

Pfizer's key operating activity is its research and development (R&D). To protect its discoveries, Pfizer holds thousands of patents and applies for hundreds more each year. However, patents don't protect Pfizer indefinitely—patents expire or fail legal challenges and, then, Pfizer's drugs face competition from other drug manufacturers. In 2007, for example, Pfizer's sales of Zoloft and Norvasc declined by about $3.5 billion because patent protection expired on both drugs. Even the company's blockbuster drug, Lipitor, with sales exceeding $10 billion in 2010 (16% of Pfizer's total revenues), is not a panacea for what ails Pfizer—the Lipitor patent expired in 2011.

Wall Street is not optimistic about Pfizer's ability to replace patents that will lapse over the next decade. While Pfizer's revenues have increased by over 40% in the past five years, its profits have decreased by about 57%, and Pfizer's stock price has fallen nearly 20% percent—see stock price chart to the right.

Although R&D activities generally yield future benefits and, thus, meet the criteria to be recorded as an asset, GAAP requires that companies expense most R&D costs. This creates balance sheets with significant "missing" assets. For example, the only asset that Pfizer has on its books specifically related to drugs that it has developed and is currently

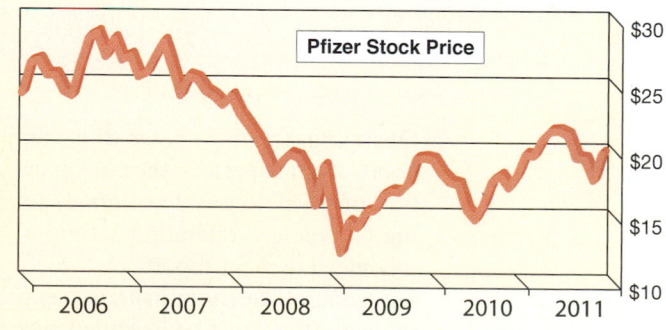

marketing is the legal cost of filing the patents with the U.S. Patent Office. Clearly this does not capture their full value to Pfizer. This module explains R&D accounting and the resulting financial statement implications.

Pfizer has restructured its business several times in an attempt to maintain operating profit. Restructurings typically involve two types of costs: severance costs relating to employee terminations and asset write-offs. GAAP grants leeway in how to account for restructuring activities. Should Pfizer expense the severance costs when the board of directors approves the

(continued on next page)

(continued from previous page)

layoffs? Or when the employees are actually paid? Or at some other point? This module discusses accounting for restructurings, including footnote disclosures that can help financial statement readers interpret restructuring activities.

A necessary part of operations is paying income taxes on profits earned. The IRS has its own rules for computing taxes owed. These rules, called the Internal Revenue Code, are different from GAAP. Thus, it is legal (and necessary) for companies to prepare two sets of financial reports, one for shareholders and one for tax authorities. In this module, we will see that tax expense reported on the income statement is not computed as a simple percentage of pretax income. The module also discusses the valuation allowance that is related to deferred tax assets, and explains how the allowance can markedly affect net income.

Earnings per share (EPS) is the most frequently quoted operating number in the financial press. It represents earnings that are available to pay dividends to common shareholders. Companies report two EPS numbers: basic and diluted. The latter represents the lower bound on EPS. It is important that we understand the difference between the two, and this module describes the two EPS computations.

Pfizer does business around the world, transacting in many currencies. Indeed, many of Pfizer's subsidiaries maintain their entire financial records in currencies other than the U.S. dollar. Consequently, to prepare its financial statements in $US, Pfizer must translate each transaction from foreign currencies into $US. This module describes the effects of foreign currency translation. When the dollar strengthens and weakens against other world currencies, a company's foreign revenues and expenses increase or decrease in $US value even if unit volumes remain unchanged. It is important to understand the mechanical relation between foreign exchange rates and income statement items if we are to properly analyze companies with global operations. This module considers these issues.

Sources: Pfizer 2010 10-K, Pfizer 2010 Annual Report; *Fortune*, January 2009; *BusinessWeek*, January 2009.

MODULE ORGANIZATION

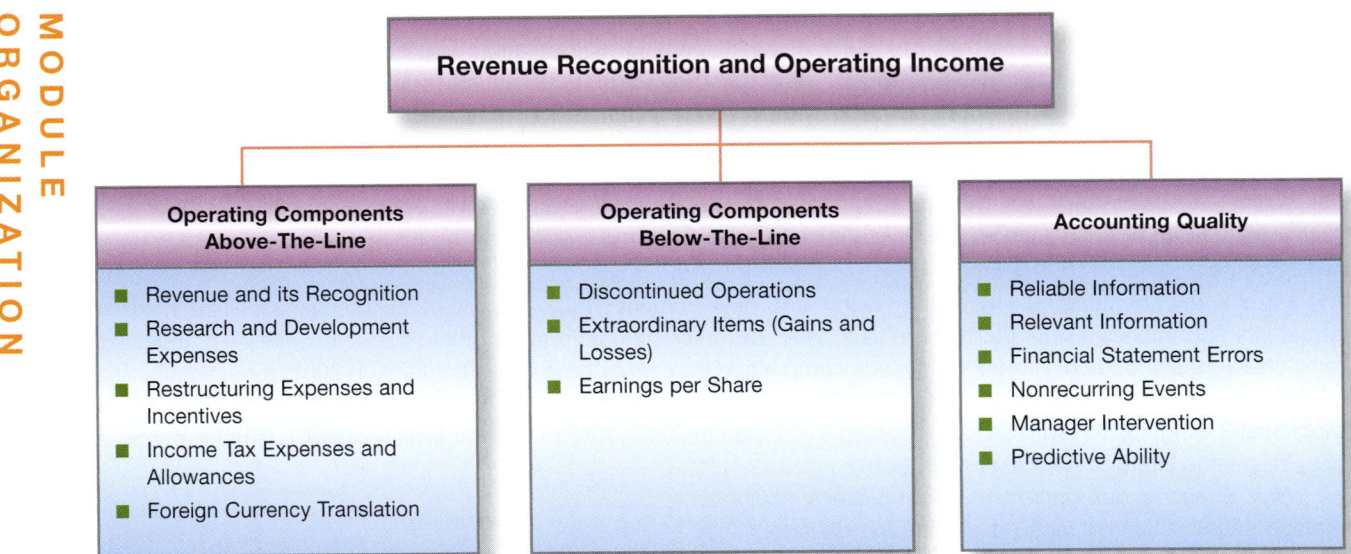

Operating activities refer to a company's primary transactions. These include the purchase of goods from suppliers, the conversion of goods into finished products, the promotion and distribution of goods, the sale of goods to customers, and post-sale customer support. For manufacturing companies, operating activities include the conversion of goods into finished products. The income statement reports on these operating activities such as sales, cost of goods sold, and selling, general, and administrative expenses. Because they are the lifeblood of any company, operating activities must be executed successfully for a company to consistently succeed.

Nonoperating activities relate to the borrowing of money and the ancillary investment activities of a company. They are not a company's primary activities.[1] These activities are typically reported in the income statement as interest revenues and expenses, dividend revenues, gains losses on sales of securities, and net income attributable to noncontrolling interest.

---

[1] Exceptions exist, for example, income derived from investments is operating income for financial-services firms such as banks and insurance companies. As another example, the income derived from financing subsidiaries of manufacturing companies, such as Ford Motor Credit and Caterpillar Financial, is part of operating income because these activities can be viewed as extensions of the sales process.

Proper identification of operating and nonoperating components is important for valuation of companies' equity (stock) and debt (notes and bonds). It is important, for example, to know whether company profitability results from operating activities, or whether poor operating performance is being masked by income from nonoperating activities. (We know that income from nonoperating activities usually depends on a favorable investment climate, which can be short-lived.)

Exhibit 5.1 classifies several common income components as operating or nonoperating.

EXHIBIT 5.1 Distinguishing Operating and Nonoperating Income Components	
Operating Activities	**Nonoperating Activities**
• Sales • Cost of goods sold • Selling, general and administrative expenses • Depreciation expense • Research and development expenses • Restructuring expenses • Income tax expenses • Extraordinary gains and losses • Gains and losses on sales of operating assets • Foreign currency translation effects • Operating asset write-downs • Other income or expenses	• Interest revenues and expenses • Dividend revenues • Gains and losses on sales of investments • Investment write-downs • Gains and losses on debt retirement • Gains and losses on discontinued operations • Allocation of profit to noncontrolling interest (previously titled "minority interest expense")

The list of operating activities above includes all the familiar operating items, as well as gains and losses on transactions relating to operating assets and the write-down of operating assets.[2] The list also includes "other" income statement items. We treat these as operating unless the income statement designates them as nonoperating or footnote information indicates that some or all of these "other" items are nonoperating. Footnotes are usually uninformative about "other" income statement items and "other" balance sheet items, and GAAP does not require specific disclosure of such items unless they are deemed *material*.[3]

We build our discussion of operating income around Pfizer's income statement (see Exhibit 5.2), which includes all of the typical operating accounts. We highlight the following topics in this module:

- Revenues
- Research and development expenses
- Restructuring expenses
- Income tax expenses

- Extraordinary gains and losses
- Earnings per share (EPS)
- Foreign currency translation effects

OPERATING INCOME COMPONENTS

Pfizer's 2010 income statement in Exhibit 5.2 highlights (in blue) the operating income components discussed in this module. We defer discussion of cost of goods sold (cost of sales) to Module 6, which focuses on inventories and other operating assets. Module 2 discusses items typically included in selling, general and administrative (SG&A) expenses, and Module 9 addresses the accounts related to acquisitions of other companies (such as amortization of intangible assets, merger-related in-process research and development charges, noncontrolling interest, and discontinued operations).

---

[2] To explain, a loss on the sale of equipment implies that the company did not depreciate the equipment quickly enough. Had the company recorded the "right" amount of depreciation over the years (that is, the amount of depreciation that perfectly matched the equipment's economic devaluation over time), the equipment's book value would have been exactly the same as its market value and no loss would have been recorded. Thus, we treat the loss on disposal in the same manner as depreciation expense—as operating. The same logic applies to write-downs of operating assets, which occur when the fair value of assets such as property and intangibles has declined below their book value.

[3] *Material* is an accounting term that means the item in question is important enough to make a difference to someone relying on the financial statements when making a business decision. Investors, for example, might find an item material if it is large enough to change their investment decision (whether to buy or sell the stock). This *materiality* judgment is in the eye of the beholder and this subjectivity makes materiality an elusive concept.

EXHIBIT 5.2	Pfizer Income Statement	
(Millions, except per share data)		**2010**
Revenues.		$67,809
Costs and expenses		
Cost of sales.		16,279
Selling, informational and administative expenses.		19,614
Research and development expenses		9,413
Amortization of intangible assets		5,404
Acquisition-related in-process research and development charges		125
Restructuring charges and acquisition-related costs.		3,214
Other deductions—net		4,338
Income from continuing operations before provision for taxes on income		9,422
Provision for taxes on income.		1,124
Income from continuing operations		8,298
Discontinued operations—net of tax		(9)
Net income before allocation to noncontrolling interests.		8,289
Less: Net income attributable to noncontrolling interests		32
Net income attributable to Pfizer Inc..		$ 8,257
Earnings per common share—basic		
Income from continuing operations attributable to Pfizer Inc. common shareholders.		$ 1.03
Discontinued operations—net of tax		—
Net income attributable to Pfizer Inc. common shareholders		$ 1.03
Earnings per common share—diluted		
Income from continuing operations attributable to Pfizer Inc. common shareholders.		$ 1.02
Discontinued operations—net of tax		—
Net income attributable to Pfizer Inc. common shareholders		$ 1.02
Weighted-average shares—basic		8,036
Weighted-average shares—diluted		8,074

We begin by discussing revenue, including the revenue recognition criteria that companies must employ and improper revenue recognition that the SEC has recently challenged. Next, we discuss Pfizer's research and development expenses, restructuring charges, provision for taxes, effects of foreign currency fluctuations, extraordinary items, and earnings per share (EPS).

Revenue and its Recognition

LO1 Explain revenue recognition criteria and identify transactions of special concern for analysis.

Pfizer reports $67,809 million in revenue. This revenue represents the culmination of a process that includes the manufacture of the drugs, their promotion, the receipt of orders, delivery to the customer, billing for the sale amount, and collection of the amounts owed. At what point in this process should Pfizer recognize its revenue and the related profit? When the drugs are delivered to the customer? When payment is received? And, how should Pfizer treat sales discounts or rights of return?

GAAP specifies two **revenue recognition criteria** that must both be met for revenue to be recognized on the income statement. Revenue must be (1) **realized or realizable**, and (2) **earned**.[4] *Realized or realizable* means that the seller's net assets (assets less liabilities) increase. That is, the seller receives an asset, such as cash or accounts receivable, or satisfies a liability, such as deferred revenue, as a result of a transaction. The company does not have to wait to recognize revenue until after it collects the accounts receivable; the increase in the account receivable (asset) means that the revenue is realizable. *Earned* means that the seller has performed its duties under the terms of the sales agreement and that title to the product sold has passed to the buyer

---

[4] SEC provides guidance for revenue recognition in *Staff Accounting Bulletin (SAB) 101* (http://www.sec.gov/interps/account/sab101.htm) that states that revenue is realized, or realizable, and earned when *each* of the following criteria are met: (1) there is persuasive evidence that a sales agreement exists; (2) delivery has occurred or services have been rendered; (3) the seller's price to the buyer is fixed or determinable; and (4) collectibility is reasonably assured.

BUSINESS INSIGHT | **Ratios Across Industries**

Over time, industries evolve and reach equilibrium levels for operating activities. For example, some industries require a high level of selling, general and administrative (SG&A) expenses, perhaps due to high advertising demands or high occupancy costs. Other industries require intense research and development (R&D) expenditures to remain competitive. To a large extent, these cost structures dictate the prices that firms in the industry charge—each industry prices its product or service to yield a sufficient level of gross profit (sales less cost of sales) to cover the operating expenses and allow the industry to remain viable. Review the following table of selected operating margins for companies in various industries (NOPM is net operating profit margin as defined in Module 3).

	Gross profit/Sales	SG&A/Sales	R&D/Sales	NOPM
Cisco Systems, Inc. (CSCO)	64.0%	26.8%	13.2%	19.0%
Intel Corporation (INTC).	65.3%	14.5%	15.1%	25.8%
Pfizer Inc. (PFE)	76.0%	28.9%	13.9%	12.2%
Target Corp. (TGT)	32.1%	20.0%	0.0%	5.0%
Best Buy Co. Inc. (BBY)	25.1%	20.5%	0.0%	2.8%
Caterpillar Inc. (CAT)	28.7%	10.0%	4.5%	6.8%
Dell Inc. (DELL)	18.5%	11.9%	1.1%	4.4%
The Home Depot, Inc. (HD)	34.3%	23.3%	0.0%	5.4%
Nike, Inc. (NKE).	45.6%	32.1%	0.0%	10.0%
Cheesecake Factory Inc. (CAKE)	42.8%	5.8%	0.0%	5.6%

We see that Cisco, Intel and Pfizer report high gross profit margins. This does not necessarily suggest they are better managed than Dell. Instead, their industries require higher levels of gross profit to cover their high levels of SG&A and R&D. Dell, on the other hand, is in a highly price-competitive segment of the computer industry. To maintain its competitive advantage, Dell must control costs. Indeed, Dell reports among the lowest SG&A-to-sales ratio of the companies listed.

---

with no right of return or other contingencies. As long as Pfizer has delivered the drugs ordered by its customers, and its customers are obligated to make payment, Pfizer can recognize revenue. The following conditions would each argue *against* revenue recognition:

- *Rights of return exist,* other than due to routine product defects covered under product warranty.

- *Consignment sales,* where products are held on consignment until ultimately sold by the consignee.

- *Continuing involvement by seller in product resale,* such as where the seller has an obligation for future performance like product updates.

- *Contingency sales,* such as when product sales are contingent on product performance or further approvals by the customer.

Revenue is not recognized in these cases until the factors inhibiting revenue recognition are resolved.

Companies are required to report their revenue recognition policies in footnotes to their 10-K reports. Pfizer recognizes its revenues as follows:

> Revenue Recognition—We record revenue from product sales when the goods are shipped and title passes to the customer. At the time of sale, we also record estimates for a variety of sales deductions, such as sales rebates, discounts and incentives, and product returns.

Pfizer adopts the position that its revenues are *earned* when its products are shipped and the risks and rewards of the merchandise passes to its customers. At that point, Pfizer has done everything required and, thus, recognizes the sale in the income statement. Most companies recognize revenues using these same criteria. Pfizer does *not* recognize revenues for the gross selling price. Instead, Pfizer deducts that portion of gross sales that is likely to be refunded to customers through sales rebates, discounts and incentives (including volume purchases). Pfizer estimates the likely cost of those price reductions and deducts that amount from gross sales. Similarly, Pfizer does not recognize revenues for those products that it estimates will be returned, possibly because the drugs hit their expiration date before they are sold by Pfizer's customers. In sum, Pfizer recognizes revenues for products delivered to customers, and for only the sales price *net* of anticipated discounts and returns. This is why we often see "Revenues, net" on companies' income statements.

IFRS INSIGHT	**Revenue Recognition and IFRS**

Revenue is generally recognized under both U.S. GAAP and IFRS when the earning process is complete (when the seller has performed all obligations under the sales arrangement and no performance obligations remain) and benefits are realized or realizable. Further, there is extensive guidance under U.S. GAAP for specific industry transactions. That guidance is not present in IFRS. Moreover, public companies in the U.S. must follow additional guidance set by the SEC. Many believe that companies recognize revenue slightly earlier under IFRS than under GAAP.

Revenue Recognition and Risk Exposure

More than 70% of SEC accounting and auditing enforcement actions involve misstated revenues. The SEC's concern about aggressive (premature) revenue recognition prompted the issuance of a special *Staff Accounting Bulletin (SAB) 101* on the matter. The SEC provides the following examples of problem areas to assist companies in properly recognizing revenue:

- *Case 1: Channel stuffing.* Some sellers use their market power over customers to induce (or even require) them to purchase more goods than they actually need. This practice, called *channel stuffing*, increases period-end sales and net income. If no side agreements exist for product returns, the practice does not violate GAAP revenue recognition guidelines, but the SEC contends that revenues are misrepresented and that the practice is a violation of securities laws.

- *Case 2: Barter transactions.* Some barter transactions are concocted to create the illusion of revenue. Examples include the advertising swaps that dot-com companies have sometimes engaged in, and the excess capacity swaps of fiber optic communications businesses. The advertising swap relates to the simultaneous sale and purchase of advertising. The excess capacity swap relates to a company selling excess capacity to a competitor and, simultaneously, purchasing excess capacity from that competitor. Both types of swaps are exchanges of nearly identical services; they do not provide income or create an expense for either party. Further, these transactions do not represent a culmination of the normal earning process and, thus, the "earned" revenue recognition criterion is not met.

- *Case 3: Mischaracterizing transactions as arm's-length.* Transfers of inventories or other assets to related entities are typically not recognized as revenue until arm's-length sales occur. Sometimes, companies disguise non-arm's-length transactions as sales to unrelated entities. This practice is improper when the buyer is related to the seller, or the buyer is unable to pay for the merchandise other than from its resale. Revenue should not be recognized unless the sales process is complete, that is, goods have been transferred and an asset has been created (future payment from a solvent, independent party).

- *Case 4: Pending execution of sales agreements.* Sometimes companies boost current-period profits by recording revenue for goods delivered for which formal customer approval has yet to be received. The SEC's position is that if the company's practice is to obtain sales authorization, then revenue is *not* earned until such approval is obtained, even though product delivery is made and customer approval is anticipated.

- *Case 5: Gross versus net revenues.* Some companies use their distribution network to sell other companies' goods for a commission. There are increasing reports of companies that inflate revenues by reporting such transactions on a gross basis (separately reporting both sales and cost of goods sold) instead of reporting only the commission (typically a percentage of sales price). The incentives for such reporting are high for some dot.com companies and start-ups that believe the market prices of their stocks are based on revenue growth and not on profitability. Reporting revenues at gross rather than net could have enormous impact on the valuations of those companies. The SEC prescribes that such sales be reported on a net basis (see Business Insight on next page).

- *Case 6: Sales on consignment.* Some companies deliver goods to other companies with the understanding that these goods will be ultimately sold to third parties. At the time of delivery, title does not pass to the second company, and the second company has no obligation to make payment to the seller until the product is sold. This type of transaction is called a *consignment sale.* The SEC's position is that a sale has not occurred, and revenue is *not* to be recognized by the original company, until the product is sold to a third party. Further, the middleman (consignee) cannot report the gross sale, and can only report its commission revenue.

- *Case 7: Failure to take delivery.* Some customers may not take delivery of the product by period-end. In this case, revenue is *not* yet earned. The earning process is only complete once the product is delivered and accepted. An example is a layaway sale. Even though the product is ordered, and even partially paid for, revenue is not recognized until the product is delivered and final payment is made or agreed to be made.

- *Case 8: Nonrefundable fees.* Sellers sometimes receive fees that are nonrefundable to the customer. An example is a health club initiation fee or a cellular phone activation fee. Some sellers wish to record these cash receipts as revenue to boost current sales and income. However, even though cash is received and nonrefundable, revenue is not recognized until the product is delivered or the service performed. Until that time, the company reports the cash received as a liability (deferred revenue). Once the obligation is settled, the liability is removed and revenue is reported.

In sum, revenue is only recognized when it is earned and when it is realized or realizable. This demands that the seller has performed its obligations (no contingencies exist) and the buyer is an independent party with the financial capacity to pay the amounts owed.

BUSINESS INSIGHT **Gross versus Net Revenues**

In 2011, **Groupon, Inc.,** announced its intentions to offer stock to the public in an initial public offering (IPO). The company's original SEC registration statement disclosed that the company recorded revenue at the gross amount it received from selling Groupons (coupons). For example, when Groupon sold a restaurant gift certificate for $20, it would record the full amount of $20 even though a hefty portion (say $9 for example) is owed the restaurant owner. By recording revenues at "gross," Groupon did not comply with GAAP because it holds no inventory, does not determine the product or service price, and does not perform the service. The SEC intervened and Groupon restated revenues in an amended SEC filing in September 2011. Groupon now reports revenues at "net," which is the commission on sales, rather than the total value of online coupons. Returning to our restaurant example, Groupon's amended revenue would be $11, not $20. Footnote 2 of its latest SEC filing reports the following. Shortly after the amended filing, Groupon's Chief Operating Officer left the firm.

Revenues ($ 000s)	2008	2009	2010
As previously reported	$ 94	$30,471	$713,365
Restatement adjustment	(89)	(15,931)	(400,424)
As restated	$ 5	$14,540	$312,941

Percentage-of-Completion Revenue Recognition

Another revenue recognition challenge arises for companies with long-term sales contracts (spanning more than one period), such as construction companies, consultants, and defense contractors. For these companies, revenue is often recognized using the percentage-of-completion method, which recognizes revenue by determining the costs incurred under the contract relative to its total expected costs.

To illustrate, assume that Bayer Construction signs a $10 million contract to construct a building. Bayer estimates construction will take two years and will cost $7,500,000. This means the contract yields an expected gross profit of $2,500,000 over two years. The following table summarizes construction costs incurred each year and the revenue Bayer recognizes.

	Construction costs incurred	Percentage complete	Revenue recognized
Year 1	$4,500,000	$\frac{\$4,500,000}{\$7,500,000} = 60\%$	$10,000,000 × 60% = $6,000,000
Year 2	$3,000,000	$\frac{\$3,000,000}{\$7,500,000} = 40\%$	$10,000,000 × 40% = $4,000,000

This table reveals that Bayer would report $6 million in revenue and $1.5 million ($6 million − $4.5 million) in gross profit on the construction project in the first year; it would report $4 million in revenue and $1 million ($4 million − $3 million) in gross profit in the second year.

Next, assume that Bayer's client makes a $1 million deposit at the signing of the contract and that Bayer submits bills to the client based on the percentage of completion. The following table reflects the bills sent to, and the cash received from, the client.

	Revenue recognized	Client billed	Cash received
At signing	$ 0	$ 0	$1,000,000
Year 1	6,000,000	5,000,000	2,000,000
Year 2	4,000,000	4,000,000	7,000,000

At the signing of the contract, Bayer recognizes no revenue because construction has not begun and thus, Bayer has not earned any revenue. By the end of the second year, Bayer has recognized all of the contract revenue and the client has paid all monies owed per the accounts receivable. The following template captures Bayer Construction's transactions over this two-year period (M indicates millions).

Transaction	Cash Asset	+	Noncash Assets	=	Liabilities	+	Contrib. Capital	+	Earned Capital		Revenues	−	Expenses	=	Net Income
Start of year 1: Record $1M deposit received at contract signing	+1M Cash			=	+1M Unearned Revenue							−		=	
Year 1: Record $4.5M construction costs	−4.5M Cash			=					−4.5M Retained Earnings			−	+4.5M Cost of Sales	=	−4.5M
Year 1: Recognize $6M revenue on partly completed contract			+5M Accounts Receivable	=	−1M Unearned Revenue				+6M Retained Earnings		+6M Revenue	−		=	+6M
Year 1: Record $2M cash received from client	+2M Cash		−2M Accounts Receivable	=								−		=	

Margin T-accounts:

Cash 1M
UR   1M
Cash
1M |
   UR
   | 1M

COGS 4.5M
Cash   4.5M
COGS
4.5M |
   Cash
   | 4.5M

AR 5M
UR 1M
REV   6M
AR
5M |
   UR
1M |
   REV
   | 6M

Cash 2M
AR   2M
Cash
2M |
   AR
   | 2M

continued

continued from prior page

Transaction	Balance Sheet								Income Statement		
	Cash Asset	+	Noncash Assets	=	Liabil- ities	+	Contrib. Capital	+	Earned Capital		
Year 2: Record $3M construction costs	−3M Cash			=					−3M Retained Earnings		
Year 2: Recognize $4M revenue for completed contract			+4M Accounts Receivable	=					+4M Retained Earnings		
Year 2: Record $7M cash received from client	+7M Cash		−7M Accounts Receivable	=							

Rev- enues	−	Expen- ses	=	Net Income
	−	+3M Cost of Sales	=	−3M
+4M Revenue	−		=	+4M
	−		=	

```
COGS   3M
   Cash      3M
       COGS
   3M |
       Cash
           3M

AR     4M
   Rev      4M
       AR
   4M |
       Rev
           4M

Cash   7M
   AR       7M
       Cash
   7M |
       AR
           7M
```

Revenue recognition policies for these types of contracts are disclosed in a manner typical to the following from the 2010 10-K report footnotes of **Raytheon Company**.

> **Revenue Recognition** We account for our long-term contracts . . . using the percentage-of-completion accounting method. Under this method, revenue is recognized based on the extent of progress towards completion of the long-term contract . . . We generally use the cost-to-cost measure of progress for all of our long-term contracts . . . Under the cost-to-cost measure of progress, the extent of progress towards completion is measured based on the ratio of costs incurred-to-date to the total estimated costs at completion of the contract.

BUSINESS INSIGHT   **Disney's Revenue Recognition**

The **Walt Disney Company** uses a method similar to percentage-of-completion to determine the amount of production cost to match against film and television revenues. Following is an excerpt from its 10-K.

> Film and television costs include capitalizable production costs, production overhead, interest, development costs, and acquired production costs and are stated at the lower of cost, less accumulated amortization, or fair value. Film and television .... costs are expensed based on the ratio of the current period's revenues to estimated remaining total revenues (Ultimate Revenues). Ultimate Revenues include revenues that will be earned within ten years from the date of the initial theatrical release or ... the delivery of the first episode.

As Disney pays production costs, it records those costs on the balance sheet as inventory. Then, as film and television revenues are recognized, the company matches a portion of production costs (from inventory) against revenues in computing income. Each period, the costs recognized are equal to the proportion of total revenues recognized in the period to the total revenues expected over the life of the film or television show. Thus, estimates of both costs and income depend on the quality of Disney's revenue estimates, which are, likely, imprecise.

The percentage-of-completion method of revenue recognition requires an estimate of total costs. This estimate is made at the beginning of the contract and is typically the one used to initially bid the contract. However, estimates are inherently inaccurate. If the estimate changes during the construction period, the percentage-of-completion is computed as the total costs incurred to date divided by the *current* estimate of total anticipated costs (costs incurred to date plus total estimated costs to complete).

If total construction costs are underestimated, the percentage-of-completion is overestimated (the denominator is too low) and revenue and gross profit to date are overstated. The estimation process inherent in this method has the potential for inaccurate or, even, improper revenue recognition. In addition, estimates of remaining costs to complete projects are difficult for the auditors to verify. This uncertainty adds additional risk to financial statement analysis.

Recognition of Unearned Revenue

In some industries it is common to receive cash before recording revenue. Customers might pay in advance for special orders, make deposits for future services, or buy concert tickets, subscriptions, or gift cards. In those cases, companies must record unearned revenues, a liability, and only record revenue when those products and services are provided. Specifically, deposits or advance payments are not recorded as revenue until the company performs the services owed or delivers the goods. Until then, the company's balance sheet shows the advance payment as a liability (called unearned revenue or deferred revenue) because the company is obligated to deliver those products and services.

Unearned revenue is particularly common among technology companies that sell goods and services as packages. These sales are called "multi-element contracts," which are sales agreements that bundle goods and services that may or may not be delivered simultaneously. When delivery is delayed the company must record unearned revenue. Consider for example, the sale of an Apple iPad. The customer not only purchases the tablet hardware but the software integral to the iPad's function, additional software, and future software upgrades. How should Apple record revenue for such a multi-element contract? The short answer is that the total sales price is allocated among the elements of the contract and revenue is recognized (as it's earned) at different points in time for each element. Allocating the total sales price presents a challenge because elements often do not have stand-alone prices. GAAP allows companies to estimate selling prices for each element if sold separately and then allocate the total selling price ratably among the elements.

More specifically, assume that on September 26, 2010 (the first day of Apple's 2011 fiscal year), Apple sells 60 iPads to a customer and charges the total invoice amount of $36,000 to the customer's credit card (a cash transaction). Apple disclosed the following in its 10K:

> Beginning with initial sales of iPad in April 2010, the Company has also indicated it may from time-to-time provide future unspecified software upgrades and features free of charge to iPad customers. The Company's estimated selling price (ESP) for the embedded software upgrade right included with the sale of each iPad is $10. Amounts allocated to the embedded unspecified software upgrade rights are deferred and recognized on a straight-line basis over 24 months.

Apple records $36,000 cash and recognizes revenue on the hardware and software components of the sale. The estimated selling price of $600 for the future software upgrades (60 units at $10 per unit) is not earned at the point of sale. Instead, Apple records a liability (unearned revenue) for this amount. This means that revenue of $35,400 is immediately reported and $600 is reported over the ensuing 24 months. Apple prepares quarterly financial statements and will recognize $75 ($600 × 3/24) of the unearned revenue each quarter for two years. As revenue is earned, the unearned revenue account on the balance sheet is reduced and revenue is recorded in the income statement. The following template reflects the initial sales transaction and the subsequent first quarter accounting adjustment.

Transaction	Balance Sheet						Income Statement		
	Cash Asset	+ Noncash Assets	= Liabil- ities	+ Contrib. Capital	+ Earned Capital		Rev- enues	− Expen- ses	= Net Income
Sep 26: Receive $36,000 cash advance for products	+36,000 Cash		= +600 Unearned Revenue		+35,400 Retained Earnings		+35,400 Revenue	−	= +35,400
Dec 26: Rec- ognize three months' of unearned revenue			= −75 Unearned Revenue		+75 Retained Earnings		+75 Revenue	−	= +75

Cash 36,000
UR 600
Revenue 35,400
Cash
36,000 |
UR
| 600
Rev
| 35,400

UR 75
Rev 75
UR
75 |
Rev
| 75

Apple's 2010 balance sheet reports the following liabilities (in millions):

Current liabilities	
Accounts payable	$12,015
Accrued expenses	5,723
Deferred revenue	2,984
Total current liabilities	20,722
Deferred revenue– non-current	1,139
Other non-current liabilities	5,531
Total liabilities	$27,392

The company reports deferred revenue as both current and noncurrent liabilities. These relate to the revenue that will be earned in the coming year ($2,984 million) and in subsequent years ($1,139). These are substantial liabilities to Apple because many of its products are sold with

BUSINESS INSIGHT   New Revenue Recognition Standard

In June 2010, the FASB and IASB published a joint exposure draft (ED) on revenue recognition, *Revenue from Contracts with Customers*. These new revenue recognition rules are similar to the rules for multi-element contracts (described above). Companies must identify separate "performance obligations" within a contract and account for each individually. A performance obligation is an enforceable promise to transfer goods or services to the customer. The challenge for companies will be to identify the various performance obligations within a single contract. The core concept is whether or not a good or service is "distinct." It is distinct if the good or service 1) can be sold separately, 2) has a distinct function, and 3) has a distinct profit margin. A distinct good or service is accounted for as a separate performance obligation. If a good or service is not distinct, it is combined with other goods or services that form a distinct good or service. Companies recognize revenue as performance obligations are satisfied, that is, when the customer obtains control of the goods or services.

For construction projects the new rules will likely yield results similar to the percentage-of-completion accounting method described above. This is due to the fact that the various construction tasks are highly interrelated and are not routinely sold independently. The critical factor is whether 1) construction tasks are distinct and 2) control over the delivered goods and services is transferred to the customer continuously during the project (as opposed to at project completion). For example, if a company bills the customer throughout the project based either on measurable outputs such as milestones or on measurable inputs such as time and materials, then transfer of control is continuous and revenue will essentially be recognized on a percentage-of-completion basis. Nonetheless, many construction firms sent comment letters to the FASB / IASB, arguing that the new rules needlessly complicate revenue recognition and impose additional costs. The new rules could be required as soon as 2012, but the ultimate requirements and adoption dates will depend on additional due process by both boards.

guaranteed future services such as software upgrades and long-term service contracts. Each quarter, the unearned revenue account increases by the new sales and decreases as revenue is earned.

Research and Development (R&D) Expenses

LO2 Describe and analyze accounting for operating expenses, including research and development, and restructuring.

R&D activities are a major expenditure for many companies, especially for those in technology and pharmaceutical industries. Pfizer's R&D costs, for example, make up 14% of revenues ($9,413 million/$67,809 million). These expenses include employment costs for R&D personnel, R&D materials and supplies, R&D related contract services, and R&D fixed-asset costs.

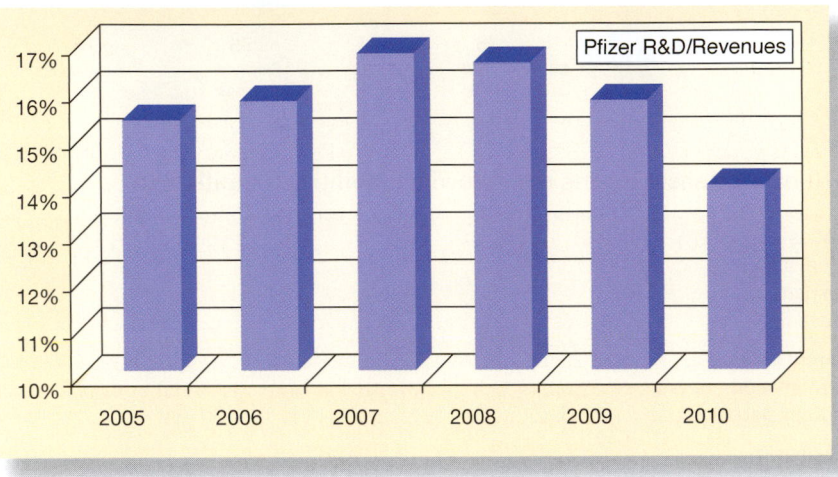

Accounting for R&D

Accounting for R&D is straightforward: R&D costs are expensed as incurred. The key issue is how to classify the expenses for financial reporting purposes. Salaries paid to researchers, and the depreciation and other expenses related to general-purpose research facilities, are accounted for in the usual manner (which is to expense salaries when paid and to capitalize and depreciate general-purpose research facilities). However, these expenses are totaled separately and are classified as R&D in the income statement rather than as SG&A. An exception to this general rule relates to the purchase of R&D assets that are only used for a specific project and then retired when that project is complete. These project-specific assets are expensed when purchased. Consequently, income is reduced in the year of acquisition (but higher in subsequent years) relative to what the company would have reported had the asset been capitalized and depreciated. (Project-specific assets are said to have no "alternate use." One alternate use could be reselling the asset. In that case, the asset is *not* considered project-specific and is accounted for like other long-term assets.)

IFRS INSIGHT	Research and Development Expenses and IFRS

IFRS accounts for research costs and development costs separately. Research costs are always expensed. Development costs must be capitalized if all of the following conditions are affirmed:

- Technical feasibility of completing the intangible asset.
- Intention to complete the intangible asset.
- Ability to use or sell the intangible asset.
- Intangible asset will generate future economic benefits (the company must demonstrate the existence of a market or, if for internal use, the usefulness of the intangible asset).
- Availability of adequate resources to complete development.
- Ability to measure reliably the expenditure attributable to the intangible asset during its development.

U.S. GAAP allows for capitalization of costs related to the development of software for sale to third parties once the software achieves "commercial feasibility," but is silent on the capitalization of other intangible assets—thus, implicitly prescribing expensing of these assets.

Following is a footnote excerpt from **Pfizer**'s 2010 annual report related to its research and development expenditures:

> Research and development (R&D) costs are expensed as incurred. These expenses include the costs of our proprietary R&D efforts, as well as costs incurred in connection with certain licensing arrangements.

Pfizer capitalizes and depreciates general research facilities (those with alternate uses). All other R&D costs are expensed as incurred.

Analysis of R&D

When R&D expenses are large, such as that for technology-based and pharmaceutical companies, a question arises as to how we should treat those expenses in our company analysis. If R&D outlays are expected to yield future benefits, companies would (conceptually) understate assets and income because GAAP requires expensing of R&D outlays. One approach is to capitalize and amortize the reported R&D expenses. To illustrate, assume that a company reports the following income statement:

Sales....................	$500
Expenses other than R&D	350
R&D expenses	**100**
Net income (per GAAP)	$ 50

Next, assume that R&D expenses create economic benefits over the next five years. Accordingly, the method would treat the $100 R&D expenditures as an asset and amortize it over its useful life. Specifically, the adjusted balance sheet would reflect the $80 of unamortized R&D assets remaining, computed as $100 in R&D asset less $20 in R&D amortization (current-year equity is also $80 greater from the $80 of expenses postponed to future years). The adjusted income statement would reflect the $20 amortization of the $100 R&D asset as follows (computed as $100/5 years):

Sales....................	$500
Expenses other than R&D ...	350
R&D amortization	**20**
Net income..............	$130

This adjusted income makes the company look more profitable than GAAP would. (However, if the company is not experiencing abnormal growth and the $100 annual R&D expenditures continue as usual, then after the five-year initial amortization period the R&D amortization in the adjusted income statement will approximate the R&D expenses in the GAAP income statement.)

While this analysis might be conceptually appealing, it has problems. First, determining the proportion of R&D expenses that creates future economic benefits is extremely subjective. GAAP income statements do not distinguish between research and that of development and, instead, report them as one combined item. As users of financial reports, we have little basis to make such an allocation, let alone decide if outlays meet certain criteria. Second, there is considerable judgment in determining the period over which future economic benefits will occur. Some intangible assets such as patents are protected for specific lengths of time, but most other intangibles have no such defined period of potential benefit. Third, the manner in which future benefits will be realized is uncertain, so amortization of an R&D asset would be arbitrary. A straight-line method (as in our example above) would be easy, but would it reflect the asset's pattern of use?

For these reasons, we do not advise routinely creating pro forma net income and balance sheet numbers by capitalizing and amortizing R&D expenses. (An exception might be for growth companies that have yet to reach a steady level of R&D outlays, for companies with product breakthroughs, and for companies that require financial comparisons to IFRS-compliant reports.) Further, for companies that spend about the same amount each year on R&D, the income statement adjustment would be small. To see this, recall our example above: if the company spends $100 on R&D each year, then after five years, the amortization of previously capitalized amounts will be $100 (5 × $20) which is exactly the same as the R&D expense itself. However, the balance sheet adjustment can be more substantial as the R&D asset is "missing" entirely from the GAAP balance sheet (in the same way that benefits from the payment of wages or advertising are missing). Hence, when we compute ratios that involve income and assets (such as ROA or RNOA) or income and equity (such as ROE), the effects of expensing R&D are likely to overstate such ratios (from the absence of R&D assets in balance sheets).

A similar conclusion is reached in a recent study (Danielson and Press, "When Does R&D Expense Distort Profitability Estimates?" *Journal of Applied Finance*, 2005):

> . . . the accounting and finance literatures provide no guidance as to when potential distortion in accounting-based return measures makes an adjustment necessary. The expensing of R&D costs affects both the income statement and balance sheet, and therefore has an uncertain impact on a firm's accounting rate of return. It is possible for the income statement and balance sheet errors to cancel out—resulting in a small difference between adjusted and unadjusted accounting rates of return—even for a firm with high R&D costs. Thus, it is not obvious when complex and time-consuming adjustments for historical R&D costs are an essential step in a profitability analysis.

The study concludes that: "unadjusted ROA and adjusted (for R&D costs) ROA typically rank firm profitability in a similar order. Thus, unadjusted ROA is a reasonable proxy for firms' underlying economic profitability in many research applications, and complex adjustment procedures are often unnecessary."

Consequently, what analysis and/or adjustment for R&D expenses should we implement? Unfortunately, there is no simple computational adjustment. Instead, we begin our quantitative analysis by comparing common-sized R&D expenditures over time and across companies in the same industry (see Business Insight below). Differences in R&D outlays and marked departures from industry benchmarks call for further analysis. For our qualitative analysis, we look to the MD&A section of the 10-K, along with external sources of information, to gauge the effectiveness of the company's R&D efforts. Pharmaceutical companies typically disclose the drugs under development ("pipeline") as well as newly patented drugs. We can also evaluate new product introductions resulting from R&D expenditures. However, the disclosures for technology companies (and most other companies) are typically not as detailed. For those companies, we must seek information about new product introductions and other successes that management highlights in the MD&A.

BUSINESS INSIGHT   **R&D at Pfizer and its Peers**

Pfizer spent $9.4 billion in 2010 for R&D compared with its revenues of $67.8 billion, or about 13.9%. This reflects a high percent of revenues devoted to R&D for the pharmaceutical industry. Following is the R&D-expense-to-sales ratio for Pfizer and some of its competitors.

	2010	2009	2008
Pfizer	13.9%	15.7%	16.5%
Bristol-Meyers Squibb	18.3	19.4	19.8
Merck	23.9	21.3	20.1
Eli Lilly	21.2	19.8	18.9
Abbott Laboratories	10.6	8.9	9.1

Restructuring Expenses and Incentives

Restructuring expenses are substantial in many income statements. Because of their magnitude, GAAP requires enhanced disclosure, either as a separate line item in the income statement or as a footnote. Restructuring costs typically include three components:

1. Employee severance or relocation costs
2. Asset write-downs
3. Other restructuring costs

The first part, **employee severance or relocation costs**, represents accrued (estimated) costs to terminate or relocate employees as part of a restructuring program. To accrue those expenses, the company must:

- Estimate total costs of terminating or relocating selected employees; these costs might include severance pay (typically a number of weeks of pay based on the employee's tenure with the company), outplacement costs, and relocation or retraining costs for remaining employees.

- Report *total* estimated costs as an expense (and a liability) in the period the restructuring program is announced. Subsequent payments to employees reduce the restructuring accrual (the liability).

The second part of restructuring costs is **asset write-downs**, also called *write-offs* or *charge-offs*. Restructuring activities usually involve closure or relocation of manufacturing or administrative facilities. This can require the write-down of assets whose fair value is less than book value. For example, restructurings can necessitate the write-down of long-term assets (such as plant assets or goodwill) and of inventories. Recall that asset cost is first recorded on the balance sheet and is subsequently transferred from the balance sheet to the income statement as expense when the asset is used. The write-down of an asset accelerates this process for a portion, or all, of the asset cost. Write-downs have no cash flow effects unless the write-down has some potential tax consequences.

The third part of restructuring costs is typically labeled "Other" and includes costs of vacating duplicative facilities, fees to terminate contracts (such as lease agreements and service contracts), and other exit costs (such as legal and asset-appraisal fees). Companies estimate and accrue these costs and reduce the restructuring liability as those costs are paid in cash.

The financial statement effects of restructuring charges can be large and frequent. We must remember that management determines the amount of restructuring costs and when to recognize them. As such, it is not uncommon for a company to time recognition of restructuring costs in a period when its income is already depressed. This behavior is referred to as a **big bath**.

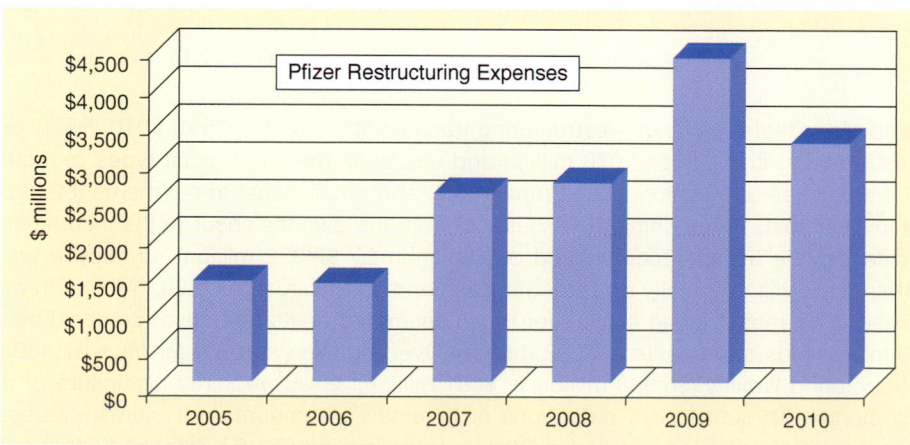

U.S. GAAP has relatively stringent rules relating to restructuring costs in an effort to mitigate abuses. For example, a company is required to have a formal restructuring plan that is approved by

BUSINESS INSIGHT Pfizer's Restructuring

Pfizer explains its restructuring efforts as follows in its 2010 10-K:

We have incurred significant costs in connection with our cost-reduction initiatives (several programs initiated since 2005) and our acquisition of Wyeth on October 15, 2009. Since the acquisition of Wyeth, our cost-reduction initiatives that were announced on January 26, 2009 have been incorporated into a comprehensive plan to integrate Wyeth's operations, generate cost savings and capture synergies across the combined company. We are focusing our efforts on achieving an appropriate cost structure for the combined company. The components of restructuring charges associated with all of our cost-reduction initiatives and the acquisition of Wyeth follow:

(Millions of dollars)	Costs Incurred 2005-2010	Activity through December 31, 2010	Accrual as of December 31, 2010
Employee termination costs.	$ 8,846	$6,688	$2,158
Asset impairments	2,322	2,322	—
Other.	902	801	101
Total	$12,070	$9,811	$2,259

Financial statement effects of Pfizer's accounting for restructuring costs are illustrated in the following template ($ millions).

	Balance Sheet						Income Statement		
Transaction	Cash Asset	+ Noncash Assets	= Liabil- ities	+ Contrib. Capital	+ Earned Capital		Rev- enues	− Expen- ses	= Net Income
2005-2010: Record total restructuring expense and liability		−2,322 Accumulated Depreciation	+9,748 Restructuring Liability		−12,070 Retained Earnings			+12,070 Restructuring Expense	−12,070
2005-2010: Paid $7,489 cash toward liability	−7,489 Cash		−7,489 Restructuring Liability					−	=

RSE   12,070
  RSL   9,748
  AD   2,322
       RSE
12,070 |
     RSL
        | 9,748
     AD
        | 2,322
RSL   7,489
  Cash   7,489
       RSL
7,489 |
     Cash
        | 7,489

The template reflects five years' restructuring transactions. From 2005 to 2010, Pfizer estimated total restructuring costs of $12,070 million and discloses the three usual types of restructuring costs of employee termination, asset impairment, and other. Asset impairments ($2,322 million) do not involve cash. Pfizer shifts the asset cost from the balance sheet to the income statement (by increasing the assets' accumulated depreciation by $2,322 million). Employee termination and other costs will eventually be settled in cash and so Pfizer accrues $9,748 million on its balance sheet as a restructuring liability for those estimated costs (employee termination costs of $8,846 million plus other costs of $902 million). Over the five years, Pfizer pays $7,489 to settle the restructuring liability ($6,688 million + $801 million). GAAP requires disclosure of the initial liability, along with subsequent reductions or reversals of amounts not ultimately used. Pfizer includes the remaining $2,259 million in *Other current liabilities* ($1.6 billion) and *Other noncurrent liabilities* ($652 million) on its 2010 balance sheet.

its board of directors before any restructuring charges are accrued. Also, a company must identify the relevant employees and notify them of its plan. In each subsequent year, the company must disclose in its footnotes the original amount of the liability (accrual), how much of that liability is settled in the current period (such as employee payments), how much of the original liability has been reversed because of original cost overestimation, any new accruals for unforeseen costs, and the current balance of the liability. This creates more transparent financial statements, which presumably deters earnings management.

RESEARCH INSIGHT   **Restructuring Costs and Managerial Incentives**

Research has investigated the circumstances and effects of restructuring costs. Some research finds that stock prices increase when a company announces a restructuring as if the market appreciates the company's candor. Research also finds that many companies that reduce income through restructuring costs later reverse a portion of those costs, resulting in a substantial income boost for the period of reversal. These reversals often occur when the company would have otherwise reported an earnings decline. Whether or not the market responds favorably to trimming the fat or simply disregards restructuring costs as transitory and, thus, as uninformative, managers have incentives to characterize such income-decreasing items as "one-time" on the income statement and routinely exclude such charges in non-GAAP, pro forma disclosures. These incentives often derive from contracts such as debt covenants and managerial bonus plans.

Restructuring costs are typically large and, as such, greatly affect reported profits. Our analysis must consider whether these costs are properly chargeable to the accounting period in which they are recognized. Following are some guidelines relating to the components of restructuring costs:

Employee Severance or Relocation Costs and Other Costs GAAP permits recognition of costs relating to employee separation or relocation that are *incremental* and that do not benefit future periods. Similarly, other accrued costs must be related to the restructuring and not to expenses that would otherwise have been incurred in the future. Thus, accrual of these costs is treated like other liability accruals. We must, however, be aware of over- or understated costs and their effect on current and future profitability. GAAP requires a reconciliation of this restructuring accrual in future years (see Business Insight on Pfizer's restructuring). A reconciliation reveals either overstatements or understatements: overstatements are followed by a reversal of the restructuring liability, and understatements are followed by further accruals. Should a company develop a reputation for recurring reversals or understatements, its management loses credibility.

Asset Write-downs Asset write-downs accelerate (or catch up) the depreciation process to reflect asset impairment. Impairment implies the loss of cash-generating capability and, likely, occurs over several years. Thus, prior periods' profits are arguably not as high as reported, and the current period's profit is not as low. This measurement error is difficult to estimate and, thus, many analysts do not adjust balance sheets and income statements for write-downs. At a minimum, however, we must recognize the qualitative implications of restructuring costs for the profitability of recent prior periods and the current period.

ANALYSIS DECISION   **You Are the Financial Analyst**

You are analyzing the 10-K of a company that reports a large restructuring expense, involving employee severance and asset write-downs. How do you interpret and treat this cost in your analysis of the company's current and future profitability? [Answer, p. 5-38]

MID-MODULE REVIEW 1

Merck & Co., Inc., reports the following income statements for 2008 through 2010.

($ in millions)	2010	2009	2008
Sales.	$45,987	$27,428	$23,850
Costs, expenses and other			
Materials and production	18,396	9,019	5,583
Marketing and administrative	13,245	8,543	7,377
Research and development	10,991	5,845	4,805
Restructuring costs.	985	1,634	1,033
Equity income from affiliates.	(587)	(2,235)	(2,561)
Other (income) expense, net.	1,304	(10,668)	(2,318)
	44,334	12,138	13,919
Income before taxes.	1,653	15,290	9,931
Taxes on income	671	2,268	1,999
Net income.	$ 982	$13,022	$ 7,932

Required

1. Merck's revenue recognition policy, as outlined in footnotes to its 10-K, includes the following: "Revenues from sales of products are recognized when title and risk of loss passes to the customer." Evaluate Merck's revenue recognition policy.
2. Merck's research and development (R&D) efforts often require specialized equipment and facilities that cannot be used for any other purpose. How does Merck account for costs related to this specialized equipment and facilities? Would Merck account for these costs differently if they had alternate uses? Explain.
3. Merck reports restructuring expense each year. What are the general categories of restructuring expenses? How do accrual accounting and disclosure requirements prevent companies from intentionally overstating restructuring expenses in one year (referred to as taking a "big bath") and reversing the unused expenses in a future year?

The solution is on page 5-60.

Income Tax Expenses and Allowances

LO3 Explain and analyze accounting for income taxes.

Companies prepare financial statements for shareholders using GAAP. When these companies file their income tax returns, they prepare financial statements using the *Internal Revenue Code (IRC)*. These two different sets of accounting rules recognize revenues and expenses differently in many cases and, as a result, can yield markedly different levels of income. In general, companies desire to report lower income to taxing authorities than they do to their shareholders so that they can reduce their tax liability and increase after-tax cash flow. This practice is acceptable so long as the financial statements are prepared in conformity with GAAP and tax returns are filed in accordance with the IRC.

As an example, consider the depreciation of long-term assets. For shareholder reports, companies typically depreciate long-term assets using straight-line depreciation (meaning the same amount of depreciation expense is reported each year over the useful life of the asset). However, for reports sent to tax authorities, companies use an *accelerated* method of depreciation (meaning more depreciation is taken in the early years of the asset's life and less depreciation in later years). When a company depreciates assets at an accelerated rate for tax purposes, the depreciation deduction for tax purposes is higher and taxable income is lower in the early years of the assets' lives. As a result, tax payments are reduced and after-tax cash flow is increased. That excess cash can then be reinvested in the business to increase its returns to shareholders.

To illustrate, assume that Pfizer purchases an asset with a five-year life. It depreciates that asset using the straight-line method (equal expense per year) when reporting to shareholders and depreciates the asset at a faster rate (accelerated depreciation) for tax purposes. Annual (full year) depreciation expense under these two methods is depicted in Exhibit 5.3.

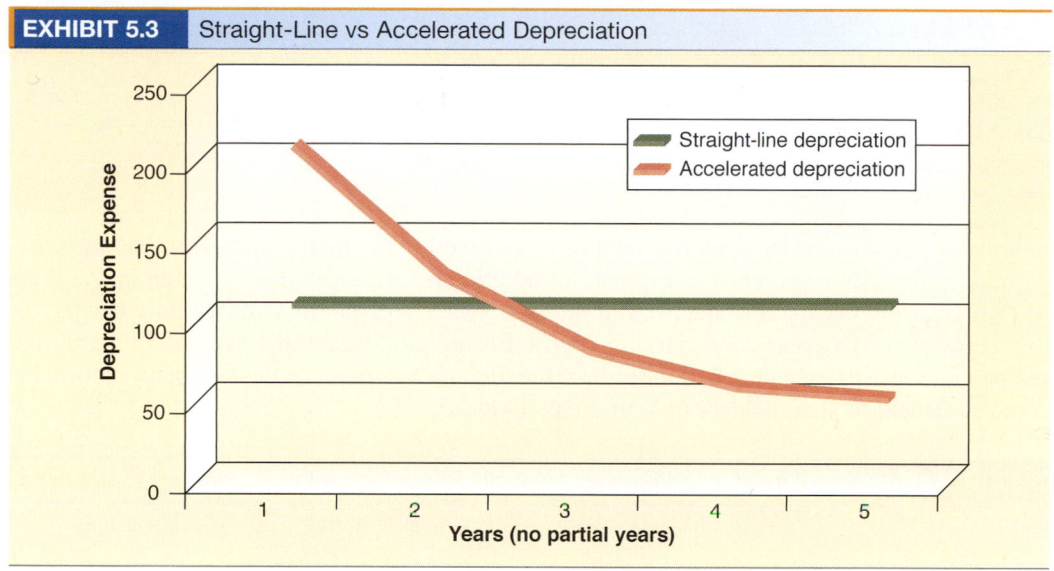

EXHIBIT 5.3   Straight-Line vs Accelerated Depreciation

During the first 2.5 years in this example, depreciation is higher in the company's tax returns than it is in its report to shareholders. In the last 2.5 years, this is reversed, with lower depreciation expense for tax purposes. Taxable income and tax payments are, therefore, higher during the last 2.5 years. The same total amount of depreciation is recognized under both methods over the five-year life of the asset. Only the timing of the recognition of the expense differs.[5]

We use this timing concept to illustrate the accounting for a **deferred tax liability**. Assume that a company purchases a depreciable asset with a cost of $100 and a two-year useful life. For financial reporting purposes (for GAAP-based reports for shareholders), it depreciates the asset using the straight-line method, which yields depreciation expense of $50 per year. For tax reporting (when filing income tax returns), it depreciates the asset on an accelerated basis, which yields depreciation deduction of $75 in the first year and $25 in the second year (the same total amount of depreciation is reported under the two depreciation methods; only the amount of depreciation reported per year differs). Assume that this company reports income before depreciation and taxes of $200 and that its tax rate is 40%. Its income statements, for both financial reporting and tax reporting, for the asset's first year are in Exhibit 5.4A.

EXHIBIT 5.4A   Year 1 Income Statements: Financial Reporting vs Tax Reporting

Year 1	Financial Reporting	Tax Reporting
Income before depreciation	$200	$200
Depreciation	50	75
Income before tax	150	125
Income tax (40%)	60 [expense]	50 [cash paid]
Net income	$ 90	$ 75

This company records income tax expense and a related deferred tax liability for the first year as reflected in the following financial statement effects template:

---

[5] The Modified Accelerated Cost Recovery System (MACRS) is the current method of accelerated asset depreciation required by the United States income tax code. Under MACRS, all assets are divided into classes that dictate the number of years over which an asset's cost is "recovered" and the percentage of the asset cost that can be depreciated per year is fixed by regulation. For a five-year asset, such as in our example, the MACRS depreciation percentages per year are 20%, 32%, 19.2%, 11.52%, 11.52%, and 5.76%. MACRS assumes that assets are acquired in the middle of the year, hence a half-year depreciation in Year 1 and a half-year depreciation in Year 6. The point at which straight-line depreciation exceeds MACRS depreciation is after about 2.5 years as assumed in the example.

Year 1

TE   60
 DTL   10
 Cash   50
        TE
 60 |
        DTL
 | 10
 Cash
 | 50

Year 1 Transaction	Balance Sheet						Income Statement		
	Cash Asset	+ Noncash Assets	= Liabil-ities	+ Contrib. Capital	+ Earned Capital		Rev-enues	− Expen-ses	= Net Income
Record tax expense: expense exceeds cash because of deferral of tax	−50 Cash		= +10 Deferred Tax Liability		−60 Retained Earnings			− +60 Tax Expense	= −60

The reduction in cash reflects the payment of taxes owed to the taxing authority. The increase in deferred tax liability represents an estimate of additional tax that will be payable in the second year (which is the tax liability deferred in the first year). This liability for a future tax payment arises because second-year depreciation expense for tax purposes will be only $25, resulting in taxes payable of $70, which is $10 more than the income tax expense the company reports in its income statement to shareholders in Year 2 (see Exhibit 5.4B).

EXHIBIT 5.4B	Year 2 Income Statements: Financial Reporting vs Tax Reporting	
Year 2	**Financial Reporting**	**Tax Reporting**
Income before depreciation	$200	$200
Depreciation	50	25
Income before tax	150	175
Income tax (40%)	60 [expense]	70 [cash paid]
Net income	$ 90	$105

At the end of Year 1, the company knows that this additional tax must be paid in Year 2 because the financial reporting and tax reporting depreciation schedules are set when the asset is placed in service. Given these known amounts, the company accrues the deferred tax liability in Year 1 in the same manner as it would accrue any estimated future liability, say for wages payable, by recognizing a liability and the related expense.

At the end of Year 2, the additional income tax is paid and the company's deferred tax liability is now satisfied. Financial statement effects related to the tax payment and expense in Year 2 are reflected in the following template:

Year 2

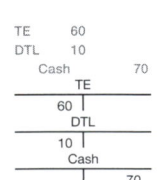

TE   60
 DTL   10
  Cash   70
        TE
 60 |
        DTL
 10 |
 Cash
 | 70

Year 2 Transaction	Balance Sheet						Income Statement		
	Cash Asset	+ Noncash Assets	= Liabil-ities	+ Contrib. Capital	+ Earned Capital		Rev-enues	− Expen-ses	= Net Income
Record tax expense: cash exceeds expense because deferred taxes are reversed	−70 Cash		= −10 Deferred Tax Liability		−60 Retained Earnings			− +60 Tax Expense	= −60

The income tax expense for financial reporting purposes is $60 each year. However, the cash payment for taxes is $70 in Year 2; the $10 excess reduces the deferred tax liability accrued in Year 1.

This example demonstrates how accelerated depreciation for tax reporting and straight-line for financial reporting creates deferred tax liabilities. Other differences between tax reporting and financial reporting create other types of deferred tax accounts. **Deferred tax assets** arise when the tax payment is *greater* than the tax expense for financial reporting purposes (opposite of the illustration above).

Restructuring accruals are one source of deferred tax assets. In the year in which a company approves a reorganization plan, it will accrue a restructuring liability for estimated employee severance payments and other costs and it will write down assets to their market values (this reduces the net book value of those assets on the balance sheet). However, tax authorities do not recognize these accrual accounting transactions until they are realized. In particular, for tax purposes, restructuring costs are not deductible until paid in the future, and asset write-downs are not deductible until the loss is realized when the asset is sold. As a result, the restructuring accrual is not a liability for tax reporting until the company makes the payment, and the write-down of assets is not a deductible expense for tax purposes until the assets are sold. Both of these differences (the liability and the assets) give rise to a deferred tax asset. The deferred tax asset cost will be transferred to the income statement in the future as an expense when the company pays the restructuring costs and sells the impaired assets for a loss.

Another common deferred tax asset relates to **tax loss carryforwards**. Specifically, when a company reports a loss for tax purposes, it can carry back that loss for up to two years to recoup previous taxes paid. Any unused losses can be carried forward for up to twenty years to reduce future taxes. This creates a benefit (an "asset") for tax reporting for which there is no corresponding financial reporting asset. Thus, the company records a deferred tax asset but only if the company is "more likely than not" to be able to recoup past taxes. This depends on the company's assessment of whether it will have sufficient profits in the future.

Companies are required to establish a *deferred tax asset valuation allowance* for deferred tax assets when the future realization of their benefits is uncertain. The effect on financial statements of establishing such an allowance is to reduce reported assets, increase tax expense, and reduce equity (this is similar to accounting for the write-down of any asset). During 2010, Pfizer increased its valuation allowance from $353 million to $894 million. Increases in the valuation allowance reduce net income on a dollar-for-dollar basis. The increase in the valuation allowance during 2010, decreased net income by $541 million ($894 million − $353 million). These effects are reversed if the allowance is reversed in the future when, and if, realization of such tax benefits becomes more likely.

Disclosures Relating to Income Taxes

Pfizer's tax footnote to its income statement is shown in Exhibit 5.5. Pfizer's $1,124 million tax expense reported in its income statement (called the provision) consists of the following two components:

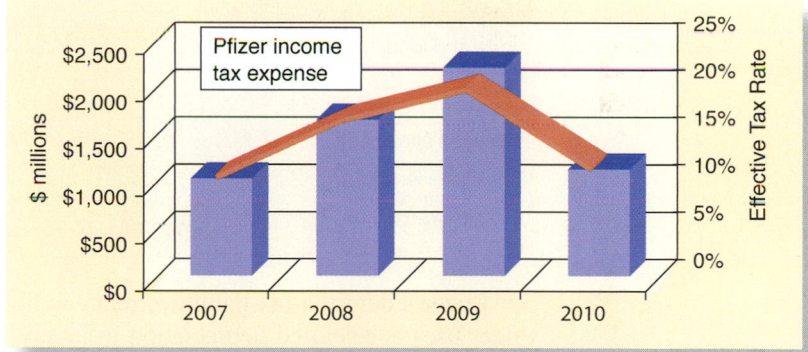

1. *Current tax expense.* Current tax expense is determined from the company's tax returns; it is the amount payable (in cash) to tax authorities (some of these taxes have been paid during the year as the company makes installments). Pfizer labels this "Current income taxes" and reports separate amounts for taxes to federal, state, local, and international tax authorities.

2. *Deferred tax expense.* Deferred tax expense is the effect on tax expense from changes in deferred tax liabilities and deferred tax assets. Pfizer labels this "Deferred income taxes" and reports separate amounts for deferrals related to U.S. and international tax rules.

In financial statement footnotes, companies must disclose the components of deferred tax liabilities and assets. Pfizer's deferred tax footnote to its balance sheet (shown in Exhibit 5.6) reports total deferred tax assets of $15,027 million and total deferred tax liabilities of $29,646 million. On the balance sheet companies report deferred tax assets and liabilities as either current or noncurrent based on when the benefit (payment) is expected to be received (made). Companies are permitted to net some deferred tax assets and liabilities, and also to combine deferred taxes with other accounts on the balance sheet. Thus, for some companies, it is impossible to completely reconcile the tax footnote to the balance sheet. Many of Pfizer's deferred tax assets relate to accrued liabilities or asset write-downs arising from expenses included in financial reporting income, but not yet recognized for tax reporting (such as employee benefits and restructuring accruals). Pfizer has recorded a valuation allowance of $894 million. These various items all yield future reductions of the company's tax payments and are, therefore, classified as assets.

EXHIBIT 5.5	Income Tax Expense Footnote for Pfizer			
Year Ended December 31 (Millions of dollars)		**2010**	**2009**	**2008**
United States				
Current income taxes				
Federal		$(2,774)	$10,169	$ 707
State and local		(313)	71	154
Deferred income taxes				
Federal		2,033	(10,002)	106
State and local		(6)	(93)	(136)
Total U.S. tax (benefit) provision		(1,060)	145	831
International				
Current income taxes		2,258	1,539	2,115
Deferred income taxes		(74)	513	(1,301)
Total international tax provision		2,184	2,052	814
Total provision for taxes on income		$ 1,124	$ 2,197	$1,645

EXHIBIT 5.6	Deferred Taxes Footnote for Pfizer			
		2010 Deferred Tax		**2009 Deferred Tax**	

(Millions of dollars)	Assets	(Liabilities)	Assets	(Liabilities)
Prepaid/deferred items	$ 1,321	$ (112)	$ 1,330	$ (60)
Inventories	132	(59)	437	(859)
Intangibles	1,165	(17,104)	949	(19,802)
Property, plant and equipment	420	(2,146)	715	(2,014)
Employee benefits	4,479	(56)	4,786	(66)
Restructurings and other charges	1,359	(70)	884	(8)
Legal and product liability reserves	1,411	—	1,010	—
Net operating loss/credit carryforwards	4,575	—	4,658	—
Unremitted earnings	—	(9,524)	—	(7,057)
State and local tax adjustments	452	—	747	—
All other	607	(575)	744	(187)
Subtotal	15,921	(29,646)	16,260	(30,053)
Valuation allowance	(894)	—	(353)	—
Total deferred taxes	$15,027	$(29,646)	$15,907	$(30,053)
Net deferred tax liability		$(14,619)		$(14,146)

Pfizer's deferred tax liabilities relate to a varied assortment of items. As we illustrate above, Pfizer uses accelerated depreciation in its tax return, which results in a deferred tax liability of $2,146 million. The deferred tax asset relating to employee benefits arises from the accrual of pension expense for financial reporting, but has not yet been funded with cash contributions. The deferred tax liability relating to unremitted earnings results from investments that Pfizer has in affiliated companies. Pfizer reports income related to those investments, but the income is not taxable until the companies actually pay dividends to Pfizer. Thus, reported profit is greater than taxable income and a deferred tax liability is recognized (we discuss accounting for intercompany investments in Module 9). Pfizer will pay taxes on the subsidiaries' profits when the subsidiaries pay dividends in the future and then the deferred tax liability will be reduced. Finally, the deferred tax asset of net operating loss carryforwards relates to losses that Pfizer has reported for tax purposes that the company is carrying forward to reduce future tax liability as explained above.

Pfizer's 2010 income before tax is $9,422 million. Its tax expense of $1,124 million represents an effective tax rate of 11.9%. The *effective tax rate* is defined as tax expense divided by pretax income ($1,124 million/$9,422 million = 11.9%).[6] By comparison, the federal *statutory tax*

---

[6] This is the effective tax rate for *all* of Pfizer's income. In Module 3 we compute the tax rate on operating profit by first deducting the taxes related to nonoperating income (or adding back the tax shield related to nonoperating expenses). The effective tax rate on total income, is a weighted average of the two rates (operating and nonoperating).

rate for corporations (the rate prescribed in tax regulations) is 35%. Companies must provide a schedule that reconciles the effective tax rate (11.9% for Pfizer) with the Federal statutory rate of 35%. Following is the schedule that **Pfizer** reports in its 10-K.

Reconciliation of the U.S. statutory income tax rate to our effective tax rate for income from continuing operations follows:

Year Ended Dec. 31	2010	2009	2008
U.S. statutory income tax rate	35.0%	35.0%	35.0%
Earnings taxed at other than U.S. statutory rate	2.5	(9.3)	(20.2)
Resolution of certain tax positions	(26.4)	—	(3.1)
Sales of biopharmaceutical companies	—	(5.1)	(4.3)
U.S. healthcare legislation	2.8	—	—
U.S. research tax credit and manufacturing deduction	(2.3)	(1.3)	(1.2)
Legal settlements	0.4	(1.6)	9.0
Acquired IPR&D	0.5	0.2	2.1
Wyeth acquisition-related costs	0.5	2.4	—
All other—net	(1.1)	—	(0.3)
Effective tax rate for income from continuing operations	11.9%	20.3%	17.0%

In addition to federal taxes (paid to the IRS), companies also pay taxes to state, local, and foreign jurisdictions where they operate. These tax rates are typically lower than the statutory rate of 35%. In 2010, Pfizer's effective tax rate was reduced by 26.4% as a result of favorable rulings in litigation with taxing authorities. Also, several miscellaneous items increased Pfizer's effective tax rate by 3.3%, resulting in a net decrease of 23.1%.

In sum, Pfizer's effective tax rate for 2010 is 11.9%, which is 23.1 percentage points below the 35% statutory rate. In 2009, however, the effective tax rate was 20.3% and in 2008 it was 17%. Fluctuations, such as these, in the effective tax rate are not uncommon and highlight the difference between income reported under GAAP and that computed using multiple tax codes and tax incentives under which companies operate. Appendix 5A explains accounting for deferred taxes in more detail.

Analysis of Income Tax Disclosures

Analysis of deferred taxes can yield useful insights. Some revenue accruals (such as accounts receivable for longer-term contracts) increase deferred tax liabilities as GAAP income exceeds tax income (similar to the effect of using straight-line depreciation for financial reporting purposes and accelerated depreciation for tax returns).

An increase in deferred tax liabilities indicates that a company is reporting higher GAAP income relative to taxable income and can indicate the company is managing earnings upwards. The difference between reported corporate profits and taxable income increased substantially in the late 1990s, just prior to huge asset write-offs. *CFO Magazine* (November 2002) implied that such differences are important for analysis and should be monitored:

> Fueling the sense that something [was] amiss [was] the growing gap between the two sets of numbers. In 1992, there was no significant difference between pretax book income and taxable net income . . . By 1996, according to IRS data, a $92.5 billion gap had appeared. By 1998 [prior to the market decline], the gap was $159 billion—a fourth of the total taxable income reported . . . If people had seen numbers showing very significant differences between book numbers for trading and tax numbers, they would have wondered if those [income] numbers were completely real.

Although an increase in deferred tax liabilities can legitimately result, for example, from an increase in depreciable assets and the use of accelerated depreciation for tax purposes, we must be aware of the possibility that such an increase arises from improper revenue recognition in that the company might not be reporting those revenues to tax authorities.

Adequacy of Deferred Tax Asset Valuation

Analysis of the deferred tax asset valuation account provides us with additional insight. This analysis involves (1) assessing the adequacy of the valuation allowance and (2) determining how and why the valuation account changed during the period and how that change affects net income.

When a company reports a deferred tax asset, the company implies that it will, more likely than not, receive a future tax benefit equal to the deferred tax asset. If the company is uncertain about the future tax benefit, it records an allowance to reduce the asset. How can we gauge the adequacy of a valuation allowance account? We might assess the reasons for the valuation account (typically reported in the tax footnote). We might examine other companies in the industry for similar allowances. We might also review the MD&A for any doubt on company prospects for future profitability.

We can quantify our analysis in at least three ways. First, we can examine the allowance as a percentage of the deferred tax assets. For **Pfizer**, this 2010 percentage is 5.62%; see below. We also want to gather data from other pharmaceutical companies and compare the sizes of their allowance accounts relative to their related deferred tax assets. The important point is that we must be comfortable with the size of the valuation account and remember that management has control over the adequacy and reporting of the allowance account (with audit assurances).

Pfizer ($ millions)	2010	2009
Deferred tax asset	$15,921	$16,260
Valuation allowance	$ 894	$ 353
Valuation allowance as a percent of total deferred tax asset	5.62%	2.17%

Second, we can examine changes in the allowance account. During a year, circumstances change and the company might be more or less assured of receiving the tax benefit. In that case, the company might decrease or increase its allowance account. The valuation allowance in 2010 is considerably larger than the previous year even though the deferred tax asset arising from net operating losses has decreased. This implies that during the year, Pfizer has revised downward the amount of net operating losses that the company expects to be able to use to reduce future taxes.

Third, we can quantify how a change in the valuation allowance affects net income and its effective tax rate (see Exhibit 5.7). To see this, recall that increases in the valuation allowance affect tax expense in the same direction, dollar for dollar. This in turn, affects net income (in the opposite direction) again, dollar for dollar. For Pfizer, its 2010 valuation allowance increased by $541 million ($353 million to $894 million), which increased tax expense and decreased net income by $541 million. This is not a large effect on income for Pfizer. However, changes in valuation allowances can have (and have had) marked effects on net income for numerous companies. One final note, reductions in the deferred tax asset valuation account can occur as a result of unused loss carryforwards; in that case, a company reduces the deferred tax asset and the related valuation allowance, which is similar in concept to the write-off of an account receivable discussed in Module 6. For our analysis, we must remember, however, that in the absence of expiring loss carryforwards, a company can increase current-period income by deliberately decreasing the valuation allowance. Knowing that such decreases can boost net income, companies might deliberately create too large a valuation allowance in one or more prior years and use it as a *cookie jar reserve* to boost income in future periods. We want to assess the details of the valuation account and changes therein from company footnotes and from the MD&A.

EXHIBIT 5.7	Effect of Deferred Tax Asset Valuation Account on Tax Expense

Pfizer ($ millions)	2010
Change in valuation allowance	$ 541
Impact of valuation allowance change on net income	$ (541)
Income before tax	$9,422
Tax expense	$1,124
Effective tax rate (Tax expense/Income before tax)	11.9%
Tax expense before change in valuation account	$ 583
Effective tax rate before change in valuation account	6.2%

IFRS INSIGHT   Income Statement Differences

IFRS allows companies to classify income statement items by nature (materials, labor, etc.) rather than by function (cost of goods sold, selling expenses, etc.). **Finmeccanica S.p.A.** is an Italian manufacturing conglomerate that operates in the defense, aerospace, transport and energy sectors. Its 2010 IFRS income statement classifies items by nature.

Finmeccanica SpA, Consolidated Income Statement (€ millions)	2010
Revenue	€18,695
Other operating income	627
Raw materials and consumables used	(6,316)
Purchase of services	(5,878)
Personnel costs	(4,772)
Amortisation, depreciation and impairment	(785)
Other operating expenses	(801)
Changes in inventories of work in progress, semi-finished and finished goods	(176)
Work performed by the Group and capitalized	638
	1,232
Finance income	850
Finance costs	(1,202)
Share of profit (loss) of equity accounted investments	(14)
Profit before taxes	866
Income taxes	(309)
Net profit	€ 557
Equity holders of the Company	€ 493
Minority interests	64
Net profit	€ 557

Because Finmeccanica classifies its income statement items by nature, there is no line item for cost of goods sold. Instead, the manufacturing and inventory costs recognized during the period are reported according to their nature (raw materials and consumables used, personnel costs, other operating expenses) along with the amount of the net change in inventories for the period. We see that other than raw materials and consumables used and the net change in inventories, all the operating costs combine product and period costs. For example, personnel costs include the salaries and wages for all staff from the manufacturing employees to the CEO.

MID-MODULE REVIEW 2

Refer to the **Merck & Co., Inc.**, 2010 income statement in Mid-Module Review 1. Merck provides the following additional information in footnotes to its 10-K.

Taxes on income consisted of:

Years Ended December 31 ($ in millions)	2010	2009	2008
Current provision			
Federal	$ 399	$ (55)	$1,054
Foreign	1,446	495	292
State	(82)	7	123
	1,763	447	1,469
Deferred provision			
Federal	764	2,095	419
Foreign	(1,777)	(437)	56
State	(79)	163	55
	(1,092)	1,821	530
	$ 671	$2,268	$1,999

Required

1. What is the total income tax expense that Merck reports in its 2010 income statement?
2. What amount of its total tax expense did (or will) Merck pay in cash (that is, what amount is currently payable)?
3. Explain how Merck calculates its income tax expense.

The solution is on page 5-60.

Foreign Currency Translation Effects

L04 Explain how foreign currency fluctuations affect the income statement.

Many companies conduct international operations and transact business in currencies other than $US. It is common for companies to purchase assets in foreign currencies, borrow money in foreign currencies, and transact business with their customers in foreign currencies. Increasingly many companies have subsidiaries whose balance sheets and income statements are prepared in foreign currencies.

Financial statements prepared according to U.S. GAAP must be reported in $US. This means that the financial statements of any foreign subsidiaries must be translated into $US before consolidation with the U.S. parent company. This translation process can markedly alter both the balance sheet and income statement. We discuss income statement effects of foreign currency translation in this module; we discuss the effects on stockholders' equity in Module 8.

Effects of Foreign Currency Transactions on Income

A change in the strength of the $US vis-à-vis foreign currencies has a direct effect on the $US equivalent for revenues, expenses, and income of the foreign subsidiary because revenues and expenses are translated at the average exchange rate for the period. Exhibit 5.8 shows those financial effects.

EXHIBIT 5.8   Income Statement Effects from Foreign Currency Movements

	Revenues	−	Expenses	=	Net Income (or Loss)
$US Weakens........	Increase		Increase		Increase
$US Strengthens	Decrease		Decrease		Decrease

Specifically, when the foreign currency strengthens (implying $US weakens), the subsidiary's revenues and expenses translate into more $US and, thus, reported income is higher than if the currencies had not fluctuated. On the other hand, when the $US strengthens, the subsidiary's revenues, expenses, and income decrease in $US terms. (The profit effect assumes that revenues exceed expenses; if expenses exceed revenues, a loss occurs, which increases if the $US weakens and decreases if the $US strengthens.)

Pfizer discusses how currency fluctuations affect its income statement in the following excerpt from footnotes to the company's 2010 10-K.

Revenues by Segment & Geographical Area ($ mil.)	Worldwide	US	International
Biopharmaceutical	$58,523	$25,962	$32,561
Diversified	8,966	2,981	5,985
Corporate and Other	320	103	217
	$67,809	$29,046	$38,763

Revenues increased . . . [partly due to] the favorable impact of foreign exchange, which increased revenues by approximately $1.1 billion, or 2%. Worldwide Biopharmaceutical revenues in 2010 were $58.5 billion, an increase of 29% compared to 2009, due to the weakening of the U.S. dollar relative to other currencies, primarily the Canadian dollar, Australian dollar, Japanese yen and Brazilian real, which favorably impacted Biopharmaceutical revenues by approximately $900 million, or 2%.

The $US weakened against many foreign currencies for several years preceding and including 2010. Thus, each unit of foreign currency purchased more $US. Therefore, revenues and expenses denominated in foreign currencies were translated to higher $US equivalents, yielding increased revenues and profits even when unit volumes remained unchanged. Pfizer also discloses that it attempts to dampen the effect that these fluctuations have on reported profit:

> **Foreign Exchange Risk**   A significant portion of our revenues and earnings is exposed to changes in foreign exchange rates. We seek to manage our foreign exchange risk in part through operational means, including managing same-currency revenues in relation to same-currency costs and same-currency assets in relation to same-currency liabilities.

The phrase "operational means" indicates that the company structures its transactions in $US rather than a foreign currency or attempts to match same-currency revenues and expenses (or assets and liabilities) to minimize the effects of currency fluctuatinos. Foreign currency financial instruments are common and include forward and futures contracts, which lock in future currency values. We explain how these instruments (called derivatives) work in Appendix 9A. In sum, we must be cognizant of the effects of currency fluctuations on reported revenues, expenses, and profits for companies with substantial foreign-currency transactions.

OPERATING COMPONENTS BELOW-THE-LINE

Pfizer's income statement includes a subtotal labeled "income from continuing operations." Historically, this presentation highlighted the nonrecurring (*transitory*) portions of the income statement so that they could be eliminated to facilitate the projection of future profitability. The word "continuing" was meant to imply that income was purged of one-time items, as these were presented "below-the-line," that is, below income from continuing operations. Two categories of items are presented below-the-line:[7]

1. **Discontinued operations**   Net income (loss) from business segments that have been or will be sold, and any gains (losses) on net assets related to those segments sold in the current period.
2. **Extraordinary items**   Gains or losses from events that are both unusual and infrequent.

Discontinued operations are generally viewed as nonoperating, and we discuss their accounting treatment in Module 9. Explanation of the accounting for extraordinary items follows.

Extraordinary Items

Extraordinary items refer to events that are both unusual *and* infrequent. Their effects are reported following income from continuing operations. Management determines whether an event is unusual and infrequent (with auditor approval) for financial reporting purposes. Further, management often has incentives to classify unfavorable items as extraordinary because they will be reported separately, after income from continuing operations (*below-the-line*). These incentives derive from managers' beliefs that investors tend to focus more on items included in income from continuing operations and less on nonrecurring items that are not included in continuing operations.

GAAP provides the following guidance in determining whether or not an item is extraordinary:

■ *Unusual nature*. The underlying event or transaction must possess a high degree of abnormality and be clearly unrelated to, or only incidentally related to, the ordinary activities of the entity.

---

[7] Prior accounting standards included a third category, **changes in accounting principles**. This category included voluntary and mandated changes in accounting policies utilized by a company, such as a change in the depreciation method. Under current GAAP, changes in accounting principles are no longer reported below-the-line. Instead, they are applied retrospectively (unless it is impractical to do so, in which case they are applied at the earliest practical date). No cumulative effect adjustment is made to income as was the case in prior standards. Instead, changes in depreciation methods are now accounted for as changes in estimates, which are applied prospectively.

- Infrequency of occurrence. The underlying event or transaction must be of a type that would not reasonably be expected to recur in the foreseeable future.

The following items are generally **not** reported as extraordinary items:

- Gains and losses on retirement of debt8
- Write-down or write-off of operating or nonoperating assets
- Foreign currency gains and losses
- Gains and losses from disposal of specific assets or business segment
- Effects of a strike
- Accrual adjustments related to long-term contracts
- Costs of a takeover defense

Extraordinary items are reported separately (net of tax) and below income from continuing operations on the income statement.

IFRS INSIGHT	**Extraordinary Items and IFRS**

IFRS does not permit the reporting of income and expense items as "extraordinary." The IASB justified its position in IAS1 as follows: "The Board decided that items treated as extraordinary result from the normal business risks faced by an entity and do not warrant presentation in a separate component of the income statement. The nature or function of a transaction or other event, rather than its frequency, should determine its presentation within the income statement. Items currently classified as 'extraordinary' are only a subset of the items of income and expense that may warrant disclosure to assist users in predicting an entity's future performance" (IAS1).

Earnings Per Share and its Analysis

LO5 Compute earnings per share and explain the effect of dilutive securities.

The income statement reports earnings per share (EPS) numbers. Most firms report two EPS numbers: basic and diluted. The difference between the two measures is shown in Exhibit 5.9.

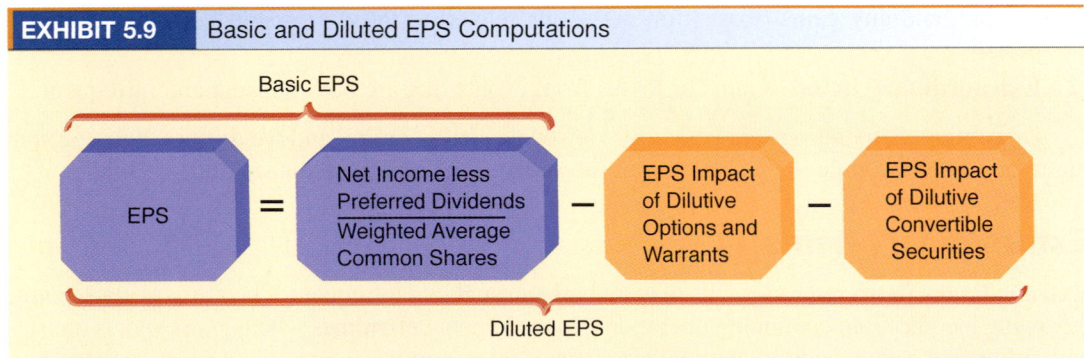

EXHIBIT 5.9	Basic and Diluted EPS Computations

Basic EPS is computed as: (Net income − Dividends on preferred stock)/Weighted average number of common shares outstanding during the year. Subtracting preferred stock dividends yields the income available for dividend payments to common shareholders. Computation of **diluted EPS** reflects the additional shares that would be issued if all stock options, warrants, and convertible securities had been converted into common shares at the beginning of the year or when issued, if issued during the year. Diluted EPS never exceeds basic EPS.

---

[8] Until recently, gains and losses on debt retirement were treated as extraordinary items. To explain, understand that debt is accounted for at historical cost, just like the accounting for equipment. The *market price* of debt, however, is determined by fluctuations in interest rates. As a result, if a company retires (pays off) its debt before maturity, the cash paid to settle the debt often differs from the debt amount reported on the balance sheet, resulting in gains and losses on retirement. These gains and losses were formerly treated as extraordinary. Following passage of SFAS 145, these gains and losses are no longer automatically treated as extraordinary, but instead must be unusual and infrequent to be designated as extraordinary.

Pfizer reports Basic EPS of $1.03 in 2010 and Diluted EPS of $1.02. Given the near identical results for basic and diluted EPS, we know that Pfizer has few dilutive securities. **PDL Biopharma, Inc.**, however, reports a dilution of 26% in its EPS as evident from its following disclosure:

Fiscal year ended December 31 (in thousands, except per share)	2010	2009	2008
Basic net income per share	$ 0.73	$ 1.59	$ 0.58
Diluted net income per share	$ 0.54	$ 1.07	$ 0.47

PDL Biopharma reports the following dilutive effects on EPS:

(In thousands)	2010	2009	2008
Numerator			
Net income	$ 91,874	$189,660	$ 68,387
Add back interest expense for convertible notes, net of tax	5,087	7,079	10,450
Income used to compute net income per dilluted share	$ 96,961	$196,739	$ 78,837
Denominator			
Total weighted-average shares used to compute income per basic share	126,578	119,402	118,728
Effect of dilutive stock options	9	18	50
Restricted stock	103	42	10
Assumed conversion of convertible notes	52,111	64,938	49,081
Shares used to compute income per dilluted share from continuing operations and net income per dilluted share	178,801	184,400	167,869

Both the numerator and the denominator in the EPS calculation are affected by dilutive securities. If all the convertible notes had been exchanged for stock at the start of the year, the company would not have had to pay interest on these notes during the year. Therefore, the after-tax interest is added to net income in the numerator.

The denominator in the diluted earnings per share calculation presumes a worst case scenario that all employees holding options exercise their right to purchase common shares and all convertible notes are converted to common shares as of the beginning of the year. In that event, PDL Biopharma will issue an additional 52,223 thousand shares, thus increasing the denominator by that amount and reducing earnings per share from $0.73 to $0.54.[9]

Analysts and investors often use EPS figures to compare operating results for companies of different sizes under the assumption that the number of shares outstanding is proportional to the income level (that is, a company twice the size of another will report double the income and will have double the common shares outstanding, leaving EPS approximately equal for the two companies). This assumption is erroneous. Management controls the number of common shares outstanding and there is no relation between firm size and number of shares outstanding. Different companies also have different philosophies regarding share issuance and repurchase. For example, consider that most companies report annual EPS of less than $5, while **Berkshire Hathaway** reported EPS of $7,928 in 2010! This is because Berkshire Hathaway has so few common shares outstanding, not necessarily because it has stellar profits.

---

[9] The effects of dilutive securities are only included if they are, in fact, dilutive. Securities that are *antidilutive* would actually increase EPS, and are, thus, excluded from the computation. An example of an antidilutive security is employee stock options whose exercise price is greater than the stock's current market price. These *underwater* (or out-of-the-money) options are antidilutive and are, therefore, excluded from the EPS computation. PDL Biopharma provides the following explanation for this exclusion in its footnotes:

"We excluded 0.3 million, 2.5 million and 10.3 million of outstanding stock options from our diluted earnings per share calculations for the years ended December 31, 2010, 2009 and 2008, respectively, because the option exercise prices were greater than the average market prices of our common stock during these periods; therefore, their effect was anti-dilutive."

ACCOUNTING QUALITY

LO6 Explain accounting quality and identify areas for analysis.

We conclude our coverage of operating income with a discussion of accounting quality. As we saw in earlier modules, there are at least two main uses of financial reports: evaluation and valuation. Financial statement readers use the reported numbers from financial statements along with information in the notes and Management Discussion and Analysis (MD&A), to evaluate company profitability, liquidity, solvency and other financial characteristics. Those users also evaluate its managers and board of directors with a view to assessing the results of past operating, investing and financing decisions. The evaluation of financial reports is also used to value the company, a process that includes forecasting operating, investing and financing results. In a later module we consider more fully the forecasting process. For now, it is important to understand that both uses of financial information (evaluation and valuation) demand high-quality accounting information.

What is high-quality accounting information? Although there is not a single definition of high quality information, there are factors that enhance information quality.

Reliable High-quality accounting information is **reliable**. In particular, information is reliable when:

- Balance sheet numbers represent economic reality: all included assets will yield future economic benefits and there are no unrecorded assets; all liabilities are recorded and measured at economically appropriate amounts. Assets and liabilities are properly labeled and classified as current or noncurrent. Accounts have not been aggregated so as to obscure their true nature.

- Income statement numbers reflect economic earnings: revenues reflect all sales activity during the period and only those sales for that period; expenses are complete and properly measured. Items are properly labeled and any netting or aggregation of numbers does not obscure their true nature or amount.

- Reported cash flows accurately portray all of the cash that flowed in and out of the company during the period.

Relevant High-quality accounting information is **relevant**. In particular information is relevant when:

- Reported earnings and cash flow numbers can be used to forecast the amount and timing of future earnings and cash flows. This attribute is referred to as "relevance" and we return to it in our forecasting module.

- Footnotes provide additional quantitative and qualitative information that is accurate and complete. Sometimes a balance sheet or income statement number is not the best indicator of current value or is not predictive of future expectations. For example, LIFO inventory is reported on the balance sheet but the footnotes augment relevance by reporting the FIFO value of inventory.

There are several ways that accounting quality is diminished. (For a good discussion of this issue, see Dechow, P., and C. Schrand. "Earnings quality," The Research Foundation of CFA Institute. Charlottesville, VA 2004).

Unintentional Errors

We must understand that there are errors in financial statements. Two reports signed by external auditors (one concerning adequacy of the company's internal controls and one disclosing the audit opinion) provide some assurance that financial statements are free from material misstatement. However, those reports do not guarantee no errors; instead, they assert that any remaining errors are not large enough to affect the decisions of financial statement readers.

One-time Events

In the ordinary course of business, companies record one-time transactions that are not expected to recur. For example, a lawsuit is settled or commodity prices spike and the company earns a windfall profit. While these nonrecurring events are reliably measured and reported, by definition they cannot be used to predict future periods' events. Those specific line items are not relevant and our expectations about future earnings must not be swayed by such events. The challenge is in determining which items reported on the income statement are truly one-time events. Often companies highlight the existence of one-time items by reporting "pro forma" earnings in company financial statements and press releases. Pro forma income commonly begins with GAAP income from continuing operations (which excludes discontinued operations and extraordinary items), and then adjusts for other one-time items including restructuring charges, large gains and losses, and acquisition expenses (goodwill amortization and other acquisition costs). SEC Regulation G requires that companies reconcile such non-GAAP information to GAAP numbers so that financial statement readers can have a basis for comparison and can determine if the excluded items truly are one-time items. For example, in 2010 Merck & Co., Inc., reported the following "pro forma" (non-GAAP) information in its Form 10-K.

($ in millions)	2010
Pretax income as reported under GAAP	$ 1,653
Increase (decrease) for excluded items:	
Purchase accounting adjustments	9,007
Restructuring costs	1,986
Merger-related costs	396
Other items:	
Vioxx Liability reserve	950
Gain on AstraZeneca asset option exercise	(443)
Gain related to the MSP Partnership	—
Gain on Merial divestiture	—
Gain on distribution from AZLP	—
	13,549
Taxes on income as reported under GAAP	671
Estimated tax benefit (expense) on excluded items	1,798
Tax benefit from foreign entity tax rate changes	391
Tax charge related to U.S. health care reform legislation	(147)
Non-GAAP taxes on income	2,713
Non-GAAP net income	$10,836

This footnote indicates that Merck considers over $10 billion of net expenses, including the $2 billion restructuring costs, as one-time charges that, if included, portray an inaccurate picture of its performance during the period. Pfizer's non-GAAP income of $10,836 million is more than ten times larger than the reported GAAP income of $982.

> **RESEARCH INSIGHT**   **Pro Forma Earnings: Incidence and Outcomes**
>
> In 2010, more than half the companies that comprise the Dow Jones Index reported non-GAAP numbers when reporting quarterly net income. *(See listing at: Larcker, D. and B. Tayan, "Pro Forma Earnings: What's Wrong with GAAP? August 20, 2010, http://ssrn.com/abstract=1678066.)* Despite the potential for abuse, investors often perceive certain non-GAAP earnings as more permanent than GAAP earnings because pro forma numbers allegedly provide better indication of future earnings power. For this reason, Wall Street analysts' earnings estimates typically use non-GAAP metrics, or "Street" earnings. Recent research reports two results that show how investors' use of pro forma earnings is changing. First, investors appear to pay more attention to pro forma earnings in the post-SOX period (after 2003), which suggests that SOX improved the credibility of non-GAAP disclosures. Second, investors discount earnings announcements in which managers make aggressive exclusions that are potentially misleading and, hence, stock values seem to reflect investors' ability to discern accounting quality. (Black, D., E. Black, T. Christensen, and W. Heninger "Has the Regulation of Pro Forma Reporting in the U.S. Changed Investors' Perceptions of Adjusted Earnings Disclosures?" November 23, 2010, http://ssrn.com/abstract=1818903)

Deliberate Manager Intervention

Ideally, all reported numbers are free from deliberate managerial intervention. This implies that the numbers are unbiased because managers have been impartial when choosing accounting policies and when exercising their discretion over reported numbers. However, history is rife with examples where this is not the case: managers can and do "manage" earnings and balance sheet numbers. Sometimes accounting quality is impugned because managers' intervention in the reporting process involves fraud. For example, in 2009, Ramalinga Raju, the CEO of Satyam (an Indian information-technology conglomerate), was arrested for reporting fictitious cash and profits of over $1 billion. However, more frequently, earnings management involves subtle, small increases in net income designed to achieve an outcome such as meeting analysts' forecasts or avoiding losses. While it is more often the case that "managed" earnings (and assets) are inflated, some managers underreport their true earnings (and assets). The highest quality accounting reports are free from biases in both directions; they are accurate because they are not over- or understated.

Reliable Numbers That Are Not Predictive

Companies can experience changes in economic events that impair the predictive ability of reliable numbers. For example, in June 2011, **Marathon Oil** announced that it was breaking the company into two new companies: **Marathon Oil**, which will engage in upstream oil and gas exploration and development activities, and **Marathon Petroleum**, which will run refineries and distribute products to retail and other customers. The company's 2010 financial statements, while reliable, were no longer relevant because the company's structure was so changed that users could not use its 2010 revenues and expenses to forecast 2011 net income. Expectations about future earnings were markedly altered.

Assessing and Remediating Accounting Quality

There is no tried and true formula for assessing accounting quality or for identifying earnings management. But, at a minimum, we can implement the following analysis and remediation techniques:

BUSINESS INSIGHT   **Meeting or Beating Analysts' Forecasts**

Missing analysts' earnings forecasts can cause stock prices to tumble. Therefore, managers aim to meet or beat the Street's expectation, sometimes resorting to earnings management involving accounting accruals, and other times using real actions (such as channel stuffing). These deliberate manager interventions reduce accounting quality. One way analysts and researchers detect potential earnings management is to identify unusual accruals and reversals (negative accruals) and quantify their effect on earnings. Of particular interest are unusual accruals that move EPS enough to meet or beat analysts' earnings forecasts; such accruals raise suspicion of managerial opportunism. Consider the case of **Green Mountain Coffee**; its consensus EPS forecast was $0.38 for the second quarter of fiscal 2011. When the company reported second-quarter earnings, they beat the consensus forecast by $0.10 per share, a 26% margin! The company's stock price shot up nearly 20% to $75.98. But a closer inspection of Green Mountain Coffee's financial statements reveals that the wide margin by which the company beat earnings forecast was not due to stellar performance but to an accounting anomaly. Its statement of cash flows reveals an unusual (negative) accrual of $22,259 thousand for sales returns for the second quarter of fiscal 2011. GAAP requires that firms report revenues net of anticipated sales returns. Companies use their historical experience with product returns to determine the sales returns expense (a debit on the income statement) with an offsetting entry to a sales-return allowance (a credit balance on the balance sheet). When customers return products, the company reduces the allowance for sales returns on the balance sheet. At the end of the quarter, the company estimates sales returns for the current quarters' sales, records the appropriate expense on the income statement, and updates the sales-return allowance. It is atypical for a company to have a negative expense for sales returns. A negative sales-return expense (a "reversal") increases revenues and earnings. This is what Green Mountain Coffee reported in 2Q 2011. On an after-tax basis, the reversal increased Green Mountain Coffee's net income by $14,468 thousand or about $0.10 per share (147,558,595 shares diluted outstanding at March 26, 2011). A skeptical analyst might conclude that it recorded a negative accrual to beat the Street's expectations. Such behavior hinders the quality of reported earnings.

- Read both reports from the external auditor and take special note of any deviation from boilerplate language.

- Peruse the footnote on accounting policies (typically footnote 1) and compare the company's policies to its industry peers. Deviations from the norm can signal opportunism.

- Examine changes in accounting policies. What would the company have reported absent the change? Did the new policy help it avoid reporting a loss or violating a debt covenant?

- Compare key ratios over time. Follow up on marked increases or decreases in ratios, read footnotes and the MD&A to see how management explains such changes. Follow up on ratios that do not change when a change is expected. For example, during the tech bubble, Worldcom, Inc., reported an expense-to-revenue ratio (ER ratio) of 42% quarter after quarter, despite the worsening of economic conditions. Later it was discovered that managers had deliberately underreported expenses to maintain the ER ratio. The lesson is that sometimes "no change" signals managerial intervention.

- Review ratios of competitors and consider macro economic conditions and how they have shifted over time. Are the ratios reasonable in light of current conditions? Are changes in the income statement aligning with changes on the balance sheet?

- Identify nonrecurring items and separately assess their impact on company performance and position. Take care when using pro forma numbers reported by the company.

- Recast financial statements as necessary to reflect an accounting policy(ies) that is more in line with competitors or one that better reflects economically relevant numbers. We illustrate recasting at several points in future modules. For example, we can convert LIFO inventory to FIFO and we can capitalize operating leases.

ANALYZING GLOBAL REPORTS

We discussed the reporting of operating income, including revenue measurement and the timing of revenue recognition. However, companies reporting under IFRS are likely to recognize revenues earlier for the following three reasons:

1. U.S. GAAP has specific guidance about what constitutes revenue, how revenue is measured, and the timing of its recognition. Also, U.S. GAAP has extensive, industry-specific revenue recognition guidelines. IFRS is not specific about the timing and measurement of revenue recognition and does not provide industry-specific guidance. With less detailed guidance, the general management preference for reporting income earlier will likely prevail.

2. A U.S. GAAP revenue-recognition criterion is that the sales price be fixed or determinable. This means that if a sale involves contingent consideration, no revenue is recognized until the contingency is resolved. IFRS considers the probability that economic benefits will flow to the seller and records such benefits as revenue if they can be reliably measured. This means contingent revenue is recognized earlier under IFRS.

3. For multiple-element contracts, both U.S. GAAP and IFRS allocate revenue based on relative fair values of the elements. However, IFRS requires fair-value estimates that are less restrictive.

For these reasons, our analysis of companies reporting under IFRS is likely to find more aggressive reporting and higher revenues (and net income). This front-loading of revenues is likely more pronounced for high revenue-growth companies and for industries with more multiple-element contracts.

We also discussed several expenses in this module, including research and development. There are differences between U.S. GAAP and IFRS for R&D. U.S. GAAP expenses all R&D costs whereas IFRS allows capitalization and subsequent amortization of certain development costs. For some companies and some industries this can create differences for both the balance sheet and income statement. For analysis purposes, we must review the R&D footnote of IFRS companies to determine the development costs capitalized for the period and the amount of amortization of previously capitalized costs. The difference between these two amounts represents the additional pretax expense that would be reported under U.S. GAAP. The IFRS intangible asset footnote reports the unamortized development costs, which represents the net asset that would not appear on a U.S. GAAP balance sheet (with the off-setting entries to deferred taxes and retained earnings).

BUSINESS INSIGHT   **Pro Forma Income and Managerial Motives**

The purported motive for reporting pro forma income is to eliminate transitory (one-time) items to enhance year-to-year comparability. Although this might be justified on the basis that pro forma income has greater predictive ability, important information is lost in the process. One role for accounting is to report how effective management has been in its stewardship of invested capital. Asset write-downs, liability accruals, and other charges that are eliminated in calculating pro forma income often reflect outcomes of poor management decisions. Our analysis must not blindly eliminate information contained in nonrecurring items by focusing solely on pro forma income. Critics of pro forma income also argue that the items excluded by managers from GAAP income are inconsistent across companies and time. They contend that a major motive for pro forma income is to mislead stakeholders. Legendary investor Warren Buffett puts pro forma in context: *"When companies or investment professionals use terms such as 'EBITDA' and 'pro forma,' they want you to unthinkingly accept concepts that are dangerously flawed."* (Berkshire Hathaway, Annual Report)

The module also considered restructuring expenses. There are differences between IFRS and U.S. GAAP on restructuring, but most are minor. The following differences relate to timing:

- Under IFRS, restructuring expense is recognized when there is a binding contract or a plan for the restructuring and if the affected employees expect the plan to be implemented. Under U.S. GAAP, restructuring expense can be recognized earlier because the trigger is managerial approval of a plan.

- Under IFRS, compensation for employees who will be terminated is recognized when employees are deemed redundant. Under U.S. GAAP, restructuring expense can be recognized later, when the employees have been informed.

The following difference relates to the restructuring expense amount:

- Consistent with other accruals under IFRS, a restructuring provision is recorded at its best estimate. This is usually the expected value or, in the case of a range of possible outcomes that are equally likely, the provision is recorded at the midpoint of the range. The U.S. GAAP estimate is at the most-likely outcome; and if there is a range of possible outcomes, the provision is recorded as the minimum amount of the range.

This means that the financial statement differences between IFRS and U.S. GAAP for restructurings cannot be predicted unequivocally. We must review the restructuring footnote; and remember that cumulative expense is the same under both reporting systems.

We also described tax expenses. There are three notable differences: two affect the income statement and one affects the balance sheet. With respect to the income statement:

1. Both U.S. GAAP and IFRS recognize deferred tax assets for timing differences and unused tax losses. However, under U.S. GAAP, a valuation allowance is set up if it is more likely than not (probability > 50%) that some portion of the deferred tax assets will not be utilized. Under IFRS, the deferred tax asset is only recognized to the extent that the future benefit is probable (probability > 50%). That is, there is no deferred tax asset if the company does not expect to earn enough taxable profit in the future to use the tax credit. This means there are no valuation allowances in IFRS (although sometimes a company reports the "unrecognized portion" of deferred tax assets). The net effect on income is identical but our review of an IFRS tax footnote will not involve assessing the adequacy of the allowance or the extent to which changes in the allowance affect net income.

2. Under IFRS, deferred tax assets on employee stock options are computed based on the options' intrinsic value at each reporting date. In contrast, GAAP uses historical value. This results in partial mark-to-market accounting for the IFRS deferred tax asset and introduces volatility in tax expense. We must review footnotes carefully to determine any potential income statement impact of IFRS revalued deferred tax assets.

With respect to the balance sheet, all deferred tax assets and liabilities are classified as long-term under IFRS. This will impact metrics and ratios that involve current assets and liabilities and could affect our comparative assessment of liquidity.

Finally, recall that separate reporting of extraordinary items is not permitted under IFRS. When comparing U.S. GAAP to IFRS, we include any extraordinary items with other expenses, according to their function.

MODULE-END REVIEW

Refer to the **Merck & Co., Inc.**, 2010 income statement in the Mid-Module Review.

Required

1. Assume that during 2010 the $US weakened with respect to the currencies in which Merck conducts its business. How would that weakening affect Merck's income statement?
2. What is the difference between basic and diluted earnings per share?

The solution is on page 5-60.

APPENDIX 5A: Expanded Explanation of Deferred Taxes

The module provided an example of how different depreciation methods for tax and financial reporting create a deferred tax liability. That example showed that total depreciation over the life of the asset is the same under both tax and financial reporting, and that the only difference is the timing of the expense or tax deduction. Because depreciation differs each year, the amount at which the equipment is reported will differ as well for book and tax purposes (cost less accumulated depreciation is called *net book value* for financial reporting purposes and *tax basis* for tax purposes). These book vs tax differences are eliminated at the end of the asset's useful life.

To understand this concept more completely, we modify the example from the module to include a third year. Assume that the company purchases PPE assets at the start of Year 1 for $120. For financial reporting purposes, the company uses straight-line depreciation and records depreciation of $40 each year (with zero salvage). For tax purposes, assume that the company takes tax depreciation deductions of $60, $50, and $10. Exhibit 5A.1 reports the annual depreciation along with the asset's net book value and its tax basis, for each year-end.

EXHIBIT 5A.1   Book and Tax Depreciation and Carrying Value

	Financial Reporting (Net Book Value)	Tax Reporting (Tax Basis)	Book vs Tax Difference	Deferred Tax Liability (Book vs Tax Difference × Tax Rate)	Deferred Tax Expense (Increase or Decrease in Deferred Tax Liability)
At purchase: PPE carrying value	$120	$120	$ 0	$ 0	
Year 1: Depreciation..............	(40)	(60)			
End of Year 1: PPE carrying value ...	80	60	$20 ($80 − $60)	$ 8 ($20 × 40%)	$ 8 ($8 − $0)
Year 2: Depreciation..............	(40)	(50)			
End of Year 2: PPE carrying value ...	40	10	$30 ($40 − $10)	$12 ($30 × 40%)	$ 4 ($12 − $8)
Year 3: Depreciation..............	(40)	(10)			
End of Year 3: PPE carrying value ...	0	0	$ 0 ($0 − $0)	$ 0	$(12) ($0 − $12)

The third column in Exhibit 5A.1 shows the "book-tax" difference, which is the difference between GAAP net book value and the tax basis at the end of each year. The fourth column shows the deferred tax liability at the end of each period, computed as the book-tax differences times the tax rate. We see from the fourth column that when the financial reporting net book value is greater than the tax basis, the company has a deferred tax liability on its balance sheet (as in Years 1 and 2). Companies' footnotes provide information about deferred taxes. For example, Pfizer's footnote reports a deferred tax liability (net) of $1,726 for its property, plant and equipment, which indicates that tax basis for PPE is less than GAAP net book value, on average, for Pfizer's PPE.

Accounting standards require a company to first compute the taxes it owes (per its tax return), then to compute any changes in deferred tax liabilities and assets, and finally to compute tax expense reported in the income statement (as a residual amount). Thus, tax expense is not computed as pretax income multiplied by the company's tax rate as we might initially expect. Instead, tax expense is computed as follows:

Tax Expense = Taxes Paid − Increase (or + Decrease) in Deferred Tax Assets + Increase (or − Decrease) in Deferred Liabilities

The far-right column in Exhibit 5A.1 shows the deferred tax expense per year, which is the amount added to, or subtracted from, taxes paid, to arrive at tax expense. If we assume this company had $100 of pre-depreciation income, its taxable income and tax expense (assuming a 40% rate) follows:

	Taxes Paid	Deferred Tax Expense	Total Tax Expense
Year 1	$16 ($100 − $60) × 40%	$ 8	$24
Year 2	$20 ($100 − $50) × 40%	$ 4	$24
Year 3	$36 ($100 − $10) × 40%	$(12)	$24

In this example, the timing difference between the financial reporting and tax reporting derives from PPE and creates a deferred tax liability. Other differences between the two sets of books create other types of deferred tax accounts. Exhibit 5A.2 shows the relation between the financial reporting and tax reporting net book values, and the resulting deferred taxes (liability or asset) on the balance sheet.

EXHIBIT 5A.2	Sources of Deferred Tax Assets and Liabilities

For Assets...

| Financial reporting net book value | > | Tax reporting net book value | → | Deferred tax liability on balance sheet |
| Financial reporting net book value | < | Tax reporting net book value | → | Deferred tax asset on balance sheet |

For Liabilities...

| Financial reporting net book value | < | Tax reporting net book value | → | Deferred tax liability on balance sheet |
| Financial reporting net book value | > | Tax reporting net book value | → | Deferred tax asset on balance sheet |

A common deferred tax asset relates to accrued restructuring costs (a liability for financial reporting purposes). Restructuring costs are not deductible for tax purposes until paid in the future and, thus, there is no accrual restructuring liability for tax reporting, which means it has a tax basis of $0. To explain how this timing difference affects tax expense, assume that a company accrues $300 of restructuring costs in Year 1 and settles the liability in Year 2 as follows:

	Financial Reporting (Net Book Value)	Tax Reporting (Tax Basis)	Book vs Tax Difference	Deferred Tax Asset (Book vs Tax Difference × Tax Rate)	Deferred Tax Expense (Decrease (or Increase) in Deferred Tax Asset)
Year 1: Accrue restructuring costs . . .	$(300)	$ 0			
End of Year 1: Liability book value . . .	$ 300	$ 0	$300 ($300 − $0)	$120 ($300 × 40%)	$(120) ($120 − $0)
Year 2: Pay restructuring costs		$(300)			
End of Year 2: Liability book value . . .	$ 0	0	$ 0 ($0 − $0)	$ 0 ($0 × 40%)	$120 ($120 − $0)

Timing differences created by the restructuring liability yield a deferred tax asset in Year 1. Timing differences disappear in Year 2 when the company pays cash for restructuring costs. To see how tax expense is determined, assume that this company has $500 of pre-restructuring income; computations follow:

	Taxes Paid	Deferred Tax Expense	Total Tax Expense
Year 1	$200 ($500 − $0) × 40%	$(120)	$ 80
Year 2	$ 80 ($500 − $300) × 40%	$ 120	$200

Deferred tax accounts derive from timing differences between GAAP expenses and tax deductions. This creates differences between the net book value and the tax basis for many assets and liabilities. Pfizer's deferred tax foot-note (see Exhibit 5.6) reports several deferred tax assets and liabilities that explain its book-tax difference and the tax basis. For example, in 2010, its deferred tax liability associated with PPE is $1,726 million ($2,146 million liability less $420 million asset). This reflects the cumulative tax savings to Pfizer from accelerated depreciation for its PPE. If we assume a tax rate of 35%, we can compute the book-tax difference for Pfizer's PPE as $4,931 million ($1,726 million/0.35). Its balance sheet reveals total PPE of $19,123, which implies that the tax basis for these assets is $14,192 million ($19,123 − $4,931).

GUIDANCE ANSWERS . . . ANALYSIS DECISION

You Are the Financial Analyst Typically, restructuring charges have three components: asset write-downs (such as inventories, property, plant, and goodwill), severance costs, and other restructuring-related expenses. Write-downs occur when the cash-flow-generating ability of an asset declines, thus reducing its current market value below its book value reported on the balance sheet. Arguably, this decline in cash-flow-generating ability did not occur solely in the current year and, most likely, has developed over several periods. It is not uncommon for companies to delay loss recognition, such as write-downs of assets. Thus, prior period income is, arguably, not as high as reported, and the current period loss is not as great as reported. Turning to severance and other costs, GAAP permits restructuring expense to include only those costs that are incremental and will not benefit future periods. The accrual of restructuring-related expenses can be viewed like other accruals; that is, it might be over- or understated. In future periods, the required reconciliation of the restructuring accrual will provide insight into the adequacy of the accrual in that earlier period.

DISCUSSION QUESTIONS

Q5-1. What are the criteria that guide firms in recognition of revenue? What does each of the criteria mean? How are the criteria met for a company like **Abercrombie & Fitch**, a clothing retailer? How are the criteria met for a construction company that builds offices under long-term contracts with developers?

ABERCROMBIE & FITCH
(ANF)

Q5-2. Why are extraordinary items reported separately from continuing operations in the income statement?

Q5-3. What are the criteria for categorizing an event as an extraordinary item? Provide an example of an event that would properly be categorized as an extraordinary item and one that would not. How does this accounting treatment differ for IFRS?

Q5-4. What is the difference between basic earnings per share and diluted earnings per share? Are potentially dilutive securities always included in the EPS computation?

Q5-5. What effect, if any, does a weakening $US have on reported sales and net income for companies operating outside the United States?

Q5-6. Identify the three typical categories of restructuring costs and their effects on the balance sheet and the income statement. Explain the concept of a big bath and why restructuring costs are often identified with this event.

Q5-7. What is the current U.S. GAAP accounting treatment for research and development costs? How does this accounting treatment differ for IFRS? Why are R&D costs normally not capitalized under U.S. GAAP?

Q5-8. Under what circumstances will deferred taxes likely result in a cash outflow?

Q5-9. What is the concept of pro forma income and why has this income measure been criticized?

Q5-10. What is unearned revenue? Provide three examples of unearned revenue.

Assignments with the ✓ logo in the margin are available in an online homework system.
See the Preface of the book for details.

MINI EXERCISES

M5-11. **Computing Percentage-of-Completion Revenues** (LO1)

Bartov Corporation agreed to build a warehouse for a client at an agreed contract price of $2,500,000. Expected (and actual) costs for the warehouse follow: 2012, $400,000; 2013, $1,000,000; and 2014, $500,000. The company completed the warehouse in 2014. Compute revenues, expenses, and income for each year 2012 through 2014 using the percentage-of-completion method. (Round percents to the nearest whole number.)

M5-12. **Applying the Financial Statement Effects Template.** (LO1)

Refer to the information for Bartov Corporation in M5-11.

a. Use the financial statement effects template to record contract revenues and expenses for each year 2012 through 2014 using the percentage-of-completion method.

b. Prepare journal entries and T-accounts to record contract revenues and expenses for each year 2012 through 2014 using the percentage-of-completion method.

M5-13. **Assessing Revenue Recognition of Companies** (LO1)

Identify and explain when each of the following companies should recognize revenue.

a. **The GAP**: The GAP is a retailer of clothing items for all ages.

b. **Merck & Company**: Merck engages in developing, manufacturing, and marketing pharmaceutical products. It sells its drugs to retailers like **CVS** and **Walgreen**.

c. **Deere & Company**: Deere manufactures heavy equipment. It sells equipment to a network of independent distributors, who in turn sell the equipment to customers. Deere provides financing and insurance services both to distributors and customers.

d. **Bank of America**: Bank of America is a banking institution. It lends money to individuals and corporations and invests excess funds in marketable securities.

e. **Johnson Controls**: Johnson Controls manufactures products for the government under long-term contracts.

M5-14. **Assessing Risk Exposure to Revenue Recognition** (LO1)

BannerAD Corporation manages a Website that sells products on consignment from sellers. It pays these sellers a portion of the sales price, and charges a commission. Identify two potential revenue recognition problems relating to such sales.

M5-15. **Estimating Revenue Recognition with Right of Return** (LO1)

The GAP offers an unconditional return policy. It normally expects 2% of sales at retail selling prices to be returned before the return period expires. Assuming that The GAP records total sales of $5 million for the current period, what amount of *net* sales should it record for this period?

M5-16. **Assessing Research and Development Expenses** (LO2)

Abbott Laboratories reports the following (summary) income statement.

Year Ended December 31 ($ millions)	2010
Net sales	$35,167
Cost of products sold	(14,665)
Research and development*	(4,038)
Selling, general and administrative	(10,376)
Pretax operating earnings	$ 6,088

* Includes acquired in process research and development.

a. Compute the percent of net sales that Abbott Laboratories spends on research and development (R&D). Compare this level of expenditure with the percentages for other companies that are discussed in the Business Insight box on page 5-4. How would you assess the appropriateness of its R&D expense level?

b. Describe how accounting for R&D expenditures affects Abbott Laboratories' balance sheet and income statement.

THE GAP
(GPS)
MERCK & COMPANY
(MRK)
DEERE & COMPANY
(DE)
BANK OF AMERICA
(BAC)
JOHNSON CONTROLS
(JCI)

THE GAP
(GPS)

ABBOTT LABORATORIES
(ABT)

M5-17. Interpreting Foreign Currency Translation Disclosure   (LO4)

Bristol-Myers Squibb (BMY) reports the following table in its 10-K report relating to the change in sales from 2009 to 2010.

	Total Change	Volume	Price	Analysis of % Change
				Foreign Exchange
	Total Change	**Volume**	**Price**	**Foreign Exchange**
U.S. net sales...................	6%	3%	3%	—
Foreign net sales	(1)%	2%	(4)%	1%
Total net sales...................	4%	2%	1%	1%

a. Did U.S. net sales increase or decrease during the year? By what percentage? How much of this change is attributable to volume versus price changes?

b. By what percentage did foreign net sales change during the year? How much of this change is attributable to volume versus price changes?

c. Why does the change in total net sales (4%) not equal the sum of the changes in U.S. (6%) and foreign net sales (−1%)?

M5-18. Analyzing Income Tax Disclosure   (LO3)

Dell Inc. reports the following footnote disclosure to its 10-K report ($ millions).

The provision for income taxes consisted of the following:

Fiscal Year Ended	January 28, 2011
Federal	
Current	$597
Deferred	(95)
	502
State	
Current	66
Deferred	9
	75
Foreign	
Current	97
Deferred	41
	138
Total	$715

a. What amount of income tax expense does Dell report in its income statement for 2011?

b. How much of Dell's income tax expense is current (as opposed to deferred)?

c. Why do deferred tax assets and liabilities arise? How do they impact the tax expense that Dell reports in its 2011 income statement?

M5-19. Defining and Computing Earnings per Share   (LO5)

Cleantech Solutions International reports the following information in footnotes to its 2010 Form 10-K.

Net income available to common shareholders for basic and diluted net income per common share............................	$11,074,332
Weighted average common shares outstanding—basic	17,879,940
Effect of dilutive securities:	
Series A convertible preferred stock	4,980,272
Warrants...	2,536,609
Weighted average common shares outstanding—diluted	25,396,821

    a.   Explain the concepts of basic and diluted earnings per share.

    b.   Compute basic and diluted EPS for 2010.

    c.   What is the effect of dilutive securities on EPS, in percentage terms?

M5-20. **Assessing Revenue Recognition for Advance Payments** (LO1)

Koonce Company operates a performing arts center. The company sells tickets for its upcoming season of six Broadway musicals and receives $420,000 cash. The performances occur monthly over the next six months.

    a.   When should Koonce record revenue for the Broadway musical series?

    b.   Use the financial statement effects template to show the $420,000 cash receipt and recognition of the first month's revenue.

M5-21. **Reporting Unearned Revenue** (LO1)

TARGET CORPORATION (TGT)

Target Corporation sells gift cards that can be used at any of the company's Target or Greatland stores. Target encodes information on the card's magnetic strip about the card's value, the date it expires (typically two years after issuance), and the store where it was purchased.

    a.   How will Target's balance sheet reflect the gift card? Will the balance sheet amount of these cards be classified as current or noncurrent?

    b.   When does Target record revenue from the gift card?

EXERCISES

E5-22. **Assessing Revenue Recognition Timing** (LO1)

Explain when each of the following businesses should recognize revenues:

LIMITED (LTD)
BOEING CO. (BA)
SUPERVALU, INC. (SVU)
MTV
BANK OF AMERICA (BAC)
HARLEY-DAVIDSON (HOG)
TIME-WARNER (TWX)

    a.   A clothing retailer like **The Limited**.

    b.   A contractor like **Boeing Company** that performs work under long-term government contracts.

    c.   A grocery store like **Supervalu**.

    d.   A producer of television shows like **MTV** that syndicates its content to television stations.

    e.   A residential real estate developer that constructs only speculative houses and later sells these houses to buyers.

    f.   A banking institution like **Bank of America** that lends money for home mortgages.

    g.   A manufacturer like **Harley-Davidson**.

    h.   A publisher of magazines such as **Time-Warner**.

E5-23. **Assessing Revenue Recognition Timing and Income Measurement** (LO1)

Explain when each of the following businesses should recognize revenue and identify any income measurement issues that could arise.

THESTREET.COM (TSCM)
ORACLE (ORCL)
INTUIT (INTU)

    a.   RealMoney.Com, a division of **TheStreet.Com**, provides investment advice to customers for an up-front fee. It provides these customers with password-protected access to its Website where customers can download investment reports. RealMoney has an obligation to provide updates on its Website.

    b.   **Oracle** develops general ledger and other business application software that it sells to its customers. The customer pays an up-front fee for the right to use the software and a monthly fee for support services.

    c.   **Intuit** develops tax preparation software that it sells to its customers for a flat fee. No further payment is required and the software cannot be returned, only exchanged if defective.

    d.   A developer of computer games sells its software with a 10-day right of return period during which the software can be returned for a full refund. After the 10-day period has expired, the software cannot be returned.

E5-24. **Constructing and Assessing Income Statements Using Percentage-of-Completion** (LO1)

GENERAL ELECTRIC COMPANY (GE)

Assume that **General Electric Company** agreed in May 2011 to construct a nuclear generator for NSTAR, a utility company serving the Boston area. The contract price of $500 million is to be paid as follows: $200 million at the time of signing; $100 million on December 31, 2011; and $200 million at completion in May 2012. General Electric incurred the following costs in constructing the generator: $100 million in 2011, and $300 million in 2012.

    a.   Compute the amount of General Electric's revenue, expense, and income for both 2011 and 2012 under the percentage-of-completion revenue recognition method.

    b.   Discuss whether or not you believe the percentage-of-completion method provides a good measure of General Electric's performance under the contract.

E5-25. **Constructing and Assessing Income Statements Using Percentage-of-Completion** (LO1)

On March 15, 2012, Frankel Construction contracted to build a shopping center at a contract price of $120 million. The schedule of expected (which equals actual) cash collections and contract costs follows:

Year	Cash Collections	Cost Incurred
2012	$ 30 million	$15 million
2013	50 million	40 million
2014	40 million	30 million
Total	$120 million	$85 million

    a.   Calculate the amount of revenue, expense, and net income for each of the three years 2012 through 2014 using the percentage-of-completion revenue recognition method. (Round percents to the nearest whole number.)

    b.   Discuss whether or not the percentage-of-completion method provides a good measure of this construction company's performance under the contract.

E5-26. **Interpreting the Income Tax Expense Footnote** (LO3)

The income tax footnote to the financial statements of **FedEx Corporation** follows.

FEDEX CORP
(FDX)

The components of the provision for income taxes for the years ended May 31 were as follows:

($ millions)	2010	2009	2008
Current provision			
Domestic			
Federal	$ 36	$ (35)	$514
State and local	54	18	74
Foreign	207	214	242
	297	197	830
Deferred provision (benefit)			
Domestic			
Federal	408	327	31
State and local	15	48	(2)
Foreign	(10)	7	32
	413	382	61
Provision for income taxes.	$710	$579	$891

    a.   What is the amount of income tax expense reported in FedEx's 2010, 2009, and 2008 income statements?

    b.   What percentage of total tax expense is currently payable in each year?

    c.   One possible reason for the $408 million federal deferred tax expense in 2010 is that deferred tax liabilities increased during that year. Provide an example that gives rise to an increase in the deferred tax liability.

E5-27. **Identifying Operating Income Components** (LO2)

Following is the income statement information from Apollo Medical Devices. Identify the components that we would consider operating.

($ in thousands)	2010
Net sales.	$5,164,771
Cost of sales before special charges.	1,382,235
Special inventory obsolescence charge.	27,876
Total cost of sales.	1,410,111
Gross profit.	3,754,660
Selling, general and administrative expense	1,770,667
Research and development expense.	631,086
Merger and acquisition costs.	46,914
In-process research and development charges.	12,244
Litigation settlement.	16,500
Operating profit	1,277,249
Interest expense.	(67,372)
Interest income.	2,076
Gain on disposal of fixed assets	4,929
Impairment of marketable securities	(5,222)
Other income (expense), net	(2,857)
Earnings before income taxes	1,208,803
Income tax expense.	301,367
Net earnings.	$ 907,436

E5-28.   Identifying Operating Income Components   (LO2)

DEERE & COMPANY
(DE)

Following is the **Deere & Company** income statement for 2010.

($ millions)	2010
Net Sales and Revenues	
Net sales.	$23,573.2
Finance and interest income	1,825.3
Other income	606.1
Total	26,004.6
Costs and Expenses	
Cost of sales.	17,398.8
Research and development expenses.	1,052.4
Selling, administrative and general expenses	2,968.7
Interest expense.	811.4
Other operating expenses	748.1
Total	22,979.4
Income of Consolidated Group before Income Taxes	3,025.2
Provision for income taxes.	1,161.6
Income of Consolidated Group	1,863.6
Equity in income of unconsolidated affiliates.	10.7
Net income.	1,874.3
Net income attributable to noncontrolling interests.	9.3
Net income attributable to Deere & Company	$ 1,865.0

Notes:

• Income statement includes John Deere commercial and consumer tractor segment, a finance subsidiary that provides loan and lease financing relating to the sales of those tractors, and a health care segment that provides managed health care services for the company and certain outside customers.

• **Equity in income of unconsolidated affiliates** refers to income John Deere has earned on investments in affiliated (but unconsolidated) companies. These are generally investments made for strategic purposes.

a. Identify the components in its income statement that you would consider operating.
b. Discuss your treatment of the company's finance and interest income that relates to financing of its John Deere lawn and garden, and commercial tractors.

E5-29.   Assessing the Income Tax Footnote   (LO3)

Colgate-Palmolive reports the following income tax footnote disclosure in its 10-K report.

Deferred Tax Balances at December 31 (In millions)	2010	2009
Deferred tax liabilities		
Intangible assets	$(463)	$(440)
Property, plant and equipment	(344)	(320)
Other	(116)	(157)
	(923)	(917)
Deferred tax assets		
Pension and other retiree benefits	471	389
Tax loss and tax credit carryforwards	130	153
Accrued liabilities	145	134
Stock-based compensation	108	103
Other	163	163
Valuation allowance	(1)	(2)
	1,016	940
Net deferred income taxes	$ 93	$ 23

a. Colgate reports $344 million of deferred tax liabilities in 2010 relating to "Property." Explain how such liabilities arise.
b. Describe how a deferred tax asset can arise from pension and other retiree benefits.
c. Colgate reports $130 million in deferred tax assets for 2010 relating to tax loss and credit carryforwards. Describe how tax loss carryforwards arise and under what conditions the resulting deferred tax assets will be realized.
d. Colgate has established a deferred tax asset valuation allowance of $1 million for 2010. What is the purpose of this allowance? How did the decrease in this allowance of $1 million from 2009 to 2010 affect net income?
e. Colgate's income statement reports income tax expense of $1,117 million. Assume that cash paid for income tax is $1,123 million and that taxes payable increased by $64 million. Use the financial statement effects template to record tax expense for 2010. (*Hint:* Show the effects of changes in deferred taxes.)

E5-30.   Analyzing and Assessing Research and Development Expenses   (LO2)

Advanced Micro Devices (AMD) and **Intel (INTC)** are competitors in the computer processor industry. Following is a table ($ millions) of sales and R&D expenses for both companies.

AMD	R&D Expense	Sales	INTC	R&D Expense	Sales
2010	$1,405	$6,494	2010	$6,576	$43,623
2009	1,721	5,403	2009	5,653	35,127
2008	1,848	5,808	2008	5,722	37,586

a. What percentage of sales are AMD and INTC spending on research and development?
b. How are AMD and INTC's balance sheets and income statements affected by the accounting for R&D costs?
c. How can one evaluate the effectiveness of R&D spending? Does the difference in R&D as a percentage of sales necessarily imply that one company is more heavily invested in R&D? Why might this not be the case?

E5-31.   Analyzing and Interpreting Foreign Currency Translation Effects   (LO4)

Kellogg Co. reports the following table and discussion in its 2010 10-K.

The following tables provide an analysis of net sales and operating profit performance for 2010 versus 2009:

(Dollars in millions)	North America	Europe	Latin America	Asia Pacific	Corporate	Consolidated
2010 net sales	$8,402	$2,230	$923	$842	$—	$12,397
2009 net sales	$8,510	$2,361	$963	$741	$—	$12,575
% change—2010 vs. 2009:						
Volume (tonnage)	−2.5%	−2.4%	−3.4%	4.3%	—	−2.1%
Pricing/mix	0.6%	−0.3%	8.2%	−2.3%	—	0.8%
Subtotal—internal business	−1.9%	−2.7%	4.8%	2.0%	—	−1.3%
Foreign currency impact. . . .	0.6%	−2.8%	−8.9%	11.7%	—	−0.1%
Total change	−1.3%	−5.5%	−4.1%	13.7%	—	−1.4%

(Dollars in millions)	North America	Europe	Latin America	Asia Pacific	Corporate	Consolidated
2010 operating profit	$1,554	$364	$153	$74	$(155)	$1,990
2009 operating profit	$1,569	$348	$179	$86	$(181)	$2,001
% change—2010 vs. 2009:						
Internal business.	−1.7%	8.2%	−2.4%	−29.5%	14.2%	−0.1%
Foreign currency impact. .	0.7%	−3.4%	−12.3%	15.2%	—	−0.5%
Total change	−1.0%	4.8%	−14.7%	−14.3%	14.2%	−0.6%

Foreign exchange risk Our Company is exposed to fluctuations in foreign currency cash flows related to third-party purchases, intercompany transactions, and when applicable, nonfunctional currency denominated third-party debt. Our Company is also exposed to fluctuations in the value of foreign currency investments in subsidiaries and cash flows related to repatriation of these investments. Additionally, our Company is exposed to volatility in the translation of foreign currency earnings to U.S. Dollars. Primary exposures include the U.S. Dollar versus the British Pound, Euro, Australian Dollar, Canadian Dollar, and Mexican Peso, and in the case of inter-subsidiary transactions, the British Pound versus the Euro. We assess foreign currency risk based on transactional cash flows and translational volatility and enter into forward contracts, options, and currency swaps to reduce fluctuations in net long or short currency positions. Forward contracts and options are generally less than 18 months duration. Currency swap agreements are established in conjunction with the term of underlying debt issuances.

a. Before the effects of foreign currency rates, total consolidated sales decreased by 1.3% during 2010. What geographic segment accounted for this overall decline?

b. How did foreign currency exchange rates affect sales at each of the geographic segments? What can we infer about the strength of the U.S. dollar vis-à-vis the currencies in Kellogg's segments?

c. Operating profit declined modestly on a consolidated basis. Which geographic segments exhibited the lowest and which the highest change in profit during the year? Explain.

d. Describe how the accounting for foreign exchange translation affects reported sales and profits.

e. How does Kellogg Co. manage the risk related to its foreign exchange exposure? Describe the financial statement effects of this risk management activity.

E5-32.   Interpreting Revenue Recognition for Gift Cards   (LO1)

BARNES & NOBLE
(BKS)

Footnotes to the 2010 annual report of **Barnes & Noble** disclose the following:

The Barnes & Noble Member program entitles Members to receive the following benefits: 40% discount off the current hardcover Barnes & Noble store bestsellers, 20% discount off all adult hardcover books, 10% discount off Barnes & Noble sale price of other eligible items, unlimited free express shipping on orders made on Barnes & Noble.com, as well as periodic special promotions at Barnes & Noble stores and online at Barnes&Noble.com. The annual fee of $25.00 is non-refundable after the first 30 days. Revenue is recognized over the twelve-month period based upon historical spending patterns for Barnes & Noble Members.

a. Explain in layman terms how Barnes & Noble accounts for the cash received for its membership program. When does Barnes & Noble record revenue from this program?
b. How does Barnes & Noble's balance sheet reflect those membership fees?
c. Does the 40% discount affect Barnes & Noble's income statement when membership fees are received?

Superscript ^{A} denotes assignments based on Appendix 5A.

PROBLEMS

P5-33. **Analyzing and Interpreting Revenue Recognition Policies and Risks** **(LO1)**
Amazon.com, Inc., provides the following explanation of its revenue recognition policies in its 10-K report.

AMAZON.COM
(AMZN)

> On January 1, 2010, we prospectively adopted ASU 2009-13, which amends Accounting Standards Codification ("ASC") Topic 605, Revenue Recognition. Under this new standard, we allocate revenue in arrangements with multiple deliverables using estimated selling prices (ESP) if we do not have vendor-specific objective evidence or third-party evidence of the selling prices of the deliverables. Estimated selling prices are management's best estimates of the prices that we would charge our customers if we were to sell the standalone elements separately.
>
> Sales of our Kindle e-reader are considered arrangements with multiple deliverables, consisting of the device, 3G wireless access and delivery for some models, and software upgrades. Under the prior accounting standard, we accounted for sales of the Kindle ratably over the average estimated life of the device. Accordingly, revenue and associated product cost of the device through December 31, 2009, were deferred at the time of sale and recognized on a straight-line basis over the two-year average estimated economic life.
>
> As of January 2010, we account for the sale of the Kindle as multiple deliverables. The revenue related to the device, which is the substantial portion of the total sale price, and related costs are recognized upon delivery. Revenue related to 3G wireless access and delivery and software upgrades is amortized over the average life of the device, which remains estimated at two years.
>
> Because we have adopted ASU 2009-13 prospectively, we are recognizing $508 million throughout 2010 and 2011 for revenue previously deferred under the prior accounting standard.

Required
a. What is a multiple-element contract? What product does Amazon sell that involves a multiple-element contract? Explain.
b. Explain how companies account for multiple-element contracts, in general.
c. Compare the accounting for the Kindle under the old and new accounting standards for revenue recognition. Amazon discloses that $508 million of previously deferred revenue will now be recognized earlier. Explain.
d. Assume that Amazon sells a Kindle with 3G capabilities for $180 and the company estimates a selling price (ESP) of $20 per unit for 3G access and future software upgrades. Compute the revenue that Amazon would recognize at the point of sale under the old and the new accounting standards.
e. Use the financial statement effects template to record the initial sale of a Kindle and the accounting adjustment required at the end of the first quarter for the new accounting standards.

P5-34. **Analyzing and Interpreting Income Tax Disclosures** **(LO3)**
The 2010 income statement for **Pfizer** is reproduced in this module. Pfizer also reports the following footnote relating to its income taxes in its 2010 10-K report.

PFIZER
(PFE)

> **Deferred Taxes** Deferred taxes arise as a result of basis differentials between financial statement accounting and tax amounts. The tax effect of the major items recorded as deferred tax assets and liabilities, shown before jurisdictional netting, as of December 31 is as follows:

continued

continued from prior page

(Millions of dollars)	2010 Deferred Tax		2009 Deferred Tax	
	Assets	(Liabilities)	Assets	(Liabilities)
Prepaid/deferred items.	$1,321	$ (112)	$1,330	$(60)
Inventories	132	(59)	437	(859)
Intangibles	1,165	(17,104)	949	(19,802)
Property, plant and equipment.	420	(2,146)	715	(2,014)
Employee benefits	4,479	(56)	4,786	(66)
Restructurings and other charges	1,359	(70)	884	(8)
Legal and product liability reserves	1,411	—	1,010	—
Net operating loss/credit carryforwards. . .	4,575	—	4,658	—
Unremitted earnings.	—	(9,524)	—	(7,057)
State and local tax adjustments.	452	—	747	—
All other	607	(575)	744	(187)
Subtotal	15,921	(29,646)	16,260	(30,053)
Valuation allowance	(894)	—	(353)	—
Total deferred taxes	$15,027	(29,646)	$15,907	(30,053)
Net deferred tax liability		$(14,619)		$(14,146)

Required

a. Describe the terms "deferred tax liabilities" and "deferred tax assets." Provide an example of how these accounts can arise.

b. Intangible assets (other than goodwill) acquired in the purchase of a company are depreciated (amortized) similar to buildings and equipment (see Module 9 for a discussion). Describe how the deferred tax liability of $17,104 million relating to intangibles arose.

c. Pfizer has many employee benefit plans, such as a long-term health plan and a pension plan. Some of these are generating deferred tax assets and others are generating deferred tax liabilities. Explain the timing of the recognition of expenses under these plans that would give rise to these different outcomes.

d. Pfizer reports a deferred tax liability labelled "unremitted earnings." This relates to an investment in an affiliated company for which Pfizer is recording income, but has not yet received dividends. Generally, investment income is taxed when received. Explain what information the deferred tax liability for unremitted earnings conveys.

e. Pfizer reports a deferred tax asset relating to net operating loss carryforwards. Explain what loss carryforwards are.

f. Pfizer reports a valuation allowance of $894 million in 2010. Explain why Pfizer has established this allowance and its effect on reported profit. Pfizer's valuation allowance was $353 million in 2009. Compute the change in its allowance during 2010 and explain how that change affected 2010 tax expense and net income.

XEROX CORPORATION
(XRX)

P5-35.   **Analyzing and Interpreting Income Components and Disclosures**   **(LO2)**
The income statement for **Xerox Corporation** follows.

Year ended December 31 (in millions)	2010	2009	2008
Revenue			
Equipment sales.	$ 3,857	$ 3,550	$ 4,679
Supplies, paper and other	3,377	3,096	3,646
Sales.	7,234	6,646	8,325
Service, outsourcing and rentals	13,739	7,820	8,485
Finance income	660	713	798
Total Revenues	21,633	15,179	17,608

continued

continued from prior page

Costs and Expenses			
Cost of sales.	4,741	4,395	5,519
Cost of service, outsourcing and rentals	9,195	4,488	4,929
Equipment financing interest	246	271	305
Research, development and engineering expenses	781	840	884
Selling, administrative and general expenses	4,594	4,149	4,534
Restructuring and asset impairment charges	483	(8)	429
Acquisition-related costs	77	72	—
Amortization of intangible assets.	312	60	54
Other expenses, net.	389	285	1,033
Total Costs and Expenses	20,818	14,552	17,687
Income (Loss) before Income Taxes, and Equity Income.	815	627	(79)
Income tax expense (benefit)	256	152	(231)
Equity in net income of unconsolidated affiliates.	78	41	113
Net income.	637	516	265
Less: Net income attributable to noncontrolling interests	31	31	35
Net income Attributable to Xerox.	$ 606	$ 485	$ 230

Notes:

- The income statement includes sales of Xerox copiers and revenue earned by a finance subsidiary that provides loan and lease financing relating to the sales of those copiers.

- **Equity in net income of unconsolidated affiliates** refers to income Xerox has earned on investments in affiliated (but unconsolidated) companies.

Required

a. Xerox reports several sources of income. How should revenue be recognized for each of these business activities? Explain.

b. Compute the relative size of Sales revenue (total) and of revenue from Service, outsourcing and rentals. Hint: Scale each type of revenue by Total revenue. Which type of revenue grew more in 2010?

c. Xerox reports research, development and engineering expenses (R&D) each year. Compare R&D spending over the three years. Hint: Scale R&D by Total revenue each year. What might explain the change in 2010?

d. Xerox reports restructuring costs each year. (1) Describe the three typical categories of restructuring costs and the accounting for each. (2) How do you recommend treating these costs for analysis purposes? (3) Should regular recurring restructuring costs be treated differently than isolated occurrences of such costs for analysis purposes? (4) What does the $(8) expense in 2009 imply about one or more previous year's accruals?

e. Xerox reports $389 million in expenses in 2010 labeled as "Other expenses, net." How can a company use such an account to potentially obscure its actual financial performance?

P5-36. **Analyzing and Interpreting Income Tax Footnote** (LO3)

Ahold, a grocery and retail company located in The Netherlands, reports the following footnote for income taxes in its 2010 annual report.

AHOLD

The following table specifies the current and deferred tax components of income taxes in the income statement:

For year ended (€ million)	2-Jan-11	3-Jan-10
Current income taxes		
Domestic taxes—the Netherlands	€169	€ 68
Foreign taxes		
United States	48	38
Europe—Other	4	11
Total current tax expense.	221	117

continued

continued from prior page

Deferred income taxes		
Domestic taxes—the Netherlands	10	52
Foreign taxes		
United States	33	4
Europe—Other	7	(25)
Total deferred tax expense.	50	31
Total income tax expense.	€271	€148

The significant components of deferred income tax assets and liabilities are as follows, as of:

	2-Jan-11	3-Jan-10
Leases and financings	€222	€197
Pensions and other post-employment benefits	46	52
Provisions.	131	137
Derivatives and loans	7	6
Interest	35	36
Other.	52	27
Total gross temporary differences	493	455
Unrecognised temporary differences.	(20)	(17)
Total recognised temporary differences.	473	438
Tax losses and credits	572	544
Unrecognised tax losses and credits.	(459)	(434)
Total recognised tax losses and credits.	113	110
Total deferred tax assets	586	548
Property, plant and equipment and intangible assets	(245)	(191)
Inventories	(103)	(92)
Other.	(5)	(9)
Total deferred tax liabilities.	(353)	(292)
Net deferred tax assets	€233	€256

Deferred income tax assets and liabilities are offset on the balance sheet when there is a legally enforceable right to offset current tax assets against current tax liabilities and when the deferred income taxes relate to income taxes levied by the same fiscal authority.

Required

a.   What income tax expense does Ahold report in its 2010 income statement? How much of this expense is currently payable?

b.   Ahold reports deferred tax liabilities relating to property, plant and equipment. Describe how these liabilities arise. How likely is it that these liabilities will be paid? Specifically, describe a scenario that will (i) defer these taxes indefinitely, and (ii) will result in these liabilities requiring payment within the near future.

c.   Ahold reports a deferred tax asset relating to provisions. Footnotes to financial statements indicate that these provisions relate, in part, to self-insurance accruals. When a company self-insures, it does not purchase insurance from a third-party insurance company. Instead, it records an expense and related liability to reflect the probable payment of losses that can occur in the future. Explain why this accrual (provision) results in a deferred tax asset.

d.   Ahold reports deferred tax assets relating to tax losses and credits. Explain how these arise and how they will result in a future benefit.

e.   The company reports unrecognized temporary differences and unrecognized tax losses and credits. These are the IFRS equivalent of valuation allowances in U.S. GAAP. Why did the company set up these unrecognised portions of deferred tax assets? How did the increase in the combined unrecognized amounts from 2009 to 2010 affect net income? How can a company use these accounts to meet its income targets in a particular year?

P5-37.[A] **Analyzing and Interpreting Tax Footnote (Financial Statement Effects Template)** (LO3)

Under Armour, Inc., reports total tax expense of $40,442 (in thousands) on its income statement for year ended December 31, 2010, and paid cash of $38,773 (in thousands) for taxes. The tax footnote in the company's 10-K filing, reports the following deferred tax information.

UNDER ARMOUR
(UA)

Deferred tax assets and liabilities consisted of the following:

December 31 (In thousands)	2010	2009
Deferred tax assets		
State tax credits, net of federal tax impact	$ 1,750	$ —
Tax basis inventory adjustment	3,052	1,874
Inventory obsolescence reserves.	2,264	2,800
Allowance for doubtful accounts and other reserves.	8,996	7,042
Foreign net operating loss carryforward	10,917	9,476
Stock-based compensation.	8,790	5,450
Intangible asset	372	1,068
Deferred rent	2,975	1,728
Deferred compensation	1,449	1,105
Other.	2,709	3,151
Total deferred tax assets	43,274	33,694
Less: valuation allowance	(1,765)	—
Total net deferred tax assets	41,509	33,694
Deferred tax liabilities		
Prepaid expenses.	(1,865)	(1,133)
Property, plant and equipment.	(3,104)	(5,783)
Total deferred tax liabilities.	(4,969)	(6,916)
Total deferred tax assets, net.	$36,540	$26,778

Required

a. Under Armour's deferred tax assets increased during the most recent fiscal year. What explains the increase?

b. Did Under Armour's deferred tax liabilities increase or decrease during the most recent fiscal year? Explain how the change arose.

c. The company recorded a valuation allowance during 2010. This allowance relates to foreign net operating tax losses. Explain how tax losses give rise to deferred tax assets. Why does the company record a valuation account? What proportion of these losses, at December 31, 2010, does the company believe will likely expire unused?

d. Explain how the valuation allowance affected 2010 net income.

e. Use the financial statement effects template to record Under Armour's income tax expense for the fiscal year 2010 along with the changes in both deferred tax assets and liabilities. Assume that the amount needed to balance the tax transaction represents the amount payable to tax authorities.

P5-38. **Analyzing and Interpreting Restructuring Costs and Effects** (LO2)

Hewlett-Packard, Inc., reports the following footnote disclosure (excerpted) in its 2010 10-K relating to its restructuring programs.

HEWLETT-
PACKARD, INC.
(HPQ)

Fiscal 2010 Acquisitions On July 1, 2010, HP completed the acquisition of Palm and initiated a plan to restructure the operations of Palm, including severance for Palm employees, contract cancellation costs and other items. The total expected cost of the plan is $46 million.

On April 12, 2010, HP completed the acquisition of 3Com. In connection with the acquisition, HP's management approved and initiated a plan to restructure the operation of 3Com, including severance costs and costs to vacate duplicative facilities. The total expected cost of the plan is $42 million. In fiscal 2010, HP recorded restructuring charges of approximately $18 million.

continued

continued from prior page

Fiscal 2010 ES Restructuring Plan On June 1, 2010, HP's management announced a plan to restructure its enterprise services business. The total expected cost of the plan that will be recorded as restructuring charges is approximately $1.0 billion, including severance costs to eliminate approximately 9,000 positions and infrastructure charges. For fiscal 2010, a restructuring charge of $650 million was recorded primarily related to severance costs. As of October 31, 2010, approximately 2,100 positions have been eliminated.

Fiscal 2009 Restructuring Plan In May 2009, HP's management approved and initiated a restructuring plan to structurally change and improve the effectiveness of several businesses. The total expected cost of the plan is $292 million in severance-related costs associated with the planned elimination of approximately 5,000 positions. As of October 31, 2010, approximately 4,200 positions had been eliminated.

Fiscal 2008 HP/EDS Restructuring Plan In connection with the acquisition of EDS on August 26, 2008, HP's management approved and initiated a restructuring plan to combine and align HP's services businesses, eliminate duplicative overhead functions and consolidate and vacate duplicative facilities. The restructuring plan is expected to be implemented over four years at a total expected cost of $3.4 billion.

The adjustments to the accrued restructuring expenses related to all of HP's restructuring plans described above for the twelve months ended October 31, 2010, were as follows:

In millions	Balance, October 31, 2009	Fiscal year 2010 charges (reversals)	Cash payments	Non-cash settlements & other adjustments	Balance, October 31, 2010
Fiscal 2010 acquisitions.........	$ —	$ 64	$ (20)	$ —	$ 44
Fiscal 2010 ES Plan:					
Severance....................	—	630	(55)	45	620
Infrastructure	—	20	(6)	(10)	4
Total 2010 ES Plan.............	—	650	(61)	35	624
Fiscal 2009 Plan...............	248	(5)	(177)	(9)	57
Fiscal 2008 HP/EDS Plan:					
Severance....................	747	236	(873)	(35)	75
Infrastructure	419	193	(185)	(19)	408
Total 2008 HP/EDS Plan........	1,166	429	(1,058)	(54)	483
Total restructuring plans........	$1,414	$1,138	$(1,316)	$(28)	$1,208

Required

a.   Briefly describe the company's 2010 restructuring program. Provide two examples of common noncash charges associated with corporate restructuring activities.

b.   Using the financial statement effects template, show the effects on financial statements of the (1) 2010 restructuring charge of $1,138 million, and (2) 2010 cash payment of $1,316 million.

c.   Assume that instead of accurately estimating the anticipated restructuring charge in 2010, the company overestimated them by $30 million. How would this overestimation affect financial statements in (1) 2010, and (2) 2011 when severance costs are paid in cash?

d.   Consider the 2010 ES restructuring. The company reports that total charges will amount to $1 billion. What is the effect on the 2010 income statement from this restructuring? Why do investors care to know the total charge if it does not impact current-period earnings?

P5-39. Analyzing and Interpreting Income Tax Footnote   (LO3)

DUPONT
(DD)

Consider the following income tax footnote information for the **E. I. du Pont de Nemours and Company**.

Provision for Income Taxes

($ millions)	2010	2009	2008
Current tax expense (benefit)			
U.S. federal.	$(109)	$23	$ 14
U.S. state and local.	—	(9)	(3)
International	454	328	327
	345	342	338
Deferred tax expense (benefit)			
U.S. federal.	245	57	210
U.S. state and local.	3	1	—
International	66	15	(167)
	314	73	43
Provision for income taxes.	$659	$415	$381

The significant components of deferred tax assets and liabilities are as follows:

($ millions)	2010		2009	
	Asset	Liability	Asset	Liability
Depreciation	$ —	$1,614	$ —	$1,515
Accrued employee benefits	3,731	81	3,899	98
Other accrued expenses	928	369	1,029	366
Inventories	273	154	197	148
Unrealized exchange gains	34	—	5	—
Tax loss/tax credit carryforwards/backs	2,680	—	3,023	—
Investment in subsidiaries and affiliates.	41	279	45	275
Amortization of intangibles.	53	636	80	558
Other.	314	144	291	152
	8,054	$3,277	8,569	$3,112
Valuation allowance	(1,666)		(1,759)	
	$3,111		$3,698	

An analysis of the company's effective income tax rate (EITR) follows:

	2010	2009	2008
Statutory U.S. federal income tax rate.	35.0%	35.0%	35.0%
Exchange gains/losses[1]	0.2	(2.6)	(0.2)
Domestic operations	(2.0)	(1.4)	(2.8)
Lower effective tax rates on international operations-net	(13.6)	(11.8)	(14.3)
Tax settlements	(1.8)	(0.2)	(1.8)
	17.8%	19.0%	15.9%

[1] Principally reflects the benefit of non-taxable exchange gains and losses resulting from remeasurement of foreign currency denominated monetary assets and liabilities.

Required

a. What is the total amount of income tax expense that DuPont reports in its 2010 income statement? What portion of this expense does DuPont expect to pay in 2011?

b. Explain how the deferred tax liability called "depreciation" arises. Under what circumstances will the company settle this liability? Under what circumstances might this liability be deferred indefinitely?

c. Explain how the deferred tax asset called "accrued employee benefits" arises. Why is it recognized as an asset?

d. Explain how the deferred tax asset called "tax loss/tax credit carryforwards/backs" arises. Under what circumstances will DuPont realize the benefits of this asset?

e. DuPont reports a 2010 valuation allowance of $1,666 million. How does this valuation allowance arise? How did the change in valuation allowance for 2010 affect net income? Valuation allowances typically relate to questions about the realizability of tax loss carryforwards. Under what circumstances might DuPont not realize the benefits of its tax loss carryforwards?

f. Dupont's footnote reports the effective income tax rates (EITR) for the three-year period. What explains the difference between the U.S. statutory rate and the company's EITR?

P5-40.   **Assessing Revenue Recognition, R&D Expense, EPS, and Income Taxes**   (LO1, 2, 3, 5)

INTUIT, INC.
(INTU)

Following are the income statement and relevant footnotes from the 10-K of Intuit, Inc.

| INTUIT INC. CONSOLIDATED STATEMENTS OF OPERATIONS | | | |
Twelve Months Ended July 31 (In millions, except per share amounts)	2010	2009	2008
Net revenue			
Product	$1,412	$1,376	$1,483
Service and other	2,043	1,733	1,510
Total net revenue	3,455	3,109	2,993
Costs and expenses			
Cost of revenue			
Cost of product revenue	144	156	154
Cost of service and other revenue	460	422	381
Amortization of acquired technology	49	59	55
Selling and marketing	976	907	841
Research and development	573	556	593
General and administrative	348	284	290
Amortization of other acquired intangible assets	42	42	35
Total costs and expenses	2,592	2,426	2,349
Operating income from continuing operations	863	683	644
Interest expense	(61)	(51)	(52)
Interest and other income	13	21	46
Gain on sale of outsourced payroll assets	—	—	52
Income from continuing operations before income taxes	815	653	690
Income tax provision	276	206	243
Net income from continuing operations	539	447	447
Net income (loss) from discontinued operations	35	—	30
Net income	$ 574	$ 447	$ 477
Basic net income per share from continuing operations	$ 1.71	$ 1.39	$ 1.36
Basic net income (loss) per share from discontinued operations	0.11	—	0.09
Basic net income per share	$ 1.82	$ 1.39	$ 1.45
Diluted net income per share from continuing operations	$ 1.66	$ 1.35	$ 1.32
Diluted net income (loss) per share from discontinued operations	0.11	—	0.09
Diluted net income per share	$ 1.77	$ 1.35	$ 1.41

The following table presents the composition of shares used in the computation of basic and diluted net income per share for the periods indicated.

Twelve Months Ended July 31 (In millions, except per share amounts)	2010	2009	2008
Denominator:			
Shares used in basic per share amounts:			
Weighted average common shares outstanding	316	322	329
Shares used in diluted per share amounts:			
Weighted average common shares outstanding	316	322	329
Dilutive common equivalent shares from stock options and restricted stock awards	9	8	10
Dilutive weighted average common shares outstanding	325	330	339

continued from prior page

Revenue Recognition

We derive revenue from the sale of packaged software products, license fees, software subscriptions, product support, hosting services, payroll services, merchant services, professional services, transaction fees and multiple element arrangements that may include any combination of these items.

Product Revenue   We recognize revenue from the sale of our packaged software products and supplies when legal title transfers, which is generally when our customers download products from the Web, when we ship the products or, when products are delivered to retailers. We sell some products on consignment to certain retailers. We recognize revenue for these consignment transactions only when the end-user sale has occurred. For products that are sold on a subscription basis and include periodic updates, we recognize revenue ratably over the contractual time period.

Service Revenue   We recognize revenue from payroll processing and payroll tax filing services as the services are performed, provided we have no other remaining obligations to these customers.

Multiple Element Arrangements   We enter into certain revenue arrangements for which we are obligated to deliver multiple products and/or services (multiple elements). For these arrangements, which generally include software products, we allocate and defer revenue for the undelivered elements based on their vendor-specific objective evidence of fair value (VSOE). VSOE is the price charged when that element is sold separately. In situations where VSOE exists for all elements (delivered and undelivered), we allocate the total revenue to be earned under the arrangement among the various elements, based on their relative fair value.

Income Taxes

Differences between income taxes calculated using the federal statutory income tax rate of 35% and the provision for income taxes from continuing operations were as follows for the periods indicated:

Twelve Months Ended July 31 (In millions)	2010	2009	2008
Income from continuing operations before income taxes	$815	$653	$690
Statutory federal income tax	$285	$229	$242
State income tax, net of federal benefit	27	9	29
Federal research and experimentation credits	(8)	(20)	(7)
Domestic production activities deduction	(14)	(11)	(12)
Share-based compensation	4	4	—
Tax exempt interest	(2)	(5)	(12)
Effects of non-U.S. operations	(20)	—	—
Other, net	4	—	3
Total provision for income taxes from continuing operations	$276	$206	$243

Significant deferred tax assets and liabilities were as follows at the dates indicated:

July 31 (In millions)	2010	2009
Deferred tax assets		
Accruals and reserves not currently deductible	$ 30	$ 31
Deferred rent	10	12
Accrued and deferred compensation	18	1
Loss and tax credit carryforwards	63	46
Property and equipment	8	5
Share-based compensation	89	92
Other, net	4	11
Total deferred tax assets	222	198
Deferred tax liabilities		
Intangible assets	55	59
Other, net	1	5
Total deferred tax liabilities	56	64
Total net deferred tax assets	166	134
Valuation allowance	(8)	(6)
Total net deferred tax assets, net of valuation allowance	$158	$128

continued

continued from prior page

> We have provided a valuation allowance related to the benefits of certain state and foreign net operating loss carryforwards that we believe are unlikely to be realized. The valuation allowance increased $2 million during the twelve months ended July 31, 2010, primarily due to state net operating loss carryforwards acquired in business combinations. These primarily California net operating loss carryforwards are unlikely to be realized as a result of the California legislation enacted in 2009 and effective for our fiscal 2012 which limits expected sources of future California taxable income for fiscal 2012 and beyond.

Required

a. Describe the differences in revenue recognition between product sales and after-sale services. How does the company recognize revenue for consignment sales? For products sold on a subscription basis? How is service revenue recognized?

b. Some of the company's sales involve multiple element arrangements. In general, what are these arrangements? How does the company account for such sales?

c. Intuit reports $573 million of Research and Development expense, up from $556 million in the prior year.
  i. What kind of research activities would we expect for a company like Intuit?
  ii. Given the kind of research activities described in part i, how does the accounting for Intuit's R&D costs differ from the way that those costs would have been accounted for had Intuit used IFRS for financial reporting?

d. Intuit's earnings per share (EPS) is $1.77 on a diluted basis, compared with its basic EPS of $1.82. What factor(s) accounts for this dilution?

e. Drawing on Intuit's income tax footnote, prepare a table in percentages showing computation of its effective tax rate for each of the three fiscal years. What tax-related items, if any, would we not expect to continue into fiscal year 2011?

f. Intuit reports deferred tax assets of $222 million.
  i. Describe how deferred tax assets relating to accruals arise.
  ii. Explain how deferred tax assets relating to loss carryforwards arise.
  iii. Intuit reports an increase of its deferred tax asset valuation allowance of $2 million in 2010. How does this affect Intuit's income?

COSTCO WHOLESALE (COST)

P5-41. Analyzing Unearned Revenue Disclosures (LO1)

The following disclosures are from the August 29, 2010, annual report of **Costco Wholesale Corporation**.

> **Revenue Recognition** We generally recognize sales, net of estimated returns, at the time the member takes possession of merchandise or receives services. When we collect payment from customers prior to the transfer of ownership of merchandise or the performance of services, the amount received is generally recorded as deferred revenue on the consolidated balance sheets until the sale or service is completed. Membership fee revenue represents annual membership fees paid by our members. We account for membership fee revenue, net of estimated refunds, on a deferred basis, whereby revenue is recognized ratably over the one-year membership period.

Revenue ($ millions)	52 weeks ended August 29, 2010	52 weeks ended August 30, 2009	52 weeks ended August 31, 2008
Net sales.	$76,255	$69,889	$70,977
Membership fees	1,691	1,533	1,506
Total revenue.	$77,946	$71,422	$72,483

continued

continued from prior page

Current Liabilities ($ millions)	August 29, 2010	August 30, 2009
Short-term borrowings....................	$ 26	$ 16
Accounts payable........................	5,947	5,450
Accrued salaries and benefits	1,571	1,418
Accrued sales and other taxes.............	322	302
Deferred membership fees................	869	824
Current portion long-term debt	0	80
Other current liabilities	1,328	1,191
Total current liabilities	$10,063	$9,281

The components of the deferred tax assets and liabilities are as follows (in $ millions):

	August 29, 2010	August 30, 2009
Equity compensation	$112	$117
Deferred income/membership fees	118	94
Accrued liabilities and reserves	392	408
Other.......................................	35	48
Total deferred tax assets	657	667
Property and equipment.......................	414	403
Merchandise inventories	170	184
Total deferred tax liabilities....................	584	587
Net deferred tax assets	$ 73	$ 80

Required

a. Explain in layman terms how Costco accounts for the cash received for its membership fees.

b. Use the balance sheet information on Costco's Deferred Membership Fees liability account and its income statement revenues related to Membership Fees earned during 2010 to compute the cash that Costco received during 2010 for membership fees.

c. Use the financial statement effects template to show the effect of the cash Costco received during 2010 for membership fees and the recognition of membership fees revenue for 2010.

d. Costco reports a deferred tax asset related to deferred income/membership fees. Explain in layman terms how this asset arises. When will Costco receive the benefit associated with this asset?

IFRS APPLICATIONS

I5-42.   Assessing Research and Development Expenses   (LO2)

Dr. Reddy's Laboratories, an Indian pharmaceutical company whose stock is traded in the U.S., reports the following (summary) income statement (reported under IFRS).

Year Ended March 31 ($ millions)	2010
Revenues	$1,563
Cost of revenues	755
Selling, general and administrative	501
Research and development	84
Other (income) expense, net	179
Results from operations...................	$ 45*

*difference due to rounding

a. Compute the percent of revenues that Dr. Reddy's Laboratories spends on research and development (R&D). Compare this level of expenditure with the percentages for other companies that are discussed in the Business Insight box on page 5-4. How would you assess the appropriateness of its R&D expense level?

b. Describe how accounting for R&D expenditures affects Dr. Reddy's Laboratories' balance sheet and income statement. How would this accounting have been different if the company had reported under U.S. GAAP?

I5-43. **Assessing Research and Development Expenses** **(LO2)**

FINMECCANICA
S.P.A.

Headquartered in Rome, Italy, **Finmeccanica S.p.A.** is a multinational conglomerate operating in the defense and aerospace sectors. The company uses IFRS for its financial reports and disclosed the following in its 2010 annual report:

Development costs, net In € millions	December 31, 2010	December 31, 2009
Balance beginning of year	624	474
Development costs capitalised during the year	182	296
Amortisation	(68)	(84)
Impairment	(53)	(18)
Sales	(12)	(44)
Balance end of year	673	624

Required

a. Under IFRS, what six criteria did Finmeccanica have to meet in order to capitalize development costs?

b. The company reported total research and development R&D expenditures of €2,030 in 2010 and €1,982 in 2009. Assume that these amounts include the development costs capitalized during the year (above). What proportion of total R&D costs did the company capitalize in each year?

c. The development costs (intangible asset) is reduced by €53 in 2010 and €18 in 2009 for impairment. Explain how an intangible asset could become impaired. How did this impairment affect Finmeccanica's income statement in 2010? Is this an operating or a nonoperating item?

d. If Finmeccanica had always used U.S. GAAP to account for research and development costs, what would have been the difference in net income for 2010?

I5-44. **Assessing Research and Development Expenses** **(LO2)**

FINMECCANICA
S.P.A.

Headquartered in Rome, Italy, **Finmeccanica S.p.A.** is a multinational conglomerate operating in the defense and aerospace sectors. The company uses IFRS for its financial reports and disclosed the following in its 2010 annual report:

Research and development costs for Finmeccanica's Energy Sector for the year ended 31 December 2010 came to €38, up 6% over 2009 (€36). Research and development activities for the Energy Sector focused primarily on the following items in 2010:

- Gas turbines: AE94.3A turbine development projects to raise power, efficiency and operational flexibility, while complying with requirements on pollutants in exhaust gas, and projects to retrofit the AE94.2 turbine to increase the power and extend the life of the Class E turbine;

- Steam turbines: international projects investigating the behaviour of special materials (extremely high temperature steels and super alloys) with a view to developing the "ultrasupercritical" turbine (with a power rating in excess of 300 MW);

- Generators: development work on the new air-cooled 400-MVA model intended to complement the large, high-performance gas turbines.

Required

a. How are R&D costs accounted for under IFRS?

b. For each of the three energy sector R&D items described above, determine if the item meets the criteria for capitalization under IFRS.

I5-45.   **Analyzing Unearned Revenue Transactions and Multiple-Element Arrangements**   (LO1)
Research in Motion reports the following financial statement data and footnote information.

Research in Motion Limited Consolidated Statements of Operations (USD $)			
	12 Months Ended		
In Millions, except per share data	Feb. 26, 2011	Feb. 27, 2010	Feb. 28, 2009
Revenue			
Hardware and other	$16,416	$12,536	$ 9,411
Service and software	3,491	2,417	1,654
Total revenue	19,907	14,953	11,065
Cost of sales			
Hardware and other	10,516	7,979	5,718
Service and software	566	390	250
Total cost of sales.	11,082	8,369	5,968
Gross margin	8,825	6,584	5,097
Operating expenses			
Research and development	1,351	965	685
Selling, marketing and administration . . .	2,400	1,907	1,495
Amortization	438	310	195
Litigation.	0	164	0
Total operating expenses	4,189	3,346	2,375
Income from operations	4,636	3,238	2,722
Investment income, net	8	28	79
Income before income taxes	4,644	3,266	2,801
Provision for income taxes.	1,233	809	908
Net income.	$ 3,411	$ 2,457	$ 1,893
Earnings per share			
Basic.	6.36	4.35	3.35
Diluted	6.34	4.31	3.30

Revenue Recognition

Multiple-element arrangements   The Company enters into revenue arrangements that may consist of multiple deliverables of its product and service offerings. The Company's typical multiple-element arrangements involve: (i) handheld devices with services and (ii) software with technical support services.

For the Company's arrangements involving multiple deliverables of handheld devices with services, the consideration from the arrangement is allocated to each respective element based on its relative selling price, using vendor-specific objective evidence of selling price (VSOE). In certain limited instances when the Company is unable to establish the selling price using VSOE, the Company attempts to establish selling price of each element based on acceptable third party evidence of selling price (TPE); however, the Company is generally unable to reliably determine the selling prices of similar competitor products and services on a stand-alone basis. In these instances, the Company uses best estimated selling price (BESP) in its allocation of arrangement consideration. The objective of BESP is to determine the price at which the Company would transact a sale if the product or service was sold on a stand-alone basis.

The Company regularly reviews VSOE, TPE and BESP, and maintains internal controls over the establishment and updates of these estimates. There were no material impacts to the amount of revenue recognized during the year, nor does the Company expect a material impact in the near term, from changes in VSOE, TPE or BESP.

Required

a.   Research in Motion has sales contracts that consist of multiple deliverables bundled for one price. What are the two typical deliverables?

b.   The footnotes report that, "Price protection is accrued as a reduction to revenue based on estimates of future price reductions, provided the price reduction can be reliably estimated and all other revenue recognition criteria have been met." Assume that the company believes that prices on the current Blackberry models will decrease by 10% in the coming year. Explain how the company would record this fact.

c. Explain in layman terms how Research in Motion records revenue from sales of bundled hardware and software.

d. Assume that a customer makes a volume purchase of 200 Blackberry Playbook tablets. The total discounted sales price is $480 per unit and the sale is on account. Because there is no reliable VSOE, RIM estimates a BESP of $476 for the hardware and services and of $84 for the software technical support. This second deliverable involves free future software upgrades for two years. Allocate the consideration received for the 200 units to each respective element in the arrangement, based on its relative selling price.

e. Use the financial statement effects template to record the original sale in part d., above, and the accounting adjustment at the end of the first fiscal year after the sale.

f. The income statement reports two types of revenue. Compare the relative magnitude of each revenue type. Hint: Scale each by total revenues.

g. The income statement reports cost of sales for both types of revenue. Which of the two has a higher gross margin? Explain why this might be the case.

DISCUSSION POINTS

D5-46. **Managing Foreign Currency Risk** **(LO4)**
Fluctuations in foreign currency exchange rates can result in increased volatility of revenues, expenses, and profits. Companies generally attempt to reduce this volatility.

a. Identify two possible solutions to reduce the volatility effect of foreign exchange rate fluctuations.
b. What costs would arise if you implemented each of your solutions?

D5-47. **Ethics and Governance: Revenue Recognition** **(LO1)**
GAAP offers latitude in determining when revenue is earned. Assume that a company that normally required acceptance by its customers prior to recording revenue as earned, delivers a product to a customer near the end of the quarter. The company believes that customer acceptance is assured, but cannot obtain it prior to quarter-end. Recording the revenue would assure "making its numbers" for the quarter. Although formal acceptance is not obtained, the sales person records the sale, fully intending to obtain written acceptance as soon as possible.

a. What are the revenue recognition requirements in this case?
b. What are the ethical issues relating to this sale?
c. Assume you are on the board of directors of this company. What safeguards can you put in place to provide assurance that the company's revenue recognition policy is followed?

D5-48. **Ethics and Governance: Earnings Management** **(LO2)**
Assume that you are CEO of a company. Your company has reported a loss for the current year. Since it cannot carry back the entire loss to recoup taxes paid in prior years, it records a loss carryforward as a deferred tax asset. Your expectation is that future profitability will be sufficient to realize the tax benefits of the carryforward. Your chief financial officer approaches you with an idea to create a deferred tax valuation allowance that will reduce the deferred tax asset, increase tax expense for the year, and increase your reported loss. He reasons that the company's stock price will not be reduced markedly by the additional reported loss since a loss year has already been factored into the current price. Further, this deferred tax valuation allowance will create a reserve that can be used in future years to increase profit (via reversal of the allowance) if needed to meet analyst expectations.

a. What stakeholders are potentially affected by the CFO's proposal?
b. How do you respond to the proposal? Justify your response.

SOLUTIONS TO REVIEW PROBLEMS

Mid-Module Review 1

Solution

1. Revenues are only recognized when the earning process is complete. Merck delivers its product before the customer is obligated to make payment. Passage of title typically constitutes delivery. Merck's policy appears to be reasonable given its product and GAAP requirements.
2. All R&D related equipment and/or facilities that have no alternative use must be expensed under GAAP. Assets that have other uses are capitalized and depreciated like other plant assets. R&D costs are aggregated into one line item (research and development expense) on Merck's income statement. Other costs are reported under materials and production and/or marketing and administrative expenses.
3. Restructuring expenses generally fall into three categories: severance costs, asset write-offs, and other costs. Restructuring programs must be approved by the board of directors before they are recognized in financial statements. Further, companies are required to disclose the initial liability accrual together with the portion that was subsequently utilized or reversed, if any. Because the restructuring accrual is an estimate, overestimates and subsequent reversals are possible. Should the company develop a reputation for recurring reversals, it will lose credibility with analysts and other stakeholders.

Mid-Module Review 2

Solution

1. Total income tax expense is $671 million.
2. $1,763 million is currently payable or has already been paid during 2010.
3. Income tax expense is the sum of current taxes (that is, currently payable as determined from the company's tax returns) plus the change in deferred tax assets and liabilities. It is a calculated figure, not a percentage that is applied to pretax income. For 2010, reported tax expense was *reduced* by the deferred provision (a liability) of $1,092 million.

Module-End Review

Solution

1. Income statement accounts that are denominated in foreign currencies must be translated into $US before the financial statements are publicly disclosed. When the $US weakens, each foreign currency unit is worth more $US. Consequently, each account in Merck's income statement is larger because the dollar weakened. Because Merck reported *positive* earnings (a profit) for 2010, net income also would be larger.
2. Basic earnings per share is equal to net income (less preferred dividends) divided by the weighted average number of common shares outstanding during the period. Diluted EPS considers the effects of dilutive securities. In diluted EPS, the denominator increases by the additional shares that would have been issued assuming exercise of all options and conversion of all convertible securities. The numerator is also adjusted for any preferred dividends and/or interest that would not have been paid upon conversion.

1. Analyze accounting for accounts receivable and the importance of the allowance for uncollectible accounts in determining profit. (p. 6-4)

2. Explain accounting for inventories and assess the effects on the balance sheet and income statement from different inventory costing methods. (p. 6-13)

3. Analyze accounting for property, plant and equipment and explain the impacts on profit and cash flows from depreciation methods, disposals and impairments. (p. 6-26)

Asset Recognition and Operating Assets

Cisco Systems, Inc., manufactures and sells networking and communications products for transporting data, voice, and video within buildings, across town, and around the world. Cisco's products are everywhere; here are a few applications:

- Schoolchildren can view a virtual science experiment from a neighborhood center's Cisco-outfitted computer room.

CISCO SYSTEMS

- Airline passengers can check flight information and print boarding passes at convenient Cisco kiosks.
- Hospital nurses check medication levels at patients' bedsides using Cisco handheld devices and wireless networks.
- Auto designers in Japan, assembly technicians in the U.S., and component makers worldwide exchange manufacturing data over a Cisco network in real time.

- Police rely on citywide Cisco wireless networks to deliver fingerprint files, mug shots, and voicemail to mobile units.
- Customers call their banks' Cisco Internet Protocol (IP) based center, where account profiles appear to call agents.
- Companies shore up their databases with Cisco network security.

Cisco reported 2010 net income of $7.7 billion on $40 billion in sales, and a return on net operating assets (RNOA) of 45%. In 2001, Cisco reported a *loss* of $1 billion after recording $2.25 billion of restructuring costs, including costs related to the severance of 6,000 employees and the write-off of obsolete inventory and other assets.

Cisco's turnaround is remarkable. Sales have increased by over 60% in the past five years, and its return on net operating assets has remained at over 40% during this period, which reflects Cisco's effective asset (balance sheet) management. Recall that RNOA comprises both a profitability component and a productivity component (see Module 3). The productivity component (reflected in net operating asset turnover, NOAT) is measured as sales divided by average net operating assets. Effective management of operating assets is crucial to achieving a high RNOA. We focus on three important operating assets in this module: accounts receivable, inventories, and property, plant and equipment (PPE).

As part of their overall marketing efforts, companies extend credit to customers. At Cisco, for example, accounts receivable are an important asset because nearly all sales are on account. While favorable credit terms stimulate sales, the resulting accounts receivable are costly. First, accounts receivable are generally non-interest bearing and tie up a company's working capital in non-earning assets. Second, receivables expose the company to collectibility risk—the risk that some customers won't pay. Third, companies incur the administrative costs associated with billing and collection. These costs must be weighed against the costs of other marketing tools, like advertising, sales incentives, and price discounts. Management of receivables is critical to financial success.

Inventories are significant assets at many companies, particularly for manufacturers such as Cisco, where inventories consist of raw materials (the basic product inputs), work in process (the cost of partially completed products), and finished goods (completed products awaiting sale). Inventories are also costly to maintain. The cost of buying and manufacturing the goods must be financed and inventories must be stored, moved, and insured. Consequently, companies prefer lower inventory levels whenever

(continued on next page)

(continued from previous page)

possible. However, companies must be careful to hold enough inventory. If they reduce inventory quantities too far, they risk inventory stock-outs, that is, not having enough inventory to meet demand. Management of inventories is also a critical activity.

Property, plant and equipment (PPE) is often the largest, and usually the most important, asset on the balance sheet. Companies need administrative offices, IT and R&D facilities, regional sales and customer service offices, manufacturing and distribution facilities, vehicles, computers, and a host of other fixed assets. Fixed asset costs are substantial and are indirectly linked to sales and profits. Consequently, fixed-asset investments are often difficult to justify and, once acquired, fixed assets are often difficult to divest. Effective management of PPE assets usually requires management review of the entire value chain.

John Chambers, CEO of Cisco, recalls a conversation he once had with the legendary Jack Welch, former Chairman of GE. Following Cisco's announced restructuring program in 2001, Welch commented, "John, you'll never have a great company until you go through the really tough times. What builds a company is not just how you handle the successes, but it's the way you handle the real challenges." Cisco survived the tech bubble burst and is now reporting impressive financial results. To ensure future financial performance, however, Cisco must effectively manage both its income statement and its operating assets.

Sources: *BusinessWeek,* 2012, 2006 and 2003; Cisco Systems 10-K, 2011; Cisco Systems Annual Report, 2011; *Fortune,* May 2009.

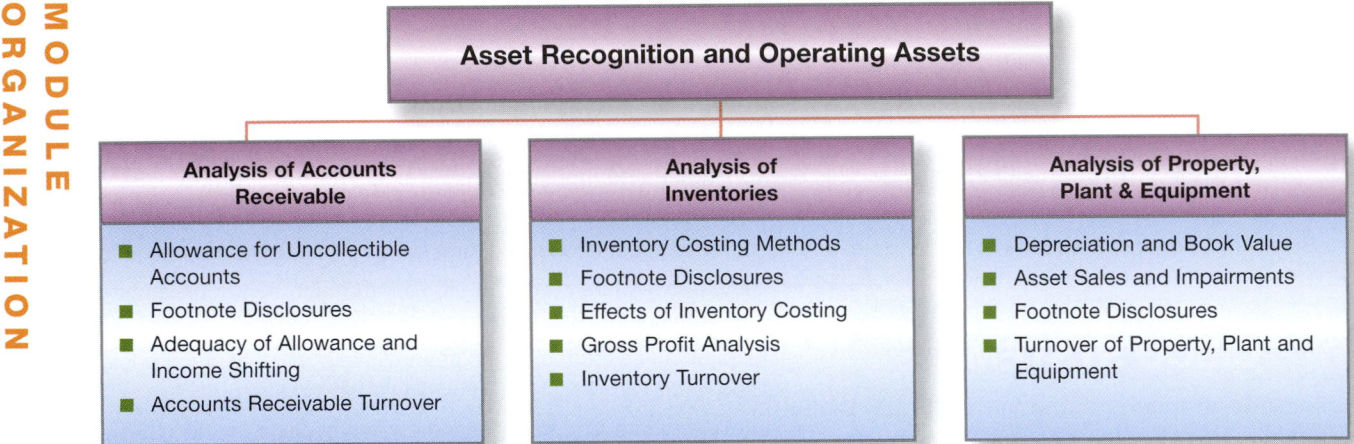

Managing net operating assets is crucial to creating shareholder value. To manage and assess net operating assets, we need to understand how they are measured and reported. This module describes the reporting and measuring of operating working capital, mainly receivables and inventories, and of long-term operating assets such as property, plant, and equipment. We do not discuss other long-term operating assets, such as equity investments in affiliated companies, investment in intangible assets, and nonoperating investments in marketable securities, as they are covered in other modules.

Receivables are usually a major part of operating working capital. They must be carefully managed as they represent a substantial asset for most companies and are an important marketing tool. GAAP requires companies to report receivables at the amount they expect to collect. This requires estimation of uncollectible accounts. The receivables reported on the balance sheet, and the expenses reported on the income statement, reflect management's estimate of uncollectible amounts. Accordingly, it is important that companies accurately assess uncollectible accounts and timely report them. It is also necessary that readers of financial reports understand management's accounting choices and their effects on reported balance sheets and income statements.

Inventory is another major component of operating working capital. Inventories usually constitute one of the three largest assets (along with receivables and long-term operating assets). Also, cost of goods sold, which flows from inventory, is the largest expense category for retailing and manufacturing companies. GAAP allows several methods for inventory accounting, and inventory-costing choices can markedly impact balance sheets and income statements, especially for companies experiencing relatively high inflation, coupled with slowly turning inventories.

Long-term plant assets are often the largest component of operating assets. Indeed, long-term operating assets are typically the largest asset for manufacturing companies, and their related depreciation expense is typically second only in amount to cost of goods sold in the income statement. GAAP allows different accounting methods for computing depreciation, which can significantly impact the income statement and the balance sheet. When companies dispose of fixed assets, a gain or loss may result. Understanding these gains and losses on asset sales is important as we assess performance. Further, asset write-downs (impairments) not only affect companies' current financial performance, but also future profitability. We must understand these effects when we forecast future income statements. This module considers all of these fixed asset accounting choices and consequences.

ANALYSIS OF ACCOUNTS RECEIVABLE

Our focus on operating assets begins with accounts receivable. To help frame our discussion, we refer to the following graphic as we proceed through the module:

LO1 Analyze accounting for accounts receivable and the importance of the allowance for uncollectible accounts in determining profit.

Income Statement
Sales
Cost of goods sold
Selling, general & administrative
Income taxes
Net income

Balance Sheet	
Cash	Current liabilities
Accounts receivable, net	Long-term liabilities
Inventory	
Property, plant, and equipment, net	Shareholders' equity
Investments	

The graphic highlights the balance sheet and income statement effects of accounts receivable. This section explains the accounting, reporting, and analysis of these highlighted items.

Retail companies transact mostly in cash. But other companies, including those that sell to other firms, usually do not expect cash upon delivery. Instead, they offer credit terms and have *credit sales* or *sales on account*.[1] An account receivable on the seller's balance sheet is always matched by a corresponding account payable on the buyer's balance sheet. Accounts receivable are reported on the seller's balance sheet at *net realizable value*, which is the net amount the seller expects to collect.

Sellers do not expect to collect all accounts receivable; they anticipate that some buyers will be unable to pay their accounts when they come due. For example, buyers can suffer business downturns that limit the cash available to meet liabilities. Then, buyers must decide which liabilities to pay. Typically, financially distressed companies decide to pay off liabilities to the IRS, to banks, and to bondholders because those creditors have enforcement powers and can quickly seize assets and disrupt operations, leading to bankruptcy and eventual liquidation. Buyers also try to cover their payroll, as they cannot exist without employees. Then, if there is cash remaining, buyers will pay suppliers to ensure continued flow of goods.

Accounts payable are *unsecured liabilities,* meaning that buyers have not pledged collateral to guarantee payment of amounts owed. As a result, when a company declares bankruptcy, accounts payable are comingled with other unsecured creditors (after the IRS and the secured creditors), and are typically not paid in full. Consequently, there is risk in the collectibility of accounts receivable. This *collectibility risk* is crucial to analysis of accounts receivable.

Cisco reports $4,929 million of accounts receivable in the current asset section of its fiscal year-end 2010 balance sheet.

$ millions	July 31, 2010
Cash and cash equivalents	$ 4,581
Investments	35,280
Accounts receivable, net of allowance for doubtful accounts of $235	4,929
Inventories	1,327
Deferred tax assets	2,126
Other current assets.	3,178
Total current assets	$51,421

Cisco reports its receivables net of allowances for doubtful (uncollectible) accounts of $235 million. This means the total amount owed to Cisco is $5,164 million ($4,929 million + $235

---

[1] An example of common credit terms are 2/10, net 30. These terms indicate that the seller offers the buyer an early-pay incentive, in this case a 2% discount off the cost if the buyer pays within 10 days of billing. If the buyer does not take advantage of the discount, it must pay 100% of the invoice cost within 30 days of billing. From the seller's standpoint, offering the discount is often warranted because it speeds up cash collections and then the seller can invest the cash to yield a return greater than the early-payment discount. The buyer often wishes to avail itself of attractive discounts even if it has to borrow money to do so. If the discount is not taken, however, the buyer should withhold payment as long as possible (at least for the full net period) so as to maximize its available cash. Meanwhile, the seller will exert whatever pressure it can to collect the amount due as quickly as possible. Thus, it is normal for there to be some tension between sellers and buyers.

million), but Cisco *estimates* that $235 million are uncollectible and reports on its balance sheet only the amount it expects to collect.

We might ask why buyers would sell to companies from whom they do not expect to collect. The answer is they would not have extended credit *if* they knew beforehand which companies would eventually not pay. For example, Cisco probably cannot identify precisely those companies that constitute the $235 million in uncollectible accounts. Yet, it knows from past experience that a certain portion of its receivables will prove uncollectible. GAAP requires companies to estimate the dollar amount of uncollectible accounts (even if managers cannot identify specific accounts that are uncollectible), and to report accounts receivable at the resulting *net realizable value* (total receivables less an allowance for uncollectible accounts).

Allowance for Uncollectible Accounts

Companies typically use an *aging analysis* to estimate the amount of uncollectible accounts. This requires an analysis of receivables as of the balance sheet date. Specifically, customer accounts are categorized by the number of days that the related invoices have been unpaid (outstanding). Based on prior experience, or on other available statistics, uncollectible percentages are applied to each category, with larger percentages applied to older accounts. The result of this analysis is a dollar amount for the allowance for uncollectible accounts (also called allowance for doubtful accounts) at the balance sheet date.

Aging Analysis

To illustrate, Exhibit 6.1 shows an aging analysis for a seller with $100,000 of gross accounts receivable at period-end. The current accounts are those that are still within their original credit period. As an example, if a seller's credit terms are 2/10, net 30, all invoices that have been outstanding for 30 days or fewer are current. Accounts listed as 1–60 days past due are those 1 to 60 days past their due date. This would include an account that is 45 days outstanding for a net 30-day invoice. This same logic applies to all categories.

EXHIBIT 6.1   Aging of Accounts Receivable

Age of Accounts	Receivable Balance	Estimated Percent Uncollectible	Estimated Uncollectible Accounts
Current	$ 50,000	2%	$1,000
1-60 days past due	30,000	3	900
61-90 days past due	15,000	4	600
Over 90 days past due	5,000	8	400
Total	$100,000		$2,900

Exhibit 6.1 also reflects the seller's experience with uncollectible accounts, which manifests itself in the uncollectible percentages for each aged category. For example, on average, 3% of buyers' accounts that are 1–60 days past due prove uncollectible for this seller. Hence, the company estimates a potential loss of $900 for the $30,000 in receivables 1 to 60 days past due.

Reporting Receivables

The seller represented in Exhibit 6.1 reports its accounts receivable on the balance sheet as follows:

Accounts receivable, net of $2,900 in allowances......... $97,100

Assume that, as of the end of the *previous* accounting period, the company had estimated total uncollectible accounts of $2,200 based on an aging analysis of the receivables at that time. Also assume that the company did not write off any accounts receivable during the period. The *reconciliation* of its allowance account for the period follows:

Beginning allowance for uncollectible accounts	$ 2,200
Add: Provision for uncollectible accounts (bad debts expense)	700
Less: Write-offs of accounts receivable	0
Ending allowance for uncollectible accounts	$ 2,900

The aging analysis revealed that the allowance for uncollectible accounts is $700 too low and therefore, the company increased the allowance accordingly. This adjustment affects the financial statements as follows:

1. Accounts receivable are reduced by an additional $700 on the balance sheet (receivables are reported *net* of the allowance account).
2. A $700 expense, called bad debts expense, is reported in the income statement (usually part of SG&A expense). This reduces pretax profit by the same amount.[2]

The allowance for uncollectible accounts, a contra-asset account, increases with new provisions (additional bad debts expense) and decreases as accounts are written off. Individual accounts are written off when the seller identifies them as uncollectible. (A write-off reduces both accounts receivable and the allowance for uncollectible accounts as described below.) As with all permanent accounts on the balance sheet, the ending balance of the allowance account is the beginning balance for next period.

Writing Off Accounts

To illustrate the write-off of an account receivable, assume that subsequent to the period-end shown above, the seller receives notice that one of its customers, owing $500 at the time, has declared bankruptcy. The seller's attorneys believe that legal costs in attempting to collect this receivable would likely exceed the amount owed. So, the seller decides not to pursue collection and to write off this account. The write-off has the following effects:

1. Gross accounts receivable are reduced from $100,000 to $99,500.
2. Allowance for uncollectible accounts is reduced from $2,900 to $2,400.

After the write-off, the seller's balance sheet appears as follows:

Accounts receivable, net of $2,400 in allowances. $97,100

Exhibit 6.2 shows the effects of this write-off on the individual accounts.

EXHIBIT 6.2	Effects of an Accounts Receivable Write-Off		
Account	**Before Write-Off**	**Effects of Write-Off**	**After Write-Off**
Accounts receivable.	$100,000	$(500)	$99,500
Less: Allowance for uncollectible accounts.	2,900	(500)	2,400
Accounts receivable, net of allowance.	$ 97,100		$97,100

The balance of net accounts receivable is the same before and after the write-off. This is always the case. The write-off of an account is a non-event from an accounting point of view. That is, total assets do not change, liabilities stay the same, and equity is unaffected as there is no net income effect. The write-off affects individual asset accounts, but not total assets.

Let's next consider what happens when additional information arrives that alters management's expectations of uncollectible accounts. To illustrate, assume that sometime after the write-off above, the seller realizes that it has underestimated uncollectible accounts and that $3,000 (not $2,400) of the remaining $99,500 accounts receivable are uncollectible. The company must increase the allowance for uncollectible accounts by $600. The additional $600 provision has the following financial statement effects:

1. Allowance for uncollectible accounts increases by $600 to the revised estimated balance of $3,000; and accounts receivable (net of the allowance for uncollectible accounts) declines by $600 from $97,100 to $96,500 (or $99,500 − $3,000).

[2] Companies can also estimate uncollectible accounts using the *percentage of sales* method. The percentage of sales method computes bad debts expense directly, as a percentage of sales and the allowance for uncollectible accounts is estimated indirectly. In contrast, the aging method computes the allowance balance directly and the bad debts expense is the amount required to bring the allowance account up to (or down to) the amount determined by the aging analysis. To illustrate, if the company in Exhibit 6.1 reports sales of $100,000 and estimates the provision at 1% of sales, it would report a bad debts expense of $1,000 and an allowance balance of $3,200 instead of the $700 bad debts expense and the $2,900 allowance as determined using the aging analysis. The two methods nearly always report different values for the allowance, net accounts receivable, and bad debts expense.

2. A $600 bad debts expense is added to the income statement, which reduces pretax income. Recall that in the prior period, the seller reported $700 of bad debts expense when the allowance account was increased from $2,200 to $2,900.

Analyzing Receivable Transactions

To summarize, recording bad debts expense increases the allowance for uncollectible accounts, which affects both the *balance sheet* and *income statement*. Importantly, the financial statement effects occur when the allowance is estimated, and not when accounts are written off. In this way, bad debts expense is matched with sales on the income statement, and accounts receivable are reported net of uncollectible accounts on the balance sheet. Exhibit 6.3 illustrates each of the transactions discussed in this section using the financial statement effects template:

EXHIBIT 6.3	Financial Statement Effects of Key Accounts Receivable Transactions

	Balance Sheet							Income Statement		
Transaction	Cash Asset	+	Noncash Assets	=	Liabil- ities	+	Contrib. Capital	+	Earned Capital	Rev- enues	−	Expen- ses	=	Net Income
a. Credit sales of $100,000			+100,000 Accounts Receivable	=					+100,000 Retained Earnings	+100,000 Sales	−		=	+100,000
b. Increase allowance for uncollectible accounts by $700			−700 Allowance for Uncollectible Accounts	=					−700 Retained Earnings		−	+700 Bad Debts Expense	=	−700
c. Write off $500 in accounts receivable			−500 Accounts Receivable +500 Allowance for Uncollectible Accounts	=							−		=	
d. Increase allowance for uncollectible accounts by $600			−600 Allowance for Uncollectible Accounts	=					−600 Retained Earnings		−	+600 Bad Debts Expense	=	−600

(margin T-accounts)

```
AR       100,000
   Sales      100,000
         AR
100,000 |
         Sales
         | 100,000

BDE      700
   AU         700
         BDE
700 |
         AU
         | 700

AU       500
   AR         500
         AU
500 |
         AR
         | 500

BDE      600
   AU         600
         BDE
600 |
         AU
         | 600
```

Footnote and MD&A Disclosures

To illustrate the typical accounts receivable disclosure, consider **Cisco**'s discussion of its allowance for uncollectible accounts (from its MD&A):

Allowances for Receivables and Sales Returns

The allowances for receivables were as follows (in millions, except percentages):

	July 31, 2010	July 25, 2009
Allowance for doubtful accounts	$235	$216
Percentage of gross accounts receivable	4.6%	6.4%
Allowance for lease receivables	$207	$213
Percentage of gross lease receivables	8.6%	10.7%
Allowance for loan receivables	$ 73	$ 88
Percentage of gross loan receivables	5.8%	10.2%

The allowances are based on our assessment of the collectibility of customer accounts. We regularly review the adequacy of these allowances by considering factors such as historical experience,

continued

Module 6 | Asset Recognition and Operating Assets **6-8**

continued from prior page

credit quality, age of the receivable balances, and economic conditions that may affect a customer's ability to pay. In addition, we perform credit reviews and statistical portfolio analysis to assess the credit quality of our receivables. We also consider the concentration of receivables outstanding with a particular customer in assessing the adequacy of our allowances. Our allowance percentages declined in fiscal 2010 compared with fiscal 2009 due to improved portfolio management as we moved out of the challenging economic environment in fiscal 2009. Our allowance percentages for accounts receivable and lease receivables represent a return to approximately the levels we experienced prior to fiscal 2009, consistent with changes we have observed in the macroeconomic environment. If a major customer's creditworthiness deteriorates, or if actual defaults are higher than our historical experience, or if other circumstances arise, our estimates of the recoverability of amounts due to us could be overstated, and additional allowances could be required, which could have an adverse impact on our revenue.

Cisco's allowance for uncollectible accounts decreased as a percentage of gross receivables from the prior year, from 6.4% to 4.6%. As the economy emerged from recession in 2010, Cisco estimated that collectibility of its receivables would improve and then reduced its estimate of uncollectible accounts. This reduction increased income for that year. However, Cisco alludes to the level of estimation required and cautions the reader that additional allowances (provisions) could be required under certain circumstances, and that would adversely affect profit.

Cisco provides a footnote reconciliation of its allowance for uncollectible (doubtful) accounts for the past three years as shown in Exhibit 6.4.

EXHIBIT 6.4	Reconciliation of Cisco's Allowance for Uncollectible Accounts
$ millions	**Allowance for Doubtful Accounts**
Year ended July 26, 2008	
Balance at beginning of fiscal year	$166
Provision	34
Write-offs and other	(23)
Balance at end of fiscal year	$177
Year ended July 25, 2009	
Balance at beginning of fiscal year	$177
Provision	54
Write-offs and other	(15)
Balance at end of fiscal year	$216
Year ended July 31, 2010	
Balance at beginning of fiscal year	$216
Provision	44
Write-offs and other	(25)
Balance at end of fiscal year	$235

Reconciling Cisco's allowance account provides insight into the level of the provision (expense) each year relative to the actual write-offs. Over the three-year period ended in 2010, Cisco wrote off $63 million of uncollectible accounts ($23 million + $15 million + $25 million) and increased its allowance by $132 million ($34 million + $54 million + $44 million), resulting in a net increase of $69 million ($235 million − $166 million). The allowance for uncollectible accounts as a percentage of gross accounts receivable was 4.6% in 2010, as the economy emerged from recession, about the same level that Cisco reported in 2008 as the economy entered recession.

Analysis Implications

This section considers analysis of accounts receivable and the allowance for uncollectible accounts.

Adequacy of Allowance Account

A company makes two representations when reporting accounts receivable (net) in the current asset section of its balance sheet:

1. It expects to collect the amount reported on the balance sheet (remember, accounts receivable are reported net of allowance for uncollectible accounts).

2. It expects to collect the amount within the next year (implied by the classification of accounts receivable as a current asset).

From an analysis viewpoint, we scrutinize the adequacy of a company's provision for its uncollectible accounts. If the provision is inadequate, the cash ultimately collected will be less than the net receivables reported on the balance sheet.

How can an outsider assess the adequacy of the allowance account? One answer is to compare the allowance account to gross accounts receivable for the company and for its competitors. For Cisco, the 2010 percentage is 4.6% (see above), a 28% decline from the level it reported in 2009. What does such a decline signify? Perhaps the overall economic environment has improved, rendering write-offs less likely. Perhaps the company has improved its credit underwriting or receivables collection efforts. The MD&A section of the 10-K report is likely to discuss such new initiatives. Or perhaps the company's customer mix has changed and it is now selling to more creditworthy customers (or, it eliminated a risky class of customers).

The important point is that we must be comfortable with the percentage of uncollectible accounts reported by the company. We must remember that management controls the size of the allowance account—albeit with audit assurances.

Income Shifting

We noted that the financial statement effects of uncollectible accounts transpire when the allowance is increased for new bad debts expense and not when the allowance is decreased for the write-off of uncollectible accounts. It is also important to note that management controls the amount and timing of the bad debts expense. Although external auditors assess the reasonableness of the allowance for uncollectible accounts, they do not possess management's inside knowledge and experience. This puts the auditors at an information disadvantage, particularly if any dispute arises.

Studies show that many companies use the allowance for uncollectible accounts to shift income from one year into another. For example, a company can increase current-period income by deliberately underestimating bad debts expense. However, in the future it will become apparent that the bad debts expense was too low when the company's write-offs exceed the balance in the allowance account. Then, the company will need to increase the allowance to make up for the earlier period's underestimate. As an example, consider a company that accurately estimates that it has $1,000 of uncollectible accounts at the end of 2011. Assume that the current balance in the allowance for uncollectible accounts is $200. But instead of recording bad debts expense of $800 as needed to have an adequate ($1,000) allowance, the company records only $100 of bad debts expense and reports an allowance of $300 at the end of 2011. Now if the company's original estimate was accurate, in 2012 it will write off accounts totaling $1,000. The write-offs ($1,000) are greater than the allowance balance ($300) and the company will need to increase the allowance by recording an additional $700 in 2012. The effect of this is that the company borrowed $700 of income from 2012 to report higher income in 2011. This is called "income shifting."

Why would a company want to shift income from a later period into the current period? Perhaps it is a lean year and the company is in danger of missing income targets. For example, internal targets influence manager bonuses and external targets set by the market influence stock prices. Or, perhaps the company is in danger of defaulting on loan agreements tied to income levels. The reality is that income pressures are great and these pressures can cause managers to bend (or even break) the rules.

Companies can just as easily shift income from the current period to one or more future periods by overestimating the current period bad debts expense and allowance for uncollectible accounts. Why would a company want to shift income to one or more future periods? Perhaps current times are good and the company wants to "bank" some of that income for future periods, sometimes called a *cookie jar reserve*. It can then draw on that reserve, if necessary, to boost income in one or more future lean years. Another reason for a company to shift income from the current period is that it does not wish to unduly inflate market expectations for future period income. Or perhaps the company is experiencing a very bad year and it feels that overestimating the provision will not drive income materially lower than it is. Thus, it decides to take a big bath (a large loss) and create a reserve that can be used in future periods. (**Sears** provides an interesting case as described in the Business Insight box.)

BUSINESS INSIGHT | **Sears' Cookie Jar**

A column several years ago in *The Wall Street Journal* reported on an equity analyst that asserted Sears' earnings growth was aided by a balance sheet maneuver of three years earlier that softened the impact of soaring levels of bad credit card debt. Namely, despite soaring credit losses, Sears had reported an earnings *increase*. How so? The analyst explained that Sears had markedly increased its allowance for uncollectible accounts in that earlier year (to a level twice that of similar companies) and had reported the related bad debts expense in that year when its earnings were high. The resulting reserve was much higher than needed. Then, when earnings were low, Sears charged its credit losses to the allowance for uncollectible accounts. However, since the balance of the allowance for uncollectible accounts was so large, no increase in that account was necessary and little or no bad debts expense was reported. Why is this a concern? The overstated reserve allowed Sears to prop up its earnings at a time when losses in its credit card unit were soaring. The analyst concluded that the increase in Sears' year-to-date earnings has depended entirely on its over-reserved allowance.

Use of the allowance for uncollectible accounts to shift income is a source of concern. This is especially so for banks where the allowance for loan losses is a large component of banks' balance sheets and loan loss expense is a major component of reported income. Our analysis must scrutinize the allowance for uncollectible accounts to identify any changes from past practices or industry norms and, then, to justify those changes before accepting them as valid.

Accounts Receivable Turnover and Average Collection Period

The net operating asset turnover (NOAT) is sales divided by average net operating assets. An important component of this measure is the **accounts receivable turnover (ART)**, which is defined as:[3]

$$\text{Accounts Receivable Turnover} = \text{Sales/Average Accounts Receivable, gross}$$

Accounts receivable turnover reveals how many times receivables have turned (been collected) during the period. More turns indicate that receivables are being collected more quickly.

A companion measure to accounts receivable turnover is the **average collection period (ACP)** for accounts receivable, also called *days sales outstanding*, which is defined as:

$$\text{Average Collection Period} = \text{Accounts Receivable, gross/Average Daily Sales}$$

where average daily sales equals sales divided by 365 days. The average collection period indicates how long, on average, the receivables are outstanding before being collected.[4]

---

[3] Technically, the numerator should be net credit sales because receivables arise from credit sales. Including cash sales in the numerator inflates the ratio. Typically, outsiders do not know the level of cash sales and, therefore, must use total sales to calculate the turnover ratio.

[4] The average collection period computation in this module uses *ending* accounts receivable. This focuses the analysis on the most current receivables. Cisco uses a variant of this approach, described in its MD&A section as follows: Accounts receivable/Average annualized 4Q sales (or AR/[(4Q Sales × 4)/365]). Arguably, Cisco's variant focuses even more on the most recent collection period because ending accounts receivable relate more closely to 4Q sales than to reported annual sales. Most analysts use the reported annual sales instead of the annualized 4Q sales because the former are easily accessed in financial statement databases. As an alternative, we could also examine average daily sales in *average* accounts receivable (Average accounts receivable/Average daily sales). The approach we use in the text addresses the average collection period of *current* (ending) accounts receivable, and the latter approach examines the average collection period of *average* accounts receivable. Finally, some analysts use "net" and not "gross" receivables. The concern with using net is that it introduces management's allowance policy as another variable in this analysis. The "correct" ratio depends on the issue we wish to investigate. It is important to choose the formula that best answers the question we are asking.

To illustrate, **Cisco**'s 2010 total net sales (products and services) are $40,040 million, gross accounts receivable are $5,164 million at year-end, and $3,393 million at the prior year-end (average is $4,278.5 million). Thus, its accounts receivable turnover is 9.36, computed as $40,040/$4,278.5, and its average collection period (days sales outstanding) is 47 days, computed as $5,164/ ($40,040/365 days).

The accounts receivable turnover and the average collection period yield valuable insights on at least two dimensions:

1. *Receivables quality* Changes in receivable turnover (and collection period) speak to accounts receivable quality. If turnover slows (collection period lengthens), the reason could be deterioration in collectibility. However, there are at least three alternative explanations:
   a. A seller can extend its credit terms. If the seller is attempting to enter new markets or take market share from competitors, it may extend credit terms to attract buyers.
   b. A seller can take on longer-paying customers. For example, facing increased competition, automobile and other manufacturing companies began leasing their products, thus reducing customers' cash outlays and stimulating sales. Moving away from cash sales and toward leasing reduced receivables turnover and increased the collection period.
   c. The seller can increase the allowance provision. Receivables turnover is sometimes computed using net receivables (after the allowance for uncollectible accounts). In this case, overestimating the provision reduces net receivables and increases the turnover ratio. Accordingly, the apparent improvement in turnover could be incorrectly attributed to improved operating performance rather than a decline in the quality of the receivables.

2. *Asset utilization* Asset turnover is an important financial performance measure used both by managers for internal performance goals, as well as by the market in evaluating companies. High-performing companies must be both effective (controlling margins and operating expenses) and efficient (getting the most out of their asset base). An increase in receivables ties up cash. As well, slower-turning receivables carry increased risk of loss. One of the first "low-hanging fruits" that companies pursue in efforts to improve overall asset utilization is efficiency in receivables collection.

The following chart shows the average collection period for accounts receivable of Cisco and four peer competitors that Cisco indentifies in its 10-K.

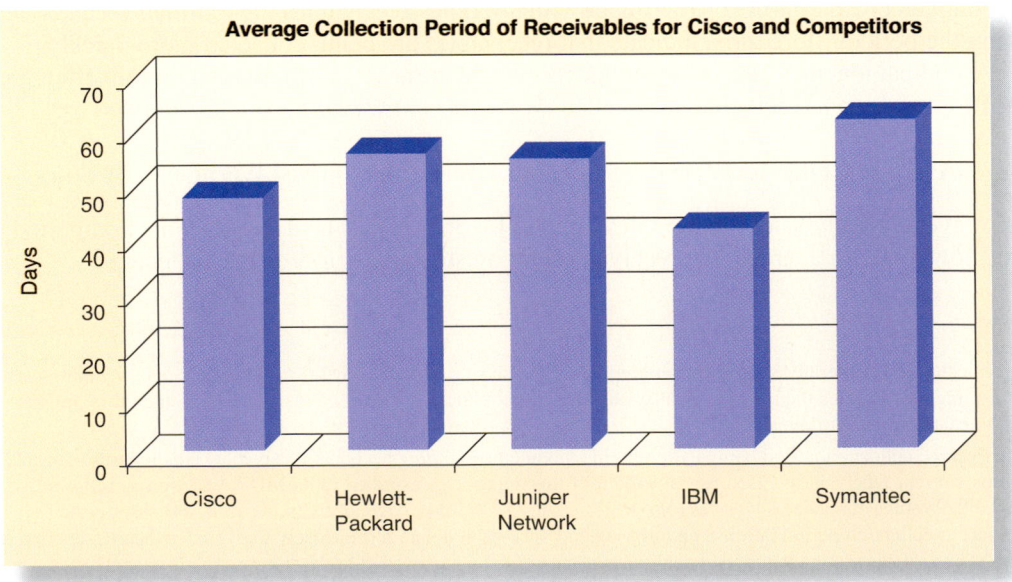

Cisco's average collection period of 47 days compares favorably with its primary competitors. Companies in this industry generally report average collection periods of 40–60 days.

To appreciate differences in average collection periods across industries, let's compare the average collection periods across a number of industries as follows:

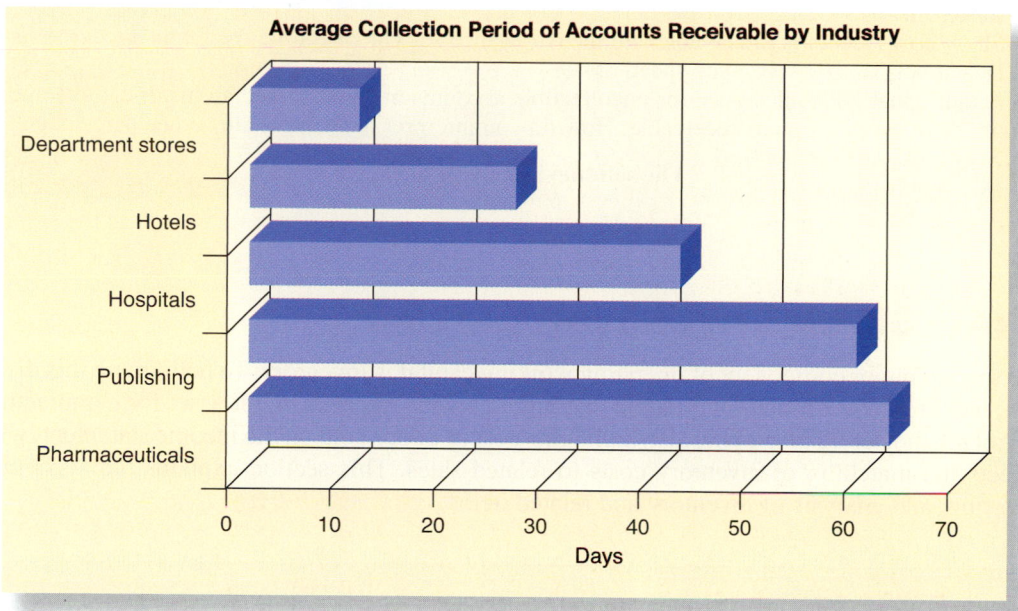

Department stores and hotels have the shortest collection periods. For those industries, receivables are minimal because sales are made mainly via cash, check or credit card. Most of the other industries in the table have collection periods ranging from 40 to 60 days. This corresponds with typical credit terms offered on commercial transactions. Pharmaceutical companies and hospitals have longer collection periods because they often require payment from third-party insurers and government agencies such as Medicare and the Veterans' Administration.

ANALYSIS DECISION	You Are the Receivables Manager

You are analyzing your receivables turnover report for the period and you are concerned that the average collection period is lengthening. What specific actions can you take to reduce the average collection period? [Answer, p. 6-37]

MID-MODULE REVIEW 1

At December 31, 2012, assume that **Hewlett-Packard** had a balance of $770,000 in its Accounts Receivable account and a balance of $7,000 in its Allowance for Uncollectible Accounts. The company then analyzed and aged its accounts receivable as shown below. Assume that HP experienced past losses as follows: 1% of current balances, 5% of balances 1-60 days past due, 15% of balances 61–180 days past due, and 40% of balances over 180 days past due. The company bases its provision for credit losses on the aging analysis.

Current	$468,000
1–60 days past due	244,000
61–180 days past due	38,000
Over 180 days past due.	20,000
Total accounts receivable.	$770,000

Required

1. What amount of uncollectible accounts (bad debts) expense will HP report in its 2012 income statement?
2. Show how Accounts Receivable and the Allowance for Uncollectible Accounts appear in its December 31, 2012, balance sheet.
3. Assume that HP's allowance for uncollectible accounts has maintained an historical average of 2% of gross accounts receivable. How do you interpret the current allowance percentage?

The solution is on page 6-52.

ANALYSIS OF INVENTORY

LO2 Explain accounting for inventories and assess the effects on the balance sheet and income statement from different inventory costing methods.

The second major component of operating working capital is inventory. To help frame this discussion, we refer to the following graphic that highlights inventory, a major asset for manufacturers and merchandisers. The graphic also highlights cost of goods sold on the income statement, which reflects the matching of inventory costs to related sales. This section explains the accounting, reporting, and analysis of inventory and related items.

Income Statement	Balance Sheet	
Sales	Cash	Current liabilities
Cost of goods sold	Accounts receivable, net	Long-term liabilities
Selling, general & administrative	**Inventory**	
Income taxes	Property, plant, and equipment, net	Shareholders' equity
Net income	Investments	

Inventory is reported on the balance sheet at its purchase price or the cost to manufacture goods that are internally produced. Inventory costs vary over time with changes in market conditions. Consequently, the cost per unit of the goods available for sale varies from period to period—even if the quantity of goods available remains the same.

When inventory is purchased or produced, it is "capitalized." That is, it is carried on the balance sheet as an asset until it is sold, at which time its cost is transferred from the balance sheet to the income statement as an expense (cost of goods sold). The process by which costs are removed from the balance sheet is important. For example, if higher cost units are transferred from the balance sheet, then cost of goods sold is higher and gross profit (sales less cost of goods sold) is lower. Conversely, if lower cost units are transferred to cost of goods sold, gross profit is higher. The remainder of this section discusses the accounting for inventory including the mechanics, reporting, and analysis of inventory costing.

Capitalization of Inventory Cost

Capitalization means that a cost is recorded on the balance sheet and is not immediately expensed on the income statement. Once costs are capitalized, they remain on the balance sheet as assets until they are used up, at which time they are transferred from the balance sheet to the income statement as expense. If costs are capitalized rather than expensed, then assets, current income, and current equity are all higher.

For purchased inventories (such as merchandise), the amount of cost capitalized is the purchase price. For manufacturers, cost capitalization is more difficult, as **manufacturing costs** consist of three components: cost of direct materials used in the product, cost of direct labor to manufacture the product, and manufacturing overhead. Direct materials cost is relatively easy to compute. Design specifications list the components of each product, and their purchase costs are readily determined. The direct labor cost per unit of inventory is based on how long each unit takes to construct and the rates for each labor class working on that product. Overhead costs are also capitalized into inventory, and include the costs of plant asset depreciation, utilities, supervisory personnel, and other costs that contribute to manufacturing activities—that is, all costs of manufacturing other than direct materials and direct labor. (How these costs are assigned to individual units and across multiple products is a *managerial accounting* topic.)

When inventories are sold, their costs are transferred from the balance sheet to the income statement as cost of goods sold (COGS). COGS is then deducted from sales to yield **gross profit**:

$$\textbf{Gross Profit} = \textbf{Sales} - \textbf{Cost of Goods Sold}$$

The manner in which inventory costs are transferred from the balance sheet to the income statement affects both the level of inventories reported on the balance sheet and the amount of gross profit (and net income) reported on the income statement.

Inventory Costing Methods

Exhibit 6.5 shows the computation of cost of goods sold.

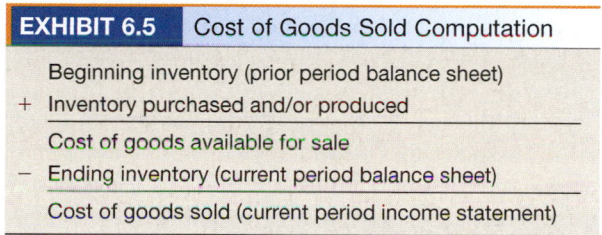

EXHIBIT 6.5	Cost of Goods Sold Computation
	Beginning inventory (prior period balance sheet)
+	Inventory purchased and/or produced
	Cost of goods available for sale
−	Ending inventory (current period balance sheet)
	Cost of goods sold (current period income statement)

The cost of inventory available at the beginning of a period is a carryover from the ending inventory balance of the prior period. Current period inventory purchases (or costs of newly manufactured inventories) are added to the beginning inventory balance, yielding the total cost of goods (inventory) available for sale. Then, the goods available are either sold, and end up in cost of goods sold for the period (reported on the income statement), or the goods available remain unsold and are still in inventory at the end of the period (reported on the balance sheet). Exhibit 6.6 shows this cost flow graphically.

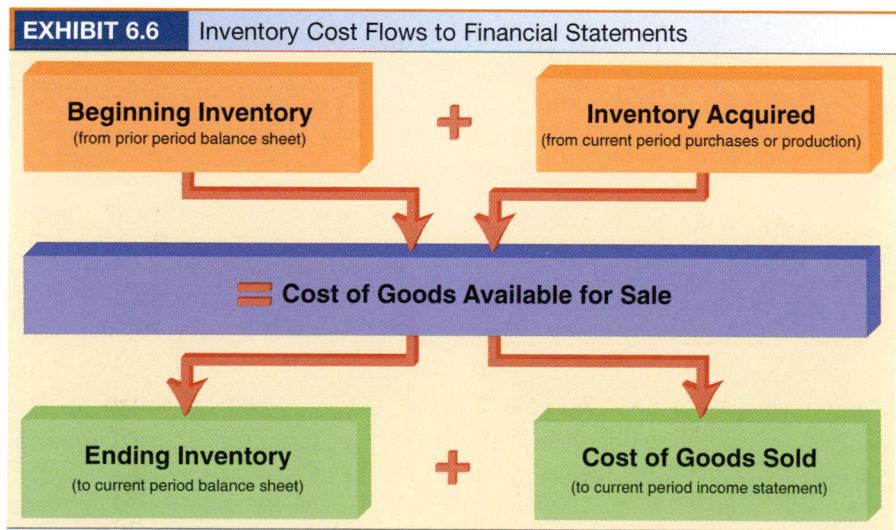

EXHIBIT 6.6 Inventory Cost Flows to Financial Statements

Understanding the flow of inventory costs is important. If all inventory purchased or manufactured during the period is sold, then COGS is equal to the cost of the goods purchased or manufactured. However, when inventory remains at the end of a period, companies must distinguish the cost of the inventories that were sold from the cost of the inventories that remain. GAAP allows for several options.

Exhibit 6.7 illustrates the partial inventory records of a company.

EXHIBIT 6.7	Summary Inventory Records			
Inventory on January 1, 2012..................	500 units	@ $100 per unit	$ 50,000
Inventory purchased in 2012	200 units	@ $150 per unit	30,000
Total cost of goods available for sale in 2012	700 units		$ 80,000
Inventory sold in 2012	450 units	@ $250 per unit	$112,500

This company began the period with 500 units of inventory that were purchased or manufactured for $50,000 ($100 each). During the period the company purchased and/or manufactured an additional 200 units costing $30,000. The total cost of goods available for sale for this period equals $80,000.

The company sold 450 units during 2012 for $250 per unit for total sales of $112,500. Accordingly, the company must remove the cost of the 450 units sold from the inventory account on the balance sheet and match this cost against the revenues generated from the sale. An important question is which costs should management remove from the balance sheet and report as cost of goods sold in the income statement? Three inventory costing methods (FIFO, LIFO and average cost) are common and all are acceptable under GAAP.

First-In, First-Out (FIFO)

The FIFO inventory costing method transfers costs from inventory in the order that they were initially recorded. That is, FIFO assumes that the first costs recorded in inventory (first-in) are the first costs transferred from inventory (first-out). Applying FIFO to the data in Exhibit 6.7 means that the costs of the 450 units sold comes from *beginning* inventory, which consists of 500 units costing $100 each. The company's cost of goods sold and gross profit, using FIFO, is computed as follows:

Sales..	$112,500
COGS (450 @ $100 each)......................	45,000
Gross profit.................................	$ 67,500

The cost remaining in inventory and reported on the 2012 year-end balance sheet is $35,000 ($80,000 goods available for sale less $45,000 COGS). The following financial statement effects template captures the transaction.

		Balance Sheet								Income Statement				
Transaction	Cash Asset	+	Noncash Assets	=	Liabil- ities	+	Contrib. Capital	+	Earned Capital		Rev- enues	−	Expen- ses	=	Net Income
Sold 450 units using FIFO costing (450 @ $100 each)			−45,000 Inventory	=					−45,000 Retained Earnings			−	+45,000 Cost of Goods Sold	=	−45,000

COGS 45,000
INV   45,000

COGS	
45,000	

	INV
	45,000

Last-In, First-Out (LIFO)

The LIFO inventory costing method transfers the most recent inventory costs from the balance sheet to COGS. That is, the LIFO method assumes that the most recent inventory purchases (last-in) are the first costs transferred from inventory (first-out). The company's cost of goods sold and gross profit, using LIFO, is computed as follows:

Sales...............................		$112,500
COGS: 200 @ $150 per unit	$30,000	
250 @ $100 per unit	25,000	55,000
Gross profit........................		$ 57,500

The cost remaining in inventory and reported on the company's 2012 balance sheet is $25,000 (computed as $80,000 − $55,000). This is reflected in our financial statements effects template as follows.

Transaction	Balance Sheet						Income Statement		
	Cash Asset	+ Noncash Assets	= Liabil- ities	+ Contrib. Capital	+ Earned Capital		Rev- enues	− Expen- ses	= Net Income
Sold 450 units using LIFO costing (200 @ $150) + (250 @ $100)		−55,000 Inventory =			−55,000 Retained Earnings			+55,000 − Cost of Goods Sold =	−55,000

```
COGS   55,000
     INV      55,000
        COGS
  55,000 |
        INV
            | 55,000
```

Average Cost (AC)

The average cost method computes the cost of goods sold as an average of the cost to purchase or manufacture all of the inventories that were available for sale during the period. To calculate the average cost of $114.286 per unit the company divides the total cost of goods available for sale by the number of units available for sale ($80,000/700 units). The company's sales, cost of sales, and gross profit follow.

Sales.....................................	$112,500
COGS (450 @ $114.286 per unit).................	51,429
Gross profit.................................	$ 61,071

The cost remaining in inventory and reported on the company's 2012 balance sheet is $28,571 ($80,000 − $51,429). This is reflected in our financial statements effects template as follows.

Transaction	Balance Sheet						Income Statement		
	Cash Asset	+ Noncash Assets	= Liabil- ities	+ Contrib. Capital	+ Earned Capital		Rev- enues	− Expen- ses	= Net Income
Sold 450 units using average cost method (450 @ $114.286)		−51,429 Inventory =			−51,429 Retained Earnings			+51,429 − Cost of Goods Sold =	−51,429

```
COGS   51,429
     INV      51,429
        COGS
  51,429 |
        INV
            | 51,429
```

It is important to understand that the inventory costing method a company chooses is independent of the actual flow of inventory. The method choice determines COGS and ending inventory but not the actual physical inventory sold. For example, many grocery chains use LIFO inventory but certainly do not sell the freshest products first. (Companies do not frequently change inventory costing methods. Companies can adopt a new inventory costing method if doing so enhances the quality of the company's financial reports. Also, IRS regulations prohibit certain inventory costing method changes.)

Lower of Cost or Market

Companies must write down the carrying amount of inventories on the balance sheet *if* the reported cost (using FIFO, for example) exceeds market value (determined by current replacement cost). This process is called reporting inventories at the **lower of cost or market** and creates the following financial statement effects:

■ Inventory book value is written down to current market value (replacement cost), reducing inventory and total assets.

■ Inventory write-down is reflected as an expense (part of cost of goods sold) on the income statement, reducing current period gross profit, income, and equity.

To illustrate, assume that a company has inventory on its balance sheet at a cost of $27,000. Management learns that the inventory's replacement cost is $23,000 and writes inventories down to a balance of $23,000. The following financial statement effects template shows the adjustment.

	Balance Sheet								Income Statement		
Transaction	Cash Asset	+	Noncash Assets	=	Liabil- ities	+	Contrib. Capital	+	Earned Capital	Rev- enues	−	Expen- ses	=	Net Income
Write down inventory from $27,000 to $23,000.			−4,000 Inventory	=					−4,000 Retained Earnings		+4,000 Cost of Goods Sold	= −4,000

```
COGS    4,000
   INV        4,000
      COGS
4,000 |
   INV
      | 4,000
```

The inventory write-down (a noncash expense) is reflected in cost of goods sold and reduces gross profit by $4,000. Inventory write-downs are included in cost of goods sold. They are *not* reported in selling, general, and administrative expenses, which is common for other asset write-downs. The most common occurrence of inventory write-downs is in connection with restructuring activities.

The write-down of inventories can potentially shift income from one period to another. If, for example, inventories were written down below current replacement cost, future gross profit would be increased via lower future cost of goods sold. GAAP anticipates this possibility by requiring that inventories not be written down below a floor that is equal to net realizable value less a normal markup. Although this still allows some discretion (and the ability to manage income), the auditors must assess net realizable value and markups.

IFRS INSIGHT **Inventory Measurement under IFRS**

Like GAAP, IFRS measures inventories at the lower of cost or market. The cost of inventory generally is determined using the FIFO (first-in, first-out) or weighted average cost method; use of the LIFO (last-in, first-out) method is prohibited under IFRS.

Footnote Disclosures

Notes to financial statements describe the inventory accounting method a company uses. To illustrate, **Cisco** reports $1,327 million in inventory on its 2010 balance sheet as a current asset. Cisco includes a general footnote on inventory along with more specific disclosures in other footnotes. Following is an excerpt from Cisco's general footnote on inventories.

> **Inventories.** Inventories are stated at the lower of cost or market. Cost is computed using standard cost, which approximates actual cost, on a first-in, first-out basis. The Company provides inventory write-downs based on excess and obsolete inventories determined primarily by future demand forecasts. The write-down is measured as the difference between the cost of the inventory and market based upon assumptions about future demand and charged to the provision for inventory, which is a component of cost of sales. At the point of the loss recognition, a new, lower-cost basis for that inventory is established, and subsequent changes in facts and circumstances do not result in the restoration or increase in that newly established cost basis.

This footnote includes at least two items of interest for our analysis of inventory:

1. Cisco uses the FIFO method of inventory costing.
2. Inventories are reported at the lower of cost or market (LCM). For example, if the current value of Cisco's inventories is less than its reported cost, Cisco would set up an "allowance" for inventories, similar to the allowance for uncollectible accounts. The inventory allowance reduces the reported inventory amount to the current (lower) market value.

Cisco also includes a more detailed inventory footnote as follows:

Inventories ($ millions)	July 31, 2010	July 25, 2009
Raw materials..	$ 217	$ 165
Work in process	50	33
Finished goods		
Distributor inventory and deferred cost of sales.......... $ 587		$ 382
Manufacturing finished goods 260		310
Total finished goods	847	692
Service-related spares	161	151
Demonstration systems	52	33
Total	$1,327	$1,074

This disclosure separately reports inventory costs by the following stages in the production cycle:

- *Raw materials and supplies* These are costs of direct materials and inputs into the production process including, for example, chemicals in raw state, plastic and steel for manufacturing, and incidental direct materials such as screws and lubricants.

- *Work in process* These are costs of partly finished products (also called work-in-progress).

- *Finished goods* These are the costs of products that are completed and awaiting sale.

Why do companies disclose such details about inventory? First, investment in inventory is typically large—markedly impacting both balance sheets and income statements. Second, risks of inventory losses are often high, due to technical obsolescence and consumer tastes. This is an important issue for a company such as Cisco that operates in a technology-sensitive industry. Indeed, Cisco reported a loss of over $2 billion in 2001 when the tech bubble burst, demand dried up, and the company had to write down unsalable inventories. Third, inventory details can provide insight into future performance—both good and bad. Fourth, high inventory levels result in substantial costs for the company, such as the following:

- Financing costs to hold inventories (when not purchased on credit or when held beyond credit period)

- Storage costs (such as warehousing and related facilities)

- Handling costs (including wages)

- Insurance costs

Consequently, companies seek to minimize inventory levels provided this does not exceed the cost of holding insufficient inventory, called stock-outs. Stock-outs result in lost sales and production delays if machines and employees must be reconfigured to fill order backlogs. Cisco's total inventories have remained at 2005 levels despite a $15.2 billion increase in sales.

Financial Statement Effects of Inventory Costing

This section describes the financial statement effects of different inventory costing methods.

Income Statement Effects

The three inventory costing methods yield differing levels of gross profit as Exhibit 6.8 shows.

EXHIBIT 6.8	Income Effects from Inventory Costing Methods		
	Sales	Cost of Goods Sold	Gross Profit
FIFO	$112,500	$45,000	$67,500
LIFO	112,500	55,000	57,500
Average cost	112,500	51,429	61,071

Recall that inventory costs rose during this period from $100 per unit to $150 per unit. The higher gross profit reported under FIFO arises because FIFO matches older, lower-cost inventory against current selling prices. To generalize: in an inflationary environment, FIFO yields higher gross profit than do LIFO or average cost methods.

In recent years, the gross profit impact from using the FIFO method has been minimal for companies due to lower rates of inflation and increased management focus on reducing inventory quantities through improved manufacturing processes and better inventory controls. The FIFO gross profit effect can still arise, however, with companies subject to high inflation and slow inventory turnover.

Balance Sheet Effects

In our illustration above, the ending inventory using LIFO is less than that reported using FIFO. In periods of rising costs, LIFO inventories are markedly lower than under FIFO. As a result, balance sheets using LIFO do not accurately represent the cost that a company would incur to replace its current investment in inventories.

Caterpillar (CAT), for example, reports 2010 inventories under LIFO costing $9,587 million. As disclosed in the footnotes to its 10-K (see below), if CAT valued these inventories using FIFO, the reported amount would be $2,575 million greater, a 27% increase. This suggests that CAT's balance sheet omits over $2,575 million in inventories.

Cash Flow Effects

Unlike for most other accounting method choices, inventory costing methods affect taxable income and, thus, taxes paid. When a company adopts LIFO in its tax filings, the IRS requires it to also use LIFO for financial reporting purposes (in its 10-K). This requirement is known as the *LIFO conformity rule*. In an inflationary economy, using FIFO results in higher taxable income and, consequently, higher taxes payable. Conversely, using LIFO reduces the tax liability.

Caterpillar, Inc., discloses the following inventory information in its 2010 10-K:

> Inventories are stated at the lower of cost or market. Cost is principally determined using the last-in, first-out (LIFO) method. The value of inventories on the LIFO basis represented about 70% of total inventories at December 31, 2010, 2009 and 2008.
>
> If the FIFO (first-in, first-out) method had been in use, inventories would have been $2,575 million, $3,022 million and $3,216 million higher than reported at December 31, 2010, 2009 and 2008, respectively.

CAT uses LIFO for most of its inventories.[5] The use of LIFO has reduced the carrying amount of 2010 inventories by $2,575 million. Had it used FIFO, its inventories would have been reported at $12,162 million ($9,587 million + $2,575 million) rather than the $9,587 million that is reported on its balance sheet as of 2010. This difference, referred to as the **LIFO reserve**, is the amount that must be added to LIFO inventories to adjust them to their FIFO value.

$$\text{FIFO Inventory} = \text{LIFO Inventory} + \text{LIFO Reserve}$$

This relation also impacts cost of goods sold (COGS) as follows:

$$\text{FIFO COGS} = \text{LIFO COGS} - \text{Increase in LIFO Reserve (or + Decrease)}$$

Use of LIFO reduced CAT's inventories by $2,575 million, resulting in a cumulative increase in cost of goods sold and a cumulative decrease in gross profit and pretax profit of that same amount.[6] Because CAT also uses LIFO for tax purposes, the decrease in pretax profits reduced

---

[5] Neither the IRS nor GAAP requires use of a single inventory costing method. That is, companies are allowed to, and frequently do, use different inventory costing methods for different types of inventory (such as spare parts versus finished goods).

[6] Recall: Cost of Goods Sold = Beginning Inventories + Purchases − Ending Inventories. Thus, as ending inventories decrease, cost of goods sold increases.

CAT's cumulative tax bill by about $901 million ($2,575 million × 35% assumed corporate tax rate). This had real cash flow consequences: CAT's cumulative operating cash flow was $901 million higher because CAT used LIFO instead of FIFO. The increased cash flow from tax savings is often cited as a compelling reason for management to adopt LIFO.

Because companies use different inventory costing methods, their financial statements are often not comparable. The problem is most serious when companies hold large amounts of inventory and when prices markedly rise or fall. To compare companies using different inventory costing methods, say LIFO and FIFO, we need to adjust the LIFO numbers to their FIFO equivalents or vice versa. For example, one way to compare CAT with another company that uses FIFO, is to add CAT's LIFO reserve to its LIFO inventory. As explained above, this $2,575 million increase in 2010 inventories would have increased its cumulative pretax profits by $2,575 million and taxes by $901 million. Thus, to adjust the 2010 balance sheet we increase inventories by $2,575 million, tax liabilities by $901 million (the extra taxes CAT would have had to pay under FIFO), and equity by the difference of $1,674 million (computed as $2,575 − $901).

To adjust CAT's 2010 income statement from LIFO to FIFO, we use the change in LIFO reserve. For CAT, the LIFO reserve decreased by $447 million during 2010, from $3,022 million in 2009 to $2,575 million in 2010. This means that had it been using FIFO, its COGS would have been $447 million higher, and 2010 gross profit and pretax income would have been $447 million lower. In 2010, CAT would have paid $156 million less in taxes had it used FIFO ($447 million × 35% assumed tax rate).

RESEARCH INSIGHT   **LIFO and Stock Prices**

The value-relevance of inventory disclosures depends at least partly on whether investors rely more on the income statement or the balance sheet to assess future cash flows. Under LIFO, cost of goods sold reflects current costs, whereas FIFO ending inventory reflects current costs. This implies that LIFO enhances the usefulness of the income statement to the detriment of the balance sheet. This trade-off partly motivates the required LIFO reserve disclosure (the adjustment necessary to restate LIFO ending inventory and cost of good sold to FIFO). Research suggests that LIFO-based income statements better reflect stock prices than do FIFO income statements that are restated using the LIFO reserve. Research also shows a negative relation between stock prices and LIFO reserve—meaning that higher magnitudes of LIFO reserve are associated with lower stock prices. This is consistent with the LIFO reserve being viewed as an inflation indicator (for either current or future inventory costs), which the market views as detrimental to company value.

Tools of Inventory Analysis

This section describes several useful tools for analysis of inventory and related accounts.

Gross Profit Analysis

The **gross profit margin (GPM)** is gross profit divided by sales. This important ratio is closely monitored by management and outsiders. Exhibit 6.9 shows the gross profit margin on Cisco's sales for the past three years.

EXHIBIT 6.9	Gross Profit Margin for Cisco		
Fiscal Year	**2010**	**2009**	**2008**
Product sales	$40,040	$36,117	$39,540
Product cost of goods sold	14,397	13,023	14,194
Gross profit.	$25,643	$23,094	$25,346
Gross profit margin.	64.0%	63.9%	64.1%

The gross profit margin is commonly used instead of the dollar amount of gross profit as the GPM allows for comparisons across companies and over time. A decline in GPM is usually cause for concern since it indicates that the company has less ability to pass on increased product cost to customers or that the company is not effectively managing product costs. Some possible reasons for a GPM decline follow:

- *Product line is stale*. Perhaps products are out of fashion and the company must resort to markdowns to reduce overstocked inventories. Or, perhaps the product lines have lost their technological edge, yielding reduced demand.

- *New competitors enter the market*. Perhaps substitute products are now available from competitors, yielding increased pressure to reduce selling prices.

- *General decline in economic activity*. Perhaps an economic downturn reduces product demand.

- *Inventory is overstocked*. Perhaps the company overproduced goods and finds itself in an overstock position. This can require reduced selling prices to move inventory.

- *Manufacturing costs have increased*. This could be due to poor planning, production glitches, or unfavorable supply chain reconfiguration.

- *Changes in product mix*. Perhaps the company is selling a higher proportion of low margin goods.

Cisco's gross profit margin on product sales increased by 0.1 percentage points (63.9% to 64.0%) over the past year. Following is **Cisco**'s discussion of its gross profit taken from its 2010 10-K:

Gross Margin In fiscal 2010, our gross margin percentage increased by 0.1 percentage points compared with fiscal 2009, driven by a slightly higher product gross margin percentage coupled with an unchanged service gross margin percentage. The higher product gross margin percentage was primarily due to lower overall manufacturing costs, higher shipment volume, and favorable product mix. Partially offsetting the product gross margin increase were higher sales discounts and rebates, and lower product pricing. The service gross margin percentage remained unchanged from period to period with the increase in gross margin from technical support services being offset by a decline in gross margin for advanced services. Our product and service gross margins may be impacted by uncertain economic conditions as well as our movement into market adjacencies and could decline if any of the factors that impact our gross margins are adversely affected in future periods.

Cisco's gross profit margin increased in 2010 because of lower manufacturing costs, higher shipment volume, and favorable product mix. This increase was partially offset by increased sales discounts. There are a number of factors that can adversely affect gross profit margins: changes in product mix, introduction of new products at lower introductory prices to gain market share, increases in production costs, sales discounts, inventory obsolescence and warranty costs, and changes in production volume.

Competitive pressures mean that companies rarely have the opportunity to completely control gross profit with price increases. Improvements in gross profit on existing product lines typically arise from better management of supply chains, production processes, or distribution networks. Companies that succeed do so because of better performance on basic business processes. This is one of Cisco's primary objectives.

Inventory Turnover

Inventory turnover (INVT) reflects the management of inventory and is computed as follows:

$$\text{Inventory Turnover} = \text{Cost of Goods Sold/Average Inventory}$$

Cost of goods sold is in the numerator because inventory is reported at cost. Inventory turnover indicates how many times inventory turns (is sold) during a period. More turns indicate that inventory is being sold more quickly, which decreases the risk of obsolete inventory and increases liquidity.

Average inventory days outstanding (AIDO), also called *days inventory outstanding*, is a companion measure to inventory turnover and is computed as follows:

Average Inventory Days Outstanding = Inventory/Average Daily Cost of Goods Sold

where average daily cost of goods sold equals cost of goods sold divided by 365 days.[7]

For Cisco, cost of products sold, in 2010, is $11,620 million, inventory at year-end is $1,327 million, inventory at prior year-end was $1,074 million (average is $1,200.5 million). Thus, its inventory turnover is 9.7, computed as $11,620 million/$1,200.5 million, which implies that, in 2010, Cisco sold its average inventory 9.7 times. Its 2010 average inventory days outstanding is 42 days, computed as $1,327 million/($11,620 million/365 days), which implies that it takes Cisco 42 days to sell its year-end inventory.

Overall, analysis of inventory turnover and days outstanding is important for at least two reasons:

1. *Inventory quality.* Inventory turnover can be compared over time and across competitors. Higher turnover is viewed favorably, because it implies that products are salable, preferably without undue discounting (we would compare profit margins to assess discounting). Conversely, lower turnover implies that inventory is on the shelves for a longer period of time, perhaps from excessive purchases or production, missed fashion trends or technological advances, increased competition, and so forth. Our conclusions about higher or lower turnover must consider alternative explanations including the following:

   - Product mix can include more (or less) higher margin, slower turning inventories. This can occur from business acquisitions that consolidate different types of inventory.

   - A company can change its promotion policies. Increased, effective advertising is likely to increase inventory turnover. Advertising expense is in SG&A, not COGS. This means the additional advertising cost is in operating expenses, but the benefit is in gross profit and turnover. If the promotion campaign is successful, the positive effects in margin and turnover should more than offset the promotion cost in SG&A.

   - A company can realize improvements in manufacturing efficiency and lower investments in direct materials and work-in-process inventories. Such improvements reduce inventory and, consequently, increase inventory turnover. Although a good sign, it does not yield any information about the desirability of a company's product line.

2. *Asset utilization.* Companies strive to optimize their inventory investment. Carrying too much inventory is expensive, and too little inventory risks stock-outs and lost sales (current and future). Companies can make the following operational changes to reduce inventory.

   - Improved manufacturing processes can eliminate bottlenecks and the consequent buildup of work-in-process inventories.

   - Just-in-time (JIT) deliveries from suppliers, which provide raw materials to the production line when needed, can reduce the level of raw materials and associated holding costs.

   - Demand-pull production, in which raw materials are released into the production process when final goods are demanded by customers instead of producing for estimated demand, can reduce inventory levels. **Dell Computer**, for example, does not manufacture a computer until it receives the customer's order; thus, Dell produces for actual, rather than estimated, demand.

Reducing inventories reduces inventory carrying costs, thus improving profitability and increasing cash flows. The reduction in inventory is reflected as an operating cash inflow in the statement of cash flows.

---

[7] Similar to the average receivables collection period, this formula examines the average daily COGS in *ending* inventories to focus analysis on current inventories. One can also examine average daily COGS in *average* inventories (Average inventories/Average daily COGS). These two approaches address different issues: the first addresses the average days outstanding of *current ending* inventories, and the second examines the average days outstanding of *average* inventories. It is important that we first identify the issue under investigation and then choose the formula that best addresses that issue.

There is normal tension between the sales side of a company that argues for depth and breadth of inventory, and the finance side that monitors inventory carrying costs and seeks to maximize cash flow. Companies, therefore, seek to *optimize* inventory investment, not minimize it.

Following is a chart comparing Cisco's average inventory days outstanding with its peer companies.

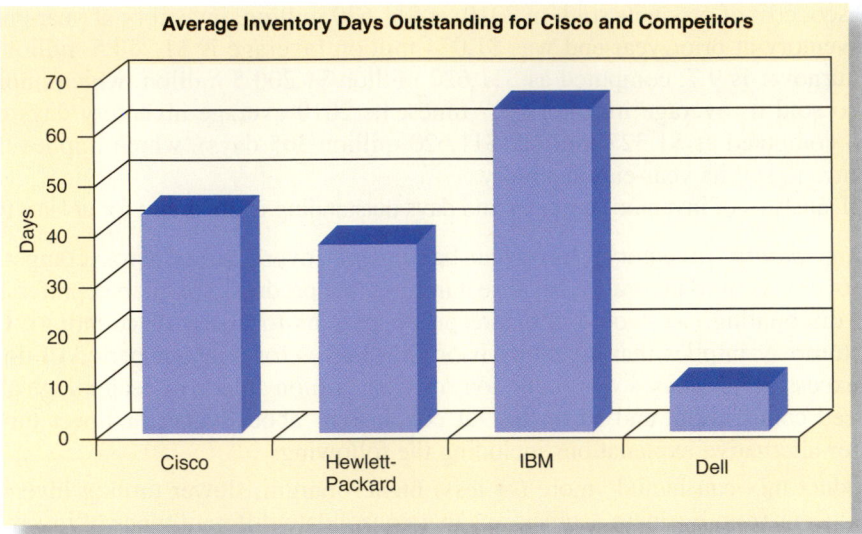

Cisco's average inventory days outstanding of 42 days compares favorably with its peers. **Cisco**'s 2010 10-K provides the following comments regarding inventory management:

> We believe that in any rapidly shifting supply and demand environment such as the one we experienced in fiscal 2010, shifts in lead times, inventory levels, purchase commitments, and manufacturing outputs will occur. During fiscal 2010, we experienced longer than normal lead times on several of our products and we continue to see challenges at some of our component suppliers. This was attributable in part to increasing demand driven by the improvement in our overall markets. In addition, and similar to what is happening throughout the industry, the longer than normal lead times also stemmed from supplier constraints based upon their labor and other actions taken during the global economic downturn. While we may continue to experience longer than normal lead times, our lead times improved on the majority of our products in the second half of fiscal 2010, and at the end of fiscal 2010, product lead times to customers were within a normal range for the majority of our products. We have increased our efforts in procuring components in order to meet customer expectations, which have contributed to an increase in purchase commitments. If, however, lead times for key components lengthen further, our operating results for a particular future period could be adversely affected if we further increase our purchase commitments, which could lead to excess and obsolete inventory charges.

Dell's average inventory days outstanding of nine days is markedly lower than other companies shown in this graph. Dell has traditionally focused on excellence in this area, and views this as a competitive advantage. Dell's 2010 10-K reports the following:

> We utilize several suppliers to manufacture sub-assemblies for our products. Our efficient supply chain management allows us to enter into flexible and mutually beneficial purchase arrangements with our suppliers in order to minimize inventory risk. Consistent with industry practice, we acquire raw materials or other goods and services, including product components, by issuing to suppliers authorizations to purchase based on our projected demand and manufacturing needs. These purchase orders are typically fulfilled within 30 days and are entered into during the ordinary course of business in order to establish best pricing and continuity of supply for our

continued

continued from prior page

production. The following table presents the components of our cash conversion cycle for the fourth quarter of each of the past three fiscal years. The slight increase in DSI from January 29, 2010, was primarily attributable to the optimization of our supply chain requiring an increase in strategic purchases of materials and finished goods inventory.

For Fiscal Quarter Ended	January 28, 2011	January 29, 2010	January 30, 2009
Days of sales outstanding	40	38	35
Days of supply in inventory	9	8	7
Days in accounts payable	(82)	(82)	(67)
Cash conversion cycle.	(33)	(36)	(25)

Dell describes its cash conversion cycle, which measures the days from initial investment of cash in inventories to collection of the receivable arising from credit sales and repayment of amounts due to inventory suppliers. Normally, this is a positive number. Companies continually strive to reduce the cash conversion cycle to reduce the amount of investment in net operating assets (NOA), thereby improving the return on net operating assets (RNOA) and increasing cash flow. For Dell, its cash conversion cycle is negative because the company takes longer to pay its suppliers than the time invested in inventories and receivables. This is mainly the result of Dell's manufacturing process that effectively reduces raw materials, work-in-process, and finished goods inventories. Bottom line: Dell's operating efficiency is generating excess cash that can be invested in operating assets to further increase profitability.

Returning to the average inventory days outstanding, it is instructive to compare this measure across selected industries.

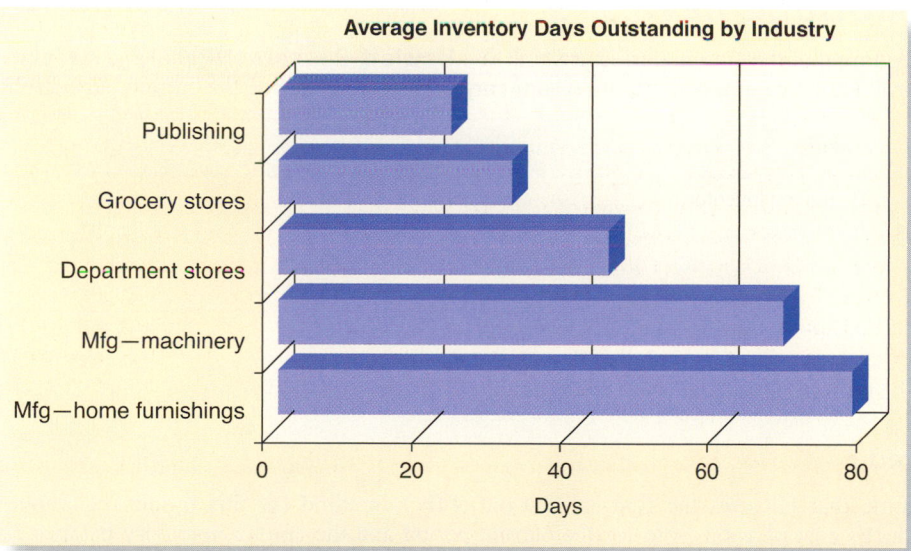

Publishing companies and grocery stores carry 20–30 days' inventory at any point in time. Inventories are low in the publishing industry because newspapers are printed and sold daily, and grocery stores do not carry large amounts of retail inventories. On the other hand, manufacturers must carry raw materials, work-in-process and finished goods inventories.

ANALYSIS DECISION   You Are the Plant Manager

You are analyzing your inventory turnover report for the month and are concerned that the average inventory days outstanding is lengthening. What actions can you take to reduce average inventory days outstanding? [Answer, p. 6-37]

LIFO Liquidations

When companies acquire inventory at different costs, they are required to account for each cost level as a separate inventory pool or layer (for example, there are the $100 and $150 units in our Exhibit 6.7 illustration). When companies reduce inventory levels, older inventory costs flow to the income statement. These older LIFO costs are often markedly different from current replacement costs. Given the usual inflationary environment, sales of older pools often yield a boost to gross profit as older, lower costs are matched against current selling prices on the income statement.

The increase in gross profit resulting from a reduction of inventory quantities in the presence of rising costs is called **LIFO liquidation**. The effect of LIFO liquidation is evident in the following footnote from **Newell Rubbermaid**'s 2010 10-K:

> Inventory costs include direct materials, direct labor and manufacturing overhead, or when finished goods are sourced, the cost is the amount paid to the third party. Cost of certain domestic inventories (approximately 52.0% and 51.7% of gross inventory costs at December 31, 2010 and 2009, respectively) was determined by the LIFO method; for the balance, cost was determined using the FIFO method. As of December 31, 2010 and 2009, LIFO reserves were $30.1 million and $24.2 million, respectively. The net income recognized by the Company related to the liquidation of LIFO based inventories in 2010 and 2009 was $8.7 million and $16.9 million, respectively.

Newell Rubbermaid reports that reductions in inventory quantities in 2010 led to the sale (at current selling prices) of products that carried lower costs from prior years. As a result of these inventory reductions, COGS were lower, which increased income by $8.7 million.

MID-MODULE REVIEW 2

At the beginning of the current period, assume that **Hewlett-Packard (HP)** holds 1,000 units of a certain product with a unit cost of $18. A summary of purchases during the current period follows:

		Units	Unit Cost	Cost
Beginning Inventory		1,000	$18.00	$18,000
Purchases:	#1.	1,800	18.25	32,850
	#2.	800	18.50	14,800
	#3.	1,200	19.00	22,800
Goods available for sale.		4,800		$88,450

During the current period, HP sells 2,800 units.

Required

1. Assume that HP uses the first-in, first-out (FIFO) method for this product. Compute the product's cost of goods sold for the current period and the ending inventory balance.
2. Assume that HP uses the last-in, first-out (LIFO) method for this product. Compute the product's cost of goods sold for the current period and the ending inventory balance.
3. Assume that HP uses the average cost (AC) method for this product. Compute the product's cost of goods sold for the current period and the ending inventory balance.
4. As manager, which of these three inventory costing methods would you choose:
    a. To reflect what is probably the physical flow of goods? Explain.
    b. To minimize income taxes for the period? Explain.
5. Assume that HP utilizes the LIFO method and delays purchasing lot #3 until the next period. Compute cost of goods sold under this scenario and discuss how the LIFO liquidation affects profit.

The solution is on page 6-52.

ANALYSIS OF PROPERTY, PLANT AND EQUIPMENT (PPE)

Many companies' largest operating asset is property, plant, and equipment. To frame our PPE discussion, the following graphic highlights long-term operating assets on the balance sheet, and selling, general and administrative expenses on the income statement. The latter includes depreciation and asset write-downs that match the assets' cost against sales derived from the assets. (Depreciation on manufacturing facilities is included in cost of goods sold.) This section explains the accounting, reporting, and analysis of PPE and related items.

LO3 Analyze accounting for property, plant and equipment and explain the impacts on profit and cash flows from depreciation methods, disposals and impairments.

Income Statement
Sales
Cost of goods sold
Selling, general & administrative
Income taxes
Net income

Balance Sheet	
Cash	Current liabilities
Accounts receivable, net	Long-term liabilities
Inventory	
Property, plant, and equipment, net	Shareholders' equity
Investments	

Capitalization of Asset Costs

Companies capitalize costs as an asset on the balance sheet only if that asset possesses both of the following characteristics:

1. The asset is owned or controlled by the company and results from a past transaction.
2. The asset provides future expected benefits.

Owning the asset means the company has title to the asset as provided in a purchase contract. (Assets acquired under leases are also capitalized if certain conditions are met—see Module 10.) Future expected benefits usually refer to future cash inflows. Companies capitalize the full cost to acquire the asset, including the purchase price, transportation, setup, and all other costs necessary to get the asset into service. This is called the asset's acquisition cost.

Companies can only capitalize asset costs that are *directly linked* to future cash inflows, and the costs capitalized as an asset can be no greater than the related expected future cash inflows. This means that if a company reports a $200 asset, we can reasonably expect that it will derive at least $200 in expected cash inflows from the use and ultimate disposal of the asset.

The *directly linked* condition for capitalization of asset cost is important. When a company acquires a machine, it capitalizes the cost because the company expects the machine's output to yield cash inflows from the sale of products associated with the machine and from the cash received when the company eventually disposes of the machine. On the other hand, when it comes to research and development (R&D) activities, it is more difficult to directly link expected cash inflows with the R&D expenditures because R&D activities are often unsuccessful. Further, companies cannot reliably estimate the future cash flows from successful R&D activities. Accordingly, GAAP requires that R&D expenditures be expensed when paid. Similar arguments are applied to advertising, promotion and wages to justify expensing of those costs. Each of these latter examples relates to items or activities that we generally think will create intangible assets. That is, we reasonably expect R&D efforts and advertising campaigns to produce results. If not, companies would not pursue them.

We also generally view employee activities as generating future benefits. Indeed, we often refer to the *human resources* (asset) of a company. However, the link between these items or activities and their outputs is not as direct as GAAP requires for capitalizing such costs. The nonrecognition of these assets is one reason why it is difficult to analyze and value knowledge-based companies and such companies are less suited to traditional ROE disaggregation analysis. Capitalization and non-capitalization of costs can markedly impact financial statements and our analysis inferences and assessment of a company as an investment prospect.

Depreciation

Once the cost of PPE is capitalized on the balance sheet as an asset, it must be systematically transferred from the balance sheet to the income statement as depreciation expense to match the asset's cost to the revenues it generates. The depreciation process requires the following estimates:

1. **Useful life**. Period of time over which the asset is expected to generate cash inflows or other measurable benefits
2. **Salvage value**. Expected disposal amount at the end of the asset's useful life
3. **Depreciation rate**. An estimate of how the asset will be used up over its useful life

Management must determine each of these factors when the asset is acquired. Depreciation commences immediately upon asset acquisition and use. Management also can revise estimates that determine depreciation during the asset's useful life.

The **depreciation base**, also called *nonrecoverable cost*, is the amount to be depreciated. The depreciation base is the acquisition cost less estimated salvage value. This means that at the end of the asset's useful life, only the salvage value remains on the balance sheet.

Depreciation method relates to the manner in which the asset is used up. Companies choose from three methods by determining which of the following assumptions best describes the asset's use:

1. Asset is used up by the same amount each period.
2. Asset is used up more in the early years of its useful life.
3. Asset is used up in proportion to its actual usage.

A company can depreciate different assets using different depreciation methods (and different useful lives). After a depreciation method is chosen, however, the company must generally stick with that method throughout the asset's useful life. This is not to say that companies cannot change depreciation methods, but changes must be justified as providing more useful financial reports.

The using up of an asset generally relates to physical or technological obsolescence. *Physical obsolescence* relates to an asset's diminished capacity to produce output. *Technological obsolescence* relates to an asset's diminished efficiency in producing output in a competitive manner.

BUSINESS INSIGHT | **WorldCom and Improper Cost Capitalization**

WorldCom's CEO, Bernie Ebbers, and chief financial officer, Scott Sullivan, were convicted in 2005 of *cooking the books* so the company would not show a loss for 2001 and subsequent quarters. Specifically, WorldCom incurred large costs in anticipation of an increase in Internet-related business that did not materialize. Instead of expensing the costs as GAAP requires and reporting a loss in the WorldCom income statement, executives shifted the costs to the balance sheet. By capitalizing these costs (recording them on the balance sheet) as PPE, WorldCom was able to disguise these costs as assets, thereby inflating current profitability. Although the WorldCom case involved massive fraud, which is difficult for outsiders to detect, an astute analyst might have suspected something was amiss from analysis of WorldCom's long-term asset turnover (Sales/ Average long-term assets) as shown below. The obvious decline in turnover reveals that World-Com's assets constituted an ever-increasing percent of total sales during periods leading up to 2002. This finding does not, in itself, imply fraud. It does, however, raise serious questions that analysts should have posed to WorldCom executives in analyst meetings.

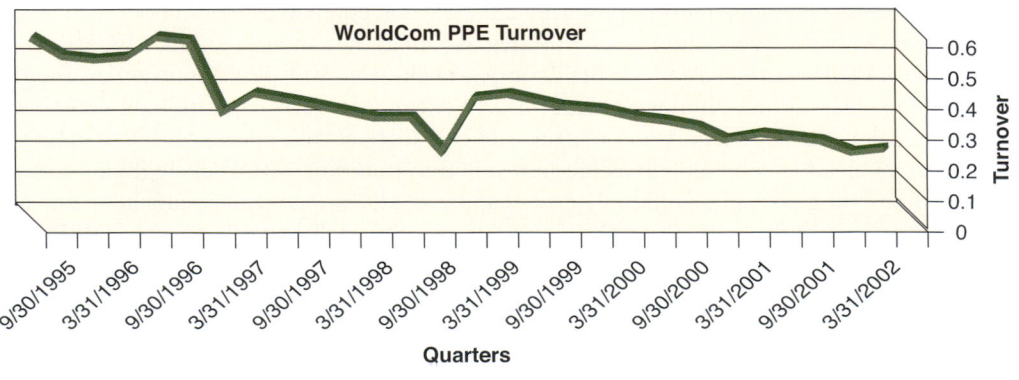

All depreciation methods have the following general formula:

$$\textbf{Depreciation Expense} = \textbf{Depreciation Base} \times \textbf{Depreciation Rate}$$

Remembering this general formula helps us understand the depreciation process. Also, each depreciation method reports the same amount of depreciation expense *over the life of the asset*. The only difference is in the amount of depreciation expense reported *for a given period*. To illustrate, consider a machine with the following details: $100,000 cost, $10,000 salvage value, and a five-year useful life. We look at two of the most common methods of depreciation.

Straight-Line Method

Under the straight-line (SL) method, depreciation expense is recognized evenly over the estimated useful life of the asset as follows:

Depreciation Base	**Depreciation Rate**
Cost − Salvage value = $100,000 − $10,000 = $90,000	1/Estimated useful life = 1/5 years = 20%

Depreciation expense per year for this asset is $18,000, computed as $90,000 × 20%. For the asset's first full year of usage, $18,000 of depreciation expense is reported in the income statement. (If an asset is purchased midyear, it is typically depreciated only for the portion of the year it is used. For example, had the asset in this illustration been purchased on May 31, the company would report $10,500 of depreciation in the first year, computed as 7/12 × $18,000, assuming the company has a December 31 year-end.) This depreciation is reflected in the company's financial statements as follows:

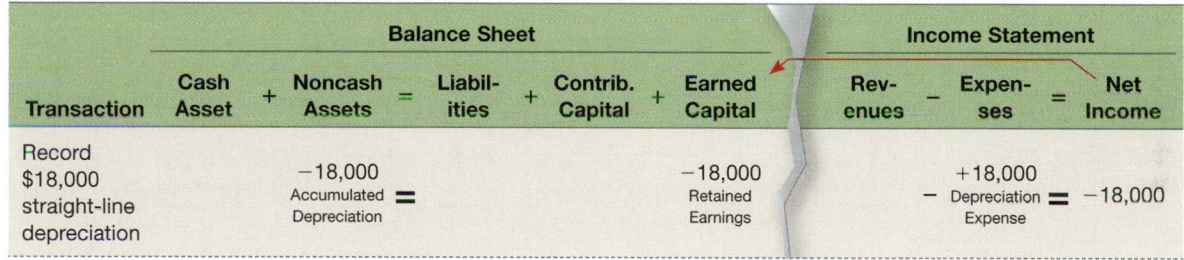
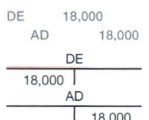

Transaction	Balance Sheet						Income Statement		
	Cash Asset	+	Noncash Assets	=	Liabil- ities	+ Contrib. Capital +	Earned Capital	Rev- enues −	Expen- ses =	Net Income
Record $18,000 straight-line depreciation			−18,000 Accumulated = Depreciation				−18,000 Retained Earnings		+18,000 − Depreciation = Expense	−18,000

The accumulated depreciation (contra asset) account increases by $18,000, thus reducing net PPE by the same amount. Also, $18,000 of the asset cost is transferred from the balance sheet to the income statement as depreciation expense. At the end of the first year the asset is reported on the balance sheet as follows:

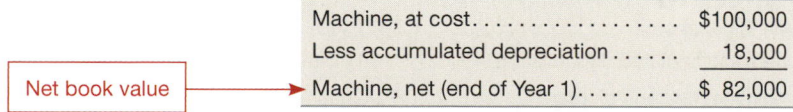

Machine, at cost..............	$100,000
Less accumulated depreciation......	18,000
Net book value → Machine, net (end of Year 1)........	$ 82,000

Accumulated depreciation is the sum of all depreciation expense that has been recorded to date. The asset **net book value (NBV)**, or *carrying value*, is cost less accumulated depreciation. Although the word value is used here, it does not refer to market value. Depreciation is a cost allocation concept (transfer of costs from the balance sheet to the income statement), not a valuation concept.

In the second year of usage, another $18,000 of depreciation expense is recorded in the income statement and the net book value of the asset on the balance sheet follows:

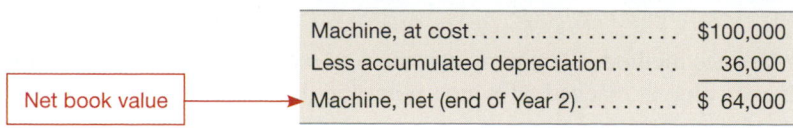

Machine, at cost..............	$100,000
Less accumulated depreciation......	36,000
Net book value → Machine, net (end of Year 2)........	$ 64,000

Accumulated depreciation of $36,000 now includes the sum of the first and second years' depreciation, and the net book value of the asset is now reduced to $64,000. After the fifth year, a total of $90,000 of accumulated depreciation will be recorded ($18,000 per year × 5 years), yielding a net book value for the machine of $10,000. The net book value at the end of the machine's useful life is exactly equal to the salvage value that management estimated when the asset was acquired.

Double-Declining-Balance Method

GAAP also allows *accelerated* methods of depreciation, the most common being the double-declining-balance method. This method records more depreciation in the early years of an asset's useful life (hence the term *accelerated*) and less depreciation in later years. At the end of the asset's useful life, the balance sheet will still report a net book value equal to the asset's salvage value. The difference between straight-line and accelerated depreciation methods is not in the total amount of depreciation, but in the rate at which costs are transferred from the balance sheet to the income statement.

For the double-declining-balance (DDB) method, the depreciation base is net book value, which declines over the life of the asset (this is why the method is called "declining balance"). The depreciation rate is twice the straight-line (SL) rate (which explains the word "double"). The depreciation base and rate for the asset in our illustrative example are computed as follows:

Depreciation Base	Depreciation Rate
Net Book Value = Cost − Accumulated Depreciation	2 × SL rate = 2 × 20% = 40%

The depreciation expense for the first year is $40,000, computed as $100,000 × 40%. This depreciation is reflected in the company's financial statements as follows:

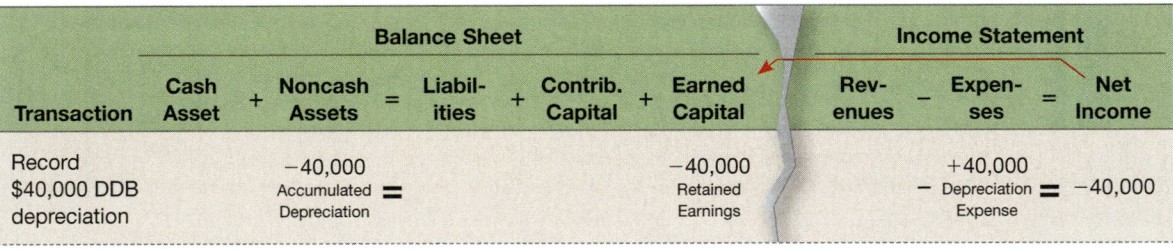

The accumulated depreciation (contra asset) account increases by $40,000 which reduces net PPE (compare this to the $18,000 depreciation under straight-line). This means that $40,000 of the asset cost is transferred from the balance sheet to the income statement as depreciation expense. At the end of the first year, the asset is reported on the balance sheet as follows:

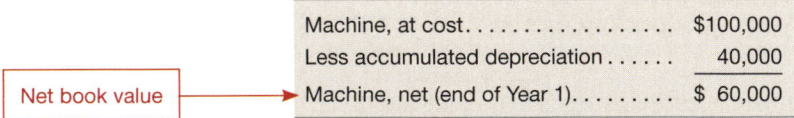

Machine, at cost..................	$100,000
Less accumulated depreciation......	40,000
Machine, net (end of Year 1).........	$ 60,000

Net book value →

In the second year, the net book value of the asset is the new depreciable base, and the company records depreciation of $24,000 ($60,000 × 40%) in the income statement. At the end of the second year, the net book value of the asset on the balance sheet is:

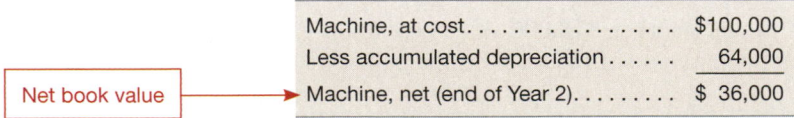

Machine, at cost..................	$100,000
Less accumulated depreciation......	64,000
Machine, net (end of Year 2).........	$ 36,000

Net book value →

Under the double-declining-balance method, a company continues to record depreciation expense in this manner until the salvage value is reached, at which point the depreciation process is discontinued. This leaves a net book value equal to the salvage value, as with the straight-line method.[8] The DDB depreciation schedule for the life of this asset is in Exhibit 6.10.

EXHIBIT 6.10	Double-Declining-Balance Depreciation Schedule		
Year	Book Value at Beginning of Year	Depreciation Expense	Book Value at End of Year
1	$100,000	$40,000	$60,000
2	60,000	24,000	36,000
3	36,000	14,400	21,600
4	21,600	8,640	12,960
5	12,960	2,960*	10,000

* The formula value of $5,184 ($12,960 × 40%) is *not* reported because it would depreciate the asset below salvage value; only the $2,960 needed to reach salvage value is reported.

Exhibit 6.11 shows the depreciation expense and net book value for both the SL and DDB methods. During the first two years, the DDB method yields a higher depreciation expense compared to the SL method. Beginning in the third year, this pattern reverses and the SL method produces higher depreciation expense. Over the asset's life, the same $90,000 of asset cost is transferred to the income statement as depreciation expense, leaving a salvage value of $10,000 on the balance sheet under both methods.

EXHIBIT 6.11	Comparison of Straight-Line and Double-Declining-Balance Depreciation			
	Straight-Line		Double-Declining-Balance	
Year	Depreciation Expense	Book Value at End of Year	Depreciation Expense	Book Value at End of Year
1	$18,000	$82,000	$40,000	$60,000
2	18,000	64,000	24,000	36,000
3	18,000	46,000	14,400	21,600
4	18,000	28,000	8,640	12,960
5	18,000	10,000	2,960	10,000
	$90,000		$90,000	

All depreciation methods yield the same salvage value

Total depreciation expense over asset life is identical for all methods

Companies typically use the SL method for financial reporting purposes and an accelerated depreciation method for tax returns.[9] The reason is that in early years the SL depreciation yields higher income on shareholder reports, whereas accelerated depreciation yields lower taxable income. Even though this relation reverses in later years, companies prefer to have the tax savings sooner rather than later so that the cash savings can be invested to produce earnings. Further, the reversal may never occur—if depreciable assets are growing at a fast enough rate, the additional first year's depreciation on newly acquired assets more than offsets the lower depreciation expense on older assets, yielding a "permanent" reduction in taxable income and taxes paid.[10]

Asset Sales and Impairments

This section discusses gains and losses from asset sales, and the computation and disclosure of asset impairments.

---

[8] A variant of DDB allows for a change from DDB to SL at the point when SL depreciation exceeds that for DDB.

[9] The IRS mandates the use of MACRS (Modified Accelerated Cost Recovery System) for tax purposes. This method specifies the useful life for various classes of assets, assumes no salvage value, and generally uses the double-declining-balance method.

[10] A third, common depreciation method is **units-of-production**, which depreciates assets according to use. Specifically, the depreciation base is cost less salvage value, and the depreciation rate is the units produced and sold during the year compared with the total expected units to be produced and sold. For example, if a truck is driven 10,000 miles out of a total expected 100,000 miles, 10% of its nonrecoverable cost is reflected as depreciation expense. This method is common for extractive industries like timber and coal.

Gains and Losses on Asset Sales

The gain or loss on the sale (disposition) of a long-term asset is computed as follows.

Gain or Loss on Asset Sale = Proceeds from Sale − Net Book Value of Asset Sold

An asset's net book value is its acquisition cost less accumulated depreciation. When an asset is sold, its acquisition cost and related accumulated depreciation are both removed from the balance sheet and any gain or loss is reported in income from continuing operations.

Gains and losses on asset sales can be large, and analysts must be aware that these gains and losses are usually *transitory operating* income components. Financial statements do not typically report gains and losses from asset sales because, if the gain or loss is small (immaterial), companies include the item in selling, general and administrative expenses. Footnotes can sometimes be informative. To illustrate, **International Paper Company** provides the following footnote disclosure relating to the sale of its forestlands ($ millions):

> In the fourth quarter, the Company completed sales of 5.1 million acres of forestlands for $6.1 billion, including $1.4 billion in cash and $4.7 billion in installment notes, resulting in pre-tax gains totaling $4.4 billion.

International Paper sold forestlands, carried on its balance sheet at a net book value of $1.7 billion (computed as $6.1 billion sale less $4.4 billion gain), for $6.1 billion. The impacts on its financial statements follow:

Cash   1.4 Bil.
N.Rec. 4.7 Bil.
   PPE   1.7 Bil.
   Gain   4.4 Bil.
———————————
        Cash
1.4 Bil. |
———————————
      Notes Rec.
4.7 Bil. |
———————————
         PPE
         | 1.7 Bil.
———————————
        Gain
         | 4.4 Bil.

	Balance Sheet						Income Statement		
Transaction	**Cash Asset**	**+ Noncash Assets**	**= Liabil- ities**	**+ Contrib. Capital**	**+ Earned Capital**		**Rev- enues**	**− Expen- ses**	**= Net Income**
Sale of forestlands	+1.4 Bil. Cash	−1.7 Bil. Forestlands (PPE) +4.7 Bil. Notes Receivable **=**			+4.4 Bil. Retained Earnings		+4.4 Bil. Gain on Asset Sale	−	**= +4.4 Bil.**

Asset Impairments

Property, plant, and equipment (PPE) assets are reported at their net book values (original cost less accumulated depreciation). This is the case even if the market values of these assets increase subsequent to acquisition. As a result, there can be unrecognized gains hidden within the balance sheet.

On the other hand, if market values of PPE assets subsequently decrease—and the asset value is deemed to be permanently impaired—then companies must write off the impaired cost and recognize losses on those assets. **Impairment** of PPE assets is determined by comparing the asset's net book value to the sum of the asset's *expected* future (undiscounted) cash flows. If the sum of expected cash flow is greater than net book value, there is no impairment. However, if the sum of the expected cash flow is less than net book value, the asset is deemed impaired and it is written down to its current fair value (generally, the present value of those expected cash flows). Exhibit 6.12 depicts this impairment analysis.

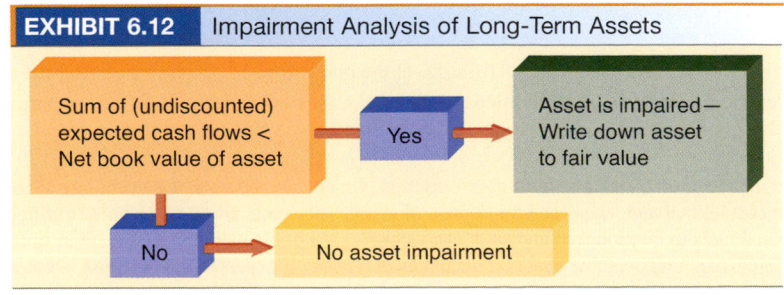

EXHIBIT 6.12 Impairment Analysis of Long-Term Assets

When a company takes an impairment charge, assets are reduced by the amount of the write-down and the loss is recognized in the income statement. To illustrate, a footnote to the 2011 10-K of **Starbucks Corporation** reports the following about asset impairments:

> **Asset Impairment** When facts and circumstances indicate that the carrying values of long-lived assets may not be recoverable, we evaluate long-lived assets for impairment. We first compare the carrying value of the asset to the asset's estimated future cash flows (undiscounted). If the estimated future cash flows are less than the carrying value of the asset, we calculate an impairment loss based on the asset's estimated fair value. For store assets, the fair value of the assets is estimated using a discounted cash flow model based on future store revenues and operating costs, using internal projections . . . We recognized net impairment and disposition losses of $67.7 million, $224.4 million and $325.0 million in fiscal 2010, 2009 and 2008, respectively, primarily due to underperforming company-operated retail stores. The net losses in fiscal 2009 and 2008 include $129.2 million and $201.6 million, respectively, of asset impairments related primarily to the US and International store closures as part of Starbucks store portfolio rationalization which began in fiscal 2008.

Starbucks's pretax write-down of impaired assets affected its financial statements as follows:

	Balance Sheet						Income Statement		
Transaction	Cash Asset	+ Noncash Assets	= Liabil- ities	+ Contrib. Capital	+ Earned Capital		Rev- enues	− Expen- ses	= Net Income
Write-down long-lived assets by $67.7 Mil.		−67.7 Mil. PPE =			−67.7 Mil. Retained Earnings			− +67.7 Mil. Asset Impairment Expense	= −67.7 Mil.

AIE   67.7 Mil.
PPE   67.7 Mil.

AIE
67.7 Mil.

PPE
67.7 Mil.

Starbucks wrote down the carrying value (net book value) of its long-lived assets by $67.7 million. This write-down accelerated the transfer of the asset's cost from the balance sheet to the income statement. Consequently, Starbucks recognized a pretax expense of $67.7 million in the current year rather than over time via the depreciation process.

It is important to note that management determines if and when to recognize asset impairments. Thus, there is room for management to opportunistically over- or underestimate asset impairments. Write-downs of long-term assets are often recognized in connection with a restructuring program.

Analysis of asset write-downs presents at least two potential challenges:

1. *Insufficient write-down.* Assets sometimes are impaired but an impairment charge is not recognized. This can arise if management is overly optimistic about future prospects or is reluctant to recognize the full impairment in income.

2. *Aggressive write-down.* This *big bath* scenario can arise if income is already very low in a given year. Management's view is that the market will not penalize the company's stock for an extra write-off when the year was already bad. Taking a larger impairment charge purges the balance sheet of costs that would otherwise hit future years' income.

GAAP does not condone either of these cases. Yet, because management must estimate future cash flows for the impairment test, it has some degree of control over the timing and amount of the asset write-off and can use that discretion to manage reported income.

IFRS INSIGHT **PPE Valuation under IFRS**

Like GAAP, companies reporting under IFRS must periodically assess long-lived assets for possible impairment. Unlike the two-step GAAP approach, IFRS use a one-step approach: firms compare an asset's net book value to its current fair value (estimated as discounted expected future cash flows) to test for impairment and then reduce net book value to that fair value. Another IFRS difference is that PPE can be revalued upwards to fair value if fair value can be measured reliably.

Footnote Disclosures

Cisco reports the following PPE asset amounts in its balance sheet:

($ millions)	July 31, 2010	July 25, 2009
Property, plant and equipment, net	$3,941	$4,043

In addition to its balance sheet disclosure, Cisco provides two footnotes that more fully describe its PPE assets:

1. *Summary of Significant Accounting Policies.* This footnote describes **Cisco**'s accounting for PPE assets in general terms:

Depreciation and Amortization Property and equipment are stated at cost, less accumulated depreciation and amortization. Depreciation and amortization are computed using the straight-line method over the following periods.

Buildings......................................	25 years
Building improvements.........................	10 years
Furniture and fixtures	5 years
Leasehold improvements......................	Shorter of remaining lease term or 5 years
Computer equipment and related software	30 to 36 months
Production, engineering, and other equipment	Up to 5 years
Operating lease assets.........................	Based on lease term—generally up to 3 years

There are two items of interest in this disclosure: (a) Cisco, like most publicly traded companies, depreciates its PPE assets using the straight-line method (for tax purposes it uses an accelerated method). (b) Cisco provides general disclosures on the useful lives of its assets: 30 months to 25 years. We will discuss a method to more accurately estimate the useful lives in the next section.

2. *Supplemental balance sheet information.* This footnote provides a breakdown of **Cisco**'s PPE assets by category as well as the balance in the accumulated depreciation account:

Property and equipment, net (millions)	July 31, 2010	July 25, 2009
Land, buildings, and building & leasehold improvements	$ 4,470	$ 4,618
Computer equipment and related software	1,405	1,823
Production, engineering, and other equipment	4,702	5,075
Operating lease assets......................................	255	227
Furniture and fixtures	476	465
	11,308	12,208
Less accumulated depreciation and amortization	(7,367)	(8,165)
Total	$ 3,941	$ 4,043

Analysis Implications

This section explains how to measure long-term asset utilization and asset age.

PPE Turnover

A crucial issue in analyzing PPE assets is determining their productivity (utilization). For example, what level of plant assets is necessary to generate a dollar of revenues? How capital intensive are the company and its competitors? To address these and similar questions, we use **PPE turnover**, defined as follows:

$$\text{PPE Turnover (PPET)} = \text{Sales/Average PPE Assets, net}$$

Cisco's 2010 PPE turnover is 10.0 ($40,040 million/[($3,941 million + $4,043 million)/2]). (We use net PPE in the computation above; arguments for using gross PPE are not as compelling as with receivables because managers have less latitude over accumulated depreciation vis-a-vis the allowance for uncollectibles.) This turnover places Cisco somewhat higher than most of its peers (see chart that follows).

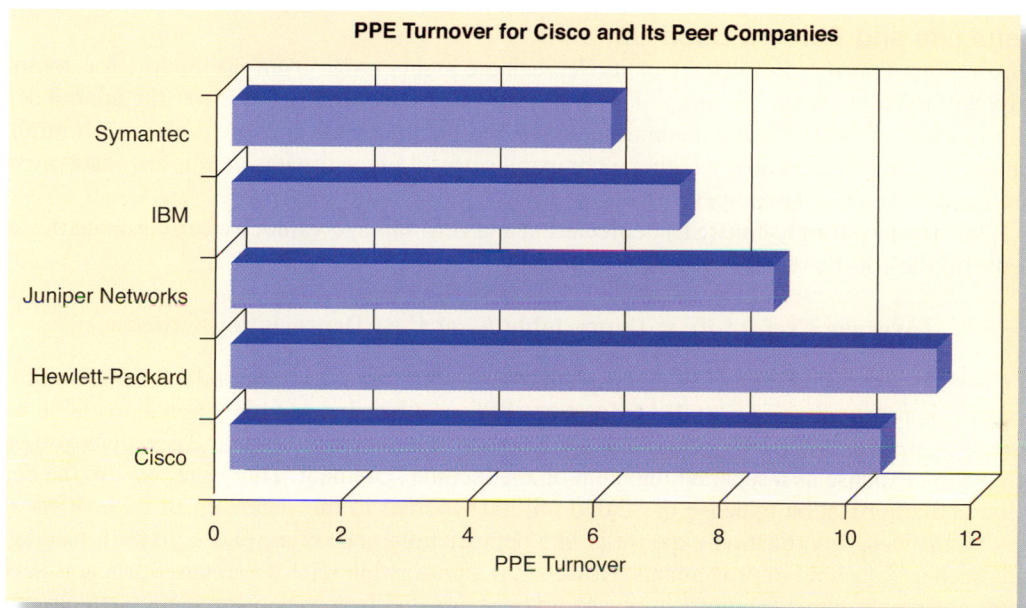

Higher PPE turnover is preferable to lower. A higher PPE turnover implies a lower capital investment for a given level of sales. Higher turnover, therefore, increases profitability because the company avoids asset carrying costs and because the freed-up assets can generate operating cash flow. (PPE turnover that is markedly higher than competitors may hint that the company leases equipment instead of owning it; see Module 10 for explanation.)

PPE turnover is lower for capital-intensive manufacturing companies than it is for companies in service or knowledge-based industries. To this point, consider the following chart of PPE turnover for selected industries.

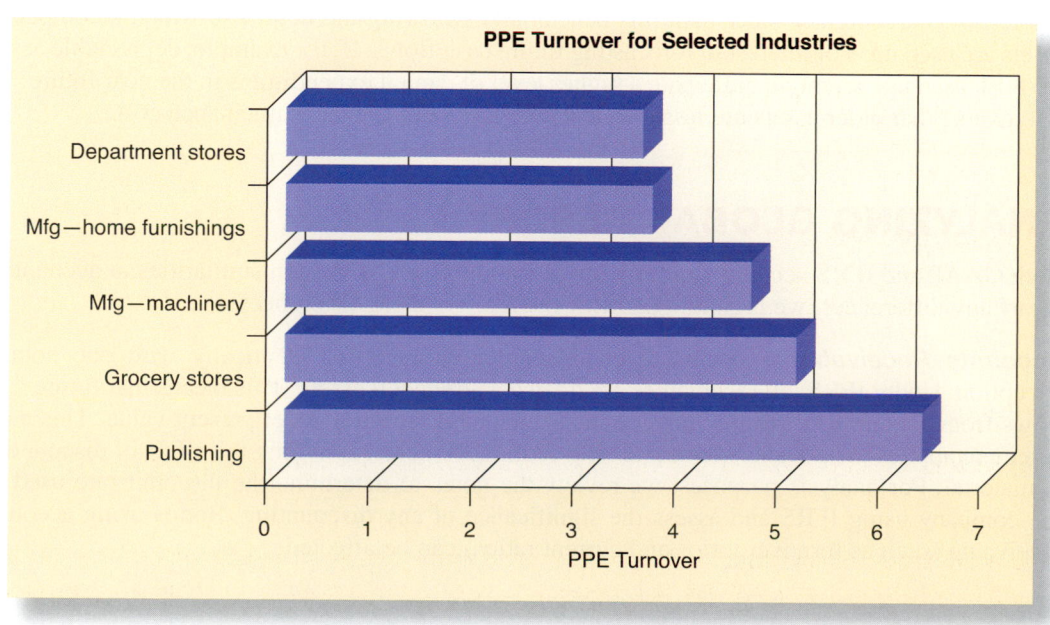

Publishers and grocery stores are not capital-intensive businesses. Their PPE turnover rates are, correspondingly, higher than for other industries.

ANALYSIS DECISION   You Are the Division Manager

You are the manager for a main operating division of your company. You are concerned that a declining PPE turnover is adversely affecting your division's return on net operating assets. What specific actions can you take to increase PPE turnover? [Answer, p. 6-37]

Useful Life and Percent Used Up

Cisco reports that the useful lives of its depreciable assets range from 30 months for computer equipment to 25 years for buildings. The longer an asset's useful life, the lower the annual depreciation expense reported in the income statement and the higher the income each year. It might be of interest, therefore, to know whether a company's useful life estimates are more conservative or more aggressive than its competitors.

If we assume straight-line (SL) depreciation and zero salvage value, we can estimate the average useful life for depreciable assets as follows:

$$\textbf{Average Useful Life = Depreciable Asset Cost/Depreciation Expense}$$

For Cisco, the estimated useful life for its plant assets is 5.6 years ($11,308 million/$2,030 million). Land cost is nearly always excluded from gross PPE cost because land is a nondepreciable asset. However, Cisco does not provide a breakout of land cost in its footnotes and Cisco does not report depreciation expense as a separate line item on the income statement. Therefore, we use the depreciation and amortization expense of $2,030 million reported in the statement of cash flows. (For many companies, amortization expense is like depreciation, and often relates, in part, to tangible assets such as leasehold improvements. However, if amortization relates to intangible assets such as patents and copyrights, the amortization should be subtracted from total depreciation and amortization before estimating useful life.)

We can also estimate the proportion of a company's depreciable assets that have already been transferred to the income statement. This ratio reflects the percent of depreciable assets that are no longer productive—as follows:

$$\textbf{Percent Used Up = Accumulated Depreciation/Depreciable Asset Cost}$$

Cisco's assets are 65% used up, computed as $7,367 million/$11,308 million. If a company replaced all of its assets evenly each year, the percent used up ratio would be 50%. Cisco's depreciable assets are slightly older than this benchmark. Knowing the degree to which a company's assets are used up is of interest in forecasting future cash flows. If, for example, depreciable assets are 80% used up, we might anticipate a higher level of capital expenditures in the near future. We also expect that older assets are less efficient and will incur higher maintenance costs.

ANALYZING GLOBAL REPORTS

Both GAAP and IFRS account similarly for operating assets. Although similarities in accounting dwarf any differences, we highlight some of the more notable differences.

Accounts Receivable Accounts receivable are accounted for identically with one notable exception. Under IFRS, all receivables are treated as *financial* assets. This means that future cash flows from accounts receivable must be discounted and reported at net present value. This measurement applies to both short-term and long-term receivables, assuming the effect of discounting is material. For analysis purposes, we review the notes to determine the discount rate used by the company using IFRS and assess the significance of any discounting. Ratios using accounts receivable (such as turnover ratios and current ratios) can be affected.

Inventory There are three notable differences in accounting for inventory:

1. IFRS does not permit use of the LIFO method; in this module, we discussed the needed adjustments when analyzing a company that uses LIFO.

2. Under U.S. GAAP, inventory is carried at lower of cost or market; under IFRS it is lower of cost or net realizable value. This means that GAAP inventory write-downs are larger than under IFRS because of the floor effect for market value, described earlier in the module. We analyze notes to determine if inventory write-downs are large. If so, GAAP cost of sales can be much higher, which can depress gross profit margins and operating income. This can impact ratios such as inventory turnover, but we cannot determine the direction, which depends on the relative size of the write-down and its impact on cost of sales versus total inventory. (When using LIFO, inventory write-downs are less frequent because the "cost" of LIFO inventory is the oldest costs, which are often low relative to current market replacement values.)

3. IFRS permits companies to reverse inventory write-downs; GAAP does not. This means that if markets recover and inventory previously "impaired" regains some or all of its value, it can be revalued upwards. IFRS notes disclose this revaluation, if material, which permits us to recompute inventory and cost of sales amounts that are comparable to GAAP.

Fixed Assets In accounting for fixed assets, four notable differences deserve mention:

1. GAAP requires the total cost of a fixed asset to be capitalized and depreciated over its useful life. Under IFRS, fixed assets are disaggregated into individual components and then each component is separately depreciated over its useful life. Thus, assets with components with vastly different useful lives, can yield depreciation expense using IFRS that is markedly different from that computed using GAAP. This means that income, and net book values of assets on the balance sheet, can differ for two otherwise identical companies using GAAP versus IFRS. Ratios using plant assets are also impacted. We must review notes regarding depreciation of asset components to make this assessment.

2. Property, plant and equipment can be carried at depreciated cost under U.S. GAAP and IFRS, but can be revalued at fair market value under IFRS. The latter will cause IFRS book values of PPE to be higher. Few companies have opted to revalue assets upwards but in some industries, such as real estate, the practice is common.

3. U.S. GAAP applies a two-step approach for determining impairments. Step 1: compare book value to *undiscounted* expected future cash flows; and Step 2: if book value is higher, measure impairment using *discounted* expected future cash flows. IFRS uses *discounted* expected future cash flows for both steps, which means IFRS uses one step. This results in more asset impairments under IFRS.

4. IFRS fair-value impairments for fixed assets can be reversed; that is, written back up after being written down. The notes to PPE articulate such reversals.

MODULE-END REVIEW

On January 2, assume that Hewlett-Packard purchases equipment that fabricates a key-product part. The equipment costs $95,000, and its estimated useful life is five years, after which it is expected to be sold for $10,000.

Required

1. Compute depreciation expense for each year of the equipment's useful life for each of the following depreciation methods:
    a. Straight-line
    b. Double-declining-balance
2. Show how HP reports the equipment on its balance sheet at the end of the third year assuming straight-line depreciation.

3. Assume that this is the only depreciable asset the company owns and that it uses straight-line depreciation. Estimate the useful life and the percent used up for this asset at the end of the third year.
4. Assume that HP estimates that, at the end of the third year, the equipment will generate $40,000 in cash flow over its remaining life and that it has a current fair value of $36,000. Is the equipment impaired? If so, what is the effect on HP's financial statements?
5. Instead of the facts in part 4, assume that, at the end of the third year, HP sells the equipment for $50,000 cash. What amount of gain or loss does HP report from this sale?

The solution is on page 6-53.

GUIDANCE ANSWERS . . . ANALYSIS DECISION

You Are the Receivables Manager First, we must realize that extending credit is an important tool in the marketing of your products, often as important as advertising and promotion. Given that receivables are necessary, there are certain ways to speed their collection. (1) We can better screen the customers to whom we extend credit. (2) We can negotiate advance or progress payments from customers. (3) We can use bank letters of credit or other automatic drafting procedures that obviate billing. (4) We can make sure products are sent as ordered, to reduce disputes. (5) We can improve administration of past-due accounts to provide for more timely notices of delinquencies and better collection procedures.

You Are the Plant Manager Companies need inventories to avoid lost sales opportunities; however, there are several ways to minimize inventory needs. (1) We can reduce product costs by improving product design to eliminate costly features that customers don't value. (2) We can use more cost-efficient suppliers; possibly producing in lower wage-rate parts of the world. (3) We can reduce raw material inventories with just-in-time delivery from suppliers. (4) We can eliminate production bottlenecks that increase work-in-process inventories. (5) We can manufacture for orders rather than for estimated demand to reduce finished goods inventories. (6) We can improve warehousing and distribution to reduce duplicate inventories. (7) We can monitor product sales and adjust product mix as demand changes to reduce finished goods inventories.

You Are the Division Manager PPE is a difficult asset to reduce. Because companies need long-term operating assets, managers usually try to maximize throughput to reduce unit costs. Also, many companies form alliances to share administrative, production, logistics, customer service, IT, and other functions. These alliances take many forms (such as joint ventures) and are designed to spread ownership of assets among many users. The goal is to identify underutilized assets and to increase capacity utilization. Another solution might be to reconfigure the value chain from raw material to end user. Examples include the sharing of IT, or manufacturing facilities, outsourcing of production or administration such as customer service centers, and the use of special purpose entities for asset securitization (see Module 10).

DISCUSSION QUESTIONS

Q6-1. Explain how management can shift income from one period into another by its estimation of uncollectible accounts.

Q6-2. Why do relatively stable inventory costs across periods reduce the importance of management's choice of an inventory costing method?

Q6-3. Explain why using the FIFO inventory costing method will increase gross profit during periods of rising inventory costs.

Q6-4. If inventory costs are rising, which inventory costing method—first-in, first-out; last-in, first-out; or average cost—yields the (a) lowest ending inventory? (b) lowest net income? (c) largest ending inventory? (d) largest net income? (e) greatest cash flow, assuming the same method is used for tax purposes?

Q6-5. Even though it may not reflect their physical flow of goods, why might companies adopt last-in, first-out inventory costing in periods when costs are consistently rising?

Q6-6. In a recent annual report, **Kaiser Aluminum Corporation** made the following statement in reference to its inventories: "The Company recorded pretax charges of approximately $19.4 million because of a reduction in the carrying values of its inventories caused principally by prevailing lower prices for alumina, primary aluminum, and fabricated products." What basic accounting principle caused Kaiser Aluminum to record this $19.4 million pretax charge? Briefly describe the rationale for this principle.

KAISER ALUMINUM CORPORATION (KALU)

Q6-7. Why is depreciation expense necessary to properly match revenues and expenses?

Q6-8. How might a company revise its depreciation expense computation due to a change in an asset's estimated useful life or salvage value?

Q6-9. When is a PPE asset considered to be impaired? How is an impairment loss computed?

Q6-10. What is the benefit of accelerated depreciation for income tax purposes when the total depreciation taken over the asset's life is identical under any method of depreciation?

Q6-11. What factors determine the gain or loss on the sale of a PPE asset?

**Assignments with the ✓ in the margin are available in an online homework system.
See the Preface of the book for details.**

MINI EXERCISES

M6-12. **Estimating Uncollectible Accounts and Reporting Accounts Receivable**   **(LO1)**
Mohan Company estimates its uncollectible accounts by aging its accounts receivable and applying percentages to various aged categories of accounts. Mohan computes a total of $2,100 in estimated uncollectible accounts as of its current year-end. Its Accounts Receivable has a balance of $98,000, and its Allowance for Uncollectible Accounts has an unused balance of $500 before any year-end adjustments.

  a. What amount of bad debts expense will Mohan report in its income statement for the current year?
  b. Determine the net amount of accounts receivable reported in current assets at year-end.

M6-13. **Interpreting the Allowance Method for Accounts Receivable**   **(LO1)**
At a recent board of directors meeting of Ascot, Inc., one of the directors expressed concern over the allowance for uncollectible accounts appearing in the company's balance sheet. "I don't understand this account," he said. "Why don't we just show accounts receivable at the amount owed to us and get rid of that allowance?" Respond to the director's question; include in your response (a) an explanation of why the company has an allowance account, (b) what the balance sheet presentation of accounts receivable is intended to show, and (c) how accrual accounting (as opposed to the cash-basis accounting) affects the presentation of accounts receivable.

M6-14. **Analyzing the Allowance for Uncollectible Accounts**   **(LO1)**
Following is the current asset section from the **Kraft Foods, Inc.**, balance sheet.

KRAFT FOODS, INC. (KFT)

$ millions	2010	2009
Cash and cash equivalents	$ 2,481	$ 2,101
Receivables (net of allowances of $246 in 2010 and $121 in 2009)	6,539	5,197
Inventories, net.	5,310	3,775
Deferred income taxes	898	730
Other current assets.	993	651
Total current assets	$16,221	$12,454

  a. Compute the gross amount of accounts receivable for both 2010 and 2009. Compute the percentage of the allowance for uncollectible accounts relative to the gross amount of accounts receivable for each of those years.
  b. Compute the relative size of net accounts receivable to total assets; the latter were $95,289 million and $66,714 million for 2010 and 2009, respectively. Interpret the quality of Kraft's receivables for 2010 compared to 2009. (As additional background, net earnings attributable to the company were $4,114 million and $3,021 million for 2010 and 2009, respectively.)

PROCTER &
GAMBLE
(PG)
COLGATE-
PALMOLIVE
(CL)

M6-15.   Evaluating Accounts Receivable Turnover for Competitors   (LO1)

Procter & Gamble (PG) and **Colgate-Palmolive** (CL) report the following sales and accounts receivable balances ($ millions) for 2010 and 2009.

$ millions	Procter & Gamble		Colgate-Palmolive	
	Sales	Accounts Receivable	Sales	Accounts Receivable
2010	$78,938	$5,335	$15,564	$1,610
2009	76,694	5,836	15,327	1,626

a.   Compute the accounts receivable turnover for both companies for 2010.

b.   Identify and discuss a potential explanation for the difference between these competitors' accounts receivable turnover.

M6-16.   Computing Cost of Goods Sold and Ending Inventory under FIFO, LIFO, and Average Cost   (LO2)

Assume that Gode Company reports the following initial balance and subsequent purchase of inventory.

Inventory balance at beginning of year	1,000 units @ $100 each	$100,000
Inventory purchased during the year	2,000 units @ $150 each	300,000
Cost of goods available for sale during the year	3,000 units	$400,000

Assume that 1,700 units are sold during the year. Compute the cost of goods sold for the year and the inventory on the year-end balance sheet under the following inventory costing methods:

a.   FIFO

b.   LIFO

c.   Average Cost

M6-17.   Computing Cost of Goods Sold and Ending Inventory under FIFO, LIFO and Average Cost   (LO2)

Bartov Corporation reports the following beginning inventory and inventory purchases.

Inventory balance at beginning of year	400 units @ $10 each	$ 4,000
Inventory purchased during the year	700 units @ $12 each	8,400
Cost of goods available for sale during the year	1,100 units	$12,400

Bartov sells 600 of its inventory units during the year. Compute the cost of goods sold for the year and the inventory on the year-end balance sheet under the following inventory costing methods:

a.   FIFO

b.   LIFO

c.   Average Cost

M6-18.   Computing and Evaluating Inventory Turnover for Two Companies   (LO2)

ABERCROMBIE &
FITCH
(ANF)
TJX COMPANIES
(TJX)

Abercrombie & Fitch (ANF) and **TJX Companies** (TJX) report the following information in their respective January 2011 10-K reports relating to their 2010 and 2009 fiscal years.

$ millions	Abercrombie & Fitch			TJX Companies		
	Sales	Cost of Goods Sold	Inventories	Sales	Cost of Goods Sold	Inventories
2010	$3,469	$1,257	$386	$21,942	$16,040	$2,765
2009	2,929	1,045	311	20,288	14,968	2,532

a.   Compute the 2010 inventory turnover for each of these two retailers.

b.   Discuss any difference you observe in inventory turnover between these two companies. Does the difference confirm your expectations given their respective business models? Explain. (Hint: ANF is a higher-end retailer and TJX sells more value-priced clothing.)

c.   Describe ways that a retailer can improve its inventory turnover.

M6-19. **Computing Depreciation under Straight-Line and Double-Declining-Balance** (LO3)

A delivery van costing $18,000 is expected to have a $1,500 salvage value at the end of its useful life of five years. Assume that the truck was purchased on January 1. Compute the depreciation expense for the first two calendar years under the following depreciation methods:

 a. Straight-line
 b. Double-declining-balance

M6-20. **Computing Depreciation under Straight-Line and Double-Declining-Balance for Partial Years** (LO3)

A company with a calendar year-end, purchases a machine costing $145,800 on May 1, 2011. The machine is expected to be obsolete after three years (36 months) and, thereafter, no longer useful to the company. The estimated salvage value is $5,400. The company's depreciation policy is to record depreciation for the portion of the year that the asset is in service. Compute depreciation expense for both 2011 and 2012 under the following depreciation methods:

 a. Straight-line
 b. Double-declining-balance

M6-21. **Computing and Comparing PPE Turnover for Two Companies** (LO3)

Texas Instruments (TXN) and Intel Corporation (INTC) report the following information.

| $ millions | Intel Corporation | | Texas Instruments | |
	Sales	Plant, Property and Equipment, net	Sales	Plant, Property and Equipment, net
2010	$43,623	$17,899	$13,966	$3,680
2009	35,127	17,225	10,427	3,158

TEXAS
INSTRUMENTS
(TXN)
INTEL
CORPORATION
(INTC)

 a. Compute the 2010 PPE turnover for both companies. Comment on any difference observed.
 b. Discuss ways in which high-tech manufacturing companies like these can increase their PPE turnover.

EXERCISES

E6-22. **Estimating Uncollectible Accounts and Reporting Accounts Receivable** (LO1)

LaFond Company analyzes its accounts receivable at December 31, and arrives at the aged categories below along with the percentages that are estimated as uncollectible.

Age Group	Accounts Receivable	Estimated Loss %
0–30 days past due	$ 90,000	1%
31–60 days past due	20,000	2
61–120 days past due	11,000	5
121–180 days past due	6,000	10
Over 180 days past due	4,000	25
Total accounts receivable	$131,000	

The unused balance of the allowance for uncollectible accounts is $520 on December 31, before any adjustments.

 a. What amount of bad debts expense will LaFond report in its income statement for the year?
 b. Use the financial statement effects template to record LaFond's bad debts expense for the year.
 c. What is the balance of accounts receivable on its December 31 balance sheet?

E6-23. **Analyzing and Reporting Receivable Transactions and Uncollectible Accounts (using percentage of sales method)** (LO1)

At the beginning of the year, Penman Company had the following account balances.

Accounts Receivable	$122,000
Allowance for Uncollectible Accounts	7,900

During the year, Penman's credit sales were $1,173,000 and collections on accounts receivable were $1,150,000. The following additional transactions occurred during the year.

Feb. 17 Wrote off Nissim's account, $3,600.
May 28 Wrote off Weiss's account, $2,400.
Dec. 15 Wrote off Ohlson's account, $900.
Dec. 31 Recorded the bad debts expense assuming that Penman's policy is to record bad debts expense as 0.8% of credit sales. (*Hint*: The allowance account is increased by 0.8% of credit sales regardless of write-offs.)

Compute the ending balances in accounts receivable and the allowance for uncollectible accounts. Show how Penman's December 31 balance sheet reports the two accounts.

E6-24. Interpreting the Accounts Receivable Footnote (LO1)

HEWLETT-
PACKARD
(HPQ)

Hewlett-Packard Company (HPQ) reports the following in its 2010 10-K report.

October 31 (In millions)	2010	2009
Accounts receivable....................................	$18,481	$16,537

HPQ footnotes to its 10-K provide the following additional information relating to its allowance for doubtful accounts.

For the fiscal years ended October 31 (In millions)	2010	2009	2008
Allowance for doubtful accounts—accounts receivable			
Balance, beginning of period	$629	$553	$226
Increase in allowance from acquisition..................	7	—	245
Addition of bad debts provision	80	282	226
Deductions, net of recoveries..........................	(191)	(206)	(144)
Balance, end of period	$525	$629	$553

a. What is the gross amount of accounts receivables for HPQ in fiscal 2010 and 2009?
b. What is the percentage of the allowance for doubtful accounts to gross accounts receivable for 2010 and 2009?
c. What amount of bad debts expense did HPQ report each year 2008 through 2010 (ignore increase in allowance from acquisitions)? How does bad debts expense compare with the amounts of its accounts receivable actually written off? (Identify the amounts and explain.)
d. Explain the changes in the allowance for doubtful accounts from 2008 through 2010. Does it appear that HPQ increased or decreased its allowance for doubtful accounts in any particular year beyond what seems reasonable? As background, total assets were $124,503, $114,799 and $113,331 for 2010, 2009 and 2008, respectively, and net earnings attributable to the company were $8,761, $7,660 and $8,329 ($ millions).

E6-25. Estimating Bad Debts Expense and Reporting Receivables (LO1)

At December 31, Sunil Company had a balance of $375,000 in its accounts receivable and an unused balance of $4,200 in its allowance for uncollectible accounts. The company then aged its accounts as follows:

Current	$304,000
1–60 days past due	44,000
61–180 days past due	18,000
Over 180 days past due...........	9,000
Total accounts receivable.........	$375,000

The company has experienced losses as follows: 1% of current balances, 5% of balances 1–60 days past due, 15% of balances 61–180 days past due, and 40% of balances over 180 days past due. The company continues to base its allowance for uncollectible accounts on this aging analysis and percentages.

a. What amount of bad debts expense does Sunil report on its income statement for the year?
b. Show how Sunil's December 31 balance sheet will report the accounts receivable and the allowance for uncollectible accounts.

E6-26. **Estimating Uncollectible Accounts and Reporting Receivables over Multiple Periods** (LO1)

Barth Company, which has been in business for three years, makes all of its sales on credit and does not offer cash discounts. Its credit sales, customer collections, and write-offs of uncollectible accounts for its first three years follow:

Year	Sales	Collections	Accounts Written Off
2009	$751,000	$733,000	$5,300
2010	876,000	864,000	5,800
2011	972,000	938,000	6,500

a. Barth recognizes bad debts expense as 1% of sales. (Hint: This means the allowance account is increased by 1% of credit sales regardless of any write-offs and unused balances.) What does Barth's 2011 balance sheet report for accounts receivable and the allowance for uncollectible accounts? What total amount of bad debts expense appears on Barth's income statement for each of the three years?

b. Comment on the appropriateness of the 1% rate used to provide for bad debts based on your analysis in part a.

E6-27. **Applying and Analyzing Inventory Costing Methods** (LO2)

At the beginning of the current period, Chen carried 1,000 units of its product with a unit cost of $20. A summary of purchases during the current period follows:

	Units	Unit Cost	Cost
Beginning Inventory	1,000	$20	$20,000
Purchases: #1...........	1,800	22	39,600
#2...........	800	26	20,800
#3...........	1,200	29	34,800

During the current period, Chen sold 2,800 units.

a. Assume that Chen uses the first-in, first-out method. Compute both cost of goods sold for the current period and the ending inventory balance. Use the financial statement effects template to record cost of goods sold for the period.

b. Assume that Chen uses the last-in, first-out method. Compute both cost of goods sold for the current period and the ending inventory balance.

c. Assume that Chen uses the average cost method. Compute both cost of goods sold for the current period and the ending inventory balance.

d. Which of these three inventory costing methods would you choose to:
1. Reflect what is probably the physical flow of goods? Explain.
2. Minimize income taxes for the period? Explain.
3. Report the largest amount of income for the period? Explain.

E6-28. **Analyzing an Inventory Footnote Disclosure** (LO2)

General Electric Company reports the following footnote in its 10-K report.

GENERAL ELECTRIC COMPANY (GE)

December 31 (In millions)	2010	2009
Raw materials and work in process	$ 6,973	$ 7,581
Finished goods....................	4,435	4,105
Unbilled shipments.................	456	759
	11,864	12,445
Less revaluation to LIFO.............	(404)	(529)
	$11,460	$11,916

The company reports its inventories using the LIFO inventory costing method.

a. What is the balance in inventories reported on GE's 2010 balance sheet?

b. What would GE's 2010 balance sheet have reported for inventories had the company used FIFO inventory costing?

c. What cumulative effect has GE's choice of LIFO over FIFO had on its pretax income as of year-end 2010? Explain.

d.   Assume GE has a 35% income tax rate. As of the 2010 year-end, how much has GE saved in taxes by choosing LIFO over FIFO method for costing inventory? Has the use of LIFO increased or decreased GE's cumulative taxes paid?

e.   What effect has the use of LIFO inventory costing had on GE's pretax income and tax expense for 2010 only (assume a 35% income tax rate)?

 E6-29.   Computing Cost of Sales and Ending Inventory   (LO2)

Stocken Company has the following financial records for the current period.

	Units	Unit Cost
Beginning inventory	100	$46
Purchases: #1.	650	42
#2.	550	38
#3.	200	36

Ending inventory is 350 units. Compute the ending inventory and the cost of goods sold for the current period using (a) first-in, first out, (b) average cost, and (c) last-in, first-out.

E6-30.   Analyzing an Inventory Footnote Disclosure   (LO2)

DEERE & CO.
(DE)

The inventory footnote from the **Deere & Company**'s 2010 10-K follows.

Inventories   Most inventories owned by Deere & Company and its U.S. equipment subsidiaries are valued at cost, on the "last-in, first-out" (LIFO) basis. Remaining inventories are generally valued at the lower of cost, on the "first-in, first-out" (FIFO) basis, or market. The value of gross inventories on the LIFO basis represented 59 percent of worldwide gross inventories at FIFO value on October 31, 2010 and 2009. If all inventories had been valued on a FIFO basis, estimated inventories by major classification at October 31 in millions of dollars would have been as follows:

($ millions)	2010	2009
Raw materials and supplies	$1,201	$ 940
Work-in-process.	483	387
Finished goods and parts.	2,777	2,437
Total FIFO value	4,461	3,764
Less adjustment to LIFO value.	1,398	1,367
Inventories	$3,063	$2,397

This footnote reveals that not all of Deere's inventories are reported using the same inventory costing method (companies can use different inventory costing methods for different inventory pools).

a.   What amount does Deere report for inventories on its 2010 balance sheet?

b.   What would Deere have reported as inventories on its 2010 balance sheet had the company used FIFO inventory costing for all of its inventories?

c.   What cumulative effect has the use of LIFO inventory costing had, as of year-end 2010, on Deere's pretax income compared with the pretax income it would have reported had it used FIFO inventory costing for all of its inventories? Explain.

d.   Assuming a 35% income tax rate, by what cumulative dollar amount has Deere's tax expense been affected by use of LIFO inventory costing as of year-end 2010? Has the use of LIFO inventory costing increased or decreased Deere's cumulative tax expense?

e.   What effect has the use of LIFO inventory costing had on Deere's pretax income and tax expense for 2010 only (assume a 35% income tax rate)?

 E6-31.   Computing Straight-Line and Double-Declining-Balance Depreciation   (LO3)

On January 2, Haskins Company purchases a laser cutting machine for use in fabrication of a part for one of its key products. The machine cost $80,000, and its estimated useful life is five years, after which the expected salvage value is $5,000. For both parts *a* and *b* below: (1) Compute depreciation expense for *each year* of the machine's five-year useful life under that depreciation method. (2) Use the financial statements effects template to show the effect of depreciation for the first year only for that method.

a.   Straight-line

b.   Double-declining-balance

E6-32. **Computing Depreciation, Net Book Value, and Gain or Loss on Asset Sale** (LO3)

Sloan Company owns an executive plane that originally cost $800,000. It has recorded straight-line depreciation on the plane for six full years, calculated assuming an $80,000 expected salvage value at the end of its estimated 10-year useful life. Sloan disposes of the plane at the end of the sixth year.

a. At the disposal date, what is the (1) cumulative depreciation expense and (2) net book value of the plane?

b. How much gain or loss is reported at disposal if the sales price is:
1. A cash amount equal to the plane's net book value.
2. $195,000 cash.
3. $600,000 cash.

E6-33. **Computing Straight-Line and Double-Declining-Balance Depreciation** (LO3)

On January 2, 2011, Dechow Company purchases a machine that manufactures a part for one of its key products. The machine cost $218,700 and is estimated to have a useful life of six years, with an expected salvage value of $23,400. Compute depreciation expense for 2011 and 2012 for the following depreciation methods. (When equipment is used exclusively in the manufacturing process, the depreciation is more accurately recorded as part of cost of goods sold and not as depreciation expense.)

a. Straight-line.
b. Double-declining-balance.

E6-34. **Computing Depreciation, Net Book Value, and Gain or Loss on Asset Sale** (LO3)

Palepu Company owns and operates a delivery van that originally cost $27,200. Palepu has recorded straight-line depreciation on the van for three years, calculated assuming a $2,000 expected salvage value at the end of its estimated six-year useful life. Depreciation was last recorded at the end of the third year, at which time Palepu disposes of this van.

a. Compute the net book value of the van on the disposal date.
b. Compute the gain or loss on sale of the van if the disposal proceeds are:
1. A cash amount equal to the van's net book value.
2. $15,000 cash.
3. $12,000 cash.

E6-35. **Estimating Useful Life and Percent Used Up** (LO3)

The property and equipment footnote from the **Deere & Company** balance sheet follows.

DEERE & CO.
(DE)

Property and Depreciation   A summary of property and equipment at October 31 follows:

Property and Equipment ($ millions)	Useful Lives (Years)	2010	2009
Land		$ 113	$ 116
Buildings and building equipment	23	2,226	2,144
Machinery and equipment	11	3,972	3,826
Dies, patterns, tools, etc.	7	1,105	1,081
All other	5	685	672
Construction in progress		478	362
Total at cost		8,579	8,201
Less accumulated depreciation		4,856	4,744
Total		$3,723	$3,457

Property and equipment is stated at cost less accumulated depreciation. Total property and equipment additions in 2010, 2009 and 2008 were $802 million, $798 million and $1,147 million and depreciation was $540 million, $513 million and $467 million, respectively.

a. Compute the estimated useful life of Deere's depreciable assets at year-end 2010. (Hint: Exclude land and construction in progress.) How does this estimate compare with the useful lives reported in Deere's footnote disclosure?

b. Estimate the percent used up of Deere's depreciable assets at year-end 2010. How do you interpret this figure?

INTEL CORP.
(INTC)

E6-36.   Computing and Evaluating Receivables, Inventory and PPE Turnovers   (LO1, 2, 3)

Intel Corporation reports the following financial statement amounts in its 2010 10-K report.

$ millions	Sales	Cost of Goods Sold	Receivables, net	Inventories	Plant, property and equipment, net
2008	$37,586	$16,742	$1,712	$3,744	$17,544
2009	35,127	15,566	2,273	2,935	17,225
2010	43,623	15,132	2,867	3,757	17,899

a.   Compute the receivables, inventory, and PPE turnover ratios for both 2009 and 2010.
b.   What changes are evident in the turnover rates of Intel for these years? Discuss ways in which a company such as Intel can improve receivables, inventory, and PPE turnover ratios.

E6-37.   Computing and Assessing Plant Asset Impairment   (LO3)

On July 1, Zeibart Company purchases equipment for $225,000. The equipment has an estimated useful life of 10 years and expected salvage value of $25,000. The company uses straight-line depreciation. Four years later, economic factors cause the fair value of the equipment to decline to $90,000. On this date, Zeibart examines the equipment for impairment and estimates $125,000 in undiscounted expected cash inflows from this equipment.

a.   Compute the annual depreciation expense relating to this equipment.
b.   Compute the equipment's net book value at the end of the fourth year.
c.   Apply the test of impairment to this equipment as of the end of the fourth year. Is the equipment impaired? Show supporting computations.
d.   If the equipment is impaired at the end of the fourth year, compute the impairment loss.

PROBLEMS

BEST BUY
(BBY)
CATERPILLAR
(CAT)
DELL
(DELL)
VERIZON
(VZ)
WALMART
(WMT)

P6-38.   Evaluating Turnover Rates for Different Companies   (LO1, 2, 3)

Following are asset turnover rates for accounts receivable; inventory; and property, plant, and equipment (PPE) for **Best Buy** (retailer), **Caterpillar** (manufacturer of heavy equipment), **Dell** (computers), **Verizon** (communications) and **Walmart** (department store).

Company Name	Accounts Receivable Turnover	Inventory Turnover	Plant, Property and Equipment Turnover
Best Buy Co	23.02	6.61	12.74
Caterpillar Inc	2.77	3.81	3.42
Dell......................	9.97	42.60	29.75
Verizon...................	8.75	34.53	1.19
Walmart..................	91.38	9.13	4.12

Required

a.   Interpret and explain difference in receivables turnover for the retailer (Best Buy) vis-à-vis that for the manufacturer (Caterpillar). What reason can you give for a 91.38 turnover for Walmart?
b.   Interpret and explain the difference in inventory turnover for Dell versus Caterpillar.
c.   Why is the PPE turnover for Caterpillar and Verizon low compared with other companies on this list?
d.   What are some general observations you might draw regarding the relative levels of these turnover rates across the different industries?

P6-39.   Interpreting Accounts Receivable and Its Footnote Disclosure   (LO1)

Following is the current asset section from the **W.W. Grainger, Inc.**, balance sheet.

W.W. GRAINGER,
INC.
(GWW)

As of December 31 ($ 000s)	2010	2009	2008
Cash and cash equivalents	$ 313,454	$ 459,871	$ 396,290
Accounts receivable (less allowances for doubtful accounts of $24,552, $25,850 and $26,481, respectively)	762,895	624,910	589,416
Inventories—net.....................	991,577	889,679	1,009,932
Prepaid expenses and other assets................	87,125	88,364	73,359
Deferred income taxes.......................	44,627	42,023	52,556
Prepaid income taxes........................	38,393	26,668	22,556
Total current assets	$2,238,071	$2,131,515	$2,144,109

Grainger reports the following footnote relating to its receivables.

Allowance for Doubtful Accounts The following table shows the activity in the allowance for doubtful accounts.

For Years Ended December 31 ($ 000s)	2010	2009	2008
Balance at beginning of period	$25,850	$26,481	$25,830
Provision for uncollectible accounts	6,718	10,748	12,924
Write-off of uncollectible accounts, less recoveries	(8,302)	(12,254)	(11,501)
Foreign currency translation impact	286	875	(772)
Balance at end of period	$24,552	$25,850	$26,481

Required

a. What amount do customers owe Grainger at each of the year-ends 2008 through 2010?
b. What percentage of its total accounts receivable does Grainger feel are uncollectible? (Hint: Percentage of uncollectible accounts = Allowance for uncollectible accounts/Gross accounts receivable)
c. What amount of bad debts expense did Grainger report in its income statement for each of the years 2008 through 2010?
d. Explain the change in the balance of the allowance for uncollectible accounts since 2008. Specifically, did the allowance increase or decrease as a percentage of gross accounts receivable, and why?
e. If Grainger had kept its 2010 allowance for uncollectible accounts at the same percentage of gross accounts receivable as it was in 2008, by what amount would its profit have changed (ignore taxes)? Explain.
f. Overall, what is your assessment of Grainger's allowance for uncollectible accounts and the related bad debts expense? As background, total assets were $3,904,377, $3,726,332 and $3,515,417 for 2010, 2009 and 2008, respectively, and net earnings attributable to the company were $510,865, $430,466 and $475,355 ($ 000s).

P6-40. **Analyzing and Interpreting Receivables and Related Ratios** (LO1)

Following is the current asset section from **Intuit**'s balance sheet.

INTUIT, INC.
(INTU)

July 31 ($ millions)	2010	2009
Cash and cash equivalents	$ 214	$ 679
Investments	1,408	668
Accounts receivable, net of allowance for doubtful accounts of $22 and $16, respectively	135	135
Income taxes receivable	27	67
Deferred income taxes	117	92
Prepaid expenses and other current assets	57	43
Current assets of discontinued operations	—	12
Current assets before funds held for customers	1,958	1,696
Funds held for customers	337	272
Total current assets	$2,295	$1,968

Total revenues were $3,455 million ($1,412 million in product sales and $2,043 million in service revenues and other) in 2010.

Required

a. What are Intuit's gross accounts receivable at the end of 2010 and 2009?
b. For both 2010 and 2009, compute the ratio of the allowance for uncollectible accounts to gross receivables. What trend do you observe?
c. Compute the receivables turnover ratio and the average collection period for 2010 based on gross receivables computed in part a. Does the collection period (days sales in receivables) appear reasonable given Intuit's lines of business (Intuit's products include QuickBooks, TurboTax and Quicken, which it sells to consumers and small businesses)? Explain.
d. Is the percentage of Intuit's allowance for uncollectible accounts to gross accounts receivable consistent with what you expect for Intuit's line of business? Explain.

e. Intuit discloses the following table related to its allowance for uncollectible accounts from its 10-K. Comment on the change in the allowance account during 2008 through 2010.

(In millions)	Balance at Beginning of Period	Additions Charged to Expense	Deductions	Balance at End of Period	Net Income	Total Assets
Year ended July 31, 2010						
Allowance for doubtful accounts	$16	$23	$(17)	$22	$574	$5,198
Year ended July 31, 2009						
Allowance for doubtful accounts	$16	$14	$(14)	$16	447	4,826
Year ended July 31, 2008						
Allowance for doubtful accounts	$15	$15	$(14)	$16	477	4,667

P6-41.   Analyzing and Interpreting Inventories and Related Ratios and Disclosures   (LO2)

DOW CHEMICAL
(DOW)

The current asset section from **The Dow Chemical Company**'s 2010 annual report follows.

December 31 (In millions)	2010	2009
Cash and cash equivalents	$ 7,039	$ 2,846
Accounts and notes receivable		
Trade (net of allowance for doubtful receivables—2010: $128; 2009: $160)	4,616	5,656
Other..	4,428	3,539
Inventories	7,087	6,847
Deferred income tax assets—current...........................	611	654
Total current assets	$23,781	$19,542

The Dow Chemical inventory footnote follows.

The following table provides a breakdown of inventories:

Inventories at December 31 (In millions)	2010	2009
Finished goods............................	$4,289	$3,887
Work in process	1,498	1,593
Raw materials.............................	644	671
Supplies	656	696
Total inventories	$7,087	$6,847

The reserves reducing inventories from a FIFO basis to a LIFO basis amounted to $1,003 million at December 31, 2010 and $818 million at December 31, 2009. Inventories valued on a LIFO basis, principally hydrocarbon and U.S. chemicals and plastics product inventories, represented 29 percent of the total inventories at December 31, 2010 and December 31, 2009.

A reduction of certain inventories resulted in the liquidation of some of the Company's LIFO inventory layers, increasing pretax income $159 million in 2010 and $84 million in 2009 and decreasing pretax income $45 million in 2008.

Required

a. What inventory costing method does Dow Chemical use? As of 2010, what is the effect on cumulative pretax income and cash flow of using this inventory costing method? (Assume a 35% tax rate.) What is the effect on 2010 pretax income and cash flow of using this inventory costing method.

b. Compute inventory turnover and average inventory days outstanding for 2010 (2010 cost of goods sold is $45,780 million). Comment on the level of these two ratios. Is the level what you expect given Dow's industry? Explain.

c. Explain why a reduction of inventory quantities increased income in 2009 and 2010, but decreased income in 2008.

P6-42. **Estimating Useful Life and Percent Used Up** (LO3)

The property and equipment section of the **Abbott Laboratories** 2010 balance sheet follows.

	December 31		
Property and equipment, at cost ($ thousands)	2010	2009	2008
Land	$ 648,988	$ 546,204	$ 509,606
Buildings.	4,334,236	4,010,439	3,698,861
Equipment	11,813,618	11,325,450	10,366,267
Construction in progress	577,460	604,813	613,939
	17,374,302	16,486,906	15,188,673
Less: accumulated depreciation and amortization . .	9,403,346	8,867,417	7,969,507
Net property and equipment	$ 7,970,956	$ 7,619,489	$ 7,219,166

The company also provides the following disclosure relating to the useful lives of its depreciable assets.

Property and Equipment—Depreciation and amortization are provided on a straight-line basis over the estimated useful lives of the assets. The following table shows estimated useful lives of property and equipment.

Classification	Estimated Useful Lives
Buildings.	10 to 50 years (average 27 years)
Equipment	3 to 20 years (average 11 years)

During 2010, the company reported $1,207,450 ($ 000s) for depreciation expense.

Required

a. Compute the estimated useful life of Abbott Laboratories' depreciable assets. How does this compare with its useful lives footnote disclosure above?

b. Compute the estimated percent used up of Abbott Laboratories' depreciable assets. How do you interpret this figure?

P6-43. **Interpreting and Applying Disclosures on Property and Equipment** (LO3)

Following are selected disclosures from the **Rohm and Haas Company** (a specialty chemical company) 2007 10-K.

Land, Building and Equipment, Net

(in millions)	2007	2006
Land	$ 146	$ 142
Buildings and improvements	1,855	1,729
Machinery and equipment	6,155	5,721
Capitalized interest.	352	340
Construction in progress	271	218
Land, buildings, and equipment, gross	8,779	8,150
Less: Accumulated depreciation	5,908	5,481
Total	$2,871	$2,669

The principal lives (in years) used in determining depreciation rates of various assets are: buildings and improvement (10–50); machinery and equipment (5–20); automobiles, trucks and tank cars (3–10); furniture and fixtures, laboratory equipment and other assets (5–10); capitalized software (5–7).

continued

continued from prior page

> The principal life used in determining the depreciation rate for leasehold improvements is the years remaining in the lease term or the useful life (in years) of the asset, whichever is shorter.
>
> **Impairment of Long-lived Assets** Long-lived assets, other than investments, goodwill and indefinite-lived intangible assets, are depreciated over their estimated useful lives, and are reviewed for impairment whenever changes in circumstances indicate the carrying value of the asset may not be recoverable. Such circumstances would include items such as a significant decrease in the market price of a long-lived asset, a significant adverse change in the manner the asset is being used or planned to be used or in its physical condition or a history of operating or cash flow losses associated with the use of the asset . . . When such events or changes occur, we assess the recoverability of the asset by comparing the carrying value of the asset to the expected future cash flows associated with the asset's planned future use and eventual disposition of the asset, if applicable . . . We utilize marketplace assumptions to calculate the discounted cash flows used in determining the asset's fair value . . . For the year ended December 31, 2007, we recognized approximately $24 million of fixed asset impairment charges.

Required

a. Compute the PPE turnover for 2007 (Sales in 2007 are $8,897 million). Does the level of its PPE turnover suggest that Rohm and Haas is capital intensive? Explain. (*Hint:* The median PPE turnover for all publicly traded companies is approximately 5.03 in 2007.)

b. Rohm and Haas reported depreciation expense of $412 million in 2007. Estimate the useful life, on average, for its depreciable PPE assets.

c. By what percentage are Rohm and Haas' assets "used up" at year-end 2007? What implication does the assets used up computation have for forecasting cash flows?

d. Rohm and Haas reports an asset impairment charge in 2007. How do companies determine if assets are impaired? How do asset impairment charges affect Rohm and Haas' cash flows for 2007? How would we treat these charges for analysis purposes?

IFRS APPLICATIONS

VOLKSWAGEN GROUP DAIMLER AG

I6-44. **Computing and Evaluating Inventory Turnover for Two Companies** (LO2)

European car makers, **Volkswagen Group** (headquartered in Wolfsburg, Germany) and **Daimler AG** (headquartered in Stuttgart, Germany) report the following information.

	Volkswagen			Daimler		
(Euros in millions)	Sales	Cost of Goods Sold	Inventories	Sales	Cost of Goods Sold	Inventories
2008	€113,808	€96,612	€17,816	€98,469	€76,910	€16,805
2009	105,187	91,608	14,124	78,924	65,567	12,845

Required

a. Compute the 2009 inventory turnover and the 2009 gross profit margin (in %) for each of these two companies.

b. Discuss any difference in inventory turnover and gross profit margin between these two companies. Does the difference confirm expectations given their respective business models? Explain.

c. How could the companies improve inventory turnover?

I6-45. **Estimating Useful Life and Percent Used Up** (LO3)

STATOIL ASA

Statoil ASA, headquartered in Stavanger, Norway, is a fully integrated petroleum company. The company uses IFRS to prepare its financial statements. During 2009, the company reported depreciation expense of NOK million 46,596. The property and equipment footnote from the Statoil balance sheet follows.

Equipment Operations (In NOK million, Norwegian Kroner)	2009	2008
Land and buildings...	15,735	16,528
Machinery, equipment, and transportation equipment	18,542	18,224
Production plants (including pipelines)	618,487	582,066
Refining and manufacturing plants	43,354	41,484
Vessels	4,079	5,604
Assets under development.................................	89,221	77,883
Total at cost	789,418	741,789
Less accumulated depreciation.............................	448,583	411,948
Total	340,835	329,841

Required

a. Compute the estimated useful life of Statoil's depreciable assets at year-end 2009. Assume that land is 25% of "Land and buildings."

b. Estimate the percent used up of Statoil's depreciable assets at year-end 2009. How do we interpret this figure?

I6-46. **Computing and Evaluating Receivables, Inventory and PPE Turnovers**   (LO1, 2, 3)

Schneider Electric is a multinational energy company headquartered in Rueil-Malmaison, France. Selected balance sheet and income statement information for 2007 through 2009 follows.

SCHNEIDER
ELECTRIC

(€ in millions)	Sales	Cost of Goods Sold	Trade Receivables	Inventories	Plant, property, and equipment, net
2007	€17,309	€10,210	€3,463	€2,481	€1,856
2008	18,311	10,879	3,537	2,584	1,970
2009	15,793	9,572	3,071	2,174	1,965

Required

a. Compute the receivables, inventory, and PPE turnover ratios for both 2008 and 2009.

b. What changes are evident in the turnover rates of Schneider Electric for these years?

c. Discuss ways in which a company such as Schneider Electric can improve receivables, inventory, and PPE turnover ratios.

I6-47. **Analyzing and Interpreting Receivables and Related Ratios**   (LO1)

Unilever is a dual-listed company consisting of **Unilever N.V.** in Rotterdam, Netherlands and **Unilever PLC** in London, UK. Both Unilever companies have the same directors and effectively operate as a single business. Following is the current asset section of Unilever's balance sheet.

UNILEVER
UNILEVER N.V.
UNILEVER PLC

(€ million)	2009	2008
Inventories	€ 3,578	€ 3,889
Trade receivables, net of allowance for doubtful accounts of €129 and €120, respectively......................................	2,314	2,788
Prepayments, accrued income, and other receivables	1,115	1,035
Current tax assets	173	234
Cash and equivalents.......................................	2,642	2,561
Other financial assets.......................................	972	632
Non-current assets held for sale	17	36
Total current assets	€10,811	€11,175

Required

a. What are Unilever's gross trade and other current receivables at the end of 2009 and of 2008?

b. For both 2009 and 2008, compute the ratio of the allowance for uncollectible accounts to gross receivables. What trend do we observe?

c. Is the ratio of Unilever's allowance for uncollectible accounts to gross accounts receivable consistent with what we expect for Unilever's line of business? Explain.

d. The company reported net sales of €39,823 in 2009. Compute the receivables turnover ratio and the average collection period for 2009 based on gross receivables computed in part *a.*

I6-48.   **Analyzing and Interpreting Inventories and Related Ratios**   **(LO2)**

Dr Reddy's Laboratories Limited is an Indian pharmaceutical manufacturer headquartered in Hyderabad, India. The company uses IFRS to prepare its financial statements. The 2010 balance sheet reported the following information.

Year ended March 31	2010 Rs. millions	2009 Rs. millions
Cash and cash equivalents	₹ 6,584	₹ 5,596
Investments	3,600	530
Trade receivables, net	11,960	14,592
Inventories	13,371	13,226
Derivative financial instruments	573	0
Current tax assets	530	58
Other current assets	5,445	5,008
Total current assets	**₹42,063**	**₹39,010**

Required

a.   Compute inventory turnover and average inventory days outstanding for 2009 (2009 cost of goods sold is Rs. Millions ₹33,937). Comment on the level of these two ratios. Is the level what we expect given Dr Reddy's industry? Explain.

b.   GAAP allows for FIFO, LIFO, and average cost inventory costing methods. How does IFRS differ?

c.   In periods of rising prices, how will net income be affected under the different inventory costing methods?

DISCUSSION POINTS

D6-49.   **Managing Operating Asset Reduction**   **(LO1, 2, 3)**

Return on net operating assets (RNOA = NOPAT/Average NOA, see Module 3) is commonly used to evaluate financial performance. If managers cannot increase NOPAT, they can still increase this return by reducing the amount of net operating assets (NOA). List specific ways that managers could reduce the following assets:

a.   Receivables
b.   Inventories
c.   Plant, property and equipment

D6-50.   **Ethics and Governance: Managing the Allowance for Uncollectible Accounts**   **(LO1)**

Assume that you are the CEO of a publicly traded company. Your chief financial officer (CFO) informs you that your company will not be able to meet earnings per share targets for the current quarter. In that event, your stock price will likely decline. The CFO proposes reducing the quarterly provision for uncollectible accounts (bad debts expense) to increase your EPS to the level analysts expect. This will result in an allowance account that is less than it should be. The CFO explains that outsiders cannot easily detect a reduction in this allowance and that the allowance can be increased next quarter. The benefit is that your shareholders will not experience a decline in stock price.

a.   Identify the parties that are likely to be affected by this proposed action.
b.   How will reducing the provision for uncollectible accounts affect the income statement and the balance sheet?
c.   How will reducing the provision for uncollectible accounts in the current period affect the income statement and the balance sheet in a future period?
d.   What argument might the CFO use to convince the company's external auditors that this action is justified?
e.   How might an analyst detect this earnings management activity?
f.   How might this action affect the moral compass of your company? What repercussions might this action have?

SOLUTIONS TO REVIEW PROBLEMS

Mid-Module Review 1

Solution

1. As of December 31, 2012:

Current	$468,000	× 1% =	$ 4,680	
1–60 days past due	244,000	× 5% =	12,200	
61–180 days past due	38,000	× 15% =	5,700	
Over 180 days past due	20,000	× 40% =	8,000	
Amount required.			30,580	
Unused allowance balance			7,000	
Provision.			$ 23,580	2012 bad debts expense

2. Current assets section of balance sheet:

Accounts receivable, net of $30,580 in allowances . . .	$739,420

3. The information here reveals that HP has markedly increased the percentage of the allowance for uncollectible accounts to gross accounts receivable; from the historical 2% to the current 4% ($30,580/$770,000). There are at least two possible interpretations:
    a. The quality of HP's receivables has declined. Possible causes include the following: (1) Sales have stagnated and the company is selling to lower-quality accounts to maintain sales volume; (2) It may have introduced new products for which average credit losses are higher; and (3) Its administration of accounts receivable has become lax.
    b. The company has intentionally increased its allowance account above the level needed for expected future losses so as to reduce current-period income and "bank" that income for future periods (income shifting).

Mid-Module Review 2

Solution

Preliminary computation: Units in ending inventory = 4,800 available − 2,800 sold = 2,000

1. First-in, first-out (FIFO)

Cost of goods sold computation:	Units		Cost		Total
	1,000	@	$18.00	=	$18,000
	1,800	@	$18.25	=	32,850
	2,800				**$50,850**

Cost of goods available for sale.	$88,450
Less: Cost of goods sold	50,850
Ending inventory ($22,800 + $14,800).	**$37,600**

2. Last-in, first-out (LIFO)

Cost of goods sold computation:	Units		Cost		Total
	1,200	@	$19.00	=	$22,800
	800	@	$18.50	=	14,800
	800	@	$18.25	=	14,600
	2,800				**$52,200**

Cost of goods available for sale.	$88,450
Less: Cost of goods sold	52,200
Ending inventory ($18,000 + [1,000 × $18.25]). . .	**$36,250**

3.   Average cost (AC)

Average unit cost	= $88,450/4,800 units	= $18.427
Cost of goods sold	= 2,800 × $18.427	= $51,596
Ending inventory	= 2,000 × $18.427	= $36,854

4.   *a.*   FIFO is normally the method that most closely reflects physical flow. For example, FIFO would apply to the physical flow of perishable units and to situations where the earlier units acquired are moved out first because of risk of deterioration or obsolescence.

   b.   LIFO results in the highest cost of goods sold during periods of rising costs (as in the HP case); and, accordingly, LIFO yields the lowest net income and the lowest income taxes.

5.   Last-in, first-out with LIFO liquidation

Cost of goods sold computation:	Units	Cost		Total
	800	@ $18.50	=	$14,800
	1,800	@ $18.25	=	32,850
	200	@ $18.00	=	3,600
	2,800			$51,250
Cost of goods available for sale (Beginning inventory + Purchase #1 + Purchase #2)	$65,650			
Less: Cost of goods sold	51,250			
Ending inventory (800 × $18).	$14,400			

The company's LIFO gross profit has increased by $950 ($52,200 − $51,250) because of the LIFO liquidation. The reduction of inventory quantities matched older (lower) cost layers against current selling prices. The company has, in effect, dipped into lower-cost layers to boost current-period profit—all from a simple delay of inventory purchases.

Module-End Review

Solution

1.   *a.*   Straight-line depreciation expense = ($95,000 − $10,000)/5 years = $17,000 per year

   b.   Double-declining-balance (note: twice straight-line rate = 2 × [100%/5 years] = 40%)

Year	Net Book Value × Rate	Depreciation Expense	Accumulated Depreciation
1	$95,000 × 0.40 =	$38,000	$38,000
2	($95,000 − $38,000) × 0.40 =	22,800	60,800
3	($95,000 − $60,800) × 0.40 =	13,680	74,480
4	($95,000 − $74,480) × 0.40 =	8,208	82,688
5	($95,000 − $82,688) × 0.40 =	2,312*	85,000

*The formula value of $4,925 is not reported for Year 5 because doing so would depreciate the asset below the estimated salvage value; only the $2,312 needed to reach salvage value is depreciated.

2.   HP reports the equipment on its balance sheet at its net book value of $44,000.

Equipment, cost	$95,000
Less accumulated depreciation ($17,000 × 3)	51,000
Equipment, net (end of Year 3)	$44,000

3.   The estimated useful life is computed as: Depreciable asset cost/Depreciation expense = $95,000/ $17,000 = 5.6 years. Because companies do not usually disclose salvage values (not required dis-

closure), the useful-life estimate is a bit high for this asset. This estimate is still informative because companies typically only provide a range of useful lives for depreciable assets in the footnotes.

The percent used up is computed as: Accumulated depreciation/Depreciable asset cost = $51,000/$95,000 = 53.7%. The equipment is more than one-half used up at the end of the third year. Again, the lack of knowledge of salvage value yields an underestimate of the percent used up. Still, this estimate is useful in that we know that the company's asset is over one-half used up and is likely to require replacement in about two years (estimated as less than one-half of its estimated useful life of 5.6 years). This replacement will require a cash outflow or financing and should be considered in our projections of future cash flows.

4. The equipment is impaired since the undiscounted expected cash flows ($40,000) are less than the net book value of the equipment ($44,000). HP must write down the equipment to its fair value of $36,000. The effect of this write-down is to reduce the net book value of the equipment by $8,000 ($44,000 − $36,000) and recognize a loss in the income statement.

5. HP must report a gain on this sale of $6,000, computed as proceeds of $50,000 less the net book value of the equipment of $44,000 (see part 2).

1. Analyze and describe the accounting for current operating liabilities, including accounts payable and accrued liabilities. (p. 7-4)

2. Analyze and explain the accounting for current and long-term nonoperating liabilities. (p. 7-10)

3. Explain how credit ratings are determined and analyze their effect on the cost of debt. (p. 7-21)

Liability Recognition and Nonowner Financing

Verizon Communications, Inc., began doing business in 2000, when **Bell Atlantic Corporation** merged with **GTE Corporation**. Verizon is one of the world's leading providers of communications services. It is the largest provider of wireline and wireless communications in the U.S., and is the largest of the "Baby Bells" as of 2010 with over $107 billion in revenues and $220 billion in assets.

VERIZON COMMUNICATIONS

When Ivan Seidenberg became sole CEO of Verizon in mid-2002 (and its chairman in late 2003), the Internet frenzy had cooled and Verizon's stock price had plunged, falling from an all-time high of $70 in late 1999 to $27 in mid-2002. Since then, the stock has fluctuated between $25 and $45 per share.

Verizon survived the Internet and telecom downturn. Now it faces a formidable new challenger: cable. Cable companies spent billions upgrading their infrastructure to offer customers discounted bundled packages of local voice, high-speed Internet connections, and video (Verizon has spent over $50 billion in the past three years). Market analysts estimate that cable companies could capture a quarter of the local voice market over the next decade as they deploy new voice over Internet protocol (VOIP) technology.

While Verizon and the other traditional phone companies see their market positions erode, they also struggle to retain their image as innovators. They face creative pressures from researchers and from companies (including Intel) who continue to develop new wireless technologies.

Competitors are rushing to build networks to deliver TV service and high-speed broadband access and Verizon is spending billions to roll out its FiOS phone, data, and video network to give its customers faster Internet service and an alternative to cable. Indeed, over the past three years, Verizon has spent $50 billion on capital expenditures. The demand for new capital spending is coming at an inopportune time. Verizon is currently saddled with a debt load of over $52 billion as of 2010 (a third of which matures over the next five years) and employee benefit obligations of over 28 billion. It is also paying over $5 billion in stock dividends annually. Faced with a question from a stockholder about why Verizon is not repurchasing its stock given its decline in value, Seidenberg said "our number-one priority for using free cash flow over the last two years has been reducing debt." To that end, over the past two years, Verizon has repaid over $15 billion of its debt.

This module focuses on liabilities; that is, short-term and long-term obligations. Liabilities are one of two financing sources for a company. The other is shareholder financing. Bonds and notes are a major part of most companies' liabilities. In this module, we show how to price liabilities and how the issuance and subsequent payment of

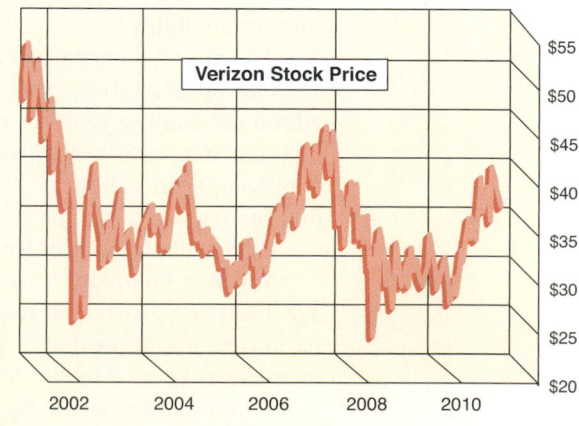

(continued on next page)

(continued from previous page)

the principal and interest affect financial statements. We also discuss the required disclosures that enable us to effectively analyze a company's ability to pay its debts as they come due.

Verizon is now working harder than ever to transform itself in an era of fiber optics and wireless communication. The dilemma facing Seidenberg is how to allocate available cash flow between strategic investment and debt payments.

Source: *Verizon* 2010 10-K and Annual Report to Shareholders.

MODULE ORGANIZATION

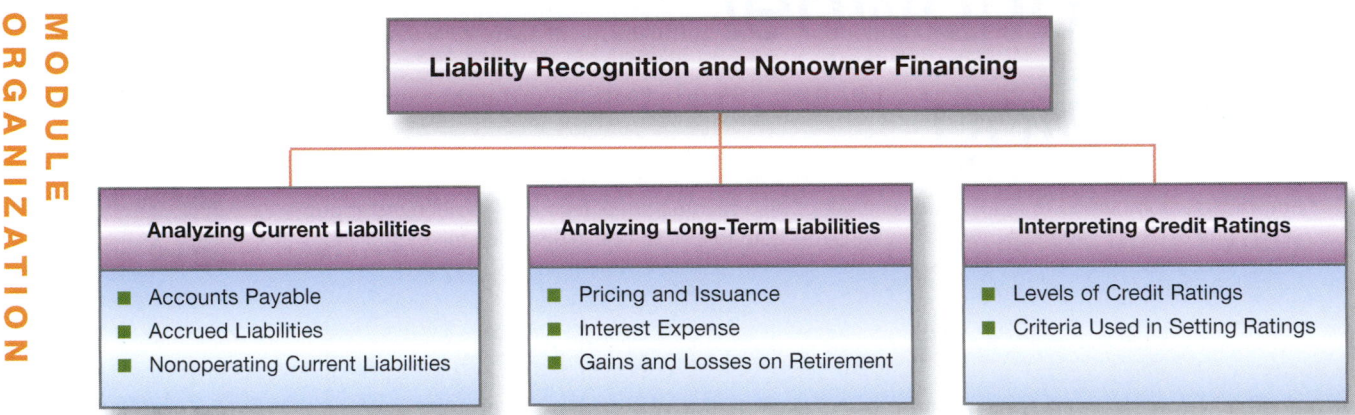

The accounting equation (Assets 5 Liabilities 1 Equity) is a useful tool in helping us think about how the balance sheet and income statement are constructed, the linkages among the financial statements, and the effects of transactions on financial statements. The accounting equation is also useful in helping us think about the statements from another perspective, namely, how the business is financed. Consider the following representation of the accounting equation:

$$\text{Assets} = \text{Liabilities} + \text{Equity}$$
$$\text{Uses of funds} = \text{Sources of funds}$$

Assets represent investments (uses of funds) that management has made. It includes current operating assets such as cash, accounts receivable, and inventories. It also includes long-term operating assets such as manufacturing and administrative facilities. Most companies also invest a portion of funds in nonoperating assets (marketable securities) that provide the liquidity a company needs to conduct transactions and to react to market opportunities and changes.

Just as asset disclosures provide us with information on where a company invests its funds, its liability and equity disclosures inform us as to how those assets are financed. These are the sources of funds. To be successful, a company must not only invest funds wisely, but must also be astute in the manner in which it raises funds. Companies strive to finance their assets at the lowest possible cost. Current liabilities (such as accounts payable and accrued liabilities) are generally non-interest-bearing. As a result, companies try to maximize the financing of their assets with these sources of funds.

Current liabilities, as the name implies, are short-term in nature, generally requiring payment within the coming year. As a result, they are not a suitable source of funding for long-term assets that generate cash flows over several years. Instead, companies often finance long-term assets with long-term liabilities that require payments over several years. Generally, companies try to link the pattern of the cash outflows of the financing source with the cash inflows of the related asset. As such, long-term financing is usually in the form of bonds, notes, and stock issuances.

When a company acquires assets, and finances them with liabilities, its financial leverage increases. Also, the required liability payments increase proportionally with the level of liabilities, and those larger payments imply a higher probability of default should a downturn in business occur. Greater levels of liabilities, then, make the company riskier to investors who, consequently, demand a higher return. Assessing the appropriate level of liabilities is part of liquidity and solvency analysis.

This module describes and analyzes *on-balance-sheet financing*, namely current and non-current liabilities that are reported on financial statements. If companies can find a way to purchase assets and have neither the asset, nor its related financing, appear on the balance sheet, they can report higher levels of asset turnover and appear less risky. This creates off-balance-sheet financing, which is the focus of Module 10.

ANALYZING CURRENT LIABILITIES

Current liabilities consist of both operating and nonoperating liabilities. Most *current operating liabilities* such as those related to inventory (accounts payable) or to utilities, wages, insurance, rent, and taxes (accrued liabilities), impact operating expenses such as cost of goods sold or selling, general and administrative expenses. *Current nonoperating liabilities* comprise short-term bank notes or the current portion of long-term debt. **Verizon**'s balance sheet reports the following current liabilities:

LO1 Analyze and describe the accounting for current operating liabilities, including accounts payable and accrued liabilities.

At December 31 ($ millions)	2010	2009
Debt maturing within one year	$ 7,542	$ 7,205
Accounts payable and accrued liabilities.	15,702	15,223
Other.	7,353	6,708
Total current liabilities.	$30,597	$29,136

Verizon reports three categories of current liabilities: (1) long-term debt obligations that are scheduled for payment in the upcoming year, (2) accounts payable and accrued liabilities, and (3) other current liabilities, which consist mainly of customer deposits, dividends payable, and miscellaneous obligations.

Analysis and interpretation of the return on net operating assets (RNOA) requires that we separate current liabilities into operating and nonoperating components. In general, these two components consist of the following:

1. **Current operating liabilities**
   - **Accounts payable** Obligations to others for amounts owed on purchases of goods and services; these are usually non-interest-bearing.
   - **Accrued liabilities** Obligations for which there is no related external transaction in the current period. These include, for example, accruals for employee wages earned but yet unpaid, accruals for taxes (usually quarterly) on payroll and current period profits, and accruals for other liabilities such as rent, utilities, and insurance. Companies make accruals to properly reflect the liabilities owed as of the financial statement date and the expenses incurred for the period.
   - **Unearned revenue** Obligations to provide goods or services in the coming year; these arise from customers' deposits, subscriptions, or prepayments.
2. **Current nonoperating liabilities**
   - **Short-term interest-bearing debt** Short-term bank borrowings and notes expected to mature in whole or in part during the upcoming year; this item can include any accrued interest payable.
   - **Current maturities of long-term debt** Long-term borrowings that are scheduled to mature in whole or in part during the upcoming year; this current portion of long-term debt includes maturing principal payments only. Any unpaid interest is usually included in the prior item.

The remainder of this section describes, analyzes and interprets current operating liabilities followed by a discussion of current nonoperating liabilities.

Accounts Payable

Accounts payable arise from the purchase of goods and services from others. Accounts payable are normally non-interest-bearing and are, thus, an inexpensive financing source. Verizon does not break out accounts payable on its balance sheet but, instead, reports them with other accruals.

It reports $15,702 million in accounts payable and accrued liabilities in 2010, and $15,223 million in 2009. The footnotes reveal that accounts payable represent $3,936 million in 2010, and $4,337 million in 2009, or 25% of the total each year.

The following financial statement effects template shows the accounting for a typical purchase of goods on credit and the ultimate sale of those goods. A series of four connected transactions illustrate the revenue and cost cycle.

		Balance Sheet						Income Statement			
Transaction	Cash Asset	+	Noncash Assets	=	Liabil- ities	+	Contrib. Capital	+	Earned Capital	Rev- enues	−	Expen- ses	=	Net Income
1. Purchase $100 inventory on credit			+100 Inventory	=	+100 Accounts Payable					−		=	
2a. Sell inventory on credit for $140			+140 Accounts Receivable	=					+140 Retained Earnings	+140 Sales	−		=	+140
2b. Record $100 cost of inventory sold in 2a			−100 Inventory	=					−100 Retained Earnings		−	+100 Cost of Goods Sold	=	−100
3. Collect $140 on accounts receivable	+140 Cash		−140 Accounts Receivable	=							−		=	
4. Pay $100 cash for accounts payable	−100 Cash			=	−100 Accounts Payable						−		=	

Left-margin T-accounts:

```
INV    100
   AP        100
      INV
 100 |
      AP
           | 100

AR     140
   Sales     140
      AR
 140 |
      Sales
           | 140

COGS   100
   INV       100
      COGS
 100 |
      INV
           | 100

Cash   140
   AR        140
      Cash
 140 |
      AR
           | 140

AP     100
   Cash      100
      AP
 100 |
      Cash
           | 100
```

The financial statement effects template reveals several impacts related to the purchase of goods on credit and their ultimate sale.

1. Purchase of inventory is reflected on the balance sheet as an increase in inventory and an increase in accounts payable.

2a. Sale of inventory involves two components—revenue and expense. The revenue part reflects the increase in sales and the increase in accounts receivable (revenue is recognized when earned, even though cash is not yet received).

2b. The expense part of the sales transaction reflects the decrease in inventory and the increase in cost of goods sold (COGS). COGS is reported in the same income statement as the related sale (this expense is recognized because the inventory asset is sold, even though inventory-related payables may not yet be paid).

3. Collection of the receivable reduces accounts receivable and increases cash. It is solely a balance sheet transaction and does not impact the income statement.

4. Cash payment of accounts payable is solely a balance sheet transaction and does not impact income statement accounts (expense relating to inventories is recognized when the inventory is sold or used up, not when the liability is paid).

Accounts Payable Turnover (APT)

Inventories are financed, in large part, by accounts payable (also called *trade credit* or *trade payables*). Such payables usually represent interest-free financing and are, therefore, less expensive than using available cash or borrowed money to finance purchases or inventory production. Accordingly, companies use trade credit whenever possible. This is called *leaning on the trade*.

The **accounts payable turnover** reflects management's success in using trade credit to finance purchases of goods and services. It is computed as:

Accounts Payable Turnover (APT) = Cost of Goods Sold/Average Accounts Payable

Payables reflect the cost of inventory, not its retail value. Thus, to be consistent with the denominator, the ratio uses cost of goods sold (and not sales) in the numerator. Management desires to use trade credit to the greatest extent possible for financing. This means that *a lower accounts payable turnover is preferable.* **Verizon**'s accounts payable turnover rate for 2010 is 10.7 times per year, computed as ($44,149 million/[($3,936 million + $4,337 million)/2]); this compares with 8.5 times three years earlier. This increase in accounts payable turnover indicates that Verizon is paying its obligations more quickly than it has in the past.

A metric analogous to accounts payable turnover is the **accounts payable days outstanding**, which is defined as follows:

Accounts Payable Days Outstanding (APDO) = Accounts Payable/Average Daily Cost of Goods Sold

Because accounts payable are a source of low-cost financing, *management desires to extend the accounts payable days outstanding as long as possible, provided that this action does not harm supply channel relations.* **Verizon**'s accounts payable remain unpaid for 32.5 days in 2010, computed as ($3,936/[$44,149/365 days]), down from 43.7 days three years earlier. Verizon is paying its suppliers more quickly than it has in the past.[1]

Accounts payable reflect a source of interest-free financing. Increased payables reduce the amount of net operating working capital as payables (along with other current operating liabilities) are deducted from current operating assets in the computation of net operating working capital. Also, increased payables mean increased cash flow (as increased liabilities increase net cash from operating activities) and increased profitability (as the level of interest-bearing debt that is required to finance operating assets declines). RNOA increases when companies make use of this low-cost financing source.[2] Yet, companies must be careful to avoid excessive "leaning on the trade" as short-term income gains can yield long-term costs such as damaged supply channels.

MID-MODULE REVIEW 1

Verizon's accounts payable turnover (Cost of goods sold/Average accounts payable) increased from 8.5 in 2007 to 10.7 in 2010.

a. Does this change indicate that accounts payable have increased or decreased relative to cost of goods sold? Explain.
b. What effect does this change have on net cash flows from operating activities?
c. What management concerns, if any, might this change in accounts payable turnover pose?

The solution is on page 7-46.

Accrued Liabilities

Accrued liabilities reflect expenses that have been incurred during the period but not yet paid in cash. Accrued liabilities can also reflect unearned revenue as explained in Module 5. **Verizon** reports details of its accrued liabilities (along with accounts payable) in the following footnote to its 2010 10-K report.

---

[1] Excessive delays in payment of payables can result in suppliers charging a higher price for their goods or, ultimately, refusing to sell to certain buyers. Although a hidden "financing" cost is not interest, it is still a real cost.

[2] Accounts payable often carry credit terms such as 2/10, net 30. These terms give the buyer, for example, 2% off the invoice price of goods purchased if paid within 10 days. Otherwise the entire invoice is payable within 30 days. By failing to take a discount, the buyer is effectively paying 2% interest charge to keep its funds for an additional 20 days. Because there are approximately 18 such 20-day periods in a year (365/20), this equates to an annual rate of interest of about 36%. Thus, borrowing funds at less than 36% to pay this liability within the discount period would be cost effective.

At December 31 ($ in millions)	2010	2009
Accounts payable............................	$ 3,936	$ 4,337
Accrued expenses	4,110	3,486
Accrued vacation, salaries and wages..............	5,686	5,084
Interest payable	813	872
Taxes payable................................	1,157	1,444
Total accounts payable and accrued liabilities........	$15,702	$15,223

Accrued Liabilities (bracket labeling: Accrued expenses, Accrued vacation, salaries and wages, Interest payable, Taxes payable)

Verizon reports one nonoperating accrual: interest payable. Its other accrued liabilities are operating accruals that include miscellaneous accrued expenses, accrued vacation pay, accrued salaries and wages, and accrued taxes. Verizon's accruals are typical. To record accruals, companies recognize a liability on the balance sheet and a corresponding expense on the income statement. This means that liabilities increase, current income decreases, and equity decreases. When an accrued liability is ultimately paid, both cash and the liability decrease (but no expense is recorded because it was recognized previously).

Accounting for Accrued Liabilities

Accounting for a typical accrued liability such as accrued wages, for two consecutive periods, follows:

	Balance Sheet						Income Statement		
Transaction	Cash Asset	+ Noncash Assets	= Liabil- ities	+ Contrib. Capital	+ Earned Capital		Rev- enues	− Expen- ses	= Net Income
Period 1: Accrued $75 for employee wages earned at period-end			= +75 Wages Payable		−75 Retained Earnings			− +75 Wages Expense	= −75
Period 2: Paid $75 for wages earned in prior period	−75 Cash		= −75 Wages Payable					−	=

WE 75
  WP 75
  WE
 75 |
   WP
      75

WP 75
  Cash 75
  WP
 75 |
   Cash
      75

The following financial statement effects result from this accrual of employee wages:

- Employees have worked during a period and have not yet been paid. The effect of this accrual is to increase wages payable on the balance sheet and to recognize wages expense on the income statement. Failure to recognize this liability and associated expense would understate liabilities on the balance sheet and overstate income in the current period and understate income in the subsequent period.

- When the company pays employees in the following period, cash and wages payable both decrease. This payment does not result in expense because the expense was recognized in the prior period when incurred.

The accrued wages illustration relates to events that are fairly certain. We know, for example, when wages are incurred but not paid. Other examples of accruals that are fairly certain are rental costs, insurance premiums, and taxes owed.

Contingent Accrued Liabilities Some accrued liabilities are less certain than others. Consider a company facing a lawsuit. Should it record the possible liability and related expense? The answer depends on the likelihood of occurrence and the ability to estimate the obligation. Specifically, if the obligation is *probable* and the amount *estimable* with reasonable certainty, then a company will recognize this obligation, called a **contingent liability**. If an obligation is only *reasonably possible* (or cannot be reliably estimated), the contingent liability is not reported on the balance sheet and is merely disclosed in the footnotes. All other contingent liabilities that are less than reasonably possible are not disclosed.

Management of Accrued Liabilities Managers have some latitude in determining the amount and timing of accruals. This latitude can lead to misreporting of income and liabilities (unintentional or otherwise). Here's how: If accruals are underestimated, then expenses are underestimated, income is overestimated, and retained earnings are overestimated. In subsequent periods when an understated accrued liability is settled (for more than the "under" estimate), reported income is lower than it should be; this is because prior-period income was higher than it should have been. (The reverse holds for overestimated accruals.) The misreporting of accruals, therefore, shifts income from one period into another. We must be keenly aware of this potential for income shifting as we analyze the financial condition of a company.

Experience tells us that accrued liabilities related to restructuring programs (including severance accruals and accruals for asset write-downs), or to legal and environmental liabilities, or business acquisitions are somewhat problematic. These accruals too often represent early recognition of expenses. Sometimes companies aggressively overestimate one-time accruals and record an even larger expense. This is called taking a *big bath*. The effect of a big bath is to depress current-period income, which relieves future periods of these expenses (thus, shifting income forward in time). Accordingly, we must monitor any change or unusual activity with accrued liabilities and view large one-time charges with skepticism.

IFRS INSIGHT	Accruals and Contingencies under IFRS

IFRS requires that a "provision" be recognized as a liability if a present obligation exists, if it is probable that an outflow of resources is required, and if the obligation can be reasonably estimated. These provisions are basically the same as accruals under GAAP. However, unlike GAAP, contingent liabilities are not recorded for IFRS. Contingencies do not meet the IFRS provisions definition because a present obligation does *not* exist as it may or may not be confirmed by uncertain future events. IFRS requires footnote disclosure of such contingent liabilities unless the eventual payment is remote in which case, no disclosure is required.

Estimating Accruals

Some accrued liabilities require more estimation than others. Warranty liabilities are an example of an accrual that requires managerial assumptions and estimates. Warranties are commitments that manufacturers make to their customers to repair or replace defective products within a specified period of time. The expected cost of this commitment can be reasonably estimated at the time of sale based on past experience. As a result, GAAP requires manufacturers to record the expected cost of warranties as a liability, and to record the related expected warranty expense in the income statement in the same period that the sales revenue is reported.

To illustrate, assume that a company estimates that its defective units amount to 1% of sales and that each unit costs $10 to replace. If sales during the period are $10,000, the estimated warranty expense is $1,000 ($10,000 × 1% × $10). The entries to accrue this liability and its ultimate payment follow.

	Balance Sheet						Income Statement			
Transaction	Cash Asset	+ Noncash Assets	= Liabil- ities	+ Contrib. Capital	+ Earned Capital		Rev- enues	− Expen- ses	= Net Income	
Period 1: Accrued $1,000 of expected warranty costs on units sold during the period			= +1,000 Warranty Payable		−1,000 Retained Earnings			− +1,000 Warranty Expense	= −1,000	
Period 2: Delivered $1,000 in replacement products to cover warranty claims	−1,000 Inventory	=	−1,000 Warranty Payable					−	=	

WRE   1,000
   WRP   1,000

WRE
1,000 |
   WRP
       | 1,000

WRP   1,000
   INV   1,000

WRP
1,000 |
   INV
       | 1,000

Accruing warranty liabilities has the same effect on financial statements as accruing wages expense in the previous section. That is, a liability is recorded on the balance sheet and an expense is reported in the income statement. When the defective product is later replaced (or repaired), the liability is reduced together with the cost of the inventory and/or the cash paid for other costs that were necessary to satisfy the claim. (Only a portion of the products estimated to fail does so in the current period; we expect other product failures in future periods. Management monitors this estimate and adjusts it if failure is higher or lower than expected.) As in the accrual of wages, the expense and the liability are reported when incurred and not when paid.

To illustrate, **Harley-Davidson** reports $54,134 thousand of warranty liability on its 2010 balance sheet. Its footnotes reveal the following additional information:

Product Warranty Estimated warranty costs are reserved for each motorcycle at the time of sale. The warranty reserve is an estimated cost per unit sold based upon historical Company claim data used in combination with other known factors that may affect future warranty claims. The Company updates its warranty estimates quarterly to ensure that the warranty reserves are based on the most current information available. The Company believes that past claim experience is indicative of future claims; however, the factors affecting actual claims can be volatile. As a result, actual claims experience may differ from estimated which could lead to material changes in the Company's warranty provision and related reserves . . . The Company currently provides a standard two-year limited warranty on all new motorcycles sold worldwide, except for Japan, where the Company provides a standard three-year limited warranty on all new motorcycles sold. The warranty coverage for the retail customer includes parts and labor and generally begins when the motorcycle is sold to a retail customer. The Company maintains reserves for future warranty claims using an estimated cost per unit sold, which is based primarily on historical Company claim information. Additionally, the Company has from time to time initiated certain voluntary safety recall campaigns. The Company reserves for all estimated costs associated with safety recalls in the period that the safety recalls are announced. Changes in the Company's warranty and safety recall liability were as follows (in thousands):

Warranty and Safety Recall Liability (in thousands)	2010	2009	2008
Balance, beginning of period	$68,044	$64,543	$70,523
Warranties issued during the period	36,785	51,336	52,645
Settlements made during the period	(58,067)	(74,022)	(71,737)
Recalls and changes to pre-existing warranty liabilities	7,372	26,187	13,112
Balance, end of period	$54,134	$68,044	$64,543

Of the $68,044 thousand balance at the beginning of 2010, Harley incurred costs of $58,067 thousand to replace or repair defective motorcycles during 2010. This reduced Harley's liability by that amount. These costs include cash paid to customers, or to employees as wages, and the cost of parts used for repairs. Harley accrued an additional $44,157 thousand ($36,785 thousand + $7,372 thousand) in new warranty liabilities in 2010. It is important to understand that only the increase in the liability resulting from additional accruals impacts the income statement, reducing income through additional warranty expense. Payments made to settle warranty claims do not affect current-period income; they merely reduce the preexisting liability.

GAAP requires that the warranty liability reflects the estimated amount of cost that the company expects to incur as a result of warranty claims. This is often a difficult estimate to make and is prone to error. There is also the possibility that a company might underestimate its warranty liability to report higher current income, or overestimate it so as to depress current income and create an additional liability on the balance sheet (*cookie jar reserve*) that can be used to absorb future warranty costs and, thus, to reduce future expenses. The overestimation would shift income from the current-period to one or more future periods. Warranty liabilities must, therefore, be examined closely and compared with sales levels. Any deviations from the historical relation of the warranty liability to sales, or from levels reported by competitors, should be scrutinized.

MID-MODULE REVIEW 2

Assume that **Verizon**'s employees worked during the current month and earned $10,000 in wages that Verizon will not pay until the first of next month. Must Verizon recognize any wages liability and expense for the current month? Explain. Use the financial statement effects template to show the effect of this accrual.

The solution is on page 7-47.

Current Nonoperating Liabilities

Current nonoperating liabilities include short-term bank loans, accrued interest on those loans, and the current maturities of long-term debt. Companies generally try to structure their financing so that debt service requirements (payments) coincide with the cash inflows from the assets financed. This means that current assets are usually financed with current liabilities, and that long-term assets are financed with long-term liabilities (and equity).

LO2 Analyze and explain the accounting for current and long-term nonoperating liabilities.

To illustrate, assume that a seasonal company's investment in current assets tends to fluctuate during the year as depicted in the graphic below:

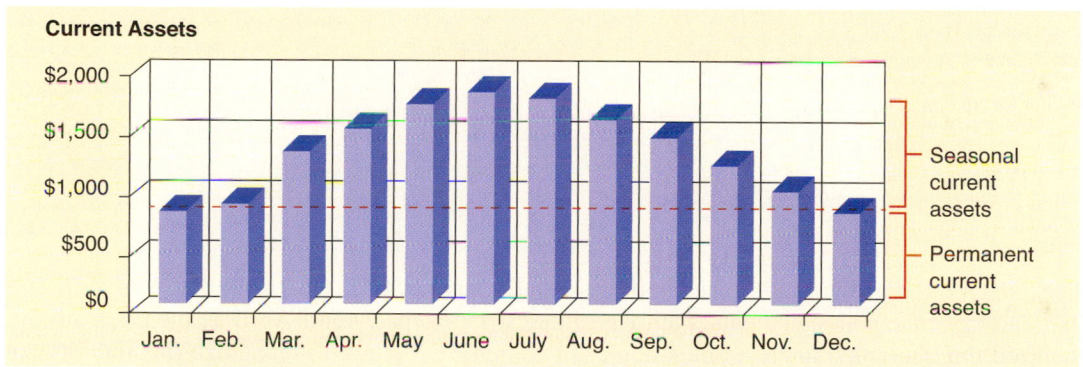

This company does most of its selling in the summer months. More inventory is purchased and manufactured in the early spring than at any other time of the year. High summer sales give rise to accounts receivable that are higher than normal during the fall. The company's working capital peaks at the height of the selling season and is lowest as the business slows in the off-season. There is a permanent level of working capital required for this business (about $750), and a seasonal component (maximum of about $1,000). Different businesses exhibit different patterns in their working capital requirements, but many have both permanent and seasonal components.

The existence of permanent and seasonal current operating assets often requires that financing sources also have permanent and seasonal components. Consider again the company depicted in the graphic above. A portion of the company's assets is in inventories that are financed, in part, with accounts payable and accruals. Thus, we expect that current operating liabilities also exhibit a seasonal component that fluctuates with the level of operations. These payables are generally non-interest-bearing and, thus, provide low-cost financing that should be used to the greatest extent possible. Additional financing needs are covered by short-term interest-bearing debt.

This section focuses on current nonoperating liabilities, which include short-term debt, current maturities of long-term liabilities, and accrued interest expenses.

Short-Term Interest-Bearing Debt

Seasonal swings in working capital are often financed with a bank line of credit (short-term debt). In this case the bank commits to lend up to a maximum amount with the understanding that the amounts borrowed will be repaid in full sometime during the year. An interest-bearing note evidences any such borrowing.

When the company borrows these short-term funds, it reports the cash received on the balance sheet together with an increase in liabilities (notes payable). The note is reported as a current liability because the company expects to repay it within a year. This borrowing has no effect on income or equity. The borrower incurs (and the lender earns) interest on the note as time passes. GAAP requires the borrower to accrue the interest liability and the related interest expense each time financial statements are issued.

To illustrate, assume that **Verizon** borrows $1,000 cash on January 1. The note bears interest at a 12% annual rate, and the interest (3% per quarter) is payable on the first of each subsequent quarter (April 1, July 1, October 1, January 1). Assuming that Verizon issues calendar-quarter financial statements, this borrowing results in the following financial statement effects for January 1 through April 1.

		Balance Sheet						Income Statement		
Transaction	Cash Asset	+ Noncash Assets	= Liabil- ities	+ Contrib. Capital	+ Earned Capital		Rev- enues	− Expen- ses	= Net Income
Jan 1: Borrow $1,000 cash and issue note payable	+1,000 Cash		= +1,000 Note Payable				−	=	
Mar 31: Accrue quarterly interest on 12%, $1,000 note payable			= +30 Interest Payable		−30 Retained Earnings		−	+30 Interest Expense =	−30
Apr 1: Pay $30 cash for interest due	−30 Cash		= −30 Interest Payable				−	=	

Margin T-accounts:

Cash 1,000
NP 1,000
Cash
1,000 |
NP
| 1,000

IE 30
IP 30
IE
30 |
IP
| 30

IP 30
Cash 30
IP
30 |
Cash
| 30

The January 1 borrowing increases both cash and notes payable. On March 31, Verizon issues its quarterly financial statements. Although interest is not paid until April 1, the company has incurred three months' interest obligation as of March 31. Failure to recognize this liability and the expense incurred would not fairly present the financial condition of the company. Accordingly, the quarterly accrued interest payable is computed as follows:

$$\text{Interest Expense} = \text{Principal} \times \text{Annual Rate} \times \text{Portion of Year Outstanding}$$
$$\$30 = \$1,000 \times 12\% \times 3/12$$

The subsequent interest payment on April 1 reduces both cash and the interest payable that Verizon accrued on March 31. There is no expense reported on April 1, as it was recorded the previous day (March 31) when Verizon prepared its financial statements. (For fixed-maturity borrowings specified in days, such as a 90-day note, we assume a 365-day year for interest accrual computations, see Mid-Module Review 3.)

Current Maturities of Long-Term Debt

Principal payments that must be made during the upcoming 12 months on long-term debt (such as for a mortgage), or on bonds and notes that mature within the next year, are reported as current liabilities called *current maturities of long-term debt*. All companies must provide a schedule of the maturities of their long-term debt in the footnotes to the financial statements. To illustrate, Verizon reports $7,542 million in long-term debt due within one year in the current liability section of the balance sheet shown earlier in the module.

MID-MODULE REVIEW 3

Assume that on January 15, **Verizon** borrowed $10,000 on a 90-day, 6% note payable. The bank accrues interest daily based on a 365-day year. Use the financial statement effects template to show the January 31 interest accrual.

The solution is on page 7-47.

ANALYZING LONG-TERM NONOPERATING LIABILITIES

Companies often include long-term nonoperating liabilities in their capital structure to fund long-term assets. Smaller amounts of long-term debt can be readily obtained from banks, private placements with insurance companies, and other credit sources. However, when a large amount of financing is required, the issuance of bonds (and notes) in capital markets is a cost-efficient way to raise funds. The following discussion uses bonds for illustration, but the concepts also apply to long-term notes.

Bonds are structured like any other borrowing. The borrower receives cash and agrees to pay it back with interest. Generally, the entire **face amount** (principal) of the bond is repaid at maturity (at the end of the bond's life) and interest payments are made in the interim (usually semiannually).

Companies that raise funds in the bond market normally work with an underwriter (like **Merrill Lynch**) to set the terms of the bond issue. The underwriter then sells individual bonds (usually in $1,000 denominations) from this general bond issue to its retail clients and professional portfolio managers (like **The Vanguard Group**), and receives a fee for underwriting the bond issue. These bonds are investments for individual investors, other companies, retirement plans and insurance companies.

After they are issued, the bonds can trade in the secondary market just like stocks. Market prices of bonds fluctuate daily despite the fact that the company's obligation for payment of principal and interest normally remains fixed throughout the life of the bond. Then, why do bond prices change? The answer is that the bond's fixed rate of interest can be higher or lower than the interest rates offered on other securities of similar risk. Because bonds compete with other possible investments, bond prices are set relative to the prices of other investments. In a competitive investment market, a particular bond will become more or less desirable depending on the general level of interest rates offered by competing securities. Just as for any item, competitive pressures will cause bond prices to rise and fall.

This section analyzes and interprets the reporting for bonds. We also examine the mechanics of bond pricing and describe the accounting for, and reporting of, bonds.

Pricing of Debt

The following two different interest rates are crucial for pricing debt.

- **Coupon (contract** or **stated) rate** The coupon rate of interest is stated in the bond contract; it is used to compute the dollar amount of interest payments that are paid to bondholders during the life of the bond issue.

- **Market (yield** or **effective) rate** This is the interest rate that investors expect to earn on the investment in this debt security; this rate is used to price the bond.

The coupon (contract) rate is used to compute interest payments and the market (yield) rate is used to price the bond. The coupon rate and the market rate are nearly always different. This is because the coupon rate is fixed prior to issuance of the bond and normally remains fixed throughout its life. Market rates of interest, on the other hand, fluctuate continually with the supply and demand for bonds in the marketplace, general macroeconomic conditions, and the borrower's financial condition.

The bond price, both its initial sales price and the price it trades at in the secondary market subsequent to issuance, equals the present value of the expected cash flows to the bondholder. Specifically, bondholders normally expect to receive two different types of cash flows:

1. **Periodic interest payments** (usually semiannual) during the bond's life; these payments are called an *annuity* because they are equal in amount and made at regular intervals.

2. **Single payment** of the face (principal) amount of the bond at maturity; this is called a *lump-sum* because it occurs only once.

The bond price equals the present value of the periodic interest payments plus the present value of the single payment. If the present value of the two cash flows is equal to the bond's face value, the bond is sold at par. If the present value is less than or greater than the bond's face value, the bond sells at a discount or premium, respectively. We next illustrate the issuance of bonds at three different prices: at par, at a discount, and at a premium.

Bonds Issued at Par

To illustrate a bond issued (also said to be sold) at par, assume that a bond with a face amount of $10 million, has a 6% annual coupon rate payable semiannually (3% semiannual rate), and a maturity of 10 years. Semiannual interest payments are typical for bonds. This means that the issuer pays bondholders two interest payments per year. Each semiannual interest payment is equal to the bond's face value times the annual rate divided by two. Investors purchasing these bonds receive the following cash flows.

	Number of Payments	Dollars per Payment	Total Cash Flows
Semiannual interest payments.....	10 years × 2 = 20	$10,000,000 × 3% = $300,000	$ 6,000,000
Principal payment at maturity......	1	$10,000,000	10,000,000
			$16,000,000

Specifically, the bond agreement dictates that the borrower must make 20 semiannual payments of $300,000 each, computed as $10,000,000 × (6%/2). At maturity, the borrower must repay the $10,000,000 face amount. To price bonds, investors identify the *number* of interest payments and use that number when computing the present value of *both* the interest payments and the principal (face) payment at maturity.

The bond price is the present value of the periodic interest payments (the annuity) plus the present value of the principal payment (the lump sum). In our example, assuming that investors desire a 3% semiannual market rate (yield), the bond sells for $10,000,000, which is computed as follows:

Present value factors are from Appendix A

Calculator
N = 20
I/Yr = 3
PMT = 300,000
FV = 10,000,000

PV = 10,000,000

	Payment	Present Value Factor[a]	Present Value
Interest	$ 300,000	14.87747[b]	$ 4,463,200[d]
Principal	$10,000,000	0.55368[c]	5,536,800
			$10,000,000

[a] Mechanics of using tables to compute present values are explained in Appendix 7A; present value factors come from Appendix A near the end of the book.

[b] Present value of an ordinary annuity for 20 periods discounted at 3% per period.

[c] Present value of a single payment in 20 periods discounted at 3% per period.

[d] Rounded.

Because the bond contract pays investors a 3% semiannual rate when investors demand a 3% semiannual market rate, given the borrower's credit rating and the time to maturity, the investors purchase those bonds at the **par (face) value** of $10 million.

Discount Bonds

As a second illustration, assume investors demand a 4% semiannual return for the 3% semiannual coupon bond, while all other details remain the same. The bond now sells for $8,640,999, computed as follows:

Calculator
N = 20
I/Yr = 4
PMT = 300,000
FV = 10,000,000

PV = 8,640,967.37*

*rounding difference

	Payment	Present Value Factor	Present Value
Interest	$ 300,000	13.59033[a]	$4,077,099
Principal	$10,000,000	0.45639[b]	4,563,900
			$8,640,999

[a] Present value of an ordinary annuity for 20 periods discounted at 4% per period.

[b] Present value of a single payment in 20 periods discounted at 4% per period.

Because the bond carries a coupon rate *lower* than what investors demand, the bond is less desirable and sells at a **discount**. More generally, bonds sell at a discount whenever the coupon rate is less than the market rate.

Premium Bonds

As a third illustration, assume that investors demand a 2% semiannual return for the 3% semiannual coupon bonds, while all other details remain the same. The bond now sells for $11,635,129,
computed as follows:

	Payment	Present Value Factor	Present Value
Interest	$ 300,000	16.35143[a]	$ 4,905,429
Principal	$10,000,000	0.67297[b]	6,729,700
			$11,635,129

[a] Present value of an ordinary annuity for 20 periods discounted at 2% per period.
[b] Present value of a single payment in 20 periods discounted at 2% per period.

Because the bond carries a coupon rate *higher* than what investors demand, the bond is more
desirable and sells at a **premium**. More generally, bonds sell at a premium whenever the coupon
rate is greater than the market rate.[3] Exhibit 7.1 summarizes this relation for bond pricing.

EXHIBIT 7.1	Coupon Rate, Market Rate, and Bond Pricing
Coupon rate > market rate →	Bond sells at a **premium** (above face amount)
Coupon rate = market rate →	Bond sells at **par** (at face amount)
Coupon rate < market rate →	Bond sells at a **discount** (below face amount)

Exhibit 7.2 shows an announcement (called a *tombstone*) of a **Union Pacific Corp** $500
million debt issuance. It has a 4% coupon rate paying 2% semiannual interest, maturing in 2021,
with an issue price of 99.525 (sold at a discount). Union Pacific Corp's underwriters took 0.65%
in fees ($3.25 million) for underwriting and selling this debt issue.[4]

Effective Cost of Debt

When a bond sells for par, the cost to the issuing company is the cash interest paid. In our first
illustration above, the *effective cost* of the bond is the 6% interest paid by the issuer.

When a bond sells at a discount, the issuer must repay more (the face value when the bond
matures) than the cash received at issuance (the discounted bond proceeds). This means that the
effective cost of a discount bond is greater than if the bond had sold at par. A discount is a cost
and, like any other cost, must eventually be transferred from the balance sheet to the income
statement as an expense.

When a bond sells at a premium, the borrower received more cash at issuance than it must
repay. The difference, the premium, is a benefit that must eventually find its way into the
income statement as a *reduction* of interest expense. As a result of the premium, the effective
cost of a premium bond is less than if the bond had sold at par.

Bonds are priced to yield the return (market rate) demanded by investors. Consequently, the
effective rate of a bond *always* equals the yield (market) rate demanded by investors, regardless
of the coupon rate of the bond. This means that companies cannot influence the effective cost
of debt by raising or lowering the coupon rate. Doing so will only result in a bond premium or
discount. We discuss the factors affecting the yield demanded by investors later in the module.

The effective cost of debt is reflected in the amount of interest expense reported in the issuer's
income statement. Because of bond discounts and premiums, interest expense is usually different

[3] Bond prices are often stated in percent form. For example, a bond sold at par is said to be sold at 100 (that is, 100%
of par). The bond sold at $8,640,999 is said to be sold at 86.41 (86.41% of par, computed as $8,640,999/$10,000,000).
The bond sold for a premium is said to be sold at 116.35 (116.35% of the bond's face value).

[4] The tombstone makes clear that if we purchase any of these notes (in denominations of $1,000) after the semiannual
interest date, we must pay accrued interest in addition to the purchase price. This interest is returned to us in the regular
interest payment. (This procedure makes the bookkeeping easier for the issuer/underwriter because all interest payments
are equal regardless of when Union Pacific actually sold the bond.)

EXHIBIT 7.2	Announcement (Tombstone) of Debt Offering to Public

$500,000,000

Union Pacific Corporation

4.00% Notes due 2021

We will pay interest on the notes each February 1 and August 1, commencing February 1, 2011. The notes will mature on February 1, 2021. We may redeem some or all of the notes at any time and from time to time at the redemption price described in this prospectus supplement. There is no sinking fund for the notes. See "Description of the Notes" for a description of the terms of the notes.

	Price to Public (1)	Underwriting Discount	Proceeds to the Company
Per Note	99.525%	0.650%	98.875%
Total	$497,625,000	$3,250,000	$494,375,000

(1) Plus accrued interest, if any, from August 2, 2010.

Neither the Securities and Exchange Commission nor any state securities commission has approved or disapproved of these securities or determined if this prospectus supplement or the accompanying prospectus is truthful or complete. Any representation to the contrary is a criminal offense. Delivery of the notes, in book-entry form only through The Depository Trust Company, will be made on or about August 2, 2010. The date of this prospectus supplement is July 28, 2010.

Joint Book-Running Managers

BofA Merrill Lynch   **J.P. Morgan**   **Morgan Stanley**

Senior Co-Managers

BNP PARIBAS   **Citi**

Co-Managers

Mitsubishi UFJ Securities   **RBS**   **Sun Trust Robinson Humphrey**
US Bancorp   **Wells Fargo Securities**

from the cash interest paid. The next section discusses how management reports, and how we interpret, bonds on the balance sheet and interest expense on the income statement.

ANALYZING DEBT FINANCING

This section identifies and describes the financial statement effects of bond transactions.

Financial Statement Effects of Debt Issuance

Bonds Issued at Par

When a bond sells at par, the issuing company receives the cash proceeds and accepts an obligation to make payments per the bond contract. Specifically, cash is increased and a long-term liability (bonds payable) is increased by the same amount. There is no revenue or expense at bond issuance. Using the facts from our $10 million bond illustration above, the issuance of bonds at par has the following financial statement effects:

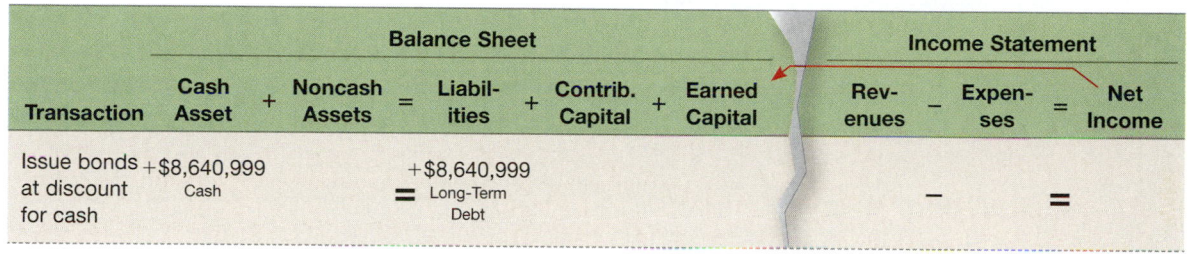

	Balance Sheet							Income Statement		
Transaction	Cash Asset	+	Noncash Assets	=	Liabil- ities	+	Contrib. Capital	+	Earned Capital	
Issue bonds at par for cash	+10,000,000 Cash				+10,000,000 Long-Term Debt					

	Rev- enues	−	Expen- ses	=	Net Income
			−		=

Cash   10,000,000
　　LTD   10,000,000
　　　Cash
10,000,000 |
　　　LTD
　　　| 10,000,000

Discount Bonds

When a bond is sold at a discount, the cash proceeds and net bond liability are recorded at the amount of the proceeds received (not the face amount of the bond). Again, using the facts above from our bond discount illustration, the financial statement effects follow:

	Balance Sheet							Income Statement		
Transaction	Cash Asset	+	Noncash Assets	=	Liabil- ities	+	Contrib. Capital	+	Earned Capital	
Issue bonds at discount for cash	+$8,640,999 Cash				+$8,640,999 Long-Term Debt					

	Rev- enues	−	Expen- ses	=	Net Income
			−		=

Cash   8,640,999
　　LTD   8,640,999
　　　Cash
8,640,999 |
　　　LTD
　　　| 8,640,999

The net bond liability (long-term debt) reported on the balance sheet consists of two components as follows:

Bonds payable, face.	$10,000,000
Less bond discount	(1,359,001)
Bonds payable, net	$ 8,640,999

Bonds are reported on the balance sheet net of any discount. When the bond matures, however, the company is obligated to repay the face amount ($10 million). Accordingly, at maturity, the bonds payable account needs to read $10 million, the amount that is owed. This means that between the bond issuance and its maturity, the discount must decline to zero. This reduction of the discount

---

BUSINESS INSIGHT   **Verizon's Zero-Coupon Debt**

Zero-coupon bonds and notes, called *zeros,* do not carry a coupon rate. Pricing of these bonds and notes is done in the same manner as those with coupon rates—the exception is the absence of an interest annuity. This means that the price is the present value of the principal payment at maturity; hence the bond is sold at a *deep discount.* **Verizon** reported on its zero-coupon debt in its 10-K (the bonds have since been paid off):

> *Zero-Coupon Convertible Notes* The previously issued $5.4 billion zero-coupon convertible notes due 2021, which resulted in gross proceeds of approximately $3 billion, were redeemable at the option of the holders on May 15th in each of the years 2004, 2006, 2011, and 2016. On May 15, 2004, $3,292 million of principal amount of the notes ($1,984 million after unamortized discount) were redeemed. On May 15, 2006, we redeemed the remaining $1,375 million accreted principal of the remaining outstanding zero-coupon convertible principal. The total payment on the date of redemption was $1,377 million.

When Verizon issued its zero-coupon convertible notes in May 2001, they had a maturity value of $5.4 billion and were slated to mature in 2021. No interest is paid in the interim. The notes sold for $3 billion. The difference between the $3 billion sales proceeds and the $5.4 billion maturity value represents Verizon's interest costs, which is the return to the investor. The effective cost of the debt is the interest rate that equates the issue price and maturity value, or approximately 3%.

over the life of the bond is called **amortization**. The next section shows how discount amortization results in additional interest expense in the income statement. This amortization causes the effective interest expense to be greater than the periodic cash interest payments.

Premium Bonds

When a bond is sold at a premium, the cash proceeds and net bond liability are recorded at the amount of the proceeds received (not the face amount of the bond). Again, using the facts above from our premium bond illustration, the financial statement effects follow:

Cash   11,635,129
  LTD   11,635,129
        Cash
11,635,129|
        LTD
           |11,635,129

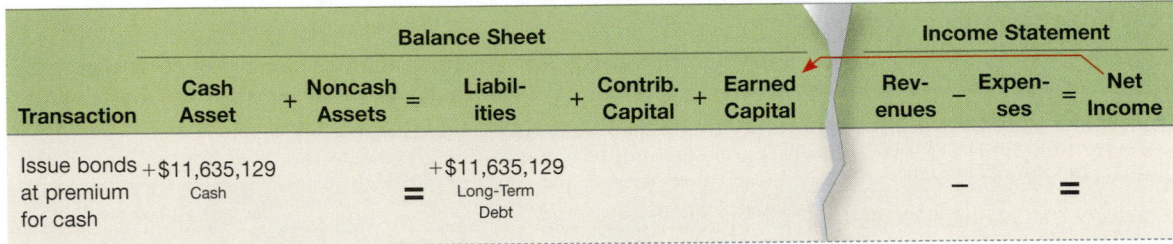

	Balance Sheet						Income Statement		
Transaction	Cash Asset	+ Noncash Assets	= Liabil- ities	+ Contrib. Capital	+ Earned Capital		Rev- enues	− Expen- ses	= Net Income
Issue bonds at premium for cash	+$11,635,129 Cash		= +$11,635,129 Long-Term Debt					−	=

The bond liability reported on the balance sheet, again, consists of two parts:

Bonds payable, face.........	$10,000,000
Add bond premium	1,635,129
Bonds payable, net	$11,635,129

The $10 million must be repaid at maturity, and the premium amortized to zero over the life of the bond. The premium represents a *benefit*, which *reduces* interest expense on the income statement.

Effects of Discount and Premium Amortization

For bonds issued at par, interest expense reported on the income statement equals the cash interest payment. However, for bonds issued at a discount or premium, interest expense reported on the income statement also includes any amortization of the bond discount or premium as follows:

Cash interest paid + Amortization of discount —————————————— Interest expense	Cash interest paid − Amortization of premium —————————————— Interest expense
	or

Specifically, periodic amortization of a discount is added to the cash interest paid to get interest expense. Amortization of the discount reflects the additional cost the issuer incurs from issuing the bonds at a discount. Over the bond's life, the discount is transferred from the balance sheet to the income statement via amortization, as an increase to interest expense. For a premium bond, the premium is a benefit the issuer receives at issuance. Amortization of the premium reduces interest expense over the bond's life. In both cases, interest expense on the income statement represents the *effective cost* of debt (the *nominal cost* of debt is the cash interest paid).

Companies amortize discounts and premiums using the effective interest method. To illustrate, assume that **Verizon** issues bonds with a face amount of $600,000, a 3% annual coupon rate payable semiannually (1.5% semiannual rate), a maturity of three years (six semiannual payment periods), and a market (yield) rate of 4% annual (2% semiannual). These facts yield a bond issue price of $583,195.71, which we round to $583,196 for the bond discount amortization table of Exhibit 7.3.

Calculator
N = 6
I/Yr = 2
PMT = 9,000
FV = 600,000

PV = 583,195.71

EXHIBIT 7.3   Bond Discount Amortization Table

Period	[A] ([E] × market%) Interest Expense	[B] (Face × coupon%) Cash Interest Paid	[C] ([A] − [B]) Discount Amortization	[D] (Prior bal − [C]) Discount Balance	[E] (Face − [D]) Bond Payable, Net
0				$16,804	$583,196
1	$11,664	$ 9,000	$2,664	14,140	585,860
2	11,717	9,000	2,717	11,423	588,577
3	11,772	9,000	2,772	8,651	591,349
4	11,827	9,000	2,827	5,824	594,176
5	11,884	9,000	2,884	2,940	597,060
6	11,940	9,000	2,940	0	600,000
	$70,804	$54,000	$16,804		

During the bond life, carrying value is adjusted to par and the discount to zero

Cash paid plus discount amortization equals interest expense

The interest period is denoted in the left-most column. Period 0 is the point at which the bond is issued, and period 1 and following are successive six-month periods (recall, interest is paid semiannually). Column [A] is interest expense, which is reported in the income statement. Interest expense is computed as the bond's net balance sheet value (the carrying amount of the bond) at the beginning of the period (column [E]) multiplied by the 2% semiannual rate used to compute the bond issue price. Column [B] is cash interest paid, which is a constant $9,000 per the bond contract (face amount × coupon rate). Column [C] is discount amortization, which is the difference between interest expense and cash interest paid. Column [D] is the discount balance, which is the previous balance of the discount less the discount amortization in column [C]. Column [E] is the net bond payable, which is the $600,000 face amount less the unamortized discount from column [D].

The table shows amounts for the six interest payment periods. The amortization process continues until period 6, at which time the discount balance is 0 and the net bond payable is $600,000 (the maturity value). Each semiannual period, interest expense is recorded at 2%, the market rate of interest at the bond's issuance. This rate does not change over the life of the bond, even if the prevailing market interest rates change. An amortization table reveals the financial statement effects of the bond for its duration. Specifically, we see the income statement effects in column [A], the cash effects in column [B], and the balance sheet effects in columns [D] and [E].

To illustrate amortization of a premium bond, we assume that Verizon issues bonds with a $600,000 face value, a 3% annual coupon rate payable semiannually (1.5% semiannual rate), a maturity of three years (six semiannual interest payments), and a 2% annual (1% semiannual) market interest rate. These facts yield a bond issue price of $617,386.43, which we round to $617,386. Exhibit 7.4 shows the premium amortization table for this bond.

Calculator
N = 20
I/Yr = 1
PMT = 300,000
FV = 10,000,000
PV = 617,386

EXHIBIT 7.4   Bond Premium Amortization Table

Period	[A] ([E] × market%) Interest Expense	[B] (Face × coupon%) Cash Interest Paid	[C] ([B] − [A]) Premium Amortization	[D] (Prior bal − [C]) Premium Balance	[E] (Face + [D]) Bond Payable, Net
0				$17,386	$617,386
1	$ 6,174	$ 9,000	$ 2,826	14,560	614,560
2	6,146	9,000	2,854	11,706	611,706
3	6,117	9,000	2,883	8,823	608,823
4	6,088	9,000	2,912	5,911	605,911
5	6,059	9,000	2,941	2,970	602,970
6	6,030	9,000	2,970	0	600,000
	$36,614	$54,000	$17,386		

During the bond life, carrying value is adjusted to par and the premium to zero

Cash paid less premium amortization equals interest expense

Interest expense is computed using the same process that we used for discount bonds. The difference is that the yield rate is 1% semiannual in the premium case. Also, cash interest paid follows from the bond contract (face amount × coupon rate), and the other columns' computations reflect the premium amortization. After period 6, the premium is fully amortized (equals zero) and the net bond payable balance is $600,000, the amount owed at maturity. Again, an amortization table reveals the financial statement effects of the bond—the income statement effects in column [A], the cash effects in column [B], and the balance sheet effects in columns [D] and [E].

Financial Statement Effects of Bond Repurchase

Companies report bonds payable at *historical (adjusted) cost*. Specifically, net bonds payable amounts follow from the amortization table, as do the related cash flows and income statement numbers. All financial statement relations are set when the bond is issued; they do not subsequently change.

Once issued, however, bonds trade in secondary markets. The yield rate used to compute bond prices for these subsequent transactions is the market interest rate prevailing at the time. These rates change daily based on the level of interest rates in the economy and the perceived creditworthiness of the bond issuer.

Companies can and sometimes do repurchase (or *redeem* or *retire*) their bonds prior to maturity. The bond indenture (contract agreement) can include provisions giving the company the right to repurchase its bonds directly from the bond holders. Or, the company can repurchase bonds in the open market. To illustrate, **Verizon**'s 10-K includes the following footnote relating to its repurchase of **MCI** debt in connection with the MCI acquisition:

> **Redemption of Debt Assumed in Merger** On January 17, 2006, Verizon announced offers to purchase two series of MCI senior notes, MCI $1,983 million aggregate principal amount of 6.688% Senior Notes Due 2009 and MCI $1,699 million aggregate principal amount of 7.735% Senior Notes Due 2014, at 101% of their par value . . . In addition, on January 20, 2006, Verizon announced an offer to repurchase MCI $1,983 million aggregate principal amount of 5.908% Senior Notes Due 2007 at 101% of their par value . . . We recorded pretax charges of $26 million ($16 million after-tax) during the first quarter of 2006 resulting from the extinguishment of the debt assumed in connection with the completion of this merger.

When a bond repurchase occurs, a gain or loss usually results, and is computed as follows:

Gain or Loss on Bond Repurchase = Net Bonds Payable − Repurchase Payment

The net bonds payable, also referred to as the *book value,* is the net amount reported on the balance sheet. If the issuer pays more to retire the bonds than the amount carried on its balance sheet, it reports a loss on its income statement, usually called *loss on bond retirement*. The issuer reports a *gain on bond retirement* if the repurchase price is less than the net bonds payable.

GAAP prescribes that gains or losses on bond repurchases be reported as part of ordinary income unless the repurchase meets the criteria for treatment as an extraordinary item (unusual and infrequent, see Module 5). Relatively few debt retirements meet these criteria and, hence, most gains and losses on bond repurchases are reported as part of income from continuing operations.

How should we treat these gains and losses for analysis purposes? That is, do they carry economic effects? The answer is no—the gain or loss on repurchase is exactly offset by the present value of the future cash flow implications of the repurchase (Appendix 7B demonstrates this).

Another analysis issue involves assessing the fair value of bonds and other long-term liabilities. This information is relevant for some investors and creditors in revealing unrealized gains and losses (similar to that reported for marketable securities). GAAP requires companies to provide information about current fair values of their long-term liabilities in footnotes (see Verizon's fair value of debt disclosure in the next section). However, these fair values are *not* reported on the balance sheet and changes in these fair values are not reflected in net income.

We must make our own adjustments to the balance sheet and income statement if we want to include changes in fair values of liabilities.

Financial Statement Footnotes

Companies are required to disclose details about their long-term liabilities, including the amounts borrowed under each debt issuance, the interest rates, maturity dates, and other key provisions. Following is **Verizon**'s disclosure for its long-term debt.

Long-Term Debt Outstanding long-term obligations are as follows:

At December 31 ($ millions)	Interest Rates %	Maturities	2010	2009
Verizon Communications—notes payable and other.	4.35 – 5.50	2011–2018	$ 6,062	$ 6,196
	5.55 – 6.90	2012–2038	10,441	10,386
	7.35 – 8.95	2012–2039	7,677	9,671
Verizon Wireless – notes payable and other.	3.75 – 5.55	2011–2014	7,000	7,000
	7.38 – 8.88	2011–2018	5,975	6,118
	Floating	2011	1,250	6,246
Verizon Wireless—Alltel assumed notes	6.50 – 7.88	2012–2032	2,315	2,334
Telephone subsidiaries—debentures	4.63 – 7.00	2011–2033	7,937	8,797
	7.15 – 7.88	2012–2032	1,449	1,449
	8.00 – 8.75	2011–2031	880	1,080
Other subsidiaries—debentures and other	6.84 – 8.75	2018–2028	1,700	1,700
Employee stock ownership plan loans.	—	—	—	23
Capital lease obligations (average rates of 6.8% and 6.3%, respectively).			332	397
Unamortized discount, net of premium			(224)	(241)
Total long-term debt, including current maturities			52,794	61,156
Less: debt maturing within one year			7,542	6,105
Total long-term debt.			$45,252	$55,051

Verizon reports a net book value for long-term debt of $52,794 million at year-end 2010. Of this amount, $7,542 million matures in the next year and is classified as a current liability (current maturities of long-term debt). The remainder of $45,252 matures after 2011. Verizon also reports $224 million in unamortized discount (net of premium) on this debt.

In addition to long-term debt amounts, rates, and due dates, and as required under GAAP, Verizon reports aggregate maturities for the five years subsequent to the balance sheet date as follows:

Maturities of Long-Term Debt Maturities of long-term debt outstanding at December 31, 2010, are as follows:

Years	(dollars in millions)
2011	$ 7,542
2012	5,902
2013	5,915
2014	3,529
2015	1,201
Thereafter	28,705

This reveals that Verizon is required to make principal payments that total $24,089 million in the next five years and an additional $28,705 million in principal payments thereafter. Such maturities are important information as a company must either meet its required payments, negotiate a rescheduling of the indebtedness, or refinance the debt to avoid default. Failing to repay debts (defaulting) usually has severe consequences as debt holders have legal remedies available to them that can bankrupt the company.

Verizon's disclosure on the fair value of its total debt follows:

At December 31, (dollars in millions)	2010		2009	
	Carrying Amount	Fair Value	Carrying Amount	Fair Value
Short- and long-term debt, excluding capital leases.....	$52,462	$59,020	$61,859	$67,359

As of 2010, indebtedness with a book value of $52,462 million had a fair value of $59,020 million, resulting in an unrecognized liability (which would be realized if Verizon redeemed the debt) of $6,558 million. The increase in fair value is due mainly to a decline in interest rates subsequent to the bonds' issuance (Verizon's credit ratings have not changed in recent years—see next section). The justification for not recognizing unrealized gains and losses on the balance sheet and income statement is that such amounts can reverse with future fluctuations in interest rates. Further, since only the face amount of debt is repaid at maturity, unrealized gains and losses that arise during intervening years do not affect the company's expected cash flows. This is the same logic for nonrecognition of gains and losses on held-to-maturity debt investments (see Module 9).

CREDIT RATINGS AND THE COST OF DEBT

LO3 Explain how credit ratings are determined and analyze their effect on the cost of debt.

Earlier in the module we explained that the effective cost of debt to the issuing company is the market (yield) rate of interest used to price the bond, regardless of the bond coupon rate. The market rate of interest is usually defined as the yield on U.S. Government borrowings such as treasury bills, notes, and bonds, called the *risk-free rate,* plus a *risk premium* (also called a *spread*).

$$\text{Yield Rate} = \text{Risk-Free Rate} + \text{Risk Premium}$$

Both the treasury yield (the so-called risk-free rate) and the corporate yield vary over time as illustrated in the following graphic.

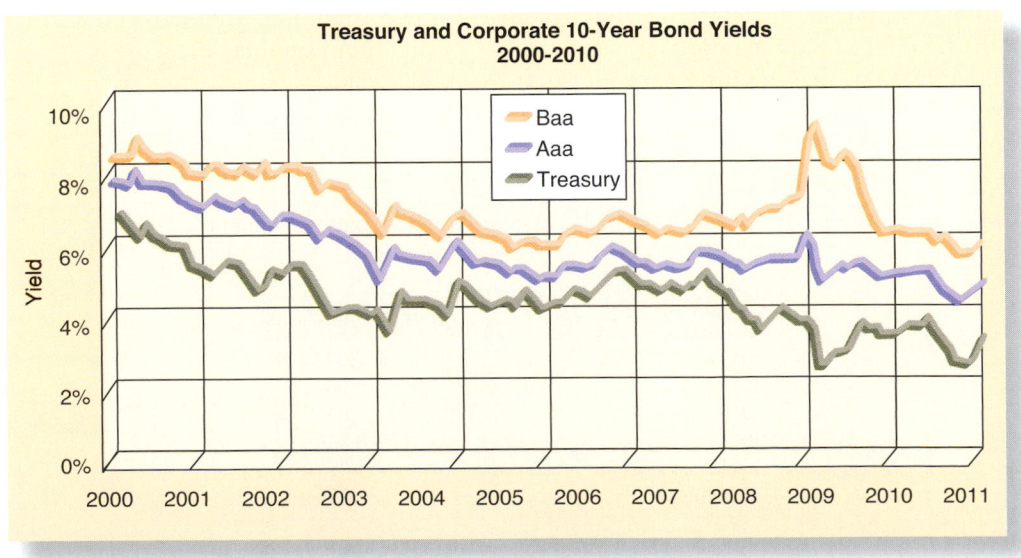

The rate of interest that investors expect for a particular bond is a function of the risk-free rate and the risk premium, where the latter depends on the creditworthiness of the issuing entity.

The yield increases (shifts upward) as debt quality moves from Treasury securities (generally considered to be risk free), which is the highest-quality debt reflected in the lowest line in the graph, to the Aaa (highest) rated corporates and, finally, to the Baa (lower-rated) corporates shown in this graph. That is, higher credit-rated issuers warrant a lower rate than lower credit-rated issuers. This difference is substantial. For example, in December of 2010, the average 10-year treasury bond yield is 3.29%, while the Aaa corporate bond yield is 5.02% and the average Baa (the lowest investment grade corporate bond) yield is 6.10%.

RESEARCH INSIGHT **Accounting Conservatism and Cost of Debt**

Research indicates that companies that use more conservative accounting policies incur a lower cost of debt. Research also suggests that while accounting conservatism can lead to lower-quality accounting income (because such income does not fully reflect economic reality), creditors are more confident in the numbers and view them as more credible. Evidence also implies that companies can lower the required return demanded by creditors (the risk premium) by issuing high-quality financial reports that include enhanced footnote disclosures and detailed supplemental reports.

What Are Credit Ratings?

A company's credit rating, also referred to as debt rating, credit quality, or creditworthiness, is related to default risk. **Default** refers to the nonpayment of interest and principal and/or the failure to adhere to the various terms and conditions (covenants) of the bond indenture. Companies that want to obtain bond financing from the capital markets, normally first seek a rating on their proposed debt issuance from one of several rating agencies such as **Standard & Poor's**, **Moody's Investors Service**, or **Fitch Ratings**. The aim of rating agencies is to rate debt so that its default risk is more accurately conveyed to, and priced by, the market. Each rating agency uses its own rating system, as Exhibit 7.5 shows. This exhibit includes the general description for each rating class—for example, AAA is assigned to debt of prime maximum safety (highest in creditworthiness).

EXHIBIT 7.5	Corporate Debt Ratings and Descriptions		
Moody's	**S&P**	**Fitch**	**Description**
Aaa	AAA	AAA	Prime Maximum Safety
Aa1	AA+	AA+	High Grade, High Quality
Aa2	AA	AA	
Aa3	AA−	AA−	
A1	A+	A+	Upper-Medium Grade
A2	A	A	
A3	A−	A−	
Baa1	BBB+	BBB+	Lower-Medium Grade
Baa2	BBB	BBB	
Baa3	BBB−	BBB−	
Ba1	BB+	BB+	Non-Investment Grade
Ba2	BB	BB	Speculative
Ba3	BB−	BB−	
B1	B+	B+	Highly Speculative
B2	B	B	
B3	B−	B−	
Caa1	CCC+	CCC	Substantial Risk
Caa2	CCC		In Poor Standing
Caa3	CCC−		
Ca			Extremely Speculative
C			May be in Default
		DDD	Default
		DD	
	D	D	

> **ANALYSIS DECISION   You Are the Vice President of Finance**
>
> Your company is currently rated B1/B+ by the Moody's and S&P credit rating agencies, respectively. You are considering restructuring to increase your company's credit rating. What types of restructurings might you consider? What benefits will your company receive from those restructurings? What costs will your company incur to implement such restructurings? [Answer, p. 7-33]

What Determines Credit Ratings?

Verizon bonds are rated A3, A−, and A by Moody's, S&P, and Fitch, respectively, as of 2010. It is this rating, in conjunction with the maturity of Verizon's bonds, that establishes the market interest rate and the bonds' selling price. There are a number of considerations that affect the rating of a bond. **Standard & Poor's** lists the following factors, categorized by business risk and financial risk, among its credit rating criteria:

Business Risk	**Financial Risk**
Industry characteristics	Financial characteristics
Competitive position (marketing, technology, efficiency, regulation)	Financial policy
	Profitability
Management	Capital structure
	Cash flow protection
	Financial flexibility

Debt ratings convey information primarily to debt investors who are interested in assessing the probability that the borrower will make interest and principal payments on time. If a company defaults on its debt, debt holders seek legal remedies, including forcing the borrower to liquidate its assets to settle obligations. However, in forced liquidations, debt holders rarely realize the entire amounts owed to them.

It's important to bear in mind that debt ratings are opinions. Rating agencies use several financial ratios to assess default risk. A partial listing of ratios utilized by Moody's, together with median averages for various ratings, is in Exhibit 7.6. In examining the ratios, recall that debt is increasingly more risky as we move from the first row, Aaa, to the last, C.

EXHIBIT 7.6	Ratio Values for Different Risk Classes of Corporate Debt*									
	EBITA/ Avg AT	**EBITA/ Int Exp**	**EBITA Margin**	**Oper Margin**	**(FFO + Int Exp)/Int Exp**	**FFO/ Debt**	**RCF/Net Debt**	**Debt/ EBITDA**	**Debt/ Book Cap**	**CAPEX/ Dep**
Aaa......	20.6%	25.6	24.9%	22.8%	23.8	129.5%	83.2%	0.7	20.7%	1.2
Aa.......	12.6%	12.5	21.6%	20.5%	13.6	51.8%	39.4%	1.6	39.3%	1.2
A........	11.8%	7.5	15.0%	14.9%	8.3	40.2%	30.7%	1.9	43.7%	1.0
Baa......	9.0%	4.4	13.1%	12.4%	6.1	27.4%	26.6%	2.7	45.4%	1.1
Ba.......	8.3%	3.1	12.4%	10.9%	4.5	22.3%	23.5%	3.3	50.8%	1.1
B........	6.6%	1.4	9.1%	7.8%	2.6	11.7%	11.6%	5.1	73.8%	0.9
C........	2.3%	0.4	2.8%	3.1%	1.4	3.1%	3.2%	7.7	100.5%	0.7

* Table reports 2010 median values; from Moody's Financial Metrics™, Key Ratios by rating and industry for North American nonfinancial corporations: December 2010 (reproduced with permission).

Ratio	Definition
EBITA/Average Assets	EBITA/Average of Current and Previous Year Assets
EBITA/Interest Expense	EBITA/Interest Expense
EBITA Margin	EBITA/Net Revenue
Operating Margin	Operating Profit/Net Revenue
(FFO + Interest Exp)/Interest Exp	(Funds From Operations + Interest Expense)/Interest Expense
FFO/Debt	Funds From Operations/(Short-Term Debt + Long-Term Debt)
RCF/Debt	(FFO − Preferred Dividends − Common Dividends − Minority Dividends)/(Short-Term Debt + Long-Term Debt)
Debt/EBITDA	(Short-Term Debt + Long-Term Debt)/EBITDA
Debt/Book Capitalization	(Short-Term Debt + Long-Term Debt)/(Short-Term Debt + Long-Term Debt + Deferred Taxes + Minority Interest + Book Equity)
CAPEX/Depreciation Exp	Capital Expenditures/Depreciation Expense

where: EBITA = Earnings from continuing operations before interest, taxes, and amortization
EBITDA = Earnings from continuing operations before interest and taxes, depreciation, and amortization
FFO = Net income from continuing operations plus depreciation, amortization, deferred income taxes, and other noncash items

A review of these ratios indicates that Moody's considers the following factors, grouped by area of emphasis, as relevant in evaluating a company's ability to meet its debt service requirements:

1. Profitability ratios (first four metrics in footnote to Exhibit 7.6)
2. Cash flow ratios (metrics five, six and seven in footnote to Exhibit 7.6)
3. Solvency ratios (last three metrics in footnote to Exhibit 7.6)

Further, these ratios are variants of many of the ratios we describe in Module 3 and elsewhere in the book. Other relevant debt-rating factors include the following:

- **Collateral** Companies can provide security for debt by pledging certain assets against the bond. This is like mortgages on assets. To the extent debt is secured, the debt holder is in a preferred position vis-à-vis other creditors.
- **Covenants** Debt agreements (indentures) can restrict the behavior of the issuing company so as to protect debt holders. For example, covenants commonly prohibit excessive dividend payment, mergers and acquisitions, further borrowing, and commonly prescribe minimum levels for key liquidity and solvency ratios. These covenants provide debt holders an element of control over the issuer's operations because, unlike equity investors, debt holders have no voting rights.
- **Options** Options are sometimes written into debt contracts. Examples are options to convert debt into stock (so that debt holders have a stake in value creation) and options allowing the issuing company to repurchase its debt before maturity (usually at a premium).

> **IFRS Alert**
> Unlike GAAP, IFRS requires that companies treat the conversion feature like an option and revalue it each period using the appropriate market rate. The difference in value each period is recorded as nonoperating revenue or expense.

RESEARCH INSIGHT | **Valuation of Debt Options**

Debt instruments can include features such as conversion options, under which the debt can be converted to common stock. Such conversion features are not accounted for separately under GAAP. Instead, convertible debt is accounted for just like debt with no conversion features (unless the conversion option can be separately traded). However, option-pricing models can be used to estimate the value of such debt features even when no market for those features exists. Empirical results suggest that those debt features represent a substantial part of debt value. These findings contribute to the current debate regarding the separation of compound financial instruments into debt and equity portions for financial statement presentation and analysis.

Any Trends with Credit Ratings?

Companies strive to maintain an "investment-grade" credit rating. This allows them to sell their bonds to institutional investors such as pension, mutual and other investment funds. Many institutional investors will not invest in bonds that are rated below investment-grade rating of Baa3 (Moody's) or BBB- (S&P and Fitch). To achieve a higher credit rating, companies must have lower financial leverage and maintain greater liquidity. This is costly to shareholders. As a result, financial managers face a difficult task in finding the optimal capital structure that maximizes returns to shareholders while reducing the cost of debt capital.

The data suggest that corporate CFOs try to maintain investment-grade bond ratings but do not rely markedly on costly equity capital. Following is a graph of the distribution of companies across bond ratings. Ratings of A and Baa account for nearly half of all corporate issuers, while those issuers in the top ratings categories (Aaa and Aa) account for 14% of corporate issuers (source: Moody's financial metrics 2010).

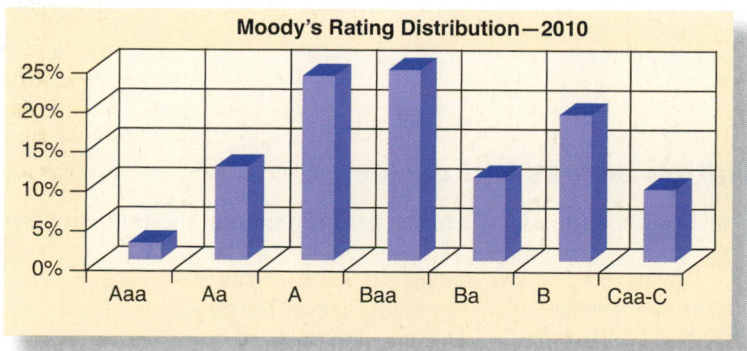

Trends in Financial Ratios Over Time

Many of the ratios we discuss above vary over time with changes in the level of macroeconomic activity. For example, financial leverage (as measured by, average assets / average equity) declined during the recovery following the recession of 2001, then increased as equity declined in the recessionary period of 2007–2008, see below. Measures of profitability and interest coverage exhibited similar trends.

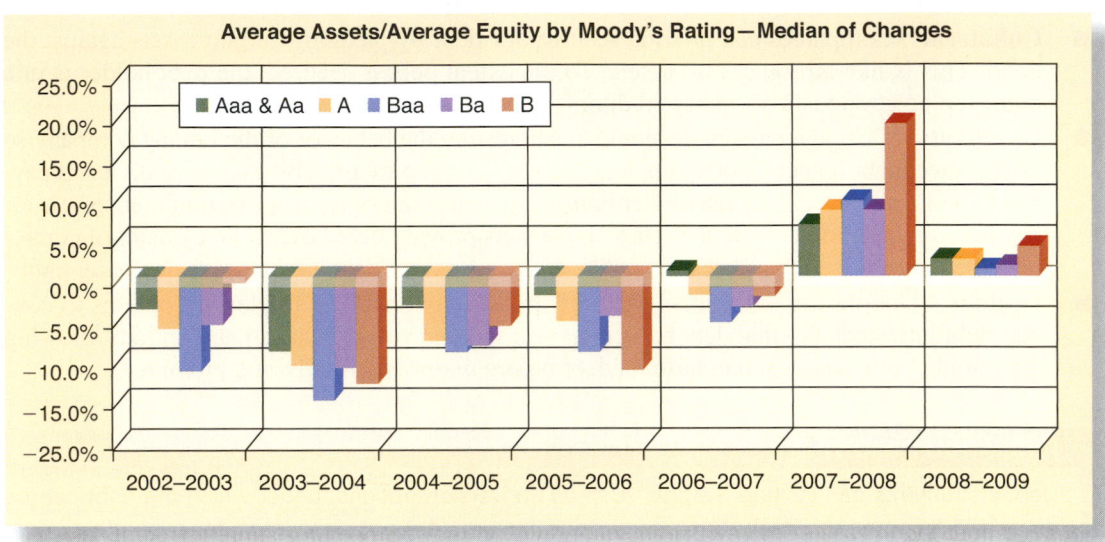

Changes in the level of financial leverage also differed across industries as shown below. Specifically, capital-intensive industries, such as transportation and capital goods reduced financial leverage during the recovery to a much greater extent than did retail and other consumer-related industries.

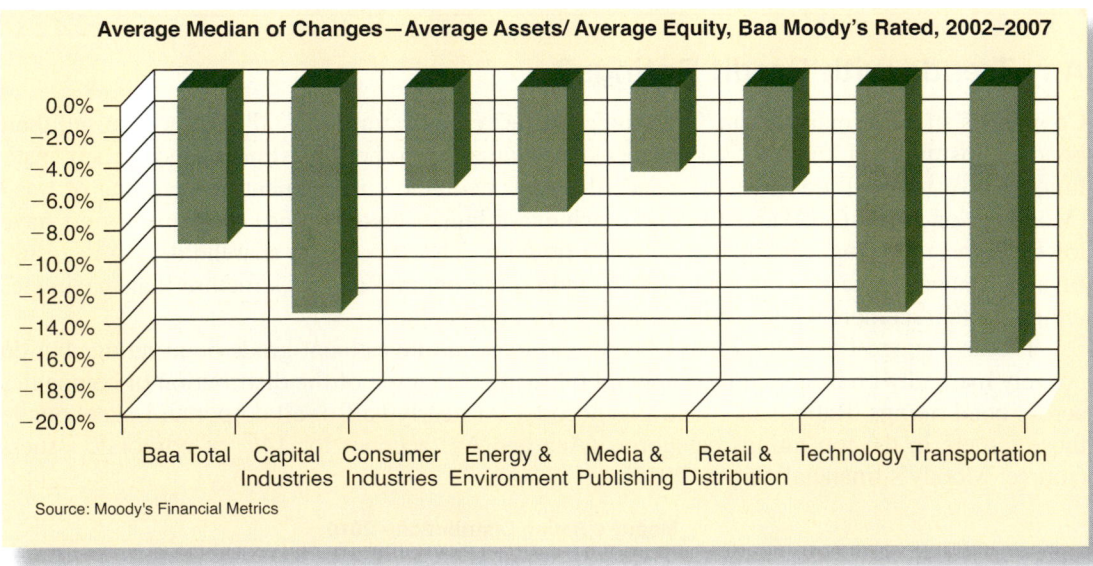

Financial Ratios across Industries

Financial ratios also differ across industries as demonstrated in the following graphic:

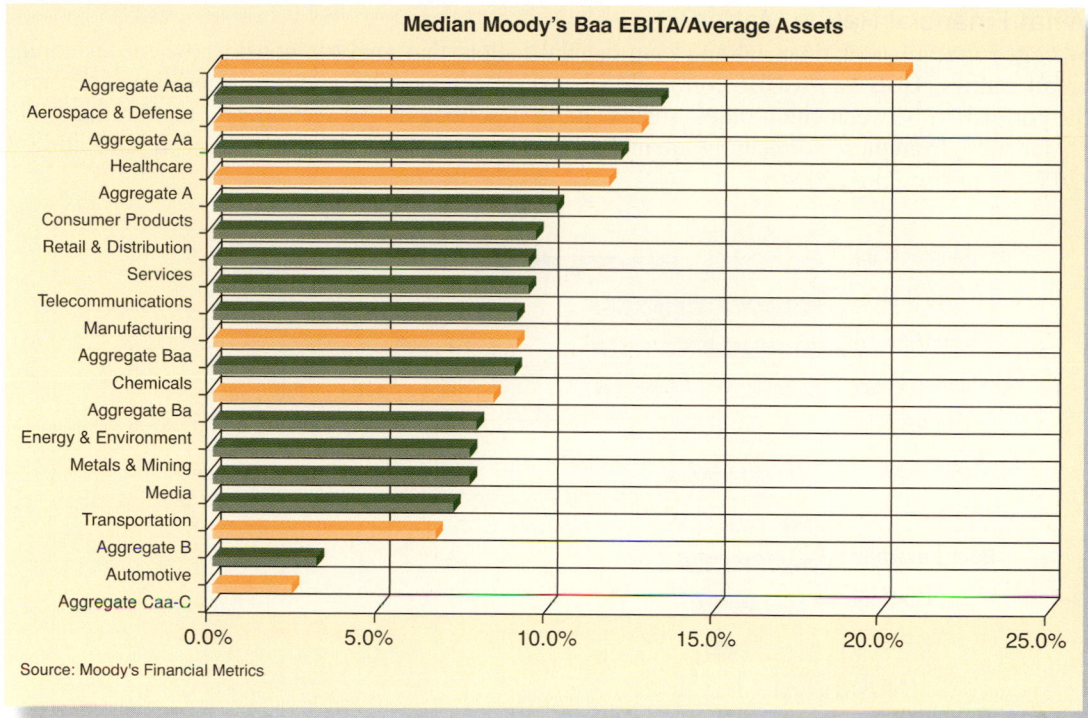

Median EBITA to average assets (a measure of return on assets) for Baa issuers is highest for defense contractors, healthcare, consumer products, and telecommunications industries. This probably reflects a larger required asset base in those industries as the median EBITA margin (EBITA as a percent of revenues) is highest for media companies, which rank much lower on the return measure, as shown in the following graphic.

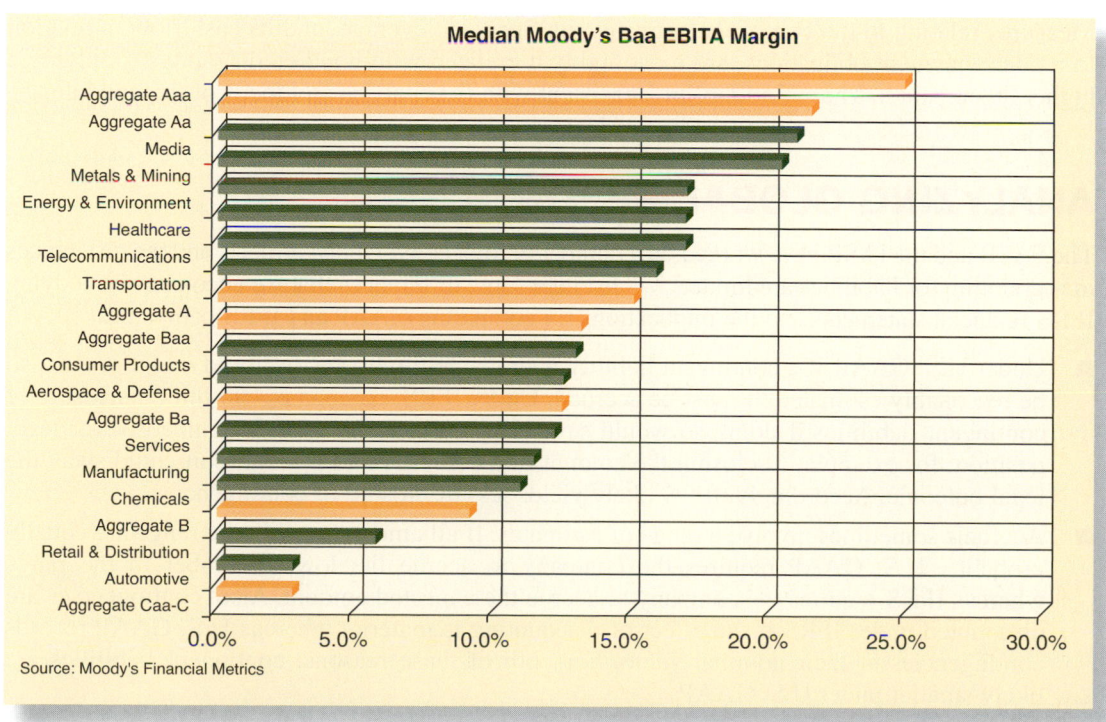

What Financial Ratios Matter?

We cited a number of financial and nonfinancial factors that analysts consider when developing credit ratings. **UBS** (www.UBS.com), global investment banking and securities firm, measured the correlation between credit ratios, such as those described in this section, and bond ratings. The "t-statistics" from those correlations are in the following chart ("The New World of Credit Ratings," *UBS Investment Bank*, 2004):

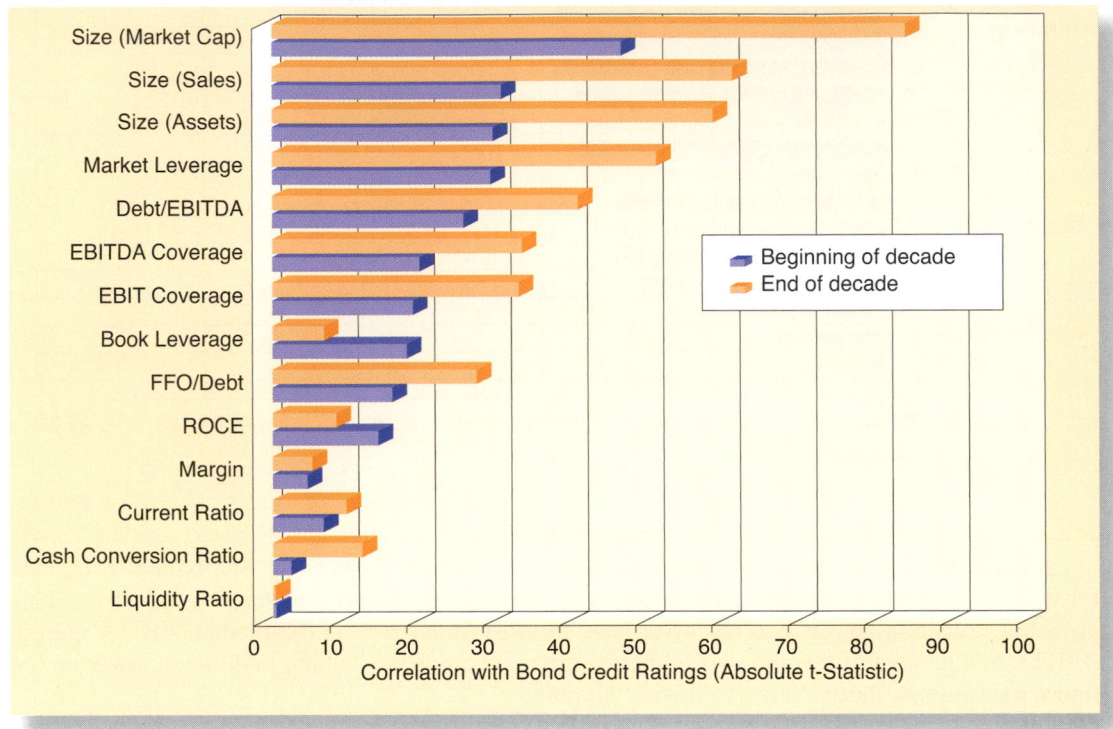

Measures relating to the size of the company, its financial leverage, and its cash flow in relation to its debt payment obligations, are most highly correlated with bond credit ratings (implying a higher "t-statistic"). These findings are consistent with the analysis and focus of this module.

ANALYZING GLOBAL REPORTS

The FASB and the IASB have worked on a number of joint convergence projects and the differences in accounting for liabilities are limited. We list here some differences that we encounter in studying IFRS financial statements and the implications for comparing GAAP and IFRS companies.

- Under U.S. GAAP, if a contingent liability is probable it must be disclosed *and* if it can also be reasonably estimated, it must be accrued. Under IFRS, companies can limit disclosure of contingent liabilities if doing so would severely prejudice the entity's competitive or legal position; for example, disclosing the amount of a potential loss on a lawsuit could sway the legal outcome. Accordingly, IFRS likely yields less disclosure of contingencies.

- Accruals sometimes involve a range of estimates. If all amounts within the range are equally probable, U.S. GAAP requires the company to accrue the lowest number in the range whereas IFRS requires the company to accrue the expected amount. Also, contingencies are discounted under IFRS if the effect of discounting is material whereas U.S. GAAP records contingencies at their nominal value. For both of these reasons, contingent liabilities are likely smaller under U.S. GAAP.

- IFRS offers more disclosure of liabilities and accruals. For each IFRS provision (the term used for accrued liabilities and expenses), the company must reconcile the opening and closing carrying amounts, describe any additional provision for the period, and explain any reversals for the period. Reconciliation is less prevalent under U.S. GAAP (required for example for allowance for doubtful accounts, warranty accruals, restructuring accruals). Recall that an over-accrual in one period shifts income to a subsequent period when the accrual is reversed. This increased transparency under IFRS might make it easier to spot earnings management.

■ U.S. GAAP classifies convertible debt as a liability. Under IFRS, convertible debt is split into two parts: debt and equity (reflecting the option to convert). The amount assigned to each part is based on fair values when the debt is issued. So, for equivalent convertible debt outstanding, IFRS balance sheets show a smaller amount for the debt portion.

MODULE-END REVIEW

On January 1, assume that **Sprint Nextel Corporation** issues $300,000 of 15-year, 10% bonds payable for $351,876, yielding an effective semiannual interest rate of 4%. Interest is payable semiannually on June 30 and December 31. (1) Show computations to confirm the issue price of $351,876, and (2) complete Sprint's financial statement effects template for (a) bond issuance, (b) semiannual interest payment and premium amortization on June 30 of the first year, and (c) semiannual interest payment and premium amortization on December 31 of the first year.

The solution is on page 7-47.

APPENDIX 7A: Compound Interest

This appendix explains the concepts of present and future value, which are useful for our analysis purposes.

Present Value Concepts

Would you rather receive a dollar now or a dollar one year from now? Most people would answer, a dollar now. Intuition tells us that a dollar received now is more valuable than the same amount received sometime in the future. Sound reasons exist for choosing the dollar now, the most obvious of which concerns risk. Because the future is uncertain, any number of events can prevent us from receiving the dollar a year from now. To avoid this risk, we choose the earlier date. Another reason is that the dollar received now could be invested. That is, one year from now, we would have the dollar and the interest earned on that dollar.

Present Value of a Single Amount

Risk and interest factors yield the following generalizations: (1) the right to receive an amount of money now, its **present value**, is worth more than the right to receive the same amount later, its **future value**; (2) the longer we must wait to receive an amount, the less attractive the receipt is; (3) the greater the interest rate the greater the amount we will receive in the future. (Putting 2 and 3 together we see that the difference between the present value of an amount and its future value is a function of both interest rate and time, that is, Principal × Interest Rate × Time); and (4) the more risk associated with any situation, the higher the interest rate.

To illustrate, let's compute the amount we would need to receive today (the present value) that would be equivalent to receiving $100 one year from now if money can be invested at 10%. We recognize intuitively that, with a 10% interest rate, the present value (the equivalent amount today) will be less than $100. The $100 received in the future must include 10% interest earned for the year. Thus, the $100 received in one year (the future value) must be 1.10 times the amount received today (the present value). Dividing $100/1.10, we obtain a present value of $90.91 (rounded). This means that we would do as well to accept $90.91 today as to wait one year and receive $100. To confirm the equality of the $90.91 receipt now to a $100 receipt one year later, we calculate the future value of $90.91 at 10% for one year as follows:

$90.91 × 1.10 × 1 year = $100 (rounded)

To generalize, we compute the present value of a future receipt by *discounting* the future receipt back to the present at an appropriate interest rate (also called the *discount rate*). We present this schematically below:

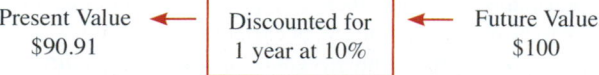

If either the time period or the interest rate were increased, the resulting present value would decrease. If more than one time period is involved, our future receipts include interest on interest. This is called *compounding*.

Time Value of Money Tables

Appendix A near the end of the book includes time value of money tables. Table 1 is a present value table that we can use to compute the present value of future amounts. A present value table provides present value factors (multipliers) for many combinations of time periods and interest rates that determine the present value of $1.

Present value tables are used as follows. First, determine the number of interest compounding periods involved (three years compounded annually are 3 periods, and three years compounded semiannually are 6 periods). The extreme left-hand column indicates the number of periods. It is important to distinguish between years and compounding periods. The table is for compounding periods (years × number of compounding periods per year).

Next, determine the interest rate per compounding period. Interest rates are usually quoted on a *per year* (annual) basis. The rate per compounding period is the annual rate divided by the number of compounding periods per year. For example, an interest rate of 10% *per year* would be 10% per period if compounded annually, and 5% *per period* if compounded semiannually.

Finally, locate the present value factor, which is at the intersection of the row of the appropriate number of compounding periods and the column of the appropriate interest rate per compounding period. Multiply this factor by the dollars that will be paid or received in the future.

All values in Table 1 are less than 1.0 because the present value of $1 received in the future is always smaller than $1. As the interest rate increases (moving from left to right in the table) or the number of periods increases (moving from top to bottom), the present value factors decline. This illustrates two important facts: (1) present values decline as interest rates increase, and (2) present values decline as the time lengthens. Consider the following three cases:

Calculator
N = 2
I/Yr = 5
PMT = 0
FV = 100

PV = 90.703

Case 1. Compute the present value of $100 to be received one year from today, discounted at 10% compounded semiannually:

> Number of periods (one year, semiannually) = 2
> Rate per period (10%/2) = 5%
> Multiplier = 0.90703
> Present value = $100.00 × 0.90703 = $90.70 (rounded)

Calculator
N = 4
I/Yr = 5
PMT = 0
FV = 100

PV = 82.270

Case 2. Compute the present value of $100 to be received two years from today, discounted at 10% compounded semiannually:

> Number of periods (two years, semiannually) = 4
> Rate per period (10%/2) = 5%
> Multiplier = 0.82270
> Present value = $100 × 0.82270 = $82.27 (rounded)

Calculator
N = 4
I/Yr = 6
PMT = 0
FV = 100

PV = 79.209

Case 3. Compute the present value of $100 to be received two years from today, discounted at 12% compounded semiannually:

> Number of periods (two years, semiannually) = 4
> Rate per period (12%/2) = 6%
> Multiplier = 0.79209
> Present value = $100 = 0.79209 = $79.21 (rounded)

In Case 2, the present value of $82.27 is less than for Case 1 ($90.70) because the time increased from two to four compounding periods—the longer we must wait for money, the lower its value to us today. Then in Case 3, the present value of $79.21 was lower than in Case 2 because, while there were still four compounding periods, the interest rate per year was higher (12% annually instead of 10%)—the higher the interest rate the more interest that could have been earned on the money and therefore the lower the value today.

Present Value of an Annuity

In the examples above, we computed the present value of a single amount (also called a lump sum) made or received in the future. Often, future cash flows involve the same amount being paid or received each period. Examples include semiannual interest payments on bonds, quarterly dividend receipts, or monthly insurance premiums. If the payment or the receipt (the cash flow) is equally spaced over time and each cash flow is the same dollar amount, we have an *annuity*. One way to calculate the present value of the annuity would be to calculate the present value of each future cash flow separately. However, there is a more convenient method.

To illustrate, assume $100 is to be received at the end of each of the next three years as an annuity. When annuity amounts occur at the *end of each period*, the annuity is called an *ordinary annuity*. As shown below, the present value of this ordinary annuity can be computed from Table 1 by computing the present value of each of the three individual receipts and summing them (assume a 5% annual rate).

Future Receipts (ordinary annuity)			PV Multiplier (Table 1)		Present Value
Year 1	**Year 2**	**Year 3**			
$100			× 0.95238	=	$ 95.24
	$100		× 0.90703	=	90.70
		$100	× 0.86384	=	86.38
			2.72325		$272.32

Calculator
N = 3
I/Yr = 5
PMT = 100
FV = 0

PV = 272.32

Table 2 in Appendix A provides a single multiplier for computing the present value of an ordinary annuity. Referring to Table 2 in the row for three periods and the column for 5%, we see that the multiplier is 2.72325. When applied to the $100 annuity amount, the multiplier gives a present value of $272.33. As shown above, the same present value (with 1 cent rounding error) is derived by summing the three separate multipliers from Table 1. Considerable computations are avoided by using annuity tables.

Bond Valuation

Recall that a bond agreement specifies a pattern of future cash flows—usually a series of interest payments and a single payment of the face amount at maturity, and bonds are priced using the prevailing market rate on the day the bond is sold. This is the case for the original bond issuance and for subsequent open-market sales. The market rate on the date of the sale is the rate we use to determine the bond's market value (its price). That rate is the bond's *yield*. The selling price of a bond is determined as follows:

1. Use Table 1 to compute the present value of the future principal payment at the prevailing market rate.
2. Use Table 2 to compute the present value of the future series of interest payments (the annuity) at the prevailing market rate.
3. Add the present values from steps 1 and 2.

EXHIBIT 7A.1 Calculation of Bond Price Using Present Value Tables

Future Cash Flows	Multiplier (Table 1)	Multiplier (Table 2)	Present Values at 4% Semiannually
(1) $100,000 of 8%, 4-year bonds with interest payable semiannually priced to yield 8%.			
Principal payment, $100,000 (a single amount received after 8 semiannual periods)	0.73069		$ 73,069
Interest payments, $4,000 at end of each of 8 semiannual periods		6.73274	26,931
Present value (issue price) of bonds			$100,000

Calculator
N = 8
I/Yr = 4
PMT = 4,000
FV = 100,000

PV = 100,000

Future Cash Flows	Multiplier (Table 1)	Multiplier (Table 2)	Present Values at 5% Semiannually
(2) $100,000 of 8%, 4-year bonds with interest payable semiannually priced to yield 10%.			
Principal payment, $100,000 (a single amount received after 8 semiannual periods)	0.67684		$ 67,684
Interest payments, $4,000 at end of each of 8 semiannual periods		6.46321	25,853
Present value (issue price) of bonds			$ 93,537

Calculator
N = 8
I/Yr = 5
PMT = 4,000
FV = 100,000

PV = 93,536.79

Future Cash Flows	Multiplier (Table 1)	Multiplier (Table 2)	Present Values at 3% Semiannually
(3) $100,000 of 8%, 4-year bonds with interest payable semiannually priced to yield 6%.			
Principal repayment, $100,000 (a single amount received after 8 semiannual periods)	0.78941		$ 78,941
Interest payments, $4,000 at end of each of 8 semiannual periods		7.01969	28,079
Present value (issue price) of bonds			$107,020

Calculator
N = 8
I/Yr = 3
PMT = 4,000
FV = 100,000

PV = 107,019.69

We illustrate in Exhibit 7A.1 the price of $100,000, 8%, four-year bonds paying interest semiannually and sold when the prevailing market rate was (1) 8%, (2) 10% or (3) 6%. Note that the price of 8% bonds sold to yield 8% is the face (or par) value of the bonds. A bond issue price of $93,537 (discount bond) yields 10%. A bond issue price of $107,020 (premium bond) yields 6%.

Time Value of Money Computations Using a Calculator

We can use a financial calculator for time value of money computations. There are five important function keys for these calculations. If we know values for four of those five, the calculator will compute the fifth. Those function keys are:

N	Number of compounding (or discounting) periods
I/Yr	Interest (yield) rate per period—entered in % terms, for example, 12% is entered as 12 and not as 0.12. This key is labeled "interest per year" but it can handle any rate per different compounding periods; for example, if we have semiannual interest payments, our compounding periods are semiannual and the interest rate is the semiannual rate.
FV	Future value of the cash flows, this is a lump sum
PMT	Annuity (coupon) per discount period
PV	Present value of the cash flows, this is a lump sum

Calculator inputs follow for the three examples in Exhibit 7A.1. In these examples, the unknown value is the bond price, which is the present value (PV) of the bond's cash flows. (For additional instruction on entering inputs into a specific calculator, or how to do more complicated computations, review the calculator's user manual or review online calculator tutorials.)

Example (1), Exhibit 7A.1: Bond priced to yield 8%.

N	=	8 (4 years × 2 periods per year = 8 semiannual periods)
I/Yr	=	4 (8% annual yield ÷ 2 periods per year = 4% semiannually)
FV	=	100,000 (face value, which is the lump sum that must be repaid in the future)
PMT	=	4,000 ($100,000 × 4% semiannual coupon rate)
PV	= 100,000	(output obtained from calculator)

Example (2), Exhibit 7A.1: Bond priced to yield 10%.

N = 8   I/Yr = 5   FV = 100,000   PMT = 4,000   PV = 93,537

Example (3), Exhibit 7A.1: Bond priced to yield 6%.

N = 8   I/Yr = 3   FV = 100,000   PMT = 4,000   PV = 107,020

Future Value Concepts

Future Value of a Single Amount

The **future value** of a single sum is the amount that a specific investment is worth at a future date if invested at a given rate of compound interest. To illustrate, suppose that we decide to invest $6,000 in a savings account that pays 6% annual interest and we intend to leave the principal and interest in the account for five years. We assume that interest is credited to the account at the end of each year. The balance in the account at the end of five years is determined using Table 3 in Appendix A, which gives the future value of a dollar, as follows:

Calculator
N = 5
I/Yr = 6
PMT = 0
PV = 6,000
FV = 8,029

$$\textbf{Principal} \times \textbf{Factor} = \textbf{Future Value}$$
$$\$6,000 \times 1.33823 = \$8,029$$

The factor 1.33823 is at the intersection of the row for five periods and the column for 6%.

Next, suppose that the interest is credited to the account semiannually rather than annually. In this situation, there are 10 compounding periods, and we use a 3% semiannual rate (one-half the annual rate because there are two compounding periods per year). The future value calculation follows:

Calculator
N = 10
I/Yr = 3
PMT = 0
PV = 6,000
FV = 8,064

$$\textbf{Principal} \times \textbf{Factor} = \textbf{Future Value}$$
$$\$6,000 \times 1.34392 = \$8,064$$

Future Value of an Annuity

If, instead of investing a single amount, we invest a specified amount *each period,* then we have an annuity. To illustrate, assume that we decide to invest $2,000 at the end of each year for five years at an 8% annual rate of return. To determine the accumulated amount of principal and interest at the end of five years, we refer to Table 4 in Appendix A, which furnishes the future value of a dollar invested at the end of each period. The factor 5.86660 is in the row for five periods and the column for 8%, and the calculation is as follows:

Periodic Payment	×	Factor	=	Future Value
$2,000	×	5.86660	=	$11,733

> **Calculator**
> N = 5
> I/Yr = 8
> PMT = 2,000
> PV = 0
>
> FV = 11,733

If we decide to invest $1,000 at the end of each six months for five years at an 8% annual rate of return, we would use the factor for 10 periods at 4%, as follows:

Periodic Payment	×	Factor	=	Future Value
$1,000	×	12.00611	=	$12,006

> **Calculator**
> N = 10
> I/Yr = 4
> PMT = 1,000
> PV = 0
>
> FV = 12,006

APPENDIX 7B: Economics of Gains and Losses on Bond Repurchases

Is a reported gain or loss on bond repurchases before maturity of economic substance? The short answer is no. To illustrate, assume that on January 1, a company issues $50 million face value bonds with an 8% annual coupon rate. The interest is to be paid semiannually (4% each semiannual period) for a term of five years (10 semiannual periods), at which time the principal will be repaid. If investors demand a 10% annual return (5% semiannually) on their investment, the bond price is computed as follows:

Present value of semiannual interest ($2,000,000 × 7.72173)	=	$15,443,460
Present value of principal ($50,000,000 × 0.61391)	=	30,695,500
Present value of bond	=	$46,138,960

> **Calculator**
> N = 10
> I/Yr = 5
> PMT = 2,000,000
> FV = 50,000,000
>
> PV = 46,138,132*
>
> *rounding difference

This bond's amortization table follows:

EXHIBIT 7B.1	Bond Discount Amortization Table

Period	[A] ([E] × market%) Interest Expense	[B] (Face × coupon%) Cash Interest Paid	[C] ([A] − [B]) Discount Amortization	[D] (Prior bal − [C]) Discount Balance	[E] (Face − [D]) Bond Payable, Net
0				$3,861,040	$46,138,960
1	$2,306,948	$2,000,000	$306,948	3,554,092	46,445,908
2	2,322,295	2,000,000	322,295	3,231,797	46,768,203
3	2,338,410	2,000,000	338,410	2,893,387	47,106,613
4	2,355,331	2,000,000	355,331	2,538,056	47,461,944
5	2,373,097	2,000,000	373,097	2,164,959	47,835,041
6	2,391,752	2,000,000	391,752	1,773,207	48,226,793
7	2,411,340	2,000,000	411,340	1,361,867	48,638,133
8	2,431,907	2,000,000	431,907	929,960	49,070,040
9	2,453,502	2,000,000	453,502	476,458	49,523,542
10	2,476,458	2,000,000	476,458	0	50,000,000

Next, assume we are at period 6 (three years after issuance) and the market rate of interest for this bond has risen from 10% to 12%. The firm decides to retire (redeem) the outstanding bond issue and finances the retirement by issuing new bonds. That is, it issues bonds with a face amount equal to the market value of the old bonds and uses the proceeds to retire the existing (old) bonds. The new bond issue will have a term of two years (four semiannual periods), the remaining life of the existing bond issue.

At the end of the third year, there are four $2,000,000 semiannual interest payments remaining on the old bonds, plus the repayment of the face amount of the bond due at the end of the fourth semiannual period. The present value of this cash flow stream, discounted at the current 12% annual rate (6% semiannual rate) is:

<table>
<tr><td>Present value of semiannual interest ($2,000,000 × 3.46511)</td><td>=</td><td>$ 6,930,220</td></tr>
<tr><td>Present value of principal ($50,000,000 × 0.79209)</td><td>=</td><td>39,604,500</td></tr>
<tr><td>Present value of bond</td><td>=</td><td>$46,534,720</td></tr>
</table>

Calculator
N = 4
I/Yr = 6
PMT = 2,000,000
FV = 50,000,000

PV = 46,534,894*

*rounding difference

This means the company pays $46,534,720 to redeem a bond that is on its books at a carrying amount of $48,226,793. The difference of $1,692,073 is reported as a gain on repurchase (also called *redemption*). GAAP requires this gain be reported in income from continuing operations unless it meets the tests for treatment as an extraordinary item (the item is both unusual and infrequent).

Although the company reports a gain in its income statement, has it actually realized an economic gain? Consider that this company issues new bonds that carry a coupon rate of 12% (6% semiannually) for $46,534,720. If we assume that those bonds are sold with a coupon rate equal to the market rate, they will sell at par (no discount or premium). The interest expense per six-month period, therefore, equals the interest paid in cash, or $2,792,083 ($46,534,720 × 6%). Total expense for the four-period life of the bond is $11,168,333 ($2,792,083 × 4). That amount, plus the $46,534,720 face amount of bonds due at maturity, results in total bond payments of $57,703,053. Had this company not redeemed the bonds, it would have paid four additional interest payments of $2,000,000 each plus the face amount of $50,000,000 at maturity, for total bond payments of $58,000,000. On the surface, it appears that the firm is able to save $296,947 by redeeming the bonds and, therefore, reports a gain. (Also, total interest expense on the new bond issue is $3,168,333 [$11,168,333 − $8,000,000] more than it would have recorded under the old issue; so, although it is recording a present gain, it also incurs future higher interest costs which are not recognized under GAAP.)

However, this gain is misleading. Specifically, this gain has two components. First, interest payments increase by $792,083 per year ($2,792,083 − $2,000,000). Second, the face amount of the bond that must be repaid in four years decreases by $3,465,280 ($50,000,000 − $46,534,720). To evaluate whether a real gain has been realized, we must consider the present value of these cash outflows and savings. The present value of the increased interest outflow, a four-period annuity of $792,083 discounted at 6% per period, is **$2,744,655** ($792,083 × 3.46511). The present value of the reduced maturity amount, $3,465,280 in four periods, is **$2,744,814** ($3,465,280 × 0.79209)—note: the two amounts differ by $159, which is due to rounding. The conclusion is that the two amounts are the same.

This analysis shows there is no real economic gain from early redemption of debt. The present value of the increased interest payments exactly offsets the present value of the decreased amount due at maturity. Why, then, does GAAP yield a gain? The answer lies in use of historical costing. Bonds are reported at amortized cost, that is, the face amount less any applicable discount or plus any premium. These amounts are a function of the bond issue price and its yield rate at issuance, which are both fixed for the life of the bond. Market prices for bonds, however, vary continually with changes in market interest rates. Companies do not adjust bond liabilities for these changes in market value. As a result, when companies redeem bonds, their carrying amount differs from market value and GAAP reports a gain or loss equal to this difference.

GUIDANCE ANSWERS . . . ANALYSIS DECISION

You Are the Vice President of Finance You might consider the types of restructuring that would strengthen financial ratios typically used to assess liquidity and solvency by the rating agencies. Such restructuring includes generating cash by reducing inventory, reallocating cash outflows from investing activities (PPE) to debt reduction, and issuing stock for cash and using the proceeds to reduce debt (an equity for debt recapitalization). These actions increase liquidity or reduce financial leverage and, thus, should improve debt rating. An improved debt rating will attract more investors because your current debt rating is below investment grade and is not a suitable investment for many professionally managed portfolios. An improved debt rating will also lower the interest rate on your debt. Offsetting these benefits are costs such as the following: (1) potential loss of sales from inventory stock-outs; (2) potential future cash flow reductions and loss of market power from reduced PPE investments; and (3) costs of equity issuances (equity costs more than debt because investors demand a higher return to compensate for added risk and, unlike interest payments, dividends are not tax deductible for the company), which can yield a net increase in the total cost of capital. All cost and benefits must be assessed before you pursue any restructuring.

Superscript ^A(^B) denotes assignments based on Appendix 7A (7B).

DISCUSSION QUESTIONS

Q7-1. What does the term *current liabilities* mean? What assets are usually used to settle current liabilities?

Q7-2. What is an accrual? How do accruals impact the balance sheet and the income statement?

Q7-3. What is the difference between a bond's coupon rate and its market interest rate (yield)?

Q7-4. Why do companies report a gain or loss when they repurchase their bonds? Is this a real economic gain or loss?

Q7-5. How do credit (debt) ratings affect the cost of borrowing for a company?

Q7-6. How would you interpret a company's reported gain or loss on the repurchase of its bonds?

Assignments with the ✅ in the margin are available in an online homework system.
See the Preface of the book for details.

MINI EXERCISES

M7-7. **Interpreting a Contingent Liability Footnote** (LO1)

NCI Building Systems reports the following footnote to one of its recent 10-Ks related to its manufacturing of metal coil coatings and metal building components.

NCI BUILDING
SYSTEMS
(NCS)

> We have discovered the existence of trichloroethylene in the ground water at our Southlake, Texas facility. Horizontal delineation concentrations in excess of applicable residential assessment levels have not been fully identified. We have filed an application with the Texas Commission of Environmental Quality ("TCEQ") for entry into the voluntary cleanup program. The cost of required remediation, if any, will vary depending on the nature and extent of the contamination. As of October 28, we have accrued $0.1 million to complete site analysis and testing. At this time, we cannot estimate a loss for any potential remediation costs, but we do not believe there will be a material adverse effect on our Consolidated Financial Statements.

a. How has NCI reported this potential liability on its balance sheet?

b. Does the $0.1 million accrual "to complete site analysis and testing" relate to a contingent liability? Explain.

M7-8. **Analyzing and Computing Financial Statement Effects of Interest** (LO2)

DeFond Company signed a 90-day, 8% note payable for $7,200 on December 16. Use the financial statement effects template to illustrate the year-end December 31 accounting adjustment DeFond must make.

M7-9. **Analyzing and Determining Liability Amounts** (LO1)

For each of the following situations, indicate the liability amount, if any, that is reported on the balance sheet of Basu, Inc., at December 31, 2012.

a. Basu owes $110,000 at year-end 2012 for inventory purchases.

b. Basu agreed to purchase a $28,000 drill press in January 2013.

c. During November and December of 2012, Basu sold products to a customer and warranted them against product failure for 90 days. Estimated costs of honoring this 90-day warranty during 2013 are $2,200.

d. Basu provides a profit-sharing bonus for its executives equal to 5% of reported pretax annual income. The estimated pretax income for 2012 is $600,000. Bonuses are not paid until January of the following year.

M7-10. **Interpreting Relations among Bond Price, Coupon, Yield, and Credit Rating** (LO2, 3)

The following appeared in Yahoo! Finance (reports.finance.yahoo.com) regarding outstanding bonds by **Boston Scientific**.

BOSTON SCIENTIFIC
(BSX)

Price	Coupon (%)	Maturity	Yield to Maturity (%)	Fitch Ratings
120.71	7.375	2040	5.873	BBB
108.42	6.000	2020	4.805	BBB

a. Discuss the relation among the coupon rate, price, and yield for the bond maturing in 2040.

b. Compare the yields on the two bonds. Why are the yields different when the credit ratings are the same?

M7-11. Determining Gain or Loss on Bond Redemption (LO2)

On April 30, one year before maturity, Nissim Company retired $200,000 of its 9% bonds payable at the current market price of 101 (101% of the bond face amount, or $200,000 × 1.01 = $202,000). The bond book value on April 30 is $197,600, reflecting an unamortized discount of $2,400. Bond interest is currently fully paid and recorded up to the date of retirement. What is the gain or loss on retirement of these bonds? Is this gain or loss a real economic gain or loss? Explain.

M7-12. Interpreting Bond Footnote Disclosures (LO2)

Bristol-Myers Squibb reports the following long-term debt as part of its MD&A in its 2010 10-K.

			Obligations Expiring by Period				
Maturity Date	**Total**	**2011**	**2012**	**2013**	**2014**	**2015**	**Later Years**
Long-term debt ...	$4,749	—	—	$597	—	—	$4,152

a. What does the $597 million in 2013 indicate about Bristol-Myers Squibb's future payment obligations?

b. What implications does this payment schedule have for our evaluation of Bristol-Myers Squibb's liquidity and solvency?

M7-13. Classifying Liability-Related Accounts into Balance Sheet or Income Statement (LO2)

Indicate the proper financial statement classification (balance sheet or income statement) for each of the following liability-related accounts.

a. Gain on Bond Retirement   *e.* Bond Interest Expense
b. Discount on Bonds Payable   *f.* Bond Interest Payable (due next period)
c. Mortgage Notes Payable   *g.* Premium on Bonds Payable
d. Bonds Payable   *h.* Loss on Bond Retirement

M7-14. Interpreting Bond Footnote Disclosures (LO2)

Comcast Corporation reports the following information from the Management Discussion and Analysis section of its 2010 10-K.

Debt Covenants We and our cable subsidiaries that have provided guarantees are subject to the covenants and restrictions set forth in the indentures governing our public debt securities and in the credit agreements governing our bank credit facilities. We and the guarantors are in compliance with the covenants, and we believe that neither the covenants nor the restrictions in our indentures or loan documents will limit our ability to operate our business or raise additional capital. We test our compliance with our credit facilities' covenants on an ongoing basis. The only financial covenant in our $6.8 billion revolving credit facility due 2013 pertains to leverage (ratio of debt to operating income before depreciation and amortization). As of December 31, 2010, we met this financial covenant by a significant margin. We do not expect to have to further reduce debt or improve operating results in order to continue to comply with this financial covenant.

a. The financial ratios to which Comcast refers are similar to those discussed in the section on credit ratings and the cost of debt. What effects might these ratios have on the degree of freedom that management has in running Comcast?

b. Violation of debt covenants can be a serious event that could limit our ability to operate our business provision in the debt contract. What pressures might management face if the company's ratios are near covenant limits?

M7-15. Analyzing Financial Statement Effects of Bond Redemption (LO2)

Holthausen Corporation issued $400,000 of 11%, 20-year bonds at 108 on January 1, 2007. Interest is payable semiannually on June 30 and December 31. Through January 1, 2012, Holthausen amortized $5,000 of the bond premium. On January 1, 2012, Holthausen retired the bonds at 103. Use the financial statement effects template to illustrate the bond retirement at January 1, 2012.

M7-16. Analyzing Financial Statement Effects of Bond Redemption (LO2)

Dechow, Inc., issued $250,000 of 8%, 15-year bonds at 96 on July 1, 2007. Interest is payable semiannually on December 31 and June 30. Through June 30, 2012, Dechow amortized $3,000 of the bond discount. On July 1, 2012, Dechow retired the bonds at 101. Use the financial statement effects template to illustrate the bond retirement.

M7-17. Analyzing and Computing Accrued Interest on Notes (LO2)

Compute any interest accrued for each of the following notes payable owed by Penman, Inc., as of December 31, 2012 (assume a 365-day year).

Lender	Issuance Date	Principal	Coupon Rate (%)	Term
Nissim......	11/21/2012	$18,000	10%	120 days
Klein.......	12/13/2012	14,000	9	90 days
Bildersee....	12/19/2012	16,000	12	60 days

M7-18. Interpreting Credit Ratings (LO3)

Cummins reports the following information in the Management Discussion & Analysis section of its 2010 10-K report.

CUMMINS (CMI)

> **Credit Ratings** A number of our contractual obligations and financing agreements, such as our revolving credit facility, have restrictive covenants and/or pricing modifications that may be triggered in the event of downward revisions to our corporate credit rating. There were no downgrades of our credit ratings in 2010 that have impacted these covenants or pricing modifications. In January 2011, Fitch affirmed our ratings and upgraded our outlook to positive. In September 2010, Standard and Poor's raised our senior unsecured debt ratings to BBB+ and changed our outlook to stable. In July 2010, Moody's Investors Service, Inc. raised our senior unsecured debt ratings to Baa2 . . . Our ratings and outlook from each of the credit rating agencies as of the date of filing are shown in the table below.
>
> | Credit Rating Agency | Senior L-T Debt Rating | S-T Debt Rating | Outlook |
> |---|---|---|---|
> | Moody's Investors Service, Inc....... | Baa2 | Non-Prime | Stable |
> | Standard and Poor's............. | BBB+ | NR | Stable |
> | Fitch......................... | BBB+ | BBB+ | Positive |

a. Cummins reduced the level of its financial leverage during 2010. Why does the reduction in financial leverage result in an increase in the credit ratings for Cummins' debt?

b. What effect will a higher credit rating have on Cummins' borrowing costs? Explain.

M7-19. Computing Bond Issue Price (LO2)

Bushman, Inc., issues $500,000 of 9% bonds that pay interest semiannually and mature in 10 years. Compute the bond issue price assuming that the prevailing market rate of interest is:

a. 8% per year compounded semiannually.

b. 10% per year compounded semiannually.

M7-20. Computing Issue Price for Zero Coupon Bonds (LO2)

Abarbanell, Inc., issues $500,000 of zero coupon bonds that mature in 10 years. Compute the bond issue price assuming that the bonds' market rate is:

a. 8% per year compounded semiannually.

b. 10% per year compounded semiannually.

M7-21. Determining the Financial Statement Effects of Accounts Payable Transactions (LO1)

Petroni Company had the following transactions relating to its accounts payable.

a. Purchases $300 of inventory on credit.

b. Sells inventory for $420 on credit.

c. Records $300 cost of sales for transaction *b*.

d. Receives $420 cash toward accounts receivable.

e. Pays $300 cash to settle accounts payable.

Use the financial statement effects template to identify the effects (both amounts and accounts) for these transactions.

M7-22. **Computing Bond Issue Price and Preparing an Amortization Table in Excel** (LO2)

On January 1, 2012, Bushman, Inc., issues $500,000 of 9% bonds that pay interest semiannually and mature in 10 years (December 31, 2021).

a. Using the Excel PRICE function, compute the issue price assuming that the bonds' market rate is 8% per year compounded semiannually. (Use 100 for the redemption value to get a price as a percentage of the face amount, and use 1 for the basis.)

b. Prepare an amortization table in Excel to demonstrate the amortization of the book (carrying) value to the $500,000 maturity value at the end of the 20th semiannual period.

EXERCISES

 E7-23. **Analyzing and Computing Accrued Warranty Liability and Expense** (LO1)

Waymire Company sells a motor that carries a 60-day unconditional warranty against product failure. From prior years' experience, Waymire estimates that 2% of units sold each period will require repair at an average cost of $100 per unit. During the current period, Waymire sold 69,000 units and repaired 1,000 of those units.

a. How much warranty expense must Waymire report in its current-period income statement?

b. What warranty liability related to current-period sales will Waymire report on its current period-end balance sheet? (*Hint:* Remember that some units were repaired in the current period.)

c. What analysis issues must we consider with respect to reported warranty liabilities?

 E7-24. **Analyzing Contingent and Other Liabilities** (LO1)

The following independent situations represent various types of liabilities. Analyze each situation and indicate which of the following is the proper accounting treatment for the company: (a) record a liability on the balance sheet, (b) disclose the liability in a financial statement footnote, or (c) neither record nor disclose any liability.

1. A stockholder has filed a lawsuit against **Clinch Corporation**. Clinch's attorneys have reviewed the facts of the case. Their review revealed that similar lawsuits have never resulted in a cash award and it is highly unlikely that this lawsuit will either.

2. **Foster Company** signed a 60-day, 10% note when it purchased items from another company.

3. The Environmental Protection Agency notifies **Shevlin Company** that a state where it has a plant is filing a lawsuit for groundwater pollution against Shevlin and another company that has a plant adjacent to Shevlin's plant. Test results have not identified the exact source of the pollution. Shevlin's manufacturing process often produces by-products that can pollute groundwater.

4. **Sloan Company** manufactured and sold products to a retailer that later sold the products to consumers. The Sloan Company will replace the product if it is found to be defective within 90 days of the sale to the consumer. Historically, 1.2% of the products are returned for replacement.

E7-25. **Recording and Analyzing Warranty Accrual and Payment** (LO1)

HARLEY-DAVIDSON
(HOG)

Refer to the discussion of and excerpt from the **Harley-Davidson** warranty reserve on page 7-9 to answer the following questions.

a. Using the financial statement effects template, record separately the accrual of warranty liability relating (1) to the "Warranties issued during the period" and (2) "Recalls and changes to preexisting warranty obligations" and (3) to the "Settlements made during the period."

b. Does the level of Harley-Davidson's warranty accrual appear to be reasonable?

 E7-26. **Analyzing and Computing Accrued Wages Liability and Expense** (LO1)

Demski Company pays its employees on the 1st and 15th of each month. It is March 31 and Demski is preparing financial statements for this quarter. Its employees have earned $25,000 since the 15th of March and have not yet been paid. How will Demski's balance sheet and income statement reflect the accrual of wages on March 31? What balance sheet and income statement accounts would be incorrectly reported if Demski failed to make this accrual (for each account indicate whether it would be overstated or understated)?

E7-27. **Analyzing and Reporting Financial Statement Effects of Bond Transactions** (LO2)

On January 1, Hutton Corp. issued $300,000 of 15-year, 10% bonds payable for $351,876, yielding an effective interest rate of 8%. Interest is payable semiannually on June 30 and December 31. (a) Show computations to confirm the issue price of $351,876. (b) Indicate the financial statement effects using the template for (1) bond issuance, (2) semiannual interest payment and premium amortization on June 30 of the first year, and (3) semiannual interest payment and premium amortization on December 31 of the first year.

E7-28. **Analyzing and Reporting Financial Statement Effects of Mortgages** (LO2)

On January 1, Piotroski, Inc., borrowed $700,000 on a 12%, 15-year mortgage note payable. The note is to be repaid in equal semiannual installments of $50,854 (payable on June 30 and December 31). Each mortgage payment includes principal and interest. Interest is computed using the effective interest method. Indicate the financial statement effects using the template for (a) issuance of the mortgage note payable, (b) payment of the first installment on June 30, and (c) payment of the second installment on December 31.

E7-29. **Assessing the Effects of Bond Credit Rating Changes** (LO3)

Ford reports the following information from the Risk Factors and the Management Discussion and Analysis sections of its 2010 10-K report.

FORD
(F)

> **Credit Ratings** Our short-term and long-term debt is rated by four credit rating agencies designated as nationally recognized statistical rating organizations ("NRSROs") by the Securities and Exchange Commission:
> - Dominion Bond Rating Service Limited ("DBRS");
> - Fitch, Inc. ("Fitch");
> - Moody's Investors Service, Inc. ("Moody's"); and
> - Standard & Poor's Rating Services, a division of The McGraw-Hill Companies ("S&P").
>
> Lower credit ratings generally result in higher borrowing costs and reduced access to capital markets. In 2005 and 2006, the credit ratings assigned to Ford Credit were lowered to below investment grade, which increased its unsecured borrowing costs and restricted its access to the unsecured debt markets. In response, Ford Credit increased its use of securitization transactions (including other structured financings) and other sources of funding. In 2010, although Ford Credit experienced several credit rating upgrades and its credit spreads narrowed considerably, its credit ratings are still below investment grade. Ford Credit's higher credit ratings have provided it more economical access to the unsecured debt markets, but it is still utilizing asset- backed securitization transactions for a substantial amount of its funding . . . Over time, and particularly in the event of any credit rating downgrades, market volatility, market disruption, or other factors, Ford Credit may reduce the amount of receivables it purchases or originates because of funding constraints . . . A significant reduction in the amount of receivables Ford Credit purchases or originates would significantly reduce its ongoing profits and could adversely affect its ability to support the sale of Ford vehicles. The following ratings actions have been taken by these NRSROs since the filing of our Quarterly Report on Form 10-Q for the quarter ended September 30, 2010:
>
> **Ford**
> - On January 28, 2011, Moody's affirmed Ford Motor Company's ratings and changed the rating outlook to positive from stable.
> - On January 28, 2011, Fitch upgraded Ford's corporate rating to BB from BB- , the senior secured rating to BBB- from BB+, and the senior unsecured rating to BB- from B. Fitch also changed the outlook to positive from stable.
> - On February 1, 2011, S&P upgraded Ford's corporate credit rating to BB- from B+, the senior secured debt rating to BB+ from BB and the senior unsecured debt rating to B+ from B. The outlook remains positive.
>
> **Ford Credit**
> - On January 28, 2011, Moody's affirmed Ford Credit's ratings and changed the rating outlook to positive from stable.
> - On January 28, 2011, Fitch upgraded Ford Credit's corporate rating to BB from BB- . Fitch also affirmed the senior unsecured rating at BB- and the short-term rating at B. Fitch changed the outlook to positive from stable.
> - On February 1, 2011, S&P upgraded Ford Credit's corporate credit rating to BB- from B+ and its senior unsecured debt rating to BB- from B+. The outlook remains positive.

a. What financial ratios do credit rating companies such as the four NRSROs listed above, use to evaluate the relative riskiness of borrowers?

b. Why might an increase in credit ratings result in lower interest costs and increase Ford's access to credit markets?

c. What type of actions can Ford take to improve its credit ratings?

E7-30. **Analyzing and Reporting Financial Statement Effects of Bond Transactions** (LO2)

Lundholm, Inc., reports financial statements each December 31 and issues $500,000 of 9%, 15-year bonds dated May 1, 2012, with interest payments on October 31 and April 30. Assuming the bonds are sold at par on May 1, 2012, complete the financial statement effects template to reflect the following events: (a) bond issuance, (b) the first semiannual interest payment, and (c) retirement of $300,000 of the bonds at 101 on November 1, 2012.

E7-31.   **Analyzing and Reporting Financial Statement Effects of Bond Transactions**   **(LO2)**
On January 1, 2012, McKeown, Inc., issued $250,000 of 8%, 9-year bonds for $220,776, which implies a market (yield) rate of 10%. Semiannual interest is payable on June 30 and December 31 of each year. (a) Show computations to confirm the bond issue price. (b) Indicate the financial statement effects using the template for (1) bond issuance, (2) semiannual interest payment and discount amortization on June 30, 2012, and (3) semiannual interest payment and discount amortization on December 31, 2012.

E7-32.   **Analyzing and Reporting Financial Statement Effects of Bond Transactions**   **(LO2)**
On January 1, 2012, Shields, Inc., issued $800,000 of 9%, 20-year bonds for $879,172, yielding a market (yield) rate of 8%. Semiannual interest is payable on June 30 and December 31 of each year. (a) Show computations to confirm the bond issue price. (b) Indicate the financial statement effects using the template for (1) bond issuance, (2) semiannual interest payment and premium amortization on June 30, 2012, and (3) semiannual interest payment and premium amortization on December 31, 2012.

E7-33.   **Determining Bond Prices, Interest Rates, and Financial Statement Effects**   **(LO2)**
Deere & Company's 2010 10-K reports the following footnote relating to long-term debt for its equipment operations subsidiary. Deere's borrowings include $300 million, 7.125% notes, due in 2031 (highlighted below).

Long-term borrowings at October 31 consisted of the following in millions of dollars:

Notes and debentures	2010	2009
6.95% notes due 2014: ($700 principal) Swapped $300 to variable interest rate of 1.25%—2009	$ 763	$ 800
4.375% notes due 2019	750	750
7-1/2% debentures due 2022	105	105
6.55% debentures due 2028	200	200
5.375% notes due 2029	500	500
8.10% debentures due 2030	250	250
7.125% notes due 2031	**300**	**300**
Other notes	461	168
Total	$3,329	$3,073

A recent price quote (from **Yahoo! Finance Bond Center**) on Deere's 7.125% notes follows.

Type	Issuer	Price	Coupon (%)	Maturity	YTM (%)	Current Yield (%)	Fitch Rating	Callable
Corp	Deere & CO	131.84	7.125	2031	4.650	5.404	A	No

This price quote indicates that Deere's 7.125% notes have a market price of 131.84 (131.84% of face value), resulting in a yield to maturity of 4.65%.

a.   Assuming that these notes were originally issued at par value, what does the market price reveal about interest rate changes since Deere issued its notes? (Assume that Deere's credit rating has remained the same.)

b.   Does the change in interest rates since the issuance of these notes affect the amount of interest expense that Deere reports in its income statement? Explain.

c.   How much cash would Deere have to pay to repurchase the 7.125% notes at the quoted market price of 131.84? (Assume no interest is owed when Deere repurchases the notes.) How would the repurchase affect Deere's current income?

d.   Assuming that the notes remain outstanding until their maturity, at what market price will the notes sell on their due date in 2031?

E7-34.ᴬ   **Computing Present Values of Single Amounts and Annuities**   **(LO2)**
Refer to Tables 1 and 2 in Appendix A near the end of the book to compute the present value for each of the following amounts:

a. $90,000 received 10 years hence if the annual interest rate is:
  1. 8% compounded annually.
  2. 8% compounded semiannually.

b. $1,000 received at the end of each year for the next eight years discounted at 10% compounded annually.

c. $600 received at the end of each six months for the next 15 years if the interest rate is 8% per year compounded semiannually.

d. $500,000 received 10 years hence discounted at 10% per year compounded annually.

E7-35.   Analyzing and Reporting Financial Statement Effects of Bond Transactions   (LO2)
On January 1, 2012, Trueman Corporation issued $600,000 of 20-year, 11% bonds for $554,860, yielding a market (yield) rate of 12%. Interest is payable semiannually on June 30 and December 31. (a) Confirm the bond issue price. (b) Indicate the financial statement effects using the template for (1) bond issuance, (2) semiannual interest payment and discount amortization on June 30, 2012, and (3) semiannual interest payment and discount amortization on December 31, 2012.

E7-36.   Analyzing and Reporting Financial Statement Effects of Bond Transactions   (LO2)
On January 1, 2012, Verrecchia Company issued $400,000 of 5-year, 13% bonds for $446,329, yielding a market (yield) rate of 10%. Interest is payable semiannually on June 30 and December 31. (a) Confirm the bond issue price. (b) Indicate the financial statement effects using the template for (1) bond issuance, (2) semiannual interest payment and premium amortization on June 30, 2012, and (3) semiannual interest payment and premium amortization on December 31, 2012.

PROBLEMS

P7-37.   Interpreting Term Structures of Coupon Rates and Yield Rates   (LO2, 3)
PepsiCo, Inc. reports $20,112 million of long-term debt outstanding as of December 2010 in the following schedule to its 10-K report.

PEPSICO, INC.
(PEP)

Debt Obligations and Commitments

Short-Term Debt Obligations ($ millions)	2010	2009
Current maturities of long-term debt	$ 113	$102
Commercial paper (0.2%)	2,632	—
Notes due 2011 (4.4%)	1,513	—
Other borrowings (5.3% and 6.7%)	640	362
	$4,898	$464

Long-Term Debt Obligations ($ millions)	2010	2009
Notes due 2012 (3.1% and 1.9%)	$ 2,437	$1,079
Notes due 2013 (3.0% and 3.7%)	2,110	999
Notes due 2014 (5.3% and 4.0%)	2,888	1,026
Notes due 2015 (2.6%)	1,617	—
Notes due 2016-2040 (4.9% and 5.4%)	10,828	4,056
Zero coupon notes, due 2011–2012 (13.3%)	136	192
Other, due 2011–2019 (4.8% and 8.4%)	96	150
	20,112	7,502
Less: current maturities of long-term debt obligations	(113)	(102)
	$19,999	$7,400

In the first quarter of 2010, we issued . . . $1.0 billion of 5.50% senior notes maturing in 2040. A portion of the net proceeds from the issuance of these notes was used to finance our acquisitions of PBG and PAS and the remainder was used for general corporate purposes.

Long-Term Contractual Commitments

Payments Due by Period ($ millions)	Total	2011	2012–2013	2014–2015	2016 and beyond
Long-term debt obligations	$20,112	$113	$4,569	$4,322	$11,108

Credit Ratings   Our objective is to maintain credit ratings that provide us with ready access to global capital and credit markets at favorable interest rates. On February 24, 2010, Moody's Inves-

continued

continued from prior page

> tors Service (Moody's) lowered the corporate credit rating of PepsiCo and its supported subsidiaries and the rating of PepsiCo's senior unsecured long-term debt to Aa3 from Aa2. Moody's rating for PepsiCo's short-term indebtedness was confirmed at Prime-1 and the outlook is stable. On March 17, 2010, Standard & Poor's Ratings Services (S&P) lowered PepsiCo's corporate credit rating to A from A+ and lowered the rating of PepsiCo's senior unsecured long- term debt to A- from A+. S&P's rating for PepsiCo's short-term indebtedness was confirmed at A-1 and the outlook is stable. Any downgrade of our credit ratings by either Moody's or S&P, including any downgrade to below invest- ment grade, could increase our future borrowing costs or impair our ability to access capital markets on terms commercially acceptable to us or at all.

As of June 2011, the price of the $1 billion 5.5% senior notes maturing in 2040 follows (from **Yahoo! Finance, reports.finance.yahoo.com**):

Type	Issuer	Price	Coupon(%)	Maturity	YTM(%)	Fitch Ratings	Callable
Corp	PEPSICO INC	108.13	5.500	15-Jan-2040	4.965	AA	No

Required

a. PepsiCo reports current maturities of long-term debt of $113 million as part of short-term debt. Why is this amount reported that way? PepsiCo reports $4,569 million of long-term debt due in 2012-2013. What does this mean? Is this amount important to our analysis of PepsiCo? Explain.

b. The $1 billion 5.50% senior notes maturing in 2040 are priced at 108.13 (108.13% of face value, or $1.0813 billion) as of June 2011, resulting in a yield to maturity of 4.965%. Assuming that the credit rating of PepsiCo has not changed, what does the pricing of this 5.5% coupon bond imply about interest rate changes since PepsiCo issued the bond?

c. What does the schedule of long-term contractual commitments reveal that might be useful in ana- lyzing PepsiCo's liquidity?

d. Moody's Investors Service lowered the corporate credit rating of PepsiCo in 2010. Why might a reduction in credit ratings result in higher interest costs and restrict PepsiCo's access to credit markets?

e. What type of actions can PepsiCo take to improve its credit ratings?

P7-38. Interpreting Debt Footnotes on Interest Rates and Interest Expense (LO2)

CVS CAREMARK CORPORATION (CVS)

CVS Caremark Corporation discloses the following as part of its long-term debt footnote in its 2010 10-K.

BORROWING AND CREDIT AGREEMENTS

The following table is a summary of the Company's borrowings as of December 31.

In millions	2010	2009
Commercial paper	$ 300	$ 315
Floating rate notes due 2010	—	350
Floating rate notes due 2010	—	1,750
5.75% senior notes due 2011	800	800
Floating rate notes due 2011	300	300
4.875% senior notes due 2014	550	550
3.250% senior notes due 2015	550	–
6.125% senior notes due 2016	700	700
5.75% senior notes due 2017	1,750	1,750
6.60% senior notes due 2019	1,000	1,000
4.75% senior notes due 2020	450	–
6.25% senior notes due 2027	1,000	1,000
6.125% note due 2039	1,500	1,500
6.302% Enhanced Capital Advantage Preferred Securities	1,000	1,000
Mortgage notes payable	6	6
Capital lease obligations	151	154
	10,057	11,175
Less:		
Short-term debt (commercial paper)	(300)	(315)
Current portion of long-term debt	(1,105)	(2,104)
	$ 8,652	$ 8,756

CVS also discloses the following information.

Interest expense, net—Interest expense, net of capitalized interest, was $539 million, $530 million and $530 million in 2010, 2009 and 2008, respectively. Interest paid totalled $583, $542 and $574 in 2010, 2009 and 2008, respectively.

Maturities of long-term debt—The aggregate maturities of long-term debt for each of the five years subsequent to December 31, 2010 are $1.1 billion in 2011, $2 million in 2012, $1 million in 2013, $550 million in 2014, and $550 million in 2015.

The price of the $1,500 million 6.125% senior note due 2039 as of 2011 follows (from **Yahoo! finance**).

Maturity Date	Issuer	Security Type	Coupon	Current Price	Current Yield	Fitch Rating	Callable
2039	CVS Caremark (NYSE: CVS)	Corporate Debentures	6.125	106.68	5.649	BBB	No

Required

a. What is the average coupon rate (interest paid) and the average effective rate (interest expense) on the long-term debt? (*Hint:* Use the disclosure for interest expense.)

b. Does your computation of the coupon rate in part *a* seem reasonable given the footnote disclosure relating to specific bond issues? Explain.

c. Explain how the amount of interest paid can differ from the amount of interest expense recorded in the income statement.

d. On its 2010 balance sheet, CVS reports current maturities of long-term debt of $1,105 million as part of short-term debt. Why is this amount reported that way? Is this amount important to our analysis of CVS? Explain.

e. The $1,500 million 6.125% senior note due in 2039 is priced at 106.68 (106.68% of face value, or $1,600.2 million) as of 2011, resulting in a yield to maturity of 5.649%. Assuming that the credit rating of CVS has not changed, what does the pricing of this 6.125% coupon bond imply about interest rate changes since CVS issued the bond?

P7-39. Analyzing Debt Terms, Yields, Prices, and Credit Ratings (LO2, 3)

Reproduced below is the debt footnote from the 2011 10-K report of **Dell Inc.**

DELL INC.
(DELL)

Long-Term Debt (In millions)	January 28, 2011	January 29, 2010
Notes		
$400 million issued on June 10, 2009, at 3.375% due June 2012 ..	$400	$401
$600 million issued on April 17, 2008, at 4.70% due April 2013	609	599
$500 million issued on September 7, 2010, at 1.40% due September 2013.....................................	499	—
$500 million issued on April 1, 2009, at 5.625% due April 2014	500	500
$700 million issued on September 7, 2010, at 2.30% due September 2015.....................................	700	—
$500 million issued on April 17, 2008, at 5.65% due April 2018	499	499
$600 million issued on June 10, 2009, at 5.875% due June 2019 ..	600	600
$400 million issued on April 17, 2008, at 6.50% due April 2038	400	400
$300 million issued on September 7, 2010, at 5.40% due September 2040.....................................	300	—
Senior Debentures		
$300 million issued on April 3, 1998 at 7.10% due April 2028	389	394
Other		
India term loan: entered into on October 15, 2009 at 8.9% due October 2011	—	24
Structured financing debt.	250	—
Total long-term debt.	5,146	3,417

continued

continued from prior page

Long-Term Debt (In millions)	January 28, 2011	January 29, 2010
Short-Term Debt		
Commercial paper	—	496
Structured financing debt.	850	164
Other.	1	3
Total short-term debt	851	663
Total debt	$5,997	$4,080

Aggregate future maturities of long-term debt at face value were as follows at January 28, 2011:

(in millions)	Maturities by Fiscal Year						
	2012	2013	2014	2015	2016	Thereafter	Total
Aggregate future maturities of long-term debt outstanding	$ —	$595	$1,155	$500	$700	$2,100	$5,050

There is an $86 difference between the total referenced in this table and the $5,146 referenced for long-term debt in the table above. The difference arises because the maturity table reports the face value of the debt $(5,050). The first table above reports the carrying value (net book value) of the debt. Many of the notes are not carried at par. The largest difference is the senior debentures that have a premium of $89 (in millions).

Reproduced below is a summary of the market values of the Dell bonds maturing from 2021 to 2040 (from Morningstar, quicktake.morningstar.com).

Name	Maturity Date	Amount $	Price	Coupon %	Yield to Maturity %
Dell 5.4%	9/10/2040	300	94.8	5.4	5.77
Dell 6.5%	4/15/2038	400	111.9	6.5	5.63
Dell 4.625%	4/1/2021	400	104.9	4.625	4.01

Required

a. What is the amount of long-term debt reported on Dell's January 28, 2011, balance sheet? What are the scheduled maturities for this indebtedness? Why is information relating to a company's scheduled maturities of debt useful in an analysis of its financial condition?

b. Dell reported $199 million in interest expense in the notes to its 2011 income statement. In the note to its statement of cash flows, Dell indicates that the cash portion of this expense is $188 million. What could account for the difference between interest expense and interest paid? Explain.

c. Dell's long-term debt is rated A2 by Moody's, A− by S&P, and A by Fitch. What factors would be important to consider in attempting to quantify the relative riskiness of Dell compared with other borrowers? Explain.

d. Dell's $300 million 5.4% notes traded at 94.8, or 94.8% of par, as of December 2010. What is the market value of these notes on that date? How is the difference between this market value and the $300 million face value reflected in Dell's financial statements? What effect would the repurchase of this entire note issue have on Dell's financial statements? What does the 94.8 price tell you about the general trend in interest rates since Dell sold this bond issue? Explain.

e. Examine the yields to maturity of the three bonds in the table above. What relation do we observe between these yields and the maturities of the bonds? Also, explain why this relation applies in general.

P7-40.   Analyzing Notes, Yields, Financial Ratios, and Credit Ratings   (LO2, 3)
Comcast Corporation reports long-term senior notes totaling over $31 billion in its 2010 10-K.

Following are selected ratios from Exhibit 7.6 computed for Comcast Corp. utilizing its 2010 data.

EBITA/Average assets	8.05%
EBITA/Interest expense	4.32
EBITA margin	24.52%
Operating margin	21.03%
(Funds from operations + Interest expense)/Interest expense.	6.19
Funds from operations/Debt	35.58%
Debt/EBITDA	2.12
Debt/Book capitalization	30.18%

Required

This debt is rated "Baa" by Moody's, which is a lower medium grade. Examine the ratios provided above. *(Hint:* Compare Comcast's ratios to the ratio values reported in Exhibit 7.6.) What factors do you believe contribute to Comcast's credit rating being less than stellar?

IFRS APPLICATIONS

I7-41. **Interpreting a Contingent Liability Footnote** **(LO1)**

BP operates off-shore drilling rigs including rigs in the Gulf of Mexico. On April 20, 2010, explosions and fire on the Deepwater Horizon rig led to the death of 11 crew members and a 200-million-gallon oil spill in the Gulf of Mexico. BP's 2010 annual report (prepared under IFRS) included the following concerning estimates of contingent liabilities (provisions):

BP P.L.C.
(BP)

> In estimating the amount of the provision, BP has determined a range of possible outcomes for Individual and Business Claims, and State and Local Claims. . . . BP has concluded that a reasonable range of possible outcomes for the amount of the provision as at 31 December 2010 is $6 billion to $13 billion. BP believes that the provision recorded at 31 December 2010 of $9.2 billion represents a reliable best estimate from within this range of possible outcomes.

How did BP record the $9.2 billion estimate in its 2010 financial statements? How would the accounting for this provision differ if BP had prepared its financial statements in accordance with U.S. GAAP?

I7-42. **Interpreting Bond Footnote Disclosures** **(LO2)**

In May 2011, French real estate company **Foncière des Régions** issued convertible bonds with a total face value of €480 million. Each €1,000 bond included a conversion option whose fair value was estimated at €13. The average proceeds per €1,000 bond was €1,028.

a. Compute the total bond proceeds.
b. What portion of the bond proceeds is accounted for as debt under IFRS?
c. Had the company reported under U.S. GAAP what amount of the bond proceeds would be accounted for as debt?

I7-43. **Assessing the Effects of Bond Credit Rating Changes for Financial Statements** **(LO3)**

Deutsche Telekom AG, headquartered in Bonn, Germany, is the largest telecommunications company in Europe. The company uses IFRS to prepare its financial statements. The company's 2009 financial statements report the following:

DEUTSCHE TELEKOM AG

> **Credit Quality** In 2009, Fitch changed our long-term rating from A- to BBB+ with a stable outlook. Moody's Investor Service and Standard and Poor's maintained our long-term rating at Baa1 and BBB+ respectively with a stable outlook. A further decrease in our credit ratings below certain thresholds by various rating agencies would result in an increase in the interest rates on certain of our bonds and medium term notes due to step-up provisions and could raise the cost of our debt refinancing activities generally.
>
> **Step-up Provisions** An improvement of our long-term senior unsecured debt ratings to A3 by Moody's and A- by Standard & Poor's would result in a 50 basis point decrease in interest rates due to relevant step-up provisions on bonds with an aggregate principal amount of approximately EUR 6.3 billion at December 31, 2009. A lowering of our long-term senior unsecured debt ratings below Baa1 by Moody's and BBB+ by Standard & Poor's would result in a 50 basis point increase in interest rates due to relevant step-up provisions on bonds and medium-term notes with an aggregate principal amount of approximately EUR 4.2 billion at December 31, 2009.

a.   What is a credit rating in layperson terms?

b.   Did the rating downgrade by Fitch move their credit rating closer to, or farther from, the Moody's and Standard & Poor's ratings? To answer this question, refer to Exhibit 7.5.

c.   Based on the company's disclosures, conjecture about the purpose of a "step-up provision." Why would creditors add such a provision to a bond issue?

d.   Compute the additional interest expense that Deutsche Telekom would incur if its credit ratings deteriorated by one notch. How much would be saved with a one-notch improvement in credit rating?

e.   The company reported interest expense of €2,896 million in 2009. Would a credit deterioration impose significant income statement consequences? What other consequences could arise?

I7-44.   **Analyzing Debt Terms, Yields, Prices, and Credit Ratings   (LO2, 3)**

STATOIL ASA
(STO)

Statoil ASA, headquartered in Stavanger, Norway, is a fully integrated petroleum company. The company uses IFRS to prepare its financial statements. Reproduced below is the long-term debt note from its 2010 annual report.

	Carrying amount in NOK million		Fair value in NOK million	
At 31 December	**2010**	**2009**	**2010**	**2009**
Total financial liabilities.........	104,424	99,230	114,911	106,966
Less current portion...........	4,627	3,268	4,627	3,268
Financial liabilities, non-current portion..........	99,797	95,962	110,284	103,698

Details of largest unsecured bonds				Carrying amount in NOK million at 31 December	
Bond agreement	**Fixed interest rate**	**Issued (year)**	**Maturity (year)**	**2010**	**2009**
USD 1500 million	5.250%	2009	2019	8.738	8.613
USD 1250 million	3.125%	2010	2017	7.278	—
USD 900 million	2.900%	2009	2014	5.251	5.174
USD 750 million	5.100%	2010	2040	4.340	—
USD 500 million	3.875%	2009	2014	2.914	2.870
USD 500 million	5.125%	2004	2014	2.927	2.887
USD 500 million	6.500%	1998	2028	2.900	2.859
USD 481 million	7.250%	2000	2027	2.814	2.776
USD 300 million	7.750%	1993	2023	1.757	1.733
EUR 1300 million	4.375%	2009	2015	10.135	10.782
EUR 1200 million	5.625%	2009	2021	9.297	9.887
EUR 500 million	5.125%	1999	2011	3.903	4.148
GBP 800 million	6.875%	2009	2031	7.224	7.421
GBP 225 million	6.125%	1998	2028	2.040	2.096

Non-current financial liabilities maturity profile		
At 31 December (in NOK million)	**2010**	**2009**
Years 2 and 3	12,555	11,757
Years 4 and 5	23,205	11,496
After 5 years......................................	64,037	72,709
Total repayment of non-current financial liabilities.......	99,797	95,962

Reproduced below is a summary of the market values, at December 2010, of the Statoil ASA bonds maturing from 2014 to 2040.

Currency	Maturity date	Amount Outstanding	Current price	Coupon	Yield
Statoil Asa USD	08/17/2017	1,250.0	101.4	3.125	2.90
Statoil Asa USD	08/17/2040	750.0	100.6	5.100	5.06
Statoil Asa USD	04/30/2014	500.0	111.2	3.875	1.74
Statoil Asa USD	04/30/2014	500.0	106.7	5.125	3.59

Required

a. What is the amount of total financial liabilities (debt) reported on Statoil's 2009 balance sheet? Of the total financial liabilities, what proportion is due within one year?

b. In what currencies has Statoil issued financial liabilities? Why do companies borrow money in foreign currencies?

c. What are the scheduled maturities for Statoil's indebtedness? Why is information relating to a company's scheduled maturities of debt useful in analyzing financial condition?

d. Statoil's long-term debt is rated AA- by Standard and Poor's and similarly by other credit agencies. What factors would be important to consider in quantifying the relative riskiness of Statoil compared to other borrowers? Explain.

e. Statoil's $1,250 million, 3.125% notes traded at 101.4, or 101.4% of par, as of December 2010. What is the market value of these notes on that date? How is the difference between this market value and the $1,250 million face value reflected on Statoil's financial statements? What does the 101.4 price tell you about the general trend in interest rates since Statoil sold this bond issue? Explain.

f. Examine the yields to maturity of the four bonds in the previous table. What relation do we observe between these yields and the maturities of the bonds? Explain why this relation applies in general.

DISCUSSION POINTS

D7-45. **Coupon Rate versus Effective Rate**   (L02)

Assume that you are the CFO of a company that intends to issue bonds to finance a new manufacturing facility. A subordinate suggests lowering the coupon rate on the bond to lower interest expense and to increase the profitability of your company. Is the rationale for this suggestion a good one? Explain.

D7-46. **Ethics and Governance: Bond Covenants**   (L02)

Because lenders do not have voting rights like shareholders do, they often reduce their risk by invoking various bond covenants that restrict the company's operating, financing and investing activities. For example, debt covenants often restrict the amount of debt that the company can issue (in relation to its equity) and impose operating restrictions (such as the ability to acquire other companies or to pay dividends). Failure to abide by these restrictions can have serious consequences, including forcing the company into bankruptcy and potential liquidation. Assume that you are on the board of directors of a company that issues bonds with such restrictions. What safeguards can you identify to ensure compliance with those restrictions?

SOLUTIONS TO REVIEW PROBLEMS

Mid-Module Review 1

Solution

a. We know that accounts payable turnover is computed as cost of goods sold divided by average accounts payable. Thus, an increase in accounts payable turnover indicates that accounts payable have decreased relative to cost of goods sold (all else equal).

b. A decrease in accounts payable results in a decrease in net cash flows from operating activities because Verizon is using cash to pay bills more quickly.

c. Decreased accounts payable increases net operating working capital (all else equal), with a consequent decrease in cash flow. While unfavorable to cash flow, the more timely payment of accounts payable can improve supplier relations. Analysts must be aware of the costs and benefits of leaning on the trade to a greater or lesser extent.

Mid-Module Review 2

Solution

Yes. Verizon must recognize liabilities and expenses when incurred, regardless of when payment is made. Accruing expenses as incurred will match the expenses to the revenues they helped generate. Failure to recognize the wages owed to employees for the period would understate liabilities and overstate income. Verizon must reflect the wages earned and the related expense in its financial statements as follows:

		Balance Sheet						Income Statement	
Transaction	Cash Asset	+ Noncash Assets	= Liabil- ities	+ Contrib. Capital	+ Earned Capital		Rev- enues	− Expen- ses	= Net Income
Accrue $10,000 in wages expense			+10,000 Wages Payable		−10,000 Retained Earnings			+10,000 Wages Expense	= −10,000

WE 10,000
  WP 10,000
     WE
10,000
    WP
       10,000

Mid-Module Review 3

Solution

		Balance Sheet						Income Statement	
Transaction	Cash Asset	+ Noncash Assets	= Liabil- ities	+ Contrib. Capital	+ Earned Capital		Rev- enues	− Expen- ses	= Net Income
Jan 31: Accrue $26 interest expense*			+26 Interest Payable		−26 Retained Earnings			+26 Interest Expense	= −26

IE 26
  IP 26
     IE
26
    IP
       26

*Accrued interest = $10,000 × 0.06 × 16/365 = $26.

Module-End Review

Solution

1.

Issue price for $300,000, 15-year bonds that pay 10% interest semiannually, discounted at 8%:
Present value of principal payment ($300,000 × 0.30832) . . . . $ 92,496
Present value of semiannual interest payments ($15,000 × 17.29203). 259,380
Issue price of bonds. $351,876

2.

Transaction	Balance Sheet						Income Statement		
	Cash Asset	+ Noncash Assets	= Liabil- ities	+ Contrib. Capital	+ Earned Capital		Rev- enues	− Expen- ses	= Net Income
January 1: Issue 10% bonds	+351,876 Cash		= +351,876 Long-Term Debt					−	=
June 30: Pay interest and amor- tize bond premium[1]	−15,000 Cash		= −925 Long-Term Debt		−14,075 Retained Earnings			− +14,075 Interest Expense	= −14,075
December 31: Pay interest and amortize bond pre- mium[2]	−15,000 Cash		= −962 Long-Term Debt		−14,038 Retained Earnings			− +14,038 Interest Expense	= −14,038

```
Cash    351,876
    LTD      351,876
         Cash
351,876 |
         LTD
         | 351,876
```

```
IE     14,075
LTD       925
    Cash    15,000
         IE
14,075 |
         LTD
   925 |
         Cash
         | 15,000
```

```
IE     14,038
LTD       962
    Cash    15,000
         IE
14,038 |
         LTD
   962 |
         Cash
         | 15,000
```

[1] $300,000 × 0.10 × 6/12 = \$15,000$ cash payment; $0.04 × \$351,876 = \$14,075$ interest expense; the difference of $925, is the bond premium amortization, which reduces the net bond carrying amount.

[2] $0.04 × (\$351,876 − \$925) = \$14,038$ interest expense. The difference between this amount and the $15,000 cash payment ($962) is the premium amortization, which reduces the net bond carrying amount.

1. Describe and analyze accounting for contributed capital, including stock sales and repurchases, and equity-based compensation. (p. 8-4)

2. Explain and analyze accounting for earned capital, including cash dividends, stock dividends, and comprehensive income. (p. 8-15)

3. Describe and interpret accounting for equity carve-outs and convertible debt. (p. 8-24)

© Getty Images

Equity Recognition and Owner Financing

8

AON CORPORATION

Aon Corporation provides risk management services, insurance and reinsurance brokerage, and human resource consulting and outsourcing. Aon aims to help its clients generate greater value from their employees by developing strategies to address human resource challenges, improve workforce performance, and streamline human resources operations. Its business has evolved as a result of organic growth and acquisitions, and it continues to extend, expand and create new human resources services that focus on its clients' changing workforce-related needs and challenges.

Aon serves its clients through the following two major segments:

- **Risk Solutions** Over 28,000 employees worldwide act as an advisor and insurance and reinsurance broker, helping clients manage their risks via consultation, as well as negotiation and placement of insurance risk with insurance carriers through its global distribution network.

- **HR Solutions** Over 29,000 worldwide partners with organizations to tackle complex benefits, talent and related financial challenges, and improve business performance by designing, implementing, communicating and administering a range of human capital, retirement, investment management, health care, compensation and talent management strategies.

Each segment aims to help clients manage the complex human elements necessary to acquire, develop, motivate and retain the talent required to meet business objectives. As of 2011, Aon employed over 59,000 employees worldwide with nearly $8.5 billion in revenues.

Aon's value lies not in plant assets, such as land and buildings, but in the knowledge capital of its employees, most of whom are Aon shareholders. This module considers how shareholders' investment is accounted for on a company's financial statements. We consider common stock features, stock options, share issuances, share repurchases, and dividend payments.

Aon has one class of stock. Of the 750 million shares that have been authorized for issuance, 385.9 million have been issued to date. It also has restricted stock and restricted stock units. This stock is awarded to employees as incentive compensation. As further incentive, it offers employee stock options. This module explains and assesses these various forms of equity-based compensation.

Aon has repurchased over 53.6 million shares of its stock at a purchase price of over $2 billion. Many companies routinely repurchase their common stock as it is the best use of excess cash when there exist no better outside investment opportunities. Some companies repurchase their stock to offset the

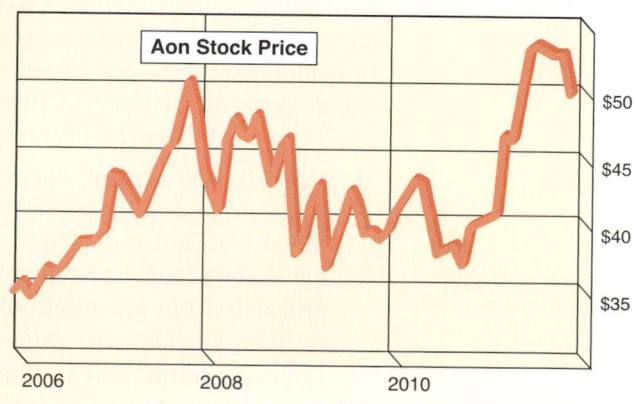

(continued on next page)

(continued from previous page)

dilutive effect of stock-based compensation programs. This module explains and analyzes stock repurchases. The module also discusses a variety of equity transactions under the general heading of equity carve-outs and convertibles. These transactions include several methods by which companies seek to unlock hidden value for the benefit of their shareholders.

Source: Aon Corporation, 2010 Form 10-K; *The Wall Street Journal,* January 2012.

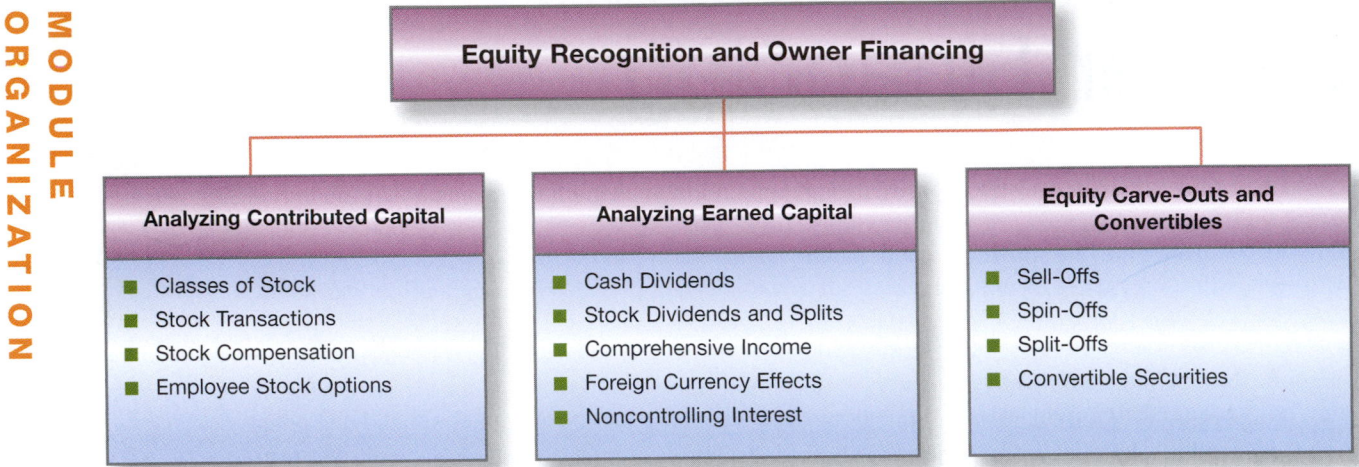

A company finances its assets through operating cash flows or it taps one or both of the following sources: either it borrows funds or it sells stock to shareholders. On average, companies obtain about half of their external financing from borrowed sources and the other half from shareholders. This module describes the issues relating to stockholders' equity, including the accounting for stock transactions (sales and repurchases of stock, dividends, stock-based compensation, and convertible securities). We also discuss equity carve-outs, a process by which companies can unlock substantial shareholder value via spin-offs and split-offs of business units into separate companies. Finally, we discuss the accumulated other comprehensive income and noncontrolling interest components of stockholders' equity.

When a company issues stock to the public, it records the receipt of cash (or other assets) and an increase in stockholders' equity, representing the shareholders' investment in the company. The increase in cash and equity is equal to the market price of the stock on the issue date multiplied by the number of shares sold.

Like bonds, stockholders' equity is accounted for at *historical cost.* Consequently, the company's financial statements do not reflect fluctuations in the market price of the stock subsequent to its issuance. The company's stock price results from market transactions that involve outside parties and not the company. However, if the company repurchases and/or resells shares of its own stock, the balance sheet will be affected because those transactions involve the company.

There is an important difference between accounting for stockholders' equity and accounting for transactions involving assets and liabilities: *there is never any gain or loss reported on the purchase and sale of a company's own stock or the payment of dividends to its shareholders.* Instead, these "gains and losses" are reflected as increases and decreases in stockholders' equity and do not affect net income (nor earned capital, see below).

The typical balance sheet has two broad categories of stockholders' equity:

1. **Contributed capital** These accounts report the proceeds received by the issuing company from original stock issuances. It often includes common stock, preferred stock, and additional paid-in capital. Netted against these contributed capital accounts is treasury stock, the amounts paid to repurchase shares of the issuer's stock from its investors, less the proceeds from the resale of such shares. Collectively, these accounts are referred to as contributed capital (or *paid-in capital*).

2. **Earned capital** This section consists of (a) retained earnings, which represent the cumulative income and losses of the company, less any dividends to shareholders, and (b) accumulated other comprehensive income (AOCI), which includes changes to equity that have not yet impacted income and are, therefore, not reflected in retained earnings.

In addition, many companies report an equity account called *noncontrolling interest*, which reflects the equity of minority shareholders. Exhibit 8.1 illustrates the stockholders' equity section of **Aon**'s balance sheet. Aon's balance sheet reports three equity accounts that make up contributed capital: common stock, additional paid-in capital, and treasury (repurchased) stock. Aon's balance sheet also reports two earned capital accounts: retained earnings and accumulated other comprehensive income (loss). The final component of Aon's stockholders' equity is the noncontrolling interest account.

EXHIBIT 8.1 Stockholders' Equity from Aon's Balance Sheet

Stockholders' Equity (In millions except per share amounts)	December 31, 2010	December 31, 2009
Contributed Capital — Common stock-$1 par value Authorized: 750 shares (issued: 2010—385.9; 2009—362.7).	$ 386	$ 363
Additional paid-in capital	4,000	3,215
Treasury stock at cost (shares: 2010—53.6; 2009—96.4)	(2,079)	(3,859)
Earned Capital — Retained earnings.	7,861	7,335
Accumulated other comprehensive loss	(1,917)	(1,675)
Noncontrolling Interest — Total Aon stockholders' equity	8,251	5,379
Noncontrolling interest	55	52
Total equity	$8,306	$5,431

* We list contributed and earned capital accounts together for learning purposes; in the Aon balance sheet, these accounts are grouped by positive and negative balances.

We analyze contributed capital, earned capital, and noncontrolling interest in order. For each section, we provide a graphic that displays the part of stockholders' equity in the balance sheet impacted by the discussion of that section.

ANALYZING CONTRIBUTED CAPITAL

Contributed capital represents the cumulative cash inflow that the company has received from the sale of various classes of stock, less the net cash that it has paid out to repurchase its stock from the market. The contributed capital of Aon is highlighted in the following graphic.

Stockholders' Equity (In millions except per share amounts)	December 31, 2010	December 31, 2009
Common stock-$1 par value Authorized: 750 shares (issued: 2010—385.9; 2009—362.7)	$ 386	$ 363
Additional paid-in capital.	4,000	3,215
Treasury stock at cost (shares: 2010—53.6; 2009—96.4)	(2,079)	(3,859)
Retained earnings	7,861	7,335
Accumulated other comprehensive loss	(1,917)	(1,675)
Total Aon stockholders' equity.	8,251	5,379
Noncontrolling interest.	55	52
Total equity.	$8,306	$5,431

In 2010, Aon's contributed capital consists of par value and additional paid-in capital for the 385.9 million shares of its common stock that Aon has issued. Its contributed capital is reduced by the cost of treasury stock for the 53.6 million shares that Aon has repurchased.

Classes of Stock

There are two general classes of stock: preferred and common. The difference between the two lies in the legal rights conferred upon each class.

Preferred Stock

Preferred stock generally has preference, or priority, with respect to common stock. Two usual preferences are:

LO1 Describe and analyze accounting for contributed capital, including stock sales and repurchases, and equity-based compensation.

1. **Dividend preference** Preferred shareholders receive dividends on their shares before common shareholders do. If dividends are not paid in a given year, those dividends are normally forgone. However, some preferred stock contracts include a *cumulative provision* stipulating that any forgone dividends (dividends in *arrears*) must first be paid to preferred shareholders, together with the current year's dividends, before any dividends are paid to common shareholders.

2. **Liquidation preference** If a company fails, its assets are sold (liquidated) and the proceeds are paid to the creditors and shareholders, in that order. Shareholders, therefore, have a greater risk of loss than creditors. Among shareholders, the preferred shareholders receive payment in full before common shareholders. This liquidation preference makes preferred shares less risky than common shares. Any liquidation payment to preferred shares is normally at par value, although sometimes the liquidation is specified in excess of par; called a *liquidating value*.

To illustrate the typical provisions contained in preferred stock agreements, consider the following stockholders' equity and related footnote disclosure from **Fortune Brands, Inc.** (2010 10-K).

December 31 (in millions, except per share amounts)	2010	2009
Fortune Brands stockholders' equity		
$2.67 convertible preferred stock	$ 4.9	$ 5.2
Common stock, par value $3.125 per share, 234.9 shares issued	734.0	734.0
Paid-in capital	820.2	755.6
Accumulated other comprehensive loss	(172.0)	(211.8)
Retained earnings	7,499.3	7,135.4
Treasury stock, at cost	(3,215.3)	(3,326.0)
Total Fortune Brands stockholders' equity	5,671.1	5,092.4
Noncontrolling interests	16.9	13.3
Total equity	$5,688.0	$5,105.7

$2.67 Convertible Preferred Stock—Redeemable at Company's Option We have 60 million authorized shares of Preferred stock. There were 160,729 and 171,138 shares of the $2.67 Convertible Preferred stock issued and outstanding at December 31, 2010 and 2009, respectively . . . The holders of $2.67 Convertible Preferred stock are entitled to cumulative dividends, three-tenths of a vote per share together with holders of common stock (in certain events, to the exclusion of the common shares), preference in liquidation over holders of common stock of $30.50 per share plus accrued dividends and to convert each share of Convertible Preferred stock into 6.601 shares of common stock . . . Holders converted 10,409 and 7,366 shares of Preferred stock into common stock during 2010 and 2009, respectively. The Company may redeem the Convertible Preferred stock at a price of $30.50 per share, plus accrued dividends. The Company paid cash dividends of $2.67 per share of Preferred stock in the aggregate amount of $0.4 million in the year ended December 31, 2010 and $0.5 million in each of the years ended December 31, 2009 and 2008.

Following are several important features of Fortune Brands' convertible preferred stock:

- Preferred stock is typically reported before common stock to indicate that these shareholders will receive payments (dividends or payments if the company is liquidated) before common shareholders.

- Holders of convertible preferred stock are entitled to $2.67 dividends per share; during 2010, the company paid dividends on preferred shares amounting to $429,146, computed as 160,729 shares × $2.67, which Fortune Brands rounds off to $0.4 million in the footnote.

- Each share of convertible preferred stock is entitled to 3/10 of a vote per share.

- Holders of convertible preferred stock have a preference in liquidation over common shareholders amounting to $30.50; this means that they receive $30.50 per share in liquidation before common shareholders receive a payment.

- Each share of convertible preferred stock is convertible into 6.601 shares of common stock. Upon conversion, the preferred shareholder tenders preferred shares to the company and receives 6.601 shares of common in return for each preferred share tendered. Subsequent to conversion, then, the shareholder loses preferences accorded to preferred shareholders (for example, in dividends and liquidation) as well as the $2.67 of dividends per share. Instead, the shareholder is now able to participate in the wealth creation of the company with unlimited upside potential both for dividends and share price appreciation.

■ Fortune Brands has an option to redeem each share at a price of $30.50; upon redemption, the preferred shareholder will receive that cash amount and will surrender that share to the company.

Fortune Brands' convertible preferred shares carry a dividend $2.67 per share. This preferred dividend compares favorably with the $0.76 of dividends per share paid to its common shareholders in 2010 (which is a return of 1.26% based on year-end stock price of $60.25). Generally, preferred stock can be an attractive investment for shareholders seeking higher dividend yields, especially when tax laws wholly or partially exempt such dividends from taxation. (In comparison, interest payments received by debt holders are not tax exempt.)

In addition to the sorts of conversion features outlined above, preferred shares sometimes carry a *participation feature* that allows preferred shareholders to share ratably with common stockholders in dividends. The dividend preference over common shares can be a benefit when dividend payments are meager, but a fixed dividend yield limits upside potential if the company performs exceptionally well. A participation feature can overcome this limitation.

> **IFRS INSIGHT** | **Preferred Stock Under IFRS**
>
> Under IFRS, preferred stock (called *preference shares*) is classified according to its underlying characteristics. Preference shares are classified as equity if they are not redeemable, or redeemable at the option of the issuer. Preference shares are classified as liabilities if the company must redeem the shares (mandatorily redeemable) or if they are redeemable at the option of the shareholder. Accounting for payments to preference shareholders follows from the balance sheet classification: cash paid out is recorded as interest expense or dividends, when the shares are classified as liabilities or equity, respectively. Under US GAAP, preferred stock is classified as equity and cash paid out to preferred shareholders is classified as a dividend.

Common Stock

Aon has one class of common stock, Class A, which has the following important characteristics:

■ Aon's Class A common stock has a par value of $1 per share. **Par value** is an arbitrary amount set by company organizers at the time of company formation and has no relation to, or impact on, the stock's market value. Generally, par value has no substance from a financial reporting perspective (there are some legal implications, which are usually minor). Its main impact is in specifying the allocation of proceeds from stock issuances between the two contributed capital accounts on the balance sheet: common stock and additional paid-in capital, as we describe below.

■ Aon has 750 million shares of stock that have been **authorized** for issuance. The company cannot issue (sell) more shares than have been authorized. So, if more shares are needed, say for an acquisition or for one of its various stock purchase programs, it must first get additional authorization by its shareholders.

■ To date, Aon's management has **issued** (sold) 385.9 million shares of stock. The number of issued shares is a cumulative amount. As of 2009, Aon had issued 362.7 million shares of stock and it issued an additional 23.2 million (385.9 million − 362.7 million) shares in 2010.

■ Aon has repurchased 53.6 million shares from its shareholders at a cumulative cost of $2,079 million. These shares are currently held in the company's treasury, hence the name treasury stock. These shares neither have voting rights nor do they receive dividends.

■ The number of **outstanding** shares is equal to the issued shares less treasury shares. There were 332.3 million (385.9 million − 53.6 million) shares outstanding at the end of 2010.

Analyzing Stock Transactions

We analyze the accounting for stock transactions in this section, including the accounting for stock issuances and repurchases.

Stock Issuance

Companies issue stock to obtain cash and other assets for use in their business. Stock issuances increase assets (cash) by the issue proceeds: the number of shares sold multiplied by the price of the stock on the issue date. Equity increases by the same amount, which is reflected in contributed capital accounts. If the stock has a par value, the common stock account increases by the number of shares sold multiplied by its par value. The additional paid-in capital account increases for the remainder. Stock can also be issued as "no-par" or as "no-par with a stated value." For no-par stock, the common stock account is increased by the entire proceeds of the sale and no amount is assigned to additional paid-in capital. For no-par stock with a stated value, the stated value is treated just like par value, that is, common stock is increased by the number of shares multiplied by the stated value, and the remainder is assigned to the additional paid-in capital account.

To illustrate, assume that Aon issues 100,000 shares of its $1 par value common stock at a market price of $43 cash per share. This stock issuance has the following financial statement effects:

Cash   4,300,000
  CS   100,000
  APIC   4,200,000

Cash
4,300,000 |
        CS
        | 100,000
        APIC
        | 4,200,000

	Balance Sheet						Income Statement		
Transaction	Cash Asset	+ Noncash Assets	= Liabil- ities	+ Contrib. Capital	+ Earned Capital		Rev- enues	− Expen- ses	= Net Income
Issue 100,000 common shares with $1 par value for $43 cash per share	+4,300,000		**=**	+100,000 Common Stock +4,200,000 Additional Paid-In Capital			−		**=**

Specifically, the stock issuance affects the financial statements as follows:

1. Cash increases by $4,300,000 (100,000 shares × $43 per share)
2. Common stock increases by the par value of shares sold (100,000 shares × $1 par value = $100,000)
3. Additional paid-in capital increases by the $4,200,000 difference between the issue proceeds and par value ($4,300,000 − $100,000)

Once shares are issued, they are traded in the open market among investors. The proceeds of those sales and their associated gains and losses, as well as fluctuations in the company's stock price subsequent to issuance, do not affect the issuing company and are not recorded in its accounting records.

Refer again to the following report of common stock on Aon's balance sheet:

IFRS Alert
Stock terminology commonly differs between IFRS and GAAP. Under IFRS, common stock is called *share capital* and additional paid-in capital (APIC) is called *share premium*. Accounting for these items is identical under both systems.

(In millions except for share amounts)	2010	2009
Common stock—$1 par value		
Authorized: 750 shares (issued: 2010—385.9; 2009—362.7)	$ 386	$ 363
Additional paid-in capital	4,000	3,215

Aon common stock, in the amount of $4,386 million, equals the number of shares issued multiplied by the common stock's par value: 385.9 million × $1 = $385.9 million (rounded to $386 million). Total proceeds from its stock issuances are $4,386, the sum of the par value and additional paid-in capital. This implies that common shares were sold, on average, for $11.37 per share ($4,386 million / 385.9 million shares).

Stock Repurchase

Aon has repurchased 53.6 million shares of its common stock for a cumulative cost of $2,079 million. One reason a company repurchases shares is because it believes that the market under-values them. The logic is that the repurchase sends a favorable signal to the market about the company's financial condition that positively impacts its share price and, thus, allows it to resell those shares for a "gain." Any such gain on resale is *never* reflected in the income statement. Instead, any excess of the resale price over the repurchase price is added to additional paid-in capital. GAAP prohibits companies from reporting gains and losses from stock transactions with their own shareholders.

Another reason companies repurchase shares is to offset the dilutive effects of an employee stock option program. When an employee exercises stock options, the number of shares outstanding increases. These additional shares reduce earnings per share and are, therefore, viewed as *dilutive*. In response, many companies repurchase an equivalent number of shares in a desire to keep outstanding shares constant.

A stock repurchase reduces the size of the company (cash declines and, thus, total assets decline). A repurchase has the opposite financial statement effects from a stock issuance. That is, cash is reduced by the price of the shares repurchased (number of shares repurchased multiplied by the purchase price per share), and stockholders' equity is reduced by the same amount. The reduction in equity is achieved by increasing a contra equity (negative equity) account called **treasury stock**, which reduces stockholders' equity. Thus, when the treasury stock contra equity account increases, total equity decreases.

When the company subsequently reissues treasury stock there is no accounting gain or loss. Instead, the difference between the proceeds received and the original purchase price of the treasury stock is reflected as an increase or decrease to additional paid-in capital.

To illustrate, assume that 3,000 common shares of Aon previously issued for $43 are repurchased for $40. This repurchase has the following financial statement effects:

	Balance Sheet						Income Statement		
Transaction	Cash Asset	+ Noncash Assets	= Liabil- ities	+ Contrib. Capital	+ Earned Capital		Rev- enues	− Expen- ses	= Net Income
Repurchase 3,000 common shares for $40 cash per share	−120,000 Cash		=	−120,000 Treasury Stock				−	=

TS 120,000
    Cash   120,000

TS
120,000 |
       Cash
       | 120,000

Assets (cash) and equity both decrease. Treasury stock (a contra equity account) increases by $120,000, which reduces stockholders' equity by that amount.

Assume that these 3,000 shares are subsequently resold for $42 cash per share. This resale of treasury stock has the following financial statement effects:

	Balance Sheet						Income Statement		
Transaction	Cash Asset	+ Noncash Assets	= Liabil- ities	+ Contrib. Capital	+ Earned Capital		Rev- enues	− Expen- ses	= Net Income
Reissue 3,000 trea- sury (com- mon) shares for $42 cash per share	+126,000 Cash		=	+120,000 Treasury Stock +6,000 Additional Paid-In Capital				−	=

Cash   126,000
TS   120,000
APIC   6,000

Cash	
126,000	

TS	
	120,000

APIC	
	6,000

Cash assets increase by $126,000 (3,000 shares × $42 per share), the treasury stock account is reduced by the $120,000 cost of the treasury shares issued (thus increasing contributed capital), and the $6,000 excess (3,000 shares × $2 per share) is reported as an increase in additional paid-in capital. (If the reissue price is below the repurchase price, then additional paid-in capital is reduced until it reaches a zero balance, after which retained earnings are reduced.) Again, there is no effect on the income statement as companies are prohibited from reporting gains and losses from repurchases and reissuances of their own stock.

The treasury stock section of **Aon**'s balance sheet is reproduced below:

> **IFRS Alert**
> Accounting for stock repurchases under IFRS is similar to GAAP except that IFRS provides little guidance on how to allocate the treasury stock to equity accounts. Thus, repurchases can be recorded as an increase to treasury stock, or as a decrease to common stock and APIC (share capital and premium), retained earnings (reserves), or some combination.

(In thousands except for share amounts)	2010	2009
Treasury stock at cost (shares: 2010 — 53.6; 2009 — 96.4)	$(2,079)	$(3,859)

Aon has repurchased a cumulative total of 53.6 million shares of its common stock for $2,079 million, an average repurchase price of $38.79 per share. This compares with total contributed capital of $4,386 million, see Exhibit 8.1. Thus, Aon has repurchased about 47% of its original contributed capital in dollar terms, which represents 14% of contributed capital in terms of shares (53.6 million / 385.9 million). Although some of Aon's treasury purchases were to meet stock option exercises, it appears that most of these purchases are motivated by a perceived low stock price by Aon management.

ANALYSIS DECISION   You Are the Chief Financial Officer

As CFO, you believe that your company's stock price is lower than its real value. You are consider- ing various alternatives to increase that price, including the repurchase of company stock in the market. What are some factors you should consider before making your decision? [Answer, p. 8-30]

Analyzing Stock-Based Compensation

Common stock has been an important component of executive compensation for decades. The general idea follows: If the company executives own stock they will have an incentive to increase its value. This aligns the executives' interests with those of other shareholders. Although the strength of this alignment is the subject of much debate, its logic compels boards of directors of most American companies to use stock-based compensation.

Employee Stock Options

One popular incentive plan is to give an employee the right to purchase common stock at a pre- specified price for a given period of time. This is called a *stock option plan*. Options allow employ- ees to purchase a predetermined number of shares at a fixed price (called the *exercise price* or *strike price*) for a specified period of time. Because there is a good chance of future stock price increases, options are valuable to employees when they receive them, even if the exercise price is exactly equal to the stock's market price the day the options are awarded. The intrinsic value of an option is the difference between the current stock price and the option's strike price. When an option is issued with a strike price equal to the current stock price, which is common practice among U.S. companies, the option has a $0 intrinsic value.

Companies use employee stock options (ESO) as a means to compensate employees and to better align the interests of employees and shareholders. The notion is that employees will work harder to increase their company's stock price when they can benefit directly from future price increases. Because an employee with stock options can purchase stock at a fixed price and resell it at the prevailing (expectedly higher) market price, the options create the possibility of a future gain. Unlike cash compensation, options give employees the same incentives as shareholders—to increase stock price.

Over the past 30 years, use of stock options has skyrocketed and options now make up the bulk of many executive compensation packages. Despite their popularity, stock options have a downside—they can create incentives for employees to increase stock price at any cost and by any means, including misstating earnings and engaging in transactions whose sole purpose is to inflate stock price. Options can also induce managerial myopia—managers want stock price to increase, at least until they can exercise their options and capture their gains.

Until recently, companies were not required to record the value of stock options as compensation expense. Previous GAAP (APB 25) held that options had value only to the extent that the predetermined purchase price (exercise price) was less than the market stock price on the date that the options were granted to the employee. If a company sets the exercise price equal to the market price on the date of grant, the view was that nothing of value had been given to the employee. This meant that no compensation expense was ever reported on such options. This reduced the quality of reported earnings because companies sheltered their income statements merely by setting the exercise price equal to the market price of the stock on the date of grant. Analysts and investors have long expressed serious concerns about accounting for stock options and the amount of unrecorded compensation expense tied to options.

Under considerable pressure and controversy, the FASB issued a pronouncement (SFAS 123R) that applies to stock options granted after 2005. Under the pronouncement, companies must expense the fair value of options and recognize an equivalent increase in stockholders' equity (to the additional paid-in capital account).

To illustrate the accounting for stock options, assume that Aon grants an employee 100,000 stock options with a strike price of $26, which will vest over a four-year period. The vesting period is the time over which an employee gains ownership of the shares, commonly over three to seven years. Employees usually acquire ownership ratably over time, such as 1/4 each year over four years, or acquire full (100%) vesting after the vesting period ends, called *cliff vesting*. Under SFAS 123R, Aon recognizes the fair value of the stock options granted over the employees' service period (generally interpreted as the options' vesting period).

A first step, then, is to determine the "fair value" of the option. SFAS 123R does not specify the method companies must use to estimate fair value, but most companies use the *Black-Scholes model* to estimate the value of exchange-traded options. This model, developed by professors Fischer Black and Myron Scholes, has six inputs, two of which are observable (the company's current stock price and the option's strike price). Companies must estimate the other four model inputs: option life, risk-free interest rate, stock price volatility, and dividend payout rate. These six inputs yield an estimate of the option's fair value. It is important we recognize that management selects the model inputs and, thus, can exercise some discretion over the reported fair value. The option's value computed using Black-Scholes increases with the estimated option life, risk-free interest rate, and stock price volatility; it decreases with the estimated dividend payout. (Free online Black-Scholes option calculators abound, which simplifies fair value estimation.) For analysis purposes, we can partly assess the quality of the reported fair values by comparing a company's model inputs to industry standards and to historical measures (of stock price volatility, for example).

Some companies have recently switched from the common Black-Scholes model to a more complicated binomial (or lattice-binomial) valuation method (currently fewer than 1,000 of the 17,000 publicly-traded U.S. companies use the binomial method). The basic mathematics of the Black-Scholes and binomial methods are identical, but the binomial method allows companies to insert additional assumptions into Black-Scholes and some claim that this provides a more accurate fair value. It also generally provides a lower fair value estimate than the Black-Scholes model, thus reducing the expense related to the options

Returning to our Aon example, assume that the Black-Scholes fair value of the 100,000 options granted is $1,000,000. Thus, Aon records fair value compensation expense of $250,000 each year (fair value of $1,000,000 spread over the four-year vesting period) and its additional paid-in capital increases by $250,000 each year (or $1,000,000 over the four years). Two points are worth noting. First, Aon expenses the entire fair value of the options granted ($1,000,000) regardless of whether the employee actually exercises the options. Second, subsequent changes in the options' value are *not* recognized in financial statements. Thus, the stock option expense and the increase to additional paid-in capital reflect the ESO fair value measured at the grant date.

As with any expense, there are tax consequences to stock option expense. That is, net income is affected on an after-tax basis—each dollar of expense is offset by a reduction in tax expense. Granting stock options creates a book-tax timing difference because the expense is recognized in the income statement at the grant date but is deductible for income tax purposes at the exercise date (see Module 5 for more details about book-tax timing differences). The general approach is that a deferred tax asset is recorded at the statutory rate for this timing difference. This difference reverses when the options are exercised. (Most companies grant *nonqualified stock options* (NQSOs), which are taxed like other compensation but *not* until the options are exercised; when NQSOs are exercised, the options' intrinsic value is taxed as ordinary income to the employee and the employer takes a corresponding tax deduction for the intrinsic value.)

Continuing with our Aon example, the company reports a deferred tax asset to recognize the future tax deduction of the compensation payment. Specifically, Aon reports a deferred tax benefit of $87,500 ($250,000 × 0.35) in each of the four years of the vesting period to reflect the expected reduction in future tax liability when the options are exercised. Thus, the after-tax stock option compensation expense is $162,500 (computed as $250,000 − $87,500). Each year, Aon increases the deferred tax asset account (on the balance sheet) by $87,500. The balance grows until the fourth year when the deferred tax asset balance is $350,000. When the employee exercises the options and Aon realizes the tax benefits, the company reduces taxes payable and reverses the deferred tax asset previously set up.[1] The financial statement effects template would record these transactions as follows in each of the four years of the vesting period.

		Balance Sheet						Income Statement		
Transaction	Cash Asset	+ Noncash Assets	= Liabil- ities	+ Contrib. Capital	+ Earned Capital		Rev- enues	− Expen- ses	= Net Income
Years 1,2,3,4: Grant 100,000 stock options with fair value of $10 per share, vesting over 4 years		+87,500 Deferred Tax Asset	=	+250,000 Additional Paid-In Capital	−162,500 Retained Earnings			+250,000 Wages Expense −87,500 Tax Expense	= −162,500 Net Income
At exercise: 100,000 stock options exer- cised at a $26 exercise price	+2,600,000 Cash		=	+2,600,000 Additional Paid-In Capital			−		=
At exercise: Tax effect of the exercised stock options		−350,000 Deferred Tax Asset	= −350,000 Taxes Payable				−		=

Journal entries (left margin):

```
WE      250,000
DTA      87,500
   TE            87,500
   APIC         250,000
         WE
250,000 |
         DTA
87,500 |
         TE
        | 87,500
         APIC
        | 250,000

Cash   2,600,000
   APIC        2,600,000
         Cash
2,600,000 |
         APIC
        | 2,600,000

TP      350,000
DTA            350,000
         TP
350,000 |
         DTA
        | 350,000
```

Aon's following footnote discloses many details of its stock option activities. Aon reports that 143,000 options were granted in 2010 with an average strike price of $38.00. These options had

---

[1] The tax benefit the company receives is based on the options' intrinsic value (current stock price less strike price) on the exercise date. Often, the exercise-date intrinsic value is greater than the grant-date fair value. Recall that deferred taxes are recorded based on grant-date fair value. Thus, the tax benefit received is often larger than the deferred tax asset on the company's balance sheet. In that case, any tax benefit in excess of the deferred tax asset is included in additional paid-in capital and not in net income. The excess tax benefit is classified as cash from financing activities on the statement of cash flows.

a fair value of $10.37 per share. The company also reports how many of its options outstanding have already vested and could potentially be exercised. (Recall that outstanding options affect the company's diluted EPS calculation, see Module 5.)

Stock Compensation Costs The Company recognizes compensation expense for all share-based payments to employees, including grants of employee stock options and restricted stock and restricted stock units ("RSUs"), as well as employee stock purchases related to the Employee Stock Purchase Plan, based on estimated fair value. Stock-based compensation expense recognized during the period is based on the value of the portion of stock-based payment awards that is ultimately expected to vest during the period, based on the achievement of service or performance conditions. Because the stock-based compensation expense recognized is based on awards ultimately expected to vest, it has been reduced for estimated forfeitures. Forfeitures are estimated at the time of grant and revised, if necessary, in subsequent periods if actual forfeitures differ from those estimates.

Stock Options Options to purchase common stock are granted to certain employees at 100% of market value on the date of grant. Commencing in 2010, the Company stopped granting stock options with the exception of historical contractual commitments . . . Aon uses a lattice-binomial option-pricing model to value stock options. Lattice-based option valuation models utilize a range of assumptions over the expected term of the options . . . The weighted average assumptions, the weighted average expected life and estimated fair value of employee stock options are summarized as follows:

	2010		2009		2008	
	All Other	**LPP**	**SSP**	**All Other**		**Key**
Years ended December 31	**Options**	**Options**	**Options**	**Options**	**Executives**	**Employees**
Weighted average volatility.....	28.5%	35.5%	34.1%	32.0%	29.4%	29.9%
Expected dividend yield.......	1.6%	1.3%	1.5%	1.5%	1.3%	1.4%
Risk-free rate	3.0%	1.5%	2.0%	2.6%	3.2%	3.0%
Weighted average expected life, in years..............	6.1	4.4	5.6	6.5	5.1	5.7
Weighted average estimated fair value per share........	$10.37	$12.19	$11.82	$12.34	$11.92	$12.87

A summary of the status of Aon's stock options and related information follows (shares in thousands).

	2010		2009		2008	
		Weighted-Average Exercise Price Per		**Weighted-Average Exercise Price Per**		**Weighted-Average Exercise Price Per**
Years ended December 31	**Shares**	**Share**	**Shares**	**Share**	**Shares**	**Share**
Beginning outstanding.............	15,937	$33	19,666	$31	26,479	$31
Options issued in connection with the Hewitt acquisition............	4,545	22	—	—	—	—
Granted.......................	143	38	1,551	38	1,539	44
Exercised	(6,197)	27	(4,475)	27	(6,779)	30
Forfeited and expired	(509)	35	(805)	38	(1,573)	41
Outstanding at end of year.........	13,919	32	15,937	33	19,666	31
Exercisable at end of year	11,293	30	9,884	31	10,357	30
Shares available for grant..........	22,777		8,257		8,140	

Option grants and option exercises both affect the statement of cash flows. At grant, there is no cash inflow or outflow. However, the noncash stock option compensation expense is added back as a reconciling item in the operating section of the statement of cash flows (indirect method). Aon reported an add-back on its 2010 statement of cash flows of $221 million.

An interesting, often underappreciated, fact is that stock option expense pervades the income statement. Below is a footnote from **Cisco System**'s 2010 10-K that details the allocation of its stock option expense to cost of sales, research and development, sales and marketing expenses, and general and administrative expenses.

Expense and Valuation Information for Share-Based Awards Share-based compensation expense consists primarily of expenses for stock options, stock purchase rights, restricted stock, and restricted stock units granted to employees. The following table summarizes share-based compensation expense (in millions):

Years Ended	July 31, 2010	July 25, 2009	July 26, 2008
Cost of sales—product	$ 57	$ 46	$ 40
Cost of sales—service	164	128	108
Share-based compensation expense in cost of sales	221	174	148
Research and development	450	382	339
Sales and marketing............................	536	441	438
General and administrative.......................	310	234	187
Share-based compensation expense in operating expenses	1,296	1,057	964
Total share-based compensation expense	$1,517	$1,231	$1,112

Restricted Stock and Restricted Stock Units

Many companies, including Aon, compensate employees with restricted stock instead of with stock options. Increasingly, firms have moved away from stock options in favor of restricted stock as compensation for several reasons. First, stock options were seen as creating excess compensation during recent stock-market booms. Second, stock options can create incentives for managers to take on excessive firm risk because the value of an option increases with firm risk. Restricted stock does not create such severe risk-taking incentives. Third, there are certain tax advantages to restricted stock vis-a-vis stock options. Under a restricted stock plan, the company transfers shares to the employee, but the shares are restricted in that they cannot be sold until the end of a vesting period. Restricted stock units differ from restricted stock in two key ways: first, the company does not distribute shares of stock to employees until certain conditions are met; and second, the number of shares ultimately given to employees is typically a function of their performance relative to specified targets. Aon describes its restricted stock unit plan as follows:

Restricted stock unit awards Employees may either receive service-based restricted stock units ("RSUs") or performance-based awards, which ultimately result in the receipt of RSUs, if the employee achieves his or her objectives . . . We account for service-based awards by expensing the total award value over the service period. We calculate the total award value by multiplying the estimated total number of shares to be delivered by the fair value on the date of grant . . . Performance-based RSUs may be immediately vested at the end of the performance period or may have a future additional service period. Generally, our performance awards are fixed, which means we determine the fair value of the award at the grant date, estimate the number of shares to be delivered at the end of the performance period, and recognize the expense over the performance or vesting period, whichever is longer . . . During 2010, the Company granted approximately 1.6 million shares in connection with the completion of the 2007 Leadership Performance Plan ("LPP") cycle and 84,000 shares related to other performance plans. During 2010, 2009 and 2008, the Company granted approximately 3.5 million, 3.7 million and 4.2 million restricted shares, respectively, in connection with the Company's incentive compensation plans.

A summary of the status of Aon's non-vested stock awards follows (shares in thousands).

	2010		2009		2008	
Years ended December 31	**Shares**	**Fair Value(1)**	**Shares**	**Fair Value(1)**	**Shares**	**Fair Value(1)**
Non-vested at beginning of year	12,850	$36	14,060	$35	14,150	$31
Granted	5,477	39	5,741	38	4,159	42
Vested........................	(6,938)	35	(6,285)	35	(3,753)	28
Forfeited.....................	(715)	35	(666)	37	(496)	(34)
Non-vested at end of year	10,674	$38	12,850	$36	14,060	$35

(1) Represents per share weighted average fair value of award at date of grant.

Information regarding Aon's performance-based plans as of December 31, 2010, 2009 and 2008 follows (shares in thousands, dollars in millions):

	2010	2009	2008
Potential RSUs to be issued based on current performance levels.......	6,095	7,686	6,205
Unamortized expense, based on current performance levels	$69	$154	$82

The fair value of awards that vested during 2010, 2009 and 2008 was $235 million, $223 million, and $107 million, respectively.

The accounting for restricted stock and restricted stock units is similar to that which we describe for stock options. Specifically, compensation expense is recognized at an amount equal to the value of the shares given to employees as those shares are earned. The consequent decline in retained earnings is offset by an increase in paid-in capital. Stockholders' equity is, therefore, unaffected.

Accounting for restricted stock is illustrated in the following template:

	Balance Sheet						Income Statement		
Transaction	**Cash Asset**	**+ Noncash Assets**	**= Liabil- ities**	**+ Contrib. Capital**	**+ Earned Capital**		**Rev- enues**	**− Expen- ses**	**= Net Income**
Year 1: Company issues 100 shares of $10 par restricted stock with a market value of $30 per share, vesting ratably over 6 years			=	+1,000 Common Stock +2,000 Additional Paid-In Capital −3,000 Deferred Compensation				−	=
Years 1,2,3,4,5,6: Record compensation expense for year			=	+500 Deferred Compensation	−500 Retained Earnings			− +500 Wage Expense	= −500

DC   3,000
　CS   1,000
　APIC   2,000
　　DC
3,000 |
　CS
　| 1,000
　APIC
　| 2,000

WE   500
　DC   500
　　WE
500 |
　DC
　| 500

The company records the restricted stock grants as a share issuance exactly as if the shares were sold. That is, the common stock account increases by the par value of the shares and additional paid-in capital increases for the remainder of the share value. However, instead of cash received, the company records a deferred compensation (contra equity) account for the value of the shares that have not yet been issued. This reduces equity. Thus, granting restricted shares leaves the total dollar amount of equity unaffected.

Subsequently, the value of shares given to employees is treated as compensation expense and recorded over the vesting period. Each year, the deferred compensation account is reduced by the vested shares and wage expense is recorded, thus reducing retained earnings. Total equity is unaffected by this transaction as the reduction of the deferred compensation contra equity account (thereby increasing stockholders' equity) is exactly offset by the decrease in retained earnings. The remaining deferred compensation account decreases total stockholders' equity until the end of the vesting period when the total restricted stock grant has been recognized as wage expense. Equity is, therefore, never increased when restricted stock is issued. As of 2010, Aon reports that "Unamortized deferred compensation expense, which includes both options and awards, amounted to $254 million as of December 31, 2010, with a remaining weighted-average amortization period of approximately 2.0 years."

MID-MODULE REVIEW 1

Part 1 Assume that **Accenture (ACN)** reported the following transactions relating to its stock accounts in 2012.

Jan 15   Issued 10,000 shares of $5 par value common stock at $17 cash per share
Mar 31   Purchased 2,000 shares of its own common stock at $15 cash per share.
June 25   Reissued 1,000 shares of its treasury stock at $20 cash per share.

Use the financial statement effects template to identify the effects of these stock transactions.

Part 2 **Accenture** reports the following table in its 10-K, which is related to its stock compensation plan.

	Number of Options	Weighted Average Exercise Price	Weighted Average Remaining Contractual Term (In Years)	Aggregate Intrinsic Value
Options outstanding as of August 31, 2009........	29,040,084	$19.35	3.6	$412,098
Granted.....................................	16,539	40.87		
Exercised	(8,010,117)	18.63		
Forfeited	(126,444)	21.72		
Options outstanding as of August 31, 2010.........	20,920,062	19.63	2.6	356,341
Options exercisable as of August 31, 2010.........	20,386,549	19.42	2.5	351,374
Options exercisable as of August 31, 2009.........	28,150,454	19.11	3.4	406,360
Options exercisable as of August 31, 2008.........	32,789,179	18.69	4.3	745,341

Required

a. Explain the terms "Granted," "Exercised," and "Forfeited." What is the meaning of "Weighted Average Exercise Price"?
b. Explain how the compensation cost related to the options above is recognized in financial statements.

The solution is on page 8-48.

The solution is on page 8-48.

LO2 Explain and analyze accounting for earned capital, including cash dividends, stock dividends, and comprehensive income.

ANALYZING EARNED CAPITAL

We now turn to the earned capital portion of stockholders' equity. Earned capital represents the cumulative profit that the company has retained. Recall that earned capital increases each period by income earned and decreases by any losses incurred. Earned capital also decreases by dividends paid to shareholders. Not all dividends are paid in the form of cash. Companies can pay dividends in many forms, including property (land, for example) or additional shares of stock. We cover both cash and stock dividends in this section. Earned capital also includes the positive or negative effects of accumulated other comprehensive income (AOCI). The earned capital of Aon is highlighted in the following graphic.

Stockholders' Equity (In millions except per share amounts)	December 31, 2010	December 31, 2009
Common stock-$1 par value Authorized: 750 shares (issued: 2010—385.9; 2009—362.7)	$ 386	$ 363
Additional paid-in capital	4,000	3,215
Treasury stock at cost (shares: 2010—53.6; 2009—96.4)	(2,079)	(3,859)
Retained earnings	**7,861**	**7,335**
Accumulated other comprehensive loss	**(1,917)**	**(1,675)**
Total Aon stockholders' equity......................................	8,251	5,379
Noncontrolling interest..	55	52
Total equity..	$8,306	$5,431

* We list contributed and earned capital accounts together for learning purposes; in the Aon balance sheet, these accounts are grouped by positive and negative balances.

Cash Dividends

Many companies, but not all, pay dividends. Their reasons for dividend payments are varied. Most dividends are paid in cash on a quarterly basis. Aon makes the following disclosure relating to dividends in its 2010 10-K:

> **Dividend**   During 2010, 2009, and 2008, Aon paid dividends on its common stock of $175 million, $165 million and $171 million, respectively. Dividends paid per common share were $0.60 for each of the years ended December 31, 2010, 2009, and 2008.

Outsiders closely monitor dividend payments. It is generally perceived that the level of dividend payments is related to the company's expected long-term recurring income. Accordingly, dividend increases are usually viewed as positive signals about future performance and are accompanied by stock price increases. By that logic, companies rarely reduce their dividends unless absolutely necessary because dividend reductions are often met with substantial stock price declines.

Financial Effects of Cash Dividends

Cash dividends reduce both cash and retained earnings by the amount of the cash dividends paid. To illustrate, assume that Aon declares and pays cash dividends in the amount of $10 million. The financial statement effects of this cash dividend payment are as follows:

	Balance Sheet					Income Statement		
Transaction	Cash Asset	+ Noncash Assets	= Liabil- ities	+ Contrib. Capital	+ Earned Capital	Rev- enues	– Expen- ses	= Net Income
Payment of $10 million in cash dividends	−10 mil. Cash	=			−10 mil. Retained Earnings		–	=

RE   10 mil.
   Cash   10 mil.

____RE____
10 mil. |
   Cash
   | 10 mil.

Dividend payments do not affect net income. They directly reduce retained earnings and bypass the income statement.

Dividends on preferred stock have priority over those on common stock, including unpaid prior years' preferred dividends (called *dividends in arrears*) when preferred stock is cumulative. To illustrate, assume that a company has 15,000 shares of $50 par value, 8% preferred stock outstanding;

assume that the preferred stock is cumulative, which means that any unpaid dividends cumulate and must be paid before common dividends. The company also has 50,000 shares of $5 par value common stock outstanding. During its first three years in business, assume that the company declares $20,000 dividends in the first year, $260,000 of dividends in the second year, and $60,000 of dividends in the third year. Cash dividends paid to each class of stock in each of the three years follows:

	Preferred Stock	Common Stock
Year 1—$20,000 cash dividends paid		
Current-year dividend (15,000 shares × $50 par × 8%; but only $20,000 paid, leaving $40,000 in arrears)	$20,000	
Balance to common		$ 0
Year 2—$260,000 cash dividends paid		
Dividends in arrears from Year 1 ([15,000 shares × $50 par × 8%] − $20,000)	40,000	
Current-year dividend (15,000 shares × $50 par × 8%)	60,000	
Balance to common		160,000
Year 3—$60,000 cash dividends paid		
Current-year dividend (15,000 shares × $50 par × 8%)	60,000	
Balance to common		0

MID-MODULE REVIEW 2

Assume that **Accenture (ACN)** has outstanding 10,000 shares of $100 par value, 5% preferred stock and 50,000 shares of $5 par value common stock. During its first three years in business, assume that Accenture declared no dividends in the first year, $300,000 of cash dividends in the second year, and $80,000 of cash dividends in the third year.

a. If preferred stock is cumulative, determine the dividends paid to each class of stock for each of the three years.
b. If preferred stock is noncumulative, determine the dividends paid to each class of stock for each of the three years.

The solution is on page 8-49.

Stock Dividends and Splits

Dividends need not be paid in cash. Many companies pay dividends in the form of additional shares of stock. Companies can also distribute additional shares to their stockholders with a stock split. We cover both of these distributions in this section.

Stock Dividends

When dividends are paid in the form of the company's stock, retained earnings are reduced and contributed capital is increased. However, the amount by which retained earnings are reduced depends on the proportion of the outstanding shares distributed to the total outstanding shares on the dividend distribution date. Exhibit 8.2 illustrates two possibilities depending on whether stock dividends are classified as small stock dividends or large stock dividends. The break point between small and large is 20–25% of the outstanding shares. When the number of additional shares issued as a stock dividend is so great that it could materially reduce share price, the transaction is akin to a stock split. The 20–25% guideline is used as a rule of thumb to distinguish material stock price effects.

For *small stock dividends,* retained earnings are reduced by the *market* value of the shares distributed (dividend shares × market price per share), and par value and contributed capital together are increased by the same amount. For *large stock dividends,* retained earnings are reduced by the *par* value of the shares distributed (dividend shares × par value per share), and common stock is increased by the same amount (no change to additional paid-in capital).

To illustrate the financial statement effects of stock dividends, assume that **BearingPoint** has 1 million shares of $5 par common stock outstanding. It then declares a small stock dividend of 15% of the outstanding shares (1,000,000 shares × 15% = 150,000 shares) when

EXHIBIT 8.2	Analysis of Stock Dividend Effects

Percentage of Outstanding Shares Distributed	Retained Earnings	Contributed Capital
Less than 20-25% (*small stock dividend treated as a dividend*)	Reduce by **market value** of shares distributed	Common stock increased by: Dividend shares × Par value per share; Additional paid-in capital increased for the balance
More than 20-25% (*large stock dividend treated as a stock split*)	Reduce by **par value** of shares distributed	Common stock increased by: Dividend shares × Par value per share

the market price of the stock is $30 per share. This small stock dividend has the following financial statement effects:

	Balance Sheet							Income Statement		
Transaction	Cash Asset	+	Noncash Assets	=	Liabil- ities	+	Contrib. Capital	+ Earned Capital	Rev- enues	− Expen- ses	= Net Income
Distribute 150,000 shares with a market value of $4.5 mil. as a small stock dividend				=			+750,000 Common Stock +$3,750,000 Additional Paid-In Capital	−$4,500,000 Retained Earnings		−	=

RE   4.5 mil.
   CS   0.75 mil.
   APIC   3.75 mil.

RE	
4.5 mil.	
	CS
	0.75 mil.
	APIC
	3.75 mil.

The company reduces retained earnings by $4,500,000, which equals the market value of the small stock dividend (150,000 shares × $30 market price per share). The increase in contributed capital is split between the par value of $750,000 (150,000 shares × $5 par value) and additional paid-in capital ($3,750,000). Similar to cash dividend payments, stock dividends, whether large or small, never impact income.

Next, assume that instead, **BearingPoint** declares a large stock dividend of 70% of the 1 million outstanding common ($5 par) shares when the market price of the stock is $30 per share. This large stock dividend is treated like a stock split and has the following financial statement effects:

	Balance Sheet							Income Statement		
Transaction	Cash Asset	+	Noncash Assets	=	Liabil- ities	+	Contrib. Capital	+ Earned Capital	Rev- enues	− Expen- ses	= Net Income
Distribute 700,000 shares as a large stock dividend				=			+$3,500,000 Common Stock	−$3,500,000 Retained Earnings		−	=

RE   3.5 mil.
   CS   3.5 mil.

RE	
3.5 mil.	
	CS
	3.5 mil.

The company's retained earnings declines by $3,500,000, which equals the par value of the large stock dividend (700,000 shares × $5 par value per share). Common stock is increased by the par value of $3,500,000. There is no effect on additional paid-in capital since large stock dividends are reported at par value.

For both large and small stock dividends, companies are required to show comparable shares outstanding for all prior periods for which earnings per share (EPS) is reported in the statements. The reasoning is that a stock dividend has no effect on the ownership percentage of each common stockholder. As such, to show a dilution in reported EPS would erroneously suggest a decline in profitability when it is simply due to an increase in shares outstanding.

Stock Splits

A stock split is a proportionate distribution of shares and, as such, is similar in substance to a large stock dividend. A typical stock split is 2-for-1, which means that the company distributes one additional share for each share owned by a shareholder. Following the distribution, each investor owns twice as many shares, so that their percentage ownership in the company is unchanged.

A stock split is not a monetary transaction and, as such, there are no financial statement effects. However, companies must disclose the new number of shares outstanding for all periods presented in the financial statements. Further, many states require that the par value of shares be proportionately adjusted as well (for example, halved for a 2-for-1 split).

If state law requires that par value not be reduced for a stock dividend, this event should be described as a *stock split affected in the form of a dividend*. The following disclosure from **John Deere**'s 2007 annual report provides such an example:

> **Stock Split in Form of Dividend** On November 14, 2007, a special meeting of stockholders was held authorizing a two-for-one stock split effected in the form of a 100 percent stock dividend to holders of record on November 26, 2007, distributed on December 3, 2007. All share and per share data (except par value) have been adjusted to reflect the effect of the stock split for all periods presented. The number of shares of common stock issuable upon exercise of outstanding stock options, vesting of other stock awards, and the number of shares reserved for issuance under various employee benefit plans were proportionately increased in accordance with terms of the respective plans.

MID-MODULE REVIEW 3

Assume that the stockholders' equity of **Arbitron, Inc.** at December 31, 2011, follows.

5% preferred stock, $100 par value, 10,000 shares authorized; 4,000 shares issued and outstanding.........................	$ 400,000
Common stock, $5 par value, 200,000 shares authorized; 50,000 shares issued and outstanding.......................	250,000
Paid-in capital in excess of par value-Preferred stock..............	40,000
Paid-in capital in excess of par value-Common stock.............	300,000
Retained earnings	656,000
Total stockholders' equity	$1,646,000

Use the template to identify the financial statement effects for each of the following transactions that occurred during 2012:

Apr. 1   Declared and issued a 100% stock dividend on all outstanding shares of common stock when the market value of the stock was $11 per share.

Dec. 7   Declared and issued a 3% stock dividend on all outstanding shares of common stock when the market value of the stock was $7 per share.

Dec. 31   Declared and paid a cash dividend of $1.20 per share on all outstanding shares.

The solution is on page 8-49.

IFRS Alert
IFRS does not use the term "other comprehensive income" but reports that account in a *statement of recognized income and expenses* (SoRIE). As with GAAP's other comprehensive income, SoRIE includes all changes to equity, other than transactions with owners.

Accumulated Other Comprehensive Income

Comprehensive income is a more inclusive notion of company performance than net income. It includes all changes in equity (assets less liabilities) that occur during a period except those resulting from contributions by and distributions to owners. It's important to note that comprehensive income includes both net income and other items, which collectively are called *other comprehensive income*.

Specifically, other comprehensive income includes (and net income excludes) foreign currency translation adjustments, unrealized changes in market values of available-for-sale securities, pension liability adjustments, and changes in market values of certain derivative investments. Comprehensive income, therefore, includes the effects of economic events that are often outside of management's control. Accordingly, some assert that net income measures management's performance, while comprehensive income measures company performance. Each period, net income or loss is added to retained earnings so that the balance sheet maintains a running total of the company's cumulative net income and losses (less any dividends paid out). In the same way, each period, comprehensive income items that are not included in net income (that is, all *other comprehensive income* items) are added to a balance sheet account called Accumulated Other Comprehensive Income (or Accumulated Other Comprehensive Loss if the comprehensive items are losses). This account maintains a running balance of the cumulative differences between net income and comprehensive income.

Aon reports the following components of its accumulated other comprehensive income in its 10-K report:

($ millions)	Net Derivative Gains (Losses)	Net Foreign Exchange Translation Adjustments*	Net Postretirement Benefit Obligations	Net Unrealized Investment Gains (Losses)	Accumulated Other Comprehensive Income
Balance as of January 1, 2008.........	$ 24	$284	$(1,110)	$76	$ (726)
Other comprehensive income	(37)	(182)	(497)	(20)	(736)
Balance as of December 31, 2008......	(13)	102	(1,607)	56	(1,462)
Other comprehensive income	13	199	(413)	(12)	(213)
Balance as of December 31, 2009......	0	301	(2,020)	44	(1,675)
Other comprehensive income	(24)	(133)	(41)	(44)**	(242)
Balance as of December 31, 2010......	$(24)	$168	$(2,061)	$ 0	$(1,917)

* Net of amount attributable to noncontrolling interest

** Relates to consolidation of a variable interest entity in 2010.

Aon's accumulated other comprehensive income for 2010 includes the four following items that affect stockholders' equity and are not reflected in net income:

1. **Net derivative losses**, $(24) million. Hedging transactions relate to the company's use of financial instruments (derivatives) to hedge exposure to various risks such as fluctuations in foreign currency exchange rates, commodity prices, and interest rates. This account relates to unrealized losses on cash flow hedges, which we discuss in the appendix to Module 9.
2. **Net foreign exchange translation adjustments**, $168 million. This is the cumulative translation adjustment for the net assets of foreign subsidiaries whose balance sheets are denominated in foreign currencies. A gain implies that the $US has weakened relative to foreign currencies; such as when assets denominated in foreign currencies translate to more $US. We discuss the effects of foreign currency translation adjustments on accumulated other comprehensive income in more detail below.
3. **Net postretirement benefit obligations**, $(2,061) million. This amount mainly relates to unrealized losses on pension investments or can derive from changes in pension plans that increase the pension liability. We discuss the accounting for pension plans and other postretirement benefit obligations in Module 10.
4. **Net unrealized investment gains**, $(0) this year. Unrealized gains and losses on available-for-sale securities are not reflected in net income. Instead, they are accumulated in a separate equity account, AOCI, until the securities are sold. We discuss the accounting for these unrealized gains (losses) in Module 9.

We discuss accounting for available-for-sale securities and derivatives in Module 9, pensions in Module 10, and the income statement effects of foreign currency translation adjustments in Module 5. In the next section, we discuss the balance sheet effects of foreign currency translation adjustments, specifically their impact on accumulated other comprehensive income. During 2010, Aon reported other comprehensive loss of $(242) million, which is the sum of the changes in each of the four components of AOCI, as shown on the statement above. This other comprehensive loss when added to the AOCI balance of $(1,675) at the beginning of the year yields the AOCI balance of $(1,917) at year-end.

Foreign Currency Translation Effects on Accumulated Other Comprehensive Income

Many companies have international transactions denominated in foreign currencies. They might purchase assets in foreign currencies, borrow money in foreign currencies, and transact business with their customers and suppliers in foreign currencies. Other companies might have subsidiaries whose entire balance sheets and income statements are stated in foreign currencies. Financial statements prepared according to U.S. GAAP must be reported in $US. This means that financial statements of foreign subsidiaries must be translated into $US before they are consolidated with those of the U.S. parent company. This translation process can markedly alter both the balance sheet and income statement. We discuss the income statement effects of foreign currency translation in Module 5 and the balance sheet effects in this section.

Consider a U.S. company with a foreign subsidiary that conducts its business in Euros. The subsidiary prepares its financial statements in Euros. Assume that the $US weakens vis-à-vis the Euro during the current period—that is, each Euro can now purchase more $US. When the balance sheet is translated into $US, the assets and liabilities are reported at higher $US than before the $US weakened. This result is shown in accounting equation format in Exhibit 8.3.[2]

EXHIBIT 8.3	Balance Sheet Effects of Changes in U.S. Dollar to Euro Exchange Rates					
Currency	**Assets**	**=**	**Liabilities**	**+**	**Equity**	
$US weakens	Increase	=	Increase	+	Increase	
$US strengthens.	Decrease	=	Decrease	+	Decrease	

The amount reflected as an increase (decrease) in equity is called a **foreign currency translation adjustment**. The *cumulative* foreign currency translation adjustment is included in accumulated other comprehensive income (or loss) as illustrated above for Aon. Foreign currency translation adjustments are direct adjustments to stockholders' equity; they do not impact reported net income. Because assets are greater than liabilities for solvent companies, the cumulative translation adjustment is positive when the $US weakens and negative when the dollar strengthens.

Referring to Aon's accumulated other comprehensive income table on the previous page, the cumulative foreign currency translation is a gain of $301 million at the beginning of 2010, which shrinks by $133 million (net of $2 million credited to noncontrolling shareholders) during the year to yield a cumulative year-end gain of $168 million. The $133 million reduction in Aon's equity reflects a strengthening of the $US vis-à-vis the foreign currencies in which Aon transacted in 2010. That is, as the $US strengthened, Aon's foreign assets and liabilities translated into fewer $US at year-end. This decreased Aon's equity (because assets are greater than liabilities for solvent companies). In general, unrealized losses (or gains) remain in other accumulated comprehensive income as long as the company owns the foreign subsidiaries to which the losses relate. The translation adjustments fluctuate between positive and negative amounts as the value of the $US fluctuates. However, when a subsidiary is sold, any remaining foreign currency translation adjustment (positive or negative) is immediately recognized in current income along with other gains or losses arising from sale of the subsidiary.

NONCONTROLLING INTEREST

Noncontrolling interest represents the equity of noncontrolling (minority) shareholders who only have a claim on the net assets of one or more of the subsidiaries in the consolidated entity. As we discuss in Module 9, if a company acquires a controlling interest in a subsidiary, it must consolidate that subsidiary when preparing its financial statements, thus reporting all of the subsidiary's assets and liabilities on the consolidated balance sheet and reporting all of the subsidiary's revenues and expenses in the consolidated income statement. If the company acquires less than 100% of the subsidiary, it must still include 100% of the subsidiary's assets, liabilities, revenues and expenses in its consolidated balance sheet and income statement, but now there are two groups of shareholders that have a claim on the net assets and earnings of the subsidiary company: the parent company and the noncontrolling shareholders (those shareholders who continue to own shares of the subsidiary company).

Consolidated stockholders' equity must now report the equity of these two groups of shareholders and consolidated net income must now be apportioned between the two groups. For Aon, the consolidated income statement apportions net income as follows:

---

[2] We assume that the company translates the subsidiary's financial statements using the more common **current rate method**, which is required for subsidiaries operating independently from the parent. Under the current rate method, most items in the balance sheet are translated using exchange rates in effect at the period-end consolidation date and the income statement is translated using the average exchange rate for the period. An alternative procedure is the *temporal method*, covered in advanced accounting courses, which uses historical exchange rates for some assets and liabilities.

Aon Consolidated Income Statement ($ millions)	
Revenues	$8,512
Expenses	7,780
Net income	732
Less: Net income attributable to noncontrolling interest	26
Net income attributable to Aon stockholders	$ 706

Net income is apportioned between the portion attributable to the noncontrolling interest and the portion attributable to the parent company's shareholders. Although it can be more complicated, in its simplest form, if the noncontrolling shareholders own 20% of a subsidiary, 20% of the subsidiary's net income is attributable to that shareholder group and the parent's shareholders received the balance of 80%.

The common stock, additional paid-in capital and retained earnings accounts we see on the consolidated balance sheet represent those of the parent's shareholders. The retained earnings attributable to the parent's shareholders is increased (decreased) by the income (loss) attributable to the parent's shareholders and is decreased by the dividends paid to the parent's shareholders in a reconciliation similar to the following for Aon:

Aon Retained Earnings Account ($ millions)	
Beginning balance of retained earnings	$7,335
Net income attributable to parent	706
Dividends	(175)
Other adjustments	(5)
Ending balance of retained earnings	$7,861

The equity of the *noncontrolling* interest, however, is only represented by one equity account labeled Noncontrolling Interest. It is updated similarly to the stockholders' equity for the parent's shareholders, that is, it is increased (decreased) by the income (loss) attributable to the noncontrolling shareholders and is decreased by the dividends paid to the noncontrolling shareholders:

Aon Noncontrolling Interest Equity Account ($ millions)	
Beginning balance (fair value at acquisition date)	$52
Net income attributable to noncontrolling interest	26
Dividends declared and paid to noncontrolling shareholders	(20)
Other adjustments	(3)
Ending balance	$55

Again, although it can be more complicated, if the noncontrolling interest owns 20% of a subsidiary company, the balance in the noncontrolling interest equity account will equal 20% of the stockholders' equity of the subsidiary company. (This is not 20% of the consolidated company, only 20% of the subsidiary company.)

Finally, the noncontrolling interest equity account is reported as a separate line in the consolidated stockholders' equity as follows:

Aon Consolidated Balance Sheet Stockholders' Equity (In millions except per share amounts)	2010
Common stock—$1 par value Authorized: 750 shares (issued: 2010—385.9; 2009—362.7)	$ 386
Additional paid-in capital	4,000
Treasury stock at cost (shares: 2010—53.6; 2009—96.4)	(2,079)
Retained earnings	7,861
Accumulated other comprehensive loss	(1,917)
Total Aon stockholders' equity	8,251
Noncontrolling interest	55
Total equity	$8,306

Analysis and Interpretation of Noncontrolling Interest

As we discuss more fully in Module 3, the return on equity (ROE) computation is usually performed from the perspective of the parent company's shareholders. Consequently, the numerator is usually the net income attributable to the parent company shareholders and the denominator includes only the equity of the parent company's shareholders (excluding noncontrolling interest equity). For the Aon financial statements shown above, that calculation follows (we use the year-end balance of equity, and not average equity, since we only illustrate one year in this example):

$$\text{ROE} = \frac{\$706}{\$8,251} = 8.6\%$$

Noncontrolling interest is reported as a component of stockholders' equity and represents the claim of the noncontrolling interest to their proportionate share of the net assets and net income *of the subsidiary in which they own stock.* These shareholders do not have a claim on the net assets or income of any other subsidiary or of the parent company. Further, their claim is a residual claim, like that of any other shareholder; that is, they are not entitled to a preference in dividends or payouts in liquidation.

Summary of Stockholders' Equity

The statement of shareholders' equity summarizes the transactions that affect stockholders' equity during the period. This statement reconciles the beginning and ending balances of important stockholders' equity accounts. Aon's statement of stockholders' equity is in Exhibit 8.4.

Aon's statement of shareholders' equity reveals the following key activities for 2010:

EXHIBIT 8.4   Aon's Statement of Stockholders' Equity

(millions)	Shares	Common Stock and Additional Paid-in Capital	Retained Earnings	Treasury Stock	Accumulated Other Comprehensive Loss, Net of Tax	Non-controlling Interest	Total	Comprehensive Income
Balance at December 31, 2009	362.7	$3,578	$7,335	$(3,859)	$(1,675)	$52	$5,431	$583
Adoption of new accounting guidance	—	—	44	—	(44)	—	—	(44)
Balance at January 1, 2010	362.7	3,578	7,379	(3,859)	(1,719)	52	5,431	539
Net income.	—	—	706	—	—	26	732	732
Shares issued—Hewitt acquisition.	61.0	2,474	—	—	—	—	2,474	—
Shares issued—employee benefit plans	2.2	135	—	—	—	—	135	—
Shares purchased	—	—	—	(250)	—	—	(250)	—
Shares reissued—employee benefit plans. . . .	—	(370)	(49)	370	—	—	(49)	—
Shares retired	(40.0)	(1,660)	—	1,660	—	—	—	—
Tax benefit—employee benefit plans.	—	20	—	—	—	—	20	—
Stock compensation expense	—	221	—	—	—	—	221	—
Dividends to stockholders	—	—	(175)	—	—	—	(175)	—
Change in net derivative gains/losses	—	—	—	—	(24)	—	(24)	(24)
Net foreign currency translation adjustments	—	—	—	—	(133)	(2)	(135)	(135)
Net postretirement benefit obligation	—	—	—	—	(41)	—	(41)	(41)
Purchase of subsidiary shares from noncontrolling interest	—	(12)	—	—	—	(3)	(15)	—
Capital contribution by noncontrolling interest	—	—	—	—	—	2	2	—
Dividends paid to noncontrolling interest on subsidiary common stock.	—	—	—	—	—	(20)	(20)	—
Balance at December 31, 2010	385.9	$4,386	$7,861	$(2,079)	$(1,917)	$55	$8,306	$532

1 Shares issued are recorded as an increase in common stock (for the par value) and additional paid-in capital (for the excess of the value of the shares issued over the par value). Aon combines common stock and additional paid-in capital accounts into one column for total proceeds. The cost of shares repurchased is recorded as treasury stock. The cost of shares reissued and/or retired is recorded as a reduction of the treasury stock account since these are treasury shares. When shares are retired, the par value of the shares retired is removed from common stock and additional paid-in capital. Aon does not provide information relating to accounting for share reissuance for the employee benefit plans.

[2] Tax benefits (in excess of the deferred tax asset previously recorded) arising from the exercise of employee stock options are recorded as an increase in additional paid-in capital (not as a reduction of tax expense).

[3] Dividends are recorded as a reduction of retained earnings.

[4] Change in the fair value of derivatives relates to cash flow derivatives. These unrealized gains (losses) are reflected as increases (decreases) in AOCI until the underlying transaction occurs, at which time they are removed from AOCI and transferred into the income statement. We discuss the accounting for derivatives in the appendix to Module 9.

[5] Net foreign currency translation adjustments relate to the translation of foreign currency-denominated balance sheets at year-end into $US. The negative amount implied that the $US has strengthened vis-à-vis the currency in which the financial statements of foreign subsidiaries are maintained with a consequent decline in the $US value of the net assets of those subsidiaries.

[6] The adjustment relating to postretirement benefit obligations relates to the financial statement effects of the changes in pension benefits or actuarial assumptions. We discuss the accounting for pension plans and other postretirement benefits in Module 10.

[7] Proceeds from sales and repurchases of the stock of noncontrolling shareholders as well as dividends paid to noncontrolling shareholders are reflected in the noncontrolling equity account.

One final point: the financial press sometimes refers to a measure called **book value per share**. This is the net book value of the company that is available to common shareholders, defined as: stockholders' equity of the parent's shareholders less preferred stock (and preferred additional paid-in capital) divided by the number of common shares outstanding (issued common shares less treasury shares). Aon's book value per share of its common stock at the end of 2010 is computed as: $8,251 million/(385.9 million shares − 53.6 million shares) = $24.83 book value per share. In contrast, Aon's **market price per share** ranged from $36.81 to $42.32 in the 4th quarter of 2010.

EQUITY CARVE-OUTS AND CONVERTIBLES

Corporate divestitures, or **equity carve-outs**, are increasingly common as companies seek to augment shareholder value through partial or total divestiture of operating units. Generally, equity carve-outs are motivated by the notion that consolidated financial statements often obscure the performance of individual business units, thus complicating their evaluation by outsiders. Corporate managers are concerned that this difficulty in assessing the performance of individual business units limits their ability to reach full valuation. Shareholder value is, therefore, not maximized. In response, conglomerates have divested subsidiaries so that the market can individually price them.

LO3 Describe and interpret accounting for equity carve-outs and convertible debt.

Sell-Offs

Equity carve-outs take many forms. The first and simplest form of divestiture is the outright sale of a business unit, called a **sell-off**. In this case, the company sells its equity interest to an unrelated party. The sale is accounted for just like the sale of any other asset. Specifically, any excess (deficit) of cash received over the book value of the business unit sold is recorded as a gain (loss) on the sale.

To illustrate, in 2010, **Conoco Phillips** sold its **Syncrude Canada Ltd.** business for $4.6 billion and recorded a pretax gain on that sale of $2.9 billion as disclosed in the following excerpt from its 2010 annual report:

> On June 25, 2010, we sold our 9.03 percent interest in the Syncrude Canada Ltd. joint venture for $4.6 billion. The $2.9 billion before-tax gain was included in the "Gain on dispositions" line of our consolidated statement of operations. The cash proceeds were included in the "Proceeds from asset dispositions" line within the investing cash flow section of our consolidated statement of cash flows. At the time of disposition, Syncrude had a net carrying value of $1.75 billion, which included $1.97 billion of properties, plants and equipment. During 2010 until its disposition, Syncrude contributed $327 million in intercompany sales and other operating revenues, and generated income before taxes of $127 million and net income of $93 million for the E&P segment.

The financial statement effects of this transaction follow:

- Conoco received $4.6 billion in cash, which it reported as a component of cash flows from investing activities in its statement of cash flows.
- The Syncrude joint venture was reported on Conoco's balance sheet at $1.75 billion on the date of sale.
- Conoco's gain on sale equaled the proceeds ($4.6 billion) less the carrying amount of the business sold ($1.75 billion), or $2.85 billion which Conoco rounds to $2.9 billion in the footnote referenced above.
- Conoco subtracts the gain on sale in computing net cash flows from operating activities to remove the gain from net income; cash proceeds are reported as a cash inflow in the investing section.

Spin-Offs

A **spin-off** is a second form of divestiture. In this case, the parent company distributes the subsidiary shares that it owns as a dividend to its shareholders who, then, own shares in the subsidiary directly rather than through the parent company. In recording this dividend, the parent company reduces retained earnings by the book value of the equity method investment, thereby removing the investment in the subsidiary from the parent's balance sheet.

The spin-off of the **Kraft Foods** subsidiary by Altria is an example of this type of equity carve-out. Altria describes its spin-off of Kraft as follows:

> **Kraft Spin-Off** On March 30, 2007 (the "Kraft Distribution Date"), Altria Group, Inc. distributed all of its remaining interest in Kraft on a pro-rata basis to Altria Group, Inc. stockholders of record as of the close of business on March 16, 2007 (the "Kraft Record Date") in a tax-free distribution. The distribution ratio was 0.692024 of a share of Kraft for each share of Altria Group, Inc. common stock outstanding. Altria Group, Inc. stockholders received cash in lieu of fractional shares of Kraft. Following the distribution, Altria Group, Inc. does not own any shares of Kraft.

Altria treats the distribution of its Kraft shares as a dividend, which Altria reports in the following excerpt from its statement of stockholders' equity.

| (In millions, except per share) | Common Stock | Additional Paid-in Capital | Earnings Reinvested in the Business | Accumulated Other Comprehensive Earnings (Losses) | | | Cost of Repurchased Stock | Total Stock-holders' Equity |
				Currency Translation Adjustments	Other	Total		
Balances, December 31, 2006	$935	$6,356	$59,879	$ (97)	$(3,711)	$(3,808)	$(23,743)	$39,619
Comprehensive earnings:								
Net earnings			9,786					9,786
Other comprehensive earnings (losses), net of income taxes:								
Currency translation adjustments				736		736		736
Change in net loss and prior service cost					744	744		744
Change in fair value of derivatrives accounted for as hedges					(18)	(18)		(18)
Total other comprehensive earnings								1,462
Total comprehensive earnings								11,248
Adoption of FIN 48 and FAS 13-2			711					711
Exercise of stock options and issuance of other stock awards		528					289	817
Cash dividends declared ($3.05 per share)			(6,430)					(6,430)
Spin-off of Kraft Foods Inc.			(29,520)	89	2,020	2,109		(27,411)
Balances, December 31, 2007	$935	$6,884	$34,426	$728	$ (965)	$ (237)	$(23,454)	$18,554

The $29,520 million book value of the Kraft subsidiary (the amount at which this equity investment is reported on Altria's balance sheet) is removed from Altria's balance sheet when the shares are distributed to Altria's shareholders, and that amount is subtracted from Altria's retained earnings (titled "Earnings Reinvested in the Business"). Altria also removes all amounts relating to Kraft that impacted its Accumulated Other Comprehensive Earnings (a net of $2,109 million). In total, the Kraft spin-off reduced Altria's equity by $27,411 million.

Split-Offs

The **split-off** is a third form of equity carve-out. In this case, the parent company buys back its own stock using the shares of the subsidiary company instead of cash. After completing this transaction, the subsidiary is an independent publicly traded company.

The parent treats the split-off like any other purchase of treasury stock. As such, the treasury stock account is increased and the equity method investment account is reduced, reflecting the distribution of that asset. The dollar amount recorded for this treasury stock depends on how the distribution is set up. There are two possibilities:

1. **Pro rata distribution**. Shares are distributed to stockholders on a pro rata basis. Namely, a shareholder owning 10% of the outstanding stock of the parent company receives 10% of the shares of the subsidiary. The treasury stock account is increased by the *book value* of the investment in the subsidiary. The accounting is similar to the purchase of treasury stock for cash, except that shares of the subsidiary are paid to shareholders instead of cash.

2. **Non pro rata distribution**. This case is like a tender offer where individual stockholders can accept or reject the distribution. The treasury stock account is recorded at the *market value* of the shares of the subsidiary distributed. Since the investment account can only be reduced by its book value, a gain or loss on distribution is recorded in the income statement for the difference. (The SEC allows companies to record the difference as an adjustment to additional paid-in capital; the usual practice, as might be expected, is for companies to report any gain as part of income.)

Bristol-Myers Squibb's non pro rata split-off of its subsidiary, **Mead Johnson**, provides an example. This transaction is described in the following excerpt from footnotes to Bristol-Myers' 10-K:

> **Mead Johnson Nutrition Company Split-off** The split-off of the remaining interest in Mead Johnson was completed on December 23, 2009. The split-off was effected through the exchange offer of previously held 170 million shares of Mead Johnson, after converting its Class B common stock to Class A common stock, for 269 million outstanding shares of the Company's stock resulting in a pre-tax gain of $7,275 million, $7,157 million net of taxes. The shares received in connection with the exchange were valued using the closing price on December 23, 2009, of $25.70 and reflected as treasury stock. The gain on the exchange was determined using the sum of the fair value of the shares received plus the net deficit of Mead Johnson attributable to the Company less taxes and other direct expenses related to the transaction, including a tax reserve of $244 million which was established.

From an accounting standpoint, the split-off of Mead Johnson is treated like the purchase of treasury stock, using the stock of Mead Johnson to fund the purchase instead of cash (such as exchanging Mead Johnson stock for Bristol-Myers stock). As a result of the transaction, the Treasury Stock account on Bristol-Myers' balance sheet increased (became more negative) by $6.9 billion (269 million shares × $25.70 per share), which reduced equity by $6.9 billion. This reduction was offset, however, by the recognition of a gain on the exchange amounting to $7.2 billion after tax. This split-off was affected by a tender offer with Bristol-Myers shareholders. Consequently, it is a non pro rata exchange and is, therefore, valued at market value with a resulting gain. The net effect on equity is minimal, but the income statement reports a substantial gain for that year.

Analysis of Equity Carve-Outs

Sell-offs, spin-offs, and split-offs all involve the divestiture of an operating segment. Although they are one-time occurrences, they can result in substantial gains that can markedly alter the income statement and balance sheet. Consequently, we need to interpret them carefully. This involves learning as many details about the carve out as possible from the annual report, the Management Discussion and Analysis, and other publicly available information.

Following an equity carve-out, the parent company loses the cash flows (positive or negative) of the divested business unit. As such, the divestiture should be treated like any other discontinued operation. Any recognized gain or loss from divestiture is treated as a nonoperating activity. The sale price of the divested unit reflects the valuation of *future expected* cash flows by the purchaser and is best viewed as a nonoperating activity. Income (and cash flows) of the divested unit up to the date of sale, however, is part of operations, although discontinued operations are typically segregated.

MID-MODULE REVIEW 4

Assume that **BearingPoint** announced the split-off of its Canadian subsidiary. BearingPoint reported a gain from the split-off. (1) Describe the accounting for a split-off. (2) Why was BearingPoint able to report a gain on this transaction?

The solution is on page 8-50.

Convertible Securities

Convertible securities are debt and equity securities that provide the holder with an option to convert those securities into other securities. In this section, we consider two specific types of convertibles: convertible debt securities, where debt is converted to common stock, and convertible preferred securities, where preferred stock is converted to common stock.

Convertible Debt Securities

Xilinx had convertible debt transactions in 2010, as explained in the following excerpt from footnotes to its 10-K report:

> **2.625% Senior Convertible Debentures** In June 2010, the Company issued $600.0 million principal amount of 2.625% Debentures to qualified institutional investors. The 2.625% Debentures are senior in right of payment to the Company's existing and future unsecured indebtedness... The 2.625% Debentures are initially convertible, subject to certain conditions, into shares of Xilinx common stock at a conversion rate of 33.0164 shares of common stock per $1 thousand principal amount of the 2.625% Debentures, representing an initial effective conversion price of approximately $30.29 per share of common stock.

The convertible debentures are reported as a long-term liability on Xilinx's balance sheet. To see the effects that conversion would have on Xilinx's financial statements, assume that the bonds are reported at their face amount of $600 (in $ millions) and that all of the bonds are subsequently converted into 19,809,840 shares ([$600 million/$1,000] × 33.0164 shares) of common stock with a par value of $0.01 per share. The financial statement effects of the conversion are as follows (Xilinx reports its balance sheet in $000s):

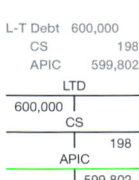

	Balance Sheet						Income Statement		
Transaction	Cash Asset	+ Noncash Assets	= Liabil- ities	+ Contrib. Capital	+ Earned Capital		Rev- enues	− Expen- ses	= Net Income
Conversion of convert- ible debt			= −600,000 Long-Term Debt	$198 Common Stock $599,802 Additional Paid-In Capital				−	=

L-T Debt 600,000
CS   198
APIC   599,802

LTD
600,000 |
           CS
           | 198
         APIC
           | 599,802

Upon conversion, the debt is removed from the balance sheet at its book value ($600 million assumed in this case) and the common stock is issued for that amount, resulting in an increase in the Common Stock account of $198,000 (assuming 19,809,840 shares issued with a par value of $0.01 per share). Additional Paid-In Capital is increased for the remaining amount. No gain or loss (or cash inflow or outflow) is recognized as a result of the conversion.

Convertible Preferred Stock

Preferred stock can also contain a conversion privilege. **Xerox** provides an example in its 2010 10-K report:

> **Series A Convertible Preferred Stock** In connection with the acquisition of ACS in February 2010 (see Note 3 Acquisitions for additional information), we issued 300,000 shares of Series A convertible perpetual preferred stock with an aggregate liquidation preference of $300 and a fair value of $349 as of the acquisition date to the holder of ACS Class B common stock. The convertible preferred stock pays quarterly cash dividends at a rate of 8 percent per year and has a liquidation preference of $1,000 per share. Each share of convertible preferred stock is convertible at any time, at the option of the holder, into 89.8876 shares of common stock for a total of 26,966 thousand shares (reflecting an initial conversion price of approximately $11.125 per share of common stock . . .). On or after the fifth anniversary of the issue date, we have the right to cause, under certain circumstances, any or all of the convertible preferred stock to be converted into shares of common stock at the then applicable conversion rate. The convertible preferred stock is also convertible, at the option of the holder, upon a change in control, at the applicable conversion rate plus an additional number of shares determined by reference to the price paid for our common stock upon such change in control. In addition, upon the occurrence of certain fundamental change events, including a change in control or the delisting of Xerox's common stock, the holder of convertible preferred stock has the right to require us to redeem any or all of the convertible preferred stock in cash at a redemption price per share equal to the liquidation preference and any accrued and unpaid dividends to, but not including the redemption date.

Accounting for the conversion of preferred stock is essentially the same as that for convertible debt that we describe above: the preferred stock account is removed from the balance sheet and common stock is issued for the dollar amount of the preferred.

Conversion privileges offer an additional benefit to the holder of a security. That is, debtholders and preferred stockholders carry senior positions as claimants in bankruptcy, and also carry a fixed interest payment or dividend yield. Thus, they are somewhat protected from losses and their annual return is guaranteed. With a conversion privilege, debtholders or preferred stockholders can enjoy the residual benefits of common shareholders should the company perform well.

A conversion option is valuable and yields a higher price for the securities than they would otherwise command. However, conversion privileges impose a cost on common shareholders. That is, the higher market price received for convertible securities is offset by the cost imposed on the subordinate (common) securities.

One final note, diluted earnings per share (EPS) takes into account the potentially dilutive effect of convertible securities. Specifically, the diluted EPS computation assumes conversion at the beginning of the year (or when the security is issued if during the year). The earnings available to common shares in the numerator are increased by any forgone after-tax interest expense or preferred dividends, and the additional shares that would have been issued in the conversion, increase the shares outstanding in the denominator (see Module 5).

IFRS INSIGHT   **Convertible Securities under IFRS**

Unlike GAAP, convertible securities (called *compound financial instruments* under IFRS) are split into separate debt and equity components. The idea is that the conversion premium is akin to a call option on the company's stock. This embedded option has a value of its own even if it is not legally detachable. Thus, under IFRS, the proceeds from the issuance are allocated between the liability component (at fair value) and an equity component (the residual amount).

ANALYZING GLOBAL REPORTS

Under IFRS, accounting for equity is similar to that under U.S. GAAP. Following are a few terminology differences:

U.S. GAAP	IFRS
Common stock	Share capital
Preferred shares	Preference shares
Additional paid-in capital	Share premium
Retained earnings	Reserves
Accumulated other comprehensive income	Other equity *or* Other components of equity
—	Revaluation surplus *or* Revaluation reserve*

* In Modules 6 and 9, we noted that certain assets including fixed assets and intangible assets may be revalued upwards (and later, revalued downwards) under IFRS. These revaluations do not affect net income or retained earnings but, instead, are reported in a separate equity account. For comparative purposes our analysis might exclude revaluations from both equity and the asset accounts to which they relate.

U.S. GAAP has a more narrow definition of liabilities than IFRS. Therefore, more items are classified as liabilities under IFRS. For example, some preferred shares are deemed liabilities under IFRS and equity under GAAP. (Both systems classify preferred shares that are mandatorily redeemable or redeemable at the option of the shareholder, as liabilities.) For comparative purposes, we look at classification of preferred shares that are not mandatorily redeemable and make the numbers consistent. To do this we add preference shares classified as liabilities under IFRS to equity.

Treasury stock transactions are sometimes difficult to identify under IFRS because companies are not required to report a separate line item for treasury shares on the balance sheet. Instead treasury share transactions reduce share capital and share premium. We must review the statement of shareholders' equity to assess stock repurchases for IFRS companies.

For example, at March 31, 2011, **British Telecom** (BT) reports the following in the equity section of its IFRS balance sheet (in £ millions):

Ordinary shares	£ 408
Share premium..........................	62
Capital redemption reserve	27
Other reserves	658
Retained earnings	770
Total parent shareholders' equity..........	**£1,925**

Its balance sheet reports no treasury stock line item, but footnotes disclose that the other reserves account (£658 million) includes the following:

(£ million)	Treasury shares
At 1 April 2010.......................	**£(1,105)**
Net issue of treasury shares..............	27
At 31 March 2011	**£(1,078)**

The footnote reports that the treasury shares reserve is used to hold BT shares purchased by the company. During 2011 the company did not purchase any additional shares but did issue 12,335,580 shares from treasury to satisfy obligations under employee share schemes and executive share awards at a cost of £27 million. At March 31, 2011, 388,570,539 shares were held as treasury shares at cost.

Share-based compensation gives rise to timing differences and both IFRS and U.S. GAAP require companies to record deferred tax assets. Under IFRS, the deferred tax asset is adjusted each period to reflect fluctuations in the market price of equity. These market-value adjustments impact the income statement via tax expense. U.S. GAAP computes the deferred tax asset using the grant-date fair value and does not adjust for stock price fluctuations. This makes IFRS tax expense more volatile.

MODULE-END REVIEW

Assume that **Express Scripts, Inc.**, has issued the following convertible debentures: each $1,000 bond is convertible into 200 shares of $1 par common. Assume that the bonds were sold at a discount, and that each bond has a current unamortized discount equal to $150. Using the financial statements effect template, illustrate the effects on the financial statements of the conversion of one of these convertible debentures.

The solution is on page 8-50.

GUIDANCE ANSWERS . . . ANALYSIS DECISION

You Are the Chief Financial Officer Several points must be considered. (1) Buying stock back reduces the number of shares outstanding, which can prop up earnings per share (EPS). However, foregone earnings from the cash used for repurchases can dampen earnings. The net effect is that EPS is likely to increase because of the reduced shares in the denominator. (2) Another motivation is that, if the shares are sufficiently undervalued (in management's opinion), the stock repurchase and subsequent resale can provide a better return than alternative investments. (3) Stock repurchases send a strong signal to the market that management feels its stock is undervalued. This is more credible than merely making that argument with analysts. On the other hand, company cash is diverted from other investments. This is bothersome if such investments are mutually exclusive either now or in the future.

DISCUSSION QUESTIONS

Q8-1. Define *par value stock*. What is the significance of a stock's par value from an accounting and analysis perspective?

Q8-2. What are the basic differences between preferred stock and common stock? What are the typical features of preferred stock?

Q8-3. What features make preferred stock similar to debt? Similar to common stock?

Q8-4. What is meant by preferred dividends in arrears? If dividends are two years in arrears on $500,000 of 6% preferred stock, and dividends are declared at the end of this year, what amount of total dividends must the company pay to preferred shareholders before paying any dividends to common shareholders?

Q8-5. Distinguish between authorized shares and issued shares. Why might the number of shares issued be more than the number of shares outstanding?

Q8-6. Describe the difference between contributed capital and earned capital. Specifically, how can earned capital be considered as an investment by the company's shareholders?

Q8-7. How does the account "additional paid-in capital" (APIC) arise? Does the amount of APIC reported on the balance sheet relative to the common stock amount provide any information about the financial condition of the company?

Q8-8. Define *stock split*. What are the major reasons for a stock split?

Q8-9. Define *treasury stock*. Why might a corporation acquire treasury stock? How is treasury stock reported in the balance sheet?

Q8-10. If a corporation purchases 600 shares of its own common stock at $10 per share and resells them at $14 per share, where would the $2,400 increase in capital be reported in the financial statements? Why is no gain reported?

Q8-11. A corporation has total stockholders' equity of $4,628,000 and one class of $2 par value common stock. The corporation has 500,000 shares authorized; 300,000 shares issued; and 40,000 shares as treasury stock. What is its book value per share?

Q8-12. What is a stock dividend? How does a common stock dividend distributed to common shareholders affect their respective ownership interests?

Q8-13. What is the difference between the accounting for a small stock dividend and the accounting for a large stock dividend?

Q8-14. Employee stock options potentially dilute earnings per share (EPS). What can companies do to offset these dilutive effects and how might this action affect the balance sheet?

Q8-15. What information is reported in a statement of stockholders' equity?

Q8-16. What items are typically reported under the stockholders' equity category of accumulated other comprehensive income (AOCI)?

Q8-17. What is the difference between a spin-off and a split-off? Under what circumstances can either result in the recognition of a gain in the income statement?

Q8-18. Describe the accounting for a convertible bond. Can the conversion ever result in the recognition of a gain in the income statement?

Assignments with the ✅ in the margin are available in an online homework system. See the Preface of the book for details.

MINI EXERCISES

M8-19. **Analyzing and Identifying Financial Statement Effects of Stock Issuances** **(LO1)**
During the current year, Beatty Company, (a) issues 8,000 shares of $50 par value preferred stock at $68 cash per share and (b) issues 12,000 shares of $1 par value common stock at $10 cash per share. Indicate the financial statement effects of these two issuances using the financial statement effects template.

M8-20. **Analyzing and Identifying Financial Statement Effects of Stock Issuances** **(LO1)**
During the current year, Magliolo, Inc., (a) issues 18,000 shares of $10 par value preferred stock at $48 cash per share and (b) issues 120,000 shares of $2 par value common stock at $37 cash per share. Indicate the financial statement effects of these two issuances using the financial statement effects template.

M8-21. **Distinguishing Between Common Stock and Additional Paid-in Capital** **(LO1)**

CISCO SYSTEMS, INC.
(CSCO)

Following is the 2010 stockholders' equity section from the **Cisco Systems, Inc.**, balance sheet.

Shareholders' Equity (in millions, except par value)	July 31, 2010
Preferred stock, no par value: 5 shares authorized; none issued and outstanding	$ —
Common stock and additional paid-in capital, $0.001 par value: 20,000 shares authorized; 5,655 and 5,785 shares issued and outstanding at July 31, 2010, and July 25, 2009, respectively	37,793
Retained earnings	5,851
Accumulated other comprehensive income.	623
Total Cisco shareholders' equity	44,267
Noncontrolling interests	18
Total equity.	$44,285

a. For the $37,793 million reported as "common stock and additional paid-in capital," what portion is common stock and what portion is additional paid-in capital?

b. Explain why Cisco does not report the two components described in part *a* separately.

M8-22. **Identifying Financial Statement Effects of Stock Issuance and Repurchase** **(LO1)**
On January 1, Bartov Company issues 5,000 shares of $100 par value preferred stock at $250 cash per share. On March 1, the company repurchases 5,000 shares of previously issued $1 par value common stock at $83 cash per share. Use the financial statement effects template to record these two transactions.

M8-23.   Assessing the Financial Statement Effects of a Stock Split   (LO2)
Medco discloses the following footnote to its 10-K report.

MEDCO HEALTH
SOLUTIONS, INC.
(MHS)

> **Stock Split** In the first quarter of 2008, we completed a two-for-one stock split, which was effected in the form of a 100% stock dividend and distributed on January 24, 2008, to shareholders of record at the close of business on January 10, 2008. All share and per share amounts have been adjusted for the increase in issued and outstanding shares after giving effect to the stock split.

What restatements has Medco made to its balance sheet as a result of the stock split?

M8-24.   Reconciling Common Stock and Treasury Stock Balances   (LO1)
Following is the stockholders' equity section from the **Abercrombie & Fitch** balance sheet.

ABERCROMBIE &
FITCH
(ANF)

Stockholders' Equity ($ thousands, except par value amounts)	January 29, 2011	January 30, 2010

Class A common stock—$.01 par value: 150,000
  shares authorized and 103,300 shares issued
  at each of January 29, 2011, and January 30, 2010 .....
	$ 1,033	$ 1,033

Paid-in capital	349,258	339,453
Retained earnings	2,272,317	2,183,690
Accumulated other comprehensive loss, net of tax........	(6,516)	(8,973)

Treasury stock at average cost: 16,054 and
  15,314 shares at January 29, 2011, and
  January 30, 2010, respectively.....................
	(725,308)	(687,286)

Total stockholders' equity	$1,890,784	$1,827,917

a.   Show the computation to yield the $1,033 balance reported for common stock.
b.   How many shares are outstanding at 2011 fiscal year-end?
c.   Use the common stock and paid-in capital accounts to determine the average price at which Abercrombie & Fitch issued its common stock.
d.   Use the treasury stock account to determine the average price Abercrombie & Fitch paid when it repurchased its common shares.

M8-25.   Identifying and Analyzing Financial Statement Effects of Cash Dividends   (LO2)
Freid Company has outstanding 6,000 shares of $50 par value, 6% preferred stock, and 40,000 shares of $1 par value common stock. The company has $328,000 of retained earnings. At year-end, the company declares and pays the regular $3 per share cash dividend on preferred stock and a $2.20 per share cash dividend on common stock. Use the financial statement effects template to indicate the effects of these two dividend payments.

M8-26.   Identifying and Analyzing Financial Statement Effects of Stock Dividends   (LO2)
Dutta Corp. has outstanding 70,000 shares of $5 par value common stock. At year-end, the company declares and issues a 4% common stock dividend when the market price of the stock is $21 per share. Use the financial statement effects template to indicate the effects of this stock dividend declaration and payment.

M8-27.   Identifying, Analyzing and Explaining the Effects of a Stock Split   (LO2)
On September 1, Weiss Company has 250,000 shares of $15 par value ($165 market value) common stock that are issued and outstanding. Its balance sheet on that date shows the following account balances relating to its common stock:

Common stock........................	$3,750,000
Paid-in capital in excess of par value........	2,250,000

On September 2, Weiss splits its stock 3-for-2 and reduces the par value to $10 per share.

a.   How many shares of common stock are issued and outstanding immediately after the stock split?
b.   What is the dollar balance of the common stock account immediately after the stock split?
c.   What is the likely reason that Weiss Company split its stock?

M8-28.   Determining Cash Dividends to Preferred and Common Shareholders   (LO2)

Dechow Company has outstanding 20,000 shares of $50 par value, 6% cumulative preferred stock and 80,000 shares of $10 par value common stock. The company declares and pays cash dividends amounting to $160,000.

a.   If there are no preferred dividends in arrears, how much in total dividends, and in dividends per share, does Dechow pay to each class of stock?

b.   If there are one year's dividends in arrears on the preferred stock, how much in total dividends, and in dividends per share, does Dechow pay to each class of stock?

M8-29.   Reconciling Retained Earnings   (LO2)

Use the following data to reconcile the 2012 retained earnings for Bamber Company (that is, explain the change in retained earnings during the year).

Total retained earnings, December 31, 2011	$347,000
Stock dividends declared and paid in 2012	28,000
Cash dividends declared and paid in 2012	35,000
Net income for 2012	94,000

M8-30.   Interpreting a Spin-Off Disclosure   (LO3)

NCR CORP.
(NCR)

NCR Corporation discloses the following in notes to its 2007 10-K report.

Spin-off of Teradata Data Warehousing Business On September 30, 2007, NCR completed the spin-off of its Teradata Data Warehousing business through the distribution of a tax-free dividend to its stockholders. NCR distributed one share of common stock of Teradata Corporation (Teradata) for each share of NCR common stock to NCR stockholders of record as of the close of business on September 14, 2007. Upon the distribution of Teradata, NCR stockholders received 100% (approximately 181 million shares) of the common stock of Teradata, which is now an independent public company trading under the symbol "TDC" on the New York Stock Exchange.

a.   Describe the difference between a spin-off and a split-off.

b.   What effects did NCR's spin-off of Teradata have on NCR's balance sheet and income statement?

M8-31.   Interpreting a Proposed Split-Off Disclosure   (LO3)

VIACOM, INC.
(VIA)

Viacom, Inc., reports the following footnote in its 2005 10-K.

Discontinued Operations In 2004, Viacom completed the exchange offer for the split-off of Blockbuster Inc. ("Blockbuster") (NYSE: BBI and BBI.B). Under the terms of the offer, Viacom accepted 27,961,165 shares of Viacom common stock in exchange for the 144 million common shares of Blockbuster that Viacom owned. Each share of Viacom Class A or Class B common stock accepted for exchange by Viacom was exchanged for 5.15 shares of Blockbuster common stock, consisting of 2.575 shares of Blockbuster Class A common stock and 2.575 shares of Blockbuster Class B common stock.

a.   Describe the accounting for a split-off.

b.   How will the proposed split-off affect the number of Viacom shares outstanding?

c.   Under what circumstances will Viacom be able to report a gain for this proposed split-off?

M8-32.   Interpreting Disclosure Related to Spin-Off   (LO3)

ALTRIA GROUP,
INC.
(MO)

Altria reports the following footnote to its 2008 10-K.

On March 28, 2008, Altria Group, Inc. distributed all of its interest in Philip Morris International Inc. ("PMI") to Altria Group, Inc. stockholders of record as of the close of business on March 19, 2008, in a tax-free distribution. Altria Group, Inc. distributed one share of PMI common stock for every share of Altria Group, Inc. common stock outstanding as of the PMI Record Date. Following the PMI Distribution Date, Altria Group, Inc. does not own any shares of PMI stock. Altria Group, Inc. has reflected the results of PMI prior to the PMI Distribution Date as discontinued operations on the consolidated statements of earnings and the consolidated statements of cash flows for all periods presented. The assets and liabilities related to PMI were reclassified and reflected as discontinued operations on the

continued

continued from prior page

consolidated balance sheet at December 31, 2007. The distribution resulted in a net decrease to Altria Group, Inc.'s total stockholders' equity of $14.4 billion on the PMI Distribution Date.

a. Describe the accounting for a spin-off.

b. What effects did this transaction have on Altria's balance sheet and income statement?

M8-33. Analyzing Financial Statement Effects of Convertible Securities (LO3)
JetBlue Airways Corporation reports the following footnote to its 2005 10-K.

JETBLUE AIRWAYS
CORPORATION
(JBLU)

In March 2005, we completed a public offering of $250 million aggregate principal amount of 3¾% convertible unsecured debentures due 2035, which are currently convertible into 14.6 million shares of our common stock at a price of approximately $17.10 per share.

a. Describe the effects on JetBlue's balance sheet if the convertible bonds are converted.

b. Would the conversion affect earnings? Explain.

EXERCISES

E8-34. Identifying and Analyzing Financial Statement Effects of Stock Transactions (LO1)
Lipe Company reports the following transactions relating to its stock accounts in the current year.

Feb. 20 Issued 10,000 shares of $1 par value common stock at $25 cash per share.
Feb. 21 Issued 15,000 shares of $100 par value, 8% preferred stock at $275 cash per share.
June 30 Purchased 2,000 shares of its own common stock at $15 cash per share.
Sep. 25 Sold 1,000 shares of its treasury stock at $21 cash per share.

Use the financial statement effects template to indicate the effects from each of these transactions.

E8-35. Identifying and Analyzing Financial Statement Effects of Stock Transactions (LO1)
McNichols Corp. reports the following transactions relating to its stock accounts in the current year.

Jan. 15 Issued 25,000 shares of $5 par value common stock at $17 cash per share.
Jan. 20 Issued 6,000 shares of $50 par value, 8% preferred stock at $78 cash per share.
Mar. 31 Purchased 3,000 shares of its own common stock at $20 cash per share.
June 25 Sold 2,000 shares of its treasury stock at $26 cash per share.
July 15 Sold the remaining 1,000 shares of treasury stock at $19 cash per share.

Use the financial statement effects template to indicate the effects from each of these transactions.

E8-36. Analyzing and Computing Average Issue Price and Treasury Stock Cost (LO1)
Following is the stockholders' equity section from the **Campbell Soup Company** balance sheet.

CAMPBELL SOUP
(CPB)

Shareowners' Equity (millions, except per share amounts)	August 1, 2010	July 2, 2009
Preferred stock: authorized 40 shares; none issued	$ —	$ —
Capital stock, $.0375 par value; authorized 560 shares; issued 542 shares	20	20
Additional paid-in capital	341	332
Earnings retained in the business	8,760	8,288
Capital stock in treasury, at cost	(7,459)	(7,194)
Accumulated other comprehensive loss	(736)	(718)
Total Campbell Soup Company shareowners' equity	926	728
Noncontrolling interest	3	3
Total equity	$ 929	$ 731

Campbell Soup Company also reports the following statement of stockholders' equity.

(Millions, except per share amounts)	Capital Stock				Additional Paid-in Capital	Earnings Retained in the Business	Accumulated Other Comprehensive Income (Loss)	Noncontrolling Interest	Total Equity
	Issued		In Treasury						
	Shares	Amount	Shares	Amount					
CAMPBELL SOUP COMPANY **Shareowners' Equity**									
Balance at August 2, 2009.........	542	$20	(199)	$(7,194)	$332	$8,288	$(718)	$ 3	$731
Comprehensive income (loss)									
Net earnings						844		—	844
Foreign currency translation adjustments, net of tax							39	—	39
Cash-flow hedges, net of tax							2		2
Pension and postretirement benefits, net of tax							(59)		(59)
Other comprehensive income (loss)...............							(18)	—	(18)
Total comprehensive income (loss) ..									826
Dividends ($1.075 per share)						(372)			(372)
Treasury stock purchased			(14)	(472)					(472)
Treasury stock issued under management incentive and stock option plans.............			7	207	9				216
Balance at August 1, 2010.........	542	$20	(206)	$(7,459)	$341	$8,760	$(736)	$ 3	$929

a. Show the computation, using par value and share numbers, to arrive at the $20 million in the common stock account.
b. At what average price were the Campbell Soup shares issued?
c. Reconcile the beginning and ending balances of retained earnings.
d. Campbell Soup reports a $39 gain as part of Accumulated Other Comprehensive Income relating to foreign currency translation adjustments. Explain what foreign currency translation adjustments represent. What effect did foreign currency translation adjustments have on net earnings for the year?
e. Campbell Soup reports an increase in stockholders' equity relating to the exercise of stock options (titled "Treasury stock issued under management incentive and stock option plans"). This transaction involves the purchase of common stock by employees at a preset price. Describe how this set of transactions affects stockholders' equity.
f. Describe the transaction relating to the "Treasury stock purchased" line in the statement of stockholders' equity.

E8-37. **Analyzing Cash Dividends on Preferred and Common Stock   (LO2)**
Moser Company began business on March 1, 2010. At that time, it issued 20,000 shares of $60 par value, 7% cumulative preferred stock and 100,000 shares of $5 par value common stock. Through the end of 2012, there has been no change in the number of preferred and common shares outstanding.

a. Assume that Moser declared and paid cash dividends of $0 in 2010, $183,000 in 2011, and $200,000 in 2012. Compute the total cash dividends and the dividends per share paid to each class of stock in 2010, 2011, and 2012.
b. Assume that Moser declared and paid cash dividends of $0 in 2010, $84,000 in 2011, and $150,000 in 2012. Compute the total cash dividends and the dividends per share paid to each class of stock in 2010, 2011, and 2012.

E8-38. **Analyzing Cash Dividends on Preferred and Common Stock   (LO2)**
Potter Company has outstanding 15,000 shares of $50 par value, 8% preferred stock and 50,000 shares of $5 par value common stock. During its first three years in business, it declared and paid no cash dividends in the first year, $280,000 in the second year, and $60,000 in the third year.

a. If the preferred stock is cumulative, determine the total amount of cash dividends paid to each class of stock in each of the three years.
b. If the preferred stock is noncumulative, determine the total amount of cash dividends paid to each class of stock in each of the three years.

E8-39. **Analyzing and Computing Issue Price, Treasury Stock Cost, and Shares Outstanding** **(LO1)**
Following is the stockholders' equity section from **Altria**'s 2010 balance sheet.

December 31 ($ million)	2010
Common stock, par value $0.33⅓ per share (2,805,961,317 shares issued)...........	$ 935
Additional paid-in capital..	5,751
Earnings reinvested in the business...	23,459
Accumulated other comprehensive losses	(1,484)
Cost of repurchased stock (717,221,651 shares in 2010).........................	(23,469)
Total stockholders' equity attributable to Altria Group, Inc.....................	5,192
Noncontrolling interests...	3
Total stockholders' equity	$ 5,195

a. Show the computation to derive the $935 million for common stock.
b. At what average price has Altria issued its common stock?
c. How many shares of Altria common stock are outstanding as of December 31, 2010?
d. At what average cost has Altria repurchased its treasury stock as of December 31, 2010?
e. Why would a company such as Altria want to repurchase $23,469 million of its common stock?
f. What does the Noncontrolling Interests account of $3 million represent?

E8-40. **Analyzing Cash Dividends on Preferred and Common Stock** **(LO2)**
Skinner Company began business on June 30, 2010. At that time, it issued 18,000 shares of $50 par value, 6% cumulative preferred stock and 90,000 shares of $10 par value common stock. Through the end of 2012, there has been no change in the number of preferred and common shares outstanding.

a. Assume that Skinner declared and paid cash dividends of $63,000 in 2010, $0 in 2011, and $378,000 in 2012. Compute the total cash dividends and the dividends per share paid to each class of stock in 2010, 2011, and 2012.
b. Assume that Skinner declared and paid cash dividends of $0 in 2010, $108,000 in 2011, and $189,000 in 2012. Compute the total cash dividends and the dividends per share paid to each class of stock in 2010, 2011, and 2012.

E8-41. **Identifying and Analyzing Financial Statement Effects of Dividends** **(LO2)**
Chaney Company has outstanding 25,000 shares of $10 par value common stock. It also has $405,000 of retained earnings. Near the current year-end, the company declares and pays a cash dividend of $1.90 per share and declares and issues a 4% stock dividend. The market price of the stock the day the dividends are declared is $35 per share. Use the financial statement effects template to indicate the effects of these two separate dividend transactions.

E8-42. **Identifying and Analyzing Financial Statement Effects of Dividends** **(LO2)**
The stockholders' equity of Pagach Company at December 31, 2011, appears below.

Common stock, $10 par value, 200,000 shares authorized; 80,000 shares issued and outstanding......................	$800,000
Paid-in capital in excess of par value..........................	480,000
Retained earnings	305,000

During 2012, the following transactions occurred:

May 12 Declared and issued a 7% stock dividend; the common stock market value was $18 per share.

Dec. 31 Declared and paid a cash dividend of 75 cents per share.

a. Use the financial statement effects template to indicate the effects of these transactions.
b. Reconcile retained earnings for 2012 assuming that the company reports 2012 net income of $283,000.

E8-43. **Identifying and Analyzing Financial Statement Effects of Dividends**   (LO2)

The stockholders' equity of Kinney Company at December 31, 2011, is shown below.

5% preferred stock, $100 par value, 10,000 shares authorized; 4,000 shares issued and outstanding.	$ 400,000
Common stock, $5 par value, 200,000 shares authorized; 50,000 shares issued and outstanding.	250,000
Paid-in capital in excess of par value—preferred stock.	40,000
Paid-in capital in excess of par value—common stock.	300,000
Retained earnings	656,000
Total stockholders' equity	$1,646,000

The following transactions, among others, occurred during 2012:

Apr. 1 Declared and issued a 100% stock dividend on all outstanding shares of common stock. The market value of the stock was $11 per share.

Dec. 7 Declared and issued a 3% stock dividend on all outstanding shares of common stock. The market value of the stock was $14 per share.

Dec. 20 Declared and paid (1) the annual cash dividend on the preferred stock and (2) a cash dividend of 80 cents per common share.

a. Use the financial statement effects template to indicate the effects of these separate transactions.

b. Compute retained earnings for 2012 assuming that the company reports 2012 net income of $253,000.

E8-44. **Identifying, Analyzing and Explaining the Effects of a Stock Split**   (LO2)

On March 1 of the current year, Zhang Company has 400,000 shares of $20 par value common stock that are issued and outstanding. Its balance sheet shows the following account balances relating to common stock.

Common stock.	$8,000,000
Paid-in capital in excess of par value.	3,400,000

On March 2, Zhang Company splits its common stock 2-for-1 and reduces the par value to $10 per share.

a. How many shares of common stock are issued and outstanding immediately after the stock split?

b. What is the dollar balance in the common stock account immediately after the stock split?

c. What is the dollar balance in the paid-in capital in excess of par value account immediately after the stock split?

E8-45. **Analyzing and Computing Issue Price, Treasury Stock Cost, and Shares Outstanding**   (LO1)

CATERPILLAR INC.
(CAT)

Following is the stockholders' equity section of the 2010 **Caterpillar Inc.**, balance sheet.

Stockholders' Equity ($ millions)	2010	2009	2008
Common stock of $1.00 par; Authorized shares: 2,000,000,000; Issued shares (2010, 2009 and 2008—814,894,624) at paid-in amount	$ 3,888	$ 3,439	$ 3,057
Treasury stock (2010—176,071,910 shares; 2009—190,171,905 shares; 2008—213,367,983 shares) at cost	(10,397)	(10,646)	(11,217)
Profit employed in the business.	21,384	19,711	19,826
Accumulated other comprehensive income (loss)	(4,051)	(3,764)	(5,579)
Noncontrolling interests	40	83	103
Total stockholders' equity	$10,864	$ 8,823	$ 6,190

a. How many shares of Caterpillar common stock are outstanding at year-end 2010?

b. What does the phrase "at paid-in amount" in the stockholders' equity section mean?

c. At what average cost has Caterpillar repurchased its stock as of year-end 2010?

d. Why would a company such as Caterpillar want to repurchase its common stock?

e. Explain how CAT's "issued shares" remains constant over the three-year period while the dollar amount of its common stock account increases.

E8-46. **Analyzing Equity Changes from Convertible Preferred Stock** (LO3)
Xerox reports the following stockholders' equity information in its 10-K report.

Shareholders' Equity (In millions, except share data in thousands)	December 31 2006	December 31 2005
Series C mandatory convertible preferred stock	$ —	$ 889
Common stock, including additional paid-in capital	4,666	4,741
Treasury stock, at cost	(141)	(203)
Retained earnings	4,202	3,021
Accumulated other comprehensive loss	(1,647)	(1,240)

(In millions, except share data in thousands)	Common Stock Shares	Common Stock Amount	Additional Paid-in Capital	Treasury Stock Shares	Treasury Stock Amount	Retained Earnings	Accumulated Other Comprehensive Loss	Total
Balance at December 31, 2005	945,106	$945	$3,796	(13,917)	$ (203)	$3,021	$(1,240)	$6,319
Net income						1,210		1,210
Translation adjustments							485	485
Minimum pension liability							131	131
Other unrealized gains							1	1
Comprehensive income								$1,827
Adjustment to initially apply FAS No. 158, net							(1,024)	(1,024)
Stock option and incentive plans, net	10,256	11	156					167
Series C mandatory convertible preferred stock dividends ($6.25 per share)						(29)		(29)
Series C mandatory convertible preferred stock conversion	74,797	75	814					889
Payments to acquire treasury stock				(70,111)	(1,069)			(1,069)
Cancellation of treasury stock	(75,665)	(75)	(1,056)	75,665	1,131			—
Other	74							—
Balance, December 31, 2006	954,568	$956	$3,710	(8,363)	$ (141)	$4,202	$(1,647)	$7,080

Preferred Stock As of December 31, 2006, we had no preferred stock shares outstanding and one class of preferred stock purchase rights. We are authorized to issue approximately 22 million shares of cumulative preferred stock, $1.00 par value.

Series C Mandatory Convertible Preferred Stock Automatic Conversion: In July 2006, 9.2 million shares of 6.25% Series C Mandatory Convertible Preferred Stock were converted at a rate of 8.1301 shares of our common stock, or 74.8 million common stock shares. The recorded value of outstanding shares at the time of conversion was $889. The conversion occurred pursuant to the mandatory automatic conversion provisions set at original issuance of the Series C Preferred Stock. As a result of the automatic conversion, there are no remaining outstanding shares of our Series C Mandatory Convertible Preferred Stock.

Common Stock We have 1.75 billion authorized shares of common stock, $1 par value. At December 31, 2006, 106 million shares were reserved for issuance under our incentive compensation plans, 48 million shares were reserved for debt to equity exchanges, 15 million shares were reserved for the conversion of the Series C Mandatory Convertible Preferred Stock and 2 million shares were reserved for the conversion of convertible debt. The 15 million shares reserved for the conversion of the Series C Mandatory Convertible Preferred Stock are expected to be released in 2007, since conversion was completed in 2006.

Required

a. At December 31, 2005, Xerox reports $889 million of 6.25% Series C Mandatory Convertible Preferred stock. What is the dollar amount of dividends that Xerox must pay on this stock (assume a par value of $100 per share)? Some have argued that securities such as this are more like debt than equity. What is the basis for such an argument?

b. Describe the effects of conversion of the Series C Mandatory Convertible Preferred stock during 2006 on Xerox's balance sheet and its income statement.

c. What is the benefit, if any, to Xerox of issuing equity securities with a conversion feature? How are these securities treated in the computation of earnings per share (EPS)?

E8-47. **Analyzing and Computing Issue Price, Treasury Stock Cost, and Shares Outstanding** (LO1)

MERCK & CO., INC.
(MRK)

Following is the stockholders' equity and minority interest sections of the 2010 **Merck & Co., Inc.,** balance sheet.

Stockholders' Equity ($ millions)	2010
Common stock, $0.50 par value; Authorized—6,500,000,000 shares; Issued—3,576,948,356 shares—2010	$ 1,788
Other paid-in capital.	40,701
Retained earnings	37,536
Accumulated other comprehensive loss	(3,216)
	76,809
Less treasury stock, at cost; 494,841,533 shares—2010	22,433
Total Merck & Co., Inc. stockholders' equity	54,376
Noncontrolling interests	2,429
Total equity	$56,805

a. Show the computation of the $1,788 million in the common stock account.
b. At what average price were the Merck common shares issued?
c. At what average cost was the Merck treasury stock purchased?
d. How many common shares are outstanding as of December 31, 2010?

PROBLEMS

P8-48. **Identifying and Analyzing Financial Statement Effects of Stock Transactions** (LO1)

The stockholders' equity section of Gupta Company at December 31, 2011, follows:

8% preferred stock, $25 par value, 50,000 shares authorized; 6,800 shares issued and outstanding.	$170,000
Common stock, $10 par value, 200,000 shares authorized; 50,000 shares issued and outstanding.	500,000
Paid-in capital in excess of par value—preferred stock.	68,000
Paid-in capital in excess of par value—common stock.	200,000
Retained earnings	270,000

During 2012, the following transactions occurred:

Jan. 10 Issued 28,000 shares of common stock for $17 cash per share.
Jan. 23 Repurchased 8,000 shares of common stock at $19 cash per share.
Mar. 14 Sold one-half of the treasury shares acquired January 23 for $21 cash per share.
July 15 Issued 3,200 shares of preferred stock for $128,000 cash.
Nov. 15 Sold 1,000 of the treasury shares acquired January 23 for $24 cash per share.

Required
a. Use the financial statement effects template to indicate the effects from each of these transactions.
b. Prepare the December 31, 2012, stockholders' equity section of the balance sheet assuming the company reports 2012 net income of $59,000.

P8-49. **Identifying and Analyzing Financial Statement Effects of Stock Transactions** (LO1, 2)

The stockholders' equity of Sougiannis Company at December 31, 2011, follows:

7% Preferred stock, $100 par value, 20,000 shares authorized; 5,000 shares issued and outstanding.	$ 500,000
Common stock, $15 par value, 100,000 shares authorized; 40,000 shares issued and outstanding.	600,000
Paid-in capital in excess of par value—preferred stock.	24,000
Paid-in capital in excess of par value—common stock.	360,000
Retained earnings	325,000
Total stockholders' equity	$1,809,000

The following transactions, among others, occurred during the following year:

> Jan. 12 Announced a 3-for-1 common stock split, reducing the par value of the common stock to $5 per share. The authorized shares were increased to 300,000 shares.
>
> Sept. 1 Repurchased 10,000 shares of common stock at $10 cash per share.
>
> Oct. 12 Sold 1,500 treasury shares acquired September 1 at $12 cash per share.
>
> Nov. 21 Issued 5,000 shares of common stock at $21 cash per share.
>
> Dec. 28 Sold 1,200 treasury shares acquired September 1 at $9 cash per share.

Required

a. Use the financial statement effects template to indicate the effects from each of these transactions.

b. Prepare the December 31, 2012, stockholders' equity section of the balance sheet assuming that the company reports 2012 net income of $83,000.

P8-50. Identifying and Analyzing Financial Statement Effects of Stock Transactions (LO1)

The stockholders' equity of Verrecchia Company at December 31, 2011, follows:

Common stock, $5 par value, 350,000 shares authorized; 150,000 shares issued and outstanding....................	$750,000
Paid-in capital in excess of par value........................	600,000
Retained earnings	346,000

During 2012, the following transactions occurred:

> Jan. 5 Issued 10,000 shares of common stock for $12 cash per share.
>
> Jan. 18 Repurchased 4,000 shares of common stock at $14 cash per share.
>
> Mar. 12 Sold one-fourth of the treasury shares acquired January 18 for $17 cash per share.
>
> July 17 Sold 500 shares of treasury stock for $13 cash per share.
>
> Oct. 1 Issued 5,000 shares of 8%, $25 par value preferred stock for $35 cash per share. This is the first issuance of preferred shares from the 50,000 authorized preferred shares.

Required

a. Use the financial statement effects template to indicate the effects of each transaction.

b. Prepare the December 31, 2012, stockholders' equity section of the balance sheet assuming that the company reports net income of $72,500 for the year.

P8-51. Identifying and Analyzing Financial Statement Effects of Stock Transactions (LO1, 2)

Following is the stockholders' equity of Dennis Corporation at December 31, 2011:

8% preferred stock, $50 par value, 10,000 shares authorized; 7,000 shares issued and outstanding.........................	$ 350,000
Common stock, $20 par value, 50,000 shares authorized; 25,000 shares issued and outstanding.........................	500,000
Paid-in capital in excess of par value—preferred stock..............	70,000
Paid-in capital in excess of par value—common stock..............	385,000
Retained earnings	238,000
Total stockholders' equity	$1,543,000

The following transactions, among others, occurred during 2012:

> Jan. 15 Issued 1,000 shares of preferred stock for $62 cash per share.
>
> Jan. 20 Issued 4,000 shares of common stock at $36 cash per share.
>
> May 18 Announced a 2-for-1 common stock split, reducing the par value of the common stock to $10 per share. The number of shares authorized was increased to 100,000 shares.
>
> June 1 Issued 2,000 shares of common stock for $60,000 cash.
>
> Sept. 1 Repurchased 2,500 shares of common stock at $18 cash per share.
>
> Oct. 12 Sold 900 treasury shares at $21 cash per share.
>
> Dec. 22 Issued 500 shares of preferred stock for $59 cash per share.

Required

Use the financial statement effects template to indicate the effects of each transaction.

THE PROCTER & GAMBLE COMPANY
(PG)

P8-52. **Analyzing and Interpreting Equity Accounts and Comprehensive Income** **(LO2)**
Following is the shareholders' equity section of the 2010 balance sheet for **Procter & Gamble Company** and its statement of shareholders' equity.

June 30 (In millions, except per share amounts)	2010	2009
Shareholders' Equity		
Convertible Class A preferred stock, stated value $1 per share (600 shares authorized)	$ 1,277	$ 1,324
Non-Voting Class B preferred stock, stated value $1 per share (200 shares authorized)	—	—
Common stock, stated value $1 per share (10,000 shares authorized; shares issued: 2010—4,007.6, 2009—4,007.3)	4,008	4,007
Additional paid-in capital	61,697	61,118
Reserve for ESOP debt retirement	(1,350)	(1,340)
Accumulated other comprehensive income (loss)	(7,822)	(3,358)
Treasury stock, at cost (shares held: 2010—1,164.1, 2009—1,090.3)	(61,309)	(55,961)
Retained earnings	64,614	57,309
Noncontrolling interest	324	283
Total shareholders' equity	$61,439	$63,382

Consolidated Statement of Shareholders' Equity

Dollars in millions; Shares in thousands	Common Shares Outstanding	Common Stock	Preferred Stock	Additional Paid-in Capital	Reserve for ESOP Debt Retirement	Accumulated Other Comprehensive Income (Loss)	Noncontrolling Interest	Treasury Stock	Retained Earnings	Total
Balance June 30, 2009	2,917,035	$4,007	$1,324	$61,118	$(1,340)	$(3,358)	$283	$(55,961)	$57,309	$63,382
Net earnings									12,736	12,736
Other comprehensive income:										
Financial statement translation						(4,194)				(4,194)
Hedges and investment securities, net of $520 tax						867				867
Defined benefit retirement plans, net of $465 tax						(1,137)				(1,137)
Total comprehensive income										$8,272
Dividends to shareholders:										
Common									(5,239)	(5,239)
Preferred, net of tax benefits									(219)	(219)
Treasury purchases	(96,759)							(6,004)		(6,004)
Employee plan issuances	17,616	1		574				616		1,191
Preferred stock conversions	5,579		(47)	7				40		—
ESOP debt impacts					(10)				27	17
Noncontrolling interest				(2)			41			39
Balance June 30, 2010	2,843,471	$4,008	$1,277	$61,697	$(1,350)	$(7,822)	$324	$(61,309)	$64,614	$61,439

Required

a.   What does the term *convertible* (in reference to the company's Class A preferred stock) mean?

b.   How many shares of common stock did Procter & Gamble issue when convertible Class A preferred stock was converted during fiscal 2010?

c.   Describe the transactions relating to employee plan issuances. At what average price was the common stock issued as of year-end 2010?

d.   What is other comprehensive income? What is the accumulated other comprehensive income account? Explain.

e.   What cash dividends did Procter & Gamble pay in 2010 for each class of stock?

P8-53. **Analyzing and Interpreting Equity Accounts and Accumulated Other Comprehensive Income** (LO2)

Following is the stockholders' equity section of **Fortune Brands** balance sheet and its statement of stockholders' equity.

FORTUNE BRANDS, INC.
(FO)

December 31 (In millions, except per share amounts)	2010	2009
Stockholders' Equity		
$2.67 convertible preferred stock	$ 4.9	$ 5.2
Common stock, par value $3.125 per share, 234.9 shares issued	734.0	734.0
Paid-in capital	820.2	755.6
Accumulated other comprehensive loss	(172.0)	(211.8)
Retained earnings	7,499.3	7,135.4
Treasury stock, at cost	(3,215.3)	(3,326.0)
Total Fortune Brands stockholders' equity	5,671.1	5,092.4
Noncontrolling interests	16.9	13.3
Total equity	$5,688.0	$5,105.7

(In millions, except per share amounts)	$2.67 Convertible Preferred Stock	Common Stock	Paid-in Capital	Accumulated Other Comprehensive Income (Loss)	Retained Earnings	Treasury Stock At Cost	Non-controlling Interests	Total
Balance at December 31, 2009	$5.2	$734.0	$755.6	$(211.8)	$7,135.4	$(3,326.0)	$13.3	$5,105.7
Comprehensive income								
Net income	—	—	—	—	487.6	—	8.4	496.0
Translation adjustments (net of tax expense of $17.3 million)	—	—	—	26.0	—	—	—	26.0
Derivative instruments (net of tax benefit of $1.5 million)	—	—	—	2.8	—	—	—	2.8
Pension and postretirement benefit adjustments (net of tax expense of $8.1 million)	—	—	—	11.0	—	—	—	11.0
Total comprehensive Income	—	—	—	39.8	487.6	—	8.4	535.8
Dividends paid to noncontrolling interests	—	—	—	—	—	—	(4.8)	(4.8)
Dividends ($0.76 per Common share and $2.67 per Preferred share)	—	—	—	—	(116.2)	—	—	(116.2)
Shares issued from treasury stock for benefit plans			5.7		—	61.4	—	67.1
Stock-based compensation	—	—	55.2	—	(7.5)	46.6	—	94.3
Tax benefit on exercise of stock options	—	—	6.1	—	—	—	—	6.1
Conversion of preferred stock	(0.3)	—	(2.4)	—	—	2.7	—	—
Balance at December 31, 2010	$ 4.9	$734.0	$820.2	$(172.0)	$7,499.3	$(3,215.3)	$16.9	$5,688.0

Required

a. Explain the "$2.67" component of the convertible preferred stock account title.

b. Show (confirm) the computation that yields the $734.0 million common stock at year-end 2010.

c. Assuming that the convertible preferred stock was sold at par value, at what average price were Fortune Brands' common shares issued as of year-end 2010?

d. What is included in Fortune Brands' other comprehensive income for 2010? What other items are typically included in other comprehensive income?

e. Explain the $6.1 million tax benefit on exercise of stock options, reported in the statement of stockholders' equity.

P8-54. **Interpreting Footnote Disclosure on Convertible Debentures** (LO3)

Alloy, Inc., reports the following footnote related to its convertible debentures in its 2007 10-K ($ thousands).

ALLOY, INC.
(ALOY)

> In August 2003, Alloy completed the issuance of $69,300 of 20-Year 5.375% Senior Convertible Debentures due August 1, 2023. If converted, bondholders would currently receive 29.851 shares of Alloy common for each $1,000 face amount bond. Alloy continues to be responsible for repaying the Convertible Debentures in full if they are not converted into shares of Alloy common stock. If not

continued

continued from prior page

previously converted to common stock, Alloy may redeem the Convertible Debentures after August 1, 2008 at 103% of their face amount from August 1, 2008 through December 31, 2008 and at declining prices to 100% in January 2011 and thereafter, with accrued interest. From August 30, 2006 through December 7, 2006, holders converted approximately $67,903 face amount of their Debentures, in accordance with their terms, into approximately 2,026,000 shares of Alloy common stock. During fiscal 2006, the Company's additional paid-in capital increased by $67,883 as a result of the conversions. At January 31, 2007, the Company had $1,397 in principal amount of outstanding Convertible Debentures. At January 31, 2007, the fair value of the Convertible Debentures was approximately $1,504, which is estimated based on quoted market prices.

Required

a. How did Alloy initially account for the issuance of the 5.375% debentures, assuming that the conversion option cannot be detached and sold separately?

b. Consider the conversion terms reported in the footnote. At what minimum stock price would it make economic sense for debenture holders to convert to Alloy common stock?

c. Use the financial statement effects template to show how Alloy accounted for the conversion of the 5.375% debentures in 2006. The par value of the company's stock is $0.01.

d. Assume that the conversion feature is valued by investors and, therefore, results in a higher initial issuance price for the bonds. What effect will the conversion feature have on the amount of interest expense and net income that Alloy reports?

e. How are the convertible debentures treated in the computation of basic and diluted earnings per share (EPS)?

P8-55. Interpreting Disclosure on Convertible Preferred Securities (LO3)

NORTHROP
GRUMMAN CORP.
(NOC)

The 2008 annual report of **Northrop Grumman Corporation** includes the following disclosure in its shareholders' equity footnote:

Conversion of Preferred Stock On February 20, 2008, the company's board of directors approved the redemption of all of the 3.5 million shares of mandatorily redeemable convertible preferred stock on April 4, 2008. Prior to the redemption date, substantially all of the preferred shares were converted into common stock at the election of shareholders. All remaining unconverted preferred shares were redeemed by the company on the redemption date. As a result of the conversion and redemption, the company issued approximately 6.4 million shares of common stock.

Required

a. Explain what is meant by "mandatorily redeemable" and "convertible" preferred stock.

b. The company's balance sheet reports preferred stock of $350 million at December 31, 2007 (and $0 at December 31, 2008). As is typical, Northrop Grumman originally sold these preferred at par. Confirm that the par value of the preferred stock is $100 per share.

c. Northrop's footnotes report that the fair value of the preferred shares was $146 per share at December 31, 2008. What would explain this large increase in its preferred stock's market price?

d. Use the financial statement effects template to record the conversion of the preferred stock on April 4, 2008. Assume that all 3.5 million shares were converted. The par value of the company's common stock is $1 per share.

P8-56. Identifying and Analyzing Financial Statement Effects of Share-Based Compensation (LO1)

Weaver Industries implements a new share-based compensation plan in 2009. Under the plan, the company's CEO and CFO each will receive non-qualified stock options to purchase 100,000, no par shares. The options vest ratably (1/3 of the options each year) over three years, expire in 10 years, and have an exercise (strike) price of $22 per share. Weaver uses the Black-Scholes model to estimate a fair value per option of $15. The company's tax rate is 40%.

Required

a. Use the financial statement effects template to record the compensation expense related to these options for each year 2009 through 2011. Include the effects of any anticipated deferred tax benefits.

b. In 2012, the company's stock price is $19. If you were the Weaver Industries CEO, would you exercise your options? Explain.

c.   In 2014, the company's stock price is $40 and the CEO exercises all of her options. Use the financial statement effects template to record the exercise.

d.   What tax benefit will Weaver Industries receive related to the CEO's exercise in part *c*? What will be the tax consequences to the CEO?

P8-57.   **Interpreting Disclosure on Employee Stock Options**   **(LO1)**

Intel Corporation reported the following in its 2010 10-K report.

Share-Based Compensation   Share-based compensation recognized in 2010 was $917 million ($889 million in 2009 and $851 million in 2008). . . . During 2010, the tax benefit that we realized for the tax deduction from share-based awards totaled $266 million ($119 million in 2009 and $147 million in 2008). . . . We use the Black-Scholes option pricing model to estimate the fair value of options granted under our equity incentive plans and rights to acquire stock granted under our stock purchase plan. We based the weighted average estimated values of employee stock option grants (excluding stock option grants in connection with the Option Exchange in 2009) and rights granted under the stock purchase plan, as well as the weighted average assumptions used in calculating these values, on estimates at the date of grant, as follows:

	Stock Options			Stock Purchase Plan		
	2010	2009	2008	2010	2009	2008
Estimated values	$4.82	$4.72	$5.74	$4.71	$4.14	$5.32
Expected life (in years)	4.9	4.9	5.0	0.5	0.5	0.5
Risk-free interest rate	2.5%	1.8%	3.0%	0.2%	0.4%	2.1%
Volatility	28%	46%	37%	32%	44%	35%
Dividend yield	2.7%	3.6%	2.7%	3.1%	3.6%	2.5%

Additional information with respect to stock option activity is as follows:

(In millions, except per option amounts)	Number of Options	Weighted Average Exercise Price
December 29, 2007	665.9	$27.76
Grants	24.9	$20.81
Exercises	(33.6)	$19.42
Cancellations and forfeitures	(42.8)	$31.14
Expirations	(2.4)	$22.84
December 27, 2008	612.0	$27.70
Grants	118.5	$18.01
Assumed in acquisition	9.0	$15.42
Exercises	(3.6)	$15.90
Cancellations and forfeitures	(29.6)	$28.16
Exchanged	(217.4)	$26.75
Expirations	(37.6)	$31.92
December 26, 2009	451.3	$25.08
Grants	20.2	$23.25
Exercises	(16.6)	$18.36
Cancellations and forfeitures	(16.1)	$24.76
Expirations	(52.4)	$60.68
December 25, 2010	386.4	$20.45
Options exercisable as of:		
December 27, 2008	517.0	$28.78
December 26, 2009	297.7	$28.44
December 25, 2010	263.0	$21.03

INTEL CORPORATION
(INTC)

Required

a. What did Intel expense for share-based compensation for 2010? How many options did Intel grant in 2010? Compute the fair value of all options granted during 2010. Why do the fair value of the option grants and the expense differ?

b. Intel used the Black-Scholes formula to estimate fair value of the options granted each year. How did the change in volatility from 2009 to 2010 affect share-based compensation in 2010? What about the change in risk-free rate?

c. How many options were exercised during 2010? Estimate the cash that Intel received from its employees when these options were exercised.

d. What was the intrinsic value per share of the options exercised in 2010? If employees who exercised options in 2010 immediately sold them, what "profit" did they make from the shares? (*Hint:* Assume that Intel grants options at-the-money.)

e. The tax benefit that Intel will receive on the options exercised is computed based on the intrinsic value of the options exercised. Estimate Intel's tax benefit from the 2010 option exercises assuming a tax rate of 37%.

f. What was the average exercise price of the options that expired in 2010? Explain why employees might have let these options expire without exercising them. (*Hint:* Assume that Intel grants options at-the-money.)

P8-58. **Interpreting Disclosure on Share-Based Compensation** **(LO1)**

INTEL CORPORATION (INTC)

Intel reported the following information in its 2010 10-K related to its restricted stock plan.

In 2009, we began issuing restricted stock units with both a market condition and a service condition (market-based restricted stock units), referred to in our 2010 Proxy Statement as outperformance stock units, to a small group of senior officers and non-employee directors. The number of shares of Intel common stock to be received at vesting will range from 33% to 200% of the target amount, based on total stockholder return (TSR) on Intel common stock measured against the benchmark TSR of a peer group over a three-year period. TSR is a measure of stock price appreciation plus any dividends paid in this performance period. As of December 25, 2010, there were 3 million market-based restricted stock units outstanding. These market-based restricted stock units accrue dividend equivalents and vest three years and one month from the grant date. Information with respect to outstanding restricted stock unit (RSU) activity is as follows:

(In Millions, Except Per RSU Amounts)	Number of RSUs	Weighted Average Grant-Date Fair Value
December 29, 2007	51.1	$20.24
Granted	32.9	$19.94
Vested	(12.1)	$19.75
Forfeited	(4.6)	$20.12
December 27, 2008	67.3	$20.18
Granted	60.0	$14.63
Assumed in acquisition	1.6	$17.52
Vested	(20.1)	$20.24
Forfeited	(3.4)	$18.19
December 26, 2009	105.4	$17.03
Granted	32.4	$22.56
Vested	(34.6)	$17.70
Forfeited	(3.4)	$17.98
December 25, 2010	99.8	$18.56
Expected to vest as of December 25, 2010	94.4	$18.54

The aggregate fair value of awards that vested in 2010 was $808 million ($320 million in 2009 and $270 million in 2008), which represents the market value of Intel common stock on the date that the restricted stock units vested. The grant date fair value of awards that vested in 2010 was $612 million ($407 million in 2009 and $239 million in 2008). The number of restricted stock units vested includes shares that we withheld on behalf of employees to satisfy the minimum statutory tax withholding

continued

continued from prior page

requirements. Restricted stock units that are expected to vest are net of estimated future forfeitures. As of December 25, 2010, there was $1.2 billion in unrecognized compensation costs related to restricted stock units granted under our equity incentive plans. We expect to recognize those costs over a weighted average period of 1.3 years.

Required

a. How do restricted stock and stock options differ? In what respects are they the same?

b. Why do companies impose vesting periods on restricted stock grants?

c. Use the financial statement effects template to record the restricted stock granted to senior executives during 2010. The common stock has a par value of $0.001 per share.

d. Use the financial statement effects template to record the 2010 compensation expense related to Intel's restricted stock awards assuming straight-line amortization of the deferred compensation over the 1.3-year amortization period.

IFRS APPLICATIONS

I8-59.   Analyzing Revaluation Reserve   (LO2)

WorkCover Queensland offers workers compensation coverage to people in Queensland, Australia. Its 2010 notes (compliant with IFRS) reported the following information on the asset revaluation reserve, which is included in stockholders' equity on the balance sheet.

WORKCOVER
QUEENSLAND

(in 000 Australian dollars)	Land	Buildings	Total
Carrying amount at the beginning of fiscal 2009	8,120	17,450	25,570
Revaluation increment (decrement)	1,000	(5,027)	(4,027)
Tax effect on revaluation.	(300)	1,508	1,208
Carrying amount at the end of fiscal 2009	8,820	13,931	22,751
Carrying amount at the beginning of fiscal 2010	8,820	13,931	22,751
Revaluation increment (decrement)	(3,000)	(2,285)	(5,285)
Tax effect on revaluation.	900	686	1,586
Carrying amount at the end of fiscal 2010	6,720	12,332	19,052

Explain the concept of asset revaluation. What happened to the fair value of land during fiscal 2009 and fiscal 2010? Were the fair values of buildings similarly affected? How was the income statement affected by these revaluations?

I8-60.   Analyzing and Computing Average Issue Price and Treasury Stock Cost and Market Cap)   (LO1, 2)

Ahold is a major international supermarket operator based in Zaandam, Netherlands. Following is information taken from Ahold's financial statements prepared in accordance with IFRS.

AHOLD

Shareholders' Equity (€ millions)	January 3, 2010	December 28, 2008
Issued and paid-in share capital	358	358
Additional paid-in capital	9,916	9,916
Legal reserves	(236)	(311)
Accumulated deficit	(5,492)	(6,353)
Net income.	894	1,077
Shareholders' equity	5,440	4,687

Footnotes to financial statements disclose the following: At January 3, 2010, and December 28, 2008, there were 1,700,000,000 authorized and 1,191,888,000 shares issued. On those respective dates, the company had treasury stock of 10,674,000 shares and 15,203,000 shares, respectively, and the amount in shareholders' equity was €(112) million and €(159) million.

Required

a. How many shares are authorized at 2009 fiscal year-end?

b. How many shares are issued at 2009 fiscal year-end? At what average price were these shares issued at fiscal year-end 2009?

c. How many treasury shares are held as of fiscal 2009 year-end? At what average price did the company repurchase treasury shares as of fiscal 2009 year-end?

d. How many shares are outstanding as of January 3, 2010?

e. At January 3, 2010, the share price for Ahold was €9.32. Compute the company's market capitalization on that date. How does this compare to the net book value of equity?

I8-61. **Analyzing and Interpreting Equity Accounts and Comprehensive Income** (LO1, 2)

HENKEL AG & CO.

Henkel AG & Co. is an international, fast-moving consumer goods (FMCG) company headquartered in Düsseldorf, Germany. Following is its shareholders' equity statement, prepared using IFRS, from its 2010 annual report (in Euros millions).

Statement of changes in equity

In millions euro	Issued capital						Other components		Shareholders of Henkel AG & Co. KGaA	Non-controlling Interests	Total
	Ordinary shares	Pre-ferred shares	Capital reserve	Trea-sury shares	Retained earnings		Transla-tion dif-ferences	Financial instru-ments			
At January 1, 2009	260	178	652	(115)	6,920		(1,199)	(212)	6,484	51	6,535
Net income					602				602	26	628
Other comprehensive income					(285)		(102)	(11)	(398)	(2)	(400)
Total comprehensive income					317		(102)	(11)	204	24	228
Distributions					(224)				(224)	(12)	(236)
Sale of treasury shares				6	4				10		10
Other changes in equity					—					7	7
At December 31, 2009/ January 1, 2010	260	178	652	(109)	7,017		(1,301)	(223)	6,474	70	6,544
Net income					1,118				1,118	25	1,143
Other comprehensive income					53		525	(59)	519	6	525
Total comprehensive income					1,171		525	(59)	1,637	31	1,668
Distribution					(225)				(225)	(19)	(244)
Sale of treasury shares				10	9				19		19
Other changes in equity					(46)				(46)	9	(37)
At December 31, 2010	260	178	652	(99)	7,926		(776)	(282)	7,859	91	7,950

Required

a. Did Henkel issue any additional ordinary or preferred shares during 2010?

b. Use the information above to infer how much Henkel paid in dividends during 2010. To whom were these dividends paid?

c. Did the company repurchase any stock during 2010? Did Henkel sell any treasury shares? If so, what did the company receive in exchange for the sale of treasury stock?

d. How much did Henkel make in economic profit or loss on the sale, relative to the original stock repurchase price? Was this recorded in net income as an accounting profit or loss?

I8-62. **Analyzing and Computing Average Issue Price and Treasury Stock Transactions** (LO 1)

THYSSENKRUPP AG

ThyssenKrupp AG, is a German steelmaker and engineering company. The equity section of the company's 2010 statement of financial position reported the following:

(In million €)	September 30, 2009	September 30, 2010
Capital stock	1,317	1,317
Additional paid in capital	4,684	4,684
Retained earnings	3,643	3,703
Cumulative other comprehensive income	(296)	192
Treasury stock (51,015,552 and 50,094,707 shares)	(1,421)	(1,396)
Equity attributable to ThyssenKrupp AG's stockholders	7,927	8,500
Noncontrolling interest	1,769	1,888
Total equity	9,696	10,388

Notes to financial statements reveal that the company sold treasury shares during 2010 for proceeds of €21 million cash. Also, on July 6, 2011, *Dow Jones Newswire* reported the following:

> Frankfurt—ThyssenKrupp AG (TKA.XE) said Wednesday it has decided to sell 49.48 million treasury shares, which correspond to 9.6% of its capital stock, as part of its strategy to reduce net debt. Analysts welcomed the share placement, saying it should help reduce debt and restore confidence in the company's balance sheet, even though it puts short-term pressure on the stock. Net financial debt stood at around EUR6.5 billion, or around twice as high as earnings before interest, taxes, depreciation and amortization at the end of the company's fiscal year 2010, ended Sept. 30. At 0830 GMT, ThyssenKrupp traded lower EUR1.80 or 5.2% at EUR32.96, underperforming a broadly firmer market.

Required

a. Consider the treasury shares at September 30, 2009. At what average price had the company repurchased these shares?

b. Use the information above to infer the number of treasury shares sold during fiscal 2010. How much cash did the company receive for these treasury shares? At what average price did the company sell these shares?

c. Use the financial statement effects template to record the sale of treasury shares during fiscal 2010.

d. Use the financial statement effects template to record the anticipated sale of treasury shares announced in July 2011. Assume that the shares will be sold for EUR32.96.

e. Assume the company uses all the anticipated proceeds to reduce debt. Quantify the effect on the total debt to total equity ratio.

DISCUSSION POINTS

D8-63.   Ethics and Governance: Equity Carve-Outs   (LO3)

Many companies use split-offs as a means to unlock shareholder value. The split-off effectively splits the company into two pieces, each of which can then be valued separately by the stock market. If managers are compensated based on reported profit, how might they strategically structure the split-off? What corporate governance issues does this present?

SOLUTIONS TO REVIEW PROBLEMS

Mid-Module Review 1

Part 1 Solution

	Balance Sheet						Income Statement			
Transaction	Cash Asset	+ Noncash Assets	= Liabil- ities	+ Contrib. Capital	+ Earned Capital		Rev- enues	− Expen- ses	= Net Income	
Jan. 15: Issue 10,000 shares, $5 par, common at $17 per share	+170,000 Cash		=	+50,000 Common Stock +120,000 Additional Paid-In Capital				−	=	
Mar. 31: Repurchase 2,000 shares of common at $15 per share	−30,000 Cash		=	−30,000 Treasury Stock				−	=	
June 25: Reissue 1,000 trea- sury shares at $20 per share	+20,000 Cash		=	+15,000 Treasury Stock +5,000 Additional Paid-In Capital				−	=	

Cash   170,000
　　CS   50,000
　　APIC   120,000

Cash	
170,000	
	CS
	50,000
	APIC
	120,000

TS   30,000
　Cash   30,000

Cash	
30,000	
	Cash
	30,000

Cash   20,000
　TS   15,000
　APIC   5,000

Cash	
20,000	
	TS
	15,000
	APIC
	5,000

Part 2 Solution

a. *Granted* relates to the number of shares under option that have been awarded to employees for the year. *Exercised* refers to the number of shares that employees have purchased that were previously under option. *Forfeited* relates to the number of shares under option that are no longer exercisable because the options were not exercised before they expired. The "Weighted Average Exercise Price" is the average price at which employees can purchase shares of stock that are under option, weighted by the number of shares at each exercise price.

b. Compensation cost is computed as the total value of employee stock options spread over the vesting period. For example, if Accenture grants employees stock options with an estimated value of $1 billion that vest over a four-year period, the expense that is recognized over the subsequent four years is $250 million per year. The "unrecognized compensation cost" is that portion of the total estimated value of the stock options that has not yet been recognized as expense in the income statement.

Mid-Module Review 2

Solution

a.

Cumulative Preferred Stock	Preferred Stock	Common Stock
Year 1—$0 cash dividends paid.	$ 0	$ 0
Year 2—$300,000 cash dividends paid		
Dividends in arrears from Year 1 ($1,000,000 × 5%).	50,000	
Current-year dividend ($1,000,000 × 5%)	50,000	
Balance to common		200,000
Year 3—$80,000 cash dividends paid		
Current-year dividend ($1,000,000 × 5%)	50,000	
Balance to common		30,000

b.

Noncumulative Preferred Stock	Preferred Stock	Common Stock
Year 1—$0 cash dividends paid.	$ 0	$ 0
Year 2—$300,000 cash dividends paid		
Current-year dividend ($1,000,000 × 5%)	50,000	
Balance to common		250,000
Year 3—$80,000 cash dividends paid		
Current-year dividend ($1,000,000 × 5%)	50,000	
Balance to common		30,000

Mid-Module Review 3

Solution

	Balance Sheet						Income Statement		
Transaction	Cash Asset	+ Noncash Assets	= Liabil- ities	+ Contrib. Capital	+ Earned Capital		Rev- enues	− Expen- ses	= Net Income
Apr. 1: Declare and issue 100% stock dividend; stock is $11 per share			=	+250,000 Common Stock	−250,000[1] Retained Earnings		−		=
Dec. 7: Declare and issue 3% stock dividend; stock is $7 per share			=	+15,000 Common Stock +6,000 Additional Paid-In Capital	−21,000[2] Retained Earnings		−		=

RE   250,000
  CS   250,000

RE
250,000 |
  CS
    | 250,000

RE   21,000
  CS   15,000
  APIC   6,000

RE
21,000 |
  CS
    | 15,000
  APIC
    | 6,000

continued

continued from prior page

	Balance Sheet						Income Statement			
Transaction	Cash Asset	+ Noncash Assets	= Liabil-ities	+ Contrib. Capital	+ Earned Capital		Rev-enues	− Expen-ses	= Net Income	
Dec. 31: Declare and pay cash dividend of $1.20 per share	−123,600 Cash		=		−123,600[3] Retained Earnings			−	=	

RE	123,600
Cash	123,600

RE	
123,600	
Cash	
	123,600

[1] This large stock dividend reduces retained earnings at the par value of shares distributed (50,000 shares × 100% × $5 par value = $250,000). Contributed capital (common stock) increases by the same amount.

[2] This small stock dividend reduces retained earnings at the market value of shares distributed (3% × 100,000 shares × $7 per share = $21,000). Contributed capital increases by the same amount ($15,000 to common stock and $6,000 to paid-in capital). Note that the number of common shares outstanding on December 7 was 100,000—the large stock dividend on April 7 doubled the number of common stock outstanding.

[3] At the time of the cash dividend, there are 103,000 shares outstanding. The cash paid is, therefore, 103,000 shares × $1.20 per share = $123,600.

Mid-Module Review 4

Solution

1. A split-off is like a treasury stock transaction, but instead of repurchasing stock with cash, shares of the parent company owned by the shareholders are exchanged for shares of the subsidiary owned by the parent. If the distribution is non pro rata, the parent can report a gain equal to the difference between the fair value of the subsidiary and its book value on the parent's balance sheet.
2. BearingPoint met the conditions for a split-off as described in part 1, which enabled it to report a gain.

Module-End Review

Solution

	Balance Sheet						Income Statement			
Transaction	Cash Asset	+ Noncash Assets	= Liabil-ities	+ Contrib. Capital	+ Earned Capital		Rev-enues	− Expen-ses	= Net Income	
Convert a bond with $850 book value into 200 common shares with $1 par value			= −850 Long-Term Debt	+200 Common Stock +650 Additional Paid-In Capital				−	=	

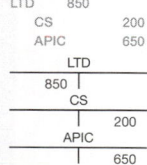

LTD	850		
		CS	200
		APIC	650

LTD	
850	
	CS
	200
	APIC
	650

1. Describe and analyze accounting for passive investments. (p. 9-5)

2. Explain and analyze accounting for equity method investments. (p. 9-11)

3. Describe and illustrate accounting for consolidations. (p. 9-17)

Intercorporate Entities

How does Google make money? A recent *BusinessWeek* article explains: "everybody knows that Google Inc.'s innovations in search technology made it the No. 1 search engine. But Google didn't make money until it started auctioning ads that appear alongside the search results. Advertising today accounts for 99% of revenue." This seems to suggest that **Google** is a media company. Indeed, with a market capitalization of about $170 billion as of mid-2011, (over four times that of **Time Warner**), Google is the world's largest media company and among America's top 30 most valuable companies. Since its IPO in 2004, Google's (GOOG) stock price has increased more than tenfold making Google one of the fastest growing companies on any stock exchange.

GOOGLE

Google's operations generated nearly $11 billion of operating cash flow in 2010, over four times the cash generated five years before. By the end of 2010, Google reported nearly $35 billion in cash and marketable securities on its balance sheet.

Google has considerable investments in government bonds. It holds these investments because it has excess cash awaiting deployment in other business activities. In the interim, the company expects to earn dividends and (potentially) capital gains from these securities. The accounting for these types of marketable securities differs markedly from the accounting for most other assets—Google's balance sheet reports these marketable securities at their current fair (or market) value instead of at their historical cost. As a result, the assets on Google's balance sheet fluctuate with the stock market. This causes stockholders' equity to fluctuate because, as we know from the accounting equation, assets equal liabilities plus equity.

We might wonder why Google would report these assets at fair value when nearly all other assets are reported at historical cost. As well, we might ask how these fluctuations in fair value affect Google's reported profit, if at all. This module answers both questions and explains the accounting for, and analysis of, such "passive" investments in marketable securities.

To expand its business activities beyond its current search-engine and advertising base, Google has strategically invested in the stock of other companies, which is a second category of investments. Through these strategic investments, Google can acquire substantial ownership of the companies such that Google can significantly influence their operations. The nature and purpose of these investments differs from Google's passive investment in marketable securities and, accordingly, the accounting reflects that difference. In particular, if Google owns enough voting stock to exert significant influence over another company, Google uses the *equity method* to account for those investments. Under the equity method, Google carries the investment on its balance sheet at an amount equal to its proportionate share of the investee company's equity. An equity method investment increases and decreases, not with changes in the stock's market value, but with changes in the investee company's stockholders' equity.

An interesting by-product of the equity method is that Google's balance sheet does not reflect the investee company's individual assets and liabilities, but only its net assets (its stockholders' equity). This is important because Google could be using the investee's assets and be responsible, to some extent, for the investee's liabilities. Yet, those liabilities are not detailed on Google's balance sheet. This creates what is called *off-balance-sheet financing*, potentially of great concern to accountants, analysts, creditors, and others who rely on financial reports. This module describes the equity method of accounting for investments, including the implications of this type of off-balance-sheet financing.

(continued on next page)

(continued from previous page)

When an investor company acquires a sufficiently large proportion of the voting stock of another company, it can effectively control the other company. At that point, the acquired company is *consolidated*. Most of the financial statements of public companies are titled "consolidated." Consolidation essentially adds together the financial statements of two or more companies. It is important that we understand what consolidated financial statements tell us and what they do not. This module covers consolidation along with a discussion of its implications for analysis.

There was much consternation among investors when Google's stock price passed $100, then $200, then $600, then $700. At each milestone, investors became increasingly concerned that Google's stock was overvalued. That concern still abounds. But, as Google

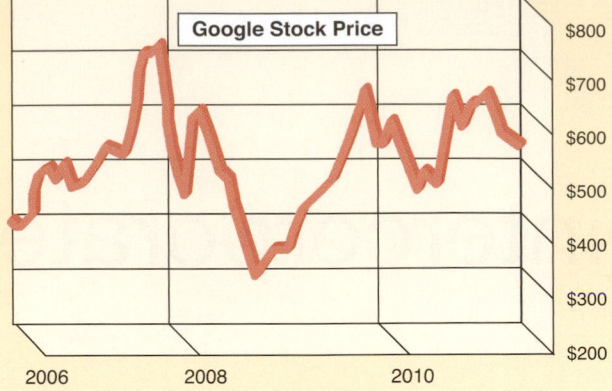

continues to make strategic investments necessary to broaden its revenue base, its share price will likely increase. Google's management believes that investments are a crucial part of the company's strategic plan. Understanding the accounting for all three types of intercorporate investment is, thus, important to our understanding of Google's (and other companies') ongoing operations.

Sources: *Google Form 10-K*, 2010; *Google Annual Report*, 2010; *BusinessWeek*, 2006; and *Fortune*, 2006 and 2011.

MODULE ORGANIZATION

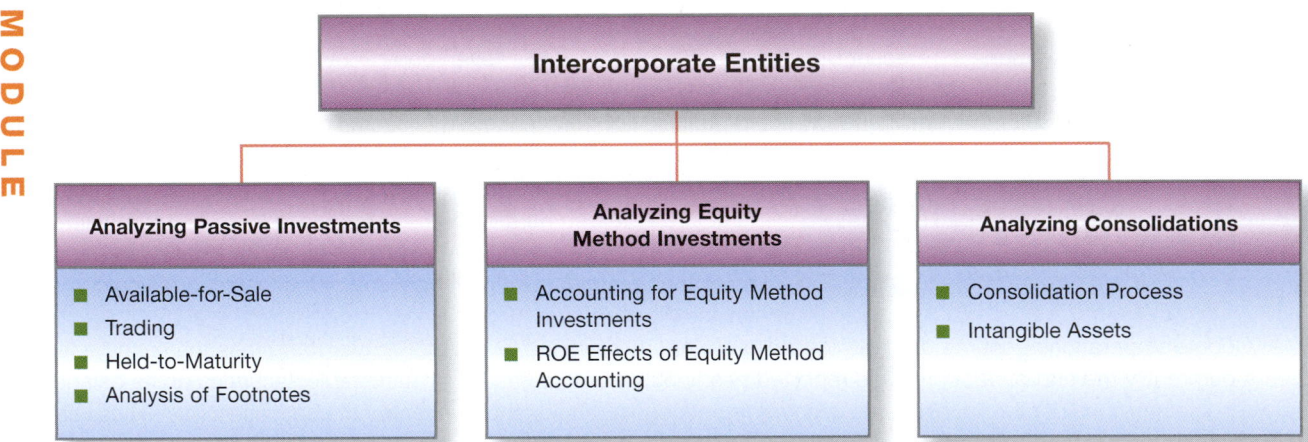

It is common for one company to purchase the voting stock of another. These purchases, called *intercorporate investments,* have the following strategic aims:

- **Short-term investment of excess cash.** Companies might invest excess cash to use during slow times of the year (after receivables are collected and before seasonal production begins) or to maintain liquidity (such as to counter strategic moves by competitors or to quickly respond to acquisition opportunities).

- **Alliances for strategic purposes.** Companies might acquire an equity interest in other companies for strategic purposes, such as gaining access to their research and development activities, to their supply or distribution markets, or to their production and marketing expertise.

- **Market penetration or expansion.** Companies might acquire control of other companies to achieve vertical or horizontal integration in existing markets or to penetrate new and growth markets.

Accounting for intercorporate investments follows one of three different methods, each of which affects the balance sheet and the income statement differently. These differences can be quite substantial. To help assimilate the materials in this module, Exhibit 9.1 graphically depicts the accounting for investments.

The degree of influence or control that the investor company (purchaser) can exert over the investee company (the company whose securities are being purchased) determines the accounting method. GAAP identifies three levels of influence/control.

1. **Passive.** A passive investment is one where the purchasing company has a relatively small investment and cannot exert influence over the investee company. The investor's goal is to real-

EXHIBIT 9.1	Accounting for Investments Based on Corporate Control

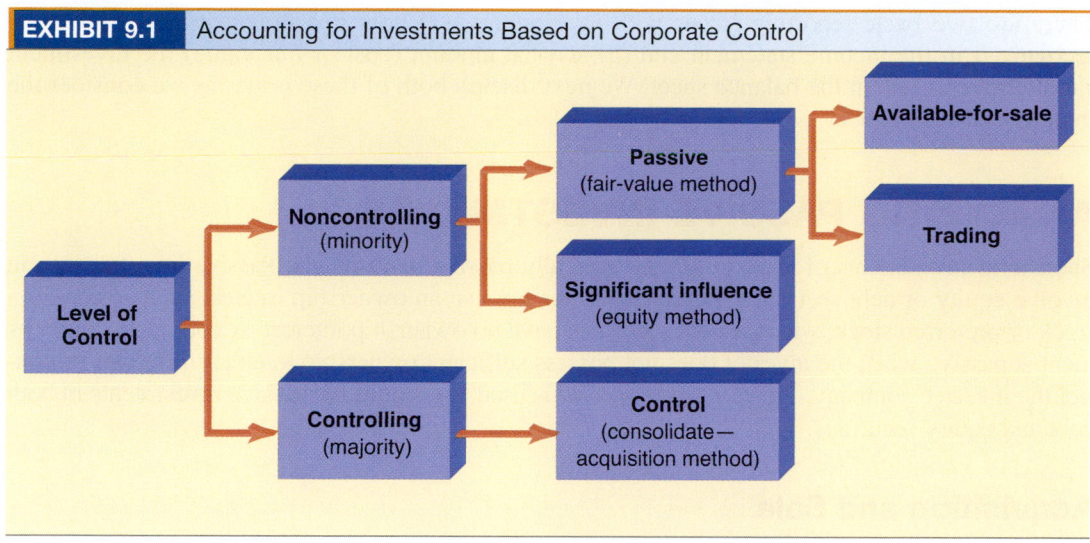

ize dividends and capital gains. Generally, the investment is considered passive if the investor company owns less than 20% of the outstanding voting stock of the investee company.

2. Significant **influence.** A company can sometimes exert significant influence over, but not control, the activities of the investee company. Significant influence can result when the percentage of voting stock owned is greater than a passive, short-term investment. However, an investment can also exhibit "significant influence" if there exist legal agreements between the investor and investee, such as a license to use technology, a formula, or a trade secret like production know-how. Absent other contractual arrangements such as those described above, significant influence is presumed at investment levels between 20% and 50%.

3. **Control.** When a company has control over another, it has the ability to elect a majority of the board of directors and, as a result, the ability to affect the investee company's strategic direction and the hiring of executive management. Control is generally presumed if the investor company owns more than 50% of the outstanding voting stock of the investee company, but can sometimes occur at less than 50% stock ownership by virtue of legal agreements, technology licensing, or other contractual means.

The level of influence/control determines the specific accounting method applied and its financial statement implications as outlined in Exhibit 9.2.

EXHIBIT 9.2	Investment Type, Accounting Treatment, and Financial Statement Effects			
	Accounting	Balance Sheet Effects	Income Statement Effects	Cash Flow Effects
Passive	Fair-value method	Investment account is reported at fair value	Interim changes in fair value reported in income *if* the investor actively trades the securities; otherwise not Dividends, if any, reported in income Sale of investment yields capital gain or loss, which is reported in income	Dividends and sale proceeds are cash inflows from investing activities Purchases are cash outflows from investing activities
Significant influence	Equity method	Investment account equals percent owned of investee company's equity*	Investor reports investment income equal to percent owned of investee income Dividends, if any, reduce investment account Sale of investment yields capital gain or loss, which is reported in income	Dividends and sale proceeds are cash inflows from investing activities Purchases are cash outflows from investing activities
Control	Consolidation	Balance sheets of investor and investee are combined	Income statements of investor and investee are combined Sale of investee yields capital gain or loss, which is reported in income	Cash flows of investor and investee are combined and retain original classification (operating, investing, or financing) Sale and purchase of investee are investing cash flows

* Investments are often acquired at purchase prices in excess of book value (the market price of S&P 500 companies was 1.9 times book value as of mid-2011). In this case the investment account exceeds the proportionate ownership of the investee's equity.

There are two basic reporting issues with investments: (1) how investment income should be recognized in the income statement and (2) at what amount (cost or fair value) the investment should be reported on the balance sheet. We next discuss both of these issues as we consider the three investment types.

ANALYZING PASSIVE INVESTMENTS

LO1 Describe and analyze accounting for passive investments.

Short-term investments of excess cash are typically passive investments. Passive investments can involve equity or debt securities. Equity securities involve an ownership interest such as common stock or preferred stock, whereas debt securities have no ownership interest. A voting stock investment is passive when the investor does not possess sufficient ownership to either influence or control the investee company. The *fair-value method* is used to account for passive investments in both debt and equity securities.

Acquisition and Sale

When a company makes a passive investment, it records the shares acquired on the balance sheet at fair value, that is, the purchase price. This is the same as accounting for the acquisition of other assets such as inventories or plant assets. Subsequent to acquisition, passive investments are carried on the balance sheet as current or long-term assets, depending on management's expectations about their ultimate holding period.

When investments are sold, any recognized gain or loss on sale is equal to the difference between the proceeds received and the book (carrying) value of the investment on the balance sheet as follows:

Gain or Loss on Sale = Proceeds from Sale − Book Value of Investment Sold

To illustrate the acquisition and sale of a passive investment, assume that **Microsoft** purchases 1,000 shares of **Skype** for $20 cash per share (this includes transaction costs such as brokerage fees). Microsoft, subsequently, sells 400 of the 1,000 shares for $23 cash per share. The following financial statement effects template shows how these transactions affect Microsoft.

	Balance Sheet										Income Statement			
Transaction	Cash Asset	+	Noncash Assets	=	Liabil- ities	+	Contrib. Capital	+	Earned Capital		Rev- enues	−	Expen- ses	=	Net Income
1. Purchase 1,000 shares of Skype common stock for $20 cash per share	−20,000 Cash		+20,000 Marketable Securities	=								−		=	
2. Sell 400 shares of Skype common stock for $23 cash per share	+9,200 Cash		−8,000 Marketable Securities	=					+1,200 Retained Earnings		+1,200 Gain on Sale	−		=	+1,200

MS   20,000
    Cash   20,000

MS
20,000 |
        Cash
                | 20,000

Cash   9,200
    MS   8,000
    GN   1,200

        Cash
9,200 |
        MS
            | 8,000
        GN
            | 1,200

Income statements include the gain or loss on sale of marketable securities as a component of *other income*, which is typically reported separately from operating income and often aggregated with interest and dividend revenue. Accounting for the purchase and sale of passive investments is the same as for any other asset. Further, there is no difference in accounting for purchases and sales across the different types of passive investments discussed in this section. However, there are differences in accounting for different types of passive investments between their purchase and their sale. We next address this issue.

Fair Value versus Cost

If a passive investment in equity securities has an active market with published prices, that investment is reported on the balance sheet at fair value. Fair value is specifically defined under GAAP. It is the value a willing party would pay to buy the asset in a well-functioning market. Quoted market prices must be used when available, which are called *Level 1 fair values*. In the absence of quoted market prices, companies can use market prices for similar assets, which are called *Level 2 fair values* or, if market prices for similar assets are not available, an estimate of investment value using financial models, which are *Level 3 fair values*. For marketable securities, **fair value** is the published price (as listed on a stock exchange) multiplied by the number of shares owned. This is one of few assets that are reported at fair value instead of historical cost.[1] For marketable securities, the current market value is almost always equal to the "fair" value and, thus, the two terms are often used interchangeably. If there exists no active market with published prices for the stock, the investment is reported at its historical cost.

Why are passive investments recorded at current fair value on the balance sheet? The answer lies in understanding the trade-off between the *objectivity* of historical cost and the *relevance* of market value. All things equal, current fair values of assets are more relevant in determining the market value of the company as a whole. However, for most assets, market values cannot be reliably determined. Adding unreliable "market values" to the balance sheet would introduce undue subjectivity into financial reports.

In the case of marketable securities, market prices result from numerous transactions between willing buyers and sellers. Market prices in this case provide an unbiased (objective) estimate of fair value to report on balance sheets. This reliability is the main reason GAAP allows passive investments to be recorded at fair value instead of at historical cost.

This fair-value method of accounting for securities causes asset values (the marketable securities) to fluctuate, with a corresponding change in equity (liabilities are unaffected). This is reflected in the following accounting equation:

Assets ↑ = Liabilities + Equity ↑   or   Assets ↓ = Liabilities + Equity ↓

An important issue is whether such changes in equity should be reported as income (with a consequent change in retained earnings), or whether they should bypass the income statement and directly impact equity via *accumulated other comprehensive income (AOCI)*. The answer differs depending on the classification of securities, which we explain next.

Investments Marked to Market

For accounting purposes, marketable securities are classified into two types, both of which are reported on the balance sheet at fair value. Remember that for marketable securities, current market value is usually synonymous with fair value, thus we say that marketable securities are *marked to market*.

1. **Available-for-sale (AFS).** These are securities that management intends to hold for capital gains and dividend revenue; although, they might be sold if the price is right.
2. **Trading (T).** These are investments that management intends to actively buy and sell for trading profits as market prices fluctuate.

Management classifies securities depending on the degree of turnover (transaction volume) it expects in the investment portfolio, which reflects management's intent to actively trade the securities or not. Available-for-sale portfolios exhibit less turnover than trading portfolios. (GAAP permits companies to have multiple portfolios, each with a different classification, and management can change portfolio classification provided it adheres to strict disclosure and reporting

---

[1] Other assets reported at fair value include (1) derivative securities (such as forward contracts, options, and futures) that are purchased to provide a hedge against price fluctuations or to eliminate other business risks (such as interest or exchange rate fluctuations), and (2) inventories and long-term assets that must be written down to market when their values permanently decline.

requirements about its expectations of turnover change.) The classification as either available-for-sale or trading determines the accounting treatment, as Exhibit 9.3 summarizes.

EXHIBIT 9.3	Accounting Treatment for Available-for-Sale and for Trading Investments	
Investment Classification	Reporting of Fair-Value Changes	Reporting of Dividends Received and Gains and Losses on Sale
Available-for-Sale (AFS)	Fair-value changes bypass the income statement and are reported in accumulated other comprehensive income (AOCI) as part of equity	Reported as *other income* in income statement
Trading (T)	Fair-value changes are reported in the income statement and impact equity via retained earnings	Reported as *other income* in income statement

The difference between the accounting treatment of available-for-sale and trading investments relates to how fair-value changes affect equity. Changes in the fair value of available-for-sale securities have no income effect; changes in fair value of trading securities have an income effect. The impact on total stockholders' equity is identical for both classifications. The only difference is whether the change is reflected in retained earnings or in the accumulated other comprehensive income (AOCI) component of stockholders' equity. Dividends and any gains or losses on security sales are reported in the other income section of the income statement for both classifications. (GAAP gives companies an option to account for available-for-sale securities like trading securities and report all changes in fair value on the income statement.) When sold, *unrealized* gains (losses) on available-for-sale investments are transferred ("reclassified") from AOCI into income and, thereby, become *realized* gains (losses).

Fair-Value Adjustments

To illustrate the accounting for changes in fair value subsequent to purchase (and before sale), assume that Microsoft's investment in Skype (600 remaining shares purchased for $20 per share) increases in value to $25 per share at year-end. The investment must be marked to market to reflect the $3,000 unrealized gain ($5 per share increase for 600 shares). The financial statement effects depend on whether the investment is classified as available-for-sale or as trading as follows:

	Balance Sheet						Income Statement		
Transaction	Cash Asset	+ Noncash Assets	= Liabil- ities	+ Contrib. Capital	+ Earned Capital		Rev- enues	− Expen- ses	= Net Income
If classified as available-for-sale									
$5 increase in fair value of Skype investment		+3,000 Marketable Securities	=		+3,000 AOCI			−	=
If classified as trading									
$5 increase in fair value of Skype investment		+3,000 Marketable Securities	=		+3,000 Retained Earnings		+3,000 Unrealized Gain	−	= +3,000

MS 3,000
  AOCI 3,000
    MS
3,000 |
    AOCI
      | 3,000

MS 3,000
  UG 3,000
    MS
3,000 |
    UG
      | 3,000

Under both classifications, the investment account increases by $3,000 to reflect the increase in the stock's market value. If Microsoft classifies these securities as available-for-sale, the unrealized gain increases the accumulated other comprehensive income (AOCI) account (which analysts typically view as a component of earned capital). However, if Microsoft classifies the securities as trading, the unrealized gain is recorded as income, thus increasing both reported income and retained earnings for the period. (Our illustration uses a portfolio with only one security for simplicity. Portfolios usually consist of multiple securities, and the unrealized gain or loss is computed based on the total cost and total market value of the entire portfolio.)

These fair-value adjustments only apply if market prices are available, that is, for publicly traded securities. Thus, this mark-to-market accounting does not apply to investments in start-up companies or privately held corporations. Investments in nonpublicly traded companies are accounted for at cost as we discuss later in this section.

> **IFRS Alert**
> IFRS permits similar accounting for financial assets, including that for trading, available-for-sale, and held-to-maturity portfolios.

Financial Statement Disclosures

Companies are required to disclose cost and fair values of their investment portfolios in footnotes to financial statements. **Google** reports the accounting policies for its investments in the following footnote to its 2010 10-K report:

> **Cash, Cash Equivalents, and Marketable Securities**   We invest our excess cash primarily in highly liquid debt instruments of the U.S. government and its agencies, municipalities in the U.S., debt instruments issued by foreign governments, time deposits, money market and other funds, including cash collateral received related to our securities lending program, mortgage-backed securities, and corporate securities. We classify all highly liquid investments with stated maturities of three months or less from date of purchase as cash equivalents and all highly liquid investments with stated maturities of greater than three months as marketable securities . . . We have classified and accounted for our marketable securities as available-for-sale . . . We carry these securities at fair value, and report the unrealized gains and losses, net of taxes, as a component of stockholders' equity, except for unrealized losses determined to be other-than-temporary which we record as interest and other income, net. We determine any realized gains or losses on the sale of marketable securities on a specific identification method, and we record such gains and losses as a component of interest and other income, net.

Google accounts for its investments in marketable securities at fair value. Because Google classifies those investments as "available-for-sale," unrealized gains and losses flow to the accumulated other comprehensive income component of stockholders' equity. When Google sells the securities, it will record any *realized* gains or losses in income.

Following is the current asset section of **Google**'s 2010 balance sheet reflecting these investments.

December 31 ($ millions)	2009	2010
Cash and cash equivalents	$10,198	$13,630
Marketable securities	14,287	21,345
Total cash, cash equivalents, and marketable securities	24,485	34,975
Accounts receivable, net of allowance of $79 and $101	3,178	4,252
Receivable under reverse repurchase agreements	0	750
Deferred income taxes, net	644	259
Income taxes receivable, net	23	0
Prepaid revenue share, expenses and other assets	837	1,326
Total current assets	$29,167	$41,562

Google's investments in marketable securities that are expected to mature within 90 days of the balance sheet date are recorded together with cash as cash equivalents. Its remaining investments are reported as marketable securities.

Footnotes to the **Google** 10-K provide further information about the composition of its investment portfolio.

As of December 31 ($ millions)	2009	2010
Cash and cash equivalents:		
Cash	$ 4,303	$ 4,652
Cash equivalents:		
Time deposits	3,740	973
Money market and other funds	2,153	7,547
U.S. government agencies	2	0
U.S. government notes	0	300
Foreign government bonds	0	150
Corporate debt securities	0	8
Total cash and cash equivalents	10,198	13,630
Marketable securities:		
Time deposits	1,250	304
Money market mutual funds	28	3
U.S. government agencies	3,703	1,857
U.S. government notes	2,492	3,930
Foreign government bonds	37	1,172
Municipal securities	2,130	2,503
Corporate debt securities	2,822	5,742
Agency residential mortgage-backed securities	1,578	5,673
Commercial mortgage-backed securities	48	0
Marketable equity security	199	161
Total marketable securities	14,287	21,345
Total cash, cash equivalents, and marketable securities	$24,485	$34,975

The majority of Google's 2010 investments are in government debt securities such as bonds and T-bills, with a relatively small portion invested in equity securities. Google accounts for all of these investments as available-for-sale and reports them in the current asset section of the balance sheet because they mature within the coming year or can be readily sold, if necessary.

Google provides additional (required) disclosures on the costs, fair values, and unrealized gains and losses for its available-for-sale investments as follows:

December 31, 2010 ($ millions)	Adjusted Cost	Gross Unrealized Gains	Gross Unrealized Losses	Fair Value
Time deposits	$ 304	$ 0	$ 0	$ 304
Money market mutual funds	3	0	0	3
U.S. government agencies	1,864	1	(8)	1,857
U.S. government notes	3,950	30	(50)	3,930
Foreign government bonds	1,154	23	(5)	1,172
Municipal securities	2,492	16	(5)	2,503
Corporate debt securities	5,600	167	(25)	5,742
Agency residential mortgage-backed securities	5,649	56	(32)	5,673
Marketable equity security	150	11	0	161
Total	$21,166	$304	$(125)	$21,345

Google's net unrealized gain of $179 million ($304 million − $125 million) is reported net of tax in the accumulated other comprehensive income (AOCI) section of its stockholders' equity as follows ($ millions):

December 31 ($ millions)	2009	2010
Class A and Class B common stock	$15,817	$18,235
Accumulated other comprehensive income	105	138
Retained earnings	20,082	27,868
Total stockholders' equity	36,004	46,241
Total liabilities and stockholders' equity	$40,497	$57,851

Google does not identify the components of its 2010 accumulated other comprehensive income of $138 except to report that the other component, beyond the unrealized gains on available-for-sale investments, is the cumulative translation adjustment relating to subsidiaries whose balance sheets are denominated in currencies other than $US. This lack of information can be confusing because the amount of unrealized gain (loss) reported in the investment footnote and the amount reported in accumulated other comprehensive income differ. Part of this difference relates to taxes: the net unrealized gain of $179 reported in the investment footnote is pretax while the amount reported in the accumulated other comprehensive income section of stockholders' equity is after-tax.

Investments Reported at Cost

Companies often purchase debt securities, including bonds issued by other companies or by the U.S. government. Such debt securities have maturity dates—dates when the security must be repaid by the borrower. If a company buys debt securities, and *management intends to hold the securities to maturity* (as opposed to selling them early), the securities are classified as **held-to-maturity** (HTM). The cost method applies to held-to-maturity securities. Exhibit 9.4 identifies the reporting of these securities.

EXHIBIT 9.4	Accounting Treatment for Held-to-Maturity Investments	
Investment Classification	**Reporting of Fair-Value Changes**	**Reporting Interest Received and the Gains and Losses on Sale**
Held-to-Maturity (HTM)	Fair-value changes are *not* reported in either the balance sheet or income statement	Interest reported as *other income* in income statement
		IF sold before maturity (the exception), any gain or loss on sale is reported in income statement

Changes in fair value do not affect either the balance sheet or the income statement. The presumption is that these investments will indeed be held to maturity, at which time their market value will be exactly equal to their face value. Fluctuations in fair value, as a result, are less relevant for this investment classification. Finally, any interest received is recorded in current income. (GAAP gives companies an option to report held-to-maturity investments at fair value; if this fair-value option is elected, the accounting for held-to-maturity securities is like that for trading securities.)

Sometimes companies acquire held-to-maturity debt securities for more or less than the security's face value. Because the value of debt securities fluctuates with the prevailing rate of interest, the market value of the security will be greater than its face value if current market interest rates are lower than what the security pays for interest. In that case, the acquirer will pay a premium for the security. Conversely, if current market interest rates exceed what the security pays in interest, the acquirer will purchase the security at a discount. (We cover premiums and discounts on debt securities in more detail in Module 7.) Either way, the company records the investment at its acquisition cost (like any other asset) and amortizes any discount or premium over the remaining life of the held-to-maturity investment. At any point in time, the acquirer's balance sheet carries the investment at "amortized cost," which is never adjusted for subsequent market value changes.

Companies can acquire equity interests in other companies that are not traded on an organized exchange. These might be start-ups that have never issued stock or established privately held companies. Because there is no market for such securities, they cannot be classified as marketable securities and are carried at historical cost on the balance sheet. **Google** references one such investment in its 2010 10-K.

Non-Marketable Equity Securities We have accounted for non-marketable equity security investments primarily at cost because we do not have significant influence over the underlying investees. We periodically review our marketable securities, as well as our non-marketable equity securities, for impairment. If we conclude that any of these investments are impaired, we determine

continued

continued from prior page

> whether such impairment is other-than-temporary. Factors we consider to make such determination include the duration and severity of the impairment, the reason for the decline in value and the potential recovery period, and our intent to sell, or whether it is more likely than not that we will be required to sell, the investment before recovery. If any impairment is considered other-than-temporary, we will write down the asset to its fair value and take a corresponding charge to our Consolidated Statements of Income.

Google uses historical cost to account for investments in non-marketable securities (equity investments where Google cannot exert significant influence over the investee company). Google monitors the value of these investments and writes them down to market value if they suffer a permanent decline in value. If such an investee company ever goes public, Google will change its accounting method. If Google's ownership percentage does not allow it to exert significant influence or control, Google will account for this investment following the procedures described above for marketable securities. However, if Google can exert significant influence or control, it will apply different accounting methods that we explain in later sections of this module.

MID-MODULE REVIEW 1

Assume that Google had the following four transactions involving investments in marketable securities. Use this information to answer requirements *a* and *b* below.

1. Purchased 1,000 shares of **Yahoo!** common stock for $15 cash per share.
2. Received cash dividend of $2.50 per share on Yahoo! common stock.
3. Year-end market price of Yahoo! common stock is $17 per share.
4. Sold all 1,000 shares of Yahoo! common stock for $17,000 cash in the next period.

Yahoo! reports the following table in the footnotes to its 2010 10-K. Use this information to answer requirements *c* and *d* below.

December 31, 2010 ($ Thousands)	Gross Amortized Costs	Gross Unrealized Gains	Gross Unrealized Losses	Estimated Fair Value
Government and agency securities	$1,353,064	$1,513	$ (514)	$1,354,063
Municipal bonds	6,609	8	—	6,617
Corporate debt securities, commercial paper, and bank certificates of deposits	740,043	1,608	(76)	741,575
Corporate equity securities	2,597	—	(1,128)	1,469
Total investments in available-for-sale securities	$2,102,313	$3,129	$(1,718)	$2,103,724

Required

a. Using the financial statement effects template, enter the effects (amount and account) relating to the four transactions assuming the investments are classified as available-for-sale.
b. Using the financial statement effects template enter the effects (amount and account) relating to the four transactions assuming that the investments are classified as trading securities.
c. What amount does Yahoo! report as investments on its balance sheet? What does this balance represent?
d. How did the net unrealized gains affect reported income in 2010?

The solution is on page 9-52.

ANALYZING INVESTMENTS WITH SIGNIFICANT INFLUENCE

LO2 Explain and analyze accounting for equity method investments.

Many companies make equity investments that yield them significant influence over the investee companies. These intercorporate investments are usually made for strategic reasons such as the following:

- **Prelude to acquisition**. Significant ownership can allow the investor company to gain a seat on the board of directors from which it can learn much about the investee company, its products, and its industry.

- **Strategic alliance**. Strategic alliances permit the investor to gain trade secrets, technical know-how, or access to restricted markets. For example, a company might buy an equity share in a company that provides inputs for the investor's production process. This relationship is closer than the usual supplier–buyer relationship and will convey benefits to the investor company.

- **Pursuit of research and development**. Many research activities in the pharmaceutical, software, and oil and gas industries are conducted jointly. The common motivation is to reduce the investor's risk or the amount of capital investment. The investment often carries an option to purchase additional shares, which the investor can exercise if the research activities are fruitful.

A crucial feature in each of these investments is that the investor company has a level of ownership that is sufficient for it to exert *significant influence* over the investee company. GAAP requires that such investments be accounted for using the *equity method*.

Significant influence is the ability of the investor to affect the financing, investing and operating policies of the investee. Ownership levels of 20% to 50% of the outstanding common stock of the investee typically convey significant influence. Significant influence can also exist when ownership is less than 20%. Evidence of such influence can be that the investor company is able to gain a seat on the board of directors of the investee by virtue of its equity investment, or the investor controls technical know-how or patents that are used by the investee, or the investor is able to exert significant influence by virtue of legal contracts with the investee. (There is growing pressure from regulators for determining significant influence by the facts and circumstances of the investment instead of a strict ownership percentage rule.)

Accounting for Investments with Significant Influence

GAAP requires that investors use the **equity method** when significant influence exists. The equity method reports the investment on the balance sheet at an amount equal to the percentage of the investee's equity owned by the investor; hence, the name equity method. (This assumes acquisition at book value. Acquisition at an amount greater than book value is covered later in this section.) Contrary to passive investments whose carrying amounts increase or decrease with the market value of the investee's stock, equity method investments increase (decrease) with increases (decreases) in the investee's stockholders' equity.

Equity method accounting is summarized as follows:

- Investments are recorded at their purchase cost.

- Dividends received are treated as a recovery of the investment and, thus, reduce the investment balance (dividends are not reported as income).

- The investor reports income equal to its percentage share of the investee's reported net income; the investment account is increased by the percentage share of the investee's income or is decreased by the percentage share of any loss.

- Changes in fair value do not affect the investment's carrying value. (GAAP gives companies an option to report equity method investments at fair value unless those investments relate to consolidated subsidiaries; we discuss consolidation later in the module.)

> **IFRS Alert**
> There is no fair-value option for investments accounted for by the equity method under IFRS.

To illustrate the equity method, consider the following scenario: Assume that **Google** acquires a 30% interest in Mitel Networks, a company seeking to develop a new technology. This investment is a strategic alliance for Google. At the acquisition date, Mitel's balance sheet reports $1,000 of stockholders' equity, and Google purchases a 30% stake for $300, giving it the ability to exert significant influence over Mitel. At the first year-end, Mitel reports profits of $100 and pays $20 in cash dividends to its shareholders ($6 to Google). Following are the financial statement effects for Google from this investment using the equity method.

9-13 **Module 9** | Intercorporate Entities

	Balance Sheet										Income Statement				
Transaction	**Cash Asset**	+	**Noncash Assets**	=	**Liabil-ities**	+	**Contrib. Capital**	+	**Earned Capital**		**Rev-enues**	−	**Expen-ses**	=	**Net Income**
1. Purchase 30% investment in Mitel for $300 cash	−300 Cash		+300 Investment in Mitel	=								−		=	
2. Mitel reports $100 income; Google's share is $30			+30 Investment in Mitel	=					+30 Retained Earnings		+30 Investment Income	−		=	+30
3. Mitel pays $20 cash dividends; $6 to Google	+6 Cash		−6 Investment in Mitel	=								−		=	
Ending balance of Google's investment account			324												

EMI 300
Cash 300

EMI	
300	

Cash	
	300

EMI 30
EI 30

EMI	
30	

EI	
	30

Cash 6
EMI 6

Cash	
6	

EMI	
	6

The investment is initially reported on Google's balance sheet at its purchase price of $300, representing a 30% interest in Mitel's total stockholders' equity of $1,000. During the year, Mitel's equity increases to $1,080 ($1,000 plus $100 income and less $20 dividends). Likewise, Google's investment increases by $30 to reflect its 30% share of Mitel's $100 income, and decreases by $6, relating to its share of Mitel's dividends. After these transactions, Google's investment in Mitel is reported on Google's balance sheet at 30% of $1,080, or $324.

Google's investment in Mitel is an asset, just like any other asset. As such, it must be tested annually for impairment. If the investment is found to be permanently impaired, Google must reduce the investment amount on the balance sheet and report a loss on the write-down of the investment in its income statement. If and when Google sells Mitel, any gain or loss on the sale is reported in Google's income statement. The gain or loss is computed as the difference between the sales proceeds and the investment's carrying value on the balance sheet. For example, if Google sold Mitel for $500, Google would report a gain on sale of $176 ($500 proceeds − $324 balance sheet value).

Companies often pay more than book value when they make equity investments. For example, if Google paid $400 for its 30% stake in Mitel, Google would initially report its investment at its $400 purchase price. The $400 investment consists of two parts: the $300 equity investment described above and the $100 additional investment. Google is willing to pay the higher purchase price because it believes that Mitel's reported equity is below its current market value. Perhaps some of Mitel's assets are reported at costs that are below market values or Mitel has intangible assets like internally generated goodwill that are missing from the balance sheet. The $300 portion of the investment is accounted for as described above. Google's management must decide how to allocate the excess of the amount paid over the book value of the investee company's equity and account for the excess accordingly. For example, if management decides that the $100 relates to depreciable assets, the $100 is depreciated over the assets' estimated useful lives. Or, if it relates to identifiable intangible assets that have a determinable useful life (like patents), it is amortized over the useful lives of the intangible assets. If it relates to goodwill, however, it is not amortized and remains on the balance sheet at $100 unless and until it is deemed to be impaired.

Two final points about equity method accounting: First, there can be a substantial difference between the book value of an equity method investment and its fair value. An increase in value is not recognized until the investment is sold. If the fair value of the investment has permanently declined, however, the investment is deemed impaired and it is written down to that lower fair value. Second, if the investee company reports income, the investor company reports its share.

Recognition of equity income by the investor, however, does not mean that it has received that income in cash. Cash is only received if the investee pays a dividend. To highlight this, the investor's statement of cash flows will include a reconciling item (a deduction from net income in computing operating cash flow) for its percentage share of the investee's net income. This is typically reported net of any cash dividends received.

RESEARCH INSIGHT   **Equity Income and Stock Prices**

Under the equity method of accounting, the investor does not recognize as income any dividends received from the investee, nor any changes in the investee's fair value, until the investment is sold. However, research has found a positive relation between investors' and investees' stock prices at the time of investees' earnings and dividend announcements. This suggests that the market includes information regarding investees' earnings and dividends when assessing the stock prices of investor companies, and implies that the market looks beyond the book value of the investment account in determining stock prices of investor companies.

Equity Method Accounting and ROE Effects

The investor company reports equity method investments on the balance sheet at an amount equal to the percentage owned of the investee company's equity when that investment is acquired at book value. To illustrate, consider the case of **Abbott Laboratories, Inc.**, which owned 50% of **TAP Pharmaceutical Products Inc.** (TAP was a joint venture with Takeda Pharmaceutical Company, Limited of Japan that was terminated in 2008.) TAP Pharmaceuticals (TAP) develops and markets pharmaceutical products mainly for the U.S. and Canada. Abbott accounts for its investment in TAP using the equity method as described in the following footnote to its 2007 10-K report:

> **Equity Method Investments ($ millions)** Abbott's 50 percent-owned joint venture, TAP Pharmaceutical Products Inc. (TAP), is accounted for under the equity method of accounting. The investment in TAP was $159, $162 and $167 at December 31, 2007, 2006 and 2005, respectively, and dividends received from TAP were $502, $487 and $343 in 2007, 2006 and 2005, respectively. Abbott performs certain administrative and manufacturing services for TAP at negotiated rates that approximate fair value.

At the end of 2007, the TAP joint venture reported stockholders' equity of $318 million and net income of $996 million. (TAP's financial statements are included in an exhibit to Abbott's 2007 10-K; not reproduced here.) In the footnote above, Abbott reports an investment balance at December 31, 2007, of $159 million (TAP equity of $318 million × 50%). In its income statement (not shown here), Abbott reports income of $498 million (TAP net income of $996 million × 50%). Provided the investment was originally acquired at book value these relations will always hold.

Let's look a bit closer at TAP. TAP's balance sheet reports assets of $1,354.2 million, liabilities of $1,036.7 million, and stockholders' equity of $317.5 million. TAP is a highly leveraged company with considerable assets. The $159 million investment balance on Abbott's balance sheet does not provide investors with any clue about the level of TAP's total assets nor about the substantial amount of TAP's financial obligations. It reflects only Abbott's share of TAP's net assets (assets less liabilities, or equity).

Further, **Abbott** makes the following additional disclosure in its footnotes relating to the cumulative payment of dividends by TAP:

> Undistributed earnings of investments accounted for under the equity method amounted to approximately $136 as of December 31, 2007.

Cumulatively, Abbott has recorded $136 million more of income than it has received in cash dividends from TAP. This shows that equity income does not necessarily equal cash inflow. This is particularly true for equity investments in growth-stage companies that do not pay dividends, or for foreign subsidiaries of U.S. nationals that might not pay dividends for tax reasons or other restrictions.

Another area of concern with equity method accounting relates to unreported liabilities. As described above, TAP reports total liabilities of $1,036.7 million as of 2007, none of which appear on Abbott's balance sheet (Abbott only reports its investment in TAP's equity as an asset). Pharmaceutical companies face large potential liabilities arising from drug sales. (For example, TAP reported a loss of $150 million relating to litigation that it settled in 2004.) Although Abbott might have no direct legal obligation for TAP's liabilities, it might need to fund settlement costs via additional investment or advances to maintain TAP's viability if the company is important to Abbott's strategic plan. Further, companies that routinely fund R&D activities through equity investments in other companies, a common practice in the pharmaceutical and software industries, can find themselves supporting underperforming equity investments to assure continued capital market funding for these entities. One cannot always assume, therefore, that the investee's liabilities will not adversely affect the investor.

The concern with unreported liabilities becomes particularly problematic when the investee company reports losses that are substantial. In extreme cases, the investee company can become insolvent (when equity is negative) as the growing negative balance in retained earnings more than offsets paid-in capital. Once the equity of the investee company reaches zero, the investor must discontinue accounting for the investment by the equity method. Instead, it accounts for the investment at cost with a zero balance and no further recognition of its proportionate share of investee company losses. In this case, the investor's income statement no longer includes the losses of the investee company and its balance sheet no longer reports the troubled investee company. Unreported liabilities can be especially problematic in this case.

To summarize, under equity method accounting, only the net equity owned is reported on the balance sheet (not the underlying assets and liabilities), and only the net equity in earnings is reported in the income statement (not the investee's sales and expenses). This is simply illustrated as follows using the (assumed) income statement and balance sheet from Mitel, the company in which Google invests $300 for a 30% ownership stake, at the end of the first year.

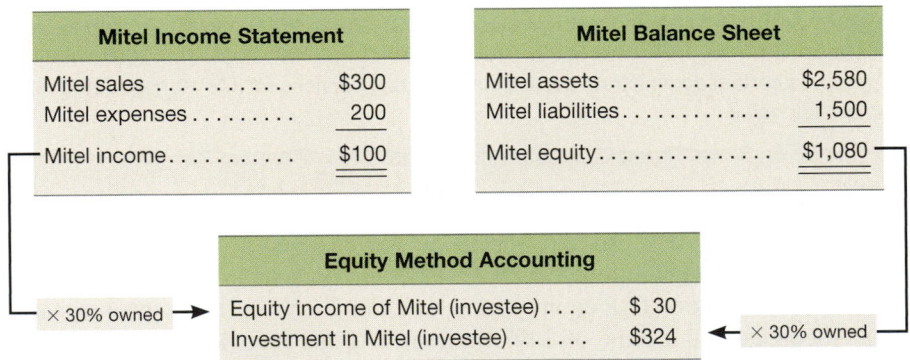

From an analysis standpoint, because the assets and liabilities are left off the Google balance sheet, and because the sales and expenses are omitted from the Google income statement, the *components* of ROE are markedly affected as follows:

■ **Net operating profit margin (NOPM = NOPAT/Sales).** Most analysts include equity income (sales less expenses) in NOPAT since it relates to operating investments. However, investee's sales are not included in the NOPM denominator. The reported NOPM is, thus, overstated.

■ **Net operating asset turnover (NOAT = Sales/Average NOA).** Investee's sales are excluded from the NOAT numerator, and net operating assets in excess of the investment balance are excluded from the denominator. This means the impact on NOAT is *indeterminate*.

■ **Financial leverage (FLEV = Net nonoperating obligations/Average equity).** Financial leverage is understated due to the absence of investee liabilities in the numerator.

Although ROE components are affected, ROE is unaffected by equity method accounting because the correct amount of investee net income and equity *is* included in the ROE numerator and denominator, respectively. Still, the evaluation of the quality of ROE is affected. Analysis using reported equity method accounting numbers would use an overstated NOPM and an understated FLEV because the numbers are based on net balance sheet and net income statement numbers. As we discuss in a later module, analysts should adjust reported financial statements for these types of items before conducting analysis. One such adjustment might be to consolidate (for analysis purposes) the equity method investee with the investor company.

IFRS INSIGHT Equity Method Investments and IFRS

Like US GAAP, IFRS requires use of the equity method for investments in "associates" where the investor has significant influence. Unlike US GAAP, IFRS does not permit an investor that continues to have significant influence over an associate to cease applying the equity method when the associate is operating under severe long-term restrictions that impair its ability to transfer funds to the investor. Instead, significant influence must be lost before the equity method ceases to apply. US GAAP allows the equity method to cease once the investee's equity reaches zero.

ANALYSIS DECISION You Are the Chief Financial Officer

You are receiving capital expenditure requests for long-term operating asset purchases from various managers. You are concerned that capacity utilization is too low. What potential courses of action can you consider? Explain. [Answer, p. 9-33]

MID-MODULE REVIEW 2

Assume that Google had the following five transactions involving investments in marketable securities accounted for using the equity method. Use this information to answer requirement *a* below.

1. Purchased 5,000 shares of **LookSmart** common stock at $10 cash per share; these shares reflect 30% ownership of LookSmart.
2. Received a $2 per share cash dividend on LookSmart common stock.
3. Recorded an accounting adjustment to reflect $100,000 income reported by LookSmart.
4. Year-end market price of LookSmart has increased to $12 per common share.
5. Sold all 5,000 shares of LookSmart common stock for $90,000 cash in the next period.

Assume that **Yahoo!** reports a $637 million equity investment in Yahoo! Japan related to its 34% ownership interest, and Yahoo!'s footnotes reveal the following financial information about Yahoo! Japan ($ millions).

Twelve Months Ended September 30	2010	2011	2012
Operating data			
Revenues	$1,367	$1,671	$1,933
Gross profit	1,252	1,584	1,836
Income from operations	656	807	984
Net income	382	451	508

September 30		2011	2012
Balance sheet data			
Current assets		$ 732	$1,131
Long-term assets		1,692	1,783
Current liabilities		535	692
Long-term liabilities		509	348

Required

a. Use the financial statement effects template to enter the effects (amount and account) for the five Google transactions, above.

b. How much income does Yahoo! report in its 2012 income statement related to this equity investment?

c. Show the computations required to yield the $637 million balance in the equity investment account on Yahoo!'s balance sheet.

The solution is on page 9-53.

ANALYZING INVESTMENTS WITH CONTROL

LO3 Describe and analyze accounting for consolidations.

This section discusses accounting for investments where the investor company "controls" the investee company. For example, in its footnote describing its accounting policies, **Google** reports the following:

> **Basis of Consolidations** The consolidated financial statements include the accounts of Google and wholly-owned subsidiaries. All intercompany balances and transactions have been eliminated.

This means that Google's financial statements are an aggregation (an adding up) of those of the parent company, Google, and all its subsidiary companies, less any intercompany activities such as intercompany sales or advances.

Accounting for Investments with Control

IFRS Alert
Consolidation accounting is generally similar with IFRS; differences exist in technical details, but not with presentation of consolidated financial statements.

Accounting for business combinations (acquiring a controlling interest) goes one step beyond equity method accounting. Under the equity method, the investor's investment balance represents the proportion of the investee's equity owned by the investor, and the investor company's income statement includes its proportionate share of the investee's income. Once "control" over the investee company is achieved, GAAP requires consolidation for financial statements issued to the public (not for the internal financial records of the separate companies). Consolidation accounting includes 100% of the investee's assets and liabilities on the investor's balance sheet and 100% of the investee's sales and expenses on the investor's income statement. Specifically, the consolidated balance sheet includes the gross assets and liabilities of the investee company, and the income statement includes the investee's gross sales and expenses rather than just the investor's share of the investee company's net assets or income. All intercompany sales and expenses, and receivables and payables, are eliminated in the consolidation process to avoid double-counting when, for example, goods are sold from the investee (called a subsidiary) to the investor (called the parent company) for resale to the parent's ultimate customers.

Investments Purchased at Book Value: Subsidiary Wholly-Owned To illustrate, consider the following scenario. Penman Company acquires 100% of the common stock of Nissim Company by exchanging newly issued Penman shares for all of Nissim's common stock. The purchase price is equal to the $3,000 book value of Nissim's stockholders' equity (contributed capital of $2,000 and retained earnings of $1,000). On its balance sheet, Penman accounts for the investment in Nissim using the equity method. This is important. Even if the investor (the parent) owns 100% of the investee, it records the investment on its (parent-company) balance sheet using the equity method described in the previous section. That is, Penman records an initial balance in the investment account of $3,000, equal to the purchase price. The balance sheets for Penman and Nissim immediately after the acquisition, together with the consolidated balance sheet, are shown in Exhibit 9.5.

Beginning on the date that Penman "controls" the activities of Nissim, GAAP requires consolidation of the two balance sheets, as well as the consolidation of the two income statements (not shown here). This process, shown in Exhibit 9.5, involves summing the individual lines for each balance sheet, after eliminating any intercompany transactions (such as investments and loans, and sales and purchases), within the consolidated group. The consolidated balances for accounts such as current assets, PPE, and liabilities are computed as the sum of those accounts from each balance sheet. The equity investment account, however, represents an intercompany transaction that Penman must eliminate during the consolidation process. This is accomplished by removing the equity investment of $3,000 (from Penman's balance sheet), and removing Nissim's stockholders' equity to which Penman's investment relates.

EXHIBIT 9.5 Mechanics of Consolidation Accounting
(Wholly-Owned Subsidiary, Purchased at Book Value)

	Penman Company	Nissim Company	Consolidating Adjustments	Consolidated
Current assets	$ 5,000	$1,000		$ 6,000
Investment in Nissim	3,000	0	(3,000)	0
PPE, net	10,000	4,000		14,000
Total assets	$18,000	$5,000		$20,000
Liabilities	$ 5,000	$2,000		$ 7,000
Contributed capital	10,000	2,000	(2,000)	10,000
Retained earnings	3,000	1,000	(1,000)	3,000
Total liabilities and equity	$18,000	$5,000		$20,000

Exhibit 9.5 shows the consolidated balance sheet in the far right column. It shows total assets of $20,000, total liabilities of $7,000 and stockholders' equity of $13,000. Notice that consolidated equity equals the equity of the parent company—this is always the case. (Likewise, consolidated net income always equals the parent company's net income as the subsidiary's net income is already reflected in the parent's income statement as equity income from its investment.)

Investments Purchased at Book Value: Subsidiary _Not_ Wholly-Owned In the event that Penman acquires less than 100% of the stock of Nissim, consolidated equity must increase to maintain the accounting equation. This equity account is titled **noncontrolling interest**. For example, assume that Penman acquires 80% of Nissim for $2,400 (80% of $3,000). The consolidating adjustments follow. The claim of noncontrolling shareholders on Nissim's net assets, is recognized in consolidated stockholders' equity, just like that of the majority shareholders. Exhibit 9.6 shows the consolidation adjustments and noncontrolling interest reported in the equity section of the consolidated balance sheet.

EXHIBIT 9.6 Mechanics of Consolidation Accounting
(Subsidiary Not Wholly-Owned, Purchased at Book Value)

	Penman Company	Nissim Company	Consolidating Adjustments	Consolidated
Current assets	$ 5,000	$1,000		$ 6,000
Investment in Nissim	2,400	0	(2,400)	0
PPE, net	10,000	4,000		14,000
Total assets	$17,400	$5,000		$20,000
Liabilities	$ 5,000	$2,000		$7,000
Contributed capital	9,400	2,000	(2,000)	9,400
Retained earnings	3,000	1,000	(1,000)	3,000
Noncontrolling interest			600	600
Total liability and equity	$17,400	$5,000		$20,000

The consolidated income statement lists the consolidated revenues, consolidated expenses, and consolidated net income. When less than 100% of the subsidiary is owned by the parent, the consolidated income statement allocates net income into that portion attributable to the parent's (controlling) shareholders and that which is attributable to the noncontrolling shareholders.

BUSINESS INSIGHT   Accounting for Noncontrolling Interests

When a company acquires less than 100% of a subsidiary, it must account for the interests of the noncontrolling shareholders separately from those of its own shareholders. This has two implications for consolidated financial statements:

1. The noncontrolling interest must be separately valued on the acquisition date. Consequently, the subsidiary is initially reported on the consolidated balance sheet at 100% of its fair value on the acquisition date (the fair value of the consideration paid plus the fair value of the noncontrolling interest on the acquisition date).

2. Consolidated net income is first computed for the company as a whole as revenues less expenses. Then, it is allocated to the portion attributable to the parent's shareholders and the noncontrolling shareholders in proportion to their respective ownership interests.

The balance of the noncontrolling interests is reported on the balance sheet in the stockholders' equity section. It is increased each year by the net income allocated to noncontrolling interests and is decreased by any dividends paid to those noncontrolling shareholders. A final point: if the subsidiary is acquired in a series of purchases, then once enough shares are purchased to gain control, the subsidiary is valued on the date control is achieved and any previously acquired shares are revalued on that acquisition date; this revaluation can result in recognition of a gain on previously acquired shares. (We describe reporting of noncontrolling interests in the balance sheet and income statement in Modules 5 and 8.)

Investments Purchased above Book Value The illustrations above assume that the purchase price of the acquisition equals the book value of the investee company. It is more often the case, however, that the purchase price exceeds the book value. This might arise, for example, if an investor company believes it is acquiring something of value that is not reported on the investee's balance sheet—such as tangible assets whose market values have risen above book value, or unrecorded intangible assets, like patents or corporate synergies. When the acquisition price exceeds book value, all net assets acquired (both tangible and intangible) must be recognized on the consolidated balance sheet.

To illustrate, assume that Penman Company acquires 100% of the voting stock of Nissim Company for $4,000. Also assume that in determining its purchase price, Penman paid the additional $1,000 because (1) Nissim's PPE is worth $300 more than its book value, and (2) Penman expects to realize $700 in additional value from corporate synergies (these "synergies" are an intangible asset with an indefinite useful life; they are classified as an asset called goodwill). The $4,000 investment account reflects two components: the book value acquired of $3,000 (as before) and an additional $1,000 of newly acquired assets. Exhibit 9.7 shows the post-acquisition balance sheets of the two companies, together with the consolidating adjustments and the consolidated balance sheet.

EXHIBIT 9.7	Mechanics of Consolidation Accounting (Purchase Price above Book Value)		
	Penman Company	**Nissim Company**	**Consolidating Adjustments**	**Consolidated**
---	---	---	---	---
Current assets	$ 5,000	$1,000		$ 6,000
Investment in Nissim	4,000	0	(4,000)	0
PPE, net	10,000	4,000	300	14,300
Goodwill			700	700
Total assets.	$19,000	$5,000		$21,000
Liabilities.	$ 5,000	$2,000		$ 7,000
Contributed capital.	11,000	2,000	(2,000)	11,000
Retained earnings	3,000	1,000	(1,000)	3,000
Total liabilities and equity	$19,000	$5,000		$21,000

The consolidated current assets and liabilities are the sum of those accounts on each company's balance sheet. The investment account, however, includes the $1,000 of additional newly acquired assets that must be reported on the consolidated balance sheet. The consolidation process in this case has two steps. First, the $3,000 equity of Nissim Company is eliminated against the investment account as before. Then, the remaining $1,000 of the investment account is eliminated and the newly acquired assets ($300 of PPE and $700 of goodwill not reported on Nissim's balance sheet) are added to the consolidated balance sheet. Thus, the consolidated balance sheet reflects the book value of Penman and the *fair market value* of Nissim (the book value plus the excess of Nissim's market value over its book value). For example, the consolidated PPE includes the book value of Penman's PPE ($10,000) along with the acquisition date fair value of Nissim's PPE ($4,300) for a total consolidated PPE of $14,300.

Consolidation is similar in successive periods. The excess purchase price assigned to depreciable assets, or identifiable intangible assets, must be amortized over the assets' useful lives. For example, if the additional $300 fair value of Nissim's PPE has an estimated life of 10 years with no salvage value, Penman would add $30 to depreciation expense on the consolidated income statement. This would reduce the consolidated PPE each year. And, as the excess of the purchase price over book value acquired is depreciated and/or amortized, the investment account on Penman's balance sheet gradually declines. Because goodwill is not amortized under GAAP, it remains at its carrying amount of $700 on the consolidated balance sheet unless it is impaired and written down (we discuss this below).

Consolidation Disclosures To illustrate consolidation mechanics with an actual case, consider the consolidated balance sheet (parent company, subsidiary, consolidating adjustments, and consolidated balance sheet) that **Caterpillar (CAT)** reports in a supplemental schedule to its 10-K report as shown in Exhibit 9.8. Caterpillar owns 100% of its financial products subsidiaries, principally Caterpillar Financial Services Corporation, whose stockholders' equity is $4,275 million as of 2010. The Investments in Financial Products account is also reported at $4,275 million on CAT's (parent company) balance sheet. This investment account is subsequently removed (eliminated) in the consolidation process, together with the equity of the subsidiaries to which it relates. Following this elimination, *and the elimination of all other intercompany transactions*, the adjusted balance sheets of the two companies are summed to yield the consolidated balance sheet that is reported in CAT's 10-K.

In sum, the consolidated balance sheet lists the consolidated assets, consolidated liabilities, and consolidated equity. (In some cases it also reports an additional equity account called *noncontrolling interests*, reflecting the ownership claim of the noncontrolling shareholders to the net assets of the subsidiary in which they are investors.)

Reporting of Acquired Intangible Assets

As previously discussed, acquisitions are routinely made at a purchase price in excess of the book value of the investee company's equity. The purchase price is first allocated to the fair values of tangible assets and liabilities. Then, the remainder is allocated to acquired intangible assets: first to identifiable intangible assets, then, any remainder is allocated to goodwill. As of the acquisition date, the purchasing company values the tangible assets acquired and liabilities assumed in the purchase and records them on the consolidated balance sheet at fair market value. Common types of intangible assets recognized during acquisitions follow:

- Marketing-related assets like trademarks and Internet domain names
- Customer-related assets like customer lists and customer contracts
- Artistic-related assets like plays, books, and videos
- Contract-based assets like licensing, lease contracts, and franchise and royalty agreements
- Technology-based assets like patents, in-process research and development, software, databases, and trade secrets

EXHIBIT 9.8 Caterpillar Consolidated Balance Sheet

At December 31, 2010 (In millions)	Machinery and Engines (Parent)	Financial Products (Subsidiary)	Consolidating Adjustments	Consolidated
Assets				
Current assets:				
Cash and short-term investments	$ 1,825	$ 1,767	$ —	$ 3,592
Receivables—trade and other	5,893	482	2,119	8,494
Receivables—finance	—	11,158	(2,860)	8,298
Deferred and refundable income taxes	823	108	—	931
Prepaid expenses and other current assets	371	550	(13)	908
Inventories	9,587	—	—	9,587
Total current assets	18,499	14,065	(754)	31,810
Property, plant and equipment—net	9,662	2,877	—	12,539
Long-term receivables—trade and other	271	236	286	793
Long-term receivables—finance	—	11,586	(322)	11,264
Investments in unconsolidated affiliated companies	156	8	—	164
Investments in Financial Products subsidiaries	4,275	—	(4,275)	—
Noncurrent deferred and refundable income taxes	2,922	90	(519)	2,493
Intangible assets	795	10	—	805
Goodwill	2,597	17	—	2,614
Other assets	314	1,224	—	1,538
Total assets	$39,491	$30,113	$(5,584)	$64,020
Liabilities				
Current liabilities:				
Short-term borrowings	$ 306	$ 4,452	$ (702)	$ 4,056
Accounts payable	5,717	177	(38)	5,856
Accrued expenses	2,422	470	(12)	2,880
Accrued wages, salaries and employee benefits	1,642	28	—	1,670
Customer advances	1,831	—	—	1,831
Dividends payable	281	—	—	281
Other current liabilities	1,142	393	(14)	1,521
Long-term debt due within one year	495	3,430	—	3,925
Total current liabilities	13,836	8,950	(766)	22,020
Long-term debt due after one year	4,543	15,932	(38)	20,437
Liability for postemployment benefits	7,584	—	—	7,584
Other liabilities	2,203	956	(505)	2,654
Total liabilities	28,166	25,838	(1,309)	52,695
Commitments and contingencies				
Redeemable noncontrolling interest*	461	—	—	461
Stockholders' equity				
Common stock	3,888	902	(902)	3,888
Treasury stock	(10,397)	—	—	(10,397)
Profit employed in the business	21,384	3,027	(3,027)	21,384
Accumulated other comprehensive income (loss)	(4,051)	263	(263)	(4,051)
Noncontrolling interests	40	83	(83)	40
Total stockholders' equity	10,864	4,275	(4,275)	10,864
Total liabilities, redeemable noncontrolling interest and stockholders' equity	$39,491	$30,113	$(5,584)	$64,020

* This $461 is reported as mezzanine (temporary) equity because it relates to a CAT subsidiary, where another company has a noncontrolling interest, for which the CAT subsidiary has an option to purchase per a redemption agreement.

To illustrate, **Procter & Gamble** (P&G) reported the following allocation of its $53.4 billion purchase price for **Gillette** in the footnotes to its 10-K report ($ millions).

Current assets	$ 5,681
Property, plant and equipment	3,655
Other noncurrent assets	382
Goodwill	35,298
Intangible assets	29,707
Total assets acquired	74,723
Current liabilities	5,346
Noncurrent liabilities	15,951
Total liabilities assumed	21,297
Net assets acquired	53,426

Tangible assets — Current assets, Property plant and equipment, Other noncurrent assets
Acquired intangible assets — Goodwill, Intangible assets
Liabilities assumed — Current liabilities, Noncurrent liabilities

Identifiable Intangible Assets (excluding goodwill) In its acquisition of **Gillette, P&G** allocated $29,707 million of its purchase price to identifiable intangible assets (other than goodwill), as described in the following footnote to **P&G**'s 10-K ($ millions):

The purchase price allocation to the identifiable intangible assets included in these financial statements is as follows:

Intangible Assets with Determinable Lives		Average Life
Brands	$ 1,627	20
Patents and technology	2,716	17
Customer relationships	1,436	27
Brands with indefinite lives	23,928	Indefinite
Total intangible assets	29,707	

The majority of the intangible asset valuation relates to brands. Our assessment as to brands that have an indefinite life and those that have a determinable life was based on a number of factors, including the competitive environment, market share, brand history, product life cycles, operating plan and macroeconomic environment of the countries in which the brands are sold. The indefinite-lived brands include Gillette, Venus, Duracell, Oral-B and Braun. The determinable-lived brands include certain brand sub-names, such as Mach3 and Sensor in the blades and razors business, and other regional or local brands. The determinable-lived brands have asset lives ranging from 10 to 40 years. The patents and technology intangibles are concentrated in the blades and razors and oral care businesses and have asset lives ranging from 5 to 20 years. The customer relationship intangible asset useful lives ranging from 20 to 30 years reflect the very low historical and projected customer attrition rates among Gillette's major retailer and distributor customers.

P&G allocated a portion of the purchase price to the following identifiable intangible assets:

- Brands
- Patents and technology
- Customer relationships

P&G deemed these identifiable intangible assets as amortizable assets, which are those having a finite useful life. P&G will subsequently amortize them over their useful lives (similar to depreciation).

IFRS Alert
When a firm purchases in-process research and development in the course of an acquisition, those costs are capitalized as an intangible asset under both IFRS and U.S. GAAP.

BUSINESS INSIGHT | **Restructuring Liabilities**

Many acquisitions are accompanied by restructuring activities that are designed to maximize asset utilization. These restructuring activities typically involve relocation and retraining or termination of employees and the exiting of less profitable product lines resulting in costs from closure of manufacturing, retailing, and administrative facilities and the write-off of assets. Acquirers can recognize restructuring liabilities when they purchase a subsidiary *only* if that subsidiary has previously accrued those liabilities. It also requires the Board of Directors to approve a formal restructuring plan and to communicate that plan to affected employees. Restructuring activities beginning *after* acquisition must be accrued and the expense recognized in post-acquisition consolidated income statements.

Goodwill Once the purchase price has been allocated to identifiable tangible and intangible assets (net of liabilities assumed), any remaining purchase price is allocated to goodwill. Goodwill, thus, represents the remainder of the purchase price that is not allocated to other assets. P&G allocated $35.3 billion (66%) of the Gillette purchase price to goodwill. The SEC scrutinizes companies that assign an excessive proportion of the purchase price to goodwill (companies might do this to avoid the future earnings drag from the amortization expense relating to identifiable intangible assets with useful lives).

BUSINESS INSIGHT | **Valuation of Earn-Outs**

Martha Stewart Living Omnimedia agreed to acquire some business units run by celebrity chef Emeril Lagasse for $50 million in cash and stock and a lucrative *earn-out* that could reach $20 million if Lagasse and company met specific profit goals. An earn-out is an incentive offered to key employees of a target company to entice them to remain with the company and increase value. Then, if the target company hits profit goals set by the buyer, the identified key employees earn a share of the profit. Under current GAAP, buyers must determine the estimated fair value of the future earn-out on the day of acquisition and record it as part of the purchase price. One impetus for an earn-out is when the buyer and seller cannot agree on a purchase price; in this way, the buyer is saying "I will pay if you make hay." Finally, any difference between the estimated fair value and the ultimate actual payout is recorded as an expense or gain.

Reporting of Goodwill

Goodwill is not amortized. Instead, GAAP requires companies to test the goodwill asset annually for impairment just like any other asset. The impairment test is a two-step process:

1. The fair value of the investee company is compared with the book value of the investor's equity investment account.[2]

2. If the fair value is less than the investment balance, the *investment* is deemed impaired. Next, one determines if the *goodwill* portion of the investment is impaired. The investor estimates the goodwill value as if the subsidiary were acquired at current fair value, and the imputed balance for goodwill becomes the balance in the goodwill account. If this imputed goodwill amount is less than its book value, the company writes goodwill down, resulting in an impairment loss on the consolidated income statement. (If not, no impairment of goodwill exists and no write-down is necessary; which, implies the impairment in this case relates to the investee's tangible assets, such as PPE, that must be tested separately for impairment.)

To illustrate the impairment computation, assume that an investment, currently reported at $1 million on the investor's balance sheet, has a current fair value of $900,000 (we know, therefore,

---

[2] GAAP allows firms to estimate fair value in three ways: using quoted market prices for identical assets, using quoted prices on similar assets, or using other valuation methods (such as the discounted cash flow model or residual operating income model—see Modules 12 through 15). The FedEx footnote, which follows, provides an example of the third method of determining fair value: an income approach. A company can avoid the goodwill impairment test if qualitative indicators (see GAAP) suggest a likelihood that the fair value of the reporting unit is greater than its carrying value; if not, then the company must apply the two-step test.

that the investment is impaired); also assume the consolidated balance sheet reports goodwill at $300,000. Management's review reveals that the current fair value of the net assets of the investee company (absent goodwill) is $700,000. This indicates that the goodwill component of the investment account is impaired by $100,000, which is computed as follows:

Fair value of investee company	$ 900,000
Fair value of net assets (absent goodwill)	(700,000)
Implied goodwill	200,000
Current goodwill balance	(300,000)
Impairment loss	$(100,000)

This analysis implies that goodwill must be written down by $100,000. The impairment loss is reported in the consolidated income statement. The related footnote disclosure would describe the reasons for the write-down and the computations involved.

FedEx provides an example of a goodwill impairment disclosure in its 10-K report:

Our operating results include a charge of approximately $891 million ($696 million, net of tax, or $2.23 per diluted share) recorded during the fourth quarter, predominantly related to noncash impairment charges associated with the decision to minimize the use of the Kinko's trade name and goodwill resulting from the Kinko's acquisition. The components of the charge include the following (in millions):

Trade name	$515
Goodwill	367
Other	9
	$891

During the fourth quarter we decided to change the name of FedEx Kinko's to FedEx Office. The impairment of the Kinko's trade name was due to the decision to minimize the use of the Kinko's trade name and rebrand our centers over the next several years. In accordance with SFAS 142, "Goodwill and Other Intangible Assets," a two-step impairment test is performed on goodwill. In the first step, we compared the estimated fair value of the reporting unit to its carrying value. The valuation methodology to estimate the fair value of the FedEx Office reporting unit was based primarily on an income approach that considered market participant assumptions to estimate fair value. Key assumptions considered were the revenue and operating income forecast, the assessed growth rate in the periods beyond the detailed forecast period, and the discount rate. In the second step of the impairment test, we estimated the current fair values of all assets and liabilities to determine the amount of implied goodwill and consequently the amount of the goodwill impairment. Upon completion of the second step of the impairment test, we concluded that the recorded goodwill was impaired and recorded an impairment charge of $367 million during the fourth quarter.

FedEx determined that goodwill, reported on its balance sheet at $1,542 million, had a current (implied) market value $1,175 million. That is, FedEx's goodwill was impaired, resulting in a write-down of $367 million. In addition, FedEx recorded a $515 million charge to write off the Kinko's trade name that it had acquired four years earlier.

IFRS INSIGHT Goodwill Impairment and Revaluation

Similar to GAAP, all long-term assets, including goodwill, must be periodically evaluated for impairment. But, under IFRS, any previous impairment losses must be reversed if the asset subsequently increases in value. However, this does not apply to goodwill; once it is impaired under IFRS, it can not be revalued upwards. This is consistent with GAAP. Impairment losses are typically larger in magnitude under IFRS because IFRS computes the impairment loss as the excess of the carrying amount of the goodwill over its recoverable amount. Under GAAP, the impairment is relative to the implied fair value of the goodwill, which by definition is higher than the recoverable amount. Thus, for identical circumstances, goodwill impairments will be larger under IFRS.

Reporting Subsidiary Stock Issuances

After subsidiaries are acquired, they can, and sometimes do, issue stock. If issued to outside investors, the result is an infusion of cash into the subsidiary and a reduction in the parent's percentage ownership. For example, **Bristol-Myers Squibb's** 10-K report discloses the following stock issuance by one of its subsidiaries.

MEAD JOHNSON NUTRITION COMPANY INITIAL PUBLIC OFFERING In February 2009, Mead Johnson completed an initial public offering (IPO), in which it sold 34.5 million shares of its Class A common stock at $24 per share. Net proceeds of $782 million, after deducting $46 million of underwriting discounts, commissions and offering expenses, were allocated to noncontrolling interest and capital in excess of par value of stock. Upon completion of the IPO, 42.3 million shares of Mead Johnson Class A common stock and 127.7 million shares of Mead Johnson Class B common stock were held by the Company, representing an 83.1% interest in Mead Johnson and 97.5% of the combined voting power of the outstanding common stock . . . Various agreements related to the separation of Mead Johnson were entered into, including a separation agreement, a transitional services agreement, a tax matters agreement, a registration rights agreement and an employee matters agreement.

Prior to the IPO, Mead Johnson was a wholly-owned subsidiary of Bristol-Myers Squibb. The IPO resulted in the issuance of 34.5 million shares by Mead, representing 16.9% of the outstanding Class A common stock, for total proceeds of $782 million. As a result of the IPO, Bristol-Myers Squibb's stockholders' equity increased by $782 million, net of the noncontrolling interest that must now be recognized to reflect the claims of the noncontrolling shareholders to the net assets of Mead Johnson. This increase in stockholders' equity as a result of the IPO is not reflected in Bristol-Myers Squibb's retained earnings since it is not reflected in net income. Rather, it is reflected as an increase in additional paid-in capital.

BUSINESS INSIGHT   **Pitfalls of Acquired Growth**

One of the greatest destructions of shareholder value occurred during the bull market between 1995 and 2001 when market exuberance fueled a tidal wave of corporate takeovers. Companies often overpaid as a result of overestimating the cost-cutting and synergies their planned takeovers would bring. Then, acquirers failed to quickly integrate operations. The result? Subsequent years' market returns of most acquirers fell below those of their peers and were often negative. Indeed, 61% of corporate buyers saw their shareholders' wealth *decrease* after the acquisition. Who won? The sellers; the target-company shareholders who sold their stock within the first week of the takeover and reaped enormous profits at the expense of the acquirers' shareholders.

Reporting the Sale of Subsidiary Companies

Discontinued operations refer to any separately identifiable business unit that the company sells or intends to sell. The income or loss of the discontinued operations (net of tax), and the after-tax gain or loss on sale of the unit, are reported in the income statement below income from continuing operations. The segregation of discontinued operations means that revenues and expenses of the discontinued business unit are *not* reported with revenues and expenses from continuing operations.

To illustrate, assume that a company's recent periods' results were generated by both continuing and discontinued operations as follows:

	Continuing Operations	Discontinued Operations	Total
Revenues	$10,000	$3,000	$13,000
Expenses	7,000	2,000	9,000
Pretax Income	3,000	1,000	4,000
Tax expense (40%).	1,200	400	1,600
Net Income.	$ 1,800	$ 600	$ 2,400

The reported income statement would appear as follows—notice the separate disclosure for discontinued operations (as highlighted).

Revenues	$10,000
Expenses	7,000
Pretax income	3,000
Tax expense (40%).	1,200
Income from continuing operations	1,800
Income from discontinued operations, net of tax	**600**
Net income.	$ 2,400

Revenues and expenses reflect those of the continuing operations only, and the (persistent) income from continuing operations is reported net of its related tax expense. Results from the (transitory) discontinued operations are collapsed into one line item and reported separately net of its own tax (this includes any gain or loss from sale of the discontinued unit's net assets). The net income figure is unchanged by this presentation.

Importantly, results of the discontinued operations are segregated from those of continuing operations. This presentation facilitates the prediction of results from the (persistent) continuing operations. Discontinued operations are segregated (reported on one line) in the current year and for the two prior years. To illustrate, **Kraft Foods** reports the following footnote to its 2010 10-K relating to the decision to divest its North American frozen pizza business ($ millions).

Pizza Divestiture On March 1, 2010, we completed the sale of the assets of our North American frozen pizza business ("Frozen Pizza") to Nestlé USA, Inc. ("Nestlé") for $3.7 billion. Our Frozen Pizza business was a component of our U.S. Convenient Meals and Canada & N. A. Foodservice segments. The sale included the DiGiorno, Tombstone and Jack's brands in the U.S., the Delissio brand in Canada and the California Pizza Kitchen trademark license. It also included two Wisconsin manufacturing facilities (Medford and Little Chute) and the leases for the pizza depots and delivery trucks. Approximately 3,600 of our employees transferred with the business to Nestlé. As a result of the divestiture, we recorded a gain on discontinued operations of $1,596 million, or $0.92 per diluted share, in 2010. Summary results of operations for the Frozen Pizza business through March 1, 2010, were as follows. The after-tax results for Kraft include both the earnings from the discontinued operations and the gain on sale for a total of $1,644 million after tax.

For Years Ended December 31, (in millions)	2010	2009	2008
Net revenues	$ 335	$1,632	$1,440
Earnings before income taxes	73	341	267
Provisions for income taxes.	(25)	(123)	(97)
Gain on discontinued operations, net of income taxes	1,596	—	—
Earnings and gain from discontinued operations, net of income taxes	$1,644	$ 218	$ 170

This footnote highlights two important items. First, in 2010, the pizza operations had revenues of $335 million and net income of $48 million ($73 million before tax less tax of $25 million). Companies often discontinue profitable operations, selling them to recoup investments and/or to focus on other lines of business. Second, the sale of the frozen pizza operations generated a gain of $1,596 million after tax. The reported gain or loss on sale is equal to the proceeds received less the balance of the equity method investment reported on the parent's balance sheet at the sale date. Both of these two components—the net income or loss from operations during the year and any gain or loss on disposal of the discontinued operations—are reported, on one line, in Kraft's income statement. For comparative years (2009 and 2008) only the first component is included in the discontinued operations line item because the frozen pizza operations were not sold until 2010.

Limitations of Consolidation Reporting

Consolidation of financial statements is meant to present a financial picture of the entire set of companies under the control of the parent. Since investors typically purchase stock in the parent company, and not in the subsidiaries, a consolidated view is more relevant than the parent company merely reporting subsidiaries as equity investments in its balance sheet. Still, we must be aware of certain limitations of consolidation:

1. Consolidated income does not imply that the parent company has received any or all of the subsidiaries' net income as cash. The parent can only receive cash from subsidiaries via dividend payments. Conversely, the consolidated cash is not automatically available to the individual subsidiaries. It is quite possible, therefore, for an individual subsidiary to experience cash flow problems even though the consolidated group has strong cash flows. Likewise, unguaranteed debts of a subsidiary are not obligations of the consolidated group. Thus, even if the consolidated balance sheet is strong, creditors of a failing subsidiary are often unable to sue the parent or other subsidiaries to recoup losses.

2. Consolidated balance sheets and income statements are a mix of the various subsidiaries, often from different industries. Comparisons across companies, even if in similar industries, are often complicated by the different mix of subsidiary companies.

3. Segment disclosures on individual subsidiaries are affected by intercorporate transfer pricing policies relating to purchases of products or services that can artificially inflate the profitability of one segment at the expense of another. Companies also have considerable discretion in the allocation of corporate overhead to subsidiaries, which can markedly affect segment profitability.

BUSINESS INSIGHT   Determining the Parent Company in an Acquisition

Sensor, Inc., is acquiring Boston Instrument Company through an exchange of stock valued at $500 million. Sensor will survive as the continuing company, and the senior management of Boston Instrument will own 65% of the outstanding stock, reflecting a premium in the exchange ratios paid by Sensor to acquire Boston Instrument. Sensor's Chairman will remain as Chairman of the company, but the purchase agreement specifies that the board of directors will elect a new Chairman within six months of the deal's close. Boston Instrument's President and CFO will assume those same positions in the new entity. Following are the market values of the tangible and intangible net assets of both companies on the date of acquisition: Sensor, $400 million; and Boston Instrument, $200 million. Which of these two companies should be viewed as the acquiring firm (parent company) for purposes of consolidation, and how does this decision affect the amount of goodwill recorded on the consolidated balance sheet? Sensor is the larger firm, its name will survive, and its Chairman will serve in that capacity in the combined company. However, most accountants would likely conclude that Boston Instrument is the parent company for purposes of consolidation. This determination is based on the 65% ownership interest of the Boston Instrument shareholders who control the new entity. Further, these shareholders will be able to elect a new Chairman within six months. The amount of goodwill recorded following the acquisition is equal to the purchase price less the fair value of the net tangible and identifiable intangible assets acquired. If Sensor is the acquiring firm, $100 million ($500 million − $400 million) of goodwill will be recorded. If Boston Instrument is the acquiring firm, $300 million ($500 million − $200 million) of goodwill will be recorded. This decision will dramatically affect both the balance sheet (relative amounts of goodwill and other assets recorded) as well as the income statement (depreciation of tangible assets and amortization of identifiable intangible assets recognized vs. annual impairment testing for goodwill).

ANALYZING GLOBAL REPORTS

Both U.S. GAAP and IFRS account similarly for investments by companies in the debt and equity securities of other companies. However, differences exist and we highlight the notable ones here.

Passive Investments   Under both U.S. GAAP and IFRS, companies classify financial (passive) instruments as trading, available-for-sale, or held-to-maturity.

■ Under IFRS the definition of financial instrument is much broader, including for example loans to customers or associates. For analysis, such instruments are disclosed in the notes, which will aid our reclassification for comparison purposes.

■ Under U.S. GAAP, unlisted securities are not considered "marketable" and are carried at cost. Under IFRS, unlisted securities can be valued at fair value, if it can be reliably measured.

■ U.S. GAAP prohibits companies from reclassifying trading securities as available-for-sale or held-to-maturity but, under certain circumstances, requires companies to reclassify securities as trading (for example, if there has been a sale of a held-to-maturity security). Under IFRS, both reclassifications to and from the trading portfolio is prohibited. This provides opportunity for strategic reporting behavior under U.S. GAAP. We should review the notes that report reclassifications to assess such behavior and identify any reporting incentives managers might have.

Equity Method Investment One important difference exists with equity method accounting between U.S. GAAP and IFRS. That is, U.S. GAAP allows only the equity method in accounting for joint ventures, whereas IFRS allows the equity method or proportionate consolidation. Under the latter, the company's share of investee's assets and liabilities (and revenues and expenses) are added line-by-line on the balance sheet (and income statement). Proportionate consolidation means that every line on the IFRS financial statement is "grossed up" as compared to GAAP. The net numbers (equity and income) are identical but comparisons of individual line items between an IFRS and a GAAP report are problematic. This is similar to our concern about the effect of equity method accounting versus consolidation. There is currently a proposal to prohibit proportionate consolidation. In the interim, as discussed in the module, GAAP notes often disclose total revenue, assets, and liabilities of equity method investees. Thus, it is possible for us to amend certain GAAP accounts for comparative analysis.

Consolidation As part of their convergence effort, the FASB and IASB engaged in a joint project for business combinations (IFRS 3 and SFAS 141). Despite the common goal to develop a consistent and comprehensive standard, a few differences remain.

■ The most notable difference is how to measure noncontrolling interests. Under IFRS, companies can measure noncontrolling interests either at fair value (full goodwill approach) or at the proportionate share of the identifiable net assets acquired (purchased goodwill approach). U.S. GAAP permits fair value only. Relative to the proportionate method, the U.S. GAAP balance sheet reports a larger goodwill and a larger noncontrolling interest in equity. This difference is most pronounced when a company acquires significantly less than 100% of the target's stock or when goodwill is a larger proportion of the cost of acquisition. This IFRS-GAAP difference affects ratios based on operating assets, such as RNOA. Because goodwill is not routinely amortized, the difference will have no income statement impact (recall from Module 3 that we exclude noncontrolling interest from our calculation of return on equity).

■ Under U.S. GAAP, parent and subsidiaries' accounting policies do not need to conform. Under IFRS, parent and subsidiaries' accounting policies must conform.

■ IFRS fair-value impairments for intangible assets, excluding goodwill, can be later reversed (that is, written back up after being written down). Companies must have reliable evidence that the value of the intangible has been restored and the reversal cannot exceed the original impairment. While the original impairment was reported as a charge on the income statement, subsequent reversals do not affect income but, instead, are added to equity through a "reserve" much like that for accumulated other comprehensive income. IFRS notes disclose any reversals of a prior impairment (again, goodwill impairments cannot be reversed).

MODULE-END REVIEW

On January 1 of the current year, assume that **Yahoo!, Inc.**, purchased all of the common shares of **EarthLink** for $600,000 cash—this is $200,000 more than the book value of EarthLink's stockholders' equity. Balance sheets of the two companies immediately after the acquisition follow:

	Yahoo! (Parent)	EarthLink (Subsidiary)	Consolidating Adjustments	Consolidated
Current assets	$1,000,000	$100,000		
Investment in EarthLink	600,000	—		
PPE, net	3,000,000	400,000		
Goodwill	—	—		
Total assets.	$4,600,000	$500,000		
Liabilities.	$1,000,000	$100,000		
Contributed capital.	2,000,000	200,000		
Retained earnings	1,600,000	200,000		
Total liabilities and equity	$4,600,000	$500,000		

During purchase negotiations, EarthLink's PPE was appraised at $500,000, and all of EarthLink's remaining assets and liabilities were appraised at values approximating their book values. Also, Yahoo! concluded that payment of an additional $100,000 was warranted because of anticipated corporate synergies. Prepare the consolidating adjustments and the consolidated balance sheet at acquisition.

The solution is on page 9-54.

APPENDIX 9A: Accounting for Derivatives

Although there is some speculative use of derivatives by U.S. companies (both industrial and financial), most companies use derivatives to shelter their income statements and cash flows from fluctuations in the market prices of currencies, commodities, and financial instruments, as well as for market rates of interest. Companies routinely face risk exposures that can markedly affect their balance sheets, profitability, and cash flows. These exposures can be grouped into two general categories:[3]

1. Exposure to changes in the **fair value** of an asset (such as accounts receivable, inventory, marketable securities, or a firm contract to sell an asset) or of a liability (such as accounts payable, a firm commitment to purchase an asset, or a fixed-rate liability).
2. Exposure to variation in **cash flows** relating to a forecasted transaction (such as *planned* inventory purchases or anticipated foreign revenues) or cash-flow exposure relating to a variable-rate debt obligation.

Both of these types of risks can be managed (hedged) with a variety of financial instruments, including futures, forward contracts, options, and swap contracts. For an example in the first risk category, consider a company with a fair-value exposure from a receivable denominated in a foreign currency. If the $US strengthens subsequently, the receivable declines in value and the company incurs a foreign-currency loss. To avoid this situation, the company can hedge the receivable with a foreign-currency derivative. Ideally, when the $US strengthens, the derivative will increase in value by an amount that exactly offsets the decrease in the value of the receivable. As a result, the company's net asset position (receivable less derivative) remains unaffected and no gain or loss arises when the $US weakens or strengthens. For accounting purposes, this is called a **fair-value hedge**.

As an example for the second risk category, consider a company that routinely purchases a food commodity used in its manufacturing process. Any price increases during the coming year will flow to cost of goods sold and profit will decrease (unless the company can completely pass the price increase along to its customers, which is rarely the case). To avoid this situation, the company can hedge the inventory purchases with a commodity derivative contract that locks in a price today. When the price of the commodity increases, the derivative contract will shelter the company and, as a result, the company's cost of goods sold remains unaffected. For accounting purposes, this is called a **cash-flow hedge**.

Accounting for derivatives essentially boils down to this: all derivatives are reported at fair value on the balance sheet. For fair-value hedges, the asset or liability being hedged (the foreign receivable in the example above), is reported on the balance sheet at fair value. If the market value of the hedged asset or liability changes, the value of the derivative changes in the opposite direction if the hedge is effective and, thus, net assets and liabilities are unaffected. Likewise, the related gains and losses are largely offsetting, leaving income unaffected.

For cash-flow hedges, there is no hedged asset or liability on the books. In our example above, it is the anticipated commodity purchases that are being hedged. Thus, the company has no inventory yet and changes in the fair

---

[3] Risks relating to changes in the fair value of a recognized asset or liability, or the variation in cash flows relating to a contractual obligation or a forecasted transaction, that results from fluctuations in the exchange value of the $US vis-à-vis other world currencies are particularly troublesome for companies. The use of derivatives to mitigate **foreign-currency risk** can fall into either of the risk categories.

value of the derivative are not met with opposite changes in an asset or liability. For these cash-flow hedges, gains or losses from the fair value of the derivative are not reported on the income statement. Instead they are held in accumulated other comprehensive income (AOCI), as part of shareholders' equity. Later, when the hedged item impacts income (say, when the commodity cost is reflected in cost of goods sold), the derivative gain or loss is reclassified from AOCI to income. If the hedge was effective, the gain or loss on the hedged transaction is offset with the loss or gain on the derivative and income is unaffected.

For both fair-value and cash-flow hedges, income is impacted only to the extent that the hedging activities are ineffective. Naturally, if derivative use is for speculative activities, gains and losses are not offset and directly flow to income. It is this latter activity, in particular, that prompted regulators to formulate newer, tougher accounting standards for derivatives.

Disclosures for Derivatives

Companies must disclose both qualitative and quantitative information about derivatives in notes to their financial statements and elsewhere (in the Management's Discussion and Analysis section). The aim of these disclosures is to inform outsiders about potential risks associated with derivative use. We present footnotes relating to fair-value hedges and cash-flow hedges below as examples of common transactions relating to use of derivatives to mitigate risk. We discuss the accounting for each and how we should interpret these disclosures in our analysis of the company.

Fair-Value Hedge

Fair-value hedges are used to mitigate risks relating to the change in the fair values of existing assets and liabilities. These fair values can change, for example, with changes in commodity prices, interest rates, or foreign exchange rates. Following is an example from the **Kellogg** 2010 10-K.

> Our Company is exposed to fluctuations in foreign currency cash flows related primarily to third-party purchases, intercompany transactions, and when applicable, nonfunctional currency denominated third-party debt . . . Additionally, our Company is exposed to volatility in the translation of foreign currency denominated earnings to U.S. dollars. Primary exposures include the U.S. dollar versus the British pound, euro, Australian dollar, Canadian dollar, and Mexican peso. We assess foreign currency risk based on transactional cash flows and translational volatility and may enter into forward contracts, options, and currency swaps to reduce fluctuations in long or short currency positions. Forward contracts and options are generally less than 18 months duration. Our Company is exposed to price fluctuations primarily as a result of anticipated purchases of raw and packaging materials, fuel, and energy. Primary exposures include corn, wheat, soybean oil, sugar, cocoa, paperboard, natural gas, and diesel fuel. We have historically used the combination of long-term contracts with suppliers, and exchange-traded futures and option contracts to reduce price fluctuations in a desired percentage of forecasted raw material purchases over a duration of generally less than 18 months.

To illustrate the accounting for the Kellogg fair-value hedge, assume that the company sells goods for €3.7 million ($5 million equivalent) on account to a customer located in Ireland. The company is concerned about the potential effects of a strengthening or weakening of the $US and enters into a forward contract to hedge that foreign-currency (FX) risk. Before the receivable is collected, the $US weakens vis-à-vis the Euro, and the Euros received (€3.7 million) converts to $5.5 million. The transactions are accounted for as follows:

	Balance Sheet						Income Statement			
Transaction	Cash Asset	+	Noncash Assets	= Liabil-ities	+	Contrib. Capital	+	Earned Capital	Rev-enues	− Expen-ses	= Net Income
1. Credit sale for €3.7 mil. ($5 mil. equivalent)			+5.0 mil. Accounts Receivable =					+5.0 mil. Retained Earnings	+5.0 mil. Sales −	=	+5.0 mil.
2a. Receive €3.7 mil. ($5.5 mil. equivalent) per transaction 1	+5.5 mil. Cash		−5.0 mil. Accounts Receivable =					+0.5 mil. Retained Earnings	+0.5 mil. Gain on Foreign Currency Transaction −	=	+0.5 mil.

AR 5.0M
 Sales 5.0M
 AR
5M
 Sales
 5M

Cash 5.5M
 AR 5.0M
 GN 0.5M
 Cash
5.5M
 AR
 5M
 Gain on FX
 0.5M

continued

continued from prior page

Transaction	Balance Sheet						Income Statement		
	Cash Asset	+ Noncash Assets	= Liabil- ities	+ Contrib. Capital	+ Earned Capital		Rev- enues	− Expen- ses	= Net Income
2b. Record loss on settlement of foreign exchange contract	−0.5 mil. Cash		=		−0.5 mil. Retained Earnings			+0.5 mil. Loss on Foreign Exchange Derivative Contract	−0.5 mil. =

LS   0.5M
    Cash   0.5M

Loss on Contract
    0.5M |
        Cash
            | 0.5M

In this transaction, the company hedged its foreign exchange exposure via a forward contract. As the $US weakens, the value of the accounts receivable increases by $0.5 million, resulting in a foreign exchange gain, and the fair value of the derivative contract decreases by $0.5 million, resulting in an offsetting loss. The net cash received is the $5.5 million from the receivable less the $0.5 million to settle the forward contract.

Why would the company want to enter into a contract such as this that resulted in a loss? After all, had the company not "hedged" the Euro receivable, the cash collected would have been $5.5 million and the company would have reported a gain. The answer is that a company does not know in advance which way currencies will move. As the Kellogg footnote indicates, sometimes the derivative suffers a loss, and at other times creates a gain. The purpose of the derivative is to lock in the operating profit on the sale and to shield the company from risk in the form of fluctuating foreign-currency exchange rates.

Cash-Flow Hedge

Following is **Tiffany & Co.**'s disclosures from its 2011 10-K report relating to its use of derivatives:

Precious Metal Collars & Forward Contracts The Company periodically hedges a portion of its fore-casted purchases of precious metals for use in its internal manufacturing operations in order to minimize the effect of volatility in precious metal prices. The Company may use a combination of call and put option contracts in net-zero-cost collar arrangements ("precious metal collars") or forward contracts. For precious metal collars, if the price of the precious metal at the time of the expiration of the precious metal collar is within the call and put price, the precious metal collar would expire at no cost to the Company. The Company accounts for its precious metal collars and forward contracts as cash flow hedges. The Company assesses hedge effectiveness based on the total changes in the precious metal collars and forward contracts' cash flows. The maximum term over which the Company is hedging its exposure to the variability of future cash flows for all forecasted transactions is 12 months. As of January 31, 2011, there were approximately 2,700 ounces of platinum and no silver precious metal derivative instruments outstanding.

Tiffany uses derivatives to hedge against the risk of fluctuations in the market price of precious metals that the company anticipates purchasing in future.

These derivatives are cash-flow hedges. Thus, unrealized gains and losses on these derivative contracts are added to the Accumulated Other Comprehensive Income (AOCI) (part of stockholders' equity) until the precious metal is purchased. Once that precious metal is purchased, any unrealized gains and losses are removed from AOCI and recognized in current-period income via cost of goods sold. The gain (loss) on the derivative contract offsets the increased (decreased) cost of the precious metal.

Although the market value of derivatives and their related assets or liabilities can be large, the net effect on stockholders' equity is usually minor. This is because companies use derivatives mainly to hedge and not to specu-late. The FASB enacted SFAS 133, "Accounting for Derivative Instruments and Hedging Activities," to respond to concerns that speculative activities were not adequately disclosed. However, subsequent to the passage of SFAS 133, the financial effects have been minimal. Either companies were not speculating to the extent suspected, or they have since reduced their level of speculation in response to increased scrutiny from better disclosures.

To illustrate the accounting for cash-flow hedge, assume that Tiffany knows that it must purchase platinum over the coming year. The platinum would cost $1 million at the current market prices but Tiffany anticipates price in-creases. Simultaneously, Tiffany purchases call options to lock in the $1 million purchase price. (Tiffany would pay an option premium which would be recorded as an asset and amortized over time; to keep the example simple, we ignore this premium.) Delivery of the platinum takes place over the year and the market price of the platinum purchases is $1.686 million. During the year, Tiffany adjusts the option to fair value, the combined mark-to-market adjustments are $0.686 million. Those transactions are accounted for as follows:

	Balance Sheet						Income Statement		
Transaction	Cash Asset	+ Noncash Assets	= Liabil-ities	+ Contrib. Capital	+ Earned Capital		Rev-enues	− Expen-ses	= Net Income
1. Record unre-alized fair-value gain on call option		+0.686 mil. Call Option =			+0.686 mil. AOCI		−	=	
2a. Purchase and use plati-num during the year	−1.686 mil. Cash	=			−1.686 mil. Retained Earnings		−	+1.686 mil. COGS =	−1.686 mil.
2b. Exercise call option as Tiffany purchases platinum	+0.686 mil. Cash	−0.686 mil. Call Option =					−	=	
2c. Recognize unrealized fair-value gain as Tiffany uses platinum		=			+0.686 mil. Retained Earnings −0.686 mil. AOCI		−	−0.686 mil. COGS =	+0.686 mil.

Call Op   0.686M
   AOCI   0.686M

Call Option
0.686M |

AOCI
  | 0.686M

FE   1.686M
  Cash   1.686M

Platinum Exp
1.686M |

Cash
  | 1.686M

Cash   0.686M
  Call Op   0.686M

Cash
0.686M |

Call Option
  | 0.686M

AOCI   0.686M
  FE   0.686M

AOCI
0.686M |

Platinum Exp
  | 0.686M

In this transaction, Tiffany has hedged its platinum purchase via call options. As the price of platinum increases, so does the value of the call option. This unrealized gain on the option is reflected in AOCI until the platinum is consumed. At that time, the unrealized gain is removed from AOCI and expenses are reduced, thereby offsetting the increase in COGS resulting from the higher platinum cost. The net effect is that Tiffany reports $1 million for COGS. The net cash outlay for platinum is also $1 million as a result of the cash inflow related to the call option. The purpose of Tiffany's derivative program is to attempt to lock in the price of platinum. This is an operating activity and the gain on the derivative contract should be included in NOPAT to offset the increased cost of the platinum. Because Tiffany hedged the fuel purchases, there is no net effect on income.

In both of our illustrations, the derivative contract is perfectly correlated with the asset or cash flow to which it relates. In practice, this is unlikely. As a result, the change in the fair value of the derivatives might not exactly offset the change in the cost of the platinum. Only the effective portion of the hedge is deferred in AOCI. The in-effective portion of the hedge affects current income. Bottom line, some of the risk will impact net income if the company cannot perfectly hedge the risk or chooses not to manage 100% of the risk.

BUSINESS INSIGHT   Counter-Party Risk

The purpose of derivative financial instruments is to transfer risk from one company to another. For example, a company might be concerned about the possible decline in the $US value of a foreign-currency-denominated account receivable. In order to hedge that risk, the company might execute a forward contract to sell the foreign currency and receive $US. That forward contract only has value, however, if the party on the other side of the transaction (the counter-party) ultimately purchases the foreign currency for $US when the contract matures. If the counter-party fails to honor its part of the agreement, the forward contract is of no value. The risk that the other party might not live up to its part of the bargain is known as *counter-party risk*. The only justification for recognizing a gain in a forward contract to offset the loss in a foreign-currency-denominated receivable is the expectation that the counter-party has the intention and ability to purchase the foreign currency in exchange for $US when the contract matures. Counter-party risk is very real. Many companies require counter-parties to back up their agreement with cash collateral or other acceptable forms of guarantees (like a bank letter of credit, for example). As a result, there is a hidden risk in companies' use of derivatives that is difficult to quantify.

Analysis of Derivatives

Derivatives relate to a specific balance sheet account or forecasted transaction. The fair value of the derivatives and their ultimate gains (losses) should be classified with the account to which they relate. For example, in the **Kellogg** example, the fair value of the foreign exchange contract is grouped with the accounts receivable to which it relates, and the gain (loss) on that derivative is considered an operating item (part of NOPAT). The commodity derivative investments that **Tiffany** uses are treated similarly. In this case, both the balance sheet accounts and income statement effects are treated as operating.

Companies also frequently use a variety of derivative instruments to hedge exposure to interest rates. Companies can, for example, use swap contracts to convert floating-rate debt to fixed-rate debt and vice-versa. In this case, the fair values of the derivatives and their ultimate income statement effects are nonoperating because they relate to interest-bearing debt.

In addition to proper classification of balance sheet and income statement accounts for computation of NOPAT and NOA, we are interested in understanding the extent to which the company is hedged. That is, are there still risks over which the company has no control and that are not hedged? Unfortunately, footnote disclosures do not provide a completely satisfactory answer. We are not privy to the internal risk analysis that the company performs. As a result, we do not know, for example, the precise extent to which the hedges are ineffective, to what degree the company has decided to hedge, and whether the company is facing risks for which a derivative instrument is not available. To gain further insight into these questions, we must often look to other sources of information such as analyst reports, the financial press, and communications from the company.

GUIDANCE ANSWERS . . . ANALYSIS DECISION

You Are the Chief Financial Officer Capacity utilization is important. If long-term operating assets are used inefficiently, cost per unit produced is too high. Cost per unit does not relate solely to manufacturing products, but also applies to the cost of providing services and many other operating activities. However, if we purchase assets with little productive slack, our costs of production at peak levels can be excessive. Further, the company may be unable to service peak demand and risks losing customers. In response, the company might explore strategic alliances. These take many forms. Some require a simple contract to use another company's manufacturing, service, or administrative capability for a fee (note: these executory contracts are not recorded under GAAP). Another type of alliance is that of a joint venture to share ownership of manufacturing or IT facilities. In this case, if demand can be coordinated with that of a partner, perhaps operating assets can be more effectively used. Finally, a special purpose entity (SPE) can be formed to acquire the asset for use by the company and its partner—explained in Module 10.

Superscript [A] denotes assignments based on Appendix 9A.

DISCUSSION QUESTIONS

Q9-1. What measure (fair value or amortized cost) is on the balance sheet for (a) trading securities, (b) available-for-sale securities, and (c) held-to-maturity securities?

Q9-2. What is an unrealized holding gain (loss)? Explain.

Q9-3. Where are unrealized holding gains and losses related to trading securities reported in the financial statements? Where are unrealized holding gains and losses related to available-for-sale securities reported in the financial statements?

Q9-4. What does significant influence imply regarding intercorporate investments? Describe the accounting procedures used for such investments.

Q9-5. On January 1 of the current year, Yetman Company purchases 40% of the common stock of Livnat Company for $250,000 cash. This 40% ownership allows Yetman to exert significant influence over Livnat. During the year, Livnat reports $80,000 of net income and pays $60,000 in cash dividends. At year-end, what amount should appear in Yetman's balance sheet for its investment in Livnat?

Q9-6. What accounting method is used when a stock investment represents more than 50% of the investee company's voting stock and allows the investor company to "control" the investee company? Explain.

Q9-7. What is the underlying objective of consolidated financial statements?

Q9-8. Finn Company purchases all of the common stock of Murray Company for $750,000 when Murray Company has $300,000 of common stock and $450,000 of retained earnings. If a consolidated balance sheet is prepared immediately after the acquisition, what amounts are eliminated in consolidation? Explain.

Q9-9. Bradshaw Company owns 100% of Dee Company. At year-end, Dee owes Bradshaw $75,000 arising from a loan made during the year. If a consolidated balance sheet is prepared at year-end, how is the $75,000 handled? Explain.

Q9-10. What are some limitations of consolidated financial statements?

Assignments with the ⊘ in the margin are available in an online homework system.
See the Preface of the book for details.

MINI EXERCISES

M9-11. Interpreting Disclosures of Available-for-Sale Securities (LO1)

Use the following year-end footnote disclosure from **Intel**'s 10-K report to answer parts *a* and *b*.

INTEL
(INTC)

(Millions of Dollars)	2010
Cost of available-for-sale equity securities	$19,677
Gross unrealized gains.	648
Gross unrealized losses	(19)
Fair value of available-for-sale equity securities	$20,306

a. What amount does Intel report on its balance sheet as available-for-sale equity securities? Explain.
b. How does Intel report the net unrealized gain of $629 million ($648 million − $19 million) in its financial statements?

M9-12. Accounting for Available-for-Sale and Trading Securities (LO1)

Assume that Wasley Company purchases 6,000 common shares of Pincus Company for $12 cash per share. During the year, Wasley receives a cash dividend of $1.10 per common share from Pincus, and the year-end market price of Pincus common stock is $13 per share. How much income does Wasley report relating to this investment for the year if it accounts for the investment as:
a. Available-for-sale investment
b. Trading investment

M9-13. Interpreting Disclosures of Investment Securities (LO1)

Amgen reports the following disclosure relating to its December 31 comprehensive income ($ millions).

AMGEN
(AMGN)

a. How is Amgen accounting for its investment in marketable equity securities? How do you know?
b. Explain how its 2010 financial statements are impacted by Amgen's investment in marketable equity securities.
c. Explain the reclassification adjustments to income of $90 million.

	Foreign Currency Translation	Cash-Flow Hedges	Available-for-Sale Securities	Other	AOCI
Balance as of December 31, 2009.	$40	$(82)	$ 95	$(8)	45
Other comprehensive income:					
Foreign currency translation adjustments . . .	(29)	—	—	—	(29)
Unrealized gains.	—	186	155	1	342
Reclassification adjustments to income.	—	(46)	(90)	—	(136)
Income taxes	11	(55)	(25)	—	(69)
Balance as of December 31, 2010.	$22	$ 3	$135	$(7)	$153

M9-14. Analyzing and Interpreting Equity Method Investments (LO2)

Stober Company purchases an investment in Lang Company at a purchase price of $1 million cash, representing 30% of the book value of Lang. During the year, Lang reports net income of $100,000 and pays cash dividends of $40,000. At the end of the year, the market value of Stober's investment is $1.2 million.
a. What amount does Stober report on its balance sheet for its investment in Lang?
b. What amount of income from investments does Stober report? Explain.
c. Stober's $182,000 unrealized gain in the market value of the Lang investment (choose one and explain):
   (1) Is not reflected on either its income statement or balance sheet.
   (2) Is reported in its current income.
   (3) Is reported on its balance sheet only.
   (4) Is reported in its accumulated other comprehensive income.

M9-15. **Computing Income for Equity Method Investments** (LO2)

Kross Company purchases an equity investment in Penno Company at a purchase price of $5 million, representing 40% of the book value of Penno. During the current year, Penno reports net income of $600,000 and pays cash dividends of $200,000. At the end of the year, the fair value of Kross's investment is $5.3 million. What amount of income does Kross report relating to this investment in Penno for the year? Explain.

M9-16. **Interpreting Disclosures on Investments in Affiliates** (LO2)

MERCK & CO., INC.
(MRK)

Merck's 10-K report included the following footnote disclosure:

> Investments in affiliates accounted for using the equity method . . . totaled $494 million at December 31, 2010...These amounts are reported in *Other assets*.

a. At what amount are the equity method investments reported on Merck's balance sheet? Does this amount represent Merck's adjusted cost or fair value?
b. How does Merck account for the dividends received on these investments?
c. What sources of income does the company report for these investments?

M9-17. **Computing Consolidating Adjustments and Noncontrolling Interest** (LO3)

Philipich Company purchases 80% of Hirst Company's common stock for $600,000 cash when Hirst Company has $300,000 of common stock and $450,000 of retained earnings. If a consolidated balance sheet is prepared immediately after the acquisition, what amounts are eliminated when preparing that statement? What amount of noncontrolling interest appears in the consolidated balance sheet?

M9-18. **Computing Consolidated Net Income** (LO3)

Benartzi Company purchased a 90% interest in Liang Company on January 1 of the current year and the purchase price reflected 90% of Liang's book value of equity. Benartzi Company had $600,000 net income for the current year *before* recognizing its share of Liang Company's net income. If Liang Company had net income of $150,000 for the year, what is the consolidated net income for the year?

M9-19. **Assigning Purchase Price in Acquisitions** (LO3)

Weaver Company acquired 80% of Koonce Company at the beginning of the current year. Weaver paid $50,000 more than the book value of Koonce's shareholders' equity and determined that this excess purchase price related to intangible assets. How does the $50,000 appear on the consolidated Weaver Company balance sheet if the intangible assets acquired related to (*a*) patents, or alternatively (*b*) goodwill? How would the consolidated income statement be affected under each scenario?

EXERCISES

 E9-20. **Assessing Financial Statement Effects of Trading and Available-for-Sale Securities** (LO1)

a. Use the financial statement effects template to record the following four transactions involving investments in marketable securities classified as trading.
  (1) Purchased 6,000 common shares of Liu, Inc., for $12 cash per share.
  (2) Received a cash dividend of $1.10 per common share from Liu.
  (3) Year-end market price of Liu common stock was $11.25 per share.
  (4) Sold all 6,000 common shares of Liu for $66,900.
b. Using the same transaction information as above, complete the financial statement effects template (with amounts and accounts) assuming the investments in marketable securities are classified as available-for-sale.

E9-21. **Assessing Financial Statement Effects of Trading and Available-for-Sale Securities** (LO1)

Use the financial statement effects template to record the accounts and amounts for the following four transactions involving investments in marketable securities:
  (1) Ohlson Co. purchases 5,000 common shares of Freeman Co. at $16 cash per share.
  (2) Ohlson Co. receives a cash dividend of $1.25 per common share from Freeman.
  (3) Year-end market price of Freeman common stock is $17.50 per share.
  (4) Ohlson Co. sells all 5,000 common shares of Freeman for $86,400 cash.
a. Assume the investments are classified as trading.
b. Assume the investments are classified as available-for-sale.

E9-22.   Interpreting Footnotes on Security Investments   (LO1)

Cisco Systems reports the following in its 10-K report.

(In millions)	Shares of Common Stock	Common Stock and Additional Paid-In Capital	Retained Earnings	Accumulated Other Comprehensive Income	Total Cisco Shareholders' Equity	Noncontrolling Interests	Total Equity
BALANCE AT JULY 25, 2009	5,785	$34,344	$3,868	$435	$38,647	$30	$38,677
Net income.	—	—	7,767	—	7,767	—	7,767
Change in:							
Unrealized gains and losses on investments.	—	—	—	195	195	(12)	183
Derivative instruments	—	—	—	48	48	—	48
Cumulative translation adjustment and other	—	—	—	(55)	(55)	—	(55)
Comprehensive income (loss)					7,955	(12)	7,943
Issuance of common stock	201	3,278	—	—	3,278	—	3,278
Repurchase of common stock.	(331)	(2,148)	(5,784)	—	(7,932)	—	(7,932)
Tax benefits from employee stock incentive plans, including transfer pricing adjustments	—	719	—	—	719	—	719
Purchase acquisitions	—	83	—	—	83	—	83
Share-based compensation expense . . .	—	1,517	—	—	1,517	—	1,517
BALANCE AT JULY 31, 2010	5,655	$37,793	$5,851	$623	$44,267	$18	$44,285

Summary of Available-for-Sale Investments

The following table summarizes the Company's available-for-sale investments (in millions):

July 31, 2010	Amortized Cost	Gross Unrealized Gains	Gross Unrealized Losses	Fair Value
Fixed income securities:				
U.S. government securities	$16,570	$ 42	$ —	$16,612
U.S. government agency securities	13,511	68	—	13,579
Non-U.S. government and agency securities. . .	1,452	15	—	1,467
Corporate debt securities.	2,179	64	(21)	2,222
Asset-backed securities	145	9	(5)	149
Total fixed income securities.	33,857	198	(26)	34,029
Publicly traded equity securities	889	411	(49)	1,251
Total	$34,746	$609	$(75)	$35,280

a.   At what amount does Cisco report its investment portfolio on its balance sheet? Does that amount include any unrealized gains or losses? Explain.

b.   How is Cisco accounting for its investment portfolio—as an available-for-sale or trading portfolio? How do you know?

c.   What does the number $195 represent in the Accumulated Other Comprehensive Income column? Explain.

E9-23.   Interpreting Footnote Disclosures for Investments   (LO1)

CNA Financial Corporation provides the following footnote to its 2010 10-K report.

Valuation of investments CNA classifies its fixed maturity securities and its equity securities as either available-for-sale or trading, and as such, they are carried at fair value. Changes in fair value of trading securities are reported within net investment income on the Consolidated Statements of Operations. Changes in fair value related to available-for-sale securities are reported as a component of other comprehensive income. . . . Investment valuations are adjusted and losses may be recognized as Net realized investment losses on the Consolidated Statements of Operations when a decline in value is determined by the Company to be other-than-temporary.

The following table provides a summary of fixed maturity and equity securities.

Summary of Fixed Maturity and Equity Securities				
December 31, 2010 (In millions)	Cost or Amortized Cost	Gross Unrealized Gains	Gross Unrealized Losses	Estimated Fair Value
Fixed maturity securities available-for-sale				
U.S. Treasury and obligations of government agencies....	$ 122	$ 16	$ 1	$ 137
Asset-backed:				
Residential mortgage-backed.......................	6,254	101	265	6,090
Commercial mortgage-backed.....................	994	40	41	993
Other asset-backed	753	18	8	763
Total asset-backed...............................	8,001	159	314	7,846
States, municipalities and political subdivisions	8,157	142	410	7,889
Foreign government...............................	602	18	—	620
Corporate and other bonds	19,492	1,603	70	21,025
Redeemable preferred stock	47	7	—	54
Total fixed maturity securities available-for-sale	36,421	1,945	795	37,571
Total fixed maturity securities trading	6	—	—	6
Equity securities available-for-sale:				
Common stock.....................................	90	25	—	115
Preferred stock...................................	332	2	9	325
Total equity securities available-for-sale	422	27	9	440
Total	$36,849	$1,972	$804	$38,017

    a.   At what amount does CNA report its investment portfolio on its balance sheet? In your answer identify the portfolio's fair value, cost, and any unrealized gains and losses.

    b.   How do CNA's balance sheet and income statement reflect any unrealized gains and/or losses on the investment portfolio?

    c.   How do CNA's balance sheet and income statement reflect gains and losses realized from the sale of available-for-sale securities?

E9-24.   **Assessing Financial Statement Effects of Equity Method Securities**   **(LO2)**

Use the financial statement effects template (with amounts and accounts) to record the following transactions involving investments in marketable securities accounted for using the equity method:

    a.   Purchased 12,000 common shares of Barth Co. at $9 per share; the shares represent 30% ownership in Barth.

    b.   Received a cash dividend of $1.25 per common share from Barth.

    c.   Barth reported annual net income of $80,000.

    d.   Sold all 12,000 common shares of Barth for $120,500.

E9-25.   **Assessing Financial Statement Effects of Equity Method Securities**   **(LO2)**

Use the financial statement effects template (with amounts and accounts) to record the following transactions involving investments in marketable securities accounted for using the equity method:

    a.   Healy Co. purchases 15,000 common shares of Palepu Co. at $8 per share; the shares represent 25% ownership of Palepu.

b.   Healy receives a cash dividend of $0.80 per common share from Palepu.
  c.   Palepu reports annual net income of $120,000.
  d.   Healy sells all 15,000 common shares of Palepu for $140,000.

E9-26.   Assessing Financial Statement Effects of Passive and Equity Method Investments   (LO1, 2)

On January 1, Ball Corporation purchased shares of Leftwich Company common stock.

  a.   Assume that the stock acquired by Ball represents 15% of Leftwich's voting stock and that Ball classifies the investment as available-for-sale. Use the financial statement effects template (with amounts and accounts) to record the following transactions:

  1. Ball purchased 10,000 common shares of Leftwich at $15 cash per share.
  2. Leftwich reported annual net income of $80,000.
  3. Ball received a cash dividend of $1.10 per common share from Leftwich.
  4. Year-end market price of Leftwich common stock is $19 per share.

  b.   Assume that the stock acquired by Ball represents 30% of Leftwich's voting stock and that Ball accounts for this investment using the equity method since it is able to exert significant influence. Use the financial statement effects template (with amounts and accounts) to record the following transactions:

  1. Ball purchased 10,000 common shares of Leftwich at $15 cash per share.
  2. Leftwich reported annual net income of $80,000.
  3. Ball received a cash dividend of $1.10 per common share from Leftwich.
  4. Year-end market price of Leftwich common stock is $19 per share.

E9-27.   Interpreting Equity Method Investment Footnotes   (LO2)

DuPont's 2010 10-K report includes information relating to the company's equity method investments ($ millions). The following footnote reports summary balance sheets for affiliated companies for which DuPont uses the equity method of accounting. The information below is shown on a 100 percent basis followed by the carrying value of DuPont's investment in these affiliates.

DUPONT
(DD)

Financial Position at December 31 (in millions)	2010	2009
Current assets	$1,972	$1,710
Noncurrent assets	1,397	1,416
Total assets	$3,369	$3,126
Short-term borrowings	$ 381	$ 375
Other current liabilities	841	768
Long-term borrowings	144	178
Other long-term liabilities	119	111
Total liabilities	$1,485	$1,432
DuPont's investment in affiliates (includes advances)	$1,041	$1,014

  a.   DuPont reports its investment in equity method affiliates on its balance sheet at $1,041 million. Does this reflect the adjusted cost or fair value of DuPont's interest in these companies?
  b.   What is the total stockholders' equity of the affiliates at the end of 2010? Approximately what percentage does DuPont own, on average, of these affiliates? Explain.
  c.   Should the balance of the equity investment be reduced to zero, say as a result of losses by the equity investee company, Dupont would cease accounting for the investment using the equity method. It would, instead, report the investments at a zero balance until the investee company would become solvent. Why might this cessation of accounting for this investment using the equity method impede our analysis and interpretation?

E9-28.   Analyzing and Interpreting Disclosures on Equity Method Investments   (LO2)

Cummins, Inc. (CMI) reports investments in affiliated companies, consisting mainly of investments in nine manufacturing joint ventures. Cummins reports those investments on its balance sheet at $734 million, and provides the following financial information of its investee companies in a footnote to its 10-K report:

CUMMINS, INC.
(CMI)

Equity Investee Financial Summary

In millions	As of and for the years ended December 31,		
	2010	2009	2008
Net sales.	$7,107	$5,554	$6,610
Gross margin	1,651	1,365	1,509
Net income.	668	427	498
Cummins share of net income	$ 321	$ 196	$ 231
Royalty and interest income.	30	18	22
Total equity, royalty and interest income from investees . . .	$ 351	$ 214	$ 253
Current assets	$2,741	$2,005	
Noncurrent assets	1,253	1,123	
Current liabilities.	(1,837)	(1,406)	
Noncurrent liabilities.	(499)	(390)	
Net assets	$1,658	$1,332	
Cummins share of net assets.	$ 744	$ 587	

a. What assets and liabilities of unconsolidated affiliates are omitted from Cummins' balance sheet as a result of the equity method of accounting for those investments?

b. Do the liabilities of the unconsolidated affiliates affect Cummins directly? Explain.

c. How does the equity method impact Cummins' ROE and its RNOA components (net operating asset turnover and net operating profit margin)?

  E9-29. **Reporting and Interpreting Stock Investment Performance** (LO1)

Kasznik Company began operations on June 15 of the current calendar year and, by year-end (December 31), had made six stock investments. Year-end information on these stock investments follows.

December 31	Cost or Equity Basis (as appropriate)	Year-End Fair Value	Market Classification
Barth, Inc.	$ 68,000	$ 65,300	Trading
Foster, Inc.	162,500	160,000	Trading
McNichols, Inc.	197,000	192,000	Available-for-sale
Patell Company	157,000	154,700	Available-for-sale
Ertimur, Inc.	100,000	102,400	Equity method
Soliman, Inc.	136,000	133,200	Equity method

a. What does Kasznik's balance sheet report for trading stock investments at December 31?

b. What does Kasznik's balance sheet report for available-for-sale investments at December 31?

c. What does Kasznik's balance sheet report for equity method investments at December 31?

d. What total amount of unrealized holding gains or unrealized holding losses related to investments appear in Kasznik's income statement?

e. What total amount of unrealized holding gains or unrealized holding losses related to investments appear in the stockholders' equity section of Kasznik's December 31 balance sheet?

f. What total amount of fair-value adjustment to investments appears in the December 31 balance sheet? Which category of investments does the fair-value adjustment relate to? Does the fair-value adjustment increase or decrease the carrying value of these investments?

E9-30. **Interpreting Equity Method Investment Footnotes** (LO2)

AT&T, INC.
(T)

AT&T reports the following footnote to its 2005 10-K report ($ millions).

Equity Method Investments We account for our nationwide wireless joint venture, Cingular, and our investments in equity affiliates under the equity method of accounting. The following table is a reconciliation of our investments in and advances to Cingular as presented on our Consolidated Balance Sheets.

continued

continued from prior page

($ millions)	2005	2004
Beginning of year........	$33,687	$11,003
Contributions	—	21,688
Equity in net income......	200	30
Other adjustments	(2,483)	966
End of year.............	$31,404	$33,687

Undistributed earnings from Cingular were $2,711 and $2,511 at December 31, 2005 and 2004. "Other adjustments" in 2005 included the net activity of $2,442 under our revolving credit agreement with Cingular, consisting of a reduction of $1,747 (reflecting Cingular's repayment of their shareholder loan during 2005) and a decrease of $695 (reflecting Cingular's net repayment of their revolving credit balance during 2005). During 2004, we made an equity contribution to Cingular in connection with its acquisition of AT&T Wireless. "Other adjustments" in 2004 included the net activity of $972 under our revolving credit agreement with Cingular, consisting of a reduction of $30 (reflecting Cingular's repayment of advances during 2004) and an increase of $1,002 (reflecting the December 31, 2004 balance of advances to Cingular under this revolving credit agreement).

We account for our 60% economic interest in Cingular under the equity method of accounting in our consolidated financial statements since we share control equally (i.e., 50/50) with our 40% economic partner in the joint venture. We have equal voting rights and representation on the Board of Directors that controls Cingular. The following table presents summarized financial information for Cingular at December 31, or for the year then ended.

Cingular ($ millions)	2005	2004	2003
Income Statements			
Operating revenues ...	$34,433	$19,565	$15,577
Operating income.....	1,824	1,528	2,254
Net income	333	201	977
Balance Sheets			
Current assets........	$ 6,049	$ 5,570	
Noncurrent assets.....	73,270	76,668	
Current liabilities......	10,008	7,983	
Noncurrent liabilities...	24,333	29,719	

We have made a subordinated loan to Cingular that totaled $4,108 and $5,855 at December 31, 2005 and 2004, which matures in June 2008. This loan bears interest at an annual rate of 6.0%. During 2005, Cingular repaid $1,747 to reduce the balance of this loan in accordance with the terms of a revolving credit agreement. We earned interest income on this loan of $311 during 2005, $354 in 2004 and $397 in 2003. This interest income does not have a material impact on our net income as it is mostly offset when we record our share of equity income in Cingular.

a. At what amount is the equity investment in Cingular reported on AT&T's balance sheet? (Hint: the table in the footnote reports AT&T's investment plus its "advances" of $4,108 to Cingular plus $311 of interest accrued on the advances.) Next, confirm (with computations) that this amount is equal to AT&T's proportionate share of Cingular's equity.

b. Did Cingular pay dividends in 2005? How do you know?

c. How much income did AT&T report in 2005 relating to this investment in Cingular?

d. Interpret the AT&T statement that "undistributed earnings from Cingular were $2,711 and $2,511 at December 31, 2005 and 2004."

e. How does use of the equity method impact AT&T's ROE and its RNOA components (net operating asset turnover and net operating profit margin)?

f. AT&T accounts for its investment in Cingular under the equity method, despite its 60% economic ownership position. Why?

g. In 2006, AT&T acquired Bell South, its joint venture partner in Cingular. What impact did this merger have on the way AT&T accounts for its investment in Cingular?

AT&T
(T)
BELL SOUTH

E9-31.   Interpreting Equity Method Investment Footnotes   (LO2)

On December 29, 2006, **AT&T** acquired **Bell South**. Prior to the acquisition, AT&T and Bell South jointly owned AT&T Mobility (formerly known as Cingular Wireless) and each accounted for its investment in AT&T Mobility under the equity method (see exercise E9-30). AT&T purchased Bell South for $66,834 million and reports the following allocation of the purchase price in its 2007 10-K:

Bell South Purchase Price Allocation ($ millions)	As of 12/31/06	Adjustments	As of 12/29/07
Assets acquired			
Current assets.	$ 4,875	$ 6	$ 4,881
Property, plant and equipment	18,498	225	18,723
Intangible assets not subject to amortization			
Trademark/name	330	—	330
Licenses	214	100	314
Intangible assets subject to amortization			
Customer lists and relationships.	9,230	(25)	9,205
Patents	100	—	100
Trademark/name	211	—	211
Investments in AT&T Mobility	32,759	2,039	34,798
Other investments.	2,446	(3)	2,443
Other assets	11,211	(168)	11,043
Goodwill	26,467	(1,554)	24,913
Total assets acquired	106,341	620	106,961
Liabilities assumed			
Current liabilities, excluding current portion of long-term debt	5,288	(427)	4,861
Long-term debt.	15,628	(4)	15,624
Deferred income taxes	10,318	(89)	10,229
Postemployment benefit obligation	7,086	163	7,249
Other noncurrent liabilities	1,223	941	2,164
Total liabilities assumed.	39,543	584	40,127
Net assets acquired	$ 66,798	$ 36	$ 66,834

a.   Describe how AT&T accounts for its investment in AT&T Mobility (formerly Cingular Wireless) following its acquisition of Bell South.

b.   AT&T had the following disclosure in its 2007 10-K regarding the reporting of its investment in AT&T Mobility: "We recorded the consolidation of AT&T Mobility as a step acquisition, retaining 60% of AT&T Mobility's prior book value and adjusting the remaining 40% to fair value." Why is AT&T only adjusting 40% of its investment in AT&T Mobility to fair value?

c.   AT&T adjusted the purchase price allocation for Bell South subsequent to the acquisition. Most of the allocation relates to an increased value placed on Bell South's equity investment in AT&T Mobility due to "increased value of licenses and customer lists and relationships acquired." Why did the increase in the allocation of the purchase price to Bell South's investment in AT&T Mobility decrease the allocation to goodwill? How will this increase in allocation to the equity investment impact AT&T's income statement?

d.   More than half of the purchase price is allocated to intangible assets and goodwill. How is the fair value of customer lists and relationships estimated? How is the fair value of goodwill estimated? Why does it matter whether the allocation of the purchase price for intangible assets relates to "customer lists and relationships" or to goodwill?

✔ **E9-32.   Constructing the Consolidated Balance Sheet at Acquisition   (LO3)**

On January 1 of the current year, Healy Company purchased all of the common shares of Miller Company for $500,000 cash. Balance sheets of the two firms immediately after the acquisition follow:

continued from prior page

	Healy Company	Miller Company	Consolidating Adjustments	Consolidated
Current assets	$1,700,000	$120,000		
Investment in Miller	500,000	—		
Plant assets, net.	3,000,000	410,000		
Goodwill	—	—		
Total assets.	$5,200,000	$530,000		
Liabilities.	$ 700,000	$ 90,000		
Contributed capital.	3,500,000	400,000		
Retained earnings	1,000,000	40,000		
Total liabilities and equity	$5,200,000	$530,000		

During purchase negotiations, Miller's plant assets were appraised at $425,000 and all of its remaining assets and liabilities were appraised at values approximating their book values. Healy also concluded that an additional $45,000 (for goodwill) demanded by Miller's shareholders was warranted because Miller's earning power was better than the industry average. Prepare the consolidating adjustments and the consolidated balance sheet at acquisition.

E9-33. **Constructing the Consolidated Balance Sheet at Acquisition** (LO3)

Rayburn Company purchased all of Kanodia Company's common stock for $600,000 cash on January 1, at which time the separate balance sheets of the two corporations appeared as follows:

	Rayburn Company	Kanodia Company	Consolidating Adjustments	Consolidated
Investment in Kanodia	$ 600,000	—		
Other assets.	2,300,000	$700,000		
Goodwill	—	—		
Total assets.	$2,900,000	$700,000		
Liabilities.	$ 900,000	$160,000		
Contributed capital.	1,400,000	300,000		
Retained earnings	600,000	240,000		
Total liabilities and equity	$2,900,000	$700,000		

During purchase negotiations, Rayburn determined that the appraised value of Kanodia's Other Assets was $720,000; and, all of its remaining assets and liabilities were appraised at values approximating their book values. The remaining $40,000 of the purchase price was ascribed to goodwill. Prepare the consolidating adjustments and the consolidated balance sheet at acquisition.

E9-34. **Assessing Financial Statement Effects from a Subsidiary Stock Issuance** (LO3)

Ryan Company owns 80% of Lev Company. Information reported by Ryan Company and Lev Company as of the current year end follows:

Ryan Company	
Shares owned of Lev	40,000
Book value of investment in Lev.	$320,000
Lev Company	
Shares outstanding.	50,000
Book value of equity.	$400,000
Book value per share	$8

Assume Lev Company issues 30,000 additional shares of previously authorized but unissued common stock solely to outside investors (none to Ryan Company) for $12 cash per share. Indicate the financial statement effects of this stock issuance on Ryan Company using the financial statement effects template.

Ryan Company's Financial Statements

	Balance Sheet						Income Statement		
Transaction	Cash Asset	+ Noncash Assets	= Liabilities	+ Contrib. Capital	+ Earned Capital		Revenues	− Expenses	= Net Income
Lev Co. issues 30,000 shares			=					−	=

E9-35. Estimating Goodwill Impairment (LO3)

On January 1 of the current year, Engel Company purchases 100% of Ball Company for $16.8 million. At the time of acquisition, the fair value of Ball's tangible net assets (excluding goodwill) is $16.2 million. Engel ascribes the excess of $600,000 to goodwill. Assume that the fair value of Ball declines to $12.5 million and that the fair value of Ball's tangible net assets is estimated at $12.3 million as of December 31.

a. Determine if the goodwill has become impaired and, if so, the amount of the impairment.
b. What impact does the impairment of goodwill have on Engel's financial statements?

E9-36. Allocating Purchase Price (LO3)

ADOBE SYSTEMS
(ADBE)

Adobe Systems, Inc., reports the following footnote to its 10-K report.

During fiscal 2006, we completed the acquisition of Macromedia, a provider of software technologies that enables the development of a wide range of Internet and mobile application solutions . . . The total $3.5 billion purchase price is allocated to the acquired net assets of Macromedia based on their estimated fair values as of December 3, 2005 and the associated estimated useful lives at that date:

(in 000s)	Amount	Estimated Useful Life
Net tangible assets.	$ 713,164	N/A
Identifiable intangible assets		
Acquired product rights	365,500	4 years
Customer contracts and relationships	183,800	6 years
Non-competition agreements.	500	2 years
Trademarks.	130,700	5 years
Goodwill	1,993,898	N/A
Stock-based compensation.	150,951	2.18 years
Total purchase price.	$3,538,513	

a. Of the total assets acquired, what portion is allocated to net tangible assets?
b. Are the assets (both tangible and intangible) of Macromedia reported on the consolidated balance sheet at the book value or at the fair value on the date of the acquisition? Explain.
c. How are the tangible and intangible assets accounted for subsequent to the acquisition?
d. Describe the accounting for goodwill. Why is an impairment test difficult to apply?

E9-37. Constructing the Consolidated Balance Sheet at Acquisition (LO3)

Easton Company acquires 100 percent of the outstanding voting shares of Harris Company. To obtain these shares, Easton pays $210,000 in cash and issues 5,000 of its $10 par value common stock. On this date, Easton's stock has a fair value of $36 per share, and Harris's book value of stockholders' equity is $280,000. Easton is willing to pay $390,000 for a company with a book value for equity of $280,000 because it believes that (1) Harris's buildings are undervalued by $40,000, and (2) Harris has an unrecorded patent that Easton values at $30,000. Easton considers the remaining balance sheet items to be fairly valued (no book-to-market difference). The remaining $40,000 of the purchase price is ascribed to corporate synergies and other general unidentifiable intangible assets (goodwill). The balance sheets at the acquisition date follow:

	Easton Company	Harris Company	Consolidating Adjustments	Consolidated
Cash.........................	$ 84,000	$ 40,000		
Receivables	160,000	90,000		
Inventory...................	220,000	130,000		
Investment in Harris	390,000	—		
Land........................	100,000	60,000		
Buildings, net	400,000	110,000		
Equipment, net.............	120,000	50,000		
Total assets...............	$1,474,000	$480,000		
Accounts payable..........	$ 160,000	$ 30,000		
Long-term liabilities	380,000	170,000		
Common stock.............	500,000	40,000		
Additional paid-in capital	74,000	—		
Retained earnings	360,000	240,000		
Total liabilities & equity......	$1,474,000	$480,000		

a. Show the breakdown of the investment into the book value acquired, the excess of fair value over book value, and the portion of the investment representing goodwill.

b. Prepare the consolidating adjustments and the consolidated balance sheet on the date of acquisition.

c. How will the excess of the purchase price over book value acquired be treated in years subsequent to the acquisition?

E9-38.[A] **Reporting and Analyzing Derivatives** (LO1)

Johnson & Johnson reports the following schedule of other comprehensive income in its 2011 10-K report ($ millions):

JOHNSON & JOHNSON
(JNJ)

(Dollars in Millions)	Foreign Currency Translation	Gains/ (Losses) on Securities	Employee Benefit Plans	Gains/ (Losses) on Derivatives & Hedges	Total Accumulated Other Comprehensive Income/(Loss)
January 3, 2010	$(508)	$(30)	$(2,665)	$145	$(3,058)
2010 changes...........................					
Unrealized gain (loss)......................	—	99	—	(333)	
Net amount reclassed to net earnings.........	—	(45)	—	288	
Net 2010 changes	(461)	54	(21)	(45)	(473)
January 2, 2011	$(969)	$24	$(2,686)	$100	$(3,531)

a. Describe how firms like Johnson & Johnson typically use derivatives.

b. How does Johnson & Johnson report its derivatives designated as cash-flow hedges on its balance sheet?

c. By what amount have the unrealized losses of $(333) million on the cash-flow hedges affected current income? What are the analysis implications?

d. What does the $288 million classified as "Net amount reclassed to net earnings" relate to? How has this affected Johnson & Johnson's profit?

PROBLEMS

P9-39. **Analyzing and Interpreting Available-for-Sale Securities Disclosures** (LO1)

Following is a portion of the investments footnote from MetLife's 2010 10-K report. Investment earnings are a crucial component of the financial performance of insurance companies such as MetLife, and investments comprise a large part of MetLife's assets. MetLife accounts for its fixed maturity (debt security or bond) investments as available-for-sale securities.

METLIFE, INC.
(MET)

December 31, 2010 (In millions)	Cost or Amortized Cost	Gross Unrealized		OTTI* Loss	Estimated Fair Value
		Gain	Temporary Loss		
Fixed Maturity Securities:					
U.S. corporate securities	$ 89,713	$ 4,486	$1,631	$ —	$ 92,568
Foreign corporate securities.	65,784	3,333	939	—	68,178
RMBS.	44,468	1,652	917	470	44,733
Foreign government securities.	42,154	1,856	610	—	43,400
U.S. Treasury, agency and government guaranteed securities	32,469	1,394	559	—	33,304
CMBS.	20,213	740	266	12	20,675
ABS	14,725	274	590	119	14,290
State and political subdivision securities.	10,476	171	518	—	10,129
Other fixed maturity securities	6	1	—	—	7
Total fixed maturity securities	$320,008	$13,907	$6,030	$601	$327,284
Equity Securities:					
Common stock.	$ 2,060	$ 146	$ 12	$ —	$ 2,194
Non-redeemable preferred stock	1,565	76	229	—	1,412
Total equity securities	$ 3,625	$ 222	$ 241	$ —	$ 3,606

* OTTI refers to "Other-Than-Temporary Impairment" that MetLife does not expect to reverse.

December 31, 2009 (In millions)	Cost or Amortized Cost	Gross Unrealized		OTTI* Loss	Estimated Fair Value
		Gain	Temporary Loss		
Fixed Maturity Securities:					
U.S. corporate securities	$ 72,075	$2,821	$2,699	$ 10	$ 72,187
Foreign corporate securities.	37,254	2,011	1,226	9	38,030
RMBS.	45,343	1,234	1,957	600	44,020
Foreign government securities	11,010	1,076	139	—	11,947
U.S. Treasury, agency and government guaranteed securities	25,712	745	1,010	—	25,447
CMBS.	16,555	191	1,106	18	15,622
ABS	14,272	189	1,077	222	13,162
State and political subdivision securities.	7,468	151	411	—	7,208
Other fixed maturity securities	20	1	2	—	19
Total fixed maturity securities	$229,709	$8,419	$9,627	$859	$227,642
Equity Securities:					
Common stock.	$ 1,537	$ 92	$ 8	$ —	$ 1,621
Non-redeemable preferred stock	1,650	80	267	—	1,463
Total equity securities	$ 3,187	$ 172	$ 275	$ —	$ 3,084

* OTTI refers to "Other-Than-Temporary Impairment" that MetLife does not expect to reverse.

Required

a. At what amount does MetLife report its fixed maturity securities on its balance sheets for 2010 and 2009?

b. What is the difference between realized and unrealized gains and losses?

c. What are the net unrealized gains (losses) for 2010 and 2009 on its fixed maturity securities? How did these unrealized gains (losses) affect the company's reported income in 2010 and 2009? (*Hint*: see the Google footnote excerpt on page 9-8 for an explanation of how OTTI losses affect income.)

P9-40.   Analyzing and Interpreting Disclosures on Equity Method Investments   (LO2)

GENERAL MILLS
(GIS)

General Mills invests in a number of joint ventures to manufacture and distribute its food products as discussed in the following footnote to its fiscal year 2010 10-K report:

INVESTMENTS IN JOINT VENTURES   Our investments in companies over which we have the ability to exercise significant influence are stated at cost plus our share of undistributed earnings or

continued

continued from prior page

losses . . . We make advances to our joint ventures in the form of loans or capital investments. We also sell certain raw materials, semi-finished goods, and finished goods to the joint ventures, generally at market prices.

We have a 50 percent equity interest in Cereal Partners Worldwide (CPW), which manufactures and markets ready-to-eat cereal products in more than 130 countries and republics outside the United States and Canada . . . We also have a 50 percent equity interest in Häagen-Dazs Japan, Inc. (HDJ).

Joint venture balance sheet activity follows:

In Millions	May 30, 2010	May 31, 2009
Cumulative investments.	$398.1	$283.3
Goodwill and other intangibles.	512.6	593.9
Aggregate advances.	238.2	114.8

Joint venture earnings and cash flow activity follows:

	Fiscal Year		
In Millions	2010	2009	2008
Sales to joint ventures	$ 10.7	$14.2	$ 12.8
Net advances (repayments)	128.1	(8.2)	(75.2)
Dividends received.	88.0	68.5	108.7

Summary combined financial information for the joint ventures on a 100 percent basis follows:

	Fiscal Year		
In Millions	2010	2009	2008
Net sales.	$2,360.0	$2,280.0	$2,207.7
Gross margin	1,053.2	873.5	906.6
Earnings before income taxes	251.2	234.7	231.7
Earnings after income taxes.	202.3	175.3	190.4

In Millions	May 30, 2010	May 31, 2009
Current assets	$ 731.7	$ 835.4
Noncurrent assets	907.3	895.0
Current liabilities.	1,322.0	1,394.6
Noncurrent liabilities.	112.1	66.9

Required

a. How does General Mills account for its investments in joint ventures? How are these investments reflected on General Mills' balance sheet, and how, generally, is income recognized on these investments?

b. General Mills reports total equity method investments on its May 30, 2010, balance sheet at $159.9 million net of advances ($398.1 million − $238.2 million). Approximately what percent of these joint ventures does General Mills own, on average?

c. Does the $159.9 million investment reported on General Mills' balance sheet sufficiently reflect the assets and liabilities required to conduct these operations? Explain.

d. Do you believe that the liabilities of these joint venture entities represent actual obligations of General Mills? Explain.

e. What potential problem(s) does equity method accounting present for analysis purposes?

P9-41. **Analyzing and Interpreting Disclosures on Consolidations** **(LO3)**

Snap-on Incorporated consists of two business units: the manufacturing company (parent corporation) and a wholly-owned finance subsidiary. These two units are consolidated in Snap-on's 10-K report. Following is a supplemental disclosure that Snap-on includes in its 10-K report that shows the separate balance sheets of the parent and the subsidiary. This supplemental disclosure is not mandated under GAAP, but is voluntarily reported by Snap-on as useful information for investors and creditors. Using this disclosure, answer the following requirements:

SNAP-ON, INC.
(SNA)

Required

a.   Do the parent and subsidiary companies each maintain their own financial statements? Explain. Why does GAAP require consolidation instead of separate financial statements of individual companies?

b.   What is the balance of Investments in Financial Services as of December 31, 2010, on the parent's balance sheet? What is the equity balance of the financial services subsidiary to which this relates as of December 31, 2010? Do you see a relation? Will this relation always exist?

c.   Refer to your answer for part a. How does the equity method of accounting for the investment in the subsidiary obscure the actual financial condition of the parent company that is revealed in the consolidated financial statements?

d.   Recall that the parent company uses the equity method of accounting for its investment in the subsidiary, and that this account is eliminated in the consolidation process. What is the relation between consolidated net income and the net income of the parent company? Explain.

e.   What is the implication for the consolidated balance sheet if the fair value of the Financial Services subsidiary (subsequent to acquisition) is greater than the book value of its stockholders' equity?

(Amounts in millions)	Operations*		Financial Services	
	2010	2009	2010	2009
ASSETS				
Current assets				
Cash and cash equivalents.	$ 462.6	$ 577.1	$109.6	$122.3
Intersegment receivables	6.7	4.8	—	0.1
Trade and other accounts receivable—net.	434.5	411.5	8.8	2.9
Finance receivables—net	—	—	215.3	122.3
Contract receivables—net	7.9	7.4	37.7	25.5
Inventories—net	329.4	274.7	—	—
Deferred income tax assets	82.4	69.3	4.6	0.2
Prepaid expenses and other assets	74.1	60.1	0.7	2.8
Total current assets.	1,397.6	1,404.9	376.7	276.1
Property and equipment—net	343.0	346.4	1.0	1.4
Investment in Financial Services	134.4	205.6	—	—
Deferred income tax assets	75.7	73.6	15.8	14.6
Long-term finance receivables—net.	—	—	345.7	177.9
Long-term contract receivables—net.	8.4	10.9	110.9	59.8
Goodwill	798.4	814.3	—	—
Other intangibles—net	192.8	206.2	—	—
Other assets	72.8	65.2	0.5	1.0
Total assets.	$3,023.1	$3,127.1	$850.6	$530.8
LIABILITIES AND SHAREHOLDERS' EQUITY				
Current liabilities				
Notes payable and current maturities of long-term debt	$ 216.0	$ 164.7	$ —	$ —
Accounts payable.	129.6	119.3	16.5	0.5
Intersegment payables	—	4.2	6.7	0.7
Accrued benefits.	45.0	48.4	—	0.3
Accrued compensation.	83.4	61.6	3.3	3.2
Franchisee deposits	40.4	40.5	—	—
Other accrued liabilities	218.1	215.7	132.0	85.7
Total current liabilities	732.5	654.4	158.5	90.4
Long-term debt and intersegment long-term debt.	418.8	674.8	536.0	227.3
Deferred income tax liabilities.	94.3	97.8	0.1	—
Retiree health care benefits	59.6	60.7	—	—
Pension liabilities	246.1	255.9	—	—
Other long-term liabilities	67.4	77.9	21.6	7.5
Total liabilities	1,618.7	1,821.5	716.2	325.2
Total shareholders' equity attributable to Snap-on Inc.	1,388.5	1,290.0	134.4	205.6
Noncontrolling interests	15.9	15.6	—	—
Total shareholders' equity	1,404.4	1,305.6	134.4	205.6
Total liabilities and shareholders' equity.	$3,023.1	$3,127.1	$850.6	$530.8

* Snap-on Incorporated with Financial Services on the equity method.

P9-42. **Analyzing Reports and Disclosures on Noncontrolling Interests** (LO3)

The following four items are reproduced from **Verizon Communications**' 2010 10-K: its income statement, its balance sheet's stockholders' equity section, its noncontrolling interest section from the statement of changes in stockholders' equity, and its footnotes relating to noncontrolling interests.

VERIZON
COMMUNICATIONS,
INC.
(VZ)

Years Ended December 31 (dollars in millions)	2010	2009	2008
Operating revenues	$106,565	$107,808	$97,354
Operating expenses			
Cost of services and sales (exclusive of items shown below)	44,149	44,579	38,615
Selling, general and administrative expense	31,366	30,717	41,517
Depreciation and amortization expense	16,405	16,534	14,610
Total operating expenses	91,920	91,830	94,742
Operating income	14,645	15,978	2,612
Equity in earnings of unconsolidated businesses	508	553	567
Other income and (expense), net	54	91	283
Interest expense	(2,523)	(3,102)	(1,819)
Income before (provision) benefit for income taxes	12,684	13,520	1,643
(Provision) benefit for income taxes	(2,467)	(1,919)	2,319
Net Income	$ 10,217	$ 11,601	$ 3,962
Net income attributable to noncontrolling interest	$ 7,668	$ 6,707	$ 6,155
Net income (loss) attributable to Verizon	2,549	4,894	(2,193)
Net Income	$ 10,217	$ 11,601	$ 3,962

At December 31 (dollars in millions, except per share amounts)	2010	2009
Equity		
Series preferred stock ($.10 par value; none issued)	$ —	$ —
Common stock ($.10 par value; 2,967,610,119 shares issued in both periods)	297	297
Contributed capital	37,922	40,108
Reinvested earnings	4,368	7,260
Accumulated other comprehensive income (loss)	1,049	(1,372)
Common stock in treasury, at cost	(5,267)	(5,000)
Deferred compensation—employee stock ownership plans and other	200	89
Noncontrolling interest	48,343	42,761
Total equity	$86,912	$84,143

Years Ended December 31 (dollars in millions)	2010	2009	2008
Noncontrolling Interest			
Balance at beginning of year	$42,761	$37,199	$32,266
Net income attributable to noncontrolling interest	7,668	6,707	6,155
Other comprehensive income (loss)	(35)	103	(30)
Total comprehensive income	7,633	6,810	6,125
Distributions and other	(2,051)	(1,248)	(1,192)
Balance at end of year	$48,343	$42,761	$37,199

Consolidation The method of accounting applied to investments, whether consolidated, equity or cost, involves an evaluation of all significant terms of the investments that explicitly grant or suggest evidence of control or influence over the operations of the investee. The consolidated financial statements include our controlled subsidiaries. For controlled subsidiaries that are not wholly owned, the noncontrolling interest is included in Net income and Total equity.

continued

continued from prior page

Noncontrolling Interest   Noncontrolling interests in equity of subsidiaries were as follows:

At December 31, (dollars in millions)	2010	2009
Noncontrolling interests in consolidated subsidiaries:		
Verizon Wireless	$47,557	$41,950
Wireless partnerships	786	811
	$48,343	$42,761

Wireless Joint Venture   Our Domestic Wireless segment, Cellco Partnership doing business as Verizon Wireless (Verizon Wireless) is a joint venture formed in April 2000 by the combination of the U.S. wireless operations and interests of Verizon and Vodafone. Verizon owns a controlling 55% interest in Verizon Wireless and Vodafone owns the remaining 45%.

Required

a.   What are noncontrolling interests and how are they accounted for?

b.   The noncontrolling interests relate primarily to a joint venture between Verizon and Vodafone described in the footnote. Why does Verizon consolidate this joint venture rather than to account for its investment using the equity method? What are the financial reporting implications for the decision to consolidate the joint venture?

c.   What does the significant amount of net income allocated to the noncontrolling interests imply about the profitability of the wireless subsidiary relative to other subsidiaries in the consolidated entity?

d.   What does the "Distributions and other" line with an amount of $(2,051) million in the noncontrolling interest portion of the statement of changes in stockholders' equity relate to?

e.   How should we treat noncontrolling interests in our return on equity (ROE) computation? Compute ROE for both the Verizon shareholders and for the noncontrolling interests.

IFRS APPLICATIONS

**GROUPE AUCHAN
SA**

I9-43.   **Interpreting Equity Method Investment Footnotes**   (LO2)
Groupe Auchan is a French retail corporation headquartered in Croix, France. The company included the following table in notes to its annual report.

Investment in Associates (in € millions)	2009	2008
At January 1	€132	€152
Results for the period (share of profit and impairment)	(55)	(10)
Dividends received	(1)	(7)
Equity interests acquired	10	25
Disposals and other	(5)	(28)
At December 31	€ 81	€132

Required

a.   Groupe Auchan holds between 20% and 50% ownership of all its investments in associates. Groupe Auchan uses the equity method to account for these investments. Why?

b.   What amount does Groupe Auchan report on its balance sheet for investments in associates at December 31, 2009? Is this a fair value or not?

c.   For the fiscal period ended December 31, 2009, were Groupe Auchan's associates profitable, in the aggregate?

d.   How do changes in the market value of the associates' stock affect the "Investment in associates" balance sheet account for Groupe Auchan?

e.   How does use of the equity method impact Groupe Auchan's ROE and its RNOA components (net operating asset turnover and net operating profit margin) as compared with the assets and liabilities and the sales and expenses that would be recorded with consolidation?

I9-44. **Interpreting Equity Method Investment Footnotes** (LO2)

Ahold, a food retailer headquartered in the Netherlands, reported in notes to its annual report that it owns 60% of the outstanding common shares in a joint venture, with **ICA**, a food retailer operating in Sweden, Norway and the Baltic states. Selected notes to Ahold's annual report (prepared under IFRS) follow:

AHOLD

> The 60% shareholding does not entitle Ahold to unilateral decision-making authority over ICA due to the shareholders' agreement with the joint venture partner, which provides that strategic, financial and operational decisions will be made only on the basis of mutual consent. On the basis of this shareholders' agreement, the Company concluded that it has no control over ICA and, consequently, does not consolidate ICA's financial statements.

Required

a. What is a joint venture?
b. Given that Ahold owns more than 50% of this joint venture, why does the company not consolidate this investment? Does this differ from U.S. GAAP?
c. What method does Ahold use to report the ICA joint venture? Explain how this method works.

I9-45. **Allocating Purchase Price Including Intangibles** (LO3)

Deutsche Telekom AG, headquartered in Bonn, Germany, is the largest telecommunications company in Europe. The company uses IFRS to prepare its financial statements. Assume that during 2011, Deutsche Telekom acquired a controlling interest in Hellenic Telecommunications Organization, S.A. (Hellenic). The table below shows the pre- and post-acquisition values of Hellenic's assets and liabilities.

DEUTSCHE
TELEKOM AG

(millions of €)	Fair value at acquisition date	Carrying amounts immediately prior to acquisition
Cash and cash equivalents	€ 1,558	€ 1,558
Non-current assets held for sale	195	158
Other assets	1,716	1,716
Current assets	3,469	3,432
Intangible assets	5,348	4,734
Goodwill	2,500	3,835
Property, plant, and equipment	6,965	5,581
Other assets	823	782
Non-current assets	15,636	14,932
Assets	€19,105	€18,364

Required

a. At the acquisition, which measurement does the company use, fair value or carrying value, to record the acquired tangible and intangible assets on its consolidated balance sheet?
b. At the acquisition date, why is fair value of goodwill less than its carrying value?
c. What are some possible reasons why intangible assets increased in value at the acquisition date?
d. Describe accounting for goodwill. Why is an impairment test difficult to apply?
e. What would Deutsche Telekom record if it determined at the end of fiscal 2011 that the goodwill purchased in the Hellenic acquisition had a reliably measured fair value of €2,000? Later, if in 2012 the company determined that the fair value of the Hellenic goodwill was €3,000, how would its balance sheet and income statement be affected?

I9-46. **Analyzing and Interpreting Available-for-Sale Securities Disclosures** (LO1)

Energias de Portugal ranks among Europe's major electricity operators, as well as being one of Portugal's largest business groups. The company is headquartered in Lisbon, Portugal. At December 31, 2009, Energias de Portugal had an available-for-sale portfolio with original cost of €251,224 (in 000s). Its 2009 annual report disclosed the following for available-for-sale investments.

ENERGIAS DE
PORTUGAL

(€ in 000s)	Fair value 1 Jan 2009	Acquisitions	Disposals	Impairment	Increase in fair value	Fair value 31 Dec 2009
Ampla Energia e Servicos, S.A.	€ 68,939	€ —	€ —	€ —	€ 94,705	€163,644
Ampla Investimentos e Servicos, S.A.	9,073	—	—	—	5,965	15,038
Banco Comercial Portugues, S.A.	122,707	—	(17,351)	(29,274)	28,036	104,118
Denerge	—	15,193	—	—	370	15,563
EDA - Electricidade dos Acores, S.A.	6,006	—	—	—	2,207	8,213
REN - Rede Electrica Nacional, S.A.	52,332	—	—	—	3,551	55,883
Sociedade Eolica de Andalucia, S.A.	10,854	209	—	—	703	11,766
Sonaecom, S.A.	28,946	—	(28,946)	—	—	—
Tagusparque, S.A.	1,097	—	—	—	965	2,062
Tejo Energia, S.A.	18,200	—	—	—	7,436	25,636
Other	32,733	14,853	(7,368)	(15)	991	41,194
	€350,887	€30,255	€(53,665)	€(29,289)	€144,929	€443,117

Required

a. What were total unrealized gains or losses in the available-for-sale portfolio at year end 2009?

b. What is the historical cost of Energias de Portugal's investment in Denerge? Is there an unrealized gain or loss on this investment at year end 2009?

c. How would pretax income be affected if Energias de Portugal had instead classified all of its available-for-sale investments as trading?

I9-47.   **Interpreting Footnote Disclosures for Acquisitions   (LO1)**

FINMECCANICA S.P.A.

Headquartered in Rome, Italy, **Finmeccanica S.p.A.** is a multinational conglomerate operating in the defense and aerospace sectors. The company uses IFRS for its financial reports and disclosed the following in its 2009 annual report.

Intangible assets acquired in the course of corporate combination operations decreased mainly as a result of amortisation and include the following items:

(€ million)	31 December 2009	31 December 2008
Know-how	€ 85	€ 88
Trademarks.	45	45
Licenses	14	16
Backlog and commercial positioning*	831	875
Total	€975	€1,024

* This represents a customer-based intangible asset

Required

a. How do Trademarks and Licenses create an intangible asset for Finnmeccanica? How do customer-based intangible assets provide value to the company?

b. Explain how the company would select an amortization policy for these intangible assets.

c. What does the carrying value of these intangible assets represent?

d. Apart from routine amortization, does the company ever adjust the assets' carrying values? (*Hint*: Consider why the company might reduce or increase the carrying value of an intangible under IFRS.)

DISCUSSION POINTS

D9-48.   **Determining the Reporting of an Investment   (LO1, 2, 3)**

Assume that your company acquires 20% of the outstanding common stock of APEX Software as an investment. You also have an option to purchase the remaining 80%. APEX is developing software (its only activity) that it hopes to eventually package and sell to customers. You do not intend to exercise your option unless its software product reaches commercial feasibility. APEX has employed your software engineers to assist in the development efforts and you are integrally involved in its software design. Your ownership interest is significant enough to give you influence over APEX's software design specifications.

Required

a. Describe the financial statement effects of the three possible methods to accounting for this investment (fair-value, equity, or consolidation).

b. What method of accounting is appropriate for this investment (fair-value, equity, or consolidation)? Explain.

D9-49. Ethics and Governance: Establishing Corporate Governance (LO2, 3)

Effective corporate governance policies are a crucial component of contemporary corporate management.

Required

What provisions do you believe should be incorporated into such a policy? How do such policies impact financial accounting?

SOLUTIONS TO REVIEW PROBLEMS

Mid-Module Review 1

a.

Transaction	Cash Asset	+	Noncash Assets	=	Liabil-ities	+	Contrib. Capital	+	Earned Capital		Rev-enues	−	Expen-ses	=	Net Income
Balance Sheet											**Income Statement**				
1. Purchased 1,000 shares of Yahoo! common stock for $15 cash per share	−15,000 Cash		+15,000 Marketable Securities	=								−		=	
2. Received cash dividend of $2.50 per share on Yahoo! common stock	+2,500 Cash			=						+2,500 Retained Earnings		+2,500 Dividend Income	−		=	+2,500
3. Year-end market price of Yahoo! common stock is $17 per share			+2,000 Marketable Securities	=						+2,000 AOCI			−		=	
4. Sold 1,000 shares of Yahoo! common stock for $17,000 cash	+17,000 Cash		−17,000 Marketable Securities	=						−2,000 AOCI +2,000 Retained Earnings		+2,000 Gain on Sale	−		=	+2,000

Transaction 1:
```
MS          15,000
   Cash          15,000
        MS
15,000 |
   Cash
       | 15,000
```

Transaction 2:
```
Cash        2,500
   DI            2,500
        Cash
2,500 |
   DI
       | 2,500
```

Transaction 3:
```
MS          2,000
   AOCI          2,000
        MS
2,000 |
   AOCI
       | 2,000
```

Transaction 4:
```
Cash        17,000
AOCI         2,000
   MS            17,000
   GN             2,000
        Cash
17,000 |
   AOCI
2,000 |
   MS
       | 17,000
   GN
       | 2,000
```

b.

	Balance Sheet						Income Statement		
Transaction	**Cash Asset**	**+ Noncash Assets**	**= Liabil- ities**	**+ Contrib. Capital**	**+ Earned Capital**		**Rev- enues**	**− Expen- ses**	**= Net Income**
1. Purchased 1,000 shares of Yahoo! common stock for $15 cash per share	−15,000 Cash	+15,000 Marketable Securities	=					−	=
2. Received cash dividend of $2.50 per share on Yahoo! com- mon stock	+2,500 Cash		=		+2,500 Retained Earnings		+2,500 Dividend Income	−	= +2,500
3. Year-end market price of Yahoo! common stock is $17 per share		+2,000 Marketable Securities	=		+2,000 Retained Earnings		+2,000 Unrealized Gain	−	= +2,000
4. Sold 1,000 shares of Yahoo! com- mon stock for $17,000 cash	+17,000 Cash	−17,000 Marketable Securities	=					−	=

Margin journal entries for b:

MS   15,000
   Cash   15,000

MS
15,000 |
       Cash
       | 15,000

Cash   2,500
   DI   2,500

Cash
2,500 |
       DI
       | 2,500

MS   2,000
   UG   2,000

MS
2,000 |
       UG
       | 2,000

Cash   17,000
   MS   17,000

Cash
17,000 |
       MS
       | 17,000

c. Yahoo! reports an investment portfolio of $2,103,724. This represents the portfolio's current market value.

d. Yahoo! classifies these investments as available-for-sale. Consequently, the net unrealized gains of $1,411 thousand (computed as gross unrealized gains of $3,129 thousand less gross unrealized losses of $1,718 thousand), had no effect on Yahoo!'s reported income. Yahoo! will realize gains and losses only when it sells the investments. Then, Yahoo! will recognize the gains or losses in current-period income.

Mid-Module Review 2

a.

	Balance Sheet						Income Statement		
Transaction	**Cash Asset**	**+ Noncash Assets**	**= Liabil- ities**	**+ Contrib. Capital**	**+ Earned Capital**		**Rev- enues**	**− Expen- ses**	**= Net Income**
1. Purchased 5,000 shares of LookSmart common stock at $10 cash per share; these shares reflect 30% ownership	−50,000 Cash	+50,000 Investments	=					−	=
2. Received a $2 per share cash dividend on Look- Smart stock	10,000 Cash	−10,000 Investments	=					−	=
3. Record 30% share of the $100,000 income reported by LookSmart		+30,000 Investments	=		+30,000 Retained Earnings		+30,000 Equity Income	−	= +30,000
4. Market value has increased to $12 per share			NOTHING RECORDED						
5. Sold all 5,000 shares of LookSmart stock for $90,000	+90,000 Cash	−70,000 Investments	=		+20,000 Retained Earnings		+20,000 Gain on Sale	−	= +20,000

Margin journal entries for a:

EMI   50,000
   Cash   50,000

EMI
50,000 |
       Cash
       | 50,000

Cash   10,000
   EMI   10,000

Cash
10,000 |
       EMI
       | 10,000

EMI   30,000
   EI   30,000

EMI
30,000 |
       EI
       | 30,000

Cash   90,000
   EMI   70,000
   GN   20,000

CASH
90,000 |
       EMI
       | 70,000
       GN
       | 20,000

b. Yahoo! reports $173 million ($508 million × 34%) of equity income related to this investment in its 2012 income statement.
c. Yahoo! Japan's stockholders' equity is $1,874 million (computed as $1,131 + $1,783 − $692 − $348, in $ millions), and Yahoo!'s investment account equals $637 million, computed as $1,874 million × 34%.

Module-End Review

Solution

	Yahoo! (Parent)	EarthLink (Subsidiary)	Consolidating Adjustments	Consolidated
Current assets	$1,000,000	$100,000		$1,100,000
Investment in EarthLink	600,000	—	$(600,000)	
PPE, net	3,000,000	400,000	100,000	3,500,000
Goodwill	—	—	100,000	100,000
Total assets.	$4,600,000	$500,000		$4,700,000
Liabilities.	$1,000,000	$100,000		$1,100,000
Contributed capital.	2,000,000	200,000	(200,000)	2,000,000
Retained earnings	1,600,000	200,000	(200,000)	1,600,000
Total liabilities and equity	$4,600,000	$500,000		$4,700,000

Explanation: The $600,000 investment account is eliminated together with the $400,000 book value of EarthLink's equity to which Yahoo's investment relates. The remaining $200,000 consists of the additional $100,000 in PPE assets and the $100,000 in goodwill from expected corporate synergies. Following these adjustments, the balance sheet items are summed to yield the consolidated balance sheet.

1. Describe and analyze the accounting for capitalized leases. (p. 10-4)

2. Describe and analyze the accounting for pensions. (p. 10-12)

3. Explain and interpret the accounting for special purpose entities (SPEs). (p. 10-24)

Off-Balance-Sheet Financing

Delta Air Lines (DAL) is solvent and profitable, but confronts competing demands for its available cash flow as a result of a heavy debt load that includes borrowed money, aircraft leases, and pension and other post-employment obligations. The magnitude of obligations arising from aircraft leases often surprises those outside the industry. Many airlines do not own the planes that they fly. To a large extent, those planes are owned by commercial leasing companies like **General Electric Commercial Credit** (GE's financial subsidiary), and are leased by the airlines.

DELTA AIR LINES

If structured in a specific way, neither the leased planes (the assets) nor the lease obligation (the liability) would be on Delta Air Lines' balance sheet. That exclusion can alter investors' perceptions of the capital investment Delta Air Lines needs to operate its business as well as the level of debt it carries. In this module, we describe an analytical procedure that provides an alternative view of the company's investing and financing activities.

The analytical adjustment increases the liability on Delta Air Lines' balance sheet: lease payment obligations on aircrafts total $7.09 billion in 2010, which is a staggering amount when compared to the company's net operating assets of $12.13 billion. This module discusses the accounting for leases and explains this analytical adjustment and how to apply it.

Pensions and long-term health care plans are another large obligation for many large companies, including Delta Air Lines. Until recently, information about these pension and health care obligations was only in footnotes. Recent accounting rule changes now require companies to report that information on the balance sheet. In particular, the balance sheet now reports the net pension and health care liabilities (the total liability less related investments that fund the liabilities).

Delta Air Lines' 2010 net pension and health care liability exceeds pension assets by $11.4 billion. That amount represents 27% of Delta's total liabilities and equity. This module explains the accounting for both pensions and health care obligations and examines footnote disclosures that convey a wealth of information relating to assumptions underlying estimates of these obligations.

Methods that companies apply to avoid reporting potential liabilities (and expenses), are commonly referred to as *off-balance-sheet financing*. Although companies have long practiced off-balance-sheet financing, more recent techniques have become increasingly complex and require careful analysis. We explain one such off-balance-sheet technique, special purpose entities (SPEs), in Appendix 10B.

Sources: Delta Air Lines 2010 Form 10-K; *The Wall Street Journal*, January 2012.

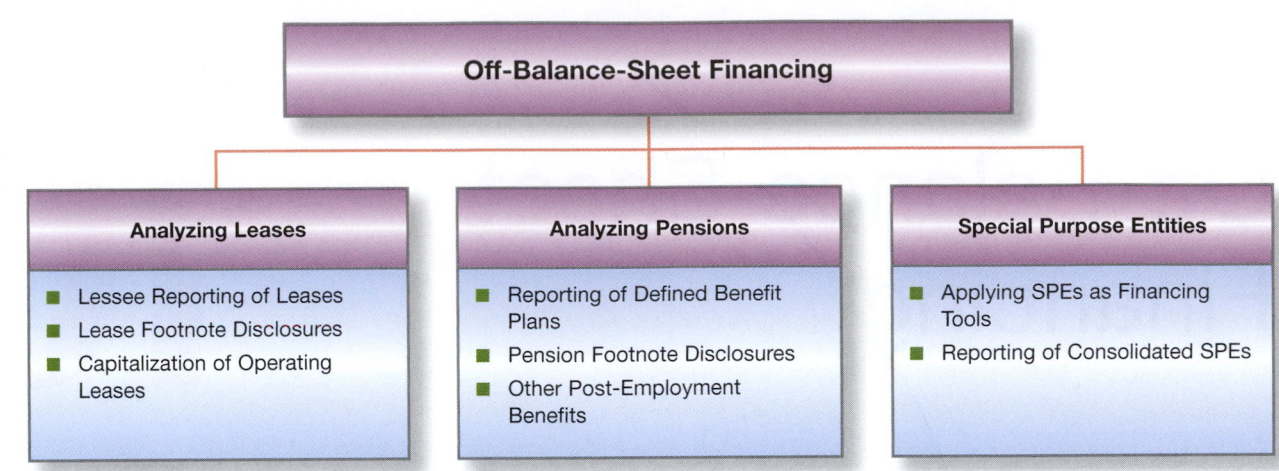

Company stakeholders pay attention to the composition of the balance sheet and its relation to the income statement. This attention extends to their analysis and valuation of both equity and debt securities. Of particular importance in this valuation process is the analysis of return on equity (ROE) and its components: return on net operating assets (RNOA)—including net operating profit margin (NOPM) and net operating asset turnover (NOAT)—and the degree of financial leverage (FLEV). Module 3 and its appendix explain these measures.

To value debt securities such as bonds and notes, one must consider a company's financial leverage (claims against assets) and the level of debt service (interest and principal payments), and compare them with expected cash flows. If analysis reveals that profitability (as measured by ROE and RNOA) and cash flows are inadequate, a company's credit rating could decline. The resulting higher cost of debt capital could limit the number of investment projects that yield a return greater than their financing cost. This restricts the company's growth and profitability.

Financial managers are aware of the importance of how financial markets perceive their companies. They also recognize the market attention directed at the quality of their balance sheets and income statements. This reality can pressure managers to *window dress* financial statements to present the company's financial condition and performance in the best possible light. To increase reported solvency and decrease the risk metrics, companies generally wish to present a balance sheet with low levels of debt. Companies that are more liquid and less financially leveraged are viewed as less likely to go bankrupt. As a result, the risk of default on their debt is less, resulting in a better credit rating and a lower interest rate.

Companies also generally wish to present a balance sheet with fewer assets. This is driven by return considerations. ROE has two components: operating return and nonoperating return. The latter is a function of the company's effective use of debt. Investors generally prefer a company's ROE to be derived from operations (RNOA) rather than from its use of debt. So, if a company can maintain a given level of profitability with fewer assets, the related increase in ROE is perceived to be driven by higher RNOA (asset turnover), and not by increased financial leverage.

Off-balance-sheet financing means that assets or liabilities, or both, are not reported on the balance sheet. Even though GAAP requires detailed footnote disclosures, managers generally believe that keeping such assets and liabilities off the balance sheet improves market perception of their operating performance and financial condition. This belief presumes that the market is somewhat inefficient, a notion that persists despite empirical evidence suggesting that analysts adjust balance sheets to include assets and liabilities that managers exclude.

This module explains and analyzes several types of off-balance-sheet financing. Major topics we discuss are leases, pensions, health care liabilities, and special purpose entities (SPEs). This is not an exhaustive list of the techniques that managers employ to achieve off-balance-sheet financing, but it includes the most common methods. We must keep one point in mind: the relevant information to assess off-balance-sheet financing is mainly in footnotes. While GAAP footnote disclosures on such financing are fairly good, we must have the analytic tools to interpret them and to understand the nature and the magnitude of assets and liabilities that managers have moved off of the balance sheet. This module provides those tools.

ANALYZING LEASES

We begin the discussion of off-balance-sheet financing with leases. The following graphic shows that leasing impacts both sides of the balance sheet (liabilities and assets) and the income statement (leasing expenses are often reported in selling, general and administrative expenses).

LO1 Describe and analyze the accounting for capitalized leases.

Income Statement
Sales
Cost of goods sold
Selling, general and administrative expenses
Income taxes
Net income

Balance Sheet	
Cash	Current liabilities
Accounts receivable	**Long-term liabilities**
Inventory	
Long-term operating assets	Shareholders' equity
Investments	

A lease is a contract between the owner of an asset (the **lessor**) and the party desiring to use that asset (the **lessee**). Since this is a private contract between two willing parties, it is governed only by applicable commercial law, and can include whatever provisions the parties negotiate.

Leases generally provide for the following terms:

- Lessor allows the lessee the unrestricted right to use the asset during the lease term.
- Lessee agrees to make periodic payments to the lessor and to maintain the asset.
- Title to the asset remains with the lessor, who usually takes physical possession of the asset at lease-end unless the lessee negotiates the right to purchase the asset at its market value or other predetermined price.

From the lessor's standpoint, lease payments are set at an amount that yields an acceptable return on investment, commensurate with the lessee's credit rating. The lessor has an investment in the lease asset, and the lessee gains use of the asset.

The lease serves as a financing vehicle, similar to a secured bank loan. However, there are several advantages to leasing over bank financing:

- Leases often require less equity investment by the lessee (borrower) compared with bank financing. Leases usually require the first lease payment be made at the inception of the lease. For a 60-month lease, this amounts to a 1/60 (1.7%) investment by the lessee, compared with a typical bank loan of 70-80% of the asset cost (thus requiring 20-30% equity investment by the borrower).
- Because leases are contracts between two parties, their terms can be structured to meet both parties' needs. For example, a lease can allow variable payments to match the lessee's seasonal cash inflows or have graduated payments for start-up companies.
- A lease can be structured such that neither the lease asset nor the lease liability is reported on the balance sheet. Accordingly, leasing can be a form of off-balance-sheet financing.

Lessee Reporting of Leases

GAAP identifies two different approaches for the reporting of leases by the lessee:

- **Capital lease method**. This method requires that both the lease asset and the lease liability be reported on the balance sheet. The lease asset is depreciated like any other long-term asset. The lease liability is amortized like debt, where lease payments are separated into interest expense and principal repayment.
- **Operating lease method**. Under this method, neither the lease asset nor the lease liability is reported on the balance sheet. Lease payments are recorded as rent expense by the lessee.

The financial statement effects for the lessee of these methods are summarized in Exhibit 10.1.

EXHIBIT 10.1	Financial Statement Effects of Lease Type for the Lessee			
Lease Type	**Assets**	**Liabilities**	**Expenses**	**Cash Flows**
Capital	Lease asset reported	Lease liability reported	Depreciation and interest expense	Payments per lease contract
Operating	Lease asset **not** reported	Lease liability **not** reported	Rent expense	Payments per lease contract

GAAP defines criteria to determine whether a lease is capital or operating.[1] Managers seeking off-balance-sheet financing structure their leases around the GAAP rules so as to fail the "capitalization tests." (A proposal currently under review by the FASB and the IASB would require companies to record the rights and obligations related to *all* leases on their balance sheets. If approved, substantially all leases would be recorded on the balance sheet as an asset and a liability.)

Under the operating method, lease assets and lease liabilities are *not* recorded on the balance sheet. The company merely discloses key details of the transaction in the lease footnote. The income statement reports the lease payment as rent expense. And, the cash outflows (payments to lessor) per the lease contract are included in the operating section of the statement of cash flows.

For capital leases, both the lease asset and lease liability are reported on the balance sheet. In the income statement, depreciation and interest expense are reported instead of rent expense. (Because only depreciation is an operating expense, NOPAT is higher when a lease is classified as a capital lease.) Further, although the cash payments to the lessor are identical whether or not the lease is capitalized on the balance sheet, the cash flows are classified differently for capital leases—that is, each payment is part interest (operating cash flow) and part principal (financing cash flow). Operating cash flows are, therefore, greater when a lease is classified as a capital lease.

Classifying leases as "operating" has four financial reporting consequences for the lessee:

1. The lease asset is not reported on the balance sheet. This means that net operating asset turnover (NOAT) is higher because reported operating assets are lower and revenues are unaffected.
2. The lease liability is not reported on the balance sheet. This means that balance sheet measures of financial leverage (like the total liabilities-to-equity ratio) are improved; many managers believe the reduced financial leverage will result in a better credit rating and, consequently, a lower interest rate on borrowed funds.
3. Without analytical adjustments (see later section on capitalization of operating leases), the portion of ROE derived from operating activities (RNOA) appears higher, which improves the perceived quality of the company's ROE.
4. During the early years of the lease term, rent expense reported for an operating lease is less than the depreciation and interest expense reported for a capital lease.[2] This means that net income is higher in those early years with an operating lease.[3] Further, if the company is growing and continually adding operating lease assets, the level of profits will continue to remain higher during the growth period.

The benefits of applying the operating method for leases are obvious to managers, thus leading some to avoid lease capitalization. Furthermore, the lease accounting standard includes rigid requirements relating to capitalization. Whenever accounting standards are rigidly defined, managers can structure transactions to meet the letter of the standard to achieve a desired accounting result when the essence of the transaction would suggest a different accounting treatment. This is *form over substance*.

---

[1] Leases must be capitalized when one or more of the following four criteria are met: (1) The lease automatically transfers ownership of the lease asset from the lessor to the lessee at termination of the lease. (2) The lease provides that the lessee can purchase the lease asset for a nominal amount (a bargain purchase) at termination of the lease. (3) The lease term is at least 75% of the economic useful life of the lease asset. (4) The present value of the lease payments is at least 90% of the fair market value of the lease asset at inception of the lease.

[2] This is true even if the company employs straight-line depreciation for the lease asset since interest expense accrues on the outstanding balance of the lease liability, which is higher in the early years of the lease life. Total expense is the same *over the life of the lease*, regardless of whether the lease is capitalized or not. That is: Total rent expense (from operating lease) = Total depreciation expense (from capital lease) + Total interest expense (from capital lease).

[3] However, NOPAT is *lower* for an operating lease because rent expense is an operating expense whereas only depreciation expense (and not interest expense) is an operating expense for a capital lease.

IFRS INSIGHT **Lease Accounting under IFRS**

U.S. GAAP and IFRS both require that leases be capitalized if the lease asset's risks and rewards are transferred to the lessee. The main difference between the two reporting systems is that IFRS are more principles based and GAAP is more rules based (as an example, see footnote 1). Given the broader application of principles, IFRS classify more leases as *finance leases* (termed "capital leases" under GAAP). Other small differences exist in the accounting for leases but these will not lead to materially different reporting outcomes in most cases.

Footnote Disclosure of Leases

Disclosures of expected payments for leases are required under both operating and capital lease methods. **Delta Air Lines** provides a typical disclosure from its 2010 annual report:

LEASE OBLIGATIONS We lease aircraft, airport terminals, maintenance facilities, ticket offices and other property and equipment from third parties. Rental expense for operating leases, which is recorded on a straight-line basis over the life of the lease term, totaled $1.2 billion, $1.3 billion and $798 million for the years ended December 31, 2010, 2009 and 2008, respectively. Amounts due under capital leases are recorded as liabilities on our Consolidated Balance Sheets. Assets acquired under capital leases are recorded as property and equipment on our Consolidated Balance Sheets. Amortization of assets recorded under capital leases is included in depreciation and amortization expense on our Consolidated Statements of Operations. The following tables summarize, as of December 31, 2010, our minimum rental commitments under capital leases and noncancelable operating leases (including certain aircraft under Contract Carrier agreements) with initial or remaining terms in excess of one year. At December 31, 2010, we operated 111 aircraft under operating leases and 113 aircraft under capital leases.

Capital Leases Year Ending December 31 (in millions)	
2011	$ 214
2012	193
2013	160
2014	130
2015	124
Thereafter	404
Total minimum lease payments	1,225
Less: amount of lease payments representing interest	(487)
Present value of minimum capital lease payments	738
Plus: unamortized premium, net	7
Less: current obligations under capital leases	(119)
Long-term capital lease obligations	$ 626

Operating Leases Year Ending December 31 (in millions)	Delta Lease Payments	Contract Carrier Aircraft Lease Payments	Total
2011	$ 899	$ 521	$ 1,420
2012	840	511	1,351
2013	816	504	1,320
2014	770	493	1,263
2015	688	481	1,169
Thereafter	7,096	1,327	8,423
Total minimum lease payments	$11,109	$3,837	$14,946

Lease disclosures such as this provide information concerning current and future payment obligations. These contractual obligations are similar to debt payments and must be factored into our evaluation of the company's financial condition.

Delta Air Lines' footnote disclosure reports minimum (base) contractual lease payment obligations for each of the next five years and the total lease payment obligations that come due in year six and beyond. This is similar to disclosures of future maturities for long-term debt. The company also must provide separate disclosures for operating leases and capital leases (Delta Air Lines has both operating and capital leases outstanding).

> **ANALYSIS DECISION**   **You Are the Division President**
>
> You are the president of an operating division. Your CFO recommends operating lease treatment for asset acquisitions to reduce reported assets and liabilities on your balance sheet. To achieve this classification, you must negotiate leases with shorter base terms and lease renewal options that you feel are not advantageous to your company. What is your response? [Answer, p. 10-29]

Capitalization of Operating Leases

U.S. GAAP as of 2011 permits the classification of leases as operating or capital as explained above. As of the publication of this textbook, U.S. standard-setters are deliberating a new accounting standard that would require all leases to be accounted for much like capital leases currently (namely, lease assets and lease liabilities would be capitalized on the balance sheet following the procedures we outline below). However, until passage of the new standard, companies will report only capital leases on their balance sheets, whereas information on their operating leases will be in footnotes such as that shown above for Delta.

Although not recognized on-balance-sheet, leased properties arguably represent assets (and create liabilities) as defined under GAAP. That is, the company controls the assets and will profit from their future benefits. Also, lease liabilities represent real contractual obligations. Although the financial statements are prepared in conformity with current (2011) GAAP, the failure to capitalize operating lease assets and lease liabilities for analysis purposes distorts ROE analysis—specifically:

- Net operating profit margin (NOPM) is understated. Over the life of the lease, rent expense under operating leases equals depreciation plus interest expense under capital leases; however, only depreciation expense is included in net operating profit (NOPAT) as interest is a nonoperating expense. Operating expense is, therefore, overstated, and NOPM is understated. While cash payments are the same whether the lease is classified as operating or capital, operating cash flow is higher with capital leases since depreciation is an add-back, and the reduction of the capital lease obligation is classified as a financing outflow. Operating cash flows are, therefore, lower with operating leases than with capital leases.

- Net operating asset turnover (NOAT) is overstated due to nonreporting of lease assets.

- Financial leverage (FLEV) is understated by the omitted lease liabilities—recall that lease liabilities are nonoperating.

Although aggregate ROE is relatively unaffected (assuming that the leases are at their midpoint on average so that rent expense is approximately equal to depreciation plus interest) failure to capitalize an operating lease results in a balance sheet that, arguably, neither reflects all of the assets that are used in the business, nor the nonoperating obligations for which the company is liable. Such noncapitalization of leases makes ROE appear to be of higher quality because it derives from higher RNOA (due to higher NOA turnover) and not from higher financial leverage. This is, of course, the main reason why some managers want to exclude leases from the balance sheet.

Lease disclosures that are required under GAAP allow us to capitalize operating leases for analysis purposes. This capitalization process involves three steps (this is the same basic process that managers will use to capitalize leases under the proposed lease-accounting standard):

1. Determine the discount rate.
2. Compute the present value of future lease payments.

3. Adjust the balance sheet to include the present value from step 2 as both a lease asset and a lease liability. Adjust the income statement to include depreciation and interest in lieu of rent expense.

Step 1. There are at least two approaches to determine the appropriate discount rate for our analysis: (1) If the company discloses capital leases, we can impute (infer) an implicit rate of return: a rate that yields the present value computed by the company given the future capital lease payments (see Business Insight box below). (2) Use the rate that corresponds to the company's credit rating or the rate from any recent borrowings involving intermediate-term secured obligations. Companies typically disclose these details in their long-term debt footnote. To illustrate the capitalization of operating leases, we use the **Delta Air Lines** lease footnote reproduced above. Step 1 estimates the implicit rate for Delta's capital leases to be 14.31% (see the following Business Insight box on computing the imputed discount rate for leases).

BUSINESS INSIGHT | **Imputed Discount Rate Computation for Leases**

When companies report both operating and capital leases, the average rate used to discount capital leases can be imputed from disclosures in the lease footnote. **Delta Air Lines** reports total undiscounted minimum capital lease payments of $1,225 million and a discounted value for those lease payments of $738 million. Using Excel, we estimate the discount rate that Delta used for its capital lease computations with the IRR function (= **IRR (values,**guess)) as shown in the following spreadsheet. The entries in cells B2 through G2 are taken from Delta's reported schedule of lease maturities in the footnote shown earlier in this section, and those in cells H2 through K2 sum to $404 million, the total lease payments due after 2015 (year 5). We assume that Delta continues to pay $124 million per year (the same as in 2015) until the $404 is used up. This yields a smaller residual payment in year 9. The spreadsheet method yields an estimate of 14.31% for the discount rate that Delta implicitly used for capitalization of its capital leases in its 2010 balance sheet.

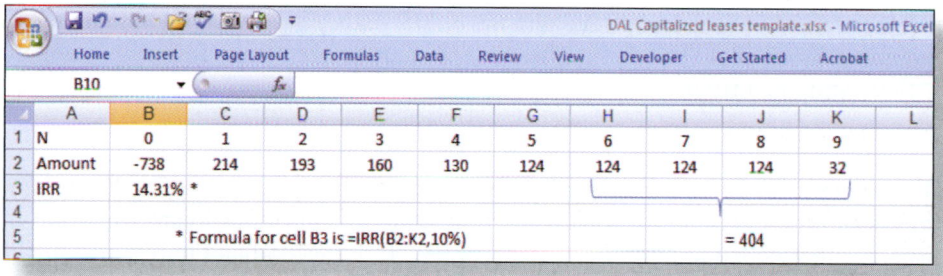

Step 2. Compute the present value of future operating lease payments using the 14.31% discount rate that we estimated in Step 1, see Exhibit 10.2. We demonstrate this computation using a spreadsheet (without rounding of numbers); we show those same computations using both a financial calculator and present value tables in Appendix 10C. The spreadsheet (and calculator) method is more exact, but may or may not yield a material difference to the number obtained when using present value tables. Given the widespread use of spreadsheets such as Excel, we use the spreadsheet method hereafter.

EXHIBIT 10.2 | Present Value of Operating Lease Payments ($ millions)

Year	Operating Lease Payment	Discount Factor ($i = 0.1431$)	Present Value
1..................	$1,420	0.87481	$1,242
2..................	1,351	0.76530	1,034
3..................	1,320	0.66949	884
4..................	1,263	0.58568	740
5..................	1,169	0.51236	599
>5..................	8,423 ($1,169 × 7.205 years)	4.32210 × 0.51236	2,589
			$7,088

Remaining life......... $8,432/$1,169 = 7.205 years

Spreadsheet Method. The present value of the operating lease payments equals the sum of the present values for each of the lease payments Year 1 through Year 5 and the present value of the lease payments after Year 5. This two-step computation follows:

1. *Present values for Years 1 through 5.* The present value of each forecasted lease payment for Years 1 through 5 is computed as the product of (a) the lease payment for that year and (b) the present value factor for that year using the following formula: $\frac{1}{(1+i)^t}$ where i is the discount factor and t is the year (1, 2, 3, 4 and 5). To illustrate using Delta, we enter the discount rate of 14.31% and the year 1, 2, 3, 4 and 5 separately for each year to obtain a present value factor for each year. For example, for Year 1 the present value factor is 0.87481, computed as $\frac{1}{(1.1431)^1}$; and, for Year 2 the present value factor is 0.76530, computed as $\frac{1}{(1.1431)^2}$; and so forth. Thus, the present value ($ in millions) of the Year 1 lease payment equals $1,242, computed from: $1,420 $\times \left[\frac{1}{(1.1431)^1}\right]$; the present value of the Year 2 lease payment equals $1,034, computed from: $1,351 $\times \left[\frac{1}{(1.1431)^2}\right]$; and so forth. In Excel, for Year 2, the present value factor is entered as: 1/1.1431^2. The present values for Year 1 through Year 5 are in the far right column of Exhibit 10.2.

2. *Present value for Year 6 and thereafter.* To compute the present value of the lease payments remaining after Year 5, we make an assumption that the company continues to make lease payments at the Year 5 level for the remainder of the lease term. The remaining lease term is, therefore, estimated as: (Total payments for Year 6 and thereafter)/(Year 5 lease payment). This means the remaining payments are an annuity for the remainder of the lease term, the present value of which equals the product of (a) the lease payment for Year 5 and (b) the present value factor for that annuity using the following formula: $\frac{1-[1/(1+i)^n]}{i} \times \frac{1}{(1+i)^5}$, where i is the discount factor and n is the remainder of the lease term. To illustrate using Delta, we enter the 14.31% discount rate and the 7.205 years estimate of the remaining lease term (computed from $8,423/$1,169). The present value of the remaining lease payments equals $2,589, computed from:

$$\$1,169 \text{ million} \times \frac{1-[1/(1.1431)^{7.205}]}{0.1431} \times \frac{1}{(1.1431)^5}$$

The first term in this computation is the assumed annual payment after Year 5; the second term is the present value factor for the remaining annuity after Year 5; and the third term discounts the second term to the present. In Excel, the second and third terms are entered as ((1−(1/(1.1431)^7.205))/0.1431) * (1/1.1431^5). The present value of the lease payments for Year 6 and thereafter is in the sixth row of the far right column of Exhibit 10.2.

We sum the present values of Year 1 through Year 5 payments and the present value of the payments in Year 6 and beyond to obtain the present value of future operating lease payments; for Delta, this totals $7,088 ($ millions), computed as $1,242 + $1,034 + $884 + $740 + $599 + $2,589.

Step 3. Use the computed present value of future operating lease payments to adjust the balance sheet, income statement, and financial ratios as we illustrate below.

Balance Sheet Effects To adjust the balance sheet, add the present value from Step 2 to both operating assets (PPE) and nonoperating liabilities (long-term debt). Exhibit 10.3 shows the adjustments for **Delta Air Lines** at year-end 2010. The capitalization of operating leases has a marked impact on Delta Airlines' balance sheet. For the airline and retailing industries, in particular, lease assets (airplanes and real estate) comprise a large portion of net operating assets, which are typically accounted for using the operating lease method. Thus, companies in these industries usually have sizeable off-balance-sheet assets and liabilities.

EXHIBIT 10.3	Adjustments to Balance Sheet from Capitalization of Operating Leases			
Delta Air Lines ($ millions)	**Reported Figures**	**Adjustments**	**Adjusted Figures**	**Percent Increase**
Net operating assets	$12,130	$7,088	$19,218	58.4%
Net nonoperating obligations. . .	11,233	7,088	18,321	63.1%
Equity	897	—	897	0.0%

Income Statement Effects Capitalizing operating leases affects the income statement via depreciation of the leased equipment and interest on the lease liability. Operating lease payments are reported as rent expense, typically included in selling, general and administrative expenses. The income statement adjustments relating to the capitalization of operating leases involve two steps:[4]

1. Remove "rent expense" of $1,420 million from operating expense.

2. Add depreciation expense from the lease assets to operating expense and add interest expense from the lease obligation as a nonoperating expense. Lease assets are estimated at $7,088 million (see Exhibit 10.3). GAAP requires companies to depreciate capital lease assets over their useful lives or the lease terms, whichever is less. For this example, we assume that the remaining lease term is 12.205 years (five years reported in the lease schedule plus 7.205 years after the fifth year). Using this term and zero salvage value results in estimated straight-line depreciation for lease assets of $581 million ($7,088 million/12.205 years). Interest expense on the $7,088 million lease liability at the 14.31% capitalization rate is $1,014 million ($7,088 million × 14.31%) for the first year.

Delta Air Lines reports NOPAT of $1,607 million, nonoperating expense of $1,014 million, and net income of $593 million. Assuming a tax rate of 37%, the net adjustment to NOPAT is $529 million ([$1,420 million rent expense − $581 million depreciation expense] × [1 − 0.37]), see Exhibit 10.4. The increase in nonoperating expense after-tax is $639 million ($1,014 × [1 − 0.37]), which is the additional after-tax interest expense on the capitalized lease obligation. Exhibit 10.4 summarizes those adjustments to Delta's profitability measures.

EXHIBIT 10.4	Adjustments to Income Statement from Capitalization of Operating Leases			
Delta Air Lines ($ millions)	**Reported Figures**	**Adjustments**	**Adjusted Figures**	**Percent Increase**
NOPAT	$1,607	$529	$2,136	32.9%
Nonoperating expense.	1,014	639	1,653	63.0%
Net income.	$ 593	$(110)	$ 483	(18.5)%

ROE and Disaggregation Effects Adjustments to capitalize operating leases can alter our assessment of ROE components. Using the adjustments we describe in Exhibits 10.3 and 10.4, the impact for ROE and its components (defined in Module 3), is summarized in Exhibit 10.5 for **Delta Air Lines**.

EXHIBIT 10.5	Ratio Effects of Adjustments from Capitalization of Operating Leases		
Delta Air Lines ($ millions)	**Reported**	**Adjusted**	**Computations for Adjusted Numbers**
NOPM.	5.1%	6.7%	$2,136/$31,755
NOAT	2.62	1.65	$31,755/$19,218*
RNOA	13.4%	11.1%	$2,136/$19,218*
Financial leverage (FLEV = NNO/Equity).	12.52	20.42	$18,321/$897
ROE	66.1%	53.8%	$483/$897*
Nonoperating return.	52.7%	42.8%	ROE − RNOA

*For simplicity, we use year-end values for the denominator in lieu of average values.

Using *year-end* (reported and adjusted) data, and Delta Air Lines' total revenues of $31,755 million, adjusted RNOA is 11.1% (down from 13.4% reported). RNOA decreased because the increase in net operating profit margin (from 5.1% to 6.7%) was more than offset by a much

---

[4] This approach uses the operating lease payments from Year 1 of the projected payments to approximate the rent expense for operating leases. This approach also uses the computed present value of future lease payments (from Step 2) to compute the depreciation and interest expense for capital leases. An alternative approach is to use *actual* rent expense for the current year (disclosed in the lease footnote) together with depreciation and interest computed based on capitalization of the *prior* year's future lease payments. Although, arguably more exact, most analysts use the simplified approach illustrated here given the extent of other estimates involved (such as discount rates, depreciation lives, and salvage values).

lower net operating asset turnover (from 2.62 to 1.65). After capitalization of its operating leases, Delta Air Lines is more profitable (from an operating standpoint) and more capital intensive than we would infer from a review of its unadjusted income statement and balance sheet.

Delta's ROE decreases by 12.3% (from 66.1% to 53.8%).[5] The analysis reveals that the nonoperating return component of its ROE decreases from 52.7% using reported figures to an adjusted 42.8%. The adjusted figures reveal that the lower spread is partially offset by much greater financial leverage from capitalized lease obligations that is not apparent prior to capitalization. Specifically, financial leverage is 20.42 times equity using adjusted figures versus 12.52 times using reported figures. Financial leverage is, therefore, revealed to play a greater role in ROE in partially offsetting the lower spread. In sum, Delta's adjusted figures reveal a company with a lower ROE and with more assets and more financial leverage than was apparent from reported figures.

Adjusted assets and liabilities arguably present a more realistic picture of the invested capital required to operate Delta Air Lines and of the amount of leverage represented by its leases. Similarly, operating profitability is revealed to be higher than reported, since a portion of Delta's rent payments represents repayment of the lease liability (a nonoperating cash outflow) rather than operating expense.

MID-MODULE REVIEW

Following is the leasing footnote disclosure from **American Airlines**' 2010 10-K report.

AMR's subsidiaries lease various types of equipment and property, primarily aircraft and airport facilities. The future minimum lease payments required under capital leases, together with the present value of such payments, and future minimum lease payments required under operating leases that have initial or remaining noncancelable lease terms in excess of one year as of December 31, 2010, were (in millions):

Year Ending December 31	Capital Leases	Operating Leases
2011	$186	$ 1,254
2012	136	1,068
2013	120	973
2014	98	831
2015	87	672
2016 and thereafter	349	6,006
	976	$10,804
Less amount representing interest	372	
Present value of net minimum lease payments	$604	

Required

1. Impute the discount rate that American uses, on average, to compute the present value of its capital leases.
2. What adjustments would we make to American's balance sheet to capitalize the operating leases at the end of 2010? (*Hint:* The implicit rate on its capital leases is approximately 13%; use this approximation to solve parts 2 and 3.)
3. Assuming the same facts as in part 2, what income statement adjustments might we consider?

The solution is on page 10-46.

---

[5] Delta's ROE (based on year-end equity) of 66.1% is high, which is an aberration resulting from the recessionary effects of the depressed economy in the late 2000s. During this period, U.S. airlines had huge losses that reduced equity and led to the bankruptcy of many carriers. Delta's high ROE for this year is due to its reduced equity base, and not to abnormally high profitability.

ANALYZING PENSIONS

Companies frequently offer pension plans as a benefit for their employees. There are two general types of pension plans:

LO2 Describe and analyze the accounting for pensions.

1. **Defined contribution plan**. This plan requires the company make periodic contributions to an employee's account (usually with a third-party trustee like a bank), and many plans require an employee matching contribution. Following retirement, the employee makes periodic withdrawals from that account. A tax-advantaged 401(k) account is a typical example. Under a 401(k) plan, the employee makes contributions that are exempt from federal taxes until they are withdrawn after retirement.

2. **Defined benefit plan**. This plan also requires the company make periodic payments to a third party, which then makes payments to an employee after retirement. Payments are usually based on years of service and the employee's salary. The company may or may not set aside sufficient funds to cover these obligations (federal law does set minimum funding requirements). As a result, defined benefit plans can be overfunded or underfunded. All pension investments are retained by the third party until paid to the employee. In the event of bankruptcy, employees have the standing of a general creditor, but usually have additional protection in the form of government pension benefit insurance.

For a defined contribution plan, the company contribution is recorded as an expense in the income statement when the cash is paid or the liability accrued. For a defined benefit plan, it is not so simple. This is because while the company contributes cash or securities to the pension investment account, the pension obligation is not satisfied until the employee receives pension benefits, which may be many years into the future. This section focuses on how a defined benefit plan impacts financial statements, and how we assess company performance and financial condition when such a plan exists.

Reporting of Defined Benefit Pension Plans

There are two accounting issues concerning the reporting of defined benefit pension plans.

1. How are pension plans (assets and liabilities) reported in the balance sheet (if at all)?
2. How is the expense relating to pension plans reported in the income statement?

The following graphic shows where pensions appear on the balance sheet (liabilities and assets) and the income statement (pension expense is reported in the same expense accounts as employee wages; for example, pension expense for manufacturing employees is in cost of goods sold, whereas pension expense for salespeople is in SG&A).

Income Statement	Balance Sheet	
Sales	Cash	Current liabilities
Cost of goods sold	Accounts receivable	**Long-term liabilities**
Selling, general and administrative expenses	Inventory	
Income taxes	**Long-term operating assets**	Shareholders' equity
Net income	Investments	

Balance Sheet Effects

Pension plan assets are primarily investments in stocks and bonds (mostly of other companies, but it is not uncommon for companies to invest pension funds in their own stock). Pension liabilities (called the **projected benefit obligation** or **PBO**) are the company's obligations to pay current and former employees. The difference between the market value of the pension plan assets and the projected benefit obligation is called the **funded status** of the pension plan. If the PBO exceeds the pension plan assets, the pension is **underfunded**. Conversely, if pension plan assets exceed the PBO, the pension plan is **overfunded**. Under current GAAP, companies are required to record only the funded status on their balance sheets (namely, the *net* amount, not the pension plan assets and PBO separately), either as an asset if the plan is overfunded, or as a liability if it is underfunded.

Pension plan assets consist of stocks and bonds whose value changes each period in three ways. First, the value of the investments increases or decreases as a result of interest, dividends, and gains or losses on the stocks and bonds held. Second, the pension plan assets increase when the company contributes additional cash or stock to the investment account. Third, the pension plan assets decrease by the amount of benefits paid to retirees during the period. These three changes in the pension plan assets are articulated below.

Pension Plan Assets
Pension plan assets, beginning balance
+ Actual returns on investments (interest, dividends, gains and losses)
+ Company contributions to pension plan
− Benefits paid to retirees
= Pension plan assets, ending balance

The pension liability, or PBO (projected benefit obligation), is computed as the present value of the expected future benefit payments to employees. The present value of these future payments depends on the number of years the employee is expected to work (years of service), the employee's salary level at retirement, and the number of years the employee will receive benefits. Consequently, companies must estimate future wage increases, as well as the number of employees expected to reach retirement age with the company and how long they are likely to receive pension benefits following retirement. Once the future retiree pool is determined, the expected future payments under the plan are discounted to arrive at the present value of the pension obligation. This is the PBO. A reconciliation of the PBO from beginning balance to year-end balance follows.

Pension Obligation
Projected benefit obligation, beginning balance
+ Service cost
+ Interest cost
+/− Actuarial losses (gains)
− Benefits paid to retirees
= Projected benefit obligation, ending balance

As this reconciliation shows, the balance in the PBO changes during the period for four reasons.

- First, as employees continue to work for the company, their pension benefits increase. The annual **service cost** represents the additional (future) pension benefits earned by employees during the current year.

- Second, **interest cost** accrues on the outstanding pension liability, just as it would with any other long-term liability (see the accounting for bond liabilities in Module 7). Because there are no scheduled interest payments on the PBO, the interest cost accrues each year, that is, interest is added to the existing liability.

- Third, the PBO can increase (or decrease) due to **actuarial losses (and gains)**, which arise when companies make changes in their pension plans or make changes in actuarial assumptions (such as the rate of wage inflation, termination and mortality rates, and the discount rate used to compute the present value of future obligations). For example, if a company increases the discount rate used to compute the present value of future pension plan payments from, say, 8% to 9%, the present value of future benefit payments declines (just like bond prices). Conversely, if the discount rate is reduced to 7%, the present value of the PBO increases. Other actuarial assumptions used to estimate the pension liability (such as the expected wage inflation rate or the expected life span of current and former employees) can also create similar actuarial losses or gains.

- Fourth, pension benefit payments to retirees reduce the PBO (just as the payments reduce the pension plan assets).

Finally, companies are permitted to net the pension plan assets and the PBO and then report this net amount on the balance sheet. This net amount is called the **funded status** and is reported as an asset if pension assets exceed the PBO, and as a liability if the PBO exceeds pension assets.

Net Pension Asset (or Liability)
Pension plan assets (at market value)
− Projected benefit obligation (PBO)
Funded status

If the funded status is positive (assets exceed liabilities such that the plan is overfunded), the overfunded pension plan is reported on the balance sheet as an asset, typically called prepaid pension cost. If the funded status is negative (liabilities exceed assets and the plan is underfunded), it is reported as a liability.[6] During the late 2000s, long-term interest rates declined drastically and many companies lowered their discount rate for computing the present value of future pension payments. Lower discount rates meant higher PBO values. This period also witnessed a bear market and pension plan assets declined in value. The combined effect of the increase in PBO and the decrease in asset values caused many pension funds to become severely underfunded. Of the 710 publicly traded companies reporting pension plans in 2010 and with revenues over $500 million, a total of 662 (93%) were underfunded. (**Delta Air Lines**, for example, reports an underfunded pension plan of $9.257 billion in 2010.)

IFRS INSIGHT Reporting of Pension Funded Status under IFRS

Like U.S. GAAP, IFRS requires companies to report the funded status of their defined benefit pension plans on the balance sheet. The IFRS calculation of the unfunded status is slightly different than under GAAP. The IFRS unfunded status is calculated as projected benefit obligation minus the fair value of plan assets; but, unlike GAAP, any actuarial gains are added (losses are subtracted). There are other differences in detailed computations, which means that for pension assets and liabilities it is difficult to reliably compare GAAP and IFRS reports.

Income Statement Effects

A company's net pension expense is computed as follows.

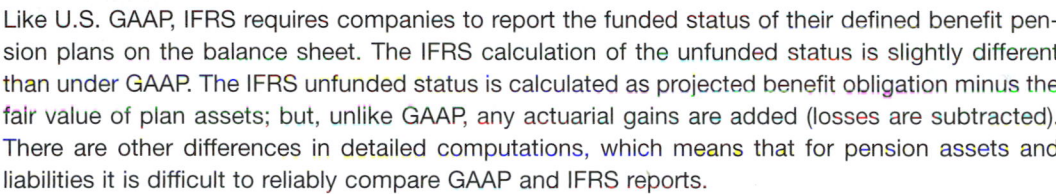

Net Pension Expense
Service cost
+ Interest cost
− *Expected* return on pension plan assets
± Amortization of deferred amounts
Net pension expense

The net pension expense is rarely reported separately on the income statement. Instead, it is included with other forms of compensation expense. However, pension expense is disclosed separately in footnotes.

The net pension expense has four components. The previous PBO section described the first two components: service costs and interest costs. The third component of pension expense relates to the return on pension plan assets, which *reduces* total pension expense. To compute this component, companies use the long-term *expected* rate of return on the pension plan assets, rather than the *actual* return, and multiply that expected rate by the prior year's balance in the pension plan assets account (usually the average balance in the prior year). Use of the expected return rather than actual return is an important distinction. Company CEOs and CFOs dislike income variability because they believe that stockholders react negatively to it, and so company executives intensely (and successfully) lobbied the FASB to use the more stable expected long-term

---

[6] Companies typically maintain many pension plans. Some are overfunded and others are underfunded. Current GAAP requires companies to separately group all of the overfunded and all of the underfunded plans, and to present a net asset for the overfunded plans and a net liability for the underfunded plans.

investment return, rather than the actual return, in computing pension expense. Thus, the pension plan assets' expected return is deducted to compute net pension expense.[7]

Any difference between the expected and the actual return is accumulated, together with other deferred amounts, off-balance-sheet and reported in the footnotes. (Other deferred amounts include changes in PBO resulting from changes in estimates used to compute the PBO and from amendments to the pension plans made by the company.) However, if the deferred amount exceeds certain limits, the excess is recognized on-balance-sheet with a corresponding amount recognized (as amortization of deferred amounts) in the income statement.[8] This amortization is the fourth component of pension expense and can be either a positive or negative amount depending on the sign of the difference between expected and actual return on plan assets. (We discuss the amortization component of pension expense further in Appendix 10A.)

A final point to consider is the operating or nonoperating nature of the components of pension expense. Most analysts consider the service cost portion of pension expense to be an operating expense, similar to salaries and other benefits. However, the interest cost component is generally viewed as a nonoperating (financing) cost. Similarly, the expected return on plan assets is considered nonoperating.

Footnote Disclosures—Components of Plan Assets and PBO

GAAP requires extensive footnote disclosures for pensions (and other post-employment benefits which we discuss later). These notes provide details relating to the net pension liability reported in the balance sheet and for the components of pension expense on the income statement.

Delta Air Lines' pension footnote below indicates that the funded status of its pension plan is $(9,257) million on December 31, 2010. This means Delta's plan is underfunded. Following are the disclosures Delta Air Lines makes in its pension footnote, $ millions.

December 31 (in millions)	2010	2009
Benefit obligation at beginning of period...................	$17,031	$15,929
Service cost..	—	—
Interest cost...	982	1,002
Actuarial loss (gain)	570	1,170
Benefits paid, including lump sums and annuities..............	(1,013)	(1,021)
Participant contributions	—	—
Plan amendments	—	—
Special termination benefits.............................	—	—
Settlements	(64)	(49)
Benefit obligation at end of period.......................	$17,506	$17,031

continued

---

[7] The IASB has amended its standard on accounting for pensions and other postretirement benefits (OPEB), which potentially has important implications for U.S. GAAP. Those amendments take effect for years starting on or after January 1, 2013, and include the following key changes:

  • *Elimination of deferred recognition.* The full value of the benefit obligation and plan assets will be reported in the balance sheet with changes arising from actuarial gains and losses recognized in full in other comprehensive income (OCI). Companies will not have an option to recognize those gains and losses in net income, either in the periods in which they occur or through amortization. Prior service cost will be recognized in full in determining net income in the period the plan amendment is made.

  • *Disaggregation of benefit cost.* The components of pension and OPEB cost (service cost, finance cost, and remeasurement cost) will be reported separately in the footnotes. Separate or aggregate presentation of service and finance cost components will be permitted in the statement of comprehensive income.

  • *Elimination of expected return on plan assets.* The discount rate would be applied to the net funded position to determine the net financing cost, which will include an implied return on assets. A separate expected long-term rate of return on plan assets will no longer be used.

[8] To avoid amortization, the deferred amounts must be less than 10% of the PBO or pension investments, whichever is less. The excess, if any, is amortized until no further excess remains. When the excess is eliminated (by investment returns or company contributions, for example), the amortization ceases.

continued from prior page

Fair value of plan assets at beginning of period	$ 7,623	$ 7,295
Actual (loss) gain on plan assets	975	1,198
Employer contributions	728	200
Participant contributions	—	—
Benefits paid, including lump sums and annuities	(1,013)	(1,021)
Settlements	(64)	(49)
Fair value of plan assets at end of period	$ 8,249	$ 7,623
Funded status at end of period	$ (9,257)	$ (9,408)

Delta Air Lines' PBO began the year with a balance of $17,031 million. It increased by the accrual of $982 million in interest cost (Delta froze its pension plans following the merger with Northwest Airlines; consequently, there is no current accrual for service cost as employees are not earning additional pension benefits). During the year, Delta realized an actuarial loss of $570 million, which increased the pension liability, and its PBO decreased as a result of $1,013 million in benefits paid to retirees, leaving a balance of $17,506 million at year-end.[9]

Pension plan assets began the year with a fair market value of $7,623 million, which increased by $975 million from investment returns and by $728 million from company contributions, and it decreased by $64 million for settlements to retirees. The company drew down its investments to make pension payments of $1,013 million to retirees. The $1,013 million payment reduced the PBO by the same amount, as discussed above, leaving the pension plan assets with a year-end balance of $8,249 million. The funded status of Delta Air Lines' pension plan at year-end was $(9,257) million, computed as $8,249 million − $17,506 million. The negative balance indicates that its pension plan is underfunded.

Delta Air Lines incurred $367 million of pension expense in 2010 and an additional $334 million of expense relating to defined contribution plans (companies typically maintain different types of retirement plans). The combined expense of $701 million is not broken out separately in the income statement. Details of this expense are found in its 2010 pension footnote, which follows ($ millions):

> We can treat the funded status as an operating item (either asset or liability).

Components of net periodic benefit cost	2010
Defined benefit plans	
Service cost	$ —
Interest cost	982
Expected return on plan assets	(677)
Amortization of prior service cost	—
Recognized net actuarial (gain) loss	48
Settlement charge, net	14
Special termination benefits	—
Net periodic cost	367
Defined contribution plan costs	334
Total cost	$701

The service and interest cost components of pension expense relate to the increase in the PBO of employees working another year for the company (expected benefits typically increase with longevity and salary, and the PBO increases because it is discounted for one less year). This expense is offset by the *expected* return on pension assets. Notice the use of expected returns rather than actual returns. Expected returns do not fluctuate as much as actual returns, and this yields a less volatile year-on-year pension expense and, consequently, less volatility in net income. The use of expected returns is in conformity with GAAP and companies lobbied for its

---

[9] This actuarial loss derives from: (1) a lower discount rate, from 5.93% to 5.69%—this change increased pension liability; and (2) a lower health care cost trend rate, from 7.5% to 7%—this change decreased pension liability. The lower discount rate dominated the lower cost trend and, thus, pension liability increased, yielding the actuarial loss.

use because of the reduced volatility for pension expense. Finally, because we cannot separate the operating and nonoperating components of a company's funded status and, hence, treat it entirely as operating, we do the same for pension expense and treat it entirely as operating. (We do this for consistency purposes even though we know that expense components related to interest cost, expected returns on plan assets, and many amortizations are nonoperating.)

RESEARCH INSIGHT   **Valuation Implications of Pension Footnote Disclosures**

The FASB requires footnote disclosure of the major components of pension cost presumably because it is useful for investors. Pension-related research has examined whether investors assign different valuation multiples to the components of pension cost when assessing company market value. Research finds that the market does, indeed, attach different interpretation to pension components, reflecting differences in information about perceived permanence in earnings.

Footnote Disclosures and Future Cash Flows

Companies use their pension plan assets to pay pension benefits to retirees. When markets are booming, as during the 1990s, pension plan assets can grow rapidly. However, when markets reverse, as in the bear markets of the early and late 2010s, the value of pension plan assets can decline. The company's annual pension plan contribution is an investment decision that is influenced, in part, by market conditions and minimum required contributions specified by law. Companies' cash contributions come from borrowed funds or operating cash flows.

RESEARCH INSIGHT   **Why Do Companies Offer Pensions?**

Research examines why companies choose to offer pension benefits. It finds that deferred compensation plans and pensions help align the long-term interests of owners and employees. Research also examines the composition of pension investments. It finds that a large portion of pension fund assets are invested in fixed-income securities, which are of lower risk than other investment securities. This implies that pension assets are less risky than nonpension assets. The FASB has mandated new pension disclosures that require firms (after 2009) to provide more detail about the types of assets held in pension plans. These disclosures presumably help investors better assess the riskiness of pension assets.

Delta Air Lines paid $1,013 million in pension benefits to retirees in 2010, yet it contributed only $728 million to pension assets that year. The remaining amount was paid out of available funds in the investment account. Cash contributions to the pension plan assets are the relevant amounts for an analysis of projected cash flows. Benefits paid in relation to the pension liability balance can provide a clue about the need for *future* cash contributions. Companies are required to disclose the expected benefit payments for five years after the statement date and the remaining obligations thereafter. Following is **Delta Air Lines**' benefit disclosure statement:

The following table summarizes the benefit payments that are scheduled to be paid in the following years ending December 31:

($ millions)	Pension
2011	$1,048
2012	1,036
2013	1,048
2014	1,059
2015	1,077
2016–2020	5,738

As of 2010, Delta Air Lines pension plan assets account reports a balance of $8,249 million, as discussed above, and during the year, the plan assets generated actual returns of $975 million. The pension plan asset account is currently generating investment returns that almost cover the $1 billion in projected benefit payments that Delta expects to pay to retirees as outlined in the schedule above. Should future investment returns decline, however, the company will have to use operating cash flow or borrow money to fund the deficit.

One application of the pension footnote is to assess the likelihood that the company will be required to increase its cash contributions to the pension plan. This estimate is made by examining the funded status of the pension plan and the projected payments to retirees. For severely underfunded plans, the projected payments to retirees might not be covered by existing pension assets and projected investment returns. In this case, the company might need to divert operating cash flow from other prospective projects to cover its pension plan. Alternatively, if operating cash flows are not available, it might need to borrow to fund those payments. This can be especially troublesome as the debt service payments include interest, which increase the required pension contribution. The decline in the financial condition and ultimate bankruptcy of **General Motors** was due in large part to its inability to meet its pension and health care obligations from pension assets. The company was forced to divert much needed operating cash flow and to borrow funds to meet its cash payment obligations.

Footnote Disclosures and Profit Implications

Recall the following earlier breakdown for pension expense:

Net Pension Expense
Service cost
+ Interest cost
− *Expected* return on pension plan assets
± Amortization of deferred amounts
Net pension expense

Interest cost is the product of the PBO and the discount rate. This discount rate is set by the company. The expected dollar return on pension assets is the product of the pension plan asset balance and the expected long-run rate of return on the investment portfolio. This rate is also set by the company. Further, PBO is affected by the expected rate of wage inflation, termination and mortality rates, all of which are estimated by the company.

GAAP requires disclosure of several rates used by the company in its estimation of PBO and the related pension expense. **Delta Air Lines** discloses the following in its pension footnote:

Net Periodic Benefit Cost (Year Ended December 31)	2010	2009	2008
Weighted average discount rate — pension benefit	5.93%	6.49%	7.19%
Weighted average discount rate — other postretirement benefit	5.75%	6.46%	6.46%
Weighted average discount rate — other postemployment benefit.	5.88%	6.50%	6.95%
Weighted average expected long-term rate of return on plan assets	8.82%	8.83%	8.96%
Assumed health care cost trend rate	7.50%	8.00%	8.00%

During 2010, Delta Air Lines decreased its discount rate (used to compute the present value of its pension obligations, or PBO) by 0.56%, while leaving essentially unchanged its estimate of the expected return on plan assets. Delta also decreased its assumed health care cost trend rate by 0.50% and said it expects further declines in that rate to a level of about 5% by 2019 from its present rate of 7.5%.

Changes in these assumptions have the following general effects on pension expense and, thus, profitability. This table summarizes the effects of increases in the various rates. Decreases have the exact opposite effects.[10]

Assumption change	Probable effect on pension expense	Reason for effect
Discount rate ▲	▲	While the higher discount rate reduces the PBO, the lower PBO is multiplied by a higher rate when the company computes the interest component of pension expense. The rate effect is larger than the discount effect, resulting in increased pension expense.
Investment return ▲	▼	The dollar amount of expected return on plan assets is the product of the plan assets balance and the expected long-term rate of return. Increasing the return increases the expected return on plan assets, thus reducing pension expense.
Wage inflation ▲	▲	The expected rate of wage inflation affects future wage levels that determine expected pension payments. An increase, thus, increases PBO, which increases both the service and interest cost components of pension expense.

In the case of **Delta Air Lines**, the decrease in both the discount rate and the assumed health care cost trend rate, coupled with no change in the expected return on investments, served to decrease pension costs and increase profitability in that year. It is often the case that companies reduce the expected investment returns with a lag, but increase them without a lag, to favorably impact profitability. We must be aware of the impact of these changes in assumptions in our evaluation of company profitability.

Analysis Implications

There are two important analysis issues relating to pensions:

1. To what extent will the company's pension plans compete with investing and financing needs for the available cash flows?

2. In what ways has the company's choice of estimates affected its profitability?

Regarding the first issue, pension plan assets are the source of funds to pay benefits to retirees, and federal law (Employee Retirement Income Security Act) sets minimum standards for pension contributions. Consequently, if investment returns are insufficient, companies must make up the shortfall with additional contributions. Any such additional contributions compete for available operating cash flows with other investing and financing activities. This can be especially severe in a business downturn when operating cash flows are depressed. As debt payments are contractual, companies can be forced to postpone needed capital investment to make the contributions necessary to ensure funding of their pension plans as required by law or labor agreements. Analysts must be aware of funding requirements when projecting future cash flows.

---

[10] The effect of two hypothetical discount rates on the PBO and interest cost is seen in the following tables using the present values from an annuity of $1 for 10 and 40 years, respectively (dollar amounts are the present value factors from Appendix A; present value of an ordinary annuity, rounded to 2 decimal places).

	Discount rate	10 Years	40 Years
PBO	5%	$7.72	$17.16
	8%	6.71	11.92

As the discount rate increases, the PBO decreases. This is the discount effect. Second, the interest cost component of pension expense is computed as the PBO × Discount rate. For the four PBO amounts and related discount rates above, interest cost follows:

	Discount rate	10 Years	40 Years
Interest cost	5%	$0.39	$0.86
	8%	0.54	0.95

Interest cost increases with increases in the discount rate, regardless of the length of the liability. This is the rate effect.

Regarding the second issue, accounting for pensions requires several assumptions, including the expected return on pension investments, the expected rate of wage inflation, the discount rate used to compute the PBO, and other actuarial assumptions that are not reported in footnotes (mortality rates, for example). Each of these assumptions affects reported profit as already explained. Analysts must be aware of changes in these assumptions and their effects on profitability. An increase in reported profit that is due to an increase in the expected return on pension investments, for example, is not related to core operating activities and, further, might not be sustainable. Such changes in estimates must be considered in our evaluation of reported profitability.

BUSINESS INSIGHT | **How Pensions Confound Income Analysis**

Overfunded pension plans and boom markets can inflate income. Specifically, when the stock market is booming, pension investments realize large gains that flow to income (via reduced pension expense). Although pension plan assets do not belong to shareholders (as they are the legal entitlement of current and future retirees), the gains and losses from those plan assets are reported in income. The following graph plots the funded status of **General Electric**'s pension plans together with pension expense (revenue) that GE reported from 1998 through 2010.

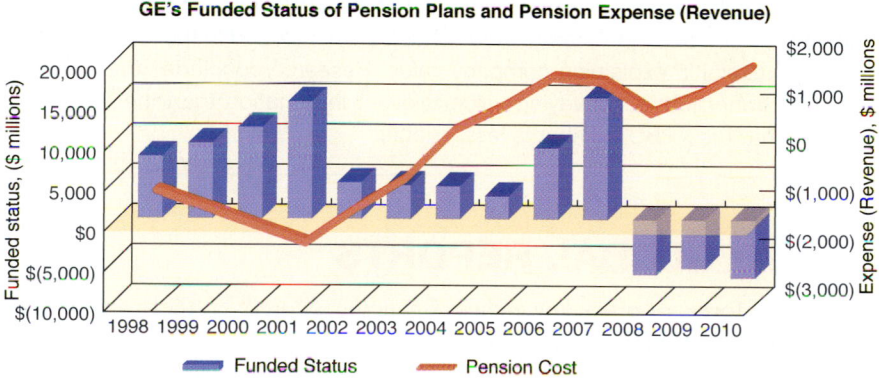

GE's Funded Status of Pension Plans and Pension Expense (Revenue)

GE's funded status has consistently been positive (indicating an overfunded plan) until the market decline of 2008. The degree of overfunding peaked in 2001 at the height of the stock market, and began to decline during the bear market of the early 2000s. GE reported pension *revenue* (not expense) during this period. In 2001, GE's reported pension *revenue* was $2,095 million (10.6% of its pretax income). Because of the plan's overfunded status, the expected return and amortization of deferred gains components of pension expense amounted to $5,288 million, far in excess of the service and interest costs of $3,193 million. In the mid to late 2000s, GE recorded pension expense (rather than revenue) as the pension plan's overfunding and expected long-term rates of return declined.

Other Post-Employment Benefits

In addition to pension benefits, many companies provide health care and insurance benefits to retired employees. These benefits are referred to as **other post-employment benefits (OPEB)**. These benefits present reporting challenges similar to pension accounting. However, companies most often provide these benefits on a "pay-as-you-go" basis and it is rare for companies to make contributions in advance for OPEB. As a result, this liability, known as the **accumulated post-employment benefit obligation (APBO)**, is largely, if not totally, unfunded. GAAP requires that the unfunded APBO liability, net of any unrecognized amounts, be reported in the balance sheet and the annual service costs and interest costs be accrued as expenses each year. This requirement is controversial for two reasons. First, future health care costs are especially difficult to estimate, so the value of the resulting APBO (the present value of the future benefits) is fraught with error. Second, these benefits are provided at the discretion of the employer and can be altered or terminated at any time. Consequently, employers argue that without a legal obligation to pay these benefits, the liability should not be reported in the balance sheet.

These other post-employment benefits can produce large liabilities. For example, **Delta Air Lines**' footnotes report a funded status for the company's health care obligation of $(2,178) million, consisting of an APBO liability of $3,298 million less health care plan investments with a market value of $1,120 million. Our analysis of cash flows related to pension obligations can be extended to other post-employment benefit obligations. For example, in addition to its pension payments, Delta Air Lines discloses that it is obligated to make health care payments to retirees totaling about $260 per year. Because health care obligations are rarely funded until payment is required (federal minimum funding standards do not apply to OPEB and there is no tax benefit to pre-funding), there are no investment returns to fund the payments. Our analysis of projected cash flows must consider this potential cash outflow in addition to that relating to pension obligations.

RESEARCH INSIGHT   Valuation of Nonpension Post-Employment Benefits

The FASB requires employers to accrue the costs of all nonpension post-employment benefits; known as *accumulated post-employment benefit obligation* (APBO). These benefits consist primarily of health care and insurance. This requirement is controversial due to concerns about the reliability of the liability estimate. Research finds that the APBO (alone) is associated with company value. However, when other pension-related variables are included in the research, the APBO liability is no longer useful in explaining company value. Research concludes that the pension-related variables do a better job at conveying value-relevant information than the APBO number alone, which implies that the APBO number is less reliable.

ANALYZING GLOBAL REPORTS

We discussed three forms of off-balance-sheet financing. Moreover, there are several differences between U.S. GAAP and IFRS on these items, which we highlight below.

Leases IFRS lease standards currently allow for operating leases, but the standards are such that it is very difficult for a lease agreement to qualify as an operating lease. IFRS standards are more principles based and so for lease accounting, there are no bright-line rules for lease classification. Instead the parties must consider the economic substance of the transaction. In addition, IFRS will classify as capital leases (labeled *financial leases*) various "arrangements" that convey the right to use an asset or compel the company to make specified payments, but that do not take the legal form of a lease. Examples include contracts where the company must make payments regardless of whether they take delivery of the contracted product or service (take-or-pay contracts) and outsourcing contracts. This will result in more capital leases under IFRS. A minor difference is that IFRS requires the separation of land and buildings for leases that involve both.

Pensions For pension accounting, there are several disclosure differences and one notable accounting difference. The accounting difference pertains to actuarial gains and losses. As discussed in Appendix 10A, U.S. GAAP permits deferral of actuarial gains and losses and then amortizes them to net income over time. A notable difference is that IFRS companies can recognize all actuarial gains and losses in comprehensive income in the year they occur. These gains and losses are not deferred, and they are *never* reported on the IFRS income statement. Many IFRS companies select this option. Turning to disclosure, one difference is that pension expense is not reported as a single item under IFRS; various components can be aggregated with other expenses. For example, interest cost can be included with other interest expenses and reported as finance expense under IFRS. A second disclosure difference is that IFRS companies do not disclose the full funded status of their pension plan on the balance sheet as U.S. GAAP requires. However, they must do so in the footnotes. These disclosure differences make it more challenging to analyze IFRS pension costs and balance sheet items. FASB and IASB continue to work toward convergence on pension accounting.

Special Purpose Entities Companies use special purpose entities (SPE) to structure projects or transactions. Under U.S. GAAP, the primary beneficiary (the party with the power to direct SPE activities and with the obligation to absorb SPE losses) is required to consolidate the SPE. At the publication of this book, the IASB has not yet addressed the issue of SPEs. Instead, IFRS focuses on the general concept of "control" to determine if the SPE is consolidated.

MODULE-END REVIEW

Following is the pension disclosure footnote from **American Airlines**' 10-K report (in millions).

Pension Obligation and Assets	2010	2009
Reconciliation of benefit obligation		
Obligation at January 1	$12,003	$10,884
Service cost	366	333
Interest cost	737	712
Actuarial (gain) loss	442	675
Plan amendments	1	—
Benefit payments	(581)	(601)
Obligation at December 31	$12,968	$12,003
Reconciliation of fair value of plan assets		
Fair value of plan assets at January 1	$ 7,051	$ 6,714
Actual return on plan assets	837	928
Employer contributions	466	10
Benefit payments	(581)	(601)
Fair value of plan assets at December 31	$ 7,773	$ 7,051
Funded status at December 31	$ (5,195)	$ (4,952)

Following is American Airlines' footnote for its pension cost as reported in its income statement (in millions).

Pension Benefits	2010	2009
Components of net periodic benefit cost		
Defined benefit plans:		
Service cost	$366	$333
Interest cost	737	712
Expected return on assets	(593)	(566)
Amortization of:		
Prior service cost	13	13
Settlement	—	—
Unrecognized net loss	154	145
Net periodic benefit cost for defined benefit plans	677	637
Defined contribution plans	168	168
	$845	$805

Required

1. In general, what factors impact a company's pension benefit obligation during a period?
2. In general, what factors impact a company's pension plan investments during a period?
3. What amount is reported on the balance sheet relating to the American Airlines pension plan?
4. How does the expected return on plan assets affect pension cost?
5. How does American Airlines' expected return on plan assets compare with its actual return (in $s) for 2010?
6. How much net pension expense is reflected in American Airlines' 2010 income statement?
7. Assess American Airlines' ability to meet payment obligations to retirees.

The solution is on page 10-47.

APPENDIX 10A: Amortization Component of Pension Expense

One of the more difficult aspects of pension accounting relates to the issue of what is recognized on-balance-sheet and what is disclosed in the footnotes off-balance-sheet. This is an important distinction, and the FASB is moving toward more on-balance-sheet recognition and less off-balance-sheet disclosure. The FASB is considering whether to eliminate deferred gains and losses, and to require recognition in the income statement of *all* changes to pension assets and liabilities. Until this standard is enacted, deferred gains and losses will only impact reported pension expense via their amortization (the fourth component of pension expense described earlier in this module).

There are three sources of *unrecognized gains and losses*:

1. The difference between actual and expected return on pension investments.

2. Changes in actuarial assumptions such as expected wage inflation, termination and mortality rates, and the discount rate used to compute the present value of the projected benefit obligation.

3. Amendments to the pension plan to provide employees with additional benefits (called **prior service costs**).

Accounting for gains and losses resulting from these three sources is the same; specifically:

■ Balance sheets report the net pension asset (overfunded status) or liability (underfunded status) irrespective of the magnitude of deferred gains and losses; that is, based solely on the relative balances of the pension assets and PBO accounts.

■ Cumulative unrecognized gains and losses from all sources are recorded in one account, called deferred gains and losses, which is only disclosed in the footnotes, not on-balance-sheet.

■ When the balance in the deferred gains and losses account exceeds prescribed levels, companies transfer a portion of the deferred gain or loss onto the balance sheet, with a matching expense on the income statement. This is the amortization process described in the text.

Recall that a company reports the *estimated* return on pension investments as a component (reduction) of pension expense. The pension assets, however, increase (decrease) by the *actual* return (loss). The difference between the two returns is referred to as a deferred (unrecognized) gain or loss. To illustrate, let's assume that the pension plan is underfunded at the beginning of the year by $200, with pension assets of $800, a PBO of $1,000, and no deferred gains or losses. Now, let's assume that actual returns for the year of $100 exceed the long-term expected return of $70. We can illustrate the accounting for the deferred gain as follows:

		On Financial Statements			Footnotes	
Year 1	**Funded Status (Liabilities)**	**Earned Capital**	**Accumulated Other Comprehensive Income (AOCI)**	**Income Statement**	**Pension Assets**	**PBO**
Balance, Jan. 1.......	$200		$ 0	$ 0	$800	$1,000
Return..............	(100)	$70 (Retained Earnings) 30 (AOCI)	30	70	100	
Balance, Dec. 31	$100	$70 (Retained Earnings) 30 (AOCI)	$30	$70	$900	$1,000

The balance sheet at the beginning of the year reports the funded status of the pension plan as a $200 liability, reflecting the underfunded status of the pension plan. Neither the $800 pension asset account, nor the $1,000 PBO appear on-balance-sheet. Instead, their balances are only disclosed in a pension footnote.

During the year, pension assets (off-balance-sheet) increase by the actual return of $100 with no change in the PBO, thus decreasing the pension liability (negative funded status) by $100. The pension expense on the income statement, however, only reflects the expected return of $70, and retained earnings increase by that amount. The remaining $30 is recognized in accumulated other comprehensive income (AOCI), a component of earned capital.

These deferred gains and losses do not affect reported profit until they exceed prescribed limits, after which the excess is gradually recognized in income.[11] For example, assume that in the following year, $5 of the $30 deferred gain is amortized (recognized on the income statement as expense, which flows to retained earnings on the balance sheet). This amortization would result in the following effects:

			On Financial Statements		Footnotes	
Year 2	**Funded Status (Liabilities)**	**Earned Capital**	**Accumulated Other Comprehensive Income (AOCI)**	**Income Statement**	**Pension Assets**	**PBO**
Balance, Jan. 1.......	$100	$70 (Retained Earnings) 30 (AOCI)	$30	$ 0	$900	$1,000
Amortization.........		$ 5 (Retained Earnings)	(5)	5		
Balance, Dec. 31	$100	$75 (Retained Earnings) 25 (AOCI)	$25	$ 5	$900	$1,000

The deferred gain is reduced by $5 and is now recognized in reported income as a reduction of pension expense. (This amortization is the fourth item in the Net Pension Expense computation table from earlier in this module.) This is the only change, as the pension assets still report a balance of $900 and the PBO reports a balance of $1,000, for a funded status of $(100) that is reported as a liability on the balance sheet.

In addition to the difference between actual and expected gains (losses) on pension assets, the deferred gains (losses) account includes increases or decreases in the PBO balance that result from changes in assumptions used to compute it, namely, the expected rate of wage inflation, termination and mortality rates for employees, and changes in the discount rate used to compute the present value of the pension obligations. Some of these can be offsetting, and all accumulate in the same deferred gains (losses) account. Justification for off-balance-sheet treatment of these items was the expectation that their offsetting nature would combine to keep the magnitude of deferred gains (losses) small. It is only in relatively extreme circumstances that this account becomes large enough to warrant amortization and, consequently, on-balance-sheet recognition. Further, the amortization portion of reported pension expense is usually small.

APPENDIX 10B: Special Purpose Entities (SPEs)

Special purpose entities (SPEs) allow companies to structure projects or transactions with a number of financial advantages. SPEs have long been used and are an integral part of corporate finance. The SPE concept is illustrated by the following graphic that summarizes information taken from **Ford**'s 2010 10-K relating to the SPE structure it uses to securitize the receivables of Ford Credit (its financing subsidiary):

L03 Explain and interpret the accounting for special purpose entities (SPEs).

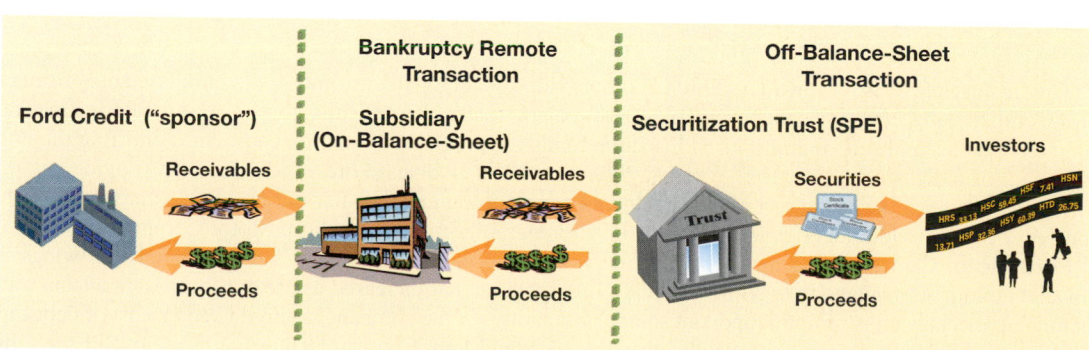

[11] The upper (lower) bound on the deferred gains (losses) account is 10% of the PBO or Plan Asset account balance, whichever is greater, at the beginning of the year. Once this limit is exceeded, the excess is amortized until the account balance is below that threshold, irrespective of whether such reduction results from amortization, or changes in the PBO or Pension Asset accounts (from changes in actuarial assumptions, company contributions, or positive investment returns).

This graphic is typical of many SPEs and has the following characteristics of all SPEs:

- A sponsoring company (here, Ford Credit) forms a subsidiary that is capitalized entirely with equity; this creates a *bankruptcy remote* structure. This means that even if Ford Credit becomes bankrupt, neither it nor its creditors will be able to access the subsidiary's assets; this reduces the risk for subsequent investors.
- The subsidiary purchases assets from the sponsoring company and sells them to a securitization (off-balance-sheet) trust (the SPE), which purchases the assets using borrowed funds (here, the SPE purchases receivables from Ford Credit's subsidiary using cash from investors).
- Cash flows from the acquired assets are used by the SPE to repay its debt (here, the SPE collects receivables and uses the funds to repay any borrowings).

The sponsoring company benefits in two ways. First, SPEs create direct economic benefits by speeding up receipt of the company's operating cash flows and by mitigating certain types of risk. Second, SPEs create indirect economic benefits by providing financial reporting benefits and alternatives. These indirect benefits derive from having assets, and their related debt, moved off-balance-sheet. Also, the SPE owns the sponsoring company's former assets. Thus, the sponsoring company enjoys an improved asset turnover ratio (assets are typically less in the denominator of the turnover ratio) and an improved financial leverage ratio (liabilities are less in the numerator of the liabilities-to-equity ratio).

Applying SPEs as Financing Tools

This section describes two common means of using SPEs as financing tools.

Asset Securitization

Consumer finance companies, retailers, and financial subsidiaries of manufacturing companies commonly use SPEs to securitize (sell) their financial assets. **Ford Credit**, the finance subsidiary of **Ford Motor Company**, provides a common example as illustrated in the MD&A of Ford's 2010 10-K report.

> **Securitization** In 2005 and 2006, the credit ratings assigned to Ford Credit were lowered to below investment grade, which increased its unsecured borrowing costs and restricted its access to the unsecured debt markets. In response, Ford Credit increased its use of securitization transactions (including other structured financings) and other sources of funding. In 2010, although Ford Credit experienced several credit rating upgrades and its credit spreads narrowed considerably, its credit ratings are still below investment grade. Ford Credit's higher credit ratings have provided it more economical access to the unsecured debt markets, but it is still utilizing asset-backed securitization transactions for a substantial amount of its funding. . .
>
> In a securitization transaction, the securitized assets are generally held by a bankruptcy-remote special purpose entity ("SPE") in order to isolate the securitized assets from the claims of Ford Credit's other creditors and ensure that the cash flows on the securitized assets are available for the benefit of securitization investors. As a result, payments to securitization investors are based on the creditworthiness of the securitized assets and any enhancements, and not on Ford Credit's creditworthiness. Senior asset-backed securities issued by the SPEs generally receive the highest short-term credit ratings and among the highest long-term credit ratings from the rating agencies that rate them.

Ford Credit's use of SPEs is typical. As Ford Credit provides financing to customers who purchase autos from Ford Motor Company, it accumulates the receivables on its balance sheet. Periodically, through a subsidiary, it packages certain receivables and sells them to its SPE, which funds the purchase by selling certificates entitling the holder to a portion of the cash receipts from eventual collection of receivables. Ford Credit does not provide any other form of protection to the outside certificate holders (its footnote indicates that the receivables are sold "without recourse," meaning without collection rights against Ford Credit or its parent, Ford Motor Company).

Ford Motor Company's credit ratings have declined in recent years, thus making its unsecured borrowings more costly and limiting its availability to borrowed funds. In response, it has increased its use of SPEs as a financing source. This funding mechanism is now an important source of liquidity for the company, as Ford Credit's cost of debt capital is substantially less, and exhibits less volatility, than that for Ford Motor Company. Thus, Ford's use of SPEs as a funding source provides necessary liquidity and also provides capital at a substantially lower interest rate. Due to the SPE's limited scope of operations, and its isolation from the general business risk of the parent company, the SPE's lenders face lower risk of default and can, therefore, charge a comparatively lower rate of interest on money they lend to the SPE.

Project and Real Estate Financing

Another common use of SPEs is to finance construction projects. For example, a sponsoring company desires to construct a manufacturing plant. It establishes an SPE and executes a contract with the SPE to build the plant and to later purchase output from the plant. The SPE uses the contract, and the newly constructed manufacturing plant assets, to collateralize debt that it issues to finance the plant's construction. The sponsoring company obtains the benefits of the plant, but does not recognize either the PPE asset or the related liability on its balance sheet. The sponsoring company has commitments with the SPE, labeled executory contracts, but GAAP currently does not require such contracts be recognized in the balance sheet, nor does it even require footnote disclosure of these contracts.

Clothing retailers such as **Gap** and **Abercrombie & Fitch** use these types of executory contracts involving outside manufacturers. The manufacturing assets, and related liabilities, are reported on the balance sheet of the SPE and not of the company itself.

A slight variation is to add leasing to this transaction. To illustrate, assume a company desires to construct an office building. It establishes an SPE to construct and finance the building and then leases the building back from the SPE under an operating lease. As we explained earlier in this module, if the lease is structured as an operating lease, neither the lease asset nor the lease obligation is reported on the company's balance sheet. Thus, the company obtains the use and benefit of the building without recording either the building or the related debt on its balance sheet.

Reporting of SPEs

Special purpose entities, such as those that Ford uses to securitize its loan and lease assets, must be consolidated by whichever company has the power to direct the activities of the SPE and the right to receive its benefits (or absorb the losses). As we discuss in Module 9, for companies that issue common stock, consolidation means that the balance sheet and income statement of the SPE are reported together with that of the parent company. The consolidation of SPEs is no different and their financial statements must be combined with those of the sponsoring company (Ford Credit in this case).

The effect of consolidation of SPEs is to report both the loan and lease receivables on Ford's consolidated balance sheet as well as the liabilities of the SPE. Similarly, the loan and lease income is reported in Ford's income statement together with the SPE's expenses, including interest expense on borrowed funds. As a result, the securitization process is fully reflected in Ford's financial statements. Further, companies are required to provide extensive disclosures relating to the magnitude of the assets securitized and the effects (and risks) on their liquidity of reliable access to securitization credit markets.

> **IFRS INSIGHT** **Consolidation of SPEs under IFRS**
>
> Under both U.S. GAAP and IFRS, SPEs are consolidated based on the transfer of risks and rewards. But unlike GAAP's more rules-based orientation, IFRS requires a more conceptual analysis of risks and rewards. This leads to consolidation of more special purpose entities under IFRS as compared to GAAP. The FASB and the IASB are working toward convergence on this standard.

Analysis Implications of SPEs

Despite that SPEs are consolidated in the financial statements of the sponsoring company, the securitization process continues to provide a lower-cost financing source to companies by reducing credit risk for the lenders. Accordingly, SPEs will continue to be part of the business landscape. As such, there are at least two analysis implications related to SPEs:

- **Cost of capital**. As discussed, SPEs reduce business risk and bankruptcy risk for their lenders. Consequently, the sponsoring company is able to obtain capital at a lower cost. Ford Motor Company (a manufacturer), for example, has witnessed a reduction in its credit ratings and a consequent increase in its cost of borrowed funds. Ordinarily, its negative credit rating would be ascribed to its subsidiaries as well, including its finance subsidiary. Using SPEs, however, the finance subsidiary, Ford Credit, is able to obtain financing at lower interest rates, which allows it to pass along that lower cost in the form of lower interest rates on auto and other loans to its customers. Without that financing source, Ford Credit would be less competitive in the marketplace vis-à-vis other, financially stronger, financial institutions.

- **Liquidity**. Financial institutions, and finance subsidiaries of manufacturing companies, rely on a business model of generating a high volume of loans, each of which carries a relatively small profit (spread of the interest rate over the cost of the funds). If they were forced to hold all of those loans on their own balance sheets, they would eventually need to raise costly equity capital to balance the increase in debt financing. That would also serve to reduce their competitiveness in the marketplace. These companies must, therefore, be able to package loans for sale, a crucial source of liquidity.

Given the importance of the cash flows contributed by its Ford Credit financing subsidiary to Ford Motor Company, analysts would be concerned about the welfare of the overall entity were there indications that its SPE financing sources would no longer be available (say, if further accounting standards limited Ford's ability to remove these loans from its consolidated balance sheet and record their transfer to the SPE as a sale). Analysts would also be concerned if the credit markets no longer favored this SPE structure as a financing mechanism (say, if the presumed bankruptcy protection of the SPEs was ultimately proven to be false following the bankruptcy of the sponsoring company and the consequent bankruptcy of an SPE that it sponsored). Neither of these events has occurred, and lenders rely on legal opinions that SPEs are "bankruptcy remote." Analysts must always assess these risks when assessing the financial strength of companies that rely on the SPE financial structure.

APPENDIX 10C: Lease Capitalization Using a Calculator and Present Value Tables

This Appendix identifies the keystrokes to compute both the present value of projected operating lease payments and the imputed discount rate using two popular financial calculators: **Hewlett-Packard 10bII** and **Texas Instruments BA II Plus**. It also computes the present value of projected lease payments using present value tables.

Hewlett-Packard 10bII: Present value of projected operating lease payments

Following are the keystrokes to compute the present value of the Delta Air Lines projected lease payments. This approach utilizes the same computational steps as our illustrations.

Enter #	Key[a]	
1	P/YR	Enter the number of periods per year
0	CF$_j$	Enter the cash flow in year 0 (current year)
1,420	CF$_j$	Enter the cash flow in year 1
1,351	CF$_j$	Enter the cash flow in year 2
1,320	CF$_j$	Enter the cash flow in year 3
1,263	CF$_j$	Enter the cash flow in year 4
1,169	CF$_j$	Enter the cash flow in year 5 (and assumed thereafter)
8	N$_j$	Enter the number of years the year 5 cash flow is repeated
240	CF$_j$	Enter the cash flow in final partial year ($1,169 × 0.205 years)
14.31	I/YR	Enter the annual discount rate
	NPV	Press **NPV** button to get present value ($7,085)

[a] To enter a number, type the number and then press the corresponding key; for example, to enter P/YR, type "1" and then press **P/YR**.

Hewlett-Packard 10bII: Imputed discount rate

This example computes the imputed discount rate given the capitalized lease disclosures in the lease footnote; we again use Delta Air Lines.

Enter #	Key[a]	
1	P/YR	Enter the number of periods per year
−738[a]	CF$_j$	Enter the cash flow in year 0 (current year)
214	CF$_j$	Enter the cash flow in year 1
193	CF$_j$	Enter the cash flow in year 2
160	CF$_j$	Enter the cash flow in year 3
130	CF$_j$	Enter the cash flow in year 4
124	CF$_j$	Enter the cash flow in year 5 (and assumed thereafter)
4	N$_j$	Enter the number of years the year 5 cash flow is repeated
32	CF$_j$	Enter the cash flow in final partial year ($124 × 0.258 years)
	IRR	Press **IRR** button to get implicit discount rate (14.31%)

[a] To enter a negative number, type in the absolute value of that number and then press +/− button; for example, to enter the initial cash flow in year 0, enter "738", press +/−, and then press **CF$_j$**.

Texas Instruments BA II Plus: Present value of projected operating lease payments

Following are the keystrokes to compute the present value of the Delta Air Lines projected lease payments. This approach utilizes the same computational steps as our illustrations.

Key	Enter #[a]	
FORMAT	0	Press the **FORMAT** button and enter decimal places desired
CF	0	Enter the cash flow in year 0 (**CF$_O$**)
↓	1,420	Enter the cash flow in year 1 (**CO1**)
↓		Frequency (**FO1**) should be pre-set at "1", so nothing need be entered
↓	1,351	Enter the cash flow in year 2 (**CO2**)
↓		Frequency (**FO2**) should be pre-set at "1"
↓	1,320	Enter the cash flow in year 3 (**CO3**)
↓		Frequency (**FO3**) should be pre-set at "1"
↓	1,263	Enter the cash flow in year 4 (**CO4**)
↓		Frequency (**FO4**) should be pre-set at "1"
↓	1,169	Enter the cash flow in year 5 (**CO5**) and assumed thereafter
↓	8	Enter the number of years the year 5 cash flow is repeated (**FO5**)
↓	240	Enter the cash flow in final partial year (1,169 × 0.205 years) (**CO6**)
↓		Frequency (**FO6**) should be pre-set at "1"
NPV	14.31	Press **NPV** button, the pre-set discount rate should say "0"; enter "14.31" the discount rate
↓, **CPT**	7,085	Press ↓ button and then press **CPT** to get present value

[a] After entering in a number from this column, press **ENTER**.

Texas Instruments BA II Plus: Imputed discount rate

Following are the keystrokes to compute the present value of the Delta Air Lines projected lease payments. This approach utilizes the same computational steps as our illustrations.

Key	Enter [a]	
CF	−738[b]	Enter the cash flow in year 0 (CF$_O$)
↓	214	Enter the cash flow in year 1 (CO1)
↓		Frequency (FO1) should be pre-set at "1"
↓	193	Enter the cash flow in year 2 (CO2)
↓		Frequency (FO2) should be pre-set at "1"
↓	160	Enter the cash flow in year 3 (CO3)
↓		Frequency (FO3) should be pre-set at "1"
↓	130	Enter the cash flow in year 4 (CO4)
↓		Frequency (FO4) should be pre-set at "1"
↓	124	Enter the cash flow in year 5 and assumed thereafter (CO5)
↓	4	Enter the number of years the year 5 cash flow is repeated (FO5)
↓	32	Enter the cash flow in final partial year (CO6)
↓		Frequency (FO6) should be pre-set at "1"
IRR		Press **IRR** button, the pre-set IRR should say "0"
↓ , CPT		Press ↓ button and then press **CPT** to get implicit discount rate

[a] After typing in a number from this column, press **ENTER**.

[b] To enter a negative number, type in the absolute value of that number and then press +/− button; for example, to enter the initial cash flow in year 0, press **CF**, enter "738", press +/−, and then press **ENTER**.

Lease Capitalization Using Present Value Tables

Present value tables list the factors for selected interest rates and discount periods (often in whole numbers). To compute the present value of the operating lease payments using those tables (see Appendix A near the end of this book), we must first round the remaining lease term (7.205 for Delta) to the nearest whole year (7), and round the discount rate (14.31% for Delta) to its nearest whole interest rate (14%). After that, computation of the present value of future operating lease payments is identical to the spreadsheet method and is shown below. We see that the present value of each projected lease payment for Years 1 through 5 is computed using the present value factor for that particular year (taken from tables similar to Appendix A, Table 1, "Present Value of Single Amount") using a discount rate of 14%. To compute the present value of the lease payments remaining after Year 5, we again assume that lease payments continue at the Year 5 amount for the remainder of the lease term. Those payments represent an annuity, $672 million for 7 years (7.205 rounded to 7), that is discounted at 14% (taken from tables similar to Appendix A, Table 2, "Present Value of Ordinary Annuity"), which is then discounted back five more years to the present.

Year ($ millions)	Operating Lease Payment	Discount Factor (*i* = 0.14)	Present Value
1.................	$1,420	0.87719	$1,246
2.................	1,351	0.76947	1,040
3.................	1,320	0.67497	891
4.................	1,263	0.59208	748
5.................	1,169	0.51937	607
>5................	8,423 [$1,169 for ~7.205 years]	4.28830 × 0.51937	2,604
			$7,136
Remaining life........	$8,423/$1,169 = 7.205 years, rounded to 7 years.		

Regardless of the method used, the computed amount is the present value of future operating lease payments. That value is $7,088 million using the spreadsheet method, $7,085 million using a calculator, and $7,136 million using present value tables.

GUIDANCE ANSWERS . . . ANALYSIS DECISION

You Are the Division President Lease terms that are not advantageous to your company but are structured merely to achieve off-balance-sheet financing can destroy shareholder value. Long-term shareholder value is created by managing your operation well, including negotiating leases with acceptable terms. Lease footnote disclosures also provide sufficient information for skilled analysts to undo the operating lease treatment. This means that you can end up with de facto capitalization of a lease with lease terms that are not in the best interests of your company and with few benefits from off-balance-sheet financing. There is also the potential for lost credibility with stakeholders.

Superscript $^{A\,(B,\,C)}$ denotes assignments based on Appendix 10A (B, C).

DISCUSSION QUESTIONS

Q10-1. What are the financial reporting differences between an operating lease and a capital lease? Explain.

Q10-2. Are footnote disclosures sufficient to overcome nonrecognition on the balance sheet of assets and related liabilities for operating leases? Explain.

Q10-3. Is the expense of a lease over its entire life the same whether or not it is capitalized? Explain.

Q10-4. What are the economic and accounting differences between a defined contribution plan and a defined benefit plan?

Q10-5. Under what circumstances will a company report a net pension asset? A net pension liability?

Q10-6. What are the components of pension expense that are reported in the income statement?

Q10-7. What effect does the use of expected returns on pension investments and the deferral of unexpected gains and losses on those investments have on income?

Q10-8. What is a special purpose entity (SPE)? Provide an example of the use of an SPE as a financing vehicle.

Q10-9. What effect does consolidating SPEs have on both accounting for SPEs and the balance sheets of companies that sponsor them?

Assignments with the ✅ in the margin are available in an online homework system.
See the Preface of the book for details.

MINI EXERCISES

M10-10. Analyzing and Interpreting Lease Footnote Disclosures   (LO1)

The GAP, Inc., discloses the following schedule to its 2011 10-K report relating to its leasing activities.

THE GAP, INC.
(GPS)

> The aggregate minimum noncancelable annual lease payments under leases in effect on January 29, 2011, are as follows:
>
> | Fiscal Year ($ millions) | |
> | --- | --- |
> | 2011 . . . . | $ 997 |
> | 2012 . . . . | 841 |
> | 2013 . . . . | 710 |
> | 2014 . . . . | 602 |
> | 2015 . . . . | 483 |
> | Thereafter . . . . | 1,483 |
> | Total minimum lease commitments . . . . . | $5,116 |

a. Compute the present value of GAP's operating leases using a 6% discount rate and round the remaining lease term to the nearest whole year.

b. What types of adjustments might we consider to GAP's balance sheet and income statement for analysis purposes?

M10-11. Analyzing and Capitalizing Operating Lease Payments Disclosed in Footnotes   (LO1)

Costco Wholesale Corporation discloses the following in footnotes to its 10-K report relating to its leasing activities.

COSTCO CORP.
(COST)

> Future minimum payments . . . during the next five fiscal years and thereafter under non-cancelable leases with terms of at least one year, at the end of 2010, were as follows ($ millions):
>
> | | |
> | --- | --- |
> | 2011 . . . . | $ 162 |
> | 2012 . . . . | 157 |
> | 2013 . . . . | 155 |
> | 2014 . . . . | 148 |
> | 2015 . . . . | 134 |
> | Thereafter . . . . | 1,572 |
> | Total minimum payments . . . . | $2,328 |

Operating leases are not reflected on-balance-sheet. In our analysis of a company, we often capitalize these operating leases, that is, add the present value of the future operating lease payments to both the reported assets and liabilities.

a. Compute the present value of Costco's operating lease payments assuming a 6% discount rate and round the remaining lease term to the nearest whole year.

b. What effect does capitalization of operating leases have on Costco's total liabilities and total assets (it reported total liabilities and total assets of $12,885 million and $23,815 million, respectively)?

M10-12. Analyzing and Interpreting Pension Disclosures—Expenses and Returns   (LO2)

StanleyBlack & Decker discloses the following pension footnote in its 10-K report.

STANLEYBLACK &
DECKER
(SWK)

($ millions)	2010
Service cost	$ 18.1
Interest cost	61.2
Expected return on plan assets	(52.5)
Amortization of prior service cost	1.0
Transition amount amortization	—
Actuarial loss amortization	2.0
Settlement/curtailment loss (gain)	(9.1)
Net periodic pension expense	$ 20.7

a. How much pension expense does StanleyBlack & Decker report in its 2010 income statement?

b. Explain, in general, how expected return on plan assets affects reported pension expense. How did expected return affect StanleyBlack & Decker's 2010 pension expense?

c. Explain use of the word "expected" as it relates to pension plan assets.

M10-13. Analyzing and Interpreting Pension Disclosures—PBO and Funded Status   (LO2)

YUM! BRANDS, INC.
(YUM)

YUM! Brands, Inc., discloses the following pension footnote in its 10-K report.

Pension Benefit Obligation ($ millions)	2010	2009
Change in benefit obligation		
Benefit obligation at beginning of year	$1,010	$ 923
Service cost	25	26
Interest cost	62	58
Participant contributions	—	—
Plan amendments	—	1
Curtailment gain	(2)	(9)
Settlement loss	1	2
Special termination benefits	1	4
Exchange rate changes	—	—
Benefits paid	(57)	(47)
Settlement payments	(9)	(10)
Actuarial (gain) loss	77	62
Benefit obligation at end of year	$1,108	$1,010

a. Explain the terms "service cost" and "interest cost."

b. How do actuarial losses arise?

c. The fair market value of YUM!'s pension assets is $907 million as of 2010. What is the funded status of the plan, and how will this be reflected on YUM!'s balance sheet?

M10-14. Analyzing and Interpreting Pension Disclosures—Plan Assets and Cash Flow   (LO2)

YUM! BRANDS, INC.
(YUM)

YUM! Brands, Inc., discloses the following pension footnote in its 10-K report.

Pension Plan Assets ($ millions)	2010	2009
Fair value of plan assets at beginning of year	$835	$513
Actual return on plan assets	108	132
Employer contributions	35	252
Participant contributions	—	—
Settlement payments	(9)	(10)
Benefits paid	(57)	(47)
Exchange rate changes	—	—
Administrative expenses	(5)	(5)
Fair value of plan assets at end of year	$907	$835

a. How does the "actual return on plan assets" of $108 million affect YUM!'s reported profits for 2010?

b.   What are the cash flow implications of the pension plan for YUM! in 2010?

c.   YUM!'s pension plan paid out $57 million in benefits during 2010. Where else is this payment reflected?

M10-15. Analyzing and Interpreting Retirement Benefit Footnote   (LO2)

Abercrombie & Fitch discloses the following footnote relating to its retirement plans in its 2010 10-K report.

> **RETIREMENT BENEFITS**   The Company maintains the Abercrombie & Fitch Co. Savings & Retirement Plan, a qualified plan. All U.S. associates are eligible to participate in this plan if they are at least 21 years of age and have completed a year of employment with 1,000 or more hours of service. In addition, the Company maintains the Abercrombie & Fitch Nonqualified Savings and Supplemental Retirement, composed of two sub-plans (Plan I and Plan II). Plan I contains contributions made through December 31, 2004, while Plan II contains contributions made on and after January 1, 2005. Participation in this plan is based on service and compensation. The Company's contributions are based on a percentage of associates' eligible annual compensation. The cost of the Company's contributions to these plans was $19.4 million in Fiscal 2010, $17.8 million in Fiscal 2009 and $24.7 million in Fiscal 2008.

a.   Does Abercrombie have a defined contribution or defined benefit pension plan? Explain.

b.   How does Abercrombie account for its contributions to its retirement plan?

c.   How does Abercrombie report its obligation for its retirement plan on the balance sheet?

M10-16. Analyzing and Interpreting Lease Disclosure   (LO1)

Dow Chemical Company provided the following footnote in its 2010 10-K report relating to operating leases.

> **Leased Property**   The Company routinely leases premises for use as sales and administrative offices, warehouses and tanks for product storage, motor vehicles, railcars, computers, office machines, and equipment under operating leases. In addition, the Company leases aircraft in the United States. At the termination of the leases, the Company has the option to purchase certain leased equipment and buildings based on a fair market value determination. In 2009, the Company purchased a previously leased ethylene plant in Canada for $713 million. Rental expenses under operating leases, net of sublease rental income, were $404 million in 2010, $459 million in 2009, and $439 million in 2008. Future minimum rental payments under operating leases with remaining noncancelable terms in excess of one year are as follows:

Minimum Operating Lease Commitments (in millions)	December 31, 2010
2011	$ 202
2012	163
2013	149
2014	126
2015	115
2016 and thereafter	1,796
Total	$2,551

Required

a.   Dow describes all of its leases as "operating." What is the significance of this designation?

b.   How might we treat these operating leases in our analysis of the company?

M10-17. Analyzing and Interpreting Disclosure on Contract Manufacturers   (LO3)

Nike reports the following information relating to its manufacturing activities in footnotes to its fiscal 2010 10-K report for the year ended May 31, 2011.

Manufacturing Virtually all of our footwear is produced by factories we contract with outside of the United States. In fiscal 2010, contract factories in Vietnam, China, Indonesia, Thailand, and India manufactured approximately 37%, 34%, 23%, 2% and 1% of total NIKE Brand footwear, respectively. We also have manufacturing agreements with independent factories in Argentina, Brazil, India, and Mexico to manufacture footwear for sale primarily within those countries. The largest single footwear factory that we have contracted with accounted for approximately 5% of total fiscal 2010 footwear production. Almost all of NIKE Brand apparel is manufactured outside of the United States by independent contract manufacturers located in 33 countries. Most of this apparel production occurred in China, Thailand, Indonesia, Malaysia, Vietnam, Sri Lanka, Turkey, Cambodia, El Salvador, Mexico, and Taiwan. The largest single apparel factory that we have contracted with accounted for approximately 7% of total fiscal 2010 apparel production.

a. What effect does the use of contract manufacturers have on Nike's balance sheet?
b. How does Nike's use of contract manufacturers affect Nike's return on net operating assets (RNOA) and its components, net operating profit margin (NOPM) and net operating asset turnover (NOAT)? Explain.
c. Nike executes agreements with its contract manufacturers to purchase their output. How are such "executory contracts" reported under GAAP? Does your answer suggest a possible motivation for the use of contract manufacturing?

M10-18. Analyzing and Interpreting Pension Plan Benefit Footnotes (LO2)

LOCKHEED MARTIN CORP. (LMT)

Lockheed Martin Corporation discloses the following funded status for its defined benefit pension plans in its 10-K report.

Defined Benefit Pension Plans (In millions)	2010	2009
Unfunded status of the plans	$(10,428)	$(10,663)

Lockheed contributed $2,240 million to its pension plan assets in 2010, up from $1,482 million in the prior year. The company also reports that it is obligated for the following expected payments to retirees in the next five years.

(In millions)	Qualified Pension Benefits
2011	$ 1,670
2012	1,740
2013	1,810
2014	1,900
2015	1,990
Years 2016–2020	11,580

a. How is this funded status reported in Lockheed's balance sheet under current GAAP?
b. How should we interpret this funded status in our analysis of the company?
c. What likely effect would a substantial decline in the financial markets have on Lockheed's contribution to its pension plans? Explain.

EXERCISES

E10-19. Analyzing and Interpreting Leasing Footnote (LO1)

LOWE'S COMPANIES (LOW)

Lowe's Companies, Inc., reports the following footnote relating to its leased facilities in its fiscal 2010 10-K report for the year ended January 28, 2011.

The Company leases facilities and land for certain facilities under agreements with original terms generally of 20 years. . . . The future minimum rental payments required under operating leases and capitalized lease obligations having initial or remaining noncancelable lease terms in excess of one year are summarized as follows:

(In millions)	Operating Leases	Capitalized Lease Obligations	Total
2011	$ 418	$ 68	$ 486
2012	416	69	485
2013	410	69	479
2014	399	64	463
2015	392	54	446
Later years	3,973	302	4,275
Total minimum lease payments	$6,008	$626	$6,634
Less amount representing interest.		(273)	
Present value of minimum lease payments		353	
Less current maturities.		(35)	
Present value of minimum lease payments, less current maturities.		$318	

a. Using your financial calculator or Excel spreadsheet, confirm that Lowe's capitalized its capital leases using a rate of 12.2%.

b. What effect does the failure to capitalize operating leases have on Lowe's balance sheet? Over the life of the lease, what effect does this classification have on net income?

c. Compute the present value of these operating leases using a discount rate of 12% and round the remaining lease term to the nearest whole year. How might we use this information in our analysis of the company?

E10-20. Analyzing and Interpreting Footnote on Operating and Capital Leases   (LO1)
Verizon Communications, Inc., provides the following footnote relating to leasing activities in its 10-K report.

VERIZON
COMMUNICATIONS,
INC.
(VZ)

The aggregate minimum rental commitments under noncancelable leases for the periods shown at December 31, 2010, are as follows:

Years (dollars in millions)	Capital Leases	Operating Leases
2011	$ 97	$ 1,898
2012	74	1,720
2013	70	1,471
2014	54	1,255
2015	42	1,012
Thereafter	81	5,277
Total minimum rental commitments	418	$12,633
Less interest and executory costs	86	
Present value of minimum lease payments	332	
Less current installments	75	
Long-term obligation at December 31, 2010 . . .	**$257**	

a. Using your financial calculator or Excel spreadsheet, confirm that Verizon capitalized its capital leases using a rate of 7.4%.

b. What effect does the failure to capitalize operating leases have on Verizon's balance sheet? Over the life of its leases, what effect does this lease classification have on net income?

c. Compute the present value of Verizon's operating leases, assuming a 7.4% discount rate and rounding the remaining lease life to three decimal places. How might we use this additional information in our analysis of the company?

E10-21. Analyzing, Interpreting and Capitalizing Operating Leases **(LO1)**

STAPLES, INC.
(SPLS)

Staples, Inc., reports the following footnote relating to its capital and operating leases in its 10-K report for the fiscal year ended January 29, 2011 ($ thousands).

Future minimum lease commitments due for retail and support facilities (including lease commitments for 76 retail stores not yet opened at January 29, 2011) and equipment leases under noncancelable operating leases are as follows (in thousands):

Year	Total
2011	$ 886,495
2012	798,958
2013	699,625
2014	594,819
2015	497,833
Thereafter	1,499,789
	$4,977,519

a. What dollar adjustment(s) might we consider to Staples' balance sheet and income statement given this information and assuming that Staples intermediate-term borrowing rate is 8% and rounding the remaining lease life to the nearest whole year? Explain.

b. Would the adjustment from part *a* make a substantial difference to Staples' total liabilities? (Staples reported total assets of nearly $14 billion and total liabilities of nearly $7 billion for 2011.)

E10-22. Analyzing, Interpreting and Capitalizing Operating Leases **(LO1)**

YUM! BRANDS, INC.
(YUM)

YUM! Brands, Inc., reports the following footnote relating to its capital and operating leases in its 2010 10-K report ($ millions).

Future minimum commitments . . . under non-cancelable leases are set forth below. At December 25, 2010, and December 26, 2009, the present value of minimum payments under capital leases was $236 million and $249 million, respectively.

Commitments ($ millions)	Capital	Operating
2011	$ 26	$ 550
2012	63	514
2013	23	483
2014	23	447
2015	23	405
Thereafter	222	2,605
	$380	$5,004

a. Confirm that the implicit rate on YUM!'s capital leases is 7.63%. Using a 7.63% discount rate, compute the present value of YUM!'s operating leases and rounding the remaining lease life to three decimal places. Describe the adjustments we might consider to YUM!'s balance sheet and income statement using that information.

b. YUM! reported total liabilities of $6,647 million for 2010. Would the adjustment from part *a* make a substantial difference to YUM!'s total liabilities? Explain.

E10-23. Analyzing, Interpreting and Capitalizing Operating Leases **(LO1)**

TJX COMPANIES
(TJX)

TJX Companies reports the following footnote relating to its capital and operating leases in its 10-K report.

Following is a schedule of future minimum lease payments for continuing operations as of January 29, 2011:

Fiscal Year ($ 000s)	Operating Leases
2012	$1,092,709
2013	1,022,364
2014	915,656
2015	794,253
2016	670,437
Later years	2,304,674
Total future minimum lease payments	$6,800,093

Required

a. Using a 7% discount rate and rounding the remaining lease life to the nearest whole year, compute the present value of TJX's operating leases. Explain the adjustments we might consider to its balance sheet and income statement using that information.

b. TJX reported total liabilities of nearly $4.9 billion for fiscal 2011. Would the adjustment from part *a* make a substantial difference to the company's total liabilities? Explain.

E10-24. Analyzing and Interpreting Pension Disclosures **(LO2)**

General Mills reports the following pension footnote in its 10-K report.

GENERAL MILLS
(GIS)

Defined Benefit Pension Plans (In millions)	Fiscal Year	
	2010	2009
Change in Plan Assets		
Fair value at beginning of year	$3,157.8	$4,128.7
Actual return on assets	535.9	(1,009.1)
Employer contributions	17.1	220.2
Plan participant contributions	3.5	3.1
Benefits payments	(182.6)	(177.4)
Foreign currency	(1.9)	(7.7)
Fair value at end of year	$3,529.8	$3,157.8
Change in Projected Benefit Obligation		
Benefit obligation at beginning of year	$3,167.3	$3,224.1
Service cost	70.9	76.5
Interest cost	230.3	215.4
Plan amendment	25.8	0.3
Curtailment/other	—	—
Plan participant contributions	3.5	3.1
Medicare Part D reimbursements	—	—
Actuarial loss (gain)	716.4	(166.8)
Benefits payments	(182.6)	(177.4)
Foreign currency	(1.6)	(7.9)
Projected benefit obligation at end of year	$4,030.0	$3,167.3

Estimated benefit payments . . . are expected to be paid from fiscal 2011–2020 as follows:

(in millions)	Defined Benefit Pension Plans
2011	$ 194.8
2012	202.8
2013	211.9
2014	221.4
2015	231.4
2016–2020	1,331.7

a. Describe what is meant by *service cost* and *interest cost*.

b. What is the total amount paid to retirees during fiscal 2010? What is the source of funds to make these payments to retirees?

c. Compute the 2010 funded status for the company's pension plan.

d. What are actuarial gains and losses? What are the plan amendment adjustments, and how do they differ from the actuarial gains and losses?

e. General Mills projects payments to retirees of over $200 million per year. How is the company able to contribute only $17.1 million to its pension plan?

f. What effect would a substantial decline in the financial markets have on General Mills' contribution to its pension plans?

E10-25. Analyzing and Interpreting Pension and Health Care Footnote   (LO2)
XEROX CORPORATION (XRX)

Xerox reports the following pension and retiree health care ("Other") footnote as part of its 10-K report.

(in millions)	Pension Benefits		Retiree Health	
	2010	2009	2010	2009
Change in Benefit Obligation				
Benefit obligation, January 1	$9,194	$8,495	$1,102	$1,002
Service cost	178	173	8	7
Interest cost	575	508	54	60
Plan participants' contributions	11	9	26	36
Plan amendments	(19)	4	(86)	1
Actuarial loss (gain)	477	209	13	124
Acquisitions	140	1	1	—
Currency exchange rate changes	(154)	373	6	15
Curtailments	(1)	—	—	—
Benefits paid/settlements	(670)	(578)	(118)	(143)
Benefit obligation, December 31	**$9,731**	**$9,194**	**$1,006**	**$1,102**
Change in Plan Assets				
Fair value of plan assets, January 1	$7,561	$6,923	$ —	$ —
Actual return on plan assets	846	720	—	—
Employer contribution	237	122	92	107
Plan participants' contributions	11	9	26	36
Acquisitions	107	—	—	—
Currency exchange rate changes	(144)	349	—	—
Benefits paid/settlements	(669)	(578)	(118)	(143)
Other	(9)	16	—	—
Fair value of plan assets, December 31	**$7,940**	**$7,561**	**$ —**	**$ —**
Net funded status at December 31	**$(1,791)**	**$(1,633)**	**$(1,006)**	**$(1,102)**

(in millions)	Pension Benefits			Retiree Health		
	2010	2009	2008	2010	2009	2008
Components of Net Periodic Benefit Cost						
Service cost	$ 178	$173	$209	$ 8	$ 7	$ 14
Interest cost	575	508	(5)	54	60	84
Expected return on plan assets	(570)	(523)	(80)	—	—	—
Recognized net actuarial loss	71	25	36	—	—	—
Amortization of prior service credit	(22)	(21)	(20)	(30)	(41)	(21)
Recognized settlement loss	72	70	34	—	—	—
Defined benefit plans	304	232	174	32	26	77
Defined contribution plans	51	38	80	—	—	—
Total net periodic benefit costs	**$ 355**	**$270**	**$254**	**$ 32**	**$ 26**	**$ 77**

continued

continued from prior page

Other Changes in Plan Assets and Benefit Obligations
Recognized in Other Comprehensive Income

Net actuarial loss (gain)	$ 198	$ 8	$1,062	$ 13	$126	$(244)
Prior service cost (credit)	(19)	—	1	(86)	1	(219)
Amortization of net actuarial (loss) gain	(143)	(95)	(70)	—	—	—
Amortization of prior service (cost) credit.	22	21	20	30	41	21
Total recognized in other comprehensive income	$ 58	$ (66)	$1,013	$ (43)	$168	$(442)

a. Describe what is meant by *service cost* and *interest cost* (the service and interest costs appear both in the reconciliation of the PBO and in the computation of pension expense).

b. What is the actual return on the pension and the health care ("Other") plan investments in 2010? Was Xerox's profitability impacted by this amount?

c. Provide an example under which an "actuarial loss," such as the $477 million loss in 2010 that Xerox reports, might arise.

d. What is the source of funds to make payments to retirees?

e. How much cash did Xerox contribute to its pension and health care plans in 2010?

f. How much cash did retirees receive in 2010 from the pension plan and the health care plan? How much cash did Xerox pay these retirees in 2010?

g. Show the computation of the 2010 funded status for the pension and health care plans.

h.[A] The company reports $198 million "Net actuarial loss (gain)" in the table relating to Other Comprehensive Income, a credit of $19 million relating to "Prior service cost," a loss of $(143) million relating to "Amortization of net actuarial (loss) gain," and a credit of 22 million relating to "Amortization of prior service (cost) credit" in the net periodic benefit cost table. Describe the process by which these amounts are transferred from Other Comprehensive Income to pension expense in the income statement.

E10-26. Analyzing and Interpreting Pension and Health Care Disclosures (LO2)
Verizon reports the following pension and health care benefits footnote as part of its 10-K report.

VERIZON
(VZ)

	Pension		Health Care and Life	
At December 31 (dollars in millions)	**2010**	**2009**	**2010**	**2009**
Change in Benefit Obligations				
Beginning of year	$ 31,818	$ 30,394	$ 27,337	$ 27,096
Service cost	353	384	305	311
Interest cost	1,797	1,924	1,639	1,766
Plan amendments	(212)	—	(2,580)	(5)
Actuarial (gain) loss, net	748	2,056	826	(469)
Benefits paid	(1,996)	(2,565)	(1,675)	(1,740)
Termination benefits	687	75	—	18
Curtailment (gain) loss, net	61	1,245	132	352
Acquisitions and divestitures, net	(581)	192	(266)	8
Settlements paid	(3,458)	(1,887)	—	—
End of year	$ 29,217	$ 31,818	$ 25,718	$ 27,337
Change in Plan Assets				
Beginning of year	$ 28,592	$ 27,791	$ 3,091	$ 2,555
Actual return on plan assets	3,089	4,793	319	638
Company contributions	138	337	1,210	1,638
Benefits paid	(1,996)	(2,565)	(1,675)	(1,740)
Settlements paid	(3,458)	(1,887)	—	—
Acquisitions and divestitures, net	(551)	123	—	—
End of year	$ 25,814	$ 28,592	$ 2,945	$ 3,091
Funded Status				
End of year	$ (3,403)	$ (3,226)	$(22,773)	$(24,246)

Years Ended December 31 (dollars in millions)	Pension			Health Care and Life		
	2010	2009	2008	2010	2009	2008
Service cost..	$ 353	$ 384	$ 382	$ 305	$ 311	$ 306
Amortization of prior service cost	109	112	62	375	401	395
Subtotal..	462	496	444	680	712	701
Expected return on plan assets	(2,176)	(2,216)	(3,444)	(252)	(205)	(331)
Interest cost......................................	1,797	1,924	1,966	1,639	1,766	1,663
Subtotal..	83	204	(1,034)	2,067	2,273	2,033
Remeasurement (gain) loss, net....................	(166)	(515)	13,946	758	(901)	1,069
Net periodic benefit (income) cost.................	(83)	(311)	12,912	2,825	1,372	3,102
Curtailment and termination benefits...............	860	1,371	32	386	532	31
Total...	$ 777	$1,060	$12,944	$3,211	$1,904	$3,133

    a.   Describe what is meant by *service cost* and *interest cost*.

    b.   What payments did retirees receive during fiscal 2010 from the pension and health care plans? What is the source of funds to make payments to retirees?

    c.   Show the computation of Verizon's 2010 funded status for both the pension and health care plans.

    d.   What expense does Verizon's income statement report for both its pension and health care plans?

HARLEY-
DAVIDSON,
INC.
(HOG)

E10-27.[B] **Analyzing and Interpreting Disclosure on Off-Balance-Sheet Financing** (LO3)

Harley-Davidson provides the following footnote in its 10-K report relating to the securitization of receivables by its finance subsidiary, Harley-Davidson Financial Services (HDFS).

Term Asset-Backed Securitization VIEs The Company transfers U.S. retail motorcycle finance receivables to SPEs which in turn issue secured notes to investors, with various maturities and interest rates, secured by future collections of the transferred U.S. retail motorcycle finance receivables. In 2010 and 2009, HDFS transferred $670.8 million and $3.08 billion, respectively, of U.S. retail motorcycle finance receivables to five separate SPEs. The SPEs in turn issued the following secured notes with the related maturity dates and interest rates (dollars in thousands):

Issue Date	Principal Amount	Weighted-Average Rate at Date of Issuance	Maturity Dates
November 2010	$600,000	1.05%	December 2011–April 2018
December 2009	562,499	1.55	December 2010–June 2017
October 2009	700,000	1.16	October 2010–April 2017
July 2009	700,000	2.11	July 2010–February 2017
May 2009	500,000	2.77	May 2010–January 2017

Each term asset-backed securitization SPE is a separate legal entity and the U.S. retail motorcycle finance receivables included in the term asset backed securitizations are only available for payment of the secured debt and other obligations arising from the term asset-backed securitization transactions and are not available to pay other obligations or claims of the Company's creditors until the associated secured debt and other obligations are satisfied. Cash and cash equivalent balances held by the SPEs are used only to support the securitizations. There are no amortization schedules for the secured notes; however, the debt is reduced monthly as available collections on the related U.S. retail motorcycle finance receivables are applied to outstanding principal. The Company was required to adopt the new guidance within ASC Topic 810 and ASC Topic 860 as of January 1, 2010. The Company determined that the formerly unconsolidated QSPEs that HDFS utilized were VIEs, of which the Company was the primary beneficiary, and consolidated them into the Company's financial statements beginning January 1, 2010.

    a.   Describe in your own words, the securitization process employed by HDFS.

    b.   What benefits does Harley-Davidson derive by securitizing receivables in this manner?

    c.   Current accounting standards require consolidation of the VIEs. What effect does this have on Harley-Davidson? Is there still a benefit to securitization? Explain.

PROBLEMS

P10-28. Analyzing, Interpreting and Capitalizing Operating Leases (LO1)
The **Abercrombie & Fitch** 10-K report contains the following footnote relating to leasing activities. This is the only information it discloses relating to its leasing activity.

At January 29, 2011, the Company was committed to noncancelable leases with remaining terms of one to 17 years. A summary of operating lease commitments under noncancelable leases follows (thousands):

Fiscal 2011	$ 331,151
Fiscal 2012	319,982
Fiscal 2013	303,531
Fiscal 2014	285,337
Fiscal 2015	262,586
Thereafter	1,110,598

Required

a. What lease assets and lease liabilities does Abercrombie report on its balance sheet? How do we know?

b. What effect does the lease classification have on A&F's balance sheet? Over the life of the lease, what effect does this classification have on the company's net income?

c. Using a 6% discount rate and rounding the remaining lease life to the nearest whole year, estimate the assets and liabilities that A&F fails to report as a result of its off-balance-sheet lease financing.

d. What adjustments would we consider to A&F's income statement corresponding to the adjustments we would make to its balance sheet in part *c*?

e. Indicate the direction (increase or decrease) of the effect that capitalizing these leases would have on the following financial items and ratios for A&F: return on equity (ROE), net operating profit after tax (NOPAT), net operating assets (NOA), net operating profit margin (NOPM), net operating asset turnover (NOAT), and measures of financial leverage.

P10-29. Analyzing, Interpreting and Capitalizing Operating Leases (LO1)
The **Best Buy** 10-K report has the following footnote related to leasing activities.

The future minimum lease payments under our capital and operating leases by fiscal year (not including contingent rentals) at February 26, 2011, were as follows:

Fiscal Year ($ millions)	Capital Leases	Operating Leases
2012	$18	$1,208
2013	16	1,166
2014	16	1,079
2015	14	992
2016	8	872
Thereafter	25	2,930
Subtotal	97	$8,247
Less: imputed interest	(18)	
Present value	$79	

Required

a. What is the balance of the lease liabilities reported on Best Buy's balance sheet?

b. What effect has the operating lease classification had on its balance sheet? Over the life of the lease, what effect does this classification have on the company's net income?

c. Confirm that the implicit discount rate used by Best Buy for its capital leases is 5.73%. Use this discount rate to estimate the assets and liabilities that Best Buy fails to report as a result of its off-balance-sheet lease financing. Round the remaining lease life to two decimals.

d. What adjustments would we make to Best Buy's income statement corresponding to the adjustments we made to its balance sheet in part *c*?

e. Indicate the direction (increase or decrease) of the effect that capitalizing the operating leases would have on the following financial items and ratios for Best Buy: return on equity (ROE), net operating profit after tax (NOPAT), net operating assets (NOA), net operating profit margin (NOPM), net operating asset turnover (NOAT), and measures of financial leverage.

P10-30. Analyzing, Interpreting and Capitalizing Operating Leases **(LO1)**

FedEx reports total assets of $24,902 and total liabilities of $11,091 for 2010 ($ millions). Its 10-K report has the following footnote related to leasing activities.

A summary of future minimum lease payments under capital leases and noncancelable operating leases with an initial or remaining term in excess of one year at May 31, 2010, is as follows (in millions):

| | | Operating Leases | | |
	Capital Leases	Aircraft and Related Equipment	Facilities and Other	Total Operating Leases
2011	$ 20	$ 526	$1,250	$ 1,776
2012	8	504	1,085	1,589
2013	119	499	926	1,425
2014	2	473	786	1,259
2015	1	455	717	1,172
Thereafter	14	2,003	4,547	6,550
Total	164	$4,460	$9,311	$13,771
Less amount representing interest	23			
Present value of net minimum lease payments	$141			

Required

a. What is the balance of lease assets and lease liabilities reported on FedEx's balance sheet? Explain.

b. Confirm that the implicit rate that FedEx uses to discount its capital leases is 4.6%. Use this discount rate and round the remaining lease life to three decimals to estimate the amount of assets and liabilities that FedEx fails to report as a result of its off-balance-sheet lease financing.

c. What adjustments would we make to FedEx's income statement corresponding to the adjustments we make to its balance sheet in part *b*?

d. Indicate the direction (increase or decrease) of the effect that capitalizing the operating leases would have on the following financial items and ratios for FedEx: return on equity (ROE), net operating profit after tax (NOPAT), net operating assets (NOA), net operating profit margin (NOPM), net operating asset turnover (NOAT), and measures of financial leverage.

e. What portion of total lease liabilities did FedEx report on-balance-sheet and what portion is off-balance-sheet?

f. Based on your analysis, do you believe that FedEx's balance sheet adequately reports its aircraft and facilities assets and related obligations? Explain.

P10-31. Analyzing and Interpreting Pension Disclosures **(LO2)**

DuPont's 10-K report has the following disclosures related to its retirement plans ($ millions).

| Obligations and Funded Status | Pension Benefits | |
December 31 ($ millions)	2010	2009
Change in benefit obligation		
Benefit obligation at beginning of year	$22,770	$21,506
Service cost	207	192
Interest cost	1,262	1,270
Plan participants' contributions	18	17
Actuarial loss	1,218	1,392
Benefits paid	(1,584)	(1,608)
Amendments	—	—
Net effects of acquisitions/divestitures	33	1
Benefit obligation at end of year	$23,924	$22,770
Change in plan assets		
Fair value of plan assets at beginning of year	$ 17,143	$ 16,209
Actual gain on plan assets	2,015	2,219
Employer contributions	782	306
Plan participants' contributions	18	17
Benefits paid	(1,584)	(1,608)
Net effects of acquisitions/divestitures	29	—
Fair value of plan assets at end of year	$ 18,403	$ 17,143
Funded status		
U.S. plans with plan assets	$ (3,408)	$ (3,594)
Non-U.S. plans with plan assets	(652)	(543)
All other plans	(1,461)	(1,490)
Total	$ (5,521)	$ (5,627)

| Components of net periodic benefit cost (credit) and amounts recognized in other comprehensive income | Pension Benefits (In millions) | | |
	2010	2009	2008
Net periodic benefit (credit) cost			
Service cost	$ 207	$ 192	$ 209
Interest cost	1,262	1,270	1,286
Expected return on plan assets	(1,435)	(1,603)	(1,932)
Amortization of loss	507	278	56
Amortization of prior service cost	16	18	18
Curtailment/settlement loss	—	—	1
Net periodic benefit (credit) cost	$ 557	$ 155	$ (362)
Changes in plan assets and benefit obligations recognized in other comprehensive income			
Net loss (gain)	634	781	6,397
Amortization of loss	(507)	(278)	(56)
Prior service cost	—	—	4
Amortization of prior service cost	(16)	(18)	(18)
Curtailment/settlement loss	—	—	(1)
Total recognized in other comprehensive income	$ 111	$ 485	$6,326
Total recognized in net periodic benefit cost and other comprehensive income	$ 668	$ 640	$5,964

| Weighted-average assumptions used to determine net periodic benefit cost for years ended December 31 | Pension Benefits | | |
	2010	2009	2008
Discount rate	5.80%	6.14%	6.01%
Expected return on plan assets	8.64%	8.75%	8.74%
Rate of compensation increase	4.24%	4.30%	4.28%

The following benefit payments, which reflect future service, as appropriate, are expected to be paid:

($ millions)	Pension Benefits
2011	$1,593
2012	1,528
2013	1,521
2014	1,527
2015	1,544
Years 2016–2020	8,002

Required

a. How much pension expense (revenue) does DuPont report in its 2010 income statement?

b. DuPont reports a $1,435 million expected return on pension plan assets as an offset to 2010 pension expense. Approximately, how is this amount computed (estimate from the numbers reported)? What is DuPont's actual gain or loss realized on its 2010 pension plan assets? What is the purpose of using this expected return instead of the actual gain or loss?

c. What main factors (and dollar amounts) affected DuPont's pension liability during 2010? What main factors (and dollar amounts) affected its pension plan assets during 2010?

d. What does the term *funded status* mean? What is the funded status of the 2010 DuPont pension plans?

e. DuPont decreased its discount rate from 6.14% to 5.80% in 2010. What effect(s) does this increase have on its balance sheet and its income statement?

f. How did DuPont's pension plan affect the company's cash flow in 2010? (Identify any inflows and outflows, including amounts.)

g. In 2010, DuPont contributed $782 million to its pension plan. Explain how the returns on pension assets affect the amount of cash that DuPont must contribute to fund the pension plan.

P10-32. **Analyzing and Interpreting Pension Disclosures** (LO2)

JOHNSON & JOHNSON (JNJ)

Johnson & Johnson provides the following footnote disclosures in its 10-K report relating to its defined benefit pension plans and its other post-retirement benefits.

($ in millions)	Retirement Plans		Other Benefit Plans	
	2010	2009	2010	2009
Change in Benefit Obligation				
Projected benefit obligation—beginning of year	$13,449	$11,923	$ 3,590	$ 2,765
Service cost	550	511	134	137
Interest cost	791	746	202	174
Plan participant contributions	42	50	—	—
Amendments	—	3	—	—
Actuarial losses	815	412	115	51
Divestitures & acquisitions	—	15	—	13
Curtailments & settlements & restructuring	(10)	(3)	—	748
Benefits paid from plan	(627)	(570)	(476)	(313)
Effect of exchange rates	(17)	362	7	15
Projected benefit obligation—end of year	$14,993	$13,449	$ 3,572	$ 3,590
Change in Plan Assets				
Plan assets at fair value—beginning of year	$10,923	$7,677	$ 16	$ 17
Actual return on plan assets	1,466	2,048	2	4
Company contributions	1,611	1,354	472	308
Plan participant contributions	42	50	—	—
Settlements	(7)	—	—	—
Benefits paid from plan assets	(627)	(570)	(476)	(313)
Effect of exchange rates	25	364	—	—
Plan assets at fair value—end of year	$13,433	$10,923	$ 14	$ 16
Funded status—end of year	$ (1,560)	$ (2,526)	$(3,558)	$(3,574)

($ in millions)	Retirement Plans			Other Benefit Plans		
	2010	**2009**	**2008**	**2010**	**2009**	**2008**
Service cost	$ 550	$511	$545	$134	$137	$142
Interest cost	791	746	701	202	174	166
Expected return on plan assets	(1,005)	(934)	(876)	(1)	(1)	(2)
Amortization of prior service cost	10	13	10	(4)	(5)	(4)
Amortization of net transition asset	1	1	2	—	—	—
Recognized actuarial losses.	236	155	62	48	55	64
Curtailments and settlements	1	(11)	7	—	(1)	—
Net periodic benefit cost	$ 584	$481	$451	$379	$359	$366

($ in millions)	Retirement Plans			Other Benefit Plans		
	2010	**2009**	**2008**	**2010**	**2009**	**2008**
U.S. Benefit Plans						
Discount rate	5.98%	6.50%	6.50%	5.98%	6.50%	6.50%
Expected long-term rate of return on plan assets.	9.00	9.00	9.00	9.00	9.00	9.00
Rate of increase in compensation levels.	4.25	4.50	4.50	4.25	4.50	4.50

Required

a.   How much pension expense does Johnson & Johnson report in its 2010 income statement?

b.   The company reports a $1,005 million expected return on pension plan assets as an offset to 2010 pension expense. Approximately, how is this amount computed? What is the actual gain or loss realized on its 2010 pension plan assets? What is the purpose of using this expected return instead of the actual gain or loss?

c.   What factors affected the company's pension liability during 2010? What factors affected the pension plan assets during 2010?

d.   What does the term *funded status* mean? What is the funded status of the 2010 pension plans and postretirement benefit plans?

e.   The company decreased its discount rate from 6.50% to 5.98% in 2010. What effect(s) does this increase have on its balance sheet and its income statement?

f.   How did Johnson & Johnson's pension plan affect the company's cash flow in 2010?

IFRS APPLICATIONS

I10-33.   Analyzing and Capitalizing Operating Lease Payments Disclosed in Footnotes   (LO1)

GlaxoSmithKline plc, headquartered in London, United Kingdom, is the world's third largest pharmaceutical company. The company's 2009 balance sheet reported total assets of £42,862 and total liabilities of £32,120 (in millions). The footnotes disclosed the following information related to leasing activities.

Commitments under non-cancellable operating leases	2009 £m	2008 £m
Rental payments due within one year	£111	£140
Rental payments due between one and two yers	72	109
Rental payments due between two and three years	50	76
Rental payments due between three and four years	21	54
Rental payments due between four and five years	14	22
Rental payments due after five years.	69	47
Total commitments under non-cancellable operating leases. . .	£337	£448

Operating leases are not reflected on-balance-sheet. In our analysis of a company, we often capitalize operating leases, that is, add the present value of the future operating lease payments to both the reported assets and liabilities.

a. Compute the present value of GlaxoSmithKline's operating payments assuming a 6% discount rate and round the remaining lease life to three decimals.

b. What effect would capitalization of operating leases have on GlaxoSmithKline's total liabilities and total assets?

I10-34. **Analyzing, Interpreting and Capitalizing Operating Leases** **(LO1)**

Total S.A. is a French multinational oil company and one of the six "supermajor" oil companies in the world. The company is headquartered in Courbevoie, France, and uses IFRS to prepare its financial statements. Total S.A. reports the following footnote relating to its finance and operating leases in its 2009 20-F report (€ millions).

> The Group leases real estate, retail stations, ships, and other equipment. The future minimum lease payments on operating and finance leases to which the Group is committed are shown as follows:
>
> | For year ended December 31, 2009 (€ million) | Operating leases | Finance leases |
> | --- | --- | --- |
> | 2010 . . . . | € 523 | € 42 |
> | 2011 . . . . | 377 | 43 |
> | 2012 . . . . | 299 | 42 |
> | 2013 . . . . | 243 | 41 |
> | 2014 . . . . | 203 | 39 |
> | 2015 and beyond . . . . | 894 | 128 |
> | Total minimum payments . . . . | €2,539 | €335 |
>
> On December 31, 2009, the present value of minimum lease payments under capital leases was €282 million.

a. Confirm that the implicit rate of Total's finance leases is 3.94%.

b. Use 3.94% as the discount rate and round the remaining lease term to three decimals to compute the present value of Total's operating leases.

c. Describe the adjustments we might consider to Total's balance sheet and income statement using the information from part b.

d. Total reported total liabilities of €74,214 million for 2009. Are these finance leases substantial? Would capitalizing the operating leases make a difference to our assessment of Total's liquidity or solvency?

I10-35. **Analyzing, Interpreting and Capitalizing Operating Leases** **(LO1)**

Air Canada is the largest Canadian airline and is the world's ninth largest passenger airline by number of destinations. The company is headquartered in Montreal, Quebec. Air Canada used Canadian GAAP to prepare its 2010 financial statements. Its footnotes include the following:

> **Operating Lease Commitments** The table below presents the future minimum lease payments under existing operating leases of aircraft and other property as at December 31, 2010.
>
> | CDN$ millions | 2011 | 2012 | 2013 | 2014 | 2015 | Thereafter | Total |
> | --- | --- | --- | --- | --- | --- | --- | --- |
> | Aircraft | 335 | 316 | 295 | 230 | 178 | 554 | 1,908 |
> | Other property | 47 | 39 | 38 | 36 | 32 | 117 | 309 |
> | | 382 | 355 | 333 | 266 | 210 | 671 | 2,217 |

Required

a. Mandatory adoption of IFRS by European companies in 2005 caused many leases previously classified as operating to be treated as capital (finance) leases. This is due to the IFRS' conceptual approach to lease classification as compared to the rules-based approach taken by many country-specific GAAP. Use a discount rate of 10% and round the remaining years to 3 decimals to estimate the amount of assets and liabilities that Air Canada would likely need to capitalize had the company used IFRS in 2010.

b. What would the income statement effect have been given the balance sheet changes from part *a*?

I10-36. Analyzing, Interpreting and Capitalizing Operating Leases (LO1)

LM Ericsson, one of Sweden's largest companies, is a provider of telecommunication and data communication systems. The company reports total assets of SEK 269,809 and total liabilities of SEK 128,782 for 2009 (in millions). Its annual report has the following footnote related to leasing activities.

As of December 31, 2009, future minimum lease payment obligations for leases were distributed as follows:

In SEK millions	Finance Leases	Operating Leases
2010	177	3,185
2011	168	2,611
2012	166	2,102
2013	164	1,270
2014	209	935
2015 and later	1,186	2,371
Total	2,070	12,474
Future finance charges	(676)	n/a
Present value of finance lease liabilities	1,394	12,474

Required

a. What is reported on Ericsson's balance sheet as leased assets and lease liabilities?

b. Confirm that the implicit rate that Ericsson uses to discount its capital leases is 7.08%. Use this discount rate and round the remaining years to 3 decimals to estimate the amount of assets and liabilities that Ericsson fails to report as a result of its off-balance-sheet lease financing.

c. What adjustments would we make to Ericsson's income statement corresponding to the balance sheet adjustments implied in part b?

d. What portion of total lease liabilities did Ericsson report on-balance-sheet and what portion is off-balance-sheet?

e. Indicate the direction (increase or decrease) of the effect that capitalizing the operating leases would have on the following financial items and ratios for Ericsson: return on equity (ROE), net operating profit after tax (NOPAT), net operating assets (NOA), net operating profit margin (NOPM), net operating asset turnover (NOAT), and measures of financial leverage.

f. Based on your analysis, do you believe that Ericsson's balance sheet adequately reports its facilities assets and related obligations? Explain.

SOLUTIONS TO REVIEW PROBLEMS

Mid-Module Review

Solution

1. The interest rate that American uses in the computation of its capital lease balance is imputed to be 12.91%; this rate is determined as follows (using a spreadsheet).

2. Using the 12.91% discount rate, the present value of American's operating leases follows ($ millions):

Year	Operating Lease Payment	Discount Factor (i = 12.91%)	Present Value
1	$ 1,254	0.88566	$1,111
2	1,068	0.78440	838
3	973	0.69471	676
4	831	0.61528	511
5	672	0.54493	366
>5	6,006	5.12909* × 0.54493	1,878**
			$5,380

Remaining life. . . . . . $6,006/$672 = 8.938 years

*The annuity factor for 9 years at 12.91% is 5.12909.

**$672 × 5.12909 × 0.54493 = $1,878

AMR's operating leases represent $5,380 million in both unreported operating assets and unreported non-operating liabilities. These amounts should be added to the balance sheet for analysis purposes.

3. Income statement adjustments relating to capitalization of operating leases involve two steps:
   a. Remove rent expense of $1,254 million from operating expense.
   b. Add depreciation expense from lease assets to operating expense and also reflect interest expense on the lease obligation as a nonoperating expense. We assume that the remaining lease term is 13.938 years (five years reported in the lease schedule plus 8.938 years after Year 5). Using this term and zero salvage value, we get an estimated straight-line depreciation for lease assets of $386 million ($5,380 million/13.938 years). Interest expense on the $5,380 million lease liability at the 12.91% capitalization rate is $695 million ($5,380 million × 12.91%). The net adjustment to NOPAT, reflecting the elimination of rent expense and the addition of depreciation expense, is $547 million, which is computed as: ($1,254 million rent expense − $386 million depreciation) × (1 − 0.37).

Module-End Review

Solution

1. A pension benefit obligation increases primarily by service cost, interest cost, and actuarial losses (which are increases in the pension liability as a result of changes in actuarial assumptions). It is decreased by the payment of benefits to retirees and by any actuarial gains.
2. Pension assets increase by positive investment returns for the period and cash contributions made by the company. Assets decrease by benefits paid to retirees and by investment losses.
3. American Airlines' funded status is $(5,195) million ($12,968 million PBO − $7,773 million Pension Assets) as of 2010. The negative amount indicates that the plan is underfunded. Consequently, this amount is reflected as a liability on American's balance sheet.
4. Expected return on plan assets acts as an offset to service cost and interest cost in computing net pension cost. As the expected return increases, net pension cost decreases.
5. American Airlines' expected return of $593 million is less than its actual return of $837 million in 2010.
6. American Airlines reports a net pension expense of $845 million in its 2010 income statement. Of this, $677 million pertained to the company's defined benefit plans, and $168 million to defined contribution plans.
7. American Airlines' funded status is negative, indicating an underfunded plan. In 2010, the company contributed $466 million to the pension plan, up from $10 million in the prior year. It is likely that the company will need to increase its future funding levels to cover the plan's requirements. This might have negative repercussions for its ability to fund other operating needs, and could eventually damage its competitive position.

© Getty Images

Forecasting Financial Statements

MODULE

11

Procter & Gamble (P&G), the world's largest consumer products company, is "one of the leaders in the race to harness massive streams of data for managing a business better. The company has been profit-forecasting on a monthly basis for about 40 years, trying to predict components such as sales, commodity prices and exchange rates. But the amount of real-time data it has been able to process has increased vastly . . . now P&G borrows liberally from tools born on the Web: ubiquitous high-speed networking, data visualization and high-speed analysis on multiple streams of information. The tools allow P&G to make in minutes the decisions that used to take weeks or months, when data had to be collated and passed through committees on their way to the top . . . . P&G is on the verge of having everyone's talents known and tracked, all information about sales decided at the executive level every week and production viewed in near real-time worldwide. The company talks in terms of increasing the amount of collected data sevenfold. The airy promises of networked technology are here, at a scale rarely, if ever, deployed before." (Forbes 2011)

PROCTER & GAMBLE (P&G)

P&G's financial performance has been impressive. In 2011, it generated over $13 billion of operating cash flow in one of the most severe recessions in recent memory. Its abundant cash flow allows it to fund the level of advertising and R&D necessary to remain a dominant force in the consumer products industry as well as to pay over $5.7 billion in dividends to shareholders.

P&G's product list is impressive. It consists of numerous well-recognized household brands. Total sales of Procter & Gamble products are distributed across its three business segments as illustrated in the chart to the side. A partial listing of its billion-dollar brands follows:

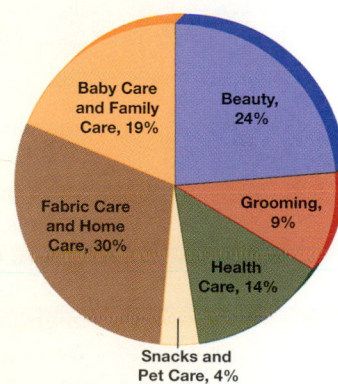

- **Beauty.** Head & Shoulders, Olay, Pantene, Wella
- **Grooming.** Braun, Fusion, Gillette, Mach3
- **Health Care.** Always, Crest, Oral-B
- **Snacks and Pet Care.** Iams, Pringles
- **Fabric Care and Home Care.** Ace, Ariel, Dawn, Downy, Duracell, Febreze, Gain, Tide
- **Baby Care and Family Care.** Bounty, Charmin, Pampers

P&G's recent successes have coincided with strong leadership. CEO Robert McDonald's innovations and market savvy have consistently propelled P&G. *BusinessWeek* explains that from its Swiffer mop to battery-powered Crest SpinBrush toothbrushes and Whitestrip tooth whiteners, P&G has outshined its peers. Since assuming the CEO job, McDonald has guided P&G to successive increases in sales, income, and cash flows. Such increases have driven impressive gains in stock price as evident from the graph below:

Still, we know that *forecasts* of financial performance drive stock price. Historical financial statements are relevant to the extent that they provide information useful to forecast financial performance. Accordingly, considerable emphasis is placed on generating reliable forecasts.

(continued on next page)

(continued from previous page)

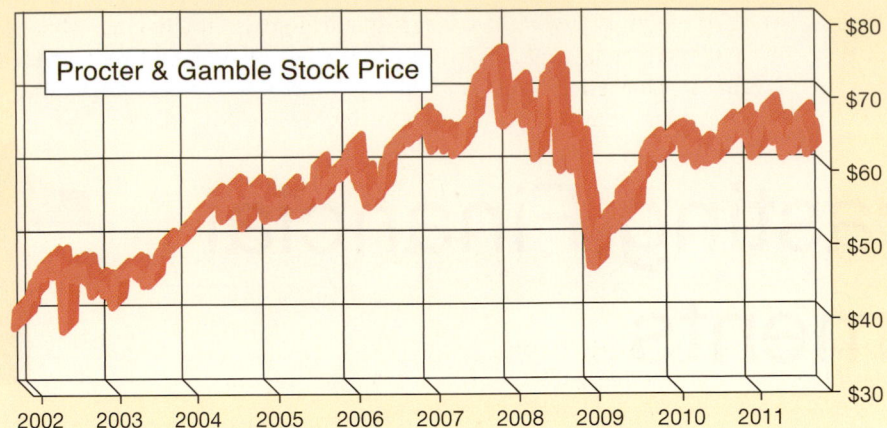

This module explains the forecasting process, including the forecasting of the income statement, the balance sheet, and the statement of cash flows. From all accounts, the rebound in P&G's stock price following the market melt-down of 2009 reflects optimism about its future financial performance and condition.

Sources: *Procter & Gamble* 2011 10-K and Annual Report; *BusinessWeek,* April 2006; *Barron's,* November 2006; *Forbes,* 2011.

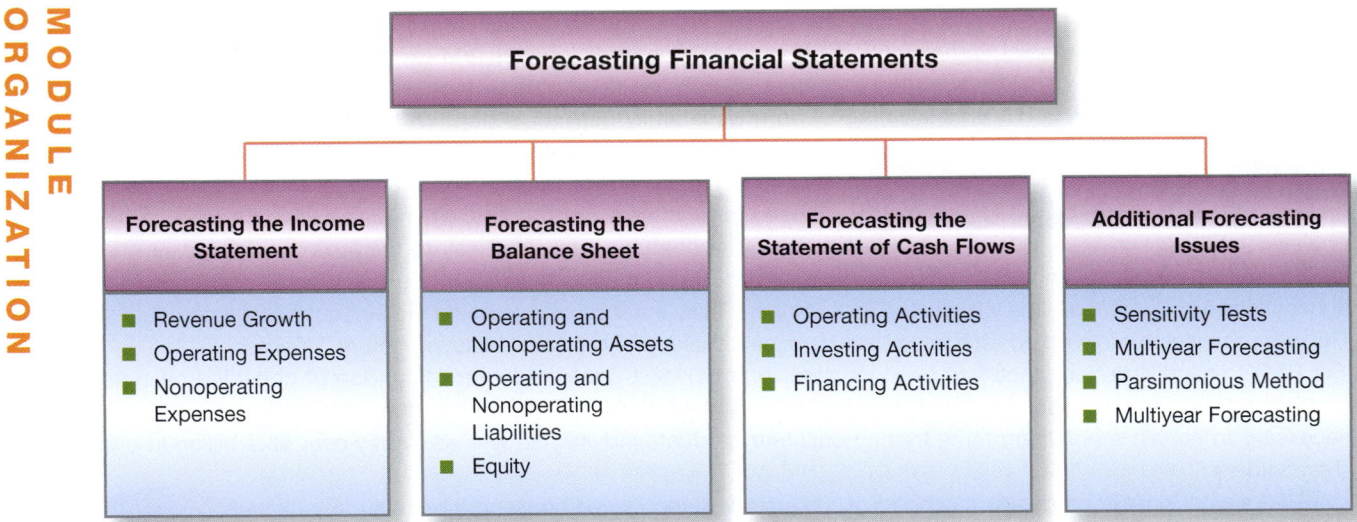

Forecasting financial performance is integral to a variety of business decisions ranging from investing to managing a company effectively. We might, for example, wish to value a company's common stock before purchasing its shares. To that end, we might use one of the valuation models we discuss in later modules that rely on financial statement forecasts as a crucial input. Or, we might be interested in evaluating the creditworthiness of a prospective borrower. In that case, we forecast the borrower's cash flows to estimate its ability to repay its obligations. We might also be interested in evaluating alternative strategic investment decisions. In this case, we can use our forecasts to evaluate the shareholder value that the strategic investment alternatives will create. All of these decisions require accurate financial forecasts. In this module, we illustrate the most common method to forecast the income statement, balance sheet, and statement of cash flows.

FORECASTING PROCESS

LO1 Explain the process of forecasting financial statements.

The forecasting process estimates future income statements, balance sheets, and statements of cash flows, in that order. The reason for this ordering is that each statement uses information from the preceding statement(s). For example, we update retained earnings on the balance sheet to reflect our forecast of the company's net income. And, the forecasted income statement and balance sheets are used in preparing forecasts for the statement of cash flows, which follows the same process described in Module 2 for preparing the historical statement of cash flows.

Overview of Forecasting Process

Before we focus on the mechanics of forecasting, we take a moment to consider some overarching principles that guide us in the forecasting process.

Reformulated (Adjusted) Financial Statements

The forecasting process begins with a retrospective analysis. That is, we analyze current and prior years' statements to be sure that they accurately reflect the company's financial condition and performance. If we believe that they do not, we adjust those statements to reflect the company's net operating assets and the operating income that we expect to persist into the future. Once we've adjusted the historical results, we are ready to forecast future results. Why would we need to adjust historical results? The answer resides in the fact that financial statements prepared in conformity with GAAP do not always accurately reflect the "true" financial condition and performance of the company. This *adjusting process*, also referred to as recasting or reformulating (or *scrubbing the numbers*), is not "black and white." It requires judgment and estimation. Repeatedly in earlier modules, we have explained estimation, accounting choice, deliberate managerial intervention in reporting, and transitory versus persistent items. These concepts are integral to adjustments we make to financial statements. It is important to distinguish between the purposes of GAAP-based financial statements and the adjusting process for purposes of forecasting. Specifically, GAAP-based statements provide more than just information for forecasting. For example, financial statements are key inputs into contracts among business parties. This means that historical results, including any transitory activities, must be reported to meet management's fiduciary responsibilities. On the other hand, to forecast future performance, we need to create a set of financial statements that focus on those items that we expect to persist, with a special emphasis on persistent operating activities.

Garbage-In, Garbage-Out

All forecasts are based on a set of forecasting assumptions. For example, to forecast the income statement, we must make assumptions about revenue growth and other assumptions about how expenses will change in relation to changes in revenues. Then, to forecast the balance sheet, we make assumptions about the relation between balance sheet accounts and changes in revenues. Consequently, before we make business decisions based on forecasted financial statements, we must understand and agree with the underlying assumptions used to produce them. The old adage, "garbage-in, garbage-out," is apt. That is, the quality of our decision is only as good as the quality of the information on which it is based. We must be sure that our forecasting assumptions are consistent with our beliefs and predictions for future growth and key financial relations.

Optimism vs Conservatism

Many people believe that it is appropriate to be overly conservative in their financial forecasts so as to minimize the likelihood of making a bad decision. "Let's be conservative in our forecasts so that we are certain our forecast will be met" is a frequent prelude to the forecasting process. Although this approach might appear reasonable, being too conservative can result in missed valuable opportunities that, in the end, can be very costly. Instead, our objective is not to be overly optimistic or overly conservative. The objective for forecasting is accuracy.

Level of Precision

Computing forecasts out to the "nth decimal place" is easy using spreadsheets. This increased precision makes the resulting forecasts appear more "professional," but not necessarily more accurate. As we discuss in this module, our financial statement forecasts are highly dependent on our revenues forecast. Whether revenues are expected to grow by 4% or 5% can markedly impact profitability and other forecasts. Estimating cost of goods sold and other items to the nth decimal place is meaningless if we have imprecise revenue forecasts. Consequently, borderline decisions that depend on a high level of forecasting precision are probably ill-advised.

Smell Test

At the end of the forecasting process, we must step back and make sure that the numbers we predict pass the *smell test*. That is, we need to assess whether our forecasts are reasonable—do they make economic sense, do they fit with the underlying relations that drive financial forecasts? For example, if our forecasts are dependent on increasing selling prices, it is wise to explore the likely consequences of a price increase. Companies cannot raise prices without a consequent loss of demand unless the product in question is protected in some way from competitive attacks. Our forecasts must appear reasonable and consistent with basic business economics.

Internal Consistency

The forecasted income statement, balance sheet, and statement of cash flows are linked in the same way that historical financial statements are. That is, they must articulate (link together within and across time) as we explain in Module 2. Preparing a forecasted statement of cash flows, although tedious, is often a useful way to uncover forecasting assumptions that are inconsistently applied across financial statements (examples are CAPEX, depreciation, debt payments, and dividends). If the forecasted cash balance on the balance sheet agrees with that on the statement of cash flows, it is likely that our income statement and balance sheet articulate properly. We also must ensure that our forecast assumptions are internally consistent. It is nonsense to forecast an increased gross profit margin during an economic recession unless we can make compelling arguments based on economics.

Crucial Forecasting Assumptions

Analysts commonly perform sensitivity analyses following preparation of their forecasts. This entails increasing and decreasing the forecast assumptions to identify those assumptions that have the greatest impact. By "impact," we mean large enough to alter business decisions. Assumptions that are identified as crucial to a decision must be investigated thoroughly to ensure that forecast assumptions are as accurate as possible.

Summary of Forecasting Process

Some professionals assert that forecasting is more art than science. Whatever it is, it must begin with a business analysis, including an assessment of general economic activity and the competitive forces within the broader business environment that we discuss in Module 1. Ideally, forecasts should be developed at an individual-product level and consider competitive advantage, trends in manufacturing costs, logistical requirements, necessary marketing support, after-sale customer service, and so forth. The narrower the focus, the more we can focus on the business environment in which the company operates and the more informed our forecasts are. Unfortunately, as external users of financial statements, we only have access to general-purpose financial statements, which we adjust as we see fit, given publicly available information and our own assessments. Then, we formulate forecast assumptions that are reasonable and consistent with the economic realities defining that company.

All-Important Revenues Forecast

The revenues (sales) forecast is, arguably, the most crucial and difficult estimate in the forecasting process. It is a crucial estimate because other income statement and balance sheet accounts derive, either directly or indirectly, from the revenues forecast. As a result, both the income statement and balance sheet grow with increases in revenues. The income statement reflects this growth concurrently. However, different balance sheet accounts reflect revenue growth in different ways. Some balance sheet accounts anticipate (or lead) revenue growth (inventories are one example). Some accounts reflect this growth concurrently (accounts receivable). And some accounts reflect revenue growth with a lag (for example, companies usually expand plant assets only after growth is deemed sustainable). Conversely, when revenues decline, so do the income statement and balance sheet, as the company shrinks to cope with adversity. Such actions include reduction of overhead costs and divestiture of excess assets. Exhibit 11.1 highlights crucial relations that are impacted by the revenues forecast for both the income statement and the balance sheet.

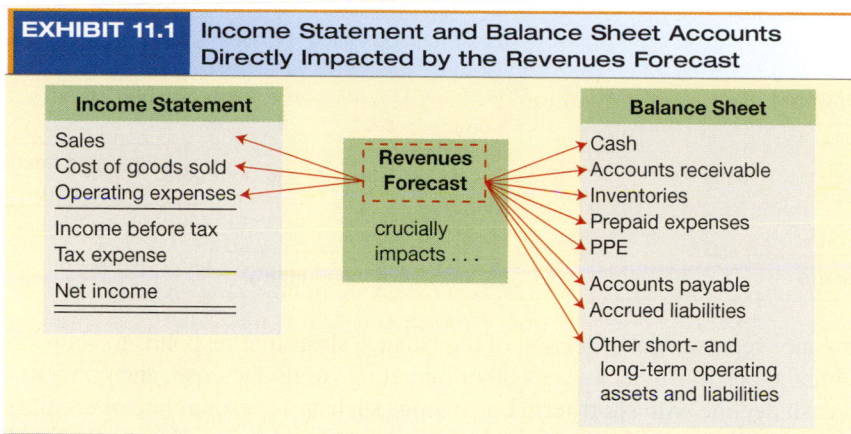

EXHIBIT 11.1 | Income Statement and Balance Sheet Accounts Directly Impacted by the Revenues Forecast

Dynamics of Income Statement (and Balance Sheet) Growth

The following accounts are impacted directly, and with a relatively short lead or lag time, by the revenues forecast (for convenience, *our discussion assumes an increase in revenues*):

- **Cost of goods sold** are impacted via increased inventory purchases, added manufacturing personnel, and greater depreciation from new manufacturing PPE.

- **Operating expenses** increase concurrently with, or in anticipation of, increased revenues; these expenses include increased costs for buyers, higher advertising costs, payments to sales personnel, costs of after-sale customer support, logistics costs, and administrative costs.

- **Cash** increases and decreases directly with increases in revenues as receivables are collected and as payables and accruals are paid.

- **Accounts receivable** increase directly with increases in revenues as more products and services are sold on credit.

- **Inventories** normally increase in anticipation of higher sales volume to ensure a sufficient stock of inventory available for sale.

- **Prepaid expenses** increase with increases in advertising and other expenditures made in anticipation of higher sales.

- **PPE** assets are usually acquired once the revenues increase is deemed sustainable and the capacity constraint is reached; thus, PPE assets increase with increased revenue, but with a lag.

- **Accounts payable** increase as additional inventories are purchased on credit.

- **Accrued liabilities** increase concurrent with increases in revenue-driven operating expenses.

- **Other operating assets and liabilities** such as deferred revenues, deferred taxes, and pensions, increase and decrease concurrent with revenues.

Dynamics of Balance Sheet Growth

To understand the dynamics of growth in the balance sheet, it is useful to view it in three sections as depicted in Exhibit 11.2. Each of these sections experiences growth at different rates. As evident from Exhibit 11.1, most net operating assets grow roughly concurrently with increases in revenues. As net operating assets are normally positive, the asset side of the balance sheet grows faster than the liability side, in dollar terms. This creates an imbalance that must be managed by the company's finance and treasury divisions.

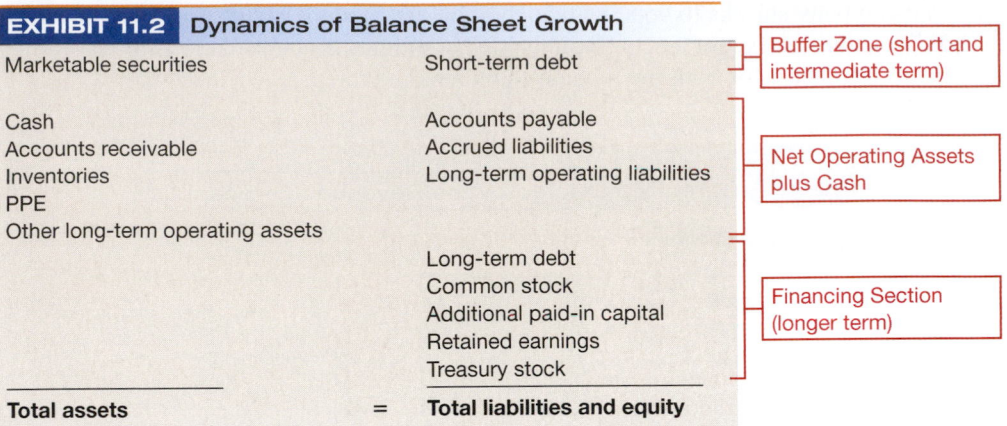

The "buffer zone" represents that section of the balance sheet that responds to short- and intermediate-term imbalances. Cash declines as other operating assets increase, and companies typically finance that cash decline with short-term borrowings such as a seasonal line of credit from a bank. Conversely, companies typically invest excess cash in marketable securities (also titled short-term investments) to provide liquidity to meet future operating needs, investment opportunities, and similar near-term demands. Companies manage the "financing section" of the balance sheet on a long-term basis to provide funding for relatively permanent increases in net assets, such as PPE or even the acquisition of other companies. Further, income is reinvested in the business, long-term debt is borrowed, and equity securities are sold in proportions that are necessary to maintain the desired financial leverage for the company. Although the cash reinvestment decision is made continually, increases in long-term debt and equity occur relatively infrequently to meet longer-term funding needs. If the store of liquidity in the buffer zone is not needed for the foreseeable future, it can be used to retire long-term debt or to repurchase the company's outstanding shares.

Dynamics of Statement of Cash Flows Growth

The dynamics of the statement of cash flows mimic the dynamics of the income statement and balance sheet. This is because the statement of cash flows is prepared using both the income statement and balance sheet. Specifically, once we have forecasts of the income statement and balance sheet, we can compute the forecasted statement of cash flows just as we would its historical counterpart.

Identifying the Forecasting Steps

We apply the forecasting process in a four-step sequence:

1. **Forecast revenues.**
2. **Forecast operating and nonoperating expenses.** We assume a relation between revenue and each specific expense account.
3. **Forecast operating and nonoperating assets, liabilities and equity.** We assume a relation between revenue and each specific balance sheet account.
4. **Adjust short-term investments or short-term debt to balance the balance sheet.** We use marketable securities and short-term debt to balance the balance sheet. We then recompute net nonoperating expense (interest/dividend income or interest expense) to reflect any adjustments we make to nonoperating asset and liability account balances.

Morgan Stanley Research Report

We illustrate the forecasting process using **Procter & Gamble** and an actual research report (along with an accompanying analysis spreadsheet) prepared by **Morgan Stanley** analysts in August 2011, which coincides with P&G's August 10 filing of its fiscal year 2011 annual report with the SEC.[1] We also benefitted from conversations with Ruma Mukerji, one of the authors of the Morgan Stanley research report, and we are grateful for the background information that she provided us for the discussion of the forecasting process in this module. We begin our discussion by explaining forecasting of the income statement. P&G's income statement is reproduced in Exhibit 11.3 as a reference point.

EXHIBIT 11.3	Procter & Gamble Income Statement			
Year ended June 30, in millions except per share amounts		**2011**	**2010**	**2009**
Net sales.		$82,559	$78,938	$76,694
Cost of products sold.		40,768	37,919	38,690
Selling, general and administrative expense		25,973	24,998	22,630
Operating income.		15,818	16,021	15,374
Interest expense.		831	946	1,358
Other nonoperating income, net		202	(28)	397
Earnings from continuing operations before income taxes		15,189	15,047	14,413
Income taxes on continuing operations.		3,392	4,101	3,733
Net earnings from continuing operations.		11,797	10,946	10,680
Net earnings from discontinued operations.		—	1,790	2,756
Net earnings.		$11,797	$12,736	$13,436
Basic net earnings per common share.		$ 4.12	$ 4.32	$ 4.49
Diluted net earnings per common share		$ 3.93	$ 4.11	$ 4.26
Dividends per common share		$ 1.97	$ 1.80	$ 1.64

STEP 1: FORECASTING REVENUES

Forecasting revenues is the most difficult and crucial step in the forecasting process. Further, many of the remaining income statement and the balance sheet accounts are forecasted based on an assumed relation with forecasted revenues. We typically utilize both financial and nonfinancial information in developing forecasts. Each account must be separately analyzed using all relevant financial and nonfinancial information, including the insights gained from earlier modules of this book.

LO2 Forecast revenues and the income statement.

To forecast revenues, then, we want to use all available, relevant information. But deciding what information is relevant and determining how to use the information varies across forecasters. As well, the level of information itself can vary across forecasters. For example, if we have access to inside information and we are developing forecasts as part of the strategic budgeting process for a company, we might have access to data regarding the competitive landscape, consumer trends and disposable income, new product introductions, production and marketing plans, and many other types of inside information. In this case, we can build our revenues forecast from the bottom up with unit sales and unit prices for each product or service sold. However, if we are a company outsider, we have much less information. In this case, we must rely on public statements by company management in conference calls and meetings in addition to the information disclosed in the management discussion and analysis (MD&A) section of the 10-K and the growth of individual product lines from segment disclosures. We also use publicly available information from competitors, suppliers, and customers for additional insight into broader trends

---

[1] Copyright 2011 Morgan Stanley. Please note that materials that are referenced comprise excerpts from research reports and should not be relied on as investment advice. This material is only as current as the publication date of the underlying Morgan Stanley research. For important disclosures, stock price charts and equity rating histories regarding companies that are the subject of the underlying Morgan Stanley research, see www.morganstanley.com/researchdisclosures. Additionally, Morgan Stanley has provided their materials here as a courtesy. Therefore, Morgan Stanley and Cambridge Business Publishers do not undertake to advise you of changes in the opinions or information set forth in these materials.

that can impact future revenues. Companies often provide "guidance" to outsiders to help refine forecasts, which is usually valuable as companies have a vested interest in correct forecasts so that their securities are accurately priced. Generally, the revenues forecast is obtained from the following formula:

$$\textbf{Forecasted revenues} = \textbf{Actual revenues} \times (\textbf{1} + \textbf{Revenue growth rate})$$

The revenue growth rate can be either positive or negative depending on numerous company and economic factors, described above. The remainder of this section identifies and explains key factors that impact revenue growth and illustrates their application to Procter & Gamble.

Factors Impacting Revenue Growth

Forecasts are made within the broader context of the general economic environment and the competitive landscape in which the company operates. There are a number of specific factors that impact a company's revenue growth.

Impact of Acquisitions   When one company acquires another, the revenues and expenses of the acquired company are consolidated but only from the date of acquisition onward (we discuss consolidation in Module 9). Acquisitions can greatly impact the acquirer's income statement, especially if the acquisition occurs toward the beginning of the acquirer's fiscal year. **Procter & Gamble**'s acquisition of Gillette in October 2005 provides an example. In its June 30, 2006, fiscal year-end income statement (ending eight months following the acquisition), P&G reported the following for sales:

Years ended June 30 ($ millions)	2006	2005	2004
Net sales.	$68,222	$56,741	$51,407

These net sales amounts include Gillette product sales from October 2005 onward (for fiscal 2006), and none of Gillette's sales are reported in fiscal 2005 or fiscal 2004. P&G's 2006 sales growth of 20.2% ([$68,222/$56,741] −1) was not P&G's organic growth, and we would have been remiss in forecasting a 20.2% increase for fiscal 2007.

Importantly, until all of the three comparative income statements in the 10-K include the acquired company, the acquirer is required to disclose what revenue and net income would have been had the acquired company been consolidated for all three years reported in the current income statement. This "what if" disclosure is called *pro forma* disclosure. Procter & Gamble's pro forma disclosure in 2006 includes the following discussion and table:

The following table provides pro forma results of operations for the years ended June 30, 2006, 2005, and 2004, as if Gillette had been acquired as of the beginning of each fiscal year presented.

Pro forma results; Years ended June 30	2006	2005	2004
Net sales (in millions)	$71,005	$67,920	$61,112
Net earnings (in millions)	8,871	8,522	7,504
Diluted net earnings per common share	2.51	2.29	1.98

Using this disclosure, we would have been able to compute the growth rate in sales for 2006 as 4.5% ([$71,005/$67,920] −1), and we would have used the pro forma net sales for 2006 as our forecasting base. That is, we would have forecasted 2007 net sales as $74,200 (calculated as $71,005 × 1.045). P&G was careful to point out, however, that the pro forma earnings estimate must be viewed with caution:

Pro forma results do not include any anticipated cost savings or other effects of the planned integration of Gillette. Accordingly, such amounts are not necessarily indicative of the results if the acquisition had occurred on the dates indicated or that may result in the future.

Impact of Divestitures Companies are required to exclude sales and expenses of discontinued operations from the continuing operations portion of their income statements, and to present the net income and gain (loss) on sale of the divested entity, net of tax, below income from continuing operations (we discuss accounting for divestitures in Module 5 and Module 9). **Procter & Gamble**'s income statement in Exhibit 11.3 reports net earnings from discontinued operations of $1,790 million and $2,756 million for fiscal years 2010 and 2009, respectively. The following footnote from PG's 2011 10-K provides information about these two discontinued operations:

Discontinued Operations In October 2009, the Company completed the divestiture of our global pharmaceuticals business to Warner Chilcott plc for $2.8 billion of cash, net of assumed and transferred liabilities . . . . The Company recorded an after-tax gain on the transaction of $1,464, which is included in net earnings from discontinued operations in the Consolidated Statement of Earnings for the year ended June 30, 2010 . . .

In November 2008, the Company completed the divestiture of our coffee business through the merger of our Folgers coffee subsidiary into The J.M. Smucker Company . . . . The Company recorded an after-tax gain on the transaction of $2,011, which is included in net earnings from discontinued operations in the Consolidated Statement of Earnings for the year ended June 30, 2009 . . . .

Following is selected financial information included in net earnings from discontinued operations for the pharmaceuticals and coffee businesses:

Year ended June 30 ($ millions)	2010			2009		
	Pharma	Coffee	Total	Pharma	Coffee	Total
Net sales.	$ 751	$ —	$ 751	$2,335	$ 668	$3,003
Earnings from discontinued operations	306	—	306	912	212	1,124
Income tax expense.	(101)	—	(101)	(299)	(80)	(379)
Gain on sale of discontinued operations	2,632	—	2,632	—	1,896	1,896
Income tax benefit (expense) on sale.	(1,047)	—	(1,047)	—	115	115
Net earnings from discontinued operations. .	$1,790	—	$1,790	$ 613	2,143	2,756

The net gain on the sale of the pharmaceuticals business, in the table above, for the year ended June 30, 2010, also includes an after-tax gain on the sale of the Actonel brand in Japan which occurred prior to the divestiture to Warner Chilcott.

The revenues, expenses, and earnings for Procter & Gamble in fiscal years 2010 and 2009, as reported in its income statement, *exclude* the revenues, expenses, and earnings from its discontinued operations. The detail relating to the revenues, expenses, and earnings of discontinued operations (and their gain on sale) is reported in the footnote disclosure shown above. This additional information allows us to better evaluate the drivers of observed growth of revenues and earnings, and we would be remiss if we included the revenues and gains relating to discontinued operations in our forecasts.

Impact of Existing vs New Store Growth Retailers typically derive revenue growth from two sources: (1) from *existing* stores (organic growth), and (2) from *new* stores. We are interested in the breakdown between these two growth sources as the latter is obtained at considerably more cost. **Target Corporation** provides the following footnote disclosure to its 10-K report.

Retail Segment Results (millions)	2010	2009	2008	Percent Change 2010/2009	Percent Change 2009/2008
Sales.	$65,786	$63,435	$62,884	3.7%	0.9%
Cost of sales.	45,725	44,062	44,157	3.8	(0.2)
Gross margin	20,061	19,373	18,727	3.5	3.5
SG&A expenses	13,367	12,989	12,838	2.9	1.2
EBITDA.	6,694	6,384	5,889	4.9	8.4
Depreciation and amortization	2,065	2,008	1,808	2.8	11.0
EBIT	$ 4,629	$ 4,376	$ 4,081	5.8%	7.3%

Retail Segment Results (millions)	2010	2009	2008
Drivers of changes in comparable-store sales:			
Number of transactions	2.0%	(0.2)%	(3.1)%
Average transaction amount.	0.1%	(2.3)%	0.2%
Units per transaction.	2.5%	(1.5)%	(2.1)%
Selling price per unit	(2.3)%	(0.8)%	2.3%

Total sales for the Retail Segment for 2010 were $65,786 million, compared with $63,435 million in 2009 and $62,884 million in 2008. All periods were 52-week years. Growth in total sales between 2010 and 2009 resulted from higher comparable-store sales and additional stores opened, whereas between 2009 and 2008, growth in total sales resulted from sales from additional stores opened, partially offset by lower comparable-store sales.

At least three points in Target's footnote disclosure are noteworthy for forecasting purposes.

1. Retailers typically operate on a 52/53 week year, closing their books on a particular day of the week rather than on a constant date. Target has the following fiscal year-end policy:

> Our fiscal year ends on the Saturday nearest January 31. Unless otherwise stated, references to years in this report relate to fiscal years, rather than to calendar years. Fiscal year 2010 ended January 29, 2011, and consisted of 52 weeks. Fiscal year 2009 ended January 30, 2010, and consisted of 52 weeks. Fiscal year 2008 ended January 31, 2009, and consisted of 52 weeks.

Target's sales for fiscal years 2008, 2009, and 2010 are all on a comparable 52-week year. Should a fiscal year include a 53-week year (as Target reported in 2006), the extra week's sales will make it appear as if sales are growing at a higher rate than they are. To accurately forecast revenue growth, we must use numbers and rates that reflect a consistent 52-week period each year. To do this, we assume that sales are recorded evenly each week and we adjust revenues for the 53-week year by multiplying reported sales by 52/53. We then use the adjusted 52-week pro forma sales to compute growth rates.

2. More than 43% ([3.7% − 2.1%]/3.7% = 43.2%) of Target's 2010 sales growth is attributable to new store openings.

3. The average per store planned capital expenditure is about $44 million ($574 million reported CAPEX for new stores/13 new stores opened in 2010 as reported in the 2011 MD&A). Although acquired growth provides the organic growth of the future, it comes at considerable cost per store.

Impact of Unit Sales and Price Disclosures Forecasts that are built from anticipated unit sales and current prices are generally more informative, and accurate, than those derived from historical dollar sales. Most companies, however, do not provide unit sales data in their 10-Ks. Apple, Inc., is an exception, and the following footnote disclosure from its 10-K provides useful information (like Target, Apple operates on a 52/53 week fiscal year):

Net Sales Fiscal years 2010, 2009 and 2008 each spanned 52 weeks. An additional week is included in the first fiscal quarter approximately every six years to realign fiscal quarters with calendar quarters.

The following table summarizes net sales and Mac unit sales by operating segment and net sales and unit sales by product during the three years ended September 25, 2010 (in millions, except unit sales in thousands and per unit amounts):

	2010	Change	2009	Change	2008
Net sales by product					
Desktops............................	$ 6,201	43%	$ 4,324	(23)%	$ 5,622
Portables...........................	11,278	18%	9,535	9%	8,732
Total Mac net sales....................	17,479	26%	13,859	(3)%	14,354
iPod	8,274	2%	8,091	(12)%	9,153
Other music related products and services....	4,948	23%	4,036	21%	3,340
iPhone and related products and services.....	25,179	93%	13,033	93%	6,742
iPad and related products and services.......	4,958	NM	0	NM	0
Peripherals and other hardware.............	1,814	23%	1,475	(13)%	1,694
Software, service, and other sales...........	2,573	7%	2,411	9%	2,208
Total net sales........................	$65,225	52%	$42,905	14%	$37,491
Unit sales by product					
Desktops...........................	4,627	45%	3,182	(14)%	3,712
Portables...........................	9,035	25%	7,214	20%	6,003
Total Mac unit sales...................	13,662	31%	10,396	7%	9,715
Net sales per Mac unit sold	$ 1,279	(4)%	$ 1,333	(10)%	$ 1,478
iPod unit sales	50,312	(7)%	54,132	(1)%	54,828
Net sales per iPod unit sold...............	$ 164	10%	$ 149	(11)%	$ 167
iPhone units sold	39,989	93%	20,731	78%	11,627
iPad units sold	7,458	NM	0	NM	0

From Apple's disclosure we can derive several useful insights for forecasting purposes.

1. On average, a Mac sells for $1,279 and the per unit selling price has decreased during the past three years; unit sales, however, have increased by 31% and 7% per year for the past two years.

2. The iPod unit sales are decreasing over the past two years, probably reflecting increased competition from other MP3 players and market saturation.

3. The average sales price of iPods in 2010 is $164, 10% higher than the average sales price in 2009.

4. iPhone unit sales are 39,989 thousand, up 93% from 2009 and 244% from 2008.

5. iPhone dollar sales are $25,179 million in 2010, 93% higher than 2009 and 273% greater than in 2008.

6. Apple has only begun to realize the effects of its iPad as of fiscal year 2010, with 7,458 thousand units sold and total revenues of about $4,958 million.

Detailed disclosures such as Apple's allow us to prepare more informed forecasts that consider both unit sales and selling prices.

Forecasting Revenue Growth

To illustrate the forecasting process, we forecast revenue growth for P&G. Our information includes public disclosures by management in meetings and conference calls with analysts and the company's published financial reports including the management discussion and analysis (MD&A) section of the 10-K. We discuss the information in each of these sources.

Public Disclosures via Meetings and Calls P&G held its first meeting with analysts on September 8, 2011, following the August 10 release of its fiscal year 2011 financial statements. Its presentation (publicly available on the "Investor Relations" section of P&G's Website) provides guidance in several areas that impact our forecasts and we include excerpts from that presentation in our discussion below.

Published Reports: Segment Disclosures and MD&A Companies are required to disclose summary financial results for each of their operating segments along with a discussion and analysis of each. (An operating segment is defined under GAAP as a component of the company for which financial information is available and disclosed to senior management.) P&G is organized into six operating segments as discussed in the following excerpt from its 2011 MD&A:

Our organizational structure is comprised of two Global Business Units (GBUs), Global Operations, Global Business Services (GBS) and Corporate Functions (CF) . . . Effective February 2011, our two GBUs are Beauty & Grooming and Household Care. The primary responsibility of the GBUs is to develop the overall strategy for our brands . . . Under U.S. GAAP, the business units comprising the GBUs are aggregated into six reportable segments: Beauty; Grooming; Health Care; Snacks and Pet Care; Fabric Care and Home Care; and Baby Care and Family Care.

Reportable Segment	% of Net Sales*	% of Net Earnings*	Categories	Billion-Dollar Brands
Beauty	24%	24%	Cosmetics, Female Antiperspirant and Deodorant, Female Personal Cleansing, Female Shave Care, Hair Care, Hair Color, Hair Styling, Pharmacy Channel, Prestige Products, Salon Professional, Skin Care	Head & Shoulders, Olay, Pantene, Wella
Grooming	9%	14%	Electronic Hair Removal Devices, Home Small Appliances, Male Blades and Razors, Male Personal Care	Braun, Fusion, Gillette, Mach3
Health Care	14%	16%	Feminine Care, Gastrointestinal, Incontinence, Rapid Diagnostics, Respiratory, Toothbrush, Toothpaste, Water Filtration, Other Oral Care	Always, Oral-B, Crest
Snacks and Pet Care	4%	2%	Pet Care, Snacks	Iams, Pringles
Fabric Care and Home Care	30%	27%	Laundry Additives, Air Care, Batteries, Dish Care, Fabric Enhancers, Laundry Detergents, Surface Care	Ace, Ariel, Dawn, Downy, Duracell, Febreze, Gain, Tide
Baby Care and Family Care	19%	17%	Baby Wipes, Diapers, Paper Towels, Tissue, Toilet Paper	Bounty, Charmin, Pampers

* Percent of net sales and net earnings from continuing operations for the year ended June 30, 2011 (excluding results held in Corporate).

P&G also reports a revenue history for each segment and its MD&A provides additional information relating to the breakdown of revenue increases for the current year into the portion relating to increases in unit volume sales, increases in prices, effects of foreign-currency translation, and changes in product mix. That disclosure and related discussion allow us to compile the following table:

Net Sales Change Drivers vs. Year Ago (2011 vs. 2010)	Volume with Acquisitions & Divestitures	Volume Excluding Acquisitions & Divestitures	Foreign Exchange	Price	Mix/ Other	Net Sales Growth
Beauty	4%	4%	1%	0%	(2)%	3%
Grooming	3%	3%	0%	2%	0%	5%
Health Care	5%	5%	0%	0%	0%	5%
Snacks and Pet Care	1%	(2)%	1%	(1)%	0%	1%
Fabric Care and Home Care	7%	5%	(1)%	0%	(2)%	4%
Baby Care and Family Care	8%	8%	(1)%	1%	(2)%	6%
Total Company	6%	5%	0%	1%	(2)%	5%

Net sales percentage changes are approximations based on quantitative formulas that are consistently applied.

P&G's total sales volume increased by 6% in 2011, or 5% excluding acquisitions and divestitures. Revenues increased by 5% in total as a result of increases in units of product sold (although marked variation is evident across products) and 1% as a result of price increases. Revenues declined, however, as a result of changes in product mix (generally relating to an increase in the relative percentage of lower-priced products). This volume/price/mix analysis is potentially important as we are often more comfortable with revenue increases resulting from increased units sold than from price increases that might be unsustainable.

Although fluctuations in foreign-exchange rates affected individual product categories in 2011, the net effects on total revenues were largely offsetting in 2011 (see Module 5 for a discussion of foreign-exchange rate effects on sales). By comparison, however, during 2008, the $US weakened vis-à-vis other major world currencies. Thus, revenues denominated in foreign currencies, including P&G's, increased when translated into $US, resulting in an increase in revenue growth of about 5%. We must be aware of these foreign exchange fluctuations as reported fluctuations in revenues might not reflect underlying fluctuations in unit volumes.

Determining the Revenue Growth Forecast

As we saw, P&G disaggregated the sales growth for each business segment into volume, foreign exchange, price, and mix effects. Morgan Stanley analysts forecast each of those factors for each of P&G's segments to obtain an aggregate forecast of sales. To illustrate, following is an excerpt from the Morgan Stanley forecast spreadsheet for P&G's total sales and for its Beauty segment (the spreadsheet has similar forecasts for each segment).

A B	AF	AK	AP	AU	AV	AW	AX	AY	AZ	BA	BB	BC	BD	BE
1 Procter & Gamble Co (PG)														
2 Segment Breakdown	FY2007	FY2008	FY2009	FY2010	Sep-10	Dec-10	Mar-11	Jun-11	FY2011	Sep-11 E	Dec-11 E	Mar-12 E	Jun-12 E	FY2012E
3 Total Sales	76,476.0	81,748.0	76,694.0	78,938.0	20,122.0	21,347.0	20,230.0	20,860.0	82,559.0	21,555.2	22,136.4	20,843.3	21,786.9	86,321.8
4 Organic Sales Growth	6.0%	5.0%	2.0%	3.4%	4.0%	3.0%	4.0%	5.0%	4.0%	3.4%	4.9%	4.8%	4.6%	4.4%
5 Volume (Organic)	5.0%	5.0%	-2.0%	4.0%	7.0%	6.0%	5.0%	3.0%	5.2%	1.3%	2.8%	2.8%	4.1%	2.8%
6 Pricing	1.0%	1.0%	5.0%	0.5%	-1.0%	0.0%	1.0%	3.0%	0.4%	3.7%	3.6%	3.7%	2.0%	3.2%
7 Mix	0.0%	-1.0%	-1.0%	-1.1%	-2.0%	-2.0%	-2.0%	-1.0%	-1.6%	-1.5%	-1.5%	-1.5%	-1.5%	-1.5%
8 FX Impact	2.0%	5.0%	-4.0%	-0.4%	-3.0%	-2.0%	1.0%	5.0%	0.2%	3.8%	-1.2%	-1.8%	0.0%	0.1%
9 Acq/Div	4.0%	-1.0%	-0.8%	-0.1%	0.6%	0.0%	0.0%	0.0%	0.3%	0.0%	0.0%	0.0%	0.0%	0.0%
10 % Sales Growth	12.1%	9.2%	-2.8%	2.9%	1.6%	1.5%	5.5%	10.2%	4.6%	7.1%	3.7%	3.0%	4.4%	4.6%
11 **Beauty**														
12 Beauty Care	17,889.0	19,515.0	18,924.0	19,491.0	4,929.0	5,290.0	4,870.0	5,068.0	20,157.0	5,259.0	5,423.1	4,965.3	5,296.1	20,943.4
13 Organic Sales Growth		4.0%	1.0%	3.2%	2.0%	3.0%	4.0%	3.0%	3.0%	3.5%	3.5%	3.5%	4.5%	3.8%
14 Volume (Organic)		2.8%	-1.0%	3.3%	4.0%	6.0%	6.0%	2.0%	4.5%	1.5%	1.5%	1.5%	4.0%	2.1%
15 Pricing		0.5%	2.0%	0.9%	0.0%	-1.0%	1.0%	2.0%	0.5%	3.0%	3.0%	3.0%	1.5%	2.6%
16 Mix		0.5%	0.0%	-0.4%	-2.0%	-2.0%	-3.0%	-1.0%	-2.0%	-1.0%	-1.0%	-1.0%	-1.0%	-1.0%
17 FX Impact		5.5%	-4.0%	0.0%	-2.0%	-1.0%	2.0%	6.0%	1.2%	3.2%	-1.0%	-1.5%	0.0%	0.1%
18 Acq/Div		-0.3%	-0.5%	-0.5%	0.0%	-1.0%	-1.0%	-2.0%	-1.0%	0.0%	0.0%	0.0%	0.0%	0.0%
19 % Sales Growth	7.2%	9.1%	-3.7%	3.0%	0.2%	1.4%	5.3%	7.1%	3.4%	6.7%	2.5%	2.0%	4.5%	3.9%
20 Grooming	7,437.0	8,254.0	7,408.0	7,631.0	1,898.0	2,164.0	1,907.0	2,056.0	8,025.0	2,074.4	2,229.4	1,958.2	2,148.5	8,410.5
21 Organic Sales Growth		4.0%	-2.0%	3.0%	6.0%	6.0%	7.0%	1.0%	5.0%	4.5%	4.5%	5.0%	4.5%	4.6%
22 Volume (Organic)		5.5%	-5.0%	0.3%	5.0%	5.0%	2.0%	1.0%	3.3%	2.5%	2.5%	3.0%	4.0%	3.0%
23 Pricing		1.3%	5.0%	3.7%	1.0%	1.0%	5.0%	2.0%	2.2%	3.0%	3.0%	3.0%	1.5%	2.6%
24 Mix		-2.3%	-2.0%	-1.0%	0.0%	0.0%	0.0%	-2.0%	-0.5%	-1.0%	-1.0%	-1.0%	-1.0%	-1.0%
25 FX Impact		6.5%	-6.0%	0.0%	-4.0%	-3.0%	1.0%	6.0%	-0.1%	4.8%	-1.5%	-2.3%	0.0%	0.2%
26 Acq/Div		-0.3%	-0.3%	0.2%	0.0%	0.0%	0.0%	0.0%	0.0%	0.0%	0.0%	0.0%	0.0%	0.0%
27 % Sales Growth	45.4%	11.0%	-8.6%	3.0%	2.2%	3.3%	8.4%	7.1%	5.2%	9.3%	3.0%	2.7%	4.5%	4.8%

For fiscal year 2012, Morgan Stanley forecasts a total sales growth rate of 4.6%, which consists of the following:

Organic sales growth		4.5%*
Volume (organic)	2.8%	
Pricing	3.2%	
Mix	(1.5)%	
Foreign exchange impact		0.1%
Acquisitions & divestitures		0.0%
Sales growth %		4.6%

* Sum of volume (2.8%), pricing (3.2%), and mix (-1.5%), which is rounded down to 4.4 in the Excel spreadsheet as more digits are used than are printed.

Morgan Stanley forecasts organic sales growth for all of P&G at 4.5%, consisting of 2.8% growth in volume, a 3.2% increase in prices, a −1.5% decline in growth due to product mix (increasing percentage of lower-priced goods). Morgan Stanley analysts also forecast an increase in sales of 0.1% resulting from a weakening of the $US in countries in which PG sells its products.

Following are a few observations that Morgan Stanley analysts conveyed to us about the way in which their sales forecasts are developed:

1. Each product forecast is built from the bottom up; that is, analysts use information about a product's market share and the forecasted growth rate for the market of each product within each country the product is sold. Development of such forecasts uses information about product market, pricing strategy, and competitive landscape. With this information, analysts forecast overall market growth, the market share for each product, changes in product pricing, and changes in the product sales mix. The total sales forecast is the sum of individual product forecasts for each product market.

2. P&G, like many companies, provides analysts with its own forecasts of sales growth by products, disaggregated into price and volume. Morgan Stanley analysts also have internally-developed databases of commodity-price indices, inflation indices, and other macroeconomic indices against which to evaluate the reasonableness of company-provided forecasts.

3. Sales forecasts are determined by quantity and price along with growth forecasts of the product markets, the company-provided future pricing strategy, and forecasts of price elasticity of demand. Analysts commonly consider, for example, the effects of a current discount pricing strategy to increase market share or to gain entrance into a new market, which are followed by price increases once volume levels and customer loyalty is solidified.

Returning to P&G, we saw that Morgan Stanley forecasted no acquisitions or divestitures. Acquisition of brands is a normal component of P&G's operating activities, yet acquisitions are one-time occurrences and come at a cost. We, like Morgan Stanley, focus on revenue growth that is not acquired, and we believe that organic sales growth is the best predictor of core operating revenue growth. P&G defines organic sales growth as follows:

Organic Sales Growth   Organic sales growth is a non-GAAP measure of sales growth excluding the impacts of acquisitions, divestitures and foreign exchange from year-over-year comparisons. We believe this provides investors with a more complete understanding of underlying sales trends by providing sales growth on a consistent basis. Organic sales is also one of the measures used to evaluate senior management and is a factor in determining their at-risk compensation.

Summary of Determining Revenue Growth Forecast   To recap, each segment is disaggregated into its business units and product lines. The presumption is that determining the revenue forecasts from the sum of product forecasts is preferable to forecasting total sales growth because the former uses more information. This implies that we use as much detailed product information as reasonable (cost vs. benefit) to forecast revenue growth. For example, we saw Morgan Stanley analysts use data on the Beauty Care and Grooming units to aggregate into the Beauty segment. We also saw that these forecasts were determined from both price and volume for each product in each market. Finally, we saw that analysts forecasted from quarterly data and determined annual forecasts as the sum of quarterly forecasts for each unit and segment.

Data Sources in Forecasting Revenue Investors use a variety of data sources. Companies provide data in conference calls and meetings with analysts. P&G, for example, provided the following guidance on organic sales growth in its Barclay's Capital Conference from 2011:

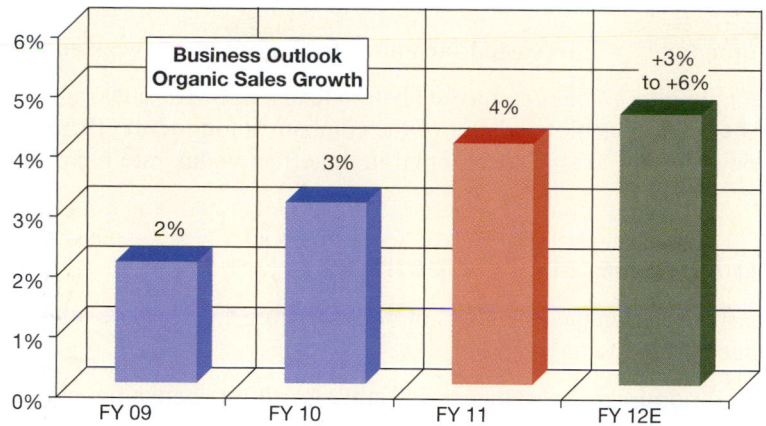

P&G's organic growth has ranged from 2% to 3% for the two most recent years, but it expects sales to recover as the world economy was expected to emerge from the recession in those previous years. Consequently, P&G's forecast of its revenue growth through fiscal year 2012 was in the range of 3% to 6%. Company expectations are an important input to our forecasts of revenue growth. Further, as we discuss above, total organic sales growth is a function of volume and price, and P&G provided the following quarterly information for forecasting these two variables:

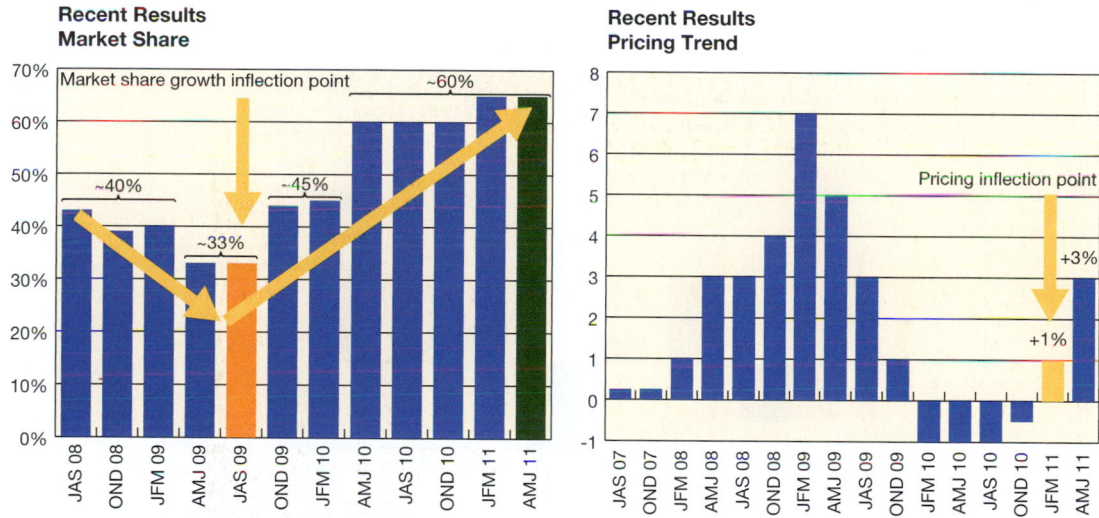

In addition to these company-provided sources of information, analysts can also use internally developed databases on macroeconomic data, commodity prices, and other inflation indices, along with data from competing companies, and other publicly available and proprietary databases. Most investors have access to similar information.

STEP 2: FORECASTING EXPENSES

The next step in the forecasting process is to predict expenses; for our purposes this includes operating expenses and nonoperating revenues and expenses.

Forecasting Operating Expenses

Generally, we use the following formula to forecast individual operating expenses:

Forecasted operating expense = Forecasted revenues × Forecasted operating expense margin

The forecasted operating expense margin is the expense expressed as a percent of sales (the common-sized expense). We normally start with the prior year's margin and then adjust it based on our business analysis. One exception to this general formula is for income taxes where we apply the following:

Forecasted income taxes = Forecasted income before taxes × Forecasted effective tax rate

In this case, we begin with forecasted income before taxes, not with sales, and the current effective tax rate is often a reasonable predictor of the company's long-term effective tax rate, taking into consideration any transitory items reported in the effective tax rate reconciliation in the tax footnote.

Forecasting Nonoperating Expenses

Generally, forecasts of individual line items of nonoperating expenses are obtained from the following "no change" forecast model:

Forecasted nonoperating expense = Nonoperating expense for prior period

This assumes no change in nonoperating expenses, with an exception of a "zero forecast" for items related to discontinued operations. If we make balance sheet financing or investment adjustments in Step 4, we must adjust one or more nonoperating expenses.

Forecasting Expenses for P&G

To illustrate the forecasting of operating expenses, we turn to Procter & Gamble. P&G's management forecasts an increase in operating profit and cash flow through fiscal year (FY) 2012 as shown in the following slide from the company's 2011 presentation to analysts.

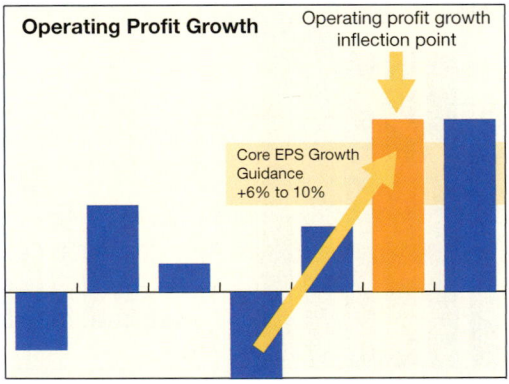

In addition to the 4.6% revenue growth, P&G's report to analysts also predicts an improved operating profit margin for FY2012.

Turning again to Morgan Stanley's analysts, we see that they forecast operating profit by business unit, consistent with how they determine sales forecasts. Following is an excerpt from the Morgan Stanley spreadsheet that has analysts' forecasts of pretax income:

	A	B	AF	AK	AP	AU	AV	AW	AX	AY	AZ	BA	BB	BC	BD	BE
1	Procter & Gamble Co (PG)															
2	Segment Breakdown		FY2007	FY2008	FY2009	FY2010	Sep-10	Dec-10	Mar-11	Jun-11	FY2011	Sep-11 E	Dec-11 E	Mar-12 E	Jun-12 E	FY2012E
66	Pretax Income By Segment		14,710.0	15,632.0	14,803.0	15,314.0	4,282.0	4,366.0	3,641.0	3,205.0	15,494.0	4,104.0	4,525.5	3,989.5	3,390.9	16,009.9
67	% Growth			6.3%	-5.3%	3.5%	2.3%	-8.1%	-3.2%	22.5%	1.2%	-4.2%	3.7%	9.6%	5.8%	3.3%
68	Beauty															
69	Beauty Care		3,440.0	3,528.0	3,558.0	3,648.0	1,081.0	1,141.0	762.0	623.0	3,607.0	982.5	1,196.8	851.4	704.0	3,734.6
70	% Growth					2.5%	5.3%	0.4%	-1.3%	-12.5%	-1.1%	-9.1%	4.9%	11.7%	13.0%	3.5%
71	Grooming		1,895.0	2,299.0	1,900.0	2,007.0	524.0	635.0	524.0	500.0	2,183.0	556.1	665.3	552.7	538.6	2,312.8
72	% Growth					5.6%	7.2%	3.6%	13.4%	12.9%	8.8%	1.0%	4.8%	5.5%	7.7%	5.9%

Total forecasted pretax income is the sum of forecasted pretax income for each business unit (which includes $3,734.6 million from the Beauty Care business unit and $2,312.8 million from the Grooming business unit as illustrated above).

Then, using the segment forecasts, Morgan Stanley analysts predict each line item of the income statement for each quarter of FY2012. We show the following excerpt from their spreadsheet as an illustration. (there are slight differences between the internal analyst spreadsheets reproduced in this module and the published report in the appendix due to timing and other differences)

	A	B	C	AQ	AV	AW	AX	AY	AZ	BA
1	Procter & Gamble Co (PG)									
2	**Income Statement**			**FY2010**	**FY2011**	**Sep-11 E**	**Dec-11 E**	**Mar-12 E**	**Jun-12 E**	**FY2012E**
3	**Sales**			**78,938.0**	**82,559.0**	**21,555.2**	**22,136.4**	**20,843.3**	**21,786.9**	**86,321.8**
4	% Growth			2.9%	4.6%	7.1%	3.7%	3.0%	4.4%	4.6%
	% Organic Growth			3.4%	4.0%	3.4%	4.9%	4.8%	4.6%	4.4%
6	Cost of Sales			-37,919.0	-40,768.0	-10,702.4	-10,833.4	-10,308.3	-11,213.5	-43.057.7
7	% of Sales			48.0%	49.4%	49.7%	48.9%	49.5%	51.5%	49.9%
8	% of Sales Bps Change			-241	134	150	75	0	-24	50
10	**Gross Profit**			**41,019.0**	**41,791.0**	**10,852.8**	**11,303.0**	**10,535.0**	**10,573.4**	**43,264.1**
11	Gross Margin %			52.0%	50.6%	50.3%	51.1%	50.5%	48.5%	50.1%
12	Gross Margin Bps Change			241	-134	-150	-75	0	24	-50
14	SG&A Expense (ex Incremental Restructuring)			-24,731.0	-25,668.0	-6,549.9	-6,575.3	-6,343.1	-6.983.1	-26,451.3
15	% of Sales			31.3%	31.1%	30.4%	29.7%	30.4%	32.1%	30.6%
16	% Growth			11.2%	3.8%	10.4%	1.2%	-1.7%	2.9%	3.1%
17	% of Sales Bps Change			233	-24	91	-72	-147	-49	-45
19	Operating Income (ex Incremental Restructuring)			16,288.0	16,123.0	4,302.9	4,727.7	4,191.9	3,590.3	16,812.7
20	Operating Margin			20.6%	19.5%	20.0%	21.4%	20.1%	16.5%	19.5%
21	% Growth			3.3%	-1.0%	-4.4%	3.6%	11.1%	9.3%	4.3%
22	Operating Margin Bps Change			8	-110	-241	-3	147	73	-5

The remainder of this section explains the details and logic behind these forecasts.

Our forecasted income statement is in Exhibit 11.4. We provide FY2011 actual income statement numbers along with our forecast assumptions and our forecasted numbers for FY2012. To simplify the exposition, we show only annual forecasts (not quarterly forecasts as estimated by Morgan Stanley analysts). Because of this simplification and rounding to whole numbers, the forecasts in this Exhibit differ slightly from those in the analysts' report in Appendix 11A.

EXHIBIT 11.4	Preliminary Forecasted Income Statement for P&G					
($ millions)		**2011**		**Forecast Assumptions**	**2012 Est.**	
Net sales.	$82,559	100.0%		$82,559 × 1.046	$86,357	100.0%
Cost of products sold.	40,768	49.4%		$86,357 × 49.9%	43,092	49.9%
Selling, general and administrative expense . .	25,973	31.5%		$86,357 × 30.6%	26,425	30.6%
Operating income.	15,818	19.2%		subtotal	16,840	19.5%
Interest expense.	831	1.0%		no change	831	1.0%
Other nonoperating income (expense), net . . .	202	0.2%		no change	202	0.2%
Earnings before income taxes	15,189	18.4%		subtotal	16,211	18.8%
Income taxes on continuing operations.	3,392	4.1%		$16,211 × 25.0%	4,053	4.7%
Net earnings.	$11,797	14.3%		subtotal	$12,158	14.1%

Operating Expenses for P&G

This section describes the process of forecasting operating expenses (*we forecast nonoperating revenues and expenses following our adjustments to the balance sheet in Step 4*).

Forecasting Net Sales Following our discussion above, we forecast net sales to increase by 4.6%, which is the forecasted outcome from a predicted 4.5% increase in organic sales, driven primarily by a 2.8% projected increase in volume and a 3.2% increase in selling prices, offset by a 1.5% decline in sales from changes in product mix (selling a greater proportion of lower priced products) and a positive 0.1% foreign exchange effect.

Forecasting Cost of Products Sold Cost of products sold as a percent of sales increased from 48.0% in 2010 to 49.4% in 2011. Morgan Stanley analysts forecast an increase in the COGS percentage by 50 bp (basis points, or 100ths of a percent) to 49.9%. That forecast considers the proportion of raw materials and labor in the production process of each product along with forecasts of changes in commodity costs and wage rates. The 50bp increase in COGS, and the resulting decline in the gross profit margin described above, are reasonable given the recessionary climate and the product markets.

Subtotaling Gross Profit Gross profit is a subtotal, forecasted sales less forecasted cost of goods sold (as an alternative, in some cases, we might choose to forecast gross profit; in that case, cost of goods sold is the "plug" figure). P&G does not report this subtotal in its current income statement and we, therefore, do not include it in our statement (there is no requirement under GAAP to provide this subtotal, yet many companies do report it).

Forecasting Selling, General and Administrative Expense P&G has reduced SG&A expenses as a percent of sales from 31.3% in 2010 to 31.1% in 2011, and it cited further expected improvement during meetings with analysts. A recessionary climate encourages P&G to focus on further overhead reduction, and coupled with P&G's continued focus on manufacturing and supply chain improvements, justifies a forecast of reduced SG&A expenses as a percent of sales. Our forecast is for SG&A expenses to be 30.6% of sales, which is a 50bp improvement on 2011, and slightly more than the 20bp improvement P&G had from 2010 to 2011. This is a trend that P&G highlighted in meetings with analysts.

Subtotaling Operating Income Operating income is a subtotal, but we still check its reasonableness. Our forecasts imply a 19.5% operating income margin, which is close to the previous year's operating income margin of 19.2%. Further, it is reasonable to expect limited improvement in operating income margin as sales increase and expenses remain under control in the post-recessionary period 2012–2014.

Nonoperating Expenses for P&G To this point, we have forecasted sales and individual operating expenses, yielding a subtotal for operating income. The nonoperating section of the income statement requires estimates of nonoperating assets (which yield interest and/or dividend income) and nonoperating liabilities (which produce interest expense). We predict nonoperating revenue and expense once we estimate nonoperating assets and liabilities at the conclusion of the next section. Also, since we do not yet have forecasts of nonoperating revenues (expenses), we cannot forecast pretax income, tax expense, and net income. Thus, we complete our forecasts for the income statement at the conclusion of Step 4.

STEP 3: FORECASTING ASSETS, LIABILITIES AND EQUITY

LO3 Forecast the balance sheet.

Step 3 is to forecast balance sheet items, which consist of assets, liabilities, and equity. Special emphasis is on forecasts of operating assets and liabilities. We generally assume no change in nonoperating assets, liabilities, and equity (we discuss exceptions to this rule in this section and further adjustments to those accounts in Step 4). Step 3 proceeds with five steps as shown in Exhibit 11.5.

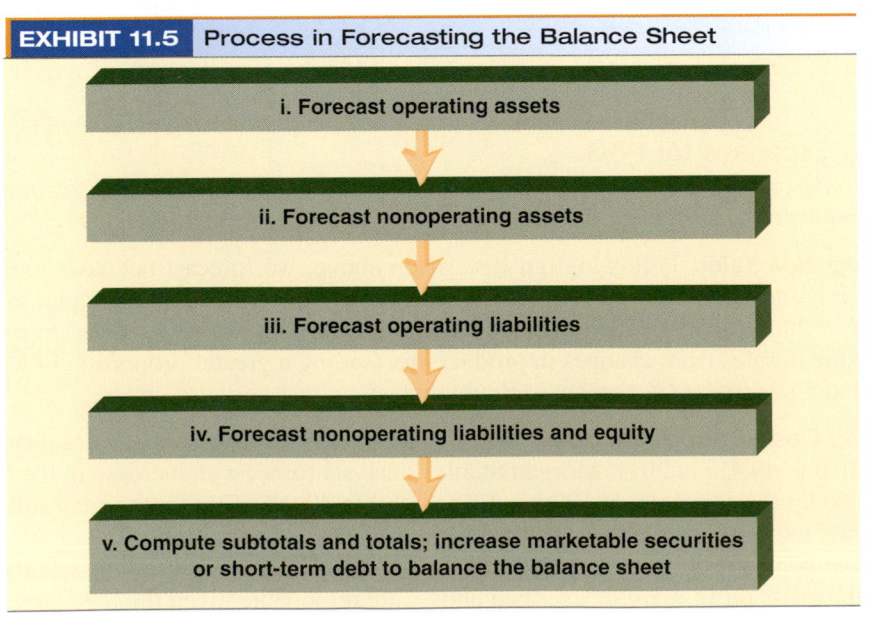

EXHIBIT 11.5   Process in Forecasting the Balance Sheet

i. Forecast operating assets

ii. Forecast nonoperating assets

iii. Forecast operating liabilities

iv. Forecast nonoperating liabilities and equity

v. Compute subtotals and totals; increase marketable securities or short-term debt to balance the balance sheet

As a starting point, we begin with **Procter & Gamble**'s balance sheet for 2011 in Exhibit 11.6. We will refer to these statements throughout this section.

EXHIBIT 11.6	Procter & Gamble Balance Sheet		
June 30, amounts in millions		**2011**	**2010**
Assets			
Current assets			
Cash and cash equivalents		$ 2,768	$ 2,879
Accounts receivable		6,275	5,335
Inventories			
Materials and supplies		2,153	1,692
Work in process		717	604
Finished goods		4,509	4,088
Total inventories		7,379	6,384
Deferred income taxes		1,140	990
Prepaid expenses and other current assets		4,408	3,194
Total current assets		21,970	18,782
Property, plant and equipment			
Buildings		7,753	6,868
Machinery and equipment		32,820	29,294
Land		934	850
Total property, plant and equipment		41,507	37,012
Accumulated depreciation		(20,214)	(17,768)
Net property, plant and equipment		21,293	19,244
Goodwill and other intangible assets			
Goodwill		57,562	54,012
Trademarks and other intangible assets, net		32,620	31,636
Net goodwill and other intangible assets		90,182	85,648
Other noncurrent assets		4,909	4,498
Total assets		$138,354	$128,172
Liabilities and shareholders' equity			
Current liabilities			
Accounts payable		$ 8,022	$ 7,251
Accrued and other liabilities		9,290	8,559
Debt due within one year		9,981	8,472
Total current liabilities		27,293	24,282
Long-term debt		22,033	21,360
Deferred income taxes		11,070	10,902
Other noncurrent liabilities		9,957	10,189
Total liabilities		70,353	66,733
Shareholders' equity			
Convertible Class A preferred stock, stated value $1 per share (600 shares authorized)		1,234	1,277
Non-voting Class B preferred stock, stated value $1 per share (200 shares authorized)		—	—
Common stock, stated value $1 per share (10,000 shares authorized;			
shares issued: 2011—4,007.9, 2010—4,007.6)		4,008	4,008
Additional paid-in capital		62,405	61,697
Reserve for ESOP debt retirement		(1,357)	(1,350)
Accumulated other comprehensive income (loss)		(2,054)	(7,822)
Treasury stock, at cost (shares held: 2011—1,242.2, 2010—1,164.1)		(67,278)	(61,309)
Retained earnings		70,682	64,614
Noncontrolling interest		361	324
Total shareholders' equity		68,001	61,439
Total liabilities and shareholders' equity		$138,354	$128,172

Process of Forecasting Balance Sheet Items

We normally make one of three general assumptions when forecasting assets, liabilities, and equity.

1. **Forecast amounts with no change.** We can use a no-change forecast, which is common for nonoperating assets (investments in securities, discontinued operations, and other nonoperating investments). After we have generated forecasts of the balance sheet, we must reexamine the no-change forecasts to see if they are reasonable or if they require adjustment.

2. **Forecast contractual or specified amounts.** We can use contractual or other specified payment tables to forecast selected balance sheet items. For example, footnote disclosures contain scheduled maturities for long-term debt, capital leases, and mandatory redeemable preferred stock for a five-year period subsequent to the financial statement date. We can use those schedules and assume that the required payments are made as projected.

3. **Forecast amounts in relation to revenues.** We can use an item's relation to revenues to forecast that item. The underlying assumption is that, as revenues change, so does that item in some predictable manner. For example, in the case of operating assets, it is reasonable to assume that the required investment in receivables, inventories, and PPE is related, in some manner, to the level of revenues. Similarly, in the case of operating liabilities, it is reasonable to expect that accounts payable will grow with COGS (which grows with revenues), and accrued liabilities will grow with increases in payroll, utilities, advertising, and other expenses (which all grow with revenues).

When forecasting amounts in relation to revenues, the third forecasting assumption above, there are three common methods: (1) forecasts using the percent of revenues, (2) forecasts using turnover rates, and (3) forecasts using days outstanding ratios.

Forecasts Using Percent of Revenues Forecasts that use the percent of revenues build on the relation between revenues and the account being forecasted; this relation follows:

$$\textbf{Forecasted account balance = Forecasted revenues} \times \left(\frac{\textbf{Actual account balance}}{\textbf{Actual revenues}} \right)$$

For example, if the relation between the actual account balance to revenues is 10%, and forecasted revenues equal $100, then the forecasted account is $10, computed as $100 × 10%.

Forecasts Using Turnover Rates Turnover rates have the following general form: Turnover rate = Revenues (or COGS)/Average account balance. Using algebra to rearrange terms, we obtain: Average account balance = Revenues (or COGS)/Turnover rate. Substituting forecasted values we get:

$$\textbf{Forecasted account balance = Forecasted revenues (or COGS)/Turnover rate}$$

Consequently, if we have forecasted revenues (or COGS) and a forecasted turnover rate, we can forecast the account balance. However, there is a problem with this method if we use turnover rates as traditionally defined using average account balances; in this case the method would forecast the *average account balance*. Balance sheets report *ending account balances*. This issue is typically resolved in one of two ways:

1. Compute the turnover rate using ending balances rather than average balances; then, our forecast is for the ending account balance.

2. Multiply the forecasted average account balance by 2 and then subtract the beginning account balance; this yields the forecast for the ending account balance.

Forecasts Using Days Outstanding Days outstanding ratios have the following general form: Days outstanding = Account balance/Average daily revenues (or COGS), where Average daily revenues (or COGS) = Revenues (or COGS)/365. We can forecast the account balance by rearranging terms as follows:

$$\textbf{Forecasted account balance = Days outstanding} \times \textbf{[Forecasted revenues (or COGS)/365]}$$

If days outstanding is computed using the ending balance of the account, the resulting forecast is for the ending balance of that account. However, some analysts prefer a shortcut method to compute days outstanding as 365/Turnover rate. Their justification is based on the mathematical equality where [365/Turnover rate] = [365/(Revenues/Account balance)] = [(Account balance × 365)/Revenues] = [Account balance/(Revenues/365)]. Importantly, however, if this turnover rate is computed in the conventional way using the *average* account balance, we would forecast the average account balance rather than the ending account balance. In this case, we must make one of the two adjustments explained in the previous section.

Equivalence of the Three Forecasting Methods If we compute the turnover rate and the days outstanding using ending account balances (meaning that we are properly forecasting the ending account balance), it does not matter which of these three forecasting methods we use. To illustrate, consider a company with current-period revenues of $1,000 and a forecasted revenue growth of 4% (or $1,040, computed as $1,000 × 1.04). Assume that the current accounts receivable ending balance is $200 and that we want to forecast accounts receivable for next year. Using each of the three methods above, our forecasted accounts receivable is $208 and is computed as follows:

Forecast Method	Forecast	Forecast Computation
Percent of revenues	$208	$1,040 × ($200/$1,000)
Turnover rate	$208	$1,040/($1,000/$200)
Days outstanding	$208	{[($200 × 365)/$1,000] × $1,040}/365

Each of these forecasting methods yields the same result. Analysts commonly use either percent of sales or days outstanding. The choice between percent of sales and days outstanding depends on the audience. Percent of sales is simple and intuitive. Days outstanding is well suited for analyses that are used in discussions with operating managers, as most managers are familiar with days outstanding ratios and can identify with projected changes (for example, what is the effect of collecting our receivables two days faster?). The choice is a matter of personal preference as all three methods yield the same result. *We use the percent of sales in our forecasts of balance sheet accounts because (1) it appears to be the most commonly used method, (2) it is the method that P&G management uses in its meetings with analysts, and (3) it is the method used by* **Morgan Stanley** *(and the majority of investment houses that we are familiar with) in the analysis illustration we provide in this module and in Appendix 11A.*

Forecasting Balance Sheet Items

We illustrate the forecasting of balance sheet items for **Procter & Gamble**.

Forecasting Operating Assets

This section describes the process of forecasting operating assets using the percent of revenues method. Morgan Stanley analysts forecast balance sheet items as a percentage of sales (except for Inventories and accounts payable that are forecasted as a percent of cost of goods sold). We provide an excerpt from the Morgan Stanley forecasting spreadsheet in Exhibit 11.7, which lists the forecasting assumptions (the entire spreadsheet is in the analysts' report in Appendix 11A).

Forecasting Accounts Receivable P&G reports accounts receivable as a percentage of sales equal to 6.8% and 7.6% at year-end 2010 and 2011, respectively. Recall that Morgan Stanley's forecasts were prepared in a recessionary environment. It was reasonable, therefore, to expect a continuing decline in the financial condition of P&G customers; meaning that some P&G customers were likely to pay more slowly, if at all. This increases predicted accounts receivable relative to sales. Accordingly, Morgan Stanley analysts forecasted a slight increase in P&G's ratio of accounts receivables to sales for 2011 quarters, but returning to the FY2011 level of ~7.7% of projected sales by year-end 2012. Using 7.7% accounts receivable-to-sales and forecasted sales of $86,357 million, we forecast accounts receivable of $6,649 million ($86,357 million × 7.7%). The 7.7% equates to an average collection period of 28.1 days (0.077 × 365 days).

Forecasting Inventories Morgan Stanley analysts forecast inventories as a percent of COGS rather than as a percent of sales. Either approach is fine and does not materially affect the forecasts as long as the method is used consistently. The motivation for use of COGS is that inventories are stated at cost, not at retail. As a result, many analysts use COGS to forecast inventories and the related accounts payable. *(In the assignments, we forecast inventories as a percent of sales so that all balance sheet items are forecasted based on the same basis.)* P&G's inventories

EXHIBIT 11.7	Morgan Stanley Forecasted Balance Sheet Percents

	A	B	C	AQ	AV	AW	AX	AY	AZ	BA
1	Procter & Gamble Co (PG)									
2				FY2010	FY2011	Sep-11 E	Dec-11 E	Mar-12 E	Jun-12 E	FY2012E
161	Cash % of Sales			3.6%	3.4%	2.9%	2.8%	3.0%	2.9%	2.9%
162	AR % of Sales			6.8%	7.6%	7.8%	7.9%	7.9%	7.6%	7.7%
163	AR Days			24.7	27.7	28.3	28.7	29.0	27.8	28.1
164	Inventories % COGS			16.8%	18.1%	18.9%	18.1%	19.1%	17.2%	17.9%
165	Inventory Days			61.5	66.1	68.9	66.2	69.9	62.6	65.2
166	Deferred Inc Tax Assets % Sales			1.3%	1.4%	1.6%	1.6%	1.6%	1.6%	1.6%
167	Other CA % Sales			4.0%	5.3%	4.8%	4.5%	4.8%	4.5%	4.5%
168	Capex, net of dispositions			-3,067.0	-3,306.0	-663.7	-874.9	-938.8	-1,295.1	-3,772.5
169	Addition to PPE as % Sales			3.9%	4.0%	3.1%	4.0%	4.5%	5.9%	4.4%
170	Depreciation % opening PPE			16.0%	14.7%	14.3%	14.3%	14.1%	14.3%	14.3%
171	Depreciation % Net PPE			16.2%	13.3%	3.6%	3.6%	3.5%	3.5%	13.8%
172	AP % COGS			19.1%	19.7%	17.0%	15.1%	15.9%	18.3%	19.1%
173	AP Days			69.8	71.8	62.2	55.2	58.2	66.8	69.6
174	Accrued and Other liabilities % Sales			10.8%	11.3%	11.6%	11.4%	12.1%	11.0%	11.1%
175	Deferred Inc Tax Liabilities % Sales			13.8%	13.4%	12.9%	12.4%	13.2%	12.7%	12.8%
176	Other Liabilities			12.9%	12.1%	11.8%	10.9%	11.7%	10.9%	11.0%
177	Dividends Paid			$1.80	$1.97	$0.53	$0.53	$0.53	$0.57	$2.15
178										
179	Total Debt			29,832.0	32,014.0	32,231.7	32,884.1	32,271.4	31,949.6	31,949.6
180	Cash			2,879.0	2,768.0	2,500.0	2,500.0	2,500.0	2,500.0	2,500.0
181	Net Debt			26,953.0	29,246.0	29,731.7	30,384.1	29,771.4	29,449.6	29,449.6
182	Interest Rate on Debt			2.8%	2.7%	2.6%	2.6%	2.6%	2.6%	2.6%
183	Interest Rate on Cash					1.5%	1.5%	1.5%	1.5%	1.5%
184	Net Debt/LTM EBITDA			1.4x	1.5x	1.6x	1.6x	1.5x	1.5x	1.5x
186	Capital Employed			109,483.0	118,274.0	119,312.2	119,958.7	119,777.8	118,945.0	118,945.0

increased in 2011 from 16.8% of COGS to 18.1% of COGS. In the MD&A section of its 10-K, P&G's management attributes the inventory increase to:

> higher commodity costs, business growth and increased stock levels in advance of initiatives and sourcing changes. Inventory days on hand increased by five days due to the impact of foreign exchange, higher commodity costs and increased safety stock levels.

Morgan Stanley analysts forecast a slight easing of these pressures to yield an annual level of 17.9% of COGS for FY2012 (they estimate inventories on a quarterly basis as: Quarterly COGS × 4 × Inventory %COGS; the year-end estimate, then, is the 4Q estimate, and the 17.9% is the ending 4Q inventory estimate divided by the annual COGS estimate). The 17.9% of COGS equates to an inventory days on hand of 65.3 (0.179 × 365 days, yielding a 0.1 rounding difference from the spreadsheet), which is down from 66.1 days at year-end 2011.

To be consistent with our approach of estimating balance sheet items in relation to the sales estimate, we forecast inventories at an equivalent rate of 8.6% of sales (computed from Morgan Stanley's estimate of ending inventories of $7,557.2 million divided by analysts' estimates of annual sales of $87,754.5 million—numbers from the FY2012E column of the forecasted balance sheet and income statement on pages 6 and 7 of the Morgan Stanley analysts' report in Appendix 11A). This results in forecasted inventories of $7,427 million ($86,357 million × 8.6%).

Forecasting Deferred Income Tax Assets and Other Current Assets Morgan Stanley analysts forecast a slight increase in deferred tax assets to 1.6% of sales (up from 1.4% of sales in FY2011) and a reduction of other current assets from 5.3% of sales to 4.5% of sales. Companies generally provide little information about these accounts in their footnote and MD&A disclosures. We assume a continuation of these percentages in FY2012.

Forecasting Capital Expenditures, PPE, and Accumulated Depreciation Capital expenditures (CAPEX) are often a large cash outflow and a major component of free cash flow, which is the focus of cash-flow-based equity valuation models. (Free cash flow is defined in Module 13 as [NOPAT − Increase in NOA] and is also defined in finance literature as [Net cash flow from operating activities − CAPEX].) CAPEX is used in forecasting PPE (gross), where Forecasted PPE (gross) = Actual PPE (gross) + Forecasted CAPEX. (We typically do not forecast dispositions of PPE unless they are specifically identified by management in the MD&A section of the 10-K or other source.) P&G reported CAPEX as a percent of sales for FY2010 of 3.9% and for FY2011 of 4.0%. In its meetings with analysts, P&G provided guidance for CAPEX as a percentage of sales of 4% to 5% of sales, and Morgan Stanley forecasts CAPEX at 4.4% of sales in their forecast. Based on our forecasted sales of $86,357 million, CAPEX is projected to be $3,800 million (computed as $86,357 million × 4.4%).

The forecast of net PPE is computed as: Beginning-year PPE, net + Forecasted CAPEX − Forecasted Depreciation. Morgan Stanley analysts combine amortization with depreciation; thus, for consistency, we will do the same. Depreciation and amortization are typically estimated by the percentage of reported depreciation and amortization expense (often reported in the statement of cash flows if not disclosed on the income statement) as a percentage of beginning-year PPE, net. This is the approach used by Morgan Stanley analysts. P&G's depreciation and amortization are 14.7% of the beginning-year balance for FY2011 ($2,838 million/$19,244 million). However, Morgan Stanley analysts forecast a slight decrease in that percentage to 14.3% for FY2012 and we use that rate in our forecast. Using the FY2011 net PPE of $21,293, our forecast of depreciation and amortization for FY2012 is $3,045 million ($21,293 million × 14.3%) and our forecast of FY2012 net PPE is $22,048 million as computed here:

Actual net PPE for FY2011.	$21,293 million	
Add: CAPEX.	3,800 million	($86,357 sales × 4.4% CAPEX-to-sales)
Less: Depreciation and amortization	(3,045) million	($21,293 PPE, net for FY2011 × 14.3%)
Forecasted net PPE for FY2012.	$22,048 million	

We applied all amortization expense to net PPE as PPE assets are sometimes amortized as well as depreciated. Often amortization expense relates to intangible assets (see next section). In that case, we apportion depreciation and amortization between depreciable and intangible assets if we have sufficient information.

Forecasting Goodwill and Other Intangible Assets and Amortization Goodwill and other intangible assets arise mainly in connection with acquisitions of other companies. Unless an acquisition is pending at year-end, and we have sufficient information about its financial impact, we forecast no change for goodwill and other intangibles. Goodwill is not amortized, but some other intangible assets are (see Module 9). If we can identify the intangible assets that are amortized and can estimate their amortization expense, we can forecast that expense and reduce the intangible assets accordingly like we did for depreciable assets above. We forecast no change in these intangible assets in this case.

Forecasting Other Noncurrent Assets Other noncurrent assets are assumed to be part of operating assets unless information suggests otherwise. Since we have no information to suggest otherwise, we forecast no change in other noncurrent assets.

Forecasting Nonoperating Assets
This section forecasts nonoperating assets for P&G. Generally, we use the no-change forecast model for nonoperating assets.

Forecasting Cash Our forecasting process assumes that the cash on the balance sheet reflects an economically appropriate balance that we forecast similarly for the next fiscal year. Procter & Gamble's 2011 fiscal year-end cash balance is $2,768 million (3.4% of sales), down from $2,879 million (3.6% of sales) in the prior year. We assume 3.4% of sales in our forecast, resulting in a forecasted cash balance of $2,936 million ($86,357 million × 3.4%) for FY2012.

Forecasting Investment Securities The no-change forecast model applies to marketable securities. For P&G, it does not report marketable securities. We adjust the level of marketable securities (cash in this case) or short-term debt in Step 4 when we balance the balance sheet.

BUSINESS INSIGHT	Does Separately Forecasting Cash and Securities Matter?

Our forecasting process, and that of the Morgan Stanley analysts, is to forecast a cash balance and adjust the level of investment securities or short-term debt to balance the balance sheet. We assume that cash consists of cash equivalents and then forecast interest income on the cash balance at the same rate as that for investment securities. Both cash and marketable securities are treated as nonoperating assets. This means it makes no difference whether we assume a larger balance for cash and a correspondingly smaller balance for investment securities or whether we assume a smaller balance for cash and a larger balance for investment securities. However, we see in recent years that cash balances have ballooned as companies face economic uncertainty. Still, we are indifferent as to whether that excess liquidity is reported as cash or as investment securities as they are both nonoperating assets. We see in Modules 13 and 14 that changes in both cash and securities increase or decrease the value of a company dollar-for-dollar. Our focus is on net operating assets (NOA), which impact company value to a much greater extent. Bottom line: do not focus on the mix between cash and securities.

Summary of Asset Forecasts To this point, we have forecasted all of P&G's operating and nonoperating assets. Following the forecast of liabilities and equity in the next section, we adjust the balance of investment securities or short-term debt to balance the balance sheet. This is Step 4.

Forecasting Operating Liabilities

This section describes the process of forecasting operating liabilities for P&G.

Forecasting Accounts Payable Morgan Stanley forecasts accounts payable as a percentage of COGS. The rationale is that inventories, which drive most accounts payable, are reported at wholesale cost and not retail. Another common method is to forecast accounts payable as a percentage of sales. Either method results in reasonable forecasts if consistently applied. For P&G, accounts payable as a percent of COGS increased from 19.1% in 2010 to 19.7% in 2011. P&G explains this increase as follows:

> Accounts payable, accrued and other liabilities increased primarily due to increased expenditures to support business growth, primarily related to the increased marketing investments.

Morgan Stanley forecasts a reduction of accounts payable as a percentage of COGS from 19.7% in FY2011 to 19.1% in FY2012. This corresponds to the reduction in inventory quantities previously discussed. As reported in Exhibit 11.7, Morgan Stanley's forecasts imply a decrease in accounts payable days outstanding from 71.8 (~19.7% × 365) to 69.6 days (~19.1% × 365). Consistent with our approach of forecasting balance sheet items in relation to forecasted sales, we forecast accounts payable at an equivalent rate of 9.2% of sales (using Morgan Stanley's estimate of accounts payable of $8,059.6 million divided by analysts' estimates of annual sales of $87,754.5 million—see the analysts' report in the appendix), resulting in an estimate for FY2012 accounts payable of $7,945 million ($86,357 million × 9.2%).

Forecasting Accrued and Other Liabilities Accruals as a percent of sales increased from 10.8% in 2010 to 11.3% in 2011. Footnotes reveal that P&G's accruals relate primarily to marketing and compensation expenses, although a large component is classified as "other." Morgan Stanley forecasts this account to remain fairly constant as a percentage of sales, decreasing slightly from 11.3% of sales to 11.1% of sales; similarly, we use 11.1% in our forecast.

Forecasting Taxes Payable Because taxes payable relate directly to tax expense, we prefer to express taxes payable as a percentage of tax expense for forecasting purposes. P&G does not separately identify income taxes payable on its balance sheet. Hence, this account is not included in our forecasts directly, but is forecasted as part of another account. When we encounter a balance sheet with taxes payable as a line item, we suggest forecasting that account using the historical percentage of taxes payable to tax expense.

Forecasting Deferred Income Tax Liabilities Deferred tax assets and deferred tax liabilities generally relate to the level of business activity. Accordingly, we can make a case to forecast these accounts as a percentage of sales. Indeed, Morgan Stanley follows this practice. That is, forecasted deferred tax liabilities are 12.8% of sales, down slightly from 13.4% of sales in FY2011.

Forecasting Other Noncurrent Liabilities Other noncurrent liabilities for P&G primarily relate to pension and other post-retirement benefits. We reasonably assume that these obligations grow with the size of the business. Following this notion, Morgan Stanley forecasts these liabilities as a percentage of sales. For P&G, these liabilities decreased as a percentage of sales, from 12.9% in FY2010 to 12.1% in FY2011. We, like Morgan Stanley, forecast a continuation of this decline to a level of 11.0% of sales for FY2012.

Forecasting Nonoperating Liabilities and Equity

This section forecasts nonoperating liabilities and equity for P&G.

Forecasting Debt Due Within One Year P&G discloses the following table for its debt due within one year:

June 30, in millions	2011	2010
Debt due within one year		
Current portion of long-term debt	$2,994	$ 564
Commercial paper	6,950	7,838
Other	37	70
Total	$9,981	$8,472

Of the $9,981 million total debt due within one year, $2,994 million represents contractual maturities of long-term debt and the $6,987 remainder represents other short-term borrowings. We assume that all contractual maturities of long-term debt will be repaid. Thus, we forecast the $2,994 million to be repaid. For the remaining short-term debt we assume no-change (Step 4 revisits this). Commercial paper represents short-term unsecured borrowings that are typically refinanced by newly issued commercial paper and are not repaid at maturity. Thus, we forecast $6,987 as short-term debt before any current portion of long-term debt. As we show below, the FY2012 current maturities of long-term debt are $3,839 million and, thus, we forecast total debt due within one year as $10,826 million ($6,987 million + $3,839 million).

Forecasting Long-Term Debt P&G's balance sheet reports long-term debt of $22,033. We use the no-change method to forecast long-term debt (and potentially modify this with optional Step 4). Companies are required to disclose the maturities of long-term debt for each of the five years subsequent to the statement date. Following is the disclosure by P&G in its long-term debt footnote:

Long-term debt maturities during the next five years are as follows:

June 30	2012	2013	2014	2015	2016
Debt maturities	$2,994	$3,839	$2,229	$3,021	$2,300

In our forecast for 2012, we classify the amount due in 2013, $3,839, as current maturities of long-term debt, and the remaining balance of $18,194 is forecasted as long-term debt. The $3,839 current maturities of long-term debt are, then, added to short-term debt as we discuss in the preceding section.

Forecasting Equity Accounts Prior to Step 4, we forecast FY2012 equity items with no change, with two exceptions. The first exception is retained earnings, which are increased by forecasted net income and are reduced by forecasted dividends. There are two approaches to forecasting dividends and either is acceptable:

1. Forecast dollar amount of dividends per share and multiply by the forecasted number of shares outstanding (and not the average number of shares outstanding as reported in the EPS calculations), or

2. Forecast a dividend payout ratio (dividends / net income) and multiply this dividend payout ratio by forecasted net income.

Morgan Stanley utilizes the first approach and forecasts dividends per share of $2.15 for the year, a 9.1% increase over the $1.97 per share paid in FY2011 (dividends per share for FY2011 increased by 9.4% over FY2010; so, this increase of 9.1% seems reasonable).

Morgan Stanley forecasts the number of shares outstanding after considering the effects of anticipated share issuances under employee stock option plans and share repurchases in treasury stock, resulting in estimated shares outstanding for FY2012 of 2,944.6 million.[2] Multiplying for forecasted dividends per share of $2.15 by the estimated number of shares outstanding of 2,944.6 million yields a forecasted dollar amount of dividends paid of $6,330.9 million. This is in line with guidance given by P&G of approximately $6 billion in dividends from its meeting with analysts.

Our initial forecast for ending FY2012 retained earnings is $76,509 million, computed as follows:

> $70,682 million beginning retained earnings
> + 12,158 million forecasted net income
> − 6,331 million forecasted dividends
> _____
> $76,509 million ending retained earnings

This forecast will likely change in Step 4 once we forecast the income (expense) related to new investments (borrowing), thus affecting our estimate of net income.

The second exception includes share repurchases (treasury stock) that are announced or planned by a company. In its Barclays capital conference, P&G provided the following slide that indicates its intentions to repurchase about $6 billion for treasury stock in the 2012 fiscal year:

Business Outlook
Cash Generation and Usage

Free Cash Flow Productivity:	+/− 90%
Capital Spending:	4% to 5% of sales
Share Repurchase:	~$6 Billion
Dividends:	~$6 Billion

This slide reflects continuation of P&G's share repurchase program that has resulted in the repurchase of $19.4 billion of treasury stock over the prior three years. Consistent with PG guidance, we forecast the purchase of treasury stock amounting to $6,000 million in 2012.

STEP 4: ADJUST FORECASTED STATEMENTS7

Our (initial) forecasted balance sheet yields total assets of $139,419 million and total liabilities and equity of $134,932 million. Because total assets exceed the total of liabilities and equity, additional financing is required and we assume an increase of $4,487 million of short-term debt to balance. Another option would have been to reduce short-term investments, but P&G did not report short-term investments on its FY2011 balance sheet.) (Note some circularity here in that adjusting debt results in changes in interest expense that results in additional debt, and so on. Morgan Stanley allows for one adjustment as we describe above, which is the $4,487 million

---

[2] Computation of shares outstanding requires estimates of anticipated share issuances and repurchases. We do not know the specific inputs that Morgan Stanley used in their computation, but can speculate that the share issuances relate to the exercise of employee stock options (footnotes usually disclose the number of shares issued for the current and prior two years). Share repurchases might be estimated by guidance provided by the company for the dollar amount of anticipated share repurchases divided by an estimate of the anticipated share price for the coming year. Thus, expected dollar amount of dividends is then: Estimate of ending basic shares outstanding (Beginning shares outstanding + Share issuances − Share repurchases) × Expected dividends per share (often disclosed by a company in guidance to analysts).

of additional debt in our example and the related interest expense. Given the estimates involved in forecasting, additional precision of further iterations is unnecessary.) Had total liabilities and equity been greater than total assets, we could have reduced short-term debt or increased short-term investments to balance.[3]

Adjust Forecasted Income Statement: Nonoperating Expenses

Given our estimates of debt as a result of the "balancing" adjustment in Step 4, we can now finish our forecasts for the income statement (which we presented in Exhibit 11.4). Specifically, we can now forecast nonoperating expense (and revenue), compute pretax income, forecast tax expense, and compute net income. This section describes the process for forecasting those remaining items on the income statement.

Forecasting Interest Expense and "Other" P&G's FY2010 interest expense of $831 million implies a 2.7% rate of interest based on average outstanding interest-bearing debt for that year of $30,923 million ([$29,832 million + $32,014 million]/2). This average interest rate was slightly less than the 2.8% rate reported for FY2010. Morgan Stanley analysts forecast a slight decline for FY2012 to 2.6% in their report (see Exhibit 11.7), and we also use 2.6% to forecast interest expense for FY2012.

Of the long-term debt outstanding as of the end of FY2011, footnotes reveal that $2,994 million is scheduled to mature during FY2012. Given our forecasted $4,487 million increase in short-term debt, then our forecast for interest expense must be adjusted accordingly (we would similarly increase interest income if we had projected an increase in short-term investments). This anticipated repayment of $2,994 million and borrowing of $4,487 million, assuming borrowing and repayment ratably over the year, results in a forecasted interest expense of $852 million ([$32,014 million + {−$2,994 million + $4,487 million}/2] × 2.6%). (Our amount is slightly higher than the Morgan Stanley estimate of $830 million, which they obtain from a detailed analysis of the debt payments and borrowings, vis-à-vis the simple average we assumed.)

Other nonoperating income for FY2011 of $202 million includes interest income on short-term investments (primarily cash balances invested in overnight investments) and net gains on divestitures. Since we are not forecasting any acquisitions or divestitures, nonoperating income is lower for FY2012. Morgan Stanley forecasts an investment rate of 1.5% on available cash balances (assumed to be approximately $2,900 million), which results in $44 million; alternatively, one can use an average of the beginning and ending balances ([$2,768 million + $2,936 million]/2 × 1.5%), which we demonstrate when computing the two-year-ahead forecasts in Exhibit 11.10.

Forecasting Income Taxes Given our forecast of interest expense, we obtain a forecasted pretax income of $16,032 million. Our general method to forecast income taxes is to predict little change, if any, in a company's effective tax rate, *assuming* it is within reasonable limits and absent the company disclosing substantial transitory tax items in the reconciliation of the effective tax rate footnote or an anticipated rate change. Morgan Stanley forecasts a 25.0% effective tax rate for 2012–14, within the range of 25.7% and 23.5% that P&G reported for FY2010 and FY2011, respectively, and we use a 25% forecasted tax rate as well. Consequently, our forecast of tax expense is $4,008 million (computed as $16,032 million of pretax income × 25% forecasted tax rate).

Net Income The resulting forecasted net income is $12,024 million for FY2012, or $4.08 per diluted share. This forecast is slightly below P&G's EPS guidance for FY2012 of $4.17–$4.33 per share, but greater than the $3.93 per diluted share reported in the P&G 10-K for FY2011.

Adjust Forecasted Balance Sheet

The forecasted balance sheet and the revised forecasted income statement for Procter & Gamble is in Exhibits 11.8A and 11.8B. We show the FY2011 balance for each account and the computations required to obtain the forecasted FY2012 balance, including the updated retained earnings computation reflecting the net income computed.

---

[3] When adjusting the balance sheet to balance, we must take care to not inadvertently alter a company's financial leverage. Recall that companies seek to maintain optimal levels of debt and equity to achieve a desired credit rating for their debt, among other objectives. Thus, we must maintain the past debt-to-equity relation within reasonable limits when balancing the forecasted balance sheet. For example, if our decision is to retire debt or to repurchase common stock, we should do it so that the historical debt-to-equity relation is roughly maintained.

EXHIBIT 11.8A	Forecasted Balance Sheet for P&G		
($ millions)	2011	Forecast Assumptions	2012 Est.
Current Assets			
Cash and cash equivalents	$ 2,768	86,357 × 3.4%	$ 2,936
Accounts receivable	6,275	86,357 × 7.7%	6,649
Inventories	7,379	86,357 × 8.6%	7,427
Deferred income taxes	1,140	86,357 × 1.6%	1,382
Prepaid expenses and other current assets	4,408	86,357 × 4.5%	3,886
Total current assets	21,970	subtotal	22,280
Net property, plant and equipment	21,293	21,293 + 3,800 − 3,045	22,048
Goodwill and other intangible assets			
Goodwill	57,562	no change	57,562
Trademarks and other intangible assets, net	32,620	no change	32,620
Net goodwill and other intangible assets	90,182	subtotal	90,182
Other noncurrent assets	4,909	no change	4,909
Total assets	$138,354	subtotal	$139,419
Current Liabilities			
Accounts payable	$ 8,022	86,357 × 9.2%	$ 7,945
Accrued and other liabilities	9,290	86,357 × 11.1%	9,586
Short-term debt (newly issued)	0	plug	4,621
Debt due within one year	9,981	9,981 − 2,994 + 3,839	10,826
Total current liabilities	27,293	subtotal	32,978
Long-term debt	22,033	22,033 − 3,839	18,194
Deferred income taxes	11,070	86,357 × 12.8%	11,054
Other noncurrent liabilities	9,957	86,357 × 11.0%	9,499
Total liabilities	70,353	subtotal	71,725
Shareholders' equity			
Preferred stock	1,234	no change	1,234
Non-voting Class B preferred stock	0	no change	0
Common stock	4,008	no change	4,008
Additional paid-in capital	62,405	no change	62,405
Reserve for ESOP debt retirement	(1,357)	no change	(1,357)
Accumulated other comprehensive income (loss)	(2,054)	no change	(2,054)
Treasury stock	(67,278)	(67,278) − 6,000	(73,278)
Retained earnings	70,682	70,682 + 12,024 − 6,331	76,375
Noncontrolling interest	361	no change	361
Total shareholders' equity	68,001	subtotal	67,694
Total liabilities and shareholders' equity	$138,354	subtotal	$139,419

EXHIBIT 11.8B	Revised Forecasted Income Statement for P&G				
($ millions)	2011		Forecast Assumptions	Revised 2012 Est.	
Net sales	$82,559	100.0%	$82,559 × 1.046	$86,357	100.0%
Cost of products sold	40,768	49.4%	$86,357 × 49.9%	43,092	49.9%
Selling, general and administrative expense	25,973	31.5%	$86,357 × 30.6%	26,425	30.6%
Operating income	15,818	19.2%	subtotal	16,840	19.5%
Interest expense	831	1.0%	(see computation in text)	852	1.0%
Other nonoperating income (expense), net	202	0.2%	(see computation in text)	44	0.1%
Earnings before income taxes	15,189	18.4%	subtotal	16,032	18.6%
Income taxes on continuing operations	3,392	4.1%	$16,032 × 25.0%	4,008	4.6%
Net earnings	$11,797	14.3%	subtotal	$12,024	13.9%

FORECASTING STATEMENT OF CASH FLOWS

LO4 Forecast the statement of cash flows.

We forecast the statement of cash flows using the forecasted income statement and forecasted balance sheet. We refer to the historical statement of cash flows mainly to check the reasonableness of our forecasts. We draw on the mechanics behind the preparation of the statement of cash flows, which we discuss in Module 2. Specifically, once we have forecasts of the balance sheet and income statement, we can compute the forecasted statement of cash flows just as we would its historical counterpart.

Process of Forecasting the Statement of Cash Flows

To illustrate the forecasting of the statement of cash flows we again turn to **Procter & Gamble**. Given its forecasted balance sheet in Exhibit 11.8A and its forecasted income statement in Exhibit 11.8B, we prepare its forecasted statement of cash flows using the procedures for preparing the statement of cash flows explained in Module 2. Our forecasted statement of cash flows is in Exhibit 11.9.

EXHIBIT 11.9	Forecasted Statement of Cash Flows for P&G	
($ millions)	**Forecast Assumptions**	**2012 Est.**
Operating activities		
Net income.	via forecasted income stmt.	$12,024
Add: Depreciation and amortization.	21,293 × 14.3%	3,045
Change in accounts receivable	6,275 − 6,649	(374)
Change in inventories.	7,379 − 7,427	(48)
Change in deferred income taxes	1,140 − 1,382	(242)
Change in prepaid expenses and other current.	4,408 − 3,886	522
Change in accounts payable	7,945 − 8,022	(77)
Change in accrued compensation and other liabilities	9,586 − 9,290	296
Change in deferred income taxes	11,054 − 11,070	(16)
Change in other noncurrent liabilities.	9,499 − 9,957	(458)
Net cash from operating activities	subtotal	14,672
Investing activities		
Capital expenditures	86,357 × 4.4%	(3,800)
Net cash from investing activities.	subtotal	(3,800)
Financing activities		
Dividends	computed as dividends per share	(6,331)
Increase in short-term debt	plug in balance sheet above	4,621
Decrease in long-term debt	current maturities via footnote	(2,994)
Purchase of treasury shares.	PG guidance to analysts	(6,000)
Net cash from financing activities	subtotal	(10,704)
Net change in cash.	subtotal	168
Beginning cash.	from 2011 balance sheet	2,768
Ending cash	subtotal	$ 2,936

Forecasting Operating Activities We begin with the operating section and the forecasted net earnings of $12,024 million, which we compute above. We, then, adjust net earnings for operating expenses and revenues that do not impact cash, and for changes in current assets and liabilities. For the first category we have depreciation and amortization, which are in SG&A expense and are added back in the statement of cash flows because they do not use cash. (Computations for these expenses are explained in our discussion of forecasting capital expenditures and PPE, and forecasting goodwill and other intangibles.) (Appendix 11A shows that Morgan Stanley also forecasts $422.3 million of compensation expense related to stock-based compensation as an add-back to net income, as it is a noncash expense; we are not privy to data that analysts had in making this estimate and do not include it in our forecasts.)

For the second category we have four current assets and four current liabilities whose cash-flow effects we must consider. For example, the forecasted increase in accounts receivable reduces the available cash. We apply this logic to each of the other current assets and liabilities. Thus, net cash flow from operating activities is forecasted at $14,672 million for 2012.

Forecasting Investing Activities The forecasted investing section reports cash expenditures for short- and long-term investments as well as the purchase and sale of long-term operating assets. The only item for P&G is the forecasted $3,800 million outflow for capital expenditures (CAPEX). We discuss the computation of this amount in the section on forecasting capital expenditures and PPE, above. The remaining long-term assets are intangible and other nonoperating assets and we assumed no changes in those assets except for amortization of intangibles. Had we forecasted other changes in those assets, we would include the cash flow effects in the investing section.

Forecasting Financing Activities The forecasted financing section includes forecasted items that impact long-term nonoperating liabilities and equity. We forecast a reduction of long-term debt in the amount of $2,994 million relating to its contractual maturities. Those maturities are reported as part of debt due within one year on the 2011 balance sheet and we assume that all contractual obligations are paid as agreed.

This concludes our initial forecasts of the financial statements for Procter & Gamble. Appendix 11A reproduces an actual analyst forecast of P&G's financial statements from **Morgan Stanley**, which applies the percent of revenues approach that we describe. (Module 13 estimates the value of P&G's stock using our forecasts and compares our estimate to one that Oppenheimer develops from its forecasts and valuation model.)

ADDITIONAL FORECASTING ISSUES

Reassessing Financial Statement Forecasts

After preparing the forecasted financial statements, it is useful to reassess whether they are reasonable in light of current economic and company conditions. This task is subjective and benefits from the forecaster's knowledge of company, industry, and economic factors. Many analysts and managers prepare "what-if" forecasted financial statements. Specifically, they change key assumptions, such as the forecasted sales growth or key cost ratios and then recompute the forecasted financial statements. These alternative forecasting scenarios indicate the sensitivity of a set of predicted outcomes to different assumptions about future economic conditions. Such sensitivity estimates can be useful for setting contingency plans and in identifying areas of vulnerability for company performance and condition.

Multiyear Forecasting of Financial Statements

LO5 Prepare multiyear forecasts of financial statements.

Many business decisions require forecasted financial statements for more than one year ahead. For example, managerial and capital budgeting, security valuation, and strategic analyses all benefit from reliable multiyear forecasts. Modules 13 and 14 use multiyear forecasts of financial results to estimate stock price for investment decisions.

Forecasting the Income Statement We forecast two years ahead using the assumptions for our one-year-ahead forecasts and adjust those assumptions as necessary. To illustrate, we forecast P&G's 2013 sales as $90,329 million, computed as our forecasted FY2012 sales of $86,357 million $\times$ 1.046, the growth rate we used for FY2012. Operating expenses are forecasted from this sales level using the methodology we describe earlier for one-year-ahead forecasts. As before, we compute nonoperating income (expense) after we estimate nonoperating liabilities and, given our estimates of nonoperating revenue (expense), we compute pretax income, tax expense and net income.

Forecasting the Balance Sheet Assuming a continuation of the percent-of-revenues relation for current assets and liabilities, we can forecast current assets and current liabilities applying the same methodology used for one-year-ahead forecasts. For example, FY2013 accounts receivable are forecasted as $6,955 million, computed as $90,329 million $\times$ 7.7% (the same percentage we used to forecast FY2012 receivables). Similarly, we forecast CAPEX at $3,974 million ($90,329 $\times$ 4.4%) and depreciation expense at $3,153 million ($22,048 in FY2012 PPE, net $\times$ 14.3% depreciation rate used previously). Forecasted net PPE is, then, equal to $22,869 million (computed as $22,048 million + $3,974 million − $3,153 million).

Operating liabilities are estimated using the same percent of estimated sales that we use in FY2012. The long-term debt footnote (presented above) reveals that contractual maturities of long-term debt for FY2013 are $2,229 million, and we forecast long-term debt at $15,965 million ($18,194 million − current maturities of $2,229 million). As before, we assume that contractual maturities of long-term debt that were scheduled for FY2012 have been paid. Consequently, we forecast debt due within one year (which includes current maturities of long-term debt) at $9,216 million ($10,826 million for FY2012 − $3,839 in prior-year current maturities + $2,229 in FY2013 current maturities).

In the stockholders' equity section, we forecast a continuation of P&G's stated objective to repurchase $6,000 million of treasury stock. Retained earnings is updated for forecasted net income and decreased by forecasted dividends. For the latter, we highlight the alternative method in this example, that is, to forecast dividends as a percent of forecasted net income. For P&G, our dividend forecast for FY2012 is $6,333 or 52.7% of forecasted net income. Applying this percentage to forecasted net income for FY2013, yields dividends of $6,633 million ($12,587 million × 52.7%).

Adjust Forecasted Statements Our initial balance sheet yields estimated total assets of $141,264 million and total liabilities and equity of $132,664 million, indicating a financing need of $8,600 million. This represents an increase of $3,979 million over the $4,621 million we forecasted for FY2012.

Our estimate of interest expense begins with our FY2012 forecast for total interest-bearing debt of $33,641 million ($4,621 million + $10,826 million + $18,194 million). This debt will decrease by scheduled payments of $3,839 million and increase by new borrowings of $3,979 million. Assuming that these payments and borrowings (netting to an increase of $140 million) occur ratably over the year and that the borrowing rate continues at 2.6%, our estimate for interest expense is $876 million ([$33,641 million + ($140 million/2)] × 2.6%). And, given our estimated cash balance of $3,071 million and a 1.5% investment rate, our estimate of interest income is $45 million ([$2,936 million + $3,071 million]/2 × 1.5%).

Our forecasted income statement and balance sheet is presented in Exhibit 11.10 (FY2012 forecasts are shown in the first column). Given our forecasted nonoperating revenue (expense), we project pretax income at $16,783 million. Assuming a continuation of the 25% effective tax rate, we forecast tax expense of $4,196 million ($16,783 × 25%) and net income of $12,587 million. Exhibit 11.10 also reports the two-year-ahead forecasted statement of cash flows which is prepared using the forecasted FY2013 and FY2012 balance sheets and our forecasted FY2013 income statement. The Morgan Stanley forecast spreadsheet which we reproduce in our Appendix 11A provides forecasts through FY2014 using similar methodology.

EXHIBIT 11.10 Forecasted Two-Year-Ahead Financial Statements for P&G

Income Statement ($ millions)	2012 Est.	Forecast Assumptions	2013 Est.
Net sales	$86,357	$86,357 × 1.046	$90,329
Cost of products sold	43,092	90,329 × 49.9%	45,074
Selling, general and administrative expense	26,425	90,329 × 30.6%	27,641
Operating income	16,840	subtotal	17,614
Interest expense	852	computed	876
Other nonoperating income/(expense), net	44	computed	45
Earnings before income taxes	16,032	subtotal	16,783
Income taxes on continuing operations	4,008	16,782 × 25.0%	4,196
Net earnings	$12,024	subtotal	$12,587

Balance Sheet ($ millions)	2012 Est.	Forecast Assumptions	2013 Est.
Current assets			
Cash and cash equivalents	$2,936	90,329 × 3.4%	$3,071
Accounts receivable	6,649	90,329 × 7.7%	6,955
Inventories	7,427	90,329 × 8.6%	7,768
Deferred income taxes	1,382	90,329 × 1.6%	1,445
Prepaid expenses and other current assets	3,886	90,329 × 4.5%	4,065
Total current assets	22,280	subtotal	23,304
Net property, plant and equipment	22,048	22,048 + 3,974 − 3,153	22,869
Goodwill and other intangible assets			
Goodwill	57,562	no change	57,562
Trademarks and other intangible assets, net	32,620	no change	32,620
Net goodwill and other intangible assets	90,182	no change	90,182
Other noncurrent assets	4,909	no change	4,909
Total assets	$139,419	subtotal	$141,264

continued

continued from prior page

EXHIBIT 11.10	Forecasted Two-Year-Ahead Financial Statements for P&G

Balance Sheet—continued ($ millions)	2012 Est.	Forecast Assumptions	2013 Est.
Current liabilities			
Accounts payable.	$ 7,945	90,329 × 9.2%	$ 8,310
Accrued and other liabilities.	9,586	90,329 × 11.1%	10,027
Short-term debt	4,621	plug	8,600
Debt due within one year	10,826	10,826 − 3,839 + 2,229	9,216
Total current liabilities.	32,978	subtotal	36,153
Long-term debt	18,194	18,194 − 2,229	15,965
Deferred income taxes.	11,054	90,329 × 12.8%	11,562
Other noncurrent liabilities	9,499	90,329 × 11.0%	9,936
Total liabilities.	71,725	subtotal	73,616
Shareholders' equity			
Preferred stock	1,234	no change	1,234
Non–Voting Class B preferred stock	0	no change	0
Common stock.	4,008	no change	4,008
Additional paid-in capital	62,405	no change	62,405
Reserve for ESOP debt retirement.	(1,357)	no change	(1,357)
Accumulated other comprehensive income (loss)	(2,054)	no change	(2,054)
Treasury stock	(73,278)	(73,278) − 6,000	(79,278)
Retained earnings	76,375	76,375 + 12,587 − 6,633	82,329
Noncontrolling interest.	361	no change	361
Total shareholders' equity	67,694	subtotal	67,648
Total liabilities and shareholders' equity.	$139,419	subtotal	$141,264

Statement of Cash Flows	2012 Est.	Forecast Assumptions	2013 Est.
Operating activities			
Net income.	$12,024	via forecasted income stmt.	$12,587
Add: Depreciation and amortization.	3,045	22,048 × 14.3%	3,153
Change in accounts receivable	(374)	6,649 − 6,955	(306)
Change in inventories.	(48)	7,427 − 7,768	(341)
Change in deferred income taxes	(242)	1,382 − 1,445	(63)
Change in prepaid expenses and other current.	522	3,886 − 4,065	(179)
Change in accounts payable	(77)	8,310 − 7,945	365
Change in accrued compensation and other liabilities . . .	296	10,027 − 9,586	441
Change in deferred income taxes	(16)	11,562 − 11,054	508
Change in other noncurrent liabilities.	(458)	9,936 − 9,499	437
Net cash from operating activities	14,672	subtotal	16,602
Investing activities			
Capital expenditures	(3,800)	90,329 × 4.4%	(3,974)
Net cash from investing activities.	(3,800)	subtotal	(3,974)
Financing activities			
Dividends	(6,331)	$12,586 × 52.7%	(6,633)
Increase in short-term debt	4,621	plug	3,979
Decrease in long-term debt	(2,994)	current maturities via footnote	(3,839)
Purchase of treasury shares.	(6,000)	subtotal	(6,000)
Net cash from financing activities	(10,704)	subtotal	(12,493)
Net change in cash.	168	subtotal	135
Beginning cash.	2,768	from balance sheet	2,936
Ending cash	$ 2,936	subtotal	$ 3,071

MID-MODULE REVIEW

Following is financial statement information from **Colgate-Palmolive Company**.

Income Statement		
For year ended December 31 ($ millions)	**2010**	**2009**
Net sales.	$15,564	15,327
Cost of sales.	6,360	6,319
Gross profit.	9,204	9,008
Selling, general and administrative expenses	5,414	5,282
Other (income) expense, net	301	111
Operating profit	3,489	3,615
Interest expense, net	59	77
Income before income taxes	3,430	3,538
Provision for income taxes.	1,117	1,141
Net income including noncontrolling interests.	2,313	2,397
Less: Net income attributable to noncontrolling interests	110	106
Net income attributable to Colgate-Palmolive Company.	$ 2,203	$ 2,291

Balance Sheet		
As of December 31 ($ millions)	**2010**	**2009**
Assets		
Cash and cash equivalents	$ 490	$ 600
Receivables (net of allowances of $53 and $52, respectively).	1,610	1,626
Inventories	1,222	1,209
Other current assets.	408	375
Total current assets	3,730	3,810
Property, plant and equipment, net	3,693	3,516
Goodwill, net	2,362	2,302
Other intangible assets, net	831	821
Other assets.	556	685
Total assets.	$11,172	$11,134
Liabilities		
Notes and loans payable	$ 48	$ 35
Current portion of long-term debt	561	326
Accounts payable.	1,165	1,172
Accrued income taxes	272	387
Other accruals	1,682	1,679
Total current liabilities.	3,728	3,599
Long-term debt	2,815	2,821
Deferred income taxes.	108	82
Other liabilities	1,704	1,375
Total liabilities.	8,355	7,877
Commitments and contingent liabilities		
Shareholders' Equity		
Preference stock	0	169
Common stock, $1 par value (2,000,000,000 shares authorized,		
732,853,180 shares issued)	733	733
Additional paid-in-capital.	1,132	1,764
Retained earnings	14,329	13,157
Accumulated other comprehensive income (loss)	(2,115)	(2,096)
Shareholders' equity before unearned compensation,		
treasury stock and noncontrolling interest	14,079	13,727
Unearned compensation	(99)	(133)
Treasury stock, at cost.	(11,305)	(10,478)
Total Colgate-Palmolive Company shareholders' equity	2,675	3,116
Noncontrolling interests	142	141
Total shareholders' equity	2,817	3,257
Total liabilities and shareholders' equity.	$11,172	$11,134

Required

Forecast the Colgate-Palmolive balance sheet, income statement, and statement of cash flows for 2011 using the following additional information; assume no change for all other accounts not listed below. All percentages, other than sales growth, are based on percent of revenues; assume all capital expenditures are purchases of PPE, and that depreciation and amortization are included as part of selling, general and administrative expenses.

Key Financial Relations and Measures ($ millions)	2010
Net sales growth.	3%
Cost of sales/Net sales	40.9%
Selling, general and administrative expenses/Net sales	34.8%
Depreciation for 2011.	$375
Amortization for 2011.	$19
Other (income) expense, net	$301
Interest expense, net	$59
Provision for income taxes/ Pretax income	32.6%
Net income attributable to noncontrolling interests	$110
Cash and cash equivalents/Net sales	3.1%
Receivables /Net sales.	10.3%
Inventories/Net sales	7.9%
Other current assets/Net sales.	2.6%
Capital expenditures for 2010	$567
Goodwill, net	$2,362
Other assets/Net sales.	3.6%
Notes and loans payable	$48
Accounts payable/Net sales.	7.5%
Accrued income taxes/Provision for income taxes	24.4%
Other accruals/Net sales	10.8%
Deferred income taxes.	$108
Other liabilities/Net sales	10.9%
Preference stock	$0
Common stock.	$733
Additional paid-in-capital.	$1,132
Accumulated other comprehensive income (loss)	$(2,115)
Unearned compensation	$(99)
Treasury stock, at cost.	$(11,305)
Noncontrolling interests	$142
Dividends/Net income	52%
Long-term debt payments required in 2012.	$359

The solution is on page 11-72.

PARSIMONIOUS MULTIYEAR FORECASTING

LO6 Implement a parsimonious method for multiyear forecasting of net operating profit and net operating assets.

The forecasting process described above uses a considerable amount of available information to derive accurate forecasts. We can, however, simplify the process by using less information. Stock valuation models commonly use more parsimonious methods to compute multiyear forecasts for an initial screening of prospective securities. For example, in Modules 13 and 14 we introduce two stock valuation models that use parsimonious forecasting methods. One model utilizes forecasted free cash flows and the other uses forecasted net operating profits after tax (NOPAT) and net operating assets (NOA); see Module 3 for descriptions of these variables. Because free cash flows are equal to net operating profits after tax (NOPAT) less the change in net operating assets (NOA), we can accommodate both stock valuation models with forecasts of NOPAT and NOA.

Parsimonious Method for Forecasting

Our parsimonious approach to forecast NOPAT and NOA requires three crucial inputs:

1. Sales growth
2. Net operating profit margin (NOPM); defined in Module 3 as NOPAT divided by sales
3. Net operating asset turnover (NOAT); defined in Module 3 as sales divided by average NOA. For forecasting purposes, we define NOAT as sales divided by *year-end* NOA instead of average NOA because we want to forecast year-end values.

Multiyear Forecasting with Parsimonious Method

The remainder of this module describes and illustrates this parsimonious approach. To illustrate, we use **Procter & Gamble**'s 2011 income statement, from Exhibit 11.3, and its 2011 balance sheet, from Exhibit 11.6, to determine the following measures. We assume that P&G's statutory tax rate is 37% on nonoperating revenues and expenses.

($ millions)	2011
Sales..	$82,559
Net operating profit after tax ($15,818 − {$3,392 + [($831 − $202) × 37%]})	$12,193
NOA (($138,354 − $2,768) − ($27,293 − $9,981) − $11,070 − $9,957)*....................	$97,247
NOPM ($12,193/$82,559)...	14.8%
NOAT ($82,559/$97,247)*..	0.85

*We use ending balance sheet amounts rather than average amounts because we forecast *ending* balance sheet amounts.

Using these inputs, we forecast P&G's sales, NOPAT, and NOA. Each year's forecasted sales is the prior-year sales multiplied successively by (1+ Growth rate) and then rounded to whole digits. Consistent with our prior revenue growth rate assumptions for P&G, we define "1 + Growth rate" as 1.046 for 2012 and onward. NOPAT is computed using forecasted (and rounded) sales each year times the 2011 NOPM of 14.8%; and NOA is computed using forecasted (and rounded) sales divided by the 2011 NOAT of 0.85. Forecasted numbers for 2012 through 2015 are in Exhibit 11.11; supporting computations are in parentheses.

This forecasting process can be continued for any desired forecast horizon. Also, the forecast assumptions such as sales growth, NOPM, and NOAT can be varied by year, if desired. This alternative, parsimonious method is much simpler than the primary method illustrated in this module. However, its simplicity does forgo information that can impact forecast accuracy.

| EXHIBIT 11.11 | Procter & Gamble Multiyear Forecasts of Sales, NOPAT and NOA |

	Reported	Forecast			
($ millions)	2011	2012 Est.	2013 Est.	2014 Est.	2015 Est.
Net sales growth.......		4.6%	4.6%	4.6%	4.6%
Net sales (unrounded) ..	$82,559	$86,356.71 ($82,559 × 1.046)	$90,329.12 ($86,356.71 × 1.046)	$94,484.26 ($90,329.12 × 1.046)	$98,830.54 ($94,484.26 × 1.046)
Net sales (rounded)	$82,559	$86,357	$90,329	$94,484	$98,831
NOPAT[1]...............	$12,193	$12,781 ($86,357 × 0.148)	$13,369 ($90,329 × 0.148)	$13,984 ($94,484 × 0.148)	$14,627 ($98,831 × 0.148)
NOA[2]................	$97,247	$101,596 ($86,357/0.85)	$106,269 ($90,329/0.85)	$111,158 ($94,484/0.85)	$116,272 ($98,831/0.85)

[1] Forecasted NOPAT = Forecasted net sales (rounded) × 2011 NOPM

[2] Forecasted NOA = Forecasted net sales (rounded)/2011 NOAT

ANALYZING GLOBAL REPORTS

There are no differences in forecasting financial statements prepared under IFRS versus U.S. GAAP. While factors influencing growth rates likely differ among countries across the globe, the method we use to assess growth is independent of the accounting principles applied. Similarly, the forecasting techniques and mechanics we describe in this module can be applied to any set of financial statements.

MODULE-END REVIEW

Johnson & Johnson (J&J) reports fiscal 2010 sales of $61,587 million, net operating profit after tax (NOPAT) of $13,065 million, and net operating assets (NOA) of $45,694 million. J&J's NOPM is computed as 21% ($13,065 million/$61,587 million) and its NOAT is computed as 1.35 ($61,587/$45,694).

Required

Use the parsimonious forecast model to project J&J's sales, NOPAT, and NOA for 2011 through 2014 assuming a sales growth rate of 4%.

The solution is on page 11-74.

APPENDIX 11A   Morgan Stanley's Forecast Report on Procter & Gamble

Morgan Stanley analysts developed their forecasts of P&G shortly after attending the analyst meetings held by P&G management. We completed our analysis and developed our forecasts at about the same time. Thus, we have an opportunity to compare the analysis in this module with the Morgan Stanley analyst report. Following is the Morgan Stanley analysts' report on Procter & Gamble Co. that the firm issued on August 7, 2011 (Pages 9-14 of the report contain the customary disclosure information typical of analyst reports). *Please note that materials that are referenced comprise excerpts from research reports and should not be relied on as investment advice. This material is only as current as the publication date of the underlying Morgan Stanley research. For important disclosures, stock price charts, and equity rating histories regarding companies that are the subject of the underlying Morgan Stanley research, see www.morganstanley.com/researchdisclosures. Additionally, Morgan Stanley has provided their materials here as a courtesy. Therefore, Morgan Stanley and Cambridge Business Publishers do not undertake to advise you of changes in the opinions or information set forth in these materials.*

Morgan Stanley

MORGAN STANLEY RESEARCH
NORTH AMERICA

Morgan Stanley & Co. LLC

Dara Mohsenian, CFA
Dara.Mohsenian@morganstanley.com
+1 212 761 6575

Ruma Mukerji, CFA
Ruma.Mukerji@morganstanley.com
+1 212 761 6754

Kevin Grundy, CPA
Kevin.Grundy@morganstanley.com
+1 212 761 3645

Alison M. Lin, CFA
Alison.Lin@morganstanley.com
+1 212 761 7250

August 7, 2011

Procter & Gamble Co.
Raising 2012e EPS Despite Low Quality Q4

Stock Rating
Overweight

Industry View
In-Line

What's New: PG reported low-quality Q4 EPS, but the stock ended up outperforming the S&P 500 as we believe investors are appropriately looking ahead to an improved pricing/commodity cost scenario in 2012, particularly with stronger than expected 3% Q4 pricing ex-mix (MS was at +1.3%). In addition, FY12 guidance was in-line with consensus. Net, we were not enthused by Q4 results given the low quality nature of Q4, and a weak developed market consumer, as well as continued commodity pressure drove below consensus Q1 guidance, but we think the worst is now behind PG with improving pricing and declining spot commodity costs, and believe undemanding valuation of 13.2 times FY13e EPS is compelling, particularly with the market adopting a more defensive orientation.

In-line but low quality Q4: Q4 EPS of $0.84 was above our $0.81 estimate and the $0.82 consensus, but was boosted 2 cents by a lower than expected tax rate and 3 cents by higher than expected other non-operating income. PG's 5% organic sales growth result (+4% excluding pre-buying ahead of price increases) was solid, but higher than expected SG&A drove a 3% operating profit miss vs. our forecast and 4% miss vs. consensus. Segment profit results were also weak, up only 4.7% y-o-y despite an easy -11.1% comparison, while pretax profit was aided by a 60% y-o-y corporate expense decline

FY12 guidance OK: PG guided to $4.17-4.33 (current consensus at $4.26) in FY12 EPS, up 6-10% y-o-y (+8-12% excluding a higher tax rate), on +3-6% organic revenue growth. However, Q1 guidance of $1.00-1.04 was below the $1.14 consensus.

Raising FY12e EPS: We are raising our FY12e EPS slightly to $4.20 from $4.16 solely on a lower than expected tax rate. On an operating basis, Q4 downside is offset by a more favorable pricing/cost outlook for FY12. We are also lowering our price target slightly to $69 (15x 2013e EPS of $4.59) from $72 to reflect a lower market multiple.

Key Ratios and Statistics

Reuters: PG.N Bloomberg: PG US
Household & Personal Care / United States of America

Price target	**$69.00**
Shr price, close (Aug 5, 2011)	$60.59
Mkt cap, curr (mm)	$180,415
52-Week Range	$67.71-59.17

Fiscal Year ending	06/10	06/11	06/12e	06/13e
ModelWare EPS ($)	**3.67**	**3.95**	**4.20**	**4.59**
Prior ModelWare EPS ($)	-	3.92	4.15	4.59
P/E	16.3	16.1	14.4	13.2
Consensus EPS ($)§	4.11	3.93	4.28	4.58
Div yld (%)	3.0	3.1	3.5	3.9

Unless otherwise noted, all metrics are based on Morgan Stanley ModelWare framework (please see explanation later in this note).
§ = Consensus data is provided by FactSet Estimates.
e = Morgan Stanley Research estimates

Quarterly ModelWare EPS

Quarter	2010	2011 Prior	2011 Current	2012e Prior	2012e Current
Q1	0.97	-	1.02	-	1.04
Q2	1.10	-	1.13	-	1.18
Q3	0.89	-	0.96	-	1.05
Q4	0.71	-	0.84	-	0.93

e = Morgan Stanley Research estimates

Morgan Stanley

MORGAN STANLEY RESEARCH

August 7, 2011
Procter & Gamble Co.

Risk-Reward Snapshot: Procter & Gamble (PG, $60.59, Overweight, PT $69)

Potential Long-Term Topline Reacceleration

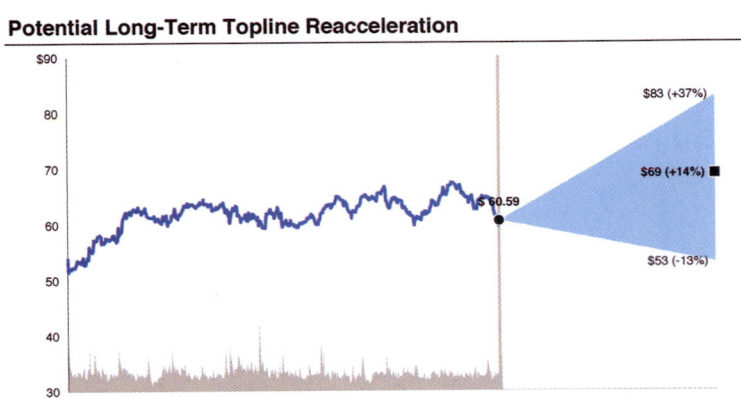

- Base Case (Aug-12)   — Historical Stock Performance   ● Current Stock Price

Price Target: $69		Based on 15x F2013e EPS, below PG's five-year historical NTM P/E average of 16.5x.
Bull Case $83	17x F2013e Bull Case EPS of $4.90	**Topline rebounds to 6% organic sales growth.** Revenue upside as PG's reinvigorated topline focus drives outsized market share gains and a macro rebound is stronger than expected. Cost cutting trims 50 bps from SG&A. Valuation expands to 17x C2012e EPS.
Base Case $69	15x F2013e Base Case EPS of $4.59	**Rebounding organic sales growth.** Organic sales growth of 4.4% through F2013, driven by emerging markets, higher marketing spending, and PG strategy changes. Average operating margin expansion of ~40 bps through F2013. Valuation expands to 15x F2013e EPS (10.2 times EV/EBITDA).
Bear Case $53	13x F2013e Bear Case EPS of $4.09	**Topline downside.** Pricing is 100 bps below our forecast due to a competitive environment and the macro rebound is slower than we expect, hurting volume by 200 bps. Margins miss by 50 bps due to negative mix. Valuation contracts to 13x F2013e EPS.

Bear to Bull: Competitive Environment and Macros Are the Key Drivers

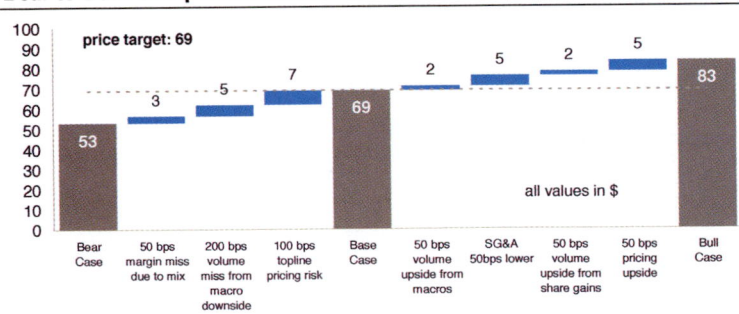

Source: Morgan Stanley Research, FactSet

Why Overweight?

- **LT Topline Re-Acceleration:** We expect PG's organic sales growth to re-accelerate to 4.5% over the next few years from 3% in F2008-11, aided by greater emerging markets focus.

- **Net Pricing/Cost Pressure Gap Eases:** With improving pricing trends despite commodity cost pressure, we expect PG's net commodity cost vs. pricing gap to ease to +1% of EPS in FY12e, versus -10% in FY11e.

- **Margin Expansion Potential:** We believe PG's focus on cost-cutting and productivity is increasing, which should provide margin flexibility to reinvest behind the business. We forecast ~50 bps of annual margin expansion in F2012-15.

Where We Could be Wrong

- **Macros Could Disappoint:** PG is sensitive to macro conditions given its skew to premium products, as each 100 basis point volume change drives an estimated 2% EPS impact.

- **Pricing:** We expect improved HPC industry pricing going forward, but if competition remains heightened, we estimate that each 100 bps of pricing pressure has a 5% EPS impact.

2

Morgan Stanley

Q4 Results Were Weak Quality

Low quality Q4 EPS is not a surprise in a difficult environment: PG F4Q11 EPS of $0.84 was above our $0.81 estimate and the $0.82 consensus, but was aided by non-operating items, including a lower than expected tax rate (worth 2 cents to EPS), and higher than expected other income (worth 3 cents), while underlying operating profit missed consensus by 4% (MS est. by 3%).

Solid organic revenue growth: Q4 organic revenue growth of 5% was PG's best result in six quarters, but would have been 4% excluding 1% benefit from retailer load in ahead of price increases. This is in-line sequentially with Q3 trends, but still a solid result given a difficult industry environment. Organic growth was driven by +3% volumes, +3% pricing, partially offset by -1% mix.

Operating profit miss driven by higher than expected SG&A: Gross margin of 48.3% was down 120 bps YoY, and was ~60bps below consensus (in-line with our forecast). However, higher than expected SG&A expense as a % of sales resulted in a 4% operating profit miss versus consensus (3% vs. our forecast), which was more than offset by other non-operating income and a lower than expected tax rate, which in aggregate added 5 cents to EPS, driving more than all of the EPS upside. PG did disclose full-year ad spending was 40 bps higher than our forecast (PG does not disclose ad spend on a quarterly basis), which does mean FY EPS is higher quality. Please refer to Exhibit 1 and Exhibit 2 for more detail on the quarter's variance versus our forecast.

Exhibit 1
4Q11 EPS Summary

$ in millions, except EPS	MS Est. vs. Actual			Year-over-Year		
	MS Est. Jun-11 E	Actual Jun-11 E	+/-	Jun-10	Actual Jun-11 E	+/-
Sales	$20,812.0	$20,860.0	0.2%	$18,926.0	$20,860.0	10.2%
% Growth	10.0%	10.2%		4.7%	10.2%	
% Organic Growth	5.0%	5.0%		4.0%	5.0%	
Cost of Sales	-10,768.3	-10,787.0	0.2%	-9,560.0	-10,787.0	0.0%
% of Sales	51.7%	51.7%	(3) bps	50.5%	51.7%	120 bps
% of Sales Bps Change	123	120			120	
Gross Profit	10,043.8	10,073.0	0.3%	9,366.0	10,073.0	7.5%
Gross Margin %	48.3%	48.3%	(56) bps	49.5%	48.3%	(120) bps
Gross Margin Bps Change	-123	-120			-120	
SG&A Expense	-6,649.7	-6,788.0	2.1%	-6,416.0	-6,788.0	5.8%
% of Sales	32.0%	32.5%	59 bps	33.9%	32.5%	(136) bps
% Growth	3.6%	5.8%			5.8%	
% of Sales Bps Change	-195	-136			-136	
Operating Income	3,394.0	3,285.0	-3.2%	2,950.0	3,285.0	11.4%
Operating Margin	16.3%	15.7%	(56) bps	15.6%	15.7%	16 bps
% Growth	15.1%	11.4%			11.4%	
Operating Margin Bps Change	72	16			16	
Interest Expense	-204.2	-212.0	3.8%	-212.0	-212.0	0.0%
Other Non-Operating Income, Net	14.0	132.0	845.6%	-121.0	132.0	-209.1%
Pretax Income	3,204	3,205	0.0%	2,617	3,205	22.5%
Taxes	-769.3	-695.0		-432.0	-695.0	0.0%
Tax Rate	24.0%	21.7%		16.5%	21.7%	518 bps
Minority Interests	0.0	0.0		0.0	0.0	
Net Income	2,434.5	2,510.0	3.1%	2,185.0	2,510.0	14.9%
EPS Diluted (Core)	$0.81	$0.84	3.3%	$0.71	$0.84	18.2%
EPS % Growth	14.4%	18.2%		-9.4%	18.2%	
Diluted Shares	2,990.2	2,983.6	-0.2%	3,068.9	2,983.6	-2.8%

Source: Company data, Morgan Stanley Research

Exhibit 2
Low Quality Q4 EPS Beat

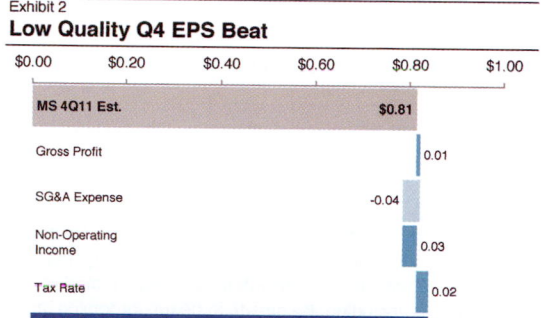

Source: Company data, Morgan Stanley Research

Q4 segment pretax profit results were weak: As shown in Exhibit 3, lower than expected revenue growth in grooming was offset by upside in baby/family. Each segment missed consensus profit estimates, except baby/ family, and total segment profit in aggregate was up only 4.7% y-o-y on an easy -11.1% comparison, offset by lower corporate pretax expense, which declined 60% y-o-y.

Exhibit 3
Segment Results – MS vs. Actual

$ in millions	MS Est. vs. Actual			Year-over-Year		
	MS Est. Jun-11 E	Actual Jun-11	+/-	Jun-10	Actual Jun-11	+/-
Total Sales	$20,812.0	$20,860.0	0.2%	$18,926.0	$20,860.0	10.2%
Organic Sales Growth	5.0%	5.0%	(4) bps	4.0%	5.0%	100bp
Volume (Organic)	4.5%	3.0%	(152) bps	8.0%	3.0%	-500bp
Pricing	1.3%	3.0%	171 bps	-1.0%	3.0%	400bp
Mix	-0.8%	-1.0%	(22) bps	-3.0%	-1.0%	200bp
FX Impact	5.0%	5.0%	0 bps	1.0%	5.0%	400bp
Segment Pretax Profit	$3,778.8	$3,492.0	-7.6%	$3,336.0	$3,492.0	4.7%
Beauty						
Beauty Care	$5,027.9	$5,068.0	0.8%	$4,730.0	$5,068.0	7.1%
Organic Sales Growth	2.0%	3.0%	100bp	5.0%	3.0%	-200bp
Pretax Profit	$691.5	$623.0	-9.9%	$712.0	$623.0	-12.5%
Grooming	$2,119.5	$2,056.0	-3.0%	$1,919.0	$2,056.0	7.1%
Organic Sales Growth	4.0%	1.0%	-300bp	12.0%	1.0%	-1100bp
Pretax Profit	$510.5	$500.0	-2.1%	$443.0	$500.0	12.9%
Household Care						
Fabric and Home Care	$6,238.9	$6,144.0	-1.5%	$5,552.0	$6,144.0	10.7%
Organic Sales Growth	7.0%	4.0%	-300bp	1.0%	4.0%	300bp
Pretax Profit	$1,190.4	$937.0	-21.3%	$965.0	$937.0	-2.9%
Baby and Family Care	$3,974.2	$4,056.0	2.1%	$3,562.0	$4,056.0	13.9%
Organic Sales Growth	7.5%	10.0%	250bp	5.0%	10.0%	500bp
Pretax Profit	$664.9	$798.0	20.0%	$571.0	$798.0	39.8%
Health & Well Being						
Health Care	$2,911.6	$2,949.0	1.3%	$2,638.0	$2,949.0	11.8%
Organic Sales Growth	5.0%	7.0%	200bp	2.0%	7.0%	500bp
Pretax Profit	$615.5	$542.0	-11.9%	$526.0	$542.0	3.0%
Snacks and Pets	$840.3	$850.0	1.2%	$798.0	$850.0	6.5%
Organic Sales Growth	1.0%	-1.0%	-200bp	3.0%	-1.0%	-400bp
Pretax Profit	$106.0	$92.0	-13.2%	$119.0	$92.0	-22.7%

Source: Company data, Morgan Stanley Research

Mixed cash flow and balance sheet results: PG reported solid Q4 cash flow results, with free cash flow up 17% y-o-y driven by sequential improvement versus weak Q3 balance sheet results and change in other assets/liabilities. Working capital results were still weak this quarter, with inventories up

Morgan Stanley

MORGAN STANLEY RESEARCH

August 7, 2011
Procter & Gamble Co.

16% and accounts receivables up 18% y-o-y, versus the 10% increase in reported sales.

Initial FY12 Guidance Relatively In-Line But Weak Q1 Guidance

PG guided to FY12 EPS of $4.17-4.33, in-line with the $4.26 consensus, up 6-10% (+8-12% excluding the higher 25% tax rate), on +3-6% organic revenue growth. Organic revenue guidance includes +3-4% pricing, -1% to -2% mix, with the rest of driven by volume. The relatively wide guidance range is driven by the current level of economic uncertainty. PG expects its organic revenue growth to be ahead of market growth of ~3%, including 4% growth in beauty/grooming, and 3% growth in household care. The company expects +1-2% growth in developed markets and +6-8% growth in emerging markets. FX is expected to contribute another +2-3% to FY12 revenue growth.

We expect PG's pricing/commodity cost gap to ease meaningfully in FY12: PG expects commodity cost inflation in FY12 to be similar to FY11 levels, which implies a $1.8B pretax headwind. PG expects to offset much of the dollar headwind through pricing, but still expects a net gross margin impact, which we estimate implies a 100-120 bps negative gross margin impact.

As shown in Exhibit 4, after assuming a 67-bp volume impact from each point of pricing, we estimate the net negative EPS impact from commodity costs versus pricing will abate

significantly to +4 cents in FY12 vs. -40 cents in FY11 (we assume 3% pricing in FY12 and commodity cost pressure in-line with what was experienced in 2011).

Exhibit 4

Price/Cost Gap (incl. Volume Impact) Should Improve Significantly in Fiscal 2012

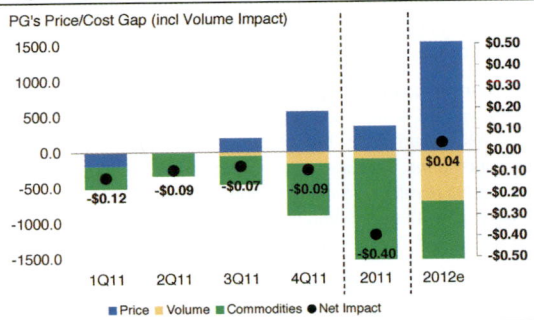

Source: Company data, Morgan Stanley Research

We are raising our FY12e EPS to $4.20 from $4.16 solely on a lower tax rate, with our Q1 estimate of $1.04 at the high end of PG's guidance.

Morgan Stanley

MORGAN STANLEY RESEARCH

August 7, 2011
Procter & Gamble Co.

Valuation and Risks

We rate PG Overweight. Our price target of $69 is based on a 15 times multiple on our FY13 EPS estimate of $4.59, below PG's 16.5x five-year average historical NTM P/E of 16.5x.

Key Risks to our Investment Thesis

Macro recovery stalls. Given Procter & Gamble's skew to premium products, the company's organic sales growth prospects will be significantly influenced by consumer spending going forward. PG's volume is sensitive to macro conditions as evidenced by its 2% volume decline in FY09. We estimate that a 100-bp change in volume is worth 2% to our FY12 EPS estimate.

Pricing environment does not improve as much as we expect. We expect improved HPC industry pricing going forward with selective list price increases in certain categories and less promotional spending. If the industry environment was more competitive than we expect, we estimate that each 100 bps of pricing pressure would be worth 5% to FY12 EPS.

Strong balance sheet could drive or hurt shareholder value. Procter & Gamble has a strong balance sheet with a net debt/EBITDA of 1.5 times at the end of F2Q11. The company has sufficient flexibility to increase its share buybacks above the $6-7 billion it did in FY11. In addition, PG may elect to pursue acquisitions which could boost or detract from shareholder value. If PG levers its balance sheet up to 2.0 times net debt/EBITDA by the end of FY12 to repurchase shares, we estimate EPS would increase by 2%.

Cost-cutting. PG's core SG&A as a percentage of sales (excluding shipping and handling, ad spending, R&D expense, and stock option expense) of 18% in FY10 was the highest in its large cap peer group despite PG's leading scale. As such, we believe PG has ample opportunity to pare back its SG&A spending, and also generate COGS cost savings/productivity. We also believe PG is more focused on cost cutting through simplifying the organization and streamlining bureaucracy, in order to better capitalize on its scale. Each 50 basis points change in core SG&A as a % of sales (about $400 million) versus our forecast would be worth an estimated 2% to FY12 EPS.

Market share vacillates. There may be upside to PG's FY12 EPS if market share gains accelerate with PG ramping up investment behind the business and a strong innovation pipeline. On the other hand, market share could stall with higher pricing. We estimate each 100 basis points of incremental volume would be worth 2% to FY12 EPS.

Currency movements. 62% of PG's FY10 sales were derived from outside the US. As such, fluctuation in currencies could materially impact our EPS estimates. We estimate that a 5% change in the USD versus PG's basket of currencies would have a 3% impact on EPS. PG is more insulated from FX risk than its peers given relatively less international exposure. In addition, PG's significant manufacturing footprint outside the US mitigates the potential transaction impact of FX.

Commodity cost volatility. While PG's diversified product portfolio spreads out its raw material exposure across a wide variety of input costs, volatile commodity costs could significantly impact EPS. In past years, PG experienced significant margin pressure from commodities with input costs increasing $2 billion and $1 billion y-o-y in FY08 and FY09, respectively. In FY11, PG again experienced $1.8B in pretax commodity cost inflation, which is in-line with PG's forecast for FY12 as well. We estimate that each 200 bps change in overall commodity costs would impact EPS by 3%.

Morgan Stanley is currently acting as financial advisor to The Procter & Gamble Company ("P&G") with respect to P&G's announced merger of its Pringle's business into Diamond Foods, Inc. ("Diamond") pursuant to a split-off.

The proposed offer is subject to the consummation of the exchange offer to exchange shares of P&G for shares of Diamond, required regulatory approvals and other customary closing conditions. This report and the information provided herein is also not intended to (i) provide advice with respect to the exchange offer, (ii) serve as an endorsement of the exchange offer, or (iii) result in the procurement, withholding or revocation of a tender in the exchange or any other action by a security holder.

P&G has agreed to pay fees to Morgan Stanley for its services, including transaction fees that are subject to the consummation of the proposed\ transaction.

Please refer to the notes at the end of the report.

Morgan Stanley

MORGAN STANLEY RESEARCH

August 7, 2011
Procter & Gamble Co.

Exhibit 5

PG Income Statement

Income Statement	FY2008	FY2009	FY2010	Sep-10	Dec-10	Mar-11	Jun-11	FY2011	Sep-11 E	Dec-11 E	Mar-12 E	Jun-12 E	FY2012E	FY2013E
Sales	81,748.0	76,694.0	78,938.0	20,122.0	21,347.0	20,230.0	20,860.0	82,559.0	21,612.4	22,828.8	21,503.0	21,810.3	87,754.5	91,795.6
% Growth	9.2%	-2.8%	2.9%	1.6%	1.5%	5.5%	10.2%	4.6%	7.4%	6.9%	6.3%	6.3%	6.3%	4.6%
% Organic Growth	5.0%	2.0%	3.4%	4.0%	3.0%	4.0%	5.0%	4.0%	3.0%	4.7%	4.7%	4.6%	4.3%	4.6%
Cost of Sales	-39,536.0	-38,690.0	-37,919.0	-9,689.0	-10,287.0	-10,005.0	-10,787.0	-40,768.0	-10,730.9	-11,172.3	-10,634.6	-11,015.2	-43,553.0	-45,099.6
% of Sales	48.4%	50.4%	48.0%	48.2%	48.2%	49.5%	51.7%	49.4%	49.7%	48.9%	49.5%	50.5%	49.6%	49.1%
% of Sales Bps Change	39		-241	70	189	135	120	134	150	75	0	-121	25	-50
Gross Profit	42,212.0	38,004.0	41,019.0	10,433.0	11,060.0	10,225.0	10,073.0	41,791.0	10,881.6	11,656.5	10,868.4	10,795.0	44,201.6	46,696.0
Gross Margin %	51.6%	49.6%	52.0%	51.8%	51.8%	50.5%	48.3%	50.6%	50.3%	51.1%	50.5%	49.5%	50.4%	50.9%
Gross Margin Bps Change	-39		241	-70	-189	-135	-120	-134	-150	-75	0	121	-25	50
SG&A Expense (ex incremental Restructuring)	-25,575.0	-22,240.0	-24,731.0	-5,932.0	-6,495.0	-6,453.0	-6,788.0	-25,668.0	-6,579.5	-6,795.8	-6,564.2	-6,966.0	-26,905.4	-27,994.9
% of Sales	31.3%	29.0%	31.3%	29.5%	30.4%	31.9%	32.5%	31.1%	30.4%	29.8%	30.5%	31.9%	30.7%	30.5%
% Growth	5.1%		11.2%	-0.5%	2.0%	7.8%	5.8%	3.8%	10.9%	4.6%	1.7%	2.6%	4.8%	4.0%
% of Sales Bps Change	-54		233	-62	14	69	-136	-24	96	-66	-137	-60	-43	-16
Operating Income (ex incremental Restructuring)	16,637.0	15,764.0	16,288.0	4,501.0	4,565.0	3,772.0	3,285.0	16,123.0	4,302.1	4,860.7	4,304.2	3,829.0	17,296.1	18,701.1
Operating Margin	20.4%	20.6%	20.6%	22.4%	21.4%	18.6%	15.7%	19.5%	19.9%	21.3%	20.0%	17.6%	19.7%	20.4%
% Growth	7.7%	-5.2%	3.3%	1.2%	-7.3%	-4.9%	11.4%	-1.0%	-4.4%	6.5%	14.1%	16.6%	7.3%	8.1%
Operating Margin Bps Change	15	20	8	-9	-202	-204	16	-110	-246	-9	137	181	18	66
Memo Item: D&A	3166	3082	3108.0	689.0	711.0	703.0	735.0	2838.0	762.4	758.2	751.9	772.1	3044.6	3141.7
Memo Item: EBITDA (excluding charges)	19,803.0	18,846.0	19,396.0	5,190.0	5,276.0	4,475.0	4,020.0	18,961.0	5,064.5	5,618.9	5,056.2	4,601.1	20,340.7	21,842.9
Memo Item: EBITDA Margin	24.2%	24.6%	24.6%	25.8%	24.7%	22.1%	19.3%	23.0%	23.4%	24.6%	23.5%	21.1%	23.2%	23.8%
Interest Expense	-1,467.0	-1,358.0	-946.0	-208.0	-209.0	-202.0	-212.0	-831.0	-208.6	-209.5	-207.6	-204.7	-830.4	-837.8
Other Non-Operating Income, Net	462.0	397.0	-28.0	-11.0	10.0	71.0	132.0	202.0	9.9	9.4	9.4	9.4	38.0	38.8
Pretax Income	15,632.0	14,803.0	15,314.0	4,282.0	4,366.0	3,641.0	3,205.0	15,494.0	4,103.4	4,660.6	4,106.1	3,633.7	16,503.8	17,902.1
Taxes	-4,309.0	-3,834.0	-3,931.0	-1,201.0	-980.0	-768.0	-695.0	-3,644.0	-1,025.8	-1,165.1	-1,026.5	-908.4	-4,125.9	-4,654.5
Tax Rate	27.6%	25.9%	25.7%	28.0%	22.4%	21.1%	21.7%	23.5%	25.0%	25.0%	25.0%	25.0%	25.0%	26.0%
Minority Interests	0.0	0.0	0.0	0.0	0.0	0.0	0.0	0.0	0.0	0.0	0.0	0.0	0.0	0.0
Net Income	11,323.0	10,969.0	11,383.0	3,081.0	3,386.0	2,873.0	2,510.0	11,850.0	3,077.5	3,495.4	3,079.6	2,725.3	12,377.8	13,247.6
EPS Diluted (Core)	$3.41	$3.48	$3.67	$1.02	$1.13	$0.96	$0.84	$3.95	$1.04	$1.18	$1.05	$0.93	$4.20	$4.59
EPS % Growth	12.2%	1.9%	5.6%	4.6%	3.0%	7.9%	18.2%	7.5%	1.8%	4.9%	9.5%	10.9%	6.5%	9.3%
Basic Shares	3,078.4	2,952.0	2,896.2	2,828.5	2,800.3	2,802.2	2,786.5	2,804.4	2,773.0	2,756.0	2,739.6	2,724.4	2,748.2	2,687.4
Diluted Shares	3,316.8	3,154.1	3,100.2	3,025.6	3,000.2	2,999.3	2,983.6	3,001.9	2,970.1	2,953.1	2,936.7	2,921.5	2,945.3	2,884.5

Source: Company data, Morgan Stanley Research estimates

6

Morgan Stanley

MORGAN STANLEY RESEARCH

August 7, 2011
Procter & Gamble Co.

Exhibit 6
PG Balance Sheet

Balance Sheet	FY2008	FY2009	FY2010	Sep-10	Dec-10	Mar-11	Jun-11	FY2011	Sep-11 E	Dec-11 E	Mar-12 E	Jun-12 E	FY2012E	FY2013E
Assets														
Surplus Cash	0.0	0.0	0.0	0.0	0.0	0.0	0.0	0.0	0.0	0.0	0.0	0.0	0.0	0.0
Cash & Equivalents	3,313.0	4,781.0	2,879.0	2,603.0	3,249.0	2,945.0	2,768.0	2,768.0	2,500.0	2,500.0	2,500.0	2,500.0	2,500.0	2,500.0
Investment Securities	228.0													
Receivables, Net	6,761.0	5,836.0	5,335.0	6,082.0	6,551.0	6,264.0	6,275.0	6,275.0	6,705.4	7,188.4	6,830.2	6,648.1	6,648.1	6,954.1
Inventories	8,416.0	6,880.0	6,384.0	7,277.0	7,423.0	7,619.0	7,379.0	7,379.0	8,102.4	8,106.5	8,141.0	7,557.2	7,557.2	7,826.8
Deferred Income Taxes	2,012.0	1,209.0	990.0	968.0	963.0	1,099.0	1,335.0	1,335.0	1,383.2	1,461.0	1,376.2	1,395.9	1,395.9	1,460.1
Prepaid Expenses and Other Current Assets	3,785.0	3,199.0	3194.0	3566.0	3644.0	3886.0	4213.0	4213.0	4175.9	4079.6	4130.5	3925.9	3925.9	4106.6
Total Current Assets	24,515.0	21,905.0	18,782.0	20,496.0	21,830.0	21,814.0	21,970.0	21,970.0	22,866.9	23,335.5	22,977.9	22,027.0	22,027.0	22,847.6
PP&E, Net	20,640.0	19,462.0	19,244.0	19,877.0	19,952.0	20,521.0	21,293.0	21,293.0	21,196.1	21,340.3	21,556.8	22,081.2	22,081.2	22,534.8
Goodwill, Net	59,767.0	56,512.0	54,012.0	56,171.0	55,760.0	57,030.0	57,030.0	57,030.0	57,030.0	57,030.0	57,030.0	57,030.0	57,030.0	57,030.0
Other Intangible Assets, Net	34,233.0	32,606.0	31,636.0	32,369.0	32,251.0	32,598.0	33,152.0	33,152.0	33,152.0	33,152.0	33,152.0	33,152.0	33,152.0	33,152.0
Other Assets	4,837.0	4,348.0	4,498.0	4,779.0	4,480.0	4,575.0	4,909.0	4,909.0	4,909.0	4,909.0	4,909.0	4,909.0	4,909.0	4,909.0
Total Assets	143,992.0	134,833.0	128,172.0	133,692.0	134,273.0	136,538.0	138,354.0	138,354.0	139,154.1	139,766.7	139,625.7	139,199.2	139,199.2	140,473.3
Liabilities														
Short-Term Debt	0.0	0.0	0.0	0.0	0.0	0.0	0.0	0.0	0.0	0.0	0.0	0.0	0.0	0.0
Notes and Loan Payable	0.0	0.0	00.0	0.0	0.0	0.0	0.0	00.0	171.4	1,675.4	980.5	789.7	789.7	1,598.2
Current Portion of Long-Term Debt	13,084.0	16,320.0	8,472.0	11,512.0	11,153.0	9,721.0	9,981.0	9,981.0	9,981.0	10,545.0	10,545.0	10,545.0	10,545.0	12,686.0
Accounts Payable	6,775.0	5,980.0	7,251.0	6,716.0	6,267.0	6,458.0	8,022.0	8,022.0	7,309.4	6,761.6	6,779.3	8,059.6	8,059.6	8,255.8
Accrued and Other Liabilities	11,099.0	8,601.0	8,559.0	9,412.0	9,816.0	9,996.0	9,290.0	9,290.0	10,022.7	10,406.0	10,410.0	9,626.0	9,626.0	9,977.8
Total Current Liabilities	30,958.0	30,901.0	24,282.0	27,640.0	27,241.0	26,175.0	27,293.0	27,293.0	27,484.5	29,388.1	28,714.8	29,020.2	29,020.2	32,517.9
Long-Term Debt	23,581.0	20,652.0	21,360.0	21,464.0	21,317.0	21,699.0	22,033.0	22,033.0	22,033.0	20,058.0	20,058.0	20,058.0	20,058.0	15,942.0
Deferred Income Taxes	11,805.0	10,752.0	10,902.0	10,709.0	10,867.0	10,923.0	10,847.2	10,847.2	11,156.4	11,347.4	11,352.3	11,079.6	11,079.6	11,589.6
Minority Interests	0.0	0.0	324.0	346.0	349.0	363.0	363.0	363.0	363.0	363.0	363.0	363.0	363.0	363.0
Other Liabilities	8,154.0	9,429.0	10,189.0	10,678.0	10,135.0	10,309.0	10,179.8	10,179.8	10,172.2	9,925.3	10,097.6	9,771.1	9,771.1	9,764.6
Total Liabilities	74,498.0	71,734.0	67,057.0	70,837.0	69,906.0	69,469.0	70,716.0	70,716.0	71,209.1	71,081.8	70,585.8	70,292.0	70,292.0	70,177.2
Shareholders' Equity														
Preferred Stock	1,366.0	1,324.0	1,277.0	1,260.0	1,253.0	1,241.0	1,241.0	1,241.0	1,241.0	1,241.0	1,241.0	1,241.0	1,241.0	1,241.0
Common Stock	4,002.0	4,007.0	4,008.0	4,008.0	4,008.0	4,008.0	4,008.0	4,008.0	4,008.0	4,008.0	4,008.0	4,008.0	4,008.0	4,008.0
Additional Paid-In Capital	60,307.0	61,118.0	61,697.0	61,839.0	61,985.0	62,180.0	62,180.0	62,180.0	62,180.0	62,180.0	62,180.0	62,180.0	62,180.0	62,180.0
Retained Earnings	48,986.0	57,309.0	64,614.0	66,282.0	68,212.0	59,692.0	71,582.7	71,582.7	73,101.0	75,045.1	76,583.8	77,629.7	77,629.7	84,087.9
Accumulated Other Comprehensive Income (Loss)	3,746.0	-3,358.0	-7,822.0	-5,007.0	-5,356.0	-3,495.0	-2,832.0	-2,832.0	-2,543.3	-2,248.4	-1,931.1	-1,609.7	-1,609.7	-379.0
Reserve for ESOP Debt Retirement	-1,325.0	-1,340.0	-1,350.0	-1,353.0	-1,355.0	-1,355.0	-1,355.0	-1,355.0	-1,355.0	-1,355.0	-1,355.0	-1,355.0	-1,355.0	-1,355.0
Treasury Stock	-47,588.0	-55,961.0	-61,309.0	-64,174.0	-64,383.0	-35,202.0	-67,186.7	-67,186.7	-68,686.7	-70,186.7	-71,686.7	-73,186.7	-73,186.7	-79,486.7
Total Shareholders' Equity	69,494.0	63,099.0	61,115.0	62,855.0	64,364.0	67,069.0	67,638.0	67,638.0	67,945.0	68,684.9	69,040.0	68,907.2	68,907.2	70,296.2
Total Liabilities & SE	143,992.0	134,833.0	128,172.0	133,692.0	134,273.0	136,538.0	138,354.0	138,354.0	139,154.1	139,766.7	139,625.7	139,199.2	139,199.2	140,473.3

Source: Company data, Morgan Stanley Research estimates

7

Morgan Stanley

MORGAN STANLEY RESEARCH

August 7, 2011
Procter & Gamble Co.

Exhibit 7

PG Cash Flow Statement

Cash Flow	FY2008	FY2009	FY2010	Sep-10	Dec-10	Mar-11	Jun-11	FY2011	Sep-11 E	Dec-11 E	Mar-12 E	Jun-12 E	FY2012E	FY2013E
Net Income	11,323.0	10,969.0	11,383.0	3,081.0	3,386.0	2,873.0	2,510.0	11,850.0	3077.5	3495.4	3079.6	2725.3	12,377.8	13,247.6
Adjustments:														
Depreciation and Amortization	3,166.0	3,082.0	3,108.0	689.0	711.0	703.0	735.0	2838.0	762.4	758.2	751.9	772.1	3044.6	3141.7
Stock-Based Compensation Expense	555.0	516.0	453.0	87.0	93.0	115.0	119.0	414.0	88.7	94.9	117.3	121.4	422.3	430.7
Deferred Income Taxes	1,214.0	596.0	36.0	48.0	94.0	44.0	-58.0	128.0	-48.2	-77.8	84.8	-19.7	-60.8	-64.3
Other	1,279.0	120.0	-1,121.0	2.0	-125.0	-797.0	680.0	-240.0	346.2	287.3	-46.0	-68.0	519.5	329.3
Changes in A/L														
Receivables	432.0	415.0	-14.0	-434.0	-497.0	436.0	69.0	-426.0	-430.4	-483.0	358.2	182.1	-373.1	-306.0
Inventories	-1,050.0	721.0	86.0	-604.0	-175.0	-38.0	316.0	-501.0	-723.4	-4.1	-34.5	583.8	-178.2	-269.6
AP, Accrued and Other Liabilities	134.0	-742.0	2446.0	-303.0	-74.0	154.0	581.0	358.0	20.1	-164.4	21.6	496.2	373.5	548.1
Other Operating Assets and Liabilities	-1,239.0	-758.0	-305.0	-114.0	-536.0	566.0	-1,106.0	-1190.0	-7.6	-246.8	172.2	-326.5	-408.7	-6.5
Cash Provided by Operations	15,814.0	14,919.0	16,072.0	2,452.0	2,877.0	4,056.0	3,846.0	13,231.0	3,085.4	3,659.7	4,505.1	4,466.8	15,717.0	17,051.1
Cash Flows from Investing Activities:														
Capital Expenditures	-3,046.0	-3,238.0	-3,067.0	-519.0	-737.0	-810.0	-1,240.0	-3,306.0	-665.5	-902.3	-968.5	-1,296.5	-3,832.8	-3,595.3
Proceeds from Asset Sales	928.0	1,087.0	3068.0	14.0	8.0	67.0	136.0	225.0	0.0	0.0	0.0	0.0	0.0	0.0
Payment for Acquisitions	-381.0	-368.0	-425.0	-398.0	-37.0	-54.0	15.0	-474.0	0.0	0.0	0.0	0.0	0.0	0.0
Other	-50.0	166.0	-173.0	-25.0	153.0	-31.0	-24.0	73.0	0.0	0.0	0.0	0.0	0.0	0.0
Cash Used for Investing Activities	-2,549.0	-2,353.0	-597.0	-928.0	-613.0	-828.0	-1113.0	-3,482.0	-665.5	-902.3	-968.5	-1296.5	-3,832.8	-3,595.3
Cash Flows from Financing Activities:														
Change in Short-Term Debt	1,844.0	-2,420.0	-1,798.0	2,412.0	-1,464.0	-1,368.0	571.0	151.0	171.4	2068.0	-694.9	-190.8	1,353.7	2,949.5
Change in Long-Term Debt	-4,659.0	2,339.0	-4,716.0	-17.0	1,393.0	-28.0	-18.0	1,330.0	0.0	-1975.0	0.0	0.0	-1,975.0	-4,116.0
Dividends Paid	-4,655.0	-5,044.0	-5,458.0	-1,422.0	-1,412.0	-1,403.0	-1530.0	-5,767.0	-1559.3	-1550.4	-1541.8	-1679.5	-6,330.9	-6,789.3
Purchase of Treasury Shares	-10,047.0	-6,370.0	-6,004.0	-3,010.0	-518.0	-1,008.0	-2,503.0	-7,039.0	-1500.0	-1500.0	-1500.0	-1500.0	-6,000.0	-6,300.0
Proceeds From Stock Options, Other	1,867.0	681.0	721.0	136.0	374.0	248.0	544.0	1302.0	200.0	200.0	200.0	200.0	800.0	800.0
Cash Used for Financing Activities	-15,650.0	-10,814.0	-17,255.0	-1,901.0	-1,627.0	-3,559.0	-2,936.0	-10,023.0	-2,687.9	-2,757.4	-3,536.7	-3,170.3	-12,152.2	-13,455.8
Cash Provided by Discontinued Operations	0.0	0.0	0.0	0.0	0.0	0.0	0.0	0.0	0.0	0.0	0.0	0.0	0.0	0.0
Exchange Rate Effect on Cash / Other	344.0	-284.0	-122.0	101.0	9.0	28.0	25.0	163.0	0.0	0.0	0.0	0.0	0.0	0.0
Net Increase (Decrease) in Cash and Cash Equivs	-2041.0	1468.0	-1902.0	-276.0	646.0	-303.0	-178.0	-111.0	-268.0	0.0	0.0	0.0	-268.0	0.0
Cash and Cash Equivs, Beg	5,354.0	3,313.0	4,781.0	2,879.0	2,603.0	3,249.0	2,946.0	2,879.0	2,768.0	2,500.0	2,500.0	2,500.0	2,768.0	2,500.0
Cash and Cash Equivs, End	3,313.0	4,781.0	2,879.0	2,603.0	3,249.0	2,946.0	2,768.0	2,768.0	2,500.0	2,500.0	2,500.0	2,500.0	2,500.0	2,500.0

Source: Company data, Morgan Stanley Research estimates

8

Morgan Stanley

Morgan Stanley

MORGAN STANLEY

ModelWare

Morgan Stanley ModelWare is a proprietary analytic framework that helps clients uncover value, adjusting for distortions and ambiguities created by local accounting regulations. For example, ModelWare EPS adjusts for one-time events, capitalizes operating leases (where their use is significant), and converts inventory from LIFO costing to a FIFO basis. ModelWare also emphasizes the separation of operating performance of a company from its financing for a more complete view of how a company generates earnings.

Disclosure Section

The information and opinions in Morgan Stanley Research were prepared by Morgan Stanley & Co. LLC, and/or Morgan Stanley C.T.V.M. S.A., and/or Morgan Stanley Mexico, Casa de Bolsa, S.A. de C.V. As used in this disclosure section, "Morgan Stanley" includes Morgan Stanley & Co. LLC, Morgan Stanley C.T.V.M. S.A., Morgan Stanley Mexico, Casa de Bolsa, S.A. de C.V. and their affiliates as necessary.
For important disclosures, stock price charts and equity rating histories regarding companies that are the subject of this report, please see the Morgan Stanley Research Disclosure Website at www.morganstanley.com/researchdisclosures, or contact your investment representative or Morgan Stanley Research at 1585 Broadway, (Attention: Research Management), New York, NY, 10036 USA.

Analyst Certification
The following analysts hereby certify that their views about the companies and their securities discussed in this report are accurately expressed and that they have not received and will not receive direct or indirect compensation in exchange for expressing specific recommendations or views in this report: Dara Mohsenian.
Unless otherwise stated, the individuals listed on the cover page of this report are research analysts.

Global Research Conflict Management Policy
Morgan Stanley Research has been published in accordance with our conflict management policy, which is available at www.morganstanley.com/institutional/research/conflictpolicies.

Important US Regulatory Disclosures on Subject Companies
Within the last 12 months, Morgan Stanley managed or co-managed a public offering (or 144A offering) of securities of Colgate-Palmolive Co, Procter & Gamble Co..
Within the last 12 months, Morgan Stanley has received compensation for investment banking services from Avon Products Inc., Clorox Co, Colgate-Palmolive Co, Newell Rubbermaid Inc., Procter & Gamble Co., Weight Watchers International.
In the next 3 months, Morgan Stanley expects to receive or intends to seek compensation for investment banking services from Avon Products Inc., Church & Dwight Co., Inc., Clorox Co, Colgate-Palmolive Co, Energizer Holdings Inc, Newell Rubbermaid Inc., Procter & Gamble Co., Tupperware Brands Corp., Weight Watchers International.
Within the last 12 months, Morgan Stanley has received compensation for products and services other than investment banking services from Avon Products Inc., Church & Dwight Co., Inc., Clorox Co, Colgate-Palmolive Co, Energizer Holdings Inc, Procter & Gamble Co., Weight Watchers International.
Within the last 12 months, Morgan Stanley has provided or is providing investment banking services to, or has an investment banking client relationship with, the following company: Avon Products Inc., Church & Dwight Co., Inc., Clorox Co, Colgate-Palmolive Co, Energizer Holdings Inc, Newell Rubbermaid Inc., Procter & Gamble Co., Tupperware Brands Corp., Weight Watchers International.
Within the last 12 months, Morgan Stanley has either provided or is providing non-investment banking, securities-related services to and/or in the past has entered into an agreement to provide services or has a client relationship with the following company: Avon Products Inc., Church & Dwight Co., Inc., Clorox Co, Colgate-Palmolive Co, Energizer Holdings Inc, Newell Rubbermaid Inc., Procter & Gamble Co., Weight Watchers International.
Morgan Stanley & Co. LLC makes a market in the securities of Avon Products Inc., Church & Dwight Co., Inc., Clorox Co, Colgate-Palmolive Co, Energizer Holdings Inc, Newell Rubbermaid Inc., Procter & Gamble Co., Tupperware Brands Corp., Weight Watchers International.
The equity research analysts or strategists principally responsible for the preparation of Morgan Stanley Research have received compensation based upon various factors, including quality of research, investor client feedback, stock picking, competitive factors, firm revenues and overall investment banking revenues.
Morgan Stanley and its affiliates do business that relates to companies/instruments covered in Morgan Stanley Research, including market making, providing liquidity and specialized trading, risk arbitrage and other proprietary trading, fund management, commercial banking, extension of credit, investment services and investment banking. Morgan Stanley sells to and buys from customers the securities/instruments of companies covered in Morgan Stanley Research on a principal basis. Morgan Stanley may have a position in the debt of the Company or instruments discussed in this report.
Certain disclosures listed above are also for compliance with applicable regulations in non-US jurisdictions.

STOCK RATINGS
Morgan Stanley uses a relative rating system using terms such as Overweight, Equal-weight, Not-Rated or Underweight (see definitions below). Morgan Stanley does not assign ratings of Buy, Hold or Sell to the stocks we cover. Overweight, Equal-weight, Not-Rated and Underweight are not the equivalent of buy, hold and sell. Investors should carefully read the definitions of all ratings used in Morgan Stanley Research. In addition, since Morgan Stanley Research contains more complete information concerning the analyst's views, investors should carefully read Morgan Stanley Research, in its entirety, and not infer the contents from the rating alone. In any case, ratings (or research) should not be used or relied upon as investment advice. An investor's decision to buy or sell a stock should depend on individual circumstances (such as the investor's existing holdings) and other considerations.

Global Stock Ratings Distribution
(as of July 31, 2011)

For disclosure purposes only (in accordance with NASD and NYSE requirements), we include the category headings of Buy, Hold, and Sell alongside our ratings of Overweight, Equal-weight, Not-Rated and Underweight. Morgan Stanley does not assign ratings of Buy, Hold or Sell to the stocks we cover. Overweight, Equal-weight, Not-Rated and Underweight are not the equivalent of buy, hold, and sell but represent recommended relative weightings (see definitions below). To satisfy regulatory requirements, we correspond Overweight, our most positive stock rating, with a buy recommendation; we correspond Equal-weight and Not-Rated to hold and Underweight to sell recommendations, respectively.

10

MorganStanley

MORGAN STANLEY RESEARCH

August 7, 2011
Procter & Gamble Co.

Stock Rating Category	Coverage Universe		Investment Banking Clients (IBC)		
	Count	% of Total	Count	% of Total IBC	% of Rating Category
Overweight/Buy	**1107**	**40%**	**451**	**48%**	**41%**
Equal-weight/Hold	**1136**	**41%**	**372**	**40%**	**33%**
Not-Rated/Hold	**114**	**4%**	**20**	**2%**	**18%**
Underweight/Sell	**384**	**14%**	**97**	**10%**	**25%**
Total	**2,741**		**940**		

Data include common stock and ADRs currently assigned ratings. An investor's decision to buy or sell a stock should depend on individual circumstances (such as the investor's existing holdings) and other considerations. Investment Banking Clients are companies from whom Morgan Stanley received investment banking compensation in the last 12 months.

Analyst Stock Ratings

Overweight (O). The stock's total return is expected to exceed the average total return of the analyst's industry (or industry team's) coverage universe, on a risk-adjusted basis, over the next 12-18 months.

Equal-weight (E). The stock's total return is expected to be in line with the average total return of the analyst's industry (or industry team's) coverage universe, on a risk-adjusted basis, over the next 12-18 months.

Not-Rated (NR). Currently the analyst does not have adequate conviction about the stock's total return relative to the average total return of the analyst's industry (or industry team's) coverage universe, on a risk-adjusted basis, over the next 12-18 months.

Underweight (U). The stock's total return is expected to be below the average total return of the analyst's industry (or industry team's) coverage universe, on a risk-adjusted basis, over the next 12-18 months.

Unless otherwise specified, the time frame for price targets included in Morgan Stanley Research is 12 to 18 months.

Analyst Industry Views

Attractive (A): The analyst expects the performance of his or her industry coverage universe over the next 12-18 months to be attractive vs. the relevant broad market benchmark, as indicated below.

In-Line (I): The analyst expects the performance of his or her industry coverage universe over the next 12-18 months to be in line with the relevant broad market benchmark, as indicated below.

Cautious (C): The analyst views the performance of his or her industry coverage universe over the next 12-18 months with caution vs. the relevant broad market benchmark, as indicated below.

Benchmarks for each region are as follows: North America - S&P 500; Latin America - relevant MSCI country index or MSCI Latin America Index; Europe - MSCI Europe; Japan - TOPIX; Asia - relevant MSCI country index.

Stock Price, Price Target and Rating History (See Rating Definitions)

Morgan Stanley

MORGAN STANLEY RESEARCH

August 7, 2011
Procter & Gamble Co.

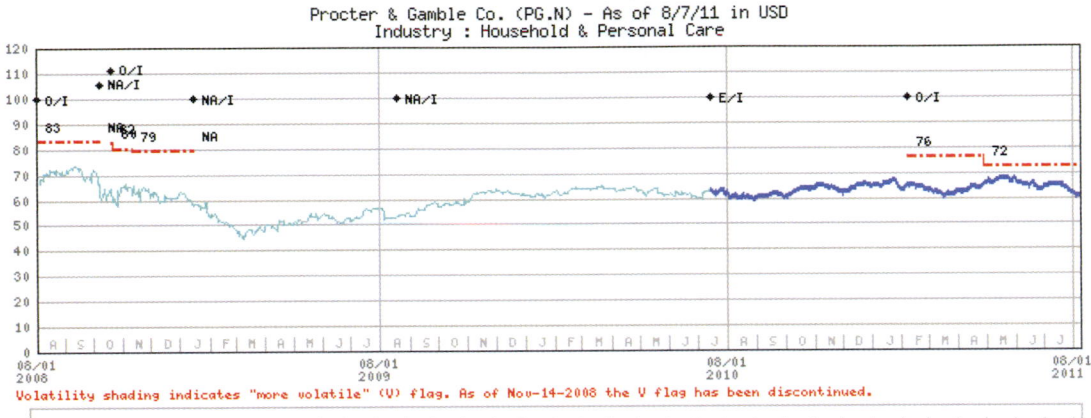

Procter & Gamble Co. (PG.N) - As of 8/7/11 in USD
Industry : Household & Personal Care

Volatility shading indicates "more volatile" (V) flag. As of Nov-14-2008 the V flag has been discontinued.

Stock Rating History: 8/1/08 : O/I; 10/8/08 : NA/I; 10/20/08 : O/I; 1/16/09 : NA/I; 8/19/09 : NA/I;
7/15/10 : E/I; 2/7/11 : O/I
Price Target History: 4/30/08 : 83; 10/8/08 : NA; 10/20/08 : 82; 10/22/08 : 80; 11/12/08 : 79; 1/16/09 : NA;
2/7/11 : 76; 4/28/11 : 72

Source: Morgan Stanley Research   Date Format : MM/DD/YY   Price Target -·-   No Price Target Assigned (NA)
Stock Price (Not Covered by Current Analyst) —   Stock Price (Covered by Current Analyst) ▬
Stock and Industry Ratings (abbreviations below) appear as ◆ Stock Rating/Industry View
Stock Ratings: Overweight (O) Equal-weight (E) Underweight (U) Not-Rated (NR) More Volatile (V) No Rating Available (NA)
Industry View: Attractive (A)   In-line (I)   Cautious (C)   No Rating (NR)

Important Disclosures for Morgan Stanley Smith Barney LLC Customers

Citi Investment Research & Analysis (CIRA) research reports may be available about the companies or topics that are the subject of Morgan Stanley Research. Ask your Financial Advisor or use Research Center to view any available CIRA research reports in addition to Morgan Stanley research reports.

Important disclosures regarding the relationship between the companies that are the subject of Morgan Stanley Research and Morgan Stanley Smith Barney LLC, Morgan Stanley and Citigroup Global Markets Inc. or any of their affiliates, are available on the Morgan Stanley Smith Barney disclosure website at www.morganstanleysmithbarney.com/researchdisclosures.

For Morgan Stanley and Citigroup Global Markets, Inc. specific disclosures, you may refer to www.morganstanley.com/researchdisclosures and https://www.citigroupgeo.com/geopublic/Disclosures/index_a.html.

Each Morgan Stanley Equity Research report is reviewed and approved on behalf of Morgan Stanley Smith Barney LLC. This review and approval is conducted by the same person who reviews the Equity Research report on behalf of Morgan Stanley. This could create a conflict of interest.

Other Important Disclosures

Morgan Stanley & Co. International PLC and its affiliates have a significant financial interest in the debt securities of Avon Products Inc., Clorox Co, Colgate-Palmolive Co, Newell Rubbermaid Inc., Procter & Gamble Co..

Morgan Stanley is not acting as a municipal advisor and the opinions or views contained herein are not intended to be, and do not constitute, advice within the meaning of Section 975 of the Dodd-Frank Wall Street Reform and Consumer Protection Act.

Morgan Stanley produces an equity research product called a "Tactical Idea." Views contained in a "Tactical Idea" on a particular stock may be contrary to the recommendations or views expressed in research on the same stock. This may be the result of differing time horizons, methodologies, market events, or other factors. For all research available on a particular stock, please contact your sales representative or go to Client Link at www.morganstanley.com.

Morgan Stanley Research does not provide individually tailored investment advice. Morgan Stanley Research has been prepared without regard to the individual financial circumstances and objectives of persons who receive it. Morgan Stanley recommends that investors independently evaluate particular investments and strategies, and encourages investors to seek the advice of a financial adviser. The appropriateness of a particular investment or strategy will depend on an investor's individual circumstances and objectives. The securities, instruments, or strategies discussed in Morgan Stanley Research may not be suitable for all investors, and certain investors may not be eligible to purchase or participate in some or all of them.

The fixed income research analysts, strategists or economists principally responsible for the preparation of Morgan Stanley Research have received compensation based upon various factors, including quality, accuracy and value of research, firm profitability or revenues (which include fixed income trading and capital markets profitability or revenues), client feedback and competitive factors. Fixed Income Research analysts', strategists' or economists' compensation is not linked to investment banking or capital markets transactions performed by Morgan Stanley or the profitability or revenues of particular trading desks.

Morgan Stanley Research is not an offer to buy or sell or the solicitation of an offer to buy or sell any security/instrument or to participate in any particular trading strategy. The "Important US Regulatory Disclosures on Subject Companies" section in Morgan Stanley Research lists all companies mentioned where Morgan Stanley owns 1% or more of a class of common equity securities of the companies. For all other companies mentioned in Morgan Stanley Research, Morgan Stanley may have an investment of less than 1% in securities/instruments or derivatives of securities/instruments of companies and may trade them in ways different from those discussed in Morgan Stanley Research. Employees of Morgan Stanley not involved in the preparation of Morgan Stanley Research may have investments in securities/instruments or derivatives of securities/instruments of companies mentioned and may trade them in ways different from those discussed in Morgan Stanley Research. Derivatives may be issued by Morgan Stanley or associated persons.

With the exception of information regarding Morgan Stanley, Morgan Stanley Research is based on public information. Morgan Stanley makes every effort to use reliable, comprehensive information, but we make no representation that it is accurate or complete. We have no obligation to tell you when opinions or information in Morgan Stanley Research change apart from when we intend to discontinue equity research coverage of a subject company. Facts and views presented in Morgan Stanley Research have not been reviewed by, and may not reflect information known to, professionals in other Morgan Stanley business areas, including investment banking personnel.

Morgan Stanley

13

Morgan Stanley

The Americas	**Europe**	**Japan**	**Asia/Pacific**
1585 Broadway	20 Bank Street, Canary Wharf	4-20-3 Ebisu, Shibuya-ku	1 Austin Road West
New York, NY 10036-8293	London E14 4AD	Tokyo 150-6008	Kowloon
United States	**United Kingdom**	**Japan**	**Hong Kong**
Tel: +1 (1) 212 761 4000	Tel: +44 (0) 20 7 425 8000	Tel: +81 (0) 3 5424 5000	Tel: +852 2848 5200

Industry Coverage:Household & Personal Care

Company (Ticker)	Rating (as of)	Price* (08/05/2011)
Dara Mohsenian, CFA		
Avon Products Inc. (AVP.N)	E (10/04/2010)	$23.21
Church & Dwight Co., Inc. (CHD.N)	E (08/19/2009)	$38.54
Clorox Co (CLX.N)	E (07/15/2011)	$67.18
Colgate-Palmolive Co (CL.N)	E (07/15/2010)	$84.15
Energizer Holdings Inc (ENR.N)	E (02/02/2011)	$78.02
Newell Rubbermaid Inc. (NWL.N)	O (12/15/2010)	$13.16
Procter & Gamble Co. (PG.N)	O (02/07/2011)	$60.59
Tupperware Brands Corp. (TUP.N)	O (08/19/2009)	$56.47
Weight Watchers International (WTW.N)	E (02/18/2011)	$61.7

Stock Ratings are subject to change. Please see latest research for each company.
* Historical prices are not split adjusted.

DISCUSSION QUESTIONS

Q11-1. Identify at least two applications that use forecasted financial statements.

Q11-2. Forecasts of the income statement typically require estimates of cost of goods sold (gross profit) and operating and nonoperating expenses (revenues) as a percentage of revenues. Identify at least three financial statement adjustments that we discuss in previous modules that might affect our forecasts for gross profit margin and operating expense percentages.

Q11-3. Forecasts of the balance sheet commonly require estimates of the relative percentage of balance sheet accounts to revenues. Identify at least three financial statement adjustments to reported balance sheet items that can impact that item's relation to revenues. These can include adjustments to recognize assets and/or liabilities that are not recognized under GAAP.

Q11-4. What does the concept of financial statement articulation mean in the forecasting process?

Q11-5. Net operating assets typically move proportionately with revenues. How do the "buffer zone" and "financing" sections of the balance sheet offset some of these changes in net operating assets?

Q11-6. Identify and describe the four major steps in forecasting financial statements.

Q11-7. In addition to recent revenues trends, what other types and sources of information can we use to help us forecast revenues?

Q11-8. Describe the rationale for use of year-end balances in the computation of turnover rates (and other percentages) that are used to forecast selected balance sheet accounts.

Q11-9. What are "comparable store sales" for retailers and why are they important?

Q11-10. Capital expenditures are usually an important cash outflow for a company, and they figure prominently into forecasts of net operating assets. What are the sources of information about capital expenditures that we can draw upon?

Assignments with the ✔ logo in the margin are available in an online homework system. See the Preface of the book for details.

MINI EXERCISES

M11-11. Forecasting an Income Statement **(LO2)**
Abercrombie & Fitch reports the following income statements.

ABERCROMBIE &
FITCH
(ANF)

Income Statement, For Fiscal Years Ended ($ thousands)	Jan. 29, 2011	Jan. 30, 2010	Jan. 31, 2009
Net sales.	$3,468,777	$2,928,626	$3,484,058
Cost of goods sold.	1,256,596	1,045,028	1,152,963
Gross profit.	2,212,181	1,883,598	2,331,095
Stores and distribution expense.	1,589,501	1,425,950	1,436,363
Marketing, general and administrative expense.	400,804	353,269	405,248
Other operating income, net	(10,056)	(13,533)	(8,778)
Operating income.	231,932	117,912	498,262
Interest expense (income), net.	3,362	(1,598)	(11,382)
Income from continuing operations before taxes.	228,570	119,510	509,644
Tax expense from continuing operations	78,287	40,557	201,475
Net income from continuing operations.	150,283	78,953	308,169
Loss from discontinued operations, net of tax.	—	(78,699)	(35,914)
Net Income.	$ 150,283	$ 254	$ 272,255

Forecast Abercrombie & Fitch's fiscal 2012 income statement assuming the following income statement relations. All percentages, other than sales growth and provision for income taxes, are based on percent of net sales.

Net Sales growth	10%
Cost of Goods Sold/Net sales	36%
Stores And Distribution Expense/Net sales	46%
Marketing, General And Administrative Expense/Net sales.	12%
Other Operating Income, Net	10,056
Interest Expense (Income), Net	3,362
Tax Expense From Continuing Operations (% Of Pretax Income).	34%
Net Loss From Discontinued Operations (Net Of Taxes)	0

M11-12. Forecasting an Income Statement   (LO2)

BEST BUY
(BBY)

Best Buy reports the following income statements.

Income Statement, Fiscal Years Ended ($ millions)	February 26, 2011	February 27, 2010	February 28, 2009
Revenue	$50,272	$49,694	$45,015
Cost of goods sold	37,611	37,534	34,017
Restructuring charges—cost of goods sold.	24	—	—
Gross profit.	12,637	12,160	10,998
Selling, general and administrative expenses	10,325	9,873	8,984
Restructuring charges	198	52	78
Goodwill and tradename impairment.	—	—	66
Operating income.	2,114	2,235	1,870
Other income (expense)			
Investment income and other	51	54	35
Investment impairment.	—	—	(111)
Interest expense	(87)	(94)	(94)
Earnings before income tax expense and equity in income of affiliates . . .	2,078	2,195	1,700
Income tax expense	714	802	674
Equity in income of affiliates.	2	1	7
Net earnings including noncontrolling interests	1,366	1,394	1,033
Net earnings attributable to noncontrolling interests	(89)	(77)	(30)
Net earnings attributable to Best Buy Co., Inc.	$ 1,277	$ 1,317	$ 1,003

Forecast Best Buy's fiscal 2012 income statement assuming the following income statement relations. All percentages (other than revenue growth, income tax expense, and net earnings attributable to non-controlling interests) are based on percent of revenue.

Revenue growth	5%
Cost of goods sold/Revenue	75%
Restructuring charges − cost of goods sold	$0
Selling, general and administrative expenses/Revenue.	21%
Restructuring charges	$0
Goodwill and tradename impairment.	$0
Investment income and other.	$51
Investment impairment.	$0
Interest expense.	$(87)
Income tax expense (% of pretax income).	34%
Equity in income of affiliates.	$2
Net earnings attributable to noncontrolling interests (% of Net earnings including noncontrolling interests).	7%

M11-13. Forecasting an Income Statement   (LO2)

GENERAL MILLS
(GIS)

General Mills reports the following fiscal year income statements.

Income Statement, Fiscal Years Ended (in millions)	May 29, 2011	May 30, 2010	May 31, 2009
Net sales....................................	$14,880.2	$14,635.6	$14,555.8
Cost of sales..............................	8,926.7	8,835.4	9,380.9
Selling, general and administrative expenses	3,192.0	3,162.7	2,893.2
Divestitures (gain), net	(17.4)	—	(84.9)
Restructuring, impairment, and other exit costs	4.4	31.4	41.6
Operating profit	2,774.5	2,606.1	2,325.0
Interest, net...............................	346.3	401.6	382.8
Earnings before income taxes and after-tax earnings from joint ventures.....................	2,428.2	2,204.5	1,942.2
Income taxes	721.1	771.2	720.4
After-tax earnings from joint ventures	96.4	101.7	91.9
Net earnings, including earnings attributable to noncontrolling interests	1,803.5	1,535.0	1,313.7
Net earnings attributable to noncontrolling interests........	5.2	4.5	9.3
Net earnings attributable to General Mills	$ 1,798.3	$ 1,530.5	$ 1,304.4

Forecast General Mills' fiscal year 2012 income statement assuming the following income statement relations. All percentages (other than net sales growth, income taxes, and net earnings attributable to noncontrolling interests) are based on percent of sales.

Net sales growth......................................	5%
Cost of sales/Net sales	60.0%
Selling, general, and administrative expenses/Net sales....................	21.5%
Divestiture (gain), net	$0.0
Restructuring, impairment, and other exit costs	$0.0
Interest, net	$346.3
Income taxes (% pretax income)	29.7%
After-tax earnings from joint ventures	$96.4
Net earnings attributable to noncontrolling interests (% net earnings before attribution).....	0.3%

M11-14. Analyzing, Forecasting, and Interpreting Working Capital Using Turnover Rates (LO3)

HARLEY-DAVIDSON
(HOG)

Harley-Davidson reports 2010 net operating working capital of $1,833 million and 2010 long-term operating assets of $2,679 million.

a. Forecast Harley-Davidson's 2011 net operating working capital and 2011 long-term operating assets. Assume forecasted 2011 net revenue of $4,938 million, net operating working capital turnover of 2.65 times, and long-term operating asset turnover of 1.81 times. (Both turnover rates are computed here using year-end balances. Finance receivables and related debt are considered operating under the assumption that they are an integral part of Harley's operating activities.)

b. Most of Harley's receivables arise from its financing activities relating to purchases of motorcycles by consumers and dealers. What effect will these receivables have on Harley's operating working capital turnover rate?

M11-15. Analyzing, Forecasting, and Interpreting Working Capital Using Turnover Rates (LO3)

NIKE
(NKE)

Nike reports 2010 net operating working capital of $2,595 million and 2010 long-term operating assets of $3,460 million.

a. Forecast Nike's 2011 net operating working capital assuming forecasted sales of $19,451 million, net operating working capital turnover of 7.33 times, and long-term operating asset turnover of 5.50 times. (Both turnover rates are computed here using year-end balances.)

b. Nike's long-term operating asset turnover rate is comparatively high. Can you suggest a possible reason given Nike's business model? Explain.

M11-16. Forecasting the Balance Sheet Using Turnover Rates (LO2, 3)

GENERAL MILLS
(GIS)

Refer to the **General Mills** information in M11-13. Assume the forecast of 2012 net sales is $15,624.2 million. Use the following financial statement relations to forecast General Mills' receivables, inventories, and accounts payable as of the end of May 2012.

Year-end turnover rates	2012
Year-end receivables/Net Sales	7.8%
Year-end inventories/Net Sales	10.8%
Year-end accounts payable/Net Sales	6.7%

KRAFT FOODS, INC.
(KFT)

M11-17. Adjusting the Income Statement (LO2)

Kraft Foods, Inc., reports the following footnote to its 2010 10-K.

Pizza Divestiture On March 1, 2010, we completed the sale of the assets of our North American frozen pizza business ("Frozen Pizza") to Nestlé USA, Inc. ("Nestlé") for $3.7 billion. Our Frozen Pizza business was a component of our U.S. Convenient Meals and Canada & North America Foodservice segments. The sale included the *DiGiorno*, *Tombstone* and *Jack's* brands in the U.S., the *Delissio* brand in Canada and the *California Pizza Kitchen* trademark license. It also included two Wisconsin manufacturing facilities (Medford and Little Chute) and the leases for the pizza depots and delivery trucks. Approximately 3,600 of our employees transferred with the business to Nestlé. Accordingly, the results of our Frozen Pizza business have been reflected as discontinued operations on the consolidated statement of earnings, and prior period results have been revised in a consistent manner.

What adjustment(s) might we consider before we forecast Kraft's income for 2011? How would we treat the cash proceeds that Kraft realized on such a sale?

EXERCISES

ABERCROMBIE & FITCH
(ANF)

E11-18. Analyzing, Forecasting, and Interpreting Income Statement and Balance Sheet (LO2, 3)

Following are the income statements and balance sheets of **Abercrombie & Fitch**.

Income Statement, For Fiscal Years Ended ($ thousands)	January 29, 2011	January 30, 2010	January 31, 2009
Net sales.	$3,468,777	$2,928,626	$3,484,058
Cost of goods sold.	1,256,596	1,045,028	1,152,963
Gross profit.	2,212,181	1,883,598	2,331,095
Stores and distribution expense.	1,589,501	1,425,950	1,436,363
Marketing, general and administrative expense.	400,804	353,269	405,248
Other operating income, net	(10,056)	(13,533)	(8,778)
Operating income.	231,932	117,912	498,262
Interest expense (income), net	3,362	(1,598)	(11,382)
Income from continuing operations before taxes.	228,570	119,510	509,644
Tax expense from continuing operations	78,287	40,557	201,475
Net income from continuing operations.	150,283	78,953	308,169
Loss from discontinued operations, net of tax.	—	(78,699)	(35,914)
Net Income.	$ 150,283	$ 254	$ 272,255

Consolidated Balance Sheets		
(Thousands, except par value amounts)	January 29, 2011	January 30, 2010
Current Assets		
Cash and equivalents.	$ 826,353	$ 669,950
Marketable securities	—	32,356
Receivables	81,264	90,865
Inventories	385,857	310,645
Deferred income taxes	60,405	44,570
Other current assets.	79,389	77,297
Total current assets	1,433,268	1,225,683
Property and equipment, net	1,149,583	1,244,019
Noncurrent marketable securities	100,534	141,794
Other assets.	264,517	210,370
Total assets.	$2,947,902	$2,821,866

continued

continued from prior page

Liabilities and stockholders' equity
Current liabilities

Accounts payable	$ 137,235	$ 150,134
Accrued expenses	306,587	246,289
Deferred lease credits	41,538	43,597
Income taxes payable	73,491	9,352
Total current liabilities	558,851	449,372

Long-term liabilities

Deferred income taxes	33,515	47,142
Deferred lease credits	192,619	212,052
Long-term debt	68,566	71,213
Other liabilities	203,567	214,170
Total long-term liabilities	498,267	544,577

Stockholders' equity:

Class A common stock—$0.01 par value: 150,000 shares authorized and 103,300 shares issued at each of January 29, 2011 and January 30, 2010	1,033	1,033
Paid-in capital	349,258	339,453
Retained earnings	2,272,317	2,183,690
Accumulated other comprehensive loss, net of tax	(6,516)	(8,973)
Treasury stock, at average cost 16,054 and 15,314 shares at January 29, 2011, and January 30, 2010, respectively	(725,308)	(687,286)
Total stockholders' equity	1,890,784	1,827,917
Total liabilities and stockholders' equity	$2,947,902	$2,821,866

a. Forecast Abercrombie & Fitch's fiscal 2012 income statement and balance sheet using the following relations (assume 'no change' for accounts not listed). Assume all capital expenditures are purchases of property and equipment.

Net sales growth	10%
Cost of goods sold/Net sales	36.20%
Stores and distribution expense/Net sales	45.80%
Marketing, general and administrative expense/Net sales	11.60%
Other operating income, net	$10,056
Interest expense (income), net	$3,362
Tax expense from continuing operations (% of pretax income)	34.30%
Net loss from discontinued operations (net of taxes)	$0
Cash and equivalents/Net sales	23.8%
Receivables/Net sales	2.3%
Inventories/Net sales	11.1%
Deferred income taxes/Net sales	1.7%
Other current assets/Net sales	2.3%
Other assets/Net sales	7.6%
Accounts payable/Net sales	4.0%
Accrued expenses/Net sales	8.8%
Deferred lease credits/Net sales	1.2%
Income taxes payable (% tax expense)	93.9%
Deferred income taxes/Net sales	1.0%
Deferred lease credits/Net sales	5.6%
Capital expenditures (% Of Sales)	4.6%
Depreciation & amortization	$229,153
Dividends (% Net income)	41.0%
Current maturities of long-term debt	$0

b. What does the forecasted adjustment to balance the accounting equation from part *a* reveal to us about the forecasted financing needs of the company? Explain.

**ABERCROMBIE &
FITCH**
(ANF)

BEST BUY CO., INC.
(BBY)

E11-19. **Forecasting the Statement of Cash Flows** **(LO4)**

Refer to the **Abercrombie & Fitch** financial information in Exercise 11-18. Prepare a forecast of fiscal 2012 statement of cash flows.

E11-20. **Analyzing, Forecasting, and Interpreting Both Income Statement and Balance Sheet** **(LO2, 3)**

Following are the income statements and balance sheets of **Best Buy Co., Inc.**

Income Statement, Fiscal Years Ended ($ millions)	February 26, 2011	February 27, 2010	February 28, 2009
Revenue	$50,272	$49,694	$45,015
Cost of goods sold	37,611	37,534	34,017
Restructuring charges—cost of goods sold	24	—	—
Gross profit	12,637	12,160	10,998
Selling, general and administrative expenses	10,325	9,873	8,984
Restructuring charges	198	52	78
Goodwill and tradename impairment	—	—	66
Operating income	2,114	2,235	1,870
Other income (expense)			
Investment income and other	51	54	35
Investment impairment	—	—	(111)
Interest expense	(87)	(94)	(94)
Earnings before income tax expense and equity in income of affiliates	2,078	2,195	1,700
Income tax expense	714	802	674
Equity in income of affiliates	2	1	7
Net earnings including noncontrolling interests	1,366	1,394	1,033
Net earnings attributable to noncontrolling interests	(89)	(77)	(30)
Net earnings attributable to Best Buy Co., Inc.	$ 1,277	$ 1,317	$ 1,003

Balance Sheet ($ millions, except per share and share amounts)	February 26, 2011	February 27, 2010
Assets		
Cash and cash equivalents	$ 1,103	$ 1,826
Short-term investments	22	90
Receivables	2,348	2,020
Merchandise inventories	5,897	5,486
Other current assets	1,103	1,144
Total current assets	10,473	10,566
Property and equipment		
Land and buildings	766	757
Leasehold improvements	2,318	2,154
Fixtures and equipment	4,701	4,447
Property under capital lease	120	95
	7,905	7,453
Less accumulated depreciation	4,082	3,383
Net property and equipment	3,823	4,070
Goodwill	2,454	2,452
Tradenames, net	133	159
Customer relationships, net	203	279
Equity and other investments	328	324
Other assets	435	452
Total assets	$17,849	$18,302

continued

continued from prior page

Liabilities and equity

Accounts payable..	$ 4,894	$ 5,276
Unredeemed gift card liabilities	474	463
Accrued compensation and related expenses................	570	544
Accrued liabilities...	1,471	1,681
Accrued income taxes	256	316
Short-term debt	557	663
Current portion of long-term debt	441	35
Total current liabilities..	8,663	8,978
Long-term liabilities	1,183	1,256
Long-term debt	711	1,104
Equity		
Best Buy Co., Inc. shareholders' equity		
Preferred stock, $1.00 par value: Authorized—400,000 shares; Issued and outstanding—none....................	—	—
Common stock, $0.10 par value: Authorized—1.0 billion shares; Issued and outstanding—392,590,000 and 418,815,000 shares, respectively.......................	39	42
Additional paid-in capital	18	441
Retained earnings..	6,372	5,797
Accumulated other comprehensive income	173	40
Total Best Buy Co., Inc. shareholders' equity...........	6,602	6,320
Noncontrolling interests	690	644
Total equity	7,292	6,964
Total liabilities and shareholders' equity.....................	$17,849	$18,302

a. Forecast Best Buy's fiscal 2012 income statement and balance sheet using the following relations (assume 'no change' for accounts not listed). Assume that all capital expenditures are purchases of property and equipment.

Revenue growth	5%
Cost of goods sold/Revenue	74.8%
Restructuring charges - cost of goods sold.................	$0
Selling, general and administrative expenses/Revenue...........	20.5%
Restructuring charges	$0
Goodwill and tradename impairment...........................	$0
Investment income and other.................................	$51
Investment impairment..	$0
Interest expense..	$(87)
Income tax expense/Pretax income)	34.4%
Equity in income of affiliates.................................	$2
Net earnings attributable to noncontrolling interests/Net earnings including noncontrolling interests	6.5%
Cash and cash equivalents/Revenue..........................	2.2%
Receivables/Revenue..	4.7%
Merchandise inventories/Revenue.............................	11.7%
Other current assets/Revenue	2.2%
CAPEX (Increase in gross Property and equipment)/Revenue........	1.5%
Goodwill..	no chg
Tradenames, Net amortization	$25
Customer relationships, Net amortization	$38
Equity and other investments.................................	no chg
Other assets/Revenue	0.9%

continued

continued from prior page

Accounts payable/Revenue	9.7%
Unredeemed gift card liabilities/Revenue	0.9%
Accrued compensation and related expenses/Revenue	1.1%
Accrued liabilities/Revenue	2.9%
Accrued income taxes/Revenue	0.5%
Long-term liabilities	no chg
Noncontrolling interests	*
Capital expenditures/Revenue	1.5%
Depreciation/Prior year gross PPE	12.0%
Amortization/Prior year intangible asset balance	18.7%
Dividends/Net income	18.6%
Long-term debt payments required in fiscal 2013	$37

* Increase by net income attributable to noncontrolling interests and assume no dividends

  b. What does the forecasted adjustment to balance the accounting equation from part *a* reveal to us about the forecasted financing needs of the company? Explain.

 **E11-21. Forecasting the Statement of Cash Flows** (LO4)

BEST BUY CO., INC.
(BBY)

Refer to the **Best Buy Co., Inc.**, financial information from Exercise 11-20. Prepare a forecast of its fiscal year 2012 statement of cash flows. (*Hint:* Use net income before noncontrolling interests to begin the statement of cash flows.)

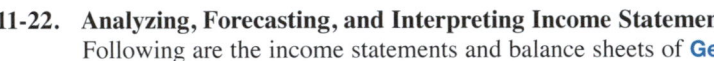 **E11-22. Analyzing, Forecasting, and Interpreting Income Statement and Balance Sheet** (LO2, 3)

GENERAL MILLS, INC.
(GIS)

Following are the income statements and balance sheets of **General Mills, Inc.**

Income Statement, Fiscal Years Ended (in millions except per share data)	May 29, 2011	May 30, 2010	May 31, 2009
Net sales	$14,880.2	$14,635.6	$14,555.8
Cost of sales	8,926.7	8,835.4	9,380.9
Selling, general and administrative expenses	3,192.0	3,162.7	2,893.2
Divestitures (gain), net	(17.4)	—	(84.9)
Restructuring, impairment, and other exit costs	4.4	31.4	41.6
Operating profit	2,774.5	2,606.1	2,325.0
Interest, net	346.3	401.6	382.8
Earnings before income taxes and after-tax earnings from joint ventures	2,428.2	2,204.5	1,942.2
Income taxes	721.1	771.2	720.4
After-tax earnings from joint ventures	96.4	101.7	91.9
Net earnings, including earnings attributable to noncontrolling interests	1,803.5	1,535.0	1,313.7
Net earnings attributable to noncontrolling interests	5.2	4.5	9.3
Net earnings attributable to General Mills	$ 1,798.3	$ 1,530.5	$ 1,304.4

Balance Sheet (In millions)	May 29, 2011	May 30, 2010
Assets		
Cash and cash equivalents	$ 619.6	$ 673.2
Receivables	1,162.3	1,041.6
Inventories	1,609.3	1,344.0
Deferred income taxes	27.3	42.7
Prepaid expenses and other current assets	483.5	378.5
Total current assets	3,902.0	3,480.0
Land, buildings and equipment	3,345.9	3,127.7
Goodwill	6,750.8	6,592.8
Other intangible assets	3,813.3	3,715.0
Other assets	862.5	763.4
Total assets	$18,674.5	$17,678.9

continued

continued from prior page

Liabilities and equity		
Accounts payable.	$ 995.1	$ 849.5
Current portion of long-term debt	1,031.3	107.3
Notes payable	311.3	1,050.1
Other current liabilities	1,321.5	1,762.2
Total current liabilities	3,659.2	3,769.1
Long-term debt	5,542.5	5,268.5
Deferred income taxes	1,127.4	874.6
Other liabilities	1,733.2	2,118.7
Total liabilities	12,062.3	12,030.9
Stockholders' equity		
Common stock, 754.6 shares issued, $0.10 par value.	75.5	75.5
Additional paid-in capital	1,319.8	1,307.1
Retained earnings.	9,191.3	8,122.4
Common stock in treasury, at cost, shares of 109.8 and 98.1	(3,210.3)	(2,615.2)
Accumulated other comprehensive loss	(1,010.8)	(1,486.9)
Total stockholders' equity.	6,365.5	5,402.9
Noncontrolling interests	246.7	245.1
Total equity	6,612.2	5,648.0
Total liabilities and equity	$18,674.5	$17,678.9

a. Forecast **General Mills'** fiscal 2012 income statement and balance sheet using the following relations (assume 'no change' for accounts not listed). Assume all capital expenditures are purchases of land, buildings and equipment, net, and that depreciation and amortization expense is included as part of selling, general and administrative expense ($ millions).

Net sales growth.	5%
Cost of sales/Net sales	60.0%
Selling, general, and administrative expenses/Net sales.	21.5%
Divestiture (gain), net	$0.0
Restructuring, impairment, and other exit costs	$0.0
Interest, net	$346.3
Income taxes/Pretax income	29.7%
After-tax earnings from joint ventures	$96.4
Net earnings attributable to noncontrolling interests/Net earnings before attribution. . .	0.3%
Cash/Net sales.	4.2%
Receivables/Net sales	7.8%
Inventories/Net sales	10.8%
Deferred income taxes/Net sales.	0.2%
Prepaid expenses and other current assets/Net sales.	3.2%
Other intangible assets.	$0 amortization
Other assets/Net sales.	5.8%
Accounts payable/Net sales.	6.7%
Other current liabilities/Net sales	8.9%
Current portion of long-term debt	$733.6
Deferred income taxes/Net sales.	7.6%
Other liabilities/Net sales	11.6%
Noncontrolling interests	*
Capital expenditures/Net sales	4.4%
Depreciation/Prior year net PPE.	20.7%
Dividends/Net income	40.6%
Current maturities of long-term debt in fiscal 2013	$733.6

* Increase by net income attributable to noncontrolling interests and assume no dividends.

b. What does the forecasted adjustment to balance the accounting equation from part *a* reveal to us about the forecasted financing needs of the company? Explain.

E11-23. **Forecasting the Statement of Cash Flows** (LO4)
Refer to the **General Mills, Inc.**, financial information from Exercise 11-22. Forecast General Mills' fiscal 2012 statement of cash flows. (Use net income before noncontrolling interests to begin the statement of cash flows.)

GENERAL MILLS,
INC.
(GIS)

E11-24. Adjusting the Balance Sheet for Operating Leases (LO1, 2, 3)

Delta Air Lines reports total net operating assets of $12,130 million, nonoperating liabilities of $11,233 million, and equity of $897 in its 2010 10-K. Footnotes reveal the existence of operating leases that have a present value of $7,088 million (see Module 10 for computations).

a. What balance sheet adjustment(s) might we consider relating to the leases before we forecast financial statements? (*Hint:* Consider the distinction between operating and nonoperating assets and liabilities.)

b. What income statement adjustment(s) might we consider? (*Hint:* Reflect on the operating and nonoperating distinction for lease-related expenses.)

ABBOTT
LABORATORIES,
INC.
(ABT)
TAP
PHARMACEUTICAL
PRODUCTS INC.

E11-25. Adjusting the Balance Sheet for Equity Method Investments (LO3)

Abbott Laboratories, Inc., reports its 50% joint venture investment in **TAP Pharmaceutical Products Inc.** using the equity method of accounting in its 2007 10-K. The Abbott balance sheet reports an investment balance of $159 million. TAP has total assets of $1,354.2 million, liabilities of $1,036.7 million, and equity of $317.5 million. Abbott's investment balance is, thus, equal to its 50% interest in TAP's equity ($317.5 million × 50% = $158.75 million, rounded to $159 million). What adjustment(s) might we consider to Abbott's balance sheet before we forecast its financial statements? (*Hint:* Consider the distinction between operating and nonoperating assets and liabilities.) What risks might Abbott Laboratories face that are not revealed on the face of its balance sheet?

WHOLE FOODS
MARKET, INC.
(WFM)

E11-26. Analyzing, Forecasting, and Interpreting Income Statement and Balance Sheet (LO2, 3)

Following are the income statement and balance sheet of **Whole Foods Market, Inc.**

Income Statement, For Years Ended (in $ 000s)	2010	2009	2008
Sales.	$9,005,794	$8,031,620	$7,953,912
Cost of goods sold and occupancy costs	5,870,393	5,277,310	5,247,207
Gross profit.	3,135,401	2,754,310	2,706,705
Direct store expenses.	2,375,716	2,145,809	2,107,940
General and administrative expenses	272,449	243,749	270,428
Pre-opening expenses	38,044	49,218	55,554
Relocation, store closures and lease termination costs. . .	11,217	31,185	36,545
Operating income.	437,975	284,349	236,238
Interest expense.	(33,048)	(36,856)	(36,416)
Investment and other income.	6,854	3,449	6,697
Income before income taxes	411,781	250,942	206,519
Provision for income taxes.	165,948	104,138	91,995
Net income.	$ 245,833	$ 146,804	$ 114,524

Assets (in $ 000s)	2010	2009
Assets		
Cash and cash equivalents	$ 131,996	$ 430,130
Short-term investments—available-for-sale securities	329,738	—
Restricted cash	86,802	71,023
Accounts receivable.	133,346	104,731
Merchandise inventories	323,487	310,602
Prepaid expenses and other current assets.	54,686	51,137
Deferred income taxes	101,464	87,757
Total current assets	1,161,519	1,055,380
Property and equipment, net of accumulated depreciation and amortization.	1,886,130	1,897,853
Long-term investments—available-for-sale securities.	96,146	—
Goodwill	665,224	658,254
Intangible assets, net of accumulated amortization.	69,064	73,035
Deferred income taxes	99,156	91,000
Other assets.	9,301	7,866
Total assets.	$3,986,540	$3,783,388

continued

continued from prior page

Liabilities and Shareholders' Equity		
Current installments of long-term debt and capital lease obligations	$ 410	$ 389
Accounts payable.	213,212	189,597
Accrued payroll, bonus and other benefits due team members	244,427	207,983
Dividends payable	—	8,217
Other current liabilities	289,823	277,838
Total current liabilities.	747,872	684,024
Long-term debt and capital lease obligations, less current installments.	508,288	738,848
Deferred lease liabilities	294,291	250,326
Other long-term liabilities.	62,831	69,262
Total liabilities.	1,613,282	1,742,460
Series A redeemable preferred stock, $0.01 par value, 425 shares authorized; zero and 425 shares issued and outstanding at 2010 and 2009, respectively	—	413,052
Shareholders' equity:		
Common stock, no par value, 300,000 shares authorized; 172,033 and 140,542 shares issued and outstanding at 2010 and 2009, respectively.	1,773,897	1,283,028
Accumulated other comprehensive income (loss)	791	(13,367)
Retained earnings	598,570	358,215
Total shareholders' equity	2,373,258	1,627,876
Total liabilities and shareholders' equity.	$3,986,540	$3,783,388

a. Forecast Whole Foods Market's 2011 income statement and balance sheet using the following relations ($ 000)—assume 'no change' for accounts not listed.

Sales growth.	10.0%
Cost of goods sold and occupancy costs/Sales	65.2%
Direct store expenses/Sales.	26.4%
General and administrative expenses/Sales	3.0%
Pre-opening expenses/Sales	0.4%
Relocation, store closure and lease termination costs	$0
Interest expense.	$(33,048)
Investment and other income.	$6,854
Provision for income taxes/Pretax income.	40.3%
Cash and cash equivalents/Sales	1.5%
Restricted cash	$86,802
Accounts receivable/Sales.	1.5%
Merchandise inventories/Sales	3.6%
Prepaid expenses and other current assets/Sales.	0.6%
Deferred income taxes (current).	$101,464
Long-term investments—available-for-sale securities.	$96,146
Goodwill	$665,224
Intangible assets, net of accumulated amortization.	$69,064
Deferred income taxes (noncurrent).	$99,156
Other assets/Sales.	0.1%
Current installments of long-term debt and capital lease obligations	$410
Accounts payable/Sales.	2.4%
Accrued payroll, bonus and other benefits due team members/Sales	2.7%
Other current liabilities/Sales	3.2%
Current maturities of long-term debt and capital lease obligations.	$410
Deferred lease liabilities	$294,291
Other long-term liabilities/Sales.	0.7%
Series A redeemable preferred stock.	$0
Common stock.	$1,773,897
Accumulated other comprehensive income (loss)	$791
Capital expenditures/Prior year net PPE	13.5%
Depreciation & amortization/Prior year net PPE.	14.5%
Dividends/Net income	3.5%

b. What does the forecasted adjustment to balance the accounting equation from part *a* reveal to us about the forecasted financing needs of the company?

E11-27. Forecasting the Statement of Cash Flows (LO4)

Refer to the **Whole Foods Market, Inc.**, financial information from Exercise 11-26. Prepare a forecast of its fiscal year 2011 statement of cash flows.

WHOLE FOODS MARKET, INC.
(WFM)

INTEL
(INTC)

E11-28. Projecting NOPAT and NOA Using Parsimonious Forecasting Method (LO6)

Following are **Intel**'s sales, net operating profit after tax (NOPAT), and net operating assets (NOA) for its year ended December 31, 2010 ($ millions).

Sales.	$43,623
Net operating profit after tax (NOPAT)	11,250
Net operating assets (NOA)	28,652

Forecast Intel's sales, NOPAT and NOA for years 2011 through 2014 using the following assumptions:

Sales growth per year.	10%
Net operating profit margin (NOPM).	25%
Net operating asset turnover (NOAT), based on NOA at December 31, 2010. . .	1.5

E11-29. Projecting NOPAT and NOA Using Parsimonious Forecasting Method (LO6)

Following are **3M**'s sales, net operating profit after tax (NOPAT), and net operating assets (NOA) for its fiscal year ended 2010 ($ millions).

3M CO.
(MMM)

Sales.	$26,662
Net operating profit after tax (NOPAT)	$ 4,266
Net operating assets (NOA)	$16,305

Forecast 3M's sales, NOPAT and NOA for fiscal years 2011 through 2014 using the following assumptions:

Sales growth per year.	15%
Net operating profit margin (NOPM).	16%
Net operating asset turnover (NOAT), based on NOA at 2010 fiscal year-end . .	1.6

PROBLEMS

P11-30. Forecasting the Income Statement, Balance Sheet, and Statement of Cash Flows (LO2, 3, 4)

Following are fiscal year financial statements of **Oracle Corporation**.

ORACLE CORPORATION
(ORCL)

Consolidated Statements of Operations			
Year ended May 31 (in millions)	2011	2010	2009
Revenues			
New software licenses	$ 9,235	$ 7,533	$ 7,123
Software license updates and product support.	14,796	13,092	11,754
Software revenues	24,031	20,625	18,877
Hardware systems products	4,382	1,506	—
Hardware systems support	2,562	784	—
Hardware systems revenues	6,944	2,290	—
Services	4,647	3,905	4,375
Total revenues	35,622	26,820	23,252

continued

continued from prior page

Operating expenses			
Sales and marketing.	6,579	5,080	4,638
Software license updates and product support	1,264	1,063	1,088
Hardware systems products	2,057	880	—
Hardware systems support	1,259	423	—
Services	3,818	3,398	3,706
Research and development	4,519	3,254	2,767
General and administrative.	970	911	785
Amortization of intangible assets	2,428	1,973	1,713
Acquisition related and other	208	154	117
Restructuring	487	622	117
Total operating expenses	23,589	17,758	14,931
Operating income.	12,033	9,062	8,321
Interest expense.	(808)	(754)	(630)
Non-operating income (expense), net	186	(65)	143
Income before provision for income taxes.	11,411	8,243	7,834
Provision for income taxes.	2,864	2,108	2,241
Net income	$ 8,547	$ 6,135	$ 5,593

Consolidated Balance Sheets		
May 31 (in millions, except per share data)	**2011**	**2010**
Assets		
Cash and cash equivalents	$16,163	$9,914
Marketable securities	12,685	8,555
Trade receivables, net of allowances for doubtful accounts of $372 and $305 as of May 31, 2011 and 2010, respectively	6,628	5,585
Inventories	303	259
Deferred tax assets	1,189	1,159
Prepaid expenses and other current assets.	2,206	1,532
Total current assets	39,174	27,004
Non-current assets		
Property, plant and equipment, net	2,857	2,763
Intangible assets, net	7,860	9,321
Goodwill	21,553	20,425
Deferred tax assets	1,076	1,267
Other assets	1,015	798
Total non-current assets.	34,361	34,574
Total assets.	$73,535	$61,578
Liabilities and equity		
Notes payable, current and other current borrowings	$1,150	$3,145
Accounts payable.	701	775
Accrued compensation and related benefits	2,320	1,895
Deferred revenues	6,802	5,900
Other current liabilities	3,219	2,976
Total current liabilities.	14,192	14,691
Non-current liabilities		
Notes payable and other non-current borrowings	14,772	11,510
Income taxes payable	3,169	2,695
Deferred tax liabilities.	59	424
Other non-current liabilities	1,098	1,059
Total non-current liabilities.	19,098	15,688

continued

continued from prior page

Oracle Corporation stockholders' equity		
Preferred stock, $0.01 par value—authorized: 1.0 shares; outstanding: none	—	—
Common stock, $0.01 par value and additional paid in capital—authorized: 11,000 shares; outstanding: 5,068 shares and 5,026 shares as of May 31, 2011 and 2010, respectively...............................	16,653	14,648
Retained earnings	22,581	16,146
Accumulated other comprehensive income........................	542	4
Total Oracle Corporation stockholders' equity........................	39,776	30,798
Noncontrolling interests...	469	401
Total equity...	40,245	31,199
Total liabilities and equity	$73,535	$61,578

Required

Forecast Oracle's fiscal 2012 income statement, balance sheet, and statement of cash flows; round forecasts to $ millions. *Hint*: We forecast total revenues by projecting a continuation of year-over-year percentage growth rates for each revenue category that Oracle includes in its income statement (rounded to the nearest whole percent). (*Note*: Oracle's long-term debt footnote reports that current maturities of long-term debt are $1,250 million for May 2012; Oracle includes the current maturities with "Notes payable, current and other current borrowings" on its balance sheet. Oracle reports capital expenditures of $450 million, dividends of $1,061 million, depreciation of $368 million, which it includes in G&A expense, and amortization of $2,428 million, which it reports separately. Identify all financial statement relations estimated and assumptions made; estimate forecasted income statement relations to 1 decimal (assume no change for: interest expense, nonoperating income, deferred tax assets and liabilities, goodwill, noncontrolling interest, common stock, and accumulated other comprehensive income). What do the forecasts imply about the financing needs of Oracle?

 P11-31. **Forecasting the Income Statement, Balance Sheet, and Statement of Cash Flows**   **(LO2, 3, 4)**

Following are the financial statements of **Nike, Inc.**

NIKE, INC.
(NKE)

Consolidated Statements of Income			
Year ended May 31 (in millions)	**2011**	**2010**	**2009**
Revenues	$20,862	$19,014	$19,176
Cost of sales..	11,354	10,214	10,572
Gross margin	9,508	8,800	8,604
Demand creation expense	2,448	2,356	2,352
Operating overhead expense...........................	4,245	3,970	3,798
Total selling and administrative expense	6,693	6,326	6,150
Restructuring charges	—	—	195
Goodwill impairment	—	—	199
Intangible and other asset impairment.....................	—	—	202
Interest expense (income), net............................	4	6	(10)
Other (income), net....................................	(33)	(49)	(89)
Income before income taxes	2,844	2,517	1,957
Income taxes	711	610	470
Net income...	$ 2,133	$ 1,907	$ 1,487

Consolidated Balance Sheets		
May 31 (in millions)	2011	2010
Assets		
Cash and equivalents...	$ 1,955	$ 3,079
Short-term investments	2,583	2,067
Accounts receivable, net	3,138	2,650
Inventories	2,715	2,041
Deferred income taxes.......................................	312	249
Prepaid expenses and other current assets............	594	873
Total current assets	11,297	10,959
Property, plant and equipment, net	2,115	1,932
Identifiable intangible assets, net........................	487	467
Goodwill..	205	188
Deferred income taxes and other assets	894	873
Total assets..	$14,998	$14,419
Liabilities and shareholders' equity		
Current portion of long-term debt	$ 200	$ 7
Notes payable	187	139
Accounts payable..	1,469	1,255
Accrued liabilities...	1,985	1,904
Income taxes payable	117	59
Total current liabilities......................................	3,958	3,364
Long-term debt	276	446
Deferred income taxes and other liabilities	921	855
Redeemable Preferred Stock...............................	—	—
Shareholders' equity		
Common stock at stated value		
Class A convertible — 90 and 90 shares outstanding..	—	—
Class B — 378 and 394 shares outstanding	3	3
Capital in excess of stated value	3,944	3,441
Accumulated other comprehensive income.............	95	215
Retained earnings	5,801	6,095
Total shareholders' equity	9,843	9,754
Total liabilities and shareholders' equity...............	$14,998	$14,419

Required

Forecast Nike's fiscal year 2012 income statement, balance sheet, and statement of cash flows. Round the revenue growth rate to the nearest whole percent, and round forecasts to $ millions. Identify all financial statement relations estimated and assumptions made; estimate forecasted income statement relations to 1 decimal (assume no change for: other expense or income, interest expense, common stock, capital in excess of stated value, and accumulated other comprehensive income). For fiscal 2011, capital expenditures are $432 million, depreciation expense is $335 million, amortization is $23 million, and dividends are $555 million. Footnotes reveal that the current portion on long-term debt due in 2013 is $48 million. What do the forecasts imply about Nike's financing needs for the upcoming year?

P11-32. **Forecasting the Income Statement, Balance Sheet, and Statement of Cash Flows** (LO2, 3, 4)

Following are the financial statements of **Home Depot, Inc.**

HOME DEPOT, INC.
(HD)

Consolidated Statements of Earnings			
	For Fiscal Year Ended		
Amounts in millions, except per share data	January 30, 2011	January 31, 2010	February 1, 2009
Net sales.	$67,997	$66,176	$71,288
Cost of sales.	44,693	43,764	47,298
Gross profit.	23,304	22,412	23,990
Operating expenses			
Selling, general and administrative	15,849	15,902	17,846
Depreciation and amortization	1,616	1,707	1,785
Total operating expenses	17,465	17,609	19,631
Operating income.	5,839	4,803	4,359
Interest and other (income) expense			
Interest and investment income.	(15)	(18)	(18)
Interest expense.	530	676	624
Other.	51	163	163
Interest and other, net	566	821	769
Earnings from continuing operations before provision for income taxes.	5,273	3,982	3,590
Provision for income taxes.	1,935	1,362	1,278
Earnings from continuing operations	3,338	2,620	2,312
Earnings (loss) from discontinued operations, net of tax.	—	41	(52)
Net earnings.	$ 3,338	$ 2,661	$ 2,260

Consolidated Balance Sheets		
	January 30, 2011	January 31, 2010
Amounts in millions, except share and per share data		
Assets		
Cash and cash equivalents	$ 545	$ 1,421
Receivables, net.	1,085	964
Merchandise inventories	10,625	10,188
Other current assets.	1,224	1,327
Total current assets	13,479	13,900
Property and equipment, at cost:		
Land	8,497	8,451
Buildings	17,606	17,391
Furniture, fixtures and equipment	9,687	9,091
Leasehold improvements	1,373	1,383
Construction in progress	654	525
Capital leases.	568	504
	38,385	37,345
Less accumulated depreciation and amortization	13,325	11,795
Net property and equipment	25,060	25,550
Notes receivable.	139	33
Goodwill	1,187	1,171
Other assets	260	223
Total assets.	$40,125	$40,877

continued

continued from prior page

Liabilities and stockholders' equity		
Accounts payable..........................	$ 4,717	$ 4,863
Accrued salaries and related expenses.........................	1,290	1,263
Sales taxes payable........................	368	362
Deferred revenue.......................	1,177	1,158
Income taxes payable......................	13	108
Current installments of long-term debt.........................	1,042	1,020
Other accrued expenses........................	1,515	1,589
Total current liabilities............................	10,122	10,363
Long-term debt, excluding current installments................	8,707	8,662
Other long-term liabilities........................	2,135	2,140
Deferred income taxes........................	272	319
Total liabilities............................	21,236	21,484
Stockholders' equity		
Common stock, par value $0.05; authorized: 10 billion shares; issued: 1.722 billion shares at January 30, 2011 and 1.716 billion shares at January 31, 2010; outstanding: 1.623 billion shares at January 30, 2011 and 1.698 billion shares at January 31, 2010......................	86	86
Paid-in-capital......................	6,556	6,304
Retained earnings......................	14,995	13,226
Accumulated other comprehensive income...............	445	362
Treasury stock, at cost, 99 million shares at January 30, 2011 and 18 million shares at January 31, 2010......................	(3,193)	(585)
Total stockholders' equity......................	18,889	19,393
Total liabilities and stockholders' equity.....................	$40,125	$40,877

Required

Forecast Home Depot's fiscal year ended January 2012 income statement, balance sheet, and statement of cash flows . Round the revenue growth rate to the nearest whole percent, and round forecasts to $ millions. Estimate forecasted income statement relations to 1 decimal (assume no change for: notes receivable, goodwill, interest income and expense, deferred income taxes, common stock and additional paid-in capital, treasury stock, and accumulated other comprehensive income). Capital expenditures were $1,096 million and dividends were $1,569 million for fiscal year ended January 2011. Home Depot's long-term debt footnote indicates maturities of long-term debt of $29 million for 2012. What is our assessment of Home Depot's financial condition over the next year?

P11-33. **Two-Year-Ahead Forecasting of Financial Statements** (LO5)

Following are the financial statements of **Target, Corp.**

TARGET CORP.
(TGT)

Consolidated Statements of Operations			
For fiscal year ended (millions, except per share data)	Jan. 29, 2011	Jan. 30, 2010	Jan. 31, 2009
Sales.........................	$65,786	$63,435	$62,884
Credit card revenues........................	1,604	1,922	2,064
Total revenues.......................	67,390	65,357	64,948
Cost of sales..........................	45,725	44,062	44,157
Selling, general and administrative expenses..............	13,469	13,078	12,954
Credit card expenses.......................	860	1,521	1,609
Depreciation and amortization.......................	2,084	2,023	1,826
Earnings before interest expense and income taxes..........	5,252	4,673	4,402
Net interest expense			
Nonrecourse debt collateralized by credit card receivables..	83	97	167
Other interest expense.........................	677	707	727
Interest income........................	(3)	(3)	(28)
Net interest expense.......................	757	801	866
Earnings before income taxes........................	4,495	3,872	3,536
Provision for income taxes........................	1,575	1,384	1,322
Net earnings.........................	$2,920	$2,488	$2,214

Consolidated Statements of Financial Position		
(millions, except footnotes)	January 29, 2011	January 30, 2010
Assets		
Cash and cash equivalents, including marketable securities of $1,129 and $1,617....	$1,712	$2,200
Credit card receivables, net of allowance of $690 and $1,016	6,153	6,966
Inventory...	7,596	7,179
Other current assets...	1,752	2,079
Total current assets	17,213	18,424
Property and equipment		
Land..	5,928	5,793
Buildings and improvements	23,081	22,152
Fixtures and equipment	4,939	4,743
Computer hardware and software	2,533	2,575
Construction-in-progress...	567	502
Accumulated depreciation	(11,555)	(10,485)
Property and equipment, net......................................	25,493	25,280
Other noncurrent assets...	999	829
Total assets..	$43,705	$44,533
Liabilities and shareholders' investment		
Accounts payable...	$6,625	$6,511
Accrued and other current liabilities..............................	3,326	3,120
Unsecured debt and other borrowings	119	796
Nonrecourse debt collateralized by credit card receivables	—	900
Total current liabilities..	10,070	11,327
Unsecured debt and other borrowings	11,653	10,643
Nonrecourse debt collateralized by credit card receivables	3,954	4,475
Deferred income taxes..	934	835
Other noncurrent liabilities	1,607	1,906
Total noncurrent liabilities.....................................	18,148	17,859
Shareholders' investment..		
Common stock...	59	62
Additional paid-in-capital..	3,311	2,919
Retained earnings	12,698	12,947
Accumulated other comprehensive loss	(581)	(581)
Total shareholders' investment.................................	15,487	15,347
Total liabilities and shareholders' investment.....................	$43,705	$44,533

Consolidated Statements of Cash Flows			
For fiscal year ended (millions)	Jan. 29, 2011	Jan. 30, 2010	Jan. 31, 2009
Operating activities			
Net earnings..	$2,920	$2,488	$2,214
Reconciliation to cash flow			
Depreciation and amortization...........................	2,084	2,023	1,826
Share-based compensation expense	109	103	72
Deferred income taxes.................................	445	364	91
Bad debt expense	528	1,185	1,251
Non-cash (gains)/losses and other, net	(145)	143	316
Changes in operating accounts:			
Accounts receivable originated at Target....................	(78)	(57)	(458)
Inventory...	(417)	(474)	77
Other current assets...................................	(124)	(129)	(99)
Other noncurrent assets................................	(212)	(114)	(55)
Accounts payable.....................................	115	174	(389)
Accrued and other current liabilities......................	149	257	(230)
Other noncurrent liabilities	(103)	(82)	(186)
Cash flow provided by operations	5,271	5,881	4,430

continued

continued from prior page

Investing activities			
Expenditures for property and equipment	(2,129)	(1,729)	(3,547)
Proceeds from disposal of property and equipment	69	33	39
Change in accounts receivable originated at third parties.	363	(10)	(823)
Other investments	(47)	3	(42)
Cash flow required for investing activities	(1,744)	(1,703)	(4,373)
Financing activities			
Reductions of short-term notes payable	—	—	(500)
Additions to long-term debt.	1,011	—	3,557
Reductions of long-term debt	(2,259)	(1,970)	(1,455)
Dividends paid	(609)	(496)	(465)
Repurchase of stock	(2,452)	(423)	(2,815)
Stock option exercises and related tax benefit	294	47	43
Other.	—	—	(8)
Cash flow required for financing activities	(4,015)	(2,842)	(1,643)
Net increase/(decrease) in cash and cash equivalents	(488)	1,336	(1,586)
Cash and cash equivalents at beginning of year	2,200	864	2,450
Cash and cash equivalents at end of year.	$ 1,712	$ 2,200	$ 864

Required

Forecast Target's fiscal year ended January 2012 and 2013 income statements, balance sheets, and state-ments of cash flow. Round the revenue growth rate to the nearest whole percent, and round forecasts to $ millions. Use the same forecasting assumptions for both years; estimate forecasted income statement relations to 1 decimal (assume no change for: interest expense, deferred income tax liability, common stock, additional paid-in capital, and accumulated other comprehensive income). Target's long-term debt footnote indicates maturities of $2,251 million in fiscal year ended January 2012, and maturities of $3,812 million in fiscal year ended January 2013. Assume return on investments of 1.5% for aver-age increase in investments. What investment or financing assumptions are required for forecasting purposes? What is our assessment of Target's financial condition over the next two years?

DISCUSSION POINTS

D11-34. Adjusting the Income Statement Prior to Forecasting (LO1, 2)

Following is the income statement of **CBS Corporation**, along with an excerpt from its MD&A section.

CBS CORPORATION
(CBS)

Income Statement Year ended December 31 ($ millions)	2005	2004	2003
Revenues	$14,536.4	$14,547.3	$13,554.5
Expenses			
Operating	8,671.8	8,643.6	8,165.4
Selling, general and administrative.	2,699.4	2,552.5	2,376.1
Impairment charges	9,484.4	17,997.1	—
Depreciation and amortization	498.7	508.6	501.7
Total expenses	21,354.3	29,701.8	11,043.2
Operating income (loss)	$ (6,817.9)	$(15,154.5)	$ 2,511.3

Operating Expenses: Table below presents consolidated operating expenses by type

Operating expenses by type Year ended December 31	2005	2004	Increase (Decrease) 2005 vs. 2004		2003	Increase (Decrease) 2004 vs. 2003	
Programming	$3,453.2	$3,441.8	$ 11.4	—%	$3,080.3	$361.5	12%
Production	2,453.5	2,584.7	(131.2)	(5)	2,661.9	(77.2)	(3)
Outdoor operations	1,134.2	1,102.7	31.5	3	1,012.6	90.1	9
Publishing operations.	525.0	517.6	7.4	1	486.3	31.3	6
Parks operations	243.8	232.7	11.1	5	212.2	20.5	10
Other.	862.1	764.1	98.0	13	712.1	52.0	7
Total operating expenses	$8,671.8	$8,643.6	$ 28.2	—%	$8,165.4	$478.2	6%

For 2005, operating expenses of $8.67 billion increased slightly over $8.64 billion in 2004. For 2004, operating expenses of $8.64 billion increased 6% over $8.17 billion in 2003. The major components and changes in operating expenses were as follows:

- Programming expenses represented approximately 40% of total operating expenses in 2005 and 2004 and 38% in 2003, and reflect the amortization of acquired rights of programs exhibited on the broadcast and cable networks, and television and radio stations. Programming expenses increased slightly to $3.45 billion in 2005 from $3.44 billion in 2004 principally reflecting higher costs for Showtime Networks theatrical titles. Programming expenses increased 12% to $3.44 billion in 2004 from $3.08 billion in 2003 reflecting higher program rights expenses for sports events and primetime series at the broadcast networks.

- Production expenses represented approximately 28% of total operating expenses in 2005, 30% in 2004, and 33% in 2003, and reflect the cost and amortization of internally developed television programs, including direct production costs, residuals and participation expenses, and production overhead, as well as television and radio costs including on-air talent and other production costs. Production expenses decreased 5% to $2.45 billion in 2005 from $2.58 billion in 2004 principally reflecting lower network costs due to the absence of *Frasier* partially offset by increased costs for new network series. Production expenses decreased 3% to $2.58 billion in 2004 from $2.66 billion in 2003 reflecting fewer network series produced in 2004 partially offset by higher news costs for political campaign coverage.

- Outdoor operations costs represented approximately 13% of total operating expenses in 2005 and 2004, and 12% in 2003, and reflect transit and billboard lease, maintenance, posting and rotation expenses. Outdoor operations expenses increased 3% to $1.13 billion in 2005 from $1.10 billion in 2004 principally reflecting higher billboard lease costs and maintenance costs associated with the impact of hurricanes in 2005. Outdoor operations costs increased 9% to $1.10 billion in 2004 from $1.01 billion in 2003 primarily reflecting higher transit and billboard lease costs.

- Publishing operations costs, which represented approximately 6% of total operating expenses in each of the years 2005, 2004 and 2003, reflect cost of book sales, royalties and other costs incurred with respect to publishing operations. Publishing operations expenses for 2005 increased 1% to $525.0 million and increased 6% to $517.6 million in 2004 from $486.3 million in 2003 primarily due to higher revenues.

- Parks operations costs, which represented approximately 3% of total operating expenses in each of the years 2005, 2004 and 2003, increased 5% to $243.8 million in 2005 from $232.7 million in 2004 principally reflecting the cost of fourth quarter 2005 winter events held at the parks and the impact of foreign currency translation. In 2004, Parks operations costs increased 10% to $232.7 million from $212.2 million in 2003 primarily from the impact of foreign currency translation.

- Other operating expenses, which represented approximately 10% of total operating expenses in 2005 and 9% in 2004 and 2003, primarily include distribution costs incurred with respect to television product, costs associated with digital media and compensation. Other operating expenses increased 13% to $862.1 million in 2005 from $764.1 million in 2004 primarily reflecting a 10% increase in distribution costs due to the DVD release of *Charmed* and increased costs associated with digital media from the inclusion of SportsLine.com, Inc. ("SportsLine.com") since its acquisition in December 2004. Other operating expenses for 2004 increased 7% to $764.1 million in 2004 from $712.1 million in 2003 principally reflecting 15% higher distribution costs due to additional volume of DVD releases of the *Star Trek* series and higher compensation.

continued

continued from prior page

Impairment Charges   SFAS 142 requires the Company to perform an annual fair value-based impairment test of goodwill. The Company performed its annual impairment test as of October 31, 2005, concurrently with its annual budgeting process which begins in the fourth quarter each year. The first step of the test examines whether or not the book value of each of the Company's reporting units exceeds its fair value. If the book value for a reporting unit exceeds its fair value, the second step of the test is required to compare the implied fair value of that reporting unit's goodwill with the book value of the goodwill. The Company's reporting units are generally consistent with or one level below the operating segments underlying the reportable segments. As a result of the 2005 annual impairment test, the Company recorded an impairment charge of $9.48 billion in the fourth quarter of 2005. The $9.48 billion reflects charges to reduce the carrying value of goodwill at the CBS Television reporting unit of $6.44 billion and the Radio reporting unit of $3.05 billion. As a result of the annual impairment test performed for 2004, the Company recorded an impairment charge of $18.0 billion in the fourth quarter of 2004. The $18.0 billion reflects charges to reduce the carrying value of goodwill at the Radio reporting unit of $10.94 billion and the Outdoor reporting unit of $7.06 billion as well as the reduction of the carrying value of intangible assets of $27.8 million related to the FCC licenses at the Radio segment. Several factors led to a reduction in forecasted cash flows and long-term growth rates for both the Radio and Outdoor reporting units. Radio and Outdoor both fell short of budgeted revenue and operating income growth targets in 2004. Competition from other advertising media, including Internet advertising and cable and broadcast television reduced Radio and Outdoor growth rates. Also, the emergence of new competitors and technologies necessitated a shift in management's strategy for the Radio and Outdoor businesses, including changes in composition of the sales force and operating management as well as increased levels of investment in marketing and promotion.

Required

Identify and explain any income statement line items over the past three years that you believe should be considered for potential adjustment in preparation for forecasting the income statement of CBS.

SOLUTIONS TO REVIEW PROBLEMS

Mid-Module Review

Solution

Forecasted 2011 financial statements for Colgate-Palmolive follow.

Forecasted Income Statement			
For year ended December 31 ($ millions)	2010	Forecast Assumptions	2011 Est.
Net sales.	$15,564	$15,564 × 1.03	$16,031
Cost of sales.	6,360	$16,031 × 40.9%	6,557
Gross profit.	9,204	subtotal	9,474
Selling, general and administrative expenses	5,414	$16,031 × 34.8%	5,579
Other (income) expense, net	301	no change	301
Operating profit	3,489	subtotal	3,594
Interest expense, net	59	no change	59
Income before income taxes	3,430	subtotal	3,535
Provision for income taxes.	1,117	$3,535 × 32.6%	1,152
Net income including noncontrolling interests.	2,313	subtotal	2,383
Less: Net income attributable to noncontrolling interests	110	no change	110
Net income attributable to Colgate-Palmolive Company.	$ 2,203	subtotal	$ 2,273

Forecasted Balance Sheet			
As of December 31 ($ millions)	**2010**	**Forecast Assumptions**	**2011 Est.**
Assets		computed	
Cash and cash equivalents	$ 490	$16,031 \times 3.1\%$	$ 497
Marketable securities......................................		plug	373
Receivables	1,610	$16,031 \times 10.3\%$	1,651
Inventories	1,222	$16,031 \times 7.9\%$	1,266
Other current assets.....................................	408	$16,031 \times 2.6\%$	417
Total current assets	3,730	subtotal	4,204
Property, plant and equipment, net	3,693	$3,693 + 567 - 375$	3,885
Goodwill, net	2,362	no change	2,362
Other intangible assets, net	831	$831 - 19$	812
Other assets...	556	$16,031 \times 3.6\%$	577
Total assets...	$11,172	subtotal	$11,840
Liabilities			
Notes and loans payable	$ 48	no change	$ 48
Current portion of long-term debt	561	footnote disclosure	359
Accounts payable.......................................	1,165	$16,031 \times 7.5\%$	1,202
Accrued income taxes	272	$1,152 \times 24.4\%$	281
Other accruals	1,682	$16,031 \times 10.8\%$	1,731
Total current liabilities..................................	3,728	subtotal	3,621
Long-term debt	2,815	$2,815 - 359$	2,456
Deferred income taxes...................................	108	no change	108
Other liabilities	1,704	$16,031 \times 10.9\%$	1,747
Total liabilities..	8,355	subtotal	7,932
Commitments and contingent liabilities			
Shareholders' Equity			
Preference stock	0	no change	0
Common stock, $1 par value (2,000,000,000 shares authorized, 732,853,180 shares issued)...................	733	no change	733
Additional paid-in-capital................................	1,132	no change	1,132
Retained earnings	14,329	$14,329 + 2,273 - 1,182$	15,420
Accumulated other comprehensive income (loss).............	(2,115)	no change	(2,115)
Shareholders' equity before unearned compensation, treasury stock and noncontrolling interest	14,079	subtotal	15,170
Unearned compensation	(99)	no change	(99)
Treasury stock, at cost..................................	(11,305)	no change	(11,305)
Total Colgate-Palmolive Company shareholders' equity	2,675	subtotal	3,766
Noncontrolling interests	142	no change	142
Total shareholders' equity	2,817	subtotal	3,908
Total liabilities and shareholders' equity....................	$11,172	subtotal	$11,840

Forecasted Statement of Cash Flows		
($ millions)	**Forecast Assumptions**	**2011 Est.**
Net income including noncontrolling interests...	via forecast income stmt.	$2,273
Add: Depreciation..........................	given	375
Add: Amortization..........................	given	19
Change in Accounts receivable.............	$1,610 − $1,651	(41)
Change in Inventories	$1,222 − $1,266	(44)
Change in Other current assets............	$408 − $417	(9)
Change in Other long-term assets	$556 − $577	(21)
Change in Accounts payable...............	$1,202 − $1,165	37
Change in Accrued income taxes	$281 − $272	9
Change in Accrued liabilities	$1,731 − $1,682	49
Change in Other long-term liabilities........	$1,747 − $1,704	43
Net cash from operating activities	subtotal	2,690
Capital expenditures	given	(567)
Increase in marketable securities...........	plug	(373)
Net cash from investing activities............	subtotal	(940)
Dividends	$2,273 × 52%	(1,182)
Payments of long-term debt	prior-year current portion	(561)
Net cash from financing activities	subtotal	(1,743)
Net change in cash......................	subtotal	7
Beginning cash..........................	via prior bal. sheet	490
Ending cash	subtotal	$ 497

Our forecasts yield liabilities in excess of assets of $373 million. In this example, we assume that marketable securities are increased by that amount. We might have also assumed repayment of debt and/or purchase of treasury stock, being careful to maintain the company's debt-to-equity ratio. One further adjustment we might make at this point would be to increase interest income assuming an investment return on the marketable securities.

Module-End Review

Solution

	2010	2011E	2012E	2013E	2014E
Sales (unrounded)	$61,587	$64,050.48	$66,612.50	$69,276.99	$72,048.07
		(61,587 × 1.04)	(64,050.48 × 1.04)	(66,612.50 × 1.04)	(69,276.99 × 1.04)
Sales (rounded)	61,587	64,050	66,612	69,277	72,048
NOPAT	13,065	13,451	13,989	14,548	15,130
		($64,050 × 0.21)	($66,612 × 0.21)	($69,277 × 0.21)	($72,048 × 0.21)
NOA	45,694	47,444	49,342	51,316	53,369
		($64,050/1.35)	($66,612/1.35)	($69,277/1.35)	($72,048/1.35)

Cost of Capital and Valuation Basics

During the bear markets of the early and late 2000s, many utility companies experienced a large market value decline. In an effort to prevent further decline, many of these utilities sold off their underperforming assets and consolidated their operations. These strategic business decisions allowed those in the utilities industry to generate positive earnings and cash flows in more recent years. Their stock prices also rebounded from the declines of the early and late 2000s.

THE SOUTHERN COMPANY

One utility company that has performed well in recent years is **The Southern Company** (SO). The Southern Company serves approximately 4.4 million customers through its various subsidiaries in Alabama, Florida, Georgia and Mississippi. The Southern Company generates, transports, and provides electricity. It also invests in, among other things, synthetic fuels and the marketing of natural gas.

The Southern Company has experienced some stock price volatility. SO's stock price on July 1, 2006, was $32.05 per share. Five years later its stock traded for $40.72 per share. Charting its price from mid-2006 through mid-2011, adjusting for stock splits, reveals a reasonable increase despite the economic downturn, which is graphically portrayed below.

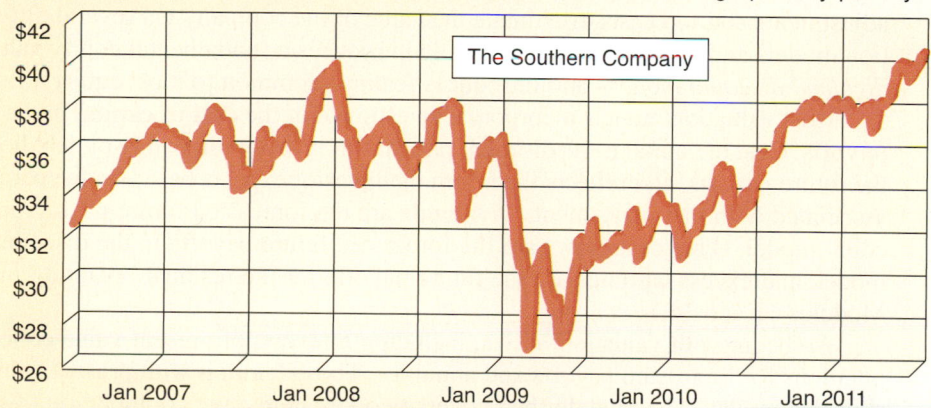

SO's dividends per share also increased during this period. Finance.Yahoo.com predicts SO's dividend stream at approximately $1.89 per share. The sum of its annual stock price change (capital gains) and its annual dividend, yields the investors' annual return from SO. Does this annual return adequately compensate investors for their risk and foregone interest return? That is, is the company fairly priced given its predicted dividend stream? This question, and those similar to it, is the focus of this module.

Sources: The Southern Company 2010 Annual Report and 10-K Filing; Finance.Yahoo.com, July 2011.

MODULE ORGANIZATION

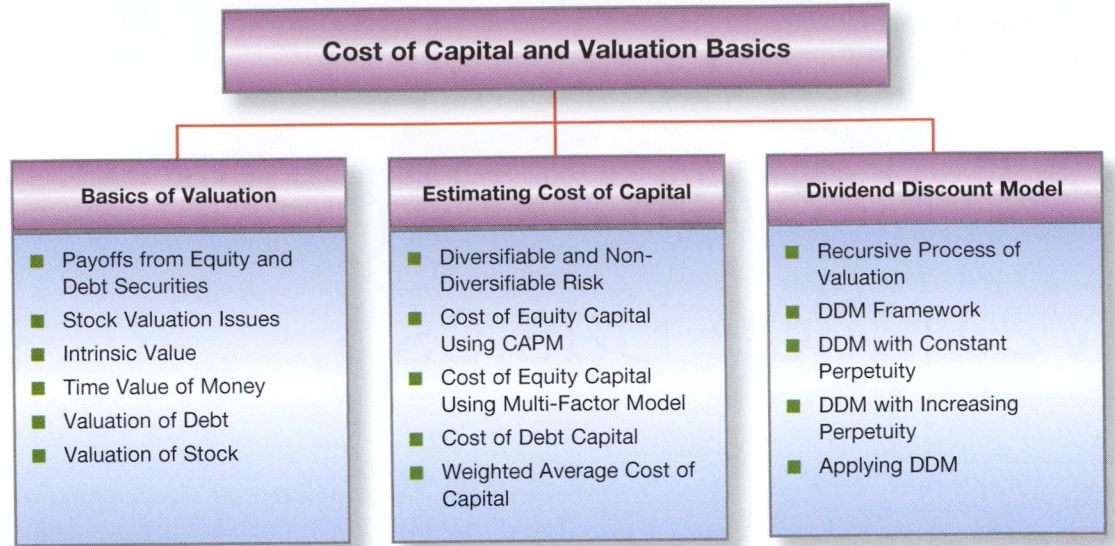

Valuation plays an important role in today's market economy. Indeed, valuation is implicit in all financial decisions and transactions in that market participants compare the value of what is given up to the value of what is received. For instance, valuation plays a central role in the following situations:

■ a merger decision depends crucially on the estimated fair value of the target company

■ the share price of an initial public offering depends on the business valuation by the issuer as well as by potential investors

■ identifying stocks or bonds that are over (or under) valued, which is a key task of a portfolio manager, depends on business valuations.

An important question is how do we value a stock, a bond, or any other financial instrument?

A *financial instrument* entitles its owner to a series of future payoffs from a company. The amount of such payoffs depends on the company's ability to generate profit through its future operations. Previous modules have dealt with the evaluation of a company's profitability and the adjusting and forecasting of financial statement numbers. In subsequent modules, we use these adjustments and forecasts to estimate the value of the company via several different equity valuation models and approaches. This module introduces a fundamental equity valuation model—the *dividend discount model*—and introduces features common to most equity valuation models.

Most valuation models incorporate an estimate of the **cost of capital** and a forecast of **future payoffs**. Cost of capital is the discount rate that an investor (an equity or debt holder) uses to value the future payoffs, and reflects the return the investor expects based on the perceived level of risk associated with that investment. **Dividends** are the forecasted future payoffs in the dividend discount model. (Free cash flows are the forecasted future payoffs in the discounted free cash flow model, and excess earnings are the future payoffs for the residual operating income model—see Modules 13 and 14.)

We begin with valuation basics, including a review of present value concepts and the computations for lump-sum payoffs and annuities. Those familiar with present value calculations can skip this review. The module then covers two key items: the computation of cost of capital and application of the dividend discount model. The cost of capital section includes discussion on the cost of equity capital, cost of debt capital, and the weighted average cost of capital. We conclude with a discussion of the pros and cons of the dividend discount model.

BASICS OF VALUATION

LO1 Explain the basics of valuation, including intrinsic value, discounting, and payoffs.

In some sense, valuing a stock is no different from valuing any another property: its price ultimately depends on demand and supply. Consider the pricing of, say, an apple. People want to buy apples mostly for nutrition. Hence the physical properties of an apple (such as its weight, freshness, taste, and appearance), as well as the overall supply of apples in the market, determine the price. The same logic holds for the pricing of stocks.

The process for valuation described in this and subsequent modules is useful for valuing securities. We can use valuation techniques to:

- Compare our stock-price estimate to the observed trading price and then decide whether to buy, sell, or hold the stock
- Set a share price in an initial public offering
- Determine the current price of a bond or other financial instrument

However, valuation methods apply more broadly than simply in securities markets. For example, this same valuation process is useful in addressing issues such as:

- Deciding whether a plant or division should be expanded or closed
- Determining how much should be paid in a merger or acquisition
- Evaluating an offer to acquire our company

Due to the availability of quoted prices as a reference, the modules focus on valuation of publicly traded stock. However, the valuation principles and methods we describe in the modules can be used to value any financial asset or liability.

Payoffs from Equity and Debt Instruments

The benefit from owning a stock or a bond comes from the cash it will bring to its owner in the future. A bond holder is entitled to receive interest payments from the company, as well as the repayment of principal after the bond matures. For stockholders, future cash flows come from two sources (i) dividends paid, if any, by the company, and (ii) cash from selling the stock to another investor, or back to the company, in the future. For Southern Company (SO), a holder of each share of its stock expects to receive $1.89 in dividend for 2011. In addition, when the stockholder sells SO's stock in the future, the holder will receive the current price of SO's stock.

Regardless of whether future cash flows come in the form of interest and principal, or dividends and proceeds from stock sales, all these cash flows have one thing in common: they occur in the future. This is the feature that makes valuing a financial instrument, such as Apple's stocks or bonds, more difficult than valuing a commodity, such as apples. When we purchase an apple, its weight, its freshness, and its appearance can be readily measured. When we buy Apple's stock, its future cash flows are yet to be determined, which makes such cash flows difficult to measure.

Steps in Stock Valuation

Because the payoffs from owning a stock or bond are in the future, such payoffs are uncertain and difficult to predict. In practice, stock valuation can be viewed as a four-step process as explained in Module 1 and depicted in the graphic on the next page.

Step 1: Understanding the business environment and accounting information. Before we can value a company, we must understand its business environment. This includes understanding competitive and macroeconomic threats, evaluating future growth opportunities, and assessing the quality of the accounting environment.

Step 2: Adjusting and assessing financial and accounting information. This includes assessing profitability and its drivers, along with understanding growth potential, strategic actions, and their implications for financial reports. This step also includes making any necessary accounting adjustments to the general-purpose financial statements.

Step 3: Forecasting financial information. Forecasting is crucial in security valuation as it provides the key inputs to valuation models. Choice of what payoffs we forecast will be determined by data availability, models utilized, and our confidence in future estimates. Without good forecasts, the output from any valuation model is dubious no matter how good the model.

Step 4: Using information for valuation. This step involves estimating the cost of capital and then applying the proper valuation model to the estimated payoffs. The cost of capital we select reflects both the *time value of money* and the *cost of risk.* Adjusting for the time value of money acknowledges that a dollar received in the future is worth less than a dollar received today. Adjusting for risk takes account of the uncertain nature of projected payoffs. Returns to investments in bonds and, especially, stocks are unpredictable and often volatile. A dollar invested in **Google** at its IPO in 2004 would have earned more than a 400% return by 2011. On the other hand, if we invested in **Enron**, our investment would have been lost. These cases reflect a saying: "life is uncertain until it is not." Most people dislike risk. In stock valuation we adjust for risk by determining a discount rate that is applied to projected payoffs. Valuation models differ in the forecasted payoffs, the forecast horizon, and the use of a discount rate. It is important to identify the crucial assumptions underlying each model, and to apply the proper model in the right way, and under the right circumstances.

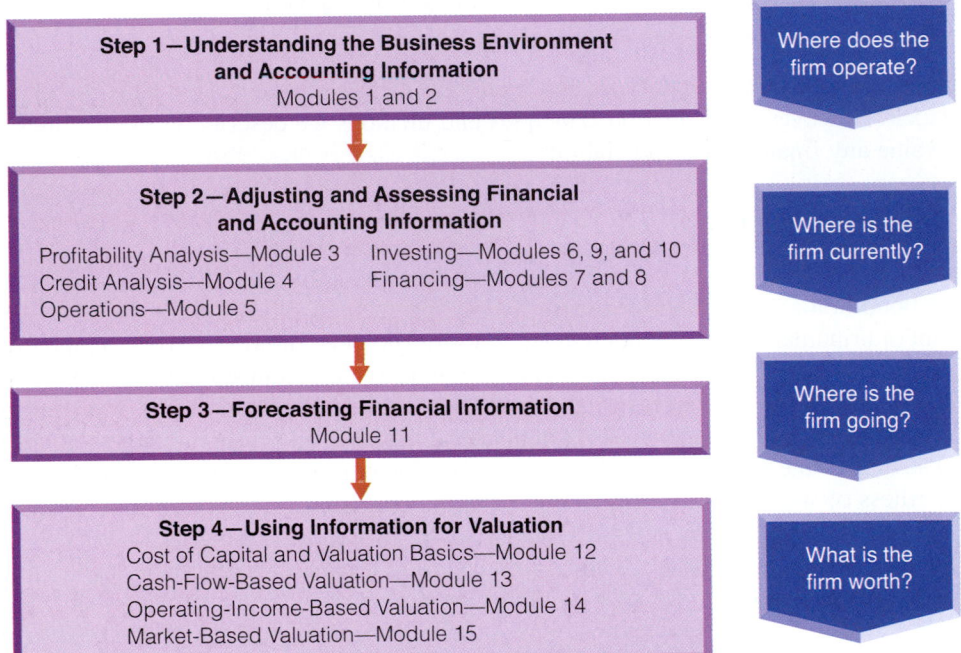

These four steps are not mutually exclusive. They are part of a valuation *process* and, as such, they are interrelated. For instance, identifying the proper valuation model is listed as part of step 4. Yet, choice of a valuation model is determined by a careful analysis of the business environment (step 1) and its impact on the accuracy of forecasts of company payoffs (step 3). Likewise, the analysis of prior results in reported financial statements (step 2) forms the foundation for what is forecasted (step 3). This interconnected series of steps provides us with a structure for understanding where the company operates, where it is currently, where it is going, and what it is worth.

Intrinsic Value

Valuation involves estimating the **intrinsic value** (IV) of a company, which is the economic value of the company assuming that actual future payoffs are known today. The following (balance sheet) equation reflects the relation between intrinsic value of the firm and the intrinsic values of debt and equity.

$$IV_{Firm} = IV_{Debt} + IV_{Equity}$$

where: IV_{Firm} = intrinsic value of the company,
IV_{Debt} = intrinsic value of company liabilities, and
IV_{Equity} = intrinsic value of company equity.

Review of Time Value of Money

This section reviews the relevant concepts associated with time value of money. Proficiency with present value calculations is a prerequisite for the materials covered in this module and the remainder of the book. If we are familiar with these materials, we can skip this section and jump to the next section on valuing debt and equity instruments.

Investors receive two kinds of payoffs (cash flows): lump sums and/or a series of equal payments, equally spaced, known as an annuity. To compute the present value of these payoffs the investor must (1) forecast the payoffs to be received and (2) determine the discount rate to be used.

Lump-Sum Payoffs

The present value factor applied to a **lump-sum** payoff is $1/(1 + r)^n$, where r is the discount rate and n is the number of periods before the payoff is received. To illustrate, what is the present value of $100 to be received two years hence at a discount rate of 11%? The present value factor is 0.81162, which is computed as $1/(1.11)^2$. This present value factor is identical to the present factor multiplier found in Table 1 of Appendix A (titled Present Value of a Single Amount). We compute the present value of the $100 payoff by multiplying it by this 0.81162 present value factor as follows:

Future payoff		Present value factor for 2 years at 11%		Present value
$100	×	0.81162	=	$81.16

We can also use a financial calculator to compute the present value. The typical financial calculator has five input buttons for time value of money calculations; we enter four values to compute a fifth value, which is the solution. We illustrate use of a calculator with the following graphic:

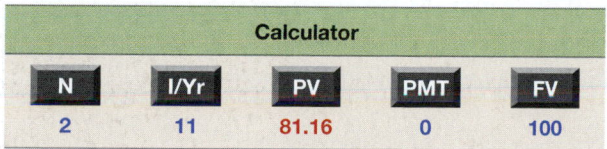

On the financial calculator, N is the number of periods (2), I/Yr is the interest rate per period (11), PV is the current or present value, PMT refers to periodic payment (0 in our example), and FV is the future value (100). Because we are solving for present value in this illustration, that value of **81.16** is highlighted in red. (Most calculators show a solution of −81.16; this is because the calculator interprets FV as a payoff to be *received* and the PV as the *investment*. So, if FV is entered as a positive amount, then PV shows negative, and vice versa.) Our solution of 81.16 implies that we are indifferent between receiving $81.16 today and receiving $100 two years from now. Stated differently, if one invests $81.16 in a bank account that earns 11% annual interest, it will grow to $100 in two years.

Continuing with the illustration above, in the first year we would earn $8.93 of interest on $81.16 invested, computed as $0.11 \times \$81.16$. In the second year, we would again earn interest, but for that year the interest would be earned on a larger amount consisting of the original $81.16 *and* the $8.93 interest earned from the first year. Exhibit 12.1 shows the 11% per year interest that would be earned on an initial investment of $81.16 over a two-year time horizon.

EXHIBIT 12.1	Investment and Interest over a Two-Year Horizon			
Time period	Investment at beginning of period	Interest rate	Interest earned	Balance at period-end
1.............	$81.16	0.11	$8.93	$ 90.09
2.............	90.09	0.11	$9.91	$100.00

Annuity Payoffs

An **annuity** is a series of equal lump sums at regular intervals. For a series of payoffs to qualify as an annuity, it must meet three criteria: (1) the series must be of equal amounts, (2) payments must occur at equal time periods, and (3) the same discount rate is applicable over the time horizon of the payoffs.

To illustrate, assume $1,000 is received at the end of each of the next four years with an 11% discount rate. Exhibit 12.2 shows the present value factors for each of the four lump-sum payments and then applies these factors to determine the four-year present value annuity factors.

EXHIBIT 12.2	Present Value Computations for an Annuity				
Time period	Interest rate	Present value formula	Present value factor	Series of Payoffs	Present value
1............	11%	$1/(1.11)^1$	0.90090	$1,000	$ 900.90
2............	11%	$1/(1.11)^2$	0.81162	1,000	811.62
3............	11%	$1/(1.11)^3$	0.73119	1,000	731.19
4............	11%	$1/(1.11)^4$	0.65873	1,000	658.73
			3.10244		$3,102.44

Exhibit 12.2 shows that a 4-year, $1,000 annuity yields a present value of $3,102.44. This can be computed in two ways. We can treat each of the four payoffs as a separate lump sum, compute the present value for each, and then sum them as follows: $900.90 + $811.62 + $731.19 + $658.73. Alternatively, we can sum the four present value factors to yield the present value factor of 3.10244 for the four-year annuity (also found in Table 2 of Appendix A), and then multiply it by the $1,000 annuity amount to yield $3,102.44.

Specifically, summing the lump-sum present value factors yields the present value annuity factor of 3.1024. Exhibit 12.2 shows that the present value of the series of four payments is computed as:

($1,000 \times 0.90090) + (\$1,000 \times 0.81162) + (\$1,000 \times 0.73119) + (\$1,000 \times 0.65873)$

Applying algebra, the $1,000 can be taken out of each of the parentheses and written as:

$1,000 \times (0.90090 + 0.81162 + 0.73119 + 0.65873)$ or $\$1,000 \times 3.10244$

The 3.10244 is the present value factor of a four-year annuity at 11%. This shows the equivalence of the two approaches.

To use a financial calculator to obtain the solution: we enter N=4, I/Yr=11, PMT=1,000, FV=0, and the solution is PV, highlighted in red. This value is more precise than the value using the tables because the factors in the tables are rounded. Our discussion proceeds with the more exact present value, $3,102.45.

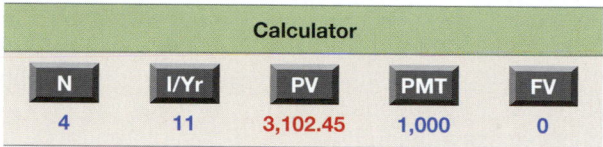

Calculator				
N	**I/Yr**	**PV**	**PMT**	**FV**
4	11	3,102.45	1,000	0

Present Value, Future Value, and Interest

In theory, we are indifferent between receiving a payoff today that is equivalent to a future payoff that is adjusted for interest. Using the payoffs in the above illustration, we are indifferent between receiving $3,102.45 today and receiving $1,000 at the end of each of the next four years.

Assuming the payoffs are invested and earn 11% annual interest, then at the end of four years they grow to $4,709.74. This is shown in Exhibit 12.3.

EXHIBIT 12.3	Lump Sum: Time Line Representation of Present and Future Values and Interest					
End of year	**0**	**1**	**2**	**3**	**4**	**...**
Lump sum (present value) ..	$3,102.45					
Interest earned		$ 341.27 $3,102.45 × 0.11	$ 378.81 $3,443.72 × 0.11	$ 420.48 $3,822.53 × 0.11	$ 466.73 $4,243.01 × 0.11	
Future value at year-end ...		$3,443.72 $3,102.45 + $341.27	$3,822.53 $3,443.72 + $378.81	$4,243.01 $3,822.53 + $420.48	**$4,709.74** $4,243.01 + $466.73	

The $4,709.74 future value four years hence is equivalent to the $3,102.45 lump sum invested today, and is also equivalent to the $1,000 annuity invested at the end of each of the next four years. The latter result is portrayed in Exhibit 12.4. Comparing Exhibits 12.3 and 12.4 shows that both of these payment patterns—the $3,102.45 invested today and the $1,000 invested at the end of each of the next four years—yield the identical future value of $4,709.74. In summary, a comparison of Exhibits 12.3 and 12.4 reveals that we are indifferent between receiving $3,102.45 today versus receiving $1,000 at the end of each of the next four years. Each of these payment patterns yields a present value of $3,102.45 and a future value of $4,709.74. These "time value of money" concepts are important to understanding valuation models and the role of discount rates.

EXHIBIT 12.4	Annuity: Time Line Representation of Present and Future Values and Interest					
End of year	**0**	**1**	**2**	**3**	**4**	**...**
Annuity		$1,000.00	$1,000.00	$1,000.00	$1,000.00	
Interest earned		$0.00	$110.00 $1,000.00 × 0.11	$232.10 $2,110.00 × 0.11	$367.63 $3,342.10 × 0.11	
Future value at year-end ...		$1,000.00 $1,000.00 + $0.00	$2,110.00 $1,000.00 + $110.00	$3,342.10 $2,110.00 + $232.10	**$4,709.73*** $3,342.10 + $367.63	
Present value	$3,102.45					

* Difference due to rounding

Using a financial calculator, we can determine that the future value of the lump sum of $3,102.45 is equal to the future value of the annuity of $1,000 per year.

Calculator				
N	**I/Yr**	**PV**	**PMT**	**FV**
4	11	3,102.45	0	4,709.74

Valuation of a Debt Instrument

Estimating the intrinsic value of a debt instrument such as a bond or note is similar to the computations in the prior section. For example, a bond stipulates a **coupon rate**, which determines the annuity payments, and the **face value** of the bond stipulates the lump-sum payment to be made at the bond's maturity. The final component necessary to determine the intrinsic value of a bond is the **market rate** of interest for the bond. The market rate is the interest rate an investor could earn by investing in other bonds with similar risks. The market rate is the discount rate used in the present value computation. (This market rate is also called the *effective rate* or the *cost of debt capital*.)

To illustrate, if we have a 3-year bond with a 9% coupon rate, a face value of $1,000, and a market rate of 10%, then the present value of the bond is $975.13. The payoffs related to this bond are determined by the coupon rate and the face value, and those payoffs are portrayed in Exhibit 12.5. (For simplicity, this section assumes no taxes; we explain the effect of taxes on the discount rate later in this module.)

EXHIBIT 12.5	Time Line Representation of Payoffs Related to a Debt Instrument				
End of year	0	1	2	3	...
Interest earned and received . . .		$90	$90	$90	
Future value at year-end		$983	$991	$1,000	
Lump sum (present value)	$975.13				

Thus, the $975.13 present value of this debt instrument is computed as the sum of (1) the $223.82 present value of the coupon payments ($90 × 2.48685) plus (2) the $751.31 present value of the maturity value ($1,000 × 0.75131). The 2.48685 present value factor is for a 3-year annuity at 10%, which is equivalent to the sum of the three lump-sum present value factors of 0.90909 + 0.82645 + 0.75131. The 0.75131 present value factor is for a lump-sum face value to be received at the end of year three. (We see that computation of future value differs from that in Exhibit 12.3 because the payoffs in Exhibit 12.5 are not reinvested but, instead, are paid out.) Using a financial calculator, we enter N=3, I/Yr=10 (market rate of interest), PMT=90 (coupon rate of 9% times $1,000 face value), FV=1,000 (face value), and then the solution is PV, highlighted in red, below.

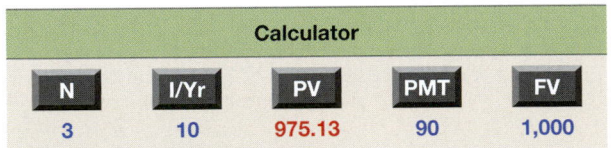

Valuation of an Equity Instrument

Estimating the intrinsic value of an equity instrument begins with the assumption that the stock pays a constant dividend each year for n future years, and then it is sold (or liquidated) with a lump-sum payment at the end of year n + 1.

To illustrate, assume that we forecast dividend payouts of $90 at the end of years 1 and 2 along with a terminal dividend of $1,090 at the end of year 3. The **terminal dividend** is the final payoff associated with the investment, and can be viewed as the proceeds from the sale of the stock or the proceeds received upon liquidation. If we assume that the discount rate is 10%, then valuation of this company is identical to that of the debt valuation illustration above. This means the value of this company's equity is $975.13. (Discount rates for debt and equity instruments of the same company differ—here we use 10% for both the debt and equity instruments to show the similarity in valuation approaches.) Again, using a financial calculator, we enter N=3, I/Yr=10 (market rate of interest), PMT=90 (annual dividend), FV=1,000 ("extra dividend" in year 3), and then the solution is PV, highlighted in red, below.

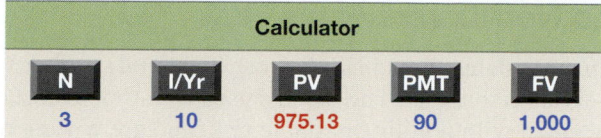

Calculator				
N	**I/Yr**	**PV**	**PMT**	**FV**
3	10	975.13	90	1,000

To this point, we have shown how to value different payoffs. We have explicitly identified the payoffs received and the discount rate used. This information can be readily programmed into a spreadsheet. However, expertise is required to project future payoffs (such as dividends, free cash flows, or earnings) for valuation purposes and to identify the proper cost of capital to use as the discount rate.

The discount rate we use depends on the payoff stream being valued. *Payoffs to debt holders* are discounted using the **cost of debt capital**. *Payoffs to equity holders* are discounted using the **cost of equity capital**. *Payoffs to the entire firm* are discounted using the **weighted average cost of capital**. We describe how investors estimate these different cost of capital measures in the next section.

ESTIMATING COST OF CAPITAL

There are different ways to estimate the cost of capital using observable market data. Investors, who price financial instruments, expect to recover two costs: the time value of money and the cost of risk. The time value of money can be viewed as the foregone interest from investing in an instrument with future payoffs. The second cost is the investor's compensation for bearing the risk associated with the uncertainty of the payoffs. These two components make up what we call the **risk-adjusted discount rate**. It is intuitive that the components of the risk-adjusted discount rate (foregone interest and compensation for risk) equal the return that investors require for investing in an asset. Hence, the risk-adjusted discount rate used in the valuation calculation, is exactly equal to the investor's required rate of return or cost of capital.

When we estimate cost of capital, we usually make the following assumptions. First, we assume that current interest rates are a good approximation of expected (future) interest rates. Second, we assume that the current risk of the firm is a good approximation of the expected firm risk. We can adjust this assumption if we know of plans to alter that risk. For example, if the firm is entering into an acquisition that will result in a new line of business with a substantially different level of risk than current operations we can adjust our expectation of future risk. When using estimates of cost of debt or equity capital, we assume that the current capital structure (mix of debt and equity financing) will persist.

BUSINESS INSIGHT   **Use of Nominal (Risk-Adjusted) vs Real Payoffs**

The value of a monetary unit commonly changes over time due to inflation or deflation. Payoffs and discount rates that include the effects of these price level changes are referred to as *nominal* or *risk-adjusted* (because they include this risk). If the effects of price level changes are not included, the payoffs and discount rates are referred to as *real*. So, should we use nominal or real amounts for valuation? Consider the following example where a nominal payoff of $200 million is expected in two years. Assume that there is 3% inflation per year expected and the nominal discount rate for this payoff is 10%, which implies a real discount rate of 6.8% ($0.068 = [(1.00 + 0.10)/(1.00 + 0.03)] - 1.00$). We can estimate the value of the expected future payoff using either nominal or real amounts as follows:

Inputs:	**Payoff**	×	**Discount Rate**	=	**Value Today**
Nominal:	$200 million	×	$1/1.10^2$	=	$165.3 million
	(nominal)		(nominal—includes inflation)		
Real:	$200 million$/1.03^2$	×	$1/1.068^2$	=	$165.3 million
	(real)		(real—excludes inflation)		

The computed value of the payoff is unaffected by whether nominal or real inputs are used in the calculation (remember that use of nominal payoffs requires use of nominal discount rates and use of real payoffs requires use of real discount rates). In practice it is easier to use nominal inputs as analysts do not forecast real payoffs nor take time to convert nominal rates to real rates. Accordingly, we use nominal inputs for valuations in this book.

Diversifiable and Non-Diversifiable Risk

To explain the use of market data to estimate the cost of capital, we must introduce the idea of diversifiable and non-diversifiable risk. The models used to estimate cost of capital assume that investors are only concerned with non-diversifiable risk, and are willing to accept diversifiable risk without compensation.

Diversifiable risk refers to risks that can be diversified away by investors. Diversification refers to the practice of holding many stocks and bonds in one's investment portfolio. How does diversification affect risk? To answer that, suppose we invest our entire worth of $1,000 into one single stock. Assume that during the previous year the volatility of the stock equals 10%, meaning, on average, the stock value could go up or down by 10% during each and every day. In contrast, if we invest our $1,000 into a portfolio (bundle) of S&P 500 stocks, the volatility of our portfolio would be, say, 4%. This is because each day some of the stocks in the S&P 500 index might go up, while others might go down. In this case these stock price movements cancel each other out, dampening large price movements. This is the basic idea of diversification. Simply put, it reflects the wisdom in the saying "don't put all your eggs in one basket." On the other hand, if we are confident that we are smarter than average (and who is not?) we might elect to put all our eggs in one basket; but, as Mark Twain cautioned, "Watch that basket!"

An important condition for diversification to reduce risk is that the returns of stocks in a portfolio must be somewhat independent. If the returns of stocks in our portfolio are correlated, meaning they tend to go up or down at the same time, then the effect of diversification on risk is reduced.

To illustrate this concept, suppose we have two stocks in our portfolio: **Pepsi** and **Coca Cola**. For these two stocks, there is the risk that some consumers switch from Coke to Pepsi, or vise versa. Since we hold both stocks, we are not bothered with this risk because with Pepsi or Coke, the consumer is drinking one of our products. However, there is also the risk that consumers choose to reduce their consumption of sodas in favor of, say, **Starbucks** coffee. If this happens, then both Pepsi and Coca Cola's sales will suffer. Diversification by investing in these two stocks (instead of only one) does not shield us from risk of product substitution. In other words, some risk is **non-diversifiable** given the pool of stocks.

It is difficult to determine whether a particular risk is diversifiable or non-diversifiable. One way to proceed in this situation is to hold what is called a "market portfolio"—meaning to hold all stocks available in the market. The underlying assumption is that, by doing this, we diversify away all the risks that are diversifiable. Hence the remaining risk in a market portfolio is "non-diversifiable." (Of course, holding the market portfolio does not diversify away the risks associated with holding stock as assets rather than some other class of assets—such as land, precious metals, foreign currencies, artwork, baseball cards, and memorabilia.)

By comparing the historical volatility of an individual stock to the historical volatility of the market portfolio, we can estimate the non-diversifiable risk in each individual stock. This is the notion behind the *capital asset pricing model*.

Cost of Equity Capital Using the Capital Asset Pricing Model

LO2 Explain and estimate the cost of equity capital.

The **capital asset pricing model (CAPM)** equates the expected return on a particular asset as the sum of three components—the risk-free rate, the *beta risk*, and the *stock-specific risk*. The first two components are used in estimating the cost of equity capital. The third component, the stock-specific risk, is the risk that is diversified away in large portfolios.

In equation form, the CAPM estimation of a company's expected return, or cost of equity capital (r_e), follows:

$$r_e = r_f + [\beta \times (r_m - r_f)] \qquad \text{12.1}$$

The first component is the expected **risk-free rate**, r_f (expectation symbols are not included in the equation). The return on ten-year U.S. treasury bills is commonly used as an estimate of r_f. The second component is the product of the market risk premium ($r_m - r_f$) and the sensitivity (β) of the asset's market return to the overall market return. The **market risk premium** is the difference between the expected market return (r_m) and the expected risk-free rate:

$$\text{Market risk premium} = r_m - r_f \qquad \text{12.2}$$

Historically, r_f has fluctuated around 5%. The overall market return, while dependent on the time period, has generally fluctuated between 9% and 13%. These figures yield a usual market risk premium of about 4% to 8%.[1] The sensitivity of the asset's market return to the overall market is referred to as the company's **market beta (β)**. Market beta is a statistical coefficient that reflects a company's historical stock price volatility relative to the overall market volatility. Market beta is commonly estimated from a regression of a company's stock returns (dependent variable) on a market index of returns (independent variable) over a representative time period (often the previous 60 months). The market index of returns represents returns from a portfolio of risky assets; an example of a market index is the S&P 500.

Market beta reflects the risk that cannot be diversified away by investing in a portfolio of risky assets (accordingly called systematic risk). In this CAPM framework, the market has a beta of 1.0. (Another way to think of this is that if we had a portfolio consisting of all available stock market assets, the value of our portfolio would move perfectly with the value of all available stock market assets.) A market beta greater than (less than) 1.0 indicates the company's stock price will change by a larger (smaller) percent with a change in the overall market. For example, according to **Finance.yahoo.com**, **The Southern Company (SO)** has a market beta of 0.35 as of mid-2011. Applying this estimate, a change in the overall market return yields a change in SO's stock that is 35% of the market change. A *negative* market beta implies that the company stock price moves contrary to the market.

Although beta is a risk measure, it is also associated with returns. The higher the risk an investor is willing to accept, the higher the expected return; and, accordingly, the lower the risk, the lower the expected return.

To illustrate, let's apply the CAPM to The Southern Company. In mid-2011, according to **bankrate.com**, the 10-year Treasury rate was 3.1%. Assuming a market risk premium of 5%, then the cost of equity capital (r_e) for Southern Company with a market beta of 0.35, is 4.9%, which is computed as $0.031 + [0.35 \times (0.081 - 0.031)]$. This estimate implies that an investor requires an expected return of 4.9% to invest in Southern Company's stock. Stated differently, the cost of equity capital is the required return to equity holders for investing in SO's stock.

BUSINESS INSIGHT | Market Beta

Numerous financial service firms and online investor Websites provide estimates of a company's market beta. Betas are commonly estimated as the slope coefficient from a linear regression of the firm's stock returns on a market index of returns over a recent time period. One common estimation method is to run a regression of a firm's monthly stock returns on the returns to the S&P 500 index over the last 60 months. Estimated betas are measured with error. In addition, those betas are backward looking estimates, but are used for decisions about the future. A key assumption in this estimation method is that a company's risk does not change substantially. Because beta is estimated from historical information, it likely fails to account for any business changes or industry shifts that alter a company's future risk. Financial service Websites for beta estimates report a range of beta estimates. These differences arise due to choices involving the time period for estimation, frequency of measurement (monthly, weekly, daily), and market index used. In mid-2011, a sampling of several beta estimates from Websites found beta estimates for Southern Company ranging from 0.31 at **Finance.Google.com** to 0.55 at **Valueline.com**.

---

[1] For readings on this topic, see E. F. Fama and K. R. French, "The Cross-Section of Expected Stock Returns," *Journal of Finance*, June 1992, pp. 427–465; W. Gebhardt, C. Lee, and B. Swaminathan, "Towards an Ex Ante Cost of Capital," *Journal of Accounting Research*, (June 2001), pp. 135–176; J. Claus and J. Thomas, "Equity Premia as low as Three Percent? Evidence from Analysts' Earnings Forecasts for Domestic and International Stock Markets," *Journal of Finance*, (October 2001), pp. 1629–1666; and P. Easton, G. Taylor, P. Shroff, and T. Sougiannis, "Using Forecasts of Earnings to Simultaneously Estimate Growth and the Rate of Return on Equity Investments," *Journal of Accounting Research*, (June 2002), pp. 657–676.

Cost of Equity Capital Using a Multi-Factor Model

Given the limitations with CAPM, researchers have developed other models to compute risk-adjusted returns. These so-called **multi-factor models** share the following basic form:

$$r_e = r_f + [\beta_1 \times r_1 + \beta_2 \times r_2 + \beta_3 \times r_3 + \ldots] \qquad \textbf{12.3}$$

The r_j represents the premium of risk factor j, and β_j captures the sensitivity of the stock to factor j, where j = 1, 2, 3, . . . The CAPM can be viewed as a special case with only one factor: the market risk premium.

Researchers have attempted to identify the risk factors. One set of research studies relies on large sample data analysis. For instance, researchers have found that stocks with a high book-to-market ratio (defined as total book value of the company divided by its total market value) tend to have higher subsequent stock returns, on average, compared with stocks with a low book-to-market ratio.

This result seems to indicate that companies with a high book-to-market ratio are regarded by investors as being more risky and the excess return simply reflects the compensation for such risk. Other risk factors identified based on similar large sample analysis include the company's size and the liquidity of its stock.

Identifying risk factors based on large sample analysis has a shortcoming; that is, we do not know why such factors matter. Why are small companies more risky than large companies? To answer this question, researchers have tried to identify risk factors based on fundamental analysis. Such risk factors can be classified as:

- *Internal risk factors*: such as operating leverage, financial leverage, effectiveness of internal control, management team, and so forth.
- *External risk factors*: such as exchange risk, political risk, supply chain risk, industry competition, and so forth.

Research on identifying and measuring risk factors is ongoing. Those factors can be viewed as part of the broader five forces that confront the company and its industry discussed in module 1.

RESEARCH INSIGHT   **CAPM and Cost of Capital**

CAPM is a misnomer in that it is not truly an asset pricing model but instead is a model used to estimate cost of capital. A strength of CAPM is its simplicity. It assumes that the only risk factor is the market return (referred to as β) and it assumes that prior period's β is a suitable estimate for future risk. However, CAPM is also criticized by academics and practitioners who argue that a firm's systematic risk varies over time and that CAPM estimates are sensitive to the particular model inputs chosen. In theory, CAPM is applied using a market index representing all available investments. Use of a stock-based index such as the S&P 500 neglects other investment opportunities. Further, CAPM attempts to measure covariance with the risk premium of the market, which is arguably time-varying with recent estimates ranging from 2% to 7% versus the 4% to 8% historical numbers. CAPM relies on one risk factor and ignores additional risk factors such as company size. Some argue that inclusion of additional risk factors yields a "better" cost of capital estimate. Due to these concerns, we must carefully consider the sensitivity of our valuation estimates to our cost of capital assumptions.

Cost of Debt Capital

LO3 Describe and estimate the cost of debt capital.

The market rate on debt instruments is known as the **cost of debt capital**. The cost of debt capital is usually reported in financial statements or can be computed using the stated coupon (interest) rate on a debt instrument along with the fair value of the debt instrument that is either recorded on the balance sheet or disclosed in its footnotes. The reported fair value of the debt instrument should approximate its present value.

A company's borrowing rate depends on its perceived level of risk by the lenders. Usual factors considered by lenders include short-term liquidity measures such as the quick ratio and interest-coverage ratio, and long-term financial stability measures such as the debt-to-equity ratio. Several companies, including **Moody's Investors Service, Standard and Poor's**, and **Fitch** provide rating services for bonds and notes. For instance, those organizations classify debt issuances into the following categories.

Moody's	S&P	Fitch	Description
Aaa	AAA	AAA	Prime Maximum Safety
Aa1	AA+	AA+	High Grade, High Quality
Aa2	AA	AA	
Aa3	AA−	AA−	
A1	A+	A+	Upper-Medium Grade
A2	A	A	
A3	A−	A−	
Baa1	BBB+	BBB+	Lower-Medium Grade
Baa2	BBB	BBB	
Baa3	BBB−	BBB−	
Ba1	BB+	BB+	Non-Investment Grade
Ba2	BB	BB	Speculative
Ba3	BB−	BB−	
B1	B+	B+	Highly Speculative
B2	B	B	
B3	B−	B−	
Caa1	CCC+	CCC	Substantial Risk
Caa2	CCC		In Poor Standing
Caa3	CCC−		
Ca			Extremely Speculative
C			May be in Default
		DDD	Default
		DD	
	D	D	

The top category is AAA, meaning the bond is very unlikely to default. Bonds with a rating of BBB− (or Baa3) and higher are referred to as *investment grade*, meaning these bonds are of high quality. In contrast, bonds with a rating of BB+ (or Ba1) and lower are referred to as a *junk bond*, reflecting the higher default risk of those bonds.[2] The cost of debt capital is closely related to the debt rating assigned to the company.

We must also consider the effect of taxes because the expected cost of debt capital is computed on an after-tax basis and is denoted r_d. Specifically, cost of debt capital is determined as follows:

$$r_d = \textbf{Pretax borrowing rate for debt} \times (1 - \textbf{Tax rate}) \qquad \textbf{12.4}$$

The after-tax cost of debt capital requires identifying the pretax (average) borrowing rate for interest-bearing debt and the income tax rate, both available from financial statement footnotes. Multiplication by the term "1 − Tax rate" yields the cost of debt after the tax savings from the interest expense deduction. Specifically, the *tax rate is often proxied by the statutory tax rate* for the company, which is the 35% federal statutory rate plus or minus the state statutory rate net of any federal benefits. (Ideally, the *marginal tax rate* is used in estimating the cost of debt capital; however, the marginal tax rate is unobservable.) The pretax borrowing rate (also called average borrowing rate) for interest-bearing debt, including both short- and long-term, is computed as:

Interest expense/Average amount of interest-bearing debt

---

[2] Differences in the borrowing rates of high grade and low grade bonds are referred to as "credit spreads." In eras of "easy money," credit spreads are low, meaning that investors do not demand much of a risk premium for lending to high risk entities. In 2007, a sudden shift in investors' appetite for risk led to a marked increase in credit spreads, and caused substantial "dislocations" in the market for certain types of high risk debt.

We encourage the use of adjusted numbers in this computation; for example, debt would include capitalized operating leases, and interest would include the adjustment to interest from any such capitalized leases.

To illustrate, we use Southern Company's tax rate and pretax borrowing rate to approximate its after-tax cost of debt capital. SO's 2010 statutory tax rate is 36.8%, consisting of the 35% federal rate and the 1.8% state rate, net of federal benefits—both reported in footnotes to its financial statements. Its pretax borrowing rate is approximately 4.6%, which is computed by dividing its 2010 interest expenses of $895 million by its average total debt of $19,350 million (see SO's 2010 statements of capitalization). Consequently, its after-tax cost of debt capital is 2.9%, computed as $0.046 \times (1 - 0.368)$.

Weighted Average Cost of Capital

LO4 Explain and estimate the weighted average cost of capital (WACC).

In our examples to this point, the discount rate for debt valuation or for equity valuation was approximated by either the cost of debt capital or the cost of equity capital, respectively. The cost of debt capital would be used to value debt instruments while the cost of equity capital would be used to discount the payoffs for an all-equity company. The nature of the stream of future payoffs that we desire to value dictates the discount rate we use to compute the present value. When valuing a debt instrument such as a bond, the cash payoffs are received by debt holders, so the cost of debt capital is used for valuation. When valuing equity instruments using the dividend discount model (discussed later in this module), the payoffs received by equity holders are discounted using the cost of equity capital.

Some valuation models, such as the discounted free cash flow and the residual operating income models, assume the payoffs (free cash flows and operating income) are distributed to both equity holders and debt holders. For these models, a company's cost of capital includes both debt *and* equity. Accordingly, cost of capital, too, must recognize that payoffs will be distributed to both debt holders and equity holders. This means that those companies' cost of capital is a weighted average of the cost of debt capital and the cost of equity capital.

To better understand the computation for the weighted average cost of capital (WACC), recall the balance sheet equation that reflects the relation between the intrinsic value of the firm and the intrinsic values of debt and equity.

$$IV_{Firm} = IV_{Debt} + IV_{Equity}$$

Where IV_{Firm} is the intrinsic value of the company, IV_{Debt} is the intrinsic value of company liabilities, and IV_{Equity} is the intrinsic value of company equity.

Multiplying the after-tax cost of debt capital (r_d) by the ratio of the company's intrinsic value that is financed by debt holders (IV_{Debt}/IV_{Firm}), and then adding this to the product of the cost of equity capital (r_e) and the ratio of the company's intrinsic value that is financed by equity holders (IV_{Equity}/IV_{Firm}) yields the **weighted average cost of capital**, denoted r_w. Specifically, the weighted average cost of capital is computed as follows:

$$r_w = \left(r_d \times \frac{IV_{Debt}}{IV_{Firm}}\right) + \left(r_e \times \frac{IV_{Equity}}{IV_{Firm}}\right) \qquad \textbf{12.5}$$

The WACC computation uses *intrinsic values* instead of numbers reported on balance sheets. However, because intrinsic values are unobservable, we typically use the market value of equity in place of the instrinsic value of equity, and the market value of debt in place of the intrinsic value of debt (or book value when market value is difficult to determine). (The market value of debt is usually reported in the 10-K footnote explaining debt.)

To clarify the relation among a company's debt and equity and the cost of capital, we must understand the difference between the sources of underlying risk and the methods by which cost of capital is estimated. Equity does not contain risk in and of itself. Rather it is risky because it represents both ownership of the firm and obligations to debtholders. Therefore, the risk in equity is driven by risks inherent in the company and its debt. Changes in either of these areas cause changes in the riskiness of equity. When we estimate cost of capital, it is straightforward to estimate cost of capital for debt and for equity. These two estimates are then applied, using the weighted average cost of capital formula, to estimate the risk of the company. The following chart helps to visualize these relations:

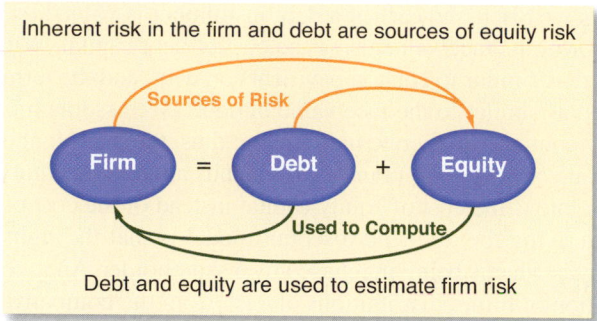

To illustrate the WACC computation, we consider **The Southern Company**. According to SO's financial statements, at December 31, 2010, the market value of its debt is approximately $20,073 million (from its 2010 10-K); the market value of its equity is $32,247 million, computed from its December 31, 2010, stock price of $38.23 times its 843.5 million shares oustanding (**Finance.Yahoo.com**). Taken together this means that SO's intrinsic value (for the entire firm) is $52,320 million. Using this information we compute SO's weighted average cost of capital as follows (SO's r_d and r_e are computed earlier in this module; $ in millions):

$$r_w = (0.029 \times [\$20{,}073/\$52{,}320]) + (0.049 \times [\$32{,}247/\$52{,}320])$$
$$= 4.1\%$$

A final point is how to treat any preferred stock. When preferred stock exists, the WACC computation includes a third term:

$$r_w = \left(r_d \times \frac{IV_{Debt}}{IV_{Firm}}\right) + \left(r_{ce} \times \frac{IV_{Common\ Equity}}{IV_{Firm}}\right) + \left(r_{pe} \times \frac{IV_{Preferred\ Equity}}{IV_{Firm}}\right)$$

This formulation separates equity into common equity, ce, and preferred equity, pe. The r_{pe} is the cost of preferred equity, which is usually the preferred dividend rate on the preferred stock. The $IV_{Preferred\ Equity}$ is the preferred stock's market value, or book value if market value is difficult to determine.

ANALYSIS DECISION **You Are an Investor**

You are considering investing in a company that has announced that it plans to alter its capital structure; that is, change its ratio of debt to equity. How might this change affect the company's weighted average cost of capital? [Answer p. 12-22]

MID-MODULE REVIEW

According to Finance.yahoo.com, **IBM** has a beta of 1.6. IBM's market value of debt is approximately $12.08 billion and its total market value of equity is $143.48 billion. IBM's average cost of debt capital (pretax) is approximately 7.5% and its marginal (statutory) income tax rate is 35%. Assume that the risk-free rate is 4.6% and the market risk premium is 5%.

Required
a. Interpret IBM's beta value.
b. Estimate its after-tax cost of debt capital.
c. Estimate its cost of equity capital.
d. Estimate its weighted average cost of capital.

The solution is on page 12-30.

DIVIDEND DISCOUNT MODEL

The **dividend discount model** (DDM) equates the value of company equity with the present value of all future dividends.[3] As we discussed earlier, a debt instrument is valued by discounting its coupon payments, if any, along with its face value using the cost of debt capital. With an equity instrument, dividends can be viewed as similar to coupon payments on debt, and the terminal dividend (the final payment) can be viewed as similar to the face value of debt. (We assume most companies are going concerns, meaning they continue to operate indefinitely; thus, the "terminal dividend" is most likely the proceeds upon the sale of the equity.) Further, dividends are paid to equity holders, which means that the proper discount rate is the cost of equity capital instead of the cost of debt capital.

The reasoning underlying the dividend discount model is that the right to the expected future payoffs from a company is what is being purchased by a shareholder. An investor gives up the use of funds today in expectation of future distributions of cash from the company. This valuation method recognizes the role of cash as the method of exchange and ties value directly to distributions of cash via dividends and/or a future selling price.

This section shows how the dividend discount model is derived. We explain how to estimate the present value of the regular dividends and the terminal dividend. We conclude this section with a discussion of issues in applying the dividend discount model.

Recursive Process of Valuation

Earlier in the module we showed how two types of payoffs in the future can be discounted to find the present value. Similarly, the intrinsic value of equity at the beginning of period one (IV_0) can be characterized as the sum of the dividends to be received during period 1 (D_1) plus the value of equity at the end of period 1 (IV_1) and then this quantity is divided by $1 + r_e$, or specifically:

$$IV_0 = \frac{D_1 + IV_1}{1 + r_e} \qquad \textbf{12.6}$$

To illustrate, suppose we decide to buy a share of stock in Western Company. What is today's intrinsic value of Western Company? If the cost of equity capital is 9%, the expected dividend for period 1 is $2, and the expected intrinsic value of equity at the end of period 1 is $41, then Western Company's intrinsic value today (IV_0) is $39.45, computed as:

$$IV_0 = \frac{D_1 + IV_1}{1 + r_e} = \frac{\$2 + \$41}{1.09} = \$39.45$$

Further, IV_1 can be equated to D_2 and IV_2; and then, IV_2 can be equated to D_3 and IV_3, and so forth. This continual substitution of future payoffs illustrates the *recursive process* of asset valuation, meaning that the price of stock today depends on the expected price of the stock tomorrow, which in turn depends on the expected price of the stock the day after tomorrow, and so forth. This process continues for infinity. (In practice, valuation is affected by the investor's time horizon and any differences in the investor's expectations about dividends and future intrinsic values compared with the market; these differences are what make a market.)

Framework of the Dividend Discount Model

One solution to the recursive process in equation 12.6 is the following:

$$IV_0 = \frac{D_1}{1 + r_e} + \frac{D_2}{(1 + r_e)^2} + \frac{D_3}{(1 + r_e)^3} + \dots \qquad \textbf{DDM}$$

---

[3] There is debate about whether taxes affect the value of dividends. It is possible that investors discount the value of dividends if dividends are taxed at a higher rate than capital gains. However, since tax exempt institutional investors make up a huge part of the market, it is argued that if taxes affected the value of dividends then tax exempt investors would have an arbitrage opportunity. It is argued that such an arbitrage opportunity, if it exists, would force dividend paying companies to yield the same return as non-dividend paying companies. Accordingly, we assume that taxes do *not* affect the value of dividends.

This DDM model equates current stock price to the present value of all future expected dividends. To apply the dividend discount model, we must forecast the company's future dividends for infinity. Two methods to forecast and discount infinite dividends are the constant perpetuity method and the increasing perpetuity method.

Dividend Discount Model with Constant Perpetuity

We can simplify the dividend discount model by assuming that the forecasted dividends stabilize at some point in the future and remain constant thereafter. The latter pattern yields a **perpetuity**, which is an ordinary annuity (meaning payments occur regularly at the end of each period) with an infinite horizon. The present value for a perpetuity of constant (non-changing) dividends equals the dividend amount divided by the discount rate (cost of equity capital). This model follows:

LO5 Describe and apply the dividend discount model with a constant perpetuity.

$$IV_0 = \frac{D_1}{r_e}$$

To illustrate use of this model, assume that we forecast a $3 per share dividend for Kimbrell Company for the initial two years, followed by a $3.50 per share dividend in the third year, and a $4 per share dividend thereafter. Assume also that we estimate the cost of equity capital for Kimbrell at 12%. As a first step, we compute the present value of the initial three years of dividends from:

$$\frac{\$3}{1.12} + \frac{\$3}{(1.12)^2} + \frac{\$3.50}{(1.12)^3} = \$2.68 + \$2.39 + \$2.49$$

Second, we compute the present value of the perpetuity of $4 to be $33.33, computed as of the end of year 3 as:

$$\frac{\$4}{0.12} = \$33.33$$

The $33.33 is the present value of the $4 perpetuity as of the end of year 3. To find the present value at the beginning of period 1 we discount the $33.33 lump-sum payment from the end of year 3 to the start of year 1. Thus, the present value of this perpetuity is $23.73, computed as ($4/0.12)/(1.12)^3. In sum, the intrinsic value of a Kimbrell share is computed as follows:

$$IV_0 = \frac{\$3}{1.12} + \frac{\$3}{(1.12)^2} + \frac{\$3.50}{(1.12)^3} + \frac{\left(\frac{\$4}{0.12}\right)}{(1.12)^3} = \$2.68 + \$2.39 + \$2.49 + \$23.73 = \$31.29$$

To generalize, the following formula reflects the dividend discount model when we assume a constant dividend beginning in period n+1 and continuing in perpetuity:

$$IV_0 = \frac{D_1}{1 + r_e} + \frac{D_2}{(1 + r_e)^2} + \frac{D_3}{(1 + r_e)^3} + \cdots \frac{D_n}{(1 + r_e)^n} + \frac{\frac{D_{n+1}}{r_e}}{(1 + r_e)^n} \quad \begin{array}{l} \textbf{Constant} \\ \textbf{Perpetuity} \\ \textbf{DDM} \end{array}$$

We typically refer to the last term as the "terminal dividend," although it is not paid out in period n + 1 and it is not terminal. A simplified application of this model is to assume the current dividend continues in perpetuity. This model was defined at the start of this section.

Dividend Discount Model with Increasing Perpetuity

Another means to simplify the dividend discount model is to assume that the forecasted dividends stabilize at some point in the future and continue to grow at some constant rate thereafter—this is referred to as the *Gordon growth model*. The latter growth pattern for dividends yields an **increasing perpetuity**, which is an ordinary annuity with an infinite horizon where the amount grows at a constant rate. The equation for the present value of an increasing perpetuity follows; in this equation,

LO6 Explain and apply the dividend discount model with an increasing perpetuity.

D_1 is the dividend amount when the constant growth period begins, r_e is the discount rate, and g is a constant growth rate.

$$IV_0 = \frac{D_1}{r_e - g}$$

If we assume that the constant growth rate equals zero, then the model reverts to the dividend discount model with constant perpetuity explained above. To illustrate use of this model for Kimbrell Company, assume that we forecast a $3 per share dividend for the initial two years, followed by a $3.50 per share dividend in the third year, and a $4 per share dividend in year four that continually grows at a 3% rate per year for year 5 and thereafter. Assume also that we estimate the cost of equity capital for Kimbrell at 12%. The present value for the initial three years is identical to that for the constant perpetuity model in the prior section. Next, the present value of an increasing perpetuity is $44.44 as of the end of year 3, computed as $D/(r - g) = \$4/(0.12 - 0.03)$. Then, we discount the $44.44 as of the end of year 3 to today's date to get $31.63, computed as ($44.44)/$(1.12)^3$. In sum, the intrinsic value of a Kimbrell share as of today is computed as:

$$IV_0 = \frac{\$3}{1.12} + \frac{\$3}{(1.12)^2} + \frac{\$3.50}{(1.12)^3} + \frac{\left(\dfrac{\$4}{0.12 - 0.03}\right)}{(1.12)^3} = \$2.68 + \$2.39 + \$2.49 + \$31.63 = \$39.19$$

To generalize, the following formula reflects the dividend discount model where the terminal dividend is assumed to continue in perpetuity and to grow at a constant rate:

$$IV_0 = \frac{D_1}{1 + r_e} + \frac{D_2}{(1 + r_e)^2} + \frac{D_3}{(1 + r_e)^3} + \cdots \frac{D_n}{(1 + r_e)^n} + \frac{\dfrac{D_n \times (1 + g)}{r_e - g}}{(1 + r_e)^n} \qquad \begin{matrix} \textbf{Gordon} \\ \textbf{Growth} \\ \textbf{DDM} \end{matrix}$$

A simplified application of this model is to assume the current dividend continues to grow in perpetuity. This model was defined at the start of this section.

Issues in Applying the Dividend Discount Model

There are several thorny issues with when applying the dividend discount model. One issue is that a large percentage of publicly traded companies do not issue dividends. Further, many of those non-dividend-paying firms will continue to have a zero payout for several years to come. Forecasting the dividend stream for those companies is challenging; that is, anyone can forecast, but generating *reliable* long-term forecasts is a different matter.

Another issue is how to deal with companies that have unusually high dividend payouts given their profit levels. For example, **Microsoft** paid a one-time dividend of $3.40 per share in 2005; its earnings that year were $1.12 per share. These companies are unlikely able to sustain such a high dividend payout, which presents another obstacle to forecasting dividends. (Some companies even borrow money to sustain dividend payments. It seems intuitive that a company that finances its dividends with debt should be valued differently than one that finances its dividends with operating profit. However, the dividend discount model does not differentiate between these cases.)

Still another issue with the dividend discount model is that it is difficult to create accurate dividend forecasts. Most analysts do not forecast dividends, especially terminal dividends (which are estimates of future prices!) Analysts focus on the wealth creation aspects of the company and forecast items such as sales and profit. Dividends are considered a financing decision, and companies generally do not create value from financing activities.

Broadly, dividends include all distributions to or from common shareholders. This includes both funds distributed to the shareholder such as cash dividends or stock repurchases as well as monies transferred from shareholders to the firm such as stock issuances (a "negative" dividend). Two approaches are used to compute the total distributions. The first approach uses cash flows:

+	Ordinary dividend payments to common shareholders
+	Net cash paid for common share repurchases
−	Net cash received from common share issuances
=	Total dividends to common shareholders

Many companies have especially low or especially high dividend payout rates. A search on <u>Finance.yahoo.com</u> finds over 500 companies with a dividend yield (dividend per share divided by price per share) of zero—see an abbreviated listing below.

Symbol	Company	Div/Yld	Symbol	Company	Div/Yld
AAPL	APPLE INC.	0.0%	LYG	LLOYDS BANKING	0.0%
BP	BP P.L.C.	0.0%	DTV	DIRECTV	0.0%
TM	TOYOTA MOTOR CORP	0.0%	HMC	HONDA MOTOR COMPANY	0.0%
C	CITIGROUP	0.0%	SNE	SONY CORPORATION	0.0%
LFC	CHINA LIFE INSURANCE	0.0%	HIT	HITACHI, LTD.	0.0%
DCM	NTT DOCOMO	0.0%	PC	PANASONIC CORP	0.0%
MTU	MITSUBISHI	0.0%	RIG	TRANSOCEAN LTD	0.0%
UBS	UBS AG COMMON STOCK	0.0%	KYO	KYOCERA CORPORATION	0.0%
NTT	NIPPON TELEGRAPH	0.0%	MBT	MOBILE TELESYSTEMS	0.0%
CAJ	CANON, INC. AMERICA	0.0%	NMR	NOMURA HOLDINGS	0.0%
AIG	AMERICAN INTL GROUP	0.0%	KB	KB FINANCIAL GROUP	0.0%
F	FORD MOTOR COMPANY	0.0%	S	SPRINT NEXTEL	0.0%

There were also 75 companies identified that had a dividend yield exceeding 10 percent—see an abbreviated listing below. This is a high dividend yield, which brings into question the ability of those companies to sustain that dividend level.

Symbol	Company	Div/Yld	Symbol	Company	Div/Yld
SDRL	SEADRILL LIMITED	10.2%	DRH	DIAMONDROCK HOSPITAL	14.5%
NLY	ANNALY CAPITAL	15.8%	PVD	ADMINISTRADORA	10.2%
AGNC	AMERICAN CAPITAL	20.5%	PHK	PIMCO HIGH INCOME	11.7%
CIM	CHIMERA INVESTMENT	17.2%	IVR	INVESCO MORTGAGE	14.2%
GOL	GOL LINHAS AEREAS	12.2%	UTF	COHEN & STEERS	16.5%
MFA	MFA FINANCIAL	10.3%	FRO	FRONTLINE LTD.	11.2%
CEL	CELLCOM ISRAEL	10.9%	CYS	CYPRESS SHARPRIDGE	17.7%
TNH	TERRA NITROGEN	10.7%	CMO	CAPSTEAD MORTGAGE	12.4%
PTNR	PARTNERCOMMUNICATION	10.3%	ENP	ENCORE ENERGY	10.8%
PVX	PROVIDENT ENERGY	11.3%	PSEC	PROSPECT CAPITAL	12.8%
HTS	HATTERAS FINANCIAL	15.3%	BGCP	BGC PARTNERS	10.3%
AINV	APOLLO INVESTMENT	11.7%	ANH	ANWORTH MORTGAGE	14.9%

The second approach uses the balance sheet:

+	Beginning common equity
−	Ending common equity
+	Comprehensive income
=	Total dividends to common shareholders

These historical distributions ("dividends") are used to forecast future dividends. Valuation using dividends requires estimating all future transfers to shareholders including the future liquidating dividend or the anticipated sale price. This creates a challenge for the analyst or investor.

There are instances, however, when the dividend discount model might perform well. If dividends are determined based on the long-run average of projected profits, they can provide a good indication of the company's long-run profitability. The model performs well in valuing companies that experience stable growth and a stable or slightly growing dividend stream. Companies in the utility industry are often cited as examples of companies for which the discount dividend model performs well. To illustrate, Southern Company's dividend for 2010 is

$1.8025 per share. Assume that its dividends will grow at a moderate 0.5% per year. Applying the Gordon Growth model, we estimate Southern Company's intrinsic value at $40.97 using a discount rate of 4.9%, computed as $1.8025/(0.049 − 0.005). This compares to its $40 stock price in mid-2011. We can also explore the sensitivity of this estimate to variations in the growth rate and discount rate. Those results are in Exhibit 12.6. We see that intrinsic value increases with rising growth rates, but decreases with rising discount rates. Further, as we see from this example and the above Kimbrell examples as well, the stock value estimate is especially sensitive to the growth assumption used to estimate the terminal dividend.

EXHIBIT 12.6	Intrinsic Value Estimates with Variation in Growth and Discount Rates		
	Growth Rate		
Discount Rate	**0.00%**	**1.00%**	**2.00%**
4.5%................	$40.06	$51.50	$72.10
5.5%................	32.77	40.06	51.50
6.5%................	27.73	32.77	40.06

In Modules 13 and 14 we use a variant of the Gordon Growth model that is written as follows:

$$IV_0 = \frac{D_1}{1 + r_w} + \frac{D_2}{(1 + r_w)^2} + \frac{D_3}{(1 + r_w)^3} + \frac{D_4}{(1 + r_w)^4} + \frac{\frac{D_4 \times (1 + g)}{r_w - g}}{(1 + r_w)^4},$$

where D represents free cash flows to the firm in Module 13, and residual operating income in Module 14. This expanded version of the model is mathematically equivalent to the equation for dividends shown here. Each of these models can be derived from equation 12.6. The choice of what payoff to use to estimate the firm's value will depend on the availability and reliability of the various forecasted payoffs.

RESEARCH INSIGHT   Circularity of Beta

The intrinsic value of both debt and equity are used in estimating the weighted average cost of capital. The market value of debt is usually reported either on the balance sheet or disclosed in footnotes and, therefore, the debt recorded on the balance sheet or the present value of debt disclosed in footnotes can be used as a proxy for the market value of debt. The market value of equity is often used as a proxy for the intrinsic value of equity. However, this creates a problem in that the market value of equity is used to determine the weighted average cost of capital which will be used to discount the payoffs in the valuation model to estimate the intrinsic value of equity. This intrinsic value of equity will then be compared to the market value of equity to determine if the company is under- or overvalued. While we might prefer to estimate the weighted average cost of capital without referring to the market value of equity, this is problematic in that cost of capital estimation requires us to estimate the intrinsic value of the company prior to discounting the company's payoffs.

MODULE-END REVIEW

Following are relevant financial details for **Harley-Davidson** (NYSE: HOG). Assume that the expected risk-free rate, r_f, is 4.6% and the expected market return is 9.6%.

Market value of equity	Total firm market value	Beta	Dividend per share	Pretax borrowing rate	Marginal (statutory) tax rate	Market price per share
$18.26 bil.	$18.30 bil.	1.42	$0.84	9%	35%	$70.47

Required
a. Estimate its after-tax cost of debt capital.
b. Estimate its cost of equity capital.
c. Estimate its weighted average cost of capital.
d. Estimate its per share intrinsic value using the dividend discount model assuming that its current dividend per share continues in perpetuity.
e. Estimate its per share intrinsic value using the dividend discount model assuming that its current dividend per share continues at $0.84 for the next two years and then grows at a continual rate of 1% for year 3 and thereafter.

The solution is on page 12-30.

GUIDANCE ANSWERS . . . ANALYSIS DECISION

You Are an Investor Altering a company's capital structure (changing its debt to equity ratio) alters its financial risk. For the shareholder, increasing leverage will increase the financial risk, which will have a corresponding increase in the expected return demanded by the shareholder. However, a company's WACC, which is the weighted average of cost of debt and cost of equity, is determined by the volatility of the company's operations. If we assume that changing the capital structure has minimal impact on company operations, ignoring any tax effects, its WACC would remain approximately the same.

QUESTIONS

Q12-1. Describe how to compute the present value of a debt security such as a bond.

Q12-2. Discuss differences between valuing a debt security and valuing the equity of a company.

Q12-3. What is a market beta? Discuss what a beta of 1.0 represents. What does a beta of 0.5 represent? A beta of 2.0?

Q12-4. Discuss the limitations associated with using beta to compute the cost of equity capital.

Q12-5. Discuss the difference between a company's intrinsic value and the company's stock price.

Q12-6. Describe how to compute the after-tax cost of debt capital.

Q12-7. Explain what the market premium represents. Describe how to compute the cost of equity capital using beta, the risk-free rate, and the market premium.

Q12-8. What is a company's cost of capital? Explain.

Q12-9. What are the three criteria for a series of payments to be considered an annuity?

Q12-10. What is a perpetuity? How is the present value of a perpetuity computed?

Q12-11. Describe how to compute the present value of an increasing perpetuity.

Q12-12. Describe the circularity that occurs when beta is used to help estimate an intrinsic value for comparison to market prices.

Assignments with the ✔ **logo in the margin are available in an online homework system.**
See the Preface of the book for details.

MINI EXERCISES

M12-13. Computing the Present Value of a Debt Security (LO1)
Compute the present value of a five-year bond with a face value of $1,000, a 10% annual coupon payment, and an 8% effective rate.

M12-14. Computing the Present Value of a Debt Security (LO1)
Compute the present value of a three-year bond with a face value of $5,000, an 8% annual coupon payment, and a 9% effective rate.

M12-15. Estimating Cost of Equity Capital (LO2)
Assume that a company's market beta equals 0.8, the risk-free rate is 5%, and the market return equals 8%. Compute the company's cost of equity capital.

M12-16. Estimating Cost of Equity Capital (LO2)

Assume that the company's market beta equals -0.8, that the risk-free rate is 5%, and the market return equals 8%. Compute the company's cost of equity capital.

M12-17. Estimating the Implied Cost of Equity Capital (LO2)

Hint: Review Equation 12.6

Assume that a company's beginning-of-period price is $10 per common share, its dividends are $0.25 per share, and its end-of-period price is $10.50 per common share. What is the company's expected cost of capital?

M12-18. Estimating the Implied End-of-Year Share Price (LO1, 2)

Assume that a company's beginning-of-period price is $15 per common share, its dividends are $1 per share, and its expected cost of equity capital is 10%. What is the expected end-of-period price per common share?

M12-19. Estimating Cost of Debt Capital (LO3)

Assume that the interest rate on a company's debt is 6% and that the company's tax rate is 35%. Compute the company's cost of debt capital.

M12-20. Estimating Cost of Debt Capital (LO3)

Assume that a company's financial statements report that its average outstanding debt totals $1.6 billion, and its total interest expense equals $80 million. If its tax rate is 35%, compute its cost of debt capital.

M12-21. Estimating Weighted Average Cost of Capital (LO4)

Assume that a company has $1.2 billion in debt, its cost of debt is 5%, it has $2 billion in equity, and its cost of equity capital is 7%. Compute the company's WACC.

M12-22. Estimating Weighted Average Cost of Capital (LO4)

Assume that a company has $1 billion in preferred stock and $3 billion in common stock. Also, it pays 6% dividends on preferred stock and its cost of equity capital is 7%. The company has no debt. Compute the company's WACC.

M12-23. Estimating Company Value using DDM with Constant Perpetuity (LO5)

Assume that a company's dividends per share are projected to remain at $1.20 each year, and that its cost of equity capital is 5%. Estimate the company's per share stock price.

M12-24. Applying DDM with Constant Perpetuity (LO5)

Assume that a company's dividends per share are projected to remain at $1.10 in perpetuity, and that its per share stock price is $22. Estimate the company's cost of equity capital.

M12-25. Estimating Company Value using DDM with Increasing Perpetuity (LO6)

Assume that a company's dividends per share are projected to grow at 2% each year, its next year's dividends per share is $1.20, and its cost of equity capital is 5%. Estimate the company's per share stock price.

M12-26. Estimating Company Value using DDM with Increasing Perpetuity (LO6)

Assume that a company paid $1.20 dividend per common share, its dividend per share is expected to grow at a constant rate of 2%, and its cost of equity capital is 5%. Estimate the company's per share stock price.

EXERCISES

E12-27. Estimating the Cost of Debt Capital (LO3)

KELLOGG COMPANY
(K)

Kellogg Company (K) manufactures cereal and other convenience food under its many well-known brands such as *Kellogg's®*, *Keebler®*, and *Cheez-It®*. The company, with more than $12 billion in annual sales worldwide, partially finances its operation through the issuance of debt. At the beginning of its 2010 fiscal year, it had $4.8 billion in total debt. At the end of fiscal year 2010, its total debt had increased to $5.9 billion. Its fiscal 2010 interest expense was $248 million, and its assumed statutory tax rate was 35%.

Required
a. Compute the company's average pretax borrowing cost. (*Hint:* Use the average amount of debt as the denominator in the computation.)
b. Assume that the book value of its debt equals its market value. Then, estimate the company's cost of debt capital.

E12-28. Estimating the Cost of Equity Capital (LO2)

KELLOGG COMPANY
(K)

Refer to information about **Kellogg Company** (K) in E12-27. Kellogg has an estimated market beta of 0.47. Assume that the expected risk-free rate is 3.1% and the expected market premium is 5%.

Required

a. What does Kellogg's market beta imply about its stock returns?

b. Estimate Kellogg's cost of equity capital.

E12-29. Estimating the Weighted Average Cost of Capital   (LO4)

Refer to information about **Kellogg Company** (K) in E12-27 and E12-28. Kellogg's stock closed at $51.08 on December 31, 2010. On that same date, the company had 419,272,027 shares issued, of which 53,667,635 shares were in treasury.

Required

a. What is Kellogg's total market capitalization as of December 31, 2010?

b. Use the information and results of E12-27 and E12-28 to compute Kellogg's WACC.

E12-30. Estimating Weighted Average Cost of Capital   (LO2, 3, 4)

Mattel, Inc. (MAT) engages in the design, manufacture, and marketing of various toy products worldwide. At December 31, 2010, Mattel's market value of equity was $8.9 billion, and its total market value was $10.1 billion. Mattel's statutory tax rate was 35%, its average pretax borrowing rate was 5.4%, and its estimated market beta was 0.99. Assume also that the expected risk-free rate is 3.1% and the expected market risk premium is 5%.

Required

a. What does Mattel's market beta imply about its stock returns?

b. Estimate Mattel's cost of debt capital, cost of equity capital, and weighted average cost of capital.

E12-31. Sensitivity of Cost of Equity Capital Estimates to Beta   (LO2)

Refer to the information about **Mattel, Inc.** (MAT) in E12-30. After further research we find that beta estimates for Mattel reported on financial Websites range from 0.85 to 1.13.

Required

a. Estimate the range of cost of equity capital estimates for Mattel implied by the different beta estimates.

b. What steps are necessary for business valuation due to the range of cost of equity capital estimates?

E12-32. Estimating Stock Value using Dividend Discount Model with Constant Perpetuity   (LO5)

Kellogg pays $1.72 in annual per share dividends to its common stockholders, and its recent stock price was $51.08. Assume that Kellogg's cost of equity capital is 5.5%.

Required

a. Estimate Kellogg's stock price using the dividend discount model with constant perpetuity.

b. Compare the estimate obtained in part a with Kellogg's $51.08 price. What does the difference between these amounts imply about Kellogg's future growth?

E12-33. Estimating Stock Value using Dividend Discount Model with Increasing Perpetuity   (LO6)

Kellogg pays $1.72 in annual per share dividends to its common stockholders, and its recent stock price was $51.08. Assume that Kellogg's cost of equity capital is 5.5%.

Required

Estimate Kellogg's expected growth rate based on its recent stock price using the dividend discount model with increasing perpetuity.

E12-34. Sensitivity of Intrinsic Value Estimates   (LO6)

Kellogg Company (K) is expected to pay $1.72 in annual dividends to its common shareholders in the future. Our best estimate of the expected cost of equity capital is 5.5% and the expected growth rate in dividends is 2%.

Required

a. Compute Kellogg's intrinsic value. Recompute intrinsic value to reflect increases and decreases of 0.5% in both (i) cost of equity capital and (ii) growth rate.

b. Given the intrinsic values computed in part a, what level of confidence do we have in the intrinsic value estimate from the dividend discount model?

E12-35. Estimating Intrinsic Share Value using Dividend Discount Model   (LO5, 6)

Mattel, Inc. (MAT) is expected to pay a $0.92 dividend per share annually. Estimate its intrinsic value per common share using the dividend discount model (DDM) under each of the following separate assumptions. (Assume MAT's cost of equity capital is 8.0%.)

Required

a. The $0.92 dividend per share occurs at the end of each of the next three years, after which there are no additional dividend payments.

b. The $0.92 dividend per share occurs at the end of each year in perpetuity.

c. The $0.92 dividend per share occurs at the end of each of the next three years, after which the dividends increase at a rate of 4% per year.

E12-36. **Assessing Terminal Dividend Assumptions for Intrinsic Value Estimates** (LO5, 6)

MATTEL, INC.
(MAT)

At December 31, 2010, **Mattel, Inc.** (MAT) was trading at a price per common share of $25.43.

Required

a. Explain how the assumption we make about a firm's terminal dividend affects the intrinsic value we compute for the firm.

b. Discuss how the terminal dividend assumption made for Mattel in E12-35 above, might explain the difference between the estimated intrinsic value and the actual trading price per common share.

E12-37. **Estimating the Market's Expected Growth Rate in Dividends** (LO5, 6)

MATTEL, INC.
(MAT)

Mattel, Inc. (MAT) was trading at a price of $25.43 per common share at December 31, 2010. Using the Gordon growth model, estimate the market's expected growth in dividends that is required to yield the $25.43 price per common share. Assume that the current dividend per share is $0.92 and is expected to grow thereafter, and that the cost of equity capital is 8.0%. (*Hint:* Use the equation for the dividend discount model with increasing perpetuity, at the top of page 12-19.)

PROBLEMS

P12-38. **Estimating Market Capitalization from Public Disclosures** (LO1)

PROCTER AND
GAMBLE
(PG)

Finance.Yahoo.com reported that **Procter and Gamble**'s (PG) market capitalization was $170.55 billion and its stock price per share was $59.98 as of June 30, 2010. The equity section from Procter and Gamble's June 30, 2010, balance sheet follows (in millions).

Convertible Class A preferred stock, stated value $1 per share (600 shares authorized)....	$ 1,277
Non-Voting Class B preferred stock, stated value $1 per share (200 shares authorized)....	—
Common stock, stated value $1 per share (10,000 shares authorized; issued: 4,007.6)	4,008
Additional paid-in capital	61,697
Reserve for ESOP debt retirement.	(1,350)
Accumulated other comprehensive income.	(7,822)
Treasury stock, at cost (shares held: 1,164.1)	(61,309)
Retained earnings	64,614
Noncontrolling interest.	324
Total Shareholders' Equity.	$61,439

Required

Verify Yahoo's computation of P&G's market capitalization using data from above.

 P12-39. **Estimating Cost of Capital Measures** (LO2, 3, 4)

SPRINT NEXTEL
(S)

Sprint Nextel Corporation (S) has $22.1 billion in total debt (which approximates its market value). Interest expense for the year was about $1.5 billion. The company's market capitalization is approximately $17.2 billion, its market beta is 2.12, and its marginal (statutory) tax rate is 35%. Assume that the risk-free rate equals 4.6% and the market premium equals 5%.

Required

a. Estimate Sprint Nextel's cost of debt capital.

b. What does a beta of 2.12 mean regarding the volatility of Sprint Nextel's stock price?

c. Estimate Sprint Nextel's cost of equity capital.

d. Estimate Sprint Nextel's weighted average cost of capital.

 **P12-40.** **Estimating Market and Book Values and Cost of Capital Measures** (LO1, 2, 3, 4)

3M COMPANY
(MMM)

The December 31, 2010, partial balance sheet of **3M Company** follows ($ millions, except per share amounts). **ycharts.com** reported that the total market capitalization of 3M was $61.86 billion and its stock price was $86.30 as of December 31, 2010. Also, **ycharts.com** estimates its total enterprise value at $63.94 billion, and its market beta at 0.83. 3M's average pretax borrowing cost is 3.7%, and its statutory tax rate is 35%. Assume that the risk-free rate equals 3.1% and the market premium equals 5%.

Liabilities
Current liabilities
  Short-term borrowings and current portion of long-term debt .... | $ 1,269
  Accounts payable.. | 1,662
  Accrued payroll.. | 778
  Accrued income taxes .... | 358
  Other current liabilities .... | 2,022

Short-term borrowings and current portion of long-term debt	$ 1,269
Accounts payable	1,662
Accrued payroll	778
Accrued income taxes	358
Other current liabilities	2,022
Total current liabilities	6,089
Long-term debt	4,183
Pension and postretirement benefits	2,013
Other liabilities	1,854
Total liabilities	$14,139

Equity
3M Company shareholders' equity:

Common stock, par value $.01 per share	$ 9
Shares outstanding — 2010: 711,977,608	
Shares outstanding — 2009: 710,599,119	
Additional paid-in capital	3,468
Retained earnings	25,995
Treasury stock	(10,266)
Accumulated other comprehensive income (loss)	(3,543)
Total 3M Company shareholders' equity	15,663
Noncontrolling interest	354
Total equity	$16,017
Total liabilities and equity	$30,156

Required

a. Verify ychart.com's computation of 3M's market capitalization using the data from its financial report excerpts above.

b. Compute the book value of 3M's long-term debt as of December 31, 2010.

c. Compute the market value of 3M's debt using the data from ychart.com.

d. Identify at least two reasons behind the difference between the amounts computed in parts *b* and *c*.

e. Compute 3M's cost of debt capital.

f. Compute 3M's cost of equity capital.

g. Compute 3M's weighted average cost of capital. Use the market capitalization from ychart.com for this calculation.

P12-41. Estimating Components of both WACC and DDM (LO2, 3, 4, 5)

Analysts estimate the cost of debt capital for **Abbott Laboratories** (NYSE: ABT) is 2.56% and that its cost of equity capital is 4.1%. Assume that ABT's statutory tax rate is 36%, the risk-free rate is 4.6%, the market risk premium is 5%, the ABT market price is $47.73 per common share, and its dividends are $1.18 per common share.

Required

a. Compute ABT's average pretax borrowing rate and its market beta.

b. Assume that its dividends continue at the current level in perpetuity. Use the constant perpetuity dividend discount model and the market price to infer the market's expected cost of equity capital. (*Hint:* Use the equation for dividend discount model with constant perpetuity, on page 12-18.)

c. Compare the inferred cost of equity capital from part *b* to the 4.1% estimated cost of equity capital from analysts. Comment on any difference.

P12-42. Estimating WACC and Expected Growth in Dividends Model (LO2, 3, 4, 5, 6)

FedEx Corporation (NYSE: FDX) was trading at $93.64 at May 31, 2011. Its dividend per share was $0.48, its market beta was estimated to be 1.19, its average pretax borrowing rate was 4.8%, and its statutory tax rate was 36.7%, consisting of the 35% federal rate plus the 1.7% state rate, net of federal benefits. FedEx's market value of equity (market capitalization) was $29.68 billion, computed as 317 million shares times its $93.64 price, and its total market value (enterprise value) was $31.77 billion, computed as $29.68 billion in equity plus $2.09 billion in long-term debt ($1.69 reported plus $0.4 fair value adjustment). Assume a risk-free rate of 3.1% and a market risk premium of 5% to answer the following requirements.

ABBOTT LABORATORIES (ABT)

FEDEX CORPORATION (FDX)

Required

a. Estimate FedEx's cost of debt capital, cost of equity capital, and weighted average cost of capital. The company's market capitalization exceeds its enterprise value. This means that the company is a "net lender" or alternately, that the company has negative net nonoperating obligations. (See Module 3 for explanation.)

b. Using the dividend discount model, and assuming a constant perpetuity at its current dividend level, estimate FedEx's intrinsic value per share.

c. Using the Gordon growth DDM, and assuming next period's dividends equal $0.52 and grow at a constant rate for each period thereafter, infer the market's expected growth in dividends that are necessary for FedEx's intrinsic value to equal $93.64 per common share. Discuss the reasonableness of this growth factor. (Assume that its cost of equity capital is 9.2%.)

 P12-43. **Estimating Cost of Capital Measures and Applying the DDM Model**   **(LO2, 5, 6)**

PROCTER AND GAMBLE
(PG)

Procter and Gamble (PG) has a June fiscal year-end. On June 30, 2006, analysts expected the company to pay $1.41 dividends per share in fiscal year 2007, and its market beta was estimated to be 0.7. Assume that the risk-free rate is 4.6% and the market premium is 5%. During fiscal year 2006, the company's sales growth was 20.2%. However, analysis reveals that P&G's fiscal 2006 sales include eight months of sales from Gillette after its acquisition by P&G during 2006. Footnotes report pro forma sales that show what the income statement would have reported had Gillette's full-year sales been included in both 2005 and 2006—specifically, P&G's sales growth would have been 4.4%.

Required

a. Estimate P&G's cost of equity capital using the CAPM model.

b. Estimate P&G's intrinsic value using the DDM assuming that dividends per share are projected at $1.41 per share after 2007. (*Hint:* Apply the DDM with constant perpetuity, shown on page 12-18.)

c. Discuss the appropriateness of the estimate computed in part b in light of the DDM assumption of zero future dividend growth.

d. If we use the Gordon growth DDM to estimate stock value per share, which of the two growth rates should we use: 20.2% or 4.4%? Explain.

e. On June 30, 2006, the stock of P&G was priced at $55.60 per share. Infer the market expectation about the future growth rate of P&G's dividend using the DDM with an increasing perpetuity (Gordon growth DDM). Comment on the reasonableness of this inferred growth rate.

P12-44. **Estimating Cost of Preferred Equity Capital and WACC**   **(LO2, 4)**

DOW CHEMICAL
(DOW)

The consolidated balance sheets of **Dow Chemical (DOW)** show that the company has 4,000,000 shares of preferred stock outstanding at the end of 2010. That preferred stock has a book value of $1,000 per share. During fiscal 2010, the company declared $340 million in dividends for its preferred stock.

Required

a. Compute the total book value of its preferred stock at the end of 2010.

b. Estimate the cost of preferred equity capital, r_{pe}.

c. Explain how to incorporate the cost of preferred equity capital into the estimation of the weighted average cost of capital. (No computations are required.)

P12-45. **Estimating Cost of Capital and the Effects of Hedging**   **(LO2, 4, 6)**

FEDEX CORPORATION
(FDX)

Refer to the information regarding **FedEx Corporation** in P12-42. Assume that FedEx is considering implementing certain transactions to hedge against potential fluctuations in gas and fuel costs and in exchange rates. It is estimated that such transactions would reduce FedEx's cash flow volatility and, thus, decrease the firm's market beta from 1.19 to 1.10.

Required

a. Estimate Fedex's cost of equity capital and its weighted average cost of capital assuming it enters into the hedges.

b. Assume that the market's expected growth in FedEx dividends is 7.5%, and that the cost of the hedge transactions would reduce FedEx's projected dividend growth by 0.20%. Using the Gordon growth DDM, infer the stock value per share.

DISCUSSION POINTS

 D12-46. **Estimating Cost of Debt Capital**   **(LO3)**

AT&T
(T)

The December 31, 2010, partial financial statements taken from the annual report for **AT&T** (T) follow.

Consolidated Statements of Income Dollars in millions except per share amounts	2010	2009
Operating revenues		
Wireless service	$ 53,510	$ 48,563
Voice	28,315	32,324
Data	27,479	25,561
Directory	3,935	4,724
Other	11,041	11,341
Total operating revenues	124,280	122,513
Operating expenses		
Cost of services and sales (exclusive of depreciation and amortization shown separately below)	52,263	50,571
Selling, general and administrative	33,065	31,427
Depreciation and amortization	19,379	19,515
Total operating expenses	104,707	101,513
Operating income	19,573	21,000
Other Income (expense)		
Interest expense	(2,994)	(3,368)
Equity in net income of affiliates	762	734
Other income, net	897	152
Total other income (expense)	(1,335)	(2,482)
Income from continuing operations before income taxes	18,238	18,518
Income tax (benefit) expense	(1,162)	6,091
Income from continuing operations	19,400	12,427
Income from discontinued operations, net of tax	779	20
Net income	$ 20,179	$ 12,447

Consolidated Balance Sheets—Liabilities and Equity Sections Dollars in millions except per share amounts, December 31	2010	2009
Current liabilities		
Debt maturing within one year	$ 7,196	$ 7,361
Accounts payable and accrued liabilities	20,055	21,260
Advanced billing and customer deposits	4,086	4,170
Accrued taxes	72	1,681
Dividends payable	2,542	2,479
Total current liabilities	33,951	36,951
Long-term debt	58,971	64,720
Deferred credits and other noncurrent liabilities		
Deferred income taxes	22,070	23,579
Postemployment benefit obligation	28,803	27,847
Other noncurrent liabilities	12,743	13,226
Total deferred credits and other noncurrent liabilities	63,616	64,652
Stockholders' equity		
Common stock ($1 par value, 14,000,000,000 authorized at December 31, 2010 and 2009: issued 6,495,231,088 at December 31, 2010 and 2009)	6,495	6,495
Additional paid-in capital	91,731	91,707
Retained earnings	31,792	21,944
Treasury stock (584,144,220 at December 31, 2010, and 593,300,187 at December 31, 2009, at cost)	(21,083)	(21,260)
Accumulated other comprehensive income	2,712	2,678
Noncontrolling interest	303	425
Total stockholders' equity	111,950	101,989
Total liabilities and stockholders' equity	$268,488	$268,312

Consolidated Statements of Stockholders' Equity—Excerpts Dollars and shares in millions except per share amounts	2010	
	Shares	Amount
Common Stock		
Balance at beginning of year	6,495	$ 6,495
Issuance of shares	–	–
Balance at end of year	6,495	$ 6,495
Treasury Shares		
Balance at beginning of year	(593)	$(21,260)
Purchase of shares.	–	–
Issuance of shares	9	177
Balance at end of year	(584)	$(21,083)
Retained Earnings		
Balance at beginning of year		$ 21,944
Net income ($3.35 per share).		19,864
Dividends to stockholders ($1.69 per share)		(9,985)
Other.		(31)
Balance at end of year		$ 31,792

Required

a.   How much interest expense did AT&T incur during 2010?

b.   What is the book value of AT&T's interest-bearing debt at the end of 2010? At the beginning of 2010?

c.   Estimate AT&T's 2010 pretax cost of debt capital.

d.   Estimate AT&T's 2010 effective (that is, average) tax rate from information in its income statement.

e.   Estimate AT&T's 2010 after-tax cost of debt capital. The company's statutory tax rate is 35%. Which tax rate, the statutory rate or the effective rate, is appropriate for computing its cost of debt capital?

D12-47.   Estimating Cost of Equity Capital and Weighted Average Cost of Capital   (LO2, 4)

AT&T
(T)

Refer to the information regarding **AT&T** in D12-46. In early 2011, **Yahoo** reports that AT&T has a market beta of 0.65, and that its closing stock price at the end of 2010 was $29.38.

Required

a.   Explain what AT&T's market beta of 0.65 implies regarding its stock price volatility.

b.   Assume that the market risk premium equals 5% and that the risk-free rate equals 3.1%. Estimate AT&T's cost of equity capital using the CAPM model.

c.   Footnote 8 of AT&T's 10-K reports that the market value of its debt approximates its book value. Assume that the company's after-tax cost of debt is 2.81%. Using this information, estimate AT&T's weighted average cost of capital.

D12-48.   Applying the Gordon Growth DDM   (LO6)

AT&T
(T)

Refer to the information regarding **AT&T** in D12-46.

Required

a.   What amount of dividends (per share) did AT&T declare for its common shareholders in 2010?

b.   AT&T's common stock was traded at $29.38 per share at the end of 2010. Use the Gordon growth model (the dividend discount model with an increasing perpetuity) to estimate the market's expectation regarding AT&T's average growth in dividends. Assume that its cost of equity capital is 5.41%.

c.   Comment on the reasonableness of the implied dividend growth rate.

D12-49.   Interpreting Market Reactions to Accounting Information   (LO1, 5)

AT&T
(T)

On December 11, 2007, AT&T announced that it would increase its dividend per share by 12.7%. At the same time the company announced a $15.2 billion stock buyback plan. The stock price of AT&T closed up 4.1% on that day.

Required

a.   Explain why AT&T's stock price reacted positively to those announcements.

b.   Speculate as to why the stock price of AT&T rose only 4.1% while its dividends per share increased 12.7%.

D12-50. **Sensitivity of Cost of Capital and Intrinsic Value Estimates** (LO2, 3, 4, 6)

At December 31, 2010, analysts estimate **Best Buy's** (BBY) beta at 1.28. The company is expected to pay $0.64 in annual dividends to its common shareholders in the foreseeable future. Assume that the market risk premium equals 5% and that the risk-free rate equals 3.1%.

BEST BUY
(BBY)

Required

a. Compute the range of estimates of Best Buy's cost of equity capital if the analysts' estimate of beta is off by as much as $+/- 0.1$.

b. Upon further consideration, we realize that a growth in dividends is necessary for an intrinsic value estimate. Determine the range of Best Buy intrinsic value estimates that are possible utilizing the cost of capital estimates from part a and an assumption that the growth rate in dividends could range from 0% to 2%.

SOLUTIONS TO REVIEW PROBLEMS

Mid-Module Review

Solution

a. Its beta value of 1.6 indicates that IBM is more volatile than the market index (in the case of **Finance. yahoo.com**, the index is the S&P 500). A beta of 1.6 implies that IBM's stock price would change as much as 160%, both up and down, with changes in the overall market index.

b. Its after-tax cost of debt capital is 4.9%, computed as $7.5\% \times (1 - 0.35)$.

c. Its cost of equity capital is 12.6%, computed as $4.6\% + (1.6 \times 5\%)$.

d. Its weighted average cost of capital is 12%, computed as:

$$r_W = \left(0.049 \times \frac{\$12.08 \text{ billion}}{\$155.56 \text{ billion}}\right) + \left(0.126 \times \frac{\$143.48 \text{ billion}}{\$155.56 \text{ billion}}\right) = 0.12$$

Module-End Review

Solution

a. Its after-tax cost of debt capital is estimated using Equation 12.4.

r_d = **Pretax average borrowing rate for debt** $\times$ **(1 − Marginal [statutory] income tax rate)**

$r_d = 0.09 \times (1 - 0.35)$

$r_d = 0.0585$

b. Its cost of equity capital is estimated using the CAPM following Equation 12.1.

$r_e = r_f + \beta \times (r_m - r_f)$

$r_e = 0.046 + [1.42 \times (0.096 - 0.046)]$

$r_e = 0.117$

c. Its weighted average cost of capital is estimated using Equation 12.5 (B is billions).

$$r_w = \left(r_d \times \frac{IV_{Debt}}{IV_{Firm}}\right) + \left(r_e \times \frac{IV_{Equity}}{IV_{Firm}}\right)$$

$$r_w = \left(0.0585 \times \frac{\$0.04B}{\$18.30B}\right) + \left(0.117 \times \frac{\$18.26B}{\$18.30B}\right)$$

$r_w = 0.0001 + 0.1167$

$r_w = 0.1168$

d. Since its payoffs (dividends) are paid to equity holders, the proper discount factor for the dividend discount model is the cost of equity capital. If intrinsic value is estimated assuming that dividend payments continue in perpetuity, its intrinsic value follows:

$$IV_{per share} = \frac{\$0.84}{0.117} = \$7.18$$

e. Here we assume that intrinsic value is estimated assuming that the dividend payments continue to grow at 1% beginning three years hence. The present value of the dividend payments for the first two years is treated as lump-sum payments. The present value of the increasing perpetuity is computed using the Gordon growth model; we obtain the present value of this perpetuity as of the end of year two, which we must then discount back two years to the present.

$$IV_{\text{per share}} = \frac{\$0.84}{1.117} + \frac{\$0.84}{(1.117)^2} + \frac{\dfrac{\$0.84}{0.117 - 0.01}}{(1.117)^2}$$

$$IV_{\text{per share}} = \$0.75 + \$0.67 + \$6.29$$

$$IV_{\text{per share}} = \$7.71$$

1. Identify equity valuation models and explain the information required to value equity securities. (p. 13-3)

2. Describe and apply the discounted free cash flow model to value equity securities. (p. 13-4)

© Getty Images

Cash-Flow-Based Valuation

During the mid-2000s, many companies experienced growth both in valuation and fundamentals. However, 2008 and 2009 brought the beginning of a recession. Many companies faced cutbacks or belt-tightening measures in an effort to respond to perceived future uncertainties. It is yet unclear whether this period marked a retrenching necessitated by unfounded expansion or the beginning of a new, positive era for businesses.

JOHNSON & JOHNSON

One industry, however, that stood apart from the crowd was that of healthcare where the market continued to grow unabated. Moreover, government spending on healthcare continues to expand and the demographics (aging population) fuel further expansion. The following graphic reveals the growth of healthcare costs relative the general business trends reflected in the Dow-Jones Industrial Average (DJIA).

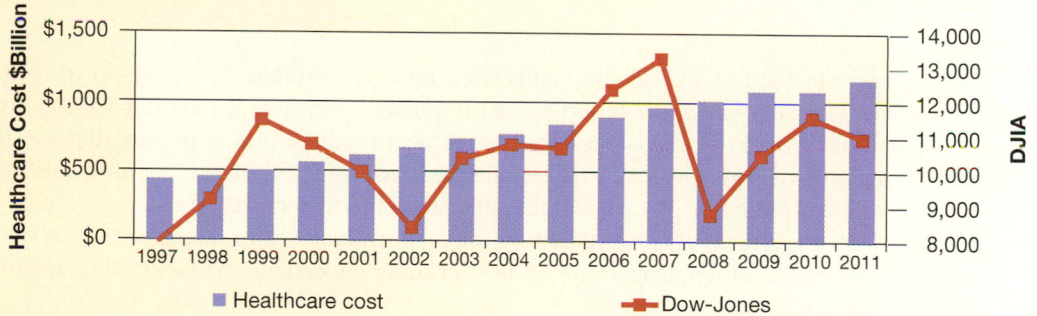

Among healthcare firms, **Johnson & Johnson (J&J)** is a common favorite for investors as it has a diversified base and plays a dominant role in the industry. For many years, J&J has engaged in the development of products that have funded both its future growth and solid returns to its shareholders. As the graph below shows, the company has witnessed steady growth in its free cash flows (FCF) over the past decade, and a steady, if not slightly upward, movement in its stock price.

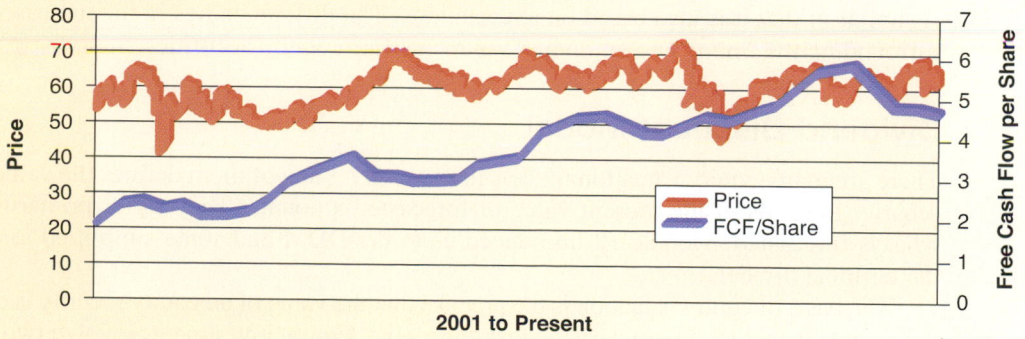

(continued on next page)

(continued from previous page)

Many investors use measures of free cash flows to form value estimates of the company. The use of free cash flows as the payoff of choice in valuation models is common in practice and their application in business valuation must be understood by market participants.

When we examine Johnson & Johnson for valuation purposes at least two questions immediately arise. First, how has Johnson & Johnson managed to create and sustain free cash flow growth over the past decade despite the economic uncertainties domestically and globally? Second, given its pattern of increasing free cash flows, why does the stock of Johnson & Johnson continue to remain entrenched in the range of $50 to $70 per share? To begin to answer these and related questions we must understand what factors drive the Johnson & Johnson stock price.

More generally, understanding cash-flow-based-valuation can yield insights into how measures of cash flow impact stock price and whether analysts expect Johnson & Johnson's price to rise or fall in the future. This module provides insights and answers to these questions. It explains how we can use forecasts of cash flows to price equity securities such as those of Johnson & Johnson's stock.

Sources: *Johnson & Johnson* 10-K and Annual Reports; Yahoo Finance, www.usgovernmentspending.com.

MODULE ORGANIZATION

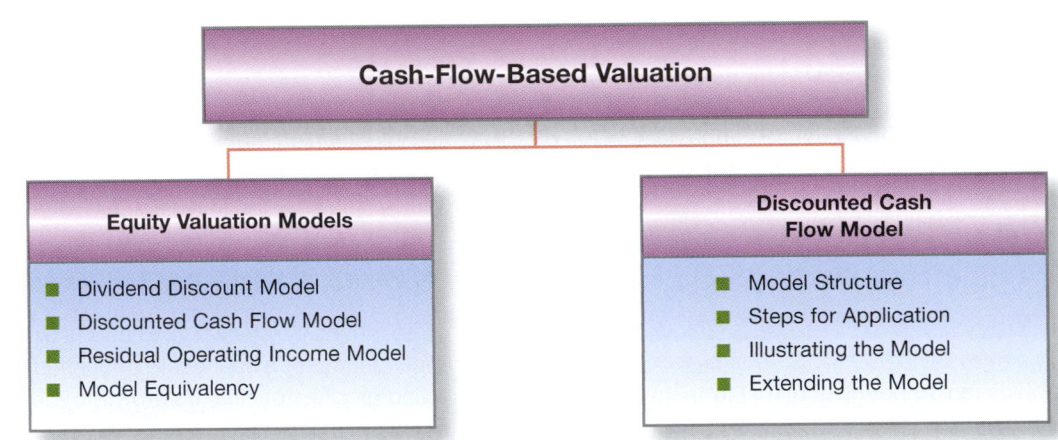

This module focuses on valuing equity securities (we explain the valuation of debt securities in Module 7). Specifically, we describe the discounted cash flow model (DCF); the residual operating income model (ROPI) is explained in the next module. It is important that we understand the determinants of equity value to make informed decisions. Employees at all levels of an organization, whether public or private, should understand the factors that create shareholder value so that they can work effectively toward that objective. For many senior managers, stock value serves as a scorecard. Successful managers are those who better understand the factors affecting that scorecard.

EQUITY VALUATION MODELS

LO1 Identify equity valuation models and explain the information required to value equity securities.

Module 7 explains that the value of a debt security is the present value of the interest and principal payments that the investor *expects* to receive in the future. The valuation of equity securities is similar in that it is also based on expectations. The difference lies in the increased uncertainty surrounding the timing and amount of payments from equity securities.

Dividend Discount Model

There are many equity valuation models in use today. Each of them defines the value of an equity security in terms of the present value of forecasted amounts. They differ primarily in terms of what is forecasted. Module 12 introduced us to the DDM and some simplified assumptions for the terminal dividend.

The basis of equity valuation is the premise that the value of an equity security is determined by the payments that the investor can expect to receive. Equity investments involve two types of payoffs: (1) dividends received during the holding period and (2) proceeds received when the security is sold.[1] The value of an equity security is, then, based on the present value of expected dividends plus the present value of the security at the end of the forecasted holding period. This **dividend discount model** is appealing in its simplicity and its intuitive focus on dividend distribution. As a practical matter, however, the model is not always useful because many companies that have a positive stock price have never paid a dividend, and are not expected to pay a dividend in the foreseeable future.

Discounted Cash Flow Model

A more practical approach to valuing equity securities focuses on the company's operating and investing activities; that is, on the *generation* of cash by the business rather than the *distribution* of cash to the shareholders. This approach is called the **discounted cash flow (DCF)** model. The focus of the forecasting process for the DCF model is the company's expected *free cash flows to the firm*, which are defined as operating cash flows net of the expected new investments in net operating assets that are required to support the business.

Residual Operating Income Model

Another approach to equity valuation also focuses on operating and investing activities. It is known as the **residual operating income (ROPI)** model. This model uses both net operating profits after tax (NOPAT) and the net operating assets (NOA) to determine equity value; see Module 3 for complete descriptions of the NOPAT and NOA measures. This approach, presented in the next module, highlights the importance of return on net operating assets (RNOA), and the disaggregation of RNOA into net operating profit margin and NOA turnover.

Model Equivalency

When the DDM was introduced in Module 12, it was based on the following relation:

$$IV_0 = \frac{D_1 + IV_1}{1 + r_e}$$

Both the DCF and ROPI models derive from this basic starting point and are, therefore, mathematically equivalent. Any differences between the estimated valuations of equity using these models arise due to implementation issues rather than the frameworks themselves. Assumptions such as forecast horizon length or terminal growth rate (discussed later in this module) can be easier to determine with less uncertainty for a particular company using a particular valuation model, which can lead to a more reliable value estimate. Following our 4-step process from Module 1, the quality of our value estimate (Step 4) is based on the quality of our forecasts of future payoffs (Step 3). Further, those forecasts are only as good as the adjustments/assessment of financial information made (Step 2) and our understanding of the company's business environment (Step 1). If the forecasts made are identical across the different payoffs, the resulting value estimates from the models will also be identical.

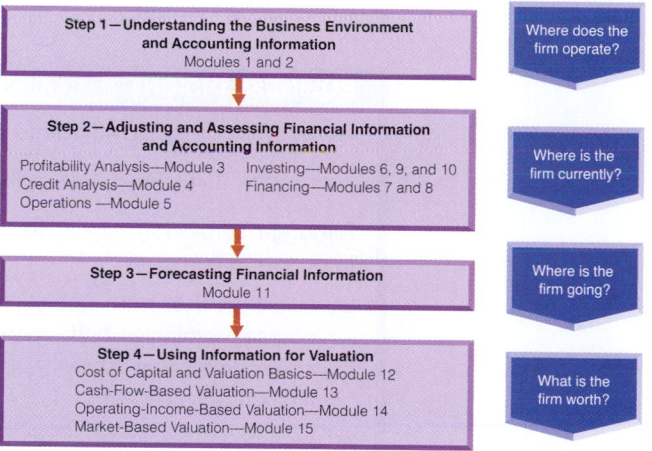

DISCOUNTED CASH FLOW (DCF) MODEL

The rationale for using the discounted cash flow (DCF) model is that cash flows are "tangible" and easy to understand. Cash is often viewed as the ultimate source of value for investors. We hold an equity security (or any asset) as an economic resource that will allow for future consumption. Thinking in terms of cash value allows us to easily quantify the amount of consumption the asset is expected to provide. Additionally, cash flows are readily comparable across differing time horizons using standard present value techniques. These characteristics lead to the widespread use of the cash-flow-based valuation model.

LO2 Describe and apply the discounted free cash flow model to value equity securities.

---

[1] The future stock price is, itself, also assumed to be related to the expected dividends that the new investor expects to receive; as a result, the expected receipt of dividends is the sole driver of stock price under this type of valuation model.

The DCF model defines firm value as follows:

$$\text{Firm Value} = \text{Present Value of Expected Free Cash Flows to Firm}$$

The expected free cash flows to the firm include cash flows arising from the operating side of the business; that is, cash generated from the firm's operating activities (but not from nonoperating activities such as interest paid on debt or dividends received on investments), and they do not include the cash flows from financing activities.

DCF Model Structure

Free cash flows to the firm (FCFF) equal net operating profit after tax that is not used to grow net operating assets. Using the terminology of Module 3 we can define FCFF as follows (see the following Business Insight box for a more traditional definition). The derivation of this equation is in Appendix 13C. That derivation shows that NOPAT – ΔNOA, where Δ represents "change," equals the sum of payments to creditors as interest and principal (NNE and –ΔNNO, respectively) and to shareholders as capital and dividend distributions (–ΔCC and DIV, respectively). This means that FCFF is the net payments to holders of both net nonoperating obligations and company equity, which can be written as follows:

$$\text{FCFF} = \text{NOPAT} - \text{Increase in NOA}$$

where

$$\text{NOPAT} = \text{Net operating profit after tax}$$

$$\text{NOA} = \text{Net operating assets}$$

Net operating profit after tax is normally positive and the net cash flows from increases in net operating assets are normally negative assuming that net operating assets increase each period. The sum of the two (positive or negative) represents the net cash flows available to creditors and shareholders. Positive FCFF imply that there are funds available for distribution to creditors and shareholders, either in the form of debt repayments, dividends, or stock repurchases (treasury stock). Negative FCFF imply that the firm requires additional funds from creditors and/or shareholders, in the form of new loans or equity investments, to support its business activities.

BUSINESS INSIGHT   **Definitions of Free Cash Flow**

We often see free cash flows to the firm (unlevered free cash flow) defined as follows:

$$\text{FCFF} = \text{Net cash flow from operating activities} - \text{Capital expenditures}$$

Although somewhat similar to the definition in this book, NOPAT – Increase in NOA, there are important differences:

- Net cash flow from operating activities uses net income as the starting point; net income, of course, comingles both operating and nonoperating components (such as selling expense and interest expense). Analysts sometimes correct for this by adding back items such as after-tax net interest expense, which is the approach used by the Oppenheimer analysts in Appendix 13B.

- Income tax expense (in net income) includes the effect of the interest tax shield (see Module 3); the usual NOPAT definition includes only the tax on operating income.

- Net cash flow from operating activities also includes nonoperating items in working capital, such as changes in interest payable and dividends payable, as well as inflows from securitization of receivables (see Module 10); NOA focuses only on operating activities.

- The FCFF definition in this box consists of net income, changes in working capital accounts, and capital expenditures; the usual NOA consists of changes in operating working capital accounts, capital expenditures, *and* changes in long-term operating liabilities.

We must be attentive to differences in definitions for free cash flow so that we understand the analytical choices we make and their implications to equity valuation. It also aids us in drawing proper inferences from analyst research reports that might apply different definitions of free cash flow.

The DCF valuation model requires forecasts of *all* future free cash flows; that is, free cash flows for the remainder of the company's life. Generating an infinite stream of forecasts is not realistic. Consequently, analysts typically estimate FCFF over a horizon period, often 4 to 10 years, and then make simplifying assumptions about the FCFF subsequent to that horizon period.

ANALYSIS DECISION **You Are the Chief Financial Officer**

Assume that you are the CFO of a company that has a large investment in plant assets and sells its products on credit. Identify steps you can take to increase your company's cash flow and, hence, your company's firm value. [Answer p. 13-15]

Steps in Applying the DCF Model

Application of the DCF model to equity valuation involves five steps:

1. Forecast and discount FCFF for the **horizon period**.[2]
2. Forecast and discount FCFF for the post-horizon period, called **terminal period**.[3]
3. Sum the present values of the horizon and terminal periods to yield firm (enterprise) value.
4. Subtract net nonoperating obligations (NNO), along with any noncontrolling interest, from firm value to yield firm equity value. If NNO is positive, the usual case, we subtract it in step 4; if NNO is negative, we add it. (For many, but not all, companies, NNO is positive because nonoperating liabilities exceed nonoperating assets; for convenience, any noncontrolling interest is often included in NNO.)
5. Divide firm equity value by the number of shares outstanding to yield stock value per share.

BUSINESS INSIGHT **Cash Flows: Nominal (Risk-Adjusted) vs Real**

Module 12 explained that the value of payoffs (such as cash flows) is unaffected by whether *nominal (risk-adjusted)* or *real* amounts are used provided that nominal cash flows are discounted using nominal discount rates and real cash flows are discounted using real discount rates. In practice, we nearly always see nominal cash flows and nominal discount rates used; analysts do not forecast real cash flows.

Illustrating the DCF Model

To illustrate, we apply the DCF model to **Johnson & Johnson**. J&J's recent financial statements are reproduced in Appendix 13A. Forecasted financials for J&J (forecast horizon of 2011–2014 and terminal period of 2015) are in Exhibit 13.1.[4] The forecasts (in bold) are for sales, NOPAT, and NOA. These forecasts assume an annual 4.0% sales growth during the horizon period, a terminal period sales growth of 1%, net operating profit margin (NOPM) of 21%, and a year-end net operating asset turnover (NOAT) of 1.3 (which is the 2010 turnover rate based on year-end

---

[2] When discounting FCFF, the appropriate discount rate (r_w) is the **weighted average cost of capital (WACC)**, where the weights are the relative percentages of debt (d) and equity (e) in the capital structure applied to the expected returns on debt (r_d) and equity (r_e), respectively: WACC $= r_w = (r_d \times \%$ of debt$) + (r_e \times \%$ of equity$)$; see footnote 7 for an example. See Module 12.

[3] For an assumed growth, g, the terminal period (T) present value of FCFF in perpetuity (beyond the horizon period) is given by, $\frac{FCFF_T}{r_w - g}$, where $FCFF_T$ is the free cash flow to the firm for the terminal period, r_w is WACC, and g is the assumed long-term growth rate of those cash flows. The resulting amount is then discounted back to the present using the horizon-end-period discount factor.

[4] We use a four-period horizon in the text and assignments to simplify the exposition and to reduce the computational burden. In practice, analysts use spreadsheets to forecast future cash flows and value the equity security, and typically have a forecast horizon of five to ten periods.

EXHIBIT 13.1	Application of Discounted Cash Flow Model					
				Horizon Period		Terminal
(In millions, except per share values and discount factors)	Reported 2010	2011	2012	2013	2014	Period
Sales (unrounded)	$ 61,587	**$64,050.48** (61,587 × 1.04)	**$66,612.50** (64,050.48 × 1.04)	**$69,277.00** (66,612.50 × 1.04)	**$72,048.08** (69,277.00 × 1.04)	**$72,768.56** (72,048.08 × 1.01)
Sales (rounded)	61,587	**64,050**	**66,612**	**69,277**	**72,048**	**72,769**
NOPAT*........................	13,065	**13,451**	**13,989**	**14,548**	**15,130**	**15,281**
NOA**.........................	45,694	**49,269**	**51,240**	**53,290**	**55,422**	**55,976**
Increase in NOA		3,575	1,971	2,050	2,132	554
FCFF (NOPAT − Increase in NOA)....		9,876	12,018	12,498	12,998	14,727
Discount factor [1/(1 + r_w)^t]‡.........		0.92593	0.85734	0.79383	0.73503	
Present value of horizon FCFF.......		9,144	10,304	9,921	9,554	
Cum present value of horizon FCFF...	$ 38,923					
Present value of terminal FCFF	154,640					
Total firm value	193,563					
Less (plus) NNO†	(10,885)					
Firm equity value	$204,448					
Shares outstanding	2,738.1					
Stock value per share.............	$ 74.67					

*Given J&J's combined federal and state statutory tax rate of 36.0% as reported in the tax footnote to its 2010 10-K, NOPAT for 2010 is computed as follows ($ millions): ($61,587 − $18,792 − $19,424 − $6,844) − ($3,613 − {0.360 × [$455 − $107 − $768]}) = $13,065. A note on rounding: To forecast sales, we multiply prior year's unrounded sales by (1 + Growth rate); this is done for the horizon and terminal periods. Then, we round each year's forecasted sales to whole units and use rounded sales to compute NOPAT and NOA, where both are rounded to whole units. At each successive step, we round the number to whole units before proceeding to the next step.

**NOA computations for 2010 follow ($ millions): ($102,908 − $19,355 − $8,303) − ($46,329 − $7,617 − $9,156) = $45,694.

†NNO is the difference between NOA and total shareholders' equity; in this case NNO ($ millions) = $45,694 − $56,579 = $(10,885). J&J's NNO is negative because it carries substantial cash and securities that exceed its debt.

‡For simplification, present value computations use discount factors rounded to 5 decimal places.

NOA; year-end amounts are used because we are forecasting year-end account balances, not average balances).[5,6]

The bottom line of Exhibit 13.1 is the estimated J&J equity value of $204,448 million, or a per share stock value of $74.67 (computed as $204,448/2,738.1 shares). The present value computations use an 8% WACC(r_w) as the discount rate.[7] Specifically, we obtain this stock valuation as follows:

[5] **NOPAT** equals revenues less operating expenses such as cost of goods sold, selling, general, and administrative expenses, and taxes. NOPAT excludes any interest revenue and interest expense and any gains or losses from financial investments. NOPAT reflects the operating side of the firm as opposed to nonoperating activities such as borrowing and security investment activities. **NOA** equals operating assets less operating liabilities. (See Module 3.)

[6] NOPAT and NOA are typically forecasted using the detailed forecasting procedures discussed in Module 11. In this module we use the parsimonious method to multiyear forecasting (see Module 11) to focus attention on the valuation process.

[7] The weighted average cost of capital (WACC) for J&J is computed using the following three-step process:

1. The cost of equity capital is given by the capital asset pricing model (CAPM): $r_e = r_f + \beta (r_m − r_f)$, where β is the beta of the stock (an estimate of stock price variability that is reported by several services such as Standard and Poors), r_f is the risk-free rate (commonly assumed as the 10-year treasury bond rate), and r_m is the expected return to the entire market. The expression $(r_m − r_f)$ is the "spread" of equities over the risk-free rate, often assumed to be about 5% to 7%. For J&J, given a beta of 1.00 and a 10-year treasury bond rate of 3.58% (r_f) as of February 28, 2011, r_e is estimated as 9.58%, computed as 3.58% + (1.00 × 6%).

2. Two alternative computations for pretax cost of debt capital are: (1) Interest expense/Average interest-bearing debt, and (2) Weighted-average effective interest rate on debt. For the latter, J&J reports its 5.25% rate in footnote 7 to its 10-K, which we use. To obtain J&J's after-tax cost of debt capital, we multiply 5.25% by 1 − 0.360, where 36.0% is the federal and state statutory tax rate from its tax footnote, yielding 3.36% (J&J's after-tax cost of debt).

3. WACC is the weighted average of the cost of equity capital and the cost of debt capital. J&J capital structure is 77% equity and 23% debt. Thus, J&J's weighted average cost of capital is (77% × 9.58%) + (23% × 3.36%) = 8.15%, rounded to 8%. (The capital structure of J&J depends on its stock price. To achieve an internally consistent value estimate, an iterative process can be used where the estimated value [in this case $74.67] is used to recompute its capital structure and get an updated WACC estimate. After several iterations, the valuation estimate and the weights used to compute WACC converge.)

1. **Compute present value of horizon period FCFF.** We compute the forecasted 2011 FCFF of $9,876 million from the forecasted 2011 NOPAT less the forecasted increase in 2011 NOA. The present value of this $9,876 million as of 2010 is $9,144.5 million, computed as $9,876 million × 0.92593 (the present value factor for one year at 8%). Similarly, the present value of 2012 FCFF (two years from the current date) is $10,303.5 million, computed as $12,018 million × 0.85734, and so on through 2014. The sum of these present values (*cumulative present value*) is $38,923 million.

2. Compute **present value of terminal period FCFF.** The present value of the terminal period FCFF is $154,640 million, computed as $\dfrac{\left(\dfrac{\$14{,}727 \text{ million}}{0.08 - 0.01}\right)}{(1.08)^4}$, or ($14,727/0.07) × 0.73503.

3. **Compute firm equity value.** Sum present values from the horizon and terminal period FCFF to get firm (enterprise) value of $193,563 million. Subtract the value of J&J's net nonoperating obligations of $(10,885) million to get firm equity value of $204,448. Dividing firm equity value by the 2,738.1 million shares outstanding (computed as 3,119,843,000 less 381,746,000) yields the estimated per share valuation of $74.67.

We perform this valuation as of February 25, 2011, which is the SEC filing date for J&J's 10-K. J&J's stock closed at $59.13 on February 25, 2011. Our valuation estimate of $74.67 indicates that the stock is undervalued as of that date. J&J's stock price climbed steadily through the spring of 2011 and was trading for $65 by July at which point J&J was still recommended as a strong BUY stock.

BUSINESS INSIGHT   **Analysts' Forecasts**

Earnings and cash-flow estimates are key to security valuation. Following are earnings estimates as of August 2011, for Johnson & Johnson from Yahoo.finance. About 20 analysts provided earnings estimates. The median (consensus) EPS estimate for 2011 (current year) is $4.97 per share, with a high of $5.02 and a low of $4.93. This compares to an actual diluted EPS of $4.78 in 2010. For 2012 (slightly more than one year ahead), the consensus EPS estimate is $5.29. The average buy rating for J&J stock is 2.2 on a scale that runs from 1.0 (Strong BUY) to 5.0 (Strong SELL).

Estimate Period	Total Analysts	Ave. EPS Est.	High EPS Est.	Low EPS Est.
2011 Fiscal Year	21	$4.97	$5.02	$4.93
2012 Fiscal Year	19	$5.29	$5.38	$5.19
Average recommendation: 2.2 (1 = Strong Buy, 3 = Hold, 5 = Strong Sell)				

Extending the DCF Model

The Johnson & Johnson illustration makes several assumptions that can be refined to derive more precise stock values. We describe some of these refinements here.

Horizon Period. The illustration uses a relatively short horizon period. It might be more reasonable to anticipate growth for longer than four years before the company achieves a long-term growth of 1%, as in our example. The downside to much longer horizon periods is that it is more difficult to accurately project growth as the time horizon extends. Thus, the shorter horizon period might provide a more conservative stock value.

Growth Rate. The illustration assumes a constant growth rate, NOPM and NOAT during the horizon period. As an alternative, we can alter these, even having different rates for each year. For example, we might assume that the recent economic downturn will depress J&J's sales for 2011 and 2012 and, thus, we might forecast a growth rate less than 4% for those two years followed by 4% growth in 2013 and 2014. Similarly, we could change NOPM and/or NOAT for each year to better match our expectations of future profitability and/or asset efficiency.

Financial Statement Forecasts. The illustration uses a parsimonious method to multiyear fore-casting to focus attention on the valuation process. As an alternative, we can prepare detailed year-by-year forecasts of the income statement and balance sheet to derive NOPAT and NOA, respectively. Year-by-year forecasts allow us to more precisely model relations on the income statement, and between the income statement and the balance sheet. For example, the parsimonious model assumes a constant NOPM of 21% for the J&J illustration. This implies that all expenses vary in exactly the same way with revenue growth. We can refine that assumption by including different growth rates for different expenses. As another example, the parsimonious model assumes one turnover rate for all net operating assets. In the J&J example, we apply a NOAT of 1.3, which is the average historic turnover rate across accounts receivable, inventory, PPE, accounts payable, and so forth. A year-by-year forecast would allow the turnover rates to vary across different operating assets and liabilities and potentially yield more precise estimates for future expected NOA.

Terminal Growth Rate. A crucial assumption in valuation is the choice of a terminal growth rate. This rate reflects all future FCFF beyond the forecast horizon, which is captured in terminal value. Many valuations are sensitive to variations in terminal growth rate. The choice of a fore-cast horizon is influenced by whether the company has achieved a long-run steady state where a pattern of future FCFF is expected to persist for the long-run of the company. Ideally, the forecast horizon is sufficiently long to allow steady state to be achieved within the horizon. The terminal growth rate can be a positive percentage (but not exceeding the discount rate), or zero, or negative (but not less than −100%). An increase in the terminal growth rate for Johnson & Johnson from 1% to 2% would increase the present value of the terminal FCFF from $154,640 to $180,413 [$14,727/(0.08 − 0.02)/1.08^4], yielding an increase in estimated value per share of $9.41 [($180,413 − $154,640)/2,738.1]. This shows the sensitivity of a valuation to a terminal growth rate. The quality of our forecasts within the horizon period directly impacts the quality of our terminal growth rate estimate.

Sensitivity Analysis of Stock Price. The illustration uses only one set of assumptions and derives only one stock price. To refine our valuation we can perform sensitivity analyses. For example, the J&J illustration uses 8% for WACC, which is our best estimate of the company's weighted average cost of capital. We might derive stock value using a larger and smaller WACC to gauge how sensitive the stock price is to changes in the discount rate. For example, the Oppen-heimer analysis simultaneously varies the growth rate and the WACC assumptions by 1 percent-age point, in 50 basis-point increments. This generates 25 different stock values—Oppenheimer displays the different assumptions as rows and columns in a table in Appendix 13B. Extending this idea, we commonly derive a "worst case" stock value by simultaneously applying the lowest reasonable assumptions for growth, NOPM, and NOAT, and the highest reasonable assumption for WACC. We also commonly derive the "best case" scenario by applying the highest reasonable assumptions for growth, NOPM, and NOAT, and the lowest reasonable assumption for WACC. This provides a range of reasonable stock values and gives us more information and confidence about potential outcomes.

Mid-Year Adjustment. Payoffs in our valuation model are assumed to occur at year-end and are discounted for the entire year. An alternative is to assume that payoffs occur evenly during the year. A common adjustment in this case is to multiply the estimated value by a *mid-year adjust-ment factor* defined as $(1 + r_w)^{0.5}$. Another common approximation of the adjustment factor is $(1 + [r_w/2])$. The Oppenheimer report in Appendix 13B applies a mid-year adjustment factor. For J&J, our WACC estimate of 8% would yield an adjustment factor of 1.04, which increases the valuation estimate to $212,626 ($204,448 × 1.04), or $77.65 per share.

Reverse Engineering. One alternative to sensitivity analysis is to use *reverse engineering* in an attempt to "unlock" the market's assumptions in determining price. The process of reverse engineering uses observed price combined with valuation assumptions to solve for one of the valuation parameters such as discount rate or terminal growth rate. If the observed market price of Johnson & Johnson of $59.13 at February 25, 2011, is used with the other assumptions in Exhibit 13.1, we can solve for the terminal growth rate (often implemented using reiterative estimation). In our case, this process yields an implied terminal growth rate of −1.6%. An investor or analyst could then decide whether he or she believes this rate to be too high or too low as a basis for determining a buy or sell decision.

Summary. In summary, the DCF model is frequently used in valuation due the appeal of relying on actual cash flows; a readily understandable concept. The model appears to avoid the need to understanding accounting's intricacies. However, when forecasting cash flows it almost always includes forecasting accounting numbers. Moreover, cash flows and accruals are simultaneously determined. For example, in Exhibit 13.1, we began by forecasting sales as a first step in implementing DCF, and some of those sales are in cash whereas some are on credit. A serious implementation issue with DCF is the choice of forecast horizon and terminal growth rate. The farther out the forecast horizon, the less reliable forecasts tend to be. Still, we demand a long enough forecast horizon to reach steady state so we can identify an appropriate terminal growth rate. This balance can make cash-flow-based valuation a difficult process to implement as FCFF often requires a very long horizon.

BUSINESS INSIGHT | **Cash Flows: Pretax vs After-Tax**

Should cash flows be computed pretax or after-tax for valuation? Let's consider an example where pretax cash flows of $100 million are expected in one year; the tax rate is 40%, so the after-tax cash flows are $60 million [$(1 - 0.40) \times \$100 = \$60$]. Further, let's assume that this company's capital structure is 70% debt with a pretax cost of debt capital of 6%, and its 30% equity has a pretax cost of equity capital of 12%. The pretax and after-tax weighted average cost of capital (WACC) follows:

	Proportion	Pretax Rate	Pretax WACC	Tax Effect	After-Tax WACC
Debt	70%	6%	4.2%	40%	2.52%
Equity	30%	12%	3.6%	–	3.60%
	100%		7.8%		6.12%

If pretax cash flows and pretax WACC are used, value is estimated as $92.8 million ($100 × 1/1.078). If after-tax cash flows and after-tax WACC are used, value is estimated as $56.5 million ($60 × 1/1.0612). We see that using pretax or after-tax numbers impacts valuation, which derives from the debt tax shield (deduction). After-tax cash flows and after-tax WACC are what we should use for valuation. When not explicitly stated, assume that after-tax numbers are used.

ANALYZING GLOBAL REPORTS

There are no differences in the method or technique of valuing equity securities using IFRS financial statements. We can use the DCF method with IFRS data as inputs and determine intrinsic values. Regarding other inputs, it is important to note that WACC varies across countries. This is readily apparent when we recognize that the risk-free rate used to compute WACC is country specific; for example, following is the yield on 10-year government debt for several countries as of October 2011 (www.bloomberg.com/markets/rates-bonds/government-bonds/). In comparison to countries such as Japan and Germany, the countries such as Greece and Brazil are riskier because of their debt levels and economic troubles. The higher the country risk, the higher the yield demanded on that country's debt.

Country	Yield to maturity	Country	Yield to maturity
Japan	0.99%	Australia	4.24%
Germany.	2.00%	Brazil.	11.52%
United States	2.06%	Greece	23.24%
United Kingdom	2.47%		

MODULE-END REVIEW

Following are forecasts of **Procter & Gamble**'s sales, net operating profit after tax (NOPAT), and net operating assets (NOA). These are taken from our forecasting process in Module 11 and now include a terminal period forecast that reflects a long-term growth rate of 1%.

(In millions)	Reported 2011	Horizon Period 2012	2013	2014	2015	Terminal Period
Sales growth..........		4.6%	4.6%	4.6%	4.6%	1%
Net sales (unrounded) ...	$ 82,559	$86,356.71 ($82,559 × 1.046)	$90,329.12 ($86,356.71 × 1.046)	$94,484.26 ($90,329.12 × 1.046)	$98,830.54 ($94,484.26 × 1.046)	$99,818.84 ($98,830.54 × 1.01)
Net sales (rounded)	$ 82,559	$ 86,357	$ 90,329	$ 94,484	$ 98,831	$ 99,819
NOPAT	12,193	12,781	13,369	13,984	14,627	14,773
NOA	97,247	101,596	106,269	111,158	116,272	117,434

Use the forecasts above to compute P&G's free cash flows to the firm (FCFF) and an estimate of its stock value using the DCF model. Make the following assumptions: discount rate (WACC) of 8%, shares outstanding of 2,765.7 million, and net nonoperating obligations (NNO) of $29,607 million (which includes $361 million in noncontrolling interest).

The solution is on page 13-27.

APPENDIX 13A: JOHNSON & JOHNSON FINANCIAL STATEMENTS

JOHNSON & JOHNSON Balance Sheet		
At Fiscal Year End ($ millions, except shares and per share)	2010	2009
Assets		
Cash and cash equivalents	$ 19,355	$15,810
Marketable securities...	8,303	3,615
Accounts receivable trade, net of allowances for doubtful accounts $340 (2009, $333)	9,774	9,646
Inventories	5,378	5,180
Deferred taxes on income	2,224	2,793
Prepaid expenses and other receivables............................	2,273	2,497
Total current assets	47,307	39,541
Property, plant and equipment, net	$ 14,553	$14,759
Intangible assets, net..	16,716	16,323
Goodwill...	15,294	14,862
Deferred taxes on income	5,096	5,507
Other assets..	3,942	3,690
Total assets..	$102,908	$94,682
Liabilities and Shareholders' Equity		
Loans and notes payable...	$ 7,617	$ 6,318
Accounts payable...	5,623	5,541
Accrued liabilities...	4,100	4,625
Accrued rebates, returns and promotions	2,512	2,028
Accrued compensation	2,642	2,777
Accrued taxes on income..	578	442
Total current liabilities..	$ 23,072	$21,731
Long-term debt	9,156	8,223
Deferred taxes on income	1,447	1,424
Employee related obligations......................................	6,087	6,769
Other liabilities	6,567	5,947
Total liabilities...	$ 46,329	$44,094

continued

continued from prior page

Shareholders' equity			
Preferred stock..	$	—	$ —
Common stock—par value $1.00 per share			
(authorized 4,320,000,000 shares; issued 3,119,843,000 shares)		3,120	3,120
Accumulated other comprehensive income.........................		(3,531)	(3,058)
Retained earnings		77,773	70,306
Less: common stock held in treasury, at cost			
(381,746,000 shares and 365,522,000 shares).......................		20,783	19,780
Total shareholders' equity		56,579	50,588
Total liabilities and shareholders' equity........................		$102,908	$94,682

JOHNSON & JOHNSON
Income Statement

For Fiscal Year Ended ($ millions)	2010	2009	2008
Sales to customers.................................	$61,587	$61,897	$63,747
Cost of products sold...............................	18,792	18,447	18,511
Gross profit..	42,795	43,450	45,236
Selling, marketing and administrative expenses	19,424	19,801	21,490
Research and development expense.......................	6,844	6,986	7,577
Purchased in-process research and development................	—	—	181
Interest income.......................................	(107)	(90)	(361)
Interest expense, net of portion capitalized................	455	451	435
Other (income) expense[1]	(768)	(526)	(1,015)
Restructuring	—	1,073	—
Earnings before provision for taxes on income	16,947	15,755	16,929
Provision for taxes on income	3,613	3,489	3,980
Net earnings...	$13,334	$12,266	$12,949

1 We classify Other (Income) Expense as nonoperating because it includes, among other items: royalty income; gains and losses related to the sale and write-down of investments in equity securities; currency gains and losses; non-controlling interests; and hedge ineffectiveness.

JOHNSON & JOHNSON
Statement of Cash Flows

For Fiscal Year Ended ($ millions)	2010	2009	2008
Cash flows from operating activities			
Net earnings..	$13,334	$12,266	$12,949
Adjustments to reconcile net earnings to cash flows:			
Depreciation and amortization of property and intangibles	2,939	2,774	2,832
Stock based compensation	614	628	627
Purchased in-process research and development....................	—	—	181
Deferred tax provision...........................	356	(436)	22
Accounts receivable allowances.......................	12	58	86
Changes in assets and liabilities, net of effects from acquisitions:			
(Increase)/decrease in accounts receivable	(207)	453	(736)
(Increase)/decrease in inventories	(196)	95	(101)
Increase/(decrease) in accounts payable and accrued liabilities	20	(507)	(272)
(Increase)/decrease in other current and noncurrent assets	(574)	1,209	(1,600)
Increase in other current and noncurrent liabilities......................	87	31	984
Net cash flows from operating activities	16,385	16,571	14,972

continued from prior page

Cash flows from investing activities			
Addition to property, plant and equipment.	(2,384)	(2,365)	(3,066)
Proceeds from the disposal of assets	524	154	785
Acquisitions, net of cash acquired.	(1,269)	(2,470)	(1,214)
Purchases of investments	(15,788)	(10,040)	(3,668)
Sales of investments	11,101	7,232	3,059
Other (primarily intangibles)	(38)	(109)	(83)
Net cash used by investing activities.	(7,854)	(7,598)	(4,187)
Cash flows from financing activities			
Dividends to shareholders	(5,804)	(5,327)	(5,024)
Repurchase of common stock.	(2,797)	(2,130)	(6,651)
Proceeds from short-term debt	7,874	9,484	8,430
Retirement of short-term debt	(6,565)	(6,791)	(7,319)
Proceeds from long-term debt.	1,118	9	1,638
Retirement of long-term debt.	(32)	(219)	(24)
Proceeds from the exercise of stock options/excess tax benefits	1,226	882	1,486
Net cash used by financing activities.	(4,980)	(4,092)	(7,464)
Effect of exchange rate changes on cash and cash equivalents.	(6)	161	(323)
Increase in cash and cash equivalents.	3,545	5,042	2,998
Cash and cash equivalents, beginning of year	15,810	10,768	7,770
Cash and cash equivalents, end of year	$19,355	$15,810	$10,768

APPENDIX 13B: OPPENHEIMER VALUATION OF PROCTER & GAMBLE

We explain the forecasting process in Module 11 and reproduce an analyst report on forecasted financial statements for **Procter & Gamble** in Appendix 11A. In this appendix, we extend that report and reproduce an analyst forecasted stock price for P&G. We include below, two excerpts from the **Oppenheimer** valuation. The first excerpt provides a qualitative and quantitative analysis from Oppenheimer's report as of October 28, 2011 (*reproduced with permission*):

Investment Thesis We remain confident in P&G's ability to execute in a challenging environment, as evidenced by its healthy organic growth outlook. In addition, P&G's anticipated pricing actions on commodity-intensive products and internal cost savings should help mitigate the risk of commodity cost inflation. Further, we expect the company to continue to gain global market share through higher spending on marketing and innovation. This growth profile and its solid handle on its cost structure should provide significant operating leverage and position the company well for meaningful EPS growth in 2011 and beyond, while valuation is compellling.

Price Target Calculation Our 12- to 18-month price target for P&G of $72 per share is derived from our five-year discounted cash flow analysis, using a weighted average cost of capital of 9.2%, a terminal (fiscal 2016) unlevered free cash flow estimate of $16.7 billion and a residual free cash flow growth rate into perpetuity of 2.50%.

Key Risks to Price Target Risks to the shares achieving our price target include, but are not limited to, management's ability to continue to deliver growth above market averages, achieve its targeted top- and bottom-line synergies from the Gillette acquisition, and weather intense competition through product innovation and marketing.

Our second excerpt is a set of assumptions and computations developed by Oppenheimer analysts to forecast P&G's target stock price reported as of October 2011 (*reproduced with permission*).

(In U.S. $ millions, except per share data)

Procter & Gamble DCF Model	F2012E	F2013E	F2014E	F2015E	F2016E
Net Income	12,435	13,318	14,141	15,017	15,955
Plus: Interest Expense (After-Tax)	598	652	730	805	870
Plus: Depreciation & Amortization	2,962	3,077	3,198	3,323	3,453
Less: Capital Expenditures	(3,845)	(3,584)	(3,724)	(3,869)	(4,021)
Plus/Less: Changes in W/C & Other	526	399	399	981	421
Unlevered Free Cash Flow	12,676	13,862	14,743	16,256	16,678
PV of Unlevered Free Cash Flow	11,603	11,615	11,308	11,414	10,719

PV of Free Cash Flow	56,659
Plus: PV of Residual Value	162,907
Enterprise Value	219,566
Less: Total Debt/Preferred	(30,480)
Equity Value	189,086
Equity Value (Adjusted)	197,633
Shares Outstanding	2,748
Value Per Share	**$72**

Assumptions:	
Risk-free Rate	5.00%
Beta	0.90
Market Risk Premium	6.00%
Cost of Equity	10.40%
Tax Rate (Statutory)	35.00%
Cost of Debt (Pre-Tax)	4.00%
Cost of Debt (After-Tax)	2.60%
Cost of Preferred	5.00%
Shares Outstanding	2,748
Price	$65
Market Cap	179,319
Total Debt	29,246
Preferred	1,234
Total Capitalization	209,799

Capitalization	Current	Target
Equity	85%	85%
Debt	14%	14%
Preferred	1%	1%
WACC		9.2%
Residual FCF Growth Rate		2.50%

Terminal Free Cash Flow Growth Rate

WACC	1.5%	2.0%	2.5%	3.0%	3.5%
8.2%	$75	$80	$87	$94	$104
8.7%	$69	$73	$79	$85	$93
9.2%	$63	$67	**$72**	$77	$83
9.7%	$59	$62	$66	$71	$76
10.2%	$55	$58	$61	$65	$69

Sources: Company financial statements and Oppenheimer & Co. Inc. estimates.

We make four observations regarding this analyst report regarding P&G's target stock price.

1. The analyst report defines unlevered (before debt) free cash flow as follows. Earlier in this module we described differences in this type of FCFF computation from our FCFF definition.

> Net income
> + Interest expense
> + Depreciation and amortization expense
> − Capital expenditures
> + Decreases in working capital
> = Unlevered free cash flow

2. This analyst report uses the same DCF computation we describe in this module. The analyst highlights the importance of the terminal year computation with a matrix that quantifies the impact on stock price of (1) growth rates subsequent to the forecasting horizon and (2) WACC. This type of sensitivity analysis is a useful way to identify crucial assumptions. We see that a 1 percentage point change in WACC results in a roughly 20% change in stock price estimate. Further, a 1 percentage point change in the terminal growth rate results in a roughly 15% change in stock price estimate.

3. The cost of equity capital is estimated using the capital asset pricing model (CAPM) as we describe in the module. The analyst's estimated WACC is 9.2%, higher than the WACC of 8% that we assumed in the module. It is not uncommon that model assumptions differ among analysts, and highlights the importance of sensitivity analyses that quantify the effects of varying model assumptions.

4. Bottom line: We see that this analyst's $72 stock price target is higher than the $51.62 stock price estimate that we independently determined in this module. There are a number of differences between our forecast and that of the Oppenheimer analyst. We assumed a constant horizon-period growth rate of 4.6% and a terminal growth rate of 1%. The Oppenheimer report shows a growth rate in unlevered free cash flow of 9.4% for 2013, 6.4% for 2014, 10.3% for 2015, and a terminal growth rate of 2.6%. These rates vary over time and are more optimistic than ours and contribute to the higher stock price target. Another difference is Oppenheimer's use of a mid-year adjustment factor (1.05 in the P&G report). The discount factors we use assume that the cash flows occur at year-end. However, firms generate cash flows throughout the year. The mid-year adjustment factor corrects for this. One simplified adjustment is to multiply the firm equity value by $\sqrt{(1 + WACC)}$ or in the P&G report by $\sqrt{(1.092)} = 1.045$, which Oppenheimer apparently rounded to 1.05. This yielded a 5% increase in the target stock price compared to our price. Again, stock prices are opinions about the intrinsic value of the stock and as with any opinion, they can differ.

APPENDIX 13C: DERIVATION OF FREE CASH FLOW FORMULA

Derivation of the free cash flow formula follows; our thanks to Professor Jim Boatsman for this exposition:

$$\text{Assets} = \text{Liabilities} + \text{Stockholders' Equity (SE)}$$
$$\text{NOA} = \text{NNO} + \text{SE}$$
$$\Delta\text{NOA} = \Delta\text{NNO} + \Delta\text{SE} \quad \text{[in change form, where } \Delta \text{ refers to change]}$$
$$\Delta\text{NOA} = \Delta\text{NNO} + \Delta\text{Contributed Capital (CC)} + \text{Net Income} - \text{Dividends (DIV)} \quad \text{[substituting for SE]}$$
$$\Delta\text{NOA} = \Delta\text{NNO} + \Delta\text{CC} + (\text{NOPAT} - \text{NNE}) - \text{DIV} \quad \text{[substituting for NI]}$$
$$-\text{NOPAT} + \Delta\text{NOA} = \Delta\text{NNO} + \Delta\text{CC} - \text{NNE} - \text{DIV} \quad \text{[rearranging terms]}$$
$$\underbrace{\text{NOPAT} - \Delta\text{NOA}}_{\substack{\text{Free cash flows} \\ \text{to the firm} \\ \text{(FCFF)}}} = \underbrace{\text{NNE} - \Delta\text{NNO} - \Delta\text{CC} + \text{DIV}}_{\substack{\text{Net payments to holders} \\ \text{of net nonoperating} \\ \text{obligations and stock}}} \quad \text{[multiplying by } -1]$$

GUIDANCE ANSWERS . . . ANALYSIS DECISION

You Are the Chief Financial Officer Cash flow can be increased by reducing assets. For example, receivables can be reduced by the following:

- Encouraging up-front payments or progress billings on long-term contracts
- Increasing credit standards to avoid slow-paying accounts before sales are made
- Monitoring account age and sending reminders to past-due customers
- Selling accounts receivable to a financial institution or special purpose entity

As another example of asset reduction, plant assets can be reduced by the following:

- Selling unused or excess plant assets
- Forming alliances with other companies to share specialized plant assets
- Owning assets in a special purpose entity with other companies
- Selling production facilities to a contract manufacturer and purchasing the output

DISCUSSION QUESTIONS

Q13-1. Explain how information contained in financial statements is useful in pricing securities. Are there some components of earnings that are more useful than others in this regard? What nonfinancial information might also be useful?

Q13-2. In general, what role do expectations play in pricing equity securities? What is the relation between security prices and expected returns (the discount rate, or WACC, in this case)?

Q13-3. What are free cash flows to the firm (FCFF) and how are they used in the pricing of equity securities?

Q13-4. Define the weighted average cost of capital (WACC).

Q13-5. Define net operating profit after tax (NOPAT).

Q13-6. Define net operating assets (NOA).

**Assignments with the ✓ logo in the margin are available in an online homework system.
See the Preface of the book for details.**

MINI EXERCISES

STARBUCKS
(SBUX)

M13-7.   Interpreting Earnings Announcement Effects on Stock Prices   (LO1, 2)
In a recent quarterly earnings announcement, **Starbucks** announced that its earnings had markedly increased (up 7 cents per share over the prior year) and were 1 cent higher than analysts' expectations. Starbucks' stock "edged higher," according to *The Wall Street Journal,* but did not markedly increase. Why do you believe that Starbucks' stock price did not markedly increase given the good news?

M13-8.   Computing Free Cash Flows to the Firm (FCFF)   (LO2)

Halliburton Company reports net operating profit after tax (NOPAT) of $2,032 million in 2010. Its net operating assets at the beginning of 2010 are $9,937 million and are $12,160 million at the end of 2010. What are Halliburton's free cash flows to the firm (FCFF) for 2010? Show computations.

HALLIBURTON
COMPANY
(HAL)

M13-9.   Estimating Share Value Using the DCF Model   (LO1, 2)

Following are forecasts of **Target Corporation**'s sales, net operating profit after tax (NOPAT), and net operating assets (NOA) as of January 29, 2011.

TARGET
CORPORATION
(TGT)

	Reported	Horizon Period				Terminal
(In millions)	2011	2012	2013	2014	2015	Period
Sales.............	$67,390	$70,086	$72,889	$75,805	$78,837	$79,625
NOPAT	3,397	3,504	3,644	3,790	3,942	3,981
NOA	29,501	30,472	31,691	32,959	34,277	34,620

Answer the following requirements assuming a terminal period growth rate of 1%, discount rate (WACC) of 7%, shares outstanding of 704 million, and net nonoperating obligations (NNO) of $14,014 million.

a. Estimate the value of a share of Target common stock using the discounted cash flow (DCF) model as of January 29, 2011.

b. Target Corporation (TGT) stock closed at $49.99 on March 18, 2011. How does your valuation estimate compare with this closing price? What do you believe are some reasons for the difference?

EXERCISES

E13-10.   Estimating Share Value Using the DCF Model   (LO1, 2)

Following are forecasts of **Abercrombie & Fitch**'s sales, net operating profit after tax (NOPAT), and net operating assets (NOA) as of January 29, 2011 (Current-year NOPAT is lower due to transitory items; we use a longer term estimate for NOPM of 8%.).

ABERCROMBIE &
FITCH
(ANF)

	Reported	Horizon Period				Terminal
(In millions)	2011	2012	2013	2014	2015	Period
Sales............	$3,469	$3,989	$4,587	$5,275	$6,066	$6,187
NOPAT	152	319	367	422	485	495
NOA	1,032	1,173	1,349	1,551	1,784	1,820

Answer the following requirements assuming a discount rate (WACC) of 10%, a terminal period growth rate of 2%, common shares outstanding of 87.2 million, and net nonoperating obligations (NNO) of $(858) million (negative NNO reflects net nonoperating assets such as investments rather than net obligations).

a. Estimate the value of a share of Abercrombie & Fitch common stock using the discounted cash flow (DCF) model as of January 29, 2011.

b. Abercrombie & Fitch (ANF) stock closed at $56.71 on March 29, 2011. How does your valuation estimate compare with this closing price? What do you believe are some reasons for the difference?

E13-11.   Estimating Share Value Using the DCF Model   (LO1, 2)

Following are forecasts of sales, net operating profit after tax (NOPAT), and net operating assets (NOA) as of February 26, 2011, for **Best Buy, Inc.**

BEST BUY
(BBY)

	Reported	Horizon Period				Terminal
(In millions)	2011	2012	2013	2014	2015	Period
Sales...........	$50,272	$52,786	$55,425	$58,196	$61,106	$61,717
NOPAT	1,389	1,584	1,663	1,746	1,833	1,852
NOA	7,876	8,248	8,660	9,093	9,548	9,643

Answer the following requirements assuming a discount rate (WACC) of 11%, a terminal period growth rate of 1%, common shares outstanding of 392.6 million, and net nonoperating obligations (NNO) of $1,274 million.

a. Estimate the value of a share of Best Buy's common stock using the discounted cash flow (DCF) model as of February 26, 2011.

b. Best Buy (BBY) stock closed at $30.20 on April 25, 2011. How does your valuation estimate compare with this closing price? What do you believe are some reasons for the difference?

E13-12. Identifying and Computing Net Operating Assets (NOA) and Net Nonoperating Obligations (NNO) (LO1, 2)

HALLIBURTON COMPANY (HAL)

Following is the balance sheet for **Halliburton Company**.

HALLIBURTON COMPANY Consolidated Balance Sheets		
At December 31 (Millions of dollars and shares)	2010	2009
Assets		
Cash and equivalents	$ 1,398	$ 2,082
Receivables, net	3,924	2,964
Inventories	1,940	1,598
Investments in markeatable securities	653	1,312
Current deferred income taxes	257	210
Other current assets	714	472
Total current assets	8,886	8,638
Property, plant and equipment—net	6,842	5,759
Goodwill	1,315	1,100
Other assets	1,254	1,041
Total assets	$18,297	$16,538
Liabilities and Stockholders' Equity		
Accounts payable	$ 1,139	$ 787
Current maturities of long-term debt	—	750
Accrued employee compensation and benefits	716	514
Deferred revenue	266	215
Other current liabilities	636	623
Total current liabilities	2,757	2,889
Long-term debt	3,824	3,824
Employee compensation and benefits	487	462
Other liabilities	842	606
Total liabilities	7,910	7,781
Shareholders' equity		
Common shares, par value $2.50 per share—authorized 2,000 shares, issued 1,069 shares and 1,067 shares	2,674	2,669
Paid-in capital in excess of par value	339	411
Accumulated other comprehensive loss	(240)	(213)
Retained earnings	12,371	10,863
Treasury stock, at cost—159 and 165 shares	(4,771)	(5,002)
Company shareholders' equity	10,373	8,728
Noncontrolling interest in consolidated subsidiaries	14	29
Total shareholders' equity	10,387	8,757
Total liabilities and shareholders' equity	$18,297	$16,538

a. Compute net operating assets (NOA) and net nonoperating obligations (NNO) for 2010.

b. For 2010, show that: NOA = NNO + Stockholders' equity.

E13-13. Identifying and Computing Net Operating Profit after Tax (NOPAT) and Net Nonoperating Expense (NNE) (LO1, 2)

Following is the income statement for **Halliburton Company**.

HALLIBURTON COMPANY Consolidated Statements of Operations			
At December 31 (millions of dollars)	2010	2009	2008
Revenue			
Services	$13,779	$ 10,832	$13,391
Product sales	4,194	3,843	4,888
Total revenue	17,973	14,675	18,279
Operating costs and expenses			
Cost of services	11,237	9,224	10,079
Cost of sales.	3,508	3,255	3,970
General and administrative.	229	207	282
Gain on sale of operating assets, net.	(10)	(5)	(62)
Total operating costs and expenses.	14,964	12,681	14,269
Operating income.	3,009	1,994	4,010
Interest expense, net of interest income			
of $11, $12, and $39.	(297)	(285)	(128)
Other nonoperating expenses, net.	(57)	(27)	(33)
Income from continuing operations before income taxes	2,655	1,682	3,849
Provision for income taxes.	(853)	(518)	(1,211)
Income from continuing operations	1,802	1,164	2,638
Income (loss) from discontinued operations, net of income tax	40	(9)	(423)
Net income.	1,842	1,155	2,215
Noncontrolling interest in net income of subsidiaries	(7)	(10)	9
Net income attributable to company	$1,835	$ 1,145	$ 2,224

Compute net operating profit after tax (NOPAT) for 2010, assuming a federal and state statutory tax rate of 35%.

E13-14. Estimating Share Value Using the DCF Model (LO1, 2)

Following are forecasts of **Halliburton Company**'s sales, net operating profit after tax (NOPAT), and net operating assets (NOA) as of December 31, 2010.

	Reported	Horizon Period				Terminal
(In millions)	2010	2011	2012	2013	2014	Period
Sales.	$17,973	$21,028	$24,603	$28,786	$33,680	$35,027
NOPAT	2,032	2,376	2,780	3,253	3,806	3,958
NOA	12,160	14,208	16,624	19,450	22,757	23,667

Answer the following requirements assuming a discount rate (WACC) of 10%, a terminal period growth rate of 4%, common shares outstanding of 910 million, and net nonoperating obligations (NNO) of $1,787 million.

a. Estimate the value of a share of Halliburton's common stock using the discounted cash flow (DCF) model as of February 17, 2011.

b. Halliburton Company (HAL) stock closed at $48.43 on February 17, 2011. How does your valuation estimate compare with this closing price? What do you believe are some reasons for the difference?

PROBLEMS

INTEL
CORPORATION
(INTC)

P13-15. Forecasting and Estimating Share Value Using the DCF Model (LO1, 2)
Following are the income statement and balance sheet for **Intel Corporation**.

INTEL CORPORATION Consolidated Statements of Income			
Year Ended (In millions)	December 25, 2010	December 26, 2009	December 27, 2008
Net revenue	$43,623	$35,127	$37,586
Cost of sales	15,132	15,566	16,742
Gross margin	28,491	19,561	20,844
Research and development	6,576	5,653	5,722
Marketing, general and administrative	6,309	7,931	5,452
Restructuring and asset impairment charges	—	231	710
Amortization of acquisition-related intangibles	18	35	6
Operating expenses	12,903	13,850	11,890
Operating income	15,588	5,711	8,954
Gains (losses) on equity method investments, net	117	(147)	(1,380)
Gains (losses) on other equity investments, net	231	(23)	(376)
Interest and other, net	109	163	488
Income before taxes	16,045	5,704	7,686
Provision for taxes	4,581	1,335	2,394
Net income	$11,464	$ 4,369	$ 5,292

INTEL CORPORATION Consolidated Balance Sheets		
As of Year-Ended (In millions, except par value)	December 25, 2010	December 26, 2009
Assets		
Current assets		
Cash and cash equivalents	$ 5,498	$ 3,987
Short-term investments	11,294	5,285
Trading assets	5,093	4,648
Accounts receivable, net	2,867	2,273
Inventories	3,757	2,935
Deferred tax assets	1,488	1,216
Other current assets	1,614	813
Total current assets	31,611	21,157
Property, plant and equipment, net	17,899	17,225
Marketable equity securities	1,008	773
Other long-term investments1	3,026	4,179
Goodwill	4,531	4,421
Other long-term assets	5,111	5,340
Total assets	$63,186	$53,095
Liabilities		
Current liabilities		
Short-term debt	$ 38	$ 172
Accounts payable	2,290	1,883
Accrued compensation and benefits	2,888	2,448
Accrued advertising	1,007	773
Deferred income on shipments to distributors	622	593
Other accrued liabilities	2,482	1,722
Total current liabilities	9,327	7,591
Long-term income taxes payable	190	193
Long-term debt	2,077	2,049
Long-term deferred tax liabilities	926	555
Other long-term liabilities	1,236	1,003
Total liabilities	13,756	11,391

continued

continued from prior page

Stockholders' equity		
Preferred stock, $0.001 par value.	—	—
Common stock, $0.001 par value, 10,000 shares authorized;		
5,581 issued and 5,511 outstanding and capital		
in excess of par value	16,178	14,993
Accumulated other comprehensive income.	333	393
Retained earnings.	32,919	26,318
Total stockholders' equity	49,430	41,704
Total liabilities and stockholders' equity.	$63,186	$53,095

[1] These investments are operating assets as they relate to associated companies.

Required

a. Compute Intel's net operating assets (NOA) for year-end 2010.

b. Compute net operating profit after tax (NOPAT) for 2010, assuming a federal and state statutory tax rate of 37%.

c. Forecast Intel's sales, NOPAT, and NOA for years 2011 through 2014 using the following assumptions:

Sales growth.	10%
Net operating profit margin (NOPM).	26%
Net operating asset turnover (NOAT) at year-end	1.50

Forecast the terminal period value assuming a 1% terminal period growth and using the NOPM and NOAT assumptions above.

d. Estimate the value of a share of Intel common stock using the discounted cash flow (DCF) model as of December 25, 2010; assume a discount rate (WACC) of 11%, common shares outstanding of 5,511 million, and net nonoperating obligations (NNO) of $(20,778) million (NNO is negative which means that Intel has net nonoperating investments).

e. Intel (INTC) stock closed at $22.14 on February 18, 2011. How does your valuation estimate compare with this closing price? What do you believe are some reasons for the difference? What investment decision is suggested from your results?

P13-16. Forecasting and Estimating Share Value Using the DCF Model   (LO1, 2)

Following are the income statement and balance sheet for **CVS Caremark**.

CVS CAREMARK
(CVS)

CVS CAREMARK INC. Balance Sheets		
December 31 (In millions, except per share amounts)	**2010**	**2009**
Assets		
Cash and cash equivalents.	$ 1,427	$ 1,086
Short-term investments	4	5
Accounts receivable, net	4,925	5,457
Inventories	10,695	10,343
Deferred income taxes	511	506
Other current assets.	144	140
Total current assets.	17,706	17,537
Property and equipment, net	8,322	7,923
Goodwill	25,669	25,680
Intangible assets, net	9,784	10,127
Other assets	688	374
Total assets.	$62,169	$61,641

continued

continued from prior page

Liabilities		
Accounts payable..	$ 4,026	$ 3,560
Claims and discounts payable	2,569	3,075
Accrued expenses	3,070	3,246
Short-term debt	300	315
Current portion of long-term debt	1,105	2,104
Total current liabilities	11,070	12,300
Long-term debt..	8,652	8,756
Deferred income taxes	3,655	3,678
Other long-term liabilities	1,058	1,102
Redeemable noncontrolling interest................................	34	37
Total liabilities	24,469	25,873
Shareholders' equity		
Common stock, par value $0.01: 3,200 shares authorized; 1,624 shares issued and 1,363 shares outstanding at December 31, 2010	16	16
Treasury stock at cost:...	(9,030)	(7,610)
Shares held in trust..	(56)	(56)
Capital surplus	27,610	27,198
Retained earnings...	19,303	16,355
Accumulated other comprehensive loss	(143)	(135)
Total shareholders' equity......................................	37,700	35,768
Total liabilities and shareholders' equity.....................	$62,169	$61,641

CVS CAREMARK INC. Consolidated Statements of Income			
For the year ended December 31 (In millions)	2010	2009	2008
Net revenues	$96,413	$98,729	$87,472
Cost of revenues	76,156	78,349	69,182
Gross profit...	20,257	20,380	18,290
Operating expenses.......................................	14,092	13,942	12,244
Operating profit	6,165	6,438	6,046
Interest expense, net	536	525	509
Income before income tax provision	5,629	5,913	5,537
Income tax provision	2,190	2,205	2,193
Income from continuing operations.......................	3,439	3,708	3,344
Loss from discontinued operations, net of income tax benefit	(15)	(12)	(132)
Net income..	3,434	3,696	3,212
Net loss attributable to noncontrolling interest	3	—	—
Preference dividends, net of income tax benefit	—	—	(14)
Net income attributable to CVS Caremark.........................	$ 3,427	$ 3,696	$ 3,198

Required

a. Compute net operating assets (NOA) as of December 31, 2010.
b. Compute net operating profit after tax (NOPAT) for fiscal year ended December 31, 2010, assuming a federal and state statutory tax rate of 37%.

c. Forecast CVS's sales, NOPAT, and NOA for 2011 through 2014 using the following assumptions:

Sales growth.	5%
Net operating profit margin (NOPM).	4%
Net operating asset turnover (NOAT) at fiscal year-end. . . .	2.10

Forecast the terminal period value assuming a 1% terminal period growth and using the NOPM and NOAT assumptions above.

d. Estimate the value of a share of CVS common stock using the discounted cash flow (DCF) model as of December 31, 2010; assume a discount rate (WACC) of 7%, common shares outstanding of 1,363 million, and net nonoperating obligations (NNO) of $8,660 million.

e. CVS's stock closed at $33.06 on February 18, 2011. How does your valuation estimate compare with this closing price? What do you believe are some reasons for the difference?

P13-17. **Forecasting and Estimating Share Value Using the DCF Model**   (LO1, 2)

Following are the income statement and balance sheet for **Abbott Laboratories (ABT)**.

ABBOTT
LABORATORIES
(ABT)

ABBOTT LABORATORIES Balance Sheet		
December 31 ($ millions)	2010	2009
Assets		
Cash and cash equivalents	$ 3,648.371	$ 8,809.339
Investments and restricted funds.	3,675.569	1,122.709
Trade receivables, net	7,184.034	6,541.941
Total inventories	3,188.734	3,264.877
Deferred income taxes.	3,076.051	2,364.142
Other prepaid expenses and receivables.	1,544.770	1,210.883
Total current assets	22,317.529	23,313.891
Investments	302.049	1,132.866
Property and equipment, net	7,970.956	7,619.489
Intangible assets, net of amortization	12,151.628	6,291.989
Goodwill.	15,930.077	13,200.174
Deferred income taxes and other assets	790.027	858.214
Total assets.	$59,462.266	$52,416.623
Liabilities and Shareholders' Investment		
Short-term borrowings.	$ 4,349.796	$ 4,978.438
Trade accounts payable.	1,535.759	1,280.542
Salaries, wages and commissions.	1,328.665	1,117.410
Other accrued liabilities	6,014.772	4,399.137
Dividends payable	680.749	620.640
Income taxes payable	1,307.723	442.140
Current portion of long-term debt	2,044.970	211.182
Total current liabilities.	17,262.434	13,049.489
Long-term debt	12,523.517	11,266.294
Post-employment and other long-term obligations.	7,199.851	5,202.111
Shareholders' investment		
Common shares, without par value. Authorized: 2,400,000,000 shares.		
Issued: 1,619,689,876 and 1,612,683,987	8,744.703	8,257.873
Common shares held in treasury: 72,705,928 and 61,516,398	(3,916.823)	(3,310.347)
Earnings employed in the business	18,927.101	17,054.027
Accumulated other comprehensive income (loss)	(1,366.846)	854.074
Total Abbott shareholders' investment.	22,388.135	22,855.627
Noncontrolling interests in subsidiaries	88.329	43.102
Total shareholders' investment.	22,476.464	22,898.729
Total liabilities and shareholders' investment.	$59,462.266	$52,416.623

ABBOTT LABORATORIES AND SUBSIDIARIES Consolidated Statement of Earnings			
Year Ended December 31 (dollars in millions)	2010	2009	2008
Net sales.....................................	$35,166.721	$30,764.707	$29,527.552
Cost of products sold........................	14,665.192	13,209.329	12,612.022
Research and development....................	3,724.424	2,743.733	2,688.811
Acquired in-process research and development.............	313.200	170.000	97.256
Selling, general and administrative	10,376.324	8,405.904	8,435.624
Total operating cost and expenses	29,079.140	24,528.966	23,833.713
Operating earnings...........................	6,087.581	6,235.741	5,693.839
Interest expense............................	553.135	519.656	528.474
Interest (income)...........................	(105.453)	(137.779)	(201.229)
(Income) from the TAP Pharmaceutical joint venture..........	—	—	(118.997)
Other (income) expense, net	(72.935)	(1,339.910)	(370.695)
Earnings from continuing operations before taxes	5,712.834	7,193.774	5,856.286
Taxes on earnings from continuing operations	1,086.662	1,447.936	1,122.070
Earnings from continuing operations..................	4,626.172	5,745.838	4,734.216
Gain on sale of discontinued operations, net of taxes.........	—	—	146.503
Net earnings...............................	$ 4,626.172	$ 5,745.838	$ 4,880.719

Required

a. Compute net operating assets (NOA) for year-end 2010.

b. Compute net operating profit after tax (NOPAT) for 2010 assuming a federal and state statutory tax rate of 35.4%.

c. Forecast Abbott Laboratories' sales, NOPAT, and NOA for 2011 through 2014 using the following assumptions:

Sales growth.......................................	10%
Net operating profit margin (NOPM)...................	14%
Net operating asset turnover (NOAT), year-end..........	1.0

   Forecast the terminal period value assuming a 1% terminal period growth and using the NOPM and NOAT assumptions above.

d. Estimate the value of a share of Abbott Laboratories' common stock using the discounted cash flow (DCF) model as of December 31, 2010; assume a discount rate (WACC) of 7%, common shares outstanding of 1,547 million, and net nonoperating obligations (NNO) of $12,061 million.

e. Abbott Laboratories (ABT) stock closed at $46.88 on February 18, 2011. How does your valuation estimate compare with this closing price? What do you believe are some reasons for the difference? What investment decision is suggested from your results?

P13-18. **Forecasting and Estimating Share Value Using the DCF Model** (LO1, 2)

KELLOGG CO.
(K)

Following are the income statement and balance sheet for **Kellogg Company**.

KELLOGG COMPANY AND SUBSIDIARIES Consolidated Statement of Income			
For Year Ended (in millions)	2010	2009	2008
Net sales.....................................	$12,397	$12,575	$12,822
Cost of goods sold............................	7,108	7,184	7,455
Selling, general and administrative expense	3,299	3,390	3,414
Operating profit	1,990	2,001	1,953
Interest expense.............................	248	295	308
Other income (expense), net	—	(22)	(14)
Income before income taxes	1,742	1,684	1,631
Income taxes	502	476	485
Net income..................................	1,240	1,208	1,146
Net loss attributable to noncontrolling interests	(7)	(4)	(2)
Net income attributable to Kellogg Company	$ 1,247	$ 1,212	$ 1,148

KELLOGG COMPANY AND SUBSIDIARIES Consolidated Balance Sheet		
(millions, except share data)	2010	2009
Current assets		
Cash and cash equivalents	$ 444	$ 334
Accounts receivable, net	1,190	1,093
Inventories	1,056	910
Other current assets.	225	221
Total current assets.	2,915	2,558
Property, net.	3,128	3,010
Goodwill	3,628	3,643
Other intangibles, net.	1,456	1,458
Other assets.	720	531
Total assets.	$11,847	$11,200
Current liabilities		
Current maturities of long-term debt	$ 952	$ 1
Notes payable	44	44
Accounts payable.	1,149	1,077
Other current liabilities	1,039	1,166
Total current liabilities	3,184	2,288
Long-term debt	4,908	4,835
Deferred income taxes.	697	425
Pension liability.	265	430
Other liabilities	639	947
Equity		
Common stock, $.25 par value, 1,000,000,000 shares authorized		
Issued: 419,272,027 shares in 2010 and 419,058,168 shares in 2009. . . .	105	105
Capital in excess of par value	495	472
Retained earnings	6,122	5,481
Treasury stock at cost: 53,667,635 shares in 2010 and 37,678,215 shares in 2009.	(2,650)	(1,820)
Accumulated other comprehensive income (loss)	(1,914)	(1,966)
Total Kellogg Company equity	2,158	2,272
Noncontrolling interests	(4)	3
Total equity.	2,154	2,275
Total liabilities and equity	$11,847	$11,200

Required

a. Compute net operating assets (NOA) as of year-end 2010.

b. Compute net operating profit after tax (NOPAT) for 2010, assuming a federal and state statutory tax rate of 36.4%.

c. Forecast Kellogg's sales, NOPAT, and NOA for 2011 through 2014 using the following assumptions:

Sales growth.	4%
Net operating profit margin (NOPM).	11%
Net operating asset turnover (NOAT), year-end	1.6

Forecast the terminal period value assuming a 1% terminal period growth and using the NOPM and NOAT assumptions above.

d. Estimate the value of a share of Kellogg common stock using the discounted cash flow (DCF) model; assume a discount rate (WACC) of 6%, common shares outstanding of 365.6 million, and net nonoperating obligations (NNO) of $5,456 million.

e. Kellogg's stock closed at $53.56 at February 28, 2011. How does your valuation estimate compare with this closing price? What do you believe are some reasons for the difference?

IFRS APPLICATIONS

TESCO, PLC

I13-19. **Forecasting and Estimating Share Value Using the DCF Model**   (L01, 2)
Following are the income statement and balance sheet for **Tesco, PLC**, a UK-based grocery chain. The company's financial statements are prepared in accordance with IFRS.

Tesco, PLC Group Income Statement		
Year ended 26 February 2011	**52 weeks 2011 £m**	**52 weeks 2010 £m**
Continuing operations		
Revenue (sales excluding VAT).	£60,931	£56,910
Cost of sales.	(55,871)	(52,303)
Gross profit.	5,060	4,607
Administrative expenses	(1,676)	(1,527)
Profit arising on property-related items	427	377
Operating profit	3,811	3,457
Share of post-tax profits of joint ventures and associates	57	33
Finance income	150	265
Finance costs.	(483)	(579)
Profit before tax	3,535	3,176
Taxation	(864)	(840)
Profit for the year	£ 2,671	£ 2,336
Attributable to:		
Owners of the parent	£ 2,655	£ 2,327
Non-controlling interests	16	9
	£ 2,671	£ 2,336

TESCO PLC Group Balance Sheet		
	26 February 2011 £m	**27 February 2010 £m**
Non-current assets		
Goodwill and other intangible assets	£ 4,338	£ 4,177
Property, plant and equipment.	24,398	24,203
Investments in joint ventures and associates.	316	152
Other investments	2,971	2,594
Financial assets	3,266	3,094
Deferred tax assets	48	38
Total non-current assets	35,337	34,258
Current assets		
Inventories	3,162	2,729
Trade and other receivables.	2,314	1,888
Financial assets	3,066	2,636
Current tax assets	4	6
Short-term investments	1,022	1,314
Cash and cash equivalents	1,870	2,819
	11,438	11,392
Non-current assets classified as held for sale	431	373
Total current assets	11,869	11,765

continued

continued from prior page

Current liabilities		
Trade and other payables	**(10,484)**	(9,442)
Financial liabilities	**(1,641)**	(1,675)
Customer prepayments and deposits	**(5,110)**	(4,387)
Current tax liabilities	**(432)**	(472)
Provisions	**(64)**	(39)
Total current liabilities	**(17,731)**	(16,015)
Non-current liabilities		
Financial liabilities	**(10,289)**	(12,520)
Post-employment benefit obligations	**(1,356)**	(1,840)
Deferred tax liabilities	**(1,094)**	(795)
Provisions	**(113)**	(172)
	(12,852)	(15,327)
Equity		
Share capital	**402**	399
Share premium account	**4,896**	4,801
Other reserves	**40**	40
Retained earnings	**11,197**	9,356
Equity attributable to owners of the parent	**16,535**	14,596
Non-controlling interests	**88**	85
Total equity	**£16,623**	£14,681

Required

a. Compute net operating assets (NOA) as of year-end 2011.

b. Compute net operating profit after tax (NOPAT) for 2011, assuming a marginal tax rate of 25%.

c. Forecast Tesco's sales, NOPAT, and NOA for 2012 through 2015 using the following assumptions:

Sales growth	6%
Net operating profit margin (NOPM)	4.8%
Net operating asset turnover (NOAT)	3.8

Estimate the terminal period value assuming a 1% terminal period growth and using the NOPM and NOAT assumptions, above.

d. Estimate the value of a share of Tesco's common stock (which trades on the London Stock Exchange) using the discounted cash flow (DCF) model; assume a discount rate (WACC) of 8%, common shares outstanding of 8,046.5 million, and net nonoperating obligations (NNO) of £(608). (Note: NNO is negative which means that Tesco has net nonoperating investments and financial assets.)

e. Tesco's stock price was £3.93 on April 19, 2011. How does your valuation estimate compare with this closing price? What do you believe are some reasons for the difference?

SOLUTIONS TO REVIEW PROBLEMS

Module-End Review

Solution

The following DCF results yield a P&G stock value estimate of $51.63 as of August 10, 2011. P&G's stock closed at $58.51 on that date. This estimate suggests that P&G's stock is marginally overvalued on that date.

(In millions, except per share values and discount factors)	Reported 2011	Horizon Period 2012	2013	2014	2015	Terminal Period
Increase in NOA[a]		$ 4,349	$ 4,673	$ 4,889	$ 5,114	$ 1,162
FCFF (NOPAT − Increase in NOA)		8,432	8,696	9,095	9,513	13,611
Discount factor [$1/(1 + r_w)^t$]		0.92593	0.85734	0.79383	0.73503	
Present value of horizon FCFF		7,807	7,455	7,220	6,992	
Cum present value of horizon FCFF	$ 29,474					
Present value of terminal FCFF	142,921[b]					
Total firm value	172,395					
Less NNO	29,607					
Firm equity value	$142,788					
Shares outstanding	2,765.7					
Stock value per share	$ 51.63					

[a] NOA increases are viewed as a cash outflow.

[b] Computed as $\left(\$\frac{3{,}611 \text{ million}}{0.0-0.01}\right)/(1.0_8)^4$, or ($13,611 million/0.07) × 0.73503, where 8% is WACC and 1% is the long-term (terminal period) growth rate.

1. Define equity valuation models and explain the information required to value equity securities. (p. 14-4)

2. Describe and apply the residual operating income model to value equity securities. (p. 14-5)

3. Explain how equity valuation models can aid managerial decisions. (p. 14-10)

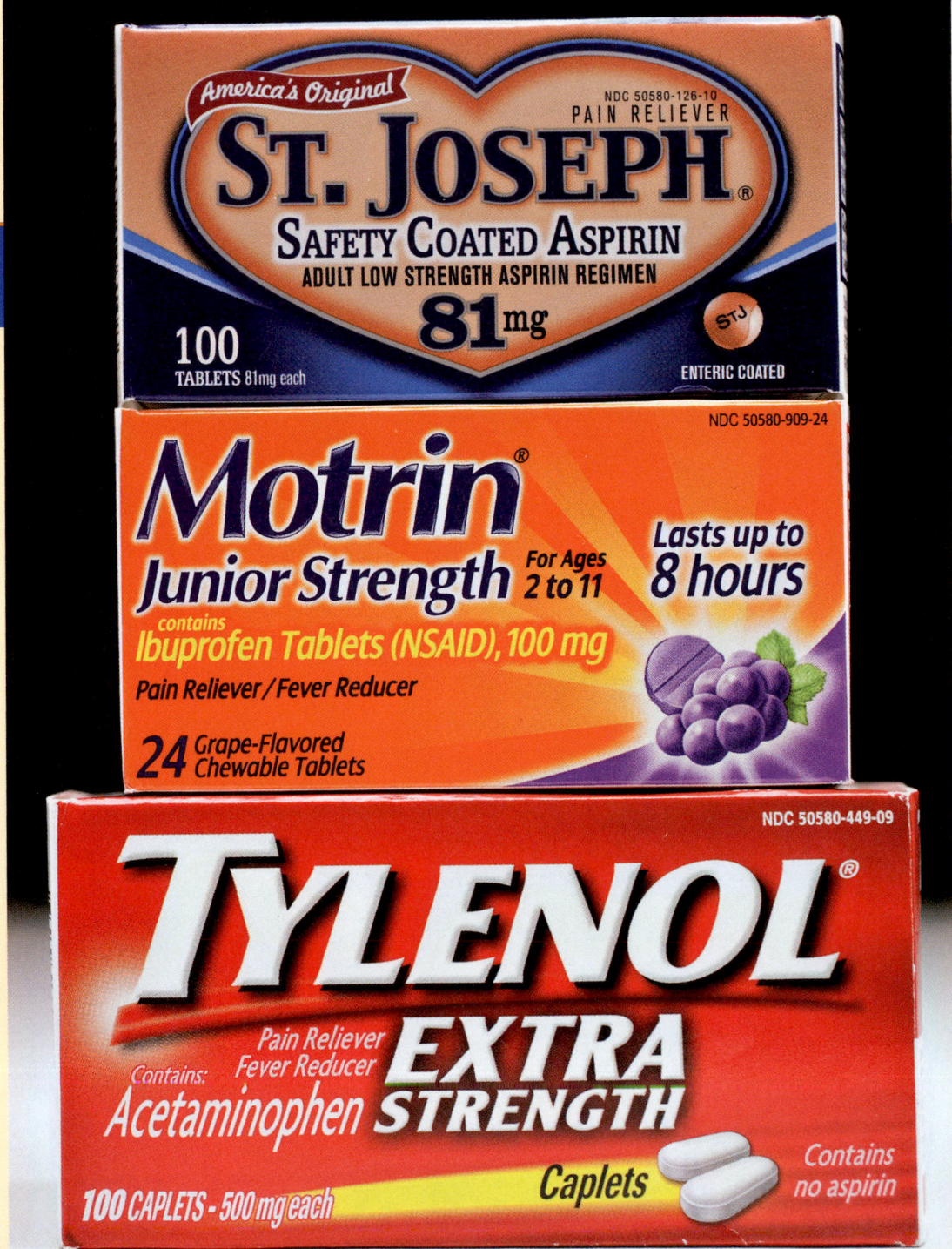

Operating-Income-Based Valuation

In the three years prior to 2008, corporate earnings were steady and climbing, stock prices grew continuously, and growth appeared limitless. Then, the recession of 2008–2009 hit. Almost all companies saw revenues and profits decline. Healthcare

JOHNSON & JOHNSON

companies, however, weathered the storm reasonably well. Compared to other sectors, healthcare tends to be less sensitive to economic changes for three reasons. First, demand for healthcare products persists as the U.S. population ages regardless of current events. Second, healthcare products are fairly immune to depressions in the economic cycle as consumers and patients need products and devices regardless of economic health. Third, government spending in healthcare is a large portion of overall healthcare spending, approaching $13 trillion in 2011. Government healthcare spending does not closely mirror economic changes as highlighted in the following graph.

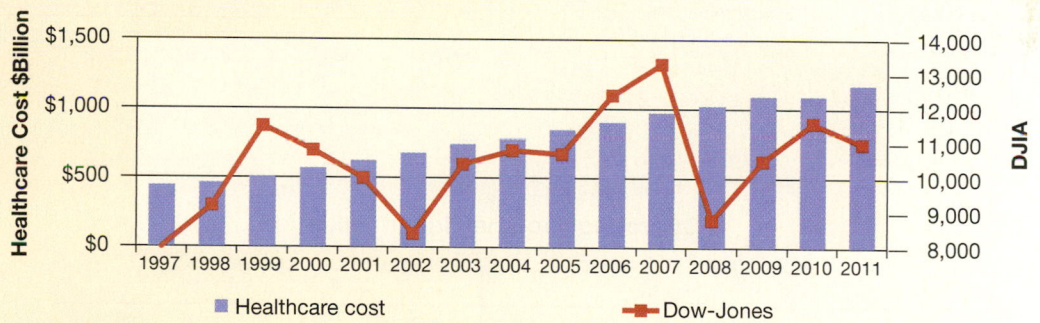

Johnson & Johnson (J&J) is a dominant company in the healthcare industry. The company engages in the research and development, manufacture, and sale of various healthcare products. Among healthcare firms, Johnson & Johnson often is a favorite for those who seek so-called ruler stocks. A *ruler stock* is one that has an earnings plot with an upward sloping line, as if drawn with a ruler. By this definition, Johnson & Johnson is a classic ruler stock, as the graph below shows.

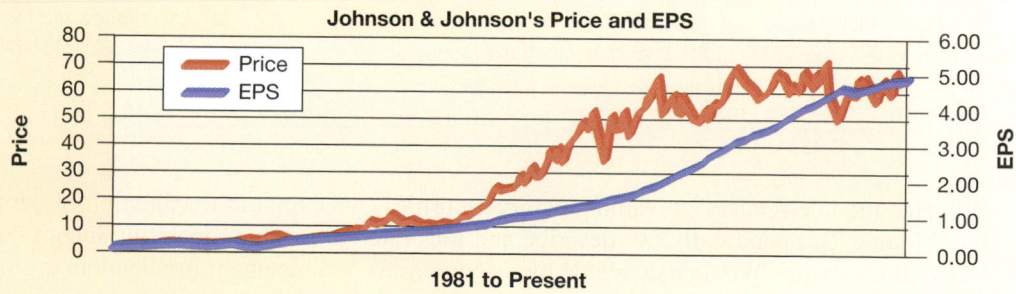

Johnson & Johnson's Price and EPS

(continued on next page)

(continued from previous page)

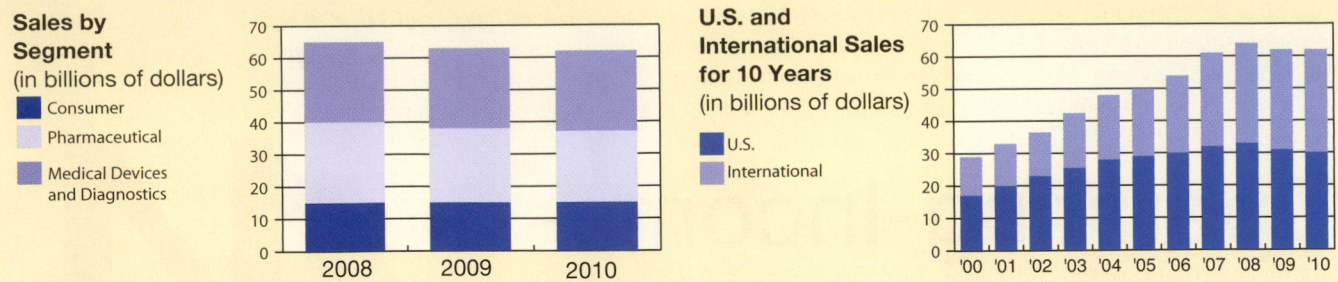

Sales by Segment (in billions of dollars)
- Consumer
- Pharmaceutical
- Medical Devices and Diagnostics

U.S. and International Sales for 10 Years (in billions of dollars)
- U.S.
- International

Ruler stocks are arguably attractive because their steady earnings growth hints at more of the same for the future. Investors often have more confidence in continued earnings growth for a ruler stock than for a company with a history of erratic earnings.

How has Johnson & Johnson managed to create and sustain such steady earnings growth? Much of the answer rests in its diversified portfolio of products, which includes consumer, pharmaceutical and medical devices. The company is also diversified geographically. The two charts above show Johnson & Johnson's balanced product portfolio and strong, growing international sales.

Johnson & Johnson's steady earnings are matched with solid dividend payments. In times of market turmoil, as during 2011, blue chip stocks with dependable dividends are perceived as providing good value to investors. Some might argue that Johnson & Johnson might not be the most "exciting" stock, but it is a solid bet in a volatile market.

Supported by its more diversified operations and fueled by a steady increase in operating profits, Johnson & Johnson's stock price has nearly completely rebounded from the decline of late 2007 and early 2008, as shown in the graph to the right.

This raises several questions. What factors drive the Johnson & Johnson stock price? Why do analysts expect its price to continue to rise? How do accounting measures of performance and financial condition impact stock price? This module provides insights and answers to these questions. It explains how we can use forecasts of operating profits and cash flows to price equity securities such as Johnson & Johnson's stock.

Sources: *Johnson & Johnson* 10-K and Annual Reports; Yahoo Finance, www.usgovernmentspending.com.

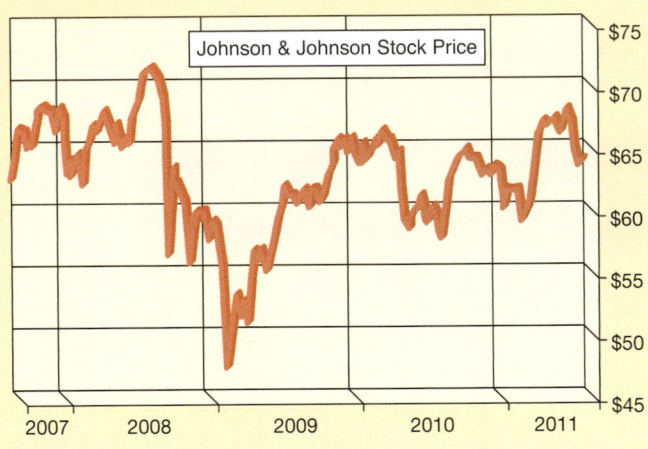

Johnson & Johnson Stock Price

MODULE ORGANIZATION

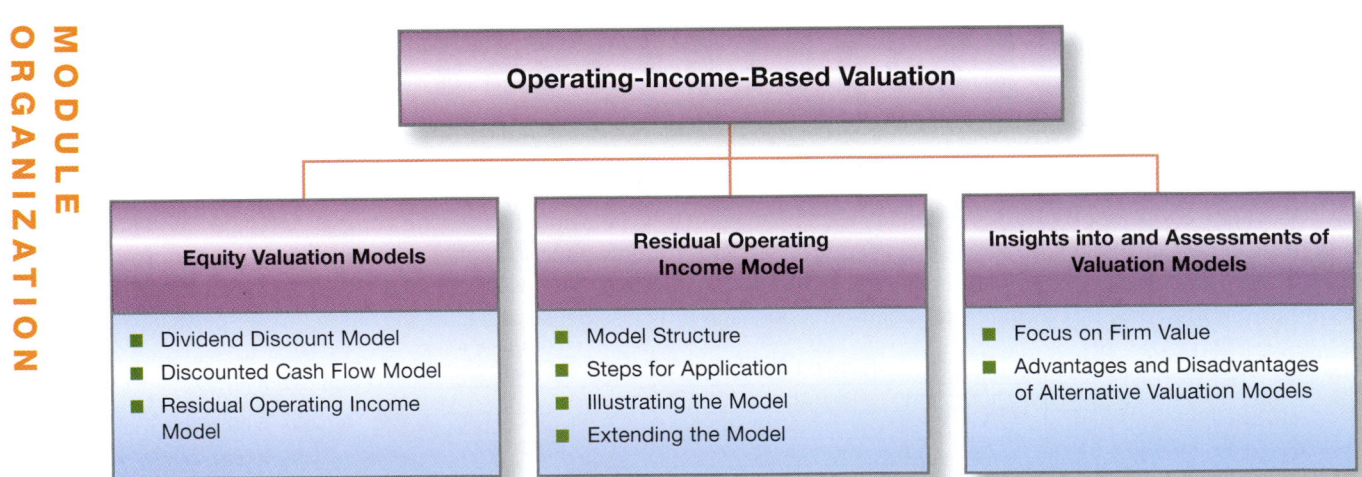

Operating-Income-Based Valuation

Equity Valuation Models	Residual Operating Income Model	Insights into and Assessments of Valuation Models
■ Dividend Discount Model ■ Discounted Cash Flow Model ■ Residual Operating Income Model	■ Model Structure ■ Steps for Application ■ Illustrating the Model ■ Extending the Model	■ Focus on Firm Value ■ Advantages and Disadvantages of Alternative Valuation Models

This module focuses on valuing equity securities (we explain the valuation of debt securities in Module 7). Specifically, we describe and illustrate the residual operating income model (ROPI) in this module. We then conclude by discussing the management implications from an increased understanding of the factors that impact values of equity securities. It is important that we understand the determinants of equity value to make informed decisions. Employees at all levels of an organization, whether public or private, should understand the factors that create shareholder value so that they can work effectively toward that objective. For many senior managers, stock value serves as a scorecard. Successful managers are those who better understand the factors affecting that scorecard.

EQUITY VALUATION MODELS

Module 7 explains that the value of a debt security is the present value of the interest and principal payments that the investor *expects* to receive in the future. The valuation of equity securities is similar in that it is also based on expectations. The difference lies in the increased uncertainty surrounding the timing and amount of payments from equity securities.

LO1 Define equity valuation models and explain the information required to value equity securities.

There are many equity valuation models in use today. Each of them defines the value of an equity security in terms of the present value of forecasted amounts. They differ primarily in terms of what is forecasted.

The basis of equity valuation is the premise that the value of an equity security is determined by the payments that the investor can expect to receive. Equity investments involve two types of payoffs: (1) dividends received during the holding period and (2) proceeds received when the security is sold. The value of an equity security is, then, based on the present value of expected dividends plus the present value of the security at the end of the forecasted holding period. This **dividend discount model** is appealing in its simplicity and its intuitive focus on dividend distribution. As a practical matter, however, the model is not always useful because many companies that have a positive stock price have never paid a dividend, and are not expected to pay a dividend in the foreseeable future.

A more practical approach to valuing equity securities focuses on the company's operating and investing activities; that is, on the *generation* of cash by the company rather than the *distribution* of cash to the shareholders. This approach is called the **discounted cash flow (DCF)** model. The focus of the forecasting process for the DCF model is the company's expected *free cash flows to the firm*, which are defined as operating cash flows net of the expected new investments in net operating assets that are required to support the business.

Another approach to equity valuation also focuses on operating and investing activities. It is known as the **residual operating income (ROPI)** model. This model uses both net operating profits after tax (NOPAT) and the net operating assets (NOA) to determine equity value; see Module 3 for complete descriptions of the NOPAT and NOA measures. This approach highlights the importance of return on net operating assets (RNOA), and the disaggregation of RNOA into net operating profit margin and NOA turnover.

When the DDM was introduced in Module 12, it was based on the following relation:

$$IV_0 = \frac{D_1 + IV_1}{1 + r_e}$$

Both the DCF and ROPI models derive from this basic starting point and are, therefore, mathematically equivalent. Any differences between the estimated valuations of equity using these models arise due to implementation issues rather than the frameworks themselves. Assumptions such as forecast horizon length or terminal growth rate (discussed later in the module) can be easier to determine with less uncertainty for a particular company using a particular valuation model, which can lead to a more reliable value estimate. Following our 4-step process from Module 1, the quality of our value estimate (Step 4) is based on the quality of our forecasts of future payoffs (Step 3). Further, those forecasts are only as good as the adjustments/assessment of financial information made (Step 2) and our understanding of the company's business environment (Step 1). If the forecasts made are identical across the different payoffs, the resulting value estimates from the models will also be identical.

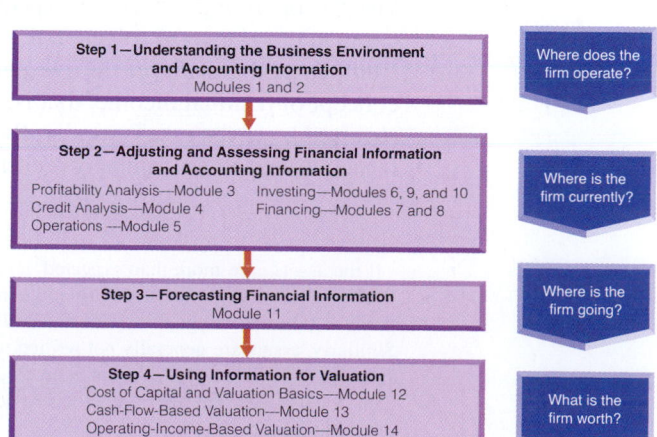

RESIDUAL OPERATING INCOME (ROPI) MODEL

LO2 Describe and apply the residual operating income model to value equity securities.

The residual operating income (ROPI) model focuses on net operating profit after tax (NOPAT) and net operating assets (NOA). This means it uses key measures from both the income statement and balance sheet in determining firm value.

The rationale for using the ROPI model is that book value provides an anchor to our valuation that is then augmented based on earnings. Accounting earnings are a measure of wealth creation, which measure economic resources generated (revenues) less economic resources consumed (expenses) regardless of whether a cash flow has concurrently occurred. The accounting earnings attempt to match accrual recognition to the timing of changes in economic value. This measure of wealth creation provides an alternative approach to valuation when compared to the measures of wealth distribution (dividends) and distributable wealth generation (free cash flows). We hold an equity security, or any asset, in the expectation that it will create additional wealth for our future consumption. This focus on wealth creation for future consumption has increased the use of earnings-based valuation in recent years.

ROPI Model Structure

The ROPI model defines firm value as the sum of two components:

$$\textbf{Firm Value} = \textbf{NOA} + \textbf{Present Value of Expected ROPI}$$

where

> **NOA = Net operating assets**
>
> **ROPI = Residual operating income**

Net operating assets (NOA) are the foundation of firm value under the ROPI model. This is potentially problematic because we measure NOA using the balance sheet, which is unlikely to fully and contemporaneously capture the true (or intrinsic) value of all of a firm's operating assets.[1] However, the ROPI model adds an adjustment that corrects for the undervaluation or overvaluation of NOA. This adjustment is the present value of expected residual operating income, and is defined as follows:

$$\textbf{ROPI} = \textbf{NOPAT} - \underbrace{(\textbf{NOA}_{\text{Beg}} \times r_w)}_{}$$

Expected NOPAT

where

> $\textbf{NOA}_{\text{Beg}}$ **= Net operating assets at beginning (*Beg*) of period**
>
> r_w **= Weighted average cost of capital (WACC)**

Residual operating income (ROPI) is the net operating profit a firm earns over and above the return that the operating assets are expected to earn given the firm's WACC. Shareholders expect the company to use NOA to generate, at least, a "hurdle" profit to cover the cost of capital (WACC). Companies that earn profits over and above that hurdle, create value for shareholders. This is the concept of residual income: that is, income earned over and above the minimum amount of return required by investors. Typically, ROPI is positive but there are two algebraic ways that ROPI can be negative: (1) if a company reports a net operating loss—that is, NOPAT is negative, or (2) if the

---

[1] If the assets earn more than expected, it could be because NOA does not capture all of the firms' assets. For example, R&D and advertising are not fully and contemporaneously reflected on the balance sheet as assets though they likely produce future earnings. Likewise, internally generated goodwill is not fully reflected on the balance sheet as an asset. Similarly, assets are generally not written up to reflect unrealized gains. Conversely, sometimes the balance sheet overstates the true value of NOA. For example, companies can delay the write-down of impaired assets and, thus, overstate their book values. These examples, and a host of others, can yield reported values of NOA that differ from the fair value of operating assets.

hurdle operating profit (NOA$_{Beg}$ × r_w) is greater than NOPAT. IN either case, we must understand the economic meaning of a negative ROPI and the valuation implications.

Specifically, recall that the NOPAT we use in the ROPI model represents future expected net operating profits to the firm. Thus, the first step in the ROPI model is to develop reasonable forecasts of NOPAT. As explained in Module 11, good forecasts begin with sound assumptions. Forecasted NOPAT can sometimes be negative for a certain period such as with new firms or with firms experiencing an economic downturn. But over the long run, firms cannot sustain continuous negative NOPAT as such firms would run short of cash and be closed or forced into bankruptcy. Similar logic leads us to infer that firms cannot generate such low NOPAT that they do not earn at least the average investor's hurdle rate. (Recall that the hurdle rate is the weighted average cost of capital.) Firms that earn profits below the hurdle rate are destroying shareholder value. If a firm consistently earns less than the hurdle rate, its shareholders would be better off if the firm liquidated because they could invest their funds elsewhere and at least expect to earn the hurdle rate. Thus, it is not economically reasonable to model ROPI that is consistently negative for a viable firm. A model that includes negative ROPI in each forecasted period, would suggest that we need to revisit our forecast assumptions. If ROPI is still negative after more careful scrutiny, the firm is likely not viable and the ROPI model valuation is inappropriate. The value of such a firm is likely equal to the fair value of its individual assets less the value to settle its liabilities.

Understanding the ROPI model helps us reap the benefits from the disaggregation of return on net operating assets (RNOA) in Module 3. In addition, the ROPI model is the foundation for many internal and external performance evaluation and compensation systems marketed by management consulting and accounting services firms.[2]

Steps in Applying the ROPI Model

Application of the ROPI model to equity valuation involves five steps:

1. Forecast and discount ROPI for the horizon period.[3]

2. Forecast and discount ROPI for the terminal period.[4]

3. Sum the present values from both the horizon and terminal periods; then add this sum to current NOA to get firm (enterprise) value.

4. Subtract net nonoperating obligations (NNO), along with any noncontrolling interest, from firm value to yield firm equity value.

5. Divide firm equity value by the number of shares outstanding to yield stock value per share.

BUSINESS INSIGHT | Earnings: Nominal (Risk-Adjusted) vs Real

Module 12 explained that the value of the payoffs (earnings) is unaffected by whether *nominal (risk-adjusted)* or *real* inputs are used in valuation provided that nominal earnings are discounted using nominal discount rates (and real earnings are discounted using real discount rates). This means that in practice, nominal earnings and nominal discount rates are used; analysts do not forecast real payoffs (earnings).

---

[2] Examples are economic value added (EVA™) from Stern Stewart & Company, the economic profit model from McKinsey & Co., the cash flow return on investment (CFROI™) from Holt Value Associates, the economic value management from KPMG, and the value builder from PricewaterhouseCoopers (PwC).

[3] When discounting ROPI, the appropriate discount rate (r_w) is the **weighted average cost of capital (WACC)**, where the weights are the relative percentages of debt (d) and equity (e) in the capital structure applied to the expected returns on debt (r_d) and equity (r_e), respectively: WACC = r_w = (r_d × % of debt) + (r_e × % of equity); see Module 12.

[4] For an assumed growth, g, the present value of the perpetuity of ROPI beyond the horizon period is given by $\frac{ROPI_T}{r_w - g}$, where ROPI$_T$ is the residual operating income for the terminal period, r_w is WACC for the firm, and g is the assumed growth rate of ROPI$_T$ following the horizon period. The resulting amount is then discounted back to the present using the WACC, computed over the length of the horizon period.

Illustrating the ROPI Model

To illustrate application of the ROPI model, we use **Johnson & Johnson**. Forecasted financials for J&J (forecast horizon of 2011–2014 and terminal period of 2015) are in Exhibit 14.1.[5] The forecasts (in bold) are for sales, NOPAT, and NOA (the same forecasts from illustration of the DCF model in Module 13). These forecasts assume an annual 4% sales growth for the horizon period, a terminal period sales growth of 1%, net operating profit margin (NOPM) of 21%, and a year-end net operating asset turnover (NOAT) of 1.30 (which is the 2010 turnover rate based on year-end NOA; year-end amounts are used because we are forecasting year-end account balances, not average balances).[6, 7]

EXHIBIT 14.1	Application of Residual Operating Income Model					
		Horizon Period				**Terminal Period**
(In millions, except per share values and discount factors)	Reported 2010	2011	2012	2013	2014	
Sales (unrounded)	$ 61,587	$64,050.48 (61,587 × 1.04)	$66,612.49 (64,050.48 × 1.04)	$69,277.00 (66,612.49 × 1.04)	$72,048.08 (69,277.00 × 1.04)	$72,768.56 (72,048.08 × 1.01)
Sales (rounded)	61,587	64,050	66,612	69,277	72,048	72,769
NOPAT*	13,065	13,451	13,989	14,548	15,130	15,281
NOA**	45,694	49,269	51,240	53,290	55,422	55,976
ROPI (NOPAT − [NOA$_{Beg}$ × r_w])		9,795	10,047	10,449	10,867	10,847
Discount factor [1/(1 + r_w)^t]‡		0.92593	0.85734	0.79383	0.73503	
Present value of horizon ROPI		9,069	8,614	8,295	7,988	
Cum present value of horizon ROPI	$ 33,966					
Present value of terminal ROPI	113,898					
NOA	45,694					
Total firm value	193,558					
Less NNO†	(10,885)					
Firm equity value	$204,443					
Shares outstanding	2,738.1					
Stock value per share	$ 74.67					

*Given J&J's combined federal and state statutory tax rate of 36.0% as reported in the tax footnote to its 2010 10-K, NOPAT for 2010 is computed as follows ($ millions): ($61,587 − $18,792 − $19,424 − $6,844) − ($3,613 − {0.360 × [$455 − $107 − $768]}) = $13,065. A note on rounding: To forecast sales, we multiply prior year's unrounded sales by (1 + Growth rate); this is done for the horizon and terminal periods. Then, we round each year's forecasted sales to whole units and use rounded sales to compute NOPAT and NOA, where both are rounded to whole units. At each successive step, we round the number to whole units before proceeding to the next step.

**NOA computations for 2010 follow ($ millions): ($102,908 − $19,355 − $8,303) − ($46,329 − $7,617 − $9,156) = $45,694.

†NNO is the difference between NOA and total shareholders' equity; in this case NNO ($ millions) = 45,694 − 56,579 = $(10,885). J&J's NNO is negative because it carries substantial cash and securities that exceed its debt.

‡For simplification, present value computations use discount factors rounded to 5 decimal places.

The bottom line of Exhibit 14.1 is the estimated J&J equity value of $204,443 million, or a per share stock value of $74.67. The present value computations use an 8% WACC as the discount rate. Specifically, we obtain this stock valuation as follows:

1. **Compute present value of horizon period ROPI.** The forecasted 2011 ROPI of $9,795 million is computed from the forecasted 2011 NOPAT ($13,451) less the product of beginning period NOA ($45,694) and WACC (0.08). The present value of this ROPI as of 2010

---

[5] We use a four-period horizon in the text and assignments to simplify the exposition and to reduce the computational burden. In practice, analysts use spreadsheets to forecast future cash flows and value the equity security, and typically have a forecast horizon of seven to ten periods.

[6] **NOPAT** equals revenues less operating expenses such as cost of goods sold, selling, general, and administrative expenses, and taxes. NOPAT excludes any interest revenue and interest expense and any gains or losses from financial investments. NOPAT reflects the operating side of the firm as opposed to nonoperating activities such as borrowing and security investment activities. **NOA** equals operating assets less operating liabilities. (See Module 3.)

[7] NOPAT and NOA are typically forecasted using the detailed forecasting procedures discussed in Module 11. In this module we use the parsimonious method to multiyear forecasting (see Module 11) to focus attention on the valuation process.

is \$9,069 million, computed as \$9,795 million $\times$ 0.92593 (the present value one year hence discounted at 8%).[8] Similarly, the present value of 2012 ROPI (two years hence) is \$8,614 million, computed as \$10,047 million $\times$ 0.85734, and so on through 2015. The sum of these present values (*cumulative present value*) is \$33,966 million.

2. Compute **present value of terminal period ROPI.** The present value of the terminal period ROPI is \$113,898 million, computed as $\dfrac{\left(\dfrac{\$10,847 \text{ million}}{0.08 - 0.01}\right)}{(1.08)^4}$, or (\$10,847/0.07) $\times$ 0.73503.

3. **Compute firm equity value.** We must sum the present values from the horizon period (\$33,966 million) and terminal period (\$113,898 million), plus NOA (\$45,694 million), to get firm (enterprise) value of \$193,558 million. We then subtract the value of net nonoperating obligations of \$10,885 million to get firm equity value of \$204,443. Dividing firm equity value by the 2,738.1 million shares outstanding yields the estimated per share valuation of \$74.67.

We perform this valuation as of February 25, 2011, which is the SEC filing date for J&J's 10-K. J&J's stock closed at \$59.13 on February 25, 2011. Our valuation estimate of \$74.67 indicates that the company's stock is undervalued as of that date. J&J's stock price climbed steadily through the spring of 2011 and was trading for \$65 by July. Our estimated price is higher than analysts' target price but J&J was still recommended as a strong BUY stock.

The ROPI model estimate for J&J is equal to that computed using the DCF model illustrated earlier in Module 13. This is the case so long as the firm is in a steady state, that is, NOPAT and NOA are growing at the same rate (for example, when RNOA is constant). When the steady-state condition is not met, for example, when a company has variable growth rates over time or when profit margins are changing from year to year, the two models yield different valuations. (The terminal period estimate of ROPI_{T+1} is normally computed as $\text{ROPI}_{T+1} = [\text{NOPAT}_T \times (1 + g)] - (\text{NOA}_T \times r_w)$. A common mistake is to compute it as $\text{ROPI}_{T+1} = [\text{ROPI}_T \times (1 + g)]$. The difference is that the latter computation requires that NOA grow at rate g from period T to T + 1, which may or may not be an intended assumption.) Analysts typically compute values from several models and use qualitative analysis to determine a final price estimate.

RESEARCH INSIGHT | **Power of NOPAT Forecasts**

Discounted cash flow (DCF) and residual operating income (ROPI) models yield identical estimates when the expected payoffs are forecasted for an infinite horizon. For practical reasons, we must use horizon period forecasts and a terminal period forecast. This truncation of the forecast horizon is a main cause of any difference in value estimates for these models. Importantly, if we can forecast (GAAP-based) NOPAT and NOA more accurately than forecasts of cash inflows and outflows, we will obtain more accurate estimates of firm value given a finite horizon.

---

[8] The weighted average cost of capital (WACC) for J&J is computed using the following three-step process:

1. The cost of equity capital is given by the capital asset pricing model (CAPM): $r_e = r_f + \beta (r_m - r_f)$, where β is the beta of the stock (an estimate of stock price variability that is reported by several services such as Yahoo! and Standard and Poors), r_f is the risk-free rate (commonly assumed as the 10-year treasury bond rate), and r_m is the expected return to the entire market. The expression $(r_m - r_f)$ is the "spread" of equities over the risk-free rate, often assumed to be about 5% to 7%. For J&J, given a beta of 1.00 and a 10-year treasury bond rate of 3.58% (r_f) as of February 28, 2011, r_e is estimated as 9.58%, computed as 3.58% + (1.00 $\times$ 6%).

2. Two alternative computations for pretax cost of debt capital are: (1) Interest expense/Average interest-bearing debt, and (2) Weighted-average effective interest rate on debt. For the latter, J&J reports its 5.25% rate in footnote 7 to its 10-K, which we use. To obtain J&J's after-tax cost of debt capital, we multiply 5.25% by 1 − 0.360, where 36.0% is the federal and state statutory tax rate from its tax footnote, yielding 3.36% (J&J's after-tax cost of debt).

3. WACC is the weighted average of the cost of equity capital and the cost of debt capital. J&J capital structure is 77% equity and 23% debt. Thus, J&J's weighted average cost of capital is (77% $\times$ 9.58%) + (23% $\times$ 3.36%) = 8.15%, rounded to 8%. (The capital structure of J&J depends on its stock price. To achieve an internally consistent value estimate, an iterative process can be used where the estimated value [in this case \$74.67] is used to recompute its capital structure and get an updated WACC estimate. After several iterations, the valuation estimate and the weights used to compute WACC converge.)

Extending the ROPI Model

The Johnson & Johnson illustration makes several assumptions that can be refined to derive more precise stock values. We describe some of these refinements here.

Horizon Period. The illustration uses a relatively short horizon period. It might be more reasonable to anticipate growth for longer than four years before the company achieves a long-term growth of 1%, as in our example. The downside to much longer horizon periods is that it is more difficult to accurately project growth as the time horizon extends. Thus, the shorter horizon period might provide a more conservative stock value.

Growth Rate. The illustration assumes a constant growth rate, NOPM and NOAT during the horizon period. As an alternative, we can alter these, even having different rates for each year. For example, we might assume that the recent economic downturn will depress J&J's sales for 2011 and 2012 and, thus, we might forecast a growth rate less than 4% for those two years followed by 4% growth in 2013 and 2014. Similarly, we could change NOPM and/or NOAT for each year to better match our expectations of future profitability and/or asset efficiency.

Financial Statement Forecasts. The illustration uses a parsimonious method to multiyear forecasting to focus attention on the valuation process. As an alternative, we can prepare detailed year-by-year forecasts of the income statement and balance sheet to derive NOPAT and NOA, respectively. Year-by-year forecasts allow us to more precisely model relations on the income statement, and between the income statement and the balance sheet. For example, the parsimonious model assumes a constant NOPM of 21% for the J&J illustration. This implies that all expenses vary in exactly the same way with revenue growth. We can refine that assumption by including different growth rates for different expenses. As another example, the parsimonious model assumes one turnover rate for all net operating assets. In the J&J example, we apply a NOAT of 1.3, which is the average historic turnover rate across accounts receivable, inventory, PPE, accounts payable, and so forth. A year-by-year forecast would allow the turnover rates to vary across different operating assets and liabilities and yield potentially more precise estimates for future expected NOA.

Terminal Growth Rate. A crucial assumption in valuation is the choice of a terminal growth rate. This rate reflects all future ROPI beyond the forecast horizon, which is captured in terminal value. Many valuations are sensitive to variations in terminal growth rate. The choice of a forecast horizon is influenced by whether the company has achieved a long-run steady state where a pattern of future ROPI is expected to persist for the long-run of the company. Ideally, the forecast horizon is sufficiently long to allow steady state to be achieved within the horizon. The terminal growth rate can be a positive percentage (but not exceeding the discount rate), or zero, or negative (but not less than −100%). An increase in the terminal growth rate in ROPI for Johnson & Johnson from 1% to 2% would increase the present value of the terminal ROPI from \$113,898 to \$132,881 [\$10,847/(0.08 − 0.02)/1.08^4], yielding an increase in estimated value per share of \$6.93 [(\$132,881 − \$113,898)/2,738.1]. This shows the sensitivity of a valuation to a terminal growth rate. The quality of our forecasts within the horizon period directly impacts the quality of our terminal growth rate estimate.

Sensitivity Analysis of Stock Price. The illustration uses only one set of assumptions and derives only one stock price. To refine our valuation we can perform sensitivity analyses. For example, the J&J illustration uses 8% for WACC, which is our best estimate of the company's weighted average cost of capital. We might derive stock value using a larger and smaller WACC to gauge how sensitive the stock price is to changes in the discount rate. Extending this idea, we commonly derive a "worst case" stock value by simultaneously applying the lowest reasonable assumptions for growth, NOPM, and NOAT, and the highest reasonable assumption for WACC. We also commonly derive the "best case" scenario by applying the highest reasonable assumptions for growth, NOPM, and NOAT, and the lowest reasonable assumption for WACC. This provides a range of reasonable stock values and gives us more information and confidence about potential outcomes.

Mid-Year Adjustment. Payoffs in our valuation model are assumed to occur at year-end and are discounted for the entire year. An alternative is to assume that payoffs occur evenly during the year. A common adjustment in this case is to multiply the estimated value by a *mid-year adjustment factor* defined as $(1 + r_w)^{0.5}$. Another common approximation of the adjustment factor is

$(1 + [r_w/2])$. The Oppenheimer report in Appendix 13B applies a mid-year adjustment factor. For J&J, our WACC estimate of 8% would yield an adjustment factor of 1.04, which increases the valuation estimate to $212,626 ($204,448 × 1.04), or $77.65 per share.

Reverse Engineering. One alternative to sensitivity analysis is to use *reverse engineering* in an attempt to "unlock" the market's assumptions in determining price. The process of reverse engineering uses observed price combined with valuation assumptions to solve for one of the valuation parameters such as discount rate or terminal growth rate. If the observed market price of Johnson & Johnson of $59.13 at February 25, 2011, is used with the other assumptions in Exhibit 14.1, we can solve for the terminal growth rate (often implemented using reiterative estimation). In our case, this process yields an implied terminal growth rate for ROPI of –3.2%. An investor or analyst could then decide whether he or she believes this rate to be too high or too low as a basis for determining a buy or sell decision.

MANAGERIAL INSIGHTS FROM THE ROPI MODEL

The ROPI model defines firm value as the sum of NOA and the present value of expected residual operating income as follows:

LO3 Explain how equity valuation models can aid managerial decisions.

$$\textbf{Firm Value} = \textbf{NOA} + \textbf{Present Value of Future } [\textbf{NOPAT} - (\textbf{NOA}_{\textbf{Beg}} \times r_w)]$$
$$\underbrace{\hspace{6cm}}_{\textbf{ROPI}}$$

Increasing ROPI, therefore, increases firm value. Managers can increase ROPI in two ways:

1. Decrease the NOA required to generate a given level of NOPAT (improve efficiency)
2. Increase NOPAT with the same level of NOA investment (improve profitability)

These are two very important observations. It means that achieving better performance requires effective management of *both* the balance sheet and the income statement. Most operating managers are accustomed to working with income statements. Further, they are often evaluated on profitability measures, such as achieving desired levels of sales and gross profit or efficiently managing operating expenses. The ROPI model focuses management attention on the balance sheet as well.

Management Focus on Improved Efficiency

The two points above highlight two paths to increase ROPI and, accordingly, firm value. First, let's consider how management can reduce the level of NOA while maintaining a given level of NOPAT. Many managers begin by implementing procedures that reduce net operating working capital, such as:

- Reducing receivables through:
    - Better assessment of customers' credit quality
    - Better controls to identify delinquencies and automated payment notices
    - More accurate and timely invoicing
- Reducing inventories through:
    - Use of less costly components (of equal quality) and production with lower wage rates
    - Elimination of product features not valued by customers
    - Outsourcing to reduce product cost
    - Just-in-time deliveries of raw materials
    - Elimination of manufacturing bottlenecks to reduce work-in-process inventories
    - Producing to order rather than to estimated demand
- Increasing payables through:
    - Extending the payment of low or no-cost payables (so long as the supplier relationships are unharmed)

Management must also look at its long-term operating assets for opportunities to reduce unnecessary operating assets, such as the:

■ Sale of unnecessary property, plant or equipment

■ Acquisition of production and administrative assets in partnership with other entities for greater throughput

■ Acquisition of finished or semifinished goods from suppliers to reduce manufacturing assets

Management Focus on Improved Profitability

The second path to increase ROPI and, accordingly, firm value is to increase NOPAT with the same level of NOA investment. Management would look to strategies that maximize NOPAT, such as:

■ Increasing gross profit dollars through:

○ Better pricing and mix of products sold

○ Reduction of raw material and labor cost without sacrificing product quality, perhaps by outsourcing, better design, or more efficient manufacturing

○ Increase of throughput to minimize overhead costs per unit (provided inventory does not build up)

■ Reducing selling, general, and administrative expenses through:

○ Better management of personnel

○ Reduction of overhead

○ Use of derivatives to hedge commodity and interest costs

○ Minimization of tax expense

Before undertaking any of these actions, managers must consider both short- and long-run implications for the company. The ROPI model helps managers assess company performance (income statement) relative to the net operating assets committed (balance sheet).

ANALYSIS DECISION   You Are the Chief Financial Officer

The residual operating income (ROPI) model highlights the importance of increasing NOPAT and reducing net operating assets, which are the two major components of the return on net operating assets (RNOA). What specific steps can you take to improve RNOA through improvement of its components: net operating profit margin and net operating asset turnover? [Answer, p. 14-15]

ASSESSMENT OF VALUATION MODELS

Exhibit 14.2 provides a brief summary of the advantages and disadvantages of the DCF and ROPI models. Neither model dominates the other in all cases, and both are theoretically equivalent. Instead, professionals must choose the model that performs best under practical circumstances.

There are numerous other equity valuation models in practice. Many require forecasting, but several others do not. A quick review of selected models follows:

The **method of comparables** (often called *multiples*) **model** predicts equity valuation or stock value using price multiples. Price multiples are defined as stock price divided by some key financial statement number. That financial number varies across investors but is usually one of the following: net income, net sales, book value of equity, total assets, or cash flow. The method then compares companies' multiples to those of their competitors to assign value.

The **net asset valuation model** draws on the financial reporting system to assign value. That is, equity is valued as reported assets less reported liabilities. Some investors adjust reported assets and liabilities for several perceived shortcomings in GAAP prior to computing net asset value. This method is commonly applied when valuing privately held companies.

EXHIBIT 14.2	Advantages and Disadvantages of DCF and ROPI Valuation Models		
Model	**Advantages**	**Disadvantages**	**Performs Best**

DCF	• Popular and widely accepted model
	• Cash flows are unaffected by accrual accounting
	• FCFF is intuitive
		• Cash investments in plant assets are treated as cash outflows, even though they create shareholder value
		• Value not recognized unless evidenced by cash flows
		• Computing FCFF can be difficult as operating cash flows are affected by
		  – Cutbacks on investments (receivables, inventories, plant assets); can yield short-run benefits at long-run cost
		  – Securitization, which GAAP treats as an operating cash flow when many view it as a financing activity
			• When the firm reports positive FCFF
			• When FCFF grows at a relatively constant rate
			• When a long-run steady-state pattern of FCFF emerges in a short horizon

ROPI	• Focuses on value drivers such as profit margins and asset turnovers • Uses both balance sheet and income statement, including accrual accounting information • Reduces weight placed on terminal period value	• Financial statements do not reflect all company assets, especially for knowledge-based industries (for example, R&D assets and goodwill) • Requires some knowledge of accrual accounting	• When financial statements reflect more of the assets and liabilities; including those items often reported off-balance-sheet • When a long-run steady-state pattern of ROPI emerges in a short horizon

The **dividend discount model** predicts that equity valuation or stock values equal the present value of expected cash dividends. This model is founded on the dividend discount formula and depends on the reliability of forecasted cash dividends.

There are additional models applied in practice that involve dividends, cash flows, research and development outlays, accounting rates of return, cash recovery rates, and real option models. Further, some practitioners, called *chartists* and *technicians,* chart price behavior over time and use it to predict equity value.

RESEARCH INSIGHT **Using Models to Identify Mispriced Stocks**

Implementation of the ROPI model can include parameters to capture differences in growth opportunities, persistence of ROPI, and the conservatism in accounting measures. Research finds differences in how such factors, across firms and over time, affect ROPI and changes in NOA. This research also hints that investors do not entirely understand the properties underlying these factors and, consequently, individual stocks can be mispriced for short periods of time. Other research contends that the apparent mispricing is due to an omitted valuation variable related to riskiness of the firm.

ANALYZING GLOBAL REPORTS

There are no differences in the method or technique of valuing equity securities using IFRS financial statements. We can use the ROPI method with IFRS data as inputs and determine intrinsic values. The extent to which NOA overstates or understates market value is corrected by the present value of future expected ROPI; this continues to hold when using different accounting standards such as IFRS. The key is accurate forecasts, which is driven by an understanding of accounting, the company, and its environment. The four steps for financial statement analysis and valuation introduced in Module 1, and reproduced at the beginning of this module, are the same regardless of the accounting standards followed.

MODULE-END REVIEW

Following are forecasts of **Procter & Gamble**'s sales, net operating profit after tax (NOPAT), and net operating assets (NOA). These are taken from our forecasting process in Module 11 and now include a terminal period forecast that reflects a long-term growth rate of 1%.

(In millions)	Reported 2011	2012	2013	2014	2015	Terminal Period
			Horizon Period			
Sales growth..........		4.6%	4.6%	4.6%	4.6%	1%
Net sales (unrounded) ...	$ 82,559	$86,356.71 ($82,559 × 1.046)	$90,329.12 ($86,356.71 × 1.046)	$94,484.26 ($90,329.12 × 1.046)	$98,830.54 ($94,484.26 × 1.046)	$99,818.84 ($98,830.54 × 1.01)
Net sales (rounded)	$ 82,559	$ 86,357	$ 90,329	$ 94,484	$ 98,831	$ 99,819
NOPAT	12,193	12,781	13,369	13,984	14,627	14,773
NOA	97,247	101,596	106,269	111,158	116,272	117,434

Drawing on these forecasts, compute P&G's residual operating income (ROPI) and an estimate of its stock value using the ROPI model. Assume the following: discount rate (WACC) of 8%, shares outstanding of 2,765.7 million, and net nonoperating obligations (NNO) of $29,607 million (which includes $361 million in noncontrolling interest).

The solution is on page 14-28.

APPENDIX 14A: JOHNSON & JOHNSON FINANCIAL STATEMENTS

JOHNSON & JOHNSON Balance Sheet		
At Fiscal Year End ($ millions, except shares and per share)	2010	2009
Assets		
Cash and cash equivalents	$ 19,355	$15,810
Marketable securities........	8,303	3,615
Accounts receivable trade, net of allowances for doubtful accounts $340 (2009, $333)	9,774	9,646
Inventories	5,378	5,180
Deferred taxes on income	2,224	2,793
Prepaid expenses and other receivables...	2,273	2,497
Total current assets	47,307	39,541
Property, plant and equipment, net	$ 14,553	$14,759
Intangible assets, net....	16,716	16,323
Goodwill	15,294	14,862
Deferred taxes on income	5,096	5,507
Other assets.....	3,942	3,690
Total assets.....	$102,908	$94,682
Liabilities and Shareholders' Equity		
Loans and notes payable.....	$ 7,617	$ 6,318
Accounts payable......	5,623	5,541
Accrued liabilities	4,100	4,625
Accrued rebates, returns and promotions	2,512	2,028
Accrued compensation	2,642	2,777
Accrued taxes on income.....	578	442
Total current liabilities.....	$ 23,072	$21,731
Long-term debt	9,156	8,223
Deferred taxes on income	1,447	1,424
Employee related obligations.....	6,087	6,769
Other liabilities	6,567	5,947
Total liabilities.....	$ 46,329	$44,094

continued

continued from prior page

Shareholders' equity		
Preferred stock.	$ —	$ —
Common stock—par value $1.00 per share		
(authorized 4,320,000,000 shares; issued 3,119,843,000 shares)	3,120	3,120
Accumulated other comprehensive income.	(3,531)	(3,058)
Retained earnings	77,773	70,306
Less: common stock held in treasury, at cost (381,746,000 shares and 365,522,000 shares). . .	20,783	19,780
Total shareholders' equity	56,579	50,588
Total liabilities and shareholders' equity.	$102,908	$94,682

JOHNSON & JOHNSON
Income Statement

For Fiscal Year Ended ($ millions)	2010	2009	2008
Sales to customers.	$61,587	$61,897	$63,747
Cost of products sold.	18,792	18,447	18,511
Gross profit.	42,795	43,450	45,236
Selling, marketing and administrative expenses	19,424	19,801	21,490
Research and development expense.	6,844	6,986	7,577
Purchased in-process research and development.	—	—	181
Interest income.	(107)	(90)	(361)
Interest expense, net of portion capitalized.	455	451	435
Other (income) expense[1]	(768)	(526)	(1,015)
Restructuring	—	1,073	—
Earnings before provision for taxes on income	16,947	15,755	16,929
Provision for taxes on income	3,613	3,489	3,980
Net earnings.	$13,334	$12,266	$12,949

[1] We classify Other (Income) Expense as nonoperating because it includes, among other items: royalty income; gains and losses related to the sale and write-down of investments in equity securities; currency gains and losses; non-controlling interests; and hedge ineffectiveness.

JOHNSON & JOHNSON
Statement of Cash Flows

For Fiscal Year Ended ($ millions)	2010	2009	2008
Cash flows from operating activities			
Net earnings.	$13,334	$12,266	$12,949
Adjustments to reconcile net earnings to cash flows:			
Depreciation and amortization of property and intangibles	2,939	2,774	2,832
Stock based compensation	614	628	627
Purchased in-process research and development.	—	—	181
Deferred tax provision.	356	(436)	22
Accounts receivable allowances.	12	58	86
Changes in assets and liabilities, net of effects from acquisitions:			
(Increase)/decrease in accounts receivable	(207)	453	(736)
(Increase)/decrease in inventories	(196)	95	(101)
Increase/(decrease) in accounts payable and accrued liabilities . . .	20	(507)	(272)
(Increase)/decrease in other current and noncurrent assets	(574)	1,209	(1,600)
Increase in other current and noncurrent liabilities.	87	31	984
Net cash flows from operating activities	16,385	16,571	14,972
Cash flows from investing activities			
Addition to property, plant and equipment.	(2,384)	(2,365)	(3,066)
Proceeds from the disposal of assets	524	154	785
Acquisitions, net of cash acquired.	(1,269)	(2,470)	(1,214)
Purchases of investments	(15,788)	(10,040)	(3,668)
Sales of investments	11,101	7,232	3,059
Other (primarily intangibles)	(38)	(109)	(83)
Net cash used by investing activities.	(7,854)	(7,598)	(4,187)

continued

continued from prior page

Cash flows from financing activities			
Dividends to shareholders	(5,804)	(5,327)	(5,024)
Repurchase of common stock	(2,797)	(2,130)	(6,651)
Proceeds from short-term debt	7,874	9,484	8,430
Retirement of short-term debt	(6,565)	(6,791)	(7,319)
Proceeds from long-term debt	1,118	9	1,638
Retirement of long-term debt	(32)	(219)	(24)
Proceeds from the exercise of stock options/excess tax benefits	1,226	882	1,486
Net cash used by financing activities	(4,980)	(4,092)	(7,464)
Effect of exchange rate changes on cash and cash equivalents	(6)	161	(323)
Increase in cash and cash equivalents	3,545	5,042	2,998
Cash and cash equivalents, beginning of year	15,810	10,768	7,770
Cash and cash equivalents, end of year	$19,355	$15,810	$10,768

GUIDANCE ANSWERS . . . ANALYSIS DECISION

You Are the Chief Financial Officer RNOA can be disaggregated into its two key drivers: net operating profit margin and net operating asset turnover. Net operating profit margin can be increased by improving gross profit margins (better product pricing, lower-cost manufacturing, etc.) and closely monitoring and controlling operating expenses. Net operating asset turnover can be increased by reducing net operating working capital (better monitoring of receivables, better management of inventories, carefully extending payables, etc.) and making more effective use of plant assets (disposing of unused assets, forming corporate alliances to increase plant asset capacity, selling productive assets to contract producers and purchasing the output, etc.). The ROPI model effectively focuses managers on the balance sheet and income statement.

DISCUSSION QUESTIONS

Q14-1. In general, what role do expectations play in pricing equity securities? What is the relation between security prices and expected returns (the discount rate, or WACC, in this case)?

Q14-2. Define the weighted average cost of capital (WACC).

Q14-3. Define net operating profit after tax (NOPAT).

Q14-4. Define net operating assets (NOA).

Q14-5. Define the concept of residual operating income. How is residual operating income used in pricing equity securities?

Q14-6. What insight does disaggregation of RNOA into net operating profit margin and net operating asset turnover provide for managing a company?

Assignments with the ✔ logo in the margin are available in an online homework system.
See the Preface of the book for details.

MINI EXERCISES

STARBUCKS
(SBUX)

M14-7.   Interpreting Earnings Announcement Effects on Stock Prices   (LO1, 2)
In a recent quarterly earnings announcement, **Starbucks** announced that its earnings had markedly increased (up 7 cents per share over the prior year) and were 1 cent higher than analysts' expectations. Starbucks' stock "edged higher," according to *The Wall Street Journal,* but did not markedly increase. Why do you believe that Starbucks' stock price did not markedly increase given the good news?

HALLIBURTON
COMPANY
(HAL)

M14-8.   Computing Residual Operating Income (ROPI)   (LO2)
Halliburton Company reports net operating profit after tax (NOPAT) of $2,032 million in 2010. Its net operating assets at the beginning of 2010 are $9,937 million. Assuming a 10% weighted average cost of capital (WACC), what is Halliburton's residual operating income for 2010? Show computations.

M14-9. **Computing, Analyzing and Interpreting Residual Operating Income (ROPI)** (LO2)

In its 2010 fiscal year annual report, **CVS** reports net operating income after tax (NOPAT) of $3,777 million. As of the beginning of fiscal year 2010 it reports net operating assets of $45,889 million.

CVS CAREMARK
(CVS)

a. Did CVS earn positive residual operating income (ROPI) in 2010 if its weighted average cost of capital (WACC) is 7%? Explain.
b. At what level of WACC would CVS not report positive residual operating income for 2010? Explain.

M14-10. **Estimating Share Value Using the ROPI Model** (LO2)

Following are forecasts of **Target Corporation**'s sales, net operating profit after tax (NOPAT), and net operating assets (NOA) as of January 29, 2011.

TARGET
CORPORATION
(TGT)

	Reported	Horizon Period				Terminal
(In millions)	2011	2012	2013	2014	2015	Period
Sales............	$67,390	$70,086	$72,889	$75,805	$78,837	$79,625
NOPAT	3,397	3,504	3,644	3,790	3,942	3,981
NOA	29,501	30,472	31,691	32,959	34,277	34,620

Answer the following requirements assuming a terminal period growth rate of 1%, discount rate (WACC) of 7%, shares outstanding of 704 million, and net nonoperating obligations (NNO) of $14,014 million.

a. Estimate the value of a share of Target common stock using the residual operating income (ROPI) model as of January 29, 2011.
b. Target Corporation (TGT) stock closed at $49.99 on March 18, 2011. How does your valuation estimate compare with this closing price? What do you believe are some reasons for the difference?

EXERCISES

E14-11. **Estimating Share Value Using the ROPI Model** (LO2)

Following are forecasts of **Abercrombie & Fitch**'s sales, net operating profit after tax (NOPAT), and net operating assets (NOA) as of January 29, 2011 (Current-year NOPAT is lower due to transitory items; we use a longer term estimate for NOPM of 8%.).

ABERCROMBIE &
FITCH
(ANF)

	Reported	Horizon Period				Terminal
(In millions)	2011	2012	2013	2014	2015	Period
Sales...........	$3,469	$3,989	$4,587	$5,275	$6,066	$6,187
NOPAT	152	319	367	422	485	495
NOA	1,032	1,173	1,349	1,551	1,784	1,820

Answer the following requirements assuming a discount rate (WACC) of 10%, a terminal period growth rate of 2%, common shares outstanding of 87.2 million, and net nonoperating obligations (NNO) of $(858) million (negative NNO reflects net nonoperating assets such as investments rather than net obligations).

a. Estimate the value of a share of Abercrombie & Fitch common stock using the residual operating income (ROPI) model as of January 29, 2011.
b. Abercrombie & Fitch stock closed at $56.71 on March 29, 2011. How does your valuation estimate compare with this closing price? What do you believe are some reasons for the difference?

E14-12. **Estimating Share Value Using the ROPI Model** (LO2)

Following are forecasts of sales, net operating profit after tax (NOPAT), and net operating assets (NOA) as of February 26, 2011, for **Best Buy, Inc.**

BEST BUY
(BBY)

	Reported	Horizon Period				Terminal
(In millions)	2011	2012	2013	2014	2015	Period
Sales...........	$50,272	$52,786	$55,425	$58,196	$61,106	$61,717
NOPAT	1,389	1,584	1,663	1,746	1,833	1,852
NOA	7,876	8,248	8,660	9,093	9,548	9,643

Answer the following requirements assuming a discount rate (WACC) of 11%, a terminal period growth rate of 1%, common shares outstanding of 392.6 million, and net nonoperating obligations (NNO) of $1,274 million.

a. Estimate the value of a share of Best Buy common stock using the residual operating income (ROPI) model as of February 26, 2011.

b. Best Buy (BBY) stock closed at $30.20 on April 25, 2011. How does your valuation estimate compare with this closing price? What do you believe are some reasons for the difference?

E14-13. **Identifying and Computing Net Operating Assets (NOA) and Net Nonoperating Obligations (NNO)** (LO1, 2)

HALLIBURTON
COMPANY
(HAL)

Following is the balance sheet for **Halliburton Company**.

HALLIBURTON COMPANY Consolidated Balance Sheets		
At December 31 (Millions of dollars and shares)	2010	2009
Assets		
Cash and equivalents...............................	$ 1,398	$ 2,082
Receivables, net....................................	3,924	2,964
Inventories	1,940	1,598
Investments in markeatable securities..............	653	1,312
Current deferred income taxes......................	257	210
Other current assets...............................	714	472
Total current assets	8,886	8,638
Property, plant and equipment—net	6,842	5,759
Goodwill	1,315	1,100
Other assets......................................	1,254	1,041
Total assets......................................	$18,297	$16,538
Liabilities and Stockholders' Equity		
Accounts payable..................................	$ 1,139	$ 787
Current maturities of long-term debt	—	750
Accrued employee compensation and benefits........	716	514
Deferred revenue	266	215
Other current liabilities	636	623
Total current liabilities............................	2,757	2,889
Long-term debt	3,824	3,824
Employee compensation and benefits................	487	462
Other liabilities	842	606
Total liabilities....................................	7,910	7,781
Shareholders' equity		
Common shares, par value $2.50 per share—authorized 2,000 shares, issued 1,069 shares and 1,067 shares......................	2,674	2,669
Paid-in capital in excess of par value................	339	411
Accumulated other comprehensive loss	(240)	(213)
Retained earnings	12,371	10,863
Treasury stock, at cost—159 and 165 shares	(4,771)	(5,002)
Company shareholders' equity	10,373	8,728
Noncontrolling interest in consolidated subsidiaries ...	14	29
Total shareholders' equity	10,387	8,757
Total liabilities and shareholders' equity............	$18,297	$16,538

a. Compute net operating assets (NOA) and net nonoperating obligations (NNO) for 2010.

b. For 2010, show that: NOA = NNO + Stockholders' equity.

E14-14. Identifying and Computing Net Operating Profit after Tax (NOPAT) and Net Nonoperating Expense (NNE) (LO1, 2)

Following is the income statement for **Halliburton Company**.

HALLIBURTON COMPANY Consolidated Statements of Operations			
At December 31 (millions of dollars)	2010	2009	2008
Revenue			
Services	$13,779	$ 10,832	$13,391
Product sales	4,194	3,843	4,888
Total revenue	17,973	14,675	18,279
Operating costs and expenses			
Cost of services	11,237	9,224	10,079
Cost of sales.	3,508	3,255	3,970
General and administrative.	229	207	282
Gain on sale of operating assets, net.	(10)	(5)	(62)
Total operating costs and expenses.	14,964	12,681	14,269
Operating income.	3,009	1,994	4,010
Interest expense, net of interest income of $11, $12, and $39.	(297)	(285)	(128)
Other nonoperating expenses, net.	(57)	(27)	(33)
Income from continuing operations before income taxes	2,655	1,682	3,849
Provision for income taxes.	(853)	(518)	(1,211)
Income from continuing operations	1,802	1,164	2,638
Income (loss) from discontinued operations, net of income tax	40	(9)	(423)
Net income.	1,842	1,155	2,215
Noncontrolling interest in net income of subsidiaries	(7)	(10)	9
Net income attributable to company	$1,835	$ 1,145	$ 2,224

Compute net operating profit after tax (NOPAT) for 2010, assuming a federal and state statutory tax rate of 35%.

E14-15. Estimating Share Value Using the ROPI Model (LO2)

Following are forecasts of **Halliburton Company**'s sales, net operating profit after tax (NOPAT), and net operating assets (NOA) as of December 31, 2010.

(In millions)	Reported 2010	Horizon Period				Terminal Period
		2011	2012	2013	2014	
Sales.	$17,973	$21,028	$24,603	$28,786	$33,680	$35,027
NOPAT	2,032	2,376	2,780	3,253	3,806	3,958
NOA	12,160	14,208	16,624	19,450	22,757	23,667

Answer the following requirements assuming a discount rate (WACC) of 10%, a terminal period growth rate of 4%, common shares outstanding of 910 million, and net nonoperating obligations (NNO) of $1,787 million.

a. Estimate the value of a share of **Halliburton Company** common stock using the residual operating income (ROPI) model as of February 17, 2011.

b. Halliburton Company stock closed at $48.43 on February 17, 2011. How does your valuation estimate compare with this closing price? What do you believe are some reasons for the difference?

E14-16. **Explaining the Equivalence of Valuation Models and the Relevance of Earnings** (LO2, 3)

Modules 13 and 14 focused on two different valuation models: the discounted cash flow (DCF) model and the residual operating income (ROPI) model. The models focus on free cash flows to the firm and on residual operating income, respectively. We stressed that these two models are theoretically equivalent.

a. What is the *intuition* for why these models are equivalent?
b. Some analysts focus on cash flows as they believe that companies manage earnings, which presumably makes earnings less relevant. Are earnings relevant? Explain.

E14-17. **Applying and Interpreting Value Driver Components of RNOA** (LO3)

The net operating profit margin and the net operating asset turnover components of return on net operating assets are often termed *value drivers*, which refers to their positive influence on stock value by virtue of their role as components of return on net operating assets (RNOA).

a. How do profit margins and asset turnover ratios influence stock values?
b. Assuming that profit margins and asset turnover ratios are value drivers, what insight does this give us about managing companies if the goal is to create shareholder value?

PROBLEMS

INTEL CORPORATION (INTC)

P14-18. **Forecasting and Estimating Share Value Using the ROPI Model** (LO2, 3)

Following are the income statement and balance sheet for **Intel Corporation**.

INTEL CORPORATION Consolidated Statements of Income			
Year Ended (In millions)	December 25, 2010	December 26, 2009	December 27, 2008
Net revenue	$43,623	$35,127	$37,586
Cost of sales	15,132	15,566	16,742
Gross margin	28,491	19,561	20,844
Research and development	6,576	5,653	5,722
Marketing, general and administrative	6,309	7,931	5,452
Restructuring and asset impairment charges	—	231	710
Amortization of acquisition-related intangibles	18	35	6
Operating expenses	12,903	13,850	11,890
Operating income	15,588	5,711	8,954
Gains (losses) on equity method investments, net	117	(147)	(1,380)
Gains (losses) on other equity investments, net	231	(23)	(376)
Interest and other, net	109	163	488
Income before taxes	16,045	5,704	7,686
Provision for taxes	4,581	1,335	2,394
Net income	$11,464	$ 4,369	$ 5,292

INTEL CORPORATION **Consolidated Balance Sheets**		
As of Year-Ended (In millions, except par value)	December 25, 2010	December 26, 2009
Assets		
Current assets		
Cash and cash equivalents...............................	$ 5,498	$ 3,987
Short-term investments	11,294	5,285
Trading assets...	5,093	4,648
Accounts receivable, net	2,867	2,273
Inventories	3,757	2,935
Deferred tax assets..	1,488	1,216
Other current assets.......................................	1,614	813
Total current assets..	31,611	21,157
Property, plant and equipment, net	17,899	17,225
Marketable equity securities	1,008	773
Other long-term investments1	3,026	4,179
Goodwill...	4,531	4,421
Other long-term assets	5,111	5,340
Total assets..	$63,186	$53,095
Liabilities		
Current liabilities		
Short-term debt	$ 38	$ 172
Accounts payable...	2,290	1,883
Accrued compensation and benefits	2,888	2,448
Accrued advertising	1,007	773
Deferred income on shipments to distributors.............	622	593
Other accrued liabilities	2,482	1,722
Total current liabilities.....................................	9,327	7,591
Long-term income taxes payable.........................	190	193
Long-term debt	2,077	2,049
Long-term deferred tax liabilities........................	926	555
Other long-term liabilities.................................	1,236	1,003
Total liabilities	13,756	11,391
Stockholders' equity		
Preferred stock, $0.001 par value......................	—	—
Common stock, $0.001 par value, 10,000 shares authorized; 5,581 issued and 5,511 outstanding and capital in excess of par value	16,178	14,993
Accumulated other comprehensive income..............	333	393
Retained earnings..	32,919	26,318
Total stockholders' equity	49,430	41,704
Total liabilities and stockholders' equity..................	$63,186	$53,095

1 These investments are operating assets as they relate to associated companies.

Required

a.   Compute Intel's net operating assets (NOA) for year-end 2010.

b.   Compute net operating profit after tax (NOPAT) for 2010, assuming a federal and state statutory tax rate of 37%.

c.   Forecast Intel's sales, NOPAT, and NOA for years 2011 through 2014 using the following assumptions:

Sales growth.	10%
Net operating profit margin (NOPM).	26%
Net operating asset turnover (NOAT) at year-end	1.50

Forecast the terminal period value assuming a 1% terminal period growth and using the NOPM and NOAT assumptions above.

d. Estimate the value of a share of Intel common stock using the residual operating income (ROPI) model as of December 25, 2010; assume a discount rate (WACC) of 11%, common shares outstanding of 5,511 million, and net nonoperating obligations (NNO) of $(20,778) million (NNO is negative which means that Intel has net nonoperating investments).

e. Intel (INTC) stock closed at $22.14 on February 18, 2011. How does your valuation estimate compare with this closing price? What do you believe are some reasons for the difference? What investment decision is suggested from your results?

P14-19. Forecasting and Estimating Share Value Using the ROPI Model   (LO2, 3)

CVS CAREMARK
(CVS)

Following are the income statement and balance sheet for **CVS Caremark**.

CVS CAREMARK INC. Balance Sheets		
December 31 (In millions, except per share amounts)	**2010**	**2009**
Assets		
Cash and cash equivalents.	$ 1,427	$ 1,086
Short-term investments	4	5
Accounts receivable, net	4,925	5,457
Inventories	10,695	10,343
Deferred income taxes	511	506
Other current assets.	144	140
Total current assets.	17,706	17,537
Property and equipment, net	8,322	7,923
Goodwill	25,669	25,680
Intangible assets, net	9,784	10,127
Other assets	688	374
Total assets.	$62,169	$61,641
Liabilities		
Accounts payable.	$ 4,026	$ 3,560
Claims and discounts payable	2,569	3,075
Accrued expenses	3,070	3,246
Short-term debt	300	315
Current portion of long-term debt	1,105	2,104
Total current liabilities	11,070	12,300
Long-term debt.	8,652	8,756
Deferred income taxes	3,655	3,678
Other long-term liabilities	1,058	1,102
Redeemable noncontrolling interest.	34	37
Total liabilities	24,469	25,873
Shareholders' equity		
Common stock, par value $0.01: 3,200 shares authorized; 1,624 shares issued and 1,363 shares outstanding at December 31, 2010	16	16
Treasury stock at cost:	(9,030)	(7,610)
Shares held in trust.	(56)	(56)
Capital surplus	27,610	27,198
Retained earnings.	19,303	16,355
Accumulated other comprehensive loss	(143)	(135)
Total shareholders' equity.	37,700	35,768
Total liabilities and shareholders' equity	$62,169	$61,641

CVS CAREMARK INC.			
Consolidated Statements of Income			
For the year ended December 31 (In millions)	**2010**	**2009**	**2008**
Net revenues	$96,413	$98,729	$87,472
Cost of revenues	76,156	78,349	69,182
Gross profit.	20,257	20,380	18,290
Operating expenses.	14,092	13,942	12,244
Operating profit	6,165	6,438	6,046
Interest expense, net	536	525	509
Income before income tax provision	5,629	5,913	5,537
Income tax provision	2,190	2,205	2,193
Income from continuing operations	3,439	3,708	3,344
Loss from discontinued operations, net of income tax benefit	(15)	(12)	(132)
Net income.	3,434	3,696	3,212
Net loss attributable to noncontrolling interest	3	—	—
Preference dividends, net of income tax benefit	—	—	(14)
Net income attributable to CVS Caremark.	$ 3,427	$ 3,696	$ 3,198

Required

a. Compute net operating assets (NOA) as of December 31, 2010.
b. Compute net operating profit after tax (NOPAT) for fiscal year ended December 31, 2010, assuming a federal and state statutory tax rate of 37%.
c. Forecast CVS's sales, NOPAT, and NOA for 2011 through 2014 using the following assumptions:

Sales growth.	5%
Net operating profit margin (NOPM).	4%
Net operating asset turnover (NOAT) at fiscal year-end.	2.10

Forecast the terminal period value assuming a 1% terminal period growth and using the NOPM and NOAT assumptions above.
d. Estimate the value of a share of CVS common stock using the residual operating income (ROPI) model as of December 31, 2010; assume a discount rate (WACC) of 7%, common shares outstanding of 1,363 million, and net nonoperating obligations (NNO) of $8,660 million.
e. CVS's stock closed at $33.06 on February 18, 2011. How does your valuation estimate compare with this closing price? What do you believe are some reasons for the difference?

P14-20. Forecasting and Estimating Share Value Using the ROPI Model   (LO2, 3)
Following are the income statement and balance sheet for **Abbott Laboratories (ABT)**.

ABBOTT LABORATORIES		
Balance Sheet		
December 31 ($ millions)	**2010**	**2009**
Assets		
Cash and cash equivalents	$ 3,648.371	$ 8,809.339
Investments and restricted funds.	3,675.569	1,122.709
Trade receivables, net	7,184.034	6,541.941
Total inventories.	3,188.734	3,264.877
Deferred income taxes.	3,076.051	2,364.142
Other prepaid expenses and receivables.	1,544.770	1,210.883
Total current assets	22,317.529	23,313.891

continued

continued from prior page

Investments	302.049	1,132.866
Property and equipment, net	7,970.956	7,619.489
Intangible assets, net of amortization	12,151.628	6,291.989
Goodwill	15,930.077	13,200.174
Deferred income taxes and other assets	790.027	858.214
Total assets	$59,462.266	$52,416.623
Liabilities and Shareholders' Investment		
Short-term borrowings	$ 4,349.796	$ 4,978.438
Trade accounts payable	1,535.759	1,280.542
Salaries, wages and commissions	1,328.665	1,117.410
Other accrued liabilities	6,014.772	4,399.137
Dividends payable	680.749	620.640
Income taxes payable	1,307.723	442.140
Current portion of long-term debt	2,044.970	211.182
Total current liabilities	17,262.434	13,049.489
Long-term debt	12,523.517	11,266.294
Post-employment and other long-term obligations	7,199.851	5,202.111
Shareholders' investment		
Common shares, without par value. Authorized: 2,400,000,000 shares.		
Issued: 1,619,689,876 and 1,612,683,987	8,744.703	8,257.873
Common shares held in treasury: 72,705,928 and 61,516,398	(3,916.823)	(3,310.347)
Earnings employed in the business	18,927.101	17,054.027
Accumulated other comprehensive income (loss)	(1,366.846)	854.074
Total Abbott shareholders' investment	22,388.135	22,855.627
Noncontrolling interests in subsidiaries	88.329	43.102
Total shareholders' investment	22,476.464	22,898.729
Total liabilities and shareholders' investment	$59,462.266	$52,416.623

ABBOTT LABORATORIES AND SUBSIDIARIES
Consolidated Statement of Earnings

Year Ended December 31 (dollars in millions)	2010	2009	2008
Net sales	$35,166.721	$30,764.707	$29,527.552
Cost of products sold	14,665.192	13,209.329	12,612.022
Research and development	3,724.424	2,743.733	2,688.811
Acquired in-process research and development	313.200	170.000	97.256
Selling, general and administrative	10,376.324	8,405.904	8,435.624
Total operating cost and expenses	29,079.140	24,528.966	23,833.713
Operating earnings	6,087.581	6,235.741	5,693.839
Interest expense	553.135	519.656	528.474
Interest (income)	(105.453)	(137.779)	(201.229)
(Income) from the TAP Pharmaceutical joint venture	—	—	(118.997)
Other (income) expense, net	(72.935)	(1,339.910)	(370.695)
Earnings from continuing operations before taxes	5,712.834	7,193.774	5,856.286
Taxes on earnings from continuing operations	1,086.662	1,447.936	1,122.070
Earnings from continuing operations	4,626.172	5,745.838	4,734.216
Gain on sale of discontinued operations, net of taxes	—	—	146.503
Net earnings	$ 4,626.172	$ 5,745.838	$ 4,880.719

Required

a. Compute net operating assets (NOA) for year-end 2010.

b. Compute net operating profit after tax (NOPAT) for 2010 assuming a federal and state statutory tax rate of 35.4%.

c. Forecast Abbott Laboratories' sales, NOPAT, and NOA for 2011 through 2014 using the following assumptions:

Sales growth.	10%
Net operating profit margin (NOPM).	14%
Net operating asset turnover (NOAT), year-end	1.0

Forecast the terminal period value assuming a 1% terminal period growth and using the NOPM and NOAT assumptions above.

d. Estimate the value of a share of Abbott Laboratories' common stock using the residual operating income (ROPI) model as of December 31, 2010; assume a discount rate (WACC) of 7%, common shares outstanding of 1,547 million, and net nonoperating obligations (NNO) of $12,061 million.

e. Abbott Laboratories (ABT) stock closed at $46.88 on February 18, 2011. How does your valuation estimate compare with this closing price? What do you believe are some reasons for the difference? What investment decision is suggested from your results?

P14-21. **Forecasting and Estimating Share Value Using the ROPI Model**   (LO2, 3)

Following are the income statement and balance sheet for **Kellogg Company**.

KELLOGG CO.
(K)

KELLOGG COMPANY AND SUBSIDIARIES			
Consolidated Statement of Income			
For Year Ended (in millions)	**2010**	**2009**	**2008**
Net sales.	$12,397	$12,575	$12,822
Cost of goods sold.	7,108	7,184	7,455
Selling, general and administrative expense	3,299	3,390	3,414
Operating profit	1,990	2,001	1,953
Interest expense.	248	295	308
Other income (expense), net	—	(22)	(14)
Income before income taxes	1,742	1,684	1,631
Income taxes	502	476	485
Net income.	1,240	1,208	1,146
Net loss attributable to noncontrolling interests	(7)	(4)	(2)
Net income attributable to Kellogg Company	$ 1,247	$ 1,212	$ 1,148

KELLOGG COMPANY AND SUBSIDIARIES		
Consolidated Balance Sheet		
(millions, except share data)	**2010**	**2009**
Current assets		
Cash and cash equivalents	$ 444	$ 334
Accounts receivable, net	1,190	1,093
Inventories	1,056	910
Other current assets.	225	221
Total current assets.	2,915	2,558
Property, net.	3,128	3,010
Goodwill	3,628	3,643
Other intangibles, net.	1,456	1,458
Other assets.	720	531
Total assets.	$11,847	$11,200

continued

continued from prior page

Current liabilities		
Current maturities of long-term debt	$ 952	$ 1
Notes payable	44	44
Accounts payable.	1,149	1,077
Other current liabilities	1,039	1,166
Total current liabilities	3,184	2,288
Long-term debt	4,908	4,835
Deferred income taxes.	697	425
Pension liability.	265	430
Other liabilities	639	947
Equity		
Common stock, $.25 par value, 1,000,000,000 shares authorized		
Issued: 419,272,027 shares in 2010 and 419,058,168 shares in 2009. . .	105	105
Capital in excess of par value	495	472
Retained earnings	6,122	5,481
Treasury stock at cost: 53,667,635 shares in 2010 and 37,678,215	(2,650)	(1,820)
shares in 2009.		
Accumulated other comprehensive income (loss)	(1,914)	(1,966)
Total Kellogg Company equity	2,158	2,272
Noncontrolling interests	(4)	3
Total equity	2,154	2,275
Total liabilities and equity	$11,847	$11,200

Required

a. Compute net operating assets (NOA) as of year-end 2010.

b. Compute net operating profit after tax (NOPAT) for 2010, assuming a federal and state statutory tax rate of 36.4%.

c. Forecast Kellogg's sales, NOPAT, and NOA for 2011 through 2014 using the following assumptions:

Sales growth.	4%
Net operating profit margin (NOPM).	11%
Net operating asset turnover (NOAT), year-end	1.6

Forecast the terminal period value assuming a 1% terminal period growth and using the NOPM and NOAT assumptions above.

d. Estimate the value of a share of Kellogg common stock using the residual operating income (ROPI) model; assume a discount rate (WACC) of 6%, common shares outstanding of 365.6 million, and net nonoperating obligations (NNO) of $5,456 million.

e. Kellogg's stock closed at $53.56 at February 28, 2011. How does your valuation estimate compare with this closing price? What do you believe are some reasons for the difference?

IFRS APPLICATIONS

TESCO, PLC

I14-22. Forecasting and Estimating Share Value Using the ROPI Model (LO2, 3)

Following are the income statement and balance sheet for **Tesco, PLC**, a UK-based grocery chain. The company's financial statements are prepared in accordance with IFRS.

Tesco, PLC Group Income Statement		
Year ended 26 February 2011	**52 weeks 2011 £m**	**52 weeks 2010 £m**
Continuing operations		
Revenue (sales excluding VAT)	£60,931	£56,910
Cost of sales	(55,871)	(52,303)
Gross profit	5,060	4,607
Administrative expenses	(1,676)	(1,527)
Profit arising on property-related items	427	377
Operating profit	3,811	3,457
Share of post-tax profits of joint ventures and associates	57	33
Finance income	150	265
Finance costs	(483)	(579)
Profit before tax	3,535	3,176
Taxation	(864)	(840)
Profit for the year	£ 2,671	£ 2,336
Attributable to:		
Owners of the parent	£ 2,655	£ 2,327
Non-controlling interests	16	9
	£ 2,671	£ 2,336

TESCO PLC Group Balance Sheet		
	26 February 2011 £m	**27 February 2010 £m**
Non-current assets		
Goodwill and other intangible assets	£ 4,338	£ 4,177
Property, plant and equipment	24,398	24,203
Investments in joint ventures and associates	316	152
Other investments	2,971	2,594
Financial assets	3,266	3,094
Deferred tax assets	48	38
Total non-current assets	35,337	34,258
Current assets		
Inventories	3,162	2,729
Trade and other receivables	2,314	1,888
Financial assets	3,066	2,636
Current tax assets	4	6
Short-term investments	1,022	1,314
Cash and cash equivalents	1,870	2,819
	11,438	11,392
Non-current assets classified as held for sale	431	373
Total current assets	11,869	11,765
Current liabilities		
Trade and other payables	(10,484)	(9,442)
Financial liabilities	(1,641)	(1,675)
Customer prepayments and deposits	(5,110)	(4,387)
Current tax liabilities	(432)	(472)
Provisions	(64)	(39)
Total current liabilities	(17,731)	(16,015)

continued

continued from prior page

Non-current liabilities		
Financial liabilities.	**(10,289)**	(12,520)
Post-employment benefit obligations	**(1,356)**	(1,840)
Deferred tax liabilities.	**(1,094)**	(795)
Provisions.	**(113)**	(172)
	(12,852)	(15,327)
Equity		
Share capital.	**402**	399
Share premium account.	**4,896**	4,801
Other reserves	**40**	40
Retained earnings	**11,197**	9,356
Equity attributable to owners of the parent	**16,535**	14,596
Non-controlling interests	**88**	85
Total equity.	**£16,623**	£14,681

Required

a. Compute net operating assets (NOA) as of year-end 2011.

b. Compute net operating profit after tax (NOPAT) for 2011, assuming a marginal tax rate of 25%.

c. Forecast Tesco's sales, NOPAT, and NOA for 2012 through 2015 using the following assumptions:

Sales growth.	6%
Net operating profit margin (NOPM).	4.8%
Net operating asset turnover (NOAT)	3.8

Estimate the terminal period value assuming a 1% terminal period growth and using the NOPM and NOAT assumptions, above.

d. Estimate the value of a share of Tesco's common stock (which trades on the London Stock Exchange) using the residual operating income (ROPI) model; assume a discount rate (WACC) of 8%, common shares outstanding of 8,046.5 million, and net nonoperating obligations (NNO) of £(608). (Note: NNO is negative which means that Tesco has net nonoperating investments and financial assets.)

e. Tesco's stock price was £3.93 on April 19, 2011. How does your valuation estimate compare with this closing price? What do you believe are some reasons for the difference?

DISCUSSION POINTS

D14-23. Operating Improvement versus Financial Engineering (LO3)

Assume that you are the CEO of a small publicly traded company. The operating performance of your company has fallen below market expectations, which is reflected in a depressed stock price. At your direction, your CFO provides you with the following recommendations that are designed to increase your company's return on net operating assets (RNOA) and your operating cash flows, both of which will, presumably, result in improved financial performance and an increased stock price.

1. To improve net cash flow from operating activities, the CFO recommends that your company reduce inventories (raw material, work-in-progress, and finished goods) and receivables (through selective credit granting and increased emphasis on collection of past due accounts).

2. The CFO recommends that your company sell and lease back its office building. The lease will be structured so as to be classified as an operating lease under GAAP. The assets will, therefore, not be included in the computation of net operating assets (NOA), thus increasing RNOA.

3. The CFO recommends that your company lengthen the time taken to pay accounts payable (lean on the trade) to increase net cash flows from operating activities.

4. Because your company's operating performance is already depressed, the CFO recommends that you take a "big bath;" that is, write off all assets deemed to be impaired and accrue excessive liabilities for future contingencies. The higher current period expense will, then, result in higher

future period income as the assets written off will not be depreciated and your company will have a liability account available to absorb future cash payments rather than recording them as expenses.

5. The CFO recommends that your company increase its estimate of expected return on pension investments. This will reduce pension expense and increase operating profit, a component of net operating profit after tax (NOPAT) and, thus, of RNOA.

6. The CFO recommends that your company share ownership of its outbound logistics (trucking division) with another company in a joint venture. This would have the effect of increasing throughput, thus spreading overhead over a larger volume base, and would remove the assets from your company's balance sheet since the joint venture would be accounted for as an equity method investment.

Evaluate each of the CFO's recommendations. In your evaluation, consider whether each recommendation will positively impact the operating performance of your company or whether it is cosmetic in nature.

SOLUTIONS TO REVIEW PROBLEMS

Module-End Review

Solution

Results from the ROPI model below yield a P&G stock value estimate of $51.62 as of August 10, 2011. P&G's stock closed at $58.51 on that date. This estimate suggests that P&G's stock is overvalued as of that date.

(In millions, except per share values and discount factors)	Reported 2011	Horizon Period				Terminal Period
		2012	2013	2014	2015	
ROPI (NOPAT − [NOA$_{Beg}$ × r_w])		$5,001	$5,241	$5,482	$5,734	$5,471
Discount factor [1/(1 + r_w)^t]		0.92593	0.85734	0.79383	0.73503	
Present value of horizon ROPI		4,631	4,493	4,352	4,215	
Cum present value of horizon ROPI	$ 17,691					
Present value of terminal ROPI	57,448[a]					
NOA	97,247					
Total firm value	172,386					
Less NNO	29,607					
Firm equity value	$142,779					
Shares outstanding (millions)	2,765.7					
Stock value per share	$ 51.62					

aComputed as $\dfrac{\frac{5{,}471 \text{ million}}{0.08 - 0.01}}{(1.08^4)}$, or ($5,471 million/0.07) × 0.73503.

The P&G stock price chart, extending from 2007 through 2011, follows.

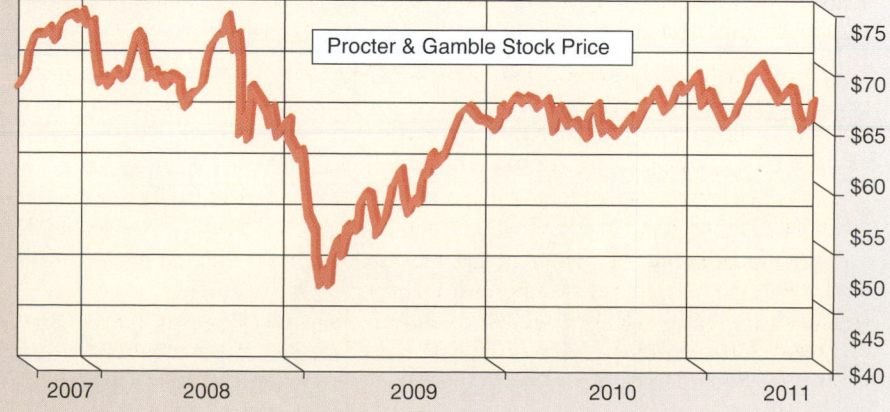

1. Explain company valuation using market multiples based on balance sheet measures. (p. 15-5)

2. Explain company valuation using market multiples based on income statement measures. (p. 15-8)

3. Identify comparable companies for use in company valuation with market multiples. (p. 15-12)

4. Interpret and reverse-engineer market multiples to assess the reliability of market expectations. (p. 15-19)

© Getty Images

Market-Based Valuation

FAMILY DOLLAR

Family Dollar operates more than 7,000 self-service retail discount stores aimed at middle-to-low-income consumers in the United States. Its annual revenues for the recent year exceeded $8 billion. During the past five years, revenues have grown by 25% and profits by 60%. Its stock price has doubled during that same period, exhibiting a three-year upward trend as revealed in the following graphic.

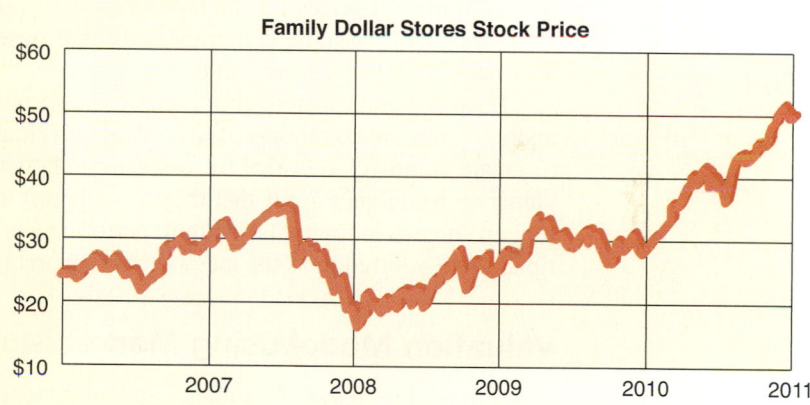

Family Dollar Stores Stock Price

During this most recent 5-year period, Family Dollar's assets increased almost 13%, while its equity was stable. We might ask: which financial metric, or combination, is a good measure of its shareholder value? Revenues? Profits? Assets? Equity? Other? Can we use one or more of these financial metrics to estimate Family Dollar's shareholder value?

To help in this valuation, what company or companies might we use to benchmark Family Dollar's performance and/or financial condition? Should we consider a competitor such as **Dollar General**? How about **Dollar Tree Stores** or **Big Lots**?

Analysts typically utilize a number of approaches to estimate the value of a company's stock price. In prior modules, we have covered two general methods that focus on expected free cash flows and residual operating income. In this module, we illustrate an alternative methodology that focuses on multiples of summary financial measures, such as assets, equity, and profit. This methodology seeks to determine the proper multiple of these summary measures to yield a value of the company's equity. This methodology is referred to as market-based valuation.

Sources: Family Dollar Corporation 2011 Annual Report and 10-K Filing.

(continued on next page)

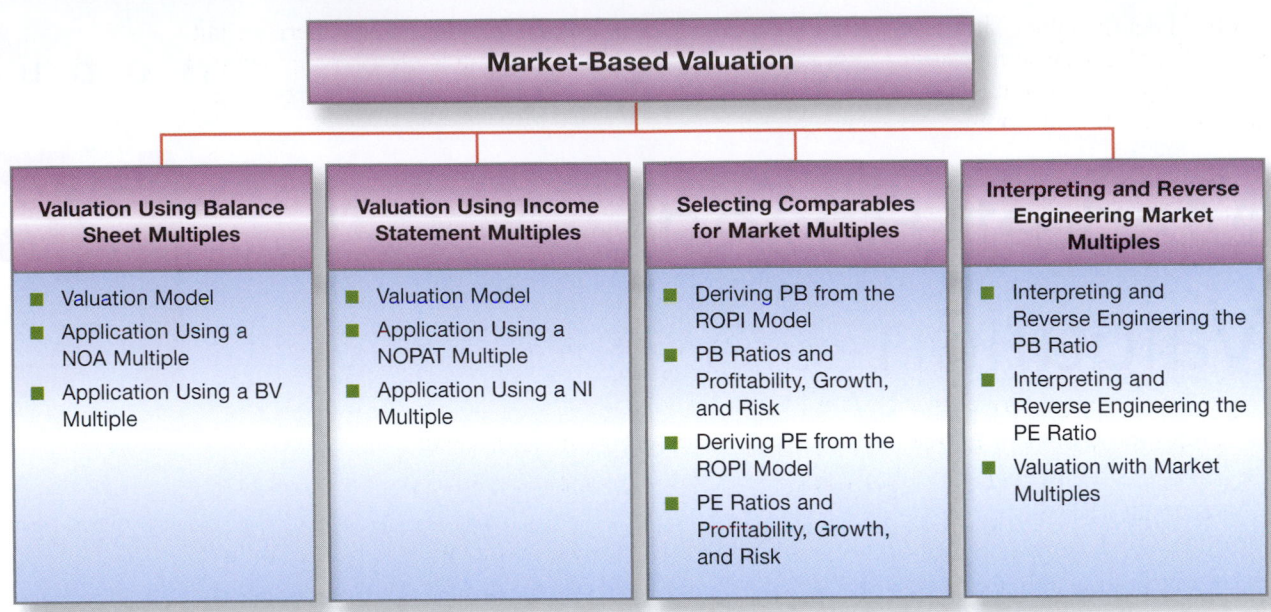

This module focuses on valuation techniques using market multiples. Unlike the valuation techniques introduced in the previous modules, valuation using market multiples does not have rigorous theoretical underpinnings. It is also problematic in that it does not require explicit forecasts of future performance for the company to be valued. Further, it requires that we assume that observed market prices for the target company are not informative about intrinsic value; and yet it requires us to assume simultaneously that observed market prices for comparable companies accurately reflect intrinsic value.

Despite these inherent shortcomings, valuation techniques using market multiples are widely applied. They are commonly used as shortcut valuation methods, as screening devices, and as means to create summary statistics for assessing relative valuations. Some who use these market-based valuation techniques argue that they are superior to other techniques precisely because they do not rely on subjective forecasts of future performance. Whatever the view, valuation using market multiples, also referred to as the method of comparables, is a common valuation technique.

Valuation Model using Market Multiples

Valuation using market multiples is popular chiefly because of its simplicity. We simply select a relevant summary measure of performance (such as earnings, book values, cash flows, or sales) from the financial statements of a target company that we wish to value. Next, we identify companies that are "comparable" to the target company on relevant dimensions (described later). For each comparable company, we compute the ratio of market value to the selected summary performance measure. The average of those ratios is the *market multiple*. (While an average of ratios from comparable companies is commonly employed, if a specific comparable company is believed to be more relevant as a benchmark, then we can place more than average weighting on its ratio.) Then, we multiply the summary measure for the target company by the market multiple—that product is the estimated value of the target company. The following model reflects this process.

$$\text{Value} = \text{Summary performance measure} \times \text{Market multiple}$$

This model does not specify whether the value obtained is the company value or equity value. Recall that the DCF and ROPI models in Modules 13 and 14 were used to value the entire company. We then find equity value by deducting the value of net nonoperating obligations (NNO) from company value. When using market multiples to estimate value, the choice of summary performance measure determines whether the output is company value or equity value. If an *equity performance measure* is selected (such as earnings or book value), then the output of the model is equity value. If a *company performance measure* is selected (such as NOPAT or NOA), then the output of the model is company value, from which we must deduct net nonoperating obligations to obtain equity value. The more commonly used market multiples are those that generate equity value directly because investors are most often interested in equity value. However, as we shall see, using market multiples to find equity value directly means capital structure must be considered in selecting comparable companies.

Application of the Model using Market Multiples

There are five steps in estimating value using a market multiple. (The steps can be applied using performance measures, or performance measures on a per share basis.)

1. Select the summary performance measure to use as the basis for valuation—such as earnings, book value, NOPAT or NOA; the model can be applied using current performance measures or forecasted performance measures.
2. Select the comparable companies to use in determining the market multiple.
3. Compute the market multiple from the comparable companies' market values and performance measures.
4. Compute the target company's value using its performance measure and the market multiple.
5. If its performance measure is an equity performance measure (such as earnings and book value), divide by shares outstanding to get equity value per share. If the performance measure is a company performance measure (such as NOPAT and NOA), subtract net nonoperating obligations, and then divide by shares outstanding to get equity value per share. (If a per share performance measure is used, we do not divide by shares outstanding.)

Although the steps are simple, key decisions are made in steps 1, 2 and 3. These decisions reveal the inherent weakness of this valuation method.

First, in step 1, which performance measure is the right one? This question has no answer as *there is no right measure.* Company value depends on future company performance. Previous modules of this book show that no single measure entirely summarizes current period performance, much less provides a sufficient basis for forecasting future company performance. Still, we could argue that particular measures are more suited to particular companies or industries. For example, book value might be more suitable for companies with assets whose reported values approximate market values such as with many financial firms. Earnings might be more suitable for companies that are growing rapidly with relatively little volatility. Free cash flows might be more suitable for companies with negative earnings.

Second, in step 2, what companies should we use as comparable companies? If comparable companies are under- or overvalued, the computed market multiple will under- or overvalue the target company. We might appeal to market efficiency and claim that the comparable companies are likely fairly priced, but this begs the question of why we are trying to find a value for our target company if it is also fairly priced? Even if comparable companies are accurately priced, when they differ in ways that matter for valuation (such as on profitability, expected growth, and risk), the computed multiple will under- or overvalue our company.

RESEARCH INSIGHT   **Efficient Markets and Valuation Using Comparables**

There is an inherent inconsistency in using market multiples to value publicly traded companies. By choosing to value a specific company using market multiples, the investor presumes that the target company is not fairly valued. However, by selecting comparable companies to determine the multiple, the investor relies on the markets to accurately value those companies. How does the investor know which companies are fairly valued and which are valued with error? Some assert that a group of companies is valued correctly on average. However, if a company deviates from the average, is that a pricing error or a valid variance from the distribution of intrinsic values?

Third, in step 3, how do we combine the comparable company data to produce a multiple? We could compute the multiple for each company and then use an equal-weighted average, or combine the data for all companies and compute a value-weighted average. Or, we could use a median of all comparable company ratios, or use an average after eliminating the highest and lowest observations.

Again, there is no correct answer to this question and the others as this valuation technique is ad hoc and the decisions commonly made to apply it are ad hoc.

Despite deficiencies in valuing companies using market multiples, it is commonly applied in practice. The following analyst report uses market multiples to explain and justify its current assessment of a company's stock price. We see references to peers, or "comparables" (comps), and the market multiple in analyzing current performance and predicting future performance, including stock price performance.

Analyst Report

Valuation of Family Dollar

We rate Family Dollar Neutral and our $49.00 December 2011 price target is predicated on a 50/50 weighted, blended P/E and EV/EBITDA multiple build. Following the recent spike in the stock subsequent to Trian's proposal to acquire the company for $55-$60 as well as our concerns that some risk exists to the company's 2H11 SSS/EPS outlook, we feel a Neutral rating is appropriate at this time.

From a fundamental perspective, we believe opportunities still remain for the company to narrow the productivity gap that exists with peer Dollar General, especially through its compelling store renovation program; however, near-term risks exist on both the top-line and margins, in our view, as 2H11 guidance was not adjusted after the 1Q/December miss. Moreover, from a valuation perspective, FDO is now trading at 15.7x, a 2-turn premium to peers Dollar General (12.8x) and Dollar Tree (13.8x), which seems a bit unwarranted.

In sum, we feel a Neutral rating is appropriate at this time. In our price target build, we layer in assumptions to include a best, base, and worst case scenario for the stock—trading multiples vary by scenario and are determined based on historical trading ranges and peer valuations. For FDO, our base case scenario (50%) is based on an absolute P/E of 13.5x and EV/EBITDA multiple of 7.0x. Our best case scenario (25%) is based on an absolute P/E of 14.5x and EV/EBITDA multiple of 7.5x. Conversely, our worst case scenario (25%) is based on a P/E of 12.5x and an EV/EBITDA multiple of 6.5x.

Family Dollar Stores, Inc (FDO; FDO US)

Company Data				2010A	2011E	2012E
Price ($)	50.11	EPS (Operating) ($)				
Date of Price	01 Mar 11	Q1 (Nov)		0.49A	0.58A	—
52-week Range ($)	55.62-32.30	Q2 (Feb)		0.81A	0.96	—
Mkt Cap ($ mn)	6,471.26	Q3 (May)		0.77A	0.98	—
Fiscal Year End	Aug	Q4 (Aug)		0.56A	0.68	—
Shares O/S (mn)	129	FY		2.62A	3.18	3.55
Price Target ($)	49.00	Bloomberg EPS FY ($)		2.58A	3.13	3.64
Price Target End Date	31 Dec 11	P/E (Operating) FY		19.1A	15.7	14.1

VALUATION USING BALANCE SHEET MULTIPLES

LO1 Explain company valuation using market multiples based on balance sheet measures.

The balance sheet is one source of performance measures to use in estimating company value. This section illustrates the mechanics of using balance sheet summary measures to estimate value. First, we estimate company value for **Family Dollar** using a multiple of net operating assets. Next, we estimate its equity value using a multiple of book value. The comparable companies we use are **Dollar General** and **Big Lots**, both of which compete with Family Dollar. Summary information for all three companies, using reported fiscal year-end data for Family Dollar (August 28, 2010), Dollar General (January 28, 2011) and Big Lots (January 29, 2011), is in Exhibit 15.1.[1] Market values for each company are collected on the fiscal year-end date from Yahoo!, Google, and/or the 10-K filing. Our task is to estimate the intrinsic value of Family Dollar's equity.

---

[1] Recall the following key definitions (readily available from services such as Yahoo! and Google):
Company assumed value = Firm value (market value of a company's net operating assets), which is also equal to the market value of its common stock and net nonoperating obligations.
Equity assumed value = Market capitalization (market value of a company's common stock)
Book value of equity = Book value of a company's common stockholders' equity

EXHIBIT 15.1	Data for Valuation Using Balance Sheet Multiples*			
(in millions)		**Family Dollar**	**Dollar General**	**Big Lots**
Company assumed value..........................		—	$12,499	$2,165
Equity assumed value		—	$ 9,699	$2,351
Net operating assets		$1,021	$ 6,854	$ 761
Book value of equity............................		$1,422	$ 4,054	$ 947
Net nonoperating obligations (assets)		$ (401)	$ 2,800	$ (186)
Common shares outstanding.....................		130.5 shares	341.5 shares	73.9 shares

From market (Company assumed value, Equity assumed value)

From financial statements (Net operating assets, Book value of equity, Net nonoperating obligations (assets), Common shares outstanding)

*Financial statements for these companies report amounts in thousands; we round to millions for ease in computation.

Valuation Using a Net Operating Asset (NOA) Multiple

We use the data from Exhibit 15.1 to compute a market multiple based on net operating assets to estimate the value of Family Dollar. We begin by determining the NOA market multiple for both Dollar General and Big Lots, which is computed as the company assumed value divided by net operating assets. Exhibit 15.2 shows the results of this computation. For example, Dollar General's NOA market multiple is 1.82, computed as $12,499/$6,854. We then average the comparables' NOA market multiples (from Dollar General and Big Lots) to get 2.33, computed as (1.82 + 2.84)/2. This market multiple is used to estimate the company intrinsic value of **Family Dollar** as follows:

$$\text{Company intrinsic value} = \text{Net operating assets} \times \text{NOA market multiple}$$
$$\$2{,}379 \qquad = \qquad \$1{,}021 \qquad \times \qquad 2.33$$

To obtain Family Dollar's equity intrinsic value we subtract net nonoperating obligations from its company value, which is then divided by shares outstanding to yield its per share intrinsic value of common equity as follows:

$$\text{Equity intrinsic value} = \text{Company intrinsic value} - \text{Net nonoperating obligations}$$
$$\$2{,}780 \qquad = \qquad \$2{,}379 \qquad - \qquad \$(401)$$

Then,

$$\text{Equity intrinsic value per share} = \frac{\text{Equity intrinsic value}}{\text{Common shares outstanding}}$$
$$\$21.30 \qquad = \qquad \frac{\$2{,}780}{130.5 \text{ shares}}$$

Family Dollar stock closed at $43.34 on Friday, August 27, 2010, the company's fiscal year-end, and at $46.37 on Tuesday, October 26, 2010, the date on which its 10-K was filed with the SEC (the *filing date*). Accordingly, this estimate suggests that Family Dollar was markedly overvalued on those dates. Of course, the estimated value would have been markedly different had we used Dollar General's market multiple alone, and yet again different if we had used Big Lots' multiple alone. This shows the key role that the market multiple plays in determining intrinsic value under this method.

EXHIBIT 15.2	Estimating Intrinsic Value using a Net Operating Asset Multiple			
(in millions, except per share amounts)		**Family Dollar**	**Dollar General**	**Big Lots**
Company assumed value............................		—	$12,499	$2,165
Net operating assets		$1,021	$ 6,854	$ 761
Common shares outstanding........................		130.5 shares	341.5 shares	73.9 shares
NOA market multiple		2.33	1.82	2.84
Company intrinsic value............................		$2,379		
Equity intrinsic value..............................		$2,780		
Equity intrinsic value per share.....................		$21.30		

Valuation Using a Book Value (BV) Multiple

We can repeat the analysis above using the book value of equity as the multiple for valuing the company. This approach yields the intrinsic value for equity, not for the entire company. This method relies on different data and, as such, we will not get the same intrinsic values as computed in the previous section.

EXHIBIT 15.3	Estimating Intrinsic Value using a Book Value Multiple		
(in millions, except per share amounts)	**Family Dollar**	**Dollar General**	**Big Lots**
Equity assumed value	—	$9,699	$2,351
Book value of equity.	$1,422	$4,054	$ 947
Common shares outstanding.	130.5 shares	341.5 shares	73.9 shares
BV market multiple.	2.44	2.39	2.48
Equity intrinsic value.	$3,470		
Equity intrinsic value per share.	$26.59		

We begin by computing the book value market multiple for both Dollar General and Big Lots, which is computed as equity assumed value divided by book value of equity. Exhibit 15.3 shows the results of this computation. For example, Dollar General's book value market multiple is 2.39, computed as $9,699/$4,054. We then average the book value market multiples (from Dollar General and Big Lots) to get 2.44, computed as (2.39 + 2.48)/2. This BV market multiple is used to estimate the equity intrinsic value of **Family Dollar** as follows:

$$\textbf{Equity intrinsic value} = \textbf{Book value of equity} \times \textbf{BV market multiple}$$
$$\textbf{\$3,470} \qquad = \qquad \textbf{\$1,422} \qquad \times \qquad \textbf{2.44}$$

To obtain Family Dollar's equity intrinsic value per share we divide by shares outstanding as follows:

$$\textbf{Equity intrinsic value per share} = \frac{\textbf{Equity intrinsic value}}{\textbf{Common shares outstanding}}$$
$$\textbf{\$26.59} \qquad = \qquad \frac{\textbf{\$3,470}}{\textbf{130.5 shares}}$$

The $26.59 stock price estimate suggests that Family Dollar stock was markedly overvalued given its $43.34 closing price at its fiscal year-end (and vis-à-vis the $46.37 price on its filing date). The estimated value would have been different had we used Dollar General's market multiple alone, and yet again different if we had used Big Lots' multiple alone. Again, this shows the key role that the market multiple plays in determining intrinsic value under this method.

It is useful for us to compare estimates of Family Dollar's intrinsic value of equity using the net operating assets multiple vis-à-vis the book value multiple. Using the NOA multiple, we estimated the intrinsic value of a share of Family Dollar to be $21.30, while the BV market multiple gave an estimate of $26.59. For Family Dollar, these estimates differ by more than 24%, which is markedly different.

How do we assess the quality of the different estimates? To answer this, let's consider the comparables. When choosing comparables, we should select companies that are similar in terms of profitability, growth, and risk. In this case, we did not control for profitability, growth, or financial risk—we did control for operating risk by choosing companies in the same industry. Still, we might have done better by choosing other retail firms with profitability, growth, and financial risk characteristics similar to those of Family Dollar. (Later in this module we provide guidance on choosing comparables for valuation purposes.) Consequently, the estimate based on the NOA market multiple is likely "better." The reason is that company financial risk does not materially affect the value of net operating assets, but it does affect the value of equity. This means the different capital structures of Family Dollar, Dollar General, and Big Lots do not matter when applying NOA multiples in valuation. But, when using book value multiples to estimate intrinsic value, it is important to select comparables with similar capital structures. (Later in this module we further explain the selection of comparables.)

ANALYSIS DECISION   **You Are an Entrepreneur**

You are the sole owner of a software firm that has developed a system to handle back-office processing for municipalities. During its first three years, your firm focused on developing the software and reported sizeable research and development expenses and annual losses. An interested buyer has approached you, and the investment bankers representing the buyer want to value your firm using market multiples. Because your firm has reported losses, they suggest basing the valuation on book value per share and using Oracle and SAP as comparables, which provide a book value multiple of 8. You believe their methodology is flawed, and their price too low. What arguments can you make in support of your position? [Answer, p. 15-23]

MID-MODULE REVIEW 1

The table below provides summary data for **Johnson & Johnson** (JNJ), along with **Procter & Gamble** and **Merck**, two large cap firms that compete in many segments of JNJ's medical and consumer products businesses.

(in millions)	Johnson & Johnson	Procter & Gamble	Merck
Company assumed value...............	—	$238,532	$ 99,560
Equity assumed value	—	$203,325	$103,315
Net operating assets	$45,894	$101,972	$ 13,809
Book value of equity....................	$39,318	$ 66,760	$ 17,560
Net nonoperating obligations (assets)	$ 6,576	$ 35,212	$ (3,750)
Common shares outstanding.............	2,893 shares	3,132 shares	2,168 shares

Required

a. Estimate the net operating assets market multiple for Procter & Gamble and Merck. Then, compute the average of these as the NOA market multiple for valuation and assess its reliability.

b. Use the results from part *a* to estimate the company intrinsic value, the equity intrinsic value, and the equity intrinsic value per share for Johnson & Johnson.

c. Compute the book value multiple (also called price-to-book or PB) for Procter & Gamble and Merck. Then, compute the average of these as the BV market multiple for valuation.

d. Use the results from part *c* to estimate equity intrinsic value and the equity intrinsic value per share for Johnson & Johnson.

The solution is on page 15-37.

VALUATION USING INCOME STATEMENT MULTIPLES

The most commonly used performance measure for estimating company value with market multiples is earnings. Price-to-earnings (PE) ratios are cited in news articles and analysts' reports, used in stocks screens and trading strategies, and even appear as the subject of academic research. The intuition in using earnings as the basis for valuing a company is straightforward—dividends are paid out of earnings, and potential dividend payouts are the basis for company value. Accordingly, we

LO2 Explain company valuation using market multiples based on income statement measures.

should pay more for companies that generate more earnings. This section illustrates the mechanics of using net operating profit after tax (NOPAT) and net income (NI) as the basis for valuation by market multiples. (For simplicity, NOPAT computations assume a tax rate of 35% for companies in this module.) First, we estimate company value for **Family Dollar** using a multiple of NOPAT. Next, we estimate its equity value using a multiple of NI. The comparable companies we again use are **Dollar General** and **Big Lots**, both of which compete with Family Dollar. Summary information for all three companies, using reported fiscal year-end data for each company (see Exhibit 15.1 for further explanation), is in Exhibit 15.4. Our task is to estimate the equity and company values for Family Dollar using Dollar General and Big Lots as comparables.

EXHIBIT 15.4   Data for Valuation Using Income Statement Multiples

(in millions)	Family Dollar	Dollar General	Big Lots
Company assumed value................................	—	$12,499	$2,165
Equity assumed value	—	$ 9,699	$2,351
Net operating profit after tax	$366	$ 816	$ 224
Net income..	$358	$ 628	$ 223
Common shares outstanding.........................	130.5 shares	341.5 shares	73.9 shares

From market — (Company assumed value, Equity assumed value)

From financial statements — (Net operating profit after tax, Net income, Common shares outstanding)

Valuation Using a Net Operating Profit After Tax (NOPAT) Multiple

We use the data from Exhibit 15.4 to compute a market multiple based on net operating profit after tax (NOPAT) to estimate the value of Family Dollar. We begin by determining the NOPAT market multiple for both Dollar General and Big Lots, which is computed as company assumed value divided by NOPAT. Exhibit 15.5 reports the results of this computation. For example, Dollar General's NOPAT market multiple is 15.32, computed as $12,499/$816. We then average the comparables' NOPAT market multiples (from Dollar General and Big Lots) to get 12.50, computed as (15.32 + 9.67)/2. This market multiple is used to estimate the company intrinsic value of **Family Dollar** as follows:

Company intrinsic value = Net operating profit after tax × NOPAT market multiple

$4,575   = $366   ×   12.50

EXHIBIT 15.5   Estimating Intrinsic Value Using a Net Operating Profit after Tax Multiple

(in millions, except per share amounts)	Family Dollar	Dollar General	Big Lots
Company assumed value...........................	—	$12,499	$2,165
Net operating profit after tax	$ 366	$ 816	$ 224
Common shares outstanding......................	130.5 shares	341.5 shares	73.9 shares
NOPAT market multiple	12.50	15.32	9.67
Company intrinsic value..........................	$4,575		
Equity intrinsic value............................	$4,976		
Equity intrinsic value per share..................	$38.13		

To obtain Family Dollar's equity intrinsic value we subtract net nonoperating obligations (in Exhibit 15.1) from company value, which is then divided by shares outstanding to yield the per share intrinsic value of its common equity as follows:

Equity intrinsic value = Company intrinsic value − Net nonoperating obligations

$4,976   = $4,575   − $(401)

Then,

$$\text{Equity intrinsic value per share} = \frac{\text{Equity intrinsic value}}{\text{Common shares outstanding}}$$

$$\$38.13 = \frac{\$4,976}{130.5 \text{ shares}}$$

This estimate suggests that Family Dollar was overvalued with respect to its $43.34 closing price at its fiscal year-end (and vis-à-vis its $46.37 price on the filing date). The estimated value would have been different had we used Dollar General's market multiple alone (Family Dollar would have been estimated to be undervalued at its fiscal year-end), and yet again different if we had used Big Lots' multiple alone, and yet again different if we had computed a weighted average. This shows the key role of the market multiple.

Valuation Using a Net Income (NI) Multiple

We can repeat the analysis above using a net income multiple as the basis for valuing the company. This approach produces the intrinsic value of the equity, not of the entire company. This method relies on different data and, as such, we will not get the same intrinsic values computed in the prior section.

EXHIBIT 15.6 Estimating Intrinsic Value Using a Net Income Multiple

(in millions, except per share amounts)	Family Dollar	Dollar General	Big Lots
Equity assumed value	—	$9,699	$2,351
Net income	$ 358	$ 628	$ 223
Common shares outstanding	130.5 shares	341.5 shares	73.9 shares
NI market multiple	12.99	15.44	10.54
Equity intrinsic value	$4,650		
Equity intrinsic value per share	$35.63		

We begin by computing the net income market multiple for both Dollar General and Big Lots, which is computed as equity assumed value divided by net income. Exhibit 15.6 shows the results of this computation. For example, Dollar General's net income market multiple is 15.44, computed as $9,699/$628. We then average the net income market multiples (from Dollar General and Big Lots) to get 12.99, computed as (15.44 + 10.54)/2. This NI market multiple is used to estimate the equity intrinsic value of **Family Dollar** as follows:

$$\textbf{Equity intrinsic value} = \textbf{Net income} \times \textbf{NI market multiple}$$
$$\$4,650 \quad = \quad \$358 \quad \times \quad 12.99$$

To obtain Family Dollar's equity intrinsic value per share we divide by shares outstanding as follows:

$$\textbf{Equity intrinsic value per share} = \frac{\textbf{Equity intrinsic value}}{\textbf{Common shares outstanding}}$$
$$\$35.63 \quad = \quad \frac{\$4,650}{130.5 \text{ shares}}$$

The $35.63 stock price estimate suggests that Family Dollar stock was slightly overvalued based on a $43.34 closing price at its fiscal year-end (and vis-à-vis its $46.37 price on the filing date). The estimated value would have been different had we used Dollar General's market multiple alone, and yet again different if we had used Big Lots' multiple alone, and again different if we had computed a weighted average.

It is again useful for us to compare estimates of Family Dollar's intrinsic value of equity using the NOPAT multiple vis-à-vis the NI multiple. Using the NOPAT multiple, we estimated the intrinsic value of a share of Family Dollar to be $38.13, while the NI market multiple gave an estimate of $35.63. How do we assess the quality of the different estimates? The estimate using the NOPAT market multiple is likely better (for the same reasons that the NOA multiple was superior to the BV multiple for balance sheet methods). That is, we did not select comparables with similar capital structures. When selecting comparables, we should select firms that are similar on profitability, growth, and risk. Although the comparables do control for operating risk, by choosing companies in the same industry, we did not control for financial risk. Consequently, because financial risk affects the equity value, but not the company value, we prefer the NOPAT multiple.

This means the different capital structures of Family Dollar, Dollar General, and Big Lots do not matter when applying NOPAT multiples in valuation. But, when using net income multiples to estimate intrinsic value, it is important to select comparables with similar capital structures.

Valuation Using Industry-Based Multiples

Some industries have specific measures related to characteristics of the industry that are closely watched by investors and analysts. For example, in the retail industry *sales per square foot of selling space* is a common measure used to understand the sales each location is able to generate relative to its size. Another example is the airline industry, which focuses on revenues, expenses or profits per *available seat mile* (one aircraft seat flown one mile, whether occupied or not). These measures can be used to create additional "industry-based" multiples that can be examined in valuing a company.

To illustrate the use of an industry-based multiple to estimate value, and using data from the MD&A section of the 10K, we find in fiscal year 2010 that Family Dollar sales per square foot of selling space was approximately $163. In contrast, Dollar General and Big Lots had sales per square foot of selling space of $201 and $166, respectively. Exhibit 15.7 shows the results of this analysis for these three companies. The $38.98 stock price estimate suggests that Family Dollar stock was slightly overvalued based on a $43.34 closing price at its fiscal year-end (and vis-à-vis its $46.37 price on the filing date).

EXHIBIT 15.7 Estimating Intrinsic Value Using an Industry-Based Multiple

(in millions, except per share amounts)	Family Dollar	Dollar General	Big Lots
Equity assumed value	—	$9,699	$2,351
Sales per square foot	$ 163	$ 201	$ 166
Common shares outstanding	130.5 shares	341.5 shares	73.9 shares
Sales per square foot market multiple	31.21	48.25	14.16
Equity intrinsic value	$5,087		
Equity intrinsic value per share	$38.98		

The limitations of the use of an industry-based multiple must be recognized. In this case, we are using a measure that focuses on sales rather than focusing on profitability. Further, if the company we are trying to value has a different cost structure than its comparables, this will add error to our estimation.

Combining Estimates from Differing Multiples

In prior sections we arrived at a variety of estimates of the value of Family Dollar. Rather than attempting to weigh the merits of the different estimates, some investors prefer to combine them in the hope that estimation error for a specific multiple is mitigated by other multiples. This combination is typically done using a simple average of the estimates. Consider the following example in Exhibit 15.8, which combines the various estimates that we previously computed for Family Dollar. In the first column we exclude the estimate based on sales-per-square-foot, whereas the second column excludes the estimate based on NOA. We do this to show the sensitivity to this combination method.

EXHIBIT 15.8 Combining Estimates of Equity Intrinsic Value per Share

Multiple Used	Estimate #1	Estimate #2
Net Operating Assets	$21.30	—
Book Value	$26.59	$26.59
Net Operating Profit after Tax	$38.13	$38.13
Net Income	$35.63	$35.63
Sales per Square Foot	–	$38.98
Average of Estimates	**$30.41**	**$34.83**

By choosing to compute an estimate that includes sales-per-square-foot and not NOA, we get an average estimate of $34.83, which is more than 10% higher than the $30.41 estimate of the intrinsic value of Family Dollar that excludes sales-per-square-foot. Before deciding what multiples to use and how we might appropriately weight them, we must understand more about the purpose and role of selecting comparable companies.

MID-MODULE REVIEW 2

The table below reports summary data for Johnson & Johnson (JNJ), along with that for Procter & Gamble and Merck, two large cap firms that compete in many segments of JNJ's medical and consumer products businesses.

(in millions)	Johnson & Johnson	Procter & Gamble	Merck
Company assumed value.	—	$238,532	$ 99,560
Equity assumed value	—	$203,325	$103,315
Net operating profit after tax	$10,563	$ 11,188	$ 4,181
Net income.	$11,053	$ 10,340	$ 4,434
Net nonoperating obligations (assets)	$ 6,576	$ 35,212	$ (3,750)
Common shares outstanding.	2,893 shares	3,132 shares	2,168 shares

Required

a. Estimate the NOPAT market multiple for Procter & Gamble and for Merck. Then, compute the average of these as the NOPAT market multiple for valuation. If we believed that one company's multiple was more reliable than another, how could be adjust our estimation?

b. Use the results from part a to estimate the company intrinsic value, the equity intrinsic value, and the equity intrinsic value per share for JNJ.

c. Compute the NI multiple (also called equity-to-income) for Procter & Gamble and for Merck. Then, compute the average of these as the NI market multiple for valuation.

d. Use the results from part c to estimate equity intrinsic value and the equity intrinsic value per share for JNJ.

The solution is on page 15-37.

SELECTING COMPARABLES FOR MARKET MULTIPLES

When valuing companies using market multiples, it is important to select comparables similar on profitability, growth, and risk. We begin this section by demonstrating how theoretically correct market multiples can be derived from the residual income operating (ROPI) model. We then examine how such multiples change with variations in key characteristics of the comparables.

LO3 Identify comparable companies for use in company valuation with market multiples.

It is important for us to remember that all market multiples, except industry-based multiples, illustrated in the previous sections can be derived from the residual income operating model. However, in this section we limit ourselves to the Price-to-Book (the BV multiple used earlier) and Price-to-Earnings (the NI multiple used earlier) multiples. The reason is that they are the multiples most commonly used in practice. This section describes how key factors—such as profitability, growth, and operating risk—should guide our selection of comparables. However, as we explained in previous sections, choosing comparables for NOA and NOPAT multiples does not depend on similar capital structures.

Deriving Price-to-Book from Residual Operating Income Model

Recall from Module 14 the following residual operating income (ROPI) model.

> **Firm value = NOA + Present value of expected ROPI, discounted using r$_w$**

Specifically, residual operating income is operating income in excess of a fair rate of return on beginning net operating assets:

$$\mathbf{ROPI} = \mathbf{NOPAT} - (\mathbf{NOA_{Beg}} \times \mathbf{r_w})$$

where

$\mathbf{NOA_{Beg}}$ = Net operating assets at beginning of period

$\mathbf{r_w}$ = Weighted average cost of capital

If we divide both sides of the ROPI model by book value of equity (OE), we have a formula for the price-to-book, or PB, ratio (we exclude the algebraic derivation):

$$\mathbf{PB} = 1 + \frac{\textbf{Present value of expected ROPI, discounted using } \mathbf{r_w}}{\mathbf{OE}}$$

This formula reveals the parameters determining PB ratios: residual operating income, the expected growth rate in residual operating income, the weighted average cost of capital, and the company's leverage—OE is less for companies with debt in their capital structure. From this formula we can show that companies which are expected to generate no future residual operating income should sell at book value and carry a PB of 1. Companies with lower profitability, lower expected growth rates, and higher discount rates should sell at lower PB ratios. Companies with higher profitability, higher expected growth rates, and lower discount rates should sell at higher PB ratios. Further, levered companies will sell at higher PB ratios than unlevered companies. We explain these relations in the next section.

PB Ratios in Relation to Profitability, Growth, and Risk

The parameters determining PB are readily identified if we assume a simple model for future residual operating income. One simple model assumes that residual operating income grows at a constant rate, g, in perpetuity. Using the formula for the present value of a perpetuity, we express the present value of residual income as follows:

$$\textbf{Present value of expected ROPI} = \frac{\textbf{Expected ROPI}}{\mathbf{r_w} - \mathbf{g}}$$

where

Expected ROPI is for period $t + 1$

g is the growth rate in ROPI each period

$\mathbf{r_w}$ is the weighted average cost of capital

We use this model in the following sections to value the present value of expected residual operating income for purposes of illustrating the relation between PB ratios and the factors of profitability, growth rates, operating risk, and leverage.

PB Increases with Company Expected Profitability

Exhibit 15.9 reports data for two companies with identical net operating assets (of $100) and identical capital structures (all equity). Company A has RNOA (and ROE) of 22%, while Company B has RNOA (and ROE) of 14%. We assume these companies have the same operating risk (with a weighted average cost of capital of 10%), and we expect perpetual growth in residual operating income equal to 2% for both.

Using the model for the present value of a perpetuity with growth of g (which is Value = Amount/[r − g]), we determine the present value of expected future ROPI for Company A as $150, computed as $12/(0.10-0.02). The present value for the low profitability Company B is $50.

EXHIBIT 15.9	PB in Relation to Profitability							
	Net operating assets	Owners' equity	RNOA	ROE	Weighted average cost of capital	Residual operating income	Expected growth rate in ROPI	Present value of expected ROPI using r_w	Value of equity
Company A: High profitability	$100	$100	22%	22%	10%	$12	2%	$150	$250
Company B: Low profitability........	$100	$100	14%	14%	10%	$ 4	2%	$ 50	$150

Next, we compute the value of the equity for the high profitability Company A as $250, computed as $100 in NOA plus the $150 present value of future ROPI. Similarly, the low profitability Company B's value of equity is $150, computed as $100 in NOA plus the $50 present value.

From these results we obtain the theoretically correct equity multiple for the high profitability Company A of 2.5, computed as 1 plus the quantity of the $150 present value divided by the $100 owners' equity. Similarly, the low profitability Company B's multiple is 1.5, computed as 1 plus the quantity of the $50 present value divided by the $100 owners' equity. These results yield the following inference: **PB increases with company expected profitability**.

PB Increases with Company Expected Growth

Exhibit 15.10 reports data for two companies with identical net operating assets ($100), capital structures, and profitability. Both companies have RNOA (and ROE) of 22%, and have similar operating risk (with a weighted average cost of capital of 10%). However, Company C is a high growth firm, with a perpetual growth rate of 4%, compared to a growth rate of 0% for Company D. (Recall that a zero growth rate in ROPI does not imply a zero growth rate in net income.)

Using the formula for the present value of a perpetuity with growth of g, we find the present value of expected future residual income for the high growth Company C is $200, computed as $12/(0.10 − 0.04). For the no growth Company D, the present value is $120, computed as $12/(0.10 − 0.00).

EXHIBIT 15.10	PB in Relation to Growth								
	Net operating assets	Owners' equity	RNOA	ROE	Weighted average cost of capital	Residual operating income	Expected growth rate in ROPI	Present value of expected ROPI using r_w	Value of equity
Company C: High growth..........	$100	$100	22%	22%	10%	$12	4%	$200	$300
Company D: Low growth..........	$100	$100	22%	22%	10%	$12	0%	$120	$220

Next, we compute the value of the equity for the high growth Company C as $300, computed as $100 in NOA plus the $200 present value. Similarly, the low growth Company D's value of equity is $220, computed as $100 in NOA plus the $120 present value.

From these results we obtain the theoretically correct equity multiple for the high growth Company C of 3.0, computed as 1 plus the quantity of the $200 present value divided by the $100 owners' equity. Similarly, the low growth Company D's multiple is 2.2, computed as 1 plus the quantity of the $120 present value divided by the $100 owners' equity. These results yield the following inference: **PB increases with company expected growth**.

PB Decreases with Increasing Company Operating Risk

Exhibit 15.11 reports data for two companies with identical net operating assets ($100), identical capital structures (no debt), and identical RNOA of 22%. However, Company E is a high operating risk firm, operating in an industry with high technological uncertainty, while Company F has low operating risk. Accordingly, high risk Company E has a higher cost of capital (15%) compared with the low risk Company F (10%).

Using the formula for the present value of a perpetuity with growth of g, we find the present value of expected future residual income for the high risk Company E is $46.7, computed as $7/(0.15 − 0.00). For the low risk Company F, the present value is $120, computed as $12/(0.10 − 0.00).

EXHIBIT 15.11	PB in Relation to Operating Risk								
	Net operating assets	Owners' equity	RNOA	ROE	Weighted average cost of capital	Residual operating income	Expected growth rate in ROPI	Present value of expected ROPI using r_w	Value of equity
Company E: High operating risk	$100	$100	22%	22%	15%	$7	0%	$46.7	$146.7
Company F: Low operating risk.....	$100	$100	22%	22%	10%	$12	0%	$120	$220

Next, we compute the value of equity for the high risk Company E as $146.7, computed as $100 in NOA plus the $46.7 present value. Similarly, the low risk Company F's value of equity is $220, computed as $100 in NOA plus the $120 present value.

From these results we obtain the theoretically correct equity multiple for the high risk Company E of 1.47, computed as 1 plus the quantity of the $46.7 present value divided by the $100 owners' equity. Similarly, the low risk Company F's multiple is 2.2, computed as 1 plus the quantity of the $120 present value divided by the $100 owners' equity. These results yield the following inference: **PB decreases as company operating risk increases**.

BUSINESS INSIGHT | **Fair Value Accounting and PB Ratios**

The FASB's recent writings suggest a preference for fair value accounting, which it regards as more relevant than historical cost accounting. Beginning in fiscal 2008, companies were permitted, but not necessarily required, to value any financial asset or liability at fair value and to record changes in fair value in income. We should consider this rule when choosing comparables for valuation by market multiples because companies using fair value accounting will tend to have lower PB ratios and more volatile earnings than those using historical cost accounting.

PB Increases with Company Leverage

PB ratios are higher than Price-to-NOA ratios when companies carry debt. The Price-to-NOA ratio is often referred to as an *unlevered PB* ratio. Exhibit 15.12 reports data for two companies with identical net operating assets ($100), identical weighted average cost of capital (10%), identical RNOA of 22%, and identical growth of 0%. However, Company G finances its operations with equity, while Company H finances its operations with $60 of 6% debt and $40 of equity. The cost of equity capital for Company G is 10%, while it is 11.5% for Company H.[2]

Using the formula for the present value of a perpetuity with growth of g, we find the present value of expected future residual income for both the unleveraged and leveraged companies is $120, computed as $12/(0.10-0.00). Consequently, the theoretically correct Price-to-NOA multiple for both companies is 2.2, computed as 1 plus the quantity of the $120 present value divided by the $100 NOA. The unleveraged Company G's PB ratio is the same as its 2.2 Price-to-NOA multiple. However, the PB multiple for the leveraged Company H is 4.0, computed as 1 plus the quantity of the $120 present value divided by the $40 owner's equity.

EXHIBIT 15.12	PB in Relation to Leverage									
	Net operating assets	Debt (6% rate)	Owners' equity	RNOA	ROE	Weighted average cost of capital	Cost of equity capital	Residual operating income	Growth rate in ROPI	Present value of expected ROPI using r_w	Value of equity
Company G: Unleveraged	$100	$ 0	$100	22%	22%	10%	10%	$12	0%	$120	$220
Company H: Leveraged	$100	$60	$ 40	22%	46%	10%	11.5%	$12	0%	$120	$160

Why would we pay more for a dollar of equity than for a dollar of net operating assets? The reason is that for every dollar of net operating assets, the company generates ROPI with a present value of $1.20 ($120/$100). However, for every dollar of equity, the company generates ROPI with a present value of $3 ($120/$40). Accordingly, this scenario shows that levered PB ratios are higher than unlevered PB ratios and yields the following inference: **PB increases with company leverage**.

In sum, when selecting comparable firms to use in valuation based on a multiple of book value, we should select firms with similar operating profitability, similar expected growth, and similar risk—both operating and financial.

---

[2] Recall from Module 12 that the weighted average cost of capital is $r_w = \left(r_d \times \dfrac{IV_{Debt}}{IV_{Firm}} \right) + \left(r_e \times \dfrac{IV_{Equity}}{IV_{Firm}} \right)$. The high leverage Company H has debt of $60, with an after-tax interest rate of 6%. That company's intrinsic value is $220, its intrinsic value of debt is $60, and its intrinsic value of equity is $160.

Quality of Comparables and Simple Controls

Selecting firms with similar operating risk, leverage, and profitability can improve our valuations. Yet, it is unlikely to compensate for the substantive deficiencies in the technique. The table below shows RNOA, leverage, and PB ratios for a set of consumer stocks (pretax ROA is between 8% and 9% for all). We see from this small sample that simple controls—for industry, current profitability, and leverage—explain little of the variation in PB ratios.

Company	RNOA	Debt-to-Equity	PB Ratio
MDC Holdings	8.6%	50.7%	0.9
Dow Jones & Company	8.6	0.0	8.6
Iconix Brand Group	8.7	127.1	2.7
Oxford Industries	8.8	44.2	1.5
Brown Shoe Company	8.8	26.8	1.6
Burger King Holdings	8.8	131.0	4.9
Cabelas	8.8	54.3	2.1
ConAgra Food	8.8	74.6	2.8
Ruddick Corporation	8.9	36.6	2.2
News Corporation	8.9	36.9	1.4
Lifetime Brands	8.9	61.7	1.7
McCormick & Schmicks Seafood Restaurant	8.9	5.2	2.1

MID-MODULE REVIEW 3

The following table reports data for Companies A through E with identical net operating assets ($100), but with differences in debt levels, returns, cost of capital, and growth.

Company	Net operating assets	Debt (6% rate)	Owners' equity	RNOA	ROE	Weighted average cost of capital	Cost of equity capital	Residual operating income	Growth rate in ROPI	Present value of expected ROPI using r_w	Value of company	Value of equity
A	$100	$ 0	$100	16%	16%	10%	10%		2%			
B	$100	$ 0	$100	12%	12%	10%	10%		2%			
C	$100	$ 0	$100	16%	16%	10%	10%		4%			
D	$100	$ 0	$100	16%	16%	12%	12%		2%			
E	$100	$60	$ 40	16%	31%	10%	12.1%		2%			

Required

a. Assume that the present value of expected ROPI follows a perpetuity with growth g (Value = Amount/[r − g]). Determine the theoretically correct PB ratio for each company A through E.

b. State the relation between the PB ratio and that of profitability, expected growth in ROPI, expected operating risk, and financial leverage. Identify two companies for each of the four relations that illustrate that relation (companies can be listed more than once).

The solution is on page 15-37.

Deriving Price-to-Earnings from Residual Operating Income Model

We can derive a model for the theoretical value of the price-to-earnings (PE) ratio using the residual operating income model in a way similar to what we did for the PB model.

$$ PE \approx \left(\frac{1 + r_e}{r_e}\right) \times \left(1 + \left[\frac{\text{Present value of expected changes in RI}}{\text{Earnings}}\right]\right) $$

The derivation is a bit complex, but the intuition is straightforward.[3] That is, the PE ratio equals (approximately[4]) the capitalized value of current income, including normal income and residual income, plus the capitalized present value of changes in future residual income. Also, because we are capitalizing total income, including its operating and nonoperating components, we use the discount rate for equity where the capitalization factor is $(1 + r_e)/r_e$.

To see how the PE formula works, we use the company data from Exhibit 15.12 to determine the theoretical expression for the PE ratio. For the unleveraged company, recall that equity value is $220, computed as the $100 net operating assets plus the $120 present value of ROPI. The cost of equity capital for the unleveraged company is 10%, which means its capitalization factor is 11, computed as $(1 + 0.10)/0.10$. Its net income is $22 (computed from RNOA × NOA), which yields a $242 company value using the capitalized total earnings ($22 × 11). This is near the $220 intrinsic value.[5]

For the leveraged company in Exhibit 15.12, recall that equity value is $160, which equals the $100 net operating assets minus the $60 debt plus the $120 present value of ROPI. The cost of equity capital for the leveraged company is 11.5%, and the capitalization factor is 9.7, computed as $(1 + 0.115)/0.115$. Its net income is $18.4 (computed from RNOA × NOA, less 6% × Debt), which implies a $178 company value using capitalized total earnings ($18.4 × 9.7). This is near the $160 intrinsic value.[6]

PE Ratios in Relation to Profitability, Growth, and Risk

We refer to the formula for the theoretical value of the PE ratio to provide insight into the factors that should affect cross-sectional variation in PE ratios. A review of the formula reveals that only growth and risk affect PE, not profitability. In contrast to the PB ratio, which increases with operating profitability, PE ratios are unaffected by RNOA. Earnings of $10 are capitalized at the same rate, regardless of whether the underlying RNOA is 5% or 50%. However, expected growth in residual income leads to higher PE ratios, and higher cost of equity capital leads to lower PE ratios. Thus, in selecting comparables to use for valuing a firm based on an earnings multiple, we should consider expected earnings growth and risk (both operating and financial risk).

---

[3] We can adapt the ROPI model to express equity value as a function of the book value of owners' equity (OE) and residual income (RI) as follows:

$$\text{Equity value} = OE + \text{Present value of expected RI, discounted using } r_e$$

where: Residual income (RI) is net income in excess of a fair rate of return on beginning equity $= NI - (OE_{Beg} \times r_e)$

  OE_{Beg} = Owners' equity at beginning of the period

  r_e = Cost of equity capital

Let's also recall that Equity value$_0 = BV_0 + \ldots \dfrac{RI_1}{1 + r_e} + \dfrac{RI_2}{(1 + r_e)^2} + \dfrac{RI_3}{(1 + r_e)^3} + \dfrac{RI_4}{(1 + r_e)^4} + \ldots$, and that $RI_t = NI_t - (r_e \times BV_{t-1})$. By adding dividends at time 0 to both sides, expanding the RI terms, and cancelling out common terms, the expression simplifies to Equity$_0 = \dfrac{1 + r_e}{r_e} \times \left(NI_0 + \dfrac{\Delta RI_1}{(1 + r_e)} + \dfrac{\Delta RI_2}{(1 + r_e)^2} + \dfrac{RI_3}{(1 + r_e)^3} + \ldots \right) - \text{Dividend}_0$.

Assuming that the current period dividend is small relative to current equity value, the theoretical PE ratio equals the capitalization factor, $(1 + r_e)/r_e$, times 1 plus the present value of changes in expected residual income.

[4] This is an approximation because on the right hand side we should subtract the current dividend payout ratio. However, in most cases, the current period dividend payout ratio is small relative to other factors, and can be ignored.

[5] This is $22 too high, which is why the expression is approximate. The "error" is because by assuming $100 beginning net operating assets, $22 income, and $100 ending net operating assets, we implicitly assume that all earnings are paid out as dividends. Such dividends are unavailable to increase future earnings, and so are not capitalized. We can correct the capitalization factor by subtracting from it the current dividend payout ratio, in this case $22/$22, or 1. This gives a capitalization factor of 10, which yields the correct intrinsic value of $220, computed as $22 × 10. In practice this correction is rarely made, because the resulting valuation errors are usually small.

[6] Again, this value approximation is high. The "error" is because we assume (see previous footnote) that all earnings are paid out as dividends and so are unavailable to increase future earnings. We can correct the capitalization factor by subtracting from it the current dividend payout ratio, in this case $18.4/$18.4, or 1. This gives the correct capitalization factor of 8.7.

If current earnings are a good forecast of future earnings, then the forward PE ratio (price divided by forecasted EPS) will be close to the trailing PE ratio (price divided by past EPS). If earnings are expected to increase, the forward PE ratio will be lower than the trailing PE ratio, and vice versa. The plot below shows the relation of forward PE ratios to trailing PE ratios in late 2007 for housing stocks. Beginning in mid-2006, home sales and mortgage originations, which had reached record highs, began to decline dramatically. What does the data suggest the market was expecting in terms of forward earnings growth for the typical housing stock? (Hint: Draw the diagonal from the coordinate (0, 0) to (20, 20) and inspect the distribution of observations above and below the line.) We see that the market expected earnings to decline as suggested by the forward PE ratio being higher than the trailing PE ratio.

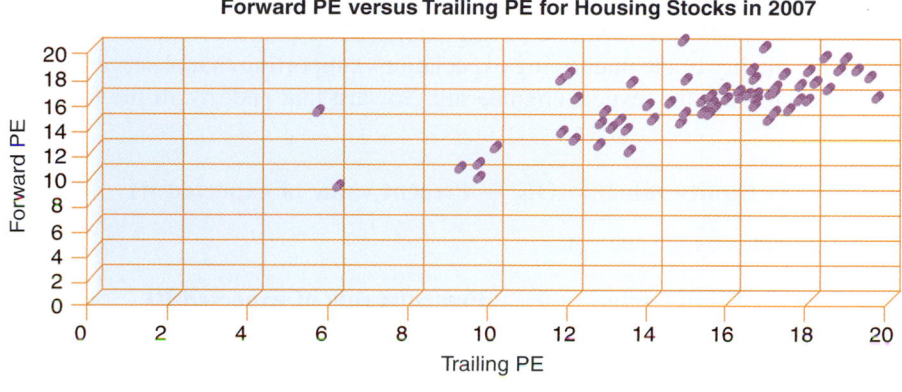

Forward PE versus Trailing PE for Housing Stocks in 2007

MID-MODULE REVIEW 4

Cummins, Inc.'s (CMI) book value of equity is $3,195 million and its forward earnings estimate is $932 million. We also collect the following information for CMI and a peer group of companies (identified by ticker symbol) from the machinery sector.

Ticker	Market Cap* (Millions)	PB (Current)	Forward PE (FY1)	5-Year Historical Growth Rate	ROE (T4Q)	Debt-to-Equity (Prior Year)
CMI.	—	—	—	52%	25%	23%
VOLVY	$35,244	2.89	14.5	45	19	44
PH.	12,512	2.75	14.1	40	19	23
CAT.	45,477	5.28	13.3	40	44	258
DE.	38,443	4.77	17.4	36	22	155
CNH	15,167	2.64	23.8	34	9	80
PCAR	20,035	3.86	16.3	31	28	69
ETN.	13,834	2.92	14.0	29	23	43
DHR	27,424	3.41	22.6	23	20	36
IR	12,186	2.35	12.5	21	30	17
ITW.	28,639	3.05	15.7	20	20	11
ITT	11,473	3.32	17.9	15	24	17

*Market cap refers to market capitalization, or firm value, as perceived by market participants.

Required

a. Identify a set of companies from this list to use as comparables for estimating the equity intrinsic value of CMI using the market multiples approach.
b. Estimate the equity intrinsic value of CMI using PB ratios from the comparable companies. For this part assume the comparables are VOLVY, PH, PCAR, ETN, DHR and IR.
c. Estimate the equity intrinsic value of CMI using PE ratios from the comparable companies. For this part assume the comparables are VOLVY, PH, PCAR, ETN, DHR and IR.

The solution is on page 15-38.

INTERPRETING AND REVERSE ENGINEERING OF MARKET MULTIPLES

Despite problems inherent in using the market multiple method to value companies, the PB and PE ratios are common in the investment world. One reason they are so widely quoted is that they economically convey the market's (combined) expectations about growth rates and discount rates for companies. By making assumptions about one of those two factors, the investor can infer expectations about the other that are impounded in current prices. The section explains how to interpret such multiples and describes the reverse engineering of market multiples to assess observed stock prices.

Interpreting and Reverse Engineering the PB Ratio

Reverse engineering is the process of observing market price metrics such as the PB and PE ratio and assessing the quality of the underlying expectations supporting that observed stock price. The PB ratio is especially apt for reverse engineering. Toward that end, recall the following relation (see footnote 4):

$$\text{Equity value} = \text{OE} + \text{Present value of expected RI}$$

If we divide both sides by OE we get:

$$\frac{\text{Equity value}}{\text{OE}} = 1 + \frac{\text{Present value of expected RI}}{\text{OE}}$$

The left hand side is PB. If we then assume that residual income is a perpetuity (that is, Present value of expected RI = $RI/[r_e - g]$), we can algebraically derive (details not shown for brevity) the following PB formula:

$$\text{PB} = 1 + \frac{\text{Expected ROE} - r_e}{r_e - g}$$

This is a tractable PB formula with three unknowns: Expected ROE, discount rate r_e, and growth rate g. We can manipulate these unknowns to infer the market's expectations about these valuation parameters. Specifically, to infer the value of a specific one we must make assumptions about the other two. This provides us a structure for reasoning about valuation parameters underlying an observed stock price. The illustrations in this module assume stability in the parameters over an infinite horizon. Additional insights are possible from varying the parameters over shorter horizons.

To illustrate, let's take a look at **Limited Brands**, the retail parent company of Victoria's Secret, White Barn Candle Company, C.O. Bigelow, Bath & Body Works, and Henri Bendel. Exhibit 15.13 presents data from Limited Brands as of mid-2011 (based on trailing four quarter data ending July 2011). **Trailing** refers to numbers reported in the prior period, whereas **forward** refers to numbers expected to be reported in the next period.

EXHIBIT 15.13	Financial Information for Limited Brands ($ millions)
Market value of equity	$11,396
Book value of equity.	$ 625
ROE (based on trailing 4 quarters).	67.5%
ROE (based on most recent quarter)	26.4%

The PB ratio for Limited Brands is 18.2, computed as $11,396/$625, which is extremely high. A PB ratio of 1 implies no future residual income and, as such, it is clear that the market expects Limited Brands to generate substantial future residual income. Looking at Limited Brands' current performance, ROE on a trailing four quarter basis is 67.5%, which is also extremely high and unlikely sustainable without the result of leverage. (Limited Brands has substantial debt, so its RNOA is much lower than the 67.5% trailing ROE.) Looking at the most recent quarter, ROE is 26.4%, which suggests a level closer to normal (the difference could also result from seasonality in Limited Brands' sales.)

To help us assess market expectations for Limited Brands we use the above PB formula to investigate scenarios using different combinations of expected ROE, growth rates, and discount rates that would justify a PB ratio of over 18 for Limited Brands. Exhibit 15.14 presents the results of one such process of reverse engineering. The results are organized into three cases, linked to a variation in one of the three parameters, and four scenarios A through D.

Case 1   Case 1 assumes that we know the market's expectation for ROE (67.5% in Scenarios A and B, and 26.4% in Scenarios C and D) and the discount rate (12% in Scenarios A and C, and 10% in Scenarios B and D), and then solve for Limited Brands' implied growth rate. Results show that to support an 18.2 PB ratio, we require a high implied growth rate, ranging from 6.7% to 11.2%, which is high; remember that this rate is assumed to exist in perpetuity.

Case 2   Case 2 assumes that we know the market's expectation for ROE (67.5% in Scenarios A and B, and 26.4% in Scenarios C and D) and the growth rate (5% in Scenarios A and C, and 4% in Scenarios B and D), and then we solve for Limited Brands' implied discount rate. Results show that to support an 18.2 PB ratio, we require a discount rate between 5.2% and 8.4%.

Case 3   Case 3 assumes that we know the market's expectation about the discount rate (10% in Scenarios A and B, and 9% in Scenarios C and D) and growth rate (7% in Scenarios A and C, and 6% in Scenarios B and D), and then we solve for Limited Brands' implied ROE. Results show that Limited Brands must maintain a high level of profitability (from 43.4% to 78.8%) in perpetuity to justify its 18.2 PB ratio.

EXHIBIT 15.14	Reverse Engineering of PB Ratio for Limited Brands			
	Scenario A	**Scenario B**	**Scenario C**	**Scenario D**
PB* (equals PB ratio observed − 1)............	17.2	17.2	17.2	17.2
Case 1: Solve for implied growth rate				
Assumed parameters				
ROE.....................................	67.5%	67.5%	26.4%	26.4%
Discount rate, r_e.........................	12.0%	10.0%	12.0%	10.0%
Implied parameter				
Growth rate, $(r_e + [PB^* \times r_e] - ROE)/PB^*$......	8.8%	6.7%	11.2%	9.0%
Case 2: Solve for implied discount rate				
Assumed parameters				
ROE.....................................	67.5%	67.5%	26.4%	26.4%
Growth rate, g...........................	5.0%	4.0%	5.0%	4.0%
Implied parameter				
Discount rate, $(ROE + [PB^* \times g])/(1 + PB^*)$.....	8.4%	7.5%	6.2%	5.2%
Case 3: Solve for implied future ROE				
Assumed parameters				
Discount rate, r_e.........................	10.0%	10.0%	9.0%	9.0%
Growth rate, g...........................	7.0%	6.0%	7.0%	6.0%
Implied parameter				
ROE, $(PB^* \times [r_e - g]) + r_e$.................	61.6%	78.8%	43.4%	60.6%

Interpreting and Reverse Engineering the PE Ratio

Reverse engineering of the PE ratio can also be applied to infer the market's expectations about future earnings, but it is not nearly as tractable as the PB ratio. For the PE ratio, recall that:

$$PE \approx \left(\frac{1 + r_e}{r_e}\right) \times \left(1 + \left[\frac{\text{Present value of expected changes in RI}}{\text{Earnings}}\right]\right)$$

where:

Residual income (RI) = NI − (OE$_{Beg}$ × r$_e$)

OE$_{beg}$ = Owners' equity at beginning of the period

r$_e$ = Cost of equity capital

This formula shows that the PE ratio approximates the capitalization factor ($[1 + r_e]/r_e$), plus an adjustment for expected increases or decreases in future residual income. To illustrate, let's assume a 10% equity cost of capital, which implies a capitalization factor of 11. If investors do not expect residual income to change, then the PE ratio should approximate 11. More precisely, investors can expect income to increase, but only at a rate equal to the change in book value times the 10% cost of equity capital. Further, if investors expect income to increase at a rate higher than 10% times the change in book value, then the PE ratio is predicted to be higher than 11; and vice versa if investors expect income to increase at a rate lower that 10% times the change in book value.

We can use the PE valuation formula and reverse engineer the market's expectations about its valuation parameters and future earnings as we did for PB ratios. However, the results when reverse engineering the PE ratio are not usually intuitive or useful. Still, we often use the PE valuation formula to help us understand why PE ratios differ among industries and companies.

Perspective on Valuation Multiples and Fundamental Analysis

We conclude this module with some perspective on using valuation multiples to value a target company. We also offer some advice on the implementation of valuation multiples.

Process of Fundamental Analysis

This module and the prior three introduced us to four different methods of valuing securities: discounted dividends, discounted cash flows, the residual operating income model, and valuation by market multiples. The first three methods require explicit modeling of a company's future performance, and the use of these forecasts for valuation. The resulting valuation can contain error because the forecasts are wrong, or because the discount rate is wrong, but not because of an inherent problem with the valuation model.

In the case of the fourth method, an investor cannot have the same assurance if market multiples are used as the valuation technique. The method does have some intuitive appeal (and it is easy!) but it does not have rigorous theoretical underpinnings. Many errors can arise. For example, the selection of comparables might not yield peers that are similar on profitability, growth, and risk. Also, the performance metric (earnings or book values) might be unstable over time and be a poor basis for assessing relative value. In addition, the market might be inefficient, so that using prices of comparables to infer the value of a target company simply compounds error. Nonetheless, market multiples are widely used and, if applied with discretion, are sometimes useful for our analysis.

Implementation of Valuation Multiples

If we use market multiples for company valuation, there are at least three steps we should take in implementing this method. First, whenever possible, use forward-looking performance measures to compute the market multiples for comparable companies. Prices are forward-looking and reflect expected future performance of a company, not past performance. Further, use an estimate of the target company's future performance to multiply by the forward-looking market multiple. Forward-looking estimates are especially important for earnings multiples as earnings are more volatile than book values. Second, select comparable companies with care so as to match them on profitability, growth, and risk profiles to those of our target company. Third, use both income-statement-based and balance-sheet-based valuation multiples, and possibly consider industry-based multiples. This might induce greater variance in the estimated value of our target company. However, as unsettling as this can be, it requires us to directly consider the reliability of those estimates and the inputs underlying them.

Fischer Black argued in an article, *The Magic in Earnings* (1980), that investors want an earnings number that they can use to determine value. He provocatively proposed that accountants adopt as their main objective the creation of an earnings number that can be multiplied by a constant (such as 10) to yield value. This accounting model would render the balance sheet superfluous to investors. He suggested that accountants were surprisingly close to producing such a number, as evidenced by the relatively low variance in PE ratios. Whatever you believe the merits of his suggestion, recent actions by the FASB to move from historical cost accounting toward fair value accounting inverts Fischer Black's suggestion in that the FASB moves the balance sheet closer to the primary indicator of company value and the income statement toward superfluous status.

MODULE-END REVIEW

Johnson & Johnson's (JNJ) current market cap is $191 billion, its book value of equity is $39.3 billion, and its trailing four quarters ROE is about 26%, with an average 13% ROE for seven health care peers. JNJ's five-year average sales growth is 10%, with an average of 13% for its peer group; and, its five-year average EPS growth is 14%, with an average of 5% for its peer group.

	Scenario A	Scenario B	Scenario C	Scenario D
PB* (equals PB ratio observed − 1)............	3.9	3.9	3.9	3.9
Case 1: Solve for implied growth rate				
Assumed parameters				
ROE.................................	26.0%	13.0%	26.0%	13.0%
Discount rate, r_e.........................	7.0%	7.0%	9.0%	9.0%
Implied parameter				
Growth rate, $(r_e + [PB^* \times r_e] - ROE)/PB^*$......	_____	_____	_____	_____
Case 2: Solve for implied discount rate				
Assumed parameters				
ROE.................................	26.0%	13.0%	26.0%	13.0%
Growth rate, g	3.0%	3.0%	5.0%	5.0%
Implied parameter				
Discount rate, $(ROE + [PB^* \times g])/(1 + PB^*)$.....	_____	_____	_____	_____
Case 3: Solve for implied future ROE				
Assumed parameters				
Discount rate, r_e.........................	7.0%	9.0%	7.0%	9.0%
Growth rate, g	3.0%	3.0%	5.0%	5.0%
Implied parameter				
ROE, $(PB^* \times [r_e - g]) + r_e$.................	_____	_____	_____	_____

Required

a. Using the assumptions in Case 1, compute the growth rate implied by JNJ's PB ratio for each Scenario A through D.

b. Using the assumptions in Case 2, compute the discount rate implied by JNJ's PB ratio for each Scenario A through D.

c. Using the assumptions in Case 3, compute the ROE implied by JNJ's PB ratio for each Scenario A through D.

d. Based on your analysis in parts *a*, *b* and *c*, do you believe the current PB ratio for JNJ reflects reasonable expectations about its future performance?

The solution is on page 15-38.

GUIDANCE ANSWERS . . . ANALYSIS DECISION

You Are an Entrepreneur You should point out that Oracle and SAP are more mature companies and probably have lower expected growth than your firm. You could find some publicly-traded start-up software firms that have also experienced losses and suggest using those as comparables. Alternatively, you could suggested a valuation based on discounted cash flows or residual income. You might also suggest that part of the buyout price be contigent on the future performance of your firm.

DISCUSSION QUESTIONS

Q15-1. Identify the advantages of valuation using market multiples compared to valuation using discounted cash flows or discounted residual operating income.

Q15-2. Identify the disadvantages of valuation using market multiples compared to valuation using discounted cash flows or discounted residual operating income.

Q15-3. This module referred to the residual operating income model described in Module 14. Explain what a company-value-to-net-operating-assets ratio equal to 1 implies about future residual operating income.

Q15-4. Describe the factors that should be considered in choosing comparable companies for computation of the market multiples company-value-to-net-operating-assets and the price-to-book-value.

Q15-5. The "E" in the PE ratio can be determined in several ways. Identify at least three different variations in measuring earnings for the PE ratio.

Q15-6. Referring to residual income, PE can be expressed in terms of cost of equity capital, the present value of expected changes in residual income, dividends, and earnings. Explain what a PE ratio of 11 implies about market growth expectations for a company with a cost of equity capital equal to 10%. Do the same analysis for a PE greater than 11 and less than 11.

Q15-7. Barron's Online posted the following headline in early October 2007: "Cisco: Goldman Ups Target On 'Stronger Multiple Outlook'." Explain what this headline means.

Assignments with the ✔ logo in the margin are available in an online homework system.
See the Preface of the book for details.

MINI EXERCISES

BURGER KING CORPORATION
(BKC)

M15-8. Valuation using a Balance Sheet Multiple (LO1)
Burger King Corporation reports total book value of $796 million and common shares outstanding of 135.7 million. The average PB ratio for restaurant companies is 7.1. Using the industry average PB ratio, estimate the intrinsic value of Burger King's equity.

BUILD-A-BEAR WORKSHOP
(BBW)

M15-9. Valuation using a Balance Sheet Multiple (LO1)
Build-a-Bear Workshop, Inc., reports a book value per share of $9.55. The industry average PB ratio for toy and hobby stores is 2.3. Using the industry average PB ratio, estimate the intrinsic value of Build-a-Bear's equity per share.

JAKKS PACIFIC
(JAKK)

M15-10. Valuation using an Income Statement Multiple (LO2)
JAKKS Pacific, Inc., a toy manufacturer, reports net income for the recent twelve months of $90 million. JAKKS' has 28.6 million shares outstanding. The industry average PE (using the trailing twelve months earnings) for its competitors is 14.25. Using this industry average PE, estimate the intrinsic value of Jakk Pacific's equity.

MOTOROLA, INC.
(MOT)

M15-11. Valuation using an Income Statement Multiple (LO2)
Motorola, Inc., was trading at $9.65 per share. Earnings estimates for the next 12 months were $0.62 per share. The industry average forward PE ratio is 10.4. Using the industry average forward PE, estimate the intrinsic value of Motorola's equity per share.

M15-12. Determining PB Ratio for Companies with Different Returns **(LO3)**

Assume that the present value of expected ROPI follows a perpetuity with growth g (Value = Amount/[r − g]). Determine the theoretically correct PB ratio for each of the following companies A and B.

Company	Net operating assets	Equity	RNOA	ROE	Weighted average cost of capital	Growth rate in ROPI
A.............	$100	$100	18%	18%	10%	2%
B.............	$100	$100	11%	11%	10%	2%

M15-13. Determining PB Ratio for Companies with Different Returns and Growth **(LO3)**

Assume that the present value of expected ROPI follows a perpetuity with growth g (Value = Amount/[r − g]). Determine the theoretically correct PB ratio for each of the following companies A and B.

Company	Net operating assets	Equity	RNOA	ROE	Weighted average cost of capital	Growth rate in ROPI
A.............	$100	$100	18%	18%	10%	2%
B.............	$100	$100	11%	11%	10%	4%

M15-14. Determining PB Ratio for Companies with Different Returns and Cost of Capital **(LO3)**

Assume that the present value of expected ROPI follows a perpetuity with growth g (Value = Amount/[r − g]). Determine the theoretically correct PB ratio for each of the following companies A and B.

Company	Net operating assets	Equity	RNOA	ROE	Weighted average cost of capital	Growth rate in ROPI
A.............	$100	$100	18%	18%	15%	2%
B.............	$100	$100	11%	11%	10%	2%

M15-15. Determining PB Ratio for Companies with Different Capitalization **(LO3)**

Assume that the present value of expected ROPI follows a perpetuity with growth g (Value = Amount/[r − g]). Determine the theoretically correct PB ratio for each of the following companies A and B.

Company	Net operating assets	Debt (6% rate)	Equity	RNOA	ROE	Weighted average cost of capital	Growth rate in ROPI
A.............	$100	$ 0	$100	11%	11.0%	10%	0%
B.............	$100	$60	$ 40	11%	18.5%	10%	0%

M15-16. Identifying Comparables for Valuation **(LO3)**

Which would be a better comparable to use in valuing **Chiquita Brands** using a PB ratio-based multiple: **Fresh Del Monte Produce** or **Lancaster Colony**? Explain your answer without reference to the actual PB ratios.

Company	5-Year Historical EPS Growth Rate	ROE T4Q	Debt-to-Equity Last Qtr	PB Current
Chiquita Brands Intl	(0.26)	(0.06)	0.89	1.05
Fresh Del Monte Produce	(0.07)	(0.03)	0.33	1.96
Lancaster Colony	(0.02)	0.10	0.12	2.71

M15-17. Identifying Comparables for Valuation   (LO3)

Which would be a better comparable to use in valuing **Synutra International** using a PE ratio-based multiple: **Sara Lee Corporation, Wimm-Bill-Dann Foods,** or **Hershey Company**? Explain your answer without reference to the actual PE ratios.

Company	Estimated Earnings Growth	ROE	Debt-to-Equity	Forward PE
Synutra International	0.39	0.34	0.24	42.94
Sara Lee Corporation	0.19	0.23	0.80	13.49
Wimm-Bill-Dann Foods	0.42	0.23	0.24	32.23
Hershey Company	(0.11)	0.36	2.16	19.88

M15-18. Identifying Comparables and Valuation using PB and PE   (LO1, 2, 3)

Panera Bread Company's book value per share is $14.17 and its forward earnings estimate per share is $2.02. The following information is also available for Panera and a peer group of companies (identified by ticker symbol) from the restaurant sector.

Ticker	Market Cap ($ mil.)	PB Current	Forward PE (FY1)	EPS 5-Year Historical Growth Rate	ROE (T 4Q)	Debt-to-Equity (Prior Year)
PNRA	—	—	—	15.3%	13.3%	0.17
PFCB	$ 689.2	2.3	21.3	6.1%	10.2%	0.32
BWLD	416.0	2.9	17.8	21.5%	15.2%	0.00
PZZA	702.2	5.5	14.4	(15.8)%	23.8%	1.06
CPKI	379.3	1.7	23.6	(7.3)%	6.8%	0.00
PEET	320.6	2.2	28.8	11.7%	6.1%	0.00
SONC	1,264.2	(12.4)	19.0	(3.3)%	(102.3)%	(7.33)
TXRH	717.6	2.0	17.1	(20.6)%	11.4%	0.18
RRGB	609.7	2.1	16.9	19.0%	11.7%	0.50

Required

a. Identify a set of three companies from this list to use as comparables for estimating the equity intrinsic value of Panera using the market multiples approach.

b. Assume that you use as comparables the following set of companies: PFCB, BWLD, and RRGB. Estimate Panera's equity intrinsic value per share using the PB ratio from these peer companies.

c. Use the same comparables as in part b and estimate Panera's equity intrinsic value per share using the PE ratio from these peer companies.

M15-19. Determining ROE and Assessing Market Expectations   (LO4)

The PB, trailing PE, and forward PE data follow for four companies. Determine the current ROE for each company. Which company do you believe the market expects to have the highest future ROE? Explain.

Company	PB	Trailing PE	Forward PE
Apple	11	48	30
Autozone	45	14	11
Coinstar	2.4	42	35
Schwab	2.1	11	21

M15-20. Determining ROE and Assessing Market Expectations   (LO4)

Refer to the information in M15-19. Which company do you believe the market expects to experience a decline in earnings? Explain.

EXERCISES

E15-21. Valuation Using Price-to-NOA Multiple   (LO1)

The following table provides summary data for **Cerner Corporation** and its competitors, **Eclipsys Corporation** and **McKesson Corporation**.

(in millions)	Cerner	Eclipsys	McKesson
Company assumed value.........................	—	$1,120	$17,519
Equity assumed value	—	$1,120	$15,570
Net operating assets	$1,328	$ 258	$ 8,454
Book value of equity............................	$1,132	$ 258	$ 6,505
Net nonoperating obligations (assets)	$ 192	$ 0	$ 1,949
Common shares outstanding......................	80.4 shares	54.0 shares	288.8 shares

Required

a.   Compute the price to net operating assets ratio for both Eclipsys and McKesson.

b.   Use Eclipsys and McKesson as comparables, along with the price to NOA ratios from part a, and then estimate for Cerner its company intrinsic value, its equity intrinsic value, and its equity intrinsic value per share.

E15-22. Valuation Using the PB Multiple   (LO1)

Refer to information in E15-21 to complete the requirements.

Required

a.   Compute the PB ratio for both Eclipsys and McKesson.

b.   Use Eclipsys and McKesson as comparables, along with the PB ratios from part b, and then estimate for Cerner its equity intrinsic value and its equity intrinsic value per share.

E15-23. Valuation Using Price-to-NOPAT Multiple   (LO2)

The following table provides summary data for **Applied Materials** and its competitors, **KLA Tencor Corporation** and **Lam Research Corporation**.

(in millions)	Applied Materials	KLA Tencor	Lam Research
Company assumed value........................	—	$6,890	$5,720
Equity assumed value	—	$6,890	$5,370
NOPAT	$1,591	$474.2	$647.3
Net Income...................................	$1,570	$474.2	$637.7
Net nonoperating obligations (assets)	$ 205	$ 0	$ 350
Common shares outstanding......................	1,350 shares	180.1 shares	135.1 shares

Required

a.   Compute the price to NOPAT ratio for both KLA Tencor Corporation and Lam Research Corporation.

b.   Use KLA Tencor Corporation and Lam Research Corporation as comparables, along with the price to NOPAT ratios from part a, and then estimate for Applied Materials its company intrinsic value, its equity intrinsic value, and its equity intrinsic value per share.

E15-24. Valuation Using the PE Multiple   (LO1)

Refer to information in E15-23 to complete the requirements.

Required

a.   Compute the price to net income ratio for both **KLA Tencor Corporation** and **Lam Research Corporation**.

b.   Use KLA Tencor Corporation and Lam Research Corporation as comparables, along with the price to net income ratios from part a, and then estimate for **Applied Materials** its equity intrinsic value and its equity intrinsic value per share.

NOKIA, INC.
(NOK)
MOTOROLA MOBILITY
(MMI)
L. M. ERICSSON
(ERIC)

E15-25. Valuation Using the PE Multiple (LO1)

Nokia, Inc., recently traded at $5.66 per share. At that time, earnings per share estimates for the next 12 months were $0.36. In addition, **Motorola Mobility** and **L.M. Ericsson** had forward PE ratios of 28.03 and 14.64, respectively.

Required

a. Using Motorola and Ericsson as comparables, estimate the intrinsic value of Nokia's equity per share.

b. Does the estimate in part *a* suggest that Nokia is undervalued or overvalued? Explain.

MCCORMICK & COMPANY
(MKC)

E15-26. Identifying Comparables and Estimating Equity Value using PB (LO1, 3)

Assume that you wish to estimate the equity intrinsic value of **McCormick & Company** using PB ratios for comparable companies. The following online data are available from companies.

Company	PB Current	EPS 5-Year Historical Growth Rate	ROE (T 4Q)	Debt-to-Equity (Prior Q)
McCormick & Co Inc	4.20	0.09	0.23	0.53
Wm Wrigley Jr Co.......	5.84	0.08	0.25	0.35
Tyson Foods Inc	1.24	(0.06)	0.05	0.54
Flowers Foods Inc	3.47	0.20	0.15	0.04

Required

a. Identify two of the three companies as better comparables for use in valuation of McCormick. Explain your reasoning. (*Hint*: Consider each company on the basis of profitability, growth, and financial risk.)

b. Explain your rationale for eliminating the third company in part *a*.

KELLOGG COMPANY
(K)

E15-27. Identifying Comparables and Estimating Equity Value using PE (LO1, 3)

Assume that you wish to estimate the equity intrinsic value of **Kellogg Company** using PE ratios for comparable companies. The following online data are available from companies.

Company	Forward PE	Estimated Earnings Growth	ROE	Debt-to-Equity
Kellogg Co..................	16.80	0.09	0.47	1.30
Bunge Limited..............	13.81	0.04	0.14	0.52
General Mills Inc............	16.61	0.10	0.22	0.63
Hormel Foods Corporation...	17.31	0.11	0.16	0.19
Ralcorp Holdings, Inc........	15.26	0.07	0.14	1.37

Required

a. Identify two of the four companies as better comparables for use in valuation of Kellogg. Explain your reasoning. (*Hint*: Consider each company on the basis of profitability, growth, and financial risk.)

b. Explain your reasoning for eliminating the two companies in part *a*.

HOT TOPIC, INC.
(HOTT)

E15-28. Identifying Comparables and Valuation using PB and PE (LO1, 2, 3)

Hot Topic, Inc.'s book value of equity is $235 million and its forward earnings estimate per share is $0.38, or $16.7 million in total earnings. The following information is also available for Hot Topic and a peer group of companies (identified by ticker symbol) from the specialty retail sector.

Ticker	Market Cap ($ mil.)	PB Current	Forward PE (FY1)	EPS 5-Year Historical Growth Rate	ROE (T 4Q)	Debt-to-Equity (Prior Year)
HOTT....	—	—	—	(21.2)%	5.9%	0.00
PLCE....	$ 595.1	1.1	14.7	11.8%	8.4%	0.00
JOSB....	439.5	1.9	9.1	14.4%	22.5%	0.00
ZUMZ ...	492.5	3.2	18.5	27.4%	19.8%	0.00
GYMB ...	1,126.3	5.7	13.0	28.5%	33.5%	0.00
MW	1,217.0	1.5	11.8	28.6%	23.5%	0.11

continued

continued from prior page

TWB.....	437.4	2.5	9.2	4.6%	17.3%	1.02
CBK.....	375.7	1.6	17.4	(11.6)%	11.8%	0.00
FINL.....	289.2	0.7	16.3	(7.7)%	(0.1)%	0.00
SSI......	515.0	1.0	11.9	(7.1)%	11.0%	0.20
DBRN ...	751.6	1.5	11.4	(0.7)%	16.9%	0.28

Required

a. Identify a set of three companies from this list to use as comparables for estimating the equity intrinsic value of Hot Topic using the market multiples approach.

b. Assume that you use as comparables the following set of companies: CBK, FINL, and SSI. Estimate Hot Topic's equity intrinsic value using the PB ratio from these peer companies.

c. Use the same comparables as in part b and estimate Hot Topic's equity intrinsic value using the PE ratio from these peer companies.

E15-29. Identifying Comparables and Valuation using PB and PE   (LO1, 2, 3)

Fossil, Inc.'s book value of equity is $772 million and its forward earnings estimate per share is $2.14, or $147 million in total. The following information is also available for Fossil and a peer group of companies (identified by ticker symbol) from the specialty retail sector.

FOSSIL, INC.
(FOSL)

Ticker	Market Cap ($ mil.)	PB Current	Forward PE (FY1)	EPS 5-Year Historical Growth Rate	ROE (T 4Q)	Debt-to-Equity (Prior Year)
FOSL.....	—	—	14.5	7.0%	18.4%	0.01
DECK.....	$1,449.4	4.9	18.2	71.5%	27.5%	0.00
KSWS	554.0	1.4	55.3	(12.6)%	10.6%	0.00
MOV......	361.2	0.8	11.2	9.2%	15.0%	0.11
ZQK......	1,223.6	1.4	17.0	(24.7)%	(15.9)%	0.85
SKX	813.1	1.3	9.3	6.7%	13.2%	0.03
PERY.....	313.0	1.2	10.8	5.7%	11.4%	0.74
UNF	865.7	1.7	14.8	11.3%	9.8%	0.45
WWW.....	1,476.3	3.1	15.6	8.1%	19.2%	0.00
MFB......	368.9	3.7	11.1	33.4%	37.6%	0.89
VLCM.....	475.1	2.7	12.9	16.8%	22.0%	0.00

Required

a. Identify a set of three companies from this list to use as comparables for estimating the equity intrinsic value of Fossil using the market multiples approach.

b. Assume that you use as comparables the following set of companies: MOV, SKX, and WWW. Estimate Fossil's equity intrinsic value using the PB ratio from these peer companies.

c. Use the same comparables as in part b and estimate Fossil's equity intrinsic value using the PE ratio from these peer companies.

E15-30. Theoretical PE for Companies with Zero Expected Growth in Residual Income   (LO3)

The cost of equity capital follows for each of five companies. For each company the expected growth in residual income is zero.

Company	Cost of equity capital
A.............	6%
B.............	9%
C.............	12%
D.............	15%
E.............	18%

a. Determine the theoretically correct PE ratio for each of the companies A through E.

b. In late 2007, approximately one-half of the companies on the New York Stock Exchange had a PE ratio between 12 and 48. Do you believe the range of those PE ratios is primarily related to differences in the cost of equity capital or to differences in expectations about future residual income? Explain.

GOOGLE
(GOOG)
YAHOO
(YHOO)
EBAY
(EBAY)

E15-31. Determining ROE to Yield Projected PB (LO4)

Google recently had a market cap of $194 billion, total equity of $46.2 billion, and 321 million shares outstanding. At about the same time, the PB of **Yahoo** and **eBay** were 1.73 and 2.4, respectively. Assume that we desire a minimum 12% annual return on our investments, and that we believe Google will sell at 2.1 times book value five years from now. What must Google earn (ROE) on average over the next 5 years to make it a worthwhile investment? (Assume that Google pays no dividends.)

E15-32. Explaining Prices relative to NOA and RNOA (LO3, 4)

Summary information for RNOA, NOA growth, price per NOA dollar for a sample of 300 companies follows. Can you explain the behavior in companies' prices from the data provided?

Number of companies	Median RNOA from year t−1 to year t	Median % growth in NOA from year t−1 to year t	Price per dollar of NOA at end of year t
150	20%	(5)%	1.80
150	20%	34%	2.10

E15-33. Linking PB and PE Ratios to ROE (LO3)

The following graphic plots the PE and PB ratio combinations for each of five separate companies A through E. Identify the company with the following description of its current and expected future performance.

_____1. High current profitability, earnings expected to decline but profitability will remain high

_____2. Average current profitability, earnings and profitability expected to remain at the average

_____3. Low current profitability, earnings expected to increase but future profitability will be about average

_____4. High current profitability, profitability will remain high

_____5. High current profitability, earnings expected to decline markedly and profitability will be low

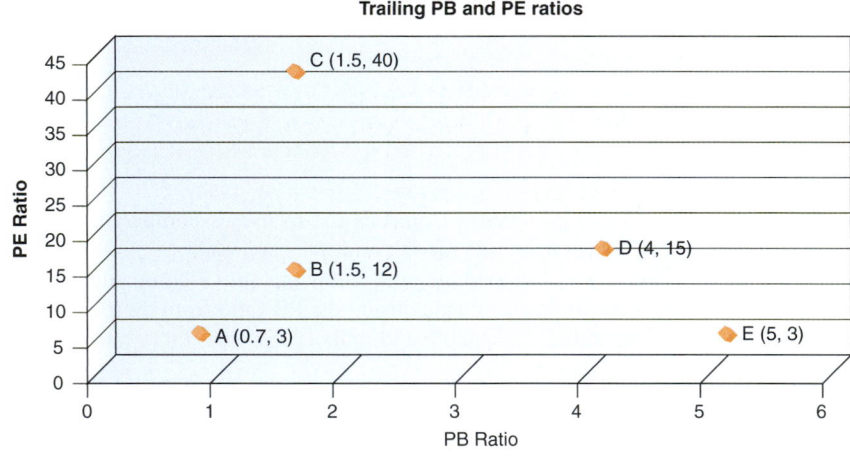

Trailing PB and PE ratios

E15-34. Computing Key Metrics from Financial Data (LO3)

For each of the following company stocks, listed among the Dow Jones Industrials, use the information provided to compute the measures *a* through *d*.

Company	Market Cap ($ mil.)	Stock Price	PB Current	BV per Share	Trailing 4-Quarter PE
Alcoa	$ 30,016	$35.39	1.89	$18.34	11.88
Boeing	67,578	87.19	10.55	8.44	16.80
Citigroup	148,886	29.89	1.17	25.86	8.03
Coca-Cola	143,928	62.28	7.32	8.51	23.59
McDonalds	69,534	58.79	4.65	12.63	21.22
3M	60,261	84.49	5.49	15.35	17.24
Wal-Mart	191,630	47.85	3.04	15.57	15.90
Exxon Mobil	503,364	92.13	4.24	21.68	13.47

a. Common shares outstanding.
b. Total book value of equity.
c. Trailing four quarters earnings per share (EPS).
d. Trailing four quarters return on equity (ROE).

PROBLEMS

P15-35. Identifying Comparables and Estimating Equity Value using PB   (LO1, 3)

Assume that your superior requests that you estimate the equity intrinsic value of **ValueClick**'s using PB ratios for comparable companies—ValueClick is one of the world's largest online marketing services companies. The following data are available on companies from the Web.

VALUECLICK
(VCLK)

Ticker	Market Cap ($ mil.)	PB Current	EPS 5-Year Historical Growth Rate	ROE (T 4Q)	Debt-to-Equity (Prior Q)
VCLK	—	—	65.4%	11.7%	0.0%
AKAM	$ 5,898.8	4.8	102.5%	7.9%	16.3%
DRIV	2,014.3	3.0	45.6%	11.0%	29.0%
EBAY	53,115.5	4.6	44.9%	12.4%	0.0%
JUPM	229.2	1.0	44.1%	0.5%	20.0%
KNOT	724.7	4.1	114.2%	15.9%	0.0%
OTEX	1,426.2	2.7	19.8%	4.5%	70.0%
RATE	913.9	4.8	24.1%	9.2%	0.0%
SRVY	431.9	2.7	11.6%	7.0%	0.0%
UNTD	1,066.3	2.9	23.8%	13.5%	0.0%
YHOO	38,003.0	4.2	44.1%	8.4%	0.0%

Required

a. Identify the set of companies you plan to use as comparables. (*Hint*: Consider each company on the basis of profitability, growth, and financial risk.)
b. Estimate the equity intrinsic value of ValueClick. It has a current book value of $707 million.
c. Prepare a memorandum to your superior identifying any issues that you believe should be considered before using the equity intrinsic value from part *b* for business decisions.

P15-36. Identifying Comparables and Estimating Equity Value using PE   (LO2, 3)

Assume that your superior requests that you estimate the equity intrinsic value of **ValueClick**'s using PE ratios for comparable companies—ValueClick is one of the world's largest online marketing services companies. The following online data are available from various companies.

VALUECLICK
(VCLK)

Ticker	Market Cap ($ mil.)	Forward PE	EPS 5-Year Historical Growth Rate	ROE (T 4Q)	Debt-to-Equity (Prior Q)
VCLK	—	—	65.4%	11.7%	0.0%
AKAM	$ 5,898.8	21.8	102.5%	7.9%	16.3%
DRIV	2,014.3	15.3	45.6%	11.0%	29.0%
EBAY	53,115.5	20.0	44.9%	12.4%	0.0%
JUPM	229.2	32.5	44.1%	0.5%	20.0%
KNOT	724.7	30.5	114.2%	15.9%	0.0%
OTEX	1,426.2	15.4	19.8%	4.5%	70.0%
RATE	913.9	24.4	24.1%	9.2%	0.0%
SRVY	431.9	24.1	11.6%	7.0%	0.0%
UNTD	1,066.3	10.7	23.8%	13.5%	0.0%
YHOO	38,003.0	43.9	44.1%	8.4%	0.0%

Required

a. Identify the set of companies you plan to use as comparables. (*Hint*: Consider each company on the basis of profitability, growth, and financial risk.)
b. Estimate the equity intrinsic value of ValueClick. Its earnings estimate is $81.5 million.
c. Prepare a memorandum to your superior identifying any issues that you believe should be considered before using the equity intrinsic value from part *b* for business decisions.

TARGET
(TGT)
KOHL'S
(KSS)
WAL-MART
(WMT)

P15-37. **Valuation Using Price-to-NOA Multiple and PB Multiple** **(LO1)**

The following table provides summary data for **Target** and its competitors, **Kohl's** and **Wal-Mart**.

(in millions)	Target	Kohl's	Wal-Mart
Company assumed value.................................	—	$23,098	$237,306
Equity assumed value	—	$22,470	$198,288
Net operating assets	$25,652	$ 6,231	$100,591
Book value of equity....................................	$15,633	$ 5,603	$ 61,573
Net nonoperating obligations (assets)	$10,109	$ 628	$ 39,018
Common shares outstanding...........................	860 shares	321 shares	41 shares

Required

a. Compute the price to net operating assets ratio for both Kohl's and Wal-Mart.

b. Use Kohl's and Wal-Mart as comparables, along with the price to NOA ratios from part *a*, and then estimate for Target its company intrinsic value, its equity intrinsic value, and its equity intrinsic value per share.

c. Compute the PB ratio for both Kohl's and Wal-Mart.

d. Use Kohl's and Wal-Mart as comparables, along with the PB ratios from part *c*, and then estimate for Target its equity intrinsic value and its equity intrinsic value per share.

TARGET
(TGT)
KOHL'S
(KSS)
WAL-MART
(WMT)

P15-38. **Valuation Using Income Statement Multiples** **(LO2)**

The following table provides summary data for **Target** and its competitors, **Kohl's** and **Wal-Mart**.

(in millions)	Target	Kohl's	Wal-Mart
Company assumed value................................	—	$23,098	$237,306
Equity assumed value	—	$22,470	$198,288
NOPAT	$ 3,159	$ 1,152	$ 13,354
Net income...	$ 2,787	$ 1,109	$ 12,178
Net nonoperating obligations (assets)	$10,109	$ 628	$ 39,018
Common shares outstanding...........................	860 shares	321 shares	41 shares

Required

a. Compute the price to NOPAT ratio for both Kohl's and Wal-Mart.

b. Use Kohl's and Wal-Mart as comparables, along with the company value to NOPAT ratios from part *a*, and then estimate for Target its company intrinsic value, its equity intrinsic value, and its equity intrinsic value per share.

c. Compute the price to net income ratio for both Kohl's and Wal-Mart.

d. Use Kohl's and Wal-Mart as comparables, along with the equity to net income ratios from part *c*, and then estimate for Target its equity intrinsic value and its equity intrinsic value per share.

P15-39. **Identifying Comparables and Valuation using PB and PE** **(LO1, 2, 3)**

MARINEMAX, INC.
(HZO)

Marinemax, Inc.'s equity book value per share is $20.11 and its forward earnings estimate per share is $0.71. The following information is also available for Marinemax and a peer group of companies (identified by ticker symbol) from the leisure goods sector.

Ticker	Market Cap ($ mil.)	PB Current	Forward PE (FY1)	EPS 5-Year Historical Growth Rate	ROE (T 4Q)	Debt-to-Equity (Prior Y)
HZO......	—	—	34.8	(11.1)%	4.8%	0.07
SHFL	$ 180.2	2.2	20.0	(15.6)%	19.0%	2.89
JAKK.....	825.0	1.2	9.9	11.7%	14.2%	0.14
POOL.....	951.1	4.6	14.8	(3.2)%	28.6%	1.34
RCRC	359.8	0.9	10.1	5.4%	4.9%	0.00
RGR......	153.6	2.0	20.9	(3.8)%	10.9%	0.00
PII........	1,395.3	8.1	12.5	(7.4)%	61.5%	1.16

Required

a. Identify a set of two companies from this list to use as comparables for estimating the equity intrinsic value of Marinemax using the market multiples approach.

b. Assume that you use as comparables the following set of companies: RCRC and RGR. Estimate Marinemax's equity intrinsic value per share using the PB ratio from these peer companies.

c. Use the same comparables as in part *b* and estimate Marinemax's equity intrinsic value per share using the PE ratio from these peer companies.

P15-40. Reverse Engineering with the PB Ratio (LO4)

The following table provides summary data for **Wolverine World Wide** (in millions). Analysts will often use the observed PB ratio to infer market expectations regarding a company's future performance under various assumptions.

Market value of equity	$1,490
Book value of equity	$ 505
ROE (based on trailing 4 quarters)	17.8%
EPS Growth (based on trailing 4 quarters)	16.0%

Required

a. Assume that the market's expectations of future ROE and the discount rate are 18% and 8%, respectively. Solve for the implied growth rate.

b. Assume that the market's expectations of future ROE and the growth rate are 18% and 3%, respectively. Solve for the implied discount rate.

c. Assume that the market's expectations of the discount rate and the growth rate are 8% and 3%, respectively. Solve for the implied future ROE.

d. Do the market expectations implied from the results of parts *a* through *c* seem reasonable? Explain.

P15-41. Reverse Engineering with the PB Ratio (LO4)

The following table provides summary data for **Family Dollar, Inc.** (in millions). Analysts will often use the observed PB ratio to infer market expectations regarding a company's future performance under various assumptions.

Market value of equity	$57,000
Book value of equity	$32,000
ROE (based on trailing 4 quarters)	11%
EPS Growth (based on trailing 4 quarters)	18%

Required

a. Assume that the market's expectations of future ROE and the discount rate are 11% and 9%, respectively. Solve for the implied growth rate.

b. Assume that the market's expectations of future ROE and the growth rate are 11% and 4%, respectively. Solve for the implied discount rate.

c. Assume that the market's expectations of the discount rate and the growth rate are 9% and 4%, respectively. Solve for the implied future ROE.

d. Do the market expectations implied from the results of parts *a* through *c* seem reasonable? Explain.

P15-42. Reverse Engineering and Interpreting the PB Ratio (LO4)

The mid-2011 market capitalization for **Google** was $163 billion, its book value of equity was $52 billion, and its trailing four-quarters ROE was 19% (while the average for the "Internet" industry was 15%). Its historical five-year average sales growth was 37% (average for the industry was 21%), its historical five-year average EPS growth was 25% (average for the industry was 35%), and analysts were forecasting a 21% annual earnings growth rate for industry over the next five years. Following are three different cases to help interpret and reverse engineer its PB ratio, including some unknown values.

PB* (equals PB ratio observed − 1)	?
Case 1: Solve for implied growth rate	
Assumed parameters	
ROE	18%
Discount rate, r_e	10%
Implied parameter	
Growth rate, $(r_e + [PB^* \times r_e] - ROE)/PB^*$	?

continued

continued from prior page

Case 2: Solve for implied discount rate
Assumed parameters
ROE 18%
Growth rate, g 15%
Implied parameter
Discount rate, $(ROE + [PB^* \times g])/(1 + PB^*)$ . . . . ?

Case 3: Solve for implied future ROE
Assumed parameters
Discount rate, r_e 16%
Growth rate, g 15%
Implied parameter
ROE, $(PB^* \times [r_e - g]) + r_e$ . . . . ?

Required

a. For Case 1, compute the growth rate implied by Google's PB ratio.
b. For Case 2, compute the discount rate implied by Google's PB ratio.
c. For Case 3, compute the ROE implied by Google's PB ratio.
d. Based on your results in parts *a* through *c*, do you believe Google's observed PB ratio implies reasonable expectations about its future performance? Explain.

P15-43. **Interpreting Analysts Reports that use Valuation with Multiples** (LO1, 2, 3, 4)

Refer to the following excerpts from an analysts' report covering **The Walt Disney Company** to complete the following requirements.

THE WALT DISNEY COMPANY
(DIS)

The Walt Disney Company (DIS)

December 8, 2011
Company Report

ANALYSIS

	Stock Type	Last Close Price	Fair Value Est
	Classic Growth	$35.92 (12/8/2011)	$45.00

Our fair value estimate for Disney is $45 per share, which implies forward price/earnings of 16 times, enterprise value/EBITDA of 8.9, and a free cash-flow yield of 6%.

We expect annual top-line growth of about 5% through fiscal 2016, including 5% sales growth in fiscal 2012. We forecast 5% annual sales growth from the media networks (7% for cable networks and 1% for ABC broadcasting), driven by affiliate fee and advertising growth. We project 65% average annual sales growth during the next five years for parks and resorts; however this segment is the most sensitive to macroeconomic headwinds. We have modeled modest 1% average annual growth assumptions for the filmed entertainment segment and 5% growth for consumer products, which should benefit from continued global growth of key Disney brands. We believe the interactive segment will continue to be a money loser, albeit a very small piece of the overall Disney pie.

We project Disney's overall operating margin to average 20% during the next five years, which is a bit higher than the recent peak margins of 19.4% in fiscal 2008. We think some additional profit expansion is reasonable, as the highest margin segment, cable networks, will grow at a faster clip than the overall firm. However, we believe operating margins at the cable networks will hover around 40% during the next five years as affiliate fee growth offsets sports programming cost inflation. We're expecting the parks and resorts segment margins to average 13.5% by 2013, still below fiscal 2008 levels of 16.5%. With the addition of Marvel and cost improvements at the Disney stores, we think consumer products margins will average 32% during the next five years, higher than the 27% margin generated in fiscal 2011.

Valuation	
Fair Value Estimate	$45.00
Stock Price	$36.61
Consider Buying	31.50
Consider Selling	60.80
Uncertainty Risk	Avg
Economic Moat	Wide
Stewardship Grade	B

Required

a. What market-based valuation multiples does this analyst reference with regard to Disney?
b. What is this analyst's price target for Disney? If Disney achieves that target in the next twelve months, what would be an investor's return? Explain.
c. Describe how this analyst justifies the price target.
d. Comment on the analysis used in this excerpt. Why is this a potentially useful way to value Disney?

DISCUSSION POINTS

D15-44. Valuation Using Balance Sheet Multiples   (LO1)

The following table provides summary data for **Limited Brands** and its competitors, **Bebe Stores** and **Gap**.

LIMITED BRANDS
(LTD)
BEBE STORES
(BEBE)
GAP
(GPS)

(in millions)	Limited Brands	Bebe Stores	Gap
Company assumed value.	—	$1,020	$14,948
Equity assumed value	—	$1,020	$14,760
Net operating assets	$4,985	$ 478	$ 4,798
Book value of equity.	$2,077	$ 478	$ 4,610
Net nonoperating obligations (assets)	$2,908	$ 0	$ 188
Common shares outstanding.	354 shares	88 shares	745 shares

Required

a. Compute the price to net operating assets ratio for both Bebe Stores and Gap.

b. Use Bebe Stores and Gap as comparables, along with the price to NOA ratios from part *a*, and then estimate for Limited Brands its company intrinsic value, its equity intrinsic value, and its equity intrinsic value per share.

c. Compute the PB ratio for both Bebe Stores and Gap.

d. Use Bebe Stores and Gap as comparables, along with the PB ratios from part *c*, and then estimate for Limited Brands its equity intrinsic value and its equity intrinsic value per share.

D15-45. Valuation Using Income Statement Multiples   (LO2)

The following table provides summary data for **Limited Brands** and its competitors, **Bebe Stores** and **Gap**.

LIMITED BRANDS
(LTD)
BEBE STORES
(BEBE)
GAP
(GPS)

(in millions)	Limited Brands	Bebe Stores	Gap
Company assumed value.	—	$1,020	$14,948
Equity assumed value	—	$1,020	$14,760
Net operating profit after tax	$ 742	$ 77	$ 805
Net income.	$ 676	$ 77	$ 778
Net nonoperating obligations (assets)	$2,908	$ 0	$ 188
Common shares outstanding.	354 shares	88 shares	745 shares

Required

a. Compute the price to NOPAT ratio for both Bebe Stores and Gap.

b. Use Bebe Stores and Gap as comparables, along with the price to NOPAT ratios from part *a*, and then estimate for Limited Brands its company intrinsic value, its equity intrinsic value, and its equity intrinsic value per share.

c. Compute the price to net income ratio for both Bebe Stores and Gap.

d. Use Bebe Stores and Gap as comparables, along with the price to net income ratios from part *c*, and then estimate for Limited Brands its equity intrinsic value and its equity intrinsic value per share.

D15-46. Assessment of Comparables, Multiples, and Observed PB   (LO3, 4)

Refer to the information in D15-44 and D15-45.

Required

a. Comment on the reasonableness of using **Bebe Stores** and **Gap** as comparables in valuing **Limited Brands**.

LIMITED BRANDS
(LTD)
BEBE STORES
(BEBE)
GAP
(GPS)

b. Assume that you are a staff analyst at a major analyst firm. Write a memorandum to your senior analyst identifying any issues you believe should be considered before using the value estimates from D15-44 and D15-45.

c. Analysts' average 5-year earnings growth forecast for Limited Brands is 13%. Which of the firms in the table below do you believe would be best for valuing Limited Brand using comparable PE ratios? Explain

Company	Analysts' 5-Year Earnings Forecasts	Debt-to-Equity	ROE	Forward PE	PB Current
J Crew Group Inc	22%	1.13	2.94	24.03	24.86
Pacific Sunwear	16%	0.05	(0.05)	23.54	1.74
Foot Locker Inc..............	13%	0.10	0.04	14.59	0.77
Home Depot Inc	11%	0.65	0.19	14.85	2.56
American Eagle Outfitters....	14%	0.00	0.29	9.90	2.61
Mens Wearhouse	17%	0.11	0.24	10.75	1.35
Aeropostale Inc.............	17%	0.00	0.39	15.84	6.90
Cabelas Inc	14%	0.77	0.11	10.41	1.19
Dress Barn Inc..............	15%	0.06	0.19	11.46	1.52
TJX Companies Inc	13%	0.40	0.30	14.52	6.61
Talbots Inc..................	14%	0.54	(0.03)	26.81	0.82
Urban Outfitters Inc	24%	0.00	0.20	25.93	6.36
Kohl's Corp	16%	0.35	0.20	12.43	2.24

d. The PB ratio for Limited Brands is 2.7, its trailing four-quarters ROE is 33% (with an industry average of 18%), its historical five-year average EPS growth is 15% (with an industry average of 16%), and analysts forecast a 14% earnings growth rate for the industry over the next five years. Using this information, reverse engineer the expectations implied by Limited's PB ratio.

PB* (equals PB ratio observed − 1).......................................	1.7
Case 1: Solve for implied growth rate	
Assumed parameters	
ROE	25%
Discount rate, r_e...	10%
Implied parameter	
Growth rate, $(r_e + [PB^* \times r_e] - ROE)/PB^*$	? %
Case 2: Solve for implied discount rate	
Assumed parameters	
ROE	25%
Growth rate, g	12%
Implied parameter	
Discount rate, $(ROE + [PB^* \times g])/(1 + PB^*)$........................	?
Case 3: Solve for implied future ROE	
Assumed parameters	
Discount rate, r_e...	10%
Growth rate, g	8%
Implied parameter	
ROE, $(PB^* \times [r_e - g]) + r_e$	? %

D15-47. Estimating Equity Value using Industry-Based Multiples (LO2, 3)

Assume that your superior requests that you apply the following multiple to value the set of companies you are currently assigned to follow.

$$\frac{\text{Price} - \text{Book Value}}{\text{R\&D Expense}}$$

The list of companies you currently follow is:

Best Buy.........................	BBY	Pfizer	PFE
Goldman Sachs Group...............	GS	P.F. Chang's China Bistro	PFCB
Home Depot......................	HD	Procter & Gamble....................	PG
JP Morgan Chase..................	JPM	Wal-Mart Stores	WMT
Kroger...........................	KR	Walt-Disney Company	DIS

Required

a. Discuss what is measured by the above multiple. Why might it be especially appropriate for certain industries?

b. Identify a set of companies from the list above for which this multiple is likely better in estimating equity value.

c.   Prepare a memorandum to the superior identifying any concerns in using the above multiple in estimating equity intrinsic value.

D15-48. Interpreting Analysts Reports that use Valuation with Multiples   (LO1, 2, 3, 4)

Refer to the following excerpts from an analysts' report (5 pages total) covering **Deckers Outdoor Corporation** to complete the following requirements.

**DECKERS OUTDOOR
CORPORATION
(DECK)**

DECKERS OUTDOOR CORP. (NNM: DECK)

February 29, 2008
Company Report

POWERFUL Q4 LED BY UGG - STRONG BUT CONSERVATIVE OUTLOOK - MUCH UPSIDE

- Based on the strong Q407 (EPS of $2.69 and Revenue of $194 million, up 48% and 56%, respectively, over Q406) results and strong FY08 guidance of a 25% increase in revenue and 20% increase in EPS to $561 million and $6.09, respectively, over FY07, we are maintaining our BUY rating and our $175 price target.
- We are slightly raising our revenue estimates for FY08 to $579 million, a 29% increase over FY07 and the company's guidance of a 25% revenue increase due to our perception (based on recent channel checks) that the momentum in UGG brand continues to increase, the Simple brand should exceed expectations, and TEVA rebirth as an outdoor brand meets with success.
- We are maintaining our $6.34 EPS estimate for FY08 which reflects a 25% increase over FY07 and above the company's guidance for a 20% growth in EPS. We are comfortable with our numbers, and continue to see upside due to Decker's track record of beating guidance:
  - o In Q4 of 2005, the company guided FY06 to revenue of $270 million, and EPS of $2.15. FY 2006 resulted in revenue of $304 million and EPS of $3.20, a guidance beat of 12.6% and 48.9%, respectively.
  - o In Q4 of 2006, the company guided FY07 revenue to $349 million and EPS to $3.36. FY07 resulted in revenue of $449 million and EPS of $5.06, a guidance beat of 28.7% and 50.5%, respectively.
- In conjunction with the aforementioned conservative guidance, DECK has also historically overestimated the EPS impact of their proposed additional SG&A spending, as we expect they have done on yesterday's call.
- We also believe the guidance to a 45% gross margin for FY08 is conservative. DECK apparently reserves some margin dollars if performance weakens. We are comfortable that such reserves were in their guidance over the past 2 years, and are baked into the FY08 guidance as well. Based on the strength and momentum of the UGG and Simple brands, and the higher gross margins in the TEVA brand, we see upside to gross margins in 2008.

FOOTWEAR & APPAREL

Fiscal Year Ends Dec	
Rating:	Buy
Price:	$126.46
Price Target:	$175
52-wk Range:	$62.11-$166.50
Market Capitalization (M):	$1,642
Shares Outstanding (M):	13.0
Assets (M):	$370.63
Debt/Equity:	0%
ROE (TTM):	26.1%
Book Value/Share:	$22.70

Earnings Summary				
FYE Dec		2007A	2008E	2009E
P/E Ratio:		25.0	19.9	16.8
Revenue (M):	Q1	$72.6	$91.4	--
	Q2	$52.7	$67.3	--
	Q3	$129.4	$169.4	--
	Q4	$194.2	$250.7	--
	Full Year	$448.9	$578.8	$668.0
EPS:	Q1	$0.73	$0.75	--
	Q2	$0.17	$0.25	--
	Q3	$1.47	$2.09	--
	Q4	$2.69	$3.21	--
	Full Year	$5.06	$6.34	$7.51

Company Description: Deckers Outdoor Corporation is a designer, producer, and brand manager of footwear for outdoor activities and casual lifestyles.   It sells its products directly to consumers, through retailers in the United States, and through distributors in a number of international countries. It markets its products under the brand names Teva, UGG, and Simple.

Keeping in mind that DECK has a history of beating even the high end of guidance, our FY08 projections are slightly above company's guidance. Our revenue projection is $578.8 million and our EPS target is $6.34. Our FY09 projections are $668 million in revenue and EPS of $7.51.

VALUATION TABLE

Company Name	Ticker	Price	Market Cap ($M)	EPS 2008 estimate	2008 P/E estimate	Cash ($M)	Debt ($M)	EV ($M)	EBITDA ($M, ttm)	EV/EBITDA ($M)
Deckers Outdoor	**DECK**	**$126.46**	**1642.6**	**$6.34**	**19.95**	**168.09**	**0.00**	**1474.50**	**93.33**	**15.80**
Columbia Sportswear	COLM	$43.27	1555.9	$3.52	12.29	191.95	21.05	1384.96	225.65	6.14
CROCS Inc.	CROX	$25.13	2049.2	$2.69	9.34	36.33	7.12	2019.98	228.95	8.82
LaCross Footwear	BOOT	$16.99	103.8	$1.27	13.38	15.39	0.39	88.83	12.74	6.97
Rocky Brands	RCKY	$5.79	31.8	$0.78	7.42	6.54	103.55	128.77	17.66	7.29
Timberland	TBL	$15.61	957.7	$0.91	17.15	43.95	46.60	960.35	134.04	7.16
Wolverine World Wide	WWW	$26.71	1410.3	$1.87	14.28	76.09	10.73	1344.93	153.7	8.75
Average (excl. DECK)					9.22					7.52

We understand that our valuation is high in the current environment, but we view DECK as an exception to the rule, as the popularity of their product lines and their propensity for beating numbers justifies the high valuation. We believe there is still significant growth ahead for UGG and that the TEVA and Simple brands are improving as well. Therefore, we view our P/E multiple of 27.6x our 2008 EPS estimate of $6.34 to reach our $175 price target as appropriate. DECK has traded at a trailing twelve month PE of 31.8x over the last three months.

Required

a.   What method is this analyst using to value Deckers?

b.   What is this analyst's price target for Deckers? If Deckers achieves that target in the next twelve months, what would be an investor's return? Explain.

c.   Describe how this analyst justifies the price target.

d.   Is there any other information in these excerpts that you might use to value Deckers? Explain.

SOLUTIONS TO REVIEW PROBLEMS

Mid-Module Review 1

Solution

a. Our estimate of the net operating assets market multiple for Procter & Gamble and Merck is 2.3 and 7.2, respectively; computed as company assumed value divided by net operating assets for each. The NOA market multiple is the average of the two ratios, or 4.8, computed as (2.3+7.2)/2. We could weight one of the two companies more heavily if we believe its ratio is more relevant for valuing Johnson & Johnson.

b. Johnson & Johnson's estimated company intrinsic value is $220,291 million, computed as $45,894 in NOA multiplied by the 4.8 NOA market multiple. Its estimated equity intrinsic value is $213,715, computed as $220,291 company intrinsic value less $6,576 in net nonoperating obligations. Its estimated equity intrinsic value per share is $73.87, computed as $213,715 in equity intrinsic value divided by 2,893 of common shares.

c. The book value multiple (price-to-book) for Procter & Gamble and Merck are 3.0 and 5.9, respectively; computed as equity assumed value divided by the book value of equity for each. The BV market multiple is the average of the two ratios, or 4.5, computed as (3.0 + 5.9)/2. We could weight one of the two companies more heavily if we believe its ratio is more relevant for valuing Johnson & Johnson.

d. Johnson & Johnson's estimated equity intrinsic value is $176,931, computed as $39,318 in book value of equity multiplied by the 4.5 BV market multiple. Its estimated equity intrinsic value per share is $61.16, computed as $176,931 in equity intrinsic value divided by 2,893 of common shares.

Mid-Module Review 2

Solution

a. Our estimate of the NOPAT market multiple for Procter & Gamble and Merck is 21.3 and 23.8, respectively; computed as company assumed value divided by net operating profit after tax for each. The NOPAT market multiple is the average of the two ratios, or 22.6, computed as (21.3 + 23.8)/2. We could weight one of the two companies more heavily if we believe its multiple is more reliable for valuing JNJ.

b. JNJ's estimated company intrinsic value is $238,724 million, computed as $10,563 in NOPAT multiplied by the 22.6 NOPAT market multiple. Its estimated equity intrinsic value is $232,148, computed as $238,724 company intrinsic value less $6,576 in net nonoperating obligations. Its estimated equity intrinsic value per share is $80.24, computed as $232,148 in equity intrinsic value divided by 2,893 of common shares.

c. The net income multiple for Procter & Gamble and Merck is 19.66 and 23.30, respectively; computed as equity assumed value divided by net income for each. The NI market multiple is the average of the two ratios, or 21.48, computed as (19.66 + 23.30)/2. We could weight one of the two companies more heavily if we believe its ratio is more relevant for valuing JNJ.

d. JNJ's estimated equity intrinsic value is $237,418, computed as $11,053 in net income multiplied by the 21.48 NI market multiple. Its estimated equity intrinsic value per share is $82.07, computed as $237,418 in equity intrinsic value divided by 2,893 of common shares.

Mid-Module Review 3

Solution

a. The following tables reports ROPI, present value of ROPI, company value, and equity value of Companies A through E (computations follow the table).

Company	Net operating assets	Debt (6% rate)	Owners' equity	RNOA	ROE	Weighted average cost of capital	Cost of equity capital	Residual operating income	Growth rate in ROPI	Present value of expected ROPI using r_w	Value of company	Value of equity
A.......	$100	$ 0	$100	16%	16%	10%	10%	$6	2%	$ 75	$175	$175
B.......	$100	$ 0	$100	12%	12%	10%	10%	$2	2%	$ 25	$125	$125
C.......	$100	$ 0	$100	16%	16%	10%	10%	$6	4%	$100	$200	$200
D.......	$100	$ 0	$100	16%	16%	12%	12%	$4	2%	$ 40	$140	$140
E.......	$100	$60	$ 40	16%	31%	10%	12.1%	$6	2%	$ 75	$175	$115

Company A:　ROPI:　　　　　$6 = (\$100 \times 16\%) - (\$100 \times 10\%)$
　　　　　　PV of ROPI　　　$75 = \$6/(10\% - 2\%)$
　　　　　　Value of equity　$175 = \$100 + \$75$
　　　　　　PB ratio　　　　1.75

Company B:　ROPI:　　　　　$2 = (\$100 \times 12\%) - (\$100 \times 10\%)$
　　　　　　PV of ROPI　　　$25 = \$2/(10\% - 2\%)$
　　　　　　Value of equity　$125 = \$100 + \$25$
　　　　　　PB ratio　　　　1.25

Company C:　ROPI:　　　　　$6 = (\$100 \times 16\%) - (\$100 \times 10\%)$
　　　　　　PV of ROPI　　　$6 = \$6/(10\% - 4\%)$
　　　　　　Value of equity　$200 = \$100 + \$100$
　　　　　　PB ratio　　　　2.00

Company D:　ROPI:　　　　　$4 = (\$100 \times 16\%) - (\$100 \times 12\%)$
　　　　　　PV of ROPI　　　$40 = \$4/(12\% - 2\%)$
　　　　　　Value of equity　$140 = \$100 + \$40$
　　　　　　PB ratio　　　　1.40

Company E:　ROPI:　　　　　$6 = (\$100 \times 16\%) - (\$100 \times 10\%)$
　　　　　　PV of ROPI　　　$75 = \$6/(10\% - 2\%)$
　　　　　　Value of company　$175 = \$100 + \$75$
　　　　　　Value of equity　$115 = \$175 - \$60$
　　　　　　PB ratio　　　　2.88

b. PB ratio increases with profitability—compare A and B.
   PB ratio increases with expected growth—compare A and C.
   PB ratio decreases as operating risk increases—compare A and D.
   Levered PB ratio is higher than unlevered PB ratio—compare A and E.

Mid-Module Review 4

Solution

a. There is more than one reasonable answer to this requirement. The important point is to select companies that are as similar as possible to CMI on the basis of profitability, growth, and risk. On this point we might eliminate CNH (low ROE) and CAT (high ROE) on the basis of profitability, ITW and ITT (two lowest 5-year growth rates) on the basis of growth, and CAT and DE (high debt-to-equity) on the basis of risk. This would leave VOLVY, PH, PCAR, ETN, DHR and IR as comparables.

b. The comparables have an average PB ratio of 3.03. Multiplying CMI's equity book value of $3,195 million by the 3.03 market multiple yields an estimate of CMI's equity intrinsic value of $9,681 million.

c. The comparables have an average forward PE ratio of 15.7. Multiplying CMI's forward earnings estimate of $932 million by the 15.7 market multiple yields as estimate of CMI's equity intrinsic value of $14,632 million.

Module-End Review

Solution

a. For Case 1, the growth rate implied by Scenarios A through D is 2.1%, 5.5%, 4.6%, and 8.0%, respectively.

b. For Case 2, the discount rate implied by Scenarios A through D is 7.7%, 5.0%, 9.3%, and 6.6%, respectively.

c. For Case 3, the future ROE implied by Scenarios A through D is 22.6%, 32.4%, 14.8%, and 24.6%, respectively.

d. We should not draw any definitive conclusions from these reverse engineering exercises. With that caveat, the implied parameters are not entirely implausible.

Compound Interest Tables

TABLE 1	Present Value of Single Amount										$p = 1/(1 + i)^t$

Interest Rate

Period	0.01	0.02	0.03	0.04	0.05	0.06	0.07	0.08	0.09	0.10	0.11	0.12
1	0.99010	0.98039	0.97087	0.96154	0.95238	0.94340	0.93458	0.92593	0.91743	0.90909	0.90090	0.89286
2	0.98030	0.96117	0.94260	0.92456	0.90703	0.89000	0.87344	0.85734	0.84168	0.82645	0.81162	0.79719
3	0.97059	0.94232	0.91514	0.88900	0.86384	0.83962	0.81630	0.79383	0.77218	0.75131	0.73119	0.71178
4	0.96098	0.92385	0.88849	0.85480	0.82270	0.79209	0.76290	0.73503	0.70843	0.68301	0.65873	0.63552
5	0.95147	0.90573	0.86261	0.82193	0.78353	0.74726	0.71299	0.68058	0.64993	0.62092	0.59345	0.56743
6	0.94205	0.88797	0.83748	0.79031	0.74622	0.70496	0.66634	0.63017	0.59627	0.56447	0.53464	0.50663
7	0.93272	0.87056	0.81309	0.75992	0.71068	0.66506	0.62275	0.58349	0.54703	0.51316	0.48166	0.45235
8	0.92348	0.85349	0.78941	0.73069	0.67684	0.62741	0.58201	0.54027	0.50187	0.46651	0.43393	0.40388
9	0.91434	0.83676	0.76642	0.70259	0.64461	0.59190	0.54393	0.50025	0.46043	0.42410	0.39092	0.36061
10	0.90529	0.82035	0.74409	0.67556	0.61391	0.55839	0.50835	0.46319	0.42241	0.38554	0.35218	0.32197
11	0.89632	0.80426	0.72242	0.64958	0.58468	0.52679	0.47509	0.42888	0.38753	0.35049	0.31728	0.28748
12	0.88745	0.78849	0.70138	0.62460	0.55684	0.49697	0.44401	0.39711	0.35553	0.31863	0.28584	0.25668
13	0.87866	0.77303	0.68095	0.60057	0.53032	0.46884	0.41496	0.36770	0.32618	0.28966	0.25751	0.22917
14	0.86996	0.75788	0.66112	0.57748	0.50507	0.44230	0.38782	0.34046	0.29925	0.26333	0.23199	0.20462
15	0.86135	0.74301	0.64186	0.55526	0.48102	0.41727	0.36245	0.31524	0.27454	0.23939	0.20900	0.18270
16	0.85282	0.72845	0.62317	0.53391	0.45811	0.39365	0.33873	0.29189	0.25187	0.21763	0.18829	0.16312
17	0.84438	0.71416	0.60502	0.51337	0.43630	0.37136	0.31657	0.27027	0.23107	0.19784	0.16963	0.14564
18	0.83602	0.70016	0.58739	0.49363	0.41552	0.35034	0.29586	0.25025	0.21199	0.17986	0.15282	0.13004
19	0.82774	0.68643	0.57029	0.47464	0.39573	0.33051	0.27651	0.23171	0.19449	0.16351	0.13768	0.11611
20	0.81954	0.67297	0.55368	0.45639	0.37689	0.31180	0.25842	0.21455	0.17843	0.14864	0.12403	0.10367
21	0.81143	0.65978	0.53755	0.43883	0.35894	0.29416	0.24151	0.19866	0.16370	0.13513	0.11174	0.09256
22	0.80340	0.64684	0.52189	0.42196	0.34185	0.27751	0.22571	0.18394	0.15018	0.12285	0.10067	0.08264
23	0.79544	0.63416	0.50669	0.40573	0.32557	0.26180	0.21095	0.17032	0.13778	0.11168	0.09069	0.07379
24	0.78757	0.62172	0.49193	0.39012	0.31007	0.24698	0.19715	0.15770	0.12640	0.10153	0.08170	0.06588
25	0.77977	0.60953	0.47761	0.37512	0.29530	0.23300	0.18425	0.14602	0.11597	0.09230	0.07361	0.05882
30	0.74192	0.55207	0.41199	0.30832	0.23138	0.17411	0.13137	0.09938	0.07537	0.05731	0.04368	0.03338
35	0.70591	0.50003	0.35538	0.25342	0.18129	0.13011	0.09366	0.06763	0.04899	0.03558	0.02592	0.01894
40	0.67165	0.45289	0.30656	0.20829	0.14205	0.09722	0.06678	0.04603	0.03184	0.02209	0.01538	0.01075

TABLE 2	Present Value of Ordinary Annuity										$p = \{1 - [1/(1 + i)^t]\}/i$

Interest Rate

Period	0.01	0.02	0.03	0.04	0.05	0.06	0.07	0.08	0.09	0.10	0.11	0.12
1	0.99010	0.98039	0.97087	0.96154	0.95238	0.94340	0.93458	0.92593	0.91743	0.90909	0.90090	0.89286
2	1.97040	1.94156	1.91347	1.88609	1.85941	1.83339	1.80802	1.78326	1.75911	1.73554	1.71252	1.69005
3	2.94099	2.88388	2.82861	2.77509	2.72325	2.67301	2.62432	2.57710	2.53129	2.48685	2.44371	2.40183
4	3.90197	3.80773	3.71710	3.62990	3.54595	3.46511	3.38721	3.31213	3.23972	3.16987	3.10245	3.03735
5	4.85343	4.71346	4.57971	4.45182	4.32948	4.21236	4.10020	3.99271	3.88965	3.79079	3.69590	3.60478
6	5.79548	5.60143	5.41719	5.24214	5.07569	4.91732	4.76654	4.62288	4.48592	4.35526	4.23054	4.11141
7	6.72819	6.47199	6.23028	6.00205	5.78637	5.58238	5.38929	5.20637	5.03295	4.86842	4.71220	4.56376
8	7.65168	7.32548	7.01969	6.73274	6.46321	6.20979	5.97130	5.74664	5.53482	5.33493	5.14612	4.96764
9	8.56602	8.16224	7.78611	7.43533	7.10782	6.80169	6.51523	6.24689	5.99525	5.75902	5.53705	5.32825
10	9.47130	8.98259	8.53020	8.11090	7.72173	7.36009	7.02358	6.71008	6.41766	6.14457	5.88923	5.65022
11	10.36763	9.78685	9.25262	8.76048	8.30641	7.88687	7.49867	7.13896	6.80519	6.49506	6.20652	5.93770
12	11.25508	10.57534	9.95400	9.38507	8.86325	8.38384	7.94269	7.53608	7.16073	6.81369	6.49236	6.19437
13	12.13374	11.34837	10.63496	9.98565	9.39357	8.85268	8.35765	7.90378	7.48690	7.10336	6.74987	6.42355
14	13.00370	12.10625	11.29607	10.56312	9.89864	9.29498	8.74547	8.24424	7.78615	7.36669	6.98187	6.62817
15	13.86505	12.84926	11.93794	11.11839	10.37966	9.71225	9.10791	8.55948	8.06069	7.60608	7.19087	6.81086
16	14.71787	13.57771	12.56110	11.65230	10.83777	10.10590	9.44665	8.85137	8.31256	7.82371	7.37916	6.97399
17	15.56225	14.29187	13.16612	12.16567	11.27407	10.47726	9.76322	9.12164	8.54363	8.02155	7.54879	7.11963
18	16.39827	14.99203	13.75351	12.65930	11.68959	10.82760	10.05909	9.37189	8.75563	8.20141	7.70162	7.24967
19	17.22601	15.67846	14.32380	13.13394	12.08532	11.15812	10.33560	9.60360	8.95011	8.36492	7.83929	7.36578
20	18.04555	16.35143	14.87747	13.59033	12.46221	11.46992	10.59401	9.81815	9.12855	8.51356	7.96333	7.46944
21	18.85698	17.01121	15.41502	14.02916	12.82115	11.76408	10.83553	10.01680	9.29224	8.64869	8.07507	7.56200
22	19.66038	17.65805	15.93692	14.45112	13.16300	12.04158	11.06124	10.20074	9.44243	8.77154	8.17574	7.64465
23	20.45582	18.29220	16.44361	14.85684	13.48857	12.30338	11.27219	10.37106	9.58021	8.88322	8.26643	7.71843
24	21.24339	18.91393	16.93554	15.24696	13.79864	12.55036	11.46933	10.52876	9.70661	8.98474	8.34814	7.78432
25	22.02316	19.52346	17.41315	15.62208	14.09394	12.78336	11.65358	10.67478	9.82258	9.07704	8.42174	7.84314
30	25.80771	22.39646	19.60044	17.29203	15.37245	13.76483	12.40904	11.25778	10.27365	9.42691	8.69379	8.05518
35	29.40858	24.99862	21.48722	18.66461	16.37419	14.49825	12.94767	11.65457	10.56682	9.64416	8.85524	8.17550
40	32.83469	27.35548	23.11477	19.79277	17.15909	15.04630	13.33171	11.92461	10.75736	9.77905	8.95105	8.24378

TABLE 3 Future Value of Single Amount

$f = (1 + i)^t$

					Interest Rate							
Period	0.01	0.02	0.03	0.04	0.05	0.06	0.07	0.08	0.09	0.10	0.11	0.12
1	1.01000	1.02000	1.03000	1.04000	1.05000	1.06000	1.07000	1.08000	1.09000	1.10000	1.11000	1.12000
2	1.02010	1.04040	1.06090	1.08160	1.10250	1.12360	1.14490	1.16640	1.18810	1.21000	1.23210	1.25440
3	1.03030	1.06121	1.09273	1.12486	1.15763	1.19102	1.22504	1.25971	1.29503	1.33100	1.36763	1.40493
4	1.04060	1.08243	1.12551	1.16986	1.21551	1.26248	1.31080	1.36049	1.41158	1.46410	1.51807	1.57352
5	1.05101	1.10408	1.15927	1.21665	1.27628	1.33823	1.40255	1.46933	1.53862	1.61051	1.68506	1.76234
6	1.06152	1.12616	1.19405	1.26532	1.34010	1.41852	1.50073	1.58687	1.67710	1.77156	1.87041	1.97382
7	1.07214	1.14869	1.22987	1.31593	1.40710	1.50363	1.60578	1.71382	1.82804	1.94872	2.07616	2.21068
8	1.08286	1.17166	1.26677	1.36857	1.47746	1.59385	1.71819	1.85093	1.99256	2.14359	2.30454	2.47596
9	1.09369	1.19509	1.30477	1.42331	1.55133	1.68948	1.83846	1.99900	2.17189	2.35795	2.55804	2.77308
10	1.10462	1.21899	1.34392	1.48024	1.62889	1.79085	1.96715	2.15892	2.36736	2.59374	2.83942	3.10585
11	1.11567	1.24337	1.38423	1.53945	1.71034	1.89830	2.10485	2.33164	2.58043	2.85312	3.15176	3.47855
12	1.12683	1.26824	1.42576	1.60103	1.79586	2.01220	2.25219	2.51817	2.81266	3.13843	3.49845	3.89598
13	1.13809	1.29361	1.46853	1.66507	1.88565	2.13293	2.40985	2.71962	3.06580	3.45227	3.88328	4.36349
14	1.14947	1.31948	1.51259	1.73168	1.97993	2.26090	2.57853	2.93719	3.34173	3.79750	4.31044	4.88711
15	1.16097	1.34587	1.55797	1.80094	2.07893	2.39656	2.75903	3.17217	3.64248	4.17725	4.78459	5.47357
16	1.17258	1.37279	1.60471	1.87298	2.18287	2.54035	2.95216	3.42594	3.97031	4.59497	5.31089	6.13039
17	1.18430	1.40024	1.65285	1.94790	2.29202	2.69277	3.15882	3.70002	4.32763	5.05447	5.89509	6.86604
18	1.19615	1.42825	1.70243	2.02582	2.40662	2.85434	3.37993	3.99602	4.71712	5.55992	6.54355	7.68997
19	1.20811	1.45681	1.75351	2.10685	2.52695	3.02560	3.61653	4.31570	5.14166	6.11591	7.26334	8.61276
20	1.22019	1.48595	1.80611	2.19112	2.65330	3.20714	3.86968	4.66096	5.60441	6.72750	8.06231	9.64629
21	1.23239	1.51567	1.86029	2.27877	2.78596	3.39956	4.14056	5.03383	6.10881	7.40025	8.94917	10.80385
22	1.24472	1.54598	1.91610	2.36992	2.92526	3.60354	4.43040	5.43654	6.65860	8.14027	9.93357	12.10031
23	1.25716	1.57690	1.97359	2.46472	3.07152	3.81975	4.74053	5.87146	7.25787	8.95430	11.02627	13.55235
24	1.26973	1.60844	2.03279	2.56330	3.22510	4.04893	5.07237	6.34118	7.91108	9.84973	12.23916	15.17863
25	1.28243	1.64061	2.09378	2.66584	3.38635	4.29187	5.42743	6.84848	8.62308	10.83471	13.58546	17.00006
30	1.34785	1.81136	2.42726	3.24340	4.32194	5.74349	7.61226	10.06266	13.26768	17.44940	22.89230	29.95992
35	1.41660	1.99989	2.81386	3.94609	5.51602	7.68609	10.67658	14.78534	20.41397	28.10244	38.57485	52.79962
40	1.48886	2.20804	3.26204	4.80102	7.03999	10.28572	14.97446	21.72452	31.40942	45.25926	65.00087	93.05097

TABLE 4 Future Value of an Ordinary Annuity

$f = [(1 + i)^t - 1]/i$

					Interest Rate							
Period	0.01	0.02	0.03	0.04	0.05	0.06	0.07	0.08	0.09	0.10	0.11	0.12
1	1.00000	1.00000	1.00000	1.00000	1.00000	1.00000	1.00000	1.00000	1.00000	1.00000	1.00000	1.00000
2	2.01000	2.02000	2.03000	2.04000	2.05000	2.06000	2.07000	2.08000	2.09000	2.10000	2.11000	2.12000
3	3.03010	3.06040	3.09090	3.12160	3.15250	3.18360	3.21490	3.24640	3.27810	3.31000	3.34210	3.37440
4	4.06040	4.12161	4.18363	4.24646	4.31013	4.37462	4.43994	4.50611	4.57313	4.64100	4.70973	4.77933
5	5.10101	5.20404	5.30914	5.41632	5.52563	5.63709	5.75074	5.86660	5.98471	6.10510	6.22780	6.35285
6	6.15202	6.30812	6.46841	6.63298	6.80191	6.97532	7.15329	7.33593	7.52333	7.71561	7.91286	8.11519
7	7.21354	7.43428	7.66246	7.89829	8.14201	8.39384	8.65402	8.92280	9.20043	9.48717	9.78327	10.08901
8	8.28567	8.58297	8.89234	9.21423	9.54911	9.89747	10.25980	10.63663	11.02847	11.43589	11.85943	12.29969
9	9.36853	9.75463	10.15911	10.58280	11.02656	11.49132	11.97799	12.48756	13.02104	13.57948	14.16397	14.77566
10	10.46221	10.94972	11.46388	12.00611	12.57789	13.18079	13.81645	14.48656	15.19293	15.93742	16.72201	17.54874
11	11.56683	12.16872	12.80780	13.48635	14.20679	14.97164	15.78360	16.64549	17.56029	18.53117	19.56143	20.65458
12	12.68250	13.41209	14.19203	15.02581	15.91713	16.86994	17.88845	18.97713	20.14072	21.38428	22.71319	24.13313
13	13.80933	14.68033	15.61779	16.62684	17.71298	18.88214	20.14064	21.49530	22.95338	24.52271	26.21164	28.02911
14	14.94742	15.97394	17.08632	18.29191	19.59863	21.01507	22.55049	24.21492	26.01919	27.97498	30.09492	32.39260
15	16.09690	17.29342	18.59891	20.02359	21.57856	23.27597	25.12902	27.15211	29.36092	31.77248	34.40536	37.27971
16	17.25786	18.63929	20.15688	21.82453	23.65749	25.67253	27.88805	30.32428	33.00340	35.94973	39.18995	42.75328
17	18.43044	20.01207	21.76159	23.69751	25.84037	28.21288	30.84022	33.75023	36.97370	40.54477	44.50084	48.88367
18	19.61475	21.41231	23.41444	25.64541	28.13238	30.90565	33.99903	37.45024	41.30134	45.59917	50.39594	55.74971
19	20.81090	22.84056	25.11687	27.67123	30.53900	33.75999	37.37896	41.44626	46.01846	51.15909	56.93949	63.43968
20	22.01900	24.29737	26.87037	29.77808	33.06595	36.78559	40.99549	45.76196	51.16012	57.27500	64.20283	72.05244
21	23.23919	25.78332	28.67649	31.96920	35.71925	39.99273	44.86518	50.42292	56.76453	64.00250	72.26514	81.69874
22	24.47159	27.29898	30.53678	34.24797	38.50521	43.39229	49.00574	55.45676	62.87334	71.40275	81.21431	92.50258
23	25.71630	28.84496	32.45288	36.61789	41.43048	46.99583	53.43614	60.89330	69.53194	79.54302	91.14788	104.60289
24	26.97346	30.42186	34.42647	39.08260	44.50200	50.81558	58.17667	66.76476	76.78981	88.49733	102.17415	118.15524
25	28.24320	32.03030	36.45926	41.64591	47.72710	54.86451	63.24904	73.10594	84.70090	98.34706	114.41331	133.33387
30	34.78489	40.56808	47.57542	56.08494	66.43885	79.05819	94.46079	113.28321	136.30754	164.49402	199.02088	241.33268
35	41.66028	49.99448	60.46208	73.65222	90.32031	111.43478	138.23688	172.31680	215.71075	271.02437	341.58955	431.66350
40	48.88637	60.40198	75.40126	95.02552	120.79977	154.76197	199.63511	259.05652	337.88245	442.59256	581.82607	767.09142

APPENDIX

B Chart of Accounts with Acronyms

Assets

Cash	Cash
MS	Marketable securities
EMI	Equity method investments
AR	Accounts receivable
AU	Allowance for uncollectible accounts
INV	Inventory (or Inventories)
SUP	Supplies
PPD	Prepaid expenses
PPDA	Prepaid advertising
PPRNT	Prepaid rent
PPI	Prepaid insurance
PPE	Property, plant and equipment (PPE)
AD	Accumulated depreciation
INT	Intangible assets
DTA	Deferred tax assets
OA	Other assets

Liabilities

NP	Notes payable
AP	Accounts payable
ACC	Accrued expenses
WP	Wages payable
SP	Salaries payable
RNTP	Rent payable
RSL	Restructuring liability
UP	Utilities payable
TP	Taxes payable
WRP	Warranty payable
IP	Interest payable
CMLTD	Current maturities of long-term debt
UR	Unearned (or deferred) revenues
LTD	Long-term debt
CLO	Capital lease obligations
DTL	Deferred tax liabilities

Equity

EC	Earned capital
CS	Common stock
APIC	Additional paid-in capital
RE	Retained earnings
DIV	Dividends
TS	Treasury stock
AOCI	Accumulated other comprehensive income
DC	Deferred compensation expense

Revenues and Expenses

Sales	Sales
REV	Revenues
COGS	Cost of goods sold (or Cost of sales)
OE	Operating expenses
WE	Wages expense
SE	Salaries expense
AE	Advertising expense
BDE	Bad debts expense
UTE	Utilities expense
DE	Depreciation expense
RDE	Research and development expense
RNTE	Rent expense
RSE	Restructuring expense
WRE	Warranty expense
AIE	Asset impairment expense
INSE	Insurance expense
SUPE	Supplies expense
GN (LS)	Gain (loss)–operating
TE	Tax expense
ONI (E)	Other nonoperating income (expense)
IE	Interest expense
UG (UL)	Unrealized gain (loss)
DI	Dividend income (or revenue)
EI	Equity income (or revenue)
GN (LS)	Gain (loss)–nonoperating

Closing Account

IS	Income summary

1. Explain and illustrate a review of financial statements and their components. (p. C-4)

2. Assess company profitability and creditworthiness. (p. C-29)

3. Forecast financial statements. (p. C-32)

4. Describe and illustrate the valuation of firm equity and stock. (p. C-35)

© Getty Images

Comprehensive Case

The past decade has seen a shift in the competitive landscape for consumer products companies. Gone are numerous competitors. Many were gobbled up in the industry's consolidation trend. Also gone is media control. Now, hundreds of different media outlets and venues compete for promotion space and scarce consumer time.

KIMBERLY-CLARK

Another development is in-store branding. Companies such as Costco, with its Kirkland Signature brand on everything from candy to apparel, threaten the powerhouse brands from Kimberly-Clark, Procter & Gamble, Colgate-Palmolive, and other consumer products companies.

Ten years ago, when Thomas J. Falk assumed the top spot at Kimberly-Clark, the nation's largest disposable diaper producer, he inherited some extra baggage: a company in the throes of an identity crisis, a decades-long rivalry with consumer-products behemoth Procter & Gamble, and a group of investors short on patience following a series of earnings misses.

In a move aimed at boosting its stock price and its return on equity, Kimberly-Clark spun off its paper and pulp businesses in 2004, and began a strategic investment and streamlining initiative in 2005. Under Falk's leadership, the company has steadily improved its focus on its health and hygiene segments.

Kimberly-Clark has also moved to shore up its brand images across its immense product line. With sales of nearly $20 billion, the company manufactures such well-recognized brands as Huggies and Pull-Ups disposable diapers, Kotex and Lightdays feminine products, Kleenex facial tissue, Viva paper towels, and Scott bathroom tissue.

The rocky ride that Kimberly-Clark investors have endured over the past few years is unlikely to subside—see the following stock price chart. Competition is fierce and well-armed, and the purchase of Gillette by Procter & Gamble further muddies the future of the industry.

On the positive side, Kimberly-Clark's earnings performance is consistent, and its financial position is solid. Kimberly-Clark's RNOA for 2010 was 17.6%, and its nonoperating return increased RNOA to yield a robust 32.6% in return on equity. It also reported $19.9 billion in assets, 42% of which is concentrated in plant, property, and equipment, and another 18.6% in intangible assets.

This module presents a financial accounting analysis and interpretation of Kimberly-Clark. It is intended to illustrate the key financial reporting topics covered in the book. We begin with a detailed review of Kimberly-Clark's financial statements and notes, followed by the forecasting of key accounts that we use to value its common stock.

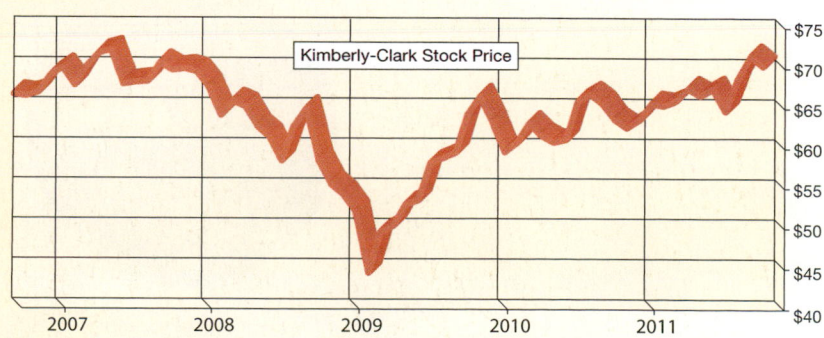

Source: *Kimberly-Clark* 10-K Filings and Annual Report to Shareholders.

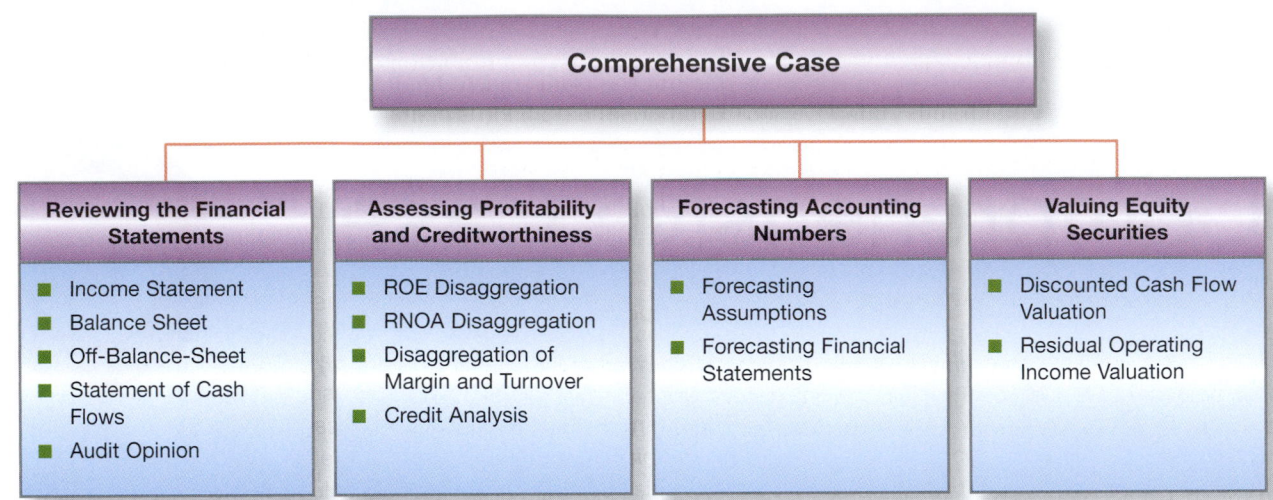

INTRODUCTION

Kimberly-Clark is one of the largest consumer products companies in the world. It is organized into four general business segments (percentages are for 2010):

- **Personal Care** (44% of sales), which manufactures and markets disposable diapers, training and youth pants, swim pants, baby wipes, feminine and incontinence care products, and related products. Products in this segment are primarily for household use and are sold under a variety of brand names, including Huggies, Pull-Ups, Little Swimmers, GoodNites, Kotex, Lightdays, Depend, Poise and other brand names.

- **Consumer Tissue** (33% of sales), which manufactures and markets facial and bathroom tissue, paper towels, napkins and related products for household use. Products in this segment are sold under the Kleenex, Scott, Cottonelle, Viva, Andrex, Scottex, Hakle, Page and other brand names.

- **Professional & Other** (16% of sales), which manufactures and markets facial and bathroom tissue, paper towels, napkins, wipes and a range of safety products for the away-from-home marketplace. Products in this segment are sold under the Kimberly-Clark, Kleenex, Scott, WypAll, Kimtech, KleenGuard, Kimcare and Jackson brand names.

- **Health Care** (7% of sales), which manufactures and markets health care products such as surgical drapes and gowns, infection control products, face masks, exam gloves, respiratory products, pain management products and other disposable medical products. Products in this segment are sold under the Kimberly-Clark, Ballard, ON-Q and other brand names.

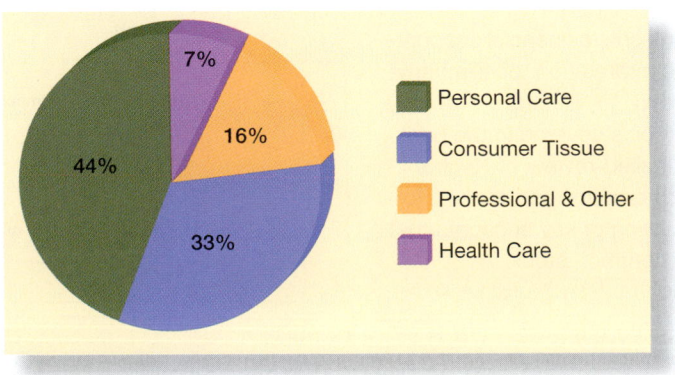

Approximately 52% of Kimberly-Clark's sales are in North America, 16% in Europe and 32% in Asia, Latin America, and other areas. Shown below is the proportion of its U.S. sales in each of these categories for each of the years 2008 through 2010:

Product Category	2010	2009	2008
Personal Care...................	43.9%	43.7%	42.6%
Consumer Tissue...............	32.9%	33.5%	34.8%
Professional & Other.............	15.8%	15.7%	16.3%
Health Care....................	7.4%	7.2%	6.3%

In addition, approximately 13% of Kimberly-Clark's sales are made to **Wal-Mart**, primarily in the personal care and consumer tissue businesses (source: Kimberly-Clark 2010 10-K).

In the MD&A section of its 10-K, Kimberly-Clark describes its competitive environment as follows:

We compete in intensely competitive markets against well-known, branded products and low-cost or private label products both domestically and internationally. Inherent risks in our competitive strategy include uncertainties concerning trade and consumer acceptance, the effects of consolidation within retailer and distribution channels, and competitive reaction. Our competitors for these markets include not only our traditional competitors but also private label manufacturers, low-cost manufacturers and rapidly-expanding international manufacturers. These competitors may have greater financial resources and greater market penetration, which enable them to offer a wider variety of products and services at more competitive prices. Alternatively, some of these competitors may have significantly lower product development and manufacturing costs, allowing them to offer products at a lower cost. The actions of these competitors could adversely affect our financial results. It may be necessary for us to lower prices on our products and increase spending on advertising and promotions, each of which could adversely affect our financial results.

Our ability to develop new products is affected by whether we can successfully anticipate consumer needs and preferences, develop and fund technological innovations, and receive and maintain necessary patent and trademark protection. In addition, we incur substantial development and marketing costs in introducing new and improved products and technologies. The introduction of a new consumer product (whether improved or newly developed) usually requires substantial expenditures for advertising and marketing to gain recognition in the marketplace. If a product gains consumer acceptance, it normally requires continued advertising and promotional support to maintain its relative market position. Some of our competitors are larger and have greater financial resources. These competitors may be able to spend more aggressively on advertising and promotional activities, introduce competing products more quickly and respond more effectively to changing business and economic conditions.

Beyond the competitive business risks described above, Kimberly-Clark faces fluctuating prices for cellulose fiber, the company's principle raw material, uncertain energy costs for manufacturing operations, foreign currency translation risks, and risks resulting from fluctuating interest rates.

Given this background, we begin the accounting analysis of Kimberly-Clark with a discussion of its financial statements.

REVIEWING THE FINANCIAL STATEMENTS

This section reviews and analyzes the financial statements of Kimberly-Clark.

L01 Explain and illustrate a review of financial statements and their components.

Income Statement Reporting and Analysis

Kimberly-Clark's income statement is reproduced in Exhibit C.1. The remainder of this section provides a brief review and analysis for Kimberly-Clark's income statement line items.

EXHIBIT C.1   Kimberly-Clark Income Statement

KIMBERLY-CLARK CORPORATION AND SUBSIDIARIES
Consolidated Income Statement

Year Ended December 31 (Millions of dollars, except per share amounts)	2010	2009	2008
Net sales	$19,746	$19,115	$19,415
Cost of products sold	13,196	12,695	13,557
Gross profit	6,550	6,420	5,858
Marketing, research and general expenses	3,673	3,498	3,291
Other (income) and expense, net	104	97	20
Operating profit	2,773	2,825	2,547
Interest income	20	26	46
Interest expense	(243)	(275)	(304)
Income before income taxes, equity interests and extraordinary loss	2,550	2,576	2,289
Provision for income taxes	(788)	(746)	(618)
Income before equity interests and extraordinary loss	1,762	1,830	1,671
Share of net income of equity companies	181	164	166
Income before extraordinary loss	1,943	1,994	1,837
Extraordinary loss, net of income taxes, attributable to Kimberly-Clark Corporation	—	—	(8)
Net income	1,943	1,994	1,829
Net income attributable to noncontrolling interests	(100)	(110)	(139)
Net income attributable to Kimberly-Clark Corporation	$ 1,843	$ 1,884	$ 1,690
Per share basis			
Basic			
Before extraordinary loss	$ 4.47	$ 4.53	$ 4.06
Extraordinary loss	—	—	(.02)
Net income attributable to Kimberly-Clark Corporation	$ 4.47	$ 4.53	$ 4.04
Diluted			
Before extraordinary loss	$ 4.45	$ 4.52	$ 4.05
Extraordinary loss	—	—	(.02)
Net income attributable to Kimberly-Clark Corporation	$ 4.45	$ 4.52	$ 4.03

Net Sales

Exhibit C.1 reveals that sales increased 3.3% in 2010 to $19,746 million, following a 1.5% sales decrease in the prior year. In its 2010 MD&A report, management attributes the increase equally to volume, price and mix effects.

Kimberly-Clark describes its revenue recognition policy as follows:

> Sales revenue is recognized at the time of product shipment or delivery, depending on when title passes, to unaffiliated customers, and when all of the following have occurred: a firm sales agreement is in place, pricing is fixed or determinable, and collection is reasonably assured. Sales are reported net of returns, consumer and trade promotions, rebates and freight allowed. Taxes imposed by governmental authorities on our revenue-producing activities with customers, such as sales taxes and value-added taxes, are excluded from net sales.

Its revenue recognition conditions are taken directly from GAAP and SEC guidelines, which recognize revenues when "earned and realizable." For Kimberly-Clark, *earned* means when title to the goods passes to the customer, and *realizable* means an account receivable whose collection is reasonably assured.

Sales for retailers and manufacturers are straightforward: revenue is recognized when the product is transferred to the buyer, an obligation for payment exists and collection of that payment is reasonably assured. In that case, the revenue is deemed to have been "earned." The primary issue for retailers and manufacturers relates to sales return allowances. These allowances pertain to product return or sales discounts (sometimes called *mark-downs*). Companies can only report sales when earned, that is, past the return allowance period. Further, companies can only report *net* sales as revenue (i.e., gross sales less any sales discounts, including volume discounts). K-C's footnotes provide the following table relating to sales allowances:

		Additions		Deductions	
December 31, 2010 ($ millions)	**Balance at Beginning of Period**	**Charged to Costs and Expenses**	**Charged to Other Accounts**	**Write-Offs and Reclassifications**	**Balance at End of Period**
Allowances for sales discounts	$21	$266	—	$269	$18

K-C's balance sheet includes a contra-asset related to sales discounts. The table indicates that the company had $21 million in sales discounts accrued at the start of the year that relate to sales in the prior year. During 2010, K-C granted its customers $266 million in additional sales discounts, $269 million of which had been taken by the customers by the end of the year. The remaining amount of $18 million, relates to discounts granted, but not yet taken, and is held over to the following year. These year-end amounts typically relate to discounts given toward the end of the year that are ultimately taken in the first quarter of the following year.

    The sales discount process affects net sales and, thus, profit. This allowance works just like any other allowance. If K-C underestimated the sales discount allowance, net sales and profit in the current year would be increased. Overestimation of the sales discount allowance would have the opposite effect: current sales and profit would be depressed. K-C's allowance has not changed appreciably in 2010 and is, therefore, not of concern.

    Revenue recognition in service industries and those industries that use the percentage-of-completion method can be problematic. Often, determining when a service contract has been "earned" can be difficult and revenue can easily be mis-estimated, either intentionally or not. Sanjay Kumar, former CEO of Computer Associates, was sentenced to 12 years in jail for his role in an accounting scandal relating primarily to misrepresentation of revenues and profit for the computer services company he headed up. The percentage-of-completion method is difficult to implement because it requires estimates of total costs or revenues of the project. Underestimation of costs results in overestimation of revenues. These estimation errors are often hidden from view because details in footnote disclosures are often vague or completely missing.

Cost of Products Sold and Gross Profit
Kimberly-Clark's 2010 gross profit margin is 33.2% ($6,550/$19,746), which is about 3.0 percentage points above what it was in 2008 (30.2%). As a benchmark, **Procter & Gamble**, the company's principle competitor, recently reported sales of $82.6 billion, over four times the level of K-C's sales, and a gross profit margin of 50.6%. This comparison highlights the intense competition that K-C faces from its much larger rival.

    The choice of inventory costing method affects cost of goods sold. K-C uses the LIFO method to cost its inventory. In 2011, the company's LIFO reserve increased by $37 million (see inventory discussion later in this Appendix). This increased cost of goods sold and reduced gross profit by $37 million. COGS can also be increased by inventory write-downs, typically related to restructuring efforts. For example, Cisco Systems, Inc. reported a $2.1 billion inventory write-down in 2001 when the tech bubble burst. This write-down increased COGS and reduced gross profit by that amount.

Marketing, Research and General Expenses
Kimberly-Clark's marketing, research and general expenses have increased to 18.6% of sales from 18.3% in the prior year. This increase resulted from general cost inflation as well as from the company's restructuring efforts designed to improve long-run manufacturing and operating costs. K-C reports 2010 net operating profit after taxes (NOPAT) of $2,083 million [($2,773 + $181) − ($788 + {$243 − $20} × 37%)] and a net operating profit margin (NOPM) of 10.5% ($2,083 million/$19,746 million)

of sales.[1] P&G, by contrast, is able to use its higher gross profit margin to fund a higher level of advertising and other SGA expenditures, resulting in a NOPM of 14.8%.

Pension Costs. Kimberly-Clark's marketing, research and general expenses include $133 million of pension expense. This is reported in the following table in the pension footnote:

Components of Net Periodic Benefit Cost						
	Pension Benefits			**Other Benefits**		
Year Ended December 31 (Millions of dollars)	**2010**	**2009**	**2008**	**2010**	**2009**	**2008**
Service cost	$ 56	$ 68	$ 73	$ 14	$ 14	$ 15
Interest cost	309	310	324	44	47	49
Expected return on plan assets	(336)	(269)	(370)	—	—	—
Curtailments	—	21	—	—	—	—
Amortization of prior service cost and transition amount	2	3	6	3	2	2
Recognized net actuarial loss	99	111	56	1	—	1
Other.	3	7	8	—	—	(1)
Net periodic benefit cost	$133	$251	$ 97	$ 62	$ 63	$ 66

For 2010, the expected return on pension investments ($336 million) provides an offset to the company's pension service and interest costs ($56 million and $309 million, respectively). Footnotes reveal that Kimberly-Clark's pension investments realized an *actual* return of $473 million in 2010 (from the pension footnote in its 10-K report). So, for 2010, use of the expected return results in an unrecognized *gain* that is deferred, along with other unrecognized gains and losses, in the computation of reported profit.

Kimberly-Clark describes how it determines the expected return in its footnotes. It is instructive to review the company's rationale and, thus, the footnote follows:

Strategic asset allocation decisions are made with the intent of maximizing return at an acceptable level of risk. Risk factors considered in setting the strategic asset allocation include, among other things, plan participants' retirement benefit security, the estimated payments of the associated liabilities, the plan funded status, and Kimberly-Clark's financial condition. The resulting strategic asset allocation is a diversified blend of equity and fixed income investments. Equity investments are typically diversified across geography and market capitalization. Fixed income investments are diversified across multiple sectors including government issues, corporate debt instruments, mortgage backed securities and asset backed securities with a portfolio duration that is consistent with the estimated payment of the associated liability. Actual asset allocation is regularly reviewed and periodically rebalanced to the strategic allocation when considered appropriate.

The expected long-term rate of return is evaluated on an annual basis. In setting this assumption, we consider a number of factors including projected future returns by asset class, current asset allocation and historical long-term market performance.

The weighted-average expected long-term rate of return on pension fund assets used to calculate pension expense for the Principal Plans was 8.19 percent in 2010 compared with 8.47 percent in 2009 and will be 7.35 percent in 2011. The expected long-term rate of return on the assets in the Principal Plans is based on an asset allocation assumption of about 60 percent with equity managers, with expected long-term rates of return ranging from 9 to 10 percent, and about 40 percent with fixed income managers, with an expected long-term rate of return ranging from 5 to 6 percent.

The expected return on pension assets offsets service and interest costs, and serves to reduce pension expense. In general, increasing (decreasing) the expected return on pension assets, increases

---

[1] We include equity income of $181 million (labeled as "share of net income of equity companies" in K-C's income statement) as operating because it relates to investments in paper-related companies and it, therefore, aligns with K-C's primary operating activities. This amount is reported by K-C net of tax, and therefore, no tax adjustment is necessary when computing NOPAT. We consider K-C's noncontrolling interests share of subsidiaries' net income, as nonoperating.

(decreases) profit. In 2010, K-C reduced its expected return from 8.17% to 7.96%. The discount rate (used to compute the PBO and the interest cost component of pension expense) declined by 55 basis points (6.40% to 5.85%). It is not uncommon for the expected return rate to be "stickier" on the downside (thus propping up profits) and more quickly adjusted on the upside (to take advantage of increasing returns). We need to be mindful of these effects when assessing operating profits.

Transitory versus Persistent Line Items

Expenses relating to restructuring activities have become increasingly common in the past two decades.

In a subsequent event footnote to its 2010 10-K, Kimberly-Clark announced the following restructuring plan:

> The restructuring plan will commence in the first quarter of 2011 and is expected to be completed by December 31, 2012. The restructuring is expected to result in cumulative charges of approximately $400 million to $600 million before tax ($280 million to $420 million after tax) over that period. We anticipate that the charges will fall into the following categories and approximate dollar ranges: workforce reduction costs ($50 million to $100 million); incremental depreciation ($300 million to $400 million); and other associated costs ($50 million to $100 million). Cash costs related to the streamlining of operations, sale or closure, relocation of equipment, severance and other expenses are expected to account for approximately 25 percent to 50 percent of the charges. Noncash charges will consist primarily of incremental depreciation.

These initiatives are designed to further improve the company's competitive position by accelerating investments in targeted growth opportunities and strategic cost reductions to streamline manufacturing and administrative operations.

Classification of these charges as transitory or persistent is a judgment call. In K-C's case, these charges relate to a multi-year program that is expected to continue through 2012. Therefore, we might classify these expenses as persistent. Our review of the financial statements did not identify any other transitory items and thus, we classified all other activity as persistent.

Earnings per Share

Net income for Kimberly-Clark has increased from $1,690 million in 2008 to $1,843 million in 2010. Basic (diluted) earnings per share, however, has increased from $4.04 ($4.03) to $4.47 ($4.45). Following is Kimberly-Clark's computation of earnings per share:

> **Earnings Per Share** A reconciliation of the average number of common shares outstanding used in the basic and diluted EPS computations follows:
>
> | (Millions) | Average Common Shares Outstanding | | |
> | --- | --- | --- | --- |
> | | 2010 | 2009 | 2008 |
> | Average shares outstanding. . . . . | 411.3 | 414.6 | 416.7 |
> | Participating securities. . . . . | 1.1 | 1.5 | 1.8 |
> | Basic. . . . . | 412.4 | 416.1 | 418.5 |
> | Dilutive effect of stock options. . . . . | 1.1 | .4 | .9 |
> | Dilutive effect of restricted share and restricted share unit awards . . . . | .9 | .3 | .2 |
> | Diluted . . . . | 414.4 | 416.8 | 419.6 |
>
> Options outstanding that were not included in the computation of diluted EPS mainly because their exercise price was greater than the average market price of the common shares are summarized below:

continued

continued from prior page

Description	2010	2009	2008
Average number of share equivalents (millions).......	**13.9**	21.8	15.6
Weighted-average exercise price..................	**$66.00**	$64.12	$66.31
Expiration date of options	**2010 to 2020**	2009 to 2019	2008 to 2018
Options outstanding at year-end (millions)...........	**14.7**	20.3	16.0

The number of common shares outstanding as of December 31, 2010, 2009 and 2008 was 406.9 million, 416.9 million and 413.6 million, respectively.

Most of the difference between basic and diluted earnings per share usually arises from the dilutive effects of employee stock options. (We should note that if stock options are *under water*, meaning that K-C's stock price is lower than the exercise price of the options, they are considered *antidilutive*, meaning that including them would increase EPS. Accordingly, they are excluded in the diluted EPS computation, but remain potentially dilutive if K-C's stock price subsequently rises above the exercise price of the options.) (Although not present for Kimberly-Clark, convertible debt and preferred shares are also potentially dilutive for many companies.)

Income Taxes

Kimberly-Clark's net income has been negatively affected over the past three years by an increase in its effective tax rate from 27.0% to 30.9% as K-C describes in the following footnote:

Year Ended December 31	2010	2009	2008
Tax at U.S. statutory rate applied to income before income taxes.....................	35.0%	35.0%	35.0%
State income taxes, net of federal tax benefit.............	1.8	(0.3)	0.9
Statutory rates other than U.S. statutory rate.............	(3.0)	(2.4)	(2.4)
Other—net..	(2.9)	(3.3)	(6.5)
Effective income tax rate...........................	30.9%	29.0%	27.0%

Common-Size Income Statement

It is useful for analysis purposes to prepare common-size statements. Exhibit C.2 shows Kimberly-Clark's common-size income statement covering the two most recent years.

EXHIBIT C.2	Kimberly-Clark Common-Size Income Statement		
Year Ended December 31		**2010**	**2009**
Net sales...		100.0%	100.0%
Cost of products sold...............................		66.8	66.4
Gross profit..		33.2	33.6
Marketing, research and general expenses................		18.6	18.3
Other (income) and expense, net......................		0.5	0.5
Operating profit....................................		14.0	14.8
Interest income.....................................		0.1	0.1
Interest expense....................................		(1.2)	(1.4)
Income before income taxes and equity interests..........		12.9	13.5
Provision for income taxes...........................		(4.0)	(3.9)
Income before equity interests........................		8.9	9.6
Share of net income of equity companies................		0.9	0.9
Net income...		9.8	10.4
Net income attributable to noncontrolling interests.........		(0.5)	(0.6)
Net income attributable to Kimberly-Clark Corporation.......		9.3%	9.9%

Note: All percentages are computed by dividing each income statement line item by that year's net sales.

The gross profit margin declined in 2010 from 33.6% in 2009 to 33.2%. This most likely reflects the competitive environment in which K-C operates. Companies typically offset a declining gross profit margin with reductions in SG&A expense. K-C has been unable to do that, however, as its marketing, research and general (SG&A) expense in 2010 actually exceeds its 2009 level as a percentage of sales. Accordingly, 2010 income before taxes declined by 0.6 percentage points relative to 2009, from 13.5% of sales to 12.9%. Further, income from equity companies (reported net of tax) remained constant as a percentage of sales at 0.9%. Finally, net income as a percentage of sales declined by 0.6 percentage points from 9.9% of sales to 9.3%.

Management Discussion and Analysis

The Management Discussion and Analysis section of a 10-K is usually informative for interpreting company financial statements and for additional insights into company operations. To illustrate, Kimberly-Clark provides the following analysis of its operating results in the MD&A section of its 2010 10-K:

Overview of 2010 Results

- Net sales increased 3.3 percent because of an increase in sales volumes, net selling prices and improvements in product mix.

- Operating profit decreased 1.8 percent, and net income attributable to Kimberly-Clark and diluted earnings per share decreased 2.2 percent and 1.5 percent, respectively. The benefits of the net sales increase, cost savings, a decrease in pension expense, and the effect of the 2009 organization optimization severance and related charges, were more than offset by inflation in key input costs, increased marketing, research and general expenses, and the charge related to the adoption of highly inflationary accounting for Venezuela.

- Cash flow from operations was $2.7 billion, a decrease of 21 percent.

Results of Operations and Related Information   *2010 versus 2009*

- Personal care net sales in North America increased about 4 percent due to an increase in sales volumes and net selling prices of 3 percent and 1 percent, respectively. The sales volume increases resulted from higher sales of feminine care and adult incontinence products, including benefits from innovation by Kotex, Poise and Depend brands and higher sales of training pants and baby wipes, partially offset by lower sales of Huggies diapers.

  In Europe, personal care net sales decreased about 2 percent due to unfavorable currency effects of 2 percent and a decrease in net selling prices of 1 percent, partially offset by increases in sales volumes of 1 percent.

  In K-C's International operations in Asia, Latin America, the Middle East, Eastern Europe and Africa ("K-C International"), net sales increased about 6 percent driven by a 5 percent increase in sales volumes and a 1 percent favorable currency effect. The growth in sales volumes was broad-based, with particular strength in Asia and Latin America, excluding Venezuela.

- Consumer tissue net sales in North America decreased 1 percent as an increase in net selling prices of 2 percent and improvements in product mix of 1 percent were more than offset by a sales volume decline of 4 percent. Sales volumes were down low single-digits in bath tissue and double-digits in paper towels, primarily as a result of continued consumer trade-down to lower-priced product offerings.

  In Europe, consumer tissue net sales decreased 2 percent due to unfavorable currency effects of 2 percent and a decrease in sales volumes of 2 percent, partially offset by an increase in net selling prices of 2 percent.

  In K-C International, consumer tissue net sales increased about 8 percent due to an increase in net selling prices of 4 percent, favorable currency effects of 2 percent and improvements in product mix of 1 percent. Increases in net selling prices were broad-based, with particular strength in Latin America and Russia.

- K-C Professional's net sales in North America increased 3 percent due to higher net selling prices of about 2 percent and favorable currency effects of 1 percent. Volume comparisons benefited from the Jackson Products, Inc. ("Jackson") acquisition in 2009 and growth in the wipes and safety categories, while washroom product volumes declined in a continued

continued

continued from prior page

> challenging economic environment. In Europe, sales of K-C Professional products decreased 1 percent, as an increase in sales volumes of 3 percent was more than offset by unfavorable currency effects of 3 percent and lower net selling prices of 1 percent.
>
> • The increased sales volumes for health care products were primarily due to a 9 percent benefit from the acquisition of I-Flow Corporation ("I-Flow") in late November 2009, as well as volume increases in other medical devices, which were more than offset by declines in supplies, including the impact from increased face mask demand in 2009 related to the H1N1 influenza virus.

Business Segments

Generally accepted accounting principles require that companies disclose the composition of their operating profit by business segment. Segments are investment centers (those having both income statement and balance sheet data) that the company routinely evaluates at the chief executive level.

We outlined and discussed Kimberly-Clark's business segments at the beginning of the appendix: personal care, consumer tissue, professional & other, and health care. Following are its GAAP disclosures for each of its business segments:

Consolidated Operations by Business Segment						
(Millions of dollars)	Personal Care	Consumer Tissue	Professional & Other	Health Care	Corporate & Other	Consolidated Total
Net sales						
2010	$8,670	$6,497	$3,110	$1,460	9	$19,746
2009	8,365	6,409	3,007	1,371	(37)	19,115
2008	8,272	6,748	3,174	1,224	(3)	19,415
Operating profit						
2010	1,764	660	468	174	(293)	2,773
2009	1,739	736	464	244	(358)	2,825
2008	1,649	601	428	143	(274)	2,547
Depreciation and amortization						
2010	277	329	142	56	9	813
2009	255	314	148	50	16	783
2008	239	319	136	52	29	775
Assets						
2010	6,316	6,106	2,962	2,410	2,070	19,864
2009	5,895	5,871	2,969	2,558	1,916	19,209
2008	5,480	5,809	2,710	2,139	1,951	18,089
Capital spending						
2010	436	331	156	40	1	964
2009	440	271	97	38	2	848
2008	375	351	130	49	1	906

Given these data, it is possible for us to perform a rudimentary return analysis for each segment. This analysis provides insight into a company's dependence on any one segment. Following is a brief summary analysis of K-C's segment return disaggregation for 2010:

(Millions of dollars)	Personal Care	Consumer Tissue	Professional & Other	Health Care
Net sales	8,670	6,497	3,110	1,460
Operating profit	1,764	660	468	174
Assets	6,316	6,106	2,962	2,410
Operating profit margin	20.3%	10.2%	15.0%	11.9%
Year-end asset turnover	1.37	1.06	1.05	0.61
Operating profit divided by year-end assets	27.9%	10.8%	15.8%	7.2%

The intensely competitive nature and capital intensity of the health care market is evident in its low profit margin (11.9%) and low return on ending operating assets (7.2%). K-C relies, to a great extent, on its personal care segment to generate income.

Balance Sheet Reporting and Analysis

Kimberly-Clark's balance sheet is reproduced in Exhibit C.3.

EXHIBIT C.3	Kimberly-Clark Balance Sheet

KIMBERLY-CLARK CORPORATION AND SUBSIDIARIES
Consolidated Balance Sheet

December 31 (Millions of dollars)	2010	2009
ASSETS		
Current assets		
Cash and cash equivalents	$ 876	$ 798
Accounts receivable, net	2,472	2,566
Note receivable	218	—
Inventories	2,373	2,033
Deferred income taxes	187	136
Other current assets	202	331
Total current assets	6,328	5,864
Property, plant and equipment, net	8,356	8,033
Investments in equity companies	374	355
Goodwill	3,403	3,275
Other intangible assets	287	310
Long-term notes receivable	393	607
Other assets	723	765
Total assets	$19,864	$19,209
LIABILITIES AND STOCKHOLDERS' EQUITY		
Current liabilities		
Debt payable within one year	$ 344	$ 610
Redeemable preferred securities of subsidiary	506	—
Trade accounts payable	2,206	1,920
Accrued expenses	1,909	2,064
Accrued income taxes	104	79
Dividends payable	269	250
Total current liabilities	5,338	4,923
Long-term debt	5,120	4,792
Noncurrent employee benefits	1,810	1,989
Long-term income taxes payable	260	168
Deferred income taxes	369	377
Other liabilities	224	218
Redeemable preferred and common securities of subsidiaries	541	1,052
Stockholders' Equity		
Kimberly-Clark Corporation stockholders' equity		
Preferred stock—no par value—authorized 20.0 million shares, none issued	—	—
Common stock—$1.25 par value—authorized 1.2 billion shares; issued 478.6 million shares at December 31, 2010 and 2009	598	598
Additional paid-in capital	425	399
Common stock held in treasury, at cost—71.7 million and 61.6 million shares at December 31, 2010 and 2009	(4,726)	(4,087)
Accumulated other comprehensive income (loss)	(1,466)	(1,833)
Retained earnings	11,086	10,329
Total Kimberly-Clark Corporation stockholders' equity	5,917	5,406
Noncontrolling interests	285	284
Total stockholders' equity	6,202	5,690
Total liabilities and stockholders' equity	$19,864	$19,209

Kimberly-Clark reports total assets of $19,864 million in 2010. Its net working capital is relatively illiquid because a large proportion of current assets consists of accounts receivable and inventories, and its cash is 4.4% ($876 million/$19,864 million) of total assets at year-end 2010, up from 4.1% in 2009. It also reports no marketable securities that can serve as another source of liquidity, if needed. The lack of liquidity is usually worrisome, but is not a serious concern in this case given Kimberly-Clark's moderate financial leverage and high level of free cash flow (see later discussion in this section).

Following is a brief review and analysis for each of Kimberly-Clark's balance sheet line items.

Accounts Receivable

Kimberly-Clark reports $2,472 million in net accounts receivable at year-end 2010. This represents 12.4% ($2,472 million/$19,864 million) of total assets, down from 13.4% in the previous year. Footnotes reveal the following additional information:

Summary of Accounts Receivable ($ millions), December 31	2010	2009
Accounts Receivable		
From customers	$2,231	$2,290
Other.	321	365
Less allowance for doubtful accounts and sales discounts.	(80)	(89)
Total.	$2,472	$2,566

Most accounts receivables are from customers. This means we must consider the following two issues:

1. **Magnitude**—Receivables are generally non-interest-bearing and, therefore, do not earn a return. Further, the company incurs costs to finance them. Accordingly, a company wants to optimize its level of investment in receivables—that is, keep them as low as possible while still meeting industry specific credit policies to meet customer demands.

2. **Collectibility**—Receivables represent unsecured loans to customers. It is critical therefore, to understand the creditworthiness of these borrowers. Receivables are reported at net realizable value, that is, net of the allowance for doubtful accounts. Kimberly-Clark reports an allowance of $80 million. In addition, the footnotes reveal the following history of the company's allowance versus its write-offs:

		Additions		Deductions	
Description (December 31, 2010)	Balance at Beginning of Period	Charged to Costs and Expenses	Charged to Other Accounts	Write-Offs and Reclassifications	Balance at End of Period
Allowance for doubtful accounts	$68	$7	—	$13	$62

The company reported a balance in the allowance for doubtful accounts of $68 million at the beginning of 2010, which is 2.6% of gross receivables [$68/($2,566 million + $68 million)]. During 2010, it increased this allowance account by $7 million. This is the amount of bad debt expense that is reported in the income statement. Write-offs and reclassifications of uncollectible accounts amounted to $13 million during the year, yielding a $62 million balance at year-end, which is 2.4% of gross receivables [$62 million/($2,472 million + $62 million)]. It appears, therefore, that the company's receivables were less adequately reserved at year-end relative to the beginning of the year, but the difference is not substantial.

The allowance for doubtful accounts should always reflect the company's best estimate of the potential loss in its accounts receivable. This amount should not be overly conservative (which would understate profit), and it should not be inadequate (which would overstate profit). K-C's estimate of its potential losses results from its own (unaudited) review of the age of its receivables (older receivables are at greater risk of uncollectibility).

Inventories

Kimberly-Clark reports $2,373 million in inventories as of 2010. Footnote disclosures reveal the following inventory costing policy:

> **Inventories and Distribution Costs**   For financial reporting purposes, most U.S. inventories are valued at the lower of cost, using the Last-In, First-Out (LIFO) method, or market. The balance of the U.S. inventories and inventories of consolidated operations outside the U.S. are valued at the lower of cost, using either the First-In, First-Out (FIFO) or weighted-average cost methods, or market. Distribution costs are classified as Cost of Products Sold.

Most of its U.S. inventories are reported on a LIFO basis. Some of its U.S. inventories, as well as those outside of the U.S., are valued at FIFO or weighted-average. The use of multiple inventory costing methods for different pools of inventories is common and acceptable under GAAP.

Kimberly-Clark provides the following footnote disclosure relating to the composition of its inventories:

	2010			2009		
Summary of Inventories ($ millions), December 31	**LIFO**	**Non-LIFO**	**Total**	**LIFO**	**Non-LIFO**	**Total**
Inventories by Major Class:						
At the lower of cost determined on the FIFO or						
weighted-average cost methods or market:						
Raw materials	$ 154	$ 350	$ 504	$ 137	$ 282	$ 419
Work in process.	195	144	339	177	111	288
Finished goods	715	763	1,478	573	685	1,258
Supplies and other	—	298	298	—	277	277
	1,064	1,555	2,619	887	1,355	2,242
Excess of FIFO or weighted-average cost over:						
LIFO cost	(246)	—	(246)	(209)	—	(209)
Total	$ 818	$1,555	$2,373	$ 678	$1,355	$2,033

Companies aim to optimize their investment in inventories because inventory is a non-income-producing asset until sold. Inventories must also be financed, stored, moved, and insured at some cost. Kimberly-Clark reports $504 million of raw materials, which is 19% of the total of $2,619 million FIFO inventories (see table above). Work-in-process inventories amount to another $339 million, and supplies and other amount to $298 million. The bulk of its inventories, or $1,478 million (56% of total inventories), is in finished goods.

Kimberly-Clark reports its total inventory cost *at FIFO* is $2,619 million then subtracts $246 million from this amount (the *LIFO reserve*) to yield the inventories balance of $2,373 million at LIFO as reported on the balance sheet. This means that, over time, Kimberly-Clark has reduced gross profit and pretax operating profit by a cumulative amount of $246 million. This has also reduced pretax income and saved federal income tax, and generated cash flow, of approximately $86.1 million (assuming a 35% statutory federal tax rate and computed as $246 million × 35%). During 2010, its LIFO reserve increased by $37 million, resulting in a $37 million decrease in gross profit and pretax operating profit, and a $13.0 million ($37 million × 35%) *increase* in cash flow from decreased federal income taxes.

Property, Plant, and Equipment

Kimberly-Clark reports Property, Plant, and Equipment, net, of $8,356 million at year-end 2010; PPE makes up 42.1% of total assets and is the largest single asset category. Given the cost of depreciable assets of $17,877 million and accumulated depreciation of $9,521 million (not reported here), PPE is 53.3% depreciated assuming straight-line depreciation ($9,521 million/$17,877 million) as of 2010. This suggests these assets are about the average age that we would expect assuming a regular replacement policy. Footnotes reveal a useful life range of 40 years for buildings and 16 to 20 years for machinery as follows:

Property and Depreciation   For financial reporting purposes, property, plant and equipment are stated at cost and are depreciated principally on the straight-line method. Buildings are depreciated over their estimated useful lives, primarily 40 years. Machinery and equipment are depreciated over their estimated useful lives, primarily ranging from 16 to 20 years. For income tax purposes, accelerated methods of depreciation are used. Purchases of computer software are capitalized. External costs and certain internal costs (including payroll and payroll-related costs of employees) directly associated with developing significant computer software applications for internal use are capitalized. Training and data conversion costs are expensed as incurred. Computer software costs are amortized on the straight-line method over the estimated useful life of the software, which generally does not exceed five years...The cost of major maintenance performed on manufacturing facilities, composed of labor, materials and other incremental costs, is charged to operations as incurred. Start-up costs for new or expanded facilities are expensed as incurred.

Again, assuming straight-line depreciation, Kimberly-Clark's 2010 depreciation expense of $790 million ($813 depreciation and amortization expense reported in its statement of cash flows, Exhibit C.5, less $23 million reported as amortization expense in footnotes not reproduced in the text, but equal to the difference in accumulated amortization) reveals that its long-term depreciable assets, as a whole, are being depreciated over an average useful life of about 21.7 years, computed as $17,877 million − $220 million of nondepreciable land and $553 million of construction in progress divided by $790 million depreciation expense.

Each year, Kimberly-Clark tests PPE for impairment and records a write-down to net realizable value if the PPE is deemed to be impaired. Following is Kimberly-Clark's discussion relating to its impairment testing:

Estimated useful lives are periodically reviewed and, when warranted, changes are made to them. Long-lived assets, including computer software, are reviewed for impairment whenever events or changes in circumstances indicate that their carrying amount may not be recoverable. An impairment loss would be indicated when estimated undiscounted future cash flows from the use and eventual disposition of an asset group, which are identifiable and largely independent of the cash flows of other asset groups, are less than the carrying amount of the asset group. Measurement of an impairment loss would be based on the excess of the carrying amount of the asset over its fair value. Fair value is measured using discounted cash flows or independent appraisals, as appropriate. When property is sold or retired, the cost of the property and the related accumulated depreciation are removed from the Consolidated Balance Sheet and any gain or loss on the transaction is included in income.

The company did not report any impairment losses in the periods covered by its recent 10-K.

If present, impairment losses should be treated as a transitory item. Further, we must consider the effects of such losses on current and future income statements. An impairment loss depresses current period income. Further, depreciation expense in future years is decreased because it is computed based on the asset's lower net book value (cost less accumulated depreciation) following the write-down. This will increase future period profitability. The net effect of an impairment charge, therefore, is to shift profit from the current period into future periods.

Investments in Equity Companies

K-C's balance sheet reports equity investments of $374 million at year-end 2010. This amount represents the book value of its investments in affiliated companies over which Kimberly-Clark can exert significant influence, but not control. Footnotes reveal investments in the following companies:

Investments in Equity Companies   Investments in companies over which we have the ability to exercise significant influence and that, in general, are at least 20 percent owned by us, are stated at cost plus equity in undistributed net income. These investments are evaluated for impairment when warranted. An impairment loss would be recorded whenever a decline in value of an equity

continued

continued from prior page

> investment below its carrying amount is determined to be other than temporary. In judging "other than temporary," we would consider the length of time and extent to which the fair value of the equity company investment has been less than the carrying amount, the near-term and longer-term operating and financial prospects of the equity company, and our longer-term intent of retaining the investment in the equity company.

Consolidation is not required unless the affiliate is "controlled." Generally, control is presumed at an ownership level of more than 50%. By this rule, Kimberly-Clark does not control any of these companies. Thus, the company uses the equity method to account for these investments. This means that only the net equity owned of these companies is reported on the balance sheet. We further discuss these investments in the section on off-balance-sheet financing.

Goodwill

Kimberly-Clark reports $3,403 million of goodwill at year-end 2010. This amount represents the excess of the purchase price for acquired companies over the fair market value of the acquired tangible and identifiable intangible assets (net of liabilities assumed). Under GAAP, goodwill is not systematically amortized, but is annually tested for impairment.

Other Assets

Kimberly-Clark reports $723 million as "other assets." There is no table detailing what assets are included in this total, but footnotes reveal the following: $15 million of long-term marketable securities, $70 million of assets related to derivative financial instruments, and $312 million of noncurrent deferred income tax assets. No information is given on the remaining $330 million of other assets, most likely because this amount represents several assets each of which is not determined to be material and, therefore, subject to disclosure.

Concerning the deferred income tax assets, Kimberly-Clark provides the following disclosure relating to its composition ($ millions):

December 31 (Millions of dollars)	2010	2009
Net current deferred income tax asset attributable to:		
Accrued expenses	$ 103	$ 102
Pension, postretirement and other employee benefits	82	86
Loss carryforwards	72	—
Installment sales	(72)	—
Inventory	(21)	(45)
Other	46	8
Valuation allowances	(23)	(15)
Net current deferred income tax asset	$ 187	$ 136
Net current deferred income tax liability included in accrued expenses	$ (28)	$ (31)
Net noncurrent deferred income tax asset attributable to:		
Tax credits and loss carryforwards	$ 447	$ 405
Pension and other postretirement benefits	153	228
Property, plant and equipment, net	(97)	(86)
Other	42	37
Valuation allowances	(233)	(211)
Net noncurrent deferred income tax asset included in other assets	$ 312	$ 373
Net noncurrent deferred income tax liability attributable to:		
Property, plant and equipment, net	$(1,081)	$(976)
Pension, postretirement and other employee benefits	550	546
Tax credits and loss carryforwards	447	462
Installment sales	(112)	(180)
Provision for unremitted earnings	(88)	(70)
Intangible assets	(43)	(63)
Other	(13)	(78)
Valuation allowances	(29)	(18)
Net noncurrent deferred income tax liability	$ (369)	$(377)

Most of this deferred tax asset (benefit) results from tax loss carryforwards. The IRS allows companies to carry forward losses to offset future taxable income, thereby reducing future tax expense. This benefit can only be realized if the company expects taxable income in the specific entity that generated the tax losses before the carryforwards expire. If the company deems it more likely than not that the carryforwards will *not* be realized, a valuation allowance for the unrealizable portion is required (this is similar to establishing an allowance for uncollectible accounts receivable). As of 2010, Kimberly-Clark has such a valuation allowance (of $285 million). Following is its discussion relating to this allowance:

> Valuation allowances increased $43 million in 2010 and decreased $75 million in 2009. Valuation allowances at the end of 2010 primarily relate to tax credits and income tax loss carryforwards of $1.2 billion. If these items are not utilized against taxable income, $210 million of the loss carryforwards will expire from 2011 through 2030. The remaining $981 million has no expiration date. Realization of income tax loss carryforwards is dependent on generating sufficient taxable income prior to expiration of these carryforwards. Although realization is not assured, we believe it is more likely than not that all of the deferred tax assets, net of applicable valuation allowances, will be realized. The amount of the deferred tax assets considered realizable could be reduced or increased due to changes in the tax environment or if estimates of future taxable income change during the carryforward period.

Tax loss carryforwards reduce income tax expense in the year they are recognized, similar to tax loss carry-backs. However, companies often establish a deferred tax asset valuation allowance which increases tax expense. It is common that companies establish both the loss carryforward and the valuation allowance concurrently. The net effect is to leave tax expense (and net income) unchanged. In future years, however, a reduction of the deferred tax asset valuation account, in anticipation of utilization of the tax carry-forwards (and not as a result of their expiration), reduces tax expense and increases net income. This is a transitory increase in profit and should not be factored into projections.

Current Liabilities

Kimberly-Clark reports current liabilities of $5,338 million on its year-end balance sheet for 2010 ($4,923 million in 2009), which consists of the following:

Current Liabilities ($ millions), December 31	2010	2009
Debt payable within one year	$ 344	$ 610
Redeemable preferred securities of subsidiary	506	—
Trade accounts payable	2,206	1,920
Accrued expenses	1,909	2,064
Accrued income taxes	104	79
Dividends payable	269	250
Total Current Liabilities	$5,338	$4,923

Regarding K-C's current liabilities, $1,119 of this amount relates to financial items, such as maturing long-term debt ($344 million), an obligation to repurchase redeemable preferred stock of a subsidiary ($506 million) and dividends payable ($269 million). The remaining items in current liabilities arise from common external transactions, such as trade accounts payable and taxes payable. These transactions are less prone to management reporting bias. We must, however, determine the presence of excessive "leaning on the trade" as a means to boost operating cash flow. K-C's trade accounts payable have increased as a percentage of total liabilities and equity from 10.0% ($1,920 million/$19,209 million) in 2009 to 11.1% ($2,206 million/$19,864 million) in 2010. While this change is not drastic, and the level is not excessive, we need to monitor K-C's balance sheet for a continuation of this trend.

The possibility of management reporting bias is typically greater for accrued liabilities, which are often estimated (and difficult to audit), involve no external transaction, and can markedly impact reported balance sheet and income statement amounts. One of Kimberly-Clark's accrued liabilities involves promotions and rebates, reported at $352 million in the footnotes as of 2010. Following is the description of its accrual policy in this area:

Promotion and Rebate Accruals Among those factors affecting the accruals for promotions are estimates of the number of consumer coupons that will be redeemed and the type and number of activities within promotional programs between us and our trade customers. Rebate accruals are based on estimates of the quantity of products distributors have sold to specific customers. Generally, the estimates for consumer coupon costs are based on historical patterns of coupon redemption, influenced by judgments about current market conditions such as competitive activity in specific product categories. Estimates of trade promotion liabilities for promotional program costs incurred, but unpaid, are generally based on estimates of the quantity of customer sales, timing of promotional activities and forecasted costs for activities within the promotional programs. Settlement of these liabilities sometimes occurs in periods subsequent to the date of the promotion activity. Trade promotion programs include introductory marketing funds such as slotting fees, cooperative marketing programs, temporary price reductions, favorable end-of-aisle or in-store product displays and other activities conducted by our customers to promote our products. Promotion accruals as of December 31, 2010 and 2009 were $352 million and $364 million, respectively. Rebate accruals as of December 31, 2010 and 2009 were $353 million and $365 million, respectively.

The company also reports accruals relating to its insurance risks as described in the following footnote:

Retained Insurable Risks Selected insurable risks are retained, primarily those related to property damage, workers' compensation, and product, automobile and premises liability based upon historical loss patterns and management's judgment of cost effective risk retention. Accrued liabilities for incurred but not reported events, principally related to workers' compensation and automobile liability, are based upon undiscounted loss development factors.

All of these accruals have similar effects on the financial statements: when the accrual is established the company recognizes both an expense in the income statement and a liability on the balance sheet. The company subsequently reduces the liability as payments are made. Companies can (and do) use accruals to shift income from one period to another, say by over-accruing in one period to intentionally depress current period profits, and later reducing the liability account, rather than recording an expense, to increase future period profits. Accruals are sometimes referred to as "pads." They represent a cost that has previously been charged to the income statement. They also represent an account that can absorb future costs. We need to monitor accrual accounts carefully for evidence of earnings management.

Long-Term Debt

Kimberly-Clark reports $5,385 million of long-term debt as of 2010. Footnotes reveal the following:

Long-term debt is composed of the following:

($ millions)	Weighted-Average Interest Rate	Maturities	December 31 2010	December 31 2009
Notes and debentures	5.97%	2012–2037	$4,286	$4,483
Dealer remarketable securities.	4.43%	2011–2016	200	—
Industrial development revenue bonds	0.35%	2015–2037	280	280
Bank loans and other financings in various currencies.	2.61%	2011–2045	619	532
Total long-term debt.			5,385	5,295
Less current portion			265	503
Long-term portion			$5,120	$4,792

Most of its long-term financing is in the form of notes and debentures, specifically $4,286 million in 2010, which mature over the next 25 years. GAAP requires disclosure of scheduled maturities for each of the five years subsequent to the balance sheet date. Kimberly-Clark's five-year maturity schedule follows:

> Scheduled maturities of long-term debt for the next five years are $265 million in 2011, $427 million in 2012, $550 million in 2013, $516 million in 2014 and $355 million in 2015.

Our concern with debt maturity dates is whether or not a company is able to repay debt as it comes due. Alternatively, a company can refinance the debt. If a company is unable or unwilling to repay or refinance its debt, it must approach creditors for a modification of debt terms for those issuances coming due. Creditors are often willing to oblige but will likely increase interest rates or impose additional debt covenants and restrictions. However, if creditors deny default waivers, the company might face the prospect of bankruptcy. This highlights the importance of long-term debt maturity disclosures.

We have little concern about Kimberly-Clark's debt maturity schedule as the company has strong cash flows. Still, it is worth noting that **Standard & Poor's** (S&P) debt rating for K-C is A. This rating is solid (described as "upper-medium grade" debt).

Noncurrent Employee Benefit and Other Obligations

Kimberly-Clark reports a (negative) funded status of its pension plan of $(1,058) million at year-end 2010 (disclosed in footnotes). This means that the company's pension plans are underfunded by that amount. This underfunding is computed as the difference between the pension benefit obligation (PBO) of $5,658 million and the fair market value of the company's pension assets of $4,600 million (these amounts are also reported in the pension footnote not reproduced here).

The central issue with respect to pensions and other post-retirement obligations is the potential demand they present on operating cash flows. Companies can tap cash from two sources to pay pension and other post-retirement obligations: from the returns on plan assets (i.e., the cumulative contributions and investment returns that have not yet been paid out to beneficiaries) and/or from operating cash flow. To the extent that plan assets are insufficient to meet retirement obligations, companies must divert operating cash flows from other investment activities, potentially reducing the dollar amount of capital projects that can be funded.

We can gain insight into potential cash flow issues by comparing expected future benefit payments to the funds available to make those payments. Companies must provide these disclosures in a schedule to the pension footnotes. K-C provides the following schedule of expected payments in the footnotes to its 10-K:

Estimated Future Benefit Payments   Over the next ten years, we expect that the following gross benefit payments and related Medicare Part D reimbursements will occur:

(Millions of dollars)	Pension Benefits	Other Benefits	Medicare Part D Reimbursements
2011	$ 360	$ 68	$ (4)
2012	362	67	(4)
2013	362	66	(5)
2014	367	67	(5)
2015	373	69	(5)
2016–2020	1,996	370	(26)

The schedule shows that K-C expects to pay out $360 million in benefits to pension beneficiaries and $68 million in health care and other post-retirement benefits (OPEB) to its former employees in 2010. The schedule also reveals that the company expects these amounts to remain fairly constant over the next five years.

K-C also reports the following table relating to its pension and other post-retirement benefit plans' assets:

Change in Plan Assets Year Ended December 31 (Millions of dollars)	Pension Benefits		Other Benefits	
	2010	2009	2010	2009
Fair value of plan assets at beginning of year	$4,244	$3,101	—	—
Actual gain on plan assets	473	520	—	—
Employer contributions	245	845	—	—
Currency and other.	(6)	134	—	—
Benefit payments	(356)	(356)	—	—
Fair value of plan assets at end of year	$4,600	$4,244	—	—

In 2010, K-C contributed $245 million to its pension plan. That amount, when combined with investment returns of $473 million, was more than sufficient to cover 2010 benefit payments of $356 million (K-C expects this amount to be $360 million in 2011). Should pension assets decline markedly as a result of severe underfunding or investment losses, K-C will need to divert operating cash flows from other investment activities into pension contributions, or to borrow funds to meet its pension obligations. Although K-C's pension obligations are under-funded (as represented by the negative funded status), its current contribution levels and investment returns are sufficient to meet its anticipated pension obligations, at least in the near future.

Other post-retirement benefit obligations (future health care payments) present a different picture. Because federal law does not require minimum funding of these plans, and companies do not receive a tax deduction for such contributions, companies rarely fund OPEB plans. All of the OPEB payments to beneficiaries, therefore, must be funded by concurrent company contributions. These payments amounted to $64 million in 2010. Given K-C's $2.7 billion in operating cash flow for 2010, the $64 million cash requirement is not material. However, OPEB funding requirements have been a burden for many companies, most notably General Motors prior to its bankruptcy.

Deferred Income Taxes

Kimberly-Clark reports deferred income tax assets and liabilities as follows:

Deferred income tax assets (liabilities) are composed of the following:

December 31 (Millions of dollars)	2010	2009
Net current deferred income tax asset attributable to:		
Accrued expenses	$ 103	$ 102
Pension, postretirement and other employee benefits.	82	86
Loss carryforwards.	72	—
Installment sales.	(72)	—
Inventory.	(21)	(45)
Other.	46	8
Valuation allowances	(23)	(15)
Net current deferred income tax asset.	$ 187	$ 136
Net current deferred income tax liability included in accrued expenses	$ (28)	$ (31)
Net noncurrent deferred income tax asset attributable to:		
Tax credits and loss carryforwards.	$ 447	$ 405
Pension and other postretirement benefits.	153	228
Property, plant and equipment, net	(97)	(86)
Other.	42	37
Valuation allowances	(233)	(211)
Net noncurrent deferred income tax asset included in other assets	$ 312	$ 373

continued

continued from prior page

Net noncurrent deferred income tax liability attributable to:		
Property, plant and equipment, net	$(1,081)	$(976)
Pension, postretirement and other employee benefits	550	546
Tax credits and loss carryforwards	447	462
Installment sales	(112)	(180)
Provision for unremitted earnings	(88)	(70)
Intangible assets	(43)	(63)
Other	(13)	(78)
Valuation allowances	(29)	(18)
Net noncurrent deferred income tax liability	$ (369)	$(377)

Most of the noncurrent deferred tax liability ($1,081 million) arises from K-C's use of straight-line depreciation for GAAP reporting and accelerated depreciation for tax reporting. As a result, tax depreciation expense is higher in the early years of the assets' lives. This will reverse in later years for individual assets, resulting in higher taxable income and tax liability. The deferred tax liability account reflects this future expected tax.

Although depreciation expense for an individual asset declines over time, thus increasing taxable income and tax liability, if K-C adds new assets at a sufficient rate, the additional first-year depreciation on those assets will more than offset the reduction of depreciation expense on older assets, resulting in a long-term reduction of tax liability. That is, the deferred tax liability is unlikely to reverse in the aggregate. For this reason, many analysts treat the deferred tax liability as a "quasi-equity" account.

Still, while deferred taxes can be postponed, they cannot be eliminated. If the company's asset growth slows markedly, it will realize higher taxable income and tax liability. We need to be mindful of the potential for a "real" tax liability (requiring cash payment) when companies begin to downsize.

K-C also reports a long-term deferred tax asset valuation allowance of $285 million for 2010 ($23 million + $233 million + $29 million), an increase of $41 million over the $244 million ($15 million + $211 million + $18 million) of the prior year. This valuation allowance is related to deferred tax assets that arise from the company's tax loss carry-forwards. The valuation allowance indicates that the company does not expect to fully realize cash flows relating to deferred tax assets, such as tax loss carry-forwards before their scheduled expiration. Increases in the deferred tax asset valuation allowance impact tax expense, and, thus, net income, dollar for dollar. K-C's net income (and net operating income after tax or NOPAT) was reduced by $41 million in 2010 as a result of the increase in this valuation allowance. In future years, we need to be aware that profit can increase if and when the allowance account is reversed with no offsetting expense (unless the reversal is related to the expiration of tax loss carryforwards).

Noncontrolling Interests in Subsidiaries

K-C reports $285 million for the equity interests of noncontrolling shareholders in subsidiaries. Noncontrolling interests are shareholder claims against the net assets and cash flows of subsidiaries of the company (after all senior claims are settled). Consequently, we treat noncontrolling interest as a component of stockholders' equity.

Redeemable Preferred Securities of Subsidiary

Redeemable preferred securities represent the sale of preferred stock by a subsidiary of Kimberly-Clark to outside interests. Because these securities are redeemable, they are not reported in K-C's stockholders' equity but, instead, are reported between liabilities and equity.

Stockholders' Equity

Kimberly-Clark reports the following statement of stockholders' equity for 2010:

Dollars in million, shares in thousands	Common Stock Issued		Additional Paid-in Capital	Treasury Stock		Retained Earnings	Accumulated Other Comprehensive Income (Loss)	Noncontrolling Interests
	Shares	Amount		Shares	Amount			
Balance at Dec. 31, 2009	478,597	$598	$399	61,649	$(4,087)	$10,329	$(1,833)	$284
Net income in stockholders' equity	—	—	—	—	—	1,843	—	44
Other comprehensive income:								
Unrealized translation	—	—	—	—	—	—	326	7
Employee postretirement benefits, net of tax	—	—	—	—	—	—	57	(2)
Other.	—	—	—	—	—	—	(16)	—
Stock-based awards exercised or vested.	—	—	(37)	(2,862)	170	—	—	—
Income tax benefits on stock-based compensation.	—	—	2	—	—	—	—	—
Shares repurchased	—	—	—	12,954	(809)	—	—	—
Recognition of stock-based compensation.	—	—	52	—	—	—	—	—
Dividends declared.	—	—	—	—	—	(1,085)	—	(47)
Other.	—	—	9	—	—	(1)	—	(1)
Balance at Dec. 31, 2010 . . .	478,597	$598	$425	71,741	$(4,726)	$11,086	$(1,466)	$285

K-C has issued 478,597,000 shares of its $1.25 par value common stock. The common stock account is, therefore, equal to $598 million, computed as 478,597,000 shares × $1.25. The additional paid-in capital (APIC) represents the excess of proceeds from stock issuance over par value. It includes adjustments relating to the recognition of stock-based compensation and the exercise of stock-based awards and other minor adjustments.

Kimberly-Clark's stockholders' equity is reduced by $809 million relating to repurchases of common stock, less the reissuance of those securities from the exercise of stock options in the amount of $170 million. These treasury shares are the result of a stock purchase plan approved by K-C's board of directors, and evidences K-C's conviction that its stock is undervalued by the marketplace. The repurchased shares are held in treasury and reduce stockholders' equity by the purchase price until such time as they are reissued, perhaps to fund an acquisition or to compensate employees under a stock purchase or stock option plan (treasury shares can also be retired).

K-C compensates employees via restricted stock in addition to other forms of compensation. Under its restricted stock plan, eligible employees are issued stock, which is restricted as to sale until fully vested (owned). When issued, the market value of the restricted stock is deducted from stockholders' equity. As the employees gain ownership of the shares (that is, the restricted stock vests), a portion of this account is transferred to the income statement as compensation expense. The consequent reduction in retained earnings offsets the reduction (and increase in equity) of the restricted stock account. Stockholders' equity is, therefore, unaffected in total, although its components change.

Retained earnings reflect a $1,843 million increase relating to net income and a $1,085 million decrease from declaration of dividends. Accumulated other comprehensive income (AOCI), which is often aggregated with retained earnings for analysis purposes, began 2010 with a balance of $(1,833) million; this negative balance reduces stockholders' equity. During the period, this AOCI account was further increased (less negative) by $326 million relating to the increase in the $US value of net assets of foreign subsidiaries. This increase in net asset value resulted from a weakened $US vis-à-vis other currencies in which the company conducts its operations in 2010. In addition, the AOCI account was increased by $57 million relating to employee postretirement benefits adjustments and decreased (made more negative) by $16 million for activities designated as "other." Finally, K-C's comprehensive income equals net income plus (minus) the components of other comprehensive income.

Common-Size Balance Sheet

Similar to our analysis of the income statement, it is useful to compute common-size balance sheets. Such statements can reveal changes or relations masked by other analyses. Kimberly-Clark's common-size balance sheet covering its recent two years is shown in Exhibit C.4.

EXHIBIT C.4 Kimberly-Clark Common-Size Balance Sheet		
December 31	**2010**	**2009**
Current assets		
Cash and cash equivalents	4.4%	4.2%
Accounts receivable, net	12.4	13.4
Note receivable	1.1	0.0
Inventories	11.9	10.6
Deferred income taxes	0.9	0.7
Other current assets	1.0	1.7
Total current assets	31.9	30.5
Property, plat and equipment, net	42.1	41.8
Investments in equity companies	1.9	1.8
Goodwill	17.1	17.0
Other intangible assets	1.4	1.6
Long-term notes receivable	2.0	3.2
Other assets	3.6	4.0
Total assets	100.0%	100.0%
Current liabilities		
Debt payable within one year	1.7%	3.2%
Redeemable preferred securities of subsidiary	2.5	0.0
Trade accounts payable	11.1	10.0
Accrued expenses	9.6	10.7
Accrued income taxes	0.5	0.4
Dividends payable	1.4	1.3
Total current liabilities	26.9	25.6
Long-term debt	25.8	24.9
Noncurrent employee benefits	9.1	10.4
Long-term income taxes payable	1.3	0.9
Deferred income taxes	1.9	2.0
Other liabilities	1.1	1.1
Redeemable preferred and common securities of subsidiaries	2.7	5.5
Stockholders' equity		
Preferred stock-no par value-authorized 20.0 million shares, none issued	0.0	0.0
Common stock- $1.25 par value-authorized 1.2 billion shares; issued 478.6 million shares at December 31, 2010 and 2009	3.0	3.1
Additional paid-in capital	2.1	2.1
Common stock held in treasury, at cost-71.7 million and 61.6 million shares at December 31, 2010 and 2009	(23.8)	(21.3)
Accumulated other comprehensive income (loss)	(7.4)	(9.5)
Retained earnings	55.8	53.8
Total Kimberly-Clark Corporation stockholders' equity	29.8	28.1
Noncontrolling interests	1.4	1.5
Total stockholders' equity	31.2	29.6
Liabilities and stockholders' equity, total	100.0%	100.0%

Note: Percentages are computed by dividing each balance sheet line item by that year's total assets.

Total current assets increased from 30.5% of total assets in 2009 to 31.9% in 2010. The 1.3% increase in inventories as a percent to total assets was largely offset by a 1.0 reduction of accounts receivable. The increase in current assets is largely due to the emergence of a note receivable in the amount of $218 million, 1.1% of total assets. Net PPE also increased as a percent of total assets, from 41.8% in 2009 to 42.1% in 2010. This was largely offset by a reduction of long-term notes receivable from 3.2% of total assets in 2009 to 2.0% in 2010.

On the liability side, current liabilities increased as a percent of the total from 25.6% in 2009 to 26.9% in 2010. This was largely due to an increase in accounts payable (from 10.0% to 11.1%) and the emergence of a current liability relating to redeemable preferred stock of a subsidiary. On balance, K-C became somewhat less financially leveraged in 2010 as stockholders' equity rose from 29.6% of the total in 2009 to 31.2%. The relative proportions of debt and equity do not appear out of line at a ratio of 2.2:1.0.

Off-Balance-Sheet Reporting and Analysis

There are numerous assets and liabilities that do not appear on the balance sheet. Some are excluded because managers and accounting professionals only report what they can reliably measure. Others are excluded because of the rigidity of accounting standards. Following are some areas we might consider in our evaluation and adjustment of the Kimberly-Clark balance sheet.

Internally Developed Intangible Assets

Many brands and their corresponding values are excluded from the balance sheet. For example, consider the brand "Kleenex." Many individuals actually refer to facial tissues as Kleenex–that is successful branding! So, is the Kleenex brand reported and valued on Kimberly-Clark's balance sheet? No. That brand value cannot be reliably measured and, hence, is not included on K-C's balance sheet.

Likewise, other valuable assets are excluded from the company's balance sheet. Examples are the value of a competent management team, high employee morale, innovative production know-how, a superior supply chain, customer satisfaction, and a host of other assets.

R&D activities often create internally generated intangible assets that are mostly excluded from the balance sheet. Footnotes reveal that Kimberly-Clark spends over $317 million (1.6% of sales) on R&D to remain competitive—and, this is for an admittedly non-high-tech company. Further, K-C reveals that it spends $698 million (3.5% of sales) on advertising. Both R&D and advertising costs are expensed under GAAP as opposed to being capitalized on the balance sheet as tangible assets. These unrecognized intangible assets often represent a substantial part of a company's market value.

Equity Method Investments

Kimberly-Clark reports equity investments of $374 million at year-end 2010. These are unconsolidated affiliates over which K-C can exert significant influence (but not control) and, hence, are accounted for using the equity method. The amount reported on the balance sheet represents the initial cost of the investment, plus (minus) the percentage share of investee earnings and losses, and minus any cash dividends received. Consequently, the investment balance equals the percentage owned of the affiliates' stockholders' equity (plus any unamortized excess purchase price).

Footnotes reveal that, in sum, these K-C affiliates have total assets of $2,117 million, liabilities of $1,502 million, and stockholders' equity of $615 million. K-C's reported investment balance of $374 in the balance sheet does not reveal the extent of the investment (assets) required to manage these companies, nor the level of potential liability exposure. For instance, if one of these affiliates falters financially, K-C might have to invest additional cash to support it rather than let it fail. Failure of an important affiliate might affect K-C's ability to finance another such venture in the future.

These investments are reported at cost, not at fair market value as are passive investments. This means that unrecognized gains and losses can be buried in such investment accounts. For example, K-C footnotes reveal the following:

> Kimberly-Clark de Mexico, S.A.B. de C.V. is partially owned by the public and its stock is publicly traded in Mexico. At December 31, 2010, our investment in this equity company was $269 million, and the estimated fair value of the investment was $3.1 billion based on the market price of publicly traded shares.

Thus, for at least one of its investments, there is an unrecognized gain of $2,831 million ($3,100 million − $269 million).

Operating Leases

Kimberly-Clark has leases classified as "operating" for financial reporting purposes. As a result, neither the lease asset nor the lease obligation are reported on its balance sheet. For example, K-C reports the following disclosure relating to its operating leases:

Leases We have entered into operating leases for certain warehouse facilities, automobiles and equipment. The future minimum obligations under operating leases having a noncancelable term in excess of one year as of December 31, 2010 are as follows:

Year Ending December 31	(Millions of dollars)
2011	$194
2012	143
2013	118
2014	103
2015	84
Thereafter	153
Future minimum obligations	$795

These leases represent an unreported asset and an unreported liability; both amounting to $711 million. This amount is computed as follows and assumes a 4% discount rate ($ millions):

Year	Operating Lease Payment	Discount Factor (i = 0.04)	Present Value
1	$194	0.96154	$187
2	143	0.92456	132
3	118	0.88900	105
4	103	0.85480	88
5	84	0.82193	69
>5	153 [$84 for ~1.821 years]	1.88609* × 0.82193	130**
			$711

Remaining life = $153/84 = 1.821 or ~2 years
*The annuity factor for 2 years at 4% is 1.88609.
**1.88609 × 0.82193 × $84 = $130

The classification of leases as operating for financial reporting purposes often involves a rigid application of accounting rules that depend solely on the structure of the lease. A large amount of assets and liabilities is excluded from many companies' balance sheets because leases are structured as operating leases. For K-C, these excluded assets amount to $711 million. The valuation of K-C common stock (shown later) uses net operating assets (NOA) as one of its inputs. Our adjustment to the K-C balance sheet, then, would entail the addition of these assets to NOA and the inclusion of $711 million in *non*operating liabilities.

Pensions

Kimberly-Clark's pension plan is underfunded as explained earlier. Total pension obligations are $5,658 million and pension assets have a market value of $4,600 million at year-end 2010. Neither of these amounts appears on the balance sheet, but are reported in the footnotes. Only the net amount of $(1,058) appears on the balance sheet via three component amounts as identified in the following footnote disclosure:

Amounts Recognized in the Balance Sheet	
Noncurrent asset—Prepaid benefit cost	$ 21
Current liability—Accrued benefit cost	(11)
Noncurrent liability—Accrued benefit cost	(1,068)
Net amount recognized	$(1,058)

Variable Interest Entities

Footnotes reveal that Kimberly-Clark owns investments in entities that are considered to be a variable interest entity (VIE) under GAAP. These entities are typically non-stock entities, such as joint ventures, partnerships and trusts, and the accounting for these entities depends upon whether the investor is deemed to be the primary beneficiary. If so, the investor must consolidate the VIE. If not, the investor accounts for its investment using the equity method. Following is K-C's footnote disclosure relating to these investments:

> We consolidate real estate entities in which we are the primary beneficiary. In most of these entities we also have voting control. We determined we are the primary beneficiary of these variable interests based on qualitative analysis. The assets of these entities are classified principally as property, plant and equipment and have a carrying amount aggregating $37 million at December 31, 2010, that serves as collateral for the obligations of these ventures. The obligations have a carrying amount aggregating $25 million, of which $23 million is included in debt payable within one year and $2 million is included in long-term debt... We have significant interests in other variable interest real estate entities in which we are not the primary beneficiary. We account for our interests in these nonconsolidated real estate entities by the equity method of accounting, and have accounted for the related income tax credits and other tax benefits as a reduction in our income tax provision. As of December 31, 2010, we had net equity of $6 million in our nonconsolidated real estate entities. We have made noncontractual cash infusions to certain of the entities aggregating $8 million principally to provide cash flow to support debt payment.

K-C invests in a number of real estate-related entities that own properties, borrow money, and provide K-C with tax benefits. These entities consist of companies that issue common stock together with partnerships and funds in which K-C is an investor. Regardless of their organizational form, and because K-C is deemed the primary beneficiary, it must consolidate the financial statements of these entities. As a result, it reports assets and liabilities of these entities of $37 million and $25 million, respectively, on its balance sheet. Had these entities *not* been consolidated, but reported as equity investments, only the proportion of the *net equity* that K-C owns would be reported in its statements (because we do not know the percentage of the entities that K-C owns, we do not know what amount would have been reported, but it would have been less than $12 million ($37 million - $25 million).

Entities that are consolidated present little analysis concerns because all of their assets and liabilities (and their revenues and expenses) are included in the financial statements of the primary beneficiary. Those that are accounted for as equity method investments, however, present analysis concerns that we must address. K-C reports the following investments in non-consolidated entities:

> We have significant interests in other variable interest real estate entities in which we are not the primary beneficiary. We account for our interests in these nonconsolidated real estate entities by the equity method of accounting . . . As of December 31, 2010, we had net equity of $6 million in our nonconsolidated real estate entities. We have made noncontractual cash infusions to certain of the entities aggregating $8 million principally to provide cash flow to support debt payments.

These nonconsolidated investments are accounted for under the equity method of accounting and, thus, K-C reports only the percentage of their equity that it owns on the balance sheet. Further, only its portion of the net income of these entities is reported in the income statement (not their revenues and expenses). K-C reports these investments at $6 million on its balance sheet. As we discuss in Module 7, however, this investment can belie a larger investment in assets and liabilities and K-C's footnote disclosures do not report the detail relating to the assets and liabilities of these entities. We do know, however, that K-C has made additional cash infusion into these entities of $8 million "to provide cash flow to support debt payments." In other words, these entities did not generate sufficient cash flow to make required debt payments and K-C felt compelled to invest additional cash into the entities to provide that funding.

Derivatives

Kimberly-Clark is exposed to a number of market risks as outlined in the following footnote to its 10-K:

> As a multinational enterprise, we are exposed to risks such as changes in foreign currency exchange rates, interest rates and commodity prices. A variety of practices are employed to manage these risks, including operating and financing activities and, where deemed appropriate, the use of derivative instruments. Derivative instruments are used only for risk management purposes and not for speculation. All foreign currency derivative instruments are entered into with major financial institutions. Our credit exposure under these arrangements is limited to agreements with a positive fair value at the reporting date. Credit risk with respect to the counterparties is actively monitored but is not considered significant since these transactions are executed with a diversified group of financial institutions.

The company hedges these risks using derivatives, including forwards, options, and swap contracts. This hedging process transfers risk from K-C to another entity (called the counterparty), which assumes that risk for a fee.

The accounting for derivatives is summarized in an appendix to Module 7. In brief, the derivative contracts, and the assets or liabilities to which they relate, are reported on the balance sheet at fair market value. Any unrealized gains and losses are ultimately reflected in net income, although they can be accumulated in AOCI for a short time. To the extent that a company's hedging activities are effective, the market values of the derivatives and the assets or liabilities to which they relate are largely offsetting, as are the net gains or losses on the hedging activities. As a result, the effect of derivative activities is generally minimal on both income and equity. (It is generally only when companies use derivatives for speculative purposes that these investments markedly affect income and equity. The aim of the derivatives standard was to highlight these speculative activities and we need to read risk footnotes carefully to assess whether companies are hedging or speculating with derivatives.)

Statement of Cash Flows Reporting and Analysis

The statement of cash flows for **Kimberly-Clark** is shown in Exhibit C.5.

In 2010, K-C generated $2,744 million of operating cash flow, primarily from income (net income plus the depreciation add-back equals $2,756 million). This amount is well in excess of K-C's capital expenditures of $964 million. K-C used excess cash to pay $1,066 million in dividends to shareholders.

Kimberly-Clark offers the following commentary regarding its 2010 operating cash flow:

> Cash provided by operations decreased $737 million primarily due to a lower level of working capital improvements as compared to the prior year, partially offset by decreased pension plan contributions.

Overall, the cash flow picture for Kimberly-Clark is strong: operating cash flows are more than sufficient to cover capital expenditures and acquisitions, leaving excess cash that is being returned to the shareholders in the form of dividends and share repurchases. The strength of its operating cash flows mitigates any concerns we might have regarding its relative lack of liquidity on the balance sheet.

| EXHIBIT C.5 | Kimberly-Clark Statement of Cash Flows |

KIMBERLY-CLARK CORPORATION AND SUBSIDIARIES
Consolidated Cash Flow Statement

Year Ended December 31 (Millions of dollars)	2010	2009	2008
Operating Activities			
Net income	$ 1,943	$ 1,994	$ 1,829
Extraordinary loss, net of income taxes, attributable to Kimberly-Clark Corporation	—	—	8
Depreciation and amortization	813	783	775
Stock-based compensation	52	86	47
Deferred income taxes	(12)	141	151
Net losses on asset dispositions	26	36	51
Equity companies' earnings in excess of dividends paid	(48)	(53)	(34)
Decrease (increase) in operating working capital	24	1,105	(335)
Postretirement benefits	(125)	(609)	(38)
Other	71	(2)	62
Cash provided by operations	2,744	3,481	2,516
Investing Activities			
Capital spending	(964)	(848)	(906)
Acquisitions of businesses, net of cash acquired	—	(458)	(98)
Investments in marketable securities	1	—	(9)
Proceeds from sales of investments	47	40	48
Investments in time deposits	(131)	(270)	(238)
Maturities of time deposits	248	223	314
Proceeds from disposition of property	9	25	28
Other	9	—	14
Cash used for investing	(781)	(1,288)	(847)
Financing Activities			
Cash dividends paid	(1,066)	(986)	(950)
Net decrease in short-term debt	(28)	(312)	(436)
Proceeds from issuance of long-term debt	515	2	551
Repayments of long-term debt	(506)	(278)	(274)
Cash paid on redeemable preferred securities of subsidiary	(54)	(53)	(47)
Proceeds from exercise of stock options	131	165	113
Acquisitions of common stock for the treasury	(803)	(7)	(653)
Shares purchased from noncontrolling interests	—	(293)	—
Other	(48)	(26)	(51)
Cash used for financing	(1,859)	(1,788)	(1,747)
Effect of exchange rate changes on cash and cash equivalents	(26)	29	(31)
Increase (decrease) in cash and cash equivalents	78	434	(109)
Cash and cash equivalents, beginning of year	798	364	473
Cash and cash equivalents, end of year	$ 876	$ 798	$ 364

Independent Audit Opinion

Kimberly-Clark is subject to various audit requirements. Its independent auditor is **Deloitte & Touche LLP**, which issued the following clean opinion on K-C's 2010 financial statements:

REPORT OF INDEPENDENT REGISTERED PUBLIC ACCOUNTING FIRM

To the Board of Directors and Stockholders of Kimberly-Clark Corporation:

We have audited the accompanying consolidated balance sheets of Kimberly-Clark Corporation and subsidiaries (the "Corporation") as of December 31, 2010 and 2009, and the related consolidated statements of income, stockholders' equity, comprehensive income, and cash flows for each of the three years in the period ended December 31, 2010. Our audits also included the financial statement

continued

continued from prior page

schedule listed in the Index at Item 15. These financial statements and financial statement schedule are the responsibility of the Corporation's management. Our responsibility is to express an opinion on the financial statements and financial statement schedule based on our audits.

We conducted our audits in accordance with the standards of the Public Company Accounting Oversight Board (United States). Those standards require that we plan and perform the audit to obtain reasonable assurance about whether the financial statements are free of material misstatement. An audit includes examining, on a test basis, evidence supporting the amounts and disclosures in the financial statements. An audit also includes assessing the accounting principles used and significant estimates made by management, as well as evaluating the overall financial statement presentation. We believe that our audits provide a reasonable basis for our opinion.

In our opinion, such consolidated financial statements present fairly, in all material respects, the financial position of Kimberly-Clark Corporation and subsidiaries as of December 31, 2010 and 2009, and the results of their operations and their cash flows for each of the three years in the period ended December 31, 2010, in conformity with accounting principles generally accepted in the United States of America. Also, in our opinion, the financial statement schedule, when considered in relation to the basic consolidated financial statements taken as a whole, presents fairly, in all material respects, the information set forth therein.

As discussed in Note 1 to the consolidated financial statements, the Corporation adopted new accounting standards for variable interest entities effective January 1, 2010. The Corporation also adopted new accounting standards for business combinations and noncontrolling interests in consolidated financial statements effective January 1, 2009.

We have also audited, in accordance with the standards of the Public Company Accounting Oversight Board (United States), the Corporation's internal control over financial reporting as of December 31, 2010, based on the criteria established in *Internal Control—Integrated Framework* issued by the Committee of Sponsoring Organizations of the Treadway Commission, and our report dated February 23, 2011, expressed an unqualified opinion on the Corporation's internal control over financial reporting.

/s/ DELOITTE & TOUCHE LLP
Deloitte & Touche LLP
Dallas, Texas
February 23, 2011

Although this report is a routine disclosure, it should not be taken for granted. Exceptions to a clean audit report must be scrutinized. Also, any disagreements between management and the independent auditor must be documented in an SEC filing. If this occurs, it is a "red flag" that must be investigated. Management activities and reports that cannot meet usual audit standards raise serious concerns about integrity and credibility. At a minimum, the riskiness of investments and relationships with such a company markedly increases.

ASSESSING PROFITABILITY AND CREDITWORTHINESS

L02 Assess company profitability and creditworthiness.

This section reports a profitability analysis of **Kimberly-Clark**. We begin by computing several key measures that are used in the ROE disaggregation, which is the overriding focus of this section. The ROE disaggregation process is defined in Module 4, and a listing of the ratio acronyms and definitions is in the review section at the end of the book.

K-C's 2010 net operating profit after-tax, or NOPAT, is $2,083 million, computed as ($2,773 million + $181 million) − ($788 million + [{$243 million − $20 million} × 37%]). In 2010, K-C's net operating assets, or NOA, total $12,106 million, computed as $19,864 − $876 − $2,206 − $1,909 − $104 − $1,810 − $260 − $369 − $224 ($ millions). For 2009, NOA totals $11,596 million.

ROE Disaggregation

Our first step is to compute the ROE and, then, disaggregate it into its operating (return on net operating assets or RNOA) and nonoperating components. Using the computations in the previous section, the 2010 disaggregation analysis of ROE for Kimberly-Clark follows. (Many of these ratios require computation of averages, such as average assets. If we wanted to compute ratios for years prior to 2010, then we would obtain information from prior 10-Ks to compute the necessary averages for these ratios.)

$$\text{ROE} = \text{RNOA} + \text{Nonoperating return}$$
$$32.55\% = 17.58\% + 14.97\%$$

where

$$\text{ROE} = \$1,843 \text{ million} / [(\$5,917 \text{ million} + \$5,406 \text{ million})/2]^*$$

$$\text{RNOA} = \$2,083 \text{ million} / [\$12,106 \text{ million} + \$11,596 \text{ million})/2]$$

*We use net income and stockholders' equity attributed to K-C shareholders.

RNOA accounts for 54% (17.58%/32.55%) of K-C's ROE. K-C successfully uses its nonoperating activities to increase its 17.58% RNOA to produce a 32.55% ROE.

Disaggregation of RNOA—Margin and Turnover

The next level analysis of ROE focuses on RNOA disaggregation. Kimberly-Clark's net operating profit margin (NOPM) and net operating asset turnover (NOAT) are as follows:

$$\text{RNOA} = \text{NOPAT/Average Net Operating Assets} = \underbrace{\text{NOPAT/Sales}}_{\text{NOPM}} \times \underbrace{\text{Sales/Average Net Operating Assets}}_{\text{NOAT}}$$

$$17.58\% = 10.55\% \times 1.67 \text{ (0.0004 rounding error)}$$

where

$$\text{NOPM} = \$2,083 \text{ million}/\$19,746 \text{ million}$$
$$\text{NOAT} = \$19,746 \text{ million}/[(\$12,106 \text{ million} + \$11,596 \text{ million})/2]$$

Kimberly-Clark's RNOA of 17.58% consists of a net operating profit margin of 10.55% and a net operating asset turnover of 1.67 times.

Disaggregation of Margin and Turnover

This section focuses on the disaggregation of profit margin and asset turnover to better understand the drivers of RNOA. Again, understanding the drivers of financial performance (RNOA) is key to predicting future company performance. Our analysis of the drivers of operating profit margin and asset turnover for Kimberly-Clark follows:

Disaggregation of NOPM	
Gross profit margin (GPM) ($6,550 mil./$19,746 mil.)	33.2%
Marketing, research and general expense margin [($3,673 mil)/$19,746 mil]	18.6%
Disaggregation of NOAT	
Accounts receivable turnover (ART) { $19,746 mil./[($2,534 mil. + $2,634 mil.)/2]}	7.64
Inventory turnover (INVT) {$13,196 mil./[($2,373 mil. + $2,033 mil.)/2]}	5.99
PPE turnover (PPET) { $19,746 mil./[($8,356 mil. + $8,033 mil.)/2]}	2.41
Accounts payable turnover (APT) {$13,196 mil./[($2,206 mil. + $1,920 mil.)/2]}	6.40
Related turnover measures	
Average collection period [$2,534 mil./($19,746 mil./365)]	46.84 days
Average inventory days outstanding [$2,373 mil./($13,196 mil./365)]	65.64 days
Average payable days outstanding [$2,206 mil./($13,196 mil./365)]	61.02 days

First, let's look at the disaggregation of NOPM. K-C reports a decrease in its gross profit margin from 33.6% in 2009 to 33.2% in 2010. As K-C points out in the excerpt from its MD&A that we reproduce on page C-4, the company operates in a very competitive market that makes gross profit margins difficult to maintain.

In its commentary, K-C explains that it might increase its advertising budget in the face of shrinking gross profit margins. That is, in fact, what happened in 2010. As gross profit margins decreased from 33.6% to 33.2%, K-C increased marketing, research and general expenses as a percentage of sales from 18.3% to 18.6%. Part of this increase was due to higher advertising expense, which increased by $139 million from 2.8% of sales to 3.5% of sales.

Next, we consider the disaggregation of NOAT. K-C's receivables turnover rate of 7.64 times corresponds to an average collection period of 46.8 days, which is reasonable considering normal credit terms. However, the more important issue here is asset productivity (turnover) instead of credit quality. This is because most of K-C's sales are to large retailers; for example, 13% of Kimberly-Clark's sales are to Wal-Mart.

Inventories turn over 5.99 times a year, resulting in an average inventory days outstanding of 65.6 days in 2010. Inventories are an important (and large) asset for companies like Kimberly-Clark. Improved turnover is always a goal so long as the company maintains sufficient inventories to meet market demand.

K-C's Property, plant, and equipment are turning over 2.41 times a year, which is about average for publicly traded companies. The issue with respect to PPET is throughput, and K-C does not discuss this aspect of its business in its financial filings.

K-C's trade accounts payable turnover is 6.40, resulting in an average payable days outstanding of 61.0 days. Since payables represent a low cost source of financing, we would prefer to see its days payable lengthened so long as K-C is not endangering its relationships with suppliers.

Credit Analysis

Credit analysis is an important part of a complete company analysis. Following is a selected set of measures for 2010 that can help us gauge the relative credit standing of Kimberly-Clark ($ millions):

Current ratio ($6,328/$5,338)	1.19
Quick ratio ([$876 + $2,472]/$5,338)	0.63
Total liabilities/Equity* ([$19,864 − $6,202]/$6,202)	2.20
Long-term debt/Equity ($5,120/$6,202)	0.83
Earnings before interest and taxes/Interest expense ($2,773/$243)	11.41
Net operating cash flows/Total liabilities ($2,744/[$19,864 − $6,202])	0.20

*Includes noncontrolling interest as equity as we analyze the company from the perspective of all equity holders; if we prefer to examine the company from the perspective of the company's equity holders only, then we would exclude noncontrolling interest.

K-C's current and quick ratios are not particularly high, and both have decreased slightly over the past two years (not shown here). These ratios do not imply any excess liquidity, and probably do not suggest any room for a further decrease in liquidity.

K-C's financial leverage, as reflected in both the liability-to-equity and long-term-debt-to-equity ratios, is slightly above the median for all publicly traded companies. Normally, this is cause for some concern. However, Kimberly-Clark has strong operating and free cash flows that mitigate this concern.

K-C's times interest earned ratio of 11.41 is healthy, indicating a sufficient buffer to protect creditors if earnings decline. It also has relatively little off-balance-sheet exposure. Thus, we do not have any serious concerns about K-C's ability to repay its maturing debt obligations.

Summarizing Profitability and Creditworthiness

An increasingly competitive environment has diminished Kimberly-Clark's gross profit margin. Operating expense reductions have not offset this decline and its NOPAT has declined slightly as a result. Its level of net operating asset turnover is acceptable, although not stellar. K-C does not provide sufficient information for us to further assess the throughput performance of its operating assets. Finally, its leverage, although higher than average, is not of great concern given K-C's strong cash flows.

FORECASTING FINANCIAL STATEMENT NUMBERS

The valuation of K-C's common stock requires forecasts of NOPAT and NOA over a forecast horizon period and a forecast terminal period. Our approach is to project individual income statement and balance sheet items using the methodology we discuss in Module 11. K-C presented its 4Q results and 2011 guidance to analysts on January 25, 2011, and provided the following slide relative to its expectations for 2011 (posted on the K-C investor relations Website).

L03 Forecast financial statements.

Planning Assumptions

- **Sales increase 3 to 4 percent**
  - Organic growth 2 to 3 percent: volume growth 1 to 2 percent, combination of net selling prices and product mix +1 percent
  - Volume estimate includes combined 1 point negative impact from continued declines in Venezuela and impact of pulp and tissue restructuring
  - Currency benefit approximately 1 percent
- **Adjusted operating profit growth 3 to 5 percent**
  - Adjusted gross profit expected to grow at a faster rate
  - Strategic marketing increase faster than sales growth
- **FORCE cost savings $200 to $250 million**

We use the mid-point of K-C's 3.5% sales growth prediction in our forecast of the company's sales for 2011. Additional slides in its presentation provide the following forecast assumptions:

1. The effective tax rate is likely to increase to 30%–32%. We use 31% in our forecast.

2. Capital spending (CAPEX) is expected to be $950–$1,050 million. In 2010, the CAPEX was 4.9% of sales. Using that percentage and expected sales growth of 3.5%, our forecast of CAPEX is $1,001 million, computed as 2010 sales of $19,746 million × 1.035 × 4.9%. Our estimate is within the range provided by K-C.

3. Share repurchases are expected to be $1,500 million per year and we use that amount in our forecast.

4. Dividends are expected to increase by 6%, resulting in forecasted dividends of $1,130 million, computed as 2010 dividends of $1,066 million × 1.06.

We assume that expenses retain their 2010 relation to sales and that all assets and liabilities, other than CAPEX referenced above, retain their relations to sales as well.

Our initial forecast results in total assets of $20,240 million and total liabilities and equity of $19,165 million. Since K-C does not report marketable securities on its balance sheet, we assume that the difference is made up with additional financing in the amount of $1,075 million. K-C reports that it issued $250 million of 3.625% Notes in the 4Q of 2010. We assume that the $1,075 million in additional financing is drawn on evenly over the year and that K-C continues to borrow at 3.625%. This means that interest expense is expected to increase by $19 million ([$1,075 million / 2] × 3.625%), from $243 million to $262 million. The resulting forecasts of the K-C income statement and balance sheet for 2011, reflecting these assumptions, are in Exhibit C.6.

The forecasted statement of cash flows is in Exhibit C.7. This forecasted statement utilizes the forecasted income statement and comparative balance sheets as presented in Exhibit C.6 and is prepared as explained in Module 11.

We forecast that K-C will generate $2,923 million in cash from operating activities in 2011, a 7% increase from the $2,744 million reported in 2010. Given projected CAPEX of $1,001 million, dividends of $1,130 million, and stock repurchases of $1,500 million, we forecast that K-C will require external financing of $1,075 million. The forecasted year-end cash balance of $899

EXHIBIT C.6	Forecasts of Income Statement and Balance Sheet of Kimberly-Clark

Consolidated Income Statement ($ millions)	2010	Forecast Assumptions	2011 Est.
Net sales...	$19,746	19,746 × 1.035	$20,437
Cost of products sold..........................	13,196	20,437 × 66.8%	13,652
Gross profit...	6,550	Subtotal	6,785
Marketing, research and general expenses	3,673	20,437 × 18.6%	3,801
Other (income) and expense, net............	104	20,437 × 0.5%	102
Operating profit	2,773	Subtotal	2,882
Interest income...................................	20	no change	20
Interest expense..................................	(243)	(243) − 19	(262)
Income before income taxes, equity interests and extraordinary loss..........	2,550	Subtotal	2,640
Provision for income taxes....................	(788)	2,640 × 31.0%	(818)
Income before equity interests and extraordinary loss	1,762	Subtotal	1,822
Share of net income of equity companies	181	no change	181
Net income...	1,943	Subtotal	2,003
Net income attributable to noncontrolling interests.....	(100)	no change	(100)
Net income attributable to Kimberly-Clark Corporation......	$ 1,843	Subtotal	$ 1,903

Consolidated Balance Sheet ($ millions)	2010	Forecast Assumptions	2011 Est.
Assets			
Cash and cash equivalents	$ 876	20,437 × 4.4%	$ 899
Accounts receivable, net	2,472	20,437 × 12.5%	2,555
Note receivable	218	no change	218
Inventories	2,373	20,437 × 12.0%	2,452
Deferred income taxes........................	187	20,437 × 0.9%	184
Other current assets...........................	202	20,437 × 1.0%	204
Total current assets	6,328	Subtotal	6,512
Property, plant and equipment, net	8,356	8,356 + 1,001 − 819	8,538
Investments in equity companies.........	374	no change	374
Goodwill..	3,403	no change	3,403
Other intangible assets.......................	287	287 − 23	264
Long-term notes receivable	393	no change	393
Other assets......................................	723	20,437 × 3.7%	756
Total assets.......................................	$19,864	Subtotal	$20,240
Liabilities and Stockholders' Equity			
New financing....................................	$ 0	plug	$ 1,075
Debt payable within one year..............	344	from debt footnote	427
Redeemable preferred securities of subsidiary	506	no change	506
Trade accounts payable.......................	2,206	20,437 × 11.2%	2,289
Accrued expenses..............................	1,909	20,437 × 9.7%	1,982
Accrued income taxes.........................	104	818 × 13.2%	108
Dividends payable	269	1,130 × 25.2%	285
Total current liabilities........................	5,338	Subtotal	6,672
Long-term debt	5,120	5,120 − 427	4,693
Noncurrent employee benefits.............	1,810	20,437 × 9.2%	1,880
Long-term income taxes payable..........	260	20,437 × 1.3%	266
Deferred income taxes........................	369	20,437 × 1.9%	388
Other liabilities..................................	224	20,437 × 1.1%	225
Redeemable preferred and common securities of subsidiaries..............	541	no change	541
Stockholders' equity			
Preferred stock, no par value, authorized 20.0 million shares, none issued	0	no change	0
Common stock, $1.25 par value, authorized 1.2 billion shares; issued 478.6 million shares at December 31, 2010 and 2009....................	598	no change	598
Additional paid-in capital	425	no change	425
Common stock held in treasury, at cost: 71.7 million and 61.6 million shares at December 31, 2010 and 2009.	(4,726)	(4,726) − 1,500	(6,226)
Accumulated other comprehensive income (loss)	(1,466)	no change	(1,466)
Retained earnings	11,086	11,086 + 1,903 − 1,130	11,859
Total Kimberly-Clark Corporation stockholders' equity	5,917	Subtotal	5,190
Noncontrolling interests	285	285 + 100	385
Total stockholders' equity	6,202	Subtotal	5,575
Liabilities and stockholders' equity, total	$19,864	Subtotal	$20,240

EXHIBIT C.7	Forecast of Statement of Cash Flows for Kimberly-Clark	
$ millions	**Forecast Assumptions**	**2011 Est.**
Operating activities		
Net income including noncontrolling interests............	via forecasted income statement	$2,003
Add: Depreciation..................................	8,356 × 9.8%	819
Add: Amortization.................................	287 × 8.1%	23
Accounts receivable...............................	2,472 − 2,555	(83)
Inventories	2,373 − 2,452	(79)
Deferred income taxes	187 − 184	3
Other current assets...............................	202 − 204	(2)
Other long-term assets............................	723 − 756	(33)
Accounts payable.................................	2,289 − 2,206	83
Accrued expenses	1,982 − 1,909	73
Accrued income taxes	108 − 104	4
Dividends payable	285 − 269	16
Noncurrent employee benefits......................	1,880 − 1,810	70
Long-term income taxes payable....................	266 − 260	6
Deferred income taxes	388 − 369	19
Other liabilities	225 − 224	1
Net cash from operating activities	subtotal	2,923
Investing activities		
Capital expenditures	20,437 × 4.9%	(1,001)
Net cash from investing activities....................	subtotal	(1,001)
Financing activities		
Dividends	1,066 × 1.06	(1,130)
Stock purchase	company guidance	(1,500)
Payments of long-term debt	prior year current maturities of LTD	(344)
New financing....................................	plug	1,075
Net cash from financing activities	subtotal	(1,899)
Net change in cash................................	subtotal	23
Beginning cash...................................	from balance sheet	876
Ending cash	subtotal	$ 899

million is equal to 4.4% of estimated sales, the same relation to sales that the company reported in 2010.

VALUING EQUITY SECURITIES

L04 Describe and illustrate the valuation of firm equity and stock.

This section estimates the values of Kimberly-Clark's equity and common stock per share.

Multiyear Forecasting

For valuation purposes we must forecast the financial statements for more than one year ahead. Exhibits C.8A and C.8B, respectively, show the 2010 reported statements and the results of forecasting the income statement and the balance sheet for four years ahead. The methods used in this forecasting process follow those described in the module on forecasting.

EXHIBIT C.8A	Four Year Ahead Forecasts of Income Statement of Kimberly-Clark				
Consolidated Income Statement ($ millions)	2010	2011E	2012E	2013E	2014E
Net sales.	$19,746	$20,437	$21,152	$21,892	$22,658
Cost of products sold.	13,196	13,652	14,130	14,624	15,136
Gross profit.	6,550	6,785	7,022	7,268	7,522
Marketing, research and general expenses	3,673	3,801	3,934	4,072	4,214
Other (income) and expense, net.	104	102	106	109	113
Operating profit	2,773	2,882	2,982	3,087	3,195
Interest income.	20	20	20	20	20
Interest expense.	(243)	(262)	(281)	(300)	(319)
Income before income taxes, equity interests and extraordinary loss	2,550	2,640	2,721	2,807	2,896
Provision for income taxes.	(788)	(818)	(844)	(870)	(898)
Income before equity interests and extraordinary loss	1,762	1,822	1,877	1,937	1,998
Share of net income of equity companies	181	181	181	181	181
Net income.	1,943	2,003	2,058	2,118	2,179
Net income attributable to noncontrolling interests	(100)	(100)	(100)	(100)	(100)
Net income attributable to Kimberly-Clark Corporation.	$ 1,843	$ 1,903	$ 1,958	$ 2,018	$ 2,079
NOPAT	$ 2,083	$ 2,155	$ 2,222	$ 2,294	$ 2,367

| EXHIBIT C.8B | Four Year Ahead Forecasts of Balance Sheet of Kimberly-Clark |

Consolidated Balance Sheet ($ millions)	2010	2011E	2012E	2013E	2014E
Assets					
Cash and cash equivalents	$ 876	$ 899	$ 931	$ 963	$ 997
Accounts receivable, net	2,472	2,555	2,644	2,737	2,832
Note receivable	218	218	218	218	218
Inventories	2,373	2,452	2,538	2,627	2,719
Deferred income taxes	187	184	190	197	204
Other current assets	202	204	212	219	227
Total current assets	6,328	6,512	6,733	6,961	7,197
Property, plant and equipment, net	8,356	8,538	8,737	8,954	9,187
Investments in equity companies	374	374	374	374	374
Goodwill	3,403	3,403	3,403	3,403	3,403
Other intangible assets	287	264	241	218	195
Long-term notes receivable	393	393	393	393	393
Other assets	723	756	783	810	838
Total assets	$19,864	$20,240	$20,664	$21,113	$21,587
Liabilities and Stockholders' Equity					
New financing	$ 0	$ 1,075	$ 2,299	$ 3,673	$ 5,043
Debt payable within one year	344	427	550	516	355
Redeemable preferred securities of subsidiary	506	506	506	506	506
Trade accounts payable	2,206	2,289	2,369	2,452	2,538
Accrued expenses	1,909	1,982	2,052	2,124	2,198
Accrued income taxes	104	108	111	115	119
Dividends payable	269	285	302	320	339
Total current liabilities	5,338	6,672	8,189	9,706	11,098
Long-term debt	5,120	4,693	4,143	3,627	3,272
Noncurrent employee benefits	1,810	1,880	1,946	2,014	2,085
Long-term income taxes payable	260	266	275	285	295
Deferred income taxes	369	388	402	416	431
Other liabilities	224	225	233	241	249
Redeemable preferred and common securities of subsidiaries	541	541	541	541	541
Stockholders' equity					
Preferred stock, no par value, authorized 20.0 million shares, none issued	0	0	0	0	0
Common stock, $1.25 par value, authorized 1.2 billion shares; issued 478.6 million shares at December 31, 2010 and 2009	598	598	598	598	598
Additional paid-in capital	425	425	425	425	425
Common stock held in treasury, at cost: 71.7 million and 61.6 million shares at December 31, 2010 and 2009	(4,726)	(6,226)	(7,726)	(9,226)	(10,726)
Accumulated other comprehensive income (loss)	(1,466)	(1,466)	(1,466)	(1,466)	(1,466)
Retained earnings	11,086	11,859	12,619	13,367	14,100
Total Kimberly-Clark Corporation stockholders' equity	5,917	5,190	4,450	3,698	2,931
Noncontrolling interests	285	385	485	585	685
Total stockholders' equity	6,202	5,575	4,935	4,283	3,616
Liabilities and stockholders' equity, total	$19,864	$20,240	$20,664	$21,113	$21,587
NOA	$12,106	$12,203	$12,345	$12,503	$12,675

Discounted Cash Flow Valuation

Exhibit C.9 shows the discounted cash (DCF) model results. In addition to the forecasted NOPAT and NOA from Exhibits C.8A and C.8B, these results use a discount (WACC) rate of 5%, shares outstanding of 406.9 million, and net nonoperating obligations (NNO) of $6,989 million. For the terminal year, we use a 1% long-term growth rate and estimate NOPAT and NOA using the NOPM and NOAT ratios from 2014 as we expained in the parsimonious forecasting method section of Module 11 as follows ($ millions): sales is $22,885 ($22,658 × 1.01), NOPAT is $2,391 ($22,885 × 10.45%, where 10.45% is from $2,367 ÷ $22,658), and NOA is $12,785 ($22,885 ÷ 1.79, where 1.79 is from $22,658/$12,675).

EXHIBIT C.9	Kimberly-Clark Discounted Cash Flow (DCF) Valuation					
(In millions, except per share values and discount factors)	**Reported 2010**	**Forecast Horizon**				**Terminal Year**
		2011	**2012**	**2013**	**2014**	
NOPAT		$2,155	$2,222	$2,294	$2,367	$2,391
Change NOA		97	142	158	172	110
FCFF (NOPAT − Increase in NOA)		2,058	2,080	2,136	2,195	2,281
Discount factor [1/(1 + r_w)^t]		0.95238	0.90703	0.86384	0.82270	
Present value of horizon FCFF		1,960	1,887	1,845	1,806	
Cum present value of horizon FCFF . . .	$ 7,498					
Present value of terminal FCFF	46,914[a]					
Total firm value	54,412					
Less (plus) NNO	6,989					
Firm equity value	47,423					
Shares outstanding	406.9					
Stock value per share.	$116.55					

[a] Computed as $\dfrac{\left(\dfrac{\$2{,}281\text{ million}}{0.05 - 0.01}\right)}{(1.05)^4}$

Residual Operating Income Valuation

Exhibit C.10 reports estimates of the values of Kimberly-Clark's equity and common stock per share using the residual operating income (ROPI) model. As with the DCF valuation, we use a discount (WACC) rate of 5%, shares outstanding of 406.9 million, and net nonoperating obligations (NNO) of $6,989 million; for the terminal year, we use a 1% long-term growth rate and estimate the following ($ millions): sales of $22,885 ($22,658 × 1.01), NOPAT of $2,391 ($22,885 × 10.45%, where 10.45% is from $2,367/$22,658), and NOA of $12,785 ($22,885/1.79, where 1.79 is from $22,658/$12,675).

EXHIBIT C.10	Kimberly-Clark Residual Operating Income (ROPI) Valuation					
(In millions, except per share values and discount factors)	**Reported 2010**	**Forecast Horizon**				**Terminal Year**
		2011	**2012**	**2013**	**2014**	
NOPAT		$ 2,155	$ 2,222	$ 2,294	$ 2,367	$ 2,391
NOA	$12,106	12,203	12,345	12,503	12,675	12,785
ROPI (NOPAT − [NOA$_{Beg}$ × r_w])		1,550	1,612	1,677	1,742	1,757
Discount factor [1/(1 + r_w)^t]		0.95238	0.90703	0.86384	0.82270	
Present value of horizon ROPI		1,476	1,462	1,448	1,433	
Cum present value of horizon ROPI	5,819					
Present value of terminal ROPI	36,137[a]					
Total firm value	54,062					
Less NNO	6,989					
Firm equity value	47,073					
Shares outstanding	406.9					
Stock value per share.	$115.69	($0.86 difference from DCF due to rounding terminal period NOPM and NOAT)				

[a] Computed as $\dfrac{\left(\dfrac{\$1{,}757\text{ million}}{0.05 - 0.01}\right)}{(1.05)^4}$

Sensitivity Analysis of Valuation Parameters

We estimate Kimberly-Clark's equity value at $47,073 million as of December 2010, which implies a per share value estimate of $115.69. As expected, equity value estimates are identical (minor difference due to rounding) for both models (because K-C is assumed to be in a steady state, that is, NOPAT and NOA growing at the same rate and, therefore, RNOA is constant).

Our stock price estimate uses only one set of assumptions and derives only one stock price. We illustrate the sensitivity of our stock price estimate to changes in input assumptions for WACC and terminal growth rate in the following table. We can expand this sensitivity analysis to any assumption or estimate we use in our financial statement adjusting, forecasting, and valuing process.

		Terminal Growth Rate				
		0.0%	0.5%	1.0%	1.5%	2.0%
W A C C	6.0%	77.62	82.78	88.97	96.53	105.98
	5.5%	86.41	92.91	100.84	110.76	123.51
	5.0%	96.97	105.28	**115.69**	129.05	146.88
	4.5%	109.87	120.76	134.77	153.45	179.60
	4.0%	126.00	140.67	160.22	187.60	228.66

Assessment of the Valuation Estimate

The closing stock price on December 31, 2010, for Kimberly-Clark (KMB) was $63.04 per share. Our model's estimates, therefore, suggest that K-C stock is undervalued as of that date. As it turns out, this valuation proved prophetic as its stock price increased to the low $70s in the continuing bear market subsequent to that date as shown in the following graph:

Summary Observations

Overall, this appendix presents a financial accounting analysis and interpretation of Kimberly-Clark's performance and position. It illustrates many of the key financial reporting topics covered in the book. We review the company's financial statements and notes, forecast key accounts, and conclude with estimates of K-C's equity value.

The Kimberly-Clark case provides an opportunity for us to apply many of the procedures conveyed in the book in a comprehensive manner. With analyses of additional companies, we become more comfortable with, and knowledgeable of, variations in financial reporting, which enhances our analysis and business decision-making skills. Our analysis of a company must go beyond the accounting numbers to include competitor and economic factors, and we must appreciate that estimation and judgment are key ingredients in financial accounting.

Glossary

A

accelerated cost recovery system (ACRS, MACRS) A system of accelerated depreciation for tax purposes introduced in 1981 (ACRS) and modified starting in 1987 (MACRS); it prescribes depreciation rates by asset classification for assets acquired after 1980

accelerated depreciation method Any depreciation method under which the amounts of depreciation expense taken in the early years of an asset's life are larger than the amounts expensed in the later years; includes the double-declining balance method

access control matrix A computerized file that lists the type of access that each computer user is entitled to have to each file and program in the computer system

account A record of the additions, deductions, and balances of individual assets, liabilities, equity, revenues, and expenses

accounting The process of measuring the economic activity of an entity in money terms and communicating the results to interested parties; the purpose is to provide financial information that is useful in making economic decisions

accounting adjustments (adjusting entries) Entries made at the end of an accounting period under accrual accounting to ensure the proper recording of expenses incurred and revenues earned for the period

accounting cycle A series of basic steps followed to process accounting information during a fiscal year

accounting entity An economic unit that has identifiable boundaries and that is the focus for the accumulation and reporting of financial information

accounting equation An expression of the equivalency of the economic resources and the claims upon those resources of a specific entity; often stated as Assets = Liabilities + Owners' Equity

accounting period The time period, typically one year (or quarter), for which periodic accounting reports are prepared

accounting system The structured collection of policies, procedures, equipment, files, and records that a company uses to collect, record, classify, process, store, report, and interpret financial data

accounts payable turnover The ratio obtained by dividing cost of goods sold by average accounts payable

accounts receivable A current asset that is created by a sale on a credit basis; it represents the amount owed the company by the customer

accounts receivable aging method A procedure that uses an aging schedule to determine the year-end balance needed in the allowance for uncollectible accounts

accounts receivable turnover Annual net sales divided by average accounts receivable (net)

accrual accounting Accounting procedures whereby revenues are recorded when they are earned and realized and expenses are recorded in the period in which they help to generate revenues

accruals Adjustments that reflect revenues earned but not received or recorded and expenses incurred but not paid or recorded

accrued expense An expense incurred but not yet paid; recognized with an accounting adjustment

accrued revenue Revenue earned but not yet billed or received; recognized with an accounting adjustment

accumulated depreciation The sum of all depreciation expense recorded to date; it is subtracted from the cost of the asset in order to derive the asset's net book value

accumulated other comprehensive income (AOCI) Current accumulation of all prior periods' other comprehensive income; *see* definition for *other comprehensive income*

adjusted trial balance A list of general ledger accounts and their balances taken after accounting adjustments have been made

adjusting The process of adjusting the historical financial statements prior to the projection of future results; also called recasting and reformulating

aging schedule An analysis that shows how long customers' accounts receivable balances have remained unpaid

allowance for uncollectible accounts A contra asset account with a normal credit balance shown on the balance sheet as a deduction from accounts receivable to reflect the expected realizable amount of accounts receivable

allowance method An accounting procedure whereby the amount of uncollectible accounts expense is estimated and recorded in the period in which the related credit sales occur

Altman's Z-score A predictor of potential bankruptcy based on multiple ratios

amortization The periodic writing off of an account balance to expense; similar to depreciation and usually refers to the periodic writing off of an intangible asset

annuity A pattern of cash flows in which equal amounts are spaced equally over a number of periods

articles of incorporation A document prepared by persons organizing a corporation in the United States that sets forth the structure and purpose of the corporation and specifics regarding the stock to be issued

articulation The linkage of financial statements within and across time

asset turnover Net income divided by average total assets

asset write-downs Adjustment of carrying value of assets down to their current fair value

assets The economic resources of an entity that are owned or controlled will provide future benefits and can be reliably measured

audit An examination of a company's financial statements by a firm of independent certified public accountants

audit report A report issued by independent auditors that includes the final version of the financial statements, accompanying notes, and the auditor's opinion on the financial statements

authorized stock The maximum number of shares in a class of stock that a corporation may issue

available-for-sale securities Investments in securities that management intends to hold for capital gains and dividend income; although it may sell them if the price is right

average cash conversion cycle Average collection period + average inventory days outstanding − average payable days outstanding

average collection period Determined by dividing accounts receivable by average daily sales, sometimes referred to as days sales outstanding or DSO

average inventory days outstanding (AIDO) An indication of how long, on average, inventories are on the shelves, computed as inventory divided by average daily cost of goods sold

B

balance sheet A financial statement showing an entity's assets, liabilities, and owners' equity at a specific date; sometimes called a statement of financial position

bearer One of the terms that may be used to designate the payee on a promissory note; means whoever holds the note

bond A long-term debt instrument that promises to pay interest periodically and a principal amount at maturity, usually issued by the borrower to a group of lenders; bonds may incorporate a wide variety of provisions relating to security for the debt involved, methods of paying the periodic interest, retirement provisions, and conversion options

book value The dollar amount carried in the accounts for a particular item; the book value of a depreciable asset is cost less accumulated depreciation; the book value of an entity is assets less liabilities

book value per share The dollar amount of net assets represented by one share of stock; computed by dividing the amount of stockholders' equity associated with a class of stock by the outstanding shares of that class of stock

borrows at a discount When the face amount of the note is reduced by a calculated cash discount to determine the cash proceeds

C

calendar year A fiscal year that ends on December 31

call provision A bond feature that allows the borrower to retire (call in) the bonds after a stated date

capital expenditures Expenditures that increase the book value of long-term assets; sometimes abbreviated as CAPEX

capital lease A lease that transfers to the lessee substantially all of the benefits and risks related to ownership of the property; the lessee records the leased property as an asset and establishes a liability for the lease obligation

capital markets Financing sources, which are formalized when companies issue securities that are traded on organized exchanges; they are informal when companies are funded by private sources

capitalization The recording of a cost as an asset on the balance sheet rather than as an expense on the income statement; these costs are transferred to expense as the asset is used up

capitalization of interest A process that adds interest to an asset's initial cost if a period of time is required to prepare the asset for use

cash An asset category representing the amount of a firm's available cash and funds on deposit at a bank in checking accounts and savings accounts

cash and cash equivalents The sum of cash plus short-term, highly liquid investments such as treasury bills and money market funds; includes marketable securities maturing within 90 days of the financial statement date

cash discount An amount that a purchaser of merchandise may deduct from the purchase price for paying within the discount period

cash-basis accounting Accounting procedures whereby revenues are recorded when cash is received and expenses are recorded when cash payments are made

cash (operating) conversion cycle The period of time (typically measured in days) from when cash is invested in inventories until inventory is sold and receivables are collected

certificate of deposit (CD) An investment security available at financial institutions generally offering a fixed rate of return for a specified period of time

change in accounting estimate Modification to a previous estimate of an uncertain future event, such as the useful life of a depreciable asset, uncollectible accounts receivable, and warranty expenses; applied currently and prospectively only

changes in accounting principles Modification of accounting methods (such as depreciation or inventory costing methods)

chart of accounts A list of all the general ledger account titles and their numerical code

clean surplus accounting Income that explains successive equity balances

closing procedures A step in the accounting cycle in which the balances of all temporary accounts are transferred to the retained earnings account, leaving the temporary accounts with zero balances

commitments A contractual arrangement by which both parties to the contract still have acts to perform

common stock The basic ownership class of corporate capital stock, carrying the rights to vote, share in earnings, participate in future stock issues, and share in any liquidation proceeds after prior claims have been settled

common-size financial statement A financial statement in which each item is presented as a percentage of a key figure such as sales or total assets

comparative financial statements A form of horizontal analysis involving comparison of two or more periods' financial statements showing dollar and/or percentage changes

compensating balance A minimum amount that a financial institution requires a firm to maintain in its account as part of a borrowing arrangement complex capital structure

comprehensive income The total change in stockholders' equity other than those arising from capital (stock) transactions; computed as net income plus other comprehensive income (OCI); typical OCI components are unrealized gains (losses) on available-for-sale securities and derivatives, minimum pension liability adjustment, and foreign currency translation adjustments

conceptual framework A cohesive set of interrelated objectives and fundamentals for external financial reporting developed by the FASB

conservatism An accounting principle stating that judgmental determinations should tend toward understatement rather than overstatement of net assets and income

consistency An accounting principle stating that, unless otherwise disclosed, accounting reports should be prepared on a basis consistent with the preceding period

consolidated financial statements Financial statements reflecting a parent company and one or more subsidiary companies and/or a variable interest entity (VIE) and its primary beneficiary

contingent liabilities A potential obligation, the eventual occurrence of which usually depends on some future event beyond the control of the firm; contingent liabilities may originate with such events as lawsuits, credit guarantees, and environmental damages

contra account An account related to, and deducted from, another account when financial statements are prepared or when book values are computed

contract rate The rate of interest stated on a bond certificate

contributed capital The net funding that a company receives from issuing and acquiring its equity shares

convertible bond A bond incorporating the holder's right to convert the bond to capital stock under prescribed terms

convertible securities Debt and equity securities that provide the holder with an option to convert those securities into other securities

copyright An exclusive right that protects an owner against the unauthorized reproduction of a specific written work or artwork

core income A company's income from its usual business activities that is expected to continue (persist) into the future

corporation A legal entity created by the granting of a charter from an appropriate governmental authority and owned by stockholders who have limited liability for corporate debt

cost of goods sold The total cost of merchandise sold to customers during the accounting period

cost of goods sold percentage The ratio of cost of goods sold divided by net sales

cost method An investment is reported at its historical cost, and any cash dividends and interest received are recognized in current income

cost principle An accounting principle stating that asset measures are based on the prices paid to acquire the assets

coupon bond A bond with coupons for interest payable to bearer attached to the bond for each interest period; whenever interest is due, the bondholder detaches a coupon and deposits it with his or her bank for collection

coupon (contract or stated) rate The coupon rate of interest is stated in the bond contract; it is used to compute the dollar amount of (semiannual) interest payments that are paid to bondholder during the life of the bond issue

covenants Contractual requirements put into loan or bond agreements by lenders

credit (entry) An entry on the right side (or in the credit column) of any account

credit card fee A fee charged retailers for credit card services provided by financial institutions; the fee is usually stated as a percentage of credit card sales

credit guarantee A guarantee of another company's debt by cosigning a note payable; a guarantor's contingent liability that is usually disclosed in a balance sheet footnote

credit memo A document prepared by a seller to inform the purchaser that the seller has reduced the amount owed by the purchaser due to a return or an allowance

credit period The maximum amount of time, usually stated in days, that the purchaser of merchandise has to pay the seller

credit rating An opinion formed by a credit-rating agency (such as Standard & Poor's, Moody's or Fitch) concerning the creditworthiness of a borrower (a corporation or a government) based on an assessment of the borrower's likelihood of default

credit terms The prescribed payment period for purchases on credit with discount specified for early payment

cumulative (preferred stock) A feature associated with preferred stock whereby any dividends in arrears must be paid before dividends may be paid on common stock

cumulative effect of a change in principle The cumulative effect on net income to the date of a change in accounting principle

cumulative translation adjustment The amount recorded in the equity section as necessary to balance the accounting equation when assets and liabilities of foreign subsidiaries are translated into $US at the rate of exchange prevailing at the statement date

current assets Cash and other assets that will be converted to cash or used up during the normal operating cycle of the business or one year, whichever is longer

current liabilities Obligations that will require within the coming year or operating cycle, whichever is longer, (1) the use of existing current assets or (2) the creation of other current liabilities

current rate method Method of translating foreign currency transactions under which balance sheet amounts are translated using exchange rates in effect at the period-end consolidation date and income statement amounts using the average exchange rate for the period

current ratio Current assets divided by current liabilities

D

days' sales in inventory Inventories divided by average cost of goods sold

debenture bond A bond that has no specific property pledged as security for the repayment of funds borrowed

debit (entry) An entry on the left side (or in the debit column) of any account

debt-to-equity ratio A firm's total liabilities divided by its total owners' equity

declining-balance method An accelerated depreciation method that allocates depreciation expense to each year by applying a constant percentage to the declining book value of the asset

default The nonpayment of interest and principal and/or the failure to adhere to the various terms and conditions of the bond indenture

deferrals Adjustments that allocate various assets and revenues received in advance to the proper accounting periods as expenses and revenues

deferred revenue A liability representing revenues received in advance; also called unearned revenue

deferred tax liability A liability representing the estimated future income taxes payable resulting from an existing temporary difference between an asset's book value and its tax basis

deferred tax valuation allowance Reduction in a reported deferred tax asset to adjust for the amount that is not likely to be realized

defined benefit plan A type of retirement plan under which the company promises to make periodic payments to the employee after retirement

defined contribution plan A retirement plan under which the company makes cash contribution into an employee's account (usually with a third-party trustee like a bank) either solely or as a matching contribution

depletion The allocation of the cost of natural resources to the units extracted and sold or, in the case of timberland, the board feet of timber cut

depreciation The decline in economic potential (using up) of plant assets originating from wear, deterioration, and obsolescence

depreciation accounting The process of allocating the cost of equipment, vehicles, and buildings (not land) to expense over the time period benefiting from their use

depreciation base The acquisition cost of an asset less estimated salvage value

depreciation rate An estimate of how the asset will be used up over its useful life—evenly over its useful life, more heavily in the early years, or in proportion to its actual usage

derivatives Financial instruments such as futures, options, and swaps that are commonly used to hedge (mitigate) some external risk, such as commodity price risk, interest rate risk, or risks relating to foreign currency fluctuations

diluted earnings per share The earnings per share computation taking into consideration the effects of dilutive securities

dilutive securities Securities that can be exchanged for shares of common stock and, thereby, increase the number of common shares outstanding

discontinued operations Net income or loss from business segments that are up for sale or have been sold in the current period

discount bond A bond that is sold for less than its par (face) value

discount on notes payable A contra account that is subtracted from the Notes Payable amount on the balance sheet; as the life of the note elapses, the discount is reduced and charged to interest expense

discount period The maximum amount of time, usually stated in days, that the purchaser of merchandise has to pay the seller if the purchaser wants to claim the cash discount

discounted cash flow (DCF) model The value of a security is equal to the present value of the expected free cash flows to the firm, discounted at the weighted average cost of capital (WACC)

discounting The exchanging of notes receivable for cash at a financial institution at an amount that is less than the face value of the notes

dividends account A temporary equity account used to accumulate owner dividends from the business

dividend discount model The value of a security today is equal to the present value of that security's expected dividends, discounted at the weighted average cost of capital

dividend payout ratio Annual dividends per share divided by the earnings per share or by net income

dividend yield Annual dividends per share divided by the market price per share

double-entry accounting system A method of accounting that recognizes the duality of a transaction such that the analysis results in a recording of equal amounts of debits and credits

E

earned When referring to revenue, the seller's execution of its duties under the terms of the agreement, with the resultant passing of title to the buyer with no right of return or other contingencies

earned capital The cumulative net income (losses) retained by the company (not paid out to shareholders as dividends)

earnings per share (EPS) Net income less preferred stock dividends divided by the weighted average common shares outstanding for the period

earnings quality The degree to which reported earnings represent how well the firm has performed from an economic standpoint

earnings smoothing Earnings management with a goal to provide an earnings stream with less variability

EBIT Earnings before interest and taxes

EBITDA Earnings before interest, taxes, depreciation and amortization

economic profit The number of inventory units sold multiplied by the difference between the sales price and the replacement cost of the inventories (approximated by the cost of the most recently purchased inventories)

economic value added (EVA) Net operating profits after tax less a charge for the use of capital equal to beginning capital utilized in the business multiplied by the weighted average cost of capital (EVA = NOPAT − [r_w × Net operating assets])

effective interest method A method of amortizing bond premium or discount that results in a constant rate of interest each period and varying amounts of premium or discount amortized each period

effective interest rate The rate determined by dividing the total discount amount by the cash proceeds on a note payable when the borrower borrowed at a discount

effective rate The current rate of interest in the market for a bond or other debt instrument; when issued, a bond is priced to yield the market (effective) rate of interest at the date of issuance

efficient markets hypothesis Capital markets are said to be efficient if at any given time, current equity (stock) prices reflect all relevant information that determines those equity prices

employee severance costs Accrued (estimated) costs for termination of employees as part of a restructuring program

employee stock options A form of compensation that grants a select group of employees the right to purchase a fixed number of company shares at a fixed price for a predetermined time period

equity carve out A corporate divestiture of operating units

equity method The prescribed method of accounting for investments in which the investor company has a significant influence over the investee company (usually taken to be ownership between 20-50% of the outstanding common stock of the investee company)

ethics An area of inquiry dealing with the values, rules, and justifications that governs one's way of life

executory contract A contract where a party has a material unperformed obligation that, if not performed, will result in a breach of contract

expenses Decreases in owners' equity incurred by a firm in the process of earning revenues

extraordinary items Revenues and expenses that are both unusual and infrequent and are, therefore, excluded from income from continuing operations

F

face amount The principal amount of a bond or note to be repaid at maturity

factoring Selling an account receivable to another company, typically a finance company or a financial institution, for less than its face value

fair value Value that an asset could be sold for (or an obligation discharged) in an orderly market, between willing buyers and sellers; often, but not always, is current market value

fair value method Method of accounting that records on the balance sheet, the asset or liabilities fair value, and records on the income statement, changes in the fair value

financial accounting The area of accounting activities dealing with the preparation of financial statements showing an entity's results of operations, financial position, and cash flows

Financial Accounting Standards Board (FASB) The organization currently responsible for setting accounting standards for reporting financial information by U.S. entities

financial assets Normally consist of excess resources held for future expansion or unexpected needs; they are usually invested in the form of other companies' stock, corporate or government bonds, and real estate

financial leverage The proportionate use of borrowed funds in the capital structure, computed as net nonoperating obligations (NNO) divided by average equity

financial reporting objectives A component of the conceptual framework that specifies that financial statements should provide information (1) useful for investment and credit decisions, (2) helpful in assessing an entity's ability to generate future cash flows, and (3) about an entity's resources, claims to those resources, and the effects of events causing changes in these items

financial statement elements A part of the conceptual framework that identifies the significant components—such as assets, liabilities, owners' equity, revenues, and expenses—used to put financial statements together

financing activities Methods that companies use to raise the funds to pay for resources such as land, buildings, and equipment

finished goods inventory The dollar amount of inventory that has completed the production process and is awaiting sale

first-in, first-out (FIFO) method One of the prescribed methods of inventory costing; FIFO assumes that the first costs incurred for the purchase or production of inventory are the first costs relieved from inventory when goods are sold

fiscal year The annual accounting period used by a business firm

five forces of competitive intensity Industry competition, bargaining power of buyers, bargaining power of suppliers, threat of substitution, threat of entry

fixed assets An alternate label for long-term assets; may also be called property, plant, and equipment (PPE)

fixed costs Costs that do not change with changes in sales volume (over a reasonable range)

forecast The projection of financial results over the forecast horizon and terminal periods

foreign currency transaction The $US equivalent of an asset or liability denominated in a foreign currency

foreign exchange gain or loss The gain (loss) recognized in the income statement relating to the change in the $US equivalent of an asset or liability denominated in a foreign currency

forward earnings Earnings expected to be reported in the next period

franchise Generally, an exclusive right to operate or sell a specific brand of products in a given geographic area

free cash flow This excess cash flow (above that required to manage its growth and development) from which dividends can be paid; computed as NOPAT − Increase in NOA

full disclosure principle An accounting principle stipulating the disclosure of all facts necessary to make financial statements useful to readers

fully diluted earnings per share *See* diluted earnings per share

functional currency The currency representing the primary currency in which a business unit conducts its operations

fundamental analysis Uses financial information to predict future valuation and, hence, buy-sell stock strategies

funded status The difference between the pension obligation and the fair value of the pension investments

future value The amount a specified investment (or series of investments) will be worth at a future date if invested at a given rate of compound interest

G

general journal A journal with enough flexibility so that any type of business transaction can be recorded in it

general ledger A grouping of all of an entity's accounts that are used to prepare the basic financial statements

generally accepted accounting principles (GAAP) A set of standards and procedures that guide the preparation of financial statements

going concern concept An accounting principle that assumes that, in the absence of evidence to the contrary, a business entity will have an indefinite life

goodwill The value that derives from a firm's ability to earn more than a normal rate of return on the fair market value of its specific, identifiable net assets; computed as the residual of the purchase price less the fair market value of the net tangible and intangible assets acquired

gross margin The difference between net sales and cost of goods sold; also called gross profit

gross profit on sales The difference between net sales and cost of goods sold; also called gross margin

gross profit margin (GPM) (percentage) The ratio of gross profit on sales divided by net sales

H

held-to-maturity securities The designation given to a portfolio of bond investments that are expected to be held until they mature

historical cost Original acquisition or issuance costs

holding company The parent company of a subsidiary

holding gain The increase in replacement cost since the inventories were acquired, which equals the number of units sold multiplied by the difference between the current replacement cost and the original acquisition cost

horizon period The forecast period for which detailed estimates are made, typically 5-10 years

horizontal analysis Analysis of a firm's financial statements that covers two or more years

I

IASB International Accounting Standards Board, independent, privately funded accounting standard-setter based in London, responsible for developing IFRS and promoting the use and application of these standards

IFRS International Financial Reporting Standards, a body of accounting standards developed by the International Accounting Standards Board and used for financial reports across much of the world

impairment A reduction in value from that presently recorded

impairment loss A loss recognized on an impaired asset equal to the difference between its book value and current fair value

income statement A financial statement reporting an entity's revenues and expenses for a period of time

indirect method A presentation format for the statement of cash flows that refers to the operating section only; that section begins with net income and converts it to cash flows from operations

intangible assets A term applied to a group of long-term assets, including patents, copyrights, franchises, trademarks, and goodwill, that benefit an entity but do not have physical substance

interest cost (pensions) The increase in the pension obligation due to the accrual of an additional year of interest

internal auditing A company function that provides independent appraisals of the company's financial statements, its internal controls, and its operations

internal controls The measures undertaken by a company to ensure the reliability of its accounting data, protect its assets from theft or unauthorized use, make sure that employees are following the company's policies and procedures, and evaluate the performance of employees, departments, divisions, and the company as a whole

inventory carrying costs Costs of holding inventories, including warehousing, logistics, insurance, financing, and the risk of loss due to theft, damage, or technological or fashion change

inventory shrinkage The cost associated with an inventory shortage; the amount by which the perpetual inventory exceeds the physical inventory

inventory turnover Cost of goods sold divided by average inventory

investing activities The acquiring and disposing of resources (assets) that a company uses to acquire and sell its products and services

investing creditors Those who primarily finance investing activities

investment returns The increase in pension investments resulting from interest, dividends, and capital gains on the investment portfolio

invoice A document that the seller sends to the purchaser to request payment for items that the seller shipped to the purchaser

invoice price The price that a seller charges the purchaser for merchandise

IOU A slang term for a receivable

IRS Internal Revenue Service, the U.S. taxing authority

issued stock Shares of stock that have been sold and issued to stockholders; issued stock may be either outstanding or in the treasury

J

journal A tabular record in which business transactions are analyzed in debit and credit terms and recorded in chronological order

just-in-time (JIT) inventory Receive inventory from suppliers into the production process just at the point it is needed

L

land improvements Improvements with limited lives made to land sites, such as paved parking lots and driveways

last-in, first-out (LIFO) method One of the prescribed methods of inventory costing; LIFO assumes that the last costs incurred for the purchase or production of inventory are the first costs relieved from inventory when goods are sold

lease A contract between a lessor (owner) and lessee (tenant) for the rental of property

leasehold The rights transferred from the lessor to the lessee by a lease

leasehold improvements Expenditures made by a lessee to alter or improve leased property

lessee The party acquiring the right to the use of property by a lease

lessor The owner of property who transfers the right to use the property to another party by a lease

leveraging The use of borrowed funds in the capital structure of a firm; the expectation is that the funds will earn a return higher than the rate of interest on the borrowed funds

liabilities The obligations, or debts, that an entity must pay in money or services at some time in the future because of past transactions or events

LIFO conformity rule IRS requirement to cost inventories using LIFO for tax purposes if they are costed using LIFO for financial reporting purposes

LIFO liquidation The reduction in inventory quantities when LIFO costing is used; LIFO liquidation yields an increase in gross profit and income when prices are rising

LIFO reserve The difference between the cost of inventories using FIFO and the cost using LIFO

liquidation value per share The amount that would be received by a holder of a share of stock if the corporation liquidated

liquidity How much cash the company has, how much is expected, and how much can be raised on short notice

list price The suggested price or reference price of merchandise in a catalog or price list

long-term liabilities Debt obligations not due to be settled within the normal operating cycle or one year, whichever is longer

lower of cost or market (LCM) GAAP requirement to write down the carrying amount of inventories on the balance sheet if the reported cost (using FIFO, for example) exceeds market value (determined by current replacement cost)

M

maker The signer of a promissory note

management discussion and anaysis (MD&A) The section of the 10-K report in which a company provides a detailed discussion of its business activities

managerial accounting The accounting activities carried out by a firm's accounting staff primarily to furnish management with accounting data for decisions related to the firm's operations

manufacturers Companies that convert raw materials and components into finished products through the application of skilled labor and machine operations

manufacturing costs The costs of direct materials, direct labor, and manufacturing overhead incurred in the manufacture of a product

market cap Market capitalization of the firm, or value as perceived by investors; computed as market value per share multiplied by shares outstanding

market (yield) rate This is the interest rate that investors expect to earn on the investment in this debt security; this rate is used to price the bond issue

market value The published price (as listed on a stock exchange)

market value per share The current price at which shares of stock may be bought or sold

matching principle An accounting guideline that states that income is determined by relating expenses, to the extent feasible, with revenues that have been recorded

materiality An accounting guideline that states that transactions so insignificant that they would not affect a user's actions or perception of the company may be recorded in the most expedient manner

materials inventory The physical component of inventory; the other components of manufactured inventory are labor costs and overhead costs

maturity date The date on which a note or bond matures

measuring unit concept An accounting guideline noting that the accounting unit of measure is the basic unit of money

merchandise inventory A stock of products that a company buys from another company and makes available for sale to its customers

merchandising firm A company that buys finished products, stores the products for varying periods of time, and then resells the products

method of comparables model Equity valuation or stock values are predicted using price multiples, which are defined as stock price

divided by some key financial statement number such as net income, net sales, book value of equity, total assets, or cash flow; companies are then compared with their competitors

minority interest *See* noncontrolling interest

modified accelerated cost recovery system (MACRS) *See* accelerated cost recovery system

multiple element arrangements Sales (revenue) arrangements containing multiple deliverables and, in some cases, multiple cash-flow streams

N

natural resources Assets occurring in a natural state, such as timber, petroleum, natural gas, coal, and other mineral deposits

net asset based valuation model Equity is valued as reported assets less reported liabilities

net assets The difference between an entity's assets and liabilities; net assets are equal to owners' equity

net book value (NBV) The cost of the asset less accumulated depreciation; also called carrying value

net income The excess of a firm's revenues over its expenses

net loss The excess of a firm's expenses over its revenues

net nonoperating expense (NNE) Nonoperating expenses and losses (plus any net income attributable to noncontrolling interest) less nonoperating revenues and gains, all measured after-tax

net nonoperating expense percentage (NNEP) Net nonoperating expense divided by net nonoperating obligations (NNO)

net nonoperating obligations (NNO) All nonoperating obligations (plus any noncontrolling interest) less nonoperating assets

net operating asset turnover (NOAT) Ratio obtained by dividing sales by net operating assets

net operating assets (NOA) Current and long-term operating assets less current and long-term operating liabilities; or net operating working capital plus long-term net operating assets

net operating profit after tax (NOPAT) Operating revenues less operating expenses (including taxes)

net operating profit margin (NOPM) Ratio obtained by dividing net operating profit after tax (NOPAT) by sales

net operating working capital (NOWC) Current operating assets less current operating liabilities

net realizable value The value at which an asset can be sold, net of any costs of disposition

net sales The total revenue generated by a company through merchandise sales less the revenue given up through sales returns and allowances and sales discounts

net working capital Current assets less current liabilities

nominal rate The rate of interest stated on a bond certificate or other debt instrument

noncash investing and financing activities Significant business activities during the period that do not impact cash inflows or cash outflows

noncontrolling interest The portion of equity (net assets) in a subsidiary not attributable, directly or indirectly, to a parent. A noncontrolling interest (formerly called minority interest) typically represents the ownership interest of shareholders other than those of the parent company.

noncurrent liabilities Obligations not due to be paid within one year or the operating cycle, whichever is longer

nonoperating expenses Expenses that relate to the company's financing activities and include interest income and interest expense, gains and losses on sales of securities, and income or loss on discontinued operations

no-par stock Stock that does not have a par value

NOPAT Net operating profit after tax

normal operating cycle For a particular business, the average period of time between the use of cash in its typical operating activity and the subsequent collection of cash from customers

note receivable A promissory note held by the note's payee

notes to financial statements Footnotes in which companies discuss their accounting policies and estimates used in preparing the statements

not-sufficient-funds check A check from an individual or company that had an insufficient cash balance in the bank when the holder of the check presented it to the bank for payment

objectivity principle An accounting principle requiring that, whenever possible, accounting entries are based on objectively determined evidence

off-balance-sheet financing The structuring of a financing arrangement so that no liability shows on the borrower's balance sheet

operating activities Using resources to research, develop, produce, purchase, market, and distribute company products and services

operating cash flow to capital expenditures ratio A firm's net cash flow from operating activities divided by its annual capital expenditures

operating cash flow to current liabilities ratio A firm's net cash flow from operating activities divided by its average current liabilities

operating creditors Those who primarily finance operating activities

operating cycle The time between paying cash for goods or employee services and receiving cash from customers

operating expense margin (OEM) The ratio obtained by dividing any operating expense category by sales

operating expenses The usual and customary costs that a company incurs to support its main business activities; these include cost of goods sold, selling expenses, depreciation expense, amortization expense, research and development expense, and taxes on operating profits

operating lease A lease by which the lessor retains the usual risks and rewards of owning the property

operating profit margin The ratio obtained by dividing NOPAT by sales

operational audit An evaluation of activities, systems, and internal controls within a company to determine their efficiency, effectiveness, and economy

organization costs Expenditures incurred in launching a business (usually a corporation), including attorney's fees and various fees paid to the state

other comprehensive income (OCI) Current period change in stockholders' equity *other than* those arising from capital (stock) transactions and those included in net income; typical OCI components are unrealized gains (losses) on available-for-sale securities and derivatives, minimum pension liability adjustment, and foreign currency translation adjustments

outstanding checks Checks issued by a firm that have not yet been presented to its bank for payment

outstanding stock Shares of stock that are currently owned by stockholders (excludes treasury stock)

owners' equity The interest of owners in the assets of an entity; equal to the difference between the entity's assets and liabilities

packing list A document that lists the items of merchandise contained in a carton and the quantity of each item; the packing list is usually attached to the outside of the carton

paid-in capital The amount of capital contributed to a corporation by various transactions; the primary source of paid-in capital is from the issuance of shares of stock

par (bonds) Face value of the bond

par value (stock) An amount specified in the corporate charter for each share of stock and imprinted on the face of each stock certificate, often determines the legal capital of the corporation

parent company A company owning one or more subsidiary companies

parsimonious method to multiyear forecasting Forecasting multiple years using only sales growth, net operating profit margin (NOPM), and the turnover of net operating assets (NOAT)

partnership A voluntary association of two or more persons for the purpose of conducting a business

password A string of characters that a computer user enters into a computer terminal to prove to the computer that the person using the computer is truly the person named in the user identification code

patent An exclusive privilege granted for 20 years to an inventor that gives the patent holder the right to exclude others from making, using, or selling the invention

payee The company or individual to whom a promissory note is made payable

payment approval form A document that authorizes the payment of an invoice

pension plan A plan to pay benefits to employees after they retire from the company; the plan may be a defined contribution plan or a defined benefit plan

percentage-of-completion method Recognition of revenue by determining the costs incurred per the contract as compared to its total expected costs

percentage of net sales method A procedure that determines the uncollectible accounts expense for the year by multiplying net credit sales by the estimated uncollectible percentage

performance obligation A promise in a contract with a customer to transfer a good or service to the customer; includes promises that are implied by business practices, published policies, or explicit statements if those promises create an expectation of the customer that the entity will perform

period statement A financial statement accumulating information for a specific period of time; examples are the income statement, the statement of owners' equity, and the statement of cash flows

permanent account An account used to prepare the balance sheet; that is, asset, liability, and equity capital (capital stock and retained earnings) accounts; any balance in a permanent account at the end of an accounting period is carried forward to the next period

physical inventory A year-end procedure that involves counting the quantity of each inventory item, determining the unit cost of each item, multiplying the unit cost times quantity, and summing the costs of all the items to determine the total inventory at cost

plant assets Land, buildings, equipment, vehicles, furniture, and fixtures that a firm uses in its operations; sometimes referred to by the acronym PPE

pooling of interests method A method of accounting for business combinations under which the acquired company is recorded on the acquirer's balance sheet at its book value, rather than market value; this method is no longer acceptable under GAAP for acquisitions occurring after 2001

position statement A financial statement, such as the balance sheet, that presents information as of a particular date

post-closing trial balance A list of general ledger accounts and their balances after closing entries have been recorded and posted

postdated check A check from another person or company with a date that is later than the current date; a postdated check does not become cash until the date of the check

preemptive right The right of a stockholder to maintain his or her proportionate interest in a corporation by having the right to purchase an appropriate share of any new stock issue

preferred stock A class of corporate capital stock typically receiving priority over common stock in dividend payments and distribution of assets should the corporation be liquidated

premium bond A bond that is sold for more than its par (face) value

present value The current worth of amounts to be paid (or received) in the future; computed by discounting the future payments (or receipts) at a specified interest rate

price-earnings ratio Current market price per common share divided by earnings per share

pro forma income A computation of income that begins with the GAAP income from continuing operations (that excludes discontinued operations, extraordinary items and changes in accounting principle), but then excludes other transitory items (most notably, restructuring charges), and some additional items such as expenses arising from acquisitions (goodwill amortization and other acquisition costs), compensation expense in the form of stock options, and research and development expenditures; pro forma income is not GAAP

promissory note A written promise to pay a certain sum of money on demand or at a determinable future time

purchase method The prescribed method of accounting for business combinations; under the purchase method, assets and liabilities of the acquired company are recorded at fair market value,

together with identifiable intangible assets; the balance is ascribed to goodwill

purchase order A document that formally requests a supplier to sell and deliver specific quantities of particular items of merchandise at specified prices

purchase requisition An internal document that requests that the purchasing department order particular items of merchandise

qualitative characteristics of accounting information The characteristics of accounting information that contribute to decision usefulness; the primary qualities are relevance and reliability

quarterly data Selected quarterly financial information that is reported in annual reports to stockholders

quick ratio Quick assets (that is, cash and cash equivalents, short-term investments, and current receivables) divided by current liabilities

realized (or realizable) When referring to revenue, the receipt of an asset or satisfaction of a liability or performance obligation as a result of a transaction or event

recognition criteria The criteria that must be met before a financial statement element may be recorded in the accounts; essentially, the item must meet the definition of an element and must be measurable

registered bond A bond for which the issuer (or the trustee) maintains a record of owners and, at the appropriate times, mails out interest payments

relevance A qualitative characteristic of accounting information; relevant information contributes to the predictive and evaluative decisions made by financial statement users

reliability A qualitative characteristic of accounting information; reliable information contains no bias or error and faithfully portrays what it intends to represent

remeasurement The computation of gain or loss in the translation of subsidiaries denominated in a foreign currency into $US when the temporal method is used

residual operating income Net operating profits after tax (NOPAT) less the product of net operating assets (NOA) at the beginning of the period multiplied by the weighted average cost of capital (WACC)

residual operating income (ROPI) model An equity valuation approach that equates the firm's value to the sum of its net operating assets (NOA) and the present value of its residual operating income (ROPI)

retailers Companies that buy products from wholesale distributors and sell the products to individual customers, the general public

retained earnings Earned capital, the cumulative net income and loss, of the company (from its inception) that has not been paid to shareholders as dividends

retained earnings reconciliation The reconciliation of retained earnings from the beginning to the end of the year; the change in retained earnings includes, at a minimum, the net income (loss) for the period and dividends paid, if any, but may include other components as well; also called statement of retained earnings

return The amount earned on an investment; also called yield

return on assets (ROA) A financial ratio computed as net income divided by average total assets

return on common stockholders' equity (ROCE) A financial ratio computed as net income less preferred stock dividends divided by average common stockholders' equity

return on equity (ROE) The ultimate measure of performance from the shareholders' perspective; computed as net income divided by average equity

return on investment The ratio obtained by dividing income by average investment; sometimes referred to by the acronym ROI

return on net operating assets (RNOA) The ratio obtained by dividing NOPAT by average net operating assets

return on sales (ROS) The ratio obtained by dividing net income by net sales

revenue recognition principle An accounting principle requiring that revenue be recognized when earned and realized (or realizable)

revenues Increases in owners' equity a firm earns by providing goods or services for its customers

sale on account A sale of merchandise made on a credit basis

salvage value The expected net recovery when a plant asset is sold or removed from service; also called residual value

secured bond A bond that pledges specific property as security for meeting the terms of the bond agreement

Securities and Exchange Commission (SEC) The commission, created by the 1934 Securities Act, that has broad powers to regulate the issuance and trading of securities, and the financial reporting of companies issuing securities to the public

segments Subdivisions of a firm for which supplemental financial information is disclosed

serial bond A bond issue that staggers the bond maturity dates over a series of years

service cost (pensions) The increase in the pension obligation due to employees working another year for the employer

share-based payment Payment for a good or service using the entity's equity securities; an example is restricted stock used to compensate employees

significant influence The ability of the investor to affect the financing or operating policies of the investee

sinking fund provision A bond feature that requires the borrower to retire a portion of the bonds each year or, in some cases, to make payments each year to a trustee who is responsible for managing the resources needed to retire the bonds at maturity

solvency The ability to meet obligations, especially to creditors

source document Any written document or computer record evidencing an accounting transaction, such as a bank check or deposit slip, sales invoice, or cash register tape

special purpose entity *See* variable interest entity

spin-off A form of equity carve out in which divestiture is accomplished by distribution of a company's shares in a subsidiary to the company's shareholders who then own the shares in the subsidiary directly rather than through the parent company

split-off A form of equity carve out in which divestiture is accomplished by the parent company's exchange of stock in the subsidiary in return for shares in the parent owned by its shareholders

spread The difference between the return on net operating activities (RNOA) and the net nonoperating expense percentage (NNEP)

stated value A nominal amount that may be assigned to each share of no-par stock and accounted for much as if it were a par value

statement of cash flows A financial statement showing a firm's cash inflows and outflows for a specific period, classified into operating, investing, and financing categories

statement of equity *See* statement of stockholders' equity

statement of financial position A financial statement showing a firm's assets, liabilities, and owners' equity at a specific date; also called a balance sheet

statement of owners' equity A financial statement presenting information on the events causing a change in owners' equity during a period; the statement presents the beginning balance, additions to, deductions from, and the ending balance of owners' equity for the period

statement of retained earnings *See* retained earnings reconciliation

statement of stockholders' equity The financial statement that reconciles all of the components of stockholders' equity

stock dividends The payment of dividends in shares of stock

stock split Additional shares of its own stock issued by a corporation to its current stockholders in proportion to their current ownership interests without changing the balances in the related stockholders' equity accounts; a formal stock split increases the number of shares outstanding and reduces proportionately the stock's per share par value

straight-line depreciation A depreciation procedure that allocates uniform amounts of depreciation expense to each full period of a depreciable asset's useful life

subsequent events Events occurring shortly after a fiscal year-end that will be reported as supplemental information to the financial statements of the year just ended

subsidiaries Companies that are owned by the parent company

subsidiary ledger A set of accounts or records that contains detailed information about the items included in the balance of one general ledger account

summary of significant accounting policies A financial statement disclosure, usually the initial note to the statements, which identifies the major accounting policies and procedures used by the firm

sum-of-the-years'-digits method An accelerated depreciation method that allocates depreciation expense to each year in a fractional proportion, the denominator of which is the sum of the years' digits in the useful life of the asset and the numerator of which is the remaining useful life of the asset at the beginning of the current depreciation period

T

T account An abbreviated form of the formal account in the shape of a T; use is usually limited to illustrations of accounting techniques and analysis

temporary account An account used to gather information for an accounting period; at the end of the period, the balance is transferred to a permanent owners' equity account; revenue, expense, and dividends accounts are temporary accounts

term loan A long-term borrowing, evidenced by a note payable, which is contracted with a single lender

terminal period The forecast period following the horizon period

times interest earned ratio Income before interest expense and income taxes divided by interest expense

total compensation cost The sum of gross pay, payroll taxes, and fringe benefits paid by the employer

trade credit Inventories purchased on credit from other companies

trade discount An amount, usually based on quantity of merchandise purchased, that the seller subtracts from the list price of merchandise to determine the invoice price

trade name An exclusive and continuing right to use a certain term or name to identify a brand or family of products

trade receivables Another name for accounts receivable from customers

trademark An exclusive and continuing right to use a certain symbol to identify a brand or family of products

trading on the equity The use of borrowed funds in the capital structure of a firm; the expectation is that the funds will earn a return higher than the rate of interest on the borrowed funds

trading securities Investments in securities that management intends to actively trade (buy and sell) for trading profits as market prices fluctuate

trailing earnings Earnings reported in the prior period

transitory items Transactions or events that are not likely to recur

translation adjustment The change in the value of the net assets of a subsidiary whose assets and liabilities are denominated in a foreign currency

treasury stock Shares of outstanding stock that have been acquired (and not retired) by the issuing corporation; treasury stock is recorded at cost and deducted from stockholders' equity in the balance sheet

trend percentages A comparison of the same financial item over two or more years stated as a percentage of a base-year amount

trial balance A list of the account titles in the general ledger, their respective debit or credit balances, and the totals of the debit and credit amounts

U

unadjusted trial balance A list of general ledger accounts and their balances taken before accounting adjustments have been made

uncollectible accounts expense The expense stemming from the inability of a business to collect an amount previously recorded as a receivable; sometimes called bad debts expense; normally classified as a selling or administrative expense

unearned revenue A liability representing revenues received in advance; also called deferred revenue

units-of-production method A depreciation method that allocates depreciation expense to each operating period in proportion to the amount of the asset's expected total production capacity used each period

useful life The period of time an asset is used by an entity in its operating activities, running from date of acquisition to date of disposal (or removal from service)

V

variable costs Those costs that change in proportion to changes in sales volume

variable interest entity (VIE) Any form of business organization (such as corporation, partnership, trust) that is established by a sponsoring company and provides benefits to that company in the form of asset securitization or project financing; VIEs were formerly known as special purpose entities (SPEs)

vertical analysis Analysis of a firm's financial statements that focuses on the statements of a single year

voucher Another name for the payment approval form

W

warranties Guarantees against product defects for a designated period of time after sale

wasting assets Another name for natural resources; *see* natural resources

weighted average cost of capital (WACC) The discount rate where the weights are the relative percentages of debt and equity in the capital structure and are applied to the expected returns on debt and equity respectively

work in process inventory The cost of inventories that are in the manufacturing process and have not yet reached completion

working capital The difference between current assets and current liabilities

Z

z-score The outcome of the Altman Z-score bankruptcy prediction model

zero coupon bond A bond that offers no periodic interest payments but that is issued at a substantial discount from its face value

Index

Note: The letter "e" refers to an exhibit on the stated page, and the letter "n" indicates that the information is included in a footnote on the given page. For example, 15n7 means footnote 7 on page 15.

Note: The letter "e" refers to an exhibit on the stated page, and the letter "n" indicates that the information is included in a footnote on the given page. For example, 15n7 means footnote 7 on page 15.

Note: The letter "e" refers to an exhibit on the stated page, and the letter "n" indicates that the information is included in a footnote on the given page. For example, 15n7 means footnote 7 on page 15.

Note: The letter "e" refers to an exhibit on the stated page, and the letter "n" indicates that the information is included in a footnote on the given page. For example, 15n7 means footnote 7 on page 15.

Note: The letter "e" refers to an exhibit on the stated page, and the letter "n" indicates that the information is included in a footnote on the given page. For example, 15n7 means footnote 7 on page 15.

Note: The letter "e" refers to an exhibit on the stated page, and the letter "n" indicates that the information is included in a footnote on the given page. For example, 15n7 means footnote 7 on page 15.

Note: The letter "e" refers to an exhibit on the stated page, and the letter "n" indicates that the information is included in a footnote on the given page. For example, 15n7 means footnote 7 on page 15.

Note: The letter "e" refers to an exhibit on the stated page, and the letter "n" indicates that the information is included in a footnote on the given page. For example, 15n7 means footnote 7 on page 15.

Note: The letter "e" refers to an exhibit on the stated page, and the letter "n" indicates that the information is included in a footnote on the given page. For example, 15n7 means footnote 7 on page 15.

Note: The letter "e" refers to an exhibit on the stated page, and the letter "n" indicates that the information is included in a footnote on the given page. For example, 15n7 means footnote 7 on page 15.

Note: The letter "e" refers to an exhibit on the stated page, and the letter "n" indicates that the information is included in a footnote on the given page. For example, 15n7 means footnote 7 on page 15.

Note: The letter "e" refers to an exhibit on the stated page, and the letter "n" indicates that the information is included in a footnote on the given page. For example, 15n7 means footnote 7 on page 15.

Note: The letter "e" refers to an exhibit on the stated page, and the letter "n" indicates that the information is included in a footnote on the given page. For example, 15n7 means footnote 7 on page 15.

Note: The letter "e" refers to an exhibit on the stated page, and the letter "n" indicates that the information is included in a footnote on the given page. For example, 15n7 means footnote 7 on page 15.

Note: The letter "e" refers to an exhibit on the stated page, and the letter "n" indicates that the information is included in a footnote on the given page. For example, 15n7 means footnote 7 on page 15.